de Gruyter Studies in Organization

An international series by internationally known authors presenting current fields of research in organization.

Organizing and organisations are substantial pre-requisites for the viability and future developments of society. Their study and comprehension are indispensable to the quality to the human life. Therefore, the series aims to:

– offer to the specialist work material in form of the most important and current problems, methods and results;
– give interested readers access to different subject areas;
– provide aids for decisions on contemporary problems and stimulate ideas.

The series will include monographs, collections of contributed papers, and handbooks.

For Bob Pinker

with many thanks

for the invitation

at LSE and in hope

of collaboration.

F. X. Kaufmann

de Gruyter Studies in Organization

An international series by internationally known authors presenting current fields of research in organization.

Organizing and organisations are substantial pre-requisites for the viability and future developments of society. Their study and comprehension are indispensable to the quality to the human life. Therefore, the series aims to:

– offer to the specialist work material in form of the most important and current problems, methods and results;
– give interested readers access to different subject areas;
– provide aids for decisions on contemporary problems and stimulate ideas.

The series will include monographs, collections of contributed papers, and handbooks.

de Gruyter Studies in Organization 4

Guidance, Control and Evaluation in the Public Sector

For Bob Pinker
with many thanks
for the invitation
at LSE and in hope
of collaboration.

F. X. Kaufmann

Guidance, Control, and Evaluation in the Public Sector

The Bielefeld Interdisciplinary Project

Edited by Franz-Xaver Kaufmann,
Giandomenico Majone, Vincent Ostrom
With Assistance of Wolfgang Wirth

Walter de Gruyter · Berlin · New York 1986

Franz-Xaver Kaufmann
Prof. Dr., Universität Bielefeld (FRG)

Giandomenico Majone
Prof. Ph. D., John F. Kennedy School of Government, Harvard University,
Cambridge, Mass. (USA)

Vincent Ostrom
Prof. Ph. D., Indiana University, Bloomington, Ind. (USA)

With 39 Figures and 37 Tables.

Gedruckt mit Unterstützung der Universität Bielefeld.

Library of Congress Cataloging-in-Publication Data

Main entry under title:
Guidance, control, and evaluation in the public sector.
  (De Gruyter studies in organization ; 4)
  Bibliography: p.
  Includes index.
  1. Public administration--Adresses, essays, lectures
2. Bureaucracy--Addresses, essays, lectures. 3. Policy sciences--Addresses, essays,
lectures. I. Kaufmann, Franz Xaver. II. Majone, Giandomenico. III. Ostrom, Vincent,
1919-. IV. Series.
JFl321.G85 1985   350.007   85–16112
ISBN 0-89925-020-3 (U.S.)

CIP-Kurztitelaufnahme der Deutschen Bibliothek

Guidance, control, and evaluation in the public sector / the Bielefeld interdisciplinary
project ed. by Franz-Xaver Kaufmann . . . with assistance of Wolfgang Wirth. – Berlin ;
New York : de Gruyter, 1985.
  (De Gruyter studies in organization ; 4)
  ISBN 3–11–009707–9
NE: Kaufmann, Franz-Xaver [Hrsg.]; GT

Preface

During the academic year 1981/82 the Center for Interdisciplinary Research at the University of Bielefeld (ZiF) hosted a research group of social scientists under the aegis of a project called "Steuerung und Erfolgskontrolle im öffentlichen Sektor" ("Guidance, Control and Performance Evaluation in the Public Sector"). The members came from eight countries and represented various academic disciplines such as economics, law, political theory, public administration and sociology. Most of them came from universities but were also acquainted with politics and public administration either through former employment, empirical research and/or consulting activities. Hence the research group was composed of people with a wide range of backgrounds and the subject to be dealt with presented no fewer complexities. The risk of on overload was high, and it is due to the extraordinarily favorable conditions ZiF could offer to the research that the present volume, an integrated account of the group's work, has been completed. Our first thanks therefore are addressed to the University of Bielefeld and the directorate and staff of ZiF, not to forget the taxpayers of the Land Nordrhein-Westfalen, who enabled us to meet for a planning session in June 1981, for months of coresidential work from October 1981 until August 1982 and for a last meeting to discuss the draft of this final report in July 1983.

Although ZiF may be called a quiet island in the stormy sea of the business modern science has increasingly become, we did no solitary work. A number of social scientists – including Winfried Brohm (Konstanz), Herbert König (Hamburg), Klaus König (Speyer), Niklas Luhmann (Bielefeld), Renate Mayntz (Köln), Ingo Metze (Münster), Fritz W. Scharpf (Berlin), Günther F. Schäfer (Maastricht), Heinrich Siedentopf (Speyer), Peter Weingart (Bielefeld) and Helmut Wollmann (Berlin) – helped to shape the focus of the research group and to find and select the most appropriate members. Several workshops were organized by members of the research group during their residence at ZiF and they brought additional expertise both from academia and political and administrative practice into the group's work. Some guests have also contributed to the present volume and additional publications further document these activities.

Wolfgang Wirth was the operative coordinator of the group's work. In the four years of planning, carrying out and finishing the group's activities he took over the bulk of stress necessarily linked to a project of this size. Most significant for the cooperative effort documented in the present volume was moreover the assistance of Hans-Jürgen Franz, Axel Groenemeyer, Lutz Leisering, Bernd Rosewitz and Hartmut Wolf, who contributed by providing documentations, taking notes and issuing protocols, not to forget all those everyday activities that linked the group with the general staff of ZiF. Hans-Jürgen Franz and Wolfgang Wirth moreover assisted the first editor during the print of this volume and prepared the indexes.

Adelheid Baker, Gillian T. Hood and Jean Randich helped the authors who were not native speakers to express their thoughts in readable English. Liselotte

Jegerlehner, Marion Kämper, Rita Nisius and Astrid Roggen patiently wrote different versions of most papers.

Werner Schuder showed his interest in publishing the volume with de Gruyter at an early stage, when nobody could know if and when we would succeed, which proved a real encouragement.

The research group expresses its gratitude to everybody who has contributed to the conditions and the outcome of its work.

Bielefeld, Autumn 1985

The Editors

Table of Contents

Part 4
Comparing Institutional Modes of Coordination

Part 1
The Challenge: Problems as Contestable Issues

1. Introduction: History of the Project and Background to the Problem

Franz-Xaver Kaufmann

Abstract

The reader is to be introduced by various ways into the topics of this volume: the context of discovery and the state of discussion which led to the project as well as the way the research group was formed and has worked is presented first. A sketch of the 'red line' of the volume follows, giving an overview of the topics of all chapters and of the structure of the volume. In the last section the pragmatic context of what the volume is aiming at is discussed: To develop conceptual frameworks which help to understand the structured complexity of relationships within the public sector as a device to redefine situations for the actors concerned. The interdisciplinary framework gives greater insight into the conditions of functioning in the public sector than traditional theories in various disciplines. Moreover the international composition of the research group helps to overcome particular perspectives of national traditions and to develop a more general framework.

1.1 Introduction

The present volume has two histories: the history of its subject and the history of its genesis as a joint effort. Both are intertwined.

The *subject* of this volume is an attempt to explain the functioning of what is conventionally called the public sector. Political theory, which traditionally focused on the state or on government, is now challenged by economic and sociological considerations broadening the scope of politics and policies into what was conventionally considered as private. This shift in academic emphasis corresponds to a growing interdependence of polity and economy, and the involvement of both with the everyday life of most people. The German distinction of *Staat* and *Gesellschaft* allows one to conceptualize this growing interdependence as the *"Verstaatlichung der Gesellschaft"* (politization of society) and the *"Vergesellschaftung des Staates"* (socialization of the state) (Habermas 1962). The English terms "welfare state" and "mixed economy" refer to similar issues, but they have not been explored as deeply in political theory. This has led some to argue as Sharkansky (1979) has done about a "withering of the state".

In political theory the 'state' or the 'government' is considered to be the steering center of a society. Classical political theories were already aware, in criticizing the absolutistic state, that the complexity of modern societies does not allow the unlimited dominance of a political center without seriously damaging their productive and adaptive capacities. The differentiation of a self-contained state and a market-regulated economy was the institutional answer of the 19th century to the problems of growth and order, but the relationship between them was always contested by the ideological mainstreams. To understand the problems of the public sector, however, it is not sufficient to deal with the relationship of economy and polity. We must incorporate a third aspect of modern societies that has been emphasized in political as well as in economic theory, a domain conventionally called the social services. They may be regarded as the organizational outcome of the welfare state and their size as well as their impact upon the everyday life of most citizens has grown substantially during the last decades. We therefore have to ask how, to what extent and under which conditions the state or the government is able to influence what happens with the provision of goods and services, taking into account the self-regulating powers of the systems concerned.

Thus the subject of our inquiry is related to (1) a better understanding of the problems of 'governability' in modern welfare states, i.e. – in terms of the present approach – the 'steerability' of public sectors; and (2) a better understanding of public sector performance which seems to be inextricably linked to the problem of the coordination of a multiplicity of actors within the public sector. Theories that have emerged in various disciplines will be screened for their possible contribution to a more comprehensive approach to the reconstruction of coordination problems in the area of guidance, control and performance evaluation. More specific issues of administrative control will also be considered.

The history of the subject is more complicated than the history of the project this volume results from. The *origins of the project* go back to January 1970, when the present author, then designated Dean, employed Friedhart Hegner as an administrative assistant in the recently founded Faculty of Sociology at the University of Bielefeld. We agreed to work together beyond the time of my responsibilities for faculty affairs, on a topic that we called "Bürgerrechte und Verwaltungsstaat" (civil rights and the administrative state). Our concern was not about the then very topical issue of democratization (as citizen participation in policy input), but about policy output and the impact of growing administration upon the lives of citizens. Together with Dieter Grunow and with support from the Stiftung Volkswagenwerk we started field research in 1972 into the relationships between tax offices and tax payers (cf. Grunow et al. 1978). In 1975 I was assigned by the Federal Ministry of Research and Technology to coordinate a research program dealing with similar issues in the field of local social policy, which included reference to several levels of policy-making. Grunow and Hegner were among the senior research staff (cf. Kaufmann 1979). In 1977 Renate Mayntz and Fritz Scharpf asked us to join a research program on implementation research (cf. Mayntz 1980, 1983). The discussions within that group sharpened my interest to a more comprehensive view of political processes. My own work was related mainly to economic sociology and to social policy; and I became aware of both shortcomings and parallels in various disciplinary approaches to analyzing the public sector. Thus, when I was asked to join the directorate of the *"Zentrum für interdisziplinäre Forschung"* (ZiF) in 1978, I put forward plans for a research group on "Guidance, Control and Performance Evaluation in the Public Sector".

The *basic idea* was simple. General agreement exists that markets have a high capacity for coordination, i.e. they are effective in allocating resources in a way that satisfies the needs of consumers and motivates producers to behave efficiently. Market mechanisms enable producers to make decisions in allocating resources to yield goods and services *(guidance)*. Markets grant benefits and impose costs that act as sanctions *(control)*. And, they give consumers an opportunity to *evaluate* products in deciding whether to buy them again or not. The major achievement of economics is in explaining how this coordination of multiple actors operates, and in specifying the necessary conditions for efficient coordination. The elegance of market theory has led the mainstream of Western economists to assume that markets are the uniquely efficient mode of coordination among multiple actors. As economic steering by markets and by central planning became distinctive features in so called capitalist and socialist societies, the thesis of Ludwig von Mises (1922) – that efficient steering of economies by political planning is impossible – became a kind of liberal dogma that affected discussions about politics in Western societies. Economic freedom was seen then as a necessary correlate and condition of political freedom (cf. e.g. Jöhr 1948; Hayek 1967). By contrast, the sociology of Max Weber emphasized the rational character of the modern state; and the emergent policy sciences, drawing upon Weber, assumed the capability of the state to exercise rational control over public policies. I was convinced neither by the case against effective political problem solving in market-theory, nor by the assumptions of goal-oriented rationality in the political realm. I wanted to understand instead why and under what conditions policies work, how they work, and why performance within the public sector seems to be neither as bad as expected by market theorists and liberals nor as efficient as hoped for by policy-scientists and socialists. I always felt that political problem solving was a different kind of problem than economic optimization. Law is its basic medium, not money, even though raising and spending money is a substantial issue in policy evaluations. Traditional political theory (including public law), however, never explained how policies worked to yield effects, but at its best suggested how they ought for perform. I therefore participated in evaluation-research and implementation-research efforts that were concerned with policy throughputs and outputs; but I also experienced difficulties in generalizing their findings and the array of facts could not be composed into a clear picture.

I therefore went back to more general questions and proposed to form a research group on guidance, control and performance evaluation in the public sector at the Center for Interdisciplinary Research (ZiF) at our university. This center for advanced studies eventually allocated funds to invite a number of scholars to come to Bielefeld for the academic year 1981/82 and to form such a research group. The subject seemed to be 'ripe' for an interdisciplinary endeavour, because there had been a growing concern about the public sector in various disciplines of the social sciences since the 1960s in the United States and since the 1970s in Germany[1].

1.2 Approaches of Various Disciplines

A short sketch of the issues may give an idea of the manifold facets of the subject that had to be taken into account. I shall try to emphasize at the same time some differences between the American and German traditions that were not consciously held at this time but became factors that were essential to intellectual progress in the research group.

It seems appropriate to begin with *Political Science and Sociology*. Several distinct approaches including the various policy sciences, theories of planning and decision-making, the social-indicator-movement, and evaluation research had developed in the United States during the sixties (see Hellstern: Ch. 14). They all aimed at direct contributions to improve the capability of governments to perform a more active part in the then desired transformation of societies. With the development of implementation research (see Sabatier: Ch. 15) political scientists became increasingly aware of the internal complexity of the political system. The need for a more complex approach became apparent (cf. Ostrom 1974). Here the linkage between the policy science approach and more elaborate concepts of the political system (seminal: Easton 1965) led to a theory of the political process that allowed topics of politics and policy analysis to be related in a common framework of problem articulation, program formulation, program implementation and evaluation (cf. May and Wildavsky 1978; Majone and Wildavsky 1978). The reception of these various ideas by German scholars (e.g. Schaefer 1974; Mayntz 1977; Hanf and Scharpf 1978), revealed an effort to link various American approaches in order to reach a higher degree of theoretical complexity[2].

Germany Public Administration is traditionally a domain of lawyers. Their work had its influence upon issues of the state and of politics in the public sector. *Administrative science* is very institutional in its approach, and only a few scholars worked on our problem in the early days (cf. K. König 1974; E. Bohne and H. König 1976). Most influential was the work of the sociologist Luhmann (1968, 1971) whose approach in terms of systems theory seemed, however, to be somewhat too general for a new paradigm of administrative science. In public law there was almost no attempt to take account of the new developments in political science that challenged the established normative reasoning by emphasizing the internal dynamics of bureaucracy and a loss in the momentum of law in processes of implementation and service delivery. This issue has been picked up on only recently (cf. Wahl 1980). Nevertheless, the continental tradition of 'steering by law' has persisted as an important line of thought, and forms a kind of contrast program to the more entrepreneurial American theories (cf. Grimm: Ch. 4).

In the field of *economics* one can observe a curious shift in interest between Europe and America. From its beginning European economic thought was concerned with the state and with economic policies.[3] After World War II this interest withered under the influence of Anglo-Saxon 'Marshallian' and 'Keynesian' economics. By contrast there was a growing concern with public finance in the United States, which eventually led to economic theories of political and administrative behavior (Downs 1957; Black 1958; Buchanan and Tullock 1962; Olson 1965; Niskanen 1971). Most of these and other approaches remained separate, and it was only in the mid-seventies that a more comprehensive approach became apparent (cf. Buchanan 1975; Müller 1976; see also Shubik: Ch. 28). Besides the mainstream of what is now called the 'new political economy', several other approaches including comparative economic systems (e.g. Neuberger and Duffy 1976), neo-institutionalism (cf. Gruchy 1972; Williamson 1975) and the economics of property-rights (cf. Furubotn and Prejovich 1974) had to be taken into account.

Thus new developments in institutional economics and in institutional analysis (cf. E. Ostrom: Ch. 22) offered opportunities for renewing interest in the steering function of rules beyond the steering function of markets.

These approaches were reluctantly received in Germany. Here, the neo-Marxist wave of the early seventies had shaped another interest in the relationship of the polity and the economy that was also called 'political economy' (cf. Frey 1974). The niche for a rather rough neo-marxist thought in Germany resulted from a growing gap between economics and sociology in Germany. The influence of American traditions, marked by a strong separation between economics and sociology, had become overwhelming; and the traditional linking of economic, political and social problems in the German historical school had broken down (cf. Kaufmann 1982a). There remained, however, some interest in problems of public enterprise (cf. Thiemeyer 1970) and in problems of economic order in the tradition of *Walter Eucken,* that now became slowly oriented to a theory of complex systems (cf. Krüsselberg 1972; Leipold 1976; Schenk 1978).

Theoretical and empirical approaches to the problems of the *welfare state* remained separate from these lines of thinking. Seminal was the tradition at the London School of Economics (Titmuss 1958; T. H. Marshall 1964; Robson 1976), American studies remained scattered (Wilensky 1975; Janowitz 1976). In Germany a great tradition had been forgotten until the mid-1970s, when research and discussion began on a large scale (cf. Kaufmann 1982b). With respect to the present volume, issues concerning the welfare state are relevant mainly to problems of coordination for the social services which have emerged from charitable institutions and the houshold's economy and have not – as it is conventionally assumed – been differentiated from the market economy (cf. Kaufmann 1979: 25). Therefore they constitute a specific segment of the public sector with their own coordination problems which should not be confused with the problems of a 'mixed economy'.

Finally there are some books which have directly inspired the present approach. Among them, Dahl and Lindblom (1953) was of paramount importance. Its complex and interdisciplinary approach was the intellectual model for what I hoped the research group would perform. Of course the thrust of Dahl and Lindblom has been seminal for much of the work of the 'new political economy', but as far as I can see, no attempt has been made to integrate the various issues of coordination and control into a common framework. Apart from this the works of Deutsch (1963) and Etzioni (1968) and of course the 'classics' of Walter Eucken (1944, 1955) have been important intellectual sources for the approach of analyzing coordination problems as problems of guidance, control and feed-back.

1.3 Drafting the Project

This very sketchy overview shows the interdisciplinary character of our subject as well as the need to include political scientists, sociologists, lawyers and economists in the research group. When I started to plan the project in 1978 I was still not prepared to enter such a wide field. In the beginnings I was thinking more of a comparative inquiry into two or three policy areas in order to describe the modes of control and evaluation used there and to explore the conditions of fit or lack of fit with the guiding goals or standards. This method of inquiry would have necessitated close cooperation between social scientists and practitioners in the research group.[4]

A growing awareness of the apparent convergence of various disciplinary approaches to public sector problems suggested a second method of inquiry, i.e., to try an interdisciplinary approach that focused directly upon theoretical issues and conceptual problems. The convergence of interest among scholars from different academic disciplines offered the prospect of an interdisciplinary community of scholars addressing a new group of problems of political, economic and social developments which had been of central concern in earlier German scholarship.

In the spring of 1980 these two approaches were discussed by a preparatory committee, which strongly recommended the more theoretical inquiry of the second approach. The project was then drafted as a proposal which I sent in the summer of 1980 to scholars whose interest I hoped to win. This proposal is given as *Appendix* to this chapter. It shows a very broadly based program, and the reader should of course not expect to find answers to all the questions raised by that proposal in this volume.

In autumn 1980 about 35 selected scholars met with the preparatory commitee at ZiF. They had been divided into two groups that met separately, and every scholar was invited to present his own possible contribution to such a research group. From these discussions a kind of short-formula for the common work emerged that focused on the question: "What institutional arrangements could provide for the way people, as representatives of organisations and actors in organisations, behave in their decisions and actions so that the resulting output of these organisations contributes to attaining those political and societal goals which legitimize their existence?"[5] This question has proved to be too narrow to encompass the interests of the participants of the group, as the reader of this volume will easily recognize.

1.4 How the Research Group Worked

The final selection of the members of the research group was, of course, a multivalent decision process which took account of the suitability of individual research interests to the general topic, of a mix among the representatives of various disciplines, of the temporal availability of the scholars and of their expected contributions to group work.

The research group met for a planning session in June 1981 and then, together with the preparatory committee and with some invited scholars, for the opening conference in October 1981. This conference dealt with five topics: (1) problems of governability, (2) typologies of different forms of public action, (3) hierarchy, markets and solidarity as modes of control, (4) approaches to the theory of bureaucracy and (5) problems of performance analysis. From November 1981 to February 1982 the permanent group was small and comprised 5–6 members from abroad and 4 members from Bielefeld University. The most intense group work was from March to July 1982, when about 12 members from abroad were permanent guests at ZiF. Four members from abroad participated without formal leave from their home employment and joined the group from time to time for several days or weeks. Moreover, some of the guests of the group became engaged for a longer time in the group's work and also contributed to the present volume. As the list of contributors shows, most participants came from Germany, the United States and the United Kingdom. Consequently, English and German served as the languages of communication. The enhancement of language skills as well as the growing understanding of different political cultures were not the least results of this joint venture.

The group met every Wednesday and more often within sub-groups interested in specific topics. Initiative was left largely to the members to plan common work, and the facilities at ZiF allowed for the organization of several workshops with scholars and practitioners from abroad.[6] This interdisciplinary interaction became a stimulating experience. But the variety and complexity of the issues involed became more and more apparent.

There was a time when the present author seriously doubted that a coherent product of the group's work would ever be attained. Consequently, his first proposal for a final report was modest and comprised a selection of the papers produced on various occasions within the group's work, ordered along the line of a general argument. But the unexpected happened: the group refused to puzzle only over the papers already written and began a joint effort to develop this line of argument more substantially. At the end of two weeks of intensive discussions, a draft for the present volume was designed and the tasks for everybody defined. This was the state of affairs when the group left in August 1982. Some uneasiness remained about whether the vision of a fully-coordinated work would be strong enough after eveybody was back at his usual desk facing different tasks. Thanks to ZiF the group met again for a week in June 1983. This meeting was to provide the occasion for a thorough discussion of the first drafts of the chapters for this volume. Most drafts came late, but they came. This caused some hectic night work, but at the end of the conference 38 papers were discussed; the structure of the volume was refined; some additional papers were commissioned and some were joined or dropped. There was a general feeling that the months spent together had improved mutual understanding. Every author received a written summary of the discussion of his paper and comments from the editors. In this way manuscripts were prepared which form the chapters of the present volume. Where necessary, authors got additional comments from the editors who met for a last time in February 1984, and revised their papers accordingly.

1.5 The Red Line

It is obviously impossible to attain the coherence of a monograph when a group of more than twenty people from various disciplines is working together. We assume however, that this volume has a line of argument that helps to clarify what the public sector is about; how its functioning can be explained; and how coordination and control among the actors involved may operate for more or less satisfactory results. The "red line" highlights the basic theme that runs through the structure and content of this volume.

Part 1 The Challenge: Problems as Contestable Issues

One of the basic experiences of the group was the multiplicity of political conceptions and institutional arrangements that may affect guidance, control and evaluation in the public sector. Traditional approaches in the social sciences, as well as political positions tend to underscore the range of possible solutions, as is revealed by a comparison of various national traditions. Even the notion of a public sector, far from being well-defined, is itself a subject of controversy with regard to its domain as well as to the role of state power in its guidance and control. The present volume makes an attempt to find a language for dealing with the political issues involved, without falling back on traditional points of view. We have tried to find levels of argumentation that allow for comparing the differences in the steering capacities involved in the constitutional and institutional arrangements of and in various countries. Awareness of differences must precede speculations about advantages and disadvantages, as the marginal effect of differences can only be construed in context.

In analyzing the public sector we could no longer think about a centralized state implementing some policy, rather we recognized a highly differentiated sector within which different forms of coordination and a redundancy of control mechanisms are operating. This means that the alternative to centralized coordination in practice is not limited to a kind of reduction of the public sector in terms of implementing more market mechanism (privatization). There are diverse forms of coordination that should be taken into account.

Chapter 1 gives an overview of the genesis and the issues of the project, including a short sketch of academic positions of interest to the present approach.

Chapter 2 deals with evidence and controversial issues of research concerning the evolution and the bureaucratization of the public sector. It sketches the 'real basis' of the *challenge* with which the research group has dealt.

Chapter 3 identifies and examines some basic assumptions of previous theoretical approaches to analyzing the modern public sector. It shows the shortcomings of policy science and public finance as a point of departure for the more complex frames of reference that are developed in later sections.

Part 2 The Public Sector: Constitutional and Conceptual Problems

In Western societies (to which our study is confined) the continental European tradition conceives the public sector as being related to a strong political center (the 'state'), whereas the Anglo-Saxon tradition conceives 'government' as being a more personalized and potentially multi-centered form of public authority.

Chapter 4 and *Chapter 5* present these two intellectual traditions of constitutional thinking and indicate their implications for basic features in the factual political constitutions of some countries in Europe and North America.

Chapter 6 analyzes the process of modernization of Western societies in terms of political and sociological theory with emphasis upon the developments of the so-called welfare state. The conception of a 'public sector' then emerges as a consequence of the growing interdependence of the highly organized activities of formally private actors and the political intervention of public actors. As this growing interdependency it itself controversial in scope and structure, the definition of the public sector becomes a contestable issue. This will be elucidated in *Chapter 7* which discusses statistical problems of the public sector both in terms of method and of content. The subsequent chapters give conceptual and empirical evidence of structural differentiation within the public sector.

Chapter 8 deals with the impact of different political structures upon the possibilities of centralized politics and analyses the patterns of coordination and the consequences of local government reform in England.

Chapter 9 shows the widening variety of organizational arrangements between pure government/state and private activities, comprising quasi-private and quasi-public activities. The difficulty of defining and delimiting "sectors" becomes apparent in this chapter.

Part 3 Guidance, Control and Evaluation

In light of the previous sections, the question of the functioning of the public sector can now be restated in terms of guidance, control and evaluation. Given a multiplicity of actors variously dependent on the powers of political core structures and potentially able to influence the operation of those powers to a varying extent, the question arises as to how their actions may be coordinated in the long chains of action typical of highly complex societies. This necessitates processes of standard setting and standard using as well as institutional arrangements providing for some forms of control, mutual adjustment and learning in intraorganizational and interorganizational relationships.

Chapter 10 gives an exposition of such ideas and shows that the coordination of guidance, control and evaluation in the public sector is more precarious than in pure market relationships, but not impossible. It requires a multiplicity of coordination mechanisms (cf. Part 4) and forms of control (cf. Part 6).

Chapter 11 deals with questions of 'oughtness' under the conditions of limited rationality. Finding acceptable criteria of choice and standard setting necessitates a normative inquiry that accounts for the fallibility of human understanding, for nonsymmetries in human relationships and for the inevitability of human order.

Chapter 12 approaches the problem of setting institutional constraints to take account of normative considerations by means of the formal theory of utilitarianism, whereas *Chapter 13* analyzes the question of how group-egoism within the public sector may be controlled by a strengthening of ethical orientation and how this could be made operative in the public context. The next chapters give an account of two mainstreams of recent policy research: evaluation research *(Chapter 14)* and implementation research *(Chapter 15)*. Their findings are related to the issue of using scientific knowledge for policy analysis as well as to the issues of guidance, control and evalution.

Finally Chapter 16 deals with problems of intraorganizational conflict und problems of multigoal achievement within the public sector. The cybernetic view gives an explanation of how conflicting goals and multi-dimensional standard-setting and standard-using may nevertheless lead to satisfying results.

Part 4 Comparing Institutional Modes of Coordination

To perform the functions of guidance, control and evaluation a multitude of procedures and institutional arrangements have emerged in the course of human history. The chapters of this section try to develop a comparative typology of characteristic institutional modes of coordination operating within the public sector. Besides the already classic types of markets and hierarchies *(Chapter 17)*, there will be an analysis of other well-known forms contributing to guidance, control and evaluation of human interaction, i.e. solidarity *(Chapter 18 and 19)*, votes and vetoes (Chapter 20) and mutual adjustment by debate and persuasion. *(Chapter 21)*. From a systematic point of view a further chapter dealing with third party intervention (e.g. adjudication, mediation, arbitration) is lacking here. The section closes with some methodological considerations of institutional analysis in terms of a configuration of rules that may also open a way to a more formal treatment of the problems of using rules to steer and order relationships in the public sector *(Chapter 22)*.

Part 5 Coordination in Interorganizational Relationships

As has already been outlined in part 2, relationships among many organized actors with separate interests, goals and strategies are the dominant feature of the public sector. Compared with interactions among individuals, interorganizational relationships involve a shift in complexity: individual motives and preferences become more patterned whereas the representatives of organizations have to consider both the opportunities of the organized environment as well as the restrictions emerging from intraorganizational relationships.

Chapter 23 analyzes federal systems as institutional arrangements for solving issues of interorganizational coordination whereas *Chapter 24* applies institutional analysis to the problem of linking action arenas.

Chapter 25 draws the lesson of a comparative approach to the solving of one type of interorganizational problem (river pollution) in three countries and shows that the achievement of specific goals is attainable through various institutional arrangements. There is no 'one best way' for organizing the public sector.

Chapter 26 focuses on the changing relationships of government and associations. It gives a survey of historic developments as well as an analysis in terms of network theory.

Chapter 27 reconsiders the problems of planning in the light of a more decentralized conception of the public sector and shows that the capacity for problem solving within the public sector is by no means bound to the limits of central control. Shortcomings have to be seen less as a consequence of perception of the problem than as a lack of interorganizational devices to promote processes of long-term mutual adjustment.

The section closes with the exposition of an ambitious program for modeling complex processes within the public sector with the help of game theory *(Chapter 28)*.

Part 6 Accountability, Performance Evaluation and Control in Public Administration

This section narrows and deepens the focus of inquiry to public administration as an essential part of the public sector. How is public administration to respond to the standards set by politics? Whereas classical theory of bureaucracy assumed conformity as self-evident, modern approaches tend to emphasize the many degrees of freedom and discretion if not arbitrariness within and among various units of administration. The proposed approach keeps within the polycentric view of the public sector previously developed and emphasizes the selectivity of various modes of control and consequently the necessity of redundancy in the structure of controls within the public sector. 'Overcontrol' is a consequence of one-sided emphasis on particular modes of control and particular standards, whereas redundancy of control means an interpolable balance of several modes of control acting often independently and focusing on different standards of performance. This idea is expanded in *Chapter 29* which also introduces various aspects of control theory.

Chapter 30 gives an introduction to evaluation problems, thus making some issues presented in part 3 more concrete. Control is useful only insofar as it uses standards that are related to those determining the guidance of processes within the public sector. The problem of multiple, non-comparable goals is discussed and considerations for a realistic design of evaluation are proposed.

The subsequent chapters deal with various, more or less institutionalized modes of control: within a single administration *(Chapter 31)*, by law courts (Chapter 32), by members of legislature *(Chapter 33)*, by audit courts *(Chapter 34)*, and by citizens who are affected by particular interventions of administrative agencies *(Chapter 35)*. Finally, an understanding of the operation of multiple forms of control is deepened by the concept of an interpolable balance of controls, that may be effected not only by formal but also by informal modes of control *(Chapter 36)*.

Part 7 By Way of Conclusion

In the concluding *chapter 37* the editors summarize the thrust of the present volume and relate it to some intellectual antecedents. They emphasize the importance of linking experience and theory in a normative inquiry about institutional design.

1.6 What About this Book

The usefulness of the social sciences is contested. Most of their research findings and writings seem to be of no practical use. Politicians and practitioners in public administration will search in vain for practical recommendations, for proposals of action or for reorganization in this book. This might be deceiving in the context of a subject that is so much related to political issues. We maintain, however, that the kind of work we have tried to do may generate practical consequences. It is the aim of the remaining pages of this Chapter to explain why and how these inquiries are related to political practice.

Today the state is under attack, at least in the countries from which most members of the research group came. Its potentialities are contested from both sides of the political spectrum and great words like 'crisis', 'bureaucracy', 'loss of legitimation', 'privatization' etc. flow easily from the lips of the protagonists. Critics 'from the Right' assume that governments have taken over too many tasks in transferring them to the public sector, and that this accounts for unemployment, the current fiscal crisis, and more generally the alleged crisis of governability in modern states (cf. e.g. Dettling 1980). The arguments referring to the latter are not always explicit, but there is always a charge against 'bureaucratization', even though the subject remains rather vague: the administration itself, the conditions of everyday life, and of society at large (cf. Grunow 1982). Critics from the Right consequently demand a reduction of the public sector, 'privatization' of public tasks, and a concomitant alleviation of the tax burden. 'Privatization' is understood mainly as a substitution for publicly planned provision of services by market provision. There should be 'more private initiative' that is assumed to be strangulated by the public tax burden as well as by the growing impact of public regulations. Governments that concentrate on their 'genuine tasks' of maintaining order and security are, however, assumed to work efficiently.

The critics from the Left strikingly resemble those from the Right. They also – and even more vigorously – claim that there is a fiscal and a political crisis in western societies, but their explanation differs. Allegedly the crisis is due to the antagonistic character of capitalist societies, to the unstable relationship between economy and polity (e.g. Gough 1979). The pretention of the state to be a *pouvoir neutre* is contested as well as its power to balance in the long run the opposite claims of various social groups. In trying to do so, they assume, democratic governments will necessarily engage more and more in new tasks and interventions and eventually be overloaded both in terms of fiscal demands and steering capacities. And when the illusion of democratic problem solving becomes apparent, they expect a loss of public authority, a gap of legitimacy that will lead to a deeper crisis in society. Within that broad view one may distinguish a traditional leftist 'orthodoxy' that continues its claim for a stronger state and for weakening the 'anarchic' forces of the market. But the stronger movement today seems to be directed against both the highly organized economy of big business and the bureaucratized state. The 'alternatives' argue neither for markets nor for the state, but for cooperation and regulations within small groups, for a 'new solidarity' (Hoefnagels 1979). The kind of progress that has been linked to organizational growth (or, as we conceive it, to a lengthening of chains of action) is assumed here to become essentially counterproductive and therefore to lead to a crisis of both, the economy and the polity.

Even reformist thinkers begin to question traditional assumptions about political potentialities for problem solving. Instead of generalizing forms of political intervention they postulate "a growing intelligence and precision of the state's stake of resources" and a "more intense and differentiated interaction among public administration, business and trade unions" (transl. from Scharpf 1979: 25). There is growing acknowledgement that the present forms of governmental intervention are reaching limits of effectiveness. Besides the scarcity of fiscal means (that should in fact surprise no one and was foreseen already by Schumpeter 1918), there is a new development that challenges the continental conception of the state and heavy reliance upon the law: the multiplication of political interventions as well as growing concern about equality and the protection of citizens against the alleged arbitrariness of public administration (cf. Böhret and Jann 1982) has led to what is called an 'inflation of laws' and the 'juridification' *(Verrechtlichung)* of society.[7] As nobody is able to gain a general overview, there exists a growing likelihood of conflicting norms and of a new form of administrative discretion, i.e. in deciding which norm should be applied in a concrete case. In many domains only a part of the norms in force are factually applied and its application controlled (cf. Wagener 1979). Moreover, at least in the federal system of West-Germany, a growing immobility results form the fiscal interdependencies of central, regional and local government (cf. Scharpf et al. 1976). There is, therefore, a growing concern about the "bureaucratic costs of the legal and social state" (Wahl 1980). Some compare the modern state with a dinosaur that has grown too big and is therefore condemned to die out.[8] At least we have to acknowledge a *growing entropy* in what is called the public sector; the amount of energy that is needed for coordination within and between public organizations is growing faster than their output in services to society. Hence a project that pretends to deal with "Guidance, Control and Evaluation in die Public Sector" may easily get credit. But will we live up to it?

The first message of this volume is a frustrating one, namely, that everything within the public sector is more complex and more complicated than 'great words' and traditional positions assume. For some this message is trivial, for the others it is discomforting and seems neither helpful nor suggestive.

The second message is a challenging one: if we don't develop theories that account for the growing complexity of the public sector, we will not be able to conceive ways out of the actual political confusion. This message challenges both social scientists and the partisans of different political creeds. And it is of course also a provocation to those for whom a politics of muddling through is the only remedy. The message says that first there should be an endeavour to redefine the situation before action is undertaken. This of course will be acknowledged as "standard scientific idiosyncrasy". Thus, the second message needs some explanation.

Human action is always related to cognition of a defined situation. Human cognition is essentially dependent upon culturally bound definitions as they are provided in everyday life by normal language[9]. We communicate within 'shared realities' and communication loses its power insofar as we are unable to relate to shared conceptions of reality. This is not only true for our everyday life but also for behavior within and among organizations. Members of an organization tend to develop shared conceptions that are particular and more or less unknown to outsiders.

Nearly all relevant interaction within what is conventionally called the public sector is *organization-related-interaction,* i.e., it takes place among the representatives of organizations or among position holders within an organization and across organizations. Even the most secret and informal contacts among persons that concern political or administrative issues will be essentially related to the positions of these persons within political and administrative frameworks. There is no position-free communication that is relevant for public issues. This of course is itself a consequence of the emergence of modern governments and administrations. Former sovereigns were more dependent on personal relationships that were extensions of households and of long-established feudal bonds.

Insofar as persons interact as representatives of organizations there will therefore always be three frames of reference operating in the mind of the actor: the frame of reference of the *individual actor as a person* (e.g. his assessment of his personal interests, his sense of justice and his identity), the frame of reference of the *organization* he is representing and the frame of reference of the *interaction* he is participating in. The latter frame consists essentially of the history of the interaction itself (and representatives normally meet repeatedly), but it is defined also by the relationships among the organizations they are representing. This interorganizational network of relationships usually exceeds the range of knowledge available to actors but they are nevertheless operative. Besides contractual rules and contested issues, a large number of explicit norms and rules normally define such interorganizational relationships. We find here an example of *the real complexity facing actors within the public sector.* But until now there has been no theory that accounts for such complexities. Theories either consider organizations as corporate actors and neglect the individuals that act as representatives, or they assume – following some of the precepts of methodological individualism – that only individual actors matter.

Analytical methodology as it is reflected in current social science research is hardly an adequate guideline for dealing with such problems. Its aim is to reach generalized conclusions by sorting out a small number (seldom more than two or three!) of dimensions or factors which are assumed to be the most relevant for a wide range of phenomena and by neglecting the context in which these factors operate. Thus, analytical models of thought remain clear, well-defined, and simple. But they cannot be helpful, if the real problem consists in a reality of overwhelming complexity which seems not to be simply contingent (and hence inaccessible to any intellecutal ordering) but structured and even more or less apparent to the relevant actors (cf. Mayntz 1985). They then do not need a small set of general assumptions (as valid as they may be) *but cognitive devices to understand better the complexities in which they act.* Therefore, the thrust of the present volume consists mainly in developing new (or at least more consistent) conceptual frameworks which attempt to give greater insight into the paramount features of and conditions of functioning in the public sector than traditional theories in various disciplines. The fact that researchers of different national and disciplinary backgrounds were able to communicate about this topic and to reach a basic understanding shared by most of them merits attention. It gives hope that these conceptions are less idiosyncratic, less one-sided and more comprehensive than those to which we are accustomed.

Whether we like it or not, we have to acknowledge that one very effective practical impact of the social sciences is their *contribution to collective conception and definitions of reality.* Our shared conceptions of 'the market', 'the state' or 'public interest' are cognitive "sediments" of former scientific inquiries that had been disseminated, became accepted by different social groups and have even become a part of general public opinion.

If therefore it is true that human beings are unable to perceive 'reality as such', but always act in defined situations where interaction takes place only upon the basis of shared conceptions, it becomes crucial that these conceptions account for the operating rules and forces that establish order in human societies. As these rules and forces as well as their interaction have grown substantially and have been transformed into organized patterns of relationships, *we also need shared conceptions that allow those changing relationships to be taken into account.* Patterns of organized complexity in modern societies are likely to manifest patterns of relationships which are counterintuitive. *Based upon 'commonsense' conceptions we imagine disorder and chaos, but further inquiry often reveals a deeper, more complex order.* Most of our conventional thinking about public and private, about planning and markets, etc., has been made obsolete by the processes of historical evolution and change. This volume should be understood as a search for the new conceptions that we need.

Shared conceptions normally derive from the way that persons experience themselves and their relationships with others. Highly organized forms of reality are, however, not accessible to direct human experience. Their conceptions are always the result of generalizations and assumptions. But different conceptions may account to varying degrees for the complexities involved. Conceptualizing a complex set of relationships requires one to work through the way that elements relate to one another in a synthetic structure. This step implies working out a complex *chain* of thought about the *configurations* of relationships that are the subject of conceptualizations. The chains of thought used to think through configurations of relationships involved in some conceptualization have theoretical significance in the way that elements and relationships work together for understanding and solving some problems. Theoretical conjectures based upon different conceptions may provide alternative approaches to understanding and resolving similar problems.

When we address ourselves to the problems of guidance, control and performance evaluation in the public sector, we have to anticipate that something referred to as "the public sector" may be conceptualized in quite different ways in different societies and in different traditions of thought within one society. The international and interdisciplinary composition of our research group increased the likelihood of confrontations about different experiences and conceptions and may, as a consequence, have contributed to a more thorough understanding of some of the basic features in addressing issues of the organized complexity of public life in modern societies.

If we conceive human beings as well as social systems not only as self-referent, but also as reflective systems, i.e. (at least potentially) endowed with the capability to conceive and hence to modify their own identity, a major function of social science for society becomes apparent: its contribution to self-understanding and hence to a higher degree of self-control in social systems (cf. Luhmann 1981: 198–228). This work, however, is more 'interpretative' than 'empirical' with the result that conjectures are less easily *refutable* than in the physical sciences.

Popper's approach to conjectures and refutations may not provide an appropriate method for proceeding with inquiry within such a subject. If acted upon, the conceptions and associated structure of elements and relationships may give rise to different realities in human societies. Our opportunity to make advances was primarily in making conjectures that clarify the similarities and differences which derive from different approaches to problems pertaining to the organization and performance of institutions in the public sector.

Such conjectures might be viewed as *contestable* rather than refutable. Arguments formulated as contestable conjectures are essential to an understanding of what can be learned from others' experiences. The contestability of conjectures should lead to a clarification of differences which are yielded when different conceptions are used as the basis for organizing different social realities.

If human societies want to learn from each other's experience, the treatment of different approaches to problems as contestable issues becomes especially important. By treating different approaches to problems as contestable issues, we can seek to clarify those similarities and differences that would permit human beings to make *informed choices* about the different opportunities that may be available to them in addressing problems pertaining to guidance, control and performance evaluation in the public sector. The more we understand the options that are available, the more choices we have in shaping our futures. The commitment of the group is to contribute to the development of such capabilities. The message of the book therefore consists not only in a trivial assertion of complexity, but in suggesting a new method of dealing with and of understanding the structured complexities in which we live.

Moreover, the reader will easily ascertain different families of thought within this volume; and he will also find contested issues being advanced by different participants. Although there was some endeavour on the part of the editors and most participants to incorporate the chapters into a general line of argument, there are still thrusts in several chapters that stand on their own. If I have emphasized the group's work in this introductory chapter this should not cast a shadow on the work of each author which deserves to be considered for its own merit.

Appendix: Proposal for the Research Group (Summer 1980)

"Different from the sector of private economy, where guidance and control of outcomes are connected systematically by market mechanisms and profits or losses, the public sector is lacking such comparably elegant feed-back-mechanisms. This, however, must not lead to the conclusion that problems of guidance would here be insolvable and that outcomes in the public sector would necessarily not be evaluable. Guidance, control and evaluation do also exist in the public sector. Normally, however, they will not occur simultaneously in different policy areas and they demand a cooperation of different mechanisms and forms of communication that have not yet been sufficiently scientifically clarified.

Apart from the early theoretical approach of R. A. Dahl and Ch. Lindblom (Politics, Economics and Welfare, 1953), an interdisciplinary approach is still lacking, although a number of recent developments within the single social sciences can be used as grounds upon which the issue should be taken up again. Such theories and developments and their disciplinary backgrounds, listed in short, are:

Economics: theory of public choice; economic theories of democracy and bureaucracy; comparative economic systems; theory of property rights.

Sociology and Political Sciences: development of the policy sciences with respect to different policy fields; integrating processes, research on implementation, evaluation and impact research; social indicators and "social reporting"; system theories and intersystem-theories; research on transfers between the scientific and the political system.

Law and Public Administration: problems of organization in public administration; problems and techniques of determining effectiveness and efficiency; development of a theory of mangement in public administration.

Often the problems appear similar in different disciplinary contexts, though the methods by which they are approached and dealt with will differ considerably. Correspondingly different aspects will be treated as particularly relevant. This constellation offers a positive basis for interdisciplinary communication.

Also within the political and administrative system the problems approached here have increasingly been given attention, whereby, however, a general orientation towards concrete problems and specific phenomena is predominant. In the Federal Republic the public sector remains largely determined by a legal (or legalistic) self-conception that only allows for dealing with the problem of control and evaluation in normative but not in functional terms. Functional aspects are merely treated as an intra-administrational problem. From that perspective guidance then happens through administrational regulations; evaluation will be a matter of "efficient" use of monetary resources. However, there are specific branch control systems within administrations. Their results function, for example, as criteria upon which financial means are allocated or individual promotion is decided.

Hitherto we do not know clearly why prevailing scientific studies attempting clarification and analytical reconstruction of inter-related policy processes within administrations have hardly been noticed or applied. Also widely unknown is how efficient the methods of control and evaluation developed and applied by practitioners are. Progress in a research field as difficult and complex as the one of present concern demands the cooperation of both scientific and practical experts. The flexible organizational facilities provided by the "Center for Interdisciplinary Research" (ZiF) appear particularly suitable to promote such progress.

The permanent group of researchers is expected to consist of 10–15 scientists who have already contributed to the problem range sketched above. The participation of colleagues with substantial research experience in specific policy areas as well as an interest in problems of theory construction in the fields of guidance, control and evaluation will be particularly appreciated. They are supposed to reside in ZiF for a period of 5–11 months. Apart from their working on individual projects they should be willing to participate actively in weekly meetings where the more general problems will be worked out collectively. Those meetings will also incorporate scientists from Bielefeld University.

Furthermore, additional workshops can be held on special topics including the possibility of inviting scientific and practical experts not belonging to the permanent research group. All publication rights concerning the works contributed in the course of the research project will principally remain with the individual authors, though we hope to have common publications of members of the research group.

The program of the group is to be determined, in detail, by the participants themselves. The following questions are only meant to indicate a few more comprehensive issues felt to be particularly relevant by the initiator of the group:

- To what extent can different disciplinary approaches to the analysis of the problem of political and administrational control and guidance be integrated?
- Can an interdisciplinary treatment of the problems of guidance lead to a higher degree of plausibility in the analysis of practical problems?
- To what extent can cybernetic models of steering and regulation be applied to political and social phenomena?
- How can theories of the political process be improved towards a development of guidance theory with respect to feed-back-mechanisms on different processual levels?
- To what extent and under what conditions can certain modes of outcome evaluation be implemented as feed-back-mechanisms?
- To what extent can a general approach in guidance theory be developed through a theory of inter-system-relationships?
- How can different techniques of control be compared with respect to their problem-solving capacity?
- How can different policy areas be compared in the aspects of guidance, control and performance evaluation?
- Which relationships exist between the legal and organizational characteristics of specific (national) political systems and their specific modes of control and performance evaluation?
- Is it possible to derive limitations regarding expansion in the public sector from guidability restrictions?
- To what extent can deficiencies in guidance and control be compensated for by possible functional equivalents?"

Acknowledgement

I am indebted to Vincent Ostrom for helpful comments and a substantial improvement in style and clarity of argument. Moreover, propositions concerning contestability (cf. page 17 s.) have been incorporated that were originally developed by him.

Notes

1   The efforts were obviously linked with political trends aiming at a more active role of government in the modernization of society. Johnson's 'war on poverty' and Brandt's 'politics for inner reform' engendered intellectual climate that challenged social science to become a part of political intelligence. Nevertheless, at the same time they fostered critical attitudes from the left and the right towards political commitments by scientists who easily became inclined to confound their hopes with their results. Some time in the seventies the intellectual climate began to change so that when the group met, the era of 'Reagonomics' and 'Thatcherism' had already begun. Even if these political efforts pretend to roll back political interventionism they remain bound to the subject of present concern. The political war-cries of 'market' versus 'state' stem from intellectual traditions that have become outmoded due to the trend of factual developments in the economy as well as in the polity.
2   For an overview of Policy Analysis in Germany see Wollmann 1982.

3 This is not only true for French mercantilism and the German "Staatswissenschaften", but also for Adam Smith (cf. Winch 1978; Kaufmann and Krüsselberg 1984).

4 Later it became evident that it is very difficult to win practitioners for a longer standing cooperation within such a research group, but this was not the reason for abandoning the plan.

5 Obviously this very un-English sentence was formulated first in German: "Wie können institutionelle Arrangements geschaffen werden, unter denen natürliche Personen als Repräsentanten von Organisationen und als Akteure in Organisationen sich in ihren Entscheidungen und Handlungen so verhalten, daß resultierende Leistungen der Organisationen denjenigen politisch/gesellschaftlichen Zielen dienen, welche deren Existenz legitimieren?"

6 These workshops included the following topics: "Auditing and Control in the Public Sector" (January 7–8, 1982), "Market, State and Solidarity in Adam Smith" (February 23–26, 1982), "Verantwortlichkeit und Erfolgskontrolle im Zeichen fiskalischer Knappheit" (June 22–23, 1982, mainly with German practitioners from administration and politics), "Analyzing Interactions Among Multiple Actors in the Public Sector" (July 1–6, 1982). For a more detailed report about the way the group worked see: *"Zentrum für interdisziplinäre Forschung der Universität Bielefeld"* 1981: 33–37, 89–92; 1982: 21–31, 39–40, 49–50, 69–72, 74–76; 1983: 54–59; see also Kaufmann 1983.

7 In the Federal Republic of Germany about 1500 laws and 2900 decrees issued by the federal government are in force. On the level of the Länder there are additional laws and above all more decrees and administrative order, e.g., in Baden-Württemberg more than 80,000. This bulk of legal norms is now supplemented by decrees issued by the authorities of the European Community. For an account of the German discussion see Kaufmann 1985.

8 This sketch of the political situation refers to one country and the lines of discussion obviously vary between countries. The problems just mentioned may be of less concern, e.g., in the American public system where the plurality of legal regulations is openly acknowledged and assumed to be settled by equity jurisprudence. There seems to be everywhere, however, a growing concern about the effectiveness of state's intervention.

9 The classic formulation of this position stems from W. I. Thomas: "If men define situations as real, they are real in their consequences." This position has now been proved by evidence of cerebrum research as well as by cognitive psychology. For the development of a sociology of knowledge that takes this state of affairs into account see P. Berger and T. Luckmann 1966. For a more elaborate application to problems of societal steering see Maturana and Varela 1980, and Willke 1983.

References

Berger, P., and T. Luckmann (1966): *The Social Construction of Reality.* Garden City, N.Y.: Doubleday.

Black, D. (1958): *The Theory of Committees and Elections.* Cambridge: Cambridge Univ. Press.

Böhret, C., and W. Jann (1982): "Verwaltungsskandale". *Aus Politik und Zeitgeschichte* B 27/1982: 35–52.

Bohne, E., and H. König (1976): "Probleme der politischen Erfolgskontrolle". *Die Verwaltung* 9/1: 19–38.

Buchanan, J. M., and G. Tullock (1962): *The Calculus of Consent. Logical Foundations of Constitutional Democracy.* Ann Arbor, Mich.: Univ. of Michigan Press.

Buchanan. J. M. (1975): "Public Finance and Public Choice." *National Tax Journal* 28/4: 383–394.

Dahl, R. A., and C. E. Lindblom (1953): *Politics, Economics and Welfare* (2nd ed.). Chicago–London 1976: Univ. of Chicago Press.

Deutsch, K. W. (1963): *The Nerves of Government: Models of Political Communication and Control*. New York: Free Press.

Dettling, W. (ed.) (1980): *Die Zähmung des Leviathan*. Baden-Baden: Nomos.

Downs, A. (1957): *An Economic Theory of Democracy*. New York: Harper.

Easton, D. (1965a): *A Framework for Political Analysis*. Englewood Cliffs, N.J.: Prentice-Hall.

Easton, D. (1965b): *A Systems-Analysis of Political Life*. New York: Wiley.

Eucken, W. (1944): *Die Grundlagen der Nationalökonomie* (4. Aufl.). Jena: Fischer.

Eucken, W. (1955): *Grundsätze der Wirtschaftspolitik* (2. Aufl.). Tübingen: Mohr.

Etzioni, A. (1968): *The Active Society. A Theory of Societal and Political Processes*. New York: Free Press.

Frey, B. S. (1974): "Die Renaissance der politischen Ökonomie." *Schweizerische Zeitschrift für Volkswirtschaft und Statistik* 110/3: 357–406.

Furubotn, E. G., and S. Pejovich (eds.) (1974): *The Economics of Property Rights*. Cambridge, Mass.: Ballinger.

Gough, I. (1979): *The Political Economy of the Welfare State*. London: MacMillan.

Gruchy, A. L. (1972): *Contemporary Economic Thought: The Contribution of Neo-Institutional Economics*. Clifton, N.J.: Kelley.

Grunow, D. (1982): *Bürokratisierung und Debürokratisierung im Wohlfahrtsstaat. Soziologische Analysen und gesellschaftliche Probleme*. Habilitationsschrift. Bielefeld.

Grunow, D., F. Hegner, and F. X. Kaufmann (1978): *Bürger und Verwaltung*. 4 Vols. Frankfurt–New York: Campus.

Habermas, J. (1962): *Strukturwandel der Öffentlichkeit*. Neuwied: Luchterhand.

Hanf, K., F. W. Scharpf (eds.) (1978): *Interorganizational Policy Making*. London: Sage.

Hayek, F. A. von (1967): *Studies in Philosophy, Politics and Economics*. London: Routledge & Paul.

Hoefnagels, H. (1979): *Die neue Solidarität – Ausweg aus der Wachstumskrise*. München: Kösel.

Janowitz, M. (1976): *Social Control of the Welfare State*. New York: Elsevier.

Jöhr, W. A. (1948): *Ist ein freiheitlicher Sozialismus möglich?* Bern: Francke.

Kaufmann, F. X. (ed.) (1979): *Bürgernahe Sozialpolitik. Planung, Organisation und Vermittlung sozialer Leistungen auf lokaler Ebene*. Frankfurt–New York: Campus.

Kaufmann, F. X. (1982a): "Wirtschaftssoziologie, allgemeine." *Handwörterbuch der Wirtschaftswissenschaft*, Vol. 9: 239–267. Stuttgart: G. Fischer.

Kaufmann, F. X. (1982b): "Sozialpolitik: Stand und Entwicklung der Forschung in der Bundesrepublik Deutschland." *Politische Vierteljahresschrift*, Sonderheft 13 Politikwissenschaft und Verwaltungswissenschaft, 344–365. Opladen: Westdeutscher Verlag.

Kaufmann, F. X. (1983): "Das Bielefelder ZiF: Ein Ort interdisziplinärer Forschung." *Merkur. Deutsche Zeitschrift für europäisches Denken* 37/4: 464–468.

Kaufmann, F. X. (1985): "Rechtsgefühl, Verrechtlichung und Wandel des Rechts." *Jahrbuch für Rechtssoziologie und Rechtstheorie*, Bd. 11. Köln–Opladen: Westdeutscher Verlag: 185–202.

Kaufmann, F. X., and H. G. Krüsselberg (eds.) (1984): *Markt, Staat und Solidarität bei Adam Smith*. Frankfurt–New York: Campus.

König, K. (1974): "Programmsteuerungen in komplexen politischen Systemen." *Die Verwaltung* 7/2: 137–158.

Krüsselberg, H. G. (1972): "Das Systemkonzept und die Ordnungstheorie: Gedanken über einige Forschungsaufgaben." In Cassel, D. G. Gutmann, and H. J. Thieme (eds.), *25 Jahre Marktwirtschaft in der Bundesrepublik Deutschland. Konzeption und Wirklichkeit*, 26–45. Stuttgart: G. Fischer.

Leipold, H. (1976): *Wirtschafts- und Gesellschaftssysteme im Vergleich: Grundzüge einer Theorie der Wirtschaftssysteme*. Stuttgart: G. Fischer.

Luhmann, N. (1968): *Zweckbegriff und Systemrationalität. Über die Funktion von Zwecken in sozialen Systemen*. Tübingen: Mohr.

Luhmann, N. (1971): *Politische Planung*. Opladen: Westdeutscher Verlag.

Luhmann, N. (1981): *Soziologische Aufklärung 3. Soziales System, Gesellschaft, Organisation*. Opladen: Westdeutscher Verlag.

Majone, G., and A. Wildavsky (1978): *"Implementation as Evolution."* In Freeman, H. (ed.), *Policy Studies Review Annual – 1978*, 103–117. Beverly Hills: Sage.

Marshall, T. H. (1964): *Class, Citizenship and Social Development*. Garden City: Doubleday.

Maturana, H. R., and F. J. Varela (1980): *Autopoiesis and Cognition: The Realization of the Living*. Dordrecht: Reidel.

May, J. V., and A. B. Wildavsky (1978): *The Policy Cycle*. Beverly Hills: Sage.

Mayntz, R. (1977): "Implementation politischer Programme: Theoretische Überlegungen zu einem neuen Forschungsgebiet." *Die Verwaltung* 10/1: 51–66.

Mayntz, R. (ed.) (1980): *Implementation politischer Programme. Empirische Forschungsberichte*. Königstein: Athenäum.

Mayntz, R. (ed.) (1983): *Implementation politischer Programme II. Ansätze zur Theoriebildung*. Opladen: Westdeutscher Verlag.

Mayntz, R. (1985): "On the Use and Non-Use of Methodological Rules in Social Research". In: Gerhardt U. E. and M. E. Wadsworth (eds.). *Stress and Stigma – Explanation and Evidence in the Sociology of Crime and Illness*, 39–52 Frankfurt: Campus, London: Macmillan and New York: St. Martins Press.

Meter, D., and C. van Horn (1975): "The Policy-Implementation-Process. A Conceptual Framework." *Administration and Society* 6/4: 445–488.

Mises, L. von (1922): *Die Gemeinwirtschaft. Untersuchungen über den Sozialismus*. Jena: Fischer.

Müller, D. (1976): "Public Choice: A Survey." *Journal of Economic Literature* 14/2: 395–433.

Neuberger, E., and W. J. Duffy (1976): *Comparative Economic Systems: A Decision-Making Approach*. Boston: Allyn & Bacon.

Niskanen, W.(1971): *Bureaucracy and Representative Government*. Chicago: Aldine.

Olson, M.(1965): *The Logic of Collective Action: Public Goods and the Theory of Groups*. Cambridge, Mass.: Harvard Univ. Press.

Ostrom, V. (1974): *The Intellectual Crisis in American Public Administration* (Rev. Ed.). Alabama: Univ. Press.

Pressmann, J., and A. Wildavsky (1973): *Implementation*. Berkeley: Univ. of Calif. Press.

Robson, W. A. (1976): *Welfare State and Welfare Society*. London: Allen & Unwin.

Schaefer, G. F. (1974): "A General Systems Approach to Public Policy Analysis." *Policy and Politics* 2/4 (June): 331–346.

Scharpf, F. W., B. Reissert, and F. Schnabel (1976): *Politikverflechtung*. Vol. 1: *Theorie und Empirie des kooperativen Föderalismus in der Bundesrepublik*. Kronberg/Ts.: Scriptor, Athenäum.

Scharpf, F. W. (1979): "Die Rolle des Staates im westlichen Wirtschaftssystem: Zwischen Krise und Neuorientierung." In Weizsäcker, C. C. v. (ed.), *Staat und Wirtschaft*. Schriften des Vereins für Socialpolitik, N. F. Bd. 102: 15–44. Berlin: Duncker & Humblot.

Schenk, K. E. (ed.) (1978): *Ökonomische Verfügungsrechte und Allokationsmechanismen in Wirtschaftssystemen*. Berlin: Duncker & Humblot.

Schumpeter, J. A. (1918): Die Krise des Steuerstaats. Repr. in *Aufsätze zur Soziologie*, 1–71. Tübingen: Mohr, 1953.

Sharkansky, I. (1979): *Wither the State? Politics and Public Enterprise in Three Countries.* Chatham, N.J.: Chatham House.

Thiemeyer, Th. (1970): *Gemeinwirtschaftlichkeit als Ordnungsprinzip. Grundlegung einer Theorie gemeinnütziger Unternehmen.* Berlin: Duncker & Humblot.

Titmuss, R. (1958): *Essays on 'The Welfare State'.* London: Allen & Unwin.

Wagener, F.(1979): "Der öffentliche Dienst im Staat der Gegenwart". In *Verhandlungen der Vereinigung deutscher Staatsrechtslehre,* Vol. 37: 215–266. Berlin–New York: De Gruyter.

Wahl, R. (1980): "Die bürokratischen Kosten des Rechts- und Sozialstaats." *Die Verwaltung* 13/3: 273–296.

Wilensky, H. L. (1975): *The Welfare State and Equality. Structural and Ideological Roots of Public Expenditures.* Berkeley–Los Angeles–London: Univ. of California Press.

Williamson, O. E. (1975): *Markets and Hierarchies. Analysis and Antitrust Implications.* New York–London: Free Press, MacMillan.

Willke, H. (1983): *Entzauberung des Staates. Überlegungen zu einer sozietalen Steuerungstheorie.* Königstein/Ts.: Athenäum.

Winch, D. (1978): *Adam Smiths Politics. An Essay in Historiography Revision.* Cambridge: Univ. Press.

Wollmann, H. (1984): "Policy Analysis: Some Observations on the West German Scene." In: *Policy Science* 17: 27–47.

Zentrum für interdisziplinäre Forschung der Universität Bielefeld: *Jahresbericht 1981.* Bielefeld.

Zentrum für interdisziplinäre Forschung der Universität Bielefeld: *Jahresbericht 1982.* Bielefeld.

Zentrum für interdisziplinäre Forschung der Universität Bielefeld: *Jahresbericht 1983.* Bielefeld. (This annual report is avialable also in Enlish.)

2. Development of the Public Sector: Trends and Issues

Dieter Grunow

Abstract

In this chapter an attempt is made to sketch a scenario of the development of "the public sector" – defined here very broadly as task fulfillment by persons and organizations under public law and/or with public funds and/or under formalized public control. Seen from a historical point of view it seems to be most satisfactory to specify this development as a multi-level and multi-dimensional process of bureaucratization. *It is argued that this process – along with others (like industrialization, urbanization, and democratization) – has shaped the world in which we live and especially the recent state of affairs in the public sector. We propose to see this general process as an* uncontestable *basis for any specific scientific query about causes, coincidences, and effects of this process. In other words, we might ignore the features of the multi-level bureaucratization process in the public sector but we cannot define its implications and consequences out of existence. Thus, besides some general longitudinal data, the reactions in and of society toward the characteristics and effects of this process can be used as a common point of departure for theoretical analysis and for the reconsidering of scientific concepts.*

2.1 Introduction

As we all know from personal experience as well as from scientific tests (e.g. Hastorf and Cantril 1954), the naive observer does not exist. In the preceding chapter it was argued that "interaction takes place only upon the basis of shared conceptions", and it was indicated that these conceptions have differed among the participants of the ZiF group. This might even lead us to the provocative question: are we talking about the same topic and about an object which can be found in the real world? In fact, it was a sincere point of discussion during the editorial conference whether it might be helpful or even possible to describe the development of "the public sector" in a way that was acceptable to all the authors of this volume – despite of very different disciplinary or theoretical perspectives. At first glance, this seemed to be possible only with recourse to plain empirical facts. But neither the data nor their interpretation can be assumed to be free of conceptualization.

It is not the intention of this chapter to explore the problems of the role of empirical data in relation to theory in detail. A pragmatic point of departure is chosen here: a) The very existence of the ZiF group and the present volume are sufficient indication for our belief that a pre-theoretical communication and understanding is possible. This refers to the fact that scientific definitions of the situation are only one class of definitions among many others, i.e. the definitions of society at large and the definitions of the groups of the population which are influenced by the structures and processes under study. b) In many instances the scientific definition of the situation is irrelevant to societal development, and the reconstruction of the history of doctrines may not allow judgments about the development of the "real world". c) Theories can be (and often are!) brought closer to reality by very different procedures: that is taking account of personal experiences and observations in one's own everyday life; using empirical evidence to confront the concepts with; considering the definition of the situation from other groups in society or even from other (recent or historical) societies.

On the basis of these demands, theories about "the public sector" show different degrees of closeness to societal developments and thus more or less practical relevance to these processes. This does not mean that the less practical theories do not have important functions in the academic discussion. It is our conviction, however, that all conceptual endeavors need to be reconsidered with regard to societal developments to prevent esoteric and unappreciative seclusions. Although the experience of the ZiF group demonstrated the difficulties of coming to a pre-theoretical understanding of the basic topics and problems we are dealing with, it did also show that it is not impossible. This experience is taken as legitimation for the following attempt to describe the emergence of the *research problem* not as result of a scientist's biography (as in the preceding chapter), but as an evolution-ary process of modern (western) societies and of the public reference to the problems which accompany this process.

2.2 The Development of the Public Sector as an Important Part of the Process of Modernization in Western Societies

As it seems to be much easier to reach a common understanding of historical phases of societal development, we will start our argument with a short outline of the origins of the modern state – following largely the analysis of Elias (1978). The modern state emerges from feudal society and its decay: The scarcity of soil for agriculture due to population growth, the limitation of internal and external expansion, the development of production technology and transport, the increas-ing division of labor and the decay of primitive economy ("Naturalwirtschaft") are important reasons for the changes in the societal powerstructure and its mainte-nance.

In this context, the emergence of the modern state is basically a process of *monopolizing physical coercion* which can be directed toward the society itself or towards enemies from outside. The build-up of a standing military force, the continuous supply of it and the acquisition of the necessary money by tax collection leads to the construction of central state organizations with far-reaching coercive power. This is of course a long lasting process with severe conflicts. But it leads to absolutistic state structures which, besides the monopoly of coercion and tax collection, have acquired a special characteristic still in action and under discussion today: the primacy of expenses over receipts (Elias 1976: 302). As can be observed in recent debates (e.g. about civil disobedience; sharing tax receipts between administrative levels; budget policies), these central characteristics of the historically developed monopolistic positions of the state are still under attack and (possibly) under revision.

With this monopolistic position the important role of the state in further societal development cannot be ignored – although the interpretation of the promoting factors may vary between different writers (e.g. Marx; Durkheim; Schumpeter). In descriptive terms, one can speak of a growth and functional differentiation of the state (Matzner 1982: 55 ff.): For example internal and external security (through police and military forces), guarantee of civil and (later) of political rights, provision of infrastructure to support economic development (especially as a prerequisite for the functioning of capitalistic market economy), provision of social security as a compensation for the negative (disintegrating) effects of industrialization, intervention in economic processes to avoid depression and to regulate the external effects of the economic process (see Musgrave 1959).

As we do not want to enter into a discussion of the causal relationships in societal development (in the sense of modernization), it should be sufficient *to speak about interdependence between the growth of population, economy, government intervention, and political participation* (Flora and Alber 1981: 38 ff.); this multidimensional growth is accompanied by a functional differentiation and division of labor between the parts of society; growing quantities lead to new qualities of interdependencies; the complexity of modern society is increased. Although "the state" is only a part of this complex structure and its development, it should be emphasized that it is neither just an independent factor of modernization (e.g. in terms of absolutistic and monolithic empowerment of the state) nor just a dependent factor (e.g. as "handy man" of capitalistic interest). For our further argument it is important to *accentuate the internal forces of the development of the state* – without ignoring other components of the modernization process. This does not lead to problems of argumentation – at least as long as the *description* of the development is predominant.

Following the conceptualization of modernization processes (e.g. Flora and Heidenheimer 1981), *we will analyze the development of "the state" as a process of bureaucratization* – which coincided with industrialization, urbanization, and democratization in western societies. It is typical of the development we can observe, that through the increasing interdependence of differentiated and specialized parts of society the characteristics of the development in one sector (i.e. the technological development with regard to communication and information processing) sooner or later influence the development in other parts of society. In very general terms, such an interpenetration is called "Vergesellschaftung des Staates" (or even colonization of the state) and "Verstaatlichung der Gesellschaft". It is a symptom of this process that "the state" is "withering away"; that we speak about a "public sector" which has only diffuse boundaries. This leaves us with two options for scientific analysis: one can try to find *exclusive* characteristics for a certain component of modernization; or one can try to make the pervasiveness of certain features of modernization visible. If our preceding arguments are basically correct, the first option might lead to highly artificial or explicit normative arguments while the second option allows for a stronger empirical orientation – but has to struggle with the complex interdependencies of "the real world".

Nevertheless the following discussion of bureaucratization will follow the second option and thus will evade, but not ignore!, simplified and unidimensional conceptualizations of the process of bureaucratization – as represented by many well-known scholars:

– Saint-Simon and his late followers (e.g. Ellul, Schelsky) see bureaucratization as a desirable (!) aspect of technological development; state authority assumes the character of technocracy.
– Elias describes bureaucratization as an undesirable (!) aspect of monopolization of expertise and power – on the way toward expertocracy.
– Marx and his late followers/interpreters (e.g. Marcuse, Habermas) describe bureaucratization as a transitory phase of state authority (which is a necessary counterpart to capitalist industrialization and production) which can be overcome in socialist and communist societies.
– Weber describes bureaucratization as the development of technically efficient bodies of administration *and* as the emergence of a legal and rational form of state authority; his value judgments about this twofold process are *ambivalent:* on the one hand, technical efficiency is an important prerequisite for problem-solving in society; on the other, the emerging administrative bodies are "dangerous" tools for the empowerment of the state, as possible factors of power and authority for their own sake – which may outrule economic *and* political forces. Thus Weber was anxious to emphasize the importance of democratic-political control of bureaucracy to prevent a continuous loss of self-determination and freedom of the citizen as a consequence of the bureaucratization of society.
– Parsons and Luhmann describe bureaucratization in the context of the increasing complexity and division of labor in modern society which necessitates hierarchical control of compliance to rules and regulations.

It is quite clear that all of these conceptualizations have some interesting questions and arguments to contribute to the discussion of the bureaucratization process. But it is also obvious that each can be criticized for many reasons (see Schluchter 1972, 1980 for such a discussion). For further analysis the *lack of empirical evidence* for their theories is the most important reason *not* to follow one of these lines of argument. *We will not separate related aspects of the development of "the state"*, but prefer to use the term "public sector" as a circumscription of those tasks, actions and institutions which are based on public law and/or public finance – which in principle are founded in the constitution. This includes many different functions and organizational forms, because sometimes public funds are the only tie which binds fields of actions into the public sector. Analyzing the development of *"the public sector"* in terms of the process of bureaucratization (as part of the modernization of societies in general) means asking very basic questions about the increase in administrative bodies of the bureaucratic-rational type (in the sense of Weber); about the quantitative expansion of the public sector as a whole; about the changing forms of empowerment of public authorities vis-à-vis the citizens and the society at large. As has been substantiated elsewhere (Grunow 1982), this task can best be accomplished by observing and describing bureaucratic phenomena and their development on different levels of sociological analysis, the individual, the organizational, the societal level, etc.

2.3 The Development of the Public Sector as a Process of Bureaucratization

Following the above arguments, bureaucratization can be defined as a long-term process in the expansion of state interventions with special, "bureaucratic" forms of societal problem-solving. During the last 100 years – which is of special interest for our analysis – these interventions have been increasingly based on positive law and are institutionalized in very different organizational structures and processes. Thus the term "public sector" seems to be most adequate for the delimitation of the field under study.

Although many historical epochs have had processes of bureaucratization (e.g. Egypt, the Roman Empire, etc.), their relevance for societal development seems to have been smaller than the impact of bureaucratization on modern (western) societies. The main reasons for this are seen (Schluchter 1979: 9 ff.) in the process of industrialization which enforced further centralization of state functions and an expansion of public responsibility for the social security of the industrial work force. Independently of special theoretical perspectives (i.e. power elite concepts, pluralism concepts, Stamokap concepts), an *increasing interdependence* and even structural similarity of politics and economy can be seen in the last 100 years (see Polanyi 1944). In ancient regimes, the contradiction between political and economic conditions limited the expansion of bureaucratic forms for societal problem-solving. For the 20th century, Weber noted basic similarities between (capitalistic) modes of production and the "rational" form of bureaucratic authority of the state. Both spheres use expertise and technical-efficient functioning intensively. Thus bureaucratization as a *quantitative* expansion of a mode of problem solving, typical of the public sector, did not have to be enforced *against* the economy but was developed with it. This – historically rather new – interdependence between the state and the private economy also has the effect that the phenomena of bureaucracy cannot be confined to the public sector. The *process* of bureaucratization can only be understood by uncovering the interrelationships (especially the reinforcing ones) *between* different societal sectors. The multi-level analysis of bureaucratization has to render this possible – whereby empirical materials will be used to underscore our attempts to draw a common, pre-theoretical picture of the development of the public sector. To avoid confusion and redundancy *we'll use mainly data from West Germany*. This does not mean that differences between western industrialized countries can and should be ignored; but it is our conviction that on our level of argumentation the empirical evidence is – often in contrast to ideological emphasis – rather similar (see, for example, Kudrle and Marmor 1981).

Organizational Bureaucratization

In almost all theories of bureaucracy and bureaucratization the organizational aspects play a major role. More and more functions for societal survival and development are carried out within organizational contexts. As Presthus (1979) remarks, we are living in an organizational society, and we are members of increasing numbers of different organizations (or secondary systems). Bureaucratization means two things in this context:

– a growing number of organizations adopt bureaucratic characteristics;
– the bureaucratic characteristics are intensified in each organization.

In the latter argument we follow the definition of the bureaucratic organization as a concept with many dimensions (Hall 1963; Litwak 1961; Pugh and Hickson 1971). These dimensions are seen as continua on which empirically based assessments of organizations can be registered. We can then differentiate between organizations with varying degrees of bureaucratic characteristics – based on scores within the following continua (according to Weber's criteria):

– *division of labor* in a more or less detailed and complicated way;
– *hierarchical chain of authority and control* with more or less hierarchical levels and a larger or smaller span of control;
– *formalization and standardization of organizational processes* with varying intensity;
– *documentation (files) about organizational decisions;*
– *impersonal forms of interaction between staff members;*
– *formal qualifications of staff members* as prerequisite for membership and advancement in the organization;
– *rational discipline* governing the behavior of the staff members by accepting the commands from above without criticism;
– *contracts for a long time* or even for the whole life span (tenure positions), but at the same time separation of the staff from the ownership of the technical infrastructure of the organization.

Although different authors might emphasize only some of these dimensions for empirical analysis (cf. Hall 1963: 34 f.), most of them agree on the general catalogue. *Organizational bureaucratization* can now be defined as the process of adopting stronger bureaucratic characteristics *within* organizations.

Intuitively it is quite clear that we can observe a process of *organizational* bureaucratization in the public sector during the last decades in western societies. But it is very difficult to prove such a process empirically. Little is known about the longterm development of public institutions with regard to bureaucratic measures: the increase of written instructions; the standardization of administrative processes; and the diversification and specialization of staff qualifications are the most obvious evidence of organizational bureaucratization:

– using the situation in Germany as an example we can show a trend toward the *growth of organizations* in the public sector (measured as the number of personnel employed). (Schmid and Treiber 1975: 84; Mayntz 1978: 50; Hamburg 1978: 25); it has to be noted, though, that the growth rates differ between specific functions of the public sector, being especially steep in the fields of social welfare;

– another very visible expansion of bureaucratic forms to solve societal problems in public organizations is the increase of rules and regulations guiding the actions of the public servants; in Germany, 1480 *"Bundesgesetze"* and 2880 *"Rechtsverordnungen des Bundes"* were effective in 1977 – only 280 (resp. 420) of them had been effective already before 1969; the German *"Bundesgesetzblatt"* contained 1082 pages in 1956 and 3886 pages in 1975 (Derlien 1980: 12; Oschatz 1979); similar trends are reported by Bennett and Johnson (1979) for the U.S.;
– the use of data processing technology in public administration (as part of the process toward impersonal expertise in the functioning of bureaucratic organizations) has increased the building of hierarchies and the trend toward centralized control (Brinckmann et al. 1981: 135); the workload of a public servant might even be put upon public display on a weekly or daily basis (Grunow et al. 1978).
– with the growth of public institutions, the specialization of the personnel has been increased ("Fachmenschentum" in the sense of Weber), and the number of professions employed within the public sector has grown (Bücker-Gärtner et al. 1977).

Although we have found a remarkable lack of precise empirical knowledge about "biographies of organizations in the public sector" (for an example see Smith 1968), the data cited above as well as everyday experience makes it plausible to speak of a trend toward *organizational* bureaucratization in the public sector during the last 5–10 decades. But the application of bureaucratic principles to newly developed fields of state interventions, such as social welfare functions, indicate quite clearly that not all dimensions of organizational bureaucratization can be intensified simultaneously and unidirectionally.

Chart 1

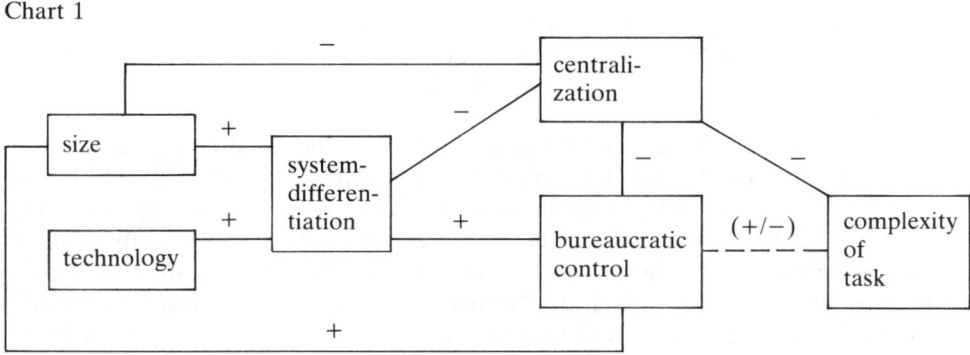

(Source: Gebert 1974:77)

The growth of organizations during the last decades can only be accepted as a partial proof for organizational bureaucratization. Neither can the age of an organization be used to infer bureaucratic characteristics, because newly built up public institutions *start* with all relevant bureaucratic measures.

Many of the data summarized by Gebert (see above) are collected outside the public sector. They indicate similar developments in state and in business organizations. It can be concluded that there is some relevant empirical evidence for *organizational bureaucratization* – but not a maximization of all bureaucratic characteristics of organizations. As has been shown by many authors, the different measures of bureaucratic organizations cannot be maximized simultaneously. An attempt to do this with one leads to contraproductivity in another or in the overall problem-solving capacity of the organization. These, then, are the topics for the "critics of bureaucracy".

The Process of Interactional Bureaucratization

Although the arguments about organizational bureaucratization are widely shared, it is very doubtful whether they give a tolerably exact or even a complete picture of the bureaucratic institutions within the public sector. Objections relate to the simplification of categories used in current methods of data collection (e.g. by asking only top administrators about "their" organization). As the importance of *informal processes in organizations* is known from human-relations studies of the thirties (Roethlisberger and Dickson 1939), the question has to be asked as to how much the structural arrangements determine the observable processes of interaction and decision making. Is it adequate to speak of a process of *interactional* bureaucratization in the public sector during the last decades?

Interactional bureaucratization is defined as intensifying the bureaucratic characteristics of interpersonal relationships and interactions, that is the introduction of impersonal, asymmetric, selective, and ritualized interaction patterns. The importance of this process becomes more obvious when we recognize that it is not restricted to the interaction between public officials but is also relevant for interactions across the boundaries (with the clientele of public administration) and for people outside public institutions. Whereas the first type of interactional bureaucratization might be expected to be a result of organizational growth and organizational bureaucratization, the other two types are much more noteworthy – although for all of them an empirical verification of the development is quite difficult.

The relevance of interactional bureaucratization in the relationship between the public sector and its clientele (cf. Grunow and Hegner 1978; Grunow 1981) stems from the authoritarian function of public institutions towards specific citizen groups or society at large. In this context the citizen is just the bottomlink in the chain of command and control. The process of interactional bureaucratization across the boundaries of organizations includes "transfers" of *internal* procedures. One that is often criticized is the use of formulas and procedures which are suitable for electronic data processing but not for dealing with the clientele of public administration. This reinforces the decrease of *personal* responsibility and accountability by the staff in public institutions.

It is not possible to prove that there has been a strong tendency towards interactional bureaucratization, but there is enough evidence (Grunow 1982: section 4.2.2.2) to make such a definition of the situation plausible. Some qualitative measures give additional support: increased contacts between citizens and large bureaucratic organizations of the public sector; the increased number of people working in such organizations and being familiar with this form of interaction; the increasing use of computer technology as the medium of interaction between public institutions and their clientele and as a symbiotic mechanism for the exertion of bureaucratic and technocratic authority; the increase in the number of rules which even regulate the *interaction* process (Grunow and Hegner 1980). Interactive control of the environment of bureaucratic organizations might even exceed boundary transactions. If people are forced to interact along bureaucratic lines so often in their everyday life, they might eventually use these actions in "private" situations as well. Although this subject has not been worked on empirically, results from other areas of research seem to support the expectation: the trend toward other-directedness (Riesman 1950); the authoritarian procedures of primary socialization (McKinley 1964); or the increase in "borderline patients" in psychiatry (Rohde-Dachser 1982). These examples do not indicate directly a transfer of specific interaction patterns from bureaucratic public institutions into the private spheres of everyday life, but a development and/or diffusion of specific personality traits within the bureaucratic context which influence interactions outside such organizations. This leads us to another level of bureaucratization analysis.

Bureaucratization of Personality

It is a well-known fact that the members of an organization adapt themselves to or are forced to comply with the bureaucratic structures and processes of their work environment. Different typologies of adaptation have been developed (Gouldner 1957; Reissman 1949; Presthus 1962) which show *different bureaucratic features of personality:* rule orientation, unconditional obedience, dogmatism, risk avoidance, need for security (Bosetzky and Heinrich 1980: 119 f.; Steinkemper 1974; Putnam 1973).

If *bureaucratization of personality* is defined as a process of increasing these features in the members of public bureaucracies, it is very difficult to find empirical evidence for it. For Germany a comparison with the Nazi regime might show a reduction of bureaucratic personality characteristics. But it might also be expected that there is a shift from obedience and dogmatism to increasing risk avoidance, lack of responsibility and need for security. Longitudinal data which might clarify this hypothesis in a strict methodological sense are not available.

But it might be more important to describe processes of the bureaucratization of personality outside organizational or occupational socialization. It is well documented that public bureaucracies "attract" certain types of personality more often than others (for West Germany, see the study of Luhmann and Mayntz 1973). These processes of *self-selection* could be a reason for the existing, and probably increasing, proportion of bureaucratic personality structures in the population at large – even before they become members of bureaucratic work organizations. Although there is no clear evidence available to prove a continuous increase in bureaucratic features of personality in western societies during the past decades, there are oscillations on a rising overall level of adherence to such personality traits.

The Process of Societal Bureaucratization

If the *distribution* of bureaucratic orientations and dispositions in society is discussed, we have to interpret this as a *societal* phenomenon, as a part of the cultural system (of norms and values). In this context we'll use the term *"collective bureaucratization of society"* to describe the increase in such features among the members of society. It exceeds the increase among public servants and other members of bureaucratic organizations. Although there are many arguments about value changes ("Wertewandel") in western societies (Inglehart 1977; Noelle-Neumann 1975; Zentralarchiv für empirische Sozialforschung 1981) – which are identified empirically as a decrease of traditional work orientations and achievement ethics as well as an increasing criticism of large-scale bureaucracies and their alienating effects – there is little explicit knowledge about the diffusion of bureaucratic orientations within the population.

As can be expected in an extremely differentiated, modern society the available empirical evidence shows a rather ambivalent picture. While the population seems to lose a consciousness of law and justice which is based on shared moral convictions, it is increasingly confronted with legal and administrative procedure (Kaufmann 1984). Laws and regulations become a pervasive tool not only for the steering of decision making in the public sector but as an everyday ingredient of public officials as well as of citizens, especially as clients of public administration (see for example, Grunow et al. 1978). Following the acquisition of this positivistic and legalistic orientation an increasing number of citizens try to regulate even their private quarrels with the neighbor by appealing to the courts. A real wave of such appeals are leaving the courts without a chance for decisions-in-time. This trend often coincides with the plea for a more authoritarian state and for more rigid public officials – especially in their relation to minority groups and the "underdogs".

But there are also countertrends visible which might result from the same experiences of societal regulation and bureaucratization. These countertrends include the growth of initiative groups and self-help-movements which are anti-etatistic, anti-bureaucratic and anti-expertocratic in their orientation and their goals. Although some of these notions might be supported by a "silent majority" of the population, the everyday activities of the citizens are giving much more evidence of further collective bureaucratization of society.

This is, in addition, reinforced by another (more often described) form of *societal* bureaucratization: the quantitative and qualitative expansion of bureaucratic organizations in the public sectors as well as an expansion of this way of societal problem solving into other sector of society, especially in the economic sector.

In other words, "the analysis" of the development of the public sector is mostly confined to what we call *societal bureaucratization by diffusion of bureaucratic organization principles*. The trend data available give empirical support to this narrow view of bureaucratization processes. But they are often of a highly aggregated nature which makes a very cautious interpretation necessary. Typical contents of this empirical material are:

– the increase in staff members of public institutions (in general) – see the graphs in the appendix, pp. 48–50 –, where besides the general trend in terms of relative and absolute growth the differences between different areas of the public sector become evident; this includes counter-trend developments (especially in the *central* administration);

– the tendency described above is also reflected in the government expenditure which is compared over the last 7 decades; if one excludes the peaks due to World War II expenditures for warfare, on overall increase, not only in absolute but also in relative terms, of public expenditure can be identified (see graphs on p. 54 in the appendix); but again, these data are not very illuminating if one does not acknowledge the differences in major areas of public tasks; the dominance of the expansion of welfare functions is again visible (see also chart 3 of appendix);

– much more evidence for the debate about the development of the public sector and its problems can be obtain by less aggregated data; the example of Hamburg (see p. 51/52 of the appendix) shows changes in the composition of personnel with reference to functions and formal training within the short period of 6 years: especially the number of teachers, doctors, nurses and social workers but also of tax administrators and data typists has increased;

– another important indicator of societal bureaucratization (with reference to the public sector) discussed here is the increase in the number of public institutions in almost all sectors of society; as they tend to remain even when they lose their functions, it is worth mentioning that since 1930 about 350 *additional* public institutions have been founded in Germany on the *national level* of public administration alone; another well-known expansion lies in the number of organizations which receive support from public finance and thus have to adapt to bureaucratic procedures of budget control and task fulfillment;

– another indication of the general trend can be seen in the quantitative and qualitative *increase of rules and regulations* in the sense that they cover *new fields* of societal structures and processes; a very obvious example has been the laws etc. on environmental protection in recent years.

Even if many of the data available are not directly usable as a measure of the development of the public sector, it can be argued – by summing up all the available evidence – that the *quantitative increase of bureaucratic organizations* within and outside the public sector and their influence on ever more aspects of people's lives and/or societal problem solving is one of the central features of societal bureaucratization. These organizations are also the main object of criticism of bureaucratization because they indicate an *increasing asymmetry of power and authority between bureaucratically organized decision making and the less organized public at large*. If one analyzes such a macro-phenomenon, it is very difficult to distinguish between the degree of bureaucratization in the public sector and in other sectors. Although there are different points of view from which this situation can be interpreted and judged, the development of a new "corporatistic" power-structure as an ingredient of societal bureaucratization is evident (Schmitter 1974).

The Process of Interorganizational Bureaucratization

Increased links between bureaucratic organizations in the public sector add a new quality to bureaucratization in addition to purely quantitative expansion. As Weber had foreseen (in principle), parallel development of bureaucratization and rationalization within the public sector (*and* the economic system) leads to *interorganizational bureaucratization* and to a new quality of empowerment of *corporate* bureaucracy.

For a more detailed analysis of interorganizational bureaucratization, three different aspects have to be considered:

- the *growth of networks of bureaucratic organizations* – either by forcing network-members to bureaucratic standards or by selecting only bureaucratic organizations for the network expansion;
- the increasing intensity and complexity of relationships between organizations in the network thus leading to a *multiplicity of dependencies;*
- the bureaucratization of the *relationships* (exchange processes, co-ordination, co-operation, etc.) between organizations as such.

The *first two aspects* are well-known trends both in the public sector ("Politikver-flechtung"; positive and negative co-ordination among public institutions, cf. Franz: Ch. 23) and in the private (esp. the economic) sector, with the latter showing very complicated, even international partner- und ownerships. As the complex interdependence of problems (environmental protection is one of the most recent examples) become more evident, the idea that everything is connected with everything else becomes a practical problem of "networking". The *third aspect* of interorganizational bureaucratization is not just a necessary result of the other two. There is no need to have *bureaucratic* relationships between two or more bureaucratic organizations; they could equally be in a situation of bargaining or of competition.

Interorganizational bureaucratization in this sense can be defined as a process by which the relationships (interaction, communication, exchange of goods, etc.) become standardized and formalized. To settle a contract by a hand-shake seems to be an anachronism within this context. Communication and control structures become hierarchical, the functional division of labor becomes more selective, the recruitment and placement principles are more and more dependent on formal qualifications and not on performance on the job, and so forth. *The relationships between fomerly independent organizations become bureaucratized.* Interorganizational networks become very similar to a *megabureaucracy.* Their notable effects lie in the relationships between organizations with different structures and styles of problem solving. Bureaucratization of interorganizational networks leads to a further standardization of organizational structures in society. Especially in the field of social policy, such trends can be observed (cf. Grunow and Hegner 1980) when voluntary organizations and private initiatives are forced to adapt to the bureaucratic rules and regulations of the public institutions, which provide the necessary financial means. Quite often, they lose their specific problem-solving competence through such an adaptation.

Summary

It is a truism that arguments about bureaucracy always depend on the definition used. But seldom enough it is concluded that the definition chosen limits scientific insight and the practical relevance of the analysis. Therefore we have emphasized that "the public sector" cannot be confined to "hierarchical decision-making processes" or to the exertion of power and authority. And vice versa: bureaucracy is not only an important characteristic of the public sector but also of other sectors in society. This special feature makes the concept of bureaucratization – as developed here – so adequate and fruitful for the description of the development of the public sector: This development is not primarily an internal change within closed boundaries of public institutions but an expansion into society and a blurring of border lines.

Bureaucratization has been defined as a long-term process involving a quantitative and qualitative increase of bureaucratic characteristics in western industrialized societies – to be observed and empirically described on different levels of sociological analysis. In general, there is little empirical material which could be used to describe these *processes* precisely. Longitudinal data or comparable studies at different stages of development are rare. Many contributions just describe the status quo. They do not include long-term comparisons and thus come to precipitate assertions about the novelty of the *current* bureaucratic phenomena. But if the following chart gives an adequate assessment of the state of bureaucratization analysis, it allows some general conclusions.

Chart 2: Synopsis of empirical evidence for bureaucratization processes

extent of empirical verification of bureaucratization processes / type of bureaucratization process	many studies available (reliable empirical verification)		only few studies available (partial empirical verification)		no studies available (no empirical verification)
	bureaucratiz. existing throughout	bureaucratiz. existing partially	extensive evidence for bureaucratization	little evidence for bureaucratization	bureaucratizat. plausibl. presumed
1 organizational bureaucratization in general/quantitative		×			
1.1 hierarchy		×			
1.2 division of labor		×			
1.3 formalization and standardization	×				

Chart 2 continued

type of bureaucratization process / extent of empirical verification of bureaucratization processes	many studies available (reliable empirical verification)		only few studies available (partial empirical verification)		no studies available (no empirical verification) bureaucratizat. plausibl. presumed
	bureaucratiz. existing throughout	bureaucratiz. existing partially	extensive evidence for bureaucratization	little evidence for bureaucratization	
1.4 impersonality of workflow		×			
1.5 emphasis on written communication	×				
1.6 formal qualification of personnel	×				
1.7 tenure position	×				
1.8 rational discipline				×	
2 interactional bureaucratization 2.1 within the organ.		×			
2.2 boundary transact.			×		
2.3 outside the organ.					×
3 person-related bureaucratization 3.1 members of organ.		×			
3.2 non-members					×
4 societal bureaucratization 4.1 bur. of the state	×				
4.2 sectoral bureauc.				×	
5 interorganizational bureaucratization 5.1 network growth			×		
5.2 bur. of relationships			×		

First of all, it must be acknowledged that the phenomena of bureaucratization cannot be understood in their overall relevance for our societies by considering one single dimension (e.g. hierarchical chain of command) in a single area of societal problem solving (e.g. in law-enforcing sections of police departments). The process of *bureaucratization has many faces and many promoting factors*. Thus, it would be insufficient to comment only on the available data on the internal changes of the public sector – mainly in the sense of organizational bureaucratization. It is our conviction that only the *multi-level-analysis* of the bureaucratization process in and across the boundaries of the public sector, as one very fundamental component of modernization in western societies, offers a sufficient basis for more detailed theoretical and empirical questions, as discussed in this volume. Although our approach has not been atheoretic, it has tried to summarize and organize multiple and diffuse notions and data about the development of the public sector.

Only by consideration of as many features as possible, might one be able to *understand* or *explain why* this overall process of bureaucratization is still going on – despite being subject to so many criticisms. It is our conviction that the forces of bureaucratization can be comprehensively described *as reinforcing effects within and between the different levels of bureaucratic phenomena*. In other words: bureaucratization will continue to expand quantitatively and qualitatively as long as these different levels have catalytic functions for each other. Bureaucratization processes will slow down if and where one feature restricts the further expansion of other manifestations of bureaucratization. Well-known pathologies of bureaucratic organizations (cf. Crozier 1964; Türk 1976; Hood 1976) or often criticized forms of *bureaucratism* (red tape; ineffectiveness; complicated communication channels, etc.) are *not* necessarily examples of the restrictions mentioned above. They might still be a stage of the bureaucratization process which can be overtaken by later developments.

However, there is no complete and empirical sound theory of bureaucratization to explain developments during the last decades in western societies. But there are many relevant hypotheses of limited range which – in toto – give a plausible interpretation of the "forces" underlying the bureaucratization processes: both unforeseen and unwanted consequences of change processes as well as obvious interest-formation and its enforcement. The complex causes of bureaucratization cannot be discussed here (cf. Grunow 1982 for further details). The following chart offers some key-terms as illustrations: the diagonal fields describe *self-contained reinforcement:* each component shows a tendency to enlarge and perfect itself; the other fields (except those on the base line) describe forms of *mutual reinforcement:* the different components of bureaucratization have a mutual catalytic function for each other by selecting or selectively supporting bureaucratic characteristics in other areas of development; the base line describes forms of *"external" reinforcement* by factors which are not genuinely elements of bureaucratization of the public sector: here demands for (further) bureaucratization come from other sectors of society (i.e. the economic system or private households). The *whole* chart offers the basic idea for the explanation of bureaucratization processes. This "idea" includes the notions of overwhelming forces of internal self-interest and external interest toward further bureaucratization on different levels as well as areas of inconsistencies, counter-trends or counter-productive effects. This makes it the

Chart 3: Central hypotheses to explain the process of bureaucratization on different levels of analysis

	Organizational bureaucratization	Interactional bureaucratization	Person-related bureaucratization	Societal bureaucratization	Interorganizat. bureaucratization
Organizational bureaucratization	growth of size; increasing concern with itself	control; schematization, standardization; automation of interaction process	selection accord. to membership requirements; behaviour control	quantitative growth of bur. organiz. f. soc. task fulfillment	co-ordination and co-optation as an attempt to control the environment
Interactional bureaucratization	furtherance of standardization and formalization of work procedures	ritualization of everyday interaction	group norms and culture of bureau as socialization agents	impersonality of relationships as behavior norm; alienation	standardization of interaction in internal and external relationships
Person-related bureaucratization	self-selection of persons for public service with bureauc. disposition	aversion to contact with people; avoidance of insecurity and conflict	reduction of (cognitive) dissonance i. fav. of bur. dispositions	transfer of agency's value orientation to primary social sphere	interorganizational incompetency and irresponsibility
Societal bureaucratization	reservoir for members of bureaucr. organiz.; social status assignment for organiz. memb.	increasing interactions with org. representatives; citizens adapt to bur. forms of interaction	prevalence of mediocrity (mediocracy); social approval of bur. person. patterns	trend towards ever greater perfection of regulation; value change	dominance of organiz. interests; adaptation pressure on non-bur. organized interes.
Interorganizational bureaucratization	obligation to adept to maximal bureaucratization within the network	tendency towards standardizing interaction styles among org. representatives	development towards the interorganization man/ client	increasing influence of corporatistic power cartels	standardization pressure of bur. relationships in interorg. networks
"External" factors of influence	national organizational culture; increase of tasks; achievement of personnel interests	pressure for rationalization; demand for formal equality of treatment	achievement of personnel interests; need for security; risk avoidance	development of social problems; market failure; dynamics of increasing demands	increasing interdependence betw. problems, policies, interests; admin.structure

more necessary to look closely into *selected fields* developed in the preceding argument.

2.4 Bureaucratization of the Public Sector, Reactions of "The Public", and Possibilities of Debureaucratization Processes

It has been argued at the beginning of this paper that the process of bureaucratization as *the most prominent element in the modernization of the public sector* might be influenced by scientific conceptualizations but is not dependent on it. Thus, the history of conceptualizations of such a process might differ markedly from the characteristics of the process itself. The size of this difference depends largely on the *empirical* references that are made when conceptualizing the development of the public sector.

The multi-level process of bureaucratization is only one type of "real-world reference field" for the specification of relevant issues of scientific analysis. It might be too broad in scope to ease the selection of "contestable issues" for an interdisciplinary group of scientists as assembled in the ZiF. Two additional points of departure can be used to support a common understanding of basic questions and problems to be worked on: a) the observation of (critical) reactions of "the public" and b) the analysis of limitations, counter-trends and counter-productive effects of the bureaucratization process. Some examples of these types of reference points for further detailed analyses are given in the following.

During the last years *debureaucratization* of the public sector has become a political and a public issue in West Germany as well as in other OECD countries. Many forces combine to promote "the career" of such an issue which is as old as public administration itself (for a historical analysis, see Jacoby 1973). These forces are related to the disappointment of the public in the results of large-scale planning in the seventies; to the fiscal crisis that has arisen especially in the context of welfare provision; to unemployment and negative "growth" in the economy; to the shift of a large majority of voters towards conservative political parties, and so forth. The "career" which the debureaucratization issue has made in the public debate is also due to the diverse use of the basic term "bureaucracy". The greater the number of groups and institutions of society which are engaged in the debate on this issue, the greater the number of connotations it will carry and the greater the diversity of practical aims underlying the arguments. This tendency very often leads to an *overestimation* of the existing forces toward change, because the attention which the public issue receives is due to *controversial and even self-defeating positions* based on a common denominator (Luhmann 1970). In West Germany, we can observe four objects of criticism in the public debate relating to debureaucratization (Grunow 1982: 65 ff.):

(a) *Single aspects of administrative activity experienced directly, as an object of the criticism of bureaucracy:* Any partial phenomenon of public administration may be the object of criticism; with particular frequency, citizens' experiences with the public officials are made the subject of discussion (that is the *direct* contact between administration and the citizen); likewise, the location of agencies, opening hours, administrative procedures, the forms used, and the like, are subject to criticism.

(b) *Administrative systems, organizational and interorganizational structures as target of the criticism of bureaucracy:* In this context, the administrative structure as a whole, that is the macro-organization (in terms of the horizontal and vertical levels of government), federalism, and the principle of departmentalization is made the object of critical considerations.

(c) *Prerequisites and the framework of administrative action:* If state activity is conceived in this context primarily as the operation and task fulfillment of public administration, its prerequisites and framework are to be found in the political subsystem, but also in other subsystems of society. The most important problems arise from the ever growing body of legislation; this development is furthermore complemented by jurisdiction which still added to the trend towards all-encompassing regulation. The problems of the financial basis of state activity have also to be taken into consideration; for instance, the costs of administration and the provision of the necessary financial means.

(d) *State activity in general as an object of the criticism of bureaucracy:* The actual debate on public bureaucracy, the costs of administration and the welfare state in general increasingly ends up with the question as to *how much state activity is necessary and desirable.* The prevailing criticism charges the state (both administration and politics) with having assumed too many tasks. Measures of regulative administration (e.g. police, tax administration, etc.) are criticized as are social security benefits and transfer payments. Still other criticisms relate to the planning and control functions which the state has assumed in various areas (in particular in the economy, in environmental protection. etc.).

It has been mentioned that the bureaucratization process has always been accompanied by severe criticism. As the manifestations of this process become more widespread in society, the *diversification* of criticism and of the underlying motives is self-evident and not surprising. Thus, it is not at all clear how the processes described can be evaluated, rejected or justified. Different, if not antagonistic interests are at stake if one argues for further bureaucratization or for an attempt towards a *de*bureaucratization. Sometimes bureaucratiziation (in the field of police law enforcement) *and de*bureaucratization (in the field of planning for economic processes or environmental protection) are demanded at the same time. If we want to formulate this argument precisely, we could say that there is *no "state of affairs" in the bureaucratization process that does not have its supporters and its opponents.* No value judgement about bureaucracy is self-evident for all members of society. The purpose of the overview given in the preceding chart is to contribute to our understanding of why this is the case. With regard to de-bureaucratization this means that single counter-trends do not necessarily imply an impact on the *overall* process of bureaucratization. But, after all, there might be self-limiting factors on all levels of bureaucratization which have prevented until now the degree of bureaucratization described in anti-utopian fiction. To explore some of the basic aspects of debureaucratization, we follow the same basic conceptual tools (i.e. multi-level analysis) as above.

In view of the small impact which criticisms of bureaucratization can secure, practical-political propositions toward debureaucratization (i.e. re-privatization of public institutions; de-regulation; decrease of public expenditure) will not serve as guidelines of our argument. Such propositions may very well be omitted because of the counter-powers (toward bureaucratization) and because the public bureaucracies themselves control the process and degree of debureaucratization. The basic premise of our analysis is the *search for self-limiting and self-defeating factors* of bureaucratization itself.

a) Two mechanisms can be described as immanently *limiting* further bureaucratization:
   - trends of quantitative and qualitative bureaucratization constitute *non-linear processes;* apart from the frequently alleged fact that in spite of ongoing bureaucratization obviously "not everything is totally bureaucratized until now" (Kamenka and Krygier 1979), there are more specific examples of such limitations: the increase in rule making, once it has passed a certain level leads to a decline in rule conformity; information overload, over-control and other characteristics of overbureaucratization entail counterproductive effects (see also Türk 1976); taken together, this can be seen as a self-limiting factor in the process of bureaucratization;
   - notwithstanding the overall tendency toward *reinforcement* which is noted between the different levels and components of the bureaucratization process, we can also observe vicious circles and contradictions existing within bureaucratic organizations as mentioned by various scholars in this field. As the most prominent ones we refer to Crozier and Merton; Crozier (1964: 194 f.) gives the following comment:

"The Clerical Agency provided the perfect example of such a generalized vicious circle of close supervision, impersonal rules, and centralization. The frustrations of the different groups, which cannot discuss the decisions that will affect them and must submit to the close supervision of their activities, build up so much that higherups do not feel solid enough to face the problem, and the whole process of decision-making tends to move one rank higher. If people who make decisions do not have to confront those who will be affected by these decisions, tensions are reduced; but frustrations go on, and so does the pressure for centralization. Of course, efforts to change the whole system, to open it up are possible; but such attempts would run counter to the general fear of dependence relationships that is a contingent cultural trait of great relevance for the understanding of the development of bureaucratic system of organization. This fear, in turn, is fed upon and reinforced by the frustrations emerging from the parallel power relationships that are likely to arise in such regulated organizations. The existence of the privileged relationships is the indirect consequence, as we have seen, of the development of impersonality and centralization; it tends to generate a very powerful secondary drive for more centralization and impersonality.

By and large, the common underlying pattern of all the vicious circles that characterize bureaucratic systems is this: the rigidity of task definition, task arrangements, and the human relations network results in a lack of communication with the environment and a lack of communication among the groups. The resulting difficulties, instead of imposing a readjustment of the model, are utilized by individuals and groups for improving their position in the power struggle within the organization. Thus a new pressure is generated for impersonality and centralization, the only solution to the problem of personal privileges."

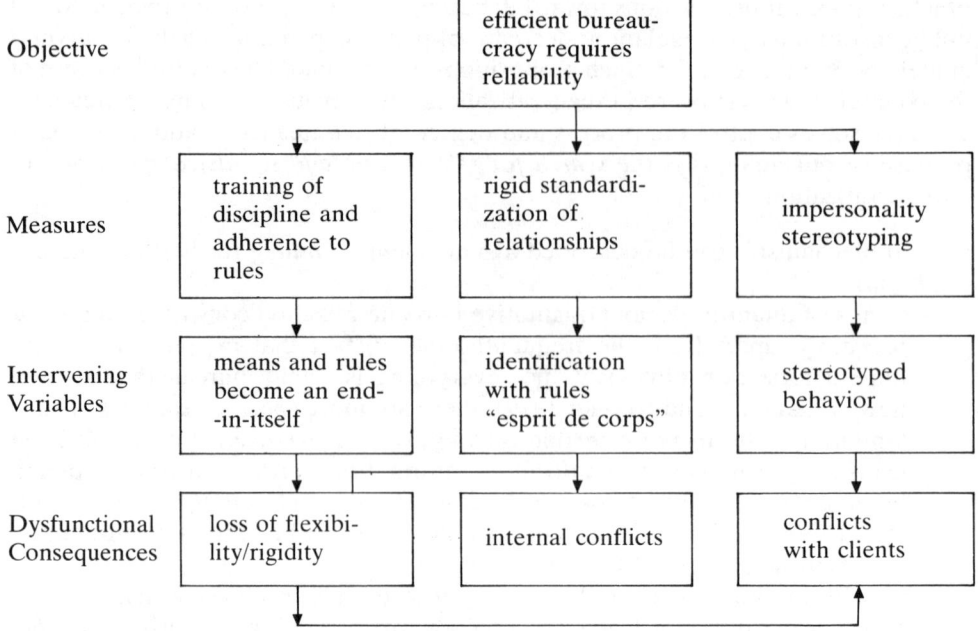

Fig. 1: Merton's Model of Structural Rigidity. *Source*: Türk (1976: 129)

The elaboration of this model towards a "bureaucratic vicious circle" is to be found in Crozier (1964) (see Fig. 2).

Another type of dilemma is typical of the public sector: it has to achieve many different formal goals (legality, economy, effectiveness, responsiveness) *which cannot be clearly (i.e. hierarchically) ordered.* This leads to a temporary adherence to one goal while others are partially ignored, according to relevant public-political demands (see Dunsire: Ch. 16). Thus neither the formal goals of performance nor the different characteristics of internal functioning can be maximized simultaneously. The emphasis on one form of bureaucratization limits of even opposes to the other modes of bureaucratization.

b) Another set of mechanisms is related to what can be called an *incomplete* bureaucratization which is a consequence of the deviant behavior of organization members,of imperfect rules and of the contingencies of external demands and internal processes occurring in public institutions; if these trends are reinforced on purpose, they might lead to a *reduction* of bureaucratic characteristics in the further development of society:

   – the trend toward *professionalization within bureaucratic organizations* (Litwak 1961; Hartmann 1968). Organization members claim greater autonomy with a view to formal rules and hierarchical chains of command;

   – the trend toward informal and *situational bureaucracy* (Müller 1973; Lawrence and Lorsch 1967). Organization members demand more personal contacts and communication and goal-related programming which leaves room for bargaining and discretion within and beyond organizational boundaries;

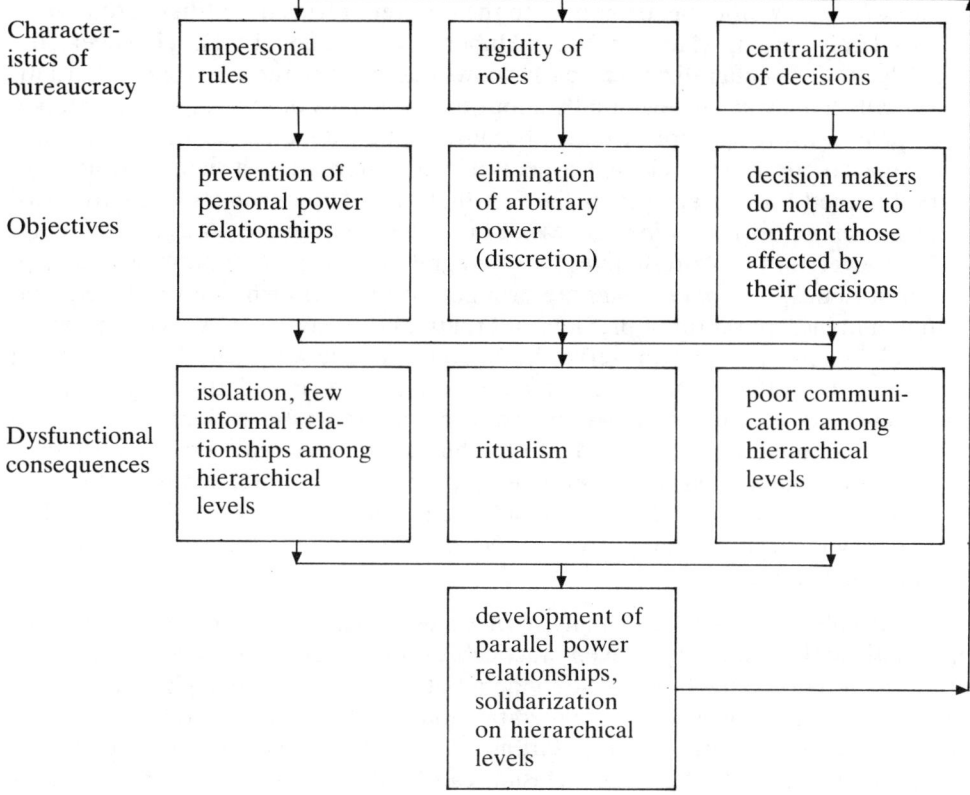

Fig. 2: Crozier's "Bureaucratic Vicious Circle". *Source*: Türk (1976: 130)

- the trend toward a *representative and "comrade" bureaucracy* (Dyson 1979; Bosetzky and Heinrich 1980). The demand for a more adequate representation of the different sections of the population within public institutions and the creation of a fellow feeling among *all* staff members which is to be effected on the basis of an intensive horizontal communication;
- the trend toward *symbolic bureaucracy* (Edelman 1975; Jacobs 1969) which is characterized by symbolic claims on organizational domains and by *non-decision making* in response to declarations concerning actions to be taken.
c) The third set of responses to the process of bureaucratization in the public sector consists of the *development of alternative modes* (i.e. non-bureaucratic forms) of problem solving within and for society. Notwithstanding the dominant trend toward bureaucratic uniformity, the bureaucratization process also "produces" some alternatives and fundamental oppositions, outsiders and dropouts, even from among central public institutions (e.g. ex-generals now participating in the peace movement.) They not merely constitute another pressure group, but seek alternative solutions to societal problems and needs. These solutions range from traditional forms of self-organization, co-operations and voluntary

work (e.g. in welfare associations) to the different forms of self-help groups and social movements (Hegner 1979; Huber 1980; Haller 1981). However, the analysis of bureaucratization clearly shows that most of these concrete alternatives will "die away" or eventually adopt the principles of the bureaucratic mode of problem solving – for instance, because of their dependence on public funds ("Staatsknete"). The relevant aspect of these alternative structures which can be retained for our analysis is the fact that in an "open society" new forms of response/opposition to the process of bureaucratization are *always* developing. Whenever former "alternatives" are integrated into the corporate structure of our societies, *new alternatives* are brought into play. Furthermore, the adaptation and incorporation of previous alternatives is of course a two-sided process: "the" system does not preserve the overall bureaucratic features it possessed before the integration process took place: new forms of thinking (whether economic or ecological) and acting (whether anti-etatistic, solidaric, responsive or competitive) are introduced *into* the bureaucratic system. Thus, alternatives not only come to pass (and eventually expand) outside bureaucratic institutions (in particular of the public sector), but also penetrate "the system" itself; and by this they might play a major role in securing "incomplete bureaucratization" as described above.

The conceptual paths to the analysis of de-bureaucratization processes are not applicable in the same way or even practicable on all levels of analysis. On the basis of the materials available we have made an attempt to indicate some interdependence between the levels of bureaucratization and the chances and prospects of effective de-bureaucratization (see Grunow 1982); it is not possible to describe and discuss them here. A general conclusion can be drawn, though: there are many paths to *de*-bureaucratization; the "overwhelming" process of bureaucratization, however, can only be effectively controlled if many paths are followed *simultaneously* and if the same goals are pursued.

2.5 Summary and Conclusion

In this paper an attempt has been made to sketch a scenario of the development of "the public sector" – defined here very broadly as task fulfillment by persons and organizations under public law and/or with public funds and/or under formalized public control. Seen from a historical point of view it seemed to be most satisfactory to specify this development as a multi-level and multi-dimensional *process of bureaucratization*. It has been argued that this process – besides others (like industrialization, urbanization, and democratization) – has shaped the world we are living in and especially the recent state of affairs in the public sector. We proposed to see this general process as an *uncontestable* basis for any specific scientific query about causes, coincidences, and effects of this process. In other words, we might ignore the features of the multi-level bureaucratization process in the public sector but we cannot define its implications and consequences away. Thus, besides some general longitudinal data, the reactions in and of society toward the characteristics and effects of this process can be used as a common point of departure for theoretical analysis and for the reconsidering of scientific concepts.

Of course, there are legitimate theoretical explorations into any subject which do not bother about what is happening in the real world – the term "Modellplatonismus" is used quite often to describe such an approach. But if it is claimed, as for the work of the ZiF group, that the scientific analyses should refer to recent or future issues and problems in the public sector development, the trends characterized above have to be seen as reference points for the "academic enterprise". In very general terms, the following reference points have been included in our discussion:

- the overall trend of quantitative expansion of the public sector and its institutions (growth of organization);
- the functional differentiation and specification of public tasks and of the structures and processes for task fulfillment, combined with differential trends (expansion *and* contraction);
- the more specific features of organizational, interactional, personal, societal, and interorganizational bureaucratization as well as the overwhelming internal and external reinforcement processes to further bureaucratization;
- the unintended or unexpected "by-products" of different forms of bureaucratization;
- the increasing diffuseness of the boundaries between the public and non-public sectors in society; that is the loss of clear-cut characteristics of "the state";
- the growing interdependence among different areas of the public sector and other sectors of society, especially the capitalist economy, combined with an increasing number of self-produced problems; through this we can expect a (growing) negative balance between societal problems/task production or demands and public-sector problem solutions.

Even if the situation defined in such general terms is acceptable, it only gives a common (sense) problem perception and does not replace a more specific selection of topics for theoretical and empirical analysis. As the present volume will show, very different reference points for this selection are used: special issues of the subject (i.e. finance control or interorganizational interface) are chosen on the basis of individual interest and former academic work; a specific approach is chosen – description of the problem field and/or attempts to explain observed phenomena and/or the proposal of better solutions. For the last mentioned perspective certain value judgments are necessary: is bureaucratization of the public sector seen as a positive, partially positive, partially negative or a negative development? What are the criteria for this judgment? Do they refer to judgments of societal groups and institutions on the public sector (criticism of bureaucratism; demand for debureaucratization)? Which set of alternatives is used for the development of criteria and the development of proposals for improvement? (better public institutions; market regulations; private self-help initiatives, etc.). The criteria and strategies for selecting such issues for academic analysis are as debatable and contestable as the findings and propositions derived from them – and in this sense they reflect the multiplicity and diversity of problems manifested and discussed in "the real world". It is still believed, though, that multi-perspective, multi-dimensional, and multi-disciplinary approaches to the field of inquiry can contribute to a better understanding of the development and problems of the public sector if seen against the background of multi-level bureaucratization which has been outlined in this paper.

2.6 Appendix: Tables and Figures

1. Germany[1]: The Relative Growth of Public Employment

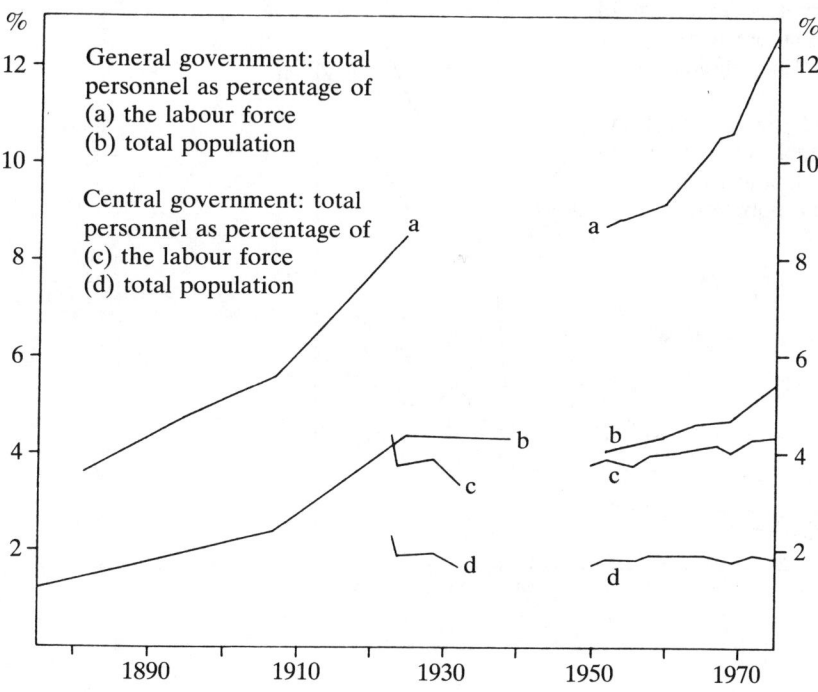

2. Structural Change of General Government

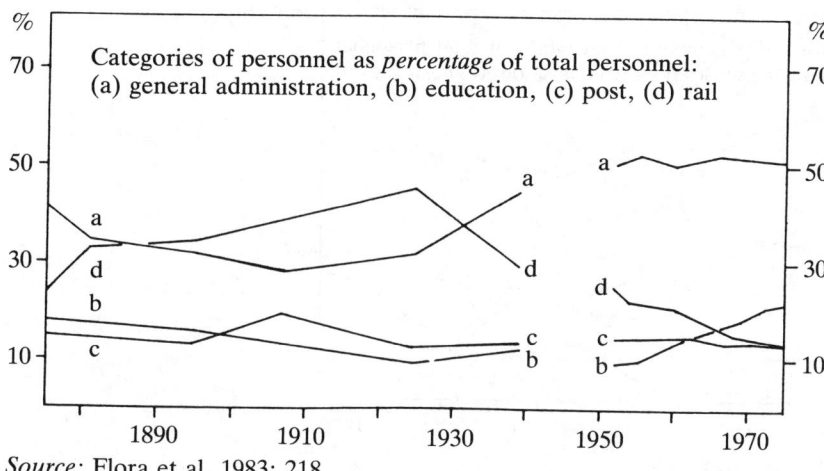

Source: Flora et al. 1983: 218

3. France[2]: The Relative Growth of Public Employment

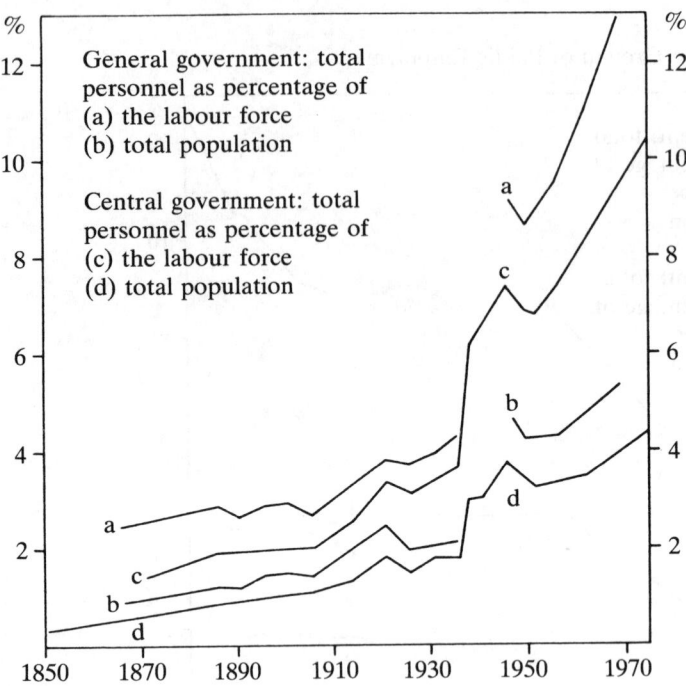

4. Structural Change of General Government

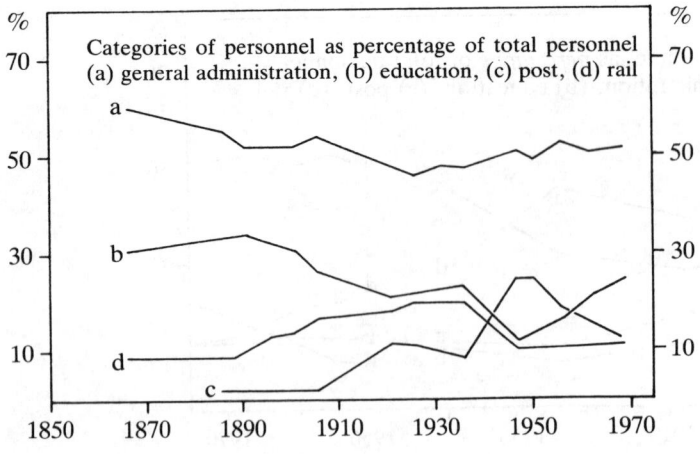

Source: Flora et al. 1983: 212.

5. Sweden[3]: The Relative Growth of Public Employment

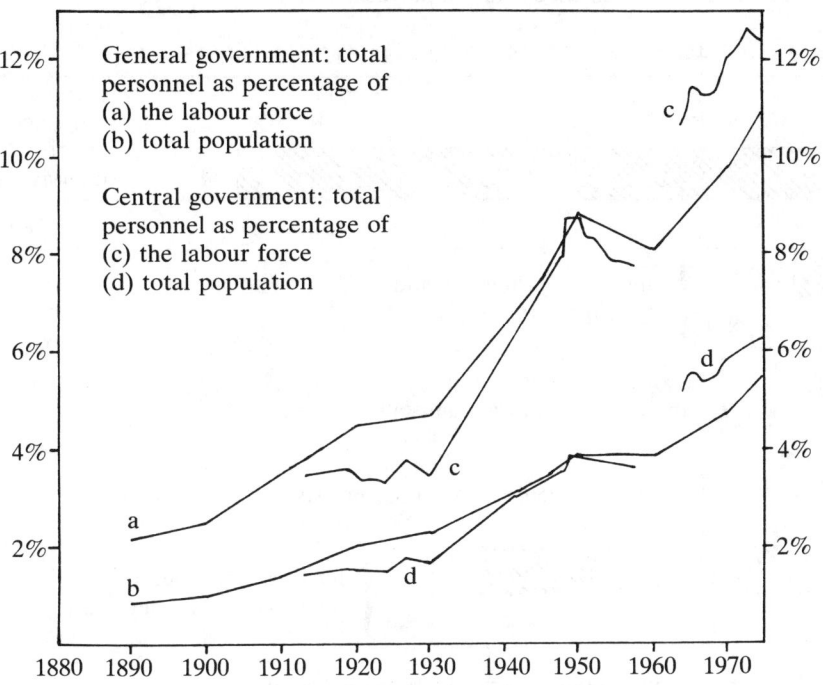

6. Structural Change of General Government

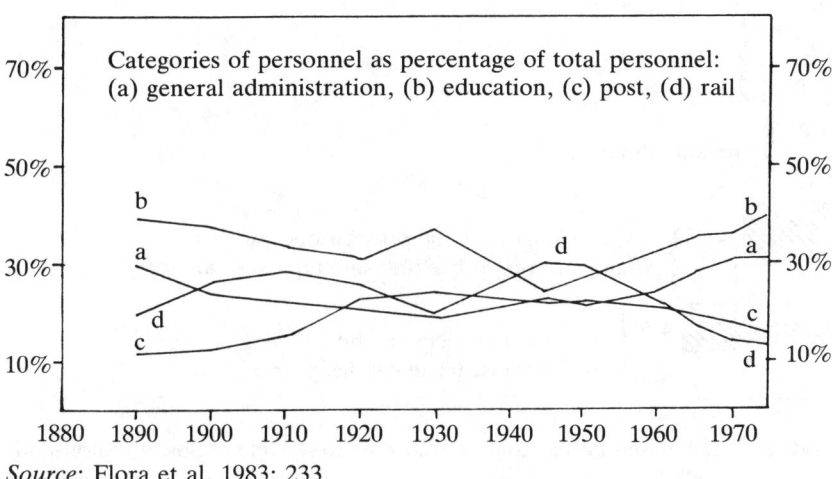

Source: Flora et al. 1983: 233.

Chart 1: Employment Development* by Occupational Groups – Comparison between 1. 4. 1970 and 31. 12. 1976 – (in thousands employees)[4]

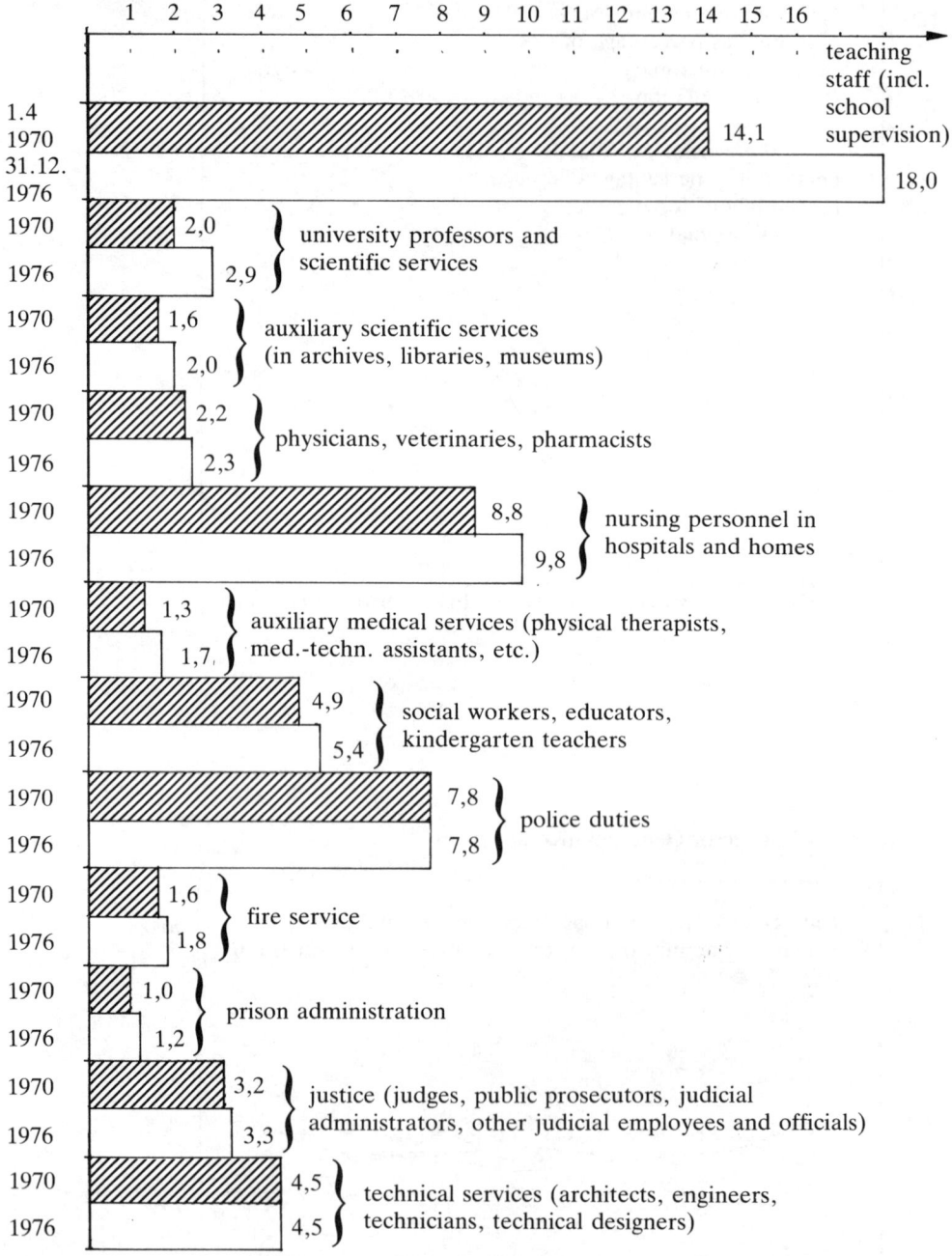

* Public authorities, agencies and Public utilities according to scheme of position/thousands employees.

Chart 1 continued

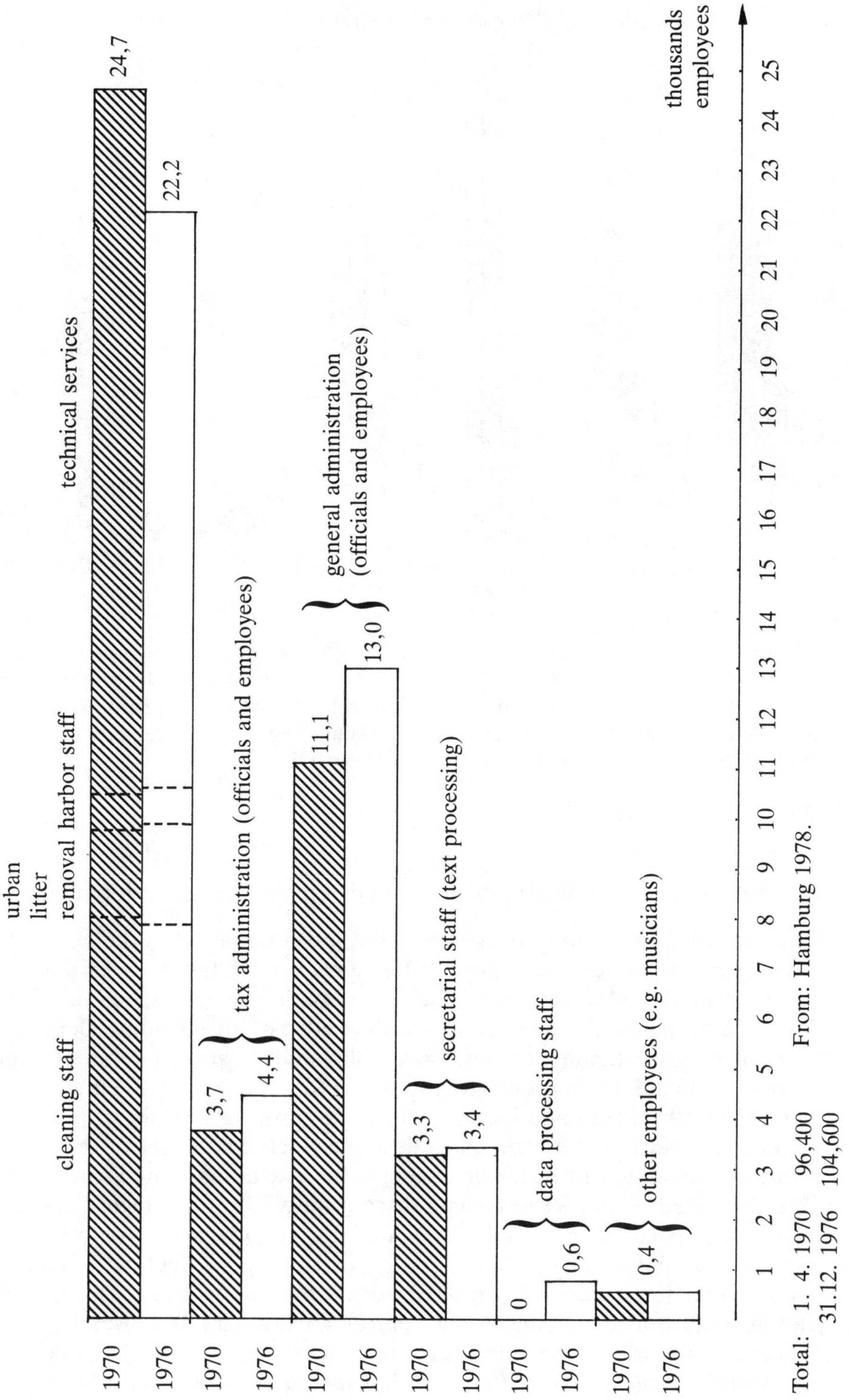

	1970	1976
technical services	24,7	22,2
cleaning staff		
urban litter removal harbor staff		
tax administration (officials and employees)	3,7	4,4
general administration (officials and employees)	11,1	13,0
secretarial staff (text processing)	3,3	3,4
data processing staff	0	0,6
other employees (e.g. musicians)	0,4	

thousands employees

1 2 3 4 5 6 7 8 9 10 11 12 13 14 15 16 17 18 19 20 21 22 23 24 25

From: Hamburg 1978.

Total: 1. 4. 1970 96,400
31.12. 1976 104,600

Chart 2: Public expenditure 1870–1970 (% of GNP)[5]

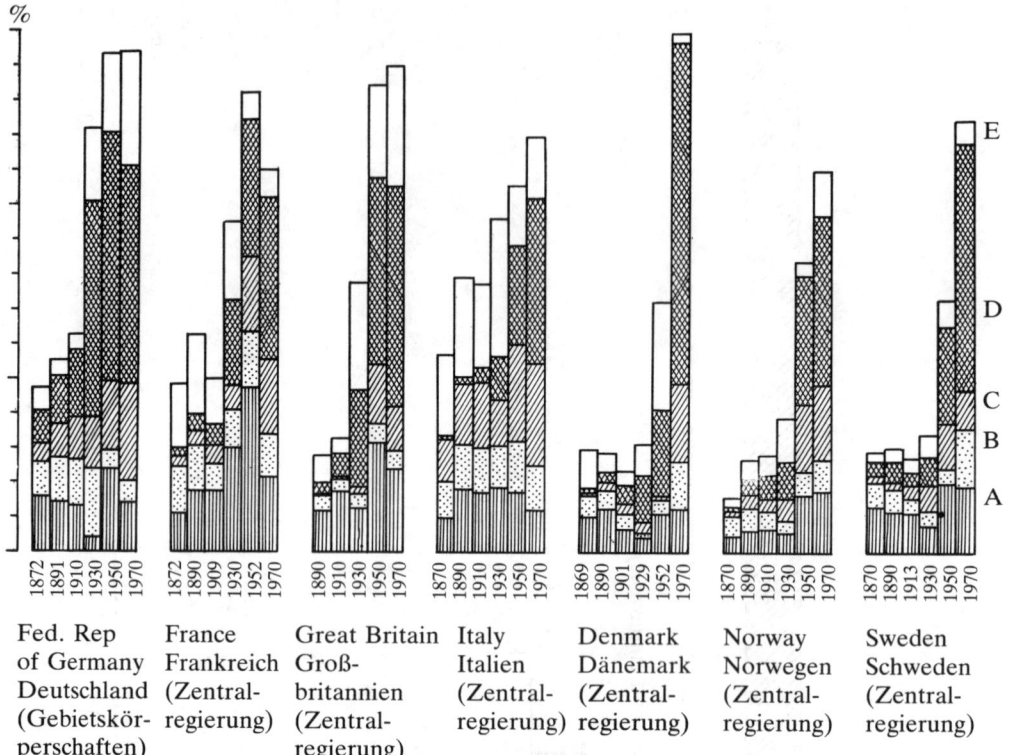

Fed. Rep
of Germany
Deutschland
(Gebietskör-
perschaften)

France
Frankreich
Groß-
britannien
(Zentral-
regierung)

Great Britain
Groß-
britannien
(Zentral-
regierung)

Italy
Italien
(Zentral-
regierung)

Denmark
Dänemark
(Zentral-
regierung)

Norway
Norwegen
(Zentral-
regierung)

Sweden
Schweden
(Zentral-
regierung)

From: Kohl (1984), Tab. 23

Comments to the preceding graphs on public employment development:

1 The following definitions are given to the indicators used in the chart:
  – general government personnel: (a) general administration = civilian employ-
    ees in public administration, excluding employees in institutions and quasi-
    public agencies; (b) education = public education, including clergy employ-
    ment by government; (c) post = employment in post, telephone, and tele-
    graph, including appropriate ministry; (d) rail = employment in public
    transportation (rail and local), including appropriate ministry;
  – central government personnel: full-time civilian employees of central govern-
    ment, including Ministries of Defense, but excluding armed forces proper.
  The data for Germany show some discontinuity due to statistical irregularities
  during the Nazi regime and World War II. For Germany we can observe a
  continuous relative growth of general government personnel: very steep relative
  to the labor force; less steep relative to the total population. This growth does
  not result from an expansion of central government because the latter has
  remained almost on the same level of percentage. As can be seen from the
  structural changes, only "education" has increased continuously during the last

Chart 3: The development of Social expenditure in the Common Market 1962–80 (% of BIP$_m$)[6]

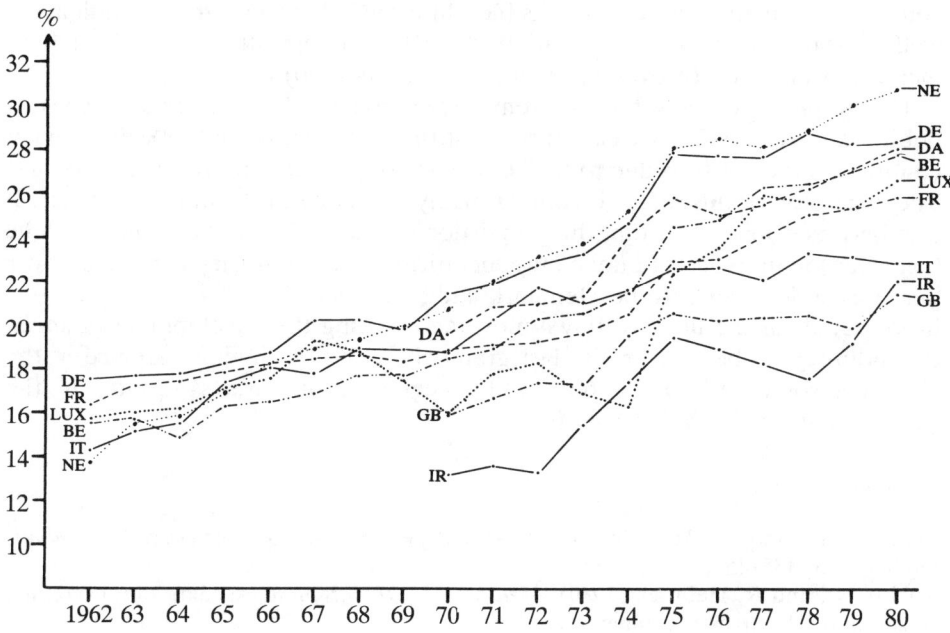

Source: Kohl (1984), Tab. 28

forty years. The relative proportion of personnel in post and rail services has decreased.

2 The data for France differ especially with regard to *central* government which has increased as much as general government; this is quite plausible for a centralized public administration like the French one. Structural changes are also somewhat different compared to the German situation: education decreased for a long period to increase only since 1950; there is also a remarkable increase of personnel in postal services during the forties and a decrease after 1950.

3 The level and relative growth of *central* government is even higher in Sweden: the curves are clearly above the curves of general government; this might in part be due to the disproportional increase of personnel in the fields of education, health and social security (see also the following charts on public expenditure.)

4 The final example of a large city (Hamburg) shows the shifts in personnel structure in detail.

Comments to the preceding graphs on public expenditure:

5 The columns contain the following types of expenditure:
A: Defense
B: General Administration, Justice, Police
C: Economic Services, Transportation
D: Social Security, Health, Education
E: Other Expenditures

The graphs show the general *relative* increase of public expenditure, which was extremely steep between 1930 and 1970 – with notable differences in different countries, though. There is a visible difference between the Scandinavian welfare states (high increase from 1950–1970) and the other countries (slight increase, stagnation or even reduction from 1950–1970).

The graphs also show the different developments of the described types of public expenditure. They clearly point out that the increase in the Scandinavian countries (1950–1970) is due to further expansions of the welfare state functions. The expansion of this sector is comparatively moderate in the other countries. It also becomes quite clear that the proportion of General Administration (B), the (expected) main place of public bureaucratization, did not vary very much over time (exceptions seem to be Denmark and Sweden).

6 More details in the up- and down-movement during the development of *social* expenditure can be seen in the last graph. It shows the higher variance in the 70ies (as compared to the 60ies): the beginning of crisis symptoms in the development of the welfare state.

References

Bennett, J. T., and M. H. Johnson (1979): "Paperwork and Bureaucracy." *Economic Inquiry* 17/3: 435–451.

Bosetzky, H., and R. Heinrich (1980): *Mensch und Organisation.* Aspekte bürokratischer Sozialisation. Stuttgart: Kohlhammer.

Brinckmann, H., K. Grimmer, K. Lenk, and D. Rave (1981): *Automatisierte Verwaltung.* Eine empirische Untersuchung über die Rationalisierung der Steuerverwaltung. Frankfurt: Campus.

Bücker-Gärtner, H., D. Grunow, F. Hegner, and G. Neubauer (1977): *Sozialwissenschaftler in der öffentlichen Verwaltung.* Ein Beitrag zur Berufsfeldanlayse von Soziologen. Frankfurt: Campus.

Crozier, M. (1964): *The Bureaucratic Phenomenon:* London: Tavistock.

Derlien, H.-U. (1980): "Bürokratisierung." In *Brockhaus-Enzyklopädie,* Vol. 25: 124–227 Wiesbaden: Brockhaus.

Dyson, K. (1979): "Die westdeutsche 'Parteibuch'-Verwaltung. Eine Auswertung." *Die Verwaltung* 12/1: 129–160.

Edelmann, M. (1975): "Symbolism in Politics." In Lindberg, L. N., A. Alford, C. Crouch, and C. Offe (eds.), *Stress and Contradiction in Modern Capitalism: Public Policy and the Theory of the State,* 309–320. Lexington, Mass.: Heath.

Elias, N. (1976): *Über den Prozeß der Zivilisation.* Frankfurt: Suhrkamp.

Flora, P. and J. Alber (1981): "Modernization, Democratization, and the Development of Welfare States in Western Europe." In Flora, P. and A. Heidenheimer (eds.), *The Development of Welfare States in Europe and America,* 37–80 New Brunswick. N.J.: Transaction Books.

Flora, P., and A. Heidenheimer (eds.) (1981): *The Development of Welfare States in Europe and America.* New Brunswick. N.J.: Transaction Books.

Flora, P., J. Alber, R. Eichenberg, J. Kohl, F. Kraus, W. Pfennig, and K. Seebohm (1983): *State, Economy, and Society in Western Europe 1815–1975.* A Data Handbook in Two Volumes. Vol. I: The Growth of Mass Democracies and Welfare States. Frankfurt: Campus.

Gebert, D. (1974): *Organisationsentwicklung.* Probleme des geplanten organisatorischen Wandels. Stuttgart: Kohlhammer.

Gouldner, A. W. (1957): "Cosmopolitans and Locals. Toward an Analysis of Latent Social Roles." *Administrative Science Quarterly* 2/3; 2/4: 281–306; 444–480.

Grunow, D. (1981): "Client-centered Research in Europe." In Goodsell, Ch. T. (ed.), *The Public Encounter: Where State and Citizen Meet,* 354–383. Bloomington, Ind.: Indiana Univ. Press.

Grunow, D. (1982): *Bürokratisierung und Debürokratisierung im Wohlfahrtsstaat.* Soziologische Analysen eines gesellschaftlichen Problems. Habilitationsschrift. Bielefeld.

Grunow, D., and F. Hegner (1978): *Die Gewährung persönlicher und wirtschaftlicher Sozialhilfe.* Untersuchungen zur Bürgernähe der kommunalen Sozialverwaltung. Bielefeld: Kleine-Verlag.

Grunow, D., and F. Hegner (1980): "Sozialpsychologische Konsequenzen der Verrechtlichung. Alltagskontakte mit der Verwaltung." In Voigt, R. (ed.), *Verrechtlichung,* 261–274. Königstein/Ts.: Athenäum.

Grunow, D., and F. Hegner (eds.) (1980): *Welfare or Bureaucracy?* Problems of Matching Social Services to Clients' Needs. Cambridge, Mass.: Oelgeschlager, Gunn & Hain.

Grunow, D., F. Hegner, and F. X. Kaufmann (1978): *Bürger und Verwaltung.* Vol. I: Steuerzahler und Finanzamt. Frankfurt: Campus.

Hall, R. (1963): "The Concept of Bureaucracy. An Empirical Assessment." *American Journal of Sociology* 69/1: 32–40.

Haller, M. (1981): "Das Dorf in der Stadt. Über 'Christiana' in Kopenhagen." In Haller, M. (ed.), *Aussteigen oder rebellieren?* Jugendliche gegen Staat und Gesellschaft, 135–155. Reinbek: Rowohlt.

Hamburg (1978): *Personalbestand im öffentlichen Dienst. Ausgewählte Struktur- und Entwicklungsdaten.* Senatsamt für den Verwaltungsdienst der Freien und Hansestadt Hamburg für die Fachtagung der Dt. Sektion des Internationalen Instituts für Verwaltungswissenschaften am 1. und 2. Juni 1978. Mannheim.

Hartmann, H. (1968): "Arbeit, Beruf, Profession." *Soziale Welt* 19/3: 193–216.

Hastorf, A. H., and H. Cantril (1954): "They Saw a Game. A Case Study." *Journal of Abnormal and Social Psychology* 49/1: 129–134.

Hegner, F. (1979): *Bürgernähe, Sozialbürgerrolle und soziale Aktion.* Bielefeld: Kleine-Verl.

Hood, C. C. (1976): *The Limits of Administration.* New York: Wiley.

Huber, J. (1980): *Wer soll das alles ändern?* Die Alternativen der Alternativbewegung. Berlin: Rotbuch Verl.

Inglehart, R. (1977): *The Silent Revolution.* Changing Values and Political Styles among Western Publics. Princeton, N.J.: Univ. Press.

Jacobs, J. (1969): "Symbolic Bureaucracy: A Case Study of a Social Welfare Agency." *Social Forces* 47/4: 413–422.

Jacoby, H. (1973): *The Bureaucratization of the World.* Berkeley: Univ. of California Press.

Kamenka, E., and M. Krygier (eds.) (1979): *Bureaucracy.* The Career of a Concept. London: Arnold.

Kaufmann, F. X. (1984): "Rechtsgefühl, Verrechtlichung und Wandel des Rechts." In *Jahrbuch für Rechtssoziologie und Rechtstheorie,* Bd. 11. Köln-Opladen: Westdeutscher Verlag. (in print)

Kohl, J. (1984): *Staatsausgaben in Westeuropa.* Analysen zur langfristigen Entwicklung der öffentlichen Finanzen. Frankfurt: Campus.

Kudrle, R. T., and R. Marmor (1981): "Die Development of Welfare States in North America." In Flora, R. and A. Heidenheimer (eds.), *The Development of Welfare States in Europe and America,* 81–121. New Brunswick, N.J.: Transaction Books.

Lawrence, P. R., and J. W. Lorsch (1967): "Differentiation and Integration in Complex Organizations." *Administrative Science Quarterly* 12/1: 1–47.

Litwak, E. (1961): "Models of Bureaucracy which Permit Conflict." *American Journal of Sociology* 67/2: 177–184.

Luhmann, N. (1970): "Die öffentliche Meinung." *Politische Vierteljahrsschrift* 11/1: 2–28.

Luhmann, N., and R. Mayntz (1973): *Personal im öffentlichen Dienst*. Eintritt und Karriere. Baden-Baden: Nomos.

Matzner, E. (1982): *Der Wohlfahrtsstaat von morgen*. Entwurf eines zeitgemäßen Musters staatlicher Interventionen. Frankfurt: Campus.

Mayntz, R. (1978): *Soziologie der öffentlichen Verwaltung*. Karlsruhe: C. F. Müller.

McKinley, D. G. (1964): *Social Class and Family Life*. New York. Free Press.

Müller, W. (1973): "Die Relativierung des bürokratischen Modells und die situative Organisation." *Kölner Zeitschrift für Soziologie und Sozialpsychologie* 25/4: 719–749.

Musgrave, R. A.(1959): *The Theory of Public Finance*. A Study in Public Economy. New York: McGraw-Hill.

Noelle-Neumann, E. (1975): "Die Schweigespirale. Was ist eigentlich öffentliche Meinung?" *Bild der Wissenschaft* 12/4: 273–283.

Oschatz, G.-B. (1979): "Erscheinungen der Verrechtlichung in der Staats- und Kommunalverwaltung." *Loccumer Protokolle* 22: 61–84.

Polanyi, K. (1944): *The Great Transformation*. The Political and Economical Origins of our Time. Boston: Beacon.

Presthus, R. (1962): *The Organizational Society*. An Analysis and a Theory (Rev. ed. 1979). New York: Vintage Books.

Pugh, D. S., and D. J. Hickson (1971): "Eine dimensionale Analyse bürokratischer Strukturen." In Mayntz, R. (ed.), *Bürokratische Organisation* (2nd ed.), 82–94. Köln: Kiepenheuer & Witsch.

Putnam, R. D. (1973): "The Political Attitudes of Senior Civil Servants in Western Europe. A Preliminary Report." *British Journal of Political Science* 3/3: 257–290.

Reissman, L. (1949): "A Study of Role Conceptions in Bureaucracy." *Social Forces* 27/3: 305–310.

Riesman, D. (1950): *The Lonely Crowd*. New York: Yale Univ. Press.

Roethlisberger, F. J., and W. J. Dickson (1939): *Management and the Worker*. Cambridge, Mass.: Harvard Univ. Press.

Rohde-Dachser, Ch. (1982): *Das Borderline-Syndrom* (2nd ed.). Bern: Huber.

Schluchter, W. (1972): *Aspekte bürokratischer Herrschaft*. Studien zur Interpretation der fortschreitenden Industriegesellschaft. München: List.

Schluchter, W. (1979): *Die Entwicklung des okzidentalen Rationalismus*. Eine Analyse von Max Webers Gesellschaftsgeschichte. Tübingen: Mohr.

Schluchter, W. (1980): *Rationalisierung der Weltbeherrschung*. Studien zu Max Weber. Frankfurt: Suhrkamp.

Schmid, G., and H. Treiber (1975): *Bürokratie und Politik*. Zur Struktur und Funktion der Ministerialbürokratie in der Bundesrepublik Deutschland. München: Fink.

Schmitter, P. C. (1974): "Still the Century of Corporatism?" *Review of Politics* 30/1: 85–131. 85–131.

Smith. J. H. (1968): "Die Entstehung einer Bürokratie." In Mayntz, R. (ed.), *Bürokratische Organisation*, 406–420. Köln: Kiepenheuer & Witsch.

Steinkemper, B. (1974): *Klassische und politische Bürokraten in der Ministerialverwaltung der Bundesrepublik Deutschland*. Köln: Heymann.

Türk, K. (1976): *Grundlagen einer Pathologie der Organisation*. Stuttgart: Enke.

Zentralarchiv für empirische Sozialforschung (1981): *Lebensziele*. Potentiale und Trends alternativen Verhaltens – 1980. Köln: Zentralarchiv für empirische Sozialforschung, Univ. zu Köln (ZA-Nr. 1136).

3. Analyzing the Public Sector: Shortcomings of Current Approaches

Giandomenico Majone, Klaus Gretschmann

Abstract

Policy Science and Public Finance are reviewed as outstanding examples of different but complementary approaches to the study of the public sector. The intellectual roots of policy science are a group of disciplines and methodologies developed during the last three decades as ways of improving the rationality of decision making in business and in government. Because of these origins, many policy scientists are committed to a teleological or end-result view of policymaking, according to which rationality simply means maximizing something. Such a view implies a stylized model of public policymaking marked by several reductionist features. All policy problems are identified with allocative decisions, policymakers are viewed as monolithic actors with unlimited information-processing capacity, political issues are treated as textbook problems for which solutions can always be found. Thus, decisionism, "unitarianism", and intellectualism are the basic shortcomings of policy science as it is taught and practiced today.

Public finance, a much older field of study, attempts to explain the development of the public sector and the structure of public revenues and expenditures by analyzing basic public functions like resource allocation, distribution, and economic stabilization. The approach of neoclassical public finance, like that of policy science, is essentially normative, decisionist, and intellectualist. The public sector is treated as a black box; institutional factors are either neglected or treated as exogenous factors. Quasi-governmental and other institutionally mixed forms between market and state are not sufficiently analyzed. At the same time, because of the methodological individualism inherited from Paretian welfare economics, corporate actors receive too little attention. Policymaking is conceived of as technocratic problem solving rather than as a political process of preference formation and consensus building. The uneasiness of neoclassical public finance in dealing with the politically important category of merit goods is indicative of this reductive view of policymaking.

These shortcomings of policy science and public finance indicate a clear need for a broader, institutionally richer approach to the study of the public sector; an approach emphasizing learning and flexibility, rather than static efficiency.

From the very beginning of the modern state, the public sector has been the object of special studies in a variety of scholarly disciplines. In Continental Europe these disciplines have traditionally included political philosophy, constitutional and administrative law, legal philosophy, administrative history, and, above all, public finance. Anglo-American influence has been more noticeable in the areas of public economics, organization theory and systems analysis, the theory of public choice, and policy science.

It is of course impossible to review critically, in a single chapter, all these different disciplines and approaches. Hence, rather than attempting a synoptic overview which would necessarily be both incomplete and superficial, we have chosen to focus on two areas of research – policy science and public finance – which in a sense best represent the two main cultural traditions.

Whereas most of the traditional disciplines approach the public sector in piecemeal fashion, tending to restrict themselves to specific groups of problems, public finance and policy science attempt to offer the broadest and most general approach to the subject. For this reason, they provide the best perspective from which to examine the current state of the art in the theoretical and applied study of the public sector. For the same reason they represent – in their premises, their modes of argument, their achievements as well as their conceptual inadequacies – the most promising starting point for a sustained effort of interdisciplinary research on public sector problems, while providing a relevant standard for evaluating such research.

Needless to say, much remains to be done in these as in all other fields of inquiry. To avoid repeating earlier mistakes, learn to ask the right questions, and thus make progress in theory development, it seems advisable to begin with a brief outline of the received view in the two disciplines, followed by a more detailed analysis of questionable assumptions and more or less obvious shortcomings and pitfalls in the treatment of various aspects of the public sector. Such an approach should prove more intelligible and provide a better idea of the state-of-the-art than a discussion of specific topics and areas of application. The two parts into which the present chapter is divided will show the reader, perhaps to his surprise, that policy science und public finance share a considerable number of common characteristics. On the other, differences in language and in points of concentration will make clear to him the differences in the conceptual premises of the two disciplines and in their historical and intellectual (Continental in one case, Anglo-American in the other) origins.

Part A. Policy Science

Giandomenico Majone

3.1 The Received View on Policy Science

The first part of this chapter is devoted to a critical assessment of a group of disciplines, collectively known as "policy science", which have been developed in the last three decades as ways of improving decision making in the public sector. Although these disciplines have emerged in different institutional contexts and evolved more or less independently, a continuous conceptual thread runs from the early studies of military and industrial operations, of strategy and logistics, through the broader concerns of systems analysis in the 1960s, to much of contemporary policy analysis. Technical efficiency as a goal or criterion of choice has been replaced by economic efficiency and this, in turn, has been tempered by considerations of equity and political feasibility. But the original analytic framework is still clearly recognizable; the initial focus on allocation problems has shifted, but it has not been supplanted.

What may be called the Received View on policy science was given emphasis and formal statement in the early 1950s, particularly at the Rand Corporation and similar policy-oriented "think tanks" in the United States. It is a conceptual compound that includes elements from operations research and management science, from microeconomics and decision theory, and a dash of social and behavioral science.

Under the Received View, ideal policymaking, rational decision making, rational problemsolving, and policy analysis are synonymous. There is a one-to-one correspondence between the stages of the policy process and the phases of analysis. For example, the following list of steps can be interpreted either as an idealized description of rational policymaking, or as a formula for conducting policy analysis: "objective-model-hypothesis control action – predict – vary hypothetical control action – revise prediction – repeat to select optimum – act – observe behaviour – refine objective – revise model – update prediction and optimization – act again – continue to observe – all in the light of changing external circumstances" (Bray 1970: 269).

Underlying the Received View and the basic categories of analysis it defines – goals, alternatives, constraints, and criteria of choice – is a deeper commitment to a teleological or "end-result" conception of policymaking. According to this conception, as formulated by John Rawls, "those institutions and acts are right which of the available alternatives produce the most good, or at least as much good as any of the other institutions and acts open as real possibilities". Rawls adds: "teleological theories have a deep intuitive appeal since they seem to embody the idea of rationality. It is natural to think that rationality is maximizing something... Indeed, it is tempting to suppose that it is self-evident that things should be arranged so as to lead to the most good" (1973: 24).

Unfortunately, this concept of rationality is not directly applicable to decision making under uncertainty, where one must choose not among single-valued alternatives, but among alternative probabilistic distributions of outcomes, but an ersatz rationality, as it were, is available in the form of consistency among one's beliefs and preferences. In the words of I. J. Good, "In a nutshell, rationality . . . means consistency. More precisely, it means consistency of one's current judgements; clearly one should not adhere to previous judgments that are no longer honestly held. This consistency must be relative to some 'theory of rationality', that is, to a theory of rational thoughts, statements, and behavior" (Good 1962: 384).

Carried to its logical extremes, the Received View would turn policy analysis either into a branch of applied mathematics – constrained optimization – or a branch of logic, the pure logic of choice, a set of self-evident propositions subject to no other test than internal consistency. Needless to say, this program has never been carried out completely, but it survives as an ideal or standard of comparison, much like the model of perfect competition used by economists to evaluate actual markets.

Despite a mounting level of criticism, the influence of this ideal on practice, research, and especially on teaching is still considerable. This is not surprising, since the emphasis of the Received View on problem-solving techniques has obvious advantages for professional training, curricular planning, and the standardization of tasks and skills. Against these advantages, one must consider the consequences of the widespread acceptance of a stylized model of public policy-making characterized by marked reductionist features.

Policy issues are identified with decision problems, which in turn are reduced to questions of allocative efficiency. The fiction of the unitary decision maker projects onto a single dimension the complexity of policy making with its multiplicity of actors and institutions, conflicting interests, and divergent evaluative criteria. A tacit belief that rationality implies infallibility and omniscience reduces social issues to purely intellectual exercises or "quizzes", policy actors to calculating machines with unlimited information processing capacities, "knowing how" (the ability to do certain things, to adapt behavior to new circumstances) to "knowing that" (conscious knowledge of general propositions and rules).

In the following pages I shall discuss separately the main reductionist features of the policy science model of policymaking.

3.2 Overemphasis on Allocation Problems

The first reductionist move has such an obvious and technically neutral appearance that it may pass almost unnoticed. It consists in taking as the paradigm problem of policy analysis how public resources ought to be allocated among competing ends. For example, a recent primer of policy analysis introduces its subject matter as follows: "How choices should be made – the whole problem of allocating scarce resources among competing ends – is the stuff of economics and the subject of this book" (Stokey and Zeckhauser 1978: 22). Similar programatic statements can be found in the writings of influential authors like Hitch and McKean (1962), Enthoven (1971), and Quade (1982).

It follows that the main task of the rational policymaker is to determine at what point further spending on a given program results in incremental gains so small that it is no longer justified. To do this, the policymaker must specify the objective or objectives that are sought; lay out the alternatives by which the objectives may be accomplished; express a consistent system of preferences; evaluate the costs and predict the consequences of each alternative; and choose the course of action that maximizes (expected) utility.

If the recipe sounds familiar this is because the logical structure of allocative decisions is the same whether the decisions are taken by individual consumers, by private entrepreneurs, or by public managers. Hence, the appeal to a generalized "logic of choice", which advocates of the Received View found, ready-made, in microeconomic theory. Is not economics, in Lionel Robbins' classic formulation (1932: 16), the science of "human behaviour as a relationship between ends and scarce means which have alternative uses"?

As Klaus Gretschmann argues in the second part of this chapter, this view of man as a "permanent calculator" guided only by his utility function and budget constraint pervades also the modern theory of public finance. But since the logic of choice has been investigated primarily in the context of private market transactions it is tempting to argue, as some authors have done, that the main if not the only object of policy analysis is to extend the principles of rational choice from the sphere of private economic transactions to the public sector. In fact, the argument continues, a good grasp of the principles of the logic of choice is even more necessary for public than for private decision makers. If, as Schumpeter once remarked, "[i]n the ordinary run of often repeated decisions the individual is subject to the salutary and rationalizing influence of favorable and unfavorable experience" (Schumpeter 1950: 258), and if competition and natural selection can be relied upon to enforce efficiency in private business, in government such influences are either much weaker or nonexistent. Hence, efficient decisions must be made consciously and, except for the simplest kind of problems, this requires systematic, and preferably quantitative, analysis.

This view of policy analysis as decision analysis "writ large" has a certain plausibility, and can even be a useful way of formulating a narrow, if practically important, range of problems: whether to use a particular vaccine to halt the spread of a threatened epidemic; where to build an urgently needed dam; how to reduce the response time of the fire department of a big city. Not surprisingly, these or similar examples are the standard illustrations used in conventional textbooks. The impression generated by such examples, however, is quite misleading.

Most problems of public policy require the use of scarce resources, but this fact justifies neither the identification of public decisions with the economist's allocative decision, nor the elevation of the criterion of allocative efficiency to a position of unique importance. To mention only one example: although economists have advocated the use of effluent charges for pollution control because of their superior allocative efficiency, legislators, regulators, industrial spokesmen, and environmentalists continue to reject such proposals, preferring to rely on the traditional, but economically less efficient, methods based on environmental standards and other administrative measures. Short of assuming a general inability to understand economic arguments, or a general conspiracy against the public interest, we must conclude that economic efficiency is not a decisive criterion of choice in public policy. Other criteria, relating for example to the *process* rather than the outcome of decision making, may be much more important. Thus, effluent charges would operate quite automatically once pollution damages and abatement costs have been determined. But this automatism, which economists value so highly, would change the nature of the regulatory process by reducing the possibility of negotiation and bargaining among representatives of the different interests. Such negation of the political nature of a process in which value judgments are at least as important as efficiency considerations (Kelman 1981), is one important reason for the lack of political appeal of the effluent charges approach.

The examples of the traditional textbooks are misleading also because their emphasis on allocative efficiency conceals the existence of other, possibly more important, kinds of efficiency. If Leibenstein is correct, even in the private economy the amount to be gained by increasing allocative efficiency is trivial, while the amount to be gained by increasing "X-efficiency" (more individual motivation. improvements in working conditions and atmosphere, better use of nonmarket inputs such as tacit knowledge, and so on) is frequently significant (Leibenstein 1976). Very likely, the role of X-efficiency in the public sector is even more important.

The mapping of policy problems onto the much smaller set of allocation problems is only the first move in the reductionist strategy. Once the economic model of choice is firmly established as the central paradigm of policy analysis, the next step – the obliteration of all differences between policies and decisions – becomes easy and, indeed, almost inevitable.

3.3 Decisionism

The doctrine of decisionism – as essential component of the Received View – attempts to force all policy problems, arguments, and deliberations into the Procustean bed of the model of choice. If policies are indistinguishable from decisions, the logic of choice must be the basic tool of analysis and decisions, the prime objects of inquiry.

But what is, precisely, a decision? The concept is not unproblematic, and the lack of conceptual clarity is the probable reason why even the most perceptive critics of the Received View tend to treat policymaking as essentially equivalent to decision making. But as Philip Selznick has observed in a different context,

"[d]ecision-making is one of those fashionable phrases that may well obscure more than it illuminates. It has an air of significance, of reference to important events; and the mere use of the phrase seems to suggest that something definite has been scientifically isolated. But decisions are with us always, at every level of experience, in every organism. The general features of all choices, or of all social choice, may some day be convincingly stated. But it will still be necessary to distinguish the more and the less trivial; and, if there is any order in this phenomenon, to identify some kinds of decisions, linking them to the distinctive problems or situations out of which they arise (Selznick 1964: 56)."

If we turn to decision theory for illumination, we find that the textbook treatments often fail to make the essential situation clear. Introductory chapters may appeal to the reader's commonsense understanding of the term "decision", but the technical discussion actually applies to decision-making situations of a rather special kind. A decision, in the sense of modern decision theory, is a choice that must be made in the situation *immediately* confronting the decision maker, taking into consideration the probable consequences of each possible course of action in his *present* situation.

Certainly there are many situations, in private life as well as in the context of business and government activities, where individuals must choose under conditions approximating the model of decision theory. The question is whether *all* problems of choice can be reasonably analyzed in such terms. For example, does the scientist's decision to accept theory A (and reject theory B) fit the decision-theoretic model? The answer of many distinguished scholars and scientists is negative. John Tukey (1960), for example, distinguishes between "decisions" and "conclusions". Conclusions (e.g., the conclusion that A is a better theory than B) differ from decisions in essential respects: they are established with careful regard to evidence, but without regard to consequences of specific actions in specific circumstances; once accepted, they are retained until strong evidence to the contrary arises; and they are judged by their immediate consequences.

In sum, a scientific conclusion is "taken into the body of knowledge, not just into the guidebook of advice for immediate action, as would be the case with a decision" (Tukey 1960: 424). Thus, although science – like any other human activity – involves many decisions, it does not live by decision alone; it draws its essential support from a different set of inferences and procedures.

Just as decision theorists tend to overlook or deny Tukey's distinction between decisions and conclusions, so the followers of the Received View on policy analysis fail to see any difference between decision making and policymaking, or even to recognize the existence of qualitatively different types of decisions. But many executive "decisions" are, in certain respects, closer to Tukey's "conclusions" than to the decision theorist's decision, as suggested by the following statement by Chester I. Barnard: *"The fine art of executive decision consists in not deciding questions that are now not pertinent, in not deciding prematurely, in not making decisions that cannot be made effective, and in not making decisions that others should make"* (quoted in Tukey 1960: 427; Barnard's italics).

Like conclusions, executive or policy decisions are not to be entered upon lightly and once reached, they become a reference point for some time as part of a growing body of institutional doctrines. The differences between the decision theorist's decisions and policy decisions is even clearer in the following passage from Theodore C. Sorensen's *Decision-Making in the White House* (1963). Having noted that the postponement of decisions often can be a weakness, and that the desire for more evidence and arguments may produce answers to questions which no longer exist, the author continues:

"Yet most presidential decisions are too far-reaching and too irrevocable to be taken in haste, when the facts are uncertain, when the choices are unclear, or when the long-range consequences are not as discernible as the immediate reactions and results. President Kennedy has said, with respect to the Cuban crisis: "If we had had to act in the first twenty-four hours, I don't think . . . we would have chosen as prudently as we finally did" (Sorensen 1963: 30).

Decisionism is closely related to another key assumption of the Received View, which is discussed below under the label of "unitarianism". The decision maker of decision theory, like the consumer and the entrepreneur of microeconomic theory, is the sole judge and executor of his choices. But even in the most tightly centralized organization, few decisions are made by only one person. Hence, to decide, even to decide correctly, is not enough. In an organizational setting there is always the additional problem of communicating and justifying executive decisions. But the transmission of decisions for information and persuasion, rather than as authoritarian directives, is often inappropriate and generally inefficient.

It is usually of little help to somebody who has to make a particular choice to know that another person, given different evidence and facing a different situation, decided to act as if such-and-such were the true state of affairs. Information is conveyed not by the choice itself, but by the reasons accepted and given. Also, to explain a decision and convince other people to acknowledge it and carry it out, the executive cannot simply appeal to the subjective reasons and personal motives that guided him in the first place. Different arguments, suitable for interpersonal communication and carefully tailored to a particular audience, must be provided. Such post-decision arguments are irrelevant to the pure logic of choice, but they are an essential element of the interactive process by which social issues are resolved (cf. Majone: Ch. 21).

A legal analogy may help to clarify this point. A judge may decide a case on the basis of his subjective notion of fairness, but his opinion must be framed in the objective categories of legal argument. Any subsequent developments in the case (e.g., an appeal) will be based on the published opinion, not on the subjective feelings and preferences of the judge. In this way, the postdecision arguments become an essential part of the judicial process. Supporting arguments, interpretations, qualifications, and indeed the entire debate following the first policy statements, become integrated into policies in similar ways, and can no longer be separated from their pristine substances. For this reason, policymakers need retrospective (postdecision) analysis at least as much as they need prospective (predecision) analysis, and probably more. That this kind of analysis is shunned by most analysts can only be explained by the constraining hold of the Received View on their minds.

3.4 Unitarianism

Experienced analysts have repeatedly pointed out that "[a]nalyses are ordinarily designed and carried out, although perhaps not always deliberately, as if they were to assist a solitary decision maker who had full authority over acceptance and implementation" (Quade 1982: 336–338). However, in the traditional literature the myth of the unitary decision maker is treated simply as a pitfall that may reduce the effective use of analysis, but does not originate within the analysis itself. I argue, instead, that "unitarianism" is not just a pitfall, but a dominant faith among supporters of the Received View and in fact, a logical consequence of the standard model of choice.

The model of the decision maker (or group acting as a unit) who lays out goals and uses the precepts of the logic of choice to select the best means to reach these goals is not immediately, if at all, applicable to situations involving two or more decision makers with different objectives. As already noted, the model has been developed for an individual who wishes to be consistent and expresses his consistency in the way he orders the consequences of different alternatives and evaluates the probabilities of uncertain events. When several decision makers are involved, there is nothing in the model that requires them to agree on their ordering either of the consequences or of the probabilities: each may be rational (i.e., consistent) in holding quite divergent views. If a joint decision is required, they will have to resolve their differences through processes (such as bargaining, negotiation, or persuasion) about which the model is silent.

Moreover, the concentration of traditional policy analysis on a mythical hero called the policymaker completely obscures the complexity of the process of policy formulation and implementation. Basic questions concerning the nature of the policymaking units are seldom raised: who are the "policymakers" in a world of large bureaucratic organizations, powerful pressure groups, and political coalitions? How does a "multi-person" policymaker operate? Who are the actors to be included in such a group? How are policies affected by existing institutions (cf. Kaufmann: Ch. 10; Ostrom: Ch. 22, Franz: Ch. 23)?

The unitary model of policymaking ignores conflicts between the interests and perceptions of different government agencies. But whenever such conflicts are present, important questions arise about the appropriate assumptions regarding the behavior of other public agencies in the formulation of policy by any particular agency. All policy instruments are effectively constrained within certain ranges by administrative and political considerations. Therefore it is important for policymakers to know which control variables are in fact within their control and to what extent, and in this respect "a feeling of oneness with the totality of the government may not be very useful" (Sen 1974: 143).

The parallelism between traditional policy analysis and the traditional theory of the firm is almost complete, This theory does not differentiate between the corner grocery store and the multinational corporation – both organizations take decisions as monolithic units and carry out their choices in a frictionless and perfectly foreseeable manner. In fact, microeconomic theory attempts to achieve simplicity and generality by *not* defining economic actors too precisely, but at the cost, as Harvey Leibenstein (1976: 47) has argued, of a silent logical leap, and at the risk of a possible logical flaw. The silent logical leap is implicit in the unexamined assumption that multiperson units behave in the same way (i.e., do not experience internal frictions and contradictions) as single-person households or firms.

The possibility of a logical flaw lies in the very nature of conventional microtheory which is essentially, to use Leibenstein's apt expression, a theory of behavior of principals. Agents, to the extent that they are considered at all in the theory, are assumed to be faithful executors of their principals' choices – their efforts are completely controlled and correctly evaluated by the firm. But there is no reason to believe that this assumption holds in general. Agents do not always act in the exclusive interest of their principals; they have their own interests and it may pay them to engage in transactions under which their principals lose. Thus, the logical pitfall consists in assuming that the essential nature of behavior does not change when we pass from single-person units to large organizations in which decisions taken by principals must be implemented by a number of agents.

Decision theory, too, is a "theory of principals" and as such it has no room for implementation problems. "It is unnecessary", as well known decision theorist informs us, "to distinguish between decision and action. A decision to wear a particular dress need not be separated from the action of wearing the dress, for if the decision did not lead to the wearing of the dress it was presumably because something intervened to prevent it and a new decision problem arose" (Lindley 1971: 4).

Given such assumptions, it is not surprising that implementation as a distinct phenomenon or stage in the policymaking process has been recognized only quite late in the development of policy analysis (cf. Sabatier: Ch. 15). Serious research on implementation problems only begun in the 1970's, particularly after publication of the seminal work of Pressman and Wildavsky (1973). Though the results so far have been rather limited – the existing literature is mostly a collection of case studies – enough has been learned to demonstrate the limited relevance of conventional policy analysis for the study of actual policymaking.

3.5 Intellectualism

The Received View tends to overintellectualize policy analysis by giving undue emphasis to the more formal or technical aspects of a subject that in fact is (or should be) concerned with the whole of the policy process.

Conventional treatments of rational decision making look upon problems of public policy as if they were puzzles for which, granted consistent premises, "correct" solutions always exist, and can be obtained by calculation rather than by the exercise of skills and by social interactions. When such views are carefully analyzed, they turn out to rest on an erroneous doctrine which Gilbert Ryle has called the intellectualist legend.

"Champions of this legend are apt to try to reassimilate knowing *how* to knowing *that* by arguing that intelligent performance involves the observance of rules, or the application of criteria. It follows that the operation which is characterized as intelligent must be preceded by an intellectual acknowledgment of these rules or criteria; that is, the agent must first go through the internal process of avowing to himself certain propositions about what is to be done ("maxims", "imperatives", or "regulative propositions" as they are sometimes called); only then can he execute his performance in accordance with those dictates. He must preach to himself before he can practice . . . To do something thinking what one is doing is, according to this legend, always to do two things; namely, to consider certain appropriate propositions, or prescriptions, and to put into practice what these propositions or prescriptions enjoin. It is to do a bit of theory and then to do a bit of practice" (Ryle 1949: 29).

The assumption that decision making (or any other type of intellectual performance) can be intelligent or rational only if it is preceded by an internal operation of planning is open to a crucial objection:

"Now very often we do go through such a process of planning what to do, and, if we are silly, our planning is silly, if shrewd, our planning is shrewd. It is also notoriously possible for us to plan shrewdly and perform stupidly, i.e., to flout our precepts in our practice. By the original argument, therefore, our intellectual planning process must inherit its title to shrewdness from yet another interior process of planning to plan, and this process could in its turn be silly or shrewd. The regress is infinite, and this reduces to absurdity the theory that for an operation to be intelligent it must be steered by a prior intellectual operation. What distinguishes sensible from silly operations is not their parentage but their procedure, and this holds no less for intellectual than for practical performances. "Intelligent" cannot be defined in terms of "intellectual" or "knowing how" in terms of "knowing *that*" . . ." (Ryle 1949: 31–32).

Somebody without a knowledge of medicine can hardly be a good surgeon, but excellence at surgery is not the same thing as knowledge of medical science, nor is it a direct result of it. Like surgery, taking decisions and giving policy advice are exercises of skills, and we do not judge skillful performance by the amount of knowledge stored in the head of the performer or by his faithful adherence to rules, but by the ability to select the relevant data and the most convincing arguments, by the timing of his decisions, the quality of his insights, the maturity of his judgment, and so on.

The emphasis on the purely intellectual aspects of policymaking is matched by an overestimation of the capacity of the human mind for formulating and solving complex problems, and a rather naive faith in the reliability of available empirical and theoretical knowledge. Authors like Herbert A. Simon and Charles E. Lindblom have repeatedly argued that the intellectual ideal of the Received View is neither adapted to man's limited problem-solving capacities and to inadequacy of information, nor to the costliness (financial as well as in terms of time and human resources) of comprehensive analysis. This disproportion between man's limited intellectual capacity and the complexity of social processes explains the failure of many attempts to find conclusive solutions to policy problems. Policy problems are never solved but only shifted and ameliorated at best. Or, rather, to the extent that a policy problem is temporarily removed from the agenda of issues under current debate, this happens because a consensus has been reached by the policy actors, not because an analytic solution has been found. But if problems are resolved by consensus reached through social interaction (bargaining, market exchange, voting, persuasion, and so on), what role is left for policy analysts to play? The answer is clear: if analysis cannot replace social interaction, then it must be subordinated and adapted to it.

Analysis can be adapted to interaction in several ways (Lindblom 1980: 26–39). First, it can take the form of partisan analysis – analysis by any participant in the policy process of how he can play his interactive role more effectively, or influence the opinions and preferences of other participants. Although partisan analysis is often viewed with suspicion, as being contrary to the public interest and to the common search for truth, it is in fact essential to the competition of ideas from which new policies emerge in a pluralist democracy. As long as the arguments of one partisan can be challenged by competing analyses, the danger of flagrant misrepresentations and outright falsifications is reduced, if not eliminated. Thus, even biased or incomplete information can contribute to the stock of knowledge that becomes the common possession of all the participants.

A second form of adaptation occurs when analysis is applied to discover ways of using existing interactions in order to achieve some public purpose, without imposing administratively determined solutions. For example, how should one modify the informational flow, institutional structure, or incentive patterns of private markets so as to reduce environmental pollution, prevent industrial accidents, or modify unhealthy life-styles? The advocates of the "public use of the private interest" (Schultze 1977) argue that it is impossible to regulate the social and economic processes of a modern industrial society by planning and administrative regulations. Social complexity can be managed only by harnessing private interests to public goals, or transforming public goals into private interests. Hence, analysis should use existing social interactions, for instance by designing market-like incentives such as pollution taxes or health vouchers.

Finally, analysis may be used to improve the basic structure of the interaction processes themselves, through institutional reform, procedural design, and, more generally, by facilitating social learning and adaptation (cf. Kaufmann: Ch. 10).

3.6 Conclusions

The policy-making view of the public sector represents an important intellectual innovation with respect to the perspectives offered by the older disciplines of economics, sociology, and political science. If the potential advantages of this approach have not yet been fully realized, despite considerable technical progress, this is because it is impossible to do useful policy analysis without an adequate theory of government, and reasonable assumptions about individual and institutional behavior.

The convenient fiction of a benevolent dictator or monolithic decision maker, and the other reductionist stratagems discussed in the preceding pages, may have played a heuristically useful role in the early stages of development of the new approach. Today, such simplified views of the policy process can only impede further progress. For example, sophisticated policy actors have always recognized the importance of roundabout methods of influencing the policy process. Instead of investing one's resources trying to secure directly some particular advantages – whether a tariff increase or a less strict environmental standard – it is often more efficient to try to change the rules and institutions which ultimately determine policy outputs.

But to take such institution-changing behavior into account, it is necessary to develop models which explicitly recognize that individuals and groups pursue their goals not only by acting within the constraints set by the given institutional framework, but also by attempting to modify those constraints in their favor. The implications of this extension of the conventional model of public choice, in which institutions are defined exogenously and, hence, taken as a constant by the policy analyst, are far-reaching. Policies which seem superior when judged by criteria relevant to the traditional approach, lose much of their attractiveness in the extended model (Majone 1976).

Thus, policy scientists must learn to base their analyses on institutionally rich models of the policy process, just as students of political processes and institutions have learned to use several formal techniques developed by decision and policy analysis. To paraphrase Kant, policy analysis without institutional analysis is empty; institutional analysis without policy analysis is blind.

Part B. Public Finance

Klaus Gretschmann

3.7 The Public Sector in the Mirror of Public Finance Theory

While modern Anglo-American public finance – like pure economics – devotes its efforts to explaining state expenditure and income under special consideration of resource allocation, distribution, and stabilization (see Musgrave 1966), the older Continental approach goes far beyond that and is characterized by broad thinking based on grand theories of the state in the Hobbesian or Hegelian tradition (see Gerloff and Meisel 1926).

One could consider this distinction programmatic: Whereas the first tradition aims at an independent theory of the public sector, the second perceives the public sector in terms of a theory of the state. The first tradition attempts to provide insights into the control requirements, the available instruments, the autonomy, the selectivity and the political effects of state activities. The state theory tradition, on the other hand, takes a more comprehensive approach, is evolutionary, interested in philosophical and constitutional questions, tries to include the reciprocal effects between state and market, and analyzes the overall economic system measuring its monetary flows and using the analysis of expenditure and taxes (Wagner 1883; Goldscheidt 1926; Bell 1974). The starting point and the center of its thinking is the State. In contrast the Anglo-American type of theory attempts, through its connection with the theoretical basis of modern welfare economics, to adopt the individualistic view, and thus uses the market ideal as a standard of reference.

Notwithstanding the fact that public finance is neither in the Anglo-American nor in the Continental version a coherent field, but rather a mixture of different research programs involving theoretical, institutional, administrative and public choice approaches, we think it is possible to focus our reflections to the hard core of the discipline, to its ideal-type common features. Although the criticism presented in what follows may not be equally applicable to all schools and theories of public finance, we feel justified in the present state of the art to sacrifice the heterogenity to concentration on common shortcomings and insufficiencies. The analysis of such shortcomings and dubious assumptions refers here largely if not exclusively to welfare (public) economics.

As far as the shortcomings to be discussed are concerned, they can generally refer to several analytical levels of a discipline:

(1) to the chosen analytical perspective and the related axiomatic foundations and premises both of which are strongly influenced by the chosen perspectives and the claims of theory. This problem will be discussed in detail in the following section 2.

(2) to the analytical tools and methodological instruments and procedures used to survey the subject area. When the analytical gate, however, is too narrow, the practical relevance of research is consequently restricted. This will be demonstrated in section 3.

(3) to the level of abstraction involving the exclusion of a number of significant aspects and the neglect of a whole series of relevant phenomena in the real world. This leads to the existence of explanatory gaps which have to be closed for a valid analysis. This will be outlined in section 4.

If our assumptions are correct, the range, the limits, the ability to develop, the fruitfulness, and thus the real strengths or conversely the weakness of a discipline are determined by these three dimensions. They will, therefore, represent the basis of the following reflections and be used as a yardstick for the appraisal of the performance of public finance economics.

3.8 Welfare Economic Foundations: Normativism and Decisionism

The Problem of State Versus Market Allocative Responsibility

Apart from the historical predecessors of modern public finance, such as the well-known Cameralism (Fürstenwohlstandslehre), the basic problem of the discipline, at least for the last hundred years, has been primarily and constantly: which "collective needs" or goods and services are, or should be, subject to the market or to the responsibility of the state.

Whereas the *positive analysis* in the Wagner tradition was content to describe and explain which tasks the state had taken over in the course of its historical development and how a secular growth of state activity and tasks (measurable by state share in GNP) had developed, modern public finance wants to apply normative criteria to determine which state activities are *legitimate* and *to what extent*. For this purpose the Theory of Collective Goods (see Schmidt 1970) or the Theory of Optimal Budget (Mackscheidt 1973) is used primarily. In these the rule has been developed that the only goods which should be the responsibility of the state are those whose properties – such as external effects, nonexcludability or joint consumption – produce a situation in which an optimal supply would not develop under the condition of individual economic rationality. Prospective users would conceal their preferences so as not to be involved in financing the product, for they would be able to use it at no cost at all as free-riders, once it were produced.

All other publicly provided goods which are basically marketable but are for historical, social or political reasons the responsibility of the state, are according to theoretical standards wrongly allocated. The reason for this is that, the perfectly competitive market, used as the standard of reference is thought to produce better results than the state[1].

As "timeless" basic rules of public finance show – for example Say's "the smallest budget is the best" or the neutrality rule of taxation: "leave them as you find them" – the choice of non-market decision processes is at most the "second best". In cases, however, where state intervention cannot be avoided, the conceptualization of the public sector should in accordance with the maxim of the pure competitive market[2], maximize the social welfare function as the summation of the self interest of individuals. In welfare economic theory of collective decisions state intervention and state's structure are normatively required to be modelled according to market foundations (Baumol 1965). This means that collective preferences are defined as analogous to individual ones: for every pair of alternatives, they state which alternative is to be preferred; the decisive problem is how a collective order can be derived from individual preferences. This is generally taken care of by using collective choice rules. The most common variant of this rule is considered to be the so-called Pareto-extension-rule, according to which alternative A is to be preferred collectively to alternative B if at least one (!) collective member regards it as better and none as worse than B. A number of additional collective choice rules can be instanced; it is important to find those that amalgamate individual preferences not only as exactly but also as smoothly as possible. This results in the basic problem of aggregation (Sen 1970). For wherever only individuals exist, society or even the state cannot reasonably develop as sui generis phenomena; at the most they can be artificially constructed. If one follows this line of reasoning, the well known choice paradoxes and impossibility theorems result. With them one can prove that a nonmarket decision situation with three persons and three alternatives cannot guarantee clear choices. This, therefore, demonstrates the decision logic inferiority of the public policy area compared to the market and thus implies normative judgments.

The determination of what should be becomes, however, a "nirvana approach" (Demsetz) in cases where the description, explanation, analysis or control of *real* phenomena is the main aim. If there are no basic differences between private und public goods in the real world, as Musgrave concedes (1971: 65); if consistent mechanisms for the aggregation of individual preferences into a social welfare function do not exist, or only under very strong assumptions; if beyond individual orientation there are common values and ideas of a general welfare which cause individuals to delegate to the state tasks beyond the public goods; if the outlined analysis lacks the application of empirical methods to survey human behavior, then Schmidt might be right that public finance, to the extent that it uses welfare economics' normative axioms to determine and legitimize the type and extent of state activity, is one of the dead ends of economics (1970: 3). *This type of normative view blocks the understanding of the real world based on empirical experience.*

Choice-Logic Versus Socio-Logic

Related to the normative welfare theory foundation of public finance sketched above, there are two sets of axiomatic behavioral assumptions relevant to its explanatory power or inadequacies:

(1) economic self interest as the exclusive basis of human action, which causes people to stand up only for their own interest and take better care of things that are theirs than of those belonging to others. Paretian welfare theory implies in its structures a type of behavior assumed in the neoclassical theory, namely the maximizing of individual economic benefits by economic agents. This assumption should guarantee an *integrated approach,* based on an ubiquitous decision-logic

rationality social and psychological factors, structural and functional differences are evened out; a society of "analytical equals" is constructed whose motivational basis is in Marcuse's words "one-dimensional".

This type of theory is thus forced neglect form a lot of influential behavioral variables, shifting them as "data constants" out of the explanatory model; it thus does not admit to explain dynamic development or evolutionary changes within the range of the theory itself. Therefore, attention is concentrated rather on static allocation and distribution problems within a fixed framework.

(2) modern public finance theory is based on a *choice-logic* model, which means that economic man, be he a producer or consumer of public goods, constantly makes decisions regarding the allocation of given scarce resources among given competing end; therefore, this model of man can be called: "egomechanic permanent calculator". Man is assumed to act principally in an isolated, monadic (Robinson Crusoe) situation, thinking in marginal terms, his only orientation being his individual preference function and his budget line. This conception – even if it is right in avoiding a bifurcated model of man (Buchanan) by modelling private and public actors in the same way – is nevertheless empirically questionable. In contrast, behavioral models based on sociology and, in particular, on game theory show a far greater variety of action orientations and are thus able to measure other kinds of action and behavior, including for example strategic behavior. As regards public finance, Schleicher in particular has demonstrated this from a game theory perspective (Schleicher 1971). Moreover Kirzner (1980: 6) has pointed out that in real life "making the right decisions . . . calls for far more than correct mathematical calculation". A shrewd and wise assessment of present and future realities is necessary in the decision context, a taking into account of uncertainty, imperfect knowledge, and particular circumstances of time and place. A concrete empirical theory of the public sector, which does not negate, but rather incorporates the choice-logic of public economics, must include *socio-logic* arguments and must supplement the goal-means rationality with "value-rationality" (Weber); it must abandon the assumption of autonomous individual action, the "immaculate conception of the indifference curve" as Boulding says. The reason for this is that in addition to the production and consumption externalities there are, particularly in the public sector, "preference externalities", a reciprocal influencing of individual preferences and of societal values. Moreover, the most recent extensive empirical study concludes with regard to public and political goods that preferences are only developed and formed by familiarity and use, and thus by practical experience of goods and services (Gretschmann and Mackscheidt 1984). The very process of consuming certain goods thus develops the preferences for these goods (and others) while welfare economics assumes preferences as given "ex ante", determining which goods will be demanded and consumed.

If, however, individual preferences have developed in and are determined by a social learning process related to specific actors on the one hand and goods on the other, then it is obviously a mistake to trace collective welfare exclusively back to autonomous, tabula rasa individual preferences. This has been recognized by students of public finance who conduct empirical research. To produce empirical results usually means that the basic preferences from actual and revealed choices regarding public goods have been inferred in each case (Engelhardt 1982: 4;

Pommerehne 1982). It is, however, a nonsequitur (post hoc ergo propter hoc) to suppose that what is supplied must have been desired. With Leibenstein (1982: 460) this method can be criticized as "bull's-eye painting economics"[3].

3.9 The "Economistically" Contracted Understanding of Policy

From the Awkward Merit Goods to the Technocratic View of Policy

In contrast to the concept of the public sector outlined above, limited to the domain of public goods only, we find goods which are in principle marketable but are nevertheless subject to state intervention because of their particular social or political importance. Musgrave has called them merit goods, an awkward classification the legitimacy of which has become the centre of an extensive debate (McLure 1968; Head 1970).

Because of the dominating share of merit goods, as opposed to "pure" public goods, in state activity or the state budget, it is clear that political leaders often practice "dirigiste" intervention, which undermines the sovereign consumer or taxpayer decision maker assumed by welfare theory. A double inconsistency, therefore, becomes evident for welfare theorists: (1) Although the goods are marketable, they are regulated by the state, and (2) although political choice by the people might be possible in this regard, bureaucratic and political elites make the decision.

The real problem of merit goods is, however, perceived wrongly as long as theory formation follows specific goods' properties being not aware of the fact that, in the last instance, it is a problem of socio-political choice and not (only) the properties of the goods themselves, which underlie the debate about merit goods.

Precisely this dimension of choice and decision making, however, points to processes of goal selection, program development, search for priorities, and the evaluation of programs – to categories which are mostly found in public finance treatment of budget and budgetary policy (see Hansmeyer and Rürup 1977), not, however, in pure public finance theory.

The discussion about the planning instruments of financial policy – such as public budgets, intermediate financial planning, PPBS, Sunset Legislation, ZBB and so forth – would have the same shortcomings of voluntarism and vagueness as the merit goods, were not a pragmatic foundation used, which I shall call the *Technocratic View*. This term may describe in a pointed way the attempt to formulate, apply and analyze appropriate and rational (financial) policy strategies. This concept is the opposite of politics which, especially in its Continental meaning, is the domain of social interaction, power, class-struggles, bargaining, clashes of interests and the success and failure of interest groups.

The concept of "politics" going back to Rousseau's model of the permanent plebiscite, represents an *"input-oriented"* idea of democracy and political processes, also found in Marx, whereas the "policy-oriented" idea of democracy concentrates *on output* and primarily on the making of binding decisions and is interested in an efficient performance of tasks.

Public finance planning discussion is clearly oriented towards the latter and assumes that for every political problem there is only *one best way,* which simply has to be found and applied. The necessary technical requirements for the structure of the political system are determined by the output, by the technical efficiency orientation. The more a policy requires intervention and social administration by the state, the less important will be the question of how the political will is formed democratically and participatively in particular cases. The harmonizing and compromising of interests – although it cannot be valued too highly – becomes a neglected factor in public finance. The chapter by Reese (Ch. 27) particularly, but also the one by Schleicher (Ch. 25) in this volume show that a number of acceptable solutions replace the one best way and, moreover, that the natural solution is determined by the strategic behavior of the persons affected as well as by the acceptability of the respective "programs".

Thus the technocratic way of looking at things prevents the realization that policy making often has to sacrifice the short term benefits of the "one best way" solution in the intererst of long term *flexibility* of the policy making capacity itself. This really makes it necessary not to select one best set of goals and instruments, working out the optimal allocation at a given time, but rather to take into account uncertainty, unforeseen events, changing social environments, and the constant development of new problems to be solved. Therefore the maximand in a public sector theory decision function cannot be of the "one best way" type aiming at short term economic welfare. It should be rather the optimizing of future flexibility (Wiedemann 1983: 161). In this connection Kaufmann points out (Ch. 10) that this is often achieved by redefining or reinterpreting goals in the process that is supposed to lead to them, the intention being to conceal obvious failures and/or to adjust the goals belatedly to what can be achieved and implemented and thus to the resistance of the persons concerned. In this way the achievement process is interpreted analytically – shooting at a moving target in which the shot determines the target.

The technocratic orientation of public finance implies an extensive form of social information gathering for the purpose of defining problems, setting goals, carrying out measures, and checking results. This can clearly become counterproductive for social reasons even though it is intended to increase efficiency: The necessary social information gathering also makes the social status quo more comprehensible. This makes citizens who are in some respect below the average or below some politically-set social standard aware of their situation, often for the first time. As a result they almost inevitably make more demands for state intervention. Through binding goal formulation, coordination and decision, the state becomes the responsible agent in processes which it in fact is not able to control. Thus state authorities may be in danger of becoming the target of performance tests and disappointed expectations, regardless of whether or not they have the means to realize the goals set for them. Moreover the increased availability of information about the state of society makes it increasingly difficult to form a consensus within the political system. This can be explained as follows: one can proceed on the assumption that social subsystems tend to operate according to the maxim of shifting their burdens inconspicuously whenever possible to the general public, but they share their advantages selectively (Hansmeyer and Mackscheidt 1977). To the extent that not only the often nonmonetary benefits of such programs, which as a rule are group specific, but also their cost incidence, which is also not necessarily monetary, become publicly known through explicit statements of goals and measurement of success, freedom of action in the formulation and execution of a policy is reduced. The trade-offs in all areas of society, which are inevitable when resources are limited but which previously were not ascertained and thus were unnoticed and without effect, now have to be included in policy control, since they can now be measured and thus made known. The consensus costs of policy decisions rise, however, in proportion to the extent that trade-offs become visible.

In so far as the theory of the public sector ignores this kind of socio-economic relationships in favor of a technocratic way of looking at things it must necessarily remain inadequate.

Costs and Prices or Public Goals: Efficiency as a Substitute for Policy

The arguments presented above are among the reasons why the significance attributed in public finance analysis of the public sector, to the theoretical problems of shadow price formation for public services, or to the cost-benefit-analysis of the performance of public tasks as decision aids and monitoring instruments, ignores the empirical importance of these concepts in practical policy. This one-sidedness is certainly typical of Anglo-American public finance but is also found increasingly in German speaking countries (Wiegard 1978; Musgrave et al. 1982; as criticism Kirsch 1975).

Whereas it certainly makes sense to carry out a financial analysis of production and cost functions of public services, particularly in times when money is scarce, the assumption of the theoretically highly valued minimum cost concept, namely that minimum cost is a good indicator of a welfare maximum in the public sector, is, to say the least, questionable. On the one hand, non-market outputs are normally hard to define, ill defined in practice, and extremely difficult to quantify or to evaluate qualitatively. On the other hand, the activities of public administration are not directed towards producing a given output with a minimum of input but rather towards achieving "monolithic" public goals.

Policy goal decisions in the public sector do not necessarily include the minimization of costs to the same extent as do the private goal decisions of market enterprises. The popular comparative efficiency studies are, therefore, only valid if a complex model is used which compares the coordination mechanisms of the public and private sectors, as well as the respective incentive structures, and analyzes, in detail the relationships of the goal spectrum, goal realization, and resource outlay to each other. It is not possible to transfer the goals of a private company directly to a public area and then draw conclusions regarding the comparative efficiency from the differences observed. To give one example, a state-owned railroad charged with the task of absorbing as many disabled former soldiers as possible while maintaining a balanced budget will have higher personnel costs than a private railroad whose stockholders insist on long term maximization of the value of their shares. An efficiency comparison is difficult because the goals are, in part at least, diametrically opposed.

A comparison would only be viable and valid within the framework of a complex model with which weights could be assigned to different goals.

If a theoretical analysis fails to consider relationships and is satisfied with a one-dimensional efficiency (monetary) criterion taken from the market – a criterion devised to solve the scarcity problem and only suitable for that – the analysis of politico-administrative processes as well as of decision and coordination structures, which make use of a large number of political, social and cultural criteria, will also be reduced to a single dimension. Efficiency thus becomes for observational and explanatory theory a mistaken substitute for policy.

Fiscalism and Budgetary Instrumentalism

Far more than its "sister", pure economics, public finance has always operated in the area where "art" and exact science overlap. Whereas the latter is normally content with description and explanation, the former is concerned with prescriptions, with goals intended to direct or control.

While public finance is basically concerned with taxes and state indebtedness on the one hand and with state expenditure on the other, its perspective is subject to two screening instruments which we shall call *fiscalism* and *budgetary instrumentalism* here.

By fiscalism we understand an analysis of the public sector mainly concerned with fiscal, i.e. monetary phenomena, effect-relationships and payment-flows. Whether in the area of the theory of control, budget incidence, willingness-to-pay models or state debt policy, this instrument always reduces policy to its fiscal equivalent or to fiscal indicators. Although public finance does recognize that certain actor relationship, coordination modalities, and control factors as well as various incentive, persuasive, and regulative policy programs underly these fiscal phenomena, it leaves the discussion to related disciplines.

In fiscalism the primary factor and object of analysis is the state budget, which not only implies that, particularly in Europe, public finance is less interested in the analysis of production and performance processes than in technical and legal aspects of budget research. This also explains the narrow viewpoint of fiscalism with regard to the public sector.

This narrowness constitutes the connection between fiscalism and budgetary instrumentalism. This instrumentalism regards as policy primarily what is reflected in the state budget itself. The public budget is considered the central control variable of the public sector; the theory of budget circulation (Haushaltskreislauf) and of the formation of budgetary goals serves as a fragmentary substitute analysis of the policy process in the politico-administrative system. State policy is budget efficient state expenditure policy; the budget becomes the verifiable government program in figures.

Zimmermann demonstrated more than a decade ago that such a budget-oriented conceptualization of policy does justice neither to the public sector as a real phenomenon nor to financial policy itself. In a widely regarded article about "Expenditure Intensity and Public Task Fulfilment" (1973) he was able to show that one and the same policy goal and the political and practical measures required to reach it could have very much, comparatively little, or no effects on the public budget and the fiscal flows. For example, if families with many children are to be helped, this can be accomplished by direct social transfer payments, which would result in an increase in public expenditure. That would not, however, be the case if tax allowances were granted or private employers were forced by law to pay wage increments for each child. State activity is thus by no means limited to budget efficient instruments, just as tax income collected under sovereign authority is not the only form of income on which a state community is dependent.

Moreover, in many an area it is possible to subject state organization to the law of the market. Instead of using planning, regulations or subsidies, the state can make economic policy as an employer (public enterprise) and thus permit the laws of market competition to work for it, with the result that all private competitors have to follow its guidelines.

Budgetary instrumentalism, which is inclined to confine its attention to budget-efficient policy processes, is thus not completely useless, but it is clearly insufficient as far as the fabric of guidance, performance and control evaluation in the public sector is concerned[4].

Public Finance Between Agents and Aggregates

Not the least important factor in the external viability and productivity of a theory is its structural methodological approach to its subject. Thus, according to Popper's spotlight theory, not only the adjustment of the spotlight is important, which as a result illuminates reality differently and creates different shadows; to continue this simile, the type of spotlight is also important – its diffuse or aimed light which determines how the area to be studied is elucidated.

In this sense the traditional public finance and economic theories are largely (macro-) *aggregate theories* which seek to provide an analysis of the monetary flows and how they affect aggregates. This is equally true of such subsectors as debt management, business cycle theory, tax theory and so forth. Only the effects of abstract control units and stock-flow yields, not types of empirical action are of interest for most public finance theories. Internal coordination and process dynamics which motivate individuals and collectives are specifically ignored. This results in a hydraulic way of theoretical thinking, a mode of analysis which is similar to a system of communicating tubes.

If one classifies the main elements of a theory according to whether they are empirically determinable action units or abstract analytical system units (regulators) which function as reference points for a complete evidence structure, it is aggregates that can be considered subject to public finance and its equation systems[5].

Accordingly, errors in financial and economic analysis usually result from four causes:

(1) the use of highly simplistic, mechanistic hypotheses concerning the type and number of aggregates (or agents) to be considered;
(2) the use of highly limited information for estimating the necessary coefficients;
(3) the common neglect of aggregation problems resulting from the use of hydraulic models;

(4) the nonobservance of different institutional arrangements, of interacting
   agents, of goods and services and so forth.

Closely related to this is a *constructivistic* way of theory formation. This means the
arbitrary use of parameters and masses of "non-essential data". In this way the
fabric of the socio-economic conditioning factors is torn apart and the determining
factors constructivistically placed on three levels:

All primary institutional structural constants of the theory (market forms,
decision technologies, motives of action, system structures and so forth), except
the explicitly mentioned variables are excluded. The variables used in the model
are divided into exogenous and endogenous ones. This implies that no attention is
paid to the short term feed-back of the exogenous to the endogenous variables or
to the long-term effect relationships between the data and the variables. In this
way, however, the discipline evades any responsibility for explaining for example
institutional and historical shifts, cannot adequately comprehend evolutionary
processes – for example institutional learning – and relegates genuine psychological, social and political influence factors to the competence of other disciplines.
Eleonor Ostrom's chapter (22) in this volume demonstrates how such a complex
problem can be solved adequately by analytical design!

3.10 The Neglect of the Real World: Institutional and Organizational Factors

Multiformity and Interdependencies Instead of a Clear Separation of Market and State

The above discussion of a variety of policy types, apart from budget efficient state
activity, reveals – beyond single personal actors on the one hand and the anonymous corpus of the state on the other – various corporate actors, i.e. institutionally
mixed forms in which the public sector presents itself. The broad spectrum of
services corresponds to the fragmented structure of state action; the original
unitarian, monolithic idea of *the* state has been split into categories. Political
science now refers to the idea of a multidimensional politico-administrative system.
The idea of the state as one institution has lost its sharp distinction, not just in our
time, as many people believe, but in the course of its historical development.
Instead of an assumed two-sector division of market against state pervading all
economic theory formation (Gretschmann 1981), which implies a clear separation,
the public sector has always encompassed a multiplicity of different organizations
and institutions which make the boundary unclear and operate in a grey zone
between the two sectors. Whereas institutionally oriented public finance, above all
in Germany, Austria and some Latin countries, has always been concerned with
mixed forms such as the institutions of fiscal federalism or the so-called parafisci
(quasi-governmental institutions), pure public finance theory tends to ignore many
less prominent mixed institutions, which are often also neglected in real institutional analyses.

Rainy, Backoff and Levine (1976: 233) have shown for the American case the varied forms an exact analysis will find; Schuppert (1981) has done the same thing for Germany. Whether it is a matter of functional bodies which have to satisfy autonomy requirements in certain marginal areas of the public sector (European radio and television for example), or a tension-relationship involving economically independent management and politically determined responsibility (such as the German Federal Railroad or the postal system) cases where the state requires to keep a low profile (foreign aid by quasi-governmental institutions) or organizational self-administration (parafisci, guilds), private organizations have always either grown into the public sector or the state has crossed its legally defined boundaries into the private sector. The direct performance of tasks by the state has become indirect; areas free of state-bureaucratic activities have developed. The state is increasingly making use of the administrative abilities of private group and companies; the pursuit of public goals is taking on a quasi-governmental character (Ronge 1980; Schuppert 1981; Huppertz 1983).

In contrast to the real world importance of such mixed "institutions" as those mentioned above, their analysis has never been a central concern of either public finance or economics as a whole. Moreover, public finance lacks a general theory of semi-public institutions. The analysis of the form, structure, and function of "Quangos" and "Quagos" is thus more than a research gap (see Hood: Ch. 9). In favor of theoretical stringency, traditional theory has banished real institutions and organizations to the analytical area reserved for "non-essential" data: The theoretician can isolate the effects and workings of "pure" economic variables only by keeping the institutional structure constant and exogenous.

This goal is achieved, however, at the cost of neglecting both the effects of these variables on the institutional structure and vice versa. This was one of Schultz's main concerns in characterizing and criticzing economic theory as institution free: "It is currently a mark of sophistication in presenting economic models not to mention institutions . . .; in thinking about institutions the analytical cupboard is bare." (1968: 1113).

What Happens in the Black Box: Phases of Functions and Process Analysis

Not only public finance and public economics are institution-free; the New Political Economy, which aims at a reintegration of policy and economics in the Downsian tradition, places, if one examines it closely, too little weight on institutions. If this shortcoming is to be eliminated, the well-known idea that political competition guarantees in most cases a close link between public services and the preferences of the citizens must be abandoned. Similarly, the equally questionable hypothesis must be dropped that the hierarchical chain of command in the politico-administrative system will not deviate significantly in the bureaucratic production of services from the wishes of the political suppliers. In this context Kaufmann stresses below (Ch. 10), that the relevant action chains have multiplied and thus become – as a result of increasing system complexity – so much longer that direct cause-effects or order-execution connections, in so far as they ever existed, are no longer present. This results primarily and increasingly in the problem of unintended consequences of individual and corporate actions aimed at particular goals.

Back to the model for the adjustment of political demand and supply. A viable theory of the public sector would, on the one hand, have to be able to determine exactly the social demand for state services, or, at least, the essential decision factors involved. To avoid oversimplification it would have to specify the internal condition variables of state services and guarantee a clear and analytical separation of suppliers, users, decision makers, lobbyists, payers, auditors, etc. as participants in the process of guidance and control of public supply and demand and as elements in the complex chains of action.

At the same time the scope for bureaucratic freedom of action and decision making must be surveyed. Oligopoly and monopoly models of the public sector do not provide an adequate analytical apparatus for this purpose. The analysis requires rather a theory of public production which permits a look into the black box of the public sector. The purpose of this would be to determine which (sets of) goals influence the orientation of the public administration in its production, cost and output decisions; how these affect the welfare position of the (potential) users, and how the latter then provide feedback; what degree of autonomy, what restrictions etc. are present (Roppel 1979).

If one wishes to do justice to these theoretical requirements, the individual functional phases of the public production process must be clearly differentiated from each other and their interdependence must be analyzed in detail. Following the example of Mackscheidt and Steinhausen (1977: 114), Matzner (1982: 151) in particular has suggested a functional phase analysis of public provision processes. He distinguishes the following phases:

(1) determination of need; (2) determining the requirements; (3) planning the concrete form of production and the necessary institutions; (4) filling the need; (5) supplying and use of services; (6) forms of financing; (7) modes of control.

Such a comprehensive analysis has not yet been made in public finance. Studies have been either limited to the analysis of selected phases, or details have been sacrificed and not treated in sufficient depth. More important, however, is the mix, the analysis of the interplay of all functional phases. A viable theory of the public sector has yet to achieve this.

3.11 Conclusion

A critical examination of the contributions of modern public finance to portraying and explaining the functioning of the public sector has detected serious inadequacies. Like many other disciplines, public finance is – partially – based on a number of controversial premises, suffers from methodological limitations, excludes a number of significant aspects, and, therefore, contains debatable findings and assertions.

All these elements discover deep gaps both in empirical research and pure theory of the public sector which at the present state of the art can only be filled by using a multidimensional approach and by applying sustained interdisciplinary effort. It has become obvious that public finance and public economics can provide only several of the stones for the mosaic – important ones to be sure, but they also leave many blank spaces.

Notes

1 The Pareto Optimum maintains that, with regard to the allocation of resources and technical productivity, an optimal situation is characterized by the fact that it is impossible to increase the production of one good without reducing that of another. Concerning the distribution of goods and the preference systems of individual economic subjects, the welfare position of one subject cannot be improved in an optimal situation without worsening that of another. If this description of an optimum becomes a politically recommended criterion, welfare economics must be considered a normative concept. Not the description of what is, but what ought to be is its subject; not describing facts but determining the best economic policy is its goal.

2 One could, on the other hand, construct the state according to the model of the family, as does Japanese sociology.

3 Leibenstein (1982: 460) reports the "story of the general who, while visiting a small town in Tsarist Russia, was very impressed by the marksmanship displayed on various barn walls. In every instance a bullet hole was found through the center of bull's eye. 'I must meet this exceptional shot,' exclaimed the general (. . .). Though the general was told that the marksman was the village idiot, he persisted until a meeting was arranged. 'Tell me,' the general commanded, 'how do you do it' (. . .) 'oh Excellency, it's not so hard. First I shoot, then I paint the bull's eye'".

4 From a critical perspective of the state this phenomenon has recently been discussed and radicalized under the term "shift of bureaucratic tasks" (Bürokratieüberwälzung). This describes a situation in which even private households and companies are required by law or decree to perform certain administrative tasks for the state without compensation (jury duty; collecting taxes; compiling statistics etc.) (see Dickertmann 1982: 153).

5 Consider for example a simple demand estimation equation for goods to be provided by the state:

$D = D (E, M, F, N, R, T, P)$

D = demand; E = externalities resulting from private sector activities; M = degree of private sector monopolization yielding producer rents; F = market frictions; N = direct needs for public goods; R = demand for redistribution; T = tax rate; P = tax prices.

References

Baumol, W. J. (1965): *Welfare Economics and the Theory of the State.* London, Bell & Sons.

Bell, D. (1974): "The Public Household – On Fiscal Sociology and the Liberal Society." *The Public Interest* 37 (Fall): 29–68.

Bray, J. (1970): *Decision in Government.* London: Gollancz.

Dickertmann, D. (1982): "Bürokratieüberwälzung aus volkswirtschaftlicher und finanzwissenschaftlicher Sicht." In Dickertmann D., H. König, and G. W. Wittkämpfer (eds.), *Bürokratieüberwälzung*, 153–182. Regensburg: Verl. Recht, Verwaltung, Wirtschaft.

Engelhardt, G. (1982): *On the Demand For Government Activities.* 38th Congress of IIFP at Copenhagen. (Mimeogr.)

Enthoven, A. C., and K. W. Smith (1971): *How Much is Enough?* New York: Harper and Row.

Gerloff, W., and F. Meisel (eds.) (1926): *Handbuch der Finanzwissenschaft* (1st ed.). Tübingen: Mohr.

Goldscheidt, R. (1926): "Staat, öffentlicher Haushalt und Gesellschaft – Wesen und Aufgabe der Finanzwissenschaft vom Standpunkt der Soziologie." *Handbuch der Finanzwissenschaft* (1st ed.), 146–184. Tübingen: Mohr.

Good, I. J. (1962): "How Rational Should a Manager Be?" *Management Science* 8/4: 383–393.

Gretschmann, K. (1981): *Steuerungsprobleme der Staatswirtschaft.* Berlin: Duncker & Humblot.

Gretschmann, K., and K. Mackscheidt (1985): *Wachsende Disharmonien zwischen öffentlichem Leistungsangebot und gesellschaftlicher Nachfrage.* Berlin: Duncker & Humblot.

Hansmeyer, K. H., and K. Mackscheidt (1977): "Finanzpsychologie." In Neumark, F. (ed.), *Handbuch der Finanzwissenschaft* (3rd. ed.), 554–586. Tübingen: Mohr.

Hansmeyer, K. H., and B. Rürup (1977): *Staatswirtschaftliche Planungsinstrumente.* Düsseldorf: Werner-Verlag.

Head, J. G. (1970): "Über meritorische Güter." In Recktenwald, H. C. (ed.), *Finanztheorie,* 64–74. Köln–Berlin: Kiepenheuer & Witsch.

Hitch, C. J., and R. McKean (1962): *The Economics of Defense in the Nuclear Age.* Cambridge, Mass.: Harvard Univ. Press.

Huppertz, P.-H. (1983): *Theorie und Politik der Parafisci – Zur Konzeption eines fiskalischen Korporatismus.* Köln. (Mimeogr.)

Kelman, S. (1981): *What Price Incentives?* Boston, Mass.: Auburn.

Kirsch, G. (1975): "Die Cost-Benefit-Analyse: Zur Kritik ihrer theoretischen Grundlagen." In Kirsch, G., and W. Wittmann (eds.), *Nationale Ziele und Soziale Indikatoren,* 69–80. Stuttgart: G. Fischer.

Kirzner, J. M. (1980): *Perception, Opportunity and Profit: Studies in the Theory of Entrepreneurship.* Chicago–London: Univ. of Chicago Press.

Leibenstein, H. (1976): *Beyond Economic Man.* Cambridge, Mass.: Harvard Univ. Press.

Leibenstein, H. (1982): "On bull's-eye-painting economics." *Journal of Postkeynesian Economics* 4/3: 460–465.

Lindblom, C. E. (1980): *The Policy-Making Process.* Englewood Cliffs, N. J.: Prentice-Hall.

Lindley, D. (1971): *Making Decisions.* London–New York: Wiley-Interscience.

Mackscheidt, K. (1973): *Zur Theorie des optimalen Budgets.* Tübingen: Mohr/Siebeck.

Mackscheidt, K., and J. Steinhausen (1977): *Finanzpolitik II. Grundfragen versorgungspolitischer Eingriffe.* Tübingen–Düsseldorf: Mohr-Siebeck-Werner.

Majone, G. (1976): "Choice among Policy Instruments for Pollution Control." *Policy Analysis* 2/3: 569–613.

Matzner, E. (1982): *Der Wohlfahrtsstaat von morgen.* Frankfurt–NewYork: Campus.

McLure, C. E. (1968): "Merit Wants – A Normatively Empty Box." *Finanzarchiv* N. F. 27/3: 474–482.

Musgrave, R. A. (1966): *Finanztheorie.* Tübingen: Mohr.

Musgrave, R. A. (1971): "Infrastruktur und die Theorie öffentlicher Güter." In Arndt, H. and D. Swatek (eds.), *Grundfragen der Infrastrukturplanung für wachsende Wirtschaften.* Schriften des Vereins für Sozialpolitik, N. F. 58: 43–54. Berlin: Duncker & Humblot.

Musgrave, R. A. (eds.) (1982): *Public Production.* Wien–New York: Springer.

Pommerehne, W. W. (1982): "Empirische Ansätze zur Erfassung der Präferenzen für öffentliche Güter." In Bombach G., B. Gahlen, and A. E. Ott (eds.), *Möglichkeiten und Grenzen der Staatstätigkeit,* 407–492. Tübingen: Mohr.

Pressman, J., A. Wildavsky (1973): *Implementation.* Berkeley, Cal.: Univ. of Calif. Press.

Quade, E. S. (1982): *Analysis for Public Decisions* (2nd ed.). New York–Amsterdam: North-Holland.

Rainey, H. G., R. W. Backoff, and C. H. Levine (1976): "Comparing Public and Private Organizations." *Public Administration Review* 36/2: 233–244.

Rawls, J.(1973): *A Theory of Justice.* New York: Oxford Univ. Press. (softcover ed.)

Robbins, L. (1932): *Politics and Economics: Papers in Political Economy.* London: MacMillan.

Ronge, V. (1980): *Am Staat vorbei*. Frankfurt a. Main– New York: Campus.

Roppel, U. (1979): *Ökonomische Theorie der Bürokratie: Beiträge zu einer Theorie des Angebotsverhaltens staatlicher Bürokratien in Demokratien*. Freiburg: Haufe.

Ryle, G. (1949): *The Concept of Mind*. London: Hutchinson.

Schleicher, H. (1971): *Staatshaushalt und Strategie*. Berlin: Duncker & Humblot.

Schmidt, K. (1970): "Kollektivbedürfnisse und Staatstätigkeit." In Haller, H. (ed.), *Theorie und Praxis des finanzpolitischen Interventionismus*, 3–27. Tübingen: Mohr/Siebeck.

Schultze, C. L. (1977): *The Public Use of Private Interest*. Washington, D.C.: The Brookings Institution.

Schumpeter, J. A. (1950): *Capitalism, Socialism and Democracy* (3rd ed.). New York: Harper & Row.

Schuppert, G. F. (1981): *Die Erfüllung öffentlicher Aufgaben durch verselbständigte Verwaltungseinheiten*. Göttingen: Schwartz.

Selznick, P. (1964): *Leadership in Administration*. New York: Harper and Row.

Sen, A. K. (1970): *Collective Choice and Social Welfare*. Edinburgh: Oliver & Boyd.

Sen, A. K. (1974): "Feasibility Constraints: Foreign Exchange and Shadow Wages." In Layard R. (ed.), *Cost-Benefit Analysis*, 140–159. Harmondsworth, Middlesex, Engl.: Penguin books.

Shultz, T. W. (1968): "Institutions and the Rising Economic Value of Man." *American Journal of Agricultural Economics* 50/5 (December): 1113–1122.

Sorensen, T. C. (1963): *Decision-Making in the White House*. New York: Columbia Univ. Press.

Stokey, E., and R. Zeckhauser (1978): *A Primer for Policy Analysis*. New York: W. W. Norton.

Tukey. J. (1960): "Conclusions versus Decisions", *Technometrics* 2/4: 423–433.

Wagner, A. (1883): *Finanzwissenschaft*. Leipzig–Heidelberg: Wintersche Verlagshandlung.

Wiedemann, P. (1983): "Policy Modeling, Planning and Flexibility." *Jahrbücher für Nationalökonomie und Statistik* Vol. 198/2: 161–172.

Wiegard, W. (1978): *Optimale Schattenpreise und Produktionsprogramme für öffentliche Unternehmen*. Frankfurt a. M.–Bern–Las Vegas: Lang.

Zimmermann, H. (1973): "Die Ausgabenintensität der öffentlichen Aufgabenerfüllung." *Finanzarchiv* N. F. 32/1: 1–20.

Part 2
The Public Sector: Constitutional and Conceptual Problems

4. The Modern State: Continental Traditions

Dieter Grimm

Abstract

The modern state emerged from the confessional civil wars of the sixteenth and seventeenth century. Its function consisted in pursuing the common best against the particular interests of society. For this purpose, the state was endowed with sovereign power over society. The monopoly of legitimate coercion thus appears as the distinguishing characteristic of the state. Originally identified with the person of the ruler, the state eventually became an impersonal, abstract entity different from government and the governed. This development was completed by the French Revolution which transferred sovereignty to the people from whom the state now derived its power. At the same time, the use of state power was limited in the liberal sense to protecting individual liberty and social autonomy. The present welfare state has again widened its functions to an all-embracing responsability for the development of society, but remains limited as to the use of coercive power. This makes the state dependent to a large extent on social cooperation, so that the identity of the state has become uncertain and a reconsideration of its role seems necessary.

4.1 The Emergence of the Absolute State from the Crisis of the Medieval Order

The State as Central Notion of Continental Politics

For more than five centuries the form of political unity on the European continent has been the state.[1] The state appears as an abstract and impersonal entity, different from government and from the governed, but embracing both of them. This entity may be conceived as a living organism, a corporate body, a machinery or apparatus, a social system. Its invariable attribute is supreme power over the people in a certain territory. The persons exercising this power act on behalf of the impersonal state. They are but organs of the latter. The supreme power may rest on different social grounds: military force, support of a dominant class, general consent, and may be organized in different ways: concentrated on an absolute ruler, or divided among several institutions. Still, it is the state that remains the constant point of reference for legitimate power in society. In this tradition, the state is not only an intellectual means of conceiving political reality, but constitutes a reality in itself. European politics cannot be fully understood when the state perspective is left out. Political institutions such as parties or administrative agencies, and political procedures like law making or government controlling adopt a different meaning in societies with or without state. On the other hand, it would be equally wrong to regard the state as a universal notion, as some European thinkers, misled by the salience of the state in their own country, did. The idea of the state as an abstract entity was unkown for a long period of time, and it is of little importance in a number of regions or countries today. The modern European state owes its existence to a particular historical experience where it seemed to be the adequate way of problem solving. This experience was the crisis of the medieval order beginning in the thirteenth century and culminating in the late fifteenth and early sixteenth century.

The Stateless Medieval Order

In the medieval world, the social order as a whole, including its moral, ecclesiastical, cultural, political, legal, economical elements, was considered part of God's creative plan. The ultimate end of the temporal order being man's eternal salvation, the order was total in the sense that it did not leave any sphere of life to the individual's will. Every authority, whether spiritual or temporal, derived its power from this end. Such a concept of social order left no room for the formation of the state because of various reasons. (1) Since the order emanated from God, an autonomous political sphere clearly distinguishable from other social functions and operating according to specific criteria could not develop. Politics remained under the guidance of religion, and the institution called to interpret God's will on earth, the church, claimed the leading role in society. (2) The total character of the order did not allow a distinction between one sphere of life where the common weal was pursued, and another where the individual could follow his private interests. Hence, no specifically public function opposed to private existence could develop. Everybody was, so to say, an agent of the divine order. (3) God's direct authorship of the order prevented any temporal authority from claiming a position above the order. Due to its divine origin, the positive order was at the same time the just order. Earthly authorities were installed for law enforcement, not for law making purposes. (4) Because of the undeveloped state of communication, the law enforcement power was not centralized, but segmented among numerous independent and equally entitled local authorities who settled their own quarrels by feud which neither the Church nor the Emperor were able to suppress. (5) Finally, these authorities did not exercise their law enforcement power as a special function for which they were installed, but as an obligation connected with a certain social status, mostly that of landownership.

The Crisis of the Medieval Order

The functioning of the medieval order depended on several conditions. Based on revelation, the system could only last when God's will or, at least, the church's authority to interpret it were uncontested. The segmental character of political authority was bound to the duration of narrow-framed units of social life with little communication across the boundaries. The lacking political disposition of the order required a certain imperviousness to social change so that new problems which seemed unsolvable under the existing order could not arise. Yet, in the later medieval period, some signs of change can be observed which affected the foundations of the system. The crusades and later the discovery of distant parts of the world widened social communication and gave rise to foreign trade and early forms of capitalism. The invention of the gun caused a revolution in war techniques and undermined the social function of the nobility and thereby the basis of feudalism. The art of printing enabled a faster dissemination of ideas. The problems arising from these developments were difficult to solve within the framework of the traditional order. Their solution presupposed an extension of political power, spatial as well as functional. Consequently, from the thirteenth century on, an accumulation of prerogatives in the hands of the princes took place. They tried to restrict the right to feud and made attempts to extend internal peace to larger units. This required, however, a basis of power independent from feudal service. The formation of a professional administration and a standing army began. Also, legislative interventions into the customary order occurred more and more frequently. The consequence was a rising demand of money. Insofar, the princes depended on the estates whose consent was necessary for levying taxes. Thus, the growing importance of the princes was accompanied by a growing importance of the estates who used this position in order to secure a share also in the legislative power.

The State as Product of the Confessional Civil Wars

The most decisive change, however, which eventually destroyed the medieval order was the Reformation. It would be inadequate to understand the Reformation only as a religious or theological event. The entire social order being based on divine revelation as transmitted by the church, a disagreement on the substance of revelation and on the pope's competence of interpreting it necessarily affected the basis of social life. While in England, the confessional change was effectuated rather smoothly, the religious dissension led to civil wars of extreme cruelty on the continent, particularly in France. In order to understand the continental political tradition, it is important to realize that the concentration and release of political power which brought about the modern state was a product of this situation. The country fell apart into hostile parties, and the prince standing on one side lost his authority for the other. The basic values of social life could no longer be secured. Different from a conflict of interests, a conflict of truths is difficult to settle by compromise. The civil war could only be ended if one confessional party succeeded in exterminating the other or if a third party rose above the enemies and forced peaceful coexistence upon them. In Germany with its multitude of political units existing under the roof of the Holy Empire, a moderate version of the first solution was adopted: the prince acquired the right to determine the confession in his territory, whereas the dissenting subjects were allowed to emigrate. In relatively centralized France, a similar solution was impossible. Therefore, the second way found growing support in the sixteenth century, particularly among a group of thinkers called "les politiques" because they advocated a political rather than a confessional solution of the crisis. It was decisive for the emergence of the modern state that Henry IV eventually adopted this suggestion.

Sovereignty as Characteristic of the State

The consequence was a complete breach with the traditional political system. Since the religiously determined order could no longer serve as common basis of social life, peace was to be restored on a new basis. In order to enable peaceful coexistence of the fighting parties, the new order had to leave open the question of truth. In principle, religious truth became a matter of private preference instead of public concern, as already prepared in the conflict of investiture some centuries ago. The social order received a secular foundation. Since such an order could not be deduced from God's will it had to be based on temporal authority. This meant nothing less than the extension of political power from law enforcement to law making, formerly reserved to God. The authorities were no longer guided by religion but could decide according to genuine political criteria, thereby enhancing the flexibility and problem solving capacity of the system. The law derived its binding force not from conformity with eternal justice but from human will. The medieval unity between law and justice broke up. The law became positive whereas the question of justice was answered by a higher ranking, but not legally binding natural law. In addition, public authority had to receive all necessary means of forcing the secular order upon the reluctant parties. In the situation of a cruel civil war, this could only be successful if the various political functions widerspread in the country were concentrated in one hand while everybody else lost his share in public power in exchange for the basic values of social life – internal peace and personal safety. The result was an all-embracing and irresistible power for which Bodin formed the notion of sovereignty, until then unkown in political theory, and defined as the exclusive right of the ruler to give laws to everybody in general and in particular without being bound by any positive law himself.

Sovereignty as Attribute of the King

Sovereignty in this sense distinguishes the modern state from the medieval community. The pre-established divine order did not allow any sovereign power. The suggestion sometimes made that, in the Middle Ages, sovereignty belonged to the law itself can hardly be upheld. Sovereignty essentially means the unconditioned right of deciding what the law shall be, and this capacity cannot be linked with the product of that decision. In the particular situation which brought forth the concept of sovereignty, the supreme power could only be attributed to the king. Standing on top of the feudal pyramid, he already occupied a central position, and he combined this position with a relatively large number of prerogatives. These two qualities elevated the king above all other authorities in the country who were either of local importance only, or, if they exercised central functions like the estates, reflected the division of the country which had to be overcome by establishing sovereign power. The king, if any, was predestinated to be endowed with sovereignty. Sovereignty originated as monarchical power. The genesis of this power made it difficult for contemporaries to distinguish between state and monarch. Sovereignty did not come into being as a systematic construction, but as the result of a historical process in which the various prerogatives of the king were gradually enlarged and finally condensed to an all-embracing supreme power. Thus, sovereignty was linked with its visible holder and appeared as the monarch's property, connected with his territory, acquired and transferred according to the rules of inheritance, exercised like other private rights, and administered by personal servants. The modern state originated, not as an impersonal, abstract entity different from the ruler, but as the ruler's patrimony, and the distinction between the person and the institution turns out to be a rather late achievement.

The Distinction Between State and Society as Consequence of Sovereignty

The new concentration of political power divided the medieval community into two different bodies: a small one consisting of the prince and his staff, characterized by the monopoly of legitimate coercive power, and a large one comprising everybody else being subject to that power. For the first body, the notion of state, formerly applied in an attributive sense only, came up in this very period. The second one used to be called society. Yet, society no longer signified the community as a whole including all political authorities, but the community without the state. The concentration of all political rights in the hands of the ruler left everybody else behind in the role of a private member. Privateness became the characteristic of society, and in this quality all members were equal notwithstanding the differences in social status. Yet, privateness under absolute power did not designate a sphere of individual self-determination protected against political interference, but the status of being subject to the state's will without having any share in its formation. Nor were private matters constituted by any pre-existing criteria but by an actual lack of political interest. In principle, there was no subject matter excluded from the ruler's determination. The legal system reflected the distinction between state and society, private and public sphere. The universal medieval law fell apart into two different sets of rules: the private law regulating the relations within society, and the public law concerning the relations between society and state. The distinction had been known to the Romans already, but used to be a merely theoretical one. In the absolute state, it won practical impact by separating questions of politics from questions of law. The competence of the courts was limited to matters of private law, whereas public law controversies were exemted from justice.

The Foundations of Monarchical Sovereignty

The leading principle for the use of political power was the common best. This formula or synonyms of it had older sources, but it adopted a new meaning in the formative period of the state. No longer pre-established by revelation and thus a matter of cognition, the common best could now vary according to time and circumstances and hence became a matter of decision. The decision belonged to the ruler who claimed knowledge of what the common best required, although he was expected to take advice. The less the common best could be traced back to God, the more did it depend on state power, and increasingly, the formula was interpreted in terms of *raison d'Etat*. In the period of transition. state power was primarily a question of independence from rivalling powers. Independence became the main concern of the absolute monarch. A standing army guaranteed independence from the feudal service of the nobility, a professional administration independence from the local authorities. The administration was recruited from jurists trained in the Roman law tradition. The Roman law as the law of a highly advanced and rationally construed empire had survived in the Roman Catholic Church. It infiltrated into temporal power just when the latter began to develop centralized rational structures following the example of the Roman Empire and the ecclesiastical hierarchy. The reception of the Roman law on the continent is explained by the higher degree of rationality and the relative independence from the local and corporate particularities which it furnished in a period where legislative techniques were still undevelopped. The training of the administrative personnel was soon taken over by the state itself, so that the emergence of the modern state was accompanied by the foundation of numerous universities securing independence from the ecclesiastical education. Most decisive and prerequisite to all the rest was, of course, the right to levy taxes independently from the consent of the estates. The mercantile policy of the absolute state must be seen as a supporting measure in order to raise the taxability of society.

The English Case in Comparison

The modern state originated in the form of absolutism, yet not by mere lust of power on the side of the princes and lack of caution on the side of society, but by a certain historical necessity arisen from the confessional civil wars. It was the concentration of power in a personal ruler which changed political reality and was then grasped by the notion of state. This explains at the same time, why in England neither the notion of state and sovereignty nor the distinction between state and society, public and private law developed in a similar way. A concentration of political functions in the hand of the king cannot be observed in England. The English crown had a prerogative, but no supreme power. A number of independent authorities continued to exist, and mainly the common law and the courts as its agency could maintain a position rather independent from the crown. The reasons can be found in an early decay of feudalism with the result that no sharp distinctions between the aristocracy and the *tiers état* developed, and the country as a whole could form a counterpart to the ruler. Parliament, thus, became virtually a representation of the people, not an assembly of estates. Moreover, this insular situation of England made a standing army for defence purposes superfluous. The main reason, however, lies in the fact that in England, the Reformation was not followed by a civil war, and hence, no historical necessity for absolutism did arise. On the contrary, Henry VIII felt it useful to secure the support of Parliament for his breach with Rome, and the Reformation which, on the continent, led to absolutism strengthened parliamentarism in England. The attempts of the Stuarts to build up a position similar to the one held by the French king could not find a historical justification. Therefore, nobility and commons together successfully resisted these plans. While the continental civil wars preceded absolutism which seemed to be the only means of restoring peace, in England, absolutism preceded the civil war, and the latter was fought to repulse it and to restore the traditional order.

The Unfinished State Building on the Continent

Yet, not every continental country, either, turned to absolute monarchy and state building. The Holy Empire completely failed to develop a supreme power, and many minor territories kept the old structures behind a façade of absolutism. Others developed republican structures, such as the Netherlands after their independence. Nor did all those countries which turned to absolutism arrive there at the same time or in the same way as this systematic outline, following the French model case, may suggest. But not even France as the leading country succeeded in concentrating all public functions in one hand and exercising them in an unlimited manner. In terms of absolutism, seventeenth century Russia may have been more advanced than any western European state. We use to call absolute a regime which did not depend on the participation of the estates in financial and legislative matters and had a standing army. But no complete power was ever won over the courts. The French parliaments maintained the right to approve or disapprove of certain legislative acts, and the courts in most other countries claimed and often exercised the right to review royal interventions into vested rights of the subjects. Furthermore, the absolute state never gained direct control over all subjects in his territory. While depriving the privileged classes of political participation, it left the social structure basically untouched so that the rural community remained subject to the landlords, not the state. Matters strongly related with religion such as family law or education, were still under the supervision of the church. The state had to content itself with regarding these powers as delegated, not original. The bureaucracy was not yet organized in a way such as to cover the whole country. It formed a staff at the royal court whereas most offices outside were venal. Statutory law was frequently issued, but badly implemented, and only late did the absolute monarchies arrive at codifying larger parts of the law such as the civil or the commercial law.

4.2 The Crisis of Absolutism and the Liberal State

The Social Contract as Justification of the State

The accumulation of secular power exercised by the monarch as his genuine right soon asked for justification. Since such justification could no longer be found in divine revelation, social philosophy turned to reason as the common endowment of mankind. Political power was deemed legitimate when in accordance with reason, and hypothetical consent of every reasonable man was considered as proof of reasonability. Rulership, then, was no longer based on divine investiture as the monarchs liked to claim, but on a fictitious social contract. The importance of contractual legitimation of public power lay in its denial of a genuine right to govern. Government was derived from the consent of the governed. This did not necessarily mean a denial of absolute monarchical power. Under the impression of civil wars, it might rather seem reasonable for men to convey all their natural rights on the ruler in order to receive safety of life and property in return, as Hobbes taught. Thus, in the beginning, the doctrine of contract furnished a justification of absolutism and strengthened the power of the state. The form of contract left, of course, room to various contents. In Holland, where the General Estates had declared their independence from the Spanish crown in 1581, sovereignty was linked theoretically with the people and not with the prince. In the long run, the contract theory undermined, in other countries, too, absolute monarchical power. The more the monarch fulfilled his function of restoring internal peace, the less did it seem plausible that he enjoyed unlimited power over society. The younger contractual theory, therefore, changed the contents of the social contract. In view of a peaceful and harmonious society, reason required the conveyance of those natural rights only which were necessary to defend natural freedom and self-determination against aggressors and criminals. This form of contract neither led to the absolute state nor to priority of the public interest, but on the contrary to preponderance of private interests and to limited state powers.

Enlightened Absolutism as Period of Transition

When this version of the social contract was first formulated by Locke it could be taken as an expression of the actual state of the English monarchy after the Glorious Revolution. In the continental situation, it had revolutionary impact and was adopted only much later when a wealthy and self-conscious bourgeoisie had emerged which felt fettered in the old system of class distinctions and state control over the economy, and which welcomed a theory justifying change. This was the case in eighteenth century France, whereas the German bourgeoisie found itself too much in retard to be prepared for liberalism. The leading role of the state was still unquestioned, and the natural law theory kept a rather etatistic outlook, as did also the physiocrate doctrine in France. In fact, it were the monarchs of the most advanced territories, Austria and Prussia, who took the initiative to abolish the feudal structures and modernize society. Philosophy gained a leading role in this process, and the enlightenment movement entered into an alliance with the absolute monarchs. Inspired by enlightenment ideas, they began to dinstinguish between the ruler and the state and understood their function as service to the state whose weal could no longer be identified with the interests of the dynasty. Likewise, the notion of common best underwent a change. It caesed to consist in the state's power alone and included individual happiness. This implied a certain amount of self-determination, so that the state prepared itself to free the subjects from feudal, corporate and ecclesiastical bonds and agreed to a certain self limitation. The rulers were not ready, however, to leave the determination of happiness to the individual will. It remained the state whose knowledge of happiness counted while the individual's understanding of his own happiness had no importance. This shows to what extent the enlightened absolutism was still absolutism.

The Emergence of the Liberal State

In France, on the contrary, the physiocratic influence on the state remained a short and unsuccessful episode. The absolute monarchy defended the old system the more tenaciously the more it was criticized by the third estate. The enlightenment movement, therefore, formed an alliance with the bourgeoisie against the state in France. In view of a stubborn state, reforms could be reached only by revolution. Revolution meant nothing else than forcible seizure of supreme power. But the French Revolution would be misunderstood if interpreted primarily as an action for political change. The ultimate end of the French bourgeoisie was a new social order which replaced class distinctions and privileges by equal rights, feudal and corporate bonds by individual liberty, economic protection by laisser faire, intellectual tutelage by freedom of conscience and thought. Political power served but as an indispensable means toward that end. The change of social order had, however, consequences for the political system, since individual freedom and absolute state power were incompatible. Therefore, the state could not remain what it had been if the renewal of society was to be successful. Taught by their historical experiences with supreme power, the main political concern of the revolutionaries was to protect liberty and equality against the state. This meant first of all a limitation of state functions. If it was true that social justice automatically emanated from individual liberty, the state lost its all-embracing responsibility for individual virtue, social welfare and economic prosperity. His only function consisted in guaranteeing the basis of the system, namely individual liberty. Secondly, safeguards preventing misuse of the remaining power were necessary. To this end, political power was linked with society in the double sense that every office holder derived his position directly or indirectly from society and that he was entitled to act only if authorized by society in the form of law.

The Maintenance of Sovereignty

With the assumption that civil society did not depend on an almighty state in order to reach social justice, the historical justification for sovereignty disappeared. Nevertheless, the French bourgeoisie was not prepared to renounce sovereignty. The reason lies in the resistance of the privileged classes of the *Ancien régime* against the liberal reforms. In this situation, the ultimate success of the revolution depended on an even increased public power which allowed to carry through the renewal of state and society. This may also explain the striking difference between the French and the American declarations of human rights. Although starting from the same fundamental principles, the French revolutionaries arrived at a sovereign state and the Americans did not. In America, where class distinctions, feudalism, state controlled economy had never been established, there was no need for a liberal reform of society. The American Revolution could limit itself to changing government and taking precautionary measures in order to prevent future abuses of political power. In France, on the contrary, political power first had to bring about the situation which, for the Americans, seemed to be the natural order. Hence, the French Revolution destroyed the absolute monarchy, but not the sovereign state. It merely changed the subject of sovereignty. Sovereignty was no longer vested in the monarch, but in the people in whose name all state functions were henceforth performed. This put a definite end to the patrimonial concept of the state. The state as impersonal entity emerged. Its national construction on the basis of written constitution perfectioned the concentration of public power by abolishing all intermediate powers between state and subject, by depriving the courts of the right to review acts of state and mainly enacted laws, and by creating an effective, centralized and non-venal civil service and a public school system. The French Revolution, far from being an antistate movement, preserved state and sovereignty as central categories of public life.

The Reversed Relation Between State and Society

Once the reform was finished, the French state, too, could limit its activity to protecting individual liberty. Compared with absolutism, this meant not only a curtailment of functions, but also degradation in rank. The liberal assumption that social justice and economic welfare were not the intended product of state action, but the automatic result of individual liberty, put an end to the former priority of the public sphere. As an invisible hand turned the pursuit of individual interests into the common best, there was no room for a state interest different from private freedom. Public interest no longer determined the range of the private sphere. On the contrary, the public sphere was now derived from the private interest. Consequently, the state lost its leadership over society and took on a service function which the individuals could not fulfill themselves, namely the protection of liberty against abuses of liberty. Likewise, public law, formally predominant over private law, was limited to a safeguard of individual rights. This change in function and rank, however, did not alter the state in substance. Its reduced function of defending individual liberty could not be performed without superior power. Therefore, the state retained the monopoly of coercion and thereby differed from society which continued to be private by nature. But the priority of society found its expression in the fact that society itself determined the conditions of the use of state power. The elected representatives of society decided in parliament what had to be considered as abuse of freedom and how the state had to react. The latter was limited to the application of the general rule. Parliament thus linked state and society together, and the individual, other than under absolute rulership, appeared in the double role of *bourgeois* and *citoyen*. The citizen's equal share in political decisions guaranteed, as explained by Rousseau, that state power could not serve other purposes than the common interest.

The Turn Toward Class State

The liberal practice used to disregard the democratic principle. The restrictions of suffrage gave to the liberal state the outlook of a rather bourgeois state. Mainly during the French "Monarchie de Juillet", one can observe that it was not always the liberal doctrine but the bourgeois interest that guided state action. By no means did the state completely refrain from intervening into the sphere of society. But it intervened only when this was required by some bourgeois interest Railway politics may serve as an example. This happened at a period when the bourgeois interest could no longer claim to be congruent with the interests of society as a whole. The industrial revolution had taken place in France and created a new class division. The fundamental assumption of liberalism that individual freedom was the precondition of social justice thereby lost its grounds. As a matter of fact, the liberal system could only function on the basis of a relative balance of power in society which did not exist. Under these circumstances, non-intervention of the state was no expression of neutrality, but of partisanship for the stronger side. The state served as a vehicle for class interests. This experience gave rise to a widespread antistate movement in political theory, and it seems not to be by chance that this movement developed particular strength among French socialists and syndicalists, many of whom saw the main obstacle for more social justice, not in the actual distribution of property or in the electoral system, but in the state as such. Independently from the marxist theory, social justice for them was a question of abolition of the state. But also Marx' theory of the state being essentially an agent of the ruling class and bound to wither away once class divisions would have been overcome, took shape in view of the French July-monarchy.

The German Model of the Separation Between State and Society

Compared with France, German socialists were more willing to expect social justice from the state. Indeed, the German state had never been a bourgeois state to the extent of the French. The German bourgeoisie welcomed the French Revolution, at least before the execution of Louis XVI, but it was not prepared to revolutionize the own country. The consitutions which, by and by, came up in Germany were not achieved by the people, but granted by the princes. They established a sphere of private interests guaranteed by fundamental rights into which government could interfere only with prior consent of representative assemblies. But the princes took care to reserve the supreme power entirely for themselves. The result was that the representative assemblies, although they were a constitutional organ, strictly speaking remained outside the state which continued to be formed exclusively by the monarch and his administrative and military staff. The people's representatives did not receive any influence on the domain of the state. Having failed to submit the state to its will, the German bourgeoisie could but try to make use of the sphere abandoned by the state and opened for private initiative. Under these circumstances, freedom did not mean participation in the formation of the common will, but absence of state intervention. On the one hand, the state lost the complete domination over society exercised during absolutism. On the other hand, society did not win domination over the state as in more democratic systems. It was this constellation which gave rise to the separation of state and society which seems typical for the German political tradition in the nineteenth century and is found neither in the Anglo-american nor in the French system. The compensation for the lack of democracy was sought in the rule of law *(Rechtsstaat)* protecting the private sphere against political intervention, and the perfection of *"Rechtsstaat"* became the chief political concern of the German bourgeoisie after the failure of the 1848 revolution.

The Idealization of the State

In this dual concept, society was considered as an accumulation of particular interests. In order to reach the higher level of a community unified under some principle or idea the people depended on the state. Thus, the elevation and idealization of the state, culminating in Hegel's philosophy, was the necessary consequence of the entirely private notion of society in Germany. The state represented all higher values of human life, and only guided and assisted by the state, was the individual able to reach his ultimate human destination. This attitude favoured, of course, a substantial rather than a functional notion of state. A state like this was neither the western European state which fulfilled some service functions for a self-sufficient society, nor the mere guardian of legality advocated by liberal philosophy, but the fulfilment of all higher aspirations of national life. On the other hand, a state of this sort could hardly be identified with the contingent person of the monarch. The pretention that it was the monarch in person from whom all decisions emanated had been given up anyway. Personal government was bound to much less complex a state of affairs. Theory followed and gave up the idea of the patrimonial state in the course of the nineteenth century. The state was now conceived in Germany, too, as an abstract personality for which the monarch only acted as the supreme organ. Although there had never been any uncertainty about the existence of sovereignty in Germany, this change in theory raised the question of its location. No doubt, it was not the people that could be called sovereign like in France, nor did it seem possible to attribute sovereignty to a mere organ of another entity. Thus, by the end of the century, German theory reached the conclusion that sovereignty belonged to the state as such, a solution which, of course, did not help when the exercise of sovereign rights was contested among different organs of the state.

Range of Action of the German State

The conspicuous position of the state in Germany was not only of theoretical interest, but had some practical implications. The fact that the old monarchical system had not been overthrown in a successful revolution but only modified by constitutional limitations, allowed the state to preserve exclusive reponsibility for the common best. Neither identified with the interests of a ruling class nor regarded as mere outcome of a struggle of interests among the different classes within society, the common best remained a value above particular interests and ascertained autonomously by the state. This is not to say that the state in fact kept the pretended neutrality toward particular interests and that state politics were without bias. But the state did enjoy a certain independence vis-à-vis particular interests, not paralleled in countries more advanced in terms of constitutional law. The German state had never become a bourgeois state like some of its western neighbours. Economic liberalism when practised remained subordinated to state purposes. It served as a means of modernizing society in the national interest. But it could be limited or given up when the national interest required other means. It seems significant that socialist ideas in Germany were much less directed against the state as such than in France. On the contrary, the solution of the problems of the working class was expected from the monarchical state. This expectation coincided with a paternalistic attitude characteristic for the absolute state, which had never been cut off completely in Germany. It revived when a whole class of the population fell in need and thereby became a menace to the regime. Relief for the working class had been demanded in other countries, too, but the apparent failure there, and the striking success here find an explanation in the different type of statehood. The fact that Germany, in spite of its constitutional backwardness, became leading in social policy was also due to the state position in this country.

The Identity of the Liberal State

The change from absolutism to liberalism which reduced the distance between England and the continent, did not affect the concept of state. On the contrary, its abstract and impersonal nature and the monopoly of power were only now achieved and secured the identity of the state as opposed to society. But the basis of identity changed. For absolutism, the identity of the state was based on its monopoly of politics which excluded society from any political share and gave it a completely private character. This monopoly broke up when the people entered into politics, either as the sovereign directing state activities like in France, or as participant in certain political decisions as in nineteenth century Germany. The people being incapable of organized political action without assistance, gave at the same time birth to non-state political organizations such as political parties and interest groups. Politics could no longer be sufficiently described by focussing on the state. Yet, in spite of the loss of its political monopoly, the state remained a distinguishable entity. In Germany, the separation of state and society brought about by a historical situation where absolutism could no longer be preserved by the princes and democracy could not yet be reached by the people, allowed a rather clearcut distinction between public and private matters. In countries where the state was based on popular sovereignty so that the German-type separation of state and society could not develop, the state was nevertheless identifiable by its function. Liberalism advocated a clear division of functions between state and society. While society was principally unlimited in activity, the state was limited to securing peace and order. The fulfilment of this task required the monopoly of legitimate power which, in turn, left back society as a sphere free of coercive means and coordinated by contractual relations only. Although transgressions of the limits could and did happen, the dividing line as such was beyond doubt.

4.3 The Crisis of Liberalism and the Welfare State

The Doubtful Identity of the Present State

Meanwhile, the certainty of former centuries about the state has been lost. It seems difficult to identify the state. The identity of the state used to be derived from its difference to society as a body in need of being governed. Such a difference was evident in the period of absolutism. All government functions had been concentrated to an all-embracing supreme power and vested in a personal holder, the monarch, who exercised them as his genuine and unlimited right, independently from consent or participation of the governed. The decisive criterion was the possession of legitimate power, and this criterion drew a line between two different groups of persons so that it seemed possible to distinguish between state and society on a physical basis: the state consisted of persons with and society of persons without political power. As soon as the unity of state and ruler had broken and the state was conceived as an abstract, impersonal entity, it became impossible to distinguish between state and society on a personal basis. This way of distinguishing failed altogether when the people assumed sovereignty. In this situation, die difference could only be found on a functional level. This was, however, facilitated by the liberal doctrine of state functions. According to this doctrine, the only purpose of the state was keeping peace, and this meant essentially defending the people against foreign aggressors and enforcing the law within society. For this limited purpose, the state was equipped with all necessary means of force, whereas any activity not disturbing social peace was left to society which, in turn, could not claim any right to use force. This distinction of functions and means still allowed a clear identification of the state. If the actual uncertainty has a real background, this must be sought in the functional relations between state and society. The existence of doubts suggests that at least some changes with respect to this relation have taken place.

The Industrial Revolution and the Crisis of Liberalism

The justification for the reduced function of the state lay in the liberal assumption that social justice and economic welfare were best produced by individual freedom. Social regulation was left to the market mechanism, whereas all state regulation appeared as disturbance of the market and therefore prejudiced the common best. The reasonableness of this assumption became more and more questioned after the industrial revolution. With regard to the functions of state, three effects of the industrial revolution should be mentioned, one of immediate effect, two with more postponed consequences. As its immediate effect, the industrial revolution set aside the market mechanism in many fields. In the first place, this was true for the labour market on which more and more people depended. The result was the emergence of the proletariat. In the process of economic concentration following the industrial revolution, the same happened with regard to large parts of the product market. More generally speaking, the industrial revolution made obvious that individual freedom led to social justice only under the additional condition of an equilibrium of social strength among the individuals. The existence of this equilibrium was a tacit assumption of the liberal doctrine which had originated before the experience of industrial society was made. To the extent that the presupposed equality of chances disappeared, freedom of property and contract could no longer guarantee a reasonable balance of interests. The principle of liberty still functioned in limiting state power, but in the social dimension, it turned out to be a means of domination in the hands of the stronger party. In the sphere freed of state power, social power structures began to develop. The liberal society deviated from its goal of general welfare and social justice.

The Growing Complexity of Industrial Society

The two other effects of the industrial revolution were of longer range. First, the still accelerating scientific and technical development is continuously increasing the domination of mankind over nature. The field of natural development constantly narrows, whereas more and more processes can be controlled by man. There is a general increase of feasibility. Feasibility, of course, opens different ways, and the direction in which to move is in most cases controversial and thus to be decided upon. From a certain degree of controversiality on, the problem becomes a political one, and the decision is transferred to the state. Insofar, there exists direct relation between technical development and state functions. The range of politics has considerably widened, compared with the times of absolutism. Secondly, the industrial revolution brought forth a still increasing specialization of social functions. This has a double effect. For once, functional specialization creates a higher degree of efficiency, but at the same token the degree of interdependence grows. Growing interdependence, in turn, means that the likelihood and the range of disturbances are increasing, too. The binary model of regulating social relations by means of free individual contracts seems not to be complex enough for the degree of social interdependence reached in the meantime. The system creates effects which exceed the control of the contracting parties and appear as external costs to be born by society as a whole. Free pursuit of individual interests no longer results in the common best. The capacity of society to secure social integration and social justice by the invisible hand goes down. The need of public control is growing.

The Increase of State Functions

While the experience of absolutism had led to the state's banishment from society, the experience of liberalism provoked its return. Beginning already in the last century, the state was expected to recover responsability for social justice and economic welfare. The more a neglect of this expectation threatened its legitimacy, the less did the state maintain its original reluctance. From the late nineteenth century on, we can observe a continuous extension of the public sector. Three stages may be distinguished. In the first one, the state began to correct the most evident abuses of economic liberty, particularly in the field of labour relations, social security and consumer and competitor protection. For this purpose, the state could rely on legislation which restricted economic freedom and thereby protected the weaker members of society. The social and economic crises following World War I led to the second stage. The state no longer limited itself to legislative corrections of laisser faire, but assisted in overcoming actual crises or calamities. This, however, could not be effected by legislation alone, but required granting aid, financial or material. By and by, the state developed a whole system of providence for the risks of poverty, unemployment, casualty, homelessness, disease etc. The growing complexity and interdependence of advanced economies, however, rendered mere corrective interventions by the state insufficient. Therefore, in the third stage, the state is expected to anticipate critical developments and avoid detriment by an effective crisis management, supply the economy with an appropriate infrastructure, initiate technological progress, and provide favorable conditions for economic growth. In addition, the welfare state philosophy requires social compensation for all sorts of individual disadvantages so that today the state can be said to bear again an all-embracing responsability for the social and cultural welfare of society.

Decomposition of Power by Increase of Functions

These three stages of extending the public sector are not to be understood as if a newly acquired function replaced the preceding one. The process was a cumulative one which led to an enormous increase of state personnel and state expenditure. It seems doubtful, however, whether the increase contributed to strengthening the identity of the state vis-à-vis society. Different from the small and homogeneous staff of the absolute ruler and even of the constitutional monarch, the present civil service is so numerous that it seems neither dirigeable from one center nor suitable for concentrated action. Rather, the social differences and tensions extend into the state itself and diminish its coherence. The same is true with regard to the multitude of state functions. The more areas are opened for state activity, the more conflicts of political aims arise. Frequently, different departments of public admin-istration counteract or cause unforeseen effects in remote fields. The demand of coordination by far exceeds the capacity of the political system. It is true that, with few exceptions, civil service is still embedded in a hierarchical organization. But from a certain size on, the top of the hierarchy is so overloaded with responsabili-ties that leadership becomes a rather symbolic affair. In addition, some modern instruments of the state like planning future development are less susceptible to hierarchical organization than the traditional state functions of securing external and internal peace. Legislative regulation of the administration cannot fill the gap. While legal determination of traditional administrative activities is rather dense, the laws regulating planning processes have only little determinative force. Thus political power is more and more decomposed and exercised rather incoherently. This makes it difficult to conceive of the present state as the homogeneous entity which it used to be in former periods.

The Abandonment of Coercive Power

Although in the range of its activities, the welfare state resembles or even exceeds the absolute state, the present state find itself much more restricted as to the means which may be used. The specific means of the state in order to perform its function correspond to its attribute, supreme power. They are command and coercion. Command and coercion are indispensable for maintaining public order. In exerci-sing global responsibility for economic development and social welfare, however, the state cannot make unlimited use of these means. The economy is constitution-ally protected against direct state control by fundamental rights, and these exclude, to the extent of the protection, the application of force. Moreover, the efficiency of social subsystems such as the economy depends on a certain autonomy allowing them to operate according to their specific criteria. This means another and sometimes even more effective limit to direct state control. In this field, the state can pursue its objectives only by using indirect means such as persuasion, financial incitement or discouragement or a change of the general framework of economic development. Functions exercised by use of indirect means have already surpassed in number the classical branches of public administration. While these keep a rather stable percentage of personnel and costs, the field where the administration plans or directs social development, supplies money, services, facilities etc. is still growing. The increase in quantity is accompanied by an increase of importance. The conditions of social life and the chances of individual development are often much more deeply affected by non obligatory act of planning than by a direct command. Inspite of the weight and effect of indirect means, the abandonment of coercive power contributes to the erosion of the state. Indirect means are not principally different from the means society can use, and thus tend to deprive the state of its hierarchical position and put it on an equal level with society.

The Growing Dependence on Social Cooperation

The increasing use of indirect means instead of command and coercion has another and even more far-reaching impact on the possibility of distinguishing between state and society and ascertaining the identity of the state. In fields where the state is limited to setting motivating data, the fulfilment of public functions does not only depend on effective state action, but in addition on the willingness of private decision-makers to follow. The dependence of the state on their cooperation brings them into a privileged position, useful in order to give special emphasis to particular interests. They can either require something in return for their coopera- tion or exercise an intensified influence on policy selection, so that decisions formally emanating from the state appear in substance as a joint venture of public and private actors. In this case, the state still determines the structure of decision making, while the process of decision making allows external participation. As a result, it is no longer possible to attribute the success or failure of a decision to either of them. In extreme cases, a state action may only be the consequence of external determination. The problem is commonly treated in terms of private influence on the state. Yet, it seems doubtful whether this still permits an adequate grasp of the problem. Influence, as strongly backed as it may be, still leaves the final decision to the state agency. When the decision making power is shared by state agencies and private actors, the latter leave the sphere of society and pass the threshold to the state. The concentration of legitimate power as main characteristic of the modern state is at stake. The system tends toward a modified corporate order, and where corporate structures develop, no clear criterion for the distinction between state and society is available. Some traits of the stateless medieval order reappear in the political system.

The External Decomposition of State Power

The internal decomposition of supreme power has an external parallel. The modern state culminated in the nation state of the nineteenth century. The national state was the domain of supreme power. External sovereignty served as protection of supreme power against the other states. This system depended on an approxima- tive congruency of political problems and problem solving units. In the course of the twentieth century, however, the growing interdependence of the national economies, the increasing density of the communication network, and the range and force of modern weapons raised the number of problems which can no longer be solved within the framework of the national state. For most of these problems, international treaties do not furnish a sufficient remedy because they usually lack an administrative infrastructure endowed with competences effective in the member states. Therefore, supranational organizations have been founded on a regional basis to which the national states transfer a number of sovereign rights. This is a process quite different from the well-known factual undermining of the sovereignty of minor states, but also from the self-limitation of states by concluding traties. Treaties leave intouched the exclusive power of the states over their subjects and thus preserve the main characteristic of statehood. Supranational organizations, on the contrary, exercise legislative, administrative and even judicial power immediately effective within the states whose own competence is inhibited to the same extent. Thereby, powers formerly regarded as genuine and unalienable state prerogatives pass to other institutions. The result resembles the one observed on the internal level: the state no longer concentrates all legitimate coercive power in itself but has to share it with other non-state, yet not private entities. The erosion is proceeding from two different points.

The End of the State

All these developments made several authors predict the decline of the state, while others have tacitly dropped the notion of state and replaced it by the "political system". The first assumption is often based on a comparison between the classical theory and the present reality of the state. If, instead, past and present realities are compared, the result is less dramatical. In the absolutist period, the ruler claimed the unlimited right to dispose of the social order, but he did not even arrive at exercising direct authority over all subjects in his territory. It was but the French Revolution and the liberal state that abolished the intermediate powers between state and individual and gained direct control over all subjects. But the liberal state did not claim the unlimited right to dispose of every sphere of life. It recognized the autonomy of social subsystems like the economy and sought its function in protecting society against disturbance. Just in this limitation, the state developped its particular strength. The present state has considerably widened its functions, but cannot fulfill all of them by applying coercive power. Yet, there remain wide areas of undoubted and effective public authority. Likewise, the state still prevails over supranational organizations. The second attitude reflects the obvious fact that politics can no longer be adequately analyzed by focussing on the state. It does, however, not answer the question whether the state still forms a distinguishable subsystem of the political system. As to this question, attention must be drawn to a striking difference within the political system. Some actors are entitled to decide with collectively binding force, and others are not. The latter may participate in the preparation of binding decisions, even to the extent that the final act appears as a mere formality. Still, they depend on the functioning of formalized structures and procedures, which indicates that it is premature to dismiss the state, if the standard is not set unrealistically high.

The Necessity of Redetermining the Role of State

It may be necessary, however, to reconsider the position and role of the state. The traditional role of the state was representing the common best vis-à-vis the particular interests assembled in society. In order to perform this role, the state occupied a hierarchical position above society and was endowed with supreme power. Meanwhile, the clear distinction between the common best and particular interests has become doubtful. On one hand, the democratic party state is not free from interests itself. On the other hand, the autonomous pursuit of particular interests also contributes to the common best. The problem is rather constituted by the nature of functional autonomy which combines high sensibility for the own concern with indifference to all others. The rising external costs of this unavoidable narrow-mindedness ask for an institution substituting the lacking sensibility of autonomous systems for their environment. This seems to be the specific role of the state in highly developped societies. Yet, legitimate autonomy limits the application of coercive power. Insofar, the state can influence the autonomous actors only by putting parts of its policy-making power to their disposal. The state is then neither acting as the exclusive representative of the common best nor out of a hierarchical position. Its position is rather that of a *primus inter pares*. Yet, not completely: the influence on the autonomous systems is partly due to the coercive power the state can exercise in the last resort. Insofar, there remains a nucleus of traditional statehood. As the Anglo-american tradition shows, this function does not have to be conceived in terms of state. The emphasis can also be put on the different governmental institutions and processes instead of the abstract entity behind them. The question is whether this conception allows a better grasp of present political reality. The answer would require a succinct comparison of the advantages and disadvantages of the two models which is beyond the framework of this paper.

Note

1 The subject matter of this paper being very broad and general, the author had the choice to either give numerous references in the text or to omit references completely. I chose the latter and hope to provide a certain compensation for the lack by a more detailed list of important books and articles.

References

Anderson, P. (1974): *Lineages of the Absolutist State*. London: New Left Books.

Aretin, K. O. (ed.) (1974): *Der Aufgeklärte Absolutismus*. Köln: Kiepenheuer & Witsch.

Berger, S. D. (ed.) (1981): *Organizing Interests in Western Europe*. Cambridge: Cambridge Univ. Press.

Böckenförde, E. W. (ed.) (1976a): *Staat und Gesellschaft*. Darmstadt: Wissenschaftliche Buchgesellschaft.

Böckenförde, E. W. (1976b): "Die Entstehung des Staates als Vorgang der Säkularisation." In Böckenförde, E. W. (ed.), *Staat – Gesellschaft – Freiheit*, 42–64. Frankfurt: Suhrkamp.

Brunner, O. (1970): *Land und Herrschaft* (6th ed.). Darmstadt: Wissenschaftliche Buchgesellschaft.

Church, W. F. (1969): *Constitutional Thought in 16th-Century France*. New York: Octagon.

Dennert, J. (1964): *Ursprung und Begriff der Souveränität*. Stuttgart: G. Fischer.

Denzer, H. (ed.) (1973): *Jean Bodin*. München: Beck.

Dyson, K. (1980): *The State Tradition in Western Europe*. Oxford: M. Robertson.

Elias, N. (1969): *Über den Prozeß der Zivilisation* (2nd ed.). Vol. II. Bern: Francke.

Forsthoff, E.(1971): *Der Staat der Industriegesellschaft.* München: Beck.

Franklin, J. H. (1973): *Jean Bodin and the Rise of Absolutist Theory.* Cambridge: Cambridge Univ. Press.

Gierke, J. (1958): *J. Althusius und die Entwicklung der naturrechtlichen Staatstheorien* (5th ed.). Berlin: Heymann.

Grimm, D. (1978): Die Trennung von privatem und öffentlichem Recht. In Dilcher, G., and N. Horn (eds.), *Sozialwissenschaften im Studium des Rechts.* Vol. IV, 55–65. München: Beck.

Habermas, J. (1973): *Legitimationsprobleme im Spätkapitalismus.* Frankfurt: Suhrkamp.

Häfelin, U. (1959): *Die Rechtspersönlichkeit des Staates.* Vol. I. Tübingen: Mohr.

Halbecq, M. (1965): *L'Etat: son autorité, son pouvoir.* Paris: Durand – Auzias.

Hartung, F. (1961): *Staatsbildende Kräfte der Neuzeit.* Berlin: Duncker & Humblot.

Hennis, W., P. Graf Kielmannsegg, and U. Matz (eds.) (1977): *Regierbarkeit.* Vol. I. Stuttgart: Klett-Cotta.

Hespe, K.(1964): *Zur Entwicklung der Staatszwecklehre in der deutschen Staatsrechtswissenschaft des 19. Jahrhunderts.* Göttingen: Schwartz.

Hintze, O. (1962): *Staat und Verfassung* (2nd ed. by G. Oestreich). Göttingen: Vandenhoek & Rupprecht.

Hofmann, H. H. (ed.) (1967): *Die Entstehung des modernen souveränen Staates.* Köln: Kiepenheuer & Witsch.

Holtzmann, W. (1953): *Das mittelalterliche Imperium und die werdenden Nationen.* Opladen: Westdeutscher Verlag.

Kantorowicz, E. H. (1957): *The King's Two Bodies.* Princeton: Princeton Univ. Press.

Kern, F. (1954): *Gottesgnadentum und Widerstandsrecht* (2nd ed.). Darmstadt: Wissenschaftliche Buchgemeinschaft.

Kern, F. (1972): *Recht und Verfassung im Mittelalter.* Darmstadt: Wissenschaftliche Buchgesellschaft.

Koselleck, R. (1959): *Kritik und Krise.* Freiburg: Alber.

Kriele, M. (1975): *Einführung in die Staatslehre.* Reinbek: Rowohlt.

Lefebvre, H. (1976–77) *De l'Etat* (3 vols.). Paris: Union Générale d'Editions.

Link, C. (1979): *Herrschaftsordnung und bürgerliche Freiheit.* Wien: Böhlau.

Lubasz, H. (ed.) (1964): *The Development of the Modern State.* New York: Mac Millan.

Luhmann, N. (1970): Soziologie des Politischen Systems. In Luhmann, N., *Soziologische Aufklärung,* 154–177. Opladen: Westdeutscher Verlag.

Luhmann, N. (1981): *Politische Theorie im Wohlfahrtsstaat,* München: Olzog.

Mager, W. (1968): *Zur Entstehung des modernen Staatsbegriffs.* Wiesbaden: Steiner.

Maier, H. (1966): *Ältere deutsche Staatslehre und westliche politische Tradition.* Tübingen: Mohr.

Meinecke, F. (1929): *Die Idee der Staatsräson in der neueren Geschichte* (3rd ed.). München: Oldenbourg.

Merk, W. (1968): *Der Gedanke des gemeinen Besten in der deutschen Staats- und Rechtsentwicklung.* Darmstadt: Wissenschaftliche Buchgesellschaft.

Nettl. J. P. (1968): "The State as a Conceptual Variable." *World Politics* XX/4: 559–592.

Oestreich, G. (1969): *Geist und Gestalt des frühmodernen Staates.* Berlin: Duncker & Humblot.

Offe, C. (1972): *Strukturprobleme des kapitalistischen Staates.* Frankfurt: Suhrkamp.

Poggi, G. (1978): *The Development of the Modern State.* London: Hutchinson.

Quaritsch, H. (1970): *Staat und Souveränität.* Frankfurt: Athenäum.

Riedel, M. (1970): *Bürgerliche Gesellschaft und Staat bei Hegel.* Neuwied: Luchterhand.

Scharpf, F. (1978): "Die Rolle des Staates im westlichen Wirtschaftssystem." Berlin: Wissenschaftszentrum, Discussion Paper Series, dp 78–81.

Scheuner, U. (1959): "Kirche und Staat in der neueren deutschen Entwicklung." In: Scheuner, U., *Schriften zum Staatskirchenrecht,* 121–168 (edited by J. Listl 1973). Berlin: Duncker & Humblot.

Scheuner, U. (1978): *Staatstheorie und Staatsrecht: Gesammelte Schriften* (ed. by Listl, J. and W. Rüfner). Berlin: Duncker & Humblot. (esp. pp. 14–133)

Scheuner, U. (1979): "Die Staatszwecke und die Entwicklung der Verwaltung im deutschen Staat des 18. Jahrhundert." In: Kleinheyer, G., and P. Mikat (eds.), *Beiträge zur Rechtsgeschichte.* Festschrift für Herman Conrad, 467–489. Paderborn: Schöningh.

Scheuner, U. (1980): *Der Beitrag der deutschen Romantik zur politischen Theorie.* Opladen: Westdeutscher Verlag.

Schieder, T. (1964): *Der Nationalstaat in Europa als historisches Phänomen.* Opladen: Westdeutscher Verlag.

Schmitt, C. (1932): *Der Begriff des Politischen.* Berlin: Duncker & Humblot.

Schmitt, C. (1934): *Politische Theologie* (2nd ed.). Berlin: Duncker & Humblot.

Schmitt, C. (1938): *Der Leviathan in der Staatslehre des Thomas Hobbes.* (Nachdr. d. Erstausg. 1982). Köln: Hohenheim-Verlag.

Schmitter, P., and G. Lehmbruch (eds.) (1979): *Trends Toward Corporatist Intermediation.* Beverly Hills, London: Sage.

Schnur, R. (1962): *Die französischen Juristen im konfessionellen Bürgerkrieg des 16. Jahrhunderts.* Berlin: Duncker & Humblot.

Schnur, R. (ed.) (1975): *Staatsräson.* Berlin: Duncker & Humblot.

Shennan, J. H. (1974): *The Origins of the Modern European State 1450–1725.* London: Hutchinson.

Strayer, J. (1970): *On the Medieval Origins of the Modern State.* Princeton: Princeton Univ. Press.

Tilly, C. (ed.) (1975): *The Formation of the National States in Western Europe.* Princeton: Princeton Univ. Press.

Ullmann, W. (1975): *Law and Politics in the Middle Ages.* Cambridge: Cambridge Univ. Press.

Weber, M. (1972): *Wirtschaft und Gesellschaft* (5th ed.). Tübingen: Mohr.

Weinacht, P. L. (1968): *Staat.* Berlin: Duncker & Humblot.

Wilks, M. J. (1963): *The Problem of Sovereignty in the Later Middle Ages.* Cambridge: Univ. Press.

Willke, H. (1983): *Entzauberung des Staates.* Frankfurt: Athenäum.

Willoweit, D. (1975): *Rechtsgrundlagen der Territorialgewalt.* Köln: Böhlau.

5. Constitutional Considerations with Particular Reference to Federal Systems

Vincent Ostrom

Abstract

The possibility that the constitution of order in human societies might be organized on different principles expressed through differing structures that yield commensurately different realities in public life is explored. A universal characteristic of human societies is the use of rules to order relationships among members of a society. The rule-ruler-ruled relationship is amenable to different patterns of organization. Hobbes's theory of sovereignty is contrasted to a theory of federal systems of government. The two models yield implications that allow for choice in the way that human societies are constituted.

5.1 Introduction

In exploring considerations pertaining to guidance, control, and performance evaluation in the public sector, a basic issue that needs to be addressed is whether public sectors represent a single type of "reality" with universal principles of organization, or multiple types of "realities" with varying principles of organization. A general tendency to use a single concept, the "state", to refer to a basic structure of authoritative relationships in a society might imply that a single type of reality exists in the governance of human societies. Alternatively, the state might be viewed as a conceptual variable including reference to "stateless societies" (Nettl 1968: 561–562).

Where language places strong reliance upon the concept of the state, such a term is usually associated with a definition that refers to a monopoly of the legitimate use of force or coercion in a society. Organization in human societies would then be dominated by a strong unitary pattern where each unit, designated as a state, would have those essential characteristics that pertain to a monopoly of authoritative relationships. Some single center of authority would exist as the basic control center in each society. The public sector would, then, be controlled by such a center and, in turn, serve as an intermediate instrumentality of control by that center, over the rest of society. Residual authority to "correct" for the weaknesses or failures of other institutions would reside with those who exercise the sovereign authority of the state to rule over society.

Other ways of conceptualizing authority relationships may exist. Different types of organization may be possible. Different conceptions and principles of organization may permit human beings to have recourse to different forms of political reality in constituting human societies. An exploration of such possibilities presents some difficult language problems. Words used in one language may be translated into equivalent terms that have quite different conceptual referents in another language. The language in a given society reflects conceptions and has connotations that fit a particular social "reality". The language appropriate to other conceptions and social "realities" may be less well developed.

The relation of conceptual sets to language and to basic patterns of organization can be illustrated by reference to some contrasting German and Swiss usages in the German language and some usages in the English language. The German term *Herrschaft* is frequently translated as the equivalent to the English term "authority". The literal reference in *Herrschaft* is to "lordship". The term has strong connotations of dominance, *Obrigkeit*. It is easy to associate patterns of dominance with a single center of ultimate authority and conceptualize the state in a unitary way. The English term authority has its root in author. The authorship in authority has an openness about the precise nature of authority relationships.

The German term for citizen is *Bürger* implying, as the English term does, reference to a *Burg* or city. A Swiss term for citizen, by contrast, is *Eidgenosse* where *Eid* refers to oath and *Genosse* refers to a companion or a comrade. A *Genossenschaft* is an association. *Eidgenossen* are companions or comrades in an association bound by oath. From this perspective a city or a *Burg* might be viewed as an association of associations. The Swiss term *Eidgenossenschaft* is used to refer to confederation with particular reference to the Swiss Confederation.

The Swiss Protestant tradition as reflected in the teachings of Zwingli, Calvin, and others is built upon associations or *Genossenschaften* as a basis for religious organization. The theological basis for this form of organization is associated with the Hebraic concept of covenant *(brit)*. One entering into a covenant is bound by oath. An *Eidgenosse* is, from this perspective, a covenanter. The term *"foedus"* in Latin means to covenant. *Foedus* is the root for such terms as confederation, federation, federal, etc.

German usage relies upon the term *Bund* in referring to federations, confederations, etc. The connotation here is more upon a union, league, or alliance. Distinctions are made between a *Staatenbund* (confederation) and a *Bundesstaat* (federal state). The emphasis in *Bundesstaat* is upon state – a state that is federal in form but still a state in contrast with the Swiss term *Eidgenossenschaft*. German and American usages that equate federal with a system of government that distributes authority between a limited national government and state or *Land* governments treats only the most superficial aspects of *Eidgenossenschaften*.

Inherent in these different language usages are basically different perspectives about authority relationships. The language of *Herrschaft* has quite different connotations than the language of *Genossen* and *Genossenschaften*. These two different sets of terms are of fundamental importance in exploring the different types of authority relationships that can be used to order relationships in human societies. *Herrschaft* is strongly associated with a unitary state that rules over society. *Genossen* and *Genossenschaften* have different implications. Structures of authority relationships reflecting comrades associating together in associations of associations are less easily thought about as *the* state.

In this essay I shall attempt to clarify basic considerations that apply to the constitution of human societies. I shall begin by identifying universal conditions that I would expect to apply to all human societies as rule-ordered relationships. Puzzles arise in specifying the nature of the ruler-ruled relationships where rules are used to order social relationships. One approach relies upon traditions of dominance inherent in the concept of *Herrschaft*. Another relies upon traditions of convenanting – of *Eidgenossenschaften*. The basic logic for these two types of solutions to the ruler-ruled relationships is well formulated respectively in Thomas *Hobbes's* "Leviathan" (1960), and in *Montesquieu's* "The Spirit of Laws" (1966), together with "The Federalist" papers written by Alexander *Hamilton* and James *Madison* (n.d.).

5.2 Human Societies as Rule-Ordered Relationships

A distinguishing characteristic of the human species is its ability to communicate through the use of a complex configuration of symbols articulated in language systems. Words are used to name sets of events and relationships; and thoughts are expressed in chains of words. This mode of communication enables human beings to transmit learning from one individual to another and, thus, to accumulate and organize knowledge across successive generations. This condition radically amplifies access to potential variety in human behavior.

In order to take advantage of each other's capabilities, it is necessary for human beings to introduce constraint into the potential variety of human behavior so that stable and predictable relationships can be maintained with one another. Language is used as an essential element in ordering social relationships. Words are used to distinguish what is allowable, and what is proscribed as not allowable, in the way that human beings relate to one another. That which is allowed defines the range of opportunities that are lawfully available to individuals in relating to one another. That which is not allowable establishes the limits or constraints that are applicable to human conduct. The basic structure of all institutional arrangements in human society is specifiable as configurations of rules that apply to the ordering of relationships among the individuals involved.

A fundamental problem in the use of rules to order relationships in human societies arises from the circumstance that rules are not self-formulating, self-applying, and self-enforcing. They are but words that have significance only by reference to the understanding that human beings share in communicating with one another. If rules are to have effect in the ordering of human relationships, they depend upon the agency of human beings to formulate rules, determine the application of rules, and enforce rules. In short, authorized relationships (authority to act) depend upon authoritative relationships (authority to formulate, apply, and enforce rules) as two distinguishable aspects of authority relationships (Commons 1959). A system of *rules* depends upon those who function as *rulers* and apply rules in relation to those who are *ruled*.

The rule-ruler-ruled relationship introduces the most fundamental source of inequalities in human societies. The enforcement of rules depends upon the potential use of sanctions to impose punishment upon those who violate rules. Rulership, thus, necessarily implies that some are lawfully vested with authority to impose deprivations in the form of punishment upon others. Some are vested with a legitimate authority to use instrumentalities of force or violence in relation to others. The concept of *Herrschaft* is implicit in rule-ordered relationships and necessarily implies a fundamental inequality between rulers and ruled.

Given the universal characteristic of relying upon language to create systems of rule-ordered relationships, we would expect all societies to manifest inequalities in their organization. In the extreme case we would expect to find no human society that maintained an absolute equality among all its members. Similarly, we would expect no human society to exist where individuals only did good in relation to one another. Instead, we would expect to find forms of both crime and punishment in all human societies. The capacity to do good depends upon potential recourse to instruments of evil in governing human relationships. These conditions are the logical correlaries of the use of language to create systems of rule-ordered relationships in human societies. Human beings must rely upon the agency of some who exercise the prerogatives of rulership in relation to others.

The general structure of the rule-ruler-ruled relationship is, however, subject to important structural variabilities that need to be specified in thinking about problems of guidance, control, and performance evaluation in human societies. In clarifying these structural variations, I shall explore only two possibilities. One is represented by Hobbes's theory of sovereignty where the ruler-ruled relationship is one of complete inequality. The other is one where prerogatives of rulership are limited by enforceable rules of constitutional law as specifying a limited fiduciary relationship between rulers and ruled. Standards of guidance and control encompassed in a system of constitutional law apply to rulers as well as those who are ruled. Once two basically different structures of rulership can be specified as theoretical possibilities, then a large number of variations might be contemplated. I confine myself to the task of clarifying the logical possibility of two different models of ruler-ruled relationships.

5.3 Hobbes's Theory of Sovereignty

In *Leviathan,* Hobbes advances a complex series of arguments in a general political theory. He formulates a theory of human nature where he postulates that individuals are motivated to seek their own good. But, without political constraint, he anticipates that individuals who seek their own good in a world of scarcity will come into conflict with one another so that each individual will be at war with every other individual. Patterns of human interaction in the absence of constraint will yield misery rather than the good that each individual is motivated to seek. Given the contradictions between motives and consequences, Hobbes argues that human beings would be led to explore the conditions of peace as an alternative to war. His analysis leads him to specify a series of rules which, if adhered to, would establish the foundation for peaceful and mutually productive relationships in human societies.

These rules, as such, are but "words", and "of no strength to secure a man at all" (Hobbes 1960: 109). The articles of peace depend upon the sword of justice to cause them to be observed. For there to be a common body of law, there must be a common source of law. It is law that transforms an aggregation of individuals into a commonwealth; and a commonwealth derives its unity from the unity of those who speak and act on its behalf as a collectivity rather than those who are the individual members of that collectivity.

Since a common system of law depends upon a common source of law and law depends upon human agents for its formulation, application, and enforcement, Hobbes conceives of a political covenant as having the form where each individual covenants with each other to assign ultimate authority to one man or one body of men to exercise the basic prerogatives of government. These prerogatives are those of sovereignty. Those who exercise them are sovereign; and all the rest are subjects. He views this as the "only way" (Hobbes 1960: 112) to create a common power sufficient to bind men to perform in accordance with rules of law. Political organization is unitary, or monocratic, in nature and those who exercise the prerogatives of rulers must, in Max Weber's terms, exercise a monopoly of the legitimate use of force in a society.

Once a presumption of monopoly, as applied to rulership, is established, then Hobbes's attributes of sovereignty follow: sovereignty is inalienable with the sovereign, unlimited and indivisible. A monopoly of authority cannot be maintained without these attributes: monopolies are single-centered and exclusive. It follows then that sovereign authority as the source of law is above the law and cannot be held accountable to law. Any effort to impose a rule of law upon a sovereign would vest ultimate authority in those who judge: problems of infinite regress would arise and be destructive of the peace of the community.

Hobbes's theory of sovereignty states the essential logic used to fashion modern nation-states in the sixteenth and seventeenth centuries. These efforts were marked, as Elias (1980, especially II: 123–311) has shown, with a monopolization of authority in a political structure that had the characteristics of an Absolutism. There can be little doubt that Hobbes's theory of sovereignty represents a logically coherent account as one way of constituting political reality. A key question is whether it is the "only way", as Hobbes asserts (1960: 112).

Hobbes's formulation is accompanied by sufficient qualification to indicate that fundamental tensions are inherent in his theoretical formulation. The exercise of sovereign prerogatives requires a high level of enlightenment: "He that is to govern a whole nation, must read in himself, not this or that particular man; but mankind" (1960: 6). The possibility of a lawful society depends upon moral virtue: ". . . injustice, ingratitude, arrogance, pride, inequity, acception of persons, and the rest, can never be made lawful. For it can never be that war shall preserve life, and peace destroy it (1960: 104). Good laws are both necessary and "good for the people". "Unnecessary laws", by contrast, "are not good laws; but traps for money . . ." (1960: 227–228). Governance in accordance with fundamental moral precepts and the "winning of favour by good offices" (1960: 236) is the highest form of worship: "For as obedience is more acceptable to God than sacrifice; so also to set light by (i.e., neglect) his commandments, is the greatest of all contumilies" (1960: 239–240). And the neglect of God's Commandments will yield for sovereigns a harvest of natural punishment that threaten the peace and stability of commonwealths:

"There is no action of man in this life, that is not the beginning of so long a chain of consequences, as no human providence is high enough, to give a man a prospect to the end.

And in this chain, there are linked together both pleasing and unpleasing events; in such manner, as he that will do anything for his pleasure, must engage himself to suffer all of the pains annexed to it; and these pains, are the natural punishments of those actions, which are the beginning of more harm than good. And hereby it comes to pass, that intemperance is naturally punished by diseases, rashness, by mischances; injustices, with the violence of enemies; pride, with ruin; cowardice, with oppression; negligent government of princes, with rebellion; and rebellion, with slaughter. For seeing punishments are consequent to the breach of laws; natural punishment must be naturally consequent to the breach of the laws of nature; and therefore follow them as their natural, not arbitrary effects" (1960: 240–241).

Sovereigns cannot be lawfully punished for a breach of the laws of which they are authors but they are accountable to the natural punishments that follow from their actions: injustices evoke the violence of enemies; the negligent government of princes, rebellion; and rebellion, slaughter. Peace again gives way to war. Hobbes views sovereignty as a necessary but not a sufficient condition for peace.

5.4 Constitutional Rule

Within the framework of Hobbes's more general formulation, it is possible to derive a solution to the problem of political organization that is an alternative to his theory of sovereignty. This requires an elaboration of a theory of democracy that is anticipated by Montesquieu and is consistent with the political theory expounded by Alexander Hamilton and James Madison in *The Federalist*. It relies more upon principles of *Eidgenossenschaften* than upon *Herrschaft*.

Hobbes conceptualizes a democracy within his theory of sovereignty where ultimate authority is exercised by an assembly of all citizens who will come together. The unitary nature of authority is preserved by reference to a single assembly of all citizens. In *De Cive,* Hobbes (1949: 91) identifies a democracy by two attributes: the *"eternal prescription of convents"* (my emphasis) and a "plurality of voices". I construe the first attribute to mean the eternal rule of assemblies; and the second to mean the exercise of power by plurality voting. This formulation neglects a critical factor that might be characterized as eternal prescriptions of convent: eternal rules of assembly.

The Rule of assemblies in democratic societies depends upon Rules of assembly. If citizens are to exercise the prerogatives of government in an assembly, there must exist, as a necessary condition, rules for establishing the qualifications of membership, the existence of a quorum, setting the time and place of meeting, conducting the business of the assembly, providing for officers to discharge specialized functions in the conduct of government, and taking decisions by forms of voting. To govern by assembly, then, requires a shared understanding about the rules that apply to the conduct of the business of an assembly.

Rules that apply to the conduct of an assembly, as an assembly, can be distinguished from those rules that apply to the discharge of authority by an assembly in relation to the exigencies of life that occur outside of any assembly. It is this distinction that marks the difference between a constitution and ordinary law. A *constitution* is that set of rules that applies to the essential conduct of government in contrast to *law* as that set of rules which applies to the exercise of subordinate authority and to ordinary relationships among members of a society.

Once this distinction is made, it would be entirely consistent with Hobbes's formulation for citizens in a democratic assembly to be zealous in the maintenance of their own authority and to be cautious in delegating authority to agents who act on their behalf. Interim authority to act in an emergency, authority to take executive action on behalf of an assembly, and authority to adjudicate cases in determining the application of law and rendering judgments in disputes might all be subject to limited authority where each official acting on authority of the assembly would be strictly accountable for the discharge of their office as a public trust. Ultimate accountability would be to the people in assembly.

In the course of time, decisions at the constitutional level have been recognized to have interesting properties provided that they can be enforced. It is possible for human beings to arrive at essentially unanimous decisions about rules that apply to the making of decisions even though particular decisions will be taken where some win and some lose (Buchanan and Tullock 1962). This principle is characteristic of many games. Each round in the play of a game involve winning and losing, yet individuals find it mutually agreeable to play a game which gives no special advantage to any particular set of players. Constitutions, as rules that apply to the conduct of government, might be formulated where each individual has equal access to different positions of authority and where the discharge of special prerogatives can be subject to an enforceable trust under mutually agreeable standards of fairness (see Rawls 1971). Such constitutions might be agreeable to everyone involved even though particular decisions may be taken where some win and some lose.

The viability of a direct democracy is subject to serious threats. These arise from limits on size. To govern by an assembly of all citizens would imply that a direct democracy must be confined to a relatively small community of people. Direct democracies would, first, be constrained by the distance that each citizen would be required to travel to attend meetings of an assembly. Proceedings within an assembly imply further constraints that are a function of size. Those proceedings depend upon only one person speaking at a time. Orderly procedures require someone to preside, recognize speakers, control the agenda, and take cumulative action. As size increases, the proportionate voice of each ordinary member declines; and the proportionate voice of the leadership increases in any democratic assembly.

This circumstance means that democratic assemblies are subject to strong oligarchical tendencies that increase with the size of an assembly. Direct democracies, thus, are subject to serious problems of institutional failure that are a function of size. They are exposed to the circumstances that officials may easily usurp the prerogatives of a large assembly. If such usurpations are acquiesced in by the citizens of a democracy, a democracy ceases to exist with the assumption of sovereign prerogatives by the usurper. It is these circumstances that led Montesquieu (1966: 126) to conclude, "If a republic be small, it is destroyed by foreign force, if it be large, it is ruined by internal imperfection." Hobbes could dismiss democracies as not being viable alternatives when monarchs reigned among the great powers of Europe.

Montesquieu conceived of confederation as providing a way out of the dilemma that implied failure for both small and large republics. He conceived of a confederate republic as enabling small republics to join in the formation of a larger confederate republic where simultaneous advantage could be gained by recourse to both small and larger scales of organization. The larger scale of a confederation would enable republics to aggregate so that they could combine sufficient force to resist external aggression and yet maintain the virtues of small republics within each member of the confederation. Should there be usurpation by officials in a single republic, Montesquieu also anticipated that the larger community of a confederate republic could provide remedies to guard against usurpation and enable the society to reform itself.

The American effort to fashion a system of constitutional republics was based upon methods similar to those conceptualized by Montesquieu. As Tocqueville emphasizes in Chapters 2, 4, and 5 of *Democracy in America,* the conceptual foundations for American democracy grew out of the convenantal theology of the Puritans. People convenanted in specifying compacts or constitutions for the organization of townships. Townships confederated to form chartered colonies in Connecticut and Rhode Island, for example, long before they became states. People were "sovereign" in their township assemblies while the King was sovereign in the Empire. The American Revolution was a contest over those conflicting principles of authority.

As Tocqueville (1945: 56) expressed it ". . . the doctrine of the sovereignty of the people came out of the townships and took possession of the state." This doctrine become "the law of the laws". These principles were reiterated in the constitution of the different units of government in the American system of governments: "the township was organized before the county, the county before the state and the state before the nation." The national government was "in fact nothing more than a summary of those republican principles which were current in the whole community before it existed and independently of its existence" (Tocqueville 1945: 59).

Critical issues pertaining to the theory and structure of confederation arose early in American efforts to create a confederate republic. These problems were addressed in the formulation of a revised constitution in 1787 to replace the Articles of Confederation as the first constitution of the American confederation. The revised theoretical formulation has come to be referred to as a "federal" system of government rather than as a confederation. But the basic conceptualization can be viewed as a variation in the structure of what Montesquieu conceptualized as a confederate republic.

One of the important problems confronting Americans during and following the Revolution was how to take joint collective action that involved the common interests of the several states and avoid the possibility of the American states warring upon one another. Unless appropriate institutions could be devised, Americans anticipated that the exigencies of war would come to dominate relationships upon the North American continent as it had done upon the European continent. In the course of time, the logic of mutually destructive conflict (Boulding 1963) would give priority to security from external attack over liberty, to the maintenance of standing armies, and to the strenghtening of executive authority in relation to legislative authority (Hamilton, Jay, and Madison n.d.: 42–43). The failure of confederation would create a "new order of things" in which "the face of

America will be but a copy of that of the continent of Europe" (Hamilton, Jay, and Madison n.d.: 263).

The first American confederation had been constituted by reference to a Congress made up of representatives of the states. Size of the delegations varied, but representatives of each state voted as a unit. Congress could act on many matters by less than a unanimous vote of the states, but all matters internal to the confederation depended upon implementation through the instrumentalities of state governments. No separate judiciary was available to adjudicate conflicts between actions of Congress and actions of the states. Funds of the confederation depended upon payments made by the states.

In his critique of confederation, Alexander Hamilton (see especially, *Federalist* 15 and 16) argued that confederation, as a form of government, was based upon a fallacious conception – a fundamental error – because it could not do what was minimally expected of a government: It could not enforce its prescriptions as law. Congress could resolve, but it depended upon the states to enforce its resolutions. The source of error, in Hamilton's analysis, turned upon the presumption that one government (the United States as a confederation), could govern other governments (the states). So long as such a conception held, the confederation was limited to the taking of *collective* sanctions in the enforcement of its prescription. Collective sanctions fail to discriminate between wrongdoers and innocent bystanders. A government of governments could not, then, meet the basic requirements of justice in the application of sanctions to those who are culpable of wrongdoing rather than to innocent bystanders. Justice requires that law be applied to individuals rather than to collectivities, as such.

This circumstance meant for Hamilton that the failure of confederation could be resolved only by a fundamental shift in structure. Each of the governments in a confederation was required to extend its authority to "the persons of the citizens", and to act in relation to "the hope and fears of individuals" (n.d.: 98–99). Rather than being a government of governments, a federal system of government should be a complex structure of governments as political associations where each individual participated in several such associations in relation to diverse, overlapping communities of interest. Each unit of government as a political association had authority to act with reference to those relationships that were shared in common by a community of people who relate themselves to a particular domain and particular sets of interest within that domain. The more encompassing community of interest prevailed in relation to matter of common concern, but other communites of interest act with autonomy in reference to other problems shared across different domains.

Federal systems, thus, represent complex structures of associations of varying scope and domain where there is a rich interpenetration of relationships to each individual member of the society. Yet each unit of government has an autonomy of its own; and society represents complex networks of concurrently organized structures where people relate to one another within the opportunities and limits afforded by diverse structures. Such structures are not unitary in having a single center of ultimate authority but are complex configurations in which inner and outer bounds can be subject to alteration and extension. The possibility of a compound structure of concurrent governments acting in relation to the interests that individuals share in diverse communities, in turn, depends upon the mainten-ance of limits in the exercise of all governmental prerogatives. Otherwise, struggles for dominance would, in the course of time, be much like that which prevailed in Europe over the millennium after the fall of Rome.

The capacity to maintain limits upon the exercise of governmental authority takes us back to a distinction between a constitution and ordinary law that is inherent in a democratic republic where citizens govern by assembly. But the reference to diverse domains inherent in a compound republic requires that the condition of direct participation by all citizens in an assembly be relaxed and that processes of governments be more carefully differentiated. The structure of constitutional rule assumes critical importance if democratic government is to mean rule of the people ("demos" = people; "cratia" = rule). Processes of constitutional decision making serve as proxy institutions for government by assembly.

If people can maintain control over processes of constitutional choice, and if constitutions serve as legal instruments for maintaining effective limits upon the exercise of governmental prerogatives, then we might conceptualize people as exercising the fundamental prerogatives of government. If all units of government in a highly federalized (or compounded) system of government can be subject to effective limits of constitutional rule, we might conceive of a system of government that can validly be construed to be a democracy. Montesquieu's conception of a method for overcoming limits of size had merit, but under somewhat more limited conditions than he indicated. These conditions were given more explicit attention in American constitutional efforts to analyze the failure of confederation and devise alternative arrangements that were consistent with the method of confedera-tion.

In what Hamilton (n.d.: 524) referred to as "the general theory of a limited constitution", several conditions are required for establishing and maintaining a system of constitutional law that can be used to enforce limits upon those who exercise governmental prerogatives. These conditions require that the attributes of sovereignty – inalienable, unlimited, indivisible exercise of authority – be fore-closed.

A general theory of the limited constitution depends first upon a fundamental distinction between a constitution and ordinary law, and between processes of constitutional decision making and governmental decision making. A constitution represents a configuration of rules that apply to the essential conduct of govern-ment. Ordinary law, by contrast, applies to the subordinate exercise of authority and to patterns of social relationships that occur in the normal exigencies of life. These distinctions, in turn, can be reinforced by distinctions in decision-making processes. A constitution, Madison (n.d.: 348) wrote, is "established by the people and unalterable by the government, and a law (is) established by the government and alterable by the government". A government in a constitutional republic does not have the prerogative of defining its own authority. That authority is formulated and revised by decision-making processes that have reference to the people acting through nongovernmental modes of decision making, such as constitutional con-ventions, initiatives, and referenda.

Once these distinctions are established, a constitution can be viewed as a legal instrument for specifying limits that apply to the exercise of governmental prerogatives. The most fundamental of those limits pertain to the prerogatives of individuals which are also specifiable as limits upon the prerogatives of government. Rights pertaining to freedom of speech, press, communication, and assembly are essential to the maintenance of an open public realm where citizens are free to communicate with one another about public affairs without governmental interference and dominance. Rights of property and freedom to contract are fundamental to voluntary association as a means of self-governance. Rights of due process of law establish the obligation of officials to discharge the prerogatives of government in accordance with lawful procedures; and these procedures require that public business be conducted in open public view subject to publicity. Further limits may be established by distinguishing governmental decision-making processes and assigning those processes to different structures. Montesquieu specified a separation of powers as a necessary attribute of the constitution of liberty (1966: Book XI); and Madison (*Federalist:* 47–51) built upon Montesquieu's formulation in distinguishing legislative from executive and judicial functions. A separation of powers implies that the general exercise of governmental prerogatives depends upon the concurrence of multiple decision-making structures. Formal limits can be established by reference to vetoes. A constitutional separation of powers implies a sharing of powers so that the political feasibility of any proposal or undertaking depends upon the concurrence of multiple decision structures. When the exercise of governmental authority by all governmental officials is subject to limits, no one exercises unlimited authority.

Constitutional provisions specifying arrangements for either the direct or indirect participation of people in the processes of government establish further constraint to the exercise of governmental prerogatives. Popular election of legislative and executive officials provide for the recurrent indirect participation of citizens in the processes of government. Proceedings by jury trial or inquiries by grand juries provide for the direct participation of citizens in the judicial process.

The principles of constitutional design that apply to a republican system of government are summarized by Madison (n.d.: 337–338) in the following way:

"In framing a government which is to be administered by men over men, the great difficulty lies in this: you must enable the government to control the governed; and in the next place oblige it to control itself. A dependence on the people is, no doubt the primary control on the government; but experience has taught mankind the necessity of auxiliary precautions.

This policy of supplying, by opposite and rival interests, the defects of better motives, might be traced through the whole system of human affairs, private as well as public. We see it particularly displayed in all of the subordinate distributions of power, where the constant aim is to divide and arrange the several offices in such a manner as that each may be a check upon the other – that the private interests of every individual may be a sentinel over the public rights. These inventions of prudence cannot be less requisite to the distribution of the supreme powers of the state."

Madison's *opposite and rival interests* are based upon the same presumption that Montesquieu (1966: Book XI) makes in prescribing that *power be used to check power.*

In such a conception, no one, or any one group of individuals, rules over society. Rather, the governance of society depends upon the concurrence of diverse groups of decision makers. Rules can be established and rules can be enforced, but no one exercises unlimited prerogatives. Everyone has access to prerogatives that can be used to challenge the improper exercise of authority by any particular official or set of officials. Such a system, organized by reference to opposite and rival interests, depends critically upon people having a shared knowledge about the basic standards of value which are used to make fundamental distinctions about the proper discharge of governmental functions. When conflicts occur, diverse decision structures provide multiple remedies for resolving conflicts and transforming them into reciprocal sets of mutually productive relationships. The structuring of opposite and rival interests can be a prelude to stalemate and unconstrained conflict unless methods of conflict resolution can be used to create or re-establish mutually productive communities of relationships.

Such a system of governance must necessarily come at a high price. Use of opposite and rival interests as the basic principle of organization implies that high levels of conflict will occur. The rhetoric associated with high levels of conflict will give an illusion of disorder. Conflict, however, is diffused as individuals seek out remedies that are available in diverse decision structures. Proportionately large amounts of time and effort will be devoted to public deliberation and to public decision making. Secrecy will be difficult to attain even in essential areas pertaining to national security. The discharge of the prerogatives of public office will be subject to public scrutiny. Processes of governance will be subject to guidance and control by those who bind themselves to standards of performance inherent in a system of constitutional rule. Citizenship might then be viewed as a companionship shared in civic associations bound to uphold standards of propriety, justice, and liberty in mutually productive communities of relationships. Methods of *Eidgenossenschaften* might be viewed as an alternative to methods of *Herrschaft* where *Herrschaft* is monopolized by a single center of authority or sovereignty.

5.5 Conclusion

The method proposed by Montesquieu for confederating or compounding republics into complex configurations of convenantal arrangements provided an alternative to Hobbes's method of having recourse to a unitary sovereign in the governance of a society. Montesquieu's method, as modified in light of Hamilton's critique, opened the possibility that democratic institutions need not be confined to small republics. In addition, Montesquieu called for a separation of powers among legislative, executive, and judicial authorities as being necessary to the constitution of liberty. Democratic institutions might attain stable forms where the autonomy of diverse self-governing communities could exist in the context of concurrent and overlapping units of government. Such a political order is many-centered and can be characterized as *polycentric,* where no single center exercises dominance over the rest (Polanyi 1951).

Reiterating principles of constitutional rule in federal systems of governance has radical implications for conceptualizing the nature of the public sector. First, there is a sense in which each unit of government acts in relation to a community of people who constitute its *public.* Each such unit is subject to regulation and control through principles of democratic organization that enable such publics to function as self-governing communities. The reiteration of patterns of self-government in multiple units of government implies that people participate in diverse publics that have a critical awareness of what it means to be self-governing.

Second, limitations upon the authority of all units of government implies that citizens and persons are generally reserved authority to participate in open public realms that are not confined to particular communites of people associated with particular units of government. It is these open public realms that serve as fora for open discussion, deliberation, and dialogue and inform the development of a *public opinion* that is independent of particular units of government. Meetings in market places, village squares, or community centers can be the occasion for discussion and the activation of opinions that are articulable through diverse instrumentalities of government.

The formulation of constitutional rights of individuals as limits upon the authority of government sometimes leads to the characterization of the nongovernmental character of this realm as "private". For example, Brecht (1970: 474) characterizes this realm as pertaining to the "private" sphere of opinion, religion, art, science. Yet, it is this *private* sphere that gives expression to "public" opinion. The liberty of the individual to participate in an open public realm and to be active in various voluntary associations is not a "private individualism" as Polanyi (1951: vii) recognizes; but an expression of a distinctive set of beliefs that establish fiduciary relationships among all members of a society. It is an open public realm where members of society openly and publicly maintain communication with one another to fashion a public opinion that is independent of particular structures of government.

Third, the development of a division of labor associated with different aspects of governmental decision making implies that the operation of any one unit of government and the concurrent operation of diverse units of government always occurs in structures of interorganizational arrangements. The dispersion of authority among diverse legislative, executive, and judicial structures implies that all organization of government occurs in an interorganizational milieu. Individuals do not stand alone against a monopoly of authority, but have the opportunity to articulate their essential interest in diversely constituted structures of authority.

This differentiation of authority in diverse decision structures has occurred to varying degrees in all modern systems of government that distinguish legislatures from courts and executive instrumentalities. All such governments can then be viewed as *simultaneously and sequentially linked patterns of interorganizational arrangements* that constitute particular forms of government. The principal distinctions rest in the nature of the linkages where parliamentary systems facilitate the formation of coalitions that can then exercise dominance through specified interorganizational linkages of a dependent type. Madison's opposite and rival interest relies more upon linkages among autonomous, interdependent units bound within the constraints of reciprocal veto capabilities. Nonetheless, all modern systems of government are multiorganizational arrangements whose distinctive characteristics turn upon the type of simultaneous and sequential linkages that occur among the different units of organization that are involved.

The way that modern societies have differentiated decision-making processes in relation to separable structures such as legislatures, courts, administrative instrumentalities, political parties, etc., implies that the unitary character of the state has, in fact, given way to substantial degrees of *polycentricity* where coordination occurs to an increasing degree through equilibrating tendencies attained by processes of mutual adjustment (Polanyi 1951). The only feature that maintains a unitary character is a presumption of supremacy that applies in the linkage of some one structure to other structures of governance. But, doctrines of parliamentary supremacy are usually accompanied by doctrines of judicial independence and executive privilege. When these different linkages are put together with multiparty electoral systems, the concept of a monopoly prevailing in the exercise of political prerogative is less and less tenable. Montesquieu, rather than Hobbes, anticipated the methods of organization that were most amenable to extending the frontiers of political artisanship in the modern world.

Fourth, highly federalized systems of government characterized by autonomy among decision structures in any unit of government and among different units of government implies that patterns of federal administration occur in an interorganizational milieu that is more characteristic of patterns of industrial organizations in market economies that in highly bureaucratized, monocentric systems of public administration (Bish 1971; Ostrom 1973; 1974). Negotiation, bargaining, contracting, and competitive rivalry are a part of the coordinating processes that characterize relationships among diversely organized administrative entities operating in the public economy of highly federalized systems of government. Multiorganizational arrangements analogous to industry structures come to characterize functional relationships among diverse agencies concerned with the supply and provision of similar types of public goods and services. Police "industries" might then take on different structural characteristics than other "industries" concerned with water supply, fire protection, waste disposal, education, welfare, or any other type of public service.

Recent work in the theory of public goods indicates that the basic problems necessitating recourse to the coercive powers of government pertain critically to organizing consumption and financing the *provision* of public goods and services. Organization of supply is amenable to a wider range of options including supply by private vendors. The availability of alternative suppliers permits choice among competitive options. Quasi-market structures can exist in the public sector even though such structures are subject to weaker competitive pressures than competitive markets in the private sector. The essential point is that nonbureaucratic modes of coordination can be used, in part, as alternatives to principles of bureaucratic organization to enhance performance capabilities in the public sector (V. Ostrom and E. Ostrom 1977).

Fifth, principles of federal organization permit multi-national communities to coexist with national and sub-national communities of interest. A theory of sovereignty only allows for movement from commonwealth to empire where a single center of authority maintains dominance. Western civilization has failed in all efforts to attain stable forms of empire. Montesquieu's method of confederating or federating together provides an opportunity of move toward nonimperial multinational communities such as the European Community.

The scope of the public sector and the way it is put together varies in proportion to the diverse communities of interests and types of organizations and enterprises that are put together to take account of interests that must rely upon the coercive powers of government as necessary elements of organization. But these factors can be put together in different ways to constitute different types of social reality. The public sector need not be monocentric in structure; and bureaucracy (hierarchy) need not be the only mode of coordination in the public sector. The public realm can be organized through diverse structures that give rise to equilibrating tendencies in polycentric orders. Basic concepts and principles that apply to the constitutional level of analysis can contribute to the development of different organizational forms and social realities. Human beings can exercise some significant degree of choice over their way of life and how they relate to one another in human societies.

References

Bish, R. (1971): *The Public Economy of Metropolitan Areas*. Chicago: Markham.

Boulding, K. E. (1963): "Toward a Pure Theory of Threat Systems." *American Economic Review* 53 (May): 424–434.

Brecht, A. (1970): *The Political Education of Arnold Brecht, An Autobiography 1884–1970*. Princeton, N. J.: Princeton Univ. Press.

Buchanan, J. and G. Tullock (1962): *The Calculus of Consent*. Logical Foundation of Constitutional Government. Ann Arbor, Mich.: Univ. of Michigan Press.

Commons, J. R. (1959): *Legal Foundations of Capitalism*. Madison, Wis.: The Univ.of Wisconsin Press.

Elias, N. (1980): *Über den Prozess der Zivilisation*. Frankfurt (Main): Suhrkamp.

Gässer, A. (1939): Geschichte der Volkfreiheit und der Demokratie. Aarm: Verlag H. R. Sauerländer + Co.

Hamilton, A., J. Jay and J. Madison (n.d.): *The Federalist*. New York: The Modern Library.

Hobbes, T. (1949): *De Cive or the Citizen*. New York: Appleton-Century-Crofts.

Hobbes, T. (1960): *Leviathan or the Matter, Forme and Power of a Commonwealth Ecclesiastical and Civil*. Oxford: Basil Blackwell.

Montesquieu, C. (1966): *The Spirit of the Laws*. New York: Hafner.

Nettl, J. P. (1968): "The State as a Conceptual Variable." *World Politics* 20/4: 559–592.

Ostrom, V. (1973): "Can Federalism Make a Difference?" *Publius* 3 (Fall): 197–238.

Ostrom, V. (1974): *The Intellectual Crisis in American Public Administration*. University, Ala.: The Univ. of Alabama Press.

Ostrom, V. (1984): *The Political Theory of a Compound Republic* (Rev. ed.). Bloomington, Ind.: Indiana Univ., Workshop in Political Theory and Policy Analysis.

Ostrom, V. and E. Ostrom (1977): "Public Goods and Public Choices." In Savas, E. S. (ed.), *Alternatives of Delivering Public Services*. Toward Improved Performance, 7–49. Boulder: Westview Press.

Polanyi, M. (1951): *The Logic of Liberty: Reflections and Rejoinders*. Chicago: The Univ. of Chicago Press.

Rawls, J. (1971): *A Theory of Justice*. Cambridge, Mass.: Harvard Univ. Press.

Tocqueville, A. (1945): *Democracy in America*. New York: Alfred A. Knopf.

6. The Blurring of the Distinction 'State Versus Society' in the Idea and Practice of the Welfare State

Franz-Xaver Kaufmann

Abstract

In this chapter the concept of the public sector is developed on its historical and comparative background. A comparison of Anglo-Saxon and German conceptions of the welfare state shows substantial differences in theory and practice of political development. The distinction between public and private is common to both political theories. There is, however, no clear boundary between public and private; the boundary itself is a politically contested issue. For scientific use 'public' and 'private' have to be considered as analytical perspectives, not as separate domains. Hence the public sector is not to be conceived as a 'boundary maintaining' system like 'state' or 'government'. The concept is broader and less limited. It includes those aspects of social reality which are related to actions of state and government, regardless of their formal public or private status.

6.1 Introduction

Modern states are said to be welfare states. Our academic understanding of what this means, however, is still in its infancy. A serious theory of the welfare state is still lacking, as several authors have emphasized in recent years (see Mommsen 1981; Luhmann 1981; Flora and Heidenheimer 1981; Alber 1982). This paper deals with some issues in defining the major problems of what is conveniently called 'the welfare state' in order to provide a better understanding of what we refer to as the public sector in this volume.

6.2 The Welfare State, a Preliminary Sketch

The first record of the use of the term 'welfare state' is supposed to stem from the British archbishop William Temple who used it in a pamphlet "Citizen and Churchmen" in the year 1941 (cf. Gregg 1967: 3).[1] This was the year in which Roosevelt and Churchill proclaimed the Atlantic Charter and asked for "freedom from fear and want" in a new society after a victorious end to World War II. One year later the Beveridge Plan, which is considered a landmark in programming the welfare state, appeared. In 1948 the General Declaration of Human Rights promulgated not only civil but also social rights like the right to social security, to work and recreation, to a decent standard of living, the protection of mothers and children as well as the right to education and to cultural participation.[2]

If one considers the welfare state as a kind of consensual definition of a society's "legal and therefore formal and explicit responsibility for the basic well-being of all of its members" (Girvetz 1968: 512), it makes sense to say that in the Anglo-Saxon world the welfare state has emerged during and since World War II, despite some preliminary innovations beginning with the British Factory Act of 1833, the Public Health Act of 1848, the Education Act of 1870, the Workmens Compensation Act of 1897 and the Old Age Pensions Act of 1908. Although Great Britain (and to some extent also France) led in the industrialization process of the 19th century and first experienced the social problems of industrial work (cf. e.g. Polanyi 1944), it was not Britain but Germany which played a pioneering role in the intellectual analysis of the new society and its problems as well as in the creation of political measures to deal with these problems.

In the thirties and forties of the 19th century a keen awarenss of the new character of industrial misery (as differentiated from pre-industrial poverty) was found in such leading theorists as Franz von Baader (1835), Robert von Mohl (1835), Lorenz von Stein (1850) and Karl Marx (1845/46: 186 f.). It is impressive to see how these thinkers, who range across the political spectrum from conservative (Baader), to liberal (Mohl), reformist, (Stein) or revolutionary (Marx) thought, converge on the diagnosis of industrial misery as stemming from a social division between the wealthier people, who are able to participate in the development of the new economic opportunities, and the "proletarians without property" (Baader), who are forced to sell their ability to work for whatever price and under whatever working conditions they can get.

The network of these new economic opportunities was called – following Hegel (1821) – "the (civil) society", and was differentiated from "the state," the constitution of self-containing legal power cf. Grimm: (Ch. 4). The new opportunities for industrialization were seen as a consequence of the withdrawal of the liberal state from economic tutelage; thus its social consequences were attributed to the *separation* between state and society and the abolition of the feudal order that accounted for economic backwardness as well as for a basic protection of the bondsmen and other early forms of social security like the guilds, local and ecclesiastical assistance, etc. It is in this context that the term 'Sozialpolitik' (meaning either social politics or social policies or both) has been asserted to denote the problem of a *mediation* between state and society in order to solve the social problems of early capitalism (cf. Pankoke 1970; Grimm 1983).

The institutional character of the term "Sozialpolitik" emerged slowly during the second part of the 19th century, and it was given academic support by the *Verein für Sozialpolitik,* an association of social scientists founded in 1872 to promote social reform by state intervention. With the unification of the German Reich in 1870/71 under the auspices of the King of Prussia the *etatistic* approach to solving social problems became stronger. The introduction of the first nationwide social security system for industrial workers in the 1880s is rightly considered a landmark in the creation of the modern welfare state. If one sees the granting of social rights as a decisive aspect in the establishment of a welfare state, Germany was a pioneer again in 1919, when the new Weimar constitution included a series of basic social rights for the first time.[3]

The widespread tendency to describe modern states as welfare states suggests that there has been a very similar political evolution in all western countries and in other parts of the world. As the recent work of some comparative researchers (Heclo 1974; Flora and Heidenheimer 1981; Köhler and Zacher 1981; Mommsen 1981; Alber 1982, 1983; Flora et al. 1983; Kohl 1985) shows, it is, however, difficult to ascertain a common pattern in the development of the social legislation and services. The genesis of welfare policies cannot be explained by valid single or even compound factor theories. There is also no consensus with respect to the core institutions of the welfare state. In the Anglo-Saxon discussion the welfare state is widely identified with the existence of certain 'social services'. In the United States the term designates five main domains of welfare institutions: education, health, income maintenance, housing and employment. In British classifications the last domain seems to be excluded. British authors, however, tend to add the newer domain of social work and counseling as "personal social services" (cf. Kaufmann 1980: 35). In the German discussion there is some tendency to identify the *Sozialstaat* with *Sozialpolitik*. This term emphasizes workers' protection and social security, i.e., activities of the central state regulated under the auspices of the Ministry of Labour, which has important corporate relationships with the employers and the unions. Whereas health and housing are sometimes included, education is regularly excluded from the concept of '*Sozialpolitik*'. Local services tend to be included only in the newer academic discussion.

These differences in emphasis should, however, not obscure the evidence that modern states show of a certain agreement with respect to the social problems regulated by government action. *Variations in the institutional embodiment seem to be bound essentially to national differences in the constitutional structure of the public sector.* The common properties of the so-called welfare states, despite certain variations in scope and institutional embodiment, can be explained by the theoretical assumption that welfare aspects of modern states are emergent properties which have developed by a process of trial and error. From the perspective of evolutionary theory one may consider various historical situations, social-political movements and conflicts as challenges and the responses of the institutionalized forms of political power (in terms of social legislation, repression or migration policies) as variations. The emergence of common properties then calls for explanation: if Western societies have adopted similar ideas and institutions for promoting what is called the welfare state, there must also be properties common to the challenges that have evoked selective responses from political institutions. The sources of the challenges can be found in the pervasive issues of industrialization and modernization.

6.3 State, Government, and Welfare

From a more analytical point of view the issues of the welfare state reflect patterns of intervention by means of the state into what is conventionally called the (civil) society (cf. Kaufmann 1982). This perspective presupposes the distinction of 'state' and 'society' which is very prominent in the German tradition (cf. Böckenförde 1976) and has also been adopted recently by Anglo-Saxon authors. There are, however, substantial differences between the original German and the current Anglo-Saxon theories that we shall try to bring out in this section.

The British literature about the welfare state suggests that the state is essentially concerned with the social welfare of its citizens. This creed may belong to the civil religion of some European countries, but it would be misleading to take it as a starting point for further analysis.[4]

First, social problems and welfare issues are only a part of political activity. It is the same government that decides about pollution control, tax reform, economic policy, defense and social security, and there are not two separate entities, one called 'welfare state' *(Sozialstaat)* and the other called political or constitutional state *(Rechtsstaat)*. A theory of the welfare state therefore cannot be restricted to welfare policies but must include the constitutional and institutional aspects of political systems which aim to promote the general welfare of the members of society. A more comprehensive view then indicates that the promotion of welfare cannot be restricted to social administration, but is also involved in full employment policy and defense, as Beveridge was clearly aware (cf. Beveridge 1943: 98 ff.).

If one wants to understand the function of welfare in politics, one may safely assume that substantial parts of modern policies are legitimated by a public concern for improving individual and/or collective welfare.[5] There is also evidence that other political concerns (e.g., economic growth, maintaining political loyalties) and interests (e.g., of professional associations or unions) are often more efficient in promoting welfare policies than commitment for welfare. Moreover, welfare policies do no always produce need-satisfaction for those individuals who are most in need of it. As they are interventions in already constituted social settings their effects depend both upon the implementation of the policy and the reactions of those concerned. Welfare effects should therefore be considered more as a by-product of policy-making in the realm of democratic control than as its essence.

The emergence of the welfare aspects of the modern state are seen mainly as a *late* feature of political development. Stein Rokkan (1975) distinguishes four basic processes of political development that seem to emerge more or less sequentially and may then be analyzed as 'phases' of an overall process of political development:

- The formation of the modern state stricto sensu, i.e., the building of military and administrative institutions related to a political center and a delimited territory. Or, in Max Weber's terms, the process of monopolization of physical power by a political center.
- Nation building as a process of political and cultural unification of the population in a state's territory.
- The establishment of political citizenship, i.e., the creation and extension of equal civil and political rights and the creation of structures for political participation (e.g., parties and representative government) leading to the political structure of mass democracies.
- The establishment of welfare states as a consequence of the evolution of mass democracy.

The work of P. Flora et al. (1983) using Rokkan's approach shows, that although this type of developmental process is indeed a valuable heuristic aid, it cannot account for the multiplicity of historical steps in the various European countries. Moreover, substantial concern was shown by the absolutistic and mercantile states, such as France or Prussia in the 18th century, for welfare policy, based on the assumption that the political and economic power of these state-societies depended upon the health and education of the population. At this point in our argument we have to consider more closely the concept of the state that we have hitherto taken for granted. As the works of Nettl (1968) and especially Dyson (1980) show, there are major differences between the theories of institutional political power in the European continental and the Anglo-Saxon tradition.

The older German tradition of policy science was already a theory of welfare policies (cf. Maier 1966). The notion of a "night-watchman" state that stands apart from civil society and does not interfere with the endeavors of the latter is essentially a creation of liberal thought (originating in the Anglo-Saxon world!) and has never been followed in continental political practice.

The concept of the state is not as universal in European history as hitherto assumed, but rather stems essentially from the continental European tradition. This is not only true for the emergence of institutions relating to positive law and stemming from the tradition of Roman law, but also applies to the history of ideas in the Anglo-Saxon tradition which takes little account of the state. The continental notion of the state has to be considered as the consequence of both institution building and formulation of theories of the state. Thus the state is

"a generalizing, integrating and legitimating concept . . . the most integrated form of political society, emphasis being placed on its association with the ideas of collectivity and the general good, on its combination of socio-cultural with a legal dimension. As an aggregate concept the state stresses the interdependency and integration of institutions as opposed to the structural differentiation typical of 'civil' society and so beloved of modern Anglo-American political science" (Dyson 1980: 208 f.).

The Anglo-Saxon concepts of government and Crown have a narrower scope, are more centered on people than on institutions and place less emphasis upon the unity of the public sector.

Nettl therefore considers England and (to a lesser degree) the United States as "stateless societies" and shows that the Anglo-Saxon social sciences consequently differ from the European tradition in their 'statelessness'.[6]

Keeping these differences in mind, the conceptual weakness of the British thinking on the 'welfare state' becomes understandable. It refers here only to a sector of the exercise of political power and not to the unifying effect of the political institutions per se. One may speculate whether the basic differences in political ideas and institutions may also explain the quite different fate of socialist ideas in the Anglo-Saxon world (and the differences with regards to the theory of the state between the late Karl Marx and Friedrich Engels).

6.4 The Public Sector

Although these differences were not quite apparent when our project was conceived, an uneasiness about conventional approaches led us in 1978 to speak about 'the public sector' (and not 'the state' or 'the welfare state'), when the first steps towards the planning of the present project were initiated.

The notion of a public sector stems both from economic and political theory. From an *economic* point of view the public sector accounts for those parts of production and/or allocation which are financed by public bodies. As the term is rather vague, it may also point to the distinction of state-regulated and market-regulated production, or to the question of public or private ownership (e.g. public enterprise).[7] These various approaches may lead to very different definitions and dimensions of the public sector. The distinction between 'public' and 'private' that is basic to the notion of the public sector has also been worked out by *political* theory. Its earliest roots go back to the distinction of *'jus publicum' ("quod ad statum rei Romanae spectat")* and *'jus privatum' ("quod ad singulorum utilitatem spectat")* in Roman law.[8] In the 18th century the term 'public opinion' emerges both in French and British political theory to emphasize the importance of the political participation of the public in the exercise of government. The public that requires the publicity of all acts of government is not a part of government (or 'state') but is conceived as an open public realm where citizens engage in free discourse, form public opinion and exercise prerogatives of citizenship where a 'public interest' is involved. In a democracy there is therefore no essential division between 'public' and 'private', rather men decide as citizens what becomes of public interest. The development of mass media has of course altered the public discourse (cf. Habermas 1962) but not the basic connotations of the term.

These sketchy remarks show the variety of dimensions inherent in the notion of what is public, but one can also ascertain common features in the economic and the political approach: although in both traditions the term 'public' is related to activities or features of state and government, it also covers a wider range of actors and activities outside of government. The fact that various – continental and Anglo-Saxon – traditions seems to agree on this basic understanding of the public sector makes the notion useful for the purposes of the present work.

One may then raise the question of the scope of the public sector. As will be shown in Chapter 7 (Gretschmann) and 9 (Hood), it is by no means easy to ascertain clear boundaries between public and private. In countries with a state tradition the distinction seems at first glance easier than in common law countries. All corporations under public law may then be said to form the public sector. In that sense the public sector covers the authorities of the central (and possibly federated) state(s). It also covers local authorities and public enterprise, and in Germany most mass media and the churches. By contrast all organizations formed under private law, e.g., large corporations or welfare associations, belong to the private sector. This clear-cut legal distinction does not account for the more substantial issues that are involved in the relationship of public and private. The question of what is of public (or only of private) interest is itself a normative and political one: liberals tend to restrict the scope of the public, socialists tend to enlarge it. If one accepts something as being public, one asserts that it is (at least virtually) subject to political intervention.

The apparent vagueness of the distinction in our times is a consequence of the very political character of the distinction. The claim for privacy in individual affairs and for publicity in government affairs was directed against the idea and practice of an absolutistic exercise of government. The resulting constitutional state was essentially a retrenchment or restriction of political power, i.e., the idea of a self-contained state which regulated the boundaries of government control as well as the boundaries of private arbitrariness. Hence the distinction public/private is closely related to that of 'state' and 'society' in the German tradition. The claim for privacy was a claim for political non-intervention, for freedom to regulate one's own affairs, even if it was in the form of a contract whose judicial forms were regulated by civil law. Hence (civil) society was perceived as the area where private subjects could develop the strength of their creative forces in order to promote knowledge, wealth and progress. The apparent inequalities resulting from or perpetuated by the struggle for survival in the growing capitalist economy, social clustering of industrial populations in the form of urbanization, and the growth of a working class led to state resp. government intervention in domains that were considered to be 'private' by those groups who were successful in achieving wealth and influence.

The forms and the justifications of the first public interventions were as various as the social problems that became the first targets for political action: the regulation of poverty, problems of public health in the cities, the deprivation of children or exploitation in factory work. On the continent problems of worker protection became paramount and led to the idea of *"Sozialpolitik"* as a 'mediation' between the forces of 'state' and 'society'. Typically, *Sozialpolitik* was not meant to expand the realm of the state itself, but rather to regulate and complement the private arrangements of work by contract and provisions for the risks of life.

It may be worthwhile to remember that after the break-down of older forms of social protection there was a strong movement towards collective self-help in Europe in the 19th century. The English 'friendly societies', the German *"Hilfskassen auf Gegenseitigkeit"* as well as the French *"mutualités"* preceded governmental initiatives to protect workers form the risks of old age and sickness. State intervention grew slowly, first in Prussia and subsequently in the German Empire. The establishment of social insurance in the 1880s took over the existing *'Hilfskassen'* which had been occasionally regulated by local and state intervention since the 1850s. They kept an autonomous status under public law and became self-administering bodies under the influence of workers and employers. Bismarck was eager, however, to subsidize them with public funds in order to convince the workers of the Empire's benevolent intentions towards them (cf. Tennstedt 1981; Köhler and Zacher 1981). The reluctant establishment of social insurance in Great Britain was also due to competition from the friendly societies and the Poor Law (cf. Thane 1982).

Similarly workers' protection was introduced mainly by granting individual and collective rights to industrial workers in relationships with their employer and not by expanding public ownership. *Thus the daily life of the industrial workers and later of the population at large became more and more dependent on a mix of public and private regulations and provisions* (cf. Rose 1985).

Besides matters of social policy there has also been a growing concern in politics with the running of the economy itself, leading to economic policies, especially after the world depression of 1929. In Keynesianism, a coherent theory of public intervention in the market economy was found that led towards what is now sometimes called a 'mixed economy'.

After World War II the area of social problems that were considered of public interest expanded substantially, covering problems of children's socializiation, of the quality of life, of care for the elderly, etc. Local social services, run by public or private agencies, became a matter of political concern for central governments (cf. Sharpe: Ch. 8). Moreover, governments tried – especially in the United Kingdom and in the United States – to solve economic and social problems by creating new agencies outside government, e.g., in the form of private corporations (cf. Hood: Ch. 9).

In Germany the tendency was more to new forms of autonomous bodies within the public service (cf. Schuppert 1981), but there were also other patterns of a public-private mix (cf. Gessner and Winter 1982). Moreover, there was a growth of legislation in most countries that regulated the activities of private corporations (e.g., in the interest of safety or consumer protection) or even forced them to provide for needs considered as 'meritorious' (e.g., fringe benefits) or to perform services for public purposes (e.g., collecting taxes, providing statistics). There is hence a *growing interdependency* of both public and private actors in economic and social policy that renders the old distinctions of 'state' and 'society' or of 'public' and 'private' as *separate domains* meaningless.

What then about the notion of a public sector? Should we accept the idea that the whole economy and all activities outside the area of mere private life have become public? This would obviously underrate activities that are not publicly regulated, financed nor publicly owned, and it could easily lead to a totalitarian view of the public domain (cf. Böckenförde 1976: 395–431). The distinction between 'public' and 'private' is still relevant, but in a different sense.

This sense is already present in the afore-mentioned quotation from Ulpian: public law is concerned with the estate of "what is common to Romans", private law is concerned with "what is of individual utility". 'Public' and 'private' are not separate domains, but *distinct perspectives* that apply in various mixtures to the social, economic and political reality. The 'purely public' (e.g., constitutional decision making) and the 'purely private' matters (e.g., gambling or love) are limiting cases, whereas most parts of social life may be considered more in a public or more in a private perspective. The predominance of one or another is rightly and in fact a normative and a political issue.

This position should, however, not obscure the fact that for a certain country at a particular time the notions of public and private are not as blurred as the above analysis suggests. Dominant views exist of what is primarily in the realm of privacy and that which primarily concerns public life. There are, however, 'grey zones' that will be explored in more detail in subsequent chapters. Welfare policies typically fall in this grey zone, and this is the reason why they are particularly suitable for exploring issues about the public sector.

6.5 Consequences for Further Research

Whereas 'state' and 'government' are rather delimited concepts whose boundaries are set essentially by law, the notion of a public sector is conceptually broader and less limited. It was the intention of the previous section to explain why this vagueness in terms of domain is a *necessary* feature of the concept. Given the fact that government influence goes far beyond the boundaries of 'the state', one needs a concept that can be adapted to describe the broadening of government influence in society and to consider this not only as a factual, but also as a *controversial* matter. The term 'public sector' *(öffentlicher Sektor, secteur public),* which is well-established in international academic and political language, exhibits precisely these features.

In the previous presentation the notion of a public sector has been developed mainly from the point of view of a growing political influence in economic and social relationships that are conventionally considered as private. This is, however, only one side of the coin. The relationship of society and state is also to be seen from the point of view of an acceptance of government. Notions of 'public opinion' and 'public interest' show that one has to consider the public sector not only in terms of policy output (in the sense of Easton 1965) but also in terms of policy input. This aspect is dealt with more generally in political science with reference to the 'political system'. Suffice it to say that the concern of this volume is about both sides of the relationships between 'private' individuals, their associations and the public realm.

This definition presupposes a structural differentiation of the political and the economic system, as it has emerged in the West and may be called an essential feature of the Western type of rationalization. In socialist societies the public sector covers the whole range of organized social relationships. From a structural point of view it is precisely the lack of a *legitimate* boundary between state and civil society that accounts for the difference from the Western or capitalist type.[9]

In the present book we are only concernd with guidance, control and performance evaluation in the public sector of *Western* societies. We therefore start from the assumption of a structural differentiation of state and civil society, or – in more modern terms – of the political, the economic, the cultural and the family system.[10] State or government then is not seen as a kind of superstructure for the whole society but as the core institution of the political system as a specialized part of society that is concerned with specific tasks, e.g., to establish and to maintain public order, to make binding decisions for all members of a society, to maintain the collective identity against external threats and to promote common welfare. These definitions obviously refer to conventional political theory in Western societies that operate on a national level. In recent years the focus upon this level has been challenged both by internationalism and regionalism. Whereas international restrictions on the exercise of national political authority cannot be dealt with adequately in the present context, our approach needs to make explicit the challenge of regionalism (or localism) to political theory (cf. Sharpe: Ch. 8).

To speak about a public sector as if it were a distinct part of modern society (as 'the state') is, however, not quite accurate. As already mentioned, the public and the private sector are not two quite separate domains, but within the basic and legitimate distinction between them there exist institutions and organizations that account for a *mix,* a conjunction or interdependence of both public and private endeavours. Karl Marx was already aware of the *analytic* character of the distinction between *"bourgeois"* and *"citoyen"*! From the perspective of individual members of society there remain, however, different forms of welfare production: public provision, the market form, the household and various forms of reciprocity and association (cf. Zapf 1982). In terms of welfare theory our concern is with the conditions under which the interplay of various forms of welfare production may yield satisfactory results. Although the issues to be dealt with in this volume do not cover the whole range of problems related to that question, we hope that the conditions and limits of public action in the production of welfare will become clearer. In order not to lose focus in our inquiry it is important to maintain the notion of (a) public sector(s) as definitely related to the core institutions of *political* life. As we have seen these are neither established nor conceptualized in the same way in any given country. It therefore makes sense to conceive of 'stateness' not as an universal, but as a variable form of political organization (cf. Nettl 1968). Our concern in the remainder of this book, however, is less with the constitutional aspects of Western societies than with the institutional arrangements that regulate interaction among the core institutions of government and the other actors in what we conventionally call the public sector.

Notes

1 However, the distinguished member of the *"Verein für Sozialpolitik",* Adolph Wagner (1876: 305) had already used the term *"Cultur- und Wohlfahrtsstaat"* to denote the extension of the activities of the state into the fields of culture and welfare, but it did not become topical in Germany. Nowadays the term *'Wohlfahrtsstaat'* has been accepted as a translation of the English term but is used in a slightly pejorative sense to denote the political and fiscal overload stemming from welfare issues. The positive equivalent is *'Sozialstaat',* see note 3.

2 See articles 22–27 of the General Declaration of Human Rights. The existence of social rights has to be considered as a basic element of the welfare state (cf. Marshall 1964).

3 These social rights could not, however, be implemented during the Weimar Republic because of economic stagnation and progressive political cleavages. This experience led the founders of the constitution of the Federal Republic to renounce the formulation of specific social rights, which have been replaced by the general rule of a 'social character' of the state (Art. 20 and 28 I *Grundgesetz*).

4 For a more detailed discussion see Kaufmann (1985).

5 In ideological debates 'welfare' is normally referred to in the sense of individual welfare, i.e. in terms of improvements of daily life for (all or particular) classes of individuals. As a matter of fact Western political systems also seem to be selective with respect to needs to be satisfied by public intervention. Individual need-satisfaction is promoted only if goods or services are judged to be 'meritorious' (Musgrave 1959: 13), i.e., that their consumption will not only satisfy individual needs but produce benevolent externalities. For example, the expansion of educational services in the 1960s was motivated by a theory of human capital formation and the sputnik shock!

6 These underlying and largely unconscious differences in basic attitudes towards the conceptualization of political institutions were vividly experienced in the discussions of the research group. It was only in the last stages of our endeavor that they became a matter of conscious awareness. The different traditions have therefore been presented

in the two preceding chapters of Grimm and V. Ostrom. For Public Finance see also Gretschmann (Ch. 3).

7   The first substantial account of these issues was given by Weidenbaum (1969).

8   See Ulpian, De justitia et jure 1,1. For a history of the form 'public' see Hölscher (1978).

9   This does not mean that there is no boundary between political and economic functions in socialist societies. The boundary is much weaker as it operates essentially on the level of organizations, but not on the institutional level. Political authorities are expected to guide and control the economy.

10 A fourfold basic differentiation of modern society in various terms is acknowledged by several 'grand theories', e.g. M. Weber, T. Parsons and N. Luhmann.

References

Alber, J. (1982): *Vom Armenhaus zum Wohlfahrtsstaat.* Frankfurt–New York: Campus.

Alber, J. (1983): "Einige Grundlagen und Begleiterscheinungen der Entwicklung der Sozialausgaben in Westeuropa, 1949–1977." *Zeitschrift für Soziologie* 12/2: 93–118.

Baader, F. von (1835): "Über das dermalige Mißverhältnis der Vermögenslosen oder Proletairs zu den Vermögen besitzenden Klassen der Societät in Betreff ihres Auskommens sowohl in materieller als intellektueller Hinsicht aus dem Standpunkte des Rechts betrachtet." (1957). In Grassel, H. (ed.), *Gesellschaftslehre,* 235–250. München. (Repr.)

Beveridge, W. (1943): *The Pillars of Security and other Wartime Essays and Adresses.* London: Allen & Unwin.

Böckenförde, E. W. (ed.) (1976): *Staat und Gesellschaft.* Darmstadt: Wissenschaftliche Buchgesellschaft.

Dyson, K. (1980): *The State Tradition in Western Europe.* Oxford: Robertson.

Easton, D. (1965): *A Systems-Analysis of Political Life.* New York: Wiley.

Flora, P., and A. Heidenheimer (eds.) (1981): *The Development of Welfare States in Europe and America.* New Brunswick–London: Transaction.

Flora, P., J. Alber, R. Eichenberg, J. Kohl, F. Kraus, W. Pfenning, and K. Seebohm (1983): *State, Economy and Society in Western Europe 1815–1975.* Vol. I. Frankfurt: Campus; London: Macmillan; Chicago: St. James Press.

Gessner, V., and G. Winter (1982): *Rechtsformen der Verflechtung von Staat und Wirtschaft.* Opladen: Westdeutscher Verlag.

Girvetz, H. K. (1968): "Welfare State." In Sills, D. L. (ed.), *International Encyclopedia of the Social Sciences.* Vol. 16: 512–521. New York: Macmillan; Free Press.

Gregg, P. (1967): *The Welfare State.* London: Harrap.

Grimm, D. (1983): "Die sozialgeschichtliche und verfassungsrechtliche Entwicklung zum Sozialstaat." In Koslowski, P., P. Kreuzer, and R. Löw (eds.), *Chancen und Grenzen des Sozialstaats,* 41–64. Tübingen: Mohr.

Habermas, J. (1962): *Strukturwandel der Öffentlichkeit.* Neuwied: Luchterhand.

Heclo, H. (1974): *Modern Social Politics in Britain and Sweden.* New Haven–London: Yale Univ. Press.

Hegel, G. W. F. (1821): *Grundlinien der Philosophie des Rechts oder Naturrecht und Staatswissenschaft im Grundrisse.* Berlin: Nicolaische Buchhandlung.

Hölscher, L. (1978): "Öffentlichkeit." In: Brunner, O., W. Conze, and R. Koselleck (eds.), *Geschichtliche Grundbegriffe. Historisches Lexikon zur politisch-sozialen Sprache in Deutschland,* Vol. 4: 413–467. Stuttgart: Klett-Cotta.

Kaufmann, F. X. (1980): "Social Policy and Social Services: Some Problems of Policy Formation, Program Implementation and Impact Evaluation." In Grunow, D., and F. Hegner (eds.), *Welfare or Bureaucracy,* 29–43. Cambridge, Mass.: Oelgeschlager, Gunn & Hain; Königstein/Ts.: A. Hain.

Kaufmann, F. X. (1982): "Elemente einer soziologischen Theorie sozialpolitischer Intervention." In: Kaufmann, F. X. (ed.), *Staatliche Sozialpolitik und Familie*, 49–86. München: Oldenbourg.

Kaufmann, F. X. (1985): "Major problems of the Welfare State: Defining the Issues." In: Eisenstadt, S. N. and O. Ahimeir (eds.), *The Welfare State and its Aftermath*. London: Croom Helm, 44–56.

Köhler, P. A., and H. F. Zacher (eds.) (1981): *Ein Jahrhundert Sozialversicherung in der Bundesrepublik Deutschland, Frankreich, Großbritannien, Österreich und der Schweiz.* Berlin: Duncker & Humblot.

Kohl, J. (1985): *Staatsausgaben in Westeuropa*. Analysen zur langfristigen Entwicklung der öffentlichen Finanzen. Frankfurt–New York: Campus.

Luhmann, N. (1981): *Politische Theorie im Wohlfahrtsstaat*. München: Olzog.

Maier, H. (1966): *Die ältere deutsche Staats- und Verwaltungslehre (Polizeiwissenschaft).* Neuwied–Berlin: Luchterhand.

Marshall, T. H. (1964): *Class, Citizenship and Social Development*. Garden City: Doubleday.

Marx, K. (1845/46) Die deutsche Ideologie, Reed. Landshut, S., *Karl Marx – Die Frühschriften* (1968). Stuttgart: Kröner.

Marx, K. (1867): *Das Kapital*. Kritik der politischen Ökonomie (Vol. 1). Hamburg: Meissner.

Mohl, R. von (1835): "Über die Nachteile, welche sowohl den Arbeitern selbst, als dem Wohlstande und der Sicherheit der gesamten bürgerlichen Gesellschaft von dem fabrikmäßigen Betriebe der Industrie zugehen und über die Notwendigkeit gründlicher Vorbeugungsmittel." In Fürstenberg, F. (ed.), *Industriesoziologie I* (2nd ed. 1966), 273–310. Neuwied: Luchterhand. (Repr.)

Mommsen, W. J. (ed.) (1981): *The Emergence of the Welfare State in Britain and Germany: 1850–1950*. London: Croom Helm.

Musgrave, R. A. (1959): *The Theory of Public Finance. A Study in Public Economy*. Tokyo: McGraw Hill.

Nettl, J. P. (1968): "The State as a Conceptual Variable." *World Politics* 20/4: 559–592.

Pankoke, E. (1970): *Sociale Bewegung – Sociale Frage – Sociale Politik*. Stuttgart: Klett.

Polanyi, K. (1944): *The Great Transformation*. New York: Rinehart & Company.

Rokkan, S. (1975): "Dimensions of State Formation and Nation-Building." In Tilly, C. (ed.), *The Formation of National States in Western Europe*, 562–600. Princeton: Princeton Univ. Press.

Rose, R. (1985): *The States contribution to the Welfare Mix*. Glasgow: Univ. of Strathclyde, Center for the Study of Public Policy.

Schiller, T. (1980): "Probleme einer Sozialstaatstheorie." In Greven, M. T., R. Prätorius, and T. Schiller, *Sozialstaat und Sozialpolitik – Krisen und Perspektiven*, 11–90. Neuwied: Luchterhand.

Schuppert, G. F. (1981): *Die Erfüllung öffentlicher Aufgaben durch verselbständigte Verwaltungseinheiten*. Göttingen: Schwartz.

Stein, L. von (1850): *Geschichte der sozialen Bewegung in Frankreich von 1789 bis auf unsere Tage*. 3 Vols. Reed. Salomon, G., München 1921.

Tennstedt, F. (1981): *Sozialgeschichte der Sozialpolitik in Deutschland*. Göttingen: Vandenhoeck & Ruprecht.

Thane, P. (1982): *Foundations of the Welfare State*. London–New York: Longman.

Wagner, A. (1876): *Allgemeine oder theoretische Volkswirtschaftslehre*. 1. Teil: Grundlegung. Heidelberg: Winter.

Weidenbaum, M. L. (1969): *The Modern Public Sector*. New York–London: Basic Books.

Zapf, W. (1984): *Welfare Production: Public versus Private. Social Indicators Research* 14: 263–274.

7. Measuring the Public Sector: A Contestable Issue

Klaus Gretschmann

Abstract

Surveying the public sector is a difficult task, since it covers a heterogeneous field of exchange, interaction and institutional arrangements, even beyond the realm of the "state". Most endeavors to measure the public sector are, therefore, reduced to monetary expenditure figures as they are the most convenient indicator. In principle, other indicators are equally suited to describe the public sector: The number and significance of public institutions and organizations, the number of public employees, the amount of legislation and regulation, the stock of wealth owned by public bodies, or the effects and range of policy programs. The fact that all of these show a high correlation not only to each other but also to their budgetary equivalent, may justify the use of expenditure shares in GNP for public sector measuring purposes, notwithstanding the serious methodological and statistical problems involved. Beyond such questions as what to include in both the numerator and denominator of such ratios or how to clear them of cyclical distortions, two limiting cases of expenditure ratios are considered in order to demonstrate that measuring the public sector not only is a controversial issue but results in different findings: The development of a "comprehensive expenditure share", including above all the so-called "hidden state demand", gives for Germany a public sector size of 70% relative to GNP, whereas the "true share", i.e. the inflation corrected disaggregated ratio, amounts to only 30%.

7.1 What Is to Be Measured: The Notion and Concept of the Public Sector

Since the days of *Adolph Wagner,* the "grand old man" of German Public Finance, the range and development of state activities have been central topics not only of a continuing public debate but also of a theoretical and empirical controversy among scholars of public finance, policy science, statistics and history.

There is, on the one hand, the issue of whether Wagner's Law of a growing demand for state expenditure, which is the fiscal expression of a more general law of expanding state activities, can be verified or disproved. On the other hand, there is the question of how to measure the actual scope of the public sector and how large it in fact is.

Unfortunately the statistical basis for empirical studies is rather weak: These are commonly reduced to monetary expenditure figures (see Pathirane and Blades 1982). What we lack, however, is broader information and data about quantity and quality of services, institutions and organizations, working mechanisms and final incidence of public sector activities.

Measurement of the public sector is a major and indispensable step in explaining the functioning of the public sector and examining the hypothesis of public sector growth. Therefore, the purpose of the following subsections is to discuss the strengths and weaknesses of various indicators and statistical measures that have been and could be used in analyzing the size of the public sector. Before we go into a detailed analysis, some general observations seem appropriate regarding the concept and notion of what is to be measured. To provide a complete picture of the subject, quantification requires first conceptualization (Rose 1984: 13). The most serious problem in measuring the public sector is *not* so much, as Eichenberger (1983) asserts, the unavailability of data but the absence of a coherent idea of what the public sector itself is. Even if, as Littmann (1964) claims, the controversy about the proper characteristics of the public sector and its limits can be regarded as an unproductive debate about categories, it nevertheless seems to be necessary within the context of this book to discuss a multifarious and multidimensional conceptualization of the public sector under the heading of how to measure it.

A first line of discussion centers upon the differentiation between the concept of "the state" and that of the "public sector". Although the term public sector is often used as a simple synonym for state or government, it in fact represents a shift in perspective. When talking about the state, we have in mind a more or less monolithic entity, assuming that government and its administration "archaically" claim full and overall sovereignty. The term state stresses a completely ordered, closed hierarchical structure whose primary and distinctive function is the maintenance of a power monopoly and of an all-embracing authority (see Elias 1969: 123 ff.). To guarantee societal order *(Ordnungsstaat)*, not to perform clearly specified tasks *(Leistungsstaat)*, has been the decisive feature of the older state concept in the Continental tradition since the 19th century.

Nowadays, the state's tasks have multiplied, the coherent picture of state-determined commonweal has faded away: public administration has been divested of its sovereign character. Public policy is shaped by party competition, multifarious group and association interests, by bureaucratic and organizational operations. The monolithic unitary state has changed into a public sector as a field for the exchange of goods, services and information as well as a domain of bargaining and conflict. It is sharing functions and responsibilities, promoting forces outside the formal government and consisting of loosely connected organizations in a confusing array of institutional arrangements.

Whereas the term state corresponds to *orderliness,* the public sector implies *openness* and includes an interwoven set of identifiable organizations which mobilize law, money and labour in order to produce public programs (Rose 1983: 167). According to the distinguished public finance economist F. K. Mann "the state" is nothing else than an artefact representing the conceptual structure of a "closed uniform system of public finance". What we are living in and what we are experiencing nowadays, however, is a constellation of various autonomous and semi-autonomous bodies and organs which take part in planning and implementing public policies, which affect regional and functional considerations of limited duration and extent. This latter is called the "coordinating political and fiscal system" (see Mann 1972: 237).

This latter concept of the public sector not only corresponds to the reality of multifarious components and elements of modern political subsystems but also opens a window to further research insofar as a lot of rather precise questions may be asked and answered: questions about information, coordination, motivations, interactions, functional prerequisites, feedback-loops and other guidance and control aspects, which do not exist in the world of "the state" but play an important role in the public sector concepts.

This way of representing the subject indicates a second way of conceptualizing the public sector. Logically it can be conceived of as the opposite of the private sector. As Kaufmann has demonstrated above (Ch. 6) there is only a rather blurred and fuzzy line between state and society or, respectively, between the public and the private sectors. As far as one does not accept the fundamentalist position, namely that there is, strictly speaking, no purely private sector at all because everything private is interwoven with public elements, or if one defines the issue the other way round, the public sector as only the pure scope of activity or authority of governments, we are in both cases faced with the problem of where to put semipublic institutions such as government owned or regulated firms, private agencies which implement public policies (Nadel 1975), public interest groups (Weisbrod, Handler and Komesar 1978), social security, national science foundations and other parastate organizations and operations which are neither fish nor fowl (see Hood: Ch. 9). According to Max Weber, the main criterion for publicness is the participation in political decisions and/or the fulfillment of public functions. In this sense Ronge has pointed out recently (1980: 11 ff.) that a large sector is developing which makes policy by private means. This phenomenon which he calls "off-state or quasi-policy" includes self-regulation of private corporations, e.g. the German deposit guaranty fund, meaning voluntary joint liability agreements of the bank industry, or the regulation of old-age social security not by state intervention, but in the context of wage contract negotiations carried out between trade-unions and employers' associations. Another example is the voluntary self-responsible stockpiling of raw materials and oil by private firms, for emergency periods, without state regulation.

In view of this development there is equal justification for interpreting such phenomena as professional organizations, unions, voluntary non-profit corporations and associations and others as satellites of either the private or the public sector. A clear-cut demarcation of the subject seems to be arbitrary. Both lines of differentiation, that of "state" versus "public sector" as well as that of "public" versus "private sectors" present serious statistical problems, as will be shown below. Statistical analysis is faced with some more problems related to these basic difficulties resulting from the inability of current statistics to demonstrate the very interaction between the private, the public and the intermediary sector.

Broadly speaking, we therefore distinguish between an *institutional* versus a *functional* (Matzner, Blaas and Schönbäck 1979) *approach* to measure the public sector. In a functional definition of the state sector all activities must be considered part of the state which perform functions that are primarily public, for example even the activities of private schools (function: education) and of security agencies (function: internal security). On the other hand, public institutions performing private functions, for example a public company producing consumer goods, should be considered part of the private sector. Such a classification is, however, of little use when the analysis is supposed to assist in distinguishing the public from the private sectors. Yet, the crucial point in the functional definition is that, differing from political system to political system, from country to country, one and the same function may be fulfilled sometimes by private, at other times by public institutions, such as education, social security, even police (Folkers 1979: 407). It was *Hegel* who nearly two hundred years ago pointed out that the state could hardly be defined with respect to its proper purposes because it is able to assuming all possible purposes, being itself the purpose of last resort.

Hence, modern official statistics are based on institutional and organizational elements of the public sector rather than on functional definitions (Littmann 1975: 20 ff.). Basically the statistical material forces us to adopt the definitions of the "state" in the sense of the "public sector" from the SNA (system of national accounts) as a starting point. According to that, the state sector includes all institutions whose tasks consist of providing services for the community and which are financed mainly by taxation, in some cases by user charges and tolls. Regional bodies and social security are part of the state. Public enterprises, regardless of their legal form are often considered to be not part of the state. Whereas, on the one hand, the ownership structure could be a reason for including public companies in the state sector, the fact that they are companies acting in accordance with the rules of private markets is, on the other hand, a good reason for placing them in the private sector.

7.2 The Menu of Choice: Looking for the "Best" Indicator

Considerable attention has been devoted during the last decades to measurement of public sector size, using public finance data, for example revenue or expenditure. R. Goldscheidt argued some seventy years ago that the budget is the skeleton of the state, stripped of all misleading ideologies (Goldscheidt 1917: 4). Similarily Schumpeter holds that the public budget, taxes and expenditure, provide the best insight into the driving forces of the fate of nations, as well as into the manner in which concrete conditions and, in particular, organizational forms grow and pass away (Schumpeter 1918: 332). The basic feature of such approaches is what we will call the "budgetary assumption", namely that *all* fields of public policy are equally related to the budget. The budget is thought of as the unifying concept and the major institution of the public sector (Colm 1955; Due and Friedlaender 1973); "there is rarely any public activity which does not affect budgetary terms" (Raabe 1976: 38).

This position can stand scrutiny only if circular flow effects on the economy or state control of GNP should be measured. What such figures do not allow is to draw conclusions regarding actual overall public activity. In other words: The budget criterion is acceptable only where the performance of public tasks is carried out through the public budget. But the real situation is quite different; government can and often does use other than fiscal resources to achieve its purposes. State activity may take the form of statutes, decrees, regulations, orders, prohibitions, procedures or persuasion, which are policy patterns with a low degree of "cost-intensity" (Zimmermann 1973): Social security for old-age can be provided either by public payments or by legal obligations to take out life insurance with private companies. Continued payments of wages in cases of illness, another example, can be ensured by legal regulation forcing the employer to continue payments as well as by public subsidies for the employer and/or the employees. The construction of a highway can be carried out by the state on its own or by private companies, which it grants concessions for the construction and permits to cover their outlays through tolls. Finally agricultural policy can be conducted by subsidies or regulating production; similarily, money and budget policy and wage and price controls are equivalent instruments for economic policy.

To summarize: The public sector as conceptualized in subsection 1 is much more than simply public finance. It is a network of formal organizations and administrative bodies (1), which employ public officials (2), which enact laws and impose regulations (3), which themselves own a stock of wealth (4), which control public enterprises (5), and which perform a whole range of services by setting and implementing programs (6). All of these elements can serve as indicators, and some will certainly argue that those are better suited to measurement purposes than pure monetary data. The valid use of these "tools" however is controversial for the following reasons:

(1) As for the public sector organizations, one undoubtedly could simply add up the number of public bodies and agencies (Rose 1976) at a certain point in time or even could set up a whole time series. Tautscher did this for West Germany covering the years 1950–1965 and found out that for that period the number of public institutions rose by some 560% (Tautscher 1969). Yet, the problem with this kind of survey is that it, on the one hand, neglects the differences in the power, size, purpose, innovative capacity, life cycle etc. of individual organizations. The same holds true for the functional differences between policy and service oriented administration (*Hoheits*- und *Leistungsverwaltung*) which is of greatest significance for range and intensity of public sector control. Moreover, the real importance of public organizations' and bureaucracies is only reflected by their frequency and intensity of interaction, portrayed in interorganizational networks (see Grunow: Ch. 2; see also section V). This fact has to be taken into account if one wishes to aggregate the different organizational subjects. Under consideration of such serious methodological problems it could more and useful for purposes of measurement to reduce organizations only to their budget size or to the staff employed.

(2) As for the public work force, the crucial point is the functional classification, namely the question of which people should indeed be counted in this category. One must ask if it makes sense to restrict the survey to public officials, how to handle part-timers and employees in the semi-public sectors, and where to put military (draftees) or educational personnel. The relevant numbers can be easily found in the SNA (for the German case see table 3 below), but nothing is said about the composition of the public work force, the qualification and productivity of employees or the quantitative relation between clients and officials (Eichenberger 1983; Nolan 1979). Here again it might be useful to measure the public sector dimension by monetary figures, e.g. by the wage sum for the publicly employed. (For an international comparison of public employment rates see table 1).

Tab. 1: Government Employment as a Percentage of Total Employment

Year	USA	Germany	UK	Italy	NL	France
1970	18.1	11.2	18.0	11.8	12.1	13.4
1971	18.0	11.6	18.8	12.5	12.4	13.8
1972	17.7	12.2	19.5	13.1	12.8	14.0
1973	17.2	12.5	19.6	13.5	13.0	14.3
1974	17.3	13.2	19.7	13.7	13.2	14.4
1975	18.0	13.9	21.0	14.1	13.5	14.9
1976	17.6	14.2	21.5	14.4	14.0	15.1
1977	17.1	14.4	21.3	14.8	14.4	15.2
1978	16.7	14.6	21.3	15.0	14.6	15.4
1979	16.4	14.8	21.4	15.1	14.7	15.4
1980	16.7	14.9	21.1	15.1	14.9	15.5

Source: OECD (1983: 64).

Tab. 2: International Comparison of Annually Enacted Laws (average covering the years 1970–1980)

USA	GB	NL	Germany	France
402	144	268	82	104

Sources: Author's own calculations on the basis of figures from the national statutes' yearbooks.

(3) To indicate the legislative activities of the public sector, either laws can be counted (see table 2 and 3) or, what has been done recently (Bernholz 1982: 38; Peterson 1982: 192), the pages added periodically to the statute book can be registered. Both indicators, however, are rather weak: They do not tell us anything about the significance, the direction, the financial or norm intensity of legislation. Moreover they neglect cases of revision, consolidation, repeal or cancellation of laws, which aggravates the problem of simple aggregation. Further, the average length of laws and statutes prejudices the numerical results insofar as it determines the number of pages. To be sure, more important than the length is the content of the laws, which can hardly be measured. Another objection to this indicator is the fact that many bills and laws aim primarily at control and regulation not of private but of public sector agencies (Kaufer 1981; Hjerppe 1980).

(4) The state and parastate stock of wealth also is a very problematic indicator, because wealth stock is a rather static, inelastic figure which reflects public *activities* only to a very small degree. Looking at the development shown in table 3 we see only smooth secular differences.

(5) The same holds true for public enterprise and nationalized industries whose significance is measured by the volume of company shares owned by state agencies.

(6) As Rose concedes, programs are the indicator most difficult to measure (Rose 1983). On the one hand, programs always show a kind of life cycle one superseding the other (Mackscheidt and Steinhausen 1977: 84). On the other hand,

Tab. 3: Development of Different Indicators for Public Sector Activities in the FRG

Year	Stock of wealth owned by the state (in billions of DM)	Public sector employees (in thousands)	Number of laws and statutory regulations	Total state expenditure (in billions of DM)
1960	50.0	2,098	↑	98.4
1961	55.4	2,228		111.9
1962	55.8	2,348	1,794	128.2
1963	60.2	2,444		138.5
1964	65.4	2,540	↓	151.7
1965	70.9	2,628	↑	168.5
1966	77.4	2,706	1,998	179.8
1967	84.3	2,777		190.5
1968	86.0	2,803	↓	202.9
1969	89.0	2,859	↑	226.4
1970	89.2	2,978	1,678	257.8
1971	94.8	3,105		296.5
1972	98.7	3,259	↓	332.2
1973	106.9	3,367	↑	376.8
1974	114.5	3,493	2,242	433.6
1975	118.5	3,576	↓	493.4
1976	121.5	3,635	↑	528.6
1977	126.1	3,660		564.4
1978	133.0	3,746	1,969	606.2
1979	140.3	3,847		653.5
1980	145.4	3,906	↓	705.7

Sources: Statistisches Bundesamt n.d. (a): various issues, SVR (1983: 295), Statistisches Bundesamt n.d. (b) (SNA): various issues, author's own calculations.

there are many programs dependent on such external variables as unemployment, inflation and other business cycle phenomena, coming and going with the existence of these transitory factors. Different origins, purposes, range and effectiveness make it extremely difficult to reduce these manifold programs to one indicator. It can be argued again that in this case it would be better to measure programs by their money inputs than by their outputs. Yet, this would be a return to the budget sphere.

Examining the individual indicators sketched above, we come to the conclusion that they do indeed develop in the same direction even though they do not show the same growth. A correlation analysis between different measures of the public sector suggests the following results (see table 4).

The examination below leads to the observation that there is no best measuring instrument for analyzing public sector activities in one index. For different contexts, different research interests and intentions, we have to choose between different concepts. But in view of the high correlation coefficients we feel free to devote our attention in the following to the most frequently used statistical measure, namely the state share in national income (see table 5), demonstrating public expenditure figures.

Tab. 4: Correlation Between Different Indicators of Public Sector Development
(1960–1980)

	x_1	x_2	x_3	x_4
x_1	–			
x_2	0.99	–		
x_3	0.68	0.69	–	
x_4	0.97	0.96	0.61	–

with x_1 = stock of wealth owned by the state
x_2 = general government employment
x_3 = laws and statutory regulations
x_4 = state expenditure

Source: See table 3.

Tab. 5: Total Outlays of Government as a Percentage of GDP

Year	USA	Germany	UK	Italy	NL	France
1960	27.6	32.5	32.6	30.1	33.7	34.6
1968	31.3	39.2	39.6	34.7	43.9	40.3
1969	30.9	38.8	41.5	34.2	44.4	39.6
1970	32.3	38.7	39.3	34.2	46.0	38.9
1971	32.3	40.2	38.4	36.6	48.0	38.3
1972	32.0	40.9	40.0	38.6	48.6	38.3
1973	31.3	41.7	41.1	37.8	49.3	38.5
1974	33.0	44.7	45.2	37.9	51.5	39.7
1975	35.5	49.0	46.9	43.2	56.6	43.5
1976	34.5	48.1	46.2	42.2	56.6	44.0
1977	33.3	48.1	44.1	42.5	54.6	44.2
1978	32.8	47.8	43.6	46.1	55.9	45.2
1979	32.9	47.7	43.3	45.2	58.0	45.5
1980	34.9	48.3	45.6	46.0	59.7	46.4

Source: OECD (1983: 64).

7.3 Value and Explanatory Power of State Expenditure Ratios

Up until now the system of national accounts (SNA) has been the main source for macro-economic, public finance and public sector statistics for economists. Although the system was created as a result of long discussions between economists and statisticians, the treatment of the state or the public sector has always remained controversial. Dealing with public expenditure, we therefore have to be aware of the enormous diversity in recording and accounting practices in different national contexts and at different times.

Moreover, for purposes of measuring public sector size *absolute* figures about government spending are not appropriate because they cannot tell us anything about the growth and development of the significance of the public sector in relation to, among other things, the private economy or the level of national income. Therefore, the most widely used instrument for describing the importance of the public sector are ratios, that is the public expenditure share of some national income aggregate such as the GNP or GDP (gross national/gross domestic product). In view of the inadequacies of the other indicators discussed above, the public expenditure/GDP ratios can be regarded as the most accurate form of statistical representation. This is certainly the main reason for their central position in individual SNAs and even in the MPSS (Manual of Public Sector Statistics) compiled by the UN statistical office in recent years. Nevertheless, the use of figures on relative public expenditure shares is controversial. The scholarly debate primarily centers around methodological problems such as the statistical demarcation of the public sector discussed above, the correct construction of the ratios, the adjustment to business cycle fluctuations or relative price influences, the consideration of sector productivity development etc.

Looking at the ratio St_E/GNP (with St_E = state expenditure) we notice that the numerator (in most OECD statistics) commonly includes general government spending, public nonfinancial corporate enterprise and public financial institutions' expenditure. It covers public sector purchases (materials and services) from private sector, outlays for the publicly employed, public investment, transfer and interest payments.

The denominator generally is represented by the GNP because (1) the depreciation (which we must deduct to arrive at the NNP (net national product) can hardly be measured exactly, and (2) because the measurable difference between the national income *at market prices* and that *at factor cost* is determined by the share of indirect taxes not representing value added which are contained in the former but not in the latter.

The construction of this kind of ratios, however, runs into serious trouble: To deal with a genuine ratio, the numerator must be fully included in the denominator, otherwise a comparison of general government expenditure with national income may be seriously misleading. If, therefore, we use a national income aggregate at market prices as the denominator, we are faced with the problem that an important part of the numerator, namely public purchases and personnel outlays, is not expressed in market prices but in terms of input cost, because market prices are not available for public output (Kuznets 1948). On the other hand, when using factor-cost as denominator, we correctly disregard indirect taxes, not taking into consideration, however, the fact that the numerator covers collective consumption which includes indirect taxes (Reich 1981: 84 ff.). In both cases we apply a different standard to both numerator and denominator.

Moreover, as far as transfer payments are included in government expenditure, the ratio can result in a distorted quotient. The exclusion of transfer payments is therefore advocated by some economists who think that the government should be regarded either as a final consumer of the goods and services purchased and used by itself or as an enterprise selling public goods and services at prices equivalent to taxes. Others consider the "consumer" or "producer" concept of government to be grossly inadequate. If one is concerned with measuring the proportion of total demand determined by the political process, then the concept of public expenditure should include transfer payments, because the incomes and the consequent demand due to transfer payments are created not by the market but by government. The purchase of goods and services *and* transfer payments are both usually financed by taxes and determined by political decisions about allocation and distribution, which contribute to the development of the public sector. The inclusion of transfer payments seems justified, provided no conclusions are drawn about the "contribution" of the public sector to national income.

Last but not least, the quotient is distorted by cyclical fluctuations: If the economy is in a depression, national income, and thus the denominator, descreases while state expenditures – representing the numerator – commonly increase in

Tab. 6: Different State Shares in National Income for the FRG (1960–1980)

Year	St_E^{1*} (VGR)	St_E^{2*} (FS)	GNP^{3*}	PC^{4*}	$\frac{St_E(VGR)}{GNP}$	$\frac{St_E(FS)}{GNP}$	$\frac{St_E(FS)}{PC}$
1960	98.4	83.9	303.0	304.0	32.48%	27.69%	27.60%
1961	111.9	95.0	331.4	334.8	33.77%	28.67%	28.38%
1962	128.2	106.5	360.5	368.3	35.56%	29.54%	28.92%
1963	138.5	116.3	382.1	397.3	36.25%	30.44%	29.27%
1964	151.7	127.2	419.6	428.9	36.15%	30.31%	29.66%
1965	168.5	139.3	458.2	466.2	36.77%	30.40%	29.88%
1966	179.8	145.0	487.4	505.3	36.89%	29.75%	28.70%
1967	190.5	153.8	493.7	529.2	38.59%	31.15%	29.06%
1968	202.9	158.8	533.7	555.4	38.02%	29.75%	28.59%
1969	226.4	174.6	597.8	599.4	37.87%	29.20%	29.13%
1970	257.8	196.3	675.7	675.3	38.15%	29.05%	29.07%
1971	296.5	226.5	751.8	763.5	39.44%	30.13%	29.67%
1972	332.2	252.1	825.1	842.0	40.26%	30.55%	29.94%
1973	376.8	280.5	918.9	932.5	41.01%	30.53%	30.08%
1974	433.6	318.3	985.6	1,025.3	43.99%	32.30%	31.04%
1975	493.4	360.5	1,028.9	1,114.6	47.95%	35.04%	32.34%
1976	528.6	376.8	1,123.0	1,176.4	47.07%	33.55%	32.03%
1977	564.6	395.2	1,196.3	1,245.2	47.20%	33.04%	31.74%
1978	606.2	431.8	1,290.0	1,322.8	45.83%	33.47%	32.64%
1979	653.5	466.7	1,395.3	1,405.3	46.84%	33.45%	33.21%
1980	705.7	504.0	1,485.7	1,501.1	47.50%	33.92%	33.58%

Sources: SVR (1983: 324), Statistisches Bundesamt n. d. (a): various issues, Bundesministerium der Finanzen n. d.: various issues, author's own calculation.

[*] In billions of DM

[1] General government expenditure including social security according to the SNA (VGR).
[2] Expenditure by federal government, states and local authorities according to the NFSt (National Financial Statistics) (FS).
[3] GDP in current prices.
[4] The nations productive capacity (*"Produktionspotential"*) in current prices.

cases where politicians follow the rules of Keynesian economic policy. Given this strategy, the public expenditure ratio is inflated artificially by business cycle effects without generating a genuine and durable increase in the public sector's relative size.

To avoid this distortion the German Sachverständigenrat (Council of Economic Advisers) has developed a statistical method which corrects the cyclical influences on the denominator. The GNP actually realized is replaced by the production potential, that is the *attainable* overall economic output at constant prices, in other words: the economy's productive capacity (PC) (see table 6). The numerator is not adjusted because it is difficult to distinguish state expenditures for economic recovery purposes from others with purely allocative or distributive functions.

In the German statistical tradition there exist two different public accounts systems, the VGR ("Volkswirtschaftliche Gesamtrechnung", that is orthodox SNA) and the FS ("Finanzstatistik", meaning public sector financial statistics). While the latter primarily defines as public sector expenditures the federal, state and municipal spending, excluding the social security system and including public enterprises, such as the Federal Railroad, the Federal Postal Service etc., only on a

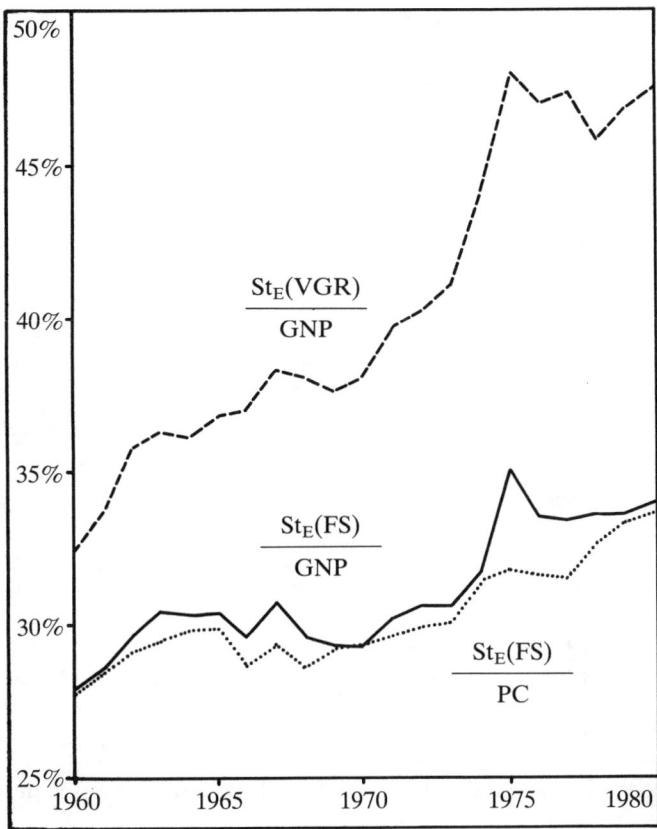

Fig. 1: Different State Expenditure Shares in GNP – The German Case

consolidated basis, that is their net surpluses or deficits, the former covers federal, state and municipal spending, including the social security system but excluding public enterprises. The FS computes all disbursement and cash expenditure; therefore public grants and loan guarantees are counted as state expenditure in St_E (FS). The VGR, on the other hand, does not include loans, debt-repayments and transfers to reserves in $St_E(VGR)$. The resulting differences in increase and volume of expenditure ratios in the two accounting systems can be derived from table 6 and are shown in figure 1.

The steeper slope and the higher level of the VGR-ratio in relation to the FS-ratio development suggest that it should be ascribed to the social security expenditure dynamics. Yet this is true only in part: As pointed out above, the FS counts

Tab. 7: Structural Composition of State Expenditure According to Public Functions in %

	Year	Germany	France	UK	USA
General Government and International Affairs	1970	21.1	–*	12.3	13.3
	1975	22.8	15.9	13.2	15.5
	1977	24.0	16.9	13.1	16.0
	1979	24.0	–*	–*	16.3
National Defense	1970	18.3	–*	21.3	33.8
	1975	17.1	17.8	18.5	24.9
	1977	16.8	17.7	20.0	23.7
	1979	16.4	–*	–*	23.5
Health	1970	5.7	–*	17.2	5.9
	1975	5.7	2.6	18.4	7.2
	1977	5.5	2.6	19.7	7.1
	1979	5.2	–*	–*	7.3
Income Security	1970	4.2	–*	4.2	6.0
	1975	4.7	5.8	5.3	8.6
	1977	4.8	6.4	5.7	9.4
	1979	4.9	–*	–*	9.6
Community and Regional Development	1970	5.7	–*	10.6	2.7
	1975	5.2	11.5	10.2	3.0
	1977	4.9	10.7	8.7	2.8
	1979	5.6	–*	–*	3.0
Fiscal Assistance for Business	1970	18.3	–*	12.0	13.3
	1975	14.2	11.6	8.9	13.0
	1977	13.4	9.4	8.2	12.6
	1979	13.7	–*	–*	12.1

Source: Eurostat (1980), Economic Report of the President, n.d.: various issues, author's own calculations.

* – = not available

public claims, for example lendings to outside parties, as part of state expenditures. This item, however, has been declining steadily since the fifties: Whereas in 1950 the claims constituted nearly 20% of the budget volume, in 1975 they only amounted to 3%. If it were possible – but unfortunately it only is in a hypothetical sense – to eliminate this factor in the FS time series, we could assume the slope of the function $St_E(FS)/GNP$ in figure 1 to be considerably steeper.

Although we certainly can derive some interesting information from statistical material as computed as they are above, we cannot gain insights into the national welfare effects of public activities, and we can say nothing about the incidence of public spending in relation both to the kind of goods and services provided and to the reaction of groups and individuals; nor can we estimate the substitution and/or complementary relationship between private and public economic activities, as long we do not disaggregate and classify St_E according *to public functions to be fulfilled.* This is done for major public activities on an international comparison level in table 7. A disaggregation of government expenditures according to *economic categories* would also be helpful in deflating public spending in a time series analysis, provided suitable price indexes for different components could be constructed.

7.4 How to "Manipulate" Expenditure Ratios: The "Real" Versus the "Comprehensive" State Share in National Income

In view of the methodological and statistical problems involved in an analysis of state activity it is not surprising that it is possible – according to one's ideological position – to produce state expenditure ratios of differing size by using specific definitions and methods. Those authors who argue that the public sector is "out of control" (Buchanan and Tullock 1977: 147) construct a high level and sharply increasing public expenditure ratio, whereas those who fear a continuous erosion of essential public goods and services employ low level and perhaps even declining quotients (see: Böttger and Gretschmann 1980). As for the first, the arguments are generally based on expenditure measures in nominal terms, that is in current prices, and some writers even advocate a "Comprehensive Expenditure Share" (CES) which includes the so-called "hidden government activities". The adherents of the second position often support their arguments by calculating a "Real State Share" (RS) which is adjusted to reflect price influence and consequently is expressed in constant prices.

Let us start by considering the first position: As outlined in some recent studies, the traditional public expenditure ratios as documented in the official SNA do not represent the actual significance of the public sector; above all they are not able to demonstrate its influence on the private economy. The following facts are disregarded: (1) The public sector can and often does impose costly burdens on private sector agencies in order to fulfill its own purposes. Examples are: Tax-self-assessment for private households, corporations' withholding of taxes, the requirement that private firms compile statistical data, the necessity for private organizations to employ people whose sole activity is to negotiate with public agencies, costs imposed on the economy by the obligatory draft of personnel for the armed forces, and legal obligations to keep books of account. Moreover, private enterprise often is (2) legally bound to provide social services. The following are typical conditions in Germany: Continued pay by the employer in case of an employee's sickness, maternity allowances also paid by employers, apprenticeship training, pension commitments or employee pension schemes covering old age, disability and survivors payments and other fringe benefits.

In order to determine the actual state share of GNP, one has to take into account the additional expenditure necessary to fulfill all the quasi-public functions listed above, which would accrue if the government assumed all these functions on its own account. In 1979 these costs were estimated for the USA at 121 billion. Consequently, we can expect that state expenditures will be substantially higher if the "hidden public demand" (Schmölders) is considered.

For example, the author of a widely recognized study (Kroker 1981) was eager to deduce a *"Comprehensive State Expenditure Ratio"* covering the hidden public demand discussed above (for data see table 8) and the activities of public enterprises measured according to their yearly sales volume (for data see table 8 also). To justify the latter, the author argues as follows: The state uses public enterprises in order to achieve certain of its performance goals in the context of its allocation,

Tab. 8: The Comprehensive State Share in GNP (German Case)

Year	(1)* Yearly total turnover of public enterprises	(2)* Private employers' social payments imposed by statutory regulations	(3)* Costs of administrative services performed by private sector institutions for government purposes	(4)* St_E (VGR)	$\Sigma 1-4$*	GNP*	Comprehensive state share %
1970	141.7	10.3	18.5	257.8	428.3	675.7	63.39
1971	165.9	12.0	21.6	296.5	496.0	751.8	65.97
1972	192.3	13.5	23.6	332.2	561.6	825.1	68.06
1973	218.7	14.8	26.3	376.8	636.6	918.9	69.28
1974	238.2	16.3	28.8	433.6	716.9	985.6	72.74
1975	252.0	15.4	29.6	493.4	790.4	1,028.9	76.82
1976	273.0	16.9	32.6	528.6	851.1	1,123.0	75.79
1977	292.1	17.8	34.3	564.6	908.8	1,196.3	79.98
1978	313.1	20.0	36.2	606.2	975.5	1,290.0	75.62
1979	340.9	21.4	39.8	653.5	1,055.6	1,395.3	75.65
1980	362.7	22.5	42.8	705.7	1,133.7	1,485.7	76.31

Source: CEEP (1978), Carlberg (1980), Kroker (1981), Klein-Blenkers (1980), author's own calculations.

* In billions of DM

distribution and stabilization policies. Instruments for such purposes are active price settings, competitive strategies, provision of urgently demanded goods and services in the necessary quality and quantity. Yet one can object that at least for the case of Germany, the public enterprises are self-managed independant bodies acting to a very large extent according to market rules.

If, however, one agrees with this approach, one simply has to add up the VGR-government expenditure, the sales volume of public enterprises, the private costs of social obligations and the private burden of "administrative delegation" of quasi-public tasks (see table 8). If we compare the comprehensive expenditures to the GNP, the result is the CES (comparative expenditure share) as shown in figure 2. According to this construction the state share in GNP is between 70 and 80%.

What has to be considered more serious than the CES method sketched above is the so-called "real expenditure ratio" (see Peffekoven 1977). Until recently most empirical studies of public spending were restricted to measuring the public sector share in nominal terms. The use of nominal ratios, however, only makes sense when price acceleration is identical for public expenditure and GNP. If in times of

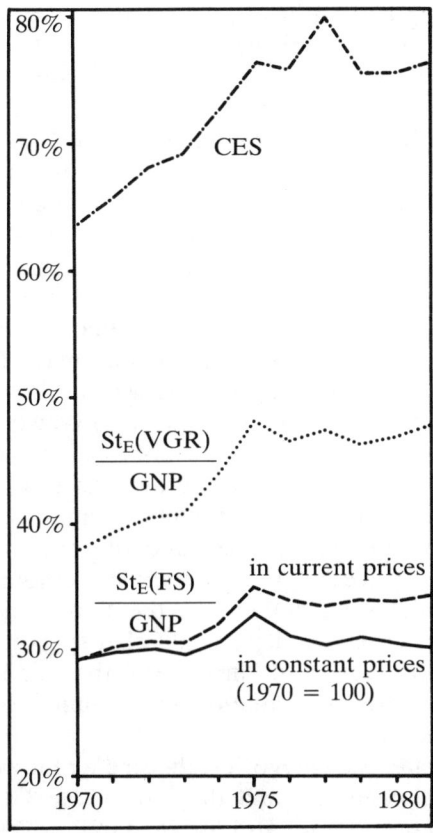

Fig. 2: The "Real" Versus the "Comprehensive" State Share in GNP (German Case)

inflation the prices for the publicly provided goods and services rise faster than the general price increases, nominal ratios do not make allowances for the resulting relative price effect, and, therefore, are unable to provide information about actual public sector activities, especially the composition and distribution of final "real" output.

In 1971, the German SVR (Council of Economic Advisers) pointed out in an empirical study that for the years 1966–1971 general government outlays in current prices had risen about 10% faster than the economy's overall price level. As early as 1963 Andic and Veverka (1963) proved that different relative price changes could explain the continuous rise in state expenditure shares to a considerable degree. A strictly theoretical economic explanation of the underlying causal relations was first offered by Baumol (1967), in Germany by Vogt (1973). Their basic argument runs as follows: A relative price effect arises from the relatively low level of technical progress and capital intensity in the public service sector compared to the highly capitalized private sector. This difference in capitalization results in a much lower increase in labor productivity in the public sector. Yet greater capitalization is not feasible because of the highly social, discontinuous and not standardizable nature of most public services. Wage increase in the public sector nevertheless exceed – unlike in the private sector – the capital determined marginal productivity of labor. This implies that, above all, relative prices for labor are constantly higher in the public than in the private sector.

It was Morris Beck (1979, 1981), who elaborated in detail the argument that in the developed countries the median ratio of government spending to GNP generally also rose in real terms from about 20% in 1950 to about 30% in 1977 (for the German case see also: Rahmeyer 1975). According to his data this trend must be ascribed to a considerable degree to the growth rate of real (deflated) transfer outlays whereas real expenditures for collective consumption had been shrinking.

In what follows we will try to find out how the deflated expenditure ratio for Germany developed during the years 1970–1980. To derive a real ratio we first have to decide which individual aggregates of government spending should be deflated by which index. Whereas the Bureau of National Accounts in the FRG has prepared a special price index of collective consumption which, however, is nowhere explained in great detail, we use – unlike Beck, who constructs two deflators for transfers and for state consumption only – a set of four different price indices each of which comes closest to the content of the aggregates mentioned above. Expenditures are itemized according to the consumption-and-investment-method of the FS: Personnel outlays are deflated by the standard wage rate index, government purchases by the producer price index, capital outlays employed to a very large extent for construction projects are deflated by the construction price index, transfer payments by the consumer price index and all other spending by the general GNP price deflator. As can be seen easily in table 9, the relative price effect is above all derived from the extreme inflation vulnerability of public construction activities and of personnel outlays.

After having deflated the disaggregated subcategories, the single real values are added up to a total of real public expenditure and divided by the GNP, also adjusted for price influences. For this purpose we also use the GNP price deflator (for the whole operation see table 9).

Tab. 9: Government Spending and Inflation – Determination of the "Real" Share in National Income for the FRG*

Year	GNP in current prices	GNP-Price Index (1970 = 100)	GNP in constant prices (1970 = 100)	St$_E$(FS) in current prices	Personnel Outlays in current prices	Standard Wage Rate Index	Personnel Outlays in constant prices	Government Purchases in current prices	Producer Price Index	Purchases in current prices	Capital outlays in current prices	Capital Construction Price Index	Capital Outlays in constant prices	Transfers in current prices	Consumer Price Index	Transfers in constant prices	Other Expenditures in current prices	Other GNP-Price Index	Other Expenditures in constant prices	"Real" State Expenditure in constant prices Column 7, 10, 13, 16, 19	"Real" State Share in GNP: Column 20/3; %
1970	675.7	100	675.7	196.3	61.4	100	61.4	33.8	100	33.8	32.2	100	32.2	44.5	100	44.5	24.4	100	24.4	196.3	29.05
1971	751.8	107.8	697.4	226.5	73.3	113.6	64.5	38.2	104.4	36.6	37.6	109.9	34.2	49.5	103.9	47.6	27.9	107.8	25.9	208.8	29.94
1972	825.1	113.6	726.3	252.1	82.0	124.5	65.9	40.0	107.0	37.4	39.1	115.4	33.9	60.2	111.1	54.2	30.8	113.6	27.1	218.5	30.08
1973	918.9	121.0	759.4	280.5	93.9	136.9	68.6	44.8	114.2	39.2	41.3	122.5	33.7	66.6	119.8	55.6	33.9	121.0	28.0	225.1	29.64
1974	985.6	129.2	762.8	318.3	108.7	142.5	76.3	49.4	129.4	38.2	46.1	131.5	35.1	75.4	127.1	59.3	38.7	129.2	30.0	238.9	31.31
1975	1,028.9	137.0	751.0	360.5	118.1	167.0	70.7	52.8	135.4	39.0	46.0	134.6	34.2	98.9	134.7	73.4	44.7	137.0	32.6	249.9	33.28
1976	1,123.0	141.6	793.1	376.8	124.0	176.4	70.3	55.9	140.4	39.8	43.6	138.9	31.4	104.9	140.4	74.7	48.4	141.6	34.2	250.4	31.57
1977	1,196.3	146.9	814.4	395.2	132.1	188.5	70.1	58.9	144.2	40.8	43.2	144.9	29.8	109.6	145.6	75.3	51.4	146.9	35.0	251.0	30.82
1978	1,290.0	153.0	843.1	431.8	140.1	198.8	70.5	65.0	145.9	44.6	47.5	153.6	30.9	121.4	149.3	81.3	57.8	153.0	37.8	265.1	31.44
1979	1,395.3	159.2	876.4	466.7	149.0	209.9	71.0	69.1	152.9	45.2	53.5	167.1	32.0	128.5	155.8	82.5	66.7	159.2	41.9	272.6	31.10
1980	1,485.7	166.3	893.4	504.0	161.1	223.9	72.1	74.2	164.5	45.1	60.7	185.6	32.7	138.1	164.3	84.1	69.9	166.3	42.0	276.0	30.89
1	1	2	3	4	5	6	7	8	9	10	11	12	13	14	15	16	17	18	19	20	

Sources: Bundesministerium der Finanzen n. d.: various issues, Statistisches Bundesamt (1982), SVR (1983), author's own calculations.

* In billions of DM

As shown in figure 2 above there was hardly any increase in the real ratio during the period of 1970–1980; with the exception of the year 1975 the quotient remained constant at the 30% line. Unlike Felderer (1976), who calculated clearly declining real expenditure ratios for the period of 1952–1972, and Beck (1981), who detected a slightly rising real public expenditure share for the period of 1950–1977 in the FRG, our own investigation concludes that public sector expenditures grew in current prices only to the extent necessary to keep real output, that is the production of state goods and services, constant during the period 1970–1980.

This result must be modified, however, because in using the FS and not the VGR we disregard the social security outlays to a large extent. Moreover the real function shown in figure 2 is basically determined by the use of a specific base year for which implicitly real and nominal state shares are thought to be identical. The Laspeyres-index construction of the function in constant prices consequently results in ratios varying to a considerable degree according to the base year used. This, however, is a general statistical problem, not a special inadequacy of deflating state expenditure shares.

Notwithstanding the enormous significance of inflation for further analysis of public sector activities, the operation of price correction is controversial. Price deflators of *marketable goods* reflect changes in the quality of products as well as in the productivity of labor. Since market prices are not available for public sector output, the common convention is to assume that output is a linear function of labor input. This implies that the productivity growth of labor in the public sector is zero. Likewise, price changes caused by changes in quality and/or in user preferences are disregarded. Such an abstraction, however, certainly distorts the price deflators used and casts doubt on the validity of the whole statistical operation.

To sum up, it can be said that there is no "one best" indicator of public sector activity nor "one best" expenditure ratio. The question of which specific data and ratios are to be used must always be decided according to the criteria of practicability, purpose, nature of the problem, questions to be answered and data and methods available. As pointed out earlier, the choice between for example the CES and the RS, as limiting cases, can significantly influence the conclusion as to whether the public sector is too large or too small. Yet in order to arrive at final conclusions we would have to investigate *not only measures but explanations* offered for the expansion of the public sector, regardless of its "right" size. Very interesting recent approaches in this regard have been presented by Gabriel (1983) and Cameron (1978). In addition models of public sector functioning, as outlined in this book, which analyze the public sector in detail and in depth, are still necessary. If the discussion of this chapter prepares the field for this kind of research, it will have fulfilled its purpose.

References

Andic, S., and J. Veverka (1963): "The Growth of Government Expenditure in Germany since the Unification." *Finanzarchiv* N. F. 23/2: 169–278.

Baumol, W. J. (1967): "Macroeconomics of Unbalanced Growth: The Anatomy of Urban Crisis." *American Economic Review* 57/3: 415–426.

Beck, M. (1979): "Public Sector Growth: A Real Perspective." *Public Finance* 34/3: 313–356.

Beck, M. (1981): *Government Spending – Trends and Issues.* New York: Praeger.

Bernholz, P. (1982): "Ausdehnung des Wohlfahrtsstaats." *Wirtschaftspolitische Blätter* 29/5: 32–46.

Böttger, G., and K. Gretschmann (1980): "Ökonomische und politische Implikationen einer mittelfristigen Erhöhung der Staatsquote." *WSI-Mitteilungen* 33/4: 216–324.

Buchanan, J. M., and G. Tullock (1977): "The Expanding Public Sector – Wagner Squared." *Public Choice* 31/(Fall): 147–151.

Bundesministerium der Finanzen (ed.) n.d. *Finanzbericht.* Bonn. (various issues)

Cameron, D. R. (1978): "The Expansion of the Public Economy: A Comparative Analysis." *The American Political Science Review* 72/4: 1243–1261.

Carlberg, M. (1980): "Öffentliche Unternehmen und Staatsquoten." *Zeitschrift für öffentliche und gemeinwirtschaftliche Unternehmen* 3/1: 1–11.

CEEP (1978): Centre d'économique europeén publique, *Die öffentliche Wirtschaft in der EG.* Brüssel.

Colm, G. (1955): *Essays in Public Finance and Fiscal Policy.* NewYork: Oxford Univ. Press.

Due, J. F., and A. F. Friedlaender (1973): *Government Finance, Economics and the Public Sector.* Homewood/Ill.: Irwin.

Economic Report of the President n.d. *Economic Report of the President.* Washington: Government Printing Office. (various issues)

Eichenberger, R. C. (1983): "Problems in Using Public Employment Data." In Taylor, Ch. L. (ed.), *Why Governments Grow – Measuring Public Sector Size,* 136–153. Beverly Hills: Sage.

Elias, N. (1969): *Über den Prozeß der Zivilisation* (Vol. 2). Bern–München: Franke.

Eurostat (1980): *Konten und Statistiken des Staates.* Brüssel.

Felderer, B. (1976): "Die reale Staatsquote." *Finanzarchiv* N. F. 35/3: 405–434.

Folkers, C. (1979): "Staatswirtschaftliche Quoten und Beziehungszahlen." *Das Wirtschaftsstudium* (WISU) 8/8: 405–409.

Gabriel, L. (1983): *Das Wachstum des Staatssektors.* Köln: Institut für Wirtschaftspolitik.

Goldscheidt, R. (1917): *Staatssozialismus oder Staatskapitalismus.* Wien–Leipzig: Schuschitzky.

Hjerppe, R. T. (1980): "The Measurement of Real Output of Public Sector Services." *The Review of Income and Wealth* 26/2: 237–250.

Kaufer, E. (1981): *Theorie der öffentlichen Regulierung.* München: Vahlen.

Klein-Blenkers, F., H. J. Mortsiefer, and W. Reske (1980): *Die Belastung von Industrieunternehmen durch administrative Leistungen für den Staat.* Göttingen: Schwartz.

Kroker, R. (1981): *Der Staat als Wirtschaftsfaktor – Zur Aussagefähigkeit der Staatsquote.* Köln: DI-Verlag.

Kuznets, S. (1948): "On the Valuation of Social Income – Reflections on Professor Hicks' Article." *Economica* 15 (February/May): 1–16; 116–131.

Littmann, K. (1964): "Strukturen und Entwicklung der staatlichen Aktivität in der Bundesrepublik Deutschland 1950–1970." In: Neumark, F. (ed.), *Strukturwandlungen einer wachsenden Wirtschaft,* 779–834. Berlin: Duncker und Humblot.

Littmann, K. (1975): *Definition und Entwicklung der Staatsquote.* Göttingen: Schwartz.

Mackscheidt, K., and J. Steinhausen (1977): *Finanzpolitik II: Grundfragen versorgungspolitischer Eingriffe.* Tübingen: Mohr/Siebeck.

Mann, F. K. (1972): "Die 'Als-Obs' in der Finanzwirtschaftslehre." *Zeitschrift für Nationalökonomie* 32/2–3: 225–240.

Matzner, E., W. Blaas, and W. Schönbäck (1979): "Die Entwicklung des Staatsanteils – eine funktionsanalytische Betrachtung." In: Weizsäcker, C. C. v. (ed.), *Staat und Wirtschaft,* 505–528. Berlin: Duncker und Humblot.

Nadel, M. V. (1975): "The Hidden Dimension of Public Policy: Private Governments and the Policy Making Process." *Journal of Politics* 37/1: 2–34.

Nolan, P. (1979): "Size and Administrative Intensity in Nations." *American Sociological Review* 44/1: 110–125.

OECD (1983): *Economic Outlook: Historical Statistics 1960–1980*. Paris.

Pathirane, L., and D. W. Blades (1982): "Defining and Measuring the Public Sector: Some International Comparison." *The Review of Income and Wealth* (Series 28): 261–289.

Pfeffekoven, R. (1977): "Begriff und Aussagefähigkeit der Staatsquote." *Wirtschaftswissenschaftliches Studium* (WiST) 6/5: 208–213.

Petersen, H. G. (1982): "Size of the Public Sector, Economic Growth and the Informal Economy." *Review of Income and Wealth* 28/2: 191–215.

Raabe, K. H. (1976): "Projektionen eines Korridors für den Staatssektor." In Duwendag, D. (ed.), *Der Staatssektor in der Sozialen Marktwirtschaft*, 37–59. Berlin: Duncker und Humblot.

Rahmeyer, F. (1975): "Preisveränderungen und Erhöhung der Staatsquote." *Konjunkturpolitik* 21: 232–253.

Reich, U. P. (1981): "Zur Berechnung der realen Staatsquote." *Ifo-Studien* 27/1: 75–102.

Ronge, V. (ed.) (1980): *Am Staat vorbei: Politik der Selbstregulierung von Kapital und Arbeit*. Frankfurt a. M.: Campus.

Rose, R. (1976): "On the Priorities of Government: A Developmental Analysis of Public Policies." *European Journal of Political Research* 4/2: 247–289.

Rose, R. (1983): "Disaggregating the Concept of Government." In Taylor, Ch. L. (ed.), *Why Governments Grow – Measuring Public Sector Size*, 157–175. Beverly Hills: Sage.

Rose, R. (1984): *Understanding Big Government – The Program Approach*. London: Sage.

Schumpeter, J. A. (1918): "Die Krise des Steuerstaats." Graz and Leipzig. Repr. in: Hickel, R. (ed.), *Die Finanzkrise des Steuerstaats – Beiträge zur politischen Ökonomie der Staatsfinanzen*, 329–379. Frankfurt a. M.: Suhrkamp.

Statistisches Bundesamt (ed.) (1982): *Lange Reihen zur Wirtschaftsentwicklung 1982*. Stuttgart, Mainz: Kohlhammer.

Statistisches Bundesamt (ed.) n.d. (a) *Statistisches Jahrbuch für die Bundesrepublik Deutschland*. Stuttgart, Mainz: Kohlhammer. (various issues)

Statistisches Bundesamt (ed.) n.d. (b) *Volkswirtschaftliche Gesamtrechnungen. Fachserie 18*. Stuttgart, Mainz: Kohlhammer. (various series and issues)

SVR (1983): Sachverständigenrat Jahresgutachten 1983/84: *Ein Schritt voran*. Stuttgart- –Mainz: Kohlhammer.

Tautscher, A. (1969): *Der ökonomische Leviathan oder die wirtschaftliche Übermacht des Staates*. Berlin: Duncker und Humblot.

Vogt, W. (1973): "Zur langfristigen ökonomischen Entwicklung eines kapitalistischen Systems." *Leviathan* 1/2: 161–188.

Weisbrod, B. A., J. F. Handler, and N. K. Komesar (eds.) (1978): *Public Interest Law*. Berkely: Univ. of California Press.

Zimmermann, H. (1973): "Die Ausgabenintensität der öffentlichen Aufgabenerfüllung." *Finanzarchiv* N. F. 32/1: 1–20.

8. Intergovernmental Policy-Making: The Limits of Subnational Autonomy

Laurence J. Sharpe

Abstract

Where central (or federal) government is responsible for public policies, but the execution of the policy is the responsibility of a decentral level of government, there may be a difference between intention and outcome: a 'control deficit'. But the decentral level may be able to frustrate central attempts to overcome the deficit by coordination. Research has shown that this phenomenon is common to many Western states. However, it may be that it will vary with structural factors, both formal and informal, and with partisan factors. The U.K., where the disposition of these factors suggests central coordination may be easier, certainly provides examples of successful central coordination especially in the field of finance, but also in factic abolishing decentral units altogether via a reorganization scheme. Enhancing the centre's capacity to coordinate may not be the only motive for reorganization, but by reducing the number of units to be coordinated it can be a very effective one. There are, however, side-effects of local re-organization which, despite claims to the contrary, entail the dilution of local service delivery both in terms of quality and access. Weakening a sense of local identity among citizens as well as losses in the "democraticness" of the national state are also probable consequences.

8.1 Introduction

Problems of scale, of service coordination at the point of consumption, and the fact of sub-national socio-economic differentiation, all require the modern state to devolve responsibility for some of its internal services to a sub-national level – sometimes two levels – of territorial general government. In Western systems, in order to operate effectively and meet prevailing democratic norms, such sub-national territorial government units are run by elected bodies and they have the right to tax. These two characteristics, together with the subnational units' role as a general government, sharply distinguishes it in power terms from other forms of decentralization – the public corporation, the quango or central field services – in the sense that such sub-national local government represents both functional and political constituencies that are independent of the central state and may therefore be *legitimately* in conflict with those of the central government of the state.

At the very least we may argue that local government is essential to the modern democratic state for three reasons. First, it recognizes that in addition to the national community, there is another community (or communities) with its own subjective loyalties and objective interdependencies at the sub-national level. In a democracy, the existence of such communities is likely to demand recognition sooner or later in some form of self-government. Second, given its range and scope no central government could cope with being directly responsible for the whole of the public sector. Thirdly, given the scale of the average Western state, the individual voter can have only the most marginal influence on his government. By creating decentralized levels of government the capacity of the individual to influence and participate in his own government is increased. Not by much, it must be admitted, but decentralization remains nonetheless one of the most important modes for mitigating the contradiction between the scale of the modern democratic state and its claim to be democratic.

It has been argued that where conflict among the central state and sub-national government does arise, the centre may be seriously impeded in fulfilling key policy tasks, with the result that there occurs "control deficits" (see Scharpf et al. 1975), or "seepage" and "momentum loss" (Sharpe 1977: 61) between the intentions of the centre and final outcomes. This disjunction between the responsibilities of central government and its capacity to fulfill them constitutes a major and possibly a growing problem for the centre (see Hanf 1978). The need for central intervention arises from the fact that the sub-national system cannot achieve the necessary coordination because power is fragmented into territorially discrete units of necessarily limited capacity and resources and yet each will possess an inevitable degree of autonomy and information monopoly. Each unit will also reflect different interests and is likely to pursue different and sometimes conflicting policies.

In this chapter the possibilities of the center to influence local government will be explored, with special reference to the British case. In order to assess the capacities of central government one has first to consider the overall structure of a political system, and the British system will prove to be rather easily susceptible to influences from the part of the center. Some of the major lines of influence will be sketched. The most intrusive form of central governments intervention is the reorganization of local government of the kind which occurred in Britain in the early 1970s. This reorganization was meant to improve the centers capacities to control local government and to improve its efficiency. We shall discuss the reasons given for this reorganization and assess the validity of these arguments as well as the evidence as to whether the stated goals of the reform could be attained.

Structural Forces and the Capacities for Central Government

The subnational system may be frustrating the achievement of national policy aims precisely when the need for such policies is becoming insistent as government becomes increasingly complex, more nationwide in scope and more interdependent. As Kenneth Hanf has noted when summarizing the conclusions of a series of studies on central-local relations, which must be regarded as one of the most important studies of its kind published in recent years, hereafter called the Hans-Scharpf study:

"A major task confronting political system in any advanced industrial country is therefore that of securing coordinated policy actions through networks of separate, but interdependent organizations where the collective capabilities of a number of participants are essential for effective problem solving, or where the activities of individual units are to be guided by more general policy considerations. Of course, even highly fragmented and pluralistic politico-administrative systems display a certain order and a "structure" of interactions which contradict the superficial appearance of complete "uncoordination". Indeed, much coordination results from the voluntary interactions among the individual units without any conscious or deliberate steering by a more inclusive decision maker, or in some way, through the systems as a whole.

For a significant range of policy problems however, the kind and amount of coordination produced through the voluntary and spontaneous actions of individual organizations is neither appropriate nor sufficient. Effective problem solving for these problems requires corrective interventions into the self-regulation of the system" (Hanf 1978: 2).

As the Hanf-Scharpf study goes on to argue, even where the capacity of the central government to exert its will over the localities appears in administrative and legal terms to be strong, local authorities enjoy considerable autonomy in practice because of their informal access to political power at the centre, their monopoly of crucial information and the fact that they and not the centre have executant responsibility.

If Hanf is right, then a key problem for the study of public policy becomes: how does the central government conduct the necessary corrective interventions in the fragmented system so that its policies are achieved? And to what extent is it able to achieve its policies without undesired side-effects? Hanf argues that such is the capacity of the sub-system to resist central interventions from above on the grounds that centralization is normatively undesirable, the centre is forced to resort to a form of bargaining: "cooperative under takings through which coordination is sought, are firmly rooted in the agreement and consent of those to be coordinated" (Hanf 1978: 3).

Hanf's conclusions are challenging, and one key variable directly affecting the centres' capacity to get its way is likely to be purely structural. That is to say we may expect the success of the centre in imposing its will may be different in a three-tier (i.e. federal) system as compared with a two-tier (i.e. unitary) system where both decentral levels participate in the implementation of the policy in question. Similarly, we may expect, that, other things being equal, the centre will have more success in a prefectoral system (e.g. France and Italy) as compared with functional systems (as in Britain and Norway), where the relationship between centre and locality is largely between functional departments and a central field agent, for general government is either totally absent or exists only in a residual form. Unitary prefectoral systems like France, or the Netherlands, should in theory provide easier conditions for corrective interventions by the centre. At the other extreme federal *and* functional systems like Australia, or the U.S., should present the very formidable difficulties for a purposive centre. Where the intermediate decentral units are relatively few and where they encompass ethnic or language enclaves which perceive themselves as being different from the core authority of the federation and are therefore disinclined to be cooperative, we may expect not only the most severe difficulty for central corrective interventions but a slow decentral shift in the inclination of the system as a whole. These are broadly the conditions pertaining in Canada and the predicted consequences seem to be following.

One additional formal structural factor that demands consideration since it is likely to impede the centre getting its way is the additional capacity of the decentralized system to resist because it enjoys institutionalized power at the centre in the form of direct representation in the Second Chamber. This is the situation in France and the United States but most decisively in West Germany.

Important as they are likely to be however, formal structural characteristics do not exhaust the possible factors that will have an important bearing on the capacity of the centre to get its way. For example, where there is a tradition of informal representation of the decentral units because local leaders also hold elective positions with the national system sometimes highly influential ones, which enable the localities the better to resist central policies with which they disagree. This is the *cumul des mandats* tradition which seems to be strongest in France. In 1971 no less than 379 of the 487 Deputies of the National Assembly and 191 of the 283 Senators plus 36 of the 41 ministers and junior ministers were elected Mayors (see Wright 1979: 213). Of the Chairmen elected to the 22 Regional Councils in 1976, 13 were Mayors, 20 were either Deputies or Senators and 13 had formerly been Ministers (see Birnbaum 1979: 123). *Multiple office holding* at different levels of government, although not perhaps as rampant as in France, is to a greater or lesser degree a feature of most Western systems with the notable exception of Britain. On one view, this parallel power structure may be just as important as the formal constitutional relationship between the centre and the localities (see Mackenzie 1954: 418).

If we add this last consideration to the others discussed earlier, we may posit that the centre is likely to have greatest difficulty in achieving its coordinative policy aims where there is a federal system together with functional articulation of services to the localities, and institutionalized representation of the sub-national levels within the national legislative process – that is to say the conditions broadly pertaining in West Germany. If this is the case, it may not be all that surprising that the bulk of the research in the Hanf-Scharpf study was on West German inter-governmental relations. In other words the difficulties the centre faces in minimiz-ing control deficits may be more a function of the structural conditions of West Germany than of Western democracies generally (see Franz: C.23).

If certain structural factors do make central coordination particularly difficult then these are good reasons for examining the experience of the centre in coordinating the subnational system in a Western state where the structural conditions are, as we have argued, somewhat less conducive to thwarting central coordinative endeavours than the West German. That is to say in a unitary rather than a federal state that also, unlike West Germany, has no institutionalized participation of the decentral level in the national legislative and policymaking process; nor any tradition such as informal participation via the *cumul des mandats*. The United Kingdom provides a good example of such a state and we will now explore some of the ways in which the British central government seeks to achieve coordination among the local government units.

8.2 Central Coordination via the Professional Community

One possible strategy that certainly seems to be open to the centre in the U.K. is an informal one which may be described as a coopting the public sector professional communities. This tactic is briefly discussed in the Hanf-Scharpf study as occurring in West Germany but as a relatively minor option and as something of a last resort (see Scharpf et al. 1978: 103).

The professional communities comprise specialist functionaries who operate at different levels of government, but because they share a common expertise form informal vertical structures. Their shared expertise provides a common interest which is probably reinforced by membership of a professional association. It is also reinforced by a desire to ensure that their sector of government maintains its share of the public budget against competition from other sectors. Taken together these professional communites form the so-called "picket fence" (Wright, D. S. 1974: 14) of "vertical functional autocracies" (Advisory Commission 1955: 7).

As vertical structures, the various communities cuts across the layers of horizontal government linking the professional cadres at each level from central policymaking to the point of service delivery. One of the functions of the community is to enhance its members inevitable quest for greater professional autonomy and in formal terms it may be posited that the horizontal layers of general government curb the normal tendency for the vertical professional communities to achieve the degree of autonomy they seek. Each layer performs this role mainly by "horizontalizing" the necessarily particularized interest of each community by being the employer of that section of the community at its level. As a general government, each level also exercizes some control over the professional communities, since each community is forced to operate alongside others and thus to take account of them. Such face-to-face relationships always dilute the pure milk of professional hubris.

The desire for autonomy of the different communities will vary and will depend on the status of the group: the higher its status the greater the desire. But there will always be some tension even in relation to the most lowly and emergent specialism and this tension is likely to be at its most intense for high status professional communities with relatively high levels of vertical cohesion for whom control by decentral units, because they lack the status of central government, is irksome in any case. Here is the centre's opportunity for it can exploit such tensions to its own advantage such that high status professional communities can be very important vehicles for effecting some types of coordinating policies by the centre. This is because the professional communities provide not merely the degree of aggregation necessary for the centre's implementation strategy, but, if the controlling echelon of each community can be won over, there is the *possibility of penetrating every unit of the sub-national system or systems.*

The controlling echelon may be won over by the provisions of incentives and possibly, in some cases, sanctions (see Webb and Wistow 1980: 76). In the British case, the centre has patronage at its disposal in the form of honours and titles that are highly prized in society at large. Such patronage cannot be matched by the sub-national system and the receipt of which is one of the attractions and career expectations of the leadership of the professional community in any case.

The *co-option* by the centre of the professional community, so as to create a sort of Trojan horse aimed at penetrating a recalcitrant sub-national system, important as it may be, is part of a more complex series of possibilities open to the centre. The leadership of the vertical professional communities, the top of the picket fence as it were, forms only part of a more ramified layer, or network, of institutions and relationships that reflect and represent the sub-national system at the national level. It includes as well as the professional communities representative pressure groups of the sub-national units, formal consultative bodies established by the centre, and the *policy community* that usually exists for each major public service. This last grouping may comprise private firms (that have a direct financial interest in the service), national media journalists, the local government press, lay pressure groups and academics. Each element of this policy community, in various ways and for various motives, seeks to promote and develop a particular public service. These policy communities vary in strength, influence and composition since some public services, for various reasons, are better suited to attracting a policy community than others. Secondary education, for example, will always have a bigger and more prominent policy community than, say, sewage disposal.

The four elements: professional community, sub-national system pressure groups, formal consultative bodies and the policy communities together form what Dunleavy has called the "national local government system". This, as he described it, is a

"set of organizations and actors which together define the rational role ard state of opinion in local government as a whole' . . . (it) determines the parameters within which local authorities operate, parameters which range from the organization of local government itself and the distribution of functions between the central state and local government to the constantly defined and redefined methods of central control, the context of central-local relations, levels of central state funding of local services, and the distribution of funding of local services, and the distribution of funding between urban areas and policy programmes. At an *ideological level* the system provides an important source of values and ideas for actors in particular localities" (Dunleavy 1981: 105, see also pp. 123 f.).

Dunleavy's study, from which this quote is taken, demonstrates convincingly how the centre used the national local government system, what we may call the *sub-national aggregation,* with great effect to promote the building by local government of high rise public housing by industrialized methods in Britain. Applying varying strategies aimed at the separate elements of the sub-national aggregation, the center was successful, if only temporarily, in effecting a very rapid and dramatic change in the dominant operating ideology of local public housing construction in urban areas in Britain.

By *operating ideology* (see Sharpe 1976: 130) we mean the generally accepted rationale and the broad modes of operation for a given service or policy; that is to say, the main elements that go to make up a specified series of actions by a public authority in response to a legally defined requirement for collective action.[1] In normal circumstances professional communities are adept in making the marginal adjustments to the operating ideology, either for entirely professional reasons, or in order to bring the operating ideology into line with majority opinion. In both cases, they maintain the illusions of technocratic dominance and, it seems, continue to confound some academic observers. Such adjustments are, after all, one of the professional community's major functions. Where public opinion shifts rapidly such adjustments require a degree of dexterity and intellectual flexibility that may not always be forthcoming.

Central governments are, of course, in *formal* terms the principal agents for making major alterations to an operating ideology since in the last resort they can legislate for the necessary change. But in order to achieve the kind of coordination which is the subject of this paper such tactics may be difficult, or risky. The conversion of the sub-national aggregation, and especially the professional and policy communities, may be a more convenient and less politically visible method of achieving the necessary coordination.

8.3 Coordination via Partisanship and Ideology

British experience also suggests that corrective interventions by the centre in order to effect coordination need not necessarily be in conflict with the interests of all the decentralized units. Some may be even more enthusiastic for certain kinds of coordination than the centre. Few policy objectives are likely to be ideologically neutral, and if central coordination makes their realization more probable then coordination itself will not be politically neutral either. Where centre and locality share the same ideological point of view, then policy objectives may be achieved simply by 'coordination from below'. Where both levels are dominated by the same political party is the most obvious example of this kind of situation. Admittedly, even where this is the case there may be difficulties because the role of the key actors at the two levels are different and institutional loyalties, even for the most partisan actors, may be difficult to overcome when there is a direct conflict of institutional interests. Nonetheless, it is clear that considerations of party loyalty places a new perspective on any discussion of the capacity of the centre to prevail over the localities. To some extent this is recognized in the Hanf-Scharpf study but never in any sense developed (see Scharpf 1978: 366)[2].

It may be said, then, that the degree of politicization of the sub-national levels could be a critical factor in reconciling the need for central concerted action and the complexity and recalcitrance of the network of intergovernmental relations via which that action has to be given effect. Partisanship, it hardly needs emphasising, can be both a negative as well as a positive factor for the capacity of the centre to achieve the necessary coordination. Where the same party is dominant at both levels there is a strong likelihood that it will be positive, where they are different it will be negative. Where elections for the central and the decentral level are held at different times, and particularly where decentral elections occur towards the end of the so-called 'honeymoon period' between the electorate and the central government, then there may be a "mid term effect", whereby the party in power naturally is punished at the polls by a disillusioned electorate and the opposition party is returned at the decentral level. Then, the negative consequences of partisanship can be decisive for central coordinative success. Where the necessary coordination has to be effected at the local government level, the partisan effect may be a peculiarity of the British local level which seems to have a particularly rigid party system. But recent research on local government policy outputs strongly suggests that even if some Western local systems appear to be less overtly partisan than the British and despite earlier research (see Fried 1973: 71 ff.), there does seem to be a clear party ideological effect in the way policy is made (see Sharpe 1981a).

Where the centre sees the partisanship of the localities as a major obstacle to achieving its major policies and its coordination aims it may seek to alter the very foundations of the central local relationship or the even more drastic remedy of altering the structure of the decentral system itself so as to render it more malleable to the centre's aims. The possibility of effecting such strategies will of course vary from country to country depending on what constraints exist on the centre's freedom of action, but it is clear that both are strategies that have been applied in the U.K.

8.4 Financial Strategy

In one sense the distinction between financial and political questions is a false one since there can hardly be any policy that does not entail a financial or resource decision as well. However, when considering the relations between a central government and a decentralized level of general government, resource and policy decisions must be distinguished simply because each level has a separate budgetary system; that is to say, two separate patterns of resource allocation. The two may be related in the sense that, as in the British case, the centre may provide a high proportion of the total resources available to the sub-national level and may, via categorical grants, strongly influence the allocation pattern of its budget. But in the nature of the case the budgets of the two levels may be viewed as being different. This difference is likely to be all the greater where central-subnational relations are conducted on functional lines as compared with systems which, in theory at least, provide a common general superior like the French prefect who has ultimate responsibility for approving all local budgets in his department.

Since it is unlikely that there will be any necessary symmetry between resource decisions at the two levels, it follows that the resource and policy strategies open to the centre for effecting the needed coordination of the decentralized level must be considered separately.

Resource strategies are important for the centre for at least two reasons: in the first place control over the level and the placing of grants may be the only form of direct control available to the centre for some policies. Secondly, the centre may provide all, or most, or the finance for the policy in question. Financial considerations may also become very prominent in periods of severe resource constraint; especially when the constraint policy has been determined by supply side economic theories that see the money supply as largely determining the stability of prices. The application of such policies by the centre may reach the point where the 'normal' relationship between financial or resource questions and service questions – that the former is merely the facilitator of the latter – become reversed. In this situation service delivery becomes an aspect of resource policy (see Webb and Wistow 1980: 80 f.).

The subordination of service to financial policy may reach the point where resources are so reduced as to raise the question whether the service can continue to be provided at all. This is not merely a function of a cut-back in central grants, since all public expenditure must be counted in the monetarist equation. Locally raised revenue is equally inimical to the supply side theory. The centre may therefore seek to erode the budgetary autonomy of the sub-national system with the precise intention of forestalling the substitution of locally derived revenue for the lost central grants. Broadly speaking, such a move by the centre has been taking place in Britain over the recent past (see Alexander 1982: Ch. 7; Burgess and Travers 1980). Given the apparent popularity of monetarist doctrines in the West generally, the same process of centralized financial policy overriding sub-national service delivery may be spreading to other countries.

Since 1945 local government has been required to take on many more tasks in the social, welfare and education fields. This expansion was such that in most Western countries local growth has been at a faster rate than that for government as a whole. Yet there has rarely been a corresponding expansion of the tax base.

Very broadly, it is this disparity between policies and resources that has produced what has been dubbed the local fiscal crisis in Western countries. The gap between the cost of the new and extended services and the lack of the means to pay for them from locally derived revenue has been filled by central grants. Western states vary enormously in the range of local tax systems. Those deriving from the British tradition still give a major role to a property tax and in them the disparity between expenditure and local revenue is at its most acute. In Scandinavia the non-progressive income tax is the major source of locally derived revenue and in that region the problem is a minor one. In most of Western Europe there is a varying mixture of income tax, property tax, and other taxes. Table 1 summarizes the composition of the local tax system for six Western European countries that includes all three types and in them there is considerable variation in the extent of the problem, but generally it is more acute than in Scandinavia but less than in the UK, the USA, Canada and Australia.

Tab. 1: Sources of Local Tax Income, 1972 (percentages)

Local Taxes	Denmark	Italy	Norway	Sweden	U.K.	W. Germany
General Tax on goods and services		10.5				
Taxes on specific goods and services	0.7	7.1		0.1		0.6
Income Tax	33.4		48.0	42.1		13.8
Corporation Tax		1.7	2.6	3.6		
Land/Property Tax	3.9	2.3	1.3		33.8	4.0
Other recurrent	0.5	3.9	2.1			
Commercial Tax		31.5				14.8*
Other mixed taxes	0.9	1.7				
Taxes on real estate transactions		1.1				1.1
total local taxes	39.4	59.7	54.0	45.8	33.8	34.3

Source: Council of Europe (1976: 43)

* Excludes tax on employers

What all Western local systems (or any other local system one suspects) lack is an income elastic tax, namely the progressive income tax, for this tax is invariably reserved for senior government.

Those dependent on the local property tax were also hard hit with the onset of relatively high levels of inflation from 1973. This was due to the basic lack of buoyancy of the property tax as compared with the centres' tax base.

Another factor that, it has been argued, has enhanced the fiscal strain or resource squeeze on local government, is derived from the relative price effect. This is based on the assumption that the productivity of government in the provision of services increases more slowly than does productivity in the private sector, yet because of a unified labour market labour costs rise at the same rate for all sectors. In consequence, more and more resources have to be devoted to government as wages and salaries merely to maintain existing levels of services (see Heller 1966: Sharpe 1981b; Newton 1981).

Productivity is lower in the public than in the private sector because the former is more labour intensive than the latter. Demonstrating that this relative price effect actually operates is fraught with difficulties, not least because we do not know whether the public and private sector are identically affected by technical change. But there is some evidence that there is a productivity lag for the public sector as a whole. Moreover, the claim that within the public sector local government is especially vulnerable to the lag is supported by some empircal analysis (see Bradford et al. 1969).

If the relative price effect thesis is correct, then there is a further reason for positing that there is a basic resource weakness in the localities vis a vis the centre, in addition to inflation and the relative lack of access to the income elastic taxes. Taken together, they constitute a degree of potential vulnerability to central control of the sub-national system that has its origins in resource and fiscal issues, but which can have consequences over a wide field of central-local relations.

8.5. The Local Reorganization Strategy in Britain and Its Goals

Where the centre does seek to change the sub-national structure itself in order to achieve its coordinative aims it is unlikely to state such motives publicly. Nor is such a drastic remedy ever likely to be the only motive; like most major policy structural change of this kind can be justified on other grounds and it is this conjunction which precipitates change. Bearing these cautionary thoughts in mind, an example of this kind of structural solution to the problem of coordinating the sub-national system may be seen in Britain where the centre 'successfully' reorganized the whole of the local government system during the early 1970s.

The new local government system in Britain was created in England and Wales by the 1972 Local Government Act and for Scotland by the Local Government (Scotland) Act of 1973. This section is concerned only with the 1972 act which had two broad objectives. First, the *socio-geographic* objective which is the attempt to bring the boundaries of local authorities more into line with present day communication patterns and linkages by joining the built-up area of cities with their hinterland. Secondly, the *service provision* objective which was sought by increas-

ing the average population size of local authorities so as to enhance their capacity
to provide services efficiently to present day standards.

Some idea of how drastic the changes wrought by the 1972 act were, is revealed
by the reduction in the total number of units, which declined from 1,391 to 422.
The various types of authority before and after reorganization may be summarized
as follows:

Old System		New System	
English County Boroughs	79	Metropolitan Counties	6
Welsh County Boroughs	4	Metropolitan Districts	36
English Counties	45	English Counties	39
Welsh Counties	13	Welsh Counties	8
English Boroughs	1086	English Districts	296
and Districts		Welsh Districts	37
Welsh Boroughs	164		
and Districts			
Total	1391	Total	422

There were other motivations, objectives and assumptions involved in the reorganization, too. Most important was the desire of the central bureaucracy and the
ministerial cadre to reduce the complexity of central coordination for service
delivery. This easing of the centres' task affected all local services, but was
especially important in education which is solely the executant responsibility of
local government and includes every aspect from kindergartens to technological
universities (polytechnics). In housing, too, reorganization was important, for
nearly one third of the housing stock has been built and is owned by local
government. For this service the centre achieved the most dramatic reduction of all
the major services from over 1200 separate local housing authorities to about 300.
Thus the effect of the reorganization was to drastically reduce the number of local
government units such that Britain has the largest (in population) local authorities
in Western Europe and probably in the Western world (see Table 2).

In addition to reducing the number of local authorities to be coordinated, the
partisan effect also played a part in this reorganization for not only was the
coordination task reduced in terms of the number to be coordinated, but the
consolidation of the old local units was applied so as to favour the party then in
power nationally – the Conservatives (see Dunleavy 1980: 89, Sharpe 1978a: 84).

Translated into local government boundaries, the *socio-geographic objective*
implied the abolition of the major urban authorities, the county boroughs, the
boundaries of which did not usually embrace even the whole of the built-up areas
of cities, and their replacement by new authorities that extended well beyond the
built-up core to some approximation of its hinterland.

The need to match the local government structure to this alleged reality rested
on three grounds. First, the objective linkage of the town plus hinterland will have
already generated a subjective community of interest among the inhabitants of the

Tab. 2: Population of Reformed Local Gorvernment Units in Western Europe

Country	Total Population	No. of Basic Units of Local Government	Approximate Average Population of Basic Units
Belgium (Communes, 1977)	9,788,248	596	16,255
Denmark (Kommuner, 1972)	4,995,653	277	17,963
France (Communes, 1968)	49,778,500	37,708	1,320
Italy (Comune, 1973)	54,136,547	8,059	6,717
Netherlands (Gemeentin, 1972)	13,599,092	841	16,170
Norway (Kommuner, 1973)	3,947,775	444	8,891
Sweden (Kommuner, 1976)	8,208,442	278	29,527
West Germany (Gemeinden & Kreisfreie Städte, 1975)	60,650,600	22,510	2,694
England & Wales (Districts incl. London Boroughs, 1972)	49,219,000	401	130,000

Source: Sharpe (1978a: 95)

spread city through the links of employment, shopping and social activities. Secondly, and more decisively, it was argued that planning and the related functions of traffic management, highways and public transport could only be effectively and efficiently undertaken if their jurisdiction covered the whole of the city and its hinterland since in planning terms service centre and hinterland are interdependent (see Royal Commission 1967a: 60 ff.). Extending the boundary was therefore an improvement on the status quo in the sense that it would come closer to internalizing the service externalities, thus making possible a sharing of the costs and the benefits of the public goods more equitably among those affected and achieving greater allocative efficiency.

The third reason why more government and more integrated government is needed in urban rather than in rural areas is derived from the fact that the centre of the towns performs a functional role on behalf of the whole built-up area and its hinterland by providing common services. The larger the urban area the wider the range of services provided by the central city. Many of these services are, of course, provided by the market and others by central government, but there remains an important range that is usually the responsibility of local government. Such services in most Western countries include further education, museums, art galleries, central libraries, theatres, markets, shopping and sports centres, parks and so forth.

The *second objective* of the new local system in Britain is that of *service efficiency* which seeks to improve the quality of local government services by enlarging the average population size of local government units. The discussion of this objective in the reform literature is a little vague and in order to achieve some clarity it is necessary to introduce a more formal mode of argument. There are two assumptions implicit in the service efficiency objective. The first is that the scale of existing units is insufficient to enable them to provide services effectively – that is, to provide the service in its full range to currently accepted standards (see Royal Commission 1967d: paras. 33–102; 1967a: paras. 256–262). The second assumption is that the units in the old system were too small to reap all the possible economies of scale, especially economies of scale in management and cost control (see Royal Commission 1967c: paras. 8–10).

The evidence that the stated objectives of the reform were, or even could, be attained is by no means convincing. Insofar as the externalities mode of argument is concerned there is no evidence that the widening of the local boundaries will reduce them substantially. The town and hinterland argument is correct only for certain services such as transportation, but their unity masks also a marked disparity in the types of settlement pattern within the area which at the extremes have very distinctive functional needs. Insofar as the service efficiency objective is concerned serious doubts may be raised as to the alleged direct relationship between population and resources as well as to the assumption of economies of scale. It apparently assumes that the long-run cost curve declines for the same level of output for all services – education, social welfare, highways, housing, police and so forth.

The pursuit of the two functionalist objectives just discussed has meant that British local authorities are, as Table 2 (see above) suggests, among the largest in the Western world. Despite the claims of the 1972 White Paper that the new units would be created "above all else" on the basis that a "genuine local democracy implies that decisions should be taken as locally as possible" (Department of Environment 1971: 6), the smallest units of the two-tier system, the districts (including the London boroughs), are on average in excess of 130,000 population. In some of the remoter rural areas this means "genuine local democracy" operates in areas of forty miles across, and districts where the seat of government is ten miles from quite large population centres within the district are common. At the county level, which provides most of the major functions, the situation is even more extraordinary. The average population of the English and Welsh counties (including the Greater London Council) is in excess of 800,000, and in some instances the seat of government is half a day's travel from the largest centres of population within the county.

The explanation for the huge local authorities in Britain is unlikely to lie in any distinctive sociogeographic characteristic. One factor which could account for larger local government units in Britain than elsewhere is the absence of an intermediate tier of administration between the localities and central government. This means that in Britain there is no alternative other than local government itself for providing non-central local services. It follows that there is much greater pressure on the local government system to be functionally appropriate. Moreover, in the absence of an intermediate tier the relationship between centre and locality is predominantly functional, every central department having its own link with the equivalent department at the local level. This enhances the tendency to view local government as first and foremost a provider of services. In France, by contrast, the small scale of the average comune is tolerable precisely because it is predominantly a political unit. With its political role overshadowed by its functional role, local government in Britain, is that much more vulnerable to the charge of functional incapacity. This peculiarity of the British system could be a factor accounting for the difference between the size of British local authorities and those of other comparable countries. There are other factors to which we have referred earlier to which we must now return.

8.6 The Penalties of Centralization

The first of these to be considered is the assumption that functional effectiveness can only be achieved by larger local authorities and that a larger unit is required in order to provide the resources and the population to make it possible to provide the full range of a given service to currently demanded levels. This looks a reasonably straightforward aim, but when it is translated into concrete services it is usually transformed so that what is being assessed is not only whether the existing structure is adequate for the performance of the main aspects of the service, but also whether it is adequate for coping with those relatively marginal additions to the service that are currently being seen as necessary for its improvement and which naturally concern the professional groups who operate it. But these relatively marginal innovations – the emblems of professionalism as it were – may be, give or take a tendency to professional modishness, essential for the improvement of the service. However, they can hardly be said to constitute the fundamentals of the service. The evidence of many of the professional groups to the *Redcliffe-Maud Commission* clearly reveals this tendency to confuse the relatively marginal with the fundamental[3] and it is perhaps best illustrated in the report of a national survey on the quality of local education authorities in relation to population size submitted to the *Commission by the Department of Education and Science*. This survey was derived from the subjective assessments Her Majesty's Inspectorate (HMI) and its principle conclusion was that: "the probability of good performance from an education authority increases with size and the probability of below acceptable performance decreases rapidly with size" (see Royal Commission 1969: 231). This is an unambiguous conclusion, yet the twelve performance indicators on which it was based could hardly be said to measure comprehensively the principle components of an education service.

The next functionalist assumption which needs a great deal more scrutiny than it seems to during the reorganization process is that which claims increased population size, seemingly any increase, brings economies of scale. Obviously a great deal more attention needs to be given to devising service performance indicators before we can say with any degree of confidence at what level of output economies are likely to occur for the major local services. Whether or not such indicators can be devised is an open question. Moreover there seems to be some fairly strong grounds for assuming that the whole discussion of economies of scale in local government is misconceived for, as we noted earlier unlike the output of a manufacturing process, which tends to be capital intensive, many local public services are inherently labour intensive. Increasing scale therefore is unlikely to lower average costs and may increase them because the need for more elaborate supervision and coordination structures occasioned by the inevitable increase in the territorial spread of the local authority arising from enlargement. This is especially so for those services which entail the provision of service delivery institutions (SDI). Such services include schools, libraries and welfare clinics. We will return to these services in a moment. If economies of scale do exist they are more likely to arise in the vertically integrated natural monopoly local services, such as water supply and sewerage.

Another possible source of increasing costs arising from the enlargement is derived from the *differing service needs of urban and rural areas*. When increasing scale involves the extention of the urban unit to include a rural and quasi-rural hinterland, it is likely that the range and the higher technological content of services that is necessary for the urban area will be extended to the rural sector as well, irrespective of need. This is because professional pressures will always be exerted in the direction of uniformity, and uniformity that is achieved by levelling up the technological input rather than levelling it down. This upward levelling process can mean that one consequence of centralization can be marked improvement in services whether or not such an improvement was demanded at the level of increased taxes it entailed. A less ambigous gain from reorganization arises where a city was previously divided into a number of separate jurisdictions. In this instance, considerable redistribution can occur since the costs of the poorer, and therefore high public consumption, areas are spread over the city as a whole.

A third possible source of increased costs has nothing necessarily to do with scale per se so much as the *costs of institutional change*. Some increases in expenditures will be inevitable because of the extra costs entailed in the process of changeover from the old institutions to the new. Such costs are likely to be quite heavy; one estimated cost of implementing the Redcliffe-Maud proposals in 1970 was put as high as £ 200,000,000 (see Cheshire County Council 1970). It may be claimed, however, that such costs must be related to the 'life' of the new system: the longer the new system lasts without change the longer the period over which the transititional costs ought to be spread. There remain, though, other costs entailed in the changeover that are not once-and-for-all-costs, but are permanent increases in local expenditure. In short, reorganization may lead to a secular upward shift in the level of expenditure. How might this come about?

We may hypothesize with a reasonable degree of confidence that for any particular public service at any point in time and at any level of output, the executants of the service (both technocrat and politician but especially the former) will favour an increase rather than a decrease in the resources allocated to that service. All government agencies, as Wildavsky (1975: 7) has emphasized, would like more resources. In the normal course of events such expansionary predispositions are seldom satisfied due to the normal processes of financial control. But when the organization comes to an end, which is what happens in a re-organization process like the 1972 Act, such normal processes of restraint can in the nature of the case no longer operate with their customary rigour and the new order offers the

Tab. 3

	Local Expenditure as a % Public Expenditure	Local Expenditure as a % of G. N. P.
Average Annual Percentage Increase 1966–1975	0.6	0.5
Percentage Increase 1974–1975	1.2	1.6

chance for all who want to increase their allocation to do so to an extent that is not possible in a stable institutional setting.

This *tendency for wholesale institutional change to lead to increased expenditure* is powerfully re-enforced by the need to maintain staff morale during the crucial transition period from the old to the new order. For during this period there are inevitable uncertainties about who among the staff of the old system is to be found a place in the new, and who is not. Moreover, not only are there uncertainties for the staff, there are also extra tasks to be undertaken since the level of services has to be maintained while at the same time the problems the changeover have to be coped with. Both additional burdens require compensating incentives and rewards for the bureaucracy and these usually take the form of overmanning in the new system, or increased remuneration, or both.

Where, as is the case in the new local government system, two conflicting objectives were pursued at the same time – enlarged master planning authorities and larger second tier units with planning control powers – exploiting economies of scale becomes doubly difficult and not only has it proved almost impossible to economize on staffs generally, land use planning staffs have had to be expanded by no less than 70 percent (see James 1975: 165).

For all these reasons it is likely that institutional change in government on the scale of the 1972 Act will lead to an increase in expenditure even when the object of the change is to reduce costs. There is certainly some prima facie evidence that the new system did increase local government expenditure. As Table 3 reveals, both as a percentage of the total public sector and as a percentage of G.N.P., local government expenditure rose in the first year of the new order more than the previous ten years average. As a percentage of public sector expenditure it was twice the previous ten year average, and as a percentage of G.N.P., it increased by no less than three times the ten year average.[4]

8.7 Service Dilution and Institutional Density

It must be emphasized that the preceding discussion of the possible diseconomies of reorganization does not imply that there will be no economies of scale to be exploited, but, rather, that greater account ought to be taken of the possible diseconomies. Nor is it claimed that the inevitable tendency to uniformity of service provision arising from joining up town and country will necessarily always entail the triumph of the urban service mode. In some cases the reverse process is likely, particularly where there is the possibility of combining cost reduction with admin-istry convenience. Even where the extension of rural standards is not a motive, a reduction in the number of SDI with lower running costs, and we may assume that the desire to do so will be all the greater precisely because costs will rise with enlarged jurisdictions for horizontally integrated services. Indeed it may well be that the reduction in the density of SDI's is assumed to be necessary in order to achieve the very economies of scale the reorganization was supposed to bring!

Besides combatting rising horizontal integration costs, a further incentive to reduce the number of SDI's is that it will also reduce the management task. Such incentives for bureaucrats and politicians should never be under-estimated and, as we noted earlier there are reasonably strong grounds for assuming that a precisely comparable incentive strongly influenced the whole reform process itself in Britain. Moreover, even if costs and management tasks were unaffected, a tendency to reduce the number of institutions will persist simply because the enlargement of area will tend over time to lower institutional density for the same reason that a reduction in the area of jurisdiction will tend to increase overall institutional density. This is because, assuming that institutional provision is mandatory, a small jurisdiction will provide at least one institution as an absolute minimum. A similar tendency may be hypothesized for senior specialist staff as well: the smaller the size of the units of administration the larger the number of such staff per capita[5].

The consequences of wider jurisdictions may be summarized as comprising a *decline in the number of service delivery points with its consequent increased travel by consumers and service dilution* because those SDI's that remain have to cope with a larger throughput without necessarily a corresponding increase in fixed capital. Reducing institutional density is politically less costly than might be supposed because the dilution of the service that results, both in terms of accessibility (longer distances to be travelled by users) or the dilution of the service itself (larger classes in schools, longer queues at library check-outs, more crowded swimming pools, larger and hence more impersonally managed residential institutions), is unlikely to be perceived by the user in the direct way that it would be perceived for those services where there is an accepted and comprehensible standard of service. Thus a longer wait at the library check-out may be unperceived, but a reduction in the number of times per week garbage is removed will create a public furore.

These effects of jurisdictional enlargement may entail improvement so that the larger and more remote institutions may have a more highly qualified staff; the more crowded swimming pool a sauna, the more centralized library a computerized checking system and a record section, and so forth. Although such technological adornments have no fundamental effect on the quality of the basic services being provided, they do serve to sugar the pill of dilution and remoteness in an age where technological innovation is highly prized.

The tendency for institutional density to decline with enlargement centralization also arises because of the psychological effect of the enlargement of jurisdiction on the decision maker's conception of the task. For although they may establish outstationed administrative machinery to reduce lines of communication, they will always tend to take the new jurisdiction as given and to view it as a manageable unit whole irrespective of its scale. This has the effect of both obscuring spatial variation and of reducing the importance of distance. Thus we may find decision-makers in the federal government in Washington discussing Texas and Alaska with the same easy familiarity that decision-makers talk about neighbourhoods in a small country town. That is the logic of their task.

Lowering institutional density will have its most adverse effect on certain client groups, such as school children with special learning problems, the inmates of old peoples and childrens homes and their relatives and friends. Such groups, it may be assumed, tend to be drawn disproportionately from that section of the population without cars so that they are dependent on some form of public transport in order to traverse the increase distances entailed. In some areas there may not be any public transport.

Similar penalties for the relatively poor and the car-less arise from centralization especially in rural areas in relation to the central institutions of the enlarged government. In Britain this is especially likely for housing, planning and the payment of local taxes. In sum, the enlargement of local government units in general, and rural ones in particular, may produce economies, but they will not be of scale, but, rather, result from shifting production costs to the consumer by reducing delivery points and diluting output. Both represent a decline in the quality of government for most and will tend to discriminate particularly against the poor.

8.8 Conclusions

In assessing the capacity of the centre to effect the necessary coordination over the sub-national system in a world in which such coordination may be becoming increasingly necessary, and yet because of the need to achieve more complex objectives increasingly difficult, there may be a temptation to overestimate the capacity of the sub-national system to thwart the centre's intentions. The formal, institutional-cum-political approach to intergovernmental relations, with its attend-ent assumption of a single, unitary and unimpeded will emanating from the centre and reaching down to every service delivery point, may well be a travesty. Whatever the attraction of exposing its errors, however, they must be resisted if the result is that in order to emphasize the interdependence and bargaining nature of all organizational relationships, however well intentioned, we dissolve away the consequences of hierarchy and authority. A French prefect, for example, may have to face both ways and in so doing become an important defender of a commune's interests. However, his ultimate dependence on, and membership of, the Ministry of the Interior means that if the Ministry is determined on action towards the communes it is better placed to achieve it than in a system where there is no equivalent of the prefect. And this will be true despite the *cumul des mandats,* for access is not automatic power. Similarly, we may presume with some degree of confidence that, despite any number of similarities, a Canadian province's capacity to count with the federal government in Ottawa when there are crucial interests at stake is not the same as the status of a Danish rural commune with the central government in Copenhagen.

The incorporation of concepts and research drawn from organizational theory has unquestionably enriched and improved our understanding of interorganizational relations[6]; especially in respect of the inherent reciprocity and inter-dependence even in what were alleged to be the most rigidly structured hierarchies (see Thoenig 1978; Ashford 1982). It may also be conceded that all interorganizational relationships are in some sense exchange relationships. But it would be pointless to press these similarities beyond their very obvious limits where applied to all forms of governmental relations between the centre and all sub-national systems. Organizational slack, information monopoly, exclusive executant responsibility, and operational expertise are crucial guides to the understanding of the inherent power of sub-national systems, but they are not of equal importance, when the centre is committed to action, as legal powers, the existence of central field agents, or fiscal capacity. Assessing the distribution of power between actors in any situation is a monstrously difficult exercise, not least because of the law of anticipated reactions. Intergovernmental relations is not in any sense exempt from this problem; if anything, the reverse. However, intractability must not be the excuse for what is essentially a diversionary tactic, however tempting that option may be. In this case adopting an essentially generalized descriptive mode for a specific explanatory purpose. Not to put too fine a point on it, *government is not just another organization.*

Equally, informal systems of power distribution arising from multiple office holding and locality rules for central legislators, can enable decentral units to by-pass formal hierarchies with striking consequences for their autonomy. But parallel informal system are just as open to the centre as to the localities, whether the chosen parallel channel is that of the political party or the national professional community, or – most effective of all – the whole sub-national aggregation.

We need perhaps to give a great deal more attention to these *informal top-down parallel power system* if we are to get to grips with the less obtrusive strategies for coordinating the sub-national system that are open to the centre. As we have seen there is, first, the possibility of appealing to party loyalty where sub-national systems are run on party lines. Second, the centre can seek to change the policy context by altering the operating ideology.

The British experience suggests, third, that the centre can exert pressure on the sub-national system even to the extent of obtruding its will into such a fundamental aspect of the sub-national system as the budget. This may be especially the case for a system like the British where the capacity for very swift and concerted action by the centre are possibly greater than in most Western systems. For there is no written constitution which delimits the power of the centre in relation to local government, moreover, the doctrine of ultra vires provides the centre with potentially unlimited power. On the other hand, there are sufficient common features of the financial structure of sub-national systems of most Western states that are likely to ease the path for the centre if it does seek to apply some form of monetarist-inspired reduction in aggregate expenditure of the sub-national system.

In extreme cases the centre may resort to changing the very sub-national structure itself so as to minimize control deficits, or, it may exploit its inherent resource advantage so as to achieve the necessary compliance. In such cases it seems the coordination of the subnational system can be achieved, but this may well be at the expense of its democratic substance as well as at the expense of its effectiveness.

For one consequence of local unit enlargement is the reduction in the accessibility, in all its senses, of the local government system to the general public. This decline is of key importance because, of all the attributes of a decentral system of government, relative accessibility as compared with national government, is inherent and as such makes a vital contribution to the 'democraticness' of the national state. For the vast majority of citizens democracy at the national level is a sham since they can have only the most marginal influence on those who govern them. A decentral level of government has the unique advantage of mitigating this fact by bringing the point of decision for collective action closer geographically to the ordinary citizen.

Moreover one important consequence of enlargement may be a general weakening among the citizenry of a sense of identity with their local government.

The decline in accessibility consequent upon enlargement also occurs in relation to the consumption of public services. For enlarged jurisdictions are likely to lead to the lowering of the density of service delivery institutions. Those who lack their own means of transport will be hardest hit and they are precisely the group which need accessibility most for a wide range of public service (lending libraries, child care homes, old age homes, welfare clinics and schools) since they cannot afford market substitutes.

The third probable consequence is the dilution of the quality of local service delivery as the new enlarged units seek to achieve the economies of scale that they assume will arise from the increased scale of service production.

As we have emphasized, the enlargement of local units has gone further in the U.K. than elsewhere, so it cannot be claimed that the British experience is typical. However, it is the extreme nature of the British change that may reveal the key problems in their starkest form that are likely to arise from the centralizing effects of all reorganization generally. Moreover, since the U.K. was the first industrialized country and is also the most urbanized (less than 2½ per cent of the workforce are engaged in agriculture) the socio-geograhic case for reorganization was, within its own terms, almost certainly stronger so it could be claimed that, on the assumption that urbanization is a function of continuing industrialization, the British experience is possibly a harbinger for other Western states.

Notes

1   Webb and Wistow (1980: 74) have called it the "guiding philosophy" by which they mean "the broad objectives, ideologies and values which are the hallmarks of policy". Davies (1977: Append. 10) has called the same phenomenon the "policcy paradigm" and in a slightly different and more refined sense that is more akin to the personal belief system of policymakers, Young (1977: 3) has coined the term "assumptive world".
2   Also see B. Hjern's essay in the same volume in which the party effect is briefly mentioned.
3   See for example, the evidence of the Association of Child Care Officers, the Town Planning Institute, the Association of Medical Officers, and the Institute of Municipal Treasurers and Accountants, all in Royal Commission (1967b).

4 I am grateful to Ken Newton for suggesting to me the possibility that the striking increase in local authority expenditure in 1974/75 might be attributable to reorganization.
5 See E. James' "Frontiers in the Welfare State" (1966). This is one of the very few pieces of systematic research that examines the negative effect of increased territorial size on the provision of local government services.
6 For a discussion of the case for applying interorganizational theory to central-local relations, see Rhodes (1979: Append. I). Also see Jones (1980) and Rhodes (1981). For some of the interorganizational literature on which the Rhodes thesis is based see Negandhi (1975).

References

Advisory Commission on Intergovernmental Relations (1955): *Report of the Advisory Committee on Local Government*. Washington D. C.

Alcaly, R. E., and D. Mermelstein (eds.) (1977): *The Fiscal Crisis of American Cities*. New York: Random House.

Alexander, A. (1982): *Local Government in Britain since Reorganization*. London: Allen & Unwin.

Ashford, D. E. (1982): *British Dogmatism and French Pragmatism*. London: Allen & Unwin.

Birnbaum, P. (1979): "'Office Holders' in the Local Politics of the French Fifth Republic." In: Lagroye, J., and V. Wright (eds.), *Local Government in Britain and France*, 114–126. London: Allen & Unwin.

Bradford, D. F., R. A. Malt, and W. E. Oates (1969): *The Rising Costs of Public Services*. In: National Tax Journal 22/2: 185–202.

Burgess, T., and T. Travers. (1980): *Ten Billions Pounds*. London: Grant McIntyre.

Cheshire County Council (1970): *Cost of Reform*. Chester.

Council of Europe (1976): The Financial Structures of Local and Regional Authorities in Europe: *Study Series on Local and Regional Authorities in Europe* 2/13: Strasbourg: Council of Europe.

Davies, R. (1977): "The Measurement of Needs and the Allocation of Grant." In *Report of the Committee of Enquiry into Local Government Finance*, Cmnd. 6453, Append. 10. London: HSMO.

Department of Environment (1971): *White Paper: Local Government in England*. Cmnd 4584. London: HSMO.

Dunleavy, P. (1980): *Urban Political Analysis*. London: Macmillan.

Dunleavy, P. (1981): *The Politics of Mass Housing in Britain 1946–1975*. Oxford: Clarendon Press.

Fried, R. (1973): *Comparative Urban Performance*. Los Angeles: Univ. of California Press.

Gunsteren, H. van (1976): *The Quest of Control*. London: Wiley.

Hanf, K. (1978): "Introduction." In Hanf, K., and F. W. Scharpf (eds.), *Interorganizational Policymaking: Limits of Coordination and Central Control*, 1–19. London: Sage.

Heller, W. W. (1966): *New Dimensions of Political Economy*. Cambridge, Mass. Harvard Univ. Press.

Hjern, B. (1978): "The Management of Financial Incentives in Social Policy." In Hanf, K., and F. W. Scharpf (eds.), *Interorganizational Policymaking*, 273–303. London: Sage.

James, E. (1966): "Frontiers of the Welfare State." *Public Administration* 44/4: 132–138.

James, J. R. (1975): "Lessons from the Past." *Town and Country Planning 43: 162–167.*

Jones, G. W. (ed.)(1980): New Approaches to the Study of Central Local Relationships. Farnborough: Gower.

Mackenzie, W. J. M. (1954): "Local Government and Parliament." *Public Administration* 32/4: 409–425.

Negandhi, A. R. (ed.) (1975): *Interorganizational Theory*. Kent, Ohio: Univ. Press.

Newton, K. (1981): *Balancing the Books*. London: Sage.

Rhodes, R. A. W. (1979): "Research into Central-Local Government Relations in Britain: A Framework for Analysis." In Rhodes, R. A. W. (ed.), *Central-Local Government Relationships,* 121–139. London. SSRC.

Rhodes, R. A. W. (1981): *Control and Power in Central-Local Relation*. Farnborough: Gower.

Royal Commission on Local Government in England (1967a): *Written Evidence of the Ministry of Housing and Local Government*. London: HSMO.

Royal Commission on Local Government in England (1967b): *Written Evidence of the Professional Associations*. London: HSMO.

Royal Commission on Local Government in England (1967c): *Written Evidence of H. M. Treasury*. London: HSMO.

Royal Commission on Local Government in England (1967d): *Written Evidence of Department of Education and Science*. London: HSMO.

Royal Commission on Local Government in England (1969): *Report* (Vol. III). Cmnd 4040. London: HSMO.

Royal Commission in Local Government in Scotland (1969): *Report*. Cmnd 4150. Edinburgh: HSMO.

Scharpf, F. W. (1978): "Interorganizational Policy Studies: Issues, Concepts and Perspectives." In Hanf, K., and F. W. Scharpf (eds.), *Interorganizational Policymaking,* 345–371. London: Sage.

Scharpf, F. W., B. Reissert, and F. Schnabel (1975): *Control Deficits in Multi-Level Problem Solving*. Berlin: International Institute of Management.

Scharpf, F. W., B. Reissert, and F. Schnabel (1978): "Policy Effectiveness and Conflict Avoidance in Intergovernmental Policy Formation." In Hanf, K., and F. W. Scharpf (eds.), *Interorganizational Policymaking,* 57–115. London. Sage.

Sharpe, L. J. (1976): "Instrumental Participation and Urban Government." In Griffith, J. A. G. (ed.), *From Policy to Administration,* 115–139. London: Allen & Unwin.

Sharpe, L. J. (1977): "Whitehall – Structures and People." In Kavanagh, D., and R. Rose (eds.), *New Trends in British Politics: Issues for Research,* 87–115. London: Sage.

Sharpe, L. J. (1978a): "'Reforming' the Grass Roots: An Alternative Analysis." In Butler, D., and A. Halsey (eds.), *Policy Politics,* 82–110. London: Macmillan.

Sharpe, L. J. (1978b): "Modernizing the Localities: Local Government Reorganization in Britain and Some Comparisons with France." In Lagroye, J., and V. Wrifht (eds.), *Local Government in Britain and France,* 42–73. London: Allen & Unwin.

Sharpe, L. J. (1979): "Decentralist Trends in Western Democracies: A First Appraisal." In Sharpe, L. J. (ed.), *Decentralist Trends in Western Democracies,* 9–79. London: Sage.

Sharpe, L. J. (1981a) "Does Politics Matter?" In Newton, K. (ed.), *Urban Political Economy,* 5–47. London: Frances Pinter.

Sharpe, L. J. (ed.) (1981b): *The Local Fiscal Crisis in Western Europe. Myths and Reality*. London: Sage.

Thoenig, J. C. (1978): "State Bureaucracies and Local Government in France." In Hanf, K., and F. W. Scharpf (eds.), *Interorganizational Policymaking,* 167–201. London: Sage.

Warren, R. L. et al. (1975): "The Interaction of Community Decision Organizations: Considerations and Empirical Findings." In Negandhi, A. R. (ed.), *Interorganizational Theory,* 145–160. Kent, Ohio: Univ. Press.

Webb, A., and G. Wistow (1980): "Implementation, Central-Local Relations and the Personal Social Services." In Jones, G. W. (ed.), *New Approaches to the Study of Central-Local Government Relationships,* 69–83. Farnborough: Gower.

Wildavsky, A. (1975): *Budgeting*. Boston: Little & Brown.

Wright, D. S. (1974): "Inter-Governmental Relations: An Analytical Overview." *The Annals* 416 (Nov.): 1–17.

Wright, V. (1979): "Regionalization Under the French Fifth Republic." In Sharpe, L. J. (ed.), *Decentralist Trends in Western Democracies*, 193–234. London: Sage.

Young, K. G. (1977): "Values in the Policy Process." *Policies and Politics* 5: 1–22.

9. The Hidden Public Sector:
The 'Quangocratization' of the World?

Christopher Hood

Abstract

This paper explores the world of 'para-government' or 'para-state' organizations (styled here as PGOs). It is in three main parts, as follows:

(1) PGOs: A Chameleon Concept? *This part stresses that what is to count as a PGO depends largely on the observer's frame of reference. This is partly a matter of different traditions of thought and partly of the different constitutional bases on which government rests in different countries.*

(2) The Animals in the Zoo. *No attempt is made to produce a Linnaean classification of PGOs; but this part of the paper attempts to demonstrate some of the variations that can exist in types of PGOs, by picking out three dimensions of difference:*

   (a) Mode of Creation – contrasting 'top-down', 'bottom-up' and 'sideways-across' styles;
   (b) Formal Status – contrasting PGOs which are unambiguously 'public' in formal status and those which are in some way constituted as private or independent enterprises;
   (c) Principal Resource – contrasting the resources of 'nodality', 'treasure', 'authority' and 'organization' as bases for PGO operations.

   Combining the first decompositions of each of these dimensions produces a 24-part typology of PGOs.

(3) PGOs in a Broader Context. *This part considers a number of different ways in which the development of PGOs can be interpreted, the relation between PGO development and government growth, and the consequences of a PGO-intensive style of government for the questions of 'control' and 'coordination' which later sections of the book attempt to analyze.*

9.1 Introduction

To explore the world of 'para-government' or 'para-state' organizations is to raise both conceptual and constitutional issues as to how the boundaries of 'government' are to be perceived or defined. The 'para-government' or 'para-state' organization (hereafter 'PGO', for convenience) is a phenomenon which is both ubiquitous and elusive (cf. Sharkansky 1979: XI). It is a chameleon, in that it is capable of appearing in a variety of ways, depending on the constitutional or conceptual frame of reference which is used by the observer.

This chapter develops that theme, in three main sections. The first shows some of the different ways in which PGOs can be defined and seen as a 'problem' for conventional ways of understanding government. The second and main section gives some indication of the diversity of enterprises which fall within this general institutional category, without attempting any rigid or exhaustive classification. The third section sets the PGO phenomenon in a broader ideological context; looks at it in the context of government growth; and briefly raises some of the issues which PGOs pose for co-ordination and control in the 'public sector', which are analyzed in the next part of this book.

9.2 PGOs: A Chameleon Concept?

The concept of a PGO is an extraordinarily slippery one, dependent as it is on what one chooses to define as the 'core' of government or of the 'state'. What is to count as a PGO depends to a very large extent on the observer's frame of reference. That frame will vary according to the particular tradition of thought from which the political world is viewed, and also according to the particular constitutional or legal base which is used to define the 'core' of government.

PGOs in a 'Liberal' Perspective

Two important ways of 'seeing' PGOs can serve to illustrate the point. One way of seeing the public sector is through the 'public/private' spectacles of liberalism – a tradition of thought which has been immensely important in shaping the way that government is viewed in modern democracies. The desirability of making a clear distinction between the province of government and that of private or independent action is a basic tenet of liberalism. Not to be able to make such a distinction, from a liberal viewpoint, is to be driven into one or both of two unacceptable positions. One is to accept the existence of *imperium in imperio,* the devolution of governmental powers to private or independent interests which are 'irresponsible' in a constitutional sense (this was, of course, the ground on which the US Supreme Court struck down Roosevelt's 'corporatist' National Recovery Administration in the 1930s, and it is a very common liberal line of attack against PGOs). The other is to adopt a totalitarian definition of the state, in which there is no 'private life', and in which *every* organization, down to and including the family, is by definition an agency of government (cf. Hayek 1944).

Liberal assumptions are deeply rooted in conventional European ideas about government. They are reflected, for instance, in conventions of national accounting, which show transactions between the 'public' and the 'private' sector – presupposing that those sectors are definable and relatively distinct – and in conventions of political responsibility which rest upon the same assumption. How then is the liberal tradition to come to terms with the blurring of the 'public/private' distinction, so commonly perceived by observers of modern mixed-economy societies? It is often asserted that we are in a hopeless mess about the use of the terms 'public' and 'private' (see, for example, Mackenzie 1967: 272) and that these traditional categories of liberal thought have lost some of their capacity to enable us to comprehend the modern world.

It is in this context – recoiling from the logic of describing as a 'government agency' *any* organization which is linked to the discharge of government functions or purposes in some way – that the liberal understanding of government can be kept alive by the invention of the concept of PGOs. Conveniently attaching a variety of 'para', 'quasi', 'semi' and other prefixes to 'government' offers at least a semantic way out of the difficulty presented by those organizations which are not easy to categorize as 'government' or as 'private or independent' – a class of institutions which are far too common in the modern world to be dismissed as occasional aberrations. Examples might include ostensibly 'private' charities which operate in practice as full-time agents of government (Bradshaw 1980; Cousins in Barker 1982: 161); 'independent' religious bodies dispensing government licensing powers which affect the livelihood of individuals (Alderman 1982); 'private' firms manipulated into existence by and dependent on government for their operations – in some cases trading with other ostensibly 'private' firms of similar provenance (Weidenbaum 1969).

Increased awareness of this class of institutional arrangements by observers of government over the past twenty years or so has led to the invention of a variety of terms and metaphors. Alan Pifer of the Carnegie Corporation coined the term 'quasi-non-government organization' in the late 1960s (Pifer 1967), as a result of observing a growing tendency for US public policy to be delivered through 'independent' not-for-profit organizations. That term was later telescoped into the notorious and much-abused buzzword 'quango', which has had an odd political history in Britain (Barker 1982: 219–25). Other terms for the phenomenon include 'the contract state', 'the new political economy' (Smith and Hague 1971), 'the modern public sector' (Weidenbaum 1969). Schuppert (1981: 278) speaks of the 'osmosis'of state and society, Sharkansky (1979: 3) of the 'incoherent' modern state. It is very significant that there is yet no generally accepted term in international discourse for the 'PGO' phenomenon.

One way of understanding the concept of PGOs is thus as an intellectual invention springing from the difficulties of those schooled (perhaps unconsciously) in liberal thought in describing the modern world of 'interpenetration' between government institutions and those of the wider society. Other intellectual traditions – Marxism, conservatism, the various theocratic creeds – scarcely need such an invention, since they take 'interpenetration' for granted and may indeed advocate it as an element of the good society. For instance, Edmund Burke believed that good government could only be guaranteed when a landed aristocracy presided over all social institutions: where 'state' ended and 'society' began was immaterial (Dyson 1980: 189). Socialist ideas of working-class dominance have similar implications.

PGOs in a 'Constitutional' Perspective

A second, slightly different, way in which PGOs can come onto an intellectual agenda is as phenomena which do not fit easily into conventional constitutional ideas of what are to be taken as the 'basic' or 'core' institutions of government. Seen from this viewpoint, PGOs do not solely – or even necessarily – consist of institutions which are awkward to place in the liberal dichotomy of 'public' versus 'private or independent'. Even unambiguously 'public' organizations may be problematic in terms of their place in the conventional framework of government, and thus come to be denoted as PGOs. Examples might include international public organizations which do not quite square with traditional (that is, French Revolutionary) doctrines of national 'sovereignty'; 'network' organizations which span different levels of government and so may be hard to reconcile with simple ideas as to how elected public officials are to be made accountable to their voters; or, in responsible-government systems, semi-independent bodies which violate the conventional idea of government responsibility to the legislature via ministers.

The 'liberal' and the 'constitutional' perspectives offer similar, but by no means identical, ways of defining PGOs, both as a population and as a 'problem'. Moreover, the constitutional perspective – beginning with assumptions about what constitutes the institutional 'core' of government or of the 'state' – will yield a different class of organizations to be defined as PGOs according to the constitutional tradition that is taken as the starting-point. The concept of PGOs does not 'travel' at all well across national boundaries if this perspective is taken.

There are, for instance, basic differences in vocabulary which reflect different assumptions about the 'core' of government. The predominant use of the term 'state' on the Continent of Europe and of 'government' in the common-law countries to refer to the ordering of the office of authority, is no mere difference of idiom. The 'state' societies of Continental Europe, building on Roman law, take 'the public power' to be a unitary, distinctive over-arching legal entity wielded by and embodied in a broad and impersonal concept of office. In the USA and Britain, the 'state' in this sense barely exists at all as a legal concept (in spite of confusing elements such as the office of Secretary of State). A number of identified public officials and authorities each 'separately and severally' act and own property in their own name; there is no concept of 'the public power' as a unity in the Roman law sense (cf. Dyson 1980). There is a presumption that each new public agency that is set up may need to have its legal powers specified *de novo* and separately in relation to every case' (Johnson 1973: 131; 1979). There is no standard framework of legal devices (such as *Anstalt* or *établissement public*) by which 'the public power' may be delegated to subordinate public agencies.

Given such differences, it is not surprising that the notion of PGOs is not freely exchangeable between the 'state' societies and the 'government' societies. The 'state' tradition of a unitary public power embodied in a general apparatus of office tends to assume that the boundaries of the public sector will normally be defined by the presence of public bureaucrats (Johnson 1973: 19–20) and that public functions will normally be discharged by public-law enterprises. Deviations from such norms – for instance in the erosion of a clear distinction between public-law and private-law organizations in the public service (cf. Schuppert 1981: 76, 149) – may be seen as belonging to an institutionally 'grey' area. But no such norms exist in the Anglo-Saxon tradition, where there is no real distinction between public and private law in the Roman-law sense and where public functions have long been discharged by institutions such as citizen powers of arrest and prosecution, lay judges, jury service (and analogous devices for the collection of taxes, used well into the present century), citizen militias – even 'private' corporations for the administration of justice, in the case of the English Inns of Court. Such things are not 'abnormal' elements challenging an orthodox idea of government's 'core': they are central to the tradition of public authority.

The 'state' societies and the 'government' societies will not therefore count the same kinds of institutions as PGOs. Moreover, the definition of a PGO will not even travel freely *within* each of these two groups, given the very different constitutional assumptions that each contains as to what constitutes the 'core' of government or of 'the state'. One obvious instance is the difference between those societies where the 'core' of government is seen as essentially unitary and those where it is seen as essentially dispersed.

Within the 'government' group, the Westminster-type responsible-government doctrine of the 'core' of government is very difficult to reconcile with autonomous public boards at national-government level; organizations of that kind have proved notoriously awkward to 'place' constitutionally in such a system, and hence may be denoted as PGOs. In a Washington-type separation-of-powers system, public boards only present a 'problem' in so far as they may be seen to cut across the doctrine of separation of powers, particularly when it comes to the exercise of regulatory powers: it is this which leads to what Freedman (1978: 9) asserts to be a persisting sense of uneasiness and concern about the place of such agencies in the machinery of US government. The quite different constitutional bases from which the discussion of PGOs proceeds in the USA and the UK is well illustrated by the curious fate of the term 'quango', which was alluded to earlier. In the USA it was used for a time to denote organizations which were hard to fit into a 'public/private' scheme of things (such as not-for-profit government contractors), but in the UK it came to be applied to unambiguously public enterprises which did not fit into the conventional 'core' doctrine of ministerial responsibility.

Similarly, within the 'state' societies, the precise connotation of 'the state' is both amorphous (d'Entreves 1967: 168) and variable: Dyson (1980: 16) remarks that 'It is clear that there is a great variety of incompatible or ill-fitting views about the concept of the state in Continental Europe'. For instance, political parties are conceived as part of the state in the German Federal Republic, but not in France, where 'state' institutions and representative institutions are seen as quite separate entities. On the other hand, the German universities are less squarely counted as part of the 'general services of the state' than is the case in France.

There is therefore no single PGO 'problem' and no single way of defining PGOs which would be meaningful for all countries. Perhaps this is one reason for the absence of a common term and of systematic cross-national research into such institutions. However, there are also some features which seem to be common to all industrialized countries. Three such features are particularly relevant to the themes of this book. First, a discussion goes on almost everywhere concerning institutional arrangements which cut perplexingly across traditional liberal distinctions of 'public' and 'private'. Second, there is similarly widespread awareness of a class of devices for discharging public business outside what have traditionally been conceived as the 'core' institutions of government in the constitutional idiom. Third, there is a widespread impression that the style of government represented by both kinds of institutions mentioned above has grown in importance everywhere. Are we really seeing 'the quangocratization of the world', to play on the title of Jacoby's (1973) interesting book *'The Bureaucratization of the World?'*

9.3 The Animals in the Zoo

I have remarked elsewhere (Hood in Barker 1982: 55) that the world of PGOs is a zoo containing many animals. Attempting to define and classify PGOs, as scholars such as Schuppert (1981) have done, is both a rewarding and a frustrating exercise (Mackenzie in Curnow and Wettenhall 1981; 408). Moreover, it is an exercise which governments themselves have to undertake whether they like it or not, if only in the making of decisions as to what is to be counted as 'public' spending, 'government' employees, 'government' responsibilities, and so forth (for example in the application of conditions of employment, pension audit arrangements). The exercise is rewarding because it sensitizes us to the wide heterogeneity of possible guises in which PGOs can appear. It is frustrating, because it also sensitizes us to the arbitrary and precarious nature of conventional definitions of the 'core' of government and to the lack of consistent or comprehensive documentation of government's margins (Sharkansky 1979).

No detailed classification of PGOs can be attempted here. But three dimensions of difference may serve initially to show some of the variety that the zoo can contain. These are (1) mode of emergence (2) legal status (3) mode of operation.

9.4 Mode of Emergence

PGOs may come into being in a variety of ways. Indeed, the development of PGOs in the modern style of government is capable of appearing 'all things to all men' for that reason. The development of PGOs can be looked at from a 'top-down' and from a 'bottom-up' view of government (cf. Barrett and Fudge 1981: 9) – and perhaps also from what might be called a 'sideways-across' perspective as well.

PGOs as a Vehicle of 'Top-Down' Government

A 'top-down' perspective on PGOs takes as its point of departure the 'centre' or apex of government and highlights the ways in which the 'core' apparatus of government may choose to do its business through unconventional or peripheral agencies – for reasons which may be good or bad, or disputed. Several authors, using this perspective, have discussed possible reasons or motivations for the development of PGOs (cf. Hood 1978: 30–46; Sharkansky 1979: 11–2, 74, 112–4; Schuppert 1981: 125 ff.). Some selective illustrations must suffice here.

There are, for instance, a cluster of 'black' motivations for the 'top-down' resort to PGOs. One is the desire to use such agencies for the pursuit of government goals by 'unacknowledgeable means' (Mackenzie 1950). Government may choose to discharge some of its business through disavowable and ostensibly independent 'front' agencies. Such agencies are commonly found in espionage (cf. Colby 1978) and foreign affairs, extending in the Israeli case to the deliberate obscuring of the parentage of government firms in order to facilitate commerce between Israel and countries that prefer to avoid officially acknowledging their dealings with Israel (Sharkansky 1979: 83). The marketing and selling of military equipment is a similar case, now widely performed by PGOs in western countries (in Britain, for example, 'International Military Supplies Ltd' supplies weapons to the world market in the guise of a private limited company – but it is wholly owned by the British government). A domestic example is the way that Italian political parties have financed themselves in part by means of donations under private company law from 'private' companies in which the Italian government has shareholdings, thus conveniently avoiding more direct 'raids' on public funds (the law was somewhat modified in 1974; see Vernon and Aharoni 1981: 72). The aim in such cases is to promote secrecy and, by building in 'deniability' (Rourke 1976: 36), avoid public responsibility or international embarrassment.

Closely related, and also a classic 'top-down' reason for resorting to PGOs is the handing of 'poisoned chalices' to outsiders as a means of taking the political 'heat' off the core institutions of government. Long ago, Machiavelli (1961: 106) observed that 'Princes give rewards and favours with their own hands, but death and punishment at the hands of others', and the same principle is often applied in the context of government intervention in sensitive fields of activity. For example, governments seeking to involve themselves in matters such as the promotion of the arts, birth control programmes, subsidy of newspapers or the provision of broadcasting facilities – areas that involve delicate and inevitably controversial issues of public taste, acceptability, 'balance' rather than 'bias' in selection, and the like – may resort to arms-length devices in an attempt to keep themselves out of first-line responsibility for such decisions. Examples are the German *Mittlerorganisationen* or the Swedish *Presstödsnämnden* which channels government money to newspapers.

Third, the 'top' or the 'centre' of government may use PGOs as vehicles for by-passing the jurisdictions of other agencies, governments, lower levels of government – even of the public auditor, where the latter's involvement might be thought to have a stultifying effect on initiative and risk-taking. The US federal government's use of 'federalism by contract' as a way of by-passing state governments in the 1960s Poverty Programme is a well-known and highly controversial example of this style of top-down PGO creation (cf. Moynihan 1970). The motivations involved in using PGOs in·this way, however, are by no means always of an unambiguously 'black' character. For instance, governments often operate through the medium of independent charitable organizations (such as the Konrad Adenauer Foundation or the Friedrich Ebert Foundation) as a means of delivering aid or relief programmes in circumstances where more direct operations by government's 'core' apparatus – in the form, say, of foreign troops operating in another government's territory – would raise many awkward political questions (cf. Eickmeier 1982: 11). For similar reasons, the organizations responsible for the maintenance of war graves abroad are deliberately placed at some remove from direct control by government's 'core' in Britain and the Federal Republic of Germany (Schuppert 1981: 29–30).

Fourth, the centre of government may turn to PGOs as a means of mobilizing what Ronge (1974) calls 'supplementary consent' for government activities. PGOs may be used as a device for co-opting interest group representatives as agents of government – a common explanation for the form of agencies such as the US Tennessee Valley Authority (Selznick 1949) and 'Concerted Action' in the Ministry of Economics in the Federal Republic of Germany (Schuppert 1981: 289–9).

Indeed, PGOs may even be used as a minor substitute for a 'spoils system' in countries which have a tradition of permanent civil service tenure – creating rewards, 'waiting rooms and exits' (Dogan 1975) for politicians and their followers. (If this were a significant factor in the development of PGOs, one might expect those countries with permanent-tenure civil sevice, such as Britain and Italy, to show the most luxuriant growth in PGOs?) Again, 'consensus-building' by such means can be 'read' in more than one way. It might be welcomed as allowing some degree of 'representative bureaucracy' and direct political oversight to be introduced into the administrative machine, following Andrew Jackson's famous doctrine of government responsiveness (Simon, Smithburg and Thompson 1950: 15). It might be attacked as a corrupt device which enables the Caligulas of modern politics to smuggle their favourite steeds into public office or to 'house-train' those who might otherwise be politically troublesome by giving them the illusion of access to power (Schuppert 1981: 163).

Fifth, and closely related, is the resort to PGOs as a means of 'load-shedding' by government's 'centre'. Sometimes, load is only 'shed' symbolically, and amounts to little more than an attempt to hide the real expansion in government's bureaucracy by inventing new categories of PGO whose staff do not appear in statistical returns for the public payroll, without any significant decentralization taking place in fact (the hiding of a large bulk of government activities by the expedient of PGOs which avoid orthodox bureaucratic reporting conventions is a theme of Sharkansky's (1979) study). There may, however, be more scope for such tactics in countries with a 'government' tradition than in countries with a 'state' tradition, since the latter tend to employ a much broader definition of the public service.

In other circumstances, the use of PGOs by the centre may represent a more serious attempt to shed load by delegation. For example, it may be seen as a way of mobilizing sources of expertise and specialist advice which lies outside government's direct domain – an application of Vannevar Bush's famous doctrine that government should 'put the contracts where the talent is'. For instance, one of the reasons for the importance of the 'semi-states' (as they are called) in the Republic of Ireland's administrative system is that, on independence from the UK in the 1920s, a vacuum at the top of the civil service resulted in rapid promotion for those with non-graduate qualifications. Subsequent trade union pressure for keeping graduates out of the Irish civil service has meant that the 'semi-states' have traditionally been the main repositories of graduate-level talent in government.

Alternatively, PGOs may be used as a means of shedding load by institutionalizing a distinction between 'executive work' and 'policy-making' in government. The doctrine that effective government requires separation of the 'policy-formulation' process from the actual 'doing' – policy 'delivery' or implementation – is a pervasive and recurrent one. It is regularly advanced by 'managerialists' like Drucker (1960) and by 'practical men' of all kinds. It is used to justify the sealing-off of many government agencies from mainstream processes of public accountability, on the grounds that such agencies can only 'get on with the job' and take a 'long view' of their subject if they are insulated to some degree from the political pressures of the moment (Hayward and Watson 1975: 161; Hogwood 1979); and, more generally, to separate the administrative 'doers' from the political dreamers and talkers (Wettenhall 1976: 2–3; Richardson 1979).

Such doctrines, immensely popular everywhere in recent years, conveniently justify the central 'core' of government in pushing out to PGOs executive tasks which had formerly been performed by mainstream agencies open to orthodox lines of public accountability – for example, in the re-styling of the British and US Post Offices in 1969 and 1970 as semi-autonomous boards rather than civil service departments, or the creation by Swedish public utilities of subsidiaries incorporated under company law, with consequently greater freedom of action than the parent institution. This doctrine is also used to justify government embarking on new ventures through the medium of PGOs (as in the traditional Australian and British doctrine of the independent public corporation as the preferred institutional arrangement for the running of government-owned industries (Wettenhall 1961); and also to justify government drawing in 'chosen instruments' from outside in the form of PGOs.

Attractive as this 'delegation' doctrine evidently is to administrative practitioners almost everywhere, it is also deeply problematic in practice. It has come under recurrent attack, mainly from intellectuals who question the basic assumption of a clear-cut 'politics-administration dichotomy' on which the doctrine rests (Schaffer 1973: 48, 110–112). In consequence, PGOs which owe their independence to this doctrine may run the risk of experiencing periodic 'legitimacy crises' (Freedman 1978).

PGOs as a Vehicle of 'Bottom-Up' Government

Many other examples could be given of the emergence of PGOs through a 'top-down' process. None of the motivations for conducting public business in this way is uncontroversial: some of those instanced above undoubtedly involve an element of 'cheating', sleight of hand, manipulation. But the 'top-down' perspective is only one way of looking at the emergence of PGOs. A different stream of developments can be perceived by using a 'bottom-up' perspective on government, which starts from totally different assumptions about the essence of public authority and the characteristics of good government (cf. Ostrom 1974). A parallel might perhaps be drawn between the status of trusts in the common-law tradition as autonomous collective entities created by citizens, and the Roman-law understanding of corporations as 'concessions' of the state (Dyson 1980: 193, 196). The former offers a basis for a 'bottom-up' understanding of the emergence of government institutions; and indeed that was exactly the basis built upon by John Locke, whose doctrines were so influential in the development of the US model of government.

Looking at the emergence of PGOs from a 'bottom-up' or 'outside-inwards' perspective produces a different class of such institutions. A 'bottom-up' perspective leads us to notice ways in which what are at one time defined as private or voluntary organizations may come to take on a 'governmental' character as they develop, or ways in which 'government' institutions can be seen to grow out of the ability of persons to contract with one another and make binding commitments to undertake joint activities. Here again, a few examples must serve to indicate this perspective on PGOs.

The observer looking at the political world through 'bottom-up' spectacles will notice many instances in which organizations beginning as independent, voluntary or 'private' institutions may come to have governmental or political significance and thus inescapably come to take on some of the aura of 'government'. It is a commonplace that the eighteenth-century age of the individual has resulted in collectivities of an unimaginable scale and that the age of independence has produced an age of interdependence (Vickers 1970). There are several possible tracks on this route to PGO status. Organizations may come to have the character of PGOs, for instance, by virtue of their simply becoming 'national institutions' which government must succour in one way or another; in effect, they nationalize themselves (Hague, Mackenzie and Barker 1975: 48–52). For example, 'private' firms regularly contracting with government may become such an integral part of government's defence capacity as to be virtually indistinguishable from full-blown public bureaucracies. The various 'armourers of the nation' (Krupps, Vickers and so on) which emerged in European countries in the nineteenth century, in the form of 'private' firms closely linked with, and supported by, their respective governments, are perhaps a case in point. The same thing may happen on a local level, for instance where voluntary associations and neighbourhood organizations run important public services, as is commonly the case in the US.

Alternatively, organizations may come to have the character of PGOs by virtue of wielding powers of decision which partake of 'government'. For example, independent bodies for the regulation of sporting events and behaviour, originating in an age of sporting amateurs or 'gentlemen', may come to take on governmental significance in an age of politicized and professionalized international sport. In such circumstances, greatly different from those prevailing at the time of their foundation, independent bodies come to be in a position of wielding powers of disciplinary action which affect a competitor's livelihood rather than his 'honour' or gentlemanly status alone; and may find themselves taking decisions which affect international relations – as in the case of promotion or approval of sporting events involving competitors from countries with regimes that are in disfavour with other groups or governments. Like it or not, organizations of this type have 'PGO' qualities thrust upon them, of a kind that would have been inconceivable when they were first founded.

Similarly, enterprises beginning as modest and independent charities or friendly societies may come to assume properties associated with 'government' institutions. Independent organizations (such as churches and welfare associations) may become closely involved with government's 'core' in the delivery of social policy (Wegener 1978). The growth of the German *Krankenkassen* on the basis of independent organizations (Tennstedt 1978) and similar insurance funds in Sweden, are cases in point. A slightly different case is the development of the 'independent' building society movement in Britain, which began on a small scale in the nineteenth century as local working-class mutual-benefit associations, but came to be the main source of finance for house purchase by the mid-twentieth century, with over 5 million mortagees in 1980. This meant that the decisions of these 'independent' organizations on interest rate changes (typically taken collectively in a 'peak' association) came to have great macroeconomic and national-politics significance, and that their decisions concerning types or areas of housing which were 'acceptable' or otherwise for loans had considerable local political significance (Barrett and Fudge 1981: 87–104). Likewise, cooperative and trade union enterprise in Germany is on such a scale that the organizations involved have experienced dramatic changes in their relationship with government over the course of the twentieth century (cf. Hesselbach 1976: 50).

Perhaps one of the most dramatic examples of this kind of 'bottom-up' development is to be found in the public services of the state of Israel, with its 'triumvirate' of public sectors. Many public services are organized at least in part by institutions which were in existence before the state of Israel was founded – principally the labour federation (Histadrut) and the Jewish Agency. These 'pre-state' organizations remain strong and in many cases act as joint participants with the conventional 'state' sector in the organization of specific public enterprises (Sharkansky 1979: Ch. 3).

A slightly different 'bottom-up' path to the development of PGOs is the case where citizen initiative under 'permissive' arrangements may create institutions with 'governmental' powers – do-it-yourself government, as it might be called. That is, 'framework' laws may enable citizens to take up power to form institutions with powers of taxation and regulation. For example, those wishing to improve the physical condition of a local residential area may be able, after securing some stipulated majority of the landlords or property-owners involved, to impose 'taxes' on those unwilling to contribute by forcing them to pay for improvements, through the medium of a neighbourhood improvement association.

Do-it-yourself government of this nature is perhaps most common in the USA, where many state constitutions provide for referendum initiatives for the creation of special districts with powers to tax. An interesting example of this line of PGO development is the Ostroms' (1972) study of water supply development in California from the 1940s to the 1960s, as a story of step-by-step institution-building that began with a voluntary association of (water) property-holders and developed by stages into the evolution of special-purpose government agencies with the unmistakeably governmental powers of taxation and of eminent domain.

'Sideways-Across' Creations

A third style of PGO creation can be contrasted *both* with the emergence of PGOs as 'top-down' creations of a government 'centre' deliberately looking outwards *and* as 'bottom-up' creations originating quite outside the 'centre' of government. This mode of emergence might – somewhat fumblingly – be termed a 'sideways-across' development, to denote the creation of 'network' organizations of a wide variety of types. Some such organizations are created to cut across national-government boundaries (these are often, confusingly, referred to as 'non-governmental' organizations in UN terminology). Cases include the St. Lawrence Bridge Authority (constituted jointly by the US and Canadian governments); SAS (the corporation which operates Scandinavian air services on a common basis and which is owned by corporations in each of the three countries involved: the Swedish owner is itself a mixed government-private enterprise); and a set of semi-independent agencies linked to the EEC, including the European Investment Bank, Euratom, the European University Institute and a wide range of 'funds', 'foundations' and 'centres'. One such is the Joint European Torus, an atomic-fusion enterprise created in Britain in 1978, which is mainly funded by the EEC and audited by the

EEC Court of Auditors, but includes members of non-EEC countries such as Sweden and Switzerland on the governing council (Hilf 1982: 102). In so far as Orwell's vision of 'Oceania' actually exists in 1984, it is a 'stateless society', and organizations such as these may constitute an important way of doing business.

Network organizations are also to be found spanning different levels of government, and connecting government agencies and authorities at the same 'horizontal' level. Examples include the US phenomenon of local authorities creating 'special districts' (for services such as sewage, transport or sport) under financial pressure to improve their tax base and borrowing limits; joint creations of local authorities, for example in associations to promote industrial investment in a particular geographical area; or the process by which PGOs themselves spawn their own subsidiaries, dependencies and side-kicks (cf. National Academy of Public Administration 1981: IV; Sharkansky 1979: 81–2) – which may themselves cross national government boundaries, as in the case of the jointly-owned subsidiaries of European nationalized industrial corporations. Almost in their nature, organizations of this kind will be extraordinarily difficult to keep track of in terms of centralized statistics or formal lists. One can quickly move from organizational 'suns' to 'planets', which may themselves turn out to be the 'suns' of other 'planets', and so on *ad infinitum*. Such *Aufgliederungstendenzen* (Hilf 1982: 254) – the endless proliferation of cross-cutting organizations – may be seen as 'organization as its own cause', to adapt Wildavsky's (1980: 62) notion of policy as its own cause.

Network organizations of this kind fit neither into a strict 'top-down' nor into a strict 'bottom-up' perspective. Some other term is needed to denote the provenance and dynamics of such organizations; and a 'sideways-across' view directs attention to those complex patterns of multiple organizational arrangements – frequently including a variety of private organizations and voluntary associations as well as formal agencies of government – that act jointly to implement some policy programme or render some type of public service.

9.5 Formal Status

Apart from the various modes in which PGOs can come into being, they can also be differentiated according to the formal or legal character of the enterprise. The discussion in the first section was intended to show that we risk confusion in the concept of PGOs if we do not distinguish that class of PGOs which are formally 'private' or independent organizations acting in practice as government-like instrumentalities for the discharge of public business, from that class of PGOs which are wholly 'public' organizations distanced from the constitutional 'core' of government in some way, by agency or arms-length arrangements.

Of itself, this distinction tells us nothing about how 'close' any given enterprise is to the 'core' of government at any given time in a sociometric sense. Moreover, there is more than one dimension on which 'public' and 'private' status can be differentiated. For instance, enterprises may be classed as 'public' or 'private' in terms of who *owns* them, who *finances* them, who *operates* them and who *oversees,* them, in senses such as audit, performance scrutiny, final authority. Given that these dimensions are to some extent independent, fourteen different combinations of mixed public-private enterprise are logically possible, in between the enterprise which is 'private' or independent on all four dimensions and that which is 'public' on all four dimensions. For instance, a government facility franchised to and outside operator might be publicly owned and overseen, but privately financed an operated; a major contractor supplying goods or services to government might be publicly financed and overseen, but privately owned and financed; an independent grant-receiving body might be publicly financed but privately (or independently) owned, operated and overseen; a government trading enterprise might be privately financed (through sales) but publicly owned, operated and overseen; and so on.

Even these simple dimensions enable us to perceive a world of public-private interfaces much more complex than applies if we are limited to a simple dichotomy between *the* 'public' and *the* 'private' sector. Moreover, these four dimensions are not the only ones that could be taken. It would be easy, for instance, to lay out different aspects of 'oversight', such as authorization (as in licensing) and performance monitoring (as in audit); and some of the other dimensions could be disaggregated as well. But to do that here would be a needless complexification: the point is simply to show that many variants can be generated on the theme of enterprises which may be hard to classify as 'public' or 'private'.

The same may apply to that class of PGOs which are unambiguously public but in some way 'deviant' in relation to the constitutional 'core' of government. For example, some such organizations may be seen as 'deviant' because they cross national boundaries, as was shown earlier; others because they cross constitutional boundaries (such as mixed judicial-executive agencies); others again because their operation is governed by special rules which run counter to the 'normal' treatment of public organization (such as secret 'unofficial' organizations or 'no-red-tape' agencies). Here, too, there are many possible types of 'hard-to-fit' organizations.

9.6 Mode of Operation

A third possible way of categorizing PGOs might be to distinguish them in terms of the resources on which they draw for their operations and which may link them to government. Four resources which are commonly used by organizations discharging public functions are 'nodality', 'treasure', 'authority' and 'organization'; indeed it might almost be said that these types of resources are so important that those who possess or use any of them to a marked degree will find it hard to avoid some kind of 'public' status. I have discussed these resources elsewhere (see Hood 1983b) and they can serve here as another way of illustrating some of the diversity in the world of PGOs.

'Nodality' is the possession of a 'mode', having the property of information-interconnectedness, of being in the middle of an information network, a junction of information channels, the hub of a wheel, the Rome to which all roads lead, 'figureheadedness'. Nodality is what gives its possessor a reason to be listened to and a reason to be offered information, without necessarily involving any element of compulsion. Nodality in this sense will tend to be a property of the 'core' of government almost by definition; but organizations outside that 'core' may take on a governmental character on account of their nodality, their position at the informational 'centre of things' in any particular field. Modern government, for instance, operates within a multiplicity of semi-official advisory networks, both for receiving and for transmitting information. Organizations with the property of nodality will tend to become at the very least advisers or intermediaries between the world of government's 'core' and the world to which their nodality relates; in some cases, their involvement with government's 'core' may go a good deal further than that.

'Treasure' denotes the possession of a stock of fungible assets, which gives its possessor the means of exchange. Again, the possession of great wealth will tend to bring any organization into some relation with government's 'core', and many organizations come to be linked with that core through the medium of 'treasure'. Major government grants or contracts, particularly where they are recurrent, are a case of 'treasure' drawing organizations into a close linkage with government's core. Some 'private' federal contractors in the USA regularly receive more money from government than the annual budgets of any of the executive departments except Defence. Indeed, there is a US administrative style of 'government by contract' in social affairs on a scale unknown in Europe, which has produced a class of nominally independent major contracting organizations for policy delivery and development, such as RAND, the Urban Institute, Mathematica, the Manpower Development Research Corporation, and so on; at the time of writing, there is talk of private contractors undertaking the running of some prisons. The 'governmental' status of such organizations may become ambiguous, particularly where contracts are of a sensitive kind, such as the administration of a missile base by a major airline. And there are, of course, many other institutional arrangements linking organizations with government's 'core' through the medium of treasure. Some independent organizations may receive special levies collected by government on their behalf, such as the German churches or the British National Film Finance Corporation. Another case is the spending 'conduit' distanced from government's core, to serve as an intermediary through which government money is given to groups such as scientists, artists, even welfare money. An example is the Swedish organization which channels government money to 'youth organizations' of all kinds, including political ones (involving discrimination between the youth organizations of 'democratic' and 'non-democratic' political parties).

'Authority' is the possession of legal power – to forbid, command, permit, command, certificate, guarantee. Authority is what gives its possessor the formal standing to determine or regulate. It is, of course, a central and defining feature of government's 'core'. But 'independent' organizations may take on the character of PGOs by virtue of the 'government-like' authority which they wield – for example in the setting of standards and the certification of competence. Government may in effect delegate legislative power to private or independent parties, as in the case of the US legislation prohibiting sale of all drugs except those recognized by the US Pharmacopoeia and similar pharmaceutical publications, on the assumption that in such cases the private parties' determinations will not be coloured by economic self-interest (Freedman 1978: 91). Even without legislation, the same thing can sometimes happen to independent organizations. The British Jockey Club (a regulatory body for horse-racing) was once – perhaps extravagantly – described as 'the most powerful body that does not possess legal powers in the world' (HC 114,

1902). By this was meant that, although the Jockey Club has no statutory powers conferred by Parliament, it is so powerfully established as the governing body for horse-racing that its regulatory powers are in practice very difficult to challenge by the establishment of rival horse-racing associations or by the mounting of races not approved by the Jockey Club. The British Boxing Board of Control is an exactly similar case, in that it wields substantial regulatory powers without any special franchise or statutory basis of authority.

'Authority' in this sense frequently constitutes the 'government-like' character of wholly public bodies which are nevertheless situated at some distance from government's core, as in the case of independent mediators (as for labour markets), regulatory bodies or special taxing authorities. A case in point is *AB Svensk Bilprovning,* the agency which tests automobile roadworthiness in Sweden: it is constituted as a company-law company but the government owns it and it is compulsory for vehicle owners to use its services (the German system is broadly the same). Likewise, through the medium of authority, government can transform the nature of what would otherwise be a private or independent organization. For example, the US government's issue of loan guarantees to the Lockheed corporation in 1975 and to the Chrysler corporation in 1979 could in a certain sense be said to turn those firms from private into quasi-public enterprise, in that their continued existence in large part turned on that exercise of authority. Another case, common in the 'state' societies, arises when government makes membership of semi-autonomous institutions compulsory for those whom it may concern – as with the German *Wassergenossenschaften,* Swedish road-repair associations, public-law chambers of commerce.

Finally, 'organization' is the direct possession of capacity for physical 'treatment' of some kind – derived from the possession of a stock of individuals, buildings, equipment, somehow arranged. Governments must by definition be capable of marshalling organization at least to the extent needed for defending their territories against outside attack and for suppressing insurrections. But many 'treatments' are of course performed for government by organizations of a private or independent kind – by volunteer, contracting or required-service arrangements. Such organizations may come to have an 'official' or 'governmental' character by virtue of the 'treatments' which they carry out: in their absence, responsibility for such treatments would fall more directly on to the shoulders of government. Examples are voluntary fire brigades or mountain rescue teams. On occasion, the link between private or independent enterprises and government's 'core' via 'organization' works the other way round, in that it is government which performs the 'treatment' – for example when government builds for and houses favoured organizations or 'services' them in some particular way, as sometimes happens with voluntary welfare organizations (see also Franz et al.: Ch. 26).

This 'resource' classification is crude, in two senses. First, the categories are not mutually exclusive, in that any given enterprise might well have links to government's 'core' by more than one of these four elements. Second, it needs to be emphasized that the point at which possession or use of resources of this kind begin to introduce an element of 'PGO' status to an ostensibly private or independent organization is necessarily a somewhat indeterminate one. Almost *every* formal organization in society will have some link with government's 'core' in terms of at least one of the four elements. This is, in fact, what extensive government involvement in modern society involves, especially in regulation and tax collection – often creating in addition a market for special 'intermediary' professions, like tax advisers, planning-law consultants, government grant specialists, which, although 'private', owe their existence to government. But to call *every* organization a PGO is to debase the term into triviality: before we can speak of private or independent organizations as PGOs in any strong sense, the links must be *intense, recurrent* or *special* to the enterprise in question. Naturally, the exact degree of 'particularity' which gives some 'para-governmental' status to an organization is a question both of fact and of evaluation on which opinions will certainly differ as between one knowledgeable observer and another, at least in individual cases.

9.7 A Varied Menagerie

There are many other dimensions on which PGOs might conceivably be ranged. But even the three taken here can give some indication of the potential variety of types. Taking only the first level of decomposition of the three dimensions discussed in this section – that is, the dichotomy of 'public' and 'private or independent' forms of PGO, the trichotomy of 'top-down', 'bottom-up' and 'sideways-across' modes of emergence, and the quatrochotomy of basic resources – and putting those dimensions together, gives 24 theoretically possible types of PGO, as shown on Figure 1. We are dealing here with a menagerie, not a single animal.

The variety of the PGO 'zoo' could certainly be expressed in classifications more refined than this one, if further dimensions or lower levels of decomposition were added. But even a crude 24-part typology can have its uses as an heuristic device for comparative analysis. It can, for instance, serve as a starting-point for an effort to pin down distinctive 'styles' of PGO operation, both between one country and another and between one field of policy, task or product and another. Which out of the 24 logically possible types are empirically rare or non-existent, and in which boxes do PGOs 'cluster' most thickly in each country?

One might expect (to take only one example) that the traditional US administrative style is to place heavy reliance on PGOs of types 7, 9, 10, 14 and 17 (as shown in Figure 1), while the Swedish profile might emphasize 7, 9 13 and 14. Type 1 PGOs are a feature of the traditional administrative style of Britain and the Federal Republic of Germany, while countries like Italy and Israel, which are often portrayed as having a high predilection for the use of company-law companies in the public services (cf. Sharkansky 1979: Ch. 3; Vernon and Aharoni 1981: 70–84), have traditionally placed more emphasis on PGOs of type 2.

Similarly, cutting to policy areas, one might expect defence everywhere to be a policy field thick with PGOs of type 14; science policy to heavily involve PGOs of types 10, 13 and 24; agricultural policy to involve a more even 'spread' of types, perhaps especially of types 1, 7, 13 and 19; and so on. Of course, national styles may well cut across 'policy field' characteristics to some extent. For instance, why are PGOs of type 22 (voluntary organizations) used for lifeboats but not (with very rare exceptions) for fire services in Britain, for rural fire services but not for

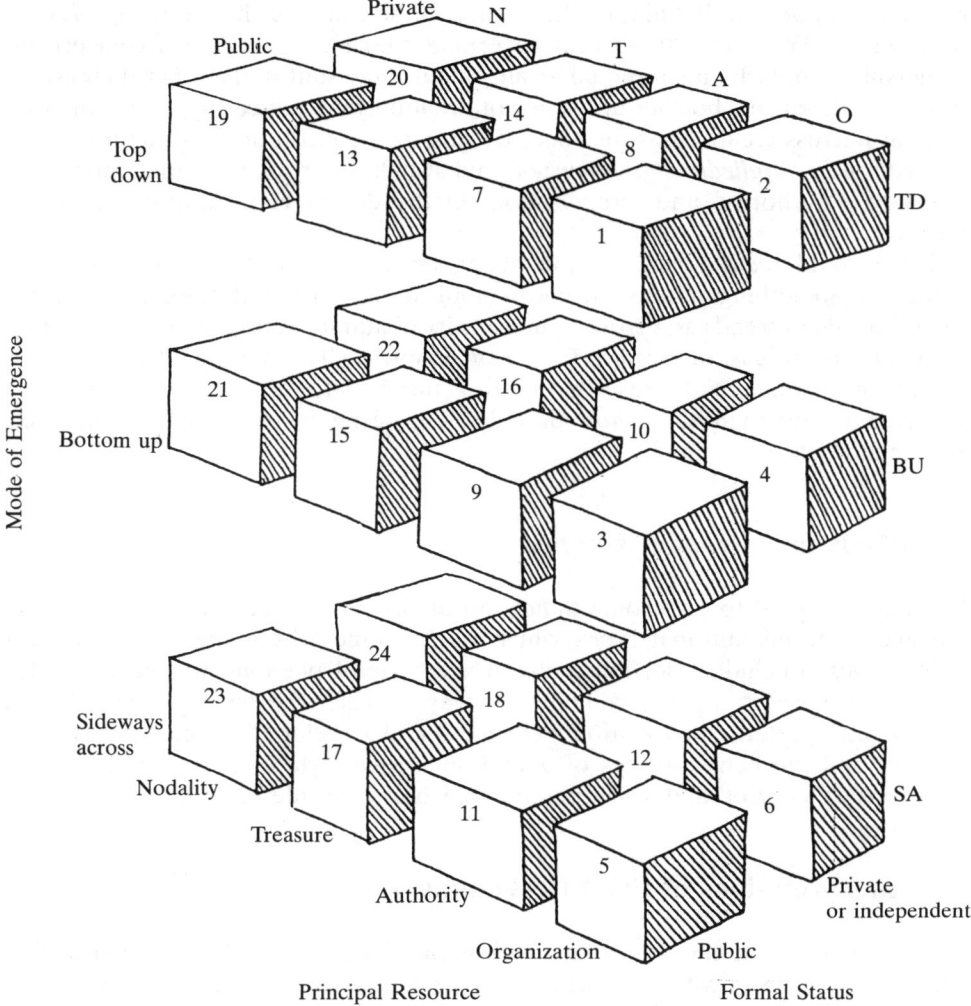

Fig. 1: A Simple Typology of PGOs

lifeboats in Sweden, and for lifeboats *and* for rural fire services in the Federal Republic of Germany?

There are also important questions to be asked concerning the dynamics of growth and change. The institutional arrangements for discharging any particular item of public business can shift from one type of PGO to another. For instance, there are many cases of the movement of public administrative tasks from private or independent PGOs to public ones (i.e. from the even numbered boxes to the odd numbered ones on Figure 1); but the direction of transfer often goes the other way too (from odd to even numbers), in the type of institutional change which is commonly (but misleadingly) designated as 'privatization'. Cases in point are private broadcasting, telecommunications and mail services eating into former public monopolies in Britain, or the change in the status of the German *Volkswagenwerk* in 1959 from 100 per cent government ownership to 60 per cent private ownership. Similarly, institutional arrangements may shift in the other dimensions too. 'Top down' or 'bottom up' styles of creation may increasingly be joined by sideways-across creations as the sheer density of the institutional structure generates complex *Aufgliederungstendenzen;* and switches may occur among 'nodality', 'treasure', 'authority' and 'organization' in the design of institutional arrangements.

If we could *really* speak of 'the quangocratization of the world' (following Jacoby) as something akin to 'the coca-colonization of the world', we might expect to find common trends as a growing uniformity of administrative style in relation to such matters, at least in Western European countries. This may well be so to some extent; but it remains the case that there is more uniformity about *what* modern governments do than about *how* they do it, in terms of institutional modes (cf. Kaufmann: Ch. 6).

9.8 PGOs in a Broader Context

Having attempted to give some indication of the rich variety to be found in the menagerie of institutional types which might come within the umbrella term 'PGO', this concluding section looks at the general phenomenon in a broader context. It considers a number of different ways in which the development of PGOs can be interpreted, the relation between PGO development and government growth, and the consequences of a PGO-intensive style of government for the questions of 'control' and 'coordination' which are considered in this volume.

9.9 Interpretations of PGO Development

It was remarked at the outset that PGOs have something of a chameleon-like character in terms of what they are, the 'problem' which they present to traditional ways of conceiving the public sector, and of the many ways in which they can be categorized. In exactly the same way, the development of this class of institution can be seen from many different points of view.

Marxists, for instance, can read government by PGOs as a way for the 'corporate bourgeoisie' to seal off public business from institutions open to popular control and so to deprive those institutions of direct control over 'the means of public administration' (Weiss and Barton 1980: 20). Here is a typical (American) example of this kind of interpretation (Perrow 1972: 262): 'The corporate bourgeoisie try to solve problems outside of the sphere of politics, within their private organizations (e.g. CED, Business Advisory Council, etc.) . . . and within the supra-municipal and state authorities (e.g. Port of New York Authority).'

From another point of view, however, PGOs can be 'read' as evidence of 'creeping socialism' the advancement of government power over social and economic matters by stealth rather than by a frontal attack (cf. Holland 1979). On these grounds, British Conservatives campaigned vigorously against the growth of 'quasi-government' institutions in the late 1960s and in the late 1970s; and the US 'alphabetocracy' of special-purpose national agencies has similarly come under attack from political forces opposed to 'big government' since the days of the New Deal (cf. Gatti 1981). But conservatives tend to be somewhat ambivalent about PGOs, since from a conservative point of view, it can be argued that if for some reason government has to intervene in some new field of social affairs, it is better to do it by means of PGOs (so as to mobilize the expertise and outlook of business experts or the voluntary or philanthropic movement) rather than by means of full-blown public bureaucracy in the Max Weber style.

Again, from the standpoint of those who see society as run by a 'power elite' (Mills 1956) – whether it be of the political right, left or centre – PGO government might be taken as evidence of a ruling elite running everything on an 'old-boy basis' behind the facade of democratic government (Mackenzie in Curnow and Wettenhall 1981: 144–59). PGOs on this view serve as convenient administrative vehicles for a smallish network of intersecting elites firmly entrenched across a wide range of social institutions. A major task of documentary research and network analysis would be needed to evaluate this kind of perspective, of a kind that has not been attempted in any country (for a very limited essay on British commercial public boards, see Hood 1983a: 1–13).

Diametrically opposed to the 'power elite' view is the idea of PGO government as an institutional expression of pluralism and social diversity, a means whereby a wide range of interest groups may come to 'own' a part of government's administrative machinery, so that there ceases to *be* any coherent ruling elite. Lowi's (1969) well-known critique of 'interest-group liberalism' argues that such an administrative style renders government impotent and undesirably buttresses the *status quo*. He asserts (Lowi 1969: 89) that 'government by and through interest groups is in its impact conservative in almost every sense of that term'. Hayward and Watson's (1975) discussion of European 'overinstitutionalization' as stifling innovation has similar implications: talk in the Federal Republic of Germany of "Herrschaft der Verbände", "Kolonisation des Staates durch Teilinteresse", "Demokratie der Interessenhaufen" (Schuppert 1981: 285) is mirrored by similar discussions in every other European country.

Another common interpretation of the development of PGOs is as evidence of the growth of a 'corporate state' (Schmitter and Lehmbruch 1979; Richardson and Jordan 1979). 'Corporate state' is a nebulous concept, which comes in many versions ('liberal' and Marxist, for example) and which has a long history, dating back well beyond Mussolini's theory of Italian fascism. In the 'corporate state' interpretation, as in the pluralist one, government institutions are 'owned' by key interest groups which straddle all the points of decision and action. But a corporatist interpretation sees a somewhat more ordered picture than does a pluralist one: in the former, political alignments are stable, 'peak' associations with more-or-less compulsory membership cover each major sector of government activity (new or other entrants to the field are barred in some way), controlling their members in a disciplined and centralized fashion in exchange for access to central power (Jordan 1982). 'Corporate' interpretations have been particularly popular in the interpretation of the government of economic affairs in industrialized countries.

Yet another broad perspective on PGOs is offered by Sharkansky (1979) and by

Schuppert (1981), who see this style of government as enabling the complexity of modern society to be given institutional expression, in a way that would not be possible with the use of 'core government' institutions alone or with the maintenance of a rigid dichotomy between 'public' and 'private' affairs. Both Sharkansky and Schuppert concede that institutional complexity brings problems as well as benefits, but they see that as unavoidable in the modern context. This interpretation is a very general one, compatible with a variety of broad ideological perspectives (see also Franz et al.: Ch. 26).

Such interpretations – and there are no doubt many other possible ones which have not been mentioned here – reflect at the least differences of emphasis. Some of them are flatly contradictory. Most of them are open to attack as presenting a distorted or incomplete picture of a highly varied phenomenon, though it is quite possible that several of them might have some validity at the same time, as explaining PGO development in different phases, in different countries or in different areas of government activity. More exploration of PGOs and how they are interpreted in a cross-national context would be needed to pursue that question.

Clearly, it is not possible within this chapter to resolve the contradictions among these interpretations or to test the adequacy of any particular one. They have been introduced here only as another way of underlining the 'chameleon-like' quality of PGOs as an institutional phenomenon. PGOs can be, and are, used for 'unmentionable' purposes – but also for unexceptionable ones. PGOs can be seen as the deliberately positioned outriders of a government centre – and also as outgrowths of voluntary, private or 'grass-roots collective' citizen activity. PGOs attract notice, support and condemnation from almost every point on the broader ideological and political spectrum. To a large extent, we see what we want to see.

9.10 PGOs in a Context of Government Growth: The Consequences for 'Co-Ordination' and 'Control'

Finally – to return to an issue raised at the end of the first section of this chapter – there are some grounds for supposing that PGOs are an important aspect of the institutional pattern of government *growth* in the recent past, in that recent government growth in western countries seems to have taken place to a considerable extent through PGOs rather than through 'core' government organizations.

The evidence for this is admittedly fragmentary and mostly confined to individual countries (cf., for example Hood 1978; Hood in Barker 1982; Heclo in King 1978: 92; Sharkansky 1979; Schuppert 1981: 3), and some caution is called for. The uniformity and novelty of this development should certainly not be exaggerated. There is no doubt that, for reasons mentioned earlier, the particular 'style' of PGO development has varied considerably from one country to another, particularly as between 'public' and 'private' types. In some countries, such as Israel or Italy, with its maze of government holding companies, many PGOs have developed in the past in the guise of government shareholdings in companies constituted under ordinary company law. This has not been the predominant pattern in the USA (partly because many US state constitutions prohibit their governments from holding stock in corporations), where the propensity for the provision of government services on contract by 'private' companies is a more noticeable characteristic. Nor, until the comparatively recent past, has this been the predominant pattern in Britain, with its traditional propensity to resort to public corporations set up by special statutes, or in Germany, with its standard legal framework for 'subordinate' state agencies.

Moreover, a little historical reflection suggests that PGOs are not in any way an invention of the twentieth century. They were well known in earlier systems of government, in forms such as tax-farming by contractors, the use of church institutions for public functions such as elementary education or population registration (still the case with the Swedish *folkbokföring:* all births deaths and marriages must be registered with the state church), the use of nominally independent 'chosen instruments' for the supply of military material to governments from the mid-nineteenth century, even 'licensed piracy', in the case of the old device of letters of marque issued by governments to 'private' warships. The mixed public-private corporation was known in the USA long before independence, and there were colonial prototypes for the combination of public and private finance used by Alexander Hamilton to create the first Bank of the United States in 1791 (National Academy of Public Administration 1981). Going further back, the monopolies under the mercantilist regimes of seventeenth-century Europe and most of the institutions in the social nexus of feudalism might also have a good claim to be considered as PGOs. Just as it is too often unreflectively assumed that 'big government' is a uniquely modern phenomenon, so there is a need for critical appraisal of the extent to which the contemporary discussion of PGOs reflects a 'new' issue, or merely an historically ever-present conceptual difficulty about what 'government' is and what its limits are (as discussed in the first section of this chapter).

Nevertheless, *if* it is 'the quangocratization of the world' or at least of the 'western world') that we are witnessing – and a good deal of hard cross-national evidence needs to be produced before that could be said with any certainty – perhaps it may be the politically chameleon-like quality of PGOs which may account for it. Moreover, there are *consequences,* as well as possible causes, of such a pattern of government growth to be considered.

The implications of a 'PGO-heavy' government structure for traditional ways of understanding 'public accountability' and 'public control' are explored later in this book. In this connection, there are two possible consequences of government growth through the medium of PGOs which may be briefly mentioned in conclusion.

First, government growth through PGOs presents a special challenge to the capacity to co-ordinate the discharge of public business, If government growth occurs to an important extent through PGOs, its nature changes (Schuppert 1981: 251): it becomes multi-bureaucratic rather than mega-bureaucratic, and the units within this multi-bureaucratic pattern, in consequence of being 'distanced' in some way from government's 'core', may possess an element of autonomy. This is reflected in a modern style of public administration theorizing which has rediscovered the 'narrow mission assignment' problem and which stresses networks, clearance points, interdependence and bargaining among semi-autonomous institutions rather than the military-style single hierarchies of the classical management school of Wilson, Willoughby, White and Gulick (cf. Pressman and Wildavsky 1973; Ostrom 1974; Friend, Power and Yewlett 1974; Hanf and Scharpf 1978; Mayntz 1980; Barrett and Fudge 1981; Booth, Pitt and Money 1982). The resulting pattern is *neither* an Adam-Smith-type market coordinated by a hidden hand *nor* a Prussian bureaucratic hierarchy *à la* Max Weber controlled by a single bureaucratic chief. The macro-steerability of a ramified system of this kind presents a challenge both for democratic theory in general and for administrative theory more narrowly conceived.

Second, the blurring of the boundaries of the 'public sector' – the *Verstaatlichung der Gesellschaft* and *Vergesellschaftung des Staates* (Dyson 1980: 243, 285) – and the growth of a network of agencies and institutions which are deliberately placed outside the 'core' institutions of government, challenges traditional ideas about how 'government' activities are controlled (cf. Schuppert 1981: 356–7). Many organizations of this kind, such as the German *Bundesbank,* have been quite deliberately contrived, as we have seen, so as to be 'out of control' in some sense (for example, in the sense of being placed outside the day-to-day ambit of scrutiny by the legislature or by the public auditor). This is likely to exacerbate the 'information-impactedness' problem inherent in all large-scale organization (Williamson 1975), meaning in this case that those on the margins are much better informed than those at the 'core' of government regarding those matters which are crucial for controlling and evaluating the margins – 'the mice in charge of the cheese', in fact.

Relatedly, the 'spreading' of government through PGOs may place some degree of strain on the data base on which control and evaluation of even the simplest kind might be built. Many observers who have explored this area, particularly in the 'government' countries (cf. Sharkansky 1979; Hood and Dunsire 1981; National Academy of Public Administration 1981: 23) have commented on the extreme sloppiness and lack of consistency with which government institutions in practice are divided into 'core' and 'marginal' types. The arbitrariness of the conventional boundary between the 'public sector' and the 'private sector' is illustrated by the so-called 'privatization' program for government corporations which was carried out in Britain between 1979 and 1983. Changing the status of organizations such as the government telephone service from statutory corporations to company-law companies in which government owned a controlling interest in the stock, was said to constitute 'privatization' – and conveniently removed the massive capital borrowing of such organizations from the official statistical returns for 'government' borrowing and 'public' expenditure. Sceptics might doubt the real extent of change which is involved in such cases, and whether the problem of control over 'public sector' organizations can be dismissed quite so simply.

Can we have the claimed advantages of PGOs without suffering side-effects of this kind in relation to co-ordination and control? Or are they simply difficulties that have to be lived with, problems that cannot be resolved – without the 'de-quangocratization of the world', that is?

Acknowledgements

Franz-Xaver Kaufmann and Vincent Ostrom have been influential in shaping my thinking for this paper. I would like to thank Bernd Rosewitz for helping me to gather materials and my other colleagues at ZiF for insights obtained in discussion. I am also indebted to Michael Ewart, Sabino Cassese, Göran Arvidsson and Andrew Dunsire for reading and commenting on a earlier draft.

References

Alderman, G. (1982): "Jews and Sunday Trading: The Use and Abuse of Delegated Legislation." *Public Administration* 60/1: 99–104.

Barker, A. (ed.) (1982): *Quangos in Britain*. London: Macmillan.

Barrett, S., and C. Fudge (1981): *Policy and Action*. London: Methuen.

Booth, S., D. C. Pitt, and W. J. Money (1982): "Organizational Redundancy? A Critical Appraisal of the GEAR Project." *Public Administration* 60/1: 56–72.

Bradshaw, J. (1980): *The Family Fund: An Initiative in Social Policy*. London: Routledge and Kegan Paul.

Colby, W., and P. Forbath (1978): *Honorable Men: My Life in the CIA*. New York: Simon and Schuster.

Curnow, G. R., and R. L. Wettenhall (eds.) (1981): *Understanding Public Administration*. Sydney: Allen and Unwin.

Eickmeier, D. (1982): "Person to Person: Development Assistance Provided by Non-Government Organizations in the Federal Republic of Germany." Bonn: inter Nationes. (mimeogr.)

d'Entreves, A. P. (1967): *The Notion of the State*. Oxford: Clarendon.

Dogan, M. (1975): *The Mandarins of Western Europe*. New York: Sage.

Drucker, P. F. (1960): *The Concept of the Corporation*. Boston: Beacon Press.

Dyson, K. (1980): *The State Tradition in Western Europe.* Oxford: Robertson.

Freedman, J. O. (1978): *Crisis and Legitimacy*. Cambridge: Cambridge Univ. Press.

Friend, J., J. M. Power, and C. Yewlett (1974): *Public Planning: The Inter-Corporate Dimension*. London: Tavistock.

Gatti, J. (ed.) (1981): *The Limits of Government Regulation*. New York: Academic Press.

Hague, D. C., W. J. M. Mackenzie, and A. Barker (eds.) (1975): *Public Policy and Private Interests*. London: Macmillan.

Hanf, K., and F. Scharpf (1978): *Interorganizational Policy-Making*. London: Sage.

Hayek, F. A. (1944): *The Road to Serfdom*. London: Routledge and Kegan Paul.

Hayward, J. E. S., and M. Watson (eds.) (1975): *Planning, Politics and Public Policy*. London: Routledge and Kegan Paul.

Hesselbach, W. (1976): *Public, Trade Union and Cooperative Enterprise in Germany* (tr. by K. Kühne). London: Frank Cass.

Hilf, M. (1982): *Die Organisationstruktur der Europäischen Gemeinschaften*. Berlin–Heidelberg–New York: Springer-Verlag.

Hogwood, B. W. (1979): "The Tartan Fringe: Quangos and Other Assorted Animals in Scotland." *Studies in Public Policy* 34. Glasgow: Centre for the Study of Public Policy, Univ. of Strathclyde.

Holland, P. (1979): *Quango Quango Quango*. London: Adam Smith Institute.

Hood, C. C. (1978): "Keeping the Centre Small: Explanations of Agency Type." *Political Studies* 26/1: 30–46.

Hood, C. C., and A. Dunsire (1981): *Bureaumetrics*. Farnborough: Gower.

Hood, C. C. (1983a): "A Tale of Two Quangocracies." *Policy and Politics* 11/1: 1–13.

Hood, C. C. (1983b): *The Tools of Government*. London: Macmillan.

Jacoby, H. (1973): *The Bureaucratization of the World* (tr. by E. L. Kanes). Berkeley: Univ. of California Press.

Johnson, N. (1973): *Government in the Federal Republic of Germany.* Oxford: Pergamon.

Johnson, N. (1979): "Quangos and the Structure of Government." (editorial) *Public Administration* 57 (Winter): 379–95.

Jordan, A. G. (1982): "Iron Triangles, Woolly Corporatism and Elastic Nets: Images of the Policy Process." *Journal of Public Policy* 1/1: 95–123.

King, A. (ed.) (1978): *The New American Political System.* Washington: American Enterprise Institute.

Lowi, T. J. (1969): *The End of Liberalism.* New York: Norton.

Machiavelli, N. (1961): *The Prince* (tr. by G. Bull). Harmondsworth: Penguin.

Mackenzie, W. J. M. (1950): "Unacknowledgeable Means." (unpubl. lecture).

Mackenzie, W. J. M. (1967): *Politics and Social Science.* Harmondsworth: Penguin.

Mayntz, R. (ed.) (1980): *Implementation politischer Programme.* Königsberg: Hain.

Mills, C. W. (1956): *The Power Elite.* New York: Oxford Univ. Press.

Moynihan, D. (1970): *Maximum Feasible Misunderstanding.* New York: Free Press.

National Academy of Public Administration (1981): *Report on Government Corporations Vol I.* Washington: Office of Management and Budget.

Ostrom, V., and E. Ostrom (1972): "Legal and Political Conditions of Water Resource Development." *Land Economics* XLVIII/1: 1–12.

Ostrom, V. (1974): *The Intellectual Crisis in American Public Administration* (rev. ed.). Alabama: Univ. of Alabama Press.

Perrow, C. (1972): *The Radical Attack on Business.* New York: Harcourt Brace Jovanovich.

Pifer, A. (1967): *The Quasi Nongovernmental Organization.* New York: Carnegie.

Pressman, J., and A. Wildavsky (1973): *Implementation.* Berkeley: Univ. of California Press.

Richardson, J. J. (1979): "Pollution Control in Sweden: Administration or Policy?" *Särtryck ur Statvetenskaplig Tidskrift* 4/2: 189–202.

Richardson, J. J., and A. G. Jordan (1979): *Governing Under Pressure: The Policy Process in a Post-Parliamentary Democrazy.* Oxford: M. Robertson.

Ronge, V. (1974): "The Politicization of Administration in Advanced Capitalist Societies." *Political Studies* 22/1: 86–93.

Rourke, F. E. (1976): *Bureaucracy, Politics and Public Policy* (2nd ed.). Boston: Little Brown.

Schaffer, B. (1973): *The Administrative Factor.* London: Cassell.

Schmitter, P. C., and G. Lehmbruch (1979): *Trends Toward Corporatist Integration.* London–Beverly Hills: Sage.

Schuppert, G. F. (1981): *Die Erfüllung öffentlicher Aufgaben durch verselbständigte Verwaltungseinheiten.* Göttingen: Verl. O. Schwartz.

Selznick, P. (1949): *TVA and the Grass Roots.* Berkeley: Univ. of California Press.

Simon, H. A., D. W. Smithburg, and V. A. Thompson (1950): *Public Administration.* New York: Knopf.

Sharkansky, I. (1979): *Wither the State? Politics and Public Enterprise in Three Countries.* Chatham, N. J.: Chatham House Publishers.

Smith, B. L. R., and D. C. Hague (eds.) (1971): *The Dilemma of Accountability in Modern Government.* London: Macmillan.

Tennstedt. F. (1978): *Soziale Selbstverwaltung.* Bonn: Verl. d. Ortskrankenkassen.

Vickers, Sir G. (1970): *Freedom in a Rocking Boat.* Harmondsworth: Penguin.

Vernon, R., and Y. Aharoni (eds.) (1981): *State-Owned Enterprise in the Western Economies.* London: Croom Helm.

Weidenbaum, M. (1969): *The Modern Public Sector: New Ways of Doing the Government's Business.* New York: Basic Books.

Wegener, R. (1978): *Staat und Verbände im Sachbereich Wohlfahrtspflege*. Berlin: Duncker and Humblot.

Weiss, C., and A. Barton (1980): *Making Bureaucracies Work*. London and Beverly Hills: Sage.

Wettenhall, R. (1961): *Railway Management and Politics in Victoria 1856–1906*. Canberra: Royal Institute of Public Administration (ACT Group).

Wettenhall, R. (1976): "Modes of Ministerialization. Part I: Towards a Typology." *Public Administration* 54 (Spring): 1–20.

Wildavsky, A. (1980): *The Art and Craft of Policy Analysis*. London: Macmillan.

Williamson, O. E. (1975): *Markets and Hierarchies*. London: Collier Macmillan.

Part 3
Guidance, Control, and Evaluation

10. The Relationship between Guidance, Control and Evaluation

Franz-Xaver Kaufmann

Abstract

A basic inquiry into the problem of coordination: How can the establishment of chains of action be explained? The focus is not on decision making but on conditions for learning. Institutional and operational coordination are distinguished, and coordination is analyzed on the individual, the interindividual, the organizational and the interorganizational level. Effective coordination involves guidance, control and feed back. These functions are explained by analyzing market relationships and processes of planning.

10.1 Introduction

Previous chapters have shown that we have to consider the public sector as the interplay of various collective actors belonging either to the state or being state-independent (private or public) actors. If therefore the public sector has to be perceived as multi-bureaucratic rather than mega-bureaucratic, i.e. as a multiplicity of actors rather than of one dominating actor, then the question about how coordination within the public sector takes place becomes a serious issue.

We shall deal with this issue in the following three parts of this book, starting from different points of view. We have first, to deepen our understanding of what the problem of coordination means, Two basic perspectives can be adopted for looking at the problem of coordination, the perspective of order and the perspective of performance and we need language to deal with both of them. Moreover, we have to take into account, that the output of what is conventionally called the public sector has to be responsive to the ends and interests of the citizens/taxpayers/consumers, and that this output as well as the needs it attempts to meet are very diverse. In a pluralistic democratic system political preferences will change over time, and there are always competing issues and multiple goals both within an between various policy areas.

It would be a false simplification to perceive "the public sector" as a boundary maintaining system, as a kind of enlarged notion of the state. It is more realistic to see it as a large number of specialized interorganizational networks, which are linked to various segments of government (cf. Franz: Ch. 23). As we have shown in chapter 6 and as has been made plain in the previous chapter by C. Hood, there is no clear empirical boundary between 'public' and 'private'. The distinction is rather a question of normative definition. There are large 'grey zones' at the boundaries, were there is e.g. a coproduction of services by (formally public or private, but always publicly regulated) organizations and purely private users. We perceive 'public' and 'private' primarily as foci of different concerns. Coordination in the public sector therefore means the coordination of actors and actions insofar as a public responsibility is concerned. We adopt the *perspective* of what may be called a *public* interest, i.e. an interest that is primarily embodied in the constitution of government. In democratic societies government is confronted with a multiplicity of claims and interests, and it is therefore impossible to define "the" public interest, e.g. in terms of an aggregation of individual interests or in terms of a higher "raison d'état". The substance of public interest is always contested, it is the domain of politics. But there is a basic agreement in democratic societies that public interest is to be related to the multiplicity of individual interests *as well* as to shared values. Government is considered as an institutional framework to further common purposes of citizens. It is a classic question of political theory how the institutional framework of the public domain may be built to actually fulfill these expectations.

In this volume a new approach is taken to that old question. We assume, that there is no one best way to solve this problem. We consider the multiplicity of institutional arrangements we find when we analyse various aspects of the public sector as an indication of the need to distinguish various patterns or modes of coordination which operate jointly or separately to maintain order, efficiency and responsiveness within the public sector. We assume that they have different merits and weaknesses which need to be assessed in order to define the conditions, under which they may lead to a more or less efficient coordination.

But before we can establish an inventory of different modes of coordination we need to understand what they have in common. It is the concern of the present chapter to develop the categories of guidance, control and evaluation in order to deepen our understanding of the coordination problem. In the broadest sense *coordination* has to do with the establishment of chains of action.[1] In the context of investigating coordination within the public sector we are interested in explaining how and under what conditions the interplay of various organized actors (e.g. ministries, local governments, political parties, business firms, welfare associations etc.) may lead to a satisfactory performance in terms of e.g. policy decisions, program implementation, resource allocation and effective satisfaction.

It is characteristic that the same organized actors may meet in different action arenas[2], e.g. in the decision process about a program and in its implementation. Coordination problems (as inter-actor coordination) are related primarily to specific action arenas. Moreover the particular actors have to coordinate their own actions among the different actions arenas (intra-actor coordination). It is reasonable to assume that consistency in various stages of the policy process is dependent on both regulations that link the processes in various action arenas, and the dynamics within the participating organized actors. As will be developed later the relationship between intra-actor coordination and inter-actor coordination is of crucial importance for understanding possibilities for and deficiencies of coordination within the public sector.

Coordination takes place on various levels of social reality: even the individual has to coordinate single acts to perform any purposeful action. Insofar as we consider two or more individuals as actors and we are interested in the outcome of their joint actions we have to ask how their actions have been coordinated. Sociological theory helps us to distinguish two basic forms of social coordination: coordination by a configuration of rules (institutional coordination) and coordination by interaction (operational coordination). Normally both forms operate in the establishment of any chain of actions where more than one person is involved.

Actors within the public sector are however not individuals but organizations. Organizations may be viewed either as social systems or as corporate actors.[3] Taking organizations as social systems emphasizes their institutional aspect. They appear as relationships of rule-ordered actions of various individual actors. Taking organizations as corporate actors emphasizes their operational aspect, they appear as a source of outputs that may be considered as elements in a chain of actions. With respect to coordination we are now confronted with two different perspectives: If we consider organizations as social systems, coordination takes place among the actions *within* the organization (intraorganizational coordination). If we consider organizations as corporate actors, coordination takes place among the actions of *different* organizations (interorganizational coordination).

We have therefore to distinguish between four levels of the coordination problem: intraindividual coordination, interindividual coordination, intraorganizational coordination and interorganizational coordination.

In order to develop the common features of the coordination problem we proceed from the most elementary level of intra-individual coordination to the more complex levels of social reality.

10.2 Individual Action

Considering an individual actor (a human being as actor), an action implies first some intention, motive(s) or goal(s), second some behavior and spending of resources for their realization and third some observation and evaluation of the effects of the behavior with respect to his intention. This normally leads either to a continuation or modification of the action (i.e. learning) or to its end (through satisfaction or by resignation).

Notice that this concept of action implies an identity of intention in the sense that the actor pursues in the course of his action a goal stated in advance. Consequently he measures its outcome using the original goal as a standard. At first glance this is nothing other than rationality – a model of rational action. The rationality implied here, however, is restricted to a definite means-end relationship. For an individual actor it may be more satisfactory to change the original goal, and hence the intention of his behavior, rather than to change his actions to achieve a more promising outcome. It is common experience that unexpected outcomes are revaluated in order to make them 'meaningful', cf. also the theory of cognitive dissonance (Festinger 1957).

As an observer we may then judge that he has changed his action, but it would be difficult to call that irrational on the part of the actor. As will be shown by Majone (Ch. 21) such 'rationalizations expost' may have an important coordinative power. If we insist upon a model of action that is formed by an identity of intention, we really do not take the position of the actor but of a generalized 'impartial observer' claiming that in the interest of third parties a consistency of explicit goals, implicit intentions, modes of behavior and evaluation of outcomes *should* be maintained in order to secure reciprocity of expectations and hence interaction in the sense of a mutually positive relationship. It is the *moral* point of view, as it has emerged in modern times, which makes man responsible for the outcome of his actions and hence imputes a consistency of intention to him.[4]

Beside the categories of *intention, realization* and *evaluation,* theories of action emphasize a fourth aspect the *situation* in which inaction takes place. In addition to the behavior of the actor, the situation determines the outcome of the action. The details of the situation may be well or badly known to the actor, but one assumes that he has a *picture of the situation* in which his action intervenes. The intention of the action is to change the situation in some respect. Hence the definition of a situation is not independent of the intention of an action. In the case of rational decision-making one wants a model of action where the intended behavior and the resources for disposal are coordinated to change the situation in the direction of the intendend goals.

Whereas older conceptions of actions and of decision theory emphasized the conditions of rationality of behavior, newer approaches emphasize the *constraints* on the actor to follow a 'fully rational' path of action:

– Individuals do not have given preferences. Even if one assumes a set of human needs and value orientations, internal conflicts exist about the priority to be given to certain needs or values with respect to given options and situations. Hence, *instability of preferences* is a normal feature of human behavior.
– Individuals have an *imperfect knowledge* of their situation. They are unable to gather all the information necessary for a fully rational decision. This stems from limitations in their cognitive capacity as well as from the variability and/or complexity of the factors that determine the situation in which they want to act.
– Individuals have a *limited capacity for information processing* in order to reach a decision. Thus only a limited number of goals may be valuated in preference building, and only a limited number of ways of action may be considered in addition to the cognitive constraints already mentioned.
– Individuals have a *limited memory.* Hence only a selection of the points of view and informations that were really taken into account in order to reach a decision are stored, other are forgotten. Even if an individual tries to be consistent in his intentions one has to assume that he/she is unable to do so perfectly.[5]

Whereas most modern theories of action focus on the *decision* aspect of action, our concern is more with its *learning* aspect. Given 'bounded rationality' it may be more successful to act and to learn from the results of one's actions than to try to improve one's decision structure in advance (see Shackle 1961). But learning from the results of one's actions implies that the individual remembers the projected action (and not only the goal of the action!) in order to compare experiences with the original project and to explain alternative outcomes. Such an 'experimental attitude' to the world is as artificial as models of rational or even 'bounded rational' decision making are. Whereas, from a decision point of view, the main constraints on rationality in human action are based on cognitive and computational limitations, instability of preferences and shortcomings of memory are the main con-straints within learning processes. Moreover learning depends on features of the situation: learning will occur more easily when actions can be iterated than in "one-off" situations.

Action is not a single act at a given time but *a process through time* (Parsons 1949: 48). A *decision* is an attempt to concentrate the features of an action into a single moment. The decision does not concern the action but only the *projection* of the action. If we analyse an action in terms of goals, means, definitions of a situation, etc., we do in fact reconstruct an imputed projection for the actor. The course of the action, i.e. the sequence of coordinated acts, does not necessarily follow the projection. It may consume more and other resources than planned. New issues may arise. Side-effects may become important etc. Thus the unifying element in an action as a process through time is not the projection itself, but the meaning or intention of the actor which defines the boundaries of an action (see Schütz 1932: 62).

This short analysis of individual actions shows that in this apparently simply case it is quite difficult for an impartial observer to ascertain the unity and the boundaries of an action. Insofar as we take the actor as autonomous master of his actions there is no reliability and hence no reliance possible among actors except in the situation of immediate exchange.

10.3 Interindividual Chains of Action

The high contingency of individual actions would be multiplied into the "double contingency of the process of interaction" (Parsons 1951: 36) and lead to chaotic situations incompatibel with human survival if they were not sufficiently controlled by elements of social order (see V. Ostrom: Ch. 5).

The idea of individual responsibility as it has emerged in early modern times is only one rather precarious form of controlling the contingencies of human interac-tions. Customs, patterns of behavior, as well as laws, courts and modern organiza-tion and the generalized media of communication like money, are other means of controlling such contingencies. They all contribute to the establishment of long chains of actions by giving more consistency but also more flexibility to human interactions. More complex and more efficient forms of human cooperation can thus be established. Our concern in this volume is to explore the possibilities of lenghtening the chains of action within the public sector.[6]

The relationship among actors is a contingent one insofar as they do not interact in a shared definition of their situation. The question of how human beings bring themselves to meaningful interaction is a classic issue of sociological theory-building that cannot be dealt with here. It can only be noted that one can distinguish three main referents for the coordination of actions: meaning, rules and interactive problem solving (e.g. by discussion, bargaining or exchange). Interac-tive problem solving always presupposes at least some shared notions of meaning and/or rules, i.e. common elements related to the interaction which are external to the actual situation. They may stem from former interactions (as is typical e.g. for family relationships), or they may be shared by a wider community, e.g. an organization, a profession, the educated of a society or everybody, who is to be accepted as a 'normal' human being. Language is of course a main constituent for interindividual coordination, but non-verbal communication may also be used.

The interindividual coordination of actions presupposes therefore:

a) *Shared elements of the defined situation* (meaning). In the context of policy making this aspect is accounted for in theories emphasizing 'belief-systems' of 'policy-communities' (cf. Sharpe: Ch. 8; Sabatier 1983).
b) *Rules of behavior.* In the context of policy making these rules stem first from public law. They may regulate policy-making in general (e.g. by defining procedures, competences and domains) or they may be specific to particular policy areas or even policy programs. But beside these formal laws a wide range of more or less explicit rules (e.g. contracted rules or custom) regulates interaction in various action arenas (cf. E. Ostrom: Ch. 22).
c) An awareness of the behavior and the interests of third parties and their interpretation in terms of the situation as well as of individual interest and adaptive reactions. In the context of policy making *mutual adjustment* seems to be a factor of paramount importance (cf. Lindblom 1965; Majone: Ch. 21).

10.4 Lengthening Chains of Action

The evolution of the human species, especially the emergence of its ability to organize into larger and more complex societies demands the development of longer chains of actions which go beyond immediate individual and interindividual experience.[7] The lengthening of chains of action corresponds to the division of labour, to the functional differentiation of society. The interdependence of a complex society can only be maintained insofar as it is possible to establish again and again the interrelatedness of necessary actions from different parts of society. As we have sketched in chapter 6 the notion of the public sector denotes problems of relationships between the political and the economic system as well as relationships between the political system and the daily life of members of society.

We are therefore concerned with the coordination of actions which are very distant in terms of structural differentiation. There are many structured boundaries to cross, if coordination is to lead to satisfactory results in terms of public interest.

The problem is however not without solutions as the mere fact of the emergence of complex societies shows. The existing complexity could not have been stabilised if the coordination problem had not been solved to a sufficient degree in practice. Our primary task is not to find out optimal modes of coordination but to explain the existing forms of coordination and their interplay. This is what parts 4 and 5 of this volume aim to do.

Simon (1977: 246) has argued, that complex systems always show a hierarchic character. He understands the term 'hierarchic' not in the narrow sense of a vertical authority structure but as "a partial ordering", e.g. the fact that complex systems show more strongly ordered parts which are only loosely coupled with other parts and together form the more complex 'hierarchic' system. This *principle of partial ordering* may be iterated and thus lead to very differentiated structures.

In the following we use the term 'hierarchy' not in this broad sense but in the conventional sense of a partial ordering *by authority*. There may be other forms of partial ordering, e.g. by exchange or by association. For our purposes it remains an open question if and to what extent the relationships among social systems emerge into a new, more comprehensive boundary maintaining system. Especially in the case of markets it is implausible to perceive them as necessarily boundary maintaining. Be as it may, the basic idea of Simon is of paramount importance for the understanding of our problem: The extraordinary lengthening of chains of action in modern societies has become possible only by partial ordering, i.e. *by the creation of formal organizations as boundary maintaining social systems.* In the case of formal organization the constituent boundary is membership, but additional organizing principles (e.g. hierarchy) are needed, if organizations grow larger.

Within an organization the most relevant social relationships are rule-ordered, i.e. they exhibit features of *institutional coordination.* Thus there exists a preliminary order that enables the members of the system under normal circumstaces to produce the output it needs to cope with the demands of its environment. For analytical as well as for practical purposes it is therefore possible to take the solution of the coordination problem within an organization for granted if one deals with interorganizational relationships. It is therefore possible to perceive the organization as a corporate actor, and in fact most organizations are constituted in the form of a legal entity, represented by individual actors acting as representatives of the organization concerned and interacting with third parties. Insofar as they represent the whole organization there seems to be no reason to take the intraorganizational transactions into account. The organization may be said to perform collective actions and the contributions of its parts may be considered as productive acts.

To perceive the organization as a corporate actor whose internal transactions are of no interest to wider systems is however a one sided perspective. For the *maintenance of internal order within a social system is not costless.* The cohesion or integration of social systems is not obtained by physical force (as in the case of material systems) but depends upon social ('homeostatic') processes within the system. A certain amount of psychological involvement and perhaps also of physical work on the part of its members is needed in all organizations to maintain internal order and to coordinate the actions necessary to cope with the various segments of the environment. The amount of this 'entropy' (to use the thermodynamic equivalent) or of 'transaction costs' (in terms of economic theory) is not fixed for a certain system but depends essentially upon the efficiency of internal coordination as well as upon external constraints. Their strengthening may result in 'organizational stress' and increase transaction costs, as every member of a University knows, when e.g. the budget is cut.

Hence every organization is confronted with a double task: to maintain its internal order and to provide output for third parties, e.g. other organizations or clients.[8] These two tasks may conflict, as the conflict of interests between mangement, personnel and clients in an organization shows (see Hegner 1978). Thus the efficiency of internal coordination is an important variable for its effectiveness as measured in terms of output to third parties. Given the necessity to cope with different external demands as well as with various internal interests it is too simple to assume an ordered hierarchy of preferences within an organization. Rather organizations tend to replicate the principle of partial-ordering in differentiating sub-systems with particular objectives. Thereby the self-regulating power of an organization is substantially enhanced (see Dunsire: Ch. 16).

The necessity for partial ordering in complex societies is also the central argument for explaining the impossibility of a centralized and authoritative steering of the whole public sector. Government is forced to grant increasing degrees of autonomy to organizations of the public sector as the complexity of its task grows. Thus the problem of *interorganizational coordination* is of paramount importance in the steering of the public sector and we will treat in extensively in part 5 of this volume. In emphasizing this level of analysis one should not forget, that this is an emergent level overlapping the three other levels mentioned.

We now proceed to the three dimensions of the coordination problem: guidance, control and evaluation. The basic idea is of course to be found in the cybernetic concepts of control and feedback, but its development aims at a more substantial sociological and political theory.

Guidance

Chains of action imply a plurality of actors. They also imply mechanisms to secure the interrelatedness of the actions of particular actors i.e. the functional equivalent of intention in individual action. Two main types of interrelatedness are discussed in the literature.[9] Following Dahrendorf (1966) we may call them market-rationality and plan-rationality. Note that we do not speak simply of 'markets' and 'hierarchies' but of specific forms of rationality indicating that the kind of interrelatedness we are interested in shows some evidence of consistency and order, i.e. *we want to understand and to define institutional arrangements under which individuals as representatives of and as actors in organizations behave in their decisions and actions in such a way that the output of the organizations concerned may correspond to some overlapping goals or standards.*

Social scientists generally agree that economic systems which are steered either by pure competition in a market-price-mechanism or by a centralised planning body are limiting cases or ideal-types seldom found in reality. Their heuristic value remains insofar as they present two different hypothetical solutions to the problem of coordinating multiple actors. In anticipation of later analysis (cf. Chapters 17–19) a short sketch of the two 'classic' coordination mechanisms is needed here for our argument.

Let us begin with *planning:* A plan is a set of goals and rules that defines the expected contribution of each actor to a chain of actions in order to reach a desired outcome.

In this case it seems possible to consider the planned chain of actions as the *projection* of a *collective action,* for which the particular contributions are elements, just as we can perceive the projections of the action of an individual as consisting of various acts to be performed through time.

Whereas the mainstream of Western economic thinking did not seriously consider the problems of a state-coordinated economic system, and hence, of mechanisms of centralised planning, a growing literature in organization theory deals with problems of inter-organizational or even societal planning (e.g. Churchman 1968; Ozbekhan 1969; Ackhoff and Emery 1972).

The common feature of these approaches lies in the assumption that planning is above all a process of coordination *of decisions* and that the criterion of consistency has to be found in a kind of *normative* inquiry, as a hierarchy among goals of action. Chains of action are here considered as following a logic of transitive goals where the more specific goals and projects contribute in obvious way to the desired outcomes defined in terms of more general goals.

Comparing this procedure with our model of individual action, we can see, that these authors emphazise the *problem of consistency of decisions* that is analogous to the problem of stability of preferences or intentions on the level of individual action. There is no doubt that in collective action the question of consistency is even more precarious than in the case of individual action. Each actor has to know what contribution is expected from him to reach the more complex outcome which should result from the coordinated acts of different actors. We call this first functional problem of the building of chains of action the *problem of guidance*. It is emphasized in the sketched approaches to normative planning, but as we shall argue, this is only the most obvious and by no means an exhaustive approach to the problem. In a more general sense the *function of guidance is performed by any process or mechanism that indicates to single actors standards by which they can ascertain the value or the expected utility of their actions in a wider context.*

In the case of the *market* there is also guidance, but no collective action. The single actors are not coordinated by a plan, but by competition and the price-mechanism. Floating prices of commodities indicate to particular actors the degree of scarcity of goods and services. By comparing the expected proceeds with the costs of production of different commodities the particular actors ascertain the utility of their products in the market economy, i.e. in terms of effective demand.

This outline of how planning processes and market mechanisms perform the function of guidance remained immanent to the two theories. There was no discussion of the question, to what extent the results of such a coordination would be generally acceptable. Planning processes may be performed by an uncontrolled elite or with the participation of all actors involved. The desired outcomes of planning processes may be in the interest of a ruling class or in the interest of the common man. Similarly coordination by markets does not, per se, maximize individual welfare in substantive terms but has external effects and needs additional mechanisms e.g. for the protection of labour or for the redistribution of income in order to achieve satisfaction of needs for the non-earning members of society. In this first step the function of guidance has no definite relationship to societal values or other standards of general acceptability. The outline of normative planning however tries to solve this problem by relating the desired outcomes of planning to societal values. We shall come back to the issues implied here.

Control, Evaluation and Feed-Back

Planning aims at the coordination of decisions, not of actions. Hence planning has to assume, that actions follow the path anticipated in the decision-situation and that the decision makers were able to consider all relevant factors for success in advance.

Three main problems remain to reveal this perception as an idealistic oversimplification. They can be derived from our analysis of individual action. First, a plan as a coordination of decisions has no immanent device to ensure the conformity of particular actors to the plan. Hence devices of control are necessary supplements for any plan that is meant to be realized. Second, decision makers are not able to gather and to process all relevant informations and to consider all issues affected by the collective action in advance. Third, collective action takes places in a (perhaps changing) situation and evolves through time. Hence modifications of the original plan may become necessary in order to attain the desired outcomes. Such modifications are possible only to the extent that a collectivity of actors is *able to learn*. Feed-back devices are needed, i.e. forms of evaluation of outcomes of particular actions as well as of chains of action in order to assess their success. However feed-back operates effectively only if there is some link between processes of evaluation and processes of control, i.e. if knowledge and power fit together.

A plan is not the collective action itself. A plan is at best the *projection* of the action – or the chain of actions – that has to be acted out by the particular actors. If we consider the contingencies implicit in the concept of individual action, it becomes clear that a theoretical reconstruction of interrelated actions has to consider the constitution of the interrelatedness as well as the constitution of the particular acts and actions that are considered elements in the chain of actions. Individual actors cannot be assumed naturally to follow a collective plan; they must either conform their intentions to the standards set by the plan or they must be motivated by factors that are not explicit in the plan, e.g. by money or by force, to incorporate the standards in their own project of action.[10] For more details, see Wirth (Ch. 29).

Hence plans have to be implemented, and this needs processes of control, of *linking decisions and output* (see Lundquist 1972). But as decisions or plans normally cannot consider the whole course of action, it is very unlikely that the desired outcomes would be reached if plans were acted out without modifications. Perfect "work to rule" would lead to a break-down of chains of action. The success of plans and decisions partially depends upon the ability of the actors to modify details or even major parts of it in the course of action, if initial assumptions prove to be incorrect or if aspects of the situation emerge that have not been taken into account at the time of the original decision. This leads to our third problem of coordinated action, i.e. the *problem of evaluation and feed-back*. To maintain the interrelatedness of a chain of actions there must exist sufficient feed-back among the participating actors to facilitate its adaptation to unanticipated problems, whether they stem from contingencies in the situation or from difficulties in the interplay of the actors themselves.

In the case of *market-relationships,* feed-back operates on two levels: First single actors are linked together by contract. This normally refers to a definite action that has been defined in advance by a contract fixing the price of that action (i.e. goods and/or services). From Roman law very sophisticated regulations have defined the rights and duties of the partners in a contract. These regulations imply an evaluation of for example the performance of the seller of a good by its buyer and define the time-limit for objecting to deficiencies in the performance as well as the methods for dealing with defective performance. Hence the laws of contract define not only a method of feed-back but also sanctions that may be imposed by the contracting parties in the case of defective performance. Hence evaluation is linked to control by law in order to maintain the anticipated relationship of actions. In case of conflict a mediation by law courts is assigned for.

But there is also feed-back on the aggregate level: The evaluation of the utility of goods and services will influence the development of future demand and hence the price-level for certain commodities. At this aggregate level evaluation is immediately linked with the operation of control by competition and by the interdependencies of pricing. By gains and losses an economic actor is informed of the evaluation of the utility of its own performance as well as of the performance of all producers of comparable goods. Even if there are strong constraints upon competition and the freedom of prices (as in oligopolistic, monopolistic or even state-controlled markets) there may be some feed-back from the development of demand and hence the profits of large corporations which need them for generate the basis of their assets (see Krüsselberg 1969 and ch. 17).

In the case of *coordination by planning* the problem of feed-back proves to be the most precarious. To clarify this point we need to consider the social *structures* required for performing a planned action. Even assuming that the participating actors are willing and intelligent, the realization of a complex plan that transcends the cognitive capacities of the particular actors needs some coordinating body to assess its course of action and to modify parts of it.[11] This coordinating body (or person) may also be the author of the plan itself. Or the plan may be established by other procedures (e.g. by all participating actors). In any case, limitations of time in the realization of a plan (that normally faces actors with different interests) force the establishment of a *coordinator*. It is therefore the growing complexity of tasks themselves (and not merely the problems of control) which account for the establishment of a kind of hierarchy and/or a mechanism of representation in the case of collective action. Moreover, the problems which stem from the contingencies of individual actors are evidenced in the facts observable in social history; that collective actions with some degree of complexity and durability are impossible without the *establishment of social structures* to bind the actors together and facilitate the problems of goal and standard setting (guidance) and of the control of the actors. We have dealt with this issue under the headline of 'partial ordering' in a preceding section.

Most of these empirical structures are *hierarchic* in character – the Weberian sociology of dominance gives a long account of its various forms. A special form of dominance has proved to be particularly suitable for planning processes as considered here, i.e. the modern forms of formal organization. By establishing a hierarchy and by separating members of an organization as in-group formally from other settings, modern organization has gained a kind of autonomy which gives it a high planning capacity. Hence the top of the organization may have effective control over the members of the organization, *but this does not improve feed-back correspondingly* mainly for two reasons: Insofar as the members of the organization conform not by commitment but by utility or fear there is no implicit consensus about the standards for an action and therefore no correspondence among the evaluation criteria. In addition the clear-cut boundaries of an organization also operate as filtering devices for information from outside so that the assessment of the impact of an organization's activities must be organized separately. This explains the frequent evidence from organization studies of a lack of information flow from the bottom to the top and corresponding difficulties in assessing the success of planned actions.

In sum there is no inherent feed-back in purely hierarchic organizations or other forms of coordination by domination. One has to assume here a *structural* variability and sometimes incompatibiliy of *evaluation criteria* by the top and the bottom of the hierarchy notwithstanding a certain complementarity of interests that may exist among them. This may provoke vicious circles of bureaucratisation (see Grunow: Ch. 2).

This seems to hold, a fortiori, in the case of planning processes where *different* organized actors are involved, as is characteristic of the public sector. If there is a strong hierarchical relationship one can expect only an amplification of the problems just sketched; if one assumes in addition a substantial autonomy of the organizations concerned one can hardly see how the interrelatedness of their actions may be explained and how these may lead to desired outcomes, acceptable from a more general point of view. The question how feed-back is operating in the public sector is therefore a focus of the present volume (cf. Hellstern: Ch. 14 and Part 6).

Under the heading of steering the most salient difference between coordination by markets and by plans is grounded in the fact that *the market mechanism links the functions of guidance, control and performance evaluation in the same process of price-regulated interactions among the concerned actors,* and that it is (or at least presumes to be) compatible with a high degree of autonomy of the particular actors and establishes chains of action at minimal cost. By contrast coordination by planning needs *separate* devices for guidance, control and performance evaluation. Hence there seems to be no inherent tendency for feed-back in organized planning processes. This is a major factor for the eulogies of economists for a market-economy. This statement should however not obscure the fact that efficiency in chains of action coordinated exclusively by markets is restricted to *economic* standards: manifest scarcity is the only guiding criterion. If one wants to introduce other standards one has to look for additional coordination devices.

10.5 Operational and Institutional Coordination

In the previous sections guidance, control and evaluation have been worked out as analytically separate functions. It has already been emphasized that the establishment of interrelated chains of actions *needs some fit of these three functions,* i.e. they must operate as ordering factors to secure the orientation of an interplay of actors towards accepted goals or standards and to improve the complementarity of the particular actions as an (often recurrent) chain or system of actions.

In this last section we have to deal with the normative issue of coordination left open until now: how is it possible to perceive processes of guidance if we cannot assume a general consensus on possible and actual goals of political action?[12] This inquiry will lead us to a better understanding of our distinction between institutional and operational coordination.

As stated by Emile Durkheim (1893), modern societies are characterized by a progressive indetermination of the 'conscience collective' insofar as the division of labour – or in a modern language the functional differentiation of society – is in progress. Consensus in modern society becomes more and more generalized and hence only visible in quite abstract ideas or general values like freedom, equality, security, health, democracy, constitutionalism etc. The universal declaration of human rights of 1948 may be cited as an example of the general standards of acceptability operating in modern societies. As already mentioned, theories, of normative planning assume that problems of guidance in planning processes can be solved by establishing transitive relationships among ultimate values, general aims for certain institutional spheres, goals for organized action and targets for particular acts. This procedure is however an exclusively theoretical one and does not account for variability in the interests of particular actors and the problems of bounded rationality (see Kaufmann 1977). Normative planning assumes an a priori fit of plan and action and considers neither the contingencies of implementation and impact nor the importance of learning through experience and the need to adapt of priorities and standards as well as resource spending in the case of ambivalent or negative feed-back. The progressive indetermination of the 'conscience collective' also means that the 'oughts' and 'ought-nots' become differentiated and have to be worked out in quite separate ways considering their normative as well as their organizational and situational relationships.

As has been demonstrated by various scholars (e.g. Luhmann 1968) the intellectual structure of a normative planning-process is too inflexible an approach for explaining the planned coordination of multiple actors and has to be replaced by a perception of sequential planning with iterative feed-back loops. No fixed hierarchy of goals can guarantee the fit of guidance and evaluation standards (see the following chapters). Differences between stated and operational goals of organizations, goal displacements and symbolic uses of politics are quite common deficiencies in the consistency of political planning processes. Notwithstanding the contingencies of the situation in which political planning interferes, inspection of the planning processes itself shows that it is often to be expected that outcomes will not be in accordance with the general aims that legitimize the establishment of these political measures.

It is therefore too simplistic as assumption to postulate a kind of 'policy cycle', in which the political articulation of problems leads to political programs which are implemented and then evaluated by the citizens in voting for or against the government in office. Feed-back by voting is much too rough a measure for guiding political decisions in major policy areas. Political voting is effective only in changing the comprehensive belief system, not in changing particular policies.

As Sabatier (1983; see also Ch. 15) shows, there is growing evidence that policies which are implemented and reinforced over a sufficiently long period may be more successful, as the early results of implementation research have suggested. If we want to understand why this is the case, we have to assume that *learning* occurs within a 'policy community', i.e. among those who are (or feel) concerned with a particular policy area or issue. The members of a 'policy community' (e.g.

politicians, administrators, representatives of professional associations, researchers or journalists concerned with particular issues) normally form one or more 'advocacy coalitions' which share particular belief systems. As Majone (1982) and Sabatier (1983) show, it is however unlikely that learning occurs within the 'core' of a belief system. The competition of belief systems and the compromises in their 'peripheries' thus sometimes account for viable policies, and this is more likely insofar as learning occurs within the policy community. Learning on the aggregate level of organizational and interorganizational relationships needs more time than on the individual level. It will therefore occur only insofar as a program or a law is operating for a sufficient period.

If we assume that *for effective policymaking it is more important to make learning processes possible than to make the best decision in advance*, we are approaching a new paradigm of political theory. We then have to ask how processes of guidance, of control and of performance evaluation may be systematically incorporated in policy areas. A realistic approach to this issue has to assume that feed-back processes as relationships of guidance, control and evaluation operate simultaneously on various levels and between different stages of the policy-making process. The idea of combining various levels of control is of course elementary to cybernetical thinking but has not yet been incorporated in a systematic way in theories of policy-making.[13]

This short outline should have already made it clear, that the idea of an exclusively operational coordination of actors with high degrees of autonomy is far too simple for understanding what really happens in political and economic coordination. Sequential planning processes cannot operate without institutional structures that guarantee basic rules for the interplay of the actors. In a certain sense the establishment of these basic structures is itself the first step in what normative planning theories consider to be the task of planning.

We prefer to distinguish institutional and operational forms of coordination. In defining domains and competent actors institutional coordination is itself a first form of guidance, which eventually may have a deeper impact on possible outcomes than the solutions produced by the actors participating in the various stages of the policy-making process. It depends also on the procedural rules which control and feed-back may operate within a constituted frame of action. Rule configurations operating to coordinate interindividual or interorganizational relationships may therefore be analysed in terms of their potential for a fit of guidance, control and evaluation as well as the interactive processes themselves. If we recall a multiplicity of independent actors with limited rationality and various preferences as the starting point of our inquiry, we can now see how important it is to find rules of institutional coordination flexible enough to enable learning by the evaluation of experiences and by redefining standards as guidelines within the process of policy making.

To understand guidance, control and evaluation in the public sector we have therefore to use the process-oriented approach of the policy sciences as well as the institutional approach as developed e.g. by theories of public choice. We have to perceive coordination as operating on various levels of social reality (individual, interindividual organizational, interorganizational) and we have to consider coordination by institutional ordering as well as coordination by interaction. The latter is emphasized by theories of policy-making, the former by institutional economics. These are two sides of the same coin.

10.6 Summary

In this chapter we were concerned with an exploration of the relationship of guidance, control and evaluation in order to explain different modes of establishing complex chains of actions as they are needed in a society that has founded its destiny upon the division of labour and consequent specialization and improvement in efficiency, as well as upon a self contained state and individual liberties with consequent pluralization of individual intentions and problems of consensus building. We have derived the three dimensions of coordination from an analysis of pure types, i.e. coordination by markets and by plans. We have analysed them from the perspective of coordinated actions and not just coordinated decisions in order to maintain an outcome-oriented approach.

To summarize: *Guidance* means the function of standard-setting for actors who are to be linked for some of their potential actions into a system in order to achieve outcomes of higher complexity. *Control* means the function of information and motivation for intelligent conformity to such a system of interrelated actions. *Evaluation* means the function of feed-back and concerns particular acts as well as the output of a whole system of action as far as it matches some desired outcomes and some mechanism of control. It is the thesis of this approach that some fit or consistency in the operating of these three functions is needed if one wants to speak about efficient coordination of a plurality of actors in terms of linked actions. This has been demonstrated by analysing the rationality of markets as well as of plans.

The unsatisfactory assumptions underlying pure market as well as pure planning theory have led in the last decades to new approaches which are important for explaining the functioning of the public sector, i.e. theories of policy making and institutional economics. They emphasize different but complementary aspects of coordination. We assert that they should converge with respect to the problem of policy-learning on the question, how may the evaluation of experience in the outcome of political and administrative decision making be incorporated more efficiently in political and administrative processes? From a conceptual point of view it is then important to distinguish forms of institutional coordination (by configurations of rules) and operational coordination (by mutual adjustment and interaction). Moreover one has to distinguish between individuals or corporate actors, i.e. organizations, because they exhibit distinctive features of social interaction.

Acknowledgement

Helpful suggestions have been made by Elinor Ostrom and Dieter Grunow on an earlier draft of this chapter.

Notes

1   Note that we do not take a decision-making-approach (for a critique see Majone: Ch.
     3), we are not interested primarily in intentions, but in outcomes. The action-oriented
     approach is more complex but also more realistic. However decision making is an
     important form of ex-ante coordination that will be dealt with too. Note also that the
     coordination problem is focused on actions and not on actors. It is only in a system-
     environment approach to organization that the analytical difference between the actor
     oriented and the action-oriented approach becomes fully understandable.

2   For the development of the term 'action arena' see E. Ostrom (Ch. 22).

3   The system-environment approach (e.g. Luhmann 1964; Thompson 1967) and the
     actor-approach (e.g. Etzioni 1968; Coleman 1974) are not incompatible but emphasize
     different aspects: if we consider organizations (or even individuals) as systems, we
     emphasize their structural aspects and their striving for internal order. If we consider
     them as actors we emphasize their ability to influence their environment by intention,
     i.e. to act in a situation (cf. also Willke 1978).

4   Former times attributed events to the gods or to destiny and therefore didn't hold
     individuals responsible for the relationship of intentions and outcomes. The ethical
     problems implied in this subject are of course numerous and cannot dealt with
     adequately here.

5   These are now common features of decision analysis (cf. first Simon 1955; March and
     Simon 1958).

6   There is another perception of our problem which emphasizes the contingency of
     intraorganizational and interorganizational relationships: The Garbage Can Model (cf.
     Olsen 1972). In the garbage can model chains of action are neither predictible nor
     ordered by rules but stem from very loosely regulated interactions as a kind of
     byproduct. Here chains of actions remain necessarily short. We therefore do not deal
     with this issues here, although it may be of practical importance in some very
     unstructured situations.

7   The idea that lengthening the chains of action ("Verlängerung der Handlungsketten")
     is an essential feature of the process of civilisation has been formulated first by Norbert
     Elias (1939). A similar idea is implicit already in Boehm-Bawerk's (1889) concept of
     roundabout production.

8   An analogous problem may occur on the individual level: the double task of production
     and reproduction, as already seen by K. Marx.

9   The initial and perhaps still the most thoughtful analysis of these two basic forms to
     solve the problem of coordinating the decisions of a multiplicity of economic actors is
     found in the work of Walter Eucken (1944; 1955). We have to generalize his approach
     in order to cover political processes.

10 Normative commitment, utilitaristic interest and fear are considered the main motives
     for conformity in the case of individuals (Etzioni 1968). The arguments against a
     predominantly normative solution as advocated by T. Parsons and theorists of norma-
     tive planning are convincing (see Ellis 1971).

11 We neglect here the simpler case of immediately joint action of a plurality of actors who
     are able to control themselves mutually and to adapt their particular action spontane-
     ously to the general purposes of the joint action. This case will be dealt with later under
     the headings of solidarity (see Kaufmann 1984; Gretschmann: Ch. 18 and Hegner: Ch.
     19). At this point we are interested in institutional arrangements that allow longer
     chains of action.

12 If a general consensus may be assumed one has to refer to solidarity as a mode of
     coordination; cf. the preceding note.

13 Note however the distinction of macro- and micro-implementation (Berman 1978), the

idea of multi-step-implementation (Majone and Wildavsky 1978) and the idea of overlapping in various stages of the policy-making process (Dahme et al. 1980), which all presuppose the existence of intermediate feed-back loops.

References

Ackhoff, R. L., and F. E. Emery (1972): *On Purposeful Systems.* Chicago: Aldine.

Berman, P. (1978): "The Study of Macro- and Microimplementation." *Public Policy* 26: 157–184.

Boehm-Bawerk, E. von (1889): *Kapital und Kapitalzins.* Vol. 2: *Positive Theorie des Kapitals* (4th ed.). Jena: G. Fischer (1921), (engl. 1959).

Churchman, C. W. (1968): *Challenge to Reason.* New York: McGraw-Hill.

Coleman, J. S. (1974): *Power and the Structure of Society.* New York: Norton.

Dahme, H.-J., D. Grunow, and F. Hegner (1980): "Aspekte der Implementation sozialpolitischer Anreizprogramme." In: Mayntz, R. (ed.), *Implementation politischer Programme,* 154–175. Königstein/Ts.: Hain.

Dahrendorf, R. (1966): *Marktrationalität und Planrationalität.* Tübingen: Mohr.

Durkheim, E. (1893): *De la division du travail social.* Paris: Alcan.

Elias, N. (1939): *Über den Prozeß der Zivilisation* (2nd enl. ed.). 2 Vols. Reed. Frankfurt a. M.: Suhrkamp, 1976. (engl. 1978: The Civilizing Process. 2 Vols. New York: Urizen Books).

Ellis, D. (1971): "The Hobbesian Problem of Order: A critical Appraisal of the Normative Solution." *American Sociological Review* 36 (Aug.): 692–703.

Etzioni, A. (1968): *The Active Society.* New York: Free Press.

Eucken, W. (1944): *Die Grundlagen der Nationalökonomie* (4th ed.). Jena: Fischer.

Eucken, W. (1955): *Grundsätze der Wirtschaftspolitik* (2nd ed.). Tübingen: Mohr.

Festinger, L. (1957): *A Theory of Cognitive Dissonance.* Evanston: Roy, Patterson.

Hegner, F. (1978): *Das bürokratische Dilemma.* Frankfurt–New York: Campus.

Kaufmann, F. X. (1977): "Zur Problematik der Effektivität und ihrer Erfassung im Bereich der sozialen Sicherung." In Külp, B. and H. D. Haas (eds.), *Soziale Probleme der modernen Industriegesellschaft,* 489–518. Berlin: Duncker & Humblot.

Kaufmann, F. X. (1984): "Solidarität als Steuerungsform, Erklärungsansätze bei Adam Smith." In Kaufmann, F. X., and H. G. Krüsselberg (eds.), *Markt, Staat und Solidarität bei Adam Smith,* 158–184. Frankfurt–New York: Campus.

Krüsselberg, H. G. (1969): *Marktwirtschaft und ökonomische Theorie.* Freiburg i. Br.: Rombach.

Lindblom, C. E. (1965): *The Intelligence of Democracy.* New York: Free Press.

Luhmann, N. (1964): *Funktion und Folgen formaler Organisation.* Berlin: Duncker & Humblot.

Luhmann, N. (1968): *Zweckbegriff und Systemrationalität.* Tübingen: Mohr.

Lundquist, L. (1972): "The Control Process: Steering and Review in Large Organizations." *Scandinavian Political Studies* 7/1: 29–43.

Majone, G. (1982): *An Evolutional Approach to Policy Change.* Paper. Bielefeld: Center for Interdisciplinary Research.

Majone, G., and A. Wildavsky (1978): *Implementation as Evolution.* New York: Sage.

March, J. G., and H. A. Simon (1958): *Organizations.* New York: Wiley.

Olsen, J. P. (1972): "Public Policy-Making and Theories of Organizational Choice." *Scandinavian Political Studies* 7/1: 45–62.

Ozbekhan, H. (1969): "Toward a General Theory of Planning." In Jantzsch, E. (ed.), *Perspectives of Planning,* 47–155, Paris. OECD.

Parsons, T. (1949): *The Structure of Social Action* (2nd ed.). New York: Free Press.

Parsons, T. (1951): *The Social System*. Toronto: Collier-MacMillan.

Sabatier, P. A. (1983): "Notes toward a Strategic Interaction Theory of Policy Evolution and Learning." Paper. Bielefeld: Center for Interdisciplinary Research.

Schütz, A. (1932): *Der sinnhafte Aufbau der sozialen Welt*. Wien: Springer.

Shackle, G. L. S. (1961): *Decision, Order and Time in Human Affairs*. Cambridge: Univ. Press.

Simon, H. A. (1955): *Models of Man*. New York: Wiley.

Simon, H. A. (1977): "The Architecture of Complexity." In Simon, H. A., *Models of Discovery and other Topics in the Methods of Science*, 212–231. Dordrecht: Reichel.

Thompson, J. D. (1967): *Organizations in Action*. New York: McGraw-Hill.

Willke, H. (1978): "Systemtheorie und Handlungstheorie – Bemerkungen zum Verhältnis von Aggregation und Emergenz." *Zeitschrift für Soziologie* 7/4: 380–389.

11. A Fallabilist's Approach to Norms and Criteria of Choice

Vincent Ostrom

Abstract

The human capability for learning, generating new knowledge, and using knowledge to transform the world in which we live means that human beings must necessarily face uncertain futures. A way of doing so is to use norms for constituting order in human societies that is open to substantial variability in what people do within those norms. The problem of normative inquiriy and the conditions of human nature that pertain to setting and using standards of oughtness in governing human relationships are examined with special reference to the contributions of Thomas Hobbes, David Hume, and Adam Smith. This method of normative inquiry provides a foundation for establishing the meaning of value terms and for setting, using, and judging criteria of choice and standards of performance.

11.1 Introduction

Homo sapiens is the species that has the greatest capability for learning and using what has been learned to transform its environs and conditions of life. A fundamental puzzle arises as a consequence of this capability. New increments to learning, in the sense of generating new knowledge, give rise to new possibilities for transforming the environs and conditions of life that could not have been anticipated without reference to those new increments of learning.[1]

This condition implies that creatures capable of generating new knowledge must necessarily face uncertain futures: the greater the rate of innovation in the generation of new knowledge, the greater the uncertainty about the future course of developments. Similarly, as increments to new knowledge increase through time, the degree of uncertainty in anticipating the future course of development increases as time horizons are extended into the future.

These conditions place radical constraints upon the viability of planning. Long-term, comprehensive planning is an impossibility. Confidence about projections into the future is inversely related to the extent of time horizons. While planning is essential to rational action it is always accompanied by the possibility of error that derives from the human capacity to learn, generate new knowledge, create new technologies, and transform the conditions of life in which human beings live.

The condition of continual striving for something better is assumed to be the most fundamental characteristic of the human species. So long as that characteristic exists, human beings can never have perfect foresight. They must go through life finding ways of ordering relationships with one another without knowing what the future holds.

What basis exists for rational choice, given these conditions of human fallibility that derive from the human quest for knowledge and enlightenment (not for ignorance)? We cannot know the future except in a very limited way. We do not know the future range of alternatives that may be available to us. A knowledge of the present range of alternatives is limited by the circumstance that we can know only some consequences associated with each alternative. We can, however, choose to order our relationships with one another with reference to rules that are open to the pursuit of a variety of options of mutual advantage, but constrain others that are likely to evoke detrimental results. Human relationships in general are organized by reference to rules. The criteria for distinguishing what is allowable and what is not allowable in the ordering of human relationships are the critical considerations that apply to the governance of human actions and transactions into complex configurations of organized activities. These criteria turn critically upon value terms that rely upon distinctions such as right or wrong, better or worse, good or bad. Questions pertaining to guidance, control, and performance evaluation require that methods are available for human beings to establish criteria of choice or standards of value that enable them to order their relationships with one another to mutual advantage.

Such an understanding would depend, at one level, upon a capacity to make interpersonal comparisons about standards of oughtness that are used in making human choices. If human beings apply the same criteria in ordering their relationships with one another, then there is a possibility of their acting in ways that can be mutually advantageous. Each needs to perceive what is of advantage to oneself and to others as well. At another level, human beings would also be required to learn about the consequences that are evoked by typical patterns of interaction with one another. Unless appropriate constraints can be maintained, human beings may react in ways that do not take adequate account of what will occur if proper foresight had been exercised.

In this essay, I shall confine myself to a consideration of the problem of normative inquiry: matters of oughtness. This problem can be posed as one of specifying what methods are available to fallible human beings for deriving norms or standards of value for informing social choices, i.e., choices that potentially affect others. Some of the basic norms or standards of value might also serve as "yardsticks" in assessing the achievements that human beings attain through the fashioning of constraints articulated as rules that apply to the ordering of their relationships. The configuration of rules for ordering human relationships is what we mean when we refer to institutional arrangements. What human beings are able to achieve by relying upon differently structured institutional arrangements might then be evaluated by some of the more basic norms or standards of value that are used to inform choice.

In exploring the methods that are available for deriving norms or standards of value, I shall rely upon the works of Thomas Hobbes, David Hume, and Adam Smith. They each make important contributions to how human beings, as fallible creatures, develop norms and criteria of choice. They take human beings as they are and draw upon their reflective capabilities to understand the human conditions and develop grounds for interpersonal comparisons. Their method avoids the fiction of an original position or a metaphysics of ethics that presents ultimate answers.

11.2 Hobbes's Contribution to a Method of Normative Inquiry

Hobbes's work is preoccupied with the problem of establishing a proper ordering of relationships in human societies. His work is more generally recognized for its merit as a positive analysis, of indicating the consequences that can be expected to result from specifiable structural conditions. But, he does recognize that order in human relationships depends critically upon making interpersonal comparisons so that any one human being can act with a cognizance of the probable effects that any act will have upon other human beings. His method of inquiry turns in substantial part upon how to make interpersonal comparisons about standards of value that enable human beings to distinguish admissible forms of conduct from inadmissible forms of conduct. Such distinctions can be made only if the *meaning* of terms referring to such criteria is *knowable*.

In this brief Introduction to *Leviathan* (1960), Hobbes states the basic presuppo-•sitions that guide his inquiry. Commonwealths are viewed as artifacts. As artifacts, commonwealths have the special characteristic that human beings are both the *matter* that comprise commonwealths and the *artificers* (artisans) who design and create commonwealths. As a consequence, knowledge of human nature is essential to those who would understand the conditions relevant to the design, creation, and governance of commonwealths so as to avoid the pathologies that contribute to their failure.

Hobbes, in the Introduction, proceeds to offer the reader a "key" that can be used to understand human nature before embarking upon this own analysis in Part I of *Leviathan*. That key is to "read thyself." This is possible because of a basic "similitude of the thoughts and passions of one man to the thoughts and passions of another" (1960: 6). Therefore, it follows that:

"whosoever looketh into himself, and considereth what he doth, when he does *think, opine, reason, hope, fear,* etc., and upon what grounds; he shall thereby read and know what are the thoughts and passions of all other men upon the like occasions" (1960: 6).

Hobbes warns, however, that this basic similitude of thoughts and passions does not extend to particular objects of thoughts and passions. Human beings cannot know *what* are the specific objects of others' thoughts and feelings except as others communicate about the objects of their thoughts and feelings. The relationship of thoughts and passions to particular objects pertain more to each individual's discrete education and experience. We can, however, come to a deeper level of understanding about *how* others think and feel in particular types of circumstances (i.e., "upon the like occasions"). A basic similitude of thoughts and passions enables human beings to pursue a reflective inquiry about the human condition through their circumstance of sharing a similar genetic endowment and arrive at generalizations that potentially have universal applicability among human beings. However, Hobbes warns that this is a difficult task, "harder than to learn any language or science"; but political inquiry "admitted of no other demonstration" (1960: 6).

Interpersonal comparisons about human subjective experiences, thus, can be made by human beings aided by this method of reflective inquiry and the use of language to communicate with others about similar experiences. The terms in a language of discourse about human subjective experiences can have meaning only to the extent that the realm of discourse is grounded in an underlying similitude of thoughts and passions that is universal among mankind. These interpersonal comparisons cannot be extended to a point of knowing what are the objects of the thoughts and passions of others, but human beings can hope to make knowledgeable comparisons at other levels of generality.

Hobbes's presentation in *Leviathan* is an application of the method of introspective inquiry to an understanding of the calculations that human beings face in the constitution of commonwealths. His first 12 chapters are critically concerned with specifying a basic structure of how human thoughts and passions enter into calculations about human choice. Reason, the expression of thought in words, is used to calculate the consequences associated with alternative possibilities. Choice occurs in the weighing of alternatives by reference to internal feelings expressed as preferences and aversions. Hobbes considers the most fundamental characteristic of human beings to be one of continual striving for something better that ceases only with death.[2]

In pursuing this analysis, Hobbes, first, explores the implications that would follow if human beings were to exist without any semblance of political order. In such circumstances, creatures who seek their own good would interact with one another in a way that would yield a mutually destructive struggle in a war of each against all. Hobbes's parable of man in a state of nature can be viewed as a proof that unconstrained pursuit of self-interest is an insufficient basis for human societies. He then sets himself the task of specifying the necessary and sufficient conditions for the creation of stable or long-lasting commonwealths.

Hobbes proceeds to specify a series of rules that would enable human beings to order their relationships with one another so that they might realize a state of peace as an alternative to war.

In the concluding remarks to Chapter 15, after having specified his basic rules as "laws of nature," Hobbes returns to methodological considerations when he asks how the *meaning* of these laws of nature are to be understood apart from their logical derivation. He did not want their meaning to turn upon a "too subtle" form of deductive inference. Hobbes is himself concerned about the abuses of language that enter into human discourse. He is thus offering the reader a clue to an understanding of the *meaning* of terms used in his laws of nature that refer to *standards of oughtness*.

His response is to suggest that each of his laws of nature can be understood in light of the Golden Rule: *"Do not that to another, which thou wouldst not have done to thyself"* (1960: 103). The Golden Rule implies a method of normative inquiry: it will "sheweth him" (1960: 103). This method can be used to understand the meaning of the laws of nature:

"he has no more to do in learning the laws of nature, but, when weighing the actions of other men with his own to put them in the other part of the balance, and his own in their place, that his own passions, and self-love, may add nothing to the weight: and then there is none of these laws of nature that will not appear unto him very reasonable" (1960: 103).

The Golden Rule has at least two interesting qualities that deserve mention. First, it presupposes a basic similitude of thoughts and passions that is characteristic of all mankind. This implies a fundamental underlying equality and universality of basic characteristics that apply to all members of the species. Second, the Golden Rule, which is often viewed as a fundamental moral precept, is itself largely devoid of moral content. Instead, it implies a method of normative inquiry that can be used to derive criteria of choice and standards of judgment. The only prescriptive connotation of the Golden Rule is that one *ought* to act in conformity with the implied method of normative inquiry (i.e., one ought to act as the method "sheweth him").

The method of normative inquiry which Hobbes derives from the Golden Rule involves several levels of calculations. His first stipulation of "read thyself" is fundamental to understanding others at a level where one is concerned with how others think and feel. Given this level of understanding, he then suggests that rules, norms, and evaluative standards that are intended to apply to human *social* relationships can be understood first by taking the perspective of others, second by discounting one's own passions and self-love so as to add no weight to the scale, and, thus, third by aspiring to impartiality. A combination of introspection, taking the perspective of others, discounting partialities, and aspiring to impartiality provides the key for making interpersonal comparisons about standards of value that apply to human social relationships. The method of normative inquiry inherent in the Golden Rule, apart from the prescriptive injunction applied to action, is potentially accessible to anyone who wishes to understand the criteria of choice and standards of judgment that are used among human communities to order their relationships with one another.

In further concluding comments to that same chapter, Hobbes argues that his laws of nature are "immutable and eternal" (1960: 104) because they reflect a basic distinction that is fundamental in human nature. Some conditions engender threat, offense, and hostility in human relationships. Other conditions engender reciprocity[3], collaboration, and mutually productive relationships among human beings. Human beings in their relationships with one another manifest basic step-wise transformations in the presence of threat or goodwill not unlike the step-wise transformations that occur among water molecules at zero degrees centigrade and at 100 degrees centigrade. Threat, offense, and hostility engender war; goodwill, reciprocity, and mutally productive relationships engender peace. Lawful relationships among human beings can occur only when conditions conducive to aggression and violence are constrained and conditions conducive to goodwill and reciprocity are facilitated. Hobbes's reference to the "immutable and eternal" indicates reference to a further criterion pertaining to universality. Normative inquiry strives toward universality rather than expedient accommodation.

The great paradox in human socieites arises from the circumstances that order in human societies is an artificial order created by human beings who rely upon *words* to specify and bind their relationships with one another. Words formulated as rules of conduct become the basis for dichotomizing the realm of all potential behaviors into those which are permissible and those which are not permissible. An effort is made to rig the game of life by facilitating patterns of reciprocal and mutually productive relationships and constraining threat, offense, and aggression.

But words are insufficient to bind men to their promises. Instead, human societies depend, in part, upon the capacity of human agents to perform tasks of governance associated with formulating, enforcing, and determining the application of rules in human relationships. This exercise of the prerogatives of governing turns critically upon the capacity of some to impose punishment upon others for their failure to conform to the requirements of law as *word-ordered* relationships. The prescriptive language of law has reference to standards of oughtness. The meaning of value terms is an essential element that enters into a comprehension of rules of law as formulated by legislators, as acted upon by individuals, and as adjusticated by those who determine the application and enforce rules of law. The problem of normative inquiry is an integral part of life in society and is fundamental to any effort to understand the basis for order in human societies.[4]

11.3 Hume's Moral Philosophy as the Science of Human Nature

When David Hume raised the fundamental issue about the relationship between "is" and "ought" propositions, he indicated no more than a need to *observe* and *explain* how "ought" propositions enter into the realm of human discourse. The point is made at the conclusion to the introductory section of Book III "Of Morals" in his *Treatise* (1948). The task he presents for himself is to provide an account for making moral distinctions after having warned that many "vulgar systems of morality" will not stand critical scrutiny because moral judgment is not grounded "merely" on relations among objects, and is not perceived by reason alone (1948: 43).

In beginning his inquiry about moral philosophy[5], Hume (1948: 49) asserts: "We must look within to find the moral quality." Human cognition is formed in part by impressions of the external realm conveyed by the senses and of the internal (or subjective) realm experienced as feelings. Learning, or thought more generally, involves the forming of associations in a two-step process. The first is the transformation of sensory impression into images retained as memory in the central nervous system. The second step is the forming of associations based upon elements, combinations, and recombinations of impressions and images that permit similarities, differences, and relationships to be established. Science is grounded in causal relationships between specifiable conditions and consequences. This is the ground for crossing the threshold from memory to expectation, and transcending the present as occurrence with reference both to a past and a future.

Human cognition of moral distinctions, if I understand Hume correctly, is grounded in feelings where virtue is initially associated with feelings of pleasure and attraction, and vice is associated with feelings of pain, aversion, and uneasiness. These are internal states that provide a first approximation for evaluating objects and events with reference broadly to desires and aversions as a crude form of benefit-cost calculations. This possibility of deriving moral distinctions turns upon a presumption that, as Hobbes would say, "a similitude of thoughts and passions" characterizes all mankind.

The most important consideration in the lives of human beings is their relationship with other human beings where they individually and jointly confront a variety of opportunities and dangers in a world plagued by scarcity. The capacity to conceptualize and distinguish ways of ordering human relationships with one another, Hume sees as being grounded in an emotional quality in which human beings experience a sentiment of sympathy or fellow feeling in relation to the emotional experience of others.[6]

This emotional quality of sympathy or fellow feeling enables an individual to project himself into the situation of others and share to some degree the emotional experience of others. There is an emotional ground for making interpersonal comparisons. The emotional sentiment of sympathy is, however, subject to psychological characteristics that are variable with proximity to others. Feelings of sympathy are more intense in relation to those who are closer to us.

Hume, however, postulates that human beings also have a propensity to generalize. This propensity to generalize is grounded in capabilities for learning. Learning depends upon associations that distinguish similarities, differences, and relationships. The expression of learning in language requires generalization. Terms that are used to name events apply to general classes of events and of general sets of relationships among events.

The capacity to share in the feelings of others permits a reflective understanding about the general tendencies that arise from particular passions. The propensity to generalize applies to all of the passions. The variability of the passions in the uniquenesses of particular circumstances is generalized as human beings express themselves in language. We "correct the momentary appearances of things" and "overlook" the uniquenesses of each particular situation as we think and communicate through the vehicle of language (Hume 1948: 138). Otherwise, it would be impossible "we could ever make use of language or communicate our sentiments to one another" (Hume 1948: 138). As a result of this psychological propensity to generalize, human beings seek for some general "standard of merit and demerit" (Hume 1948: 139) that is less subject to the variability of each specific emotional experience:

"the intercourse of sentiments, therefore, in society and in conversation, makes us form some general unalterable standard by which we may approve or disapprove of characters and manners" (Hume 1948: 220).

The intercourse of sentiments grounded in sympathy or fellow feeling is transformed through generalization into sentiments of approval and disapproval for general standards of conduct. There are psychological grounds for human beings to make interpersonal comparisons about subjective experiences and to arrive at a shared basis for distinguishing right from wrong and deriving other standards of oughtness that pertain to the proper ordering of human relationships.

Hume summarizes the basic elements in his argument in a brief statement in *An Enquiry Concerning the Principles of Morals* (1948: 254):

"The distinction, therefore, between these species of sentiment [i.e., sympathy, or fellow feeling *vs.* 'those connected with any other passion' (Hume 1948: 253) being so great and evident, language must soon be moulded upon it and must invent a peculiar set of terms in order to express those universal sentiments of censure and approbation which arise from humanity or from views of general usefulness or its contrary. Virtue and Vice become known; morals are recognized; certain general rules are framed of human conduct and behavior; such measures are expected of men in such situations. This action is determined to be conformable to our abstract rule; that other, contrary. And by such universal principles are the particular sentiments of self-love frequently controlled and limited."

The moral quality arises from fellow feelings expressed as general rules: *Virtue and Vice become known; morals are recognized; certain general rules are framed of human conduct; such measures are expected of men in such situations. This action is determined to be conformable to our abstract rule; that other, contrary.*[7]

Feelings of sympathy permit human beings to take the perspective of others and to share in their emotional experience. When raised to a level of generality that discounts the uniquenesses of particular circumstances, taking the perspective of others permits the sympathetic observer to move to a level of impartiality in rendering judgments both in relation to one's own conduct and in relation to the conduct of others. The standards of evaluation derived from this method provide the normative foundation of human community.

A major portion of Hume's treatment of morals is concerned with the virtue of justice. He views justice as an artificial virtue created as a derivative of efforts to establish an artificial order that permits human beings to take advantage of mutually productive relationships with one another. The distinction between justice and injustice becomes an extension of the distinction between right and wrong as applied to rule-ruler-ruled relationships.

In general, Hume gives a deeper psychological and epistemological grounding to Hobbes's method of normative inquiry. The basic calculations remain. Learning to "read thyself" provides grounds for understanding others. The method of the Golden Rule permits one to take the perspectives of others, discount partialities, aspire to impartiality, and to derive standards of oughtness that can be used to formulate abstract rules that apply to the proper ordering of relationships among human beings. These are the grounds for ordering human relationships where both rulers and ruled can be held accountable to the same standards of oughtness that apply in the choices that people make and in evaluating performances.

11.4 Smith's Theory of Moral Sentiments

Adam Smith's *Theory of Moral Sentiments* (n.d.) can be viewed as a further elaboration of the basic method of normative inquiry advanced by both Hobbes and Hume. Smith (n.d.: 49) conceives sympathy to be "our fellow feeling with any passion whatever" as expressed in situations that excite particular passions. An expression of sympathy and its reciprocal expression by those being sympathized with yield a moderation of feelings that come to be expressed in a sense of propriety. "Every faculty in one man is the measure by which he judges the like faculty in another" (Smith n.d.: 62). A shared sense of propriety is the basis for making moral distinctions. Sympathy and the capacity to take the perspective of others enables human beings to function as spectators capable of forming judgments of approval and disapproval about the way that people act and order their relationships with one another with reference to general standards of propriety (i.e., right and wrong).

Smith sees this capacity to take the perspective of a spectator as applying to an individual's own conduct:

"And, in the same manner, we either approve or disapprove of our own conduct, according as we feel that, when we place ourselves in the situation of another man, and view it, as it were, with his eyes and from his station, we either can or cannot enter into and sympathize with the sentiments and motives which influenced it. We can never survey our own sentiments and motives, we can never form any judgment concerning them, unless we remove ourselves, as it were, from our own natural station, and endeavour to view them as at a certain distance from us. But we can do this in no other way than by endeavouring to view them with the eyes of other people, or as other people are likely to view them . . . We endeavour to examine our own conduct as we imagine any other fair and impartial spectator would examine it" (n.d.: 204).

Smith now adds to Hobbes's formulation that human beings can come to a better understanding of themselves by taking the perspective of others to "scrutinize the propriety of their own conduct" (Smith n.d.: 206). By viewing one's own conduct from the perspective of others, one can better "read thyself," as Hobbes would put it. The pattern of reflection is extended. One uses indications of approbation and disapprobation by others as a mirror to reflect upon one's own conduct. In doing so, one takes the perspective of others which is informed by one's understanding of oneself and others to give credence to their censure or applause in order to better *read* oneself and judge one's own conduct.

This taking the perspective of the other to assess one's own conduct leads Smith to specify more carefully the concept of the impartial observer or the impartial spectator which he formulates in the following terms:

"When I endeavour to examine my own conduct, when I endeavour to pass judgment upon it, and either to approve or to condemn it, it is evident that, in all such cases, I divide myself, as it were, into two persons; and that I, the examiner and the judge, represent a different character from the other I, the person whose conduct is examined into and judged of. The first is the spectator, whose sentiments with regard to my own conduct I endeavour to enter into, by placing myself in his situation, and by considering how it would appear to me, when seen from that particular point of view. The second is the agent whom I properly call myself, and of whose conduct, under the character of a spectator, I was endeavouring to form some opinion. The first is the judge; the second is the person judged of. But that the judge should in every respect, be the same with the person judged of, is as impossible as that the cause should, in every respect, be the same with the effect" (n.d.: 206–207).

An individual actor is characterized by elements of uniqueness and partialities that pertain to the particular experiences, education, and constitution of that individual. Taking the perspective of the other is a cognitive process, an act of the imagination, that, on the part of any organism capable of learning, must necessarily classify and distinguish in ways that loses details of uniquenesses by which everything would be viewed in their distinct individualities. Human cognition is otherwise and is informed by propensities to classify and to generalize. Mutual sympathy evokes a sense of propriety and generalizing the perspective of others evokes impartiality. Smith provides a psychological explanation for the development of a moral conscience in the human animal. Taking the perspective of others and aspiring to impartiality grounded in sympathetic understanding enables human beings to formulate criteria of choice or standards of oughtness that move toward universality. In principle, at least, Smith's impartial observer is consistent with

Kant's categorical imperative which requires that one act in a way that is consistent with a universal rule of conduct.

Smith argues that human beings lay down rules to bind ourselves to what is fit and proper and reduce the self-deceit that comes from delusions of self-love. Justice is, for Smith, a virtue that hinders us from hurting others. Benevolence is a virtue that extends goodwill where one seeks to please others and is deserving of gratitude. Justice, in particular, is the virtue most closely bound by rules:

"The rules of justice may be compared to the rules of grammar; the rules of the other virtues to the rules which critics lay down for the attainment of what is sublime and elegant. The one are precise, accurate and indispensable. The others are loose, vague and indeterminate, and present us with a general idea of the perfection we ought to aim at . . ." (n.d.: 290).

Smith's *Theory of Moral Sentiments*, thus, contains reference to a method of normative inquiry that provides a basis for individual self-governance which Smith refers to as self-command and for the governance of social relationships in human society. The exercise of liberty in individual conduct has reference then, at a minimal level, to the standards of choice that apply to prudence and justice in human social relationships. Standards of liberty and justice are consonant with one another and are informed by standards of propriety grounded in distinctions between right and wrong. Proper benevolence, for Smith, is essential to a higher level of moral achievement, but benevolence has meaning only if freely given. A free society, thus, best allows for the exercise of liberty as an expression of prudence, justice, *and* proper benevolence.

Smith emphasizes that the development of criteria derived from taking the perspective of others leads to two different levels of consideration. The first is carried to perfection; the second is cognizant of a proximity to an ideal "which the actions of the greater part of men commonly arrive at" (Smith n.d.: 74). What goes beyond the mean toward the ideal, Smith characterizes as deserving of applause; and what falls short of the level which the "greater part of men commonly arrive at" is deserving of blame. A cognizance of these two levels of evaluation is especially important in the conduct of empirical inquiry. Measuring human achievement against the level of perfection will always lead to an assessment that human beings and human institutions are wanting. A comparative assessment of performance can only be made by comparing human achievements (i.e., what men arrive at) with one another in light of the relevant measure or perfection.

Reference to the ideal as a measure of perfection can give rise to serious errors of judgment which Smith attributes to "the man of system." His observation is deserving of an extended quotation:

"The man of system, on the contrary, is apt to be very wise in his own conceit, and is often so enamoured with the supposed beauty of his own ideal plan of government, that he cannot suffer the smallest deviation from any part of it. He goes on to establish it completely and in all its parts, without any regard either to the great interests or to the strong prejudices which may oppose it: he seems to imagine that he can arrange the different members of a great society with as much ease as the hand arranges the different pieces upon a chess-board; he does not consider that the pieces upon the chess-board have no other principle of motion besides that which the hand impresses upon them; but that, in the great chess-board of human society, every single piece has a principle of motion of its own, altogether different from that which the legislature might choose to impress upon it. If those two principles coincide and act in the same direction, the game of human society will go on easily and harmoniously, and is very likely to be happy and successful. If they are opposite or different, the game will go on miserably, and the society must be at all times in the highest degree of disorder.

Some general, and even systematical, idea of the perfection of policy and law, may no doubt be necessary for directing the views of the statesman. But to insist upon establishing, and upon establishing all at once, and in spite of all opposition, every thing which that idea may seem to require, must often be the highest degree of arrogance. It is to erect his own judgment into the supreme standard of right and wrong. It is to fancy himself the only wise and worthy man in the commonwealth, and that his fellow-citizens should accommodate themselves to him, and not he to them. It is upon this account that of all political speculators sovereign princes are by far the most dangerous. This arrogance is perfectly familiar to them. They entertain no doubt of the immense superiority of their own judgment. When such imperial and royal reformers, therefore, condescend to contemplate the constitution of the country which is committed to their government, they seldom see any thing so wrong in it as the obstructions which it may sometimes oppose to the execution of their own will" (n.d.: 380–381).

From this observation, I conclude that the condition of human fallibility necessarily implies limits to human cognition and judgment. These limits are such that human beings can only aspire to but cannot attain standards of rightness, truth, or justice carried to perfection. Their appeal in considering the appropriateness of a standard is to their fellow human beings. Human dialogue informed by appropriate methods of normative inquiry is a basis for deriving levels of understanding and agreement which can form the foundations for human communities. In turn, we might expect the conceptions, methods, and evaluative criteria used in normative inquiry to be reflected in the achievements attained by human communities. The warrantability for conceptions, methods, and evaluative standards is established by what is achieved, even though that achievement is short of perfection.

11.5 Conclusion

Hobbes, Hume, and Smith each contribute to a method of normative inquiry that enables fallible human beings to derive norms or standards of oughtness that apply both to making choices and evaluating performance. That method is grounded in the ancient moral precept of the Golden Rule. The first level of inquiry pertains to"read thyself" and through that reading to come to understand how others think and feel "on the like occasions," to use Hobbes's terms. To extend one's understanding of what is shared in common by human beings, a second level of inquiry is implied by sympathetically taking the perspective of others and inquiring into the shared meaning of value terms used in a language of discourse so that individual partialities are discounted and a fair and impartial view is attained. Using the perspective of the impartial observer permits human beings to derive standards of oughtness that might aspire to universality or to being "immutable and eternal," as Hobbes expresses this criterion.

The criterion of universality has two potentially different referents. One is to the generality of the proposition. The universe of discourse is not confined to particular communities. While the human condition for each individual is culture bound, this does not foreclose the possibility that human beings in their methods of normative inquiry might aspire to formulate general criteria of choice that have universal import. It is not enough simply to be other-directed.

The other referent to universality pertains to a potential for common understanding and agreement. Hobbes's presumption about a basic similitude of thoughts and passions characteristic of all mankind implies grounds for consensus reflected in common understanding and agreement. His method of normative inquiry provides a basis for human enlightenment where Hobbes would anticipate that the exercise of political authority can be potentially reconciled with the consent of those who are governed. Mere applause and censureship, however, is not an appropriate proxy for enlightened consensus. While human beings might aspire to standards of universality and agreement, they cannot, as fallible creatures, attain immutability and eternity. They can aspire to something better, but they cannot attain perfection. A continual striving to enhance human understanding is accompanied by a burden to engage in a dialogue with one another where we develop standards of judgments that apply to assertions about both is-ness and ought-ness. The standards and norms, that inform human choice and are the grounds for human community, will always be subject to reconsideration so long as human beings use the frail structure of words, and the meaning we attribute to words in our efforts to communicate with one another, and order our relationships with one another.

When meanings turn critically upon sentiments or feelings, human beings cannot rely solely upon the formal definition of words to convey meaning. Rather, it is necessary to put oneself, and how one experiences oneself, in the place of others. In this way, it becomes possible to understand how others think and feel and how others relying upon such methods of mutual understanding might derive common criteria to use in relating themselves to one another. Standards for distinguishing right from wrong, justice from injustice, true from false, and benefit from harm can be generated by such methods. Human beings can come to know how such criteria enter into calculations in relation both to the choices that are made and in evaluating achievement in human societies. Formal definitions and rigorous specifications of rules can never substitute for methods of inquiry where human beings draw upon their own experience in understanding the meaning of terms that apply to human conduct.[8]

This implies that a failure to use appropriate methods of normative inquiry and a misspecification of essential relationships may contribute to serious sources of misunderstanding in formulating appropriate standards of oughtness. If justice, for example, is the application of standards of propriety of rule-ruler-ruled relationships, there is danger of misspecifying essential relationships if only subject-to-subject relationships are considered. Assuming that the offices of citizen and subject refer to the same individuals, there are critical issues in a democratic society about the standards of propriety that apply to citizen-official relationships and how officials can be held accountable to principles of justice in their proper discharge of the prerogatives in official-subject relationships. It is considerations like these which mean that standards may themselves change in the course of time. Fallible creatures might still use appropriate methods of inquiry to reconsider what standards of oughtness are to apply to the way that human beings relate themselves to one another.

General standards of oughtness that can be derived from using the methods of normative inquiry are of basic importance in setting standards that are applicable to guidance, control, and performance evaluation in the public sector. This is the basis for making normative distinctions about what is to be permitted and what is not to be permitted as a function of rule-ordering. Finer degrees of distinction about what is preferred among the permissible options must then rely upon particular institutional arrangements that enable human beings to communicate their preferences to one another. Prices in a market economy provide signalling mechanisms to allow people to express their preferences for the array of options that are available in the very large realm of possibilities that meet the criterion of being "goods". Money, as a medium of exchange, becomes a measure of value for everything exchanged for money. Similarly, elections enable people to communicate some order of preferences in the taking of collective decisions about goods and services to be provided in the public sectors. Debate in parliamentary proceedings, discussions in public fora and in the press, protest meetings, and many other institutional arrangements enable people to inform one another about their preferences and aversions and take one another into account under circumstances where no one need have fear of others, and where each acts in relation to general rules of conduct that take account of the interests of others.

Standard setting and standard using are of fundamental importance in establishing the way that human beings order their relationships with one another. How people relate to one another is as important as what they accomplish in their joint and interdependent activities. Standards of propriety and of justice are as essential to governing the conditions of life in human communities as the goods, services, and states of affairs that are yielded by their joint endeavours. The ordering of means is as essential to respectful relationships among human beings as the ends that are accomplished.[9]

Reference to a means-ends calculus pertaining to the attainment of goals is apt to confuse different forms of calculation that enter into assessments of performance in human societies. One form of means-ends calculation is analogous to that which enters into the production of any economic good. The factors and technologies of production are the means that enter into the production of a good as an end. Preferences are reflected in demand with reference to supply and are expressable in price. These are taken into account in a benefit-cost calculus. A competitive market is expected to yield results where marginal cost is equal to price. A net surplus of value accrues wherever subjective preferences exceed prices. The rule that benefits should be equal to or greater than cost is the equivalent economic calculation for a public economy. But, difficulties arise in attaching measurable benefits to goods and services that are not subject to marketable transactions or may not be measurable in cardinal units of measurement. Thus, serious difficulties arise in applying an economic calculus to measure public-sector performance.

Where criteria of choice apply to the basic value terms used in any system of law to distinguish permitted from proscribed patterns of behavior, quite different forms of calculation arise. Criteria for distinguishing right from wrong, lawful from unlawful, become the basis for judgment. These criteria may coincide with a broad spectrum of economic calculations in as much as most economic "goods" are within the set that is identified as lawful and which are amenable to a rightful possession and/or use.

Presumably, criteria informed by normative inquiry and moral judgment can be viewed as means for ordering relationships that would yield some resultant social state of affairs. As an act of imagination, such a state might be conceived as the "good life" (e.g., E. Jordan 1949: Ch. 22). Images of the "good life" are likely to reflect moral criteria carried to perfection in Smith's formulation rather than those social states of affairs that are manifestations of what human beings commonly achieve.

Fundamental tensions must exist in all human societies between what is achieved and what is aspired to. As efforts are made to objectify the "good life" as specifiable states of affairs, strong differences must necessarily exist about *what* is preferred in contrast to *how* people relate to one another. A community of saints may be at peace with themselves under "objective" conditions that others would view as a prison. Tensions also arise from the human propensity to strive for something better. The image of the "good life" is likely to be transformed with each human achievement. In addition, the use of instruments of coercion to do good is likely to seduce all who strive to attain the "good life" into a serious neglect of the costs entailed. The most oppressive tyrants are those who are most strongly persuaded that they know *what* is good for others.

We, thus, confront the circumstance that the tools we use and the calculations we make are only imperfect measures of performance that depend for their meaning upon shared communities of understanding and agreement. These calculations work tolerably well when people can keep one another reasonably well informed about their intentions and the way they relate to one another. Human communities depend critically upon communication where sympathy, mutual understanding, and goodwill provide the foundation for productive relationships.

Notes

1   F. A. Hayek in *Rules and Order,* the first volume in *Law, Legislation and Liberty,* recognizes the uncertainty that derives from human capabilities to generate new knowledge. I have pursued some of the implications that follow in an essay on "Some Paradoxes for Planners: Human Knowledge and Its Limitations" (in Chickering 1976: 243–253).

   Most theories of cultural evolution are grounded upon assumptions about a capacity of human beings to transmit learning by the use of language from one individual to another in contemporary and succeeding generations and upon a capacity to generate new knowledge that expands the basic repertoire of adaptive potential. This would imply that human beings must necessarily face uncertain futures. See, for example, Julian Huxley, *Knowledge, Morality and Destiny;* Pierre Teilhard de Chardin, *The Phenomenon of Man;* and V. F. Turchin, *The Phenomenon of Science.*

2   The relevant passage in Hobbes (1960: 64) is: "So that in the first place, I put for a general inclination of all mankind, a perpetual and restless desire for power after power, that ceaseth only with death." Power is defined as as "present means to obtain some future apparent good." I interpret his statement to mean that human beings are motivated by a perpetual and restless desire to use present means to attain some future apparent good that is continuously reiterated so long as life endures: A universal rule

that applies to all mankind is a continual striving for something better. This applies to the saint as well as the tyrant. Striving for excellence is striving nonetheless.

3   There is some difficulty in communicating about these terms and knowing what is meant by the different perspectives taken in the German and English languages. Reciprocity is usually translated as *"Gegenseitigkeit"* or *"die gegenseitige Beziehung"* (the reciprocal relation). The intuitive sense of *gegenseitig* pertains to opposite or countervailing. The intuitive sense of the English term reciprocity is sharing in a common relationship marked by goodwill. When I use the term reciprocity, I refer to sharing in a common relationship marked by mutual goodwill rather than one that is opposite or countervailing. My usage implies something that is more like solidarity and less like *Gegenseitigkeit*.

4   I have not addressed Hobbes's theory of sovereignty. This is referred to in Chapter 5 of this volume on "Constitutional Considerations with Special Reference to Federal Systems." Hobbes's theory of sovereignty is the most vulnerable part of his analysis, and his formulation depends for its sufficiency upon a sovereign's accountability to God. The sufficiency of his formulation collapses in the absence of that condition.

5   The first sentence in Hume's *An Inquiry Concerning Human Understanding* reads as follows: "Moral philosophy or the science of human nature may be treated after two different manners, each of which has its peculiar merit and may contribute to the entertainment, instruction, and reformation of mankind" (1955: 15).

I assume that this is to be read as meaning that Hume regards moral philosophy to be "the science of human nature."

6   This emotional quality is perhaps best illustrated by the human experience of watching images from photographs of a drama projected upon a movie screen. Everyone knows that the drama is fiction, and that the images on a screen are no more than patterned light. Yet, spectators are able to project themselves into the circumstances of the drama so that watching a motion picture can be a compelling, emotional experience that ranges from uncontrollable laughter to tears. There is, thus, a secondary order of emotional experience in which human beings are capable of sharing in the emotional experiences of others. This is what Hume means by sympathy or fellow feeling. He uses the two terms equivalently.

7   These observations by Hume indicate that Hume had formulated what Harsanyi (1977: 648–652) refers to as rule utilitarianism as contrasted to act utilitarianism. One might also argue that Hume's conception of justice as an artificial virtue is an expression of institutional utilitarianism as Reinhard Selten (cf. Ch. 12) distinguishes institutional utilitarianism from rule utilitarianism in his essay that follows this one. See especially Hume's discussion "Of Justice" in Part III of the *Enquiry* (1948: 185–206).

8   Hume, in *An Inquiry Concerning Human Understanding* (1955: 190–191), provides an illustration of the difficulties of relying upon definitions to refer to the subjective level of phenomena that pertains to how human beings think. His task is to distinguish the term "belief" from a contrary term "fiction." He has to point to the common experiences that human beings have with reference to patterns of thought. He indicates how the human imagination can associate images (his "ideas") by an unlimited power of dividing, combining, and mixing images (ideas). All kinds of fictions can be imagined. But, belief is attached to a pattern of thought by a sense of being plausible, i.e., by being a conception that is realizable and can become a part of tangible experience associated with "reality."

We are apparently confronted with the circumstance that some human beings can lose touch with reality sufficiently to believe themseves to be another human being. Such human beings, however, are considered to be mentally incompetent. Most human beings are able to distinguish fiction from belief once one examines one's own thought processes in a way that one's experience permits the distinction to be made. Simple definitions do not suffice.

9   The essential place of means in the ordering of human relationships can, perhaps, he indicated by a recognition that human behavior is commonly conceived to be purposive or goal directed. The critical focus in ordering human relationships bears upon the coordination of activities or actions. Motives and the purpose or goal to be achieved are important in construing the meaning and social significance of actions. The critical issue in social organization is, however, the coordination or ordering of activities, i.e., the means that are used to achieve purposes or goals.

Patterns of social organization are relatively open systems of order that can accommodate significant variability in the way these patterns are used as instruments to accomplish diverse purposes and objectives. Traffic on highways can be ordered with references to a few relatively simple rules rather than having to program the origin, movement, and destination of every vehicle in a fully determinant way. People motivated by different purposes can use the rules of the road to reach their respective destinations by giving proper attention to the way they order their actions to take account of the expected actions of others. Institutions operating in the public sector manifest characteristic patterns of relationships that can be used for a variety of different purposes. There are, thus, important degrees of latitude in pursuing any particular purpose. These degrees of latitude allow for choice in the ordering of activities as means. The degrees of latitude are never complete because human action would then be independent of purposiveness. It is still possible, for example, for people dedicated to the destruction of "capitalism" to pursue that goal and still not be destructive of the maintenance of civil relationships in what is presumed to be a "capitalist" society. Human beings can forebear and take account of one another in ways that permit an ordering of activities in relation to one another that has some measure of independence of the particular purpose or goal that is being sought. The ordering of means then has a primacy that bears upon the proper exercise of authority relationships in human societies. The order in human societies is an open order that is bounded by constraints. Principles of indeterminacy apply such that a fully determinate complex of simple cause and effect relationships (one-one transformations) cannot be assumed to exist. Choice is possible within constraints. Many-one and one-many transformations can be assumed to exist.

References

Beck, L. W. (1978): *Essays on Kant and Hume*. New Haven, Conn.: Yale Univ. Press.

Chickering, A. L. (ed.) (1976): *The Politics of Planning*. San Francisco: Institute for Contemporary Studies.

Harsanyi, J. C. (1977): "Morality and the Theory of Rational Behavior." *Social Research* 44/4: 623–656.

Hayek, F. A. von (1973): *Law, Legislation and Liberty* (3 vols., 1973–1979). Chicago, Ill.: Univ. of Chicago Press.

Hobbes, T. (1960): *Leviathan or the Matter, Forme and Power of a Commonwealth Ecclesiastical and Civil*. Oxford: Basil Blackwell.

Hume, D. (1948): *Hume's Moral and Political Philosophy*. New York: Hafner Publishing Company.

Hume, D. (1955): *An Inquiry Concerning Human Understanding*. New York: Liberal Arts Press.

Huxley, J. (1960): *Knowledge, Morality and Destiny*. New York: Mentor Book.

Jordan, E. (1949): *The Good Life*. Chicago, Ill.: Univ. of Chicago Press.

Polanyi, M. (1958): *Personal Knowledge*. Chicago, Ill.: Univ. of Chicago Press.

Smith, A. (n. d.): *The Theory of Moral Sentiments*. Indianapolis, Ind.: Liberty Press.

Teilhard de Chardin, P. (1961): *The Phenomenon of Man*. New York: Harper & Row.

Turchin, V. F. (1977): *The Phenomenon of Science*. New York: Columbia Univ. Press.

Appendix 1
A Note on Biology, Time and the Golden Rule

Martin Shubik

On Nonsymmetry

One of the central axioms of Hobbes, Hume, and Smith in *The Theory of Moral Sentiments* and similar works is the Golden Rule. This is usually phrased as "Do not unto others as you would not have them do unto you." This rule is a manifestation of the important role of symmetry in normative arguments in the social sciences.

Symmetry plays a key role in many of the arguments in game theory concerning fair division and value. Tied in with the assumption of symmetry, unless otherwise explicitly specified is the assumption of equal information, perception, and ability to grasp information.

There is an aesthetic attractiveness to the Golden Rule; and the exercise of seeing how far we can proceed within extremely parsimonious set of axioms is attractive to both the philosopher and to the mathematical social scientist. Although this exercise is attractive, it can be dangerously misleading in the development of the social sciences and even ethics. The reasons are simple and based upon simple features of biology and time. The Golden Rule is not an abstract verity but an inadequate approximation in transactions between the sexes, for example. This also holds true in transactions between individuals of sufficiently different ages.

We need to consider two sexes and possibly eight or nine age groups in order to modify the Golden Rule in applications. The age categories might be: (1) baby, (2) child, (3) adolescent, (4) young middle-aged, (5) old middle-aged, (6) old, (7) senile, (8) dead, (9) foetus, and (10) generations unborn.

What is being suggested is not just an added complication that can be taken care of by easy modification of the initial model. New problems are posed. In particular, if we regard men and women as related but different "machines," we cannot expect M to be able to simulate W and W to simulate M *simultaneously*.

When we consider a male adolescent and his father, the "machines" may be approximately the same, but the amount of programming and historical inputs are different. In particular, the middle-aged father may be able to "put himself in the son's place" because he has been there. But the reverse does not hold. Machine, M, who differs from M1 primarily by having more programs, can simulate M1 over a broader range than M1 can simulate M.

The categories "senile" and "dead" noted in the age breakdown are not strictly chronological with the others, but in carrying out the machine analogy they appear to be worth noting. In particular, biological degeneration may destroy the ability of the senile individual to "put herself in a younger woman's shoes."

The final category "dead" was included to raise questions concerning the usefulness of counterfactuals such as "If Jefferson were President now rather than Reagan, what would he have done about Lebanon?," and also to argue that the dead, although not relevant to direct Golden Rule considerations, do figure indirectly in the inputs that accrue in cultural history. Thus, honor to ancestors and responsibility to generations unborn are not based upon a one-to-one introspection between two actors but are phrases involving one individual with a coding of history and a volitional projection of the future.

A different set of criteria might involve race and species. If our drive for symmetry is so large, should we put ourselves in the other dog or dolphin's place? Although this question is not pursued further, it is raised nevertheless to remind us that even in the purest form, the Golden Rule has some form of empirical assumptions which rules out dogs, dolphins, the dead, and the unborn and inanimate objects.

Woman and Men: Two-Way Nonsymmetry

The empirical questions at the biological level include differences in sexual role, brain function, maturation, longevity, health, and what they imply in terms of preferences and decision structure.

Suppose that we knew precisely how to characterize the biological differences between machine W and M and what they imply in terms of preference and choice. If W and M each know these differences, how does W use her knowledge to put herself in the position of M and vice-versa? This may be the point at which culture, history, and society come into play on the individual. In the game of man with man in many situations we can factor out culture, history, and society. When M1 puts himself in M2's position, he can conceptualize within an equivalence class of machines. When M tries to put himself in the position of W, a filter function of some variety, probably based upon historically developed cultural norms, is used as a proxy procedure to try to conceptualize a point of view he himself can *never* experience. Figure 1 indicates the distinction:

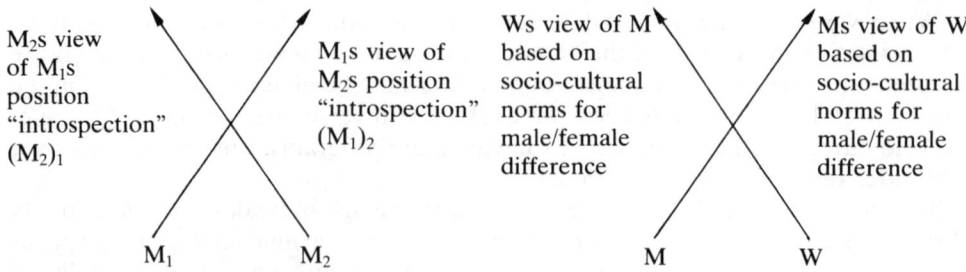

Fig. 1

Mothers and Daughters: One-Way Nonsymmetry

As a first order approximation we may assume that a mother "who has been there" can simulate, or put herself in the position of her teen-aged daughter. But her daughter without the experience that she will have obtained in 25 years time must use a sociocultural norm as is shown in Figure 2.

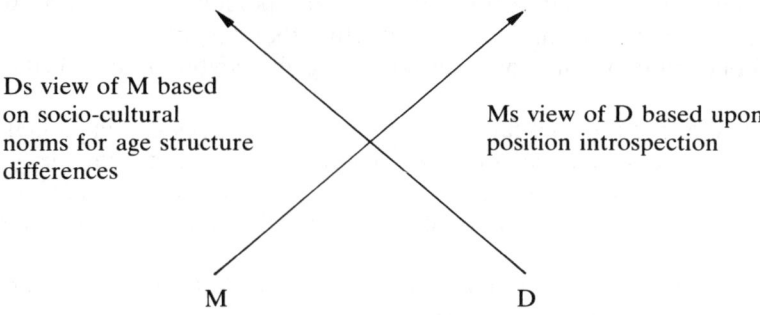

Ds view of M based on socio-cultural norms for age structure differences

Ms view of D based upon position introspection

M   D

Fig. 2

Some Questions and Implications

At the level of application the above comments suggest, for example, that unless sociocultural norms are appropriate, a society supplying social services has a better chance of success if the social workers and managers are roughly of the same age structure and are of the same sex as their clients. For example, a requirement that the personal attendants and managers at an old-age home be older than 50 might help.

At a different level we need to consider age requirements for officials and legislators. How much of a bureaucratic age structure can or should be dependent on the biology of aging as contrasted with the sociocultural norms concerning the links between age and honor, seniority and status?

The questions raised here call for several different investigations. One in particular is the interpreting and sorting out of biological and sociocultural sexual differences.

Gaming experiments may be worthwhile. It might be feasible to control for sociocultural factors utilizing experimental games.

The problems with the development of formal game theoretical and ethical models which reflect the essential nonsymmetries noted are not theoretical but empirical and conceptual. *If* all players could be regarded as intrinsically fungible or symmetric then a symmetric fair division will emerge. If all are not equal, the fair division theory will provide a nonsymmetric answer, but the problem we are faced with is how does the nonsymmetry depend upon the intrinsic inequalities in the players.

A philosopher's solution might be to argue original position and say, for example, that each individual has an equal chance of being born male or female and that the game should be played among the unborn. I believe that it is more reasonable to start with what is, rather than with such a counterfactual.

My argument is not with abstract equity theory. Full symmetry as an axiom based upon a Golden Rule to be applied to a counterfactual unisex population of the same age appears to me to be a perfectly reasonable research assumption for logical development. What bothers me is what I perceive to be a *non sequitar* in reasoning or an extra normative counterfactual that "people should be born equal or should play an impossible original-position game devoid of historical or societal context."

I believe that the abstract fair-division theories in ethics and in formal development of game theory has been of great value. But I suggest that the going from unisex, ageless, *in vitro,* normative theory to application or to inferences about society or the political economy requires an explicit understanding of sex and age differences.

The modification calls for not merely biological knowledge, but how unlike individuals form Golden Rule inferences about each other in the absence of introspective similarity.

Acknowledgement

The author wishes to acknowledge several stimulating conversations with Vincent Ostrom and Seymour Sorenson.

Appendix 2
Nonsymmetries in Making Interpersonal Comparisons

Vincent Ostrom

Grounds for making interpersonal comparisons are the essential foundation for setting and using standards to order relationships in human societies, to judge conduct in relation to standards, and to use standards to evaluate performance. The existence of nonsymmetries suggests that methods for making interpersonal comparisons based upon moral precepts, like the Golden Rule, are subject to serious limits. Two methods would seem to be available to attempt to correct for nonsymmetries. One is communication across the thresholds created by the nonsymmetries of life and experience by those who are involved. Another method is to attempt to devise an appropriate cognitive structure for understanding others and then to proceed by conjecture to test the fit of one's conjectural model with observed behavioral patterns or evidence about behavioral patterns.

The problem is an unavoidable one that plagues all efforts at human understanding. Human actions, efforts, and achievements are purposive and reflect human thought and choice. The meaning or significance of human effort always reflect a union of fact and value and is never value-free. The meaning of value terms in human discourse depend upon learning how to make interpersonal comparisons. Both symmetries and nonsymmetries in interpersonal comparisons would appear to have critical importance for methodological problems in the social sciences and humanities where scholars must attempt to cross the thresholds of biological, environmental, social, cultural, and historical nonsymmetries in the conduct of their investigations. Similar problems would appear to be critical in experimental gaming in efforts to account for discrepancies between "rational" solutions and experimental results. Finally, a wide range of practical problems arise with regard to communication, discourse, and argumentation in decision-making processes that depend upon human beings crossing nonsymmetrical thresholds to establish commonly shared grounds for judgments and decisions. Once we understand the symmetries that provide the foundations for making interpersonal comparisons, we still face the task of clarifying nonsymmetries and how they limit interpersonal comparisons.

Acknowledgement

Discussions with Martin Shubik about nonsymmetries in making interpersonal comparisons point to a universe of inquiry to which I can only make the briefest response.

12. Institutional Utilitarianism

Reinhard Selten

Abstract

Institutional utilitarianism as an ethical theory is based on the idea that the institutions of society should be such that a maximum of total utility is achieved under the condition that every individual mainly follows his self-interest. Some problems of utilitarianism in general as well as specific problems of rule utilitarianism and institutional utilitarianism are exposed and new perspectives of research opened. The appendix gives an example of how utilitarian analysis and cost-benefit analysis may lead to different results in judging institutional arrangements.

12.1 Introduction and Overview

Utilitarianism is a philosophical position in ethical theory which holds that moral judgements should be derived from a principle of joint utility maximization. Joint utility is the sum (or the average) of the utilities of all individuals in society or mankind or some other universe of moral subjects.

When the idea of utilitarianism was introduced by Bentham, no attention was payed to the scale on which utility is supposed to be measured. Obviously, adding up utilities does not make sense unless cardinal measurement is possible.

With the rise of Paretian economics more and more economists began to look at utility as an ordinal concept. Moreover, utility was thought of as purely subjective and a comparison of utility levels of different persons was held to be impossible. Since utilitarianism crucially depends on cardinality and interpersonal comparability it appeared to be an outmoded theory of merely historical interest.

The idea of cardinal utility was reintroduced into economics by von Neumann and Morgenstern who axiomatized expected utility maximization in their famous "Theory of Games and Economic Behavior" (1944). Since then it is well understood that rational behavior in the presence of risk must be based on a concept of utility with measurability on an interval scale. The unit of measurement and the zero point are arbitrary, but this exhausts the degrees of freedom of numerical representation.

The reestablishment of cardinal utility removed one objection to utilitarianism but the situation remained essentially unchanged as long as the impossibility of interpersonal comparisons was considered to be self-evident by the vast majority of economic theorists. Utilitarianism continued to be looked upon as an untenable position.

In 1955 John Harsanyi published a relatively short paper on "Cardinal Welfare, Individualistic Ethics and Interpersonal Comparisons of Utility" whose fundamental significance was at first hardly noticed but became more and more apparent in the following decades. Harsanyi challenged the dogma of the impossibility of interpersonal utility comparisons by a convincing philosophical argument and thereby reestablished utilitarianism as a respectable ethical position. Modern textbooks on social choice do not any more reject interpersonal utility comparisons as impossible (Sen 1970). Such comparisons are recognized as the basis of ethical judgement, not only by utilitarianism, but also by competing ethical positions like Rawlsian egalitarianism (Rawls 1972).

Ethical theories based on utility judgments may be called "economic" since they fit into the framework of modern economic theory. Utilitarianism and Rawlsian egalitarianism are representatives of the economic type of ethical theories. Other types of ethical theories emphasize fundamental values like "freedom" or"human dignity" as goals to be achieved independently of whether they are valued by individuals or not. Such ideas have not yet been worked out in a way which permits them to be used as a tool of economic analysis. Some ethical theorists are more concerned with logical structures of ethical reasoning than with the content of moral judgement. They look at systems of statements about actions which "ought to be taken" are "forbidden" or "permitted" and their logical relationships (Hare 1971, von Wright 1963). This type of logicist ethics has little to offer to economic theory, even if it may be of interest for other reasons. Of course, these short remarks cannot do full justice to a vast body of literature on non-economic ethical theories but they may serve to indicate the basis of the author's preference for theories based on interpersonal utility comparisons.

Rawlsian egalitarianism maintains that the minimal utility obtained by any individual should be as high as possible. One can speak of an ethical maxmin-criterion. However, this view is incompatible with the idea that society as a whole should exhibit the same kind of rationality as a rational individual according to Bayesian decision theory (Harsanyi 1975). The author thinks that this argument decides the issue of utilitarianism versus Rawlsian egalitarianism in favor of utilitarianism. However, this view is by no means shared by all social choice theorists. It must be expected that the debate between both schools of thought will continue for some time.

Utilitarianism is maybe the most elaborate consistent view of ethical theory. Nevertheless, it has its internal problems. Different versions of utilitarian ethics must be distinguished. It is necessary to contrast act utilitarianism with rule utilitarianism. Act utilitarianism maintains that every single action should be judged in terms of the maximization of the sum of all utilities whereas rule utilitarianism rejects judgements on isolated actions in favor of the evaluation of generalized rules of moral behavior.

In this chapter it will be argued that another distinction between personal and institutional utilitarianism needs also to be made. The term "personal" is meant to characterize ethical imparatives directly applied to individual behavior in everyday life. Personal utilitarianism is an appeal to every human being to act ethically wherever he or she has a choice to make.

Institutional utilitarianism is based on a pessimistic attitude towards the effectiveness of moral appeals. It ist based on the idea that the institutions of society should be such that a maximum of total utility is achieved under the condition that every individual mainly follows his self-interest. Moral appeals, even if they could have some limited effectiveness, should not be necessary for a satisfactory functioning of society.

After this broad overview it may be useful to cover some of the issues which have been raised above in somewhat more detail, even if it cannot be the aim of a relatively short chapter to offer a thorough discussion of utilitarianism and its problems.

12.2 Harsanyi's Argument for Interpersonal-Comparability

Suppose that there are n individuals $i = 1, \ldots, n$ each of whom has a von Neumann-Morgenstern utility function u_i defined on all possile futures of the world. We can think of a possible future of the world as described by a huge set of parameters $x_1, \ldots, x_m$. Individual i's utility has the form:

$$u_i = f_i (x_1, \ldots, x_m)$$

Preferences are determined by natural law. If the genetic structure and the past history of individual i are given, complete knowledge of natural law would permit the prediction of f_i. Suppose that hereditary and environmental influences on i are described by a set of parameters $P_{i1}, \ldots, P_{ik}$. Then player i's utility is a function of $x_1, \ldots, x_m$ and $P_{i1}, \ldots, P_{ik}$:

$$u_i = f(x_1, \ldots, x_m; P_{i1}, \ldots, P_{ik})$$

Note that the function f is the same for every individual. f will be called the universal utility function.

The mere fact that individual utilities can be expressed by a universal utility function does not yet establish interpersonal comparability. One needs an additional assumption which shall be called the "principle of hypothetical preference judgments". This principle assumes that an individual can make meaningful preference comparisons involving different values of the parameters P_{ij} and that these judgements are correctly expressed by f.

One of the parameters P_{ij} may be the size of a person. Somebody may say: I would be happy to loose 20% of my income if in exchange I could be 10 centimeters taller. This is a meaningful preference judgement, even if the person is fully grown. In fact, some such comparisons may be much easier than other comparisons which are not merely hypothetical. Since accidents do happen one must develop an estimate of the loss of utility involved in blindness in order to evaluate some possible futures.

Examples of this kind show that interpersonal comparisons are not really different from intrapersonal comparisons. An estimate of my utility loss in case of blindnesss is very similar to an interpersonal comparison with a blind twin, who is identical with me in every other respect.

The principle of hypothetical preference judgments contains a consistency assumption: preferences between different hypothetical positions do not depend on the actual position. Ceteris paribus, the utility loss involved in blindness should not depend on whether the person is not blind and considers hypothetical blindness or whether the situation is the other way around. It is not unreasonable to think of this assumption as satisfied for fully rational individuals.

12.3 Act Utilitarianism and Rule Utilitarianism

Harsanyi has shown that contrary to earlier philosophical opinions there is an important difference between act utilitarianism and rule utilitarianism (Harsanyi 1977). In order to illustrate the fact that both views may have different consequences it is useful to look at an example. Suppose that there are 1000 individuals who have to vote on a measure of great common benefit. At least 501 of these must take part in the vote in order to secure the desired outcome. Taking part in the vote involves a utility loss which is small compared to the common benefit but not negligible. Consider a rule which commands every one of the 1000 individuals to take part in the vote. If one of the individuals, say individual 1, is an act utilitarian who expects the others to follow the rule, he will not vote, since thereby total utility is increased.

Obviously, if all 1000 individuals are act utilitarians they cannot follow the rule that everyone should vote. On the other hand, a society of rule utilitarians can adopt this rule if it is the best one available.

The example assumes that the 1000 individuals cannot communicate in order to coordinate their behavior; it also neglects the possibility of mixed strategies.

An act utilitarian looks at the expected behavior of all other individuals and maximizes total utility taking this behavior as fixed. A society of rule utilitarians looks at the situation as a problem of joint optimization where the behavior is varied for all individuals simultaneously.

12.4 Personal Utilitarianism and Institutional Utilitarianism

As has been explained above institutional utilitarianism takes a pessimistic view towards the effectiveness of moral appeals. Probably, personal utilitarianism would advise us, who are lucky enough to live in countries with high income per head, to sacrifice a large part of our salaries to the hungry people in underdeveloped parts of the world. We cannot really expect that moral rules of this kind will be followed. Within very narrow limits people are willing to sacrifice some of their own utility for the common good. Therefore, moral appeals, e.g. an appeal to save water in a time of drought may work if it does not cost too much to obey. In exceptional situations like natural catastrophes the willingness may increase beyond the usual level but even then we cannot expect too much of the average person.

Institutional utilitarianism takes the behavior of people as given and tries to find those institutions which produce the best result under this restriction. The description of human behavior on which the optimization is based should neither neglect nor overestimate the limited effectiveness of moral appeals.

In fact, institutional utilitarianism could not hope to produce practical results if people would be exclusively motivated by self-interest. If those who decide on the change of social institutions cannot be influenced by moral considerations, then any attempt of improvement is bound to fail.

If moral considerations have some weight they will strengthen the position of those whose self-interest points in the right direction. Moreover, desirable changes like the abolition of slavery may be brougt about by many morally motivated people each of whom is willing to sacrifice a little. Of course, those who derive their income from slavery must be expected to resist the change and moral interests alone may not be powerful enough to achieve the purpose.

12.5 The Universe of Morally Relevant Individuals

It is a serious problem of utilitarianism to describe the set of all individuals whose utilities should enter the total utility to be maximized. We call this set the universe of morally relevant individuals. Most theorists would agree that all human beings living now belong to this universe. But what about unborn children and members of future generations? Maybe one has to include everybody who may live in the future but should we weigh everybody equally or should we apply a time discount?

In connection with measures which influence the size of the population, it also becomes important to decide whether one really wants to maximize the sum of all utilities or whether it is maybe preferable to maximize average utility.

Institutional utilitarianism should be mainly concerned with the long run consequences of social institutions. In principle, those institutions are best which produce the highest total utility in the long run. However, costs of transition cannot be completely ignored. An adequate solution of this problem seems to require some kind of time discount.

12.6 The Purification Problem

It has been pointed out by many philosophers, e.g. by Leonhard Nelson whose ethical view is similar to utilitarianism that a distinction must be made between justified and unjustified interests (Nelson 1972). It cannot be morally right to hang an innocent man in order to satisfy the desires of many sadistic onlookers even if their total utility gain outweighs the utility loss of the hanged one. Not only interests in the suffering of others but to a certain extent also interests in the well-being of others have to be excluded from consideration. Somebody who has hundred aunts who love him dearly should not be unduly preferred over others merely because of this fact.

In order to overcome these difficulties one may propose to "purify" the individual utility functions of preferences concerning the well-being of others, before they are added up in order to obtain total utilities. As far as the author knows no satisfactory formal theory of utility purification has been developed up to now, but the problem is by no means hopeless and may be solved eventually.

The structure of the purification problem

Further insight into the purification problem can be gained by a decomposition into two subproblems. The first subproblem will be referred to as the identification of justified interests. The identification of justified interests concerns the question which aspects of possible futures should be included or excluded in the determination of purified utilities.

The second subproblem arises once the first one has been solved. One has to find a way to construct purified utility functions on the basis of the original ones, given a specification of those influences which should be included in the determination of purified utilities. This subproblem will be referred to as the construction of purified utilities.

The decomposition of the purification problem into these two subproblems provides a workable approach to the development of a purification theory. Of course, there may be other approaches which structure the problem in a different way. The separation of the identification of justified interests from the subsequent construction of purified utility functions has the advantage that it helps to clarify the nature of the moral judgements involved.

12.8 The Identification of Justified Interests

Purification is concerned with the elimination of preferences concerning the well-being of others. Therefore, influences which primarily concern the welfare of other persons should not be taken into account by purified utilities.

As an example one may look at a policy measure which helps to avoid accidents on public playing grounds. A measure of this kind primarily benefits the children's welfare. The fact that the parents value the life and the health of their children should not lead to an undesirable double counting of the beneficial effects. Of course, there may be direct effects on the parents' welfare like diminished costs for health care,etc. which should be taken into account in the parents' purified utilities. However, it is clear that the mere fact that the parents love their children should not increase the gain in total purified utility attributed to the policy measure. Otherwise, one might come to the conclusion that accident preventing improvements are less important for playgrounds used exclusively by orphans.

As soon as one looks at practical examples it seems to be quite clear which influences on an individual's utility should enter or not enter the determination of purified utilities. If one wants to explore questions of institutional change in the framework of a formal theoretical model, it can be decided on an ad hoc basis which variables should be included as influences on purified utilities. This means that the identification of justified interests is settled by the moral judgment of the modeller. As long as a more elaborate theoretical framework for the identification of justified interests is not available, it is reasonable to take this approach.

It would be desirable to develop a formal theory on the basis of which the identification of justified interests could be obtained by derivation from general postulates in every particular case. However, this seems to be a very difficult task. It is not even clear what kind of theoretical framework could be used in order to give a precise meaning to the questions to be asked by a general theory for the identification of justified interests.

12.9 The Construction of Purified Utility Functions

An individual's utility function evaluates possible futures of the world described by a huge set of parameters. The identification of justified interests determines a subset of parameters on which the purified utility function is permitted to depend. It will be convenient to refer to this subset as the individual's purified parameter subset. Of course, every individual has a different purified parameter subset.

In order to solve the problem posed by the construction of purified utility functions one needs a mathematical rule which can be applied to a given utility function and a given purified parameter subset in order to obtain the purified utility function. A rule of this kind will be called a purification rule.

A reasonable purification rule should be based on an axiomatic theory which derives the precise form of the rule from basic postulates which express intuitively desirable requirements.

Unlike the development of a general theory for the identification of justified interests the axiomatic characterization of a purification rule is a reasonably well defined research task.

12.10 The Rationality Problem

Utilitarianism assumes individuals with von Neumann-Morgenstern utility functions. However, it is doubtful whether human beings are rational enough to permit this description.

In a world of limited rationality where people fail to maximize utility not only utilitarianism but also most of economic theory is an inadequate instrument of analysis. Unfortunatey, the theory of limited rationality is not yet sufficiently developed to be able to replace our traditional picture of man as an infinitely clever optimizer. However, it is not inconceivable that the fundamental ideas of utilitarianism can be reconciled with a sufficiently elaborate theory of limited rationality once it will have been developed.

The basic problem to be solved by a formal theory of limited rationality is the replacement of the utility maximization hypothesis by an alternative mathematical description of human decision making. From this point of view it is important that the utility maximization hypothesis can be decomposed into two parts: existence of utility and maximization of utility.

Of course, one cannot assume maximization of utility without presupposing existence of utility but the reverse is not true. Existence of utility simply means that a decision-maker has the capability to make consistent preference judgments. This does not imply that such judgments are easy to obtain. The decision-maker may have to employ a difficult, painful and time consuming cognitive process in order to form consistent preference judgments. If this is the case he may not go into the trouble unless a very important occasion arises and even then he may fail to make as many preference comparisons as are necessary in order to obtain an optimal decision.

A theory of limited rationality may be utility based in the sense that it makes use of the utility concept without the assumption that utility is maximized. In order to see this one may look at learning as an alternative to optimization. Learning is guided by reinforcement and it is not unreasonable to think of reinforcement as related to utility. A utility based learning theory would look at utility as something which is experienced rather than known in advance.

It is clear that institutional utilitarianism is easily reconcilable with utility based theories of limited rationality. It does not matter whether the decision-makers maximize utilities or not. As long as utilities exist one can try to design institutions which improve utilitarian welfare in a world of limited rationality.

Unfortunately, the existence of utility is a doubtful assumption. It may be true that at least in some situations of practical importance human beings are unable to form consistent preference judgements, even if they try very hard. The consistency requirements in the axiomatic characterization of von Neumann-Morgenstern utility are very severe. They are known to be violated in many experiments. In the long run, it can easily turn out to be unavoidable to develop a theory of limited rationality which is not utility based.

It is not easy to see how institutional utilitarianism can be combined with a theory of limited rationality which is not utility based. However, even there the situation is not hopeless. It may be possible to reconstruct utility as an individual welfare measure based on behavioral tendencies.

12.11 Utilitarian Comparison of Institutional Arrangements

Generally, a section of reality like the provision of health care is shaped by a multitude of legal and organizational facts which are constraints on individual behavior and create incentives and disincentives. Thereby, individual behavior is limited and guided by a system of rules. The use of the words institutional arrangement refers to a rule system of this kind.

It is important to compare the social desirability of different institutional arrangements which can be proposed for the same section of social reality. This is a task which can be approached in the spirit of institutional utilitarianism. In order to do this, one has to construct formal models of the institutional arrangements under consideration. The consequences of individual decision behavior within these models must be explored and the overall effect on utilitarian welfare must be assessed. Utilitarian welfare is the sum (or the average) of the purified utilities of all individuals concerned.

The comparison of the utilitarian welfare obtained for different institutional arrangements indicates which one of them is best from the point of view of institutional utilitarianism. Of course, such conclusions depend on the assumption that the formal models reflect reality sufficiently well.

An extremely simple example for this kind of theoretical analysis will be given in the appendix. The example does not intend to be more than an expositional exercise.

The usual methods of cost benefit analysis are not in total agreement with the spirit of utilitarianism. Cost benefit analysis employs welfare measures like consumer's rent which do not necessarily correctly express gains or losses in total utility. Consumer's rent measures the public's willingness to pay. Since the willingness to pay depends not only on utility but also on income it may happen that cost benefit comparisons give less weight to the utility gains of low income receivers than to those of high income receivers. This point is illustrated by the example in the appendix.

In practice, the utilitarian approach meets the difficulty that in most cases empirical knowledge on interpersonally comparable utilities is unavailable. Under such circumstances, the methods of cost benefit analysis can be looked upon as an approximation to utilitarianism.

The difficulties of practical application do not diminish the theoretical importance of utilitarian comparisons. Hypothetical exercises in the framework of abstract models without immediate empirical application enhance the understanding of reality by a clarification of conceptual issues. Moreover, the results of purely theoretical investigations may inspire the improvement of empirical research techniques.

12.12 Concluding Remarks

Utilitarianism is a well worked out ethical theory which can be used to judge the moral desirability of social institutions. It is well adapted to the present methodology of formal modelling and analysis of economics. This methodology has proved to be successful not only in economics but also in other social sciences.

References

Hare, R.M. (1971): *Practical Inferences*. London: MacMillan.
Harnsanyi, J.C. (1955): "Cardinal Welfare, Individualistic Ethics and Interpersonal Comparisons of Utility." *The Journal of Political Economy* 63 (Aug.): 309-321.
Harsanyi, J.C. (1975): "Can the Maximin Principle Serve as a Basis for Morality: A Critique of John Rawl's Theory." *American Political Science Review* 69/2: 594-607.
Harsanyi, J.C. (1977): "Rule Utilitarianism and Decision Theory". *Erkenntnis* 11: 25-53.
Nelson, L. (1972): *Kritik der praktischen Vernunft* (2nd ed.). Hamburg: Meiner.
Neumann, J. von, and O. Morgenstern (1944): *Theory of Games and Economic Behavior*. Princeton: Univ. Press
Rawls, J. (1972): *A Theory of Justice*. London-Oxford-New York: Clarendon Press.
Sen, A.K. (1970): *Collective Choice and Social Welfare*. San Francisco: Holden Day.
Wright, G.H. von (1963): *Norm and Action. A Logical Inquiry*. London: Routledge & Paul.

Appendix: Should We Pass an Open Space Ordinance?
A Hypothetical Example

Imagine a posted forest area near a community of n low income receivers 1, . . .,n. The forest area is owned by a single individual A. The question arises whether an open space ordinance should be passed which opens access to the forest area for recreational use. Up to now, the area is fenced in and nobody except A has access to the forest.

Recreational use of the forest by the n individuals would cause damages of D money units. Individual A has to bear this cost if the ordinance is passed. For the sake of simplicity it is assumed that it is legally impossible to compensate the owner by a payment from public funds. It is also not practicable to take an entrance fee. The administrative costs are too high.

The n + 1 individuals 1, . . .,n and A are the only ones whose welfare is influenced by the ordinance. It is assumed that all individuals including A have the same utility function. An individual's utility U depends on his or her income y. The utility of income is a monotonically increasing strictly concave function u(y). This utility is increased by a positive constant v if the individual has access to the forest area

$$U = \begin{cases} u(y) & \text{without access to the forest area} \\ u(y) + v & \text{with access to the forest area} \end{cases}$$

It is assumed that each of the individuals i = 1, . . .,n has the same income x. Individual A's income is X. The idea that A is relatively rich is epressed by following inequality:

$$X - D > x$$

This means that A remains richer than the other individuals, even if he has to bear the damage D.

Utilitarian analysis: Let W be the sum of all utilities of the n + 1 individuals 1, . . .,n and A. Suppose that the ordinance is not passed. Then we have:

$$W = nu(x) + u(X) + v$$

In this case only A has access to the forest. Each of the individuals 1, . . .,n has utility u(x) and A has utility u(X) + v. Now consider the case that the ordinance is passed. Then we have:

$$W = nu(x) + u(X-D) + (n+1)\, v.$$

The comparison between both cases yields the conclusion that the ordinance should be passed if the following inequality (a) holds:

(a) $nv > u(X) - u(X-D)$

On the left hand side, we find the utility gain nv of the individuals 1, . . .,n and the right hand side shows the utility loss of individual A. The ordinance should not be passed if the reverse inequality holds.

Cost benfit analysis:In order to compute the gain in consumers' rent obtained by the n individuals, if the ordinance is passed, one has to determine the highest price p which these individuals would be willing to pay for getting access. Suppose that an individual i with i = 1, . . .,n has to pay p in order to get access. Then the income which still can be spent for other purposes is x-p. This is the relevant income to be inserted for y in the utility function. The highest price p which individual i is willing to pay for access is determined by the following equation:

$$v + u(x{-}p) = u(x)$$

On the left hand side, we find his utility if he buys access. The right hand side shows his utility for the case that he does not buy access. At the highest price he would be willing to pay both utilities must be equal.

The gain in consumers' rent obtained by individuals 1, . . .,n is np. This gain must be compared with the damage D. This yields the conclusion that the cost benefit comparison works in favor of the open space ordinance if we have:

(b) $np > D.$

According to the cost benefit comparison the ordinance should be passed if this inequality (b) holds and it should not be passed if the reverse inequality is satisfied.

Comparison of the two criteria: We have obtained two different criteria for passing the ordinance, the utilitarian criterion (a) and the cost benefit criterion (b). It is our intention to show that there is a substantial difference between the two criteria. The utilitarian criterion is more favorable to the open space ordinance. Wherever the two criteria disagree, the utilitarian criterion recommends the ordinance and the cost benefit criterion rejects it. The following figure illustrates the derivation of this result.

The criteria (a) and (b) can be re-written as follows.

(a') $n > \dfrac{u(X) - u(X{-}D)}{v}$

(b') $n > \dfrac{D}{p}$

This shows that the utilitarian criterion is more favorable to the ordinance if we have:

(c) $\dfrac{u(X) - u(X{-}D)}{v} < \dfrac{D}{p}$

If (c) holds then the utilitarian criterion leaves more room for a favorable decision. (c) is equivalent to the following inequality:

(c') $\dfrac{u(X) - u(X{-}D)}{D} < \dfrac{v}{p}$

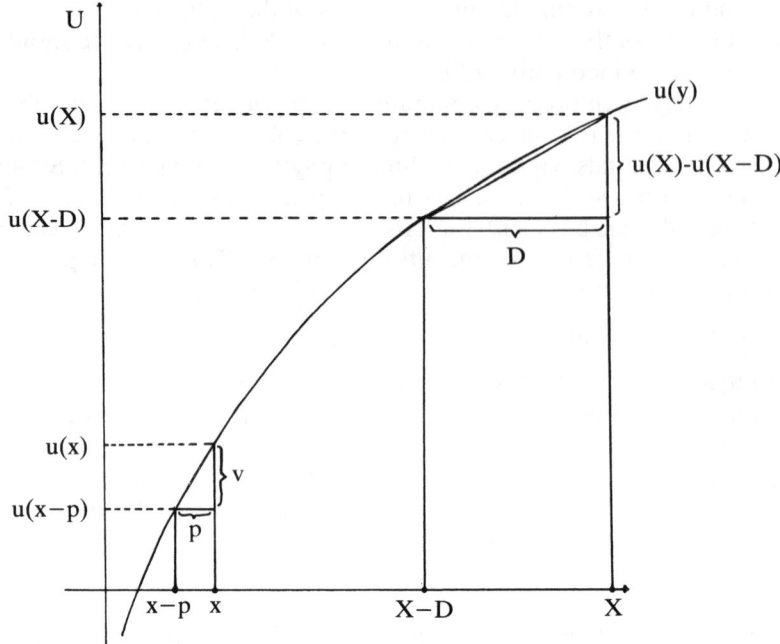

Fig.1: Comparison between the utilitarian criterion and the cost benefit criterion

In view of the strict concavity of u and the assumption $X-D > x$ inequality (c') holds. This can be seen immediately with the help of the figure. We can conclude that the utilitarian criterion is more favorable to the open space ordinance than the cost benefit criterion.

In order to make the result more clear it may be helpful to look at it in a slightly different way. Suppose that the utility function and the income levels x and X are kept fixed and that D is gradually increased. Obviously, p does not depend on D and remains fixed, too, if only D is varied. As long as D is smaller than np both criteria recommend the ordinance. As soon as D surpasses the critical level $D_1 =$ np the cost benefit criterion begins to disfavor the ordinance. The utilitarian criterion continues to recommend the ordinance until a second critical level D_2 of D is reached where the utility gain nv exactly equals the utility loss $u(X) - u(X-D_2)$. For $D \geq D_2$ both criteria reject the ordinance. The difference between both criteria matters in the interval $D_1 < D < D_2$. There the utilitarian criterion recommends the ordinance whereas the cost benefit criterion rejects it.

The example illustrates a general point. If marginal utility of income is decreasing then the utilitarian welfare theorist must have the suspicion that cost benefit comparisons underemphasize the interests of poor people. Consumers' rent measures the willingness to pay. If marginal utility of income is decreasing then a poor individual is willing to pay less for the same utility gain than a rich one.

The conclusion reached in the example also depends on the assumption that the owner remains richer than the other individuals even if the ordinance is passed.

Therefore, the assumption of decreasing marginal utility of income has the consequence that the owner's utility loss per dollar shown on the left hand side of (c') is smaller than the other individuals' utility gain per dollar, shown on the right hand side of (c'). As we have seen, inequality (c') is crucial for the result that the utilitarian criterion is more favorable to the ordinance than the cost benefit criterion.

13. The Ethical Context of Bureaucracy and Performance Analysis

Herman R. van Gunsteren

Abstract

The tendency to locate ethics in the private sphere has made it increasingly difficult to deal with ethical questions that are necessarily involved in evaluation of public policies and activities. Attention is drawn to the possibility of an autonomous ethics for public life. Plural societies are developing a public ethics of responsibility that evolves over time and is connected to processes of public learning in which citizens, in their double capacities as rulers and ruled, are involved. Such learning characteristically takes place in responsibility fora in which individuals are urged to account for their actions as holders of public authority. The author briefly analyzes the working of such fora, the significance of notions of individual responsibilities in societies in which many actors are not individuals but organizations, and the problems involved in translating ethical conclusions into effective bureaucratic actions.

> Il faut savoir ce qui doit être pour bien
> juger de ce qui est; la plus grande diffi-
> culté pour éclaircir ces importantes ma-
> tières est d'intéresser un particulier à
> les discuter, de répondre à ces deux
> questions: Que m'importe? et: Qu'y
> puis-je faire? Nous avons mis notre
> Emile en état de se répondre à toutes
> deux.
>
> *Rousseau (1971: 311)*

13.1 Introduction

Performance evaluation of bureaucratic actions is a good thing – in principle. It is feedback that invites learning. Learning, however, is not always for the better. One may learn to do evil. Thus, a commitment to performance evaluation leaves the question of what it is that is being learned unanswered. Whose voice is being listened to and who is ignored? Which signals, messages, are headed, which values and routines determine their routing in the bureaucratic system? In terms of what values is the outcome of bureaucratic learning conceived? Do bureaucratic actions, as a result of learning, become more efficient, more adequate, humane, professional, just, democratic?

In liberal democracies democratic feedback is of primary importance, (although not always decisive – neither normatively nor in fact). The citizens decide in what terms bureaucratic performance is to be evaluated. This democratic feedback reaches bureaucrats by way of elected representative bodies and political superiors. The capacity of this constitutional channel is insufficient to carry the bulk of the messages that citizens are sending out to the bureaucracy, even when one takes into account the amplification of messages through legal proceedings. Citizen messages reach the bureaucracy also through advisory committees, pressure groups, data on consumer behavior, tax evasion, migration, through opinion polls, the media, public opinion, and finally in the form of direct complaints and criticism of individual citizens (see Wirth: Ch. 35).

These messages, in particular complaints and criticism of citizens aimed directly at behavior of bureaucracies and bureaucrats, are often couched in ethical terms. This poses an acute problem for the responsible and democratically minded civil servant. While he may sympathise or agree with the messages, or at least consider them legitimate, he also knows from experience that systemic bureaucratic responses to precisely such messages are notoriously inadequate, if not nonexistent. The loss is at least twofold: in terms of democracy and of intelligence (because a potentially valuable source of feedback is ignored). In order to help improve this sad state of affairs I shall try to understand what is involved in ethical criticism of bureaucratic actions and in the bureaucratic processing of such ethical messages.

13.2 Citizen Complaints

Some not uncommon accusations against civil servants are: indifference, non-responsiveness, lack of humanity, laziness, bribery, partisanship, pestering, hunger for power, incompetence. Usually these qualifications of bureaucratic behavior imply ethical condemnation: the behavior is judged to be bad, wrong. Sometimes, without further thinking or experience, most of the wrongdoer's colleagues are included in the condemnation as well. One may dismiss this as nonconsequential dinner table talk, which has nothing to do with considered opinions and real grievances. But one may also remember that language, what we say and how we say it, does in varying ways or degrees shape thought and action, what we do. Even if dinner table talk about bureaucratic behavior does not faithfully, literally, express the talkers' considered opinions and attitudes, one can safely assume that some relation between these exists. *Was sich liebt, das neckt sich* (teasing is a sign of love). But irritation and ethical indignation, which so often result from encounters between citizens and bureaucrats, as well as from talk about such encounters with fellow citizens, can hardly be taken as signs of affection.

Further accusations against civil servants concern their active or passive (remaining silent) complicity in crimes that the state they serve commits. Think of Eichmann, Vietnam, Watergate, the treatment of prisoners, the "psychiatric" treatment of dissidents. In our first category of cases the focus is primarily on the individual civil servant's actions and only secondarily on the conditions (organisational, political, cultural, constitutional, etc) that make such actions possible. In the second category the focus is primarily on the actions, official and unofficial, of (parts of) the state or its apparatuses, and only secondarily on the individual civil servant's contribution that helps to make such actions possible.

A third category of complaints concerns bureaucratic ineffectiveness and inefficiency. Since it is bureaucracy as a whole that is being condemned it is difficult to understand to whom the ethical accusations are directed. That they are of an ethical nature cannot be doubted. "Look at what "they" are doing with our money and with the constitutional authority that was entrusted to them!"

More sophisticated but otherwise quite similar accusations against bureaucracy can be found in works of social science and journalism. Technocracy; "efficiency for what"; bureaucracy is ungovernable and insensitive to democratic/political directives; in the welfare state public bureaucracies hold, or rather administer, a knowledge-power through which the souls and minds of individual citizens, including citizens who happen to be civil servants, are disciplined (an internal constraint that is said to have replaced the formerly predominantly external relation of constraint between ruler and ruled – in an unexpected way we have become Aristotelian citizens after all, knowing both how to rule and to be ruled); bureaucratic work is debilitating, it prevents people from doing the good they are capable of. Although such statements and analyses are usually couched in descriptive terms, their ethical meaning can hardly be missed.

13.3 Bureaucratic Responses: A Double Bind?

How should civil servants respond to such criticism? To specific accusations, e.g. of laziness or bribery, adequate reactions are often not too difficult to find. Other cases, like complicity in criminal state actions, are more problematic, because the harm can seldom be undone. Future oriented reactions, which significantly reduce the likelihood that similar bureaucratic wrongdoings will occur, are difficult to devise, but in principle also not impossible. Fundamental difficulties arise, however, when the civil servant must decide how to react to a common core of many of these critical citizen messages, namely that he should become more humane, more ethical, in the exercise of his function. As a civil servant he has obligations beyond those to individual citizens. He is bound by a professional code of conduct and to the law which makes him one link in a hierarchical chain of command. Central concepts used in judging his actions within this frame of reference are objectivity, neutrality, efficiency, effectiveness, legality, the primacy of law and political decision making. Adherence to professional codes of conduct and hierarchical chains of command are for civil servants not merely formal obligations, but also ethical duties.

The very same citizens who criticise civil servants for being cold, not humane, for their lack of ethical concern, would readily criticise civil servants for lack of neutrality, *détournement de pouvoir,* for using their authority for other purposes than the ones for which it was conferred, if civil servants really started reacting to the first kind of criticism by trying to follow personal ethical convictions in the exercise of their functions. Thus society, the citizens in their collective and individual capacities, makes inconsistent demands on civil servants. On the one hand they are assigned a position that is designed to prevent their personal ethical convictions from influencing the way they function. Civil servants should be competent and be guided by nothing but the law, not by personal convictions, be they ethical or not. On the other hand citizens insist that civil servants should become more ethical. Thus civil servants are in a double bind situation: they are simultaneously required and forbidden to let ethical conviction influence them in the exercise of their functions. Seen in this light, ethical disaffection with the behaviour of civil servants is not merely a problem of them, of the civil servants who faultily implement the good ethical intentions of us, the citizens, but also, and primarily, a problem of inconsistent demands that *we* place upon civil servants. I shall return to this dilemma, and to possible ways out of it, later on. First I want to reconsider some long standing and general questions about the application of ethics to public action.

13.4 Private Ethics and Public Life

In the fifties, after the second world war, ethicalisation of the public sphere, both in politics and in administration, was thought to be dangerous. Those who engaged in public careers with the firm ethical resolve to do good were bound to end up doing evil. More, and more serious, evil than done by those who had entered public careers with less high minded ethical intentions. Such were the lessons drawn from recent experience and from such contributions as Max Weber's remarks on *Gesinnungsethik*, Karl Popper's theory of "The open society and its enemies", Daniel Bell's proclamation of "The end of ideology", studies of totalitarianism and of "Totalitarian Democracy". The emerging consensus on the dangers of ethicalisation of the public sphere was reinforced and spread by influential journals like "Encounter" and influential social scientists like Edward Shils.

The sixties saw a shattering of this consensus, not so much through criticism of the arguments on which it rested, as through direct ethical/political protest of citizens against specific government policies and through general ethical condemnations of "the system" and those who associated their careers, happiness and identity with its future. During the seventies protests subsided somewhat, and certainly became more routinized and less influential. But the owl of political philosophy began to wake up and spread its wings in books and journals. Particularly in a journal like "Philosophy and Public Affairs" one discerns a rivival of the almost forgotten discipline of making ethical arguments and judgments about public policies.

Of course looking at activities of public officials from an ethical standpoint is, and has always been, a legitimate enterprise. Quite another matter is it, however, to ask what advantages would result if public officials would really start following the advice of the ethical theorists, if their activities became more ethicalized. And what disadvantages. Still another matter is it to look for factors that actually foster an ethicalisation of public action. Within this last enterprise one can distinguish between different strategies for bringing about the desired changes, like persuasion, indoctrination, altering incentive structures, changing the laws, forcing people through threats, direct or indirect, of violence, appeals to self-respect and a sense of responsibility and solidarity. I shall not go into these distinctions here. Not because they are unimportant, but because I only brought them up here in order to show that the status of writings of the "Philosophy and Public Affairs" type is questionable as soon as they pretend to go beyond the first kind of enterprise. That is, as soon as they assume, explicitly or implicitly, that an ethicalisation of public life is a good thing, they have to face up to the serious arguments that were raised precisely against this assumption in the fifties. This they often fail to do, that is, they ignore these "outdated" arguments.

Before I go on to consider the question of whether ethicalisation of public life is a good thing I wish to make one more distinction. Namely between morality in the sense of a code of specific rules of behavior and morality in the sense of action dictated by conscience." Morality-conscience concerns the voluntary actions of some people towards others. And those who perform the actions know whether their actions will do other people good or ill, and in what proportion. An action is moral if its author is free to choose whether to perform it or not, and if it does not cause harm to others." (Zinoviev 1981: 799). Every society has morality in the first sense. Whether it is a good or a bad one, whether and to what extent it has morality in the second sense, remains to be determined. In ethically plural societies substantive codes of conduct, morality in the first sense, will by definition stand little chance of being accepted by all members. Therefore ethical theories that are intended to be applicable to such societies generally deemphasize substantive moral codes and argue instead for the importance of morality-conscience, of correct procedures and attitudes (one should be "responsible") when choosing one's individual moral position. This procedural and individualistic trend of contemporary ethical theory is in itself not bad, but surely cannot go on indefinitely. A purely individualistic and procedural ethical theory will end up with the anomalies of Max Stirner's *Der Einzige und sein Eigentum* and with the absurd admission that decisions like those of Hitler are ethically good if they are taken by individual human beings who followed the right procedures when consulting their private consience. When, later on in this chapter I advocate responsibility fora, a theory of reserve-circuits, and flexible notions of personal responsibility of public officials, I follow contemporary ethical theorists in the procedural and individualistic direction. That there are limits to this approach I do not doubt. Where they lie and of what nature they are, I do not know. I suspect that in liberal democracies they have to do with the ethical commitment to a system of laws that guarantees public opinion and individual moral choice. But this must remain a subject for further study.

Let us look then at the question of whether ethicalisation of public life is a good thing. The question concerns, more precisely, the applicability to actions of public officials of an ethics that has its source outside the public sphere. In our time this appears as the question of the applicability of private ethics to public life. From Augustine to Machiavelli the question was about the relation of Christian ethics and politics. If one wants to be precise one can point out that Christian ethics was, during that period, not located outside the public realm, but that both political (king) and Christian (Pope) sources of authority and codes of conduct were located in a public realm of some sort, the community of Christians. Against this one can point out, however, that even in Augustine there is a source of Christian ethics, a society that is not visible in this world, that lies outside the realm in which worldly and ecclesiastical rulers are engaged in politics.

Both Augustine and Machiavelli pose the problem of dirty hands: in order to be effective in politics one must be prepared to act badly in Christian/ethical terms. Those who are not prepared to do this will be wiped off the public stage pretty soon by those who, with regret or not, violate the dictates of Christan ethics. The analyses of Augustine and Machiavelli are remarkably similar. But not their evaluations. For Augustine the problem of dirty hands constitutes one more expression of the condition of fallen man, who must sin while living in this world. The situation is tragic: Christians are obliged to serve the State (which is both an expression of God's punishment and of His grace), but in doing so they must necessarily commit sins. Machiavelli sees rather the triumph of the strong, "virtuous", ruler, or, some would say, of the emerging sovereign modern state. One can applaud Machiavelli for relocating the source of political virtue where it belongs, namely inside the public realm. The trouble is, however, that this notion of political virtue is so oriented towards effectiveness, towards success at all cost, that many would hesitate to speak here of an autonomous ethics of and for the public sphere. According to quite a few commentators, among them Hannah Arendt (1959), the Greeks knew such an autonomous political ethics. But there also, as A. W. H. Adkins (1960) has shown in his beautiful book *"Merit and Responsibility"*, this autonomous political ethics gained at best a tenuous foothold after much effort to strip the notion of virtue (aretè) of its dominant connotation of success in battle. It seems that if an autonomous political ethics can be at all developed, power and success will certainly remain more determinative for virtue there than they are in the sphere of private or Christian ethics.

Be that as it may, with the Reformation and the rise of social contract theories the line of Machiavelli was not continued. The source of ethical norms became firmly located outside the public sphere. Virtue was privatised and individualized and its content became variable. Efforts to create an autonomous public ethics, as those of Rousseau with his civil religion or of Auguste Comte, were frowned upon. The only civil religions, that were accepted as long as they did not reveal themselves as such, were the Rule of Law, the Authority of Science, and the Rationality of increasing Efficiency. (Expect in some backward or regressive societies where ideological movements were taken seriously as sources of a political ethics). Thus the question of an autonomous ethics for the public sphere was not openly posed, and the problems of the relation between ethics and public action were reduced to the question if, and if so to what extent, private ethics should be applied to public actions.

13.5 Towards an Autonomous Ethics for Public Life

Now there are many good arguments against the direct applicability of private ethics to public life. Private ethics does not exist any longer, except in the form of moral decisions taken by individuals, or in the form of a bewildering plurality of private ethical codes. If the requirements that these different ethics make of public officials contradict each other, as they often in fact do, which are to be applied and which are to be ignored? The direct application of private ethics to public action will often lead to the oppression of ethical minorities. It will also render the making of compromises for cooperation between a plurality of people and groups virtually impossible. That is, it prevents the finding of solutions to the problem of many hands. And finally, its ignores, and thereby fails to deal with, the unavoidable problem of dirty hands.

Notwithstanding these powerful arguments the conclusion is seldom drawn that private ethics should be kept away from the public sphere altogether. Why is this so? I think because private ethics is seen as the only real kind of ethics, all other kinds of ethics being derived from it. Thus basically the choice becomes one between the application of private ethics to public action or no ethics in the public realm at all. As long as we continue to see the public sphere as derivative from the private sphere, as long as we see democracy as the translation of private wants into public demands, and democratic control as evaluation based on private ethical opinions, we will not find a genuine public ethics. What presents itself as public ethics will be unmasked either as derivative from private ethics, or as a means toward some end that lies beyond this ethics. It follows from these considerations that, instead of continuing these halfhearted efforts to apply private ethics to public action, it might be worthwhile to reconsider the possibility of an autonomous public ethics.

This will, like all moral selfunderstanding, as Kolakowski (1973: 39) has argued, necessarily be based on some kind of myth. Causal explanations of one's own

moral understandings are self-defeating. It is not possible to have moral understandings and at the same time to causally explain them. The temptation to reify
moral selfunderstanding is particularly acute in the public sphere. There we want to
be objective, rational, democratic, and thus try to "explain" (justify) public ethics
in terms of private wants, thereby committing the scientistic mistake Kolakowski
warned us for.

It must be pointed out here that not all the authors who during the fifties argued
against the ethicalisation of public life wanted to do away with ethics altogether.
Their argument was, we can now see, in fact directed against the direct application
of private ethics to public action. It is true that some of them put too much trust in
science, pragmatism and democratic mechanism, thus hoping to be able to do
without ethics in the public sphere altogether. But others, notably Edward Shils
(1972) with his passionate plea for and analysis of "civility", did in fact argue for an
autonomous ethics for the public sphere. Not any ethics, but an ethics of free
political systems. That is, an ethics that assigns a prominent and protected place to
private ethical opinions and judgments, without, however, making them eo ipso
always decisive. If one follows this approach to problems of ethics and public
action, which I do, then one will look for and foster processes (rituals for example)
that (re)produce such an autonomous public ethics and the myths that sustain it.
Private ethics will not become irrelevant to the public sphere. But instead of
engaging in halfhearted direct application of private ethical judgments to the public
sphere, one will investigate how and under what conditions and transformations
they are (to be) admitted into the public sphere.

An autonomous public ethics should, however, not only be formulated but also
practised. Suppose that we have formulated a viable public ethics and that there is
one civil servant who genuinely wants to act in accordance with it. How can the
good that he wants to achieve be given a reasonable chance of becoming effective?
This requires 1) that he have the courage to act differently from his colleagues; 2)
that he be not immediately punished or eliminated for doing so and 3) that the
contributions of other civil servants to the case at hand do not contradict or thwart
his good intention (the problem of many hands). The fulfillment of each of these
conditions is unlikely, the fulfillment of all three unlikely to the third degree.
Moreover, efforts to work towards the fulfillment of those conditions are themselves often ethically questionable. For the fulfillment of condition 1) ethical education may be needed. By whom, in what ethics? Fulfillment of the second condition involves more freedom to act according to the civil servant's own insight, more
discretion. But this freedom cannot be extended exclusively toward the side of the
good without also increasing the freedom to do evil. Demarcating a bottomline
above which there is freedom, an approach that often works in the ordering of
private life, does not work here, because when a civil servant uses the freedom
above such a borderline he can eo ipso be accused of favoritism and of producing
inequality before the law. Fulfillment of the third condition can be promoted by
way of law making and of hierarchical instructions. But this implies a loss of
situation specific flexibility and makes the fulfillment of the first two conditions
even more difficult.

I shall not work out these difficulties here. I mention them only because I want
to point out that, although I favour the development of an autonomous public

ethics, I also realize that efforts to bring about such development by way of simple social engineering are self-defeating, because contradictory (like the will to forget, or the command to love). Thus I propose to look for alternatives other than social engineering and spontaneous generation. For instance persuasion by one's fellow citizens and civil servants.

13.6 Mixed Systems, Reserve Circuits and Bureaucratic Learning

Remember the double bind situation in which civil servants find themselves stuck. The problem, I said, does not so much lie with the bureaucrats as with conflicting demands that we, the citizens, make upon them. On the one hand we demand that civil servants be ethically autonomous, responsible and flexible, on the other we want them to be neutral, loyal and technically competent servants. Would we be happy with a purely Weberian bureaucracy? No, because it would be insensitive, inhumane, rigid, obedient but without initiative, and above all, insensitive to ethical criticism, except when it arrives in the form of the law or instructions from superiors. Would we be happy with a purely "human", flexible and situation-oriented bureaucracy (if that is not a contradiction in terms)? No, because of inequality before the law, lack of coordination and disobedience to political directives concerning broad lines of policy. Both types are far from ideal. Is it amazing, then, that after having listened to these inconsistent demands and expectations, many civil servants simply raise their eyebrows and go their own ways? (Thus confirming our prejudice that they do not want to listen to ethical criticism).

It is time to acknowledge the mixture that lies between these two extreme types as a legitimate form of bureaucracy in its own right and to work out improvements and controls of this in principle legitimate mixture. Compare the progress that became possible once pluralistic political systems, that were neither pure democracies nor pure autocracies, became acknowledged as legitimate mixed systems, as polyarchies that do not fulfill the democratic ideal but that are the best that can be reached in the given circumstances. (Some – though not Robert Dahl (1982) – idealized this system of polyarchy, forgetting that circumstances may change, and thereby also what is best in the given circumstances). It would be a step forward if the bureaucratic forms that lie between Weberian and humane bureaucracy were no longer perceived as guilt-ridden mixtures, like the black market, but as legitimate ones like markets and polyarchies. Thus it would become conceivable to meet the citizens' ethical criticisms that I mentioned earlier, without having to fall back upon the non viable extremes of Weberian bureaucracy and humane ad hoc administration. As long as these remain the only alternatives, criticism of existing bureaucratic practices, which has to situate itself in either of these two, will remain unconvincing. This will change when the above mentioned mixture is accepted as legitimate; legitimate but not perfect, so that improvements are possible.

How can such a mixture between formal-hierarchical and flexible-humane administration be conceived? I propose by considering formal hierarchies in administration not as descriptions of reality, nor as norms which prescribe behavior, but as reserve-circuits that one can fall back upon in emergencies, that is, when daily administrative interaction, which usually does not conform to the formal hierarchical model, gets stuck, leads to conflicts it cannot solve. Thus valuable elements of Weberian bureaucracy are retained while at the same time civil servants are given the freedom for semi-autonomous decision making (see Majone: Ch. 21), which is required both from an ethical and a cybernetic point of view. (Central rule of complex systems in turbulent environments is cybernetically unsound, because the centre's variety, its capacity for learning, is too small for the task at hand (van Gunsteren 1976)). Of course "mistakes" in the way civil servants use their discretion should be clearly brought to light, but beyond this one must be very reluctant to inflict additional forms of "punishment" upon the "wrongdoer". Anxiety and learning do not go well together. And there is a definite need for more public space in which anxiety-free learning, in both a cybernetic/technical and an ethical sense, can actually take place.

13.7 The Concept of Responsibility

What about the content of an autonomous ethics of the public sphere? There can be no question of a monolithic substantive code of ethics that applies directly to all activities of all civil servants. This would not fit with the conception of considerable discretion for administrative subunits and individual civil servants backed up by a formal reserve-circuit. It also would not fit with the contemporary trend in ethical theory away from substantive moral codes and towards morality-conscience. But there can also be no question of accepting actions of civil servants that are dictated by a purely subjective ethics. In a situation of ethical relativism and rapidly changing circumstances we need substantive ethical orientation from sources that lie somewhere between a monolithic and a subjective ethics. The concept of responsibility (Hart 1968: 210–237) refers to this intermediate ethical orientation. Someone who acts responsibly acts ethically, but not necessarily in accordance with the ethical norms which I would have followed had I acted in his place. In order to be qualified as responsible, his action must be such that it can be understood as the outcome of a choice based on ethically respectable values and reasonable perception of the relevant facts. Thus the move from substantive ethics towards an ethics of responsibility does not imply that anything goes. Some valuations (e.g. people over 60 are a nuisance and therefore should be killed) and some misperceptions of facts (e.g. I did not see that the baby on my desk was burning to death) remain ethically unacceptable. A responsible person would not make such valuations nor fail to notice and act upon such facts.

13.8 Responsibility Fora

Where and how are notions of responsibility learned, reproduced, and transformed? In typical interaction structures that I propose to call responsibilitiy fora. Empirically this type of interaction structure is found in courts in law, professional journals and associations, official and semi-official meetings with peers or with superiors, and sometimes in contacts between civil servants and citizens. A responsibility forum is a cultural area which is marked off from the world of everyday activities by clear boundaries and controlled points of entry and exit. Boundaries, exit, and entry may, but need not, be marked by visible symbols or physical constructions. In responsibility fora the stream of daily activities is temporarily halted, suspended. People come together and ask each other: what have you done? Why did you do it, how can your action be ethically justified? The person who is interrogated is obliged to answer. He cannot simply say "This is what I chose to do". He is forced to remember, to reconstruct the past, to give plausible reasons for his acting as he did. And to admit, when he is unable to give such reasons, that he was wrong, that he acted irresponsibly. Thus in a responsibility forum the participants transform the past from a succession of blind events into a history that is the outcome of human choice and action. They reconstruct the past in order to induce people to act more responsibly in the future. Out of many possible connections between actions and events – too many to be handled – some are selected as foci of attention of responsible actors, others are ignored for the time being.

Through such accusatory dialogues in responsibility fora civil servants learn what it is to act responsibly, what they are responsible for, what responsibilities they have, and finally what their substantive ethical duties are. Responsibility fora are institutions for the enactment of rituals through which the myth of history as the outcome of human choice is regenerated. There we engage in never entirely successful efforts to bring this myth and reality in accordance with each other.

13.9 Organizational Action and Individual Responsibility

If one accepts this conception of responsibility fora the initially puzzling phenomenon of responsibility without control, the fact that civil servants are sometimes held responsible for events that lie somewhat outside their formal or informal range of control, becomes understandable. The point of responsibility fora is not punishment but learning; inviting, persuading, sometimes forcing, people to learn what it is to act responsibly. Learning may be a painful activity; it is doing something which you are not yet capable of doing.

In responsibility fora individual civil servants are held personally accountable for actions of the organization to which they belong. One may say that this is mistaken, because when we have to do with actions of legally chartered organizations one can only hold the organization as such responsible, not individual members of it. Although this view has some prima facie plausibility, I think that it is mistaken. It is true that it is often not easy to find a person who can be held responsible for what the organization does. In the case of Lieutenant Calley in the Vietnam war his defenders argued that he couldn't be held responsible because he was a rather unimportant cog in the big machine of the American army. He was too close to the actual killings. But on the other hand his superiors argued that they didn't know and couldn't know what was going on at the local level. They were too far away from the actual action. Thus both proximity and distance were exculpating circumstances. A magnificent arrangement in which everyone is safe except the victims. It seems that the bigger the organization the fewer persons can be held responsible for its actions. These problems are addressed by Hannah Arendt in her incisive considerations on Eichmann (Arendt 1964). She emphasizes that Eichmann, precisely because he was a conformist and man of clichés who didn't think independently, was able to commit crimes by simply doing his bureaucratic work in accordance with the instructions of his superiors. Eichmann, she says, was right in maintaining that he wasn't guilty in the sense of the indictment. He had not broken the law of his own country, but rather committed a novel kind of crime of legal obedience.

These horrible and famous cases exemplify a very common phenomenon. When being interpellated in a forum, members of organizations shove responsibility for the actions of their organisation from one to another. When one person is finally held responsible he feels himself to be the scapegoat. "It's not me but the president, (or the man who actually paid the bribe or fired the pistol,) who is responsible." The fallacious assumption that is involved here is that responsibility is a transferable and fixed quantity. It is true that under certain circumstances responsibility can be transferred from one person to another and that in some cases when this happens the responsibility of the one who has made the transfer ends. It also cannot be denied that decisions and actions of organisations are often difficult to ascribe to specific persons and that this ascription has always a conventional character. Finally it is true that one cannot hold each und every member of an organization responsible for each and every action of the organization. Responsibility must remain specific. But from all this it doesn't follow that responsibility is a kind of ball that can go from hand to hand. Transferring responsibility is not transferring a thing, but changing relations between people. By sharing or delegating responsibility one usually increases the total volume of responsibility. One remains oneself responsible to some degree and someone else becomes responsible as well. The well known feeling "the bigger the organization, the less responsibility" can thus be seen to depend on an inadequate conception of what it is to transfer and share responsibility. The correct maxim is: the bigger the organization the greater the sum total of responsibilities.

For brevity's sake I refer here to Dennis Thompson (1980) who convincingly argues that a situation of "many hands" need not prevent us from holding civil servants personally responsible. Collective or hierarchical responsibilities do not necessarily exclude personal responsibility.

13.10 From Ethical Complaint to Bureaucratic Action

Civil servants should not only listen to ethical messages from citizens, but also translate them so that the administration can process them and finally produce responses that are adequate both from the administrative (good management) and ethical point of view. This is not easy. Let me give two examples. Look again at the citizen complaints about civil servants that I listed at the beginning of this chapter. For instance the complaint about unresponsiveness. Does an ethics centered around personal responsibility provide a direct answer or solution? Hardly. In order to elicit an adequate response from the administration one usually needs to know one's way about in the bureaucratic labyrinths. As long as one does not possess this expert knowledge, bureaucracy and bureaucrats will often remain unresponsive. Ethical accusations against individual civil servants, who themselves are cogs in a machine, will seldom help. Some citizens can afford to hire such expert knowledge. And as a result the administration and individual civil servants are often responsive. But most citizens do not have, nor can afford to buy, such expert knowledge. But there is worse: the same goes for many individual civil servants. They do not know their own bureaucracy. And here lies their ethical wrongdoing. Their understanding of the bureaucratic labyrinth of which they form a part is often too negative and defeatist. "This is the way things go." "I cannot help you." What citizens require from individual civil servants is that they act as reliable guides in the bureaucratic labyrinth and that they only leave their clients/ citizens when they have handed them over to equally reliable collegues. This is one example of what I refer to as the "translation" of ethical citizen complaints.

For a second example, look again at the list of complaints. Activities of civil servants *are* controlled by politics, law, morality, public opinion. All we have to do, it seems, is to reinforce and/or control these controls somewhat. But the complaints keep coming in. How come? This is so, it seems to me, because in polities like the Netherlands the controls are relatively effective in checking individual corruption, but ineffective with regard to a specific and hidden form of collective corruption. This form of "corruption" consists in the vigorous and ruthless pursuit of the interest of one's own administrative (sub)unit. What we have here is not the pursuit of naked self-interest, but of self-interest dressed up as the interest of some collectivity or institution. Direct peergroup control is ineffective here, because the members of the group are all involved in the "selfless" pursuit of some transpersonal interest, hoping to receive their personal share of the spoils later on.

I suspect that in The Netherlands this form of corruption is widespread and serious, and that existing controls are until now relatively ineffective in the face of it (van Gunsteren 1983). This form of corruption is a source of ungovernability, an obstacle to administrative reform and cooperation, and often the true source of individual actions of civil servants that receive ethical criticism from citizens. I have proposed an administrative "translation" of such criticism here. Obviously, actually producing adequate administrative and ethical responses to them will be a much more difficult task (see Argyris 1982).

13.11 Conclusion

Citizens usually evaluate public actions of bureaucrats in ethical terms. Therefore, in liberal democracies, those who are committed to public learning through performance analysis cannot bypass the thorny problems of the relations between ethics and public life. Good arguments have been advanced against a direct application of private ethical convictions to public actions. But leaving public life without any ethical anchoring point altogether is equally unacceptable. Therefore I have drawn attention to the possibility of an autonomous ethics for public life, in which private ethical judgments are neither ingored nor eo ipso decisive.

The development of such an ethics for public life will be hampered as long as we do not accept mixtures between Weberian and subjective-humane bureaucracy as in principle legitimate. In ethically plural societies, where no one substantive private ethical code should be dominant, the emphasis will have to be on a public ethics of responsibility, that evolves over time and is connected to processes of public learning in which citizens, in their double capacities as rulers and ruled, are involved. Learning about individual responsibility for public actions characteristically takes place in responsibility fora, in which individuals are urged to account for their actions as holders of public authority. In such fora blind events that happened in the past are reinterpreted as actions of responsible individuals. Thus notions of responsibility are being reset in order to increase human control over what will happen in the world. The fact that ours have become organizational societies (Coleman 1982) sets specific problems for the development of notions of individual responsibility, but makes such notions neither superfluous nor impossible. While the task of translating individual convictions and actions into organizational/ systemic ones and vice versa has become more complicated it has also become more urgent. Efforts to improve systems and organizational controls cannot claim to be rational as long as they are not anchored in the life-worlds of speaking and evaluating citizens (Habermas 1981).

References

Adkins, A. W. H. (1960): *Merit and Responsibility*. Oxford: Oxford Univ. Press.
Arendt, H. (1959): *The Human Condition*. Garden City: Anchor Books.
Arendt, H. (1964): *Eichmann in Jerusalem*. New York: Viking.
Argyris, C. (1982): *Reasoning, Learning, and Action*. San Francisco: Jossey-Bass.
Bell, D. (1960): *The End of Ideology*. Glencoe. Free Press.
Coleman, J. S. (1982): *The Assymmetric Society*. Syracuse: Syracuse Univ. Press.
Dahl, R. A. (1982): *Dilemmas of Pluralist Democracy*. New Haven: Yale Univ. Press.
Gunsteren, H. van (1976): *The Quest for Control*. London: Wiley.
Gunsteren, H. van (1983): "Effiency en Corruptie." *Bestuurswetenschappen*. 5 (June): 281–285.
Habermas, J. (1981): *Theorie des kommunikativen Handelns*. Frankfurt: Suhrkamp.
Hart, H. L. A. (1968): *Punishment and Responsiblity*. Oxford: Clarendon Press.
Kolakowski, L. (1973): *Die Gegenwärtigkeit des Mythos*. München: Piper.
Popper, K. (1945): *The Open Society and its Enemies*. London: Routledge & Kegan Paul.
Rousseau, J. J. (1971): *Emile ou de l'Education* In Rousseau, J. J. *Œuvres Complètes*. Part III. Paris: Seuil.
Shils, E. (1972): *The Intellectuals and the Powers*. Chicago: Chicago Univ. Press.
Stirner, M. (1972): *Der Einzige und sein Eigentum*. Stuttgart: Reclam.
Thompson, D. (1980): "Moral Responsibility of Public Officials: The Problem of Many Hands." *American Political Science Review* 74/6: 905–946.
Weber, M. (1968): *Politik als Beruf*. Berlin: Duncker & Humblot.
Zinoviev, A. (1981): *The Yawning Heights*. Harmondworth: Penguin.

14. Assessing Evaluation Research

Gerd-Michael Hellstern

Abstract

Modern interdependent societies are in need of self-reflexive mechanisms. Particularly in western societies, evaluation has become a major tool rising from scattered beginnings to widespread institutionalization at different institutions and levels.

The success in institutionalization is not matched by an equal success in utilization. Rather, its meteoric rise has been accompanied by repeated critique and crisis questioning the content and substance of evaluations and pointing to its lack of relevance and utility despite promises. Evaluation researchers responded by designing manifold strategies to adapt their research to the changing demands of the political and administrative environments. They moved from narrow goal achievement measurements and experimental designs to comprehensive models of evaluation comprising strategies allowing for situational responsiveness. As evaluation is maturing, research integration, aiming to drive out competing evidence and build up more systemic knowledge from which future theory-driven approaches may derive, gains in prominence. By turning to an understanding of the philosophical basis of judging and valuation, evaluation research may overcome past failures to integrate theory into the analysis of shifting problem fields.

14.1 Introduction

From sporadic exercise, evaluation research grew in the mid-sixties and seventies at a meteoric rate in Western Europe and North America (OECD 1980; Levine et al. 1981). For some time the experimenting society, which systematically tries to exploit a rational mode of analysis and learning, seems to become true (Campbell 1969; Riecken and Boruch 1974; Bennet and Lumsdaine 1975). Those times have passed. The late seventies and the early eighties have shaken the optimistic picture and given rise to a more gloomy picture. Science has lost part of its credibility (Deutsch and Markovits 1980), and the experimental mode of thinking has given way to a more practical thinking stressing individual, idiosyncratic knowledge and common-sense experience, recognizing that all knowledge is based on values and rests on critical assumptions regarding human information processing capabilities (Lindblom and Cohen 1979). For some time the traditional and classical mode of rational policy thinking of which evaluation research formed part seemed to fade away (Aaron 1978; Cronbach 1980; Guba and Lincoln 1981). But despite mounting evidence of its limited relevance and utility, and peripheral influence on decisions, evaluation as a tool to assess the worth and effects of programs continues to grow (Dunn et al. 1981). Since the arrival of the first policy units in government, it has been well established (Chelimsky 1983; Brewer 1984). The intense discussion on technically incompetent research (Bernstein and Freeman 1975), on under- and misutilization (Patton 1978) and inadequate theoretical grounding (Cronbach et al. 1980) has been answered by improvements in technical quality (Cook and Campbell 1979), a search for new techniques (Smith 1981, 1982) and models (House 1980, 1983) and theoretical reconceptualizations (Raizen and Rossi 1981; Evaluation Research Society 1983). After each set-back evaluation research seems to emerge with a more focused identity, a clearer paradigm and a more powerful set of technologies.

Despite all signs of maturation in evaluation research the debate on how to improve the utility and relevance of evaluations continues (Bryk 1983). The current interest in raising the responsibility and accountability of government by integrating Quality Control and Cost-Effectiveness Measures into the evaluation frame (Smith and Caroll 1982; HMSO 1982), and the intensified discussion on standards for evaluation, ethical issues and basic principles of evaluation research (Joint Committee 1981, Evaluation Research Society, Standards Committee 1983) signal efforts to fit the demands posed by a complex and turbulent environment into theoretical models of evaluation. Unconventional and sophisticated techniques, the rise of multidimensional, multi method evaluations (Connor 1984) demonstrate the unbroken ability of the young evaluation profession to integrate new concepts and techniques in order to match an inherently ecological, evolutionary and pluralistic arena (Connor 1984; Rossi and Wright 1984). The recent arrival of secondary analysis, meta-analysis and research integration to drive out conflicting and competing evidence and codify the agreed reliable knowledge reconfirms those observations (Glass et al. 1981; Wortmann 1983). The tension between knowledge production and the dynamics of the policy fields, between the social and political powers shaping events and the limited contribution evaluation researcher can supply to raise the cognitive standards for judgements about effects by applying rigourous scientific standards lead to a continuous search and redefinition of tasks and instruments (Kaufmann and Strohmeier 1981).

To assess evaluation research one has to sort out the more ephemeral oscillations from the core issues. This requires a reflection of the historical evolution of evaluation, the nature and magnitude of its growth (see section 2 of this chapter) and an understanding of the diverse reasons why evaluations are used by different participants (section 3). From such a perspective the reason for the metamorphosis of evaluation may be better understood (section 4) and the value of its different approaches assessed (section 5), preparing the ground for conclusions about future opportunities in the evaluation field (section 6).

14.2 The Rise and Recurrent Crisis of Evaluation

Institutional Success

Initially evaluation originated from diverse disciplinary field – economics – psychology – sociology and even anthropology. Since the mid-seventies it has begun to form a distinct profession and has become institutionalized. A number of journals emerged *"Evaluation Magazine"*, *"Evaluation News"*, *"Evaluation and Program*

Planning", "Evaluation Review", "Evaluation and Education", "Evaluation and the Health Profession", "Studies in Educational Evaluation" for communication and dissimination of results and techniques. Numerous monographs and readers were published and some topical series started like the *"Progress Series in Evaluation"*, the *"New Direction for Program Evaluation"* and a yearly *"Evaluation Studies Review Annual"*. In fact, it seems no longer possible to keep up with the pace of publications. Major documentation centers like *ERIC* – in education – in the USA or the *IZ* (Information Center for Social Science) in Germany list some 35,000, 10,000 items respectively of reports, publications connected to evaluation research. For 1973–1975 the *"US-Congressional Sourcebook on Federal Program Evaluations"* contains 1,700 and for the period 1981–1983 2,650 evaluation studies respectively. The main evaluation agency in the US, the *GAO* (General Accounting Office) counts 1,000 reports for 1982. Smaller number are reported from Europe. In the United Kingdom 150 committees for scrutiny (Rayner-Committees) have been formed two years after their introduction by the Conservative government in 1979. In Sweden a growing part of the work of the more than 200 commissions in 1982 is taken up by evaluations, and in the Federal Republic of the 50 annual reports a growing number is based on some kind of evaluative research, sometimes kept from the broader public and the research community. National societies developed *(ENET, Canadian Evaluation Research Society, Evaluation Research Society)*, setting up committees to control the standards for conducting evaluations (Joint Committee 1981). In the US some states have begun or are considering the certification of evaluators, and the GAO, in a ten-year program turned its accountants into evaluators. Some universities have started their own courses and degree programs in evaluation, after governmental research and training institutes in Germany, the United Kingdom, the USA and Sweden as well as the International Institute of Administration have already developed some training courses and evaluation institutes.

Taking a longer view on the formation of the evaluation field, one could cite a number of early studies, which critically assessed the scope, practice and impact of governments, of which those by Bentham, Mill and, in Germany, Humboldt should be named. Those early evaluations marked a critical turn in state history, but they were rarely guided by a conscious effort to provide information for decision-making or intended to demand a testing of policies. Such goals are first encountered around the turn of the 20th century in some efforts of the social, often charity, movements and educational reformers. Such forerunners of evaluation appear again in the thirties when governments became involved in recovery programs like the New Deal in the USA (Caro 1978). But massive engagement started only with the growing amount of money spent on social programs and international aid in the early sixties. Yet, it took another decade for evaluation research to emerge as a distinct profession and to become institutionalized on a larger scale. Often it started with convential R & D-(Research and Development) Programs given to innovative private research institutions like the Tavistock Institute and later the Policy Studies Institute in Britain, Infratest and Prognos in the Federal Republic, Abt Ass., Systems Development Corporations, Mitre, Rand or Stanford International (SIR) in the USA. Only later it spread to university institutes as well, forming a policy network of attentive administrators, interested university researchers and entrepreneurial private research organizations. Reliable figures on the size of the field are difficult to arrive at as evaluations are often carried out internally and jointly with other tasks, but turnover may be compared to some smaller industrial sectors (see Freeman and Salomon 1981). Today evaluation is institutionalized in all 23 organizations of the UNO, most notably at the World Bank, the WHO, FAO, UNESCO, UNDP, ILO, UNIDO, and pressures are continuing to intensify those activities (UNO 1984). In most western countries some form of evaluation research is conducted, rarely systematic and more often ad-hoc. Few have developed comprehensive systems as the Canadian government, rarely is it carried through centrally as in the United Kingdom. More often functions are split between diverse institutions and agencies as in Sweden between the Commissions doing policy and program evaluation, and the National Audit Bureau and National Agencies engaged in mangement and efficiency evaluations (see Arvidsson: Ch. 30).

Limited Utility

Institutionalization provides for the necessary climate and context to allow evaluation researchers to work, but it derives its value only from the hypothesized link between successful institutionalization as a prerequisite for the use of evaluations. To apply the use test has been the main drive and deeper cause of all controversies about selection of appropriate methods, concepts and theories in evaluation (Weiss and Bucavalas 1981).

A specific journal dedicates itself to the task of asking how evaluation can produce usable knowledge (Knowledge: Creation-Diffusion-Utilization). There exists widespread agreement that evaluation is wanting in this respect – a finding which has given rise to a series of controversies and intense disputes, causing numerous attempts to reform and reconceptualize evaluation research, claiming that the task of evaluation was not well understood, and knowledge of how to conduct evaluations was lacking (Scriven, Eisner, Patton, Cronbach). Some of those disputes seem to have been resolved by the maturation of evaluation research, but some problems have proved to be persistent, and the debate continues to pose critical questions relating to:

Science, Policy and Ethics: What is the role of evaluation in respect to the policy process? Should evaluation simply inform or attempt to influence policies? What kind of information is needed to gain in importance? what are the consequences for the conduct of evaluation research of taking over the clients' perspective? Is the evaluator, to take a popular phrase the "Client's prostitute or critical lover"? What can be derived from those questions for the scientific standards and ethical behavior in evaluation?

Methods and Techniques: Why did evaluations not have any or only small effects when evaluating government programs? Is the experimental design adequate to deal with a complex environment and an unstable treatment? How can evaluators take account of unstable and indeterminant forces which make predictions of behavior so uncertain? Do they not neglect synergetic and historical facts in the process of decompartmentalization of a complex structural entity? Are they neglecting multiple interacting effects? Which are the assumptions underlying their models, and how do they shape the results?

Communication and Transfer: Can transfer techniques help to disseminate results, or are the problems of communicating results less a problem of diffusion techniques than of underlying differences in values and perspectives? Where are the limits of marketing results? Is acceptance a problem of knowledge or politics? What are the limits of client-oriented evaluations? Who should be the audience for evaluations? What are the tasks of dissemination phases in the evaluation research and of transfer institutions?

Conflicting Rationalities? A rising number of scholars have begun to question the ability of the political and administrative system to process information stemming from evaluation rationally (e.g. Banfield, Scharpf, Wilson). Differences in rules and principles governing the world of science and the world of politics – truth-seeking vs. power politics, universal generalization vs. situational bargaining prevent an active utilization of evaluations. As different incentives operate in both systems an integration of the different rationales is not feasible. Others have argued that unexplained assumptions govern evaluations and are the source of non-utilization. Evaluators usually take a top-down public management outlook, and are concerned with micro-individual reform, thus neglecting a more structural analysis of forces shaping societal institutions. The concentration on program issues is misleading as programs are changing. It would need more longitudinal research to take a broader perspective, transcending the focus of the clients' immediate interests to discover the basic problems and test the appropriateness of solutions. If this does not happen, each change in government or shifts in values and the political climate will make instrumental and program-related evaluations obsolete.

Softer Methods? The rationale for program evaluation sprung from the convincingly simple and effective model of experimental science. If models of actions could be tested and later replicated, policies might eliminate ineffective steps and choose the most efficient ones. Large-scale experiments have been conducted and produced informative knowledge, but their results, like in the National Income Maintenance Experiment, have not been used. This may partly be due to difficulties in implementing successful experiments. Often little effects have been found; it proved difficult to avoid losses in the membership of an adequate control group and regression artifacts may have occurred. But more often it sems to be the case that the goals and assumptions of the actors in a policy field differed from the goals and assumptions used in the analysis. Like in welfare economics, empirical interests were replaced by assumed ones; instead of motivational and pragmatic interests stated "legislated" goals were used. Formal evaluations of those goals produces little interest. On the other hand, decision theoretical approaches based on actors' interests using multi-attribute utility approaches have been difficult to conduct (Edwards 1983). Therefore more and more researchers started to question the use of established methods and techniques, demanding more field-related qualitative approaches fitting the action and living context of their research environment, building on feedback of everyday experiences from practitioners, concentrating on descriptions of relevant events and more localized situations. Strategic mixing of different research methods like triangulation emerged from the discussion without proving to meet better, by "utilization-focused", "creative" strategies, the utility criteria of different audiences and to be able to bridge the gap between research evidence and its usage (Denzin 1978, Patton 1978, 1980).

Targeting Evaluation Transfer? The lack in utilization has turned attention to the dissemination and diffusion of research results. For some programs (e.g. in Education) Research Diffusion Centers who certify the quality of and disseminate research results, have been established. The turn to contextual methods has raised the awareness of differences in the informational needs. Knowledgeable gatekeepers and committed innovators have been discovered as important links between researchers and practitioners. More important, different types of information – instrumental and conceptual – have been discovered, and conscious efforts undertaken to fit evaluation to the differential needs of specific policy stages and clients. The internal evaluators, who possess intimate knowledge about political and administrative contexts, have gained in importance despite arguments of a loss of quality and of independency of evaluations.

Despite these diverse efforts users of evaluations and evaluators continue to express concern about the limited ability of evaluations to meet the needs and influence policies. Whereas criticism continues, evaluation research still manages to survive and continues to spread to other institutions and nations.

14.3 Why Has Evaluation Research Become Popular?

Converging Forces

If evaluation research has failed so often, why has it become so successful? In the early sixties and seventies public attention was not primarily on evaluation research, but on the institutionalization of political planning, budgetary programming systems linking task and financial systems, optimizing techniques of operation research, and rational choice models to coordinate activities (Levine et al. 1981). Manifold attempts to institutionalize political planning in central institutions in governments, numerous ideas to establish planning agencies at all levels of government emerged and are well documented. In the design of these rational planning models, evaluation served as a part of model rhetoric rather than as an ongoing activity. As an idealized feedback loop of managerial cybernetic cycles – popular in textbook models at the time, evaluation was supposed to link past information for future planning. The detailed analysis of problems generated in the feedback loop created little interest despite early organizational studies on the defects of management information systems and distorted communication channels between levels of hierarchies. The purpose of evaluation was primarily understood as a technical (posterior) problem which an empirical science could easily overcome later. What was more, the concept of evaluation was, in a strange way, kept seperate and supposed not to interfere with the fragile distribution of power and the difficult questions of social and political control. How evaluation might change the delicate fabric of different and manifold control mechanisms operating in the policy field, set by the constitution, traditional norms, political issues, administrative routines and social cultures, was not at stake. Even in the futile attempts of policy reformers to gain control of a reluctant administration in a turbulent environment, evaluations were not considered to play a major role. The basic spirit of evaluation models was being considered technical, rational, related to narrow goal achievements and program substance, and not interwoven with the actors' divergent interests. That evaluations might infringe on the complex and fragmented decision-making structure and influence administrative implementation processes seems to have been less obvious, despite early textbooks' warnings about the potential conflict inherent in evaluations (Campbell 1969; Caro 1972; Weiss 1972). Evaluation was conceived to create a basis of technical knowledge, to inform on goal achievements, provide evidence of the succesful introduction of innovations, e.g. in curricula or comprehensive school systems. At best, it could help to devise allocations more rationally like in regional economic policies. The institutionalizing of supportive information systems (Management Information Systems) to be used to monitor rule compliance and the development of participation devices like in Community Development Programs, was introduced only later to overcome data deficiencies and implementation failures. Neither the relation of evaluation research to the traditional forms and means of control nor the possible contribution of evaluation as a system to guide actions were at issue – despite the Popperian rhetoric in many – mainly social democratic-party programs of a cumulative, progressive and gradual learning process (see Kaufmann: Ch. 10).

Whereas the early planning models failed, partly due to unrecognized impracticability, to technical complexity, and political vulnerability, evaluation changed its form from narrow experimental testing of outcomes to creative broadly-gauged participative approaches, and even grew in importance. The spread of its influence should not be understood as a rational, systematically planned or comprehensive strategy to institutionalize social science-based knowledge about the effects and outcomes of policies. Rather, and more realistically, evaluation research crept into the arena of policy analysis, and was forced on the programs by hopeful political and administrative innovators and enhanced by entrepreneurial social science promises, and then disseminated bit by bit, like all new innovations, to different institutional contexts under varied methodological forms of disguise, supplementing and amending traditional routine information processing.

Guiding the development of evaluation technologies were experiences from various disciplines and different policy fields. In the late fifties *educational testing* has been developed in response to the Sputnik shock to mobilize human resources. Conscious planning and testing should help to modernize science study programs, mathematics, and social studies. In economics, *project appraisal* techniques to judge the return on the international economic aid programs to the developing new nations were supported by national governments and international organizations like the UN and her affiliates. In social science, *survey techniques* and sampling procedures were refined enabling to measure the impact of new media and market promotional activities. When in the sixties and, in Europe, in the seventies new social programs emerged, they could draw on those scattered early experiences, although no systematic meta-evaluation of those early predecessors has been undertaken, and often the close connection between the breakthrough in different fields and the emergent evaluation research has not been recognized. It were science entrepreneurs, often with a broadly based knowledge of strategic planning like the *Rand Corporation*, the *Systems Development Corporation (SDC)*, or newly formed research enterprises like *Abt Ass., Stanford Research International (SRI)* which seized the opportunity to apply those techniques and methodological tools to new fields, but crucially neglecting the link with broader social science knowledge and concepts as it turned out. For the first time social scientists, albeit mainly economists and educational psychologists in certain fields, seemed to make a measurable, relevant, acknowledged as well as paid contribution to public policies by providing the technical basis for measuring effects and effectiveness of programs. Fertilized by the growing movement for social indicators and the analytical successes of causal data analysis, evaluation – confined, in the beginning, to high-priority and politically sensitive arenas – expanded its scope of application to nearly all fields and at all levels of government, and was conducted regularly as an internal evaluation or on a consultancy basis. Campbell's moving vision of a learning, progressive forward-moving reformed society did not seem to be unrealistic:

"The United States and other modern nations should be ready for an experimental approach to social reform, an approach, in which we try out new programs designed to cure specific social problems, in which we learn whether or not these programs are effective, and in which we retain, imitate and modify, or discard them on the basis of apparent effectiveness on the multiple imperfect criteria available." (Campbell 1969: 409 ff.)

Two trends seem to have converged:

(1) *The increasing sophistication and maturation of social science* as an empirical scientific activity after World War II, the increasing ability of social scientists to apply new sophisticated measurement tools to decipher social reality and, to a lesser degree, form causal theories which underly interconnected actions in the institutions of societies. For the various interests in social sciences the new field provided different opportunities:
   – for the ivory-tower social scientists the new field provided a prospect for testing theories in practice and gaining access to empirical "real world" data,
   – for the methodologists it meant the certification and the public recognition of the power of their newly acquired tools and the necessary support to refine them,
   – for the graduating young social scientists evaluations opened the prospect for a useful contribution to society, outside the realm of the university, blending employment opportunities, policy relevance and his own social concern.

(2) *The growth of organizational density in modern societies* stemming from increasing differentiation and division of work, which necessitates the growth of independent capacities to coordinate actions. This requires to take into account the consequences of actions and replace more individualized experiences and task-oriented personalized information and knowledge production by a more systematic process of knowledge production. A set of different societal forces operated to stimulate the public interest in the use of social science based evaluations, interests:
   – to guide behavioral and institutional change, to understand impediments to reform and resistance in an uncontrollable environment,
   – to provide feedback on reform failures as informations were lacking about the results of implementations in a system characterized by division of functions, responsibilities and power,
   – to support processes of consensus building and argumentation to decrease the level of conflict and protest by rationalizing the discussion process,

– to shift power as, due to the changing functions of government, traditional division of powers were in danger of being undermined, evaluations should help to keep the executive and the administration accountable.

From Dashed Hopes To Multiple Evaluations

In the beginning evaluation research could build on a broad consensus. The insertion of evaluation clauses like in Title I ESEA (Elementary and Secondary Education Act) to provide compensatory eduction to disadvantaged chrildren in 1964 in the USA, or the start of Comprehensive School Experiments in the Federal Republic of Germany in 1969 could rely on widespread agreement. Albeit, different reasons underlay the formal consensus for evaluation. Every actor hoped that evaluations would yield something different. To those favoring the introduction of new social programs, evaluations promised support or at least some information (perhaps) of use to the program; in essence evaluation would make policies more rational, defendable and easier to justify and legitimize in the public and administrative political arena. To opponents it opened convenient avenues for future challenge and termination of the opposed program, since by way of evaluation, ammunition to criticize a program should or could be provided, at least final decisions could be postponed. To both sides evaluations promised to be a more rational and reliable tool to build evidence and attain decisions than the past ad-hoc information – gathering and knowledge – building procedures. Few argued about the limits and inherent conservative bias of evaluations; neglecting established programs, concentrating on social programs and providing arguments for those who pay. Especially to those responsible for a program, evaluation research seemed to posses some convincing characteristics:

(1) it could serve as an important tool *to learn* about a program's operation and its effects, which could be important in reviewing decisions for drafting new guidelines, allocating resources and monitoring claims,
(2) at the same time it could provide a means *to control* the implementing organization, a constant challenge in centralized as well as federal states due either to regionally decentralized program delivery structures or coproduction needs in a pluralistic society,
(3) evaluations could be used as *persuasive* instruments to influence public debates, create a supportive outside constituency by raising awareness and providing information; evaluations can increase the credibility of the program agencies vis-à-vis a suspicious parliament or critical public opinion and confirm the competent and professional delivery of a program.

Often those hopes did not materialize. A lack of technical skills, political understanding or substantive knowledge initially led to a poor reputation of evaluation. More often than not evaluation potential has not been used, the results have been kept secret, were shelved or even suppressed. Many administrators and evaluators, well aware of the potential risks that evaluations might pose in terms of influencing the political environment, feared the uncontrollability of evaluations. As the case of Head-Start demonstrates when Nixon attempted to influence the public debate by the release of the early negative findings, the purposeful use of evaluations may fail and produce the opposite results. Head-Start continued to grow. Even those evaluations, timed to channel public awareness, e.g. at pre-election time, like in the Ruhrprogramm in the Federal Republic, have been kept at a low profile to avoid repercussions. Suchman's warning that evaluation may be used to white or eye-wash a program, is met with less often than the attempt to hide the findings (Suchman 1967).

To avoid political maneuvering, misuse and no use of evaluations and gear evaluations to immediate improvements and melioriation in programs, the *self-evaluating* organization which monitors its own activities has been suggested. Indeed, in many programs self-evaluation schemes have been mandated – mainly in local school and community development programs. In a real life context, where evaluations always can become the source of sanctions and discrimination, results, as a matter of self-interest, tend to be subverted. Evaluations as a program of learning by implementators in the process of implementation, breaks down as soon as the mutual trust of the participating group breaks down (Wildavsky 1972).

A more realistic model emerges from the interaction between the divergent mix of distinct evaluations by different interest groups. Evalution may work, if it is functioning in a larger context of competing evidence. *Multiple evaluations* are in the process of evolving in most nations. A rich set of various instruments and institutions has developed. Political maneuvering has strengthened the General Accounting Office (GAO) as an independent evaluation agency in the U.S. providing evaluations for Congress. Administrative fragmentation has intensified interest in evaluation in Germany. Private interest groups have become aware of the potential of evaluations for checking adverse effects of pending regulations and programs. Depending on constitutional arrangements, historical experiences, policy fields and power distributions, we find different forms of evaluations enacted:

– *in parliament:* legal evaluation requirements (and sunsetting practices) are more common today. Evaluative reports have become a universal request. Their fulfillment is controlled in the USA by the *Congressional Research Service* and the *GAO,* in Germany by the *Parliamentary Advisory Services.* In addition Hearings, Commissions, the institutionalization of Ombudsmen are some of the more frequently used instruments (Hellstern: Ch. 33).
– *in administrative agencies* and for the executive, information systems like the *MINIS (Management Information Systems for Ministers)* in Great Britain, procedural tools like *impact statements* on environmental, social, technological, fiscal or land-use effects are increasingly utilized either regularly or in preparing a new law. For larger projects, Cost-Benefit Analysis has become a legal requirement in some nations (OECD 1980).
– *interest groups:* public and private interest groups have begun to develop their own evaluation tools. Trade Unions in Norway and Sweden, the health producer groups in the United States and Germany are examples. If independent evaluations are not feasible, these groups ask for participation in commissions or the commission of adversary evaluations and review panels.

Institutional and methodological leadership may exist in different institutions. In the U.S. it has moved to the GAO and Congress. In Great Britain it is still with the executive which has an interest that parliamentary commission conduct efficiency scrutinies (Rayner Scrutinies). In Germany ministerial research institutions and intergovernmental boards like the Federal-State-Commission on Educational Planning and Research and interministerial working groups, e.g. on legislation and cost-benefit analysis, play a leading role. In Sweden independent commissions and boards like the Commission for Higher Education predominantly support evaluations. In France and Canada evaluation is part of the administrative and financial control system; in Canada the Treasury and its wing, the Accounting Office, have probably developed the most comprehensive evaluation system to date. As a result of these multiple employments of divergent evaluations, evaluation research

Tab. 1: Main Focus of Evaluations in Different Nations

Country	Canada	Germany F. R.	Great Britain	Sweden	USA
Types	Comprehensive, Administrative	Intergovernmental, Program-Related	Adversary Review Commissions	Independent Boards	Adversary multiple Evaluations
Areas	Public Utilities, Governmental Activities	Joint Programs (Regional Policy etc), Comprehensive, Higher Education Humanizing the Labor World, Labor Market New Technologies	All ministerial activities, Nationalised Industries, Inner Cities Regional Policy	Education Occupational Safety, Social Welfare	Social Programms e.g.: Community Programms, Rehabilitation, Education, Health Provision, Criminal Justice
Consumer Audience	Executive	Administration	Executive	Cabinet	Congress
Base	Inside Research and Monitoring	Institutional Research	Informed Criticisms	Professional Review Panels	Contractual Research
Methods	Management Analysis	Action Research, Process Evaluations	Judgemental Scrutinies Monitoring	Judgemental Consensus	Experimental Outcome
Impetus	Efficiency, Effectiveness, Integration	Change Acceptance	Efficiency Cost-saving	Consensus Orientation	Reform Outcome
Focus[1]	T–S_2	S_1–S_2	T	S_2	S_1–S_2 — C

[1] S_2 ex-ante situation, S_2 current situation, T program activities, C Control Group

emerged as a far more varied, rich and informative activity as could be envisioned in the early days. The main types and methods used, and the main areas differ from one country to another (see Tab. 1). Imitation and learning occur across policy fields and nations.

At the same time evaluation designs became a more complex undertaking. Results were regarded as less assertive. The uncertainties surrounding the findings were subjected to public discussion questioning the credibility and interests of evaluation researchers. Policymakers developed a critical sensitivity about the limits of social scientists, and evaluators became painfully aware of the shifting and differential information needs and usages of their results by policymakers and an interested public. Any main differences may not be found to relate to nations, but rather to different policy fields and institutional levels.

14.4 Do Evaluation Concepts Fit the Policy Field's Quest?

Historic specific constellations of specific needs, different actors, and different techniques have led to what may be called the *"heterogenity"* of evaluation research (Rossi 1981). A varied set of evaluation models emerged in an attempt to fit concepts and techniques of the social sciences to the turbulence and dynamics of the policy field. The evaluation models differ according to "what purpose", "for whom", "how" and "whose" evaluation research should be conducted. This made it difficult to define clearly the boundaries of the field and identify the substantive core of evaluative activities. The infinite potential configurations of purpose, techniques, concepts, actors served and institutionalized forms led to a great number and wide variety of research models. The evaluators' attentive sensitivity to the *need for utilization* as the basic aim of evaluation has led to successive waves of diverse strategies to find a *fit* between the conceptual requirements of science models, and the conditions and constraints of a particular policy field (see the following summary of evaluation models).

Underlying the majority of models is the assumption that an ordinary, clear sequence of events takes place as programs are designed, implemented, evaluated and replanned. From the planning stage it is assumed that some theoretical knowledge exists from which a model of intervention or a *theory of action* and its consequences stem. This model relates to some known needs which are measured and for which implementation guidelines and strategies are developed; *process evaluation* safeguards the implementation, monitors first results, and later *impact evaluations* assess the outcome of the program results for the participants, ideally evaluating *cost and benefits* for the different actors. If such a model is tested beforehand, it may later be *generalized* and achieve persuasive predictable results (Rossi et al. 1979). Several authors have noted that the *rationality* governing the creation of such classical evaluation models is severely limited for widespread application in policy fields. In order to work the "classical" evaluation research model needs the, what is highly improbable, trustful collaboration of legislators who establish clear goals, an executive which converts the legislative intents into specific program guidelines, evaluators who develop adequate evaluative criteria from the program objectives and are able to monitor implementation and effectiveness as well as examine the range of stimulated effects. Ideally such a rational model is first tested, replicated and later *disseminated*. As comprehensive evaluation which covers all aspects and meets all assumptions can rarely be conducted, evaluations are usually eclectic and concentrate on selected, critical phases of a program. Simplifications are necessary to implement the evaluation research design. As it may be difficult to have agreed program goals, and the necessary implementation may not be achieved (e.g. random assignments of control groups to permit systematic comparison), implementation failures occur frequently, prevent the test of the theoretical model and lead to inconclusive findings. To save the rationale of evaluation some have argued clearer program objectives, a firm application of enforcements and sanctions for better implementation, all of which may lead to more reliable evaluations (Sabatier: Ch. 15).

The compliance cost of such actions may be severely underestimated. A more realistic analysis of evaluation researcher's activities points to the basic divergence between different modes of knowing. Operational wisdom, general knowledge-building, and the everyday interactive problem-solving capacities may require different models of information processing and production. The science model is only one and poorly equipped to deal with everyday problems. Technical knowledge in a complex environment with shifting tasks and constant change has sometimes less value than common sense experiences (Lindblom and Cohen 1979).

Underlying those arguments is the conclusion that "technical" program evaluations may be seriously limited as soon as they enter the less well specified "life" context of a program. Whereas the science approach may prove to be successful for *well-defined problems* with clear goals and clear causal relations, most problems do not fall in this category. They are not well structured and cannot be broken down easily into their components (see Table 2).

Furthermore, the causal context surrounding those problems cannot be kept separate to allow for causal explanations which take into account the consequences emerging from an action over time. Most problems for which evaluation research could be useful for policymakers and clients, are *ill-structured problems*, with substantive problems varying from actor to actor and over time; they are dynamic. Such problems are not mechanical and cannot be separated from the context. The definition " of what constitutes the problem" differs from actor to actor. A transfer of results is rarely possible; rather, a re-invention and adaptation to the special situation is necessary. The traditional investigation and generalization techniques of social science research fit such an outlook even less. Most problems in the public

Tab. 2: Evaluation Types Derived from Different Knowledge Needs in Well – and Ill-Structured Problem Settings

Goals	Cause-Effect-Relationships	
	Complete Knowledge	Incomplete Knowledge
Crystalized	Goal-Monitoring	Experimental Evaluation
Ambiguous	Consensus (Judgement Building)	Naturalistic Evaluation (Qualitative and Case Approach)

policy area are ill-structured. Unlike with well-structured problems, clear-cut decision rules are less likely. What makes a "better" model rests on how one defines "better", a question ultimately relating to philosophical values.

The assumption behind the classical evaluation models argues that organizations are created mainly as instruments for certain goals and that evaluation research in those models may be characterized as empirically-oriented, using systematic methods for observations and concentrating on *individual* change. This characterization holds for those evaluation research models which belong to the *"system-analytical, behavioral objective* and *decision-making models"*. For many social entities which need to accommodate many different interests and at the same time require some shared consensus, such a conception of rational aggregation may not hold true as time, history, culture involve intervening factors which make an instrumentalized use difficult and rational value aggregation unnecessary. The idea that different approaches are needed to answer different questions has received broad support among evaluation researchers. They urge the adoption of methods to meet the needs arising in particular evaluative situations (Patton 1980). A range of unconventional *"responsive-natural"* models like the *"art-critical"*, *"accreditibility"* and *"polarized"* evaluation models assume that criteria for decisions are intuitively based and not available to rational procedures of aggregating and weighting as required by behavioral and decision-oriented quantitative models based on utilitarian and objectivist goals (see Table 3 below). Early evaluation models have been classified according to the degree to which they aim at narrow (set) goals or undertake to discover broader systemic and unknown effects (e.g. Etzioni 1968; Kersaw 1975; Scriven 1980). Later evaluations were categorized according to a phase model which sets the range of evaluation activities to stretch from input/needs-assessments to process-/monitoring approaches, to outcome/impact measurements and, more recently, to include cost-analysis (Landsberg et al. 1979; Rossi, Freeman and Wright 1979; Suchman 1967; Wholey et al. 1979). More recent have classifications emphasized the use of particular methods, techniques and theories to stress the specific mode of thinking and perspective involved in evaluation (Crane 1982; Guba and Lincoln 1981; Patton 1978, see also Tab. 3 below).

More recent evaluation models are questioning the need for concentrating on manipulation and related assumptions *(instrumentality, policy optimism and problem-solving determinism)*, stressing the importance of understanding and identifying the underlying assumptions which may lead to the definition of an issue, guide the motivation of the different actors and their interactions, in order to recognize more clearly the different levels of analysis and the multidimensionality of public policies. As a direct response, multidimensional concepts and techniques have been developed, which integrate different subjective data – like in the discrepancy model of perception and expectations – and design the cognitive maps of actors according to their chains of arguments and the systematization of anecdotes.

As preferences are conceived as moving, changing and developing over time, meshing very different dimensions, and difficult to explicate in advance, more evaluations have used models which allow for the implicit use of accumulated experiences like expert judgments in *peer review systems* or workmen's assessments in *quality control circles* (see Majone: Ch. 21).

Tab. 3: Synopsis of Major Classifications of Evaluation Models

Stage Models	Methods Orientation	Theory and Knowledge Classification
Suchman 1967 (also Attkinson/Hargreavas et al. 1978) Evaluation of Effort Evaluation of Performance Evaluation of Adequacy Evaluation of Efficiency Evaluation of Process	*Edwards/Guttenberg 1975* Field Experiments *(Campbell/Cook)* Pragmatic Evaluations (usual practice *Kiresuk)* Decision theoretical Approach *(Multiattribute/Bayesian)*	*Chelimsky 1977* A Knowledge Perspective A Management Perspective An Accountability Perspective
Etzioni 1969 Goal-Attainment Model Systems Model *Wholey 1970/1981* Program Outcome Evaluation Program Strategy Evaluation Project Evaluation Evaluability Assessment Rapid Feedback Evaluation Performance Monitoring Intensive Evaluation	*House 1980* Systems Analysis Behavioral Objectives Decision Making Goal-free Art Criticism Accreditation Adversary Transaction	*Crane 1982* Scientific Theory Testing Applied Scientific Methods *(Rossi)* Utilization-focused Evaluation *(Alkin/Patton)* Evaluation as Education *(Cronbach)* Qualitative Casestudy *(Parlett/Hamilton* Egalitarian Evaluations *(Rawls)* Utilitarian Evaluation *Edwards/Guttantag*
Perkins (vgl. a. Landsberg/Deigher) 1977 Strategic Compliance Program Design Management Intervention Effect Program Impact	*Guba/Lincoln 1981* Discrepancy Model *(Provus)* Countenance Model *(Stoke)* Context-Input-Process-Product Model *(CIPP Stufflebeam)* Connoissearslang Model *(Eisner)* Goal-free Model *(Scriven)* Responsive and Naturalistic Model *(Cuba)*	
Cook et al. 1978 (vgl. Scriven 1971) Formative Evaluation Summative Evaluation *Rossi/Freeman 1979* Needs Assessment (Program planning questions) Monitoring policy Implementation Impact Assessment Economic Efficiency Questions		

The new *responsive models* may signal not only an advance, but also a danger. As the classical models are no longer used as yardsticks, the tension still existing between the problem field (and its needs) and the scientific approach of defining, measuring and searching for solutions may lead to a loss of importance of scientific research due to the political climate, and to methodological laissez-faire, introducing an uncontrolled bias. As comprehensive evaluations which use different models are too costly and time-consuming, and *eclectic use* is made of evaluations, different modes and criteria are needed for selecting models which meet information needs in particular situation and keep up the scientific standards. The introduction of *quality controls* for evaluations by setting agreed standards have been the concern of a growing movement inside the evaluation profession. At each stage of the evaluation research process, from negotiating the contract and formulating the research question to the stage to utilization and dissemination of results, criteria have been developed which evaluators should strive to meet. Those criteria relate to the *accuracy* of evaluations, to respecting *proprieties* in conducting evaluations, to a recognition of the limits of evaluations *(feasibility)* and to a commitment to meet information needs as requested *(utility)*. It is hoped that funding agencies will adhere to these standards, and that the standards will become a common good applied in reviewing research by the community of evaluators and used in the training of young evaluation professionals (Evaluation Research Society 1980; Rossi 1982).

14.5 Assessing Strategies

Policy context and evaluation research strategies are closely related. The set of past (and the set of possible) models is too large systematicaly to evaluate all of them; but the problems and values of different strategies may well be condensed in three sets of evaluation research strategies which have evolved historically in stages as discussed below:
(1) the evolution of the *goal-oriented model,* the search for measuring and identifying goals
(2) the use of the *experimental research design* for evaluation as an attempt to solve the causal problems, relating treatment to outcomes
(3) the discovery of *interactive research models* to take administrative and political constraints into account more explicitly.

The Search for Goals

Despite variations in definitions most textbooks take it for granted that evaluation measures the extent to which a program realizes certain goals. Technically speaking, the evaluation process assigns a value to some *set* objectives and determines the degree of success of a policy action or program in terms of the achievement of those objectives.

This requires two tasks of the evaluator:

(1) to establish the goals

(2) to "separate out" specific effects attributable to a given policy action from a program's total output as the main tasks of evaluation research (e.g. Suchmann 1967; Weiss 1972; Rossi et al. 1979).

Most textbooks follow this view. After describing and standardizing program activities (What constitutes a program?), it is attempted to elicit goals and to measure preferences to which program changes could be compared. The concern for goals seems a logical one, its deceptive simplicity may be less straightforward than initially imagined. There are four major problems associated with the conceptualization of goals:

(1) the problems of identifying and gaining access to goals
(2) the fact of multiple goals for people, programs and groups
(3) the question of whose goals are to be represented (client demand, official goals, leader values etc.)
(4) the fact that goals change over time and priorities may be reset over time, a fact which, if one takes into account multiple actors with differing goals and values and preferences can easily defy any calculation procedure.

Even, if goals could be agreed, the standards for such goals may be difficult to arrive at and could become vexed evaluation questions:

(a) *historical standards:* e.g. this year's performance versus last year's performance
(b) *normative standards:* e.g. a program's performance versus the performance of a similar or comparable program or versus regional, national, or international standards
(c) *theoretical standards:* the design or "if everything went right" standard, given the existing resource limitations
(d) *absolute standards:* e.g. the zero defect standard independent of resource limitations
(e) *negotiated or compromised standards:* based on a standard-setting process such as managing by objectives.

In view of the deep concern evaluators have expressed for practical relevance, experts of the goal model are trying hard to establish the right goals to ensure that the results of their research will influence agency policy formulation or induce changes. But a hopeful model, in which: a top executive supports and uses the results of evaluations to make important decisions; a program manager encourages and supports the evaluation of his program; and an evaluator produces pertinent recommendations and changes relating to the efficiency and effectiveness of the program, defies the program reality of goal evaluation which more realistically includes a top executive who lacks time and interest to define "his goals" as he has to build coalitions and accommodate differing goals; program managers who use tactics to hide goals, mislead the goal-setting process as they know of the variety of goals; and evaluators whose efforts are equally divided between survival and the advocacy of honest evaluations with little time left for understanding the process of goal changes and cooperation to search for the underlying assumption and interests of given goals. Since they are rarely geared to the normative interest of the participants evaluation results are therefore either selectively used or ingored by agency policymakers. Even when evaluation research results were intended for use in policy-making, a different political motive may emerge and transcend the desire to use the research results.

The problems involved in goal questions center on the following three issues:

Time. Evaluation takes place in a process which evolves over time; sometimes the program to be valuated has evolved in a long historical process which has already produced many ideas, theories and assumptions which in turn have been internalized in the way the program is viewed and acted upon. To take a set of goals would neglect those connotations; it would neglect the evolving and often – in respect to different situations and configurations of actors-moving goals. Even for a single actor-analysis the assumption of clear stable goals is rarely met. ("We wish many conflicting things over time.") Their analysis is difficult to conduct and – as could be shown – in a sense may be irrational and unethical as the setting and achievements of goals may depend upon a whole complex of dynamic interacting structural factors which change over time and are not under individual or program control.

Substance. Some policy situations simply do not allow a clear specification of objectives. Due to the complexity of the arena or the problem itself, it may not be very clear "which way to go", but depending on what the situation demands, steps for actions must be taken. To commit oneself in such a situation to binding goals would necessitate knowing the legal, social, and political implications and risks involved. Instead cognitive limits and a kind of economizing make it often seem more useful to proceed on the basis of rather loosely organized goals or even contradicting goals – a situation consistent with many government programs – and adapt goals later as problems and issues become clearer.

Actors and Interactions. In some situations it seems to be absurd to ask for a commitment to goals. In case of highly politicized issues the exclusion of the basic discussion may be the only rational strategy to achieve some kind of preliminary yet necessary compromise. As Festinger points out cognitive dissonance cannot be endured for long. Explicit goal-setting would in many fields certainly lead to such an (unnecessary) conflict situation and produce rigid behavior. The need for consensus-building and the ability to take advantage of future opportunities for (better) argumentation and legitimation may be the reason for much of the open goal-processing going on in human interaction. The more precise the goals the more the action space, the maneuvering of actors will be limited. In a situation with unequal or balanced distribution of power resources, dominating goals and enforcing goals would prevail over change. Innovation and creative adaption would be difficult to develop.

In many situations evaluation strategies relying on clear goal setting like *goal attainment scaling* (GAS) are adequate and useful. Depending on substance, time, the multiplicity of interdependent policies and actors it may often be advisable, in respect of a given cognitive capacity, contextual situation and power distribution, not to proceed with clear goal-setting procedures. Yet, if *formal* goal-setting seems not to be useful, *goal clarification* seems all the more important. The task of the evaluation then becomes one of recording and observing the process of goal evolution, of interpreting and analyzing the changes and explaining the preference for general or unclear goals.

Evaluability Assessments

Having recognized the central issue of goal-setting, the former Assistant Secretary for evaluation in the largest evaluation unit in the U.S. (ASPE, Dep. HEW) has argued that in future evaluations to be conducted a *pre-evaluation* should take place, which assesses the evaluability of a program and decides on the kind of evaluation to be undertaken. In the *evaluability assessment,* he recommends three conditions to be met:

(1) Program objectives to be well-defined
(2) Program assumptions/objectives should be well-defined
(3) The evaluations' intended uses must be well-defined.

Only if these preconditions are met, Wholey sees a chance that evaluation research may be of more use. His model which has been used extensively at ASPE in the former U.S.-Department of Health, Education and Welfare (HEW) contains eight steps:

(1) *Define the program* to be evaluated. Evaluators and managers decide what the program is which will be evaluated.
(2) *Collect information* in the intendend program. Evaluator documents program objectives, how they are achieved, and how they are measured.
(3) Develop concise description of the program *(logic modeling).* Evaluator grahically represents program's locigal structure.
(4) Document the extent to which program activities and objectives are defined in *measurable terms.* Evaluator determines whether management has measures for all major components of the logic model.
(5) Collect information on *program reality.* Feasibility and *cost* of collecting program information is determined.
(6) Synthesize program information to clarify feasibility of performance measurements and plausibility of program objectives *(equivalency modeling).* A model is designed, clarifying what field data are available. Feasibility of obtaining program objectives is also determined.
(7) Identify evelution/management *options.* Using the three criteria outlined above, the portion of the program that is "ready for useful evaluation" is determined.
(8) *Present information* to Management. Management verifies initial findings and determines next steps. (see Wholey 1979)

Although the attempt to obtain a prior evaluability assessment seems to be an improvement, some questions need yet to be asked. Wholey's mode helps to economize on evaluation information; but limiting himself to issues of goal clarification, he may also limit himself to programs which are of lesser interest or those with paper goals, while the actual goals remain hidden. His dependence on the stated goals may prevent him from asking more informative questions about goals.

Wholey's essentially *participatory program clarification model* is an implicit acknowledgment of the limits of program evaluation. Evaluation is only meaningful, if there is someone with power who is interested in its results. But this approach is a rather narrow one.

1. According to his model *only* those programs with *clear goals* will be evaluated, and those without will fail to get evaluated, even if there is a need for this.

2. In getting objectives agreed, the most important task of current evaluation research to analyze *unintendend* aspects of a program may *fail* since managers have the say about which objectives should be considered the goals of a program.

3. *Goal evaluation* is only one part of the evaluation game, equally important is the critical description of the *treatment* and service delivery activities, or of the *constituencies* of a program. In a dynamic and political environment the limitation of one's view to goal evaluation aspects ignores the need for goal change and goal diversity. Using evaluability assessment may not enhance the production of useful information; to outline and unterstand factors and effects accompanying change in a bureaucratic environment may be more important than a limited goal agreement statement.

Testing Alternatives One strategy has been to follow up the *theoretical modelling processes* which increasingly take into account prior information and value distributions. In expanding the more traditional *multi-utility* and *Bayesian model* to embrace fuzzy problems, the limited application possibilities of the early approaches may be well extended (Menges 1982; Edwards and Newman 1983). Although they are theoretically clear, the empirical results cannot convince, as often, after preferences have been assembled, calculated and corrected, the participants cannot identify with the aggregate results (Love 1982).

A less technical, but equally sophisticated analytical evaluation process underlies the approach favored by the *US-National Institute of Evaluation (NIE)*. The *"stakeholder"* concepts try to avoid the "narrow, unrealistic, irrelevant, unfair and unused" approaches implied by simple goal-directed evaluation procedures. By taking explicitly into account all the needs of those groups which have a "stake" in the evaluation, it is hoped to sensitize evaluators to different local needs and the conflicting values of different "user groups". Pilot evaluations of educational programs showed that the assumptions of the stakeholder approach that the "stakeholders" can be identified and will participate, are often not very realistic. And if so, the stakeholders often do not know what kind of information they want, could need, and what are the future decisions to be taken for which evaluation should produce useful results. As a possible controlled strategy to move from formal goal-setting procedures to a better understanding of the multiple and shifting goals in an interactive setting, the approach seems promising. Practical experiences with participative strategies suggest that evaluation may sink into a political action strategy without control of the underlying assumptions and rules, if these strategies are not guided by theoretical understanding and testing (Bryk 1983).

Interesting and feasible strategies to supplement the stakeholder approach have emerged from the organizational consulting practice and linguistics which investigate the differences between the goals *exposed* and underlying assumptions (or goals *used*). In *argumentative* analysis the concepts and interpretations which underly the goals of different actors are systematically decomposed, by following the sequential structure of discourse. In these strategies, the goals in question are challenged by the theoretically derived interpretation, and the logical tools of science are utilized to control this process. Goal-setting and measuring activities are replaced or supplemented by a systematic *goal clarification analysis*. A better understanding of the changing, evolutionary and contingent character of goals may thus emerge (Argyris 1982; Soeffner 1979).

The Experimental Model Revived?

Since Campbell and Stanley's first systematic study into the use of *social experimentation* (Campbell and Stanley 1966; later Campbell and Cook 1976; Cook and Campbell 1979), experimental or quasi-experimental designs have been regarded as the main strategy evaluators should aim for (Caporaso and Roos 1973; Riecken and Boruch 1974; Bennett and Lumsdaine 1975; Boruch and Riecken 1975; Rivlin and Timpane 1975; Fairweather and Tornatzky 1977; Ferber and Hirsch 1982). The idea of an "experimental society" (Campbell 1969; Rivlin 1971) succeeded insofar as, in the early seventies, some large-scale experiments in the fields of education, housing, health manpower and income maintenance policies have been launched following the urgent advice of evaluators (Rossi and Lyall 1976; Caro 1977; Arrow et al. 1979; OECD 1980).

As with the goal approach, experimenters expect that a program has well-defined objectives and that the effectiveness can be determined by measuring the extent to which objectives are achieved. This requires the following:

– objectives have to be clear, and precise statements on the goals and objectives of a program are necessary,
– situations or settings in which the pogram operate need to be reasonably controlled, they should not be subject to disruption or obscure influence by diffusion and mutual cross-site learning,
– the treatment should be uniform. If the treatment varies in an unplanned or unintended fashion and for different subjects or locations at different times (or is not delivered at all), it is impossible to say what has caused what; therefore specified stable program components are required in a classical evaluation experiment,
– the treatment should be applied to a large number of cases to provide an adequate sample, and it should be large enough to create an effect.

The four *Income Maintenance Experiments* in *New Jersey, Denver/Seattle, Gary* and in *Iowa (Rural Experiments)* demonstrate well the substantive and methodological potentials and restrictions of experimental approaches (Kershaw and Fair 1975; Watts and Rees 1976; Robins et al. 1980). After the sequence of different experiments were completed a more agreed upon theory and better empirical estimates of the magnitude of work incentives by a potential Income Maintenance Program emerged. Work disincentives are smaller than expected, they depend on life-cycle, family situation and race. Besides, estimations of the magnitudes of effects under differing constraints, calculations on the probable consequences for the budget and the economy could be given. In addition, some surprising benefits of the program were found. Those range from better nutrition to improved school attendance. Some perplexing effects of the program discovered like the increase in marital break-ups as a result of welfare payments, have stimulated widespread discussion. The debate helped to clarify the theory behind such effects, e.g. that income maintenance allow women more self-determination, and the normative implications of decisions (how to weigh women's personal self-realization against the problem of family break-ups?) (Rossi and Lyall 1976; Haveman 1980; Ferber and Hirsch 1982). The existence of relatively robust treatments (money) explain the partial success of those experiments compared to educational experiments, which tend to be converted into action research.

The limits of the experiments emerged through their connection to the policy cycle. Between the start and the time agreed results showed up a decade passed, and policies change in the meantime. The problem of a new US national welfare program has largely been submerged by the issue of how to create more jobs. The possibilities for immediate usage of the main results of the experiments disappeared. If evaluations are intended to lead to an improvement of policies, the cost of experiments whose results are never utilized is quite high. Taking the expenses for the three largest experiments, the *National Income Maintenance,* the *National Health* (probably the best conducted) and the *National Housing Allowance Experiments* as realistic cost estimates for social experiments, we find that experiments costing less than 100 million Dollar will probably not be conducted. Still, remember that compared to the cost of less well-specified policies these costs are minor ones, the questions remains of how we can change the experimental design to fit the evolutionary and cyclical character of policies in a better way.

Regarding the *design* it may be argued that we have learned so much about the design needs and the implementation problems of large-scale experiments that it is very likely that in future experiments profitable outcomes may increase sequential experimentations, using pilot experiments as in the *National Health Insurance* Study or in the first *National Income Maintenance Program* – if one views the *New Jersey* experiment as a learning pilot program for others – may help to improve results and reduce cost.

Such strategies seem to be necessary as firm conclusions have emerged that the number of arbitrary decisions in experiments, contrary to the calculated and precise impression of experimental approaches, is quite substantial. These decisions are difficult to control; they concern the number of variables to be added for control, the need for different forms of (theoretically-oriented) specification and the consideration of possible interaction effects (which again influence the size of the often underrated sample). Time effects play a crucial role, e.g. the effects of program duration on individual behavior have been difficult to disentangle. *Windfall effects* evoked by those who wish to take advantage of the program perceiving the limited duration as minimizing risks and *resistance effects* as adaptation costs due to the shortage of the benefits given are valued high, may level out. More difficulties than expected have also been created by attempts to *implement* the experimental programs. In the *Rural Experiment* of the *National Income Maintenance Experiment* the sample size sometimes turned out to be too small to allow for any reliable conclusions to be drawn. The main reason were difficulties in attracting participants, and the loss of participants in the control group over time. In one experiment of 1,300 male family heads only 345 could be retained after the end of the program. Further more, misunderstandings and changes in the report form rendered many calculations from the results questionable. In the *Rural Experiment* the content of many filled-out report forms has been questioned as farmers "learned" rather quickly to make the most advantageous use of the experiments. This learning, which occurred during the conduct of the program, may be difficult to control and test in an experiment. The *Administrative Experiment* in the *National Housing Allowances Experiments* derived from such occurrences a recognition of the problems involved in implementation.

Serious problems also arose after the completion of the experiments. Many questioned the attempt to *derive conclusions* from the few sites of the experiments for the national level. Can we design experiments to find out how effects would differ, if experiments were nationalized? It may well occur that effects in routine programs are quite different due to less calculable implementations and the reduction of alternative opportunities open to participants. Therefore, experimenting with a variety of intervention combinations and the process of generalization to the national level may require different sets of research methodologies and theories even if a representative (random) selection could be conducted.

As in the goal model the typical legislator and program manager were frequently disappointed by the results of scientific experiments since the latter were by design oriented toward measuring narrow goals; they were abstract, and frequently too impersonal and too sophisticated to impact on their decision agenda, and often focused on analytical techniques rather than program content and substantive issues of concern. Many of the smaller experiments, especially in education (e.g. the performance contracting experiment in the U.S.), were considered a failure. Often, the design was either not implemented, results were inconclusive, showed no effect or took too much time to be recognized as relevant (Pincus 1980).

As many view it, the dominance of the classical experimental "impact" *paradigm* may be a hindrance for a successful utilization of evaluations (Patton 1978). The "no effect" results in early evaluation research was explained as being due to the isolative "variable" approach, an assumption which contradicts real-world experiences and neglects synergetic and long-term accumulative effects (Cronbach et al. 1980).

In a now classical article Rein and Weiss (1969) have criticized the paradigm, others like Scriven (1971); Patton (1978), Cronbach (1980) followed, emphasizing:

– programs are usually a *complex, dynamic entity;* to define its elements (what constitutes a program) is a complicated question. In a program multiple, conflicting goals exist; often, those goals are not quantifiable; they are not sufficiently clear for measuring, but rather broadly based, open and dynamic
– programs have *multiple and different means* to achieve or accomplish program (or hidden individual) objectives
– program *settings vary in size,* location and situation
– *variation in treatment delivery* occur constantly, the delivery is usually left to local or individual discretion
– resources and *impacts are small* in relation to the types of changes expected, too small to be disentangled from other effects
– data are often *unreliable,* the available administrative data and records are often in poor shape, indicators constructed often lack a close connection to what should be measured
– the *chain of effects* is difficult to disentangle, synergetic effects and *time dimension* of effects are difficult to discover; the concentration on objectives leads to the neglect of far more important questions about "side and unintended" effects
– existing programs cannot be subjected to experimental treatment and crossprogram and policy evaluation is rarely possible.

There are, however, a number of achievements and advantages with this type of evaluation:

(1) Experiments frequently presented a new analytical perspective of progress which questions traditional experiences and routines,
(2) they re-established the credibility of the analysts since many were technically sound and helped to establish an improved data base,
(3) they provided "state-of-the-art" application of skills and opportunities and, in turn, attracted technically competent analysts to the evaluation staff,
(4) they added to general theory and led to the building-up of information.

The mixed evaluation of the experimental design is well reflected in the diverse reactions of the commenting and participating researchers:

After the first results of the large-scale experiments showed up in U.S. programs, experiments drew a general critique, even by the proponents of the experimental approaches (Rossi and Lyall 1976; Cronbach 1980, 1982; Campbell and Cook 1976). After more evidence has been accumulated, results compared and aggregated, the differences in the results have become understandable. The proponents of well-conducted, scientific experiments returned to their prior commitments. The best results, it is now maintained, may only be attained by the more rigorous use of the best (experimental) design (Cook and Campbell 1979; Caro 1980; Mosteller 1981). This changing view does not only hold true for the U.S., but also applies to other countries with experiments conducted in a similar way (The Netherlands, Germany, Norway). There is no question that giving evaluators more leverage and using more rigorous (and better theory-based) program designs, may lead to better evaluations; but is it a sufficient condition for the generation of better knowledge and its use? Even a sophisticated methodology is no guarantee of an effective usage of evaluation research, the most valid data base and the best results are ineffective, if results are not presented in time, if they are not relevant to decision-making, and if they are not practicable and understandable to evaluation users. Therefore, validity criteria, relevance criteria and (information) cost-effectiveness have to be balanced in choosing an optimal evaluation strategy (Rich 1979; Alkin et al. 1979).

Probably, the combination of what has emerged from the critique levelled at experimental programs, the increased use of *longitudinal analysis* of records, the conduct of *computer simulations,* and the inreased usage of *secondary analysis* (to provide for a more specified and theoretically-grounded experimental strategy) may be the prerequisites to lead experimental designs from their "pseudo-evaluation function" (Dunn) to a more relevant and fruitful evaluation strategy.

Situational Responsiveness by Interactive Approaches?

The constraints and restrictions which in the classical approaches are viewed as limits or "validity threats" (Cook and Campbell 1979) form the basis of emerging alternatives (Dunn et al. 1981; Guba and Lincoln 1981; Patton 1978, 1980, 1981; Smith 1981, 1982).

The reason for their rise has been the increasing awareness that in most cases only parts of the problems have been studied by applying statistical or more classical experimental designs. To gain a more holistic *"Gestalt"* understanding seems to be essential as different evaluators often "touch" different features of a problem and, in consequence come up with different ideas about the problem, which are difficult to reconcile and often too abstract to allow for practical strategies to be derived. This has given rise to what have been considered alternative approaches which try to accommodate for diverse experiences, wants and needs, in what is essentially regarded no longer as a research strategy oriented toward the intensification of interventions, but takes into account the more structural "system" characteristics of problems (Dunn et al. 1981). Part of this approach is the recognition that program and management-centered problem-orientation may become obsolete fast as new programs or politicians appear. To derive knowledge based on newly or established programs may be less helpful in a long term historical view as a more systematic attempt to understand the problem and the shifts in its solutions.

Such an approach contains some critical steps like delineating the arena, identifying the "stakeholders", analyzing the assumption underlying the argumentation, trying to test the assumptions and arguments against actual policies and integrate the diverse results (Table 4).

Tab. 4: Redesigning Evaluation Steps

	Activities	Purpose
(1)	Decomposition of policy arenas and problems.	Observing of interactions. System boundaries and – functions.
(2)	Stakeholder identification.	Search for vested interests, groups and actors
(3)	Analysis of assumptions.	Identification of premises.
(4)	Priorization of assumptions, structured debate.	Determination of status of knowledge claims.
(5)	Argumentation analysis.	Determination of the relationships between assumptions and claims.
(6)	Knowledge synthesis.	Knowledge integration.

cf. Ahonen 1983; Dunn 1981.

The aim of those "natural", "responsive", "creative", "multidimensional" approaches in evaluation is to take advantage of the differences in aims, intentions, the varying settings, the different data sources, the accumulation of events by developing an evaluation strategy which explores the experience of the actors, acknowledging their detailed substantial knowledge to a greater extent than the researcher has. Such an approach concentrates on the processes which influence outcomes, demonstrates how different factors cumulate through time, and follows their sequential activitation in order to identify causal efficacy relative to the variation in outcome. It aims at discovering effects and causal connections instead of being confined and restricted to pre-categorized analytical tables. – Adequate techniques have been developed more rapidly during recent years (Denzin 1978; Filstead 1970; Lofland 1971). The ideas behind these approaches are:

(1) *getting close* to the people actually doing and acting, and develop familiarity with the substance of their problems
(2) *focusing* on their basic *situations* and acting role at different (group, organization, world etc.) *levels*
(3) *delineating* their *interaction and strategies,* tactics and argumentations
(4) *assembling* and analyzing the abundance of *episodes* or events in terms of disciplined abstractions by judgments
(5) studying the *assumptions* of argumentations of different actors and their different perspectives and motivations
(6) *comparing* events and episodes with the argumentation and their assumptions.

The combined use, the *"triangulation"* or *"methodological mix"* of a variety of data-gathering methods, including participant observations, interviewing, group discussions and the analysis of documents and official or private records, are necessary for this approach. This advantage is crucial, for it means that evaluators use a variety of approaches to examine subtle differences which would otherwise escape attention, like those between private attitudes and public behavior, or the unnoticed assumptions of voiced arguments. This requires further that the investigator selects from his research repertoire those methods that are most appropriate to the study of a given situation from different angles. As such an evaluation is related to the "real life" experiences and perspectives of actors, the results will be better valued and can be transferred personally to the peculiar local situations to be tested more easily by the practioners for their credibility. This better understanding of real-life situations helps to improve communication with practitioners. The gain in mutual understanding may well offset the suspected losses in accurate measurement or make-believe objectivity.

The pledge for new approaches should not disguise that for many questions the uses of "minority paradigms" like phenomenological sociology, symbolic interactionism (Mead) seem to be inferior to classical designs. Strategies which conceive research reactions as instances of ordinary interactions and try to analyze them in such terms, may loose the rigor of complex models of theory-testing which enable maintaining a fundamentally nomological orientation. Often, softer approaches lack preciseness in disentagling effects and confound situational with systemic effects; so there are no clear results to be used for program design. The strategy of some impact researchers to confine the demonstration of the validity of their findings to statistical tables and measures from which they draw their conclusions, may confront a similar dilemma as soon as they have to defend the assumptions and definitions of their categories. Few evaluators find the time to interrelate quantitative and qualitative approaches, using substantive theories outlining the relationships between the theoretical constructs, applying measurement theories detailing assumptions about the quality of particular selected indicators related to the constructs, and developing statements about the effects and causes of systemic measurement errors. To *combine methods* would enable a check across different interpretations and *validating* special eclectic evaluation results. Interlocking methods can also provide a check on bias by juxtaposing two or more sets of data on the same problem, like the observation records of a meeting and the individual perspectives of that meeting. Thus, it can be determined whether the perceptions correlate highly with the recorded data (Denzin 1978; Hamilton 1978).

But the broadest potential seems to lie in the close connection to substantive findings which are indispensable bases for the formulation of theories which may be useful. Integrating methods like action research, ethnomethodology, oral history into the research design enables us – last not least – to adress actors in a way allowing for interactional validation and for *organizational learning,* both prerequisites for increased utilizations of results (Alkin et al. 1979; Hellstern 1984).

14.6 Future Concern and Perspectives

After almost two decades of rapid growth evaluators have still not reached consensus about the basic purposes and substance of their enterprise. The controversies and shifting concepts reflect the need for adaptation to changing events and conditions necessitating different analytical tools, rather than a difference in basic opinions.

1. Originally, e.g. in the U.S. and some European countries, evaluation research sprung up from a *reform perspective.* It was meant to replace dated tradition-based authoritative opinions by establishing scientific information processing and learning capabilities within the policy process (Etheridge 1984; Pressman and Wildavsky 1973). The post World War II commitments to achieving social change through the extension of government interventions created the environment in which hopes that new programs may be tested, monitored and corrected seemed to be feasible. In practice, the experimental testing models were often superseded by *action research* geared to support a program.

2. Since the late seventies and early eighties evaluators have increasingly turned to optimizing the return from public expenditure by assessing utility and costs of programs. Evaluation changed from outcome to *process-evaluations* and *implementation assessments,* from contractual research to *internal monitoring.* Strategies to minimize costs of services and the development of *accountability* and *quality control procedures* should ensure responsibility and responsiveness. The change had its roots in the growing economic and financial constraints, and the new preferences of incoming governments, signaling change. Apart from rhetoric about the evaluator's role as the *hatchet man* for the termination of programs, for cutback-management and financial management control systems misconstrued evaluation's role in the curtailment of programs. The political clout of evaluators and their liberal outlook prevented their participation in the political bargaining on cutbacks. Rather, evaluators were used to search for *alternative options* in service delivery, especially in the non-profit sector and by the use of volunteers in the self-help-movements.

3. Today, evaluation is in the process of being integrated into administrative routine on many levels and in different institutions. In federal nations the emphasis has shifted to the states and localities. The limits are better known, and it is recognized that a *variety of approaches* is necessary. Evaluations are used in many shapes and sizes, small and large, inside and outside of government. Their purpose includes: describing a program (process or formative evaluation), analyzing its assumptions and their relationships with program activities (evaluability assessments), identifying program effects (outcome, impact or summary evaluations),

comparing alternative programs or synthesizing findings from different evaluations (meta-evaluation). In the building of evaluation theory the process of valuing and the formation of judgments and their aggregation have gained more attention. Innovative use, dissemination and transfer techniques are being explored and in developing designs the multidimensional and multidisciplinary character of evaluation is stressed (Chelimsky 1983).

4. In the future the number of institutions – outside the governmental institutions – which recognize the critical need for evaluations in a increasingly interdependent society will be growing. In a pluralistic society with multiple forces shaping the decisions, the representative mechanism alone cannot achieve accountability and establish trust and legitimacy. In avoiding unintended consequences in a situation in which each action evokes a chain of frequently uncontrollable reactions, about whose extension and intensity limited knowledge exists, the responsibilities of evaluators have increased. With more actors requiring participation, more values and interests have to be taken into account; the impacts and risks of steps have to be carefully calculated. The appropriateness of a program or step, the level of effort needed, the expected size and nature of effects, the strength of causal connections between outcome and actions and the cost-effectiveness of different steps need informed attention.

Controversies about the use of appropriate methods, the proper role of evaluations, and the basic principles which should guide evaluations will certainly continue. The fragile balance between the power-driven request for *immediate, relevant* evaluations, and the need to further *independent, long-term* evaluation research to establish credibility and long-term validity will continue to undergo constant modification and compromise. A number of characteristics and activities need special concern:

Agenda building: One important function of evaluations has been to define the boundaries of a public debate. As new issues arise evaluations help to guide those debates. They help to settle some factual disputes and gradually to shift the debate to open questions and solvable problems.

Variety and integration: Evaluators can rarely supply sufficient information to point to an unequivocal solution. Even in broadly-gauged comprehensive evaluations – which are rarely conducted – only a subset of questions can realistically be answered. Therefore evaluations have to establish criteria for the *eclectic* use of evaluations according to the existing uncertainty and risks involed, costs and yield of information and potential use and technical feasibility. In the process of evaluation they need to apply a) a variety of approaches and include a variety of perspectives employing a more conceptual framework, searching for multidimensional concepts, and b) strategies which integrate past research results and resolve conflicting evidence.

Normative concern and evaluation standards: Evaluation in the past often proved to be more worthwhile in helping to structure new programs. In ongoing programs the evaluators insistence on restructuring has rarely been successful. But it has helped to keep the quest for responsibility alive as programs were delivered and flowed through the maze of representative institutions and bureaucratic structures. By demonstrating models and successful alternatives, options continued to be publicly discussed: Evaluators could do so only by establishing a measure of independence from the political processes and prove the quality of their evidence. To establish standards which assure the appropriateness of a design, the reliability of its execution and the absence of major errors and arbitrariness is a prerequisite for the long – term utility of evaluations.

Assumptional analysis and feedback: More recent evaluations have stressed the role of positional thinking, the understanding of different views, positions and perspectives. In addition, they began to employ social theories to check the different assumptions and opinions surrounding programs. In conducting evaluations, sequential research strategies were followed which enable the counteracting of imbalance and bias in design and subjecting the evaluation process to an interactive feedback process involving clients and their views. Some caveats are necessary:

Evaluations across programs: Use of evaluations in the past has been severely limited by the concentration on programs and program effects. This has often prevented the mapping of how different programs and rules interact. Evaluations which center on a problem or issue and investigate the intermingling of different programs in one policy arena or in a problem field, have rarely been conducted. This has narrowed the use of evaluation to focusing on management concerns, often replicating the idiosyncratic specialization and sectorialization found in the field. It undermined the value of evaluations for alternative policy choices.

Opportunity structures: Evaluation is basically an instrument to enable learning from past failures and successes. Unfortunately, past outcomes have often been treated as statistical entities and not as something subjected to change over time. Instead of decision-free and sequential thinking evaluators have used effect measures taken from regression analysis and proposed static replications instead of informed variations based on probabilities. To take into account processes of change and evolution could help to conceive the current activities as undergoing constant transformation, building up new opportunities for which evaluation may build up a self-reflexive capacity.

System-thinking: Past evaluations have tended to illuminate certain aspects to the neglect of others without developing criteria for isolating the investigated elements. This tendency has been supported by the specialization of evaluators and the fragmentation of the political and administrative system. For many questions the structural entities of a system and their consequences have to be taken into account. To avoid the trap of episodic and atomistic evaluations, holistic thinking and interdisciplinary cooperation have to embrace the more isolated evaluation modules, an approach which should not preclude quantitative and mathematical efforts.

Time-related effects: Evaluations of past programs showed a remarkable difference between short-term and long-term effects. Pre-school "Head Start" programs, urban renewal projects and manpower training programs demonstrated the importance of distinguishing between short-term and long-term achievements. Neither proper indicators nor adequate discounting strategies to value the different effects have been developed.

Evaluation synthesis: Future evaluations will continue to be partial and eclectic. Local self-evaluations will gain prominence, small-scale evaluations better fit the interests of program managers and clients. At the same time it may be difficult to establish authoritative evidence since those evaluations may produce conflicting evidence and often tend to be based on qualitative techniques tending to confound effects. To resolve conflicts and to establish a set of knowledge which allows for a long-time cumulation of experience and improves the rationality of programs and their evaluations, evaluation synthesis is needed: Secondary analysis to establish validity of research and reduce cost of evaluations, replications to test the generalizibility of more localized evaluations, research integration and meta-analysis which help to establish a set of reliable theories and, consequently, reduce bias inherent in individual studies.

Past concern in the evaluation field has been on strategies, then on design issues and the selection of adequate evaluation models fitting the situational context, more recently on principles and rules which 1) establish criteria for the selection of the needed evaluation focus and 2) govern the process of human valuation, the assignment of worth and the aggregation of different values. It seems a historical irony that in some countries evaluation is stagnating at a time when it seems to be better equipped than ever to conduct useful evaluations. The current trend to internalize evaluation research activities needs careful observation to avoid an obsolence and trivialization of evaluation. Evaluation, if it is to be of long-term use, needs to continue to take into account different perspectives without devaluing research standards of sample-selection, data-collection and analysis. It even needs to improve the use of theory-oriented evaluation conceptions, and, at the same time, to take advantage of the increasing knowledge of human information processing to develop methods to fit evaluation research strategies to organizational and social learning, in order to continue the process of evaluation research routinization.

References

Aaron, H. J. (1978): *Politics and the Professors: The Great Society in Perspective.* Washington, D. C.: The Brookings Institutions.

Ahonen, P. (1983): *Public Policy Evaluation as Discourse.* Helsinki: The Finnish Political Science Association.

Alkin, M. C., R. Daillak and P. White (1979): *Using Evaluations: Does Evaluation Make a Difference?* Beverly Hills–London: Sage.

Anderson, S., and S. Ball (1978): *The Profession and Practice of Program Evaluation.* San Francisco: Jossey-Bass.

Argyris, C. (1982): *Reasoning, Learning and Action.* San Francisco, Washington, London: Jossey-Bass.

Argyris, C., and S. A. Schon (1978): *Organizational Learning: A Theory of Action Perspective.* Reading, Mass.: Addison-Wesley.

Arrow, K. J., C. Abt, and St. J. Fitzsimmons (eds.) (1979): *Applied Research for Social Policy.* Cambridge, Mass.: Abt Books.

Attkinson, C. C., W. A. Hargreaves, M. Horowitz, and J. E. Sorensen (eds.) (1978): *Evaluation of Human Service Programs.* New York. Academic Press.

Bennet, C., and A. A. Lymsdaine (eds.) (1975): *Evaluation and Experiment.* New York. Academic Press.

Bernstein, I. N., and H. E. Freeman (1975): *Academic and Entrepreneurial Research.* New York: Russell-Sage Foundation.

Boruch, R. F. (1982): "Experimental Tests in Education: Recommendations from the Holtzman Report." *The American Statistician* 36/1: 1–14.

Boruch, R. F., and H. W. Riecken (eds.) (1975): *Experimental Testing of Social Policy*. Boulder, Co.: West View Press.

Boruch, R. F., P. M. Wortman, and D. S. Cordray (1981): *Reanalyzing Program Evaluations*. San Francisco: Jossey-Bass.

Boruch, R. F., and D. S. Cordray (eds.) (1982): *An Appraisal of Educational Program Evaluations: Federal, State and Local Agencies*. New York: Cambridge University Press.

Brewer, M. B. (1984): Evaluation: Past and Present. In: Struening, E. L., and M. B. Brewer (eds.), *The University Edition of the Handbook of Evaluation Research*, 15–27. Beverly Hills–London–New Delhi: Sage Publ.

Bryk, A. S. (ed.) (1983): *Stakeholder-Based Evaluation. New Directions for Program Evaluation* 17. San Francisco: Jossey-Bass.

Campbell, D. T. (1969): "Reforms as Experiments". *American Psychologist* 24: 409–429.

Campbell, D. T., and J. C. Stanley (1963): *Experimental and Quasi-Experimental Designs for Research*. Chicago: Rand McNally.

Caporaso, L. A., and L. L. Roos (1973): *Quasiexperimental Research*. Evanston: Northwestern Univ. Press.

Caro, F. G. (ed.) (1977): *Readings in Evaluation Research* (2nd ed.). New York: Russel-Sage-Foundation.

Chelimsky, E. A. (1977): *A Symposium on the Use of Evaluations by Federal Agencies* (Vol. 1). McLean, Va.: Mitre Corporation.

Chelimsky, E. A. (1983): Program Evaluation and Appropriate Governmental Change. *Annals* Vol. 466 (March): 103–118.

Connor, R. (ed.) (1984): *Evaluation Studies Review Annual* (Vol. 9). Beverly Hills–London: Sage.

Cook, T. D., and D. T. Campbell (1976): "The Design and Conduct of Quasi-Experiments and True Experiments in Field Settings." In Dunnette, M. (ed.), *Handbook of Industrial and Organizational Psychology*, 223–327. Chicago: Rand McNally.

Cook, T. D., and D. T. Campbell (1979): *Quasi-Experimentation: Design and Analysis Issues for Field Settings*, Chicago: Rand McNally.

Crane, J. A. (1982): *The Evaluation of Social Policies*. Boston–The Hague–London: Kluwer-Nijhoff.

Cronbach L. J. (1980): *Toward Reform of Program Evaluation*. San Francisco: Jossey-Bass.

Cronbach, L. J. (1982): *Designing Evaluations of Educational and Social Programs*. San Francisco: Jossey-Bass.

Datta, L. E. (ed.) (1982): *Evaluation in Change. Meeting New Government Needs*. Beverly Hills–London: Sage.

Denzin, N. K. (1978): *The Research Act*. New York: McGraw-Hill.

Deutsch, K. W., and A. Markovits (eds.) (1980): *Fear of Science vs. Trust in Science*. Königstein/Ts.: Athenäum.

Dunn, W. N., I. I. Mitroff, and St. J. Deutsch (1981): "The Obscolescence of Evaluation Research." *Evaluation and Program Planning* 4/3: 207–218.

Edwards, W., and J. R. Newman (1983): "Multiattribute Evaluation." The Sage University Paper Series *Quantitative Applications in the Social Sciences* 26. Beverly Hills–London: Sage.

Ethridge, L. S. (1984): *Governmental Learning*. Basel–New York: Dekker. (forthcoming)

Etzioni, A. (1968): *The Active Society. A Theory of Social and Political Processes*. New York: Free Press.

Evaluation Research Society (Standards Committee) (1983): *Standards for Program Evaluation*. Potomac, Md.: Evaluation Research Society.

Fairweather, G. W., and L. G. Tornatzky (1977): *Experimental Methods for Social Policy Research*. New York: Pergamon Press.

Ferber, R., and W. Z. Hirsch (1982): *Social Experimentation and Economic Policy*. Cambridge–London–New York: Cambridge Univ. Press.

Filstead. W. J. (ed.) (1970): *Qualitative Methodology*. Chicago: Markham.

Freeman, H. E., and M. A. Solomon (1981): "The Next Decade in Evaluation Research." In R. A. Levine et al. (eds.), *Evaluation Research and Practice*, 12–26. Beverly Hills–London: Sage.

Glass, G. V., B. McGaw, and M. L. Smith (1981): *Meta-Analysis in Social Research*. Beverly Hills–London: Sage.

Gray, A., and B. Jenkins (eds.) (1983): *Policy Analysis and Evaluation ind British Government*. London: Royal Institute of Public Administration.

Guba, E. G., and Y. S. Lincoln (1981): *Effective Evaluation. Improving the Usefulness of Evaluation Results through Responsive and Naturalistic Approaches*. San Francisco: Jossey-Bass.

Guttentag, M., and E. L. Struening (eds.) (1975): *Handbook of Evaluation Research* (Vol. 2). Beverly Hills–London: Sage.

Hamilton, D., (1978): *Beyond the Numbers Game*. Berkely: McCutchan.

Haveman, R. H. (ed.) (1977): *A Decade of Antipoverty Programs*. New York: Academic Press.

Hellstern, G. M. (1984): "What have we learned from Evaluation Research." In Edlund, C., and G. Hermeren (eds.), *Evaluation Research. Metoder för Utvärdering av Reformer i Arbetslivet*, 58–80. Lund: Filosofiska institutionen.

Hellstern, G. M., and H. Wollmann (1983): *Experimentelle Politik – Reformstrohfeuer oder Lernstrategie*. Opladen. Westdeutscher Verlag.

Hellstern, G. M., and H. Wollmann (1984): *Evaluierungsforschung*. Basel–New York: Birkhäuser.

Her Majesty Stationary Office (HMSO) (1982): *Efficiency and Effectiveness in the Civil Service*. London: HC 236 Cmnd. 8616.

House, E. R. (ed.) (1983): *Philosophy of Evaluation*. San Francisco–Beverly Hill–London: Sage.

Joint Committee on Standards for Educational Evaluation (1981): *Standards for Evaluation of Educational Programs, Projects and Material*. New York: McGraw-Hill.

Kaufmann, F. X., and K. P. Strohmeier (1981): "Evaluation as Meaningful Social Research." In Levine, R. A. et al. (eds.), *Evaluation Research and Practice*, 146–167. Beverly Hills–London: Sage.

Kershaw, D., and J. Fair (1975): *The New Jersey Income Maintenance Experiments* (Vol. 1). New York: Academic Press.

Landsberg, G., W. D. Neigher, R. J. Hammer, C. H. Windle, and J. R. Way (eds.) (1979): *Evaluation in Practice*. Washington, D. C.: U.S. Dept. of Health and Human Services.

Levine, R. A., M. A. Solomon, G.-M. Hellstern, and H. Wollmann (1981): *Evaluation Research and Practice. A Comparative and International Perspective*. Beverly Hills–London: Sage.

Lindblom, C. E., and D. K. Cohen (1979): *Usable Knowledge. Social Science and Social Problem Solving*. New Haven, Conn.–London: Yale Univ. Press.

Lofland, J. (1971): *Analyzing Social Settings*. Belmont, Cal.: Wandsworth.

Love, A. J. (ed.) (1983): *Developing Effective Internal Evaluation*. San Francisco: Jossey Bass.

Madaus, G. F., M. Scriven, and D. L. Stufflebeam (1983): *Evaluation Models: Viewpoints on Educational and Human Services Evaluation*. Boston: Kluwer: Nijhoff.

Menges, G. (1982): "Wege in die Realität." *Zeitschrift für die gesamte Staatswissenschaft* 138/4: 646–663.

Merton, R. K. (1936): "The unanticipated consequences of purposive social action." *American Sociology Review* 1/6: 894–904.

Mitroff, I. I. (1983): "Beyond Experimentation. New Methods for a New Age." In: Seidman, E. (ed.), *Handbook of Social Intervention,* 163–177. Beverly Hills, Cal.–London–New Delhi: Sage.

Morell, J. A. (1979): *Program Evaluation in Social Research.* New York: Pergamon Press.

Mosteller, F. (1981): "Innovation and Evaluation." *Science* 211/6: 881–886.

Nachmias, D. (ed.) (1980): *The practice of Policy Evaluation.* New York: St. Martins Press.

Organisation for Economic Cooperation and Development (OECD) (1980): The Utilisation of the Social Sciences in the United States. Paris: OECD.

Patton, M. Q. (1978): *Utilization-Focused Evaluation.* Beverly Hill–London: Sage.

Patton, M. Q. (1980): *Qualitative Evaluation.* Beverly Hills–London: Sage.

Pincus, J. (ed.) (1980): *Educational Evaluation in the Public Policy Setting.* Santa Monica: Rand Corp.

Pressmann, J., and A. Wildavsky (1973): *Implementation.* Berkeley: Univ.of Cal. Press.

Raizen, S. A., and P. H. Rossi (eds.) (1981): *Program Evaluation in Education: When? How? To what Ends?* Washington, D. C.: National Academy Press.

Riecken, H. W., and R. F. Boruch (eds.) (1974): *Social Experimentation.* New York: Academic Press.

Rich, R. F. (ed.) (1979): *Translating Evaluation Into Policy.* Beverly Hills–London: Sage.

Rivlin, A. M. (1971): *Systematic Thinking for Social Action.* Washinton, D. C.: The Bookings Inst.

Rivlin, A. M., and P. M. Timpane (eds.) (1975): *Planned Variation in Education.* Washington, D. C.: The Brookings Inst.

Robins, P. K., R. G. Spiegelman, S. Weiner, and J. G. Bell (eds.) (1980): *A Guaranteed Annual Income: Evidence from a Social Experiment.* New York: Academic Press.

Rossi, P. H. (ed.) (1982): *Standards for Evaluation Practice.* (New Directions for Program Evaluation, Vol. 15) San Francisco: Jossey-Bass.

Rossi, P. H., H. E. Freeman, and S. R. Wright (1979): *Evaluation: A Systematic Approach.* Beverly Hills–London: Sage Publ.

Rossi, P. H., K. C. Lyall (1976): *Reforming Public Welfare.* New York: Russel Sage Found.

Rossi, P. H., and J. D. Wright (1984): "Evaluation Research: An Assessment." *Annual Review of Sociology* Vol. 10: 331–352.

Scriven, M. (1980): *The Logic of Evaluation.* Inverness: Edgepress.

Simon, H. A. (1972): "The Theory of Problem Solving." *Information Processing* 71/3: 261–277.

Smith, B. L. R., and J. D. Carroll (eds.) (1982): *Improving the Accountability and Performance of Government.* Washington. D. C.: The Brookings Inst.

Smith, N. L. (ed.) (1981): *Metaphors for Evaluation: Sources of New Methods.* Beverly Hills–London: Sage.

Smith, N. L. (ed.) (1982): "Field assessments of innovative evaluation methods." *New Directions for Program Evaluation* Vol. 13. San Francisco: Jossey-Bass.

Soeffner, H.-G. (ed.) (1979): *Interpretative Verfahren in den Sozial- und Textwissenschaften.* Stuttgart: Metzler.

Suchman, E. A. (1967): *Evaluative Research: Principles and Practice in Service and Social Action Programs.* New York: Russel-Sage Foundation.

Toulmin, S., (1979): *An Introduction to Reasoning.* New York: MacMillan.

United States. General Accounting Office (US. GAO) (1983): *The Evaluation Synthesis,* Methods Paper I. Washington, D. C.: Institute for Program Evaluation.

Waller, J. D., J. W. Scanlon, D. M. Kemp, and P. G. Nally (1978): *Developing Useful Evaluation Capability: Lessons From the Model Evaluation Program.* Washington, D. C.: Urban Institute.

Watts, H. W., and A. Rees (1976): *The New Jersey Income-Maintenance Experiment* (Vol. 2). New York: Academic Press.

Weiss, C. H. (1972): *Evaluation Research: Methods of Assessing Program Effectiveness.* Englewood Cliffs, N. J.: Prentice-Hall.

Weiss, C. H. (ed.) (1977): *Using Social Research in Public Policy Making.* Lexington, Mass.: Lexington Books.

Weiss, C. H., and M. J. Bucuvalas (1980): *Social Science Research and Decision-Making.* New York–Guildford–Surrey: Columbia Univ. Press.

Weiss, R. S., and M. Rein (1969): "The Evaluation of Broad-Aim Programs: A Cautionary Case and a Moral." *Annals of the American Academy of Political and Social Science* 385: 133–142.

Wissenschaftszentrum Berlin (ed.) (1977): *Interaktion von Wissenschaft und Politik.* Frankfurt–New York: Campus.

Wildavsky, A. (1972): The Self-Evaluating Organization. *Public Administration Review* 32/5: 509–520.

Wholey, J. S. (1979): *Evaluation: Promise and Performance.* Washington D. C.: The Urban Inst.

Wortman, P. (1983): "Evaluation Research: A Methodological Perspective." *Annual Review of Psychology* 34: 223–260.

15. What Can We Learn from Implementation Research?

Paul A. Sabatier

Abstract

This paper analyzes the extensive literature on policy implementation which has developed in Europe and North America over the past decade. It concludes that 1) official policy-makers often have only a rather limited ability to control the behavior of street-level bureaucrats, particularly when the latter are rather high-status professionals; 2) a time-frame of at least 5–10 years is generally required to avoid premature conclusions concerning a program's effects and to permit some appreciation of the extent of policy-oriented learning; 3) erroneous causal assumptions are often among the most important factors explaining performance gaps in governmental policies; and 4) it may be preferable in many instances to start from the actors involved in policy problems *rather than those involved in implementing a policy* decision.

On the basis of such conclusions, several scholars have moved from implementation research into an analysis of policy evolution and learning.

15.1 Introduction

The 1960s and early 1970s represented a rather remarkable era of policy innovation in Western Europe and North America. Virtually every country instituted one or more reforms to expand educational opportunity, to reduce interregional economic disparties, to expand health and social security programs, to reduce air and water pollution, to improve consumer protection, to protect the rights of minority groups, etc. A decade of relative prosperity made these reforms possible. Activist governments provided the political will. And social scientists and other professionals provided many of the ideas.

It soon became clear, however, that many of the programs were not working as intended. Implementation research arose largely as an effort to explain these apparent failures.

One of the early studies – Pressman and Wildavsky's (1973) analysis of the abortive effort by the Federal Government to create 3,000 jobs in Oakland – was to have an enormous impact on the first generation of implementation research, particularly in the United States. First, starting from the dictionary definition of "implementation" as the "carrying out of a decision," it focused inquiry on the extent to which, and the reasons for which, the formal objectives of a policy decision were (or were not) attained. It thus focused attention squarely on one of the principal topics of this volume, namely, the extent to which official policy-makers can use a variety of control mechanisms and institutional arrangements to guide social change (Kaufmann: Ch. 10).

Moreover, Pressman and Wildavsky went beyond the bounds of traditional public administration in several critical ways. In so doing, they provided the new field with a separate identity. For one thing, they focused attention on "the complexity of joint action," i.e. the enormous number of clearance points in various bureaucracies and target groups at various levels of government whose assent, if not active cooperation, are usually required for a program to achieve its objectives. They thus pointed to the importance of interorganizational relations and policy networks, a distinguishing feature of implementation research (in contrast to the single-organization focus of traditional administrative studies).

In addition, Pressman and Wildavsky chose as their dependent variable not the behavior or decisions of implementing agencies but rather policy *outcomes*, e.g. the number of jobs created or improvements in air quality. In so doing, they identified a program's *causal theory* as a critical explanatory variable. For example, the Oakland program was based on the premise that trickle down effects from public works projects are an efficient strategy for creating jobs. While this may be true for underdeveloped regions like Appalachia, it is hardly appropriate for the highly developed San Francisco Bay Area – where a much more precise targeting is required. Thus, even if the implementing agencies had behaved in a manner completely consistent with legislative intent, the program would not have achieved its objectives – or would have done so only very inefficiently – because it was based on an inadequate model of the critical factors affecting the problem. As we shall see, this focus on a program's underlying causal assumptions was as to become one of the major contributions of implementation research.

In the decade since publication of their classic, a number of approaches to implementation analysis have emerged. Suffice it to say that the "top-down" approach of Pressman and Wildavsky – which starts from a policy decision and then explores the extent to which, and the reasons for which, its objectives are attained – has been refined and tested by a number of scholars (Rodgers and Bullock 1976; Mayntz 1978; Van Horn 1979; Mazmanian and Sabatier 1981; 1983). It has also been subjected to considerable criticism. Some has been relatively friendly, e.g. the need to incorporate longer time-frames than the 2–4 years common of most early studies (Kirst and Jung 1982), and the need to give greater attention to the legal structuring of the implementation process. In addition, Wildavsky and others have expressed reservations about the frequency with which one can usefully make a clear conceptual distinction between formulation/adoption, on the one hand, and implementation, on the other (Majone and Wildavsky 1978; Barrett and Fudge 1981).

But by far the most fundamental critique has come from a group of largely European scholars who have labeled themselves "bottoms uppers" (Hanf 1982). They got their start from a number of studies showing very substantial limits on the ability of central governments to guide the behavior of local implementors and target groups (Derthick 1972; Berman and McLaughlin 1976; Williams and Elmore 1976; Weatherly and Lipsky 1977; Hanf and Scharpf 1978; Barrett and Fudge 1981). When combined with doubts about the utility of separating formulation from implementation, what emerged was a perspective which argued that the appropriate starting point should not be a policy decision but rather the actors involved in addressing a *policy problem*. From this arguably emerges a more accurate portrait of the role of various governmental programs – vis a vis other factors – in guiding behavior "on the ground." While the "bottom uppers" have developed some rather imaginative descriptive tools (see Elmore 1979; Hjern and Porter 1981), thus far they have largely been unable to transform their network analyses into a viable causal model which incorporates the often indirect effects which legal and socio-economic factors can have on individual behavior.[1]

It is not the purpose of this chapter to review the voluminous literature on implementation. That has been done elsewhere (Barrett and Fudge 1981; Sabatier and Mazmanian 1983a). Instead, it attempts to draw a number of conclusions from this literature which are particularly relevant to an understanding of the problems of guidance, control, and performance evaluation in the public sector. In addition, the concluding section suggests a promising strategy for combining the best features of the "top down" and "bottom up" approaches in order to understand the factors affecting the ability of governments to guide/change target group behavior over time.

15.2 Implications of the Implementation Literature for Guidance and Control in the Public Sector

The Importance of Street-Level Bureaucrats in Program Delivery

Implementation studies frequently have found that the most important actors are not the official policy-makers in the capital but rather the street-level bureaucrats – classroom teachers, social workers, pollution control inspectors – who interact directly with target groups (e.g. secondary school students, polluting industries). Legislative intent is usually sufficiently vague and the amount of hierarchical control within organizations sufficiently weak that street-level implementing officials have very substantial discretion (Williams and Elmore 1976; Berman and McLaughlin 1976; Weatherly and Lipsky 1977; Hanf and Scharpf 1978; Barrett and Fudge 1981). This is even more so in programs which require a high degree of commitment and skill from on-the-ground professionals: Such commitment normally is contingent upon a rather large domain in which they can exercise their professional judgment.

In short, elected policy-makers – whether they be a local city council or a national cabinet – can seldom exercise effective control over street-level bureaucrats in the sense of keeping the latter's behavior within tightly circumscribed limits. In any but the smallest bureaucracy, problems of communication and control are far from trivial (March and Simon 1958; Grunow: Ch. 31). Even if the top knows that the bottom is doing – which is often not the case – any attempt to tightly circumscribe the behavior of professionals is likely to be counterproductive (Elmore 1978). Finally, many implementation efforts involve not simply a singly organization but rather a loosely-coupled network of organizations from different levels of government, none of which is preeminent (Hjern and Porter 1981). In such a situation, the "program" may actually consist of the sum of negotiated settlements among street-level bureaucrats and target groups – largely irrespective of what is written in the law books (see Wirth: Ch. 35).

While implementation scholars agree about the substantial discretion usually exercised by street-level bureaucrats, they disagree concerning the ability of elected officials to guide the behavior of implementors and target groups so as to bring their actions within the limits defined as legally acceptable over time.

On the one hand are scholars like Hanf and Scharpf (1978: Ch. 1), Elmore (1979), Barrett and Fudge (1981), and probably Berman (1980) who suggest that control by formal policy-makers is virtually impossible and/or undesirable.[2] Thus one should give street-level professionals the resources they need and trust them to do a good job. The evidence suggests that this strategy is used with some frequency in certain countries – most notably, Britain (Hill 1982) – and in policy areas such as mental health with strong professional associations and few clear standards. It is also a preferred strategy in cases – e.g. sulfur oxide emissions in Europe – in which policy-makers are preoccupied with not putting "their" target groups at a competitive disadvantage vis-a-vis those in other regions or countries (Knoepfel and Weidner 1982b).

Nevertheless, there are a number of reasons for believing that formal policy-makers are not nearly so impotent as Hanf et al. might suggest.

First, while it would seem obvious that any implementation study should contain a careful content analysis of the formal policy decision being implemented, skeptics of formal guidance mechanisms have not always done so. For example, Berman and McLaughlin's (1976) multi-volume analysis of the implementation of Federally-sponsored educational innovations by local school districts during the early 1970s contained only the most cursory discussion of the formal decisions of federal authorities: Were these statutorially-mandated programs or the result of purely administrative rule-making? Were the programs in any sense mandatory, or were they merely innovations offered to local districts for their consideration? Careful analysis of such questions would seem critical to any judgments concerning the relative influence of federal vs. loal officials, yet the studies were largely silent on these topics. Similarly, decent scholarship requires that clear distinctions be made between campaign manifestos and the speeches of public officials, on the one hand, and official governmental policy decisions, on the other. The former often contain promises which are not reflected in the negotiated settlements characteristic of most legislative and cabinet decisions. Only the latter, of course, are officially binding on street-level implementors and target groups. To use the former as the benchmark for measuring the shortfall between "policy" and outcome – and thus as an indicator of the power of street-level implementors – is really quite misleading.[3] In sum, any assessment of the (in)capacity of official policy-makers to guide local implementors would seem to require a more careful analysis of their stated intent – as contained in the official policy decisions – than has often been the case.

Second, it should be obvious that the ability of central authorities to alter the behavior of local officials varies with a number of factors. The excellent chapter by Sharpe in this volume (Ch. 8) argues that these include the number of formal levels in a political system, the representation of local officials at the center via one of the legislative houses or the *cumul de mandats,* the presence of vertically integrating professional communities or political parties, and the financial autonomy of localities. These factors operate primarily at the systemic (nation-state) level, although a few also vary by policy area within countries. In addition, Mazmanian and Sabatier (1981, 1983) have suggested a number of specific mechanisms available to official policy-makers which can improve their ability to guide the behavior of street-level implementors: These include the clarity of the policy directives; the number of veto/clearance points involved; the financial resources available; the formal access of various interests to the implementation process; and, to some extent, the policy preferences of implementing officials. Moreover, at least in the U.S., federal and state officials have some ability to affect the degree of local constituency group support for a program (Sabatier 1975).

In short, the degree of autonomy of street-level bureaucrats *varies* from country to country, policy area to policy area, program to program. It is virtually never either trivial or total. Hanf et al. emphasize that implementation involves a multitude of locally-negotiated settlements. While true, this really doesn't say very much. The trick is to relate the negotiated outcomes to the ability of various interests to participate in the negotiations; the legal, political, technical, and financial resources available to each; and the willingness of each to expend those resources in a particular case. One must not assume that official policy makers have only a trivial ability to affect such locally negotiated settlements (see Franz: Ch. 23).

The initial preoccupation of implementation scholars with explaining program failures led to an unrepresentative set of policy cases, and almost certainly exaggerated the autonomy of street-level implementors vis-a-vis formal policy-makers. For example, the vast majority of early studies dealt with social programs initiated by federal authorities in the U.S. and the German Federal Republic (Derthick 1972; Pressman and Wildavsky 1973; Williams and Elmore 1975; Berman and McLaughlin 1976; Hanf and Scharpf 1978). A moment's application of the Sharpe and Mazmanian/Sabatier variable lists suggests that these should be among the weakest cases of guidance by formal policy-makers: Not only did they involve the entire panoply of veto points inherent in federal systems, but they generally also involved programs in which federal officials had only modest ideas of where they wanted to go or how to get there, as well as very little local political support. Small wonder that one found substantial local discretion and variation in program performance. Subsequent research has revealed a number of cases of basically successful program implementation – the 1965 Voting Rights Acts (Rodgers and Bullock 1976), the British Open University (Cerych and Sabatier 1985), the California coastal commissions (Sabatier and Mazmanian 1983b) – due in no small part to the ability of official policy makers to enunciate reasonably clear objectives, to affect the preferences of key implementing officials, to reduce the number of negotiators to a manageable level, and to assure that many of them would be supportive of the program.

In sum, while street-level implementators are always important, official policy-makers are not always as impotent to affect the outcome of local negotiations as Hanf et al. seem to suggest. Our understanding of the actual distribution of influence will be veiled in ignorance pending more careful analyses of a cross section of important policy decisions in several countries.

The Need to Take into Account a Fairly Long Time-span

Most of the early implementation studies attempted to reach judgments concerning a program's outcomes, and the factors affecting them, within 2–4 years of the basic policy decision (usually in the form of a new law). Examples include Derthick's (1972) analysis of new towns within U.S. cities, the Pressman and Wildavsky (1973) classic, and the initial studies of the federal compensatory education legislation (Murphy 1971).

This time-span was explicable given the felt need to explain the apparent inability of programs to meet their mandated objectives. Both policy-makers and academics wanted to know why. In some cases, e.g. the Oakland study, the time-frame was perfectly appropriate because it coincided roughly with the program's demise.

But in many other cases this limited time-span proved to be quite misleading. First, it led to premature assessments of a program's effects. In the case of ambitious efforts to significantly change the behavior of large numbers of people, it is clear in retrospect that a 2–4 year time-frame is completely inappropriate. It takes a year or two to get a program to hire personnel, draft the basic implementing regulations, and otherwise get off the ground. To expect major changes after only a few years is quite unrealistic – and perhaps a peculiarly American failing. When it doesn't happen, we are quick to judge a program to have failed. In several cases, such judgments have turned out to be premature and unfair. Second, and directly related, a short time-frame neglects the possibility that program proponents will identify and overcome a series of impediments over a period of years. In such cases, the result can be *cumulative incremental change:* After a decade or so, the program proves to be much closer to achieving its mandated objectives than it was after 2–4 years. In short, an abbreviated time-span blinds us to the potential for *policy-oriented learning* and *policy evolution/change.*

An excellent example is Title I of ESEA, the U.S.'s compensatory education program. It was supposed to funnel federal funds to school districts with large numbers of disadvantaged children in order to improve their educational performance. Studies conducted a few years after passage of the 1965 legislation revealed a dismal failure, with widespread evidence that schools were not targeting the funds on disadvantaged students and, not surprisingly, that such students were showing no improvement in basic learning skills (Murphy 1971; McLaughlin 1975). Yet studies conducted 6–8 years later – i.e. after a decade or so of implementation – revealed substantial improvements in targeting funds and a number of instances of significant improvements in educational performances (Kirst and Jung 1982).

While a complex story, the improvements can basically be attributed, first, to continued Congressional commitment to compensatory eduction throughout the 1965–78 period and, second, to a gradual learning process by program proponents (Mazmanian and Sabatier 1983: Ch. 6). For example, early audits – leaked to the press in 1968 by dissatisfied implementing officials – revealed widespread misuse of funds by local school districts. These were attributed to ambiguities in the legislation, to a general unwillingness of federal officials to monitor and improve local compliance, and to the political weakness of program beneficiaries (e.g. the poor) in most local school districts. The resulting scandal led to Congressional clarification of intent, to a strengthening of the authority of program proponents within the federal education ministry, to a variety of efforts to develop supportive constituencies in state and local school agencies (e.g. via the hiring of parents as teachers' aides), and to a tightening of federal regulations concerning targeting of funds. It also became increasingly obvious that educators really had very little idea about *how* to teach children from disadvantaged backgrounds. This led to a rather substantial federal research program designed to identify successful techniques and to promote their adoption by local school districts. That turned out to be a slow and difficult process, in part because of the gradual realization that one could not force innovation upon teachers – an example of the need for professional discretion mentioned earlier.

There are still lots of questions concerning the sustainability of educational improvements once students leave the compensatory education program. And the compensatory education coalition in Congress has been directly challenged since 1981 by President Reagan. Nevertheless, for over a decade there was a pattern of learning by program proponents as they identified obstacles and then devised a series of strategies to deal with them. The result was a cumulative incremental – and, at the end of 12 years, dramatic – improvement in the targeting of funds and some fairly substantial evidence of at least short-term improvements in students' educational performance.

Of course, there are also numerous cases of initially effective programs whose performance declines over time. For example, there is a substantial American literature indicating that attempts to regulate business in order to benefit consumers are subject to a "cycle of decay" over time (Bernstein 1955; Sabatier 1975; Quirk 1981).

In sum, the direction of program change is subject to changes in socio-economic conditions, interest group support, elections, and learning by both proponents and opponents. But there is a rather remarkable consensus among implementation scholars concerning the desirability of taking a fairly long-term perspectives, e.g. 10–15 years, in order to understand the ability of the public sector to guide target group behavior (Majone and Wildavsky 1978; Barrett and Fudge 1981; Mazmanian and Sabatier 1983). Shorter time intervals are likely to produce erroneous conclusions about program effects and to mask the critical process of policy evolution and learning.

The Importance of Basing a Program on Sound Causal Assumptions

As previously indicated, one of Pressman and Wildavsky's major contributions to the implementation literature – and to our understanding of the factors affecting governmental efforts to guide behavior in order to obtain desired outcomes – was their focus on the causal assumptions behind a program.

There are several different ways of conceptualizing the notion of a program's (often implicit) causal model. Some authors, including Pressman and Wildavsky (1973) and Bardach (1977), are concerned with understanding the factors contributing to efficiency at least as much as with those affecting efficacy. Others, such as Berman (1978) and Sabatier and Mazmanian (1981, 1983a), focus purely on those contributing to effectiveness. For example, the latter authors have developed a concept of a program's (implicit) causel model which includes two aspects:

(1) The cognitive component: To what extent did the policy formulators understand the principal problem-related factors and institutional linkages affecting goal attainment?
(2) The jurisdictional component: To what extent did they give implementing agencies jurisdiction over sufficient linkages to have at least the potential of attaining legal goals?

Their emphasis, then, is on the theory actually *incorporated* into the legislation or other authoritative policy decision rather than merely on the one that some policy formulators may have had in mind (which comprises the cognitive component).

Whatever the precise nature of the concept of causal model (assumptions) underlying a program used by various authors, study after study has shown this to be a critical variable explaining program outcomes. For example, an analysis of the implementation of the 1972 California Coastal Zone Conservation Act revealed the implementing agencies were much more successful in protecting *visual* access to the ocean than in promoting *physical* access (Sabatier and Mazmanian 1983b). The differential was almost wholly attributable to the validity of the causal assumptions behind each program. The legislation contained implicit assumptions that both types of access would be provided if the principal implementing agency were granted jurisdiction over all new development within 1000 yards of the ocean. That assumption proved valid with respect to protecting scenic access because the coastal agency had the authority to deny (or impose conditions on) any proposed building which endangered coastal views, e.g. from the road paralleling the ocean. But the legislative assumptions were quite inadequate with respect to physical access to the beach because they did not deal with (provide jurisdiction over) all sorts of additional factors necessary for the provision of physical access: The coastal agency could deny permits for new developments which did not, for example, deed a public access easement. But the legislation allocated no authority to provide the insurance and other services necessary for the actual opening of any accessway, nor did it allocate authority to acquire (and manage) land for parks. In short, the 1972 legislation incorporated wholly inadequate assumptions about what was necessary to provide physical access.

Other examples of the importance of underlying models come from a study of the implementation of European higher education reforms (Cerych and Sabatier 1985). In 1968, the planners of the British Open University (OU) predicted an enrollment of approximately 25,000 students in the 1970 entering class. Actual enrollment turned out to be 24,000. Two years before, planners of the French university institutes of technology predicted enrollments in 1972 – the fifth year of the program – would attain 160,000 students. The actual figure turned out to be 34,000. The principal reason for this enormous variation in ability to attain projected enrollments was simply that the British planners were using more accurate causal assumptions and better data than their French colleagues. The French based their projections on an extremely general model indicating the types of manpower training needed for targeted levels of economic development. It implicitly assumed, among other things, that students would radically alter their historic preference for 4-year university (as opposed to short-cycle, technical) education and that the competing short-cycle institutions would simply disappear. Not surprisingly, these turned out to be quite erroneous. In contrast, British planners of the OU calculated the pool of potential applicants from specific subgroups of the population (e.g. teachers without a university degree), made a conservative estimate (e.g. 10%) of the percentage likely to enroll, and then supplemented this analysis with a survey of the British population soliciting their degree of interest in attending the OU in the near future. They then interpreted these results in a likewise conservative fashion and, not surprisingly, came up with quite accurate projections.

Again, however, an adequate time horizon is critical for understanding guidance mechanisms. For one of the things which happend in many of these cases is that program proponents gradually improved their causal assumptions over time. The leaders of the California coastal agencies soon realized that their access authority was inadequate, and thus proposed to the legislature in 1976 that management and acquisition authority be provided. Similarly, French educational planners began exploring the reasons behind their grossly inadequate projections. This led to the development of much more differentiated (by region and by market sector) manpower training models; to several unsuccessful attempts to eliminate the competing short-cycle institutions; and finally to what Wildavsky (1979) has termed "a strategic retreat on objectives." Projected enrollments were gradually revised downwards untill by 1979 they finally matched the actual enrollment of 52,000 students.

Do not Assume that Governmental Action is a Critical Factor

As will be recalled, "top down" implementation approaches start with a policy decision and then examine the extent to which, and the reasons for which, legal and other objectives are attained over time. One of the principal shortcomings of this approach is a danger of overemphasizing the importance of the program under study in affecting target group behavior and ultimate outcomes. This can be dealt with through careful research design – ideally, an interrupted time series with a pretest-posttest control group. But such quasi-experimental designs frequently present all sorts of practical problems given the time and resource constraints of real-world research. At any rate, numerous implementation studies – e.g. Pressman and Wildavsky (1973), Bardach (1977), Cerych and Sabatier (1985) – have not always been as carefully designed as they might have been. As a result, one suspects that the influence of the governmental program under study has sometimes been overemphasized.

In this respect, the bottom-up approach presents some methodological advantages (Hjern and Hull 1982). By starting with the actors involved in a policy problem and investigating their perceptions of the range of factors affecting their activities, the researcher is less likely to underestimate the importance of market forces or the unanticipated consequences of programs in other policy areas. For example, the comparative study of sulfur oxide emissions in several European countries directed by Knoepfel and Weidner (1982b) frequently found that purely market forces (e.g. the efficiency of different production processes) and governmental programs in other policy areas (particularly energy) had at least as much effect on firms' emissions as did pollution control policy.

Of course, pure bottom-up approaches have their own methodological shortcomings, e.g. a tendency to ignore why potentially-important actors are *not* in a given implementation network. In addition, their reliance on actors' perceptions produces a tendency to neglect how a variety of legal and socio-economic factors may structure actors' participation, resources, and preferences without their explicit knowledge. But these deficiences can largely be corrected once more explicit and elaborate causal models get added to the networking technique.

15.3 Where Do We Go from Here?

This chapter has argued that a decade of implementation research in the U.S. and Europe has at least four implications for our understanding of guidance and control in the public sector:

(1) Street-level bureaucrats – classroom teachers, social workers, pollution control inspectors – play a critical role in the provision of governmental services and in attempts to regulate private behavior. Particularly in the case of professionals, it is probably illusory for official policy-makers to think they can *tightly control* the behavior of their supposed subordinates. On the other hand, policy-makers can affect what happens on the ground by structuring the implementation process through relatively clear directives and through affecting the number, the resources, and, to some extent, the preferences of street-level bureaucrats and target groups. But the efficacy of such mechanisms will vary by country, policy area, and program.
(2) In assessing the effectiveness of various attempts at guidance and control, one needs to take into account a reasonably long time-period, at least 5–10 years. Shorter time-frames may produce quite erroneous conclusions concerning a program's effects. More importantly, they neglected the importance of learning, as various actors respond to perceptions of performance gaps and to changing conditions by devising a series of strategies to address them.
(3) The causal assumptions behind a program are a critical factor affecting performance. They are also one of the factors most susceptible to policy learning.
(4) Rather than start with a *policy decision* and then examine its implementation, it is probably preferable to begin with a *policy problem* and then examine the variety of actors actually and potentially involved in addressing it. But such an approach must be built upon an explicit causal theory of the factors affecting the participation rates, resources, and preferences of various actors if it is to rise beyond purely descriptive network analysis.

Starting from these conclusions, one very promising approach is to develop strategic interaction models of policy evolution and learning. Majone (1982) has begun to sketch the rudiments of a model of policy evolution analogous in structure to theories of biological evolution. Thus it focuses on mechanisms which generate variation, produce selection, and pass on selected traits over time. In an alternative model, Sabatier (1983) tries to separate policy-oriented learning from the more general process of policy change. He proposes that actors within a policy community can be aggregated into a few advocacy coalitions, each with its own belief system, which seek to have their core beliefs enacted into governmental action programs and to experiment with various strategies of realizing core values over time. A major focus of this model is the strategic interaction process whereby different coalitions attempt to modify perceptions of the causal factors affecting a problem area.

An important factor affecting the extent of policy-oriented learning seems to be the existence of reasonably well-structured communication fora (the cognitive equivalent of van Gunsteren's responsibility fora, see chapter 13) in which professionals and other experts from different advocacy coalitions are forced to confront each other's arguments in a relatively depoliticized setting. Thus, despite the partisan nature of policy making and severe cognitive limits on rationality, actors' desires to realize core values in a world of limited resources provide strong incentives to learn more about the magnitude of salient problems, the factors affecting them, and the consequences of policy alternatives.

Such models of policy evolution and learning are still quite tentative. But when elaborated, tested, and refined, they should make a major contribution to our understanding of guidance, control, and performance evaluation in the public sector.

Notes

1 For examples of almost purely discriptive case studies of "implementation networks," see Hanf and Scharpf (1978: Ch. 12), the symposium by Hjern and Hull (1972), and the cases in Barrett and Fudge (1981). Of efforts to develop causal models, that of Scharpf (Hanf and Scharpf 1978: Ch. 13) based on exchange theory is suggestive but rudimentary, while that of Knoepfel and Weidner (1982a) is comprehensive but completely lacking in parsimony and, at times, virtually unintelligible.

2 In addition, private conversations indicate that Benny Hjern probably belongs in this list. Berman's (1980) inclusion is subject to debate. His article on "programmed" and "adaptive" approaches seems rather balanced at first glance. But the description of programmed approaches is a caricature – note the complete absence of any footnotes to real-life proponents – and the whole article is very ambiguous concerning the conditions appropriate to various points on the programmed-adaptive scale. Private conversations and his earlier work with McLaughlin on the Rand change agency study suggest to me that he has strong affinity for this position.

3 For example, Burgess has criticized the British Open University for having failed in its (alleged) mission of attracting a significantly greater percentage of working class students than more traditional British universities. While he provides no citations concerning the source of this supposed mission, it was probably Labour's 1966 campaign manifesto. Yet a careful analysis of the *governmental* policy documents – most notably, the 1968 Planning Committee Report – reveal that they were utterly silent on the topic of class representation, while being very explicit that the OU was to be open to anyone on a firstcome, first-serve basis (Cerych and Sabatier 1985). In short, not only was Burgess incorrect in contending that the OU was intended to significantly increase working class access to higher education, any attempt to impose quotas for various classes would arguably have been counter to its legal mandate.

References

Bardach, E. (1977): *The Implementation Game.* Cambridge: MIT Press.

Barrett, S., and C. Fudge (eds.) (1981): *Policy and Action.* London: Methuen.

Berman, P. (1978): "The Study of Macro- and Micro-Implementation." *Public Policy* 26 (Spring): 157–184.

Berman, P. (1980): "Thinking about Programmed and Adaptive Implementation." In Ingram, H., and D. Mann (eds.), *Why Polities Succeed or Fail,* 205–231. Beverly Hills: Sage.

Berman, P., and M. McLaughlin (1976): "Implementation of ESEA Title I." *Teacher College Record* 17 (Feb.): 397–415.

Bernstein, M. (1955): *Regulating Business by Independent Commission.* Princeton: Princeton Univ. Press.

Cerych, L., and P. Sabatier (1985): *The Implementation of European Higher Education Reforms.* Stoke-on Trent: Trentham.

Derthick, M. (1972): *New Towns In-Town.* Washington: Urban Institute.

Elmore, R. (1978): "Organizational Models of Social Program Implementation," *Public Policy* 26 (Spring): 185–228.

Elmore, R. (1979): "Backward Mapping." *Political Science Quarterly* 94/4: 601–616.

Hanf, K. (1982): "The Implementation of Regulatory Policy: Enforcement as Bargaining." *European Journal of Political Research* 10 (June): 159–172.

Hanf, K., and F. W. Scharpf (eds.) (1978): *Interorganizational Policy Making: Limits to Coordination and Central Control:* London: Sage.

Hill, M. (1982): "The Role of the British Alkali and Clean Air Inspectorate in Air Pollution Control." *Policy Studies Journal* 11 (Sept.): 165–174.

Hjern, B., and D. Porter (1981): "Implementation Structures: A New Unit of Administrative Analysis." *Organization Studies* 2/3: 211–227.

Hjern, B., and C. Hull (1982): "Implementation Research as Empirical Constitutionalism." *European Journal of Political Research* 10 (June): 105–116.

Horn, C. van (1979): *Policy Implementation in the Federal System.* Lexington, Mass.: D. C. Heath.

Kirst, M., and R. Jung (1982): "The Utility of a Longitudinal Approach in Assessing Implementation: Title I, ESEA." In Williams, W. (ed.), *Studying Implementation,* 119–148. Chatham, N. J.: Chatham House.

Knoepfel, P., and H. Wiedner (1982a): "A Conceptual Framework for Studying Implementation." In Downing, P., and K. Hanf (eds.), *The Implementation of Pollution Control Programs,* 7–31. Tallahassee: Policy Sciences Program.

Knoepfel, P., and H. Wiedner (1982b): "Implementing Air Quality Control Programs in Europe." *Policy Studies Journal* 11 (Sept.): 103–115.

Majone, G. (1982): *"An Evolutional Approach to Policy Chance."* Paper presented at the ZIF, University of Bielefeld, German Federal Republic.

Majone, G., and A. Wildavsky (1978): "Implementation as Evolution." In Freeman, H. (ed.), *Policy Studies Review Annual – 1978,* 103–117. Beverly Hills: Sage.

March, J. G., and H. A. Simon (1958): *Organizations.* New York: Wiley.

Mayntz, R. (1978): "Intergovernmental Implementation of Environmental Policy." In Hanf, K., and F. W. Scharpf (eds.), *Interorganizational Policy Making,* 201–214. London: Sage.

Mazmanian, D., and P. Sabatier (eds.) (1981): *Effective Policy Implementation.* Lexington, Mass.: D. C. Heath.

Mazmanian, D., and P. Sabatier (1983): *Implementation and Public Policy.* Chicago: Scott Foresman.

McLaughlin, M. (1975): *Evaluation and Reform: ESEA, Title I.* Cambridge: Ballinger.

Murphy, J. (1971): "Title I of ESEA: The Politics of Implementing Federal Education Reform." *Harvard Educational Review* 41/1: 35–63.

Pressman, J., and A. Wildavsky (1973): *Implementation*. Berkeley: Univ. of California Press.

Quirk, P. (1981): *Industry Influence in Federal Regulatory Agencies*. Princeton: Princeton Univ. Press.

Rodgers, H., and C. Bullock (1976): *Coercion to Compliance*. Lexington, Mass.: D. C. Heath.

Sabatier, P. A. (1975): "Social Movements and Regulatory Agencies." *Political Science* 6 (Sept.): 301–342.

Sabatier, P. A. (1983): "Toward a Strategic Interaction Theory of Policy Evaluation and Learning." Paper submitted for Publication to *Policy Sciences*.

Sabatier, P. A., and D. Mazmanian (1983a): "Policy Implementation." In Nagel, S. (ed.), *Encyclopedia of Public Policy,* 143–169. New York: M. Dekkar.

Sabatier, P. A., and D. Mazmanian (1983b): *Can Regulation Work? The Implementation of the 1972 California Coastal Initiative*. New York: Plenum.

Weatherly, R., and M. Lipsky (1977): "Street Level Bureaucrats and Institutional Innovation: Implementing Special Education Reform." *Harvard Educational Review* 47 (May): 171–197.

Wildavsky, A. (1979): *Speaking Truth to Power*. Boston: Little, Brown.

Williams, W. (1980): *The Implementation Perspective*. Berkeley: Univ. of California Press.

Williams, W., and R. Elmore (1976): *Social Program Implementation*. New York: Academic Press.

16. A Cybernetic View of Guidance, Control and Evaluation in the Public Sector

Andrew Dunsire

Abstract

Three problems of controlling the public sector are identified: its inertia, its complexity, and its multivalence. Public policy goals are essentially mutually incompatible, and easy reversibility of policy priorities explains evaluation weakness. But procedural objectives are both sectorwide and enduring: control in the public sector is predominantly procedural control. The mutual incompatibility of procedural goals, many of them embodied in specific control divisions and agencies, presents itself to the decision-maker as polylemma. *Tensions produced by polylemma in a system where control is otherwise very distributed, give steering-power to superiors in each bureaucracy, by selecting which procedural objectives to stress or relax. In the public sector as a whole substitutes for hierarchical authority operate. An inherently-unstable equilibrium is kept within bounds by opposed forces of attraction/repulsion and can be biased within limits. In different cultures, these limits (before destabilization) may be wider than in others.*

16.1 Introduction

The word 'public' in the phrase 'the public sector' has a lot to answer for. Because it is 'public', there is a presumption that, however large and complex it is, the public sector is (or certainly should be) under control; in contrast to the 'private sector', where the impersonal amoral forces of 'the market' operate, the workings of the public sector are not only assumed to be governed by political intent and choice (or culpable neglect), for which *someone* is responsible; but also to be open to scrutiny in its inner processes – its procedures as well as its substantive results, its means as well as its ends, its correctness as well as its effectiveness. There is a good deal of myth about it; but although the boundary between 'public' and 'private' sectors is by no means as easy to draw as the stereotypes suggest, it remains true that there is a premium upon guidance, evaluation and control in the public sector. And responsibility argues for control as well as *vice versa*.

I propose for the purposes of this chapter to characterise the problems of bringing and keeping the public sector under control (by those who are responsible for it) as falling under these three heads:

(1) the size or massiveness of the public sector; or, if one thinks of it in movement, its huge inertia or momentum;
(2) the complexity of the public sector, the bewildering variety of agencies, programmes, policies, instruments, techniques, rules, operations;

(3) the lack of a common yardstick of success and failure, compared with the 'profitability' criterion for the private sector; indeed, the problem is that there are several mutually *conflicting* yardsticks.

Cybernetics (Gk *kubernetes,* L *gubernator,* steersman) is the science of guidance, evaluation and control, claiming to deal in principles that are of application whether the material manifestations are those of inanimate matter (galaxies, man-made machines), organic matter ("Nature", including the human organism), or complex interactions of both (terrestrial weather, animal societies). In this chapter no justice can be done to such claims, but the reader will judge whether the cybernetic view on the topics of this book is of use in giving some enlightenment on the problems just outlined. (For an introduction to cybernetics, see Ashby 1956; Beer 1959. The pioneers of control theory were Maxwell 1868; Wiener 1948; Shannon and Weaver 1949; Ashby 1952. See also Wiener 1950; Beer 1966, 1972; Deutsch 1963; Kalmus 1967; Kuhn 1974; Steinbruner 1976.)

16.2 The Massiveness of the Public Sector

Citizens often perceive 'government' as a set of massive forces they imperfectly understand, in face of which they are relatively powerless; as with stormy weather, the safest strategy seems to be to keep out of it, to be exposed to it as little as possible, to construct retreats and defences; if the worst comes to the worst, to mount rescue services. But those who actually work in the public sector know well that the public sector is *not* like the weather. TV satellite pictures have begun to familiarise us all with the idea of 'our' weather being just that small part which happens to concern us, from out of a phenomenon for which there are no real boundaries: the system is a global one, and totally interactive. If barometric pressure goes up in one area, it must go down in one or more other areas to compensate; if it rains a lot here, there must be increased transpiration or absorption of water vapour from the land there, or from the oceans, to make up; temperature varies greatly from place to place and from time to time, but the *mean* temperature of the Earth as a whole varies very little. Thus the weather at any one place is a local manifestation of a global adjustment and compensating process, an equilibrating of atmospheric forces which never settles down to mean values because it is constantly 'disturbed' by solar and planetary changes; and yet demonstrates a system 'under control' in one sense – not running away out of control, keeping within limits, adjusting, compensating. Which is not to say that someone is controlling it.

Actually, *any* 'natural' system will always be under control in this sense – at some level of system. To understand the terrestrial weather system's dynamics, we have to take the Sun into account – we have to consider our Earth as an element in the planetary system of Sol (one 'level of system' up) (Stanley-Jones 1960).

The public sector, on the other hand, is not a 'natural system', and doesn't keep itself under control in this way; it, surely, has to 'be controlled'. Nor is the public sector a seamless web, a continuous system like global weather; on the contrary, part of the 'size' problem is the number of distinct organisations it comprises, each organisation enveloped in all-too-real boundaries across which communication and exchange is often difficult, time- and energy-consuming. Moreover, a considerable number of these organisations are large in themselves; frequently larger, in terms of staff employed, than the largest organisations in the private sector. So we are undoubtedly dealing with massive structures, whether we think of the public sector as a whole (employing every fifth person employed, in many countries), or the major organisations of which it is composed.

One feature of massive structures considered dynamically, in motion or in operation, is again something we all recognise. It is their great inertia or momentum. The elephant, for instance, cannot *dart;* you can almost observe the sequence of its muscle movements, as you can in a slow-motion film of a running human; but equally, it is hard to stop once it is moving at speed. Everyone is now familiar with the phenomenon of the 150,000-tonne supertanker vessel, which requires so many minutes and so many miles of sea-room to alter direction, that a helmsman can only avoid present peril by turning the helm half-an-hour ago, as it were. At the other end of the scale, the movements of a small lizard may be so quick that we cannot follow them; the computer's response to a command so instantaneous as to disconcert us (some manufacturers make their machines more 'user-friendly' by interposing a quite artificial delay).

We are noting differences in the time-scale of change from one state of a system to the next, or 'volatility'. Our standard is the time-scale of change with which we are most familiar: that which we experience with our own conscious mind in relation to our normal surroundings (call it awareness at whole-organism level for humans). Now, the human body itself operates at more than one time-scale (or 'sensitivity'): the speed of a reflex response is considerably greater than that of a deliberate action mediated by the forepart of the brain. And in comparison with the internal body-speeds of insects, the human is slow – elephantine, in fact.

For the same kind of reason, getting a change through a bureaucratic decision-process is slow. Bureaucracies, by their nature and not because of the laziness or wickedness of the people in them, are like supertankers more than they are like computers (and the larger, the more so). In organisation theory terms, if they were able to respond to environmental or other change rapidly, they would simply not be bureaucracies; the compensating loss would be in the predictability and economy of routine (Burns and Stalker 1961).

We can hypothesise, therefore, that if the public sector as a whole is being controlled by the same sort of mechanism by which a supertanker is steered, it is at best a slow-acting control, not very sensitive to snap judgements or changes of mind by those attempting to exert control. Harold Macmillan once compared managing the British economy with trying to catch a train using last year's timetable; the information one was receiving actually referred to the situation as it was six months previously, and an adjustment made now might seriously overcorrect a trend if in fact the trend had already begun to correct itself.

But *is* a public sector controlled by the same sort of mechanism (cybernetically viewed) as is a supertanker? That would argue for a central control room somewhere, into which all relevant information came, and from which the commands issued to effect any necessary 'changes of course'. In organisation theory terms, the entire public sector would have to be arranged as a hierarchy, with the command centre at the top; an image conflicting somewhat with an earlier remark that the public sector is made up of a large number of organizations with communication problems between them – the image *there* being of an interorganisational *network,* not a hierarchy. But that could be cleared up (we shall come across this ambiguity of portrayal, between 'hierarchy' and 'network', again: the writer's position is that real systems often have *both* kinds of characteristic, and that it is not feasible to portray them adequately using only one set of imagery).

What is just contrary to common sense, however, is any notion that the President or Prime Minister and other Ministers *directly* control the activities of the entire government machine in anything like the way the helmsman himself controls the movements of the rudder. They wouldn't have the time. They have to delegate. But can you delegate control, and yet retain it? How, moreover, do you cope with the enormous *complexity* of the public sector, how do you keep control over so many different kinds of specialist and expert? This is the next topic; but first we shall elucidate a few basic ideas about *control* as such.

16.3 The Complexity of the Public Sector

The cyberneticist takes the view that if anyone is going to control anything directly, there are three indispensable elements: (1) a clear picture of what must be going on if given purposes are to be attained; (2) good and recent information about what actually *is* going on; and (3) some effective means of reducing any discrepancy between (2) and (1). The paradigm is the activity, mentioned several times already, of the helmsman on a ship, where (1) is the given course heading, (2) is the actual direction being taken as registered by the compass; and (3) is the helm and rudder, plus power to provide forward motion. These three requisites of direct (or simple) control are sometimes called Director, Detector, and Effector; but they correspond broadly to Guidance, Evaluation, and 'Controls'. The three processes can be demonstrated in any purposive regulatory system (budgetary control, inventory control, immigration control, etc.). Technically, control is maintained separately on each value or variable: one criterion, one correcting device – though of course they can be linked in arrays and sequences. So any control system such as budgetary control will involve a number of distinct standards, monitorings and adjustments, depending upon the complexity of the problems being tackled.

The cyberneticist's measure for complexity is called *variety,* and it is a count of the number of alternative states a system might be found in. This number can be high, even in a system with a small number of variables. Suppose a closed entity with seven elements, each element linked to every other by two channels, one in each direction; and each channel incorporating an on/off switch. A 'state' of this system is a configuration of which channels are 'on' and 'off'. There are 2^{42} (two to the power of forty-two) different possible states, or well over a million million (Beer 1966: 251). That is the *variety* of that system.

The basic law of cybernetics is W Ross Ashby's 'Law of Requisite Variety' (Ashby 1952), which in one of its several formulations says that you can only fully control something if you can match its variety in your controlling device. In fencing parlance, you must have a parry for its every thrust. In another illustration owed to

Stafford Beer (1966), the variety generated by the possible movements of eleven men on a football field would be impossible to match if you didn't happen to have a control device consisting of another eleven men, each a variety generator of comparable capacity.

The variety of a system on the scale of the public sector is a number which is itself so large as to be inconceivable. Yet the corresponding theoretically required control capacity is the same number.

There are only two ways forward: either increase the capacity of the controllers (whom we here envisage as the Ministers of the Government) by providing them with massive 'variety generators' of some kind; or somehow reduce the variety of the system to be controlled by them; or, of course, both.

Let us tackle the second possibility: reducing the variety of the system to be controlled. If we want a suggestion as to how this might be done, we all actually have a good model very close to hand. One brain (admittedly a most complex organ) is required to control the (even more complex) system that is our own human body, as well as cope with a changing environment. But it does not do so all by itself, directly. We are all aware of some events in our body over which we are not in direct control (heartbeat, sweating, flow of stomach acid); and we know, intellectually, that there are many bodily functions going on inside the skin-envelope of which we are *not* aware – regarding which we, as 'persons', at whole-organism level, do not even receive internal communications. We cannot *feel* the state of our bone marrow or what is going on in the kidneys. We cannot, by thinking about it, know the pH factor of our blood or how much of a number of different trace metals we are retaining or getting rid of each day. We can now *arrange* for these things to be monitored, and effect changes in them, by external intervention, if 'health' demands it. But normal functioning depends upon millions of such monitoring operations in our 'inner regions' that are quite shut off from consciousness – from the thinking part of the brain. If we did have to 'control' everything that goes on inside us, by thinking about it and issuing 'instructions', the complexity would overwhelm us. That we do not have to, and yet persist, is evidence that the variety of the system to be controlled has been reduced for us in some way.

To see more clearly *how*, it will be better to shift attention to an *action*, a simple use of the motor nervous system and musculature of the limbs, etc. Pick up a pencil. You can do it without thinking – without even looking, if you laid it down only a moment ago. You form the intention, and your arm moves, positioning itself relevantly in three-dimensional space, the fingers open in suitable configuration, feel whether the pencil is appropriately placed to grasp and if not, either reposition the fingers or nudge the pencil until it is; close the fingers, withdraw hand and arm, probably manipulating the ensemble as you do so as to bring the pencil into an apt orientation for writing – and so on. Robots can be designed to do it. My point is that, so far as the 'reasoning' part of the brain is concerned, the arms, hands, fingers and associated sensing mechanisms might as well belong to a robot. They have long ago been programmed to behave in this manner without needing to be 'told' every time by the thinking part of the brain.

Of course, the behaviour is not 'automatic' (like an automaton): it was learnt, and since the arms, fingers, etc. are all very much 'multipurpose', they can do many other things. Nor is the picking up of a pencil a *reflex* action: it was a controlled action; but the thousands of micro-operations of which it was composed were under the control of the entire central nervous system, not of one part of the brain only. The two separate nerve systems (motor 'out' and sense-data 'back') were cooperating in switching operations performed in several different 'control centres': at each joint of the fingers, at the wrist, the shoulder, the top of the spinal cord, the cerebellum. But there is even more to it. A movement of the arm involves not only the activating of the flexor muscles (those that cause bending of a limb) and the inhibiting of a number of extensor muscles (those that straighten it), but also the activity of some muscles in the trunk and in the abdominal wall, to provide 'anchorage'; and if you are not sitting down, you may need to set some thigh and leg muscles to work as well, to maintain balance as your centre of gravity shifts.

We *learned* how to do all this in extreme infancy, so that 'movements' are 'packaged', and triggered off in packages by a single volley of signals flashed out over the whole network and 'read' by those lower-order centres which, as it were, recognise their call-sign. By adulthood, not only does the forepart of the brain not have to do any more than trigger off such programmes of packaged signals, it cannot do any more than that. The brain cannot 'speak' to a finger directly, only via the hierarchy of control centres. Each centre only communicates with the centre of next lower (or higher) order. That is the principle of 'discontinuous transmission' which characterises all nervous communication. Messages do not flow from the brain to the fingers: messages are received and retransmitted, received and retransmitted, neuron by neuron; and the message transmitted onwards by each control centre is its own characteristic message, not simply a copy of the stimulus. Similarly, feedback information is discontinuously transmitted 'upwards' from many original tactile sensing points, coalescing and being reduced in total volume as several input signals to a synapse are coded into one output impulse.

The effect is to reduce the information load on the higher order centres to a tiny fraction of the information actually in the system, in any particular operation – and yet provide them with a 'summary' of it. Thus the variety of the system with which the highest-order centres are faced is such as they are able to cope with – because they are enjoying the benefit of the control capacity being deployed in many centres of lower order. The brain's control capacity is multiplied by the capacities of its subordinate centres. (For further reading on control in the human body, accessible to non-specialists, see Stanley-Jones 1960; Kennedy 1967; Nathan 1969; etc. The pioneer in this field was Cannon 1932.)

A cyberneticist is committed to the view that this description of control mechanisms in the human motor nervous system is not simply that, *sui generis;* but that it is an illustration of control principles, of laws or truths that apply in other material contexts – in machines, or human social groupings – where the information transfer and interpretation processes are *cybernetically* indistinguishable, whatever the appearances. It is not necessary, however, for the reader to be committed in this way, to accept the homology; it will be quite enough if an analogy is admitted.

In my books *Implementation in a Bureaucracy* and *Control in a Bureaucracy* (1978) I have shown, I think, that a bureaucracy of the familiar Weberian type is, by its nature, analogous. The system hierarchy of Ministry, department, branch, division, section and so on (however named) corresponds to the system hierarchy of whole-organism, consciousness-mediating lobes of the brain, cerebellum and other areas of the brain, spinal cord, limb centres, digit centres and so on. Internal transmissions of information in a bureaucracy can be shown to be discontinuous, developing the analysis suggested by March and Simon (1958), Cyert and March (1963) and others; communications outwards/downwards have to be *operational-ised* or spelt out, communications inwards/upwards are 'distilled', and subject to *uncertainty absorption*. On this basis control capacity in a bureaucracy can be expected to be distributed also; and of course it is. Each head of section is responsible for the control of his own section; each head of division for the control of her division and so on. The bureaucracy is controllable because each of its constituent parts, level by level, is *self*-controlling.

In cybernetic terms, the organisation as a whole is composed of servomecha-nisms-within-servomechanisms. A servomechanism is a machine which monitors departures of a sensed value from a set value (or a sensed rate of change from a set rate of change, etc.), and takes corrective action without human intervention. The paradigm is James Watt's 'governor' for a steam-engine, which monitored the speed of rotation of the main output shaft: if the speed increased (either because the load on the shaft lessened, or because the boiler produced more steam), the familiar pair of flexibly-coupled brass weights would fly outwards under centrifugal force, this action causing the steam inlet valve to close a litte; if speed decreased (either because the load was greater, or because the boiler produced less steam) the opposite would occur. Thus the 'governor' kept the output of the engine constant within a designed range, between a pair of thresholds rather than around a given point.

In the usual terminology, the output variance was *fed back* to the input with the sign (+ or −) reversed; hence *negative feedback,* the essential feature of all self-regulation. Servomechanisms were the foundation of industrial mechanisation; the modern automated plant incorporates several hierarchical levels of (mainly elec-tronic) regulatory devices in control systems-within-systems. (For reading on the history of negative feedback devices, see Mayr 1971; Bennett 1979; in administra-tion, Kaufman 1973; Meyer 1973).

But there is no *cybernetic* distinction between a control device which incorpo-rates a human operator and one which does not. Let me give an illustration of another kind.

In some very old automobiles, the ignition-advance and fuel/air-mixture controls were driver-operated, by means of levers on the steering column: now, in some cars, both are entirely automatic, taken care of by devices within the engine compartment – the driver has lost direct control of them and relies on the servomechanisms. Brakes, accelerator and steering are also often 'servo-assisted' in the modern car, but the driver retains direct control of their essential function. But from the point of view of a traffic policeman on traffic-control duty at a street intersection, it matters not at all whether the ignition-advance controls in a car he is signalling to stop or come on are driver-operated or automatic; nor, indeed, whether the brakes, accelerator and steering are driver-operated or not – provided the vehicle obeys his signals. He wishes to control vehicle-movements, not drivers (let alone ignition).

From the point of view of a District Traffic Controller a mile or two away, sitting at a bank of television monitor screens covering a dozen key junctions, a junction which is being kept under control, whether by a policeman on point-duty or by automatic traffic light signals, is one that is self-regulating. It can not only be 'left to its own devices': it can be *used,* incorporated into his wider vistas of traffic management for the whole city, by adjustments to the timing circuits of the lights, or radio instructions to the policeman, so as to favour one traffic stream against another. A reliable self-regulating subsystem can be regarded as a resource. A superior can harness the control his subordinates are maintaining. And each superior in a hierarchy is himself or herself a subordinate, and vice-versa (except at the bottom and the top – if there *is* a top in this regard).

These principles apply to a branch of a single organisation as described, to the Police Department as a whole, to the complex of organisations (or 'multiorganisation') which is a city government, and ultimately by the intervening levels of system to control of the public sector as a whole. If the public sector is not disintegrating or in chaos, that is evidence that it is 'under control', not running away out of control. It has infinite capacity to vary, but a myriad factors are operating to correct departures from set values, thresholds or patterns, to preserve governing relations. There is control, available for harnessing. And the source of this relative stability is to be found in the fact that all the elements of the public sector, hierarchically arranged in systems-within-systems-within-systems, are self-controlling units.

However, mere maintenance of existing governing relations (that pattern of values which happens to be being maintained at any one moment) is hardly *sufficient* control in the hands of those responsible if, as with the weather, some distributions of the variables and values are preferable to others. Those responsible need the capability to steer the system (even if it has to be 'slowly', as we saw earlier). Indeed, those responsible for any *part* need the same capability, just as the district traffic controller needed to be able to alter the governing values at particular junctions.

There is another aspect. You can leave an objective, goal, or governing value as it is presently set, but relax or tighten up the rigour with which it is maintained, the speed at which errors are corrected, the degree of latitude allowed before correction begins. For control is not an either/or matter (as if you either have control or you do not). You can have weak control or strong, loose or tight, broad or fine – or somewhere between in each case. These ordinary-speech terms have technical referents which we need not go into here: briefly, it depends on whether the three mechanisms of a control device (director, detector, effector) are well matched and tuned to the same range of sensitivity. You can, for instance, have very powerful sanctions coupled with a very clear and unambiguous requirement, but if your detecting device – that which tells you what is going on – is weak, then your control over the situation is weak. It is difficult to keep a car on the road in a fog; it is difficult to prevent smuggling, etc. The same goes, *mutatis mutandis,* for poor directors or inadequate effectors. A control device is only as good as its weakest element.

'Improving' control (achieving closer or more precise and prompt regulation at less cost) may therefore require sharpening up the designation of the *datum* (the given standard, thresholds, or pattern against which performance is to be measured), or increasing the supply of and up-to-dateness of relevant information about current performance, or stepping up the impact and speed of acting of the means of correcting errors and reducing discrepancies (or perhaps choosing different means). But strict and exact regulation may not always be what is desired. Loose control is 'better than nothing' in most situations; but besides that, a loose control, incorporating a large degree of latitude or flexibility in the hands of the controller, is sometimes better than more rigorous monitoring (as generations of 'Human Relations' management theorists have impressed on us). Those responsible for results need the capability to 'tune' a control system to the strength desired.

We shall see later how these two desiderata – steering the system into preferable configurations, and tuning the controls to the strength preferred – can be achieved. But first it is necessary to describe the nature of public sector objectives, goals, and values in some greater detail, since this has a vital bearing on the matter.

16.4 The Multivalence of the Public Sector

It is not the case, of course, that the activities of the private sector are subject to one overriding criterion of value: that of 'profitability'. Quite apart from the criteria that a Government typically imposes (which must override profitability), such as on fraudulent practice or on injury to the environment, commercial firms have at the very least to choose between short-, medium- and long-term profitability. One might argue that the overriding criterion is really *survival,* in a competitive world where you *have* to make profits; but that is itself subject to Aquinas' critique, that if the captain of a ship rated survival higher than all other values, he would keep his ship in harbour. Nevertheless, one of the touchstones often advanced to distinguish private sector from public sector organisations is that the latter 'cannot go bankrupt' – except that attention *has* been given to the senses in which government *can* go bankrupt (Rose and Peters 1978).

Whatever be the case, as a formal proposition, for 'survival' as the *ultimate* test for an organisation, it can be stated with some confidence that whether in the private or the public sector an organisation will be at any one time subject to several more *proximate* obligations, demands and pressures which, formally or informally, impose criteria of choice on its decision-makers. And it is of the nature of such obligations, demands and pressures that some of them will be incompatible with others.

All objectives of public policy are, to some extent, in competition with all others for scarce resources; not only for money, but for land, labour, energy, etc. Thus motorways compete with hospitals and schools, and defence takes resources that might have gone into geriatric welfare (and vice versa). Even within any single policy field, several objectives compete. These problems are well known and, beyond a point at least, inescapable. The political process is to a large degree concerned with establishing the priorities among competing objectives which will govern, in turn, the *datums* (the 'givens') of the control mechanisms.

Moreover, each policy field has its competing advocates and interested parties, some so entrenched and powerful that they themselves become not so much influences on politicians' choice but *constraints* on it, limits to the selection of priorities (e.g. professional bodies in the health sector). And of course decisions within the political system of the country are subject to constraints imposed from outside the system – from the international political economic system, for example.

On any of these levels, we can view the 'decision-making process' as if it were like the weather; i.e. we *can* make the inference that the 'decision' to rain, let's say, at a particular place and time, is the outcome of the configuration of temperatures, pressures and humidities at that place at that time; and the analogy is that an organizational decision-maker's decision is an outcome likewise, though perhaps involving many many more variables, including personal motivations. The 'pluralist' or 'mutual partisan adjustment' (Lindblom 1965) view of the political system tends towards this 'dynamic equilibrium' zero-sum model, and properly integrated into its larger-system and smaller subsystem network/hierarchy, it can be a powerful concept. The price of not developing the thought here (for the reason that we do not really need it in the present analysis) is that we have to postulate a difference of *kind* between the activities of standard-setting and of standard-maintaining, of determining the 'given' in a control mechanism and of detecting and correcting deviations from it; whereas the difference is really one of system-viewpoint – and the same person may well carry out both tasks.

As a theoretical proposition it is the case that the 'givens' of a situation are set for a control mechanism at the level of system immediately above (or the next *larger* system); recall the District Traffic Controller in relation to the traffic controller at street level. But a superior in an organisational hierarchy *is a member of* the next larger system, is himself/herself part of the self-regulating system at that level, as well as within his own jurisdiction. And the tighter the control in that jurisdiction, the more reliable he or she is at the higher level, and the more power he or she can wield in the political process at that level, i.e. in decision-making. (The opposite effect is expressible in proverb form: "A man with unreliable servants is an unreliable man: put not your trust in that man's master either.")

So a public sector under steerable and tunable control will be a reliable implement in government's attempts e.g. to control the economy, or make any other moves at the national political level. To the extent that control in the public sector is weak, to that extent government will have less leverage in its own decisions, and at international level. But these are commonplace observations.

Control will be weak, as already indicated, if the datum are unclear, or constantly changing. If the selection of priorities among policy goals is but temporary, or easily reversible, because of the operation of the political system, the performance evaluation and correction mechanisms either never get installed, or get little chance to work. Thus the price of political reversibility may be taken in lack of policy evaluation. Moreover, for many political purposes, the trumpeted designation of the selected policy objective *is* the pay-off, and subsequent performance (implementation, 'success') in respect of that policy is either too remote a consideration to be of present interest, or it is positively unwelcome. Few politicians like to allow of doubt that their policy is the right one, or to be told that it has not worked. Where the objectives of public policy are the legitimate prizes of politics, and the fairly rapid alternation in office of political parties with opposed value-systems is regarded as a *virtue,* then there is simply not a big enough premium on policy evaluation and correction by feedback mechanisms.

Only if datums (standards, targets, thresholds) stay relatively stable, commensurate with the relatively-ponderous time-scale-of-change in bureaucratic operations, can policy norms control be perfected. If you wish to explore the possibilities of improving policy evaluation, select a policy field which does not alter much in decades (i.e. is of little 'political' interest). (Alternatively, select your polity carefully. The author is writing these words in Singapore, where both sides of this assertion can be demonstrated: the regime of Mr Lee Kuan Yew has been in continuous power for nearly two decades, and policy evaluation mechanisms *are* being installed, in several fields of policy, and taken into account in policy-making.)

In most democratic regimes, control in the public sector in respect of substantive policy objectives is demonstrably weak. It is not so weak that policy 'at the delivery end' is random, or bears no relation at all to the policy norm set at the centre; but as many implementation and evaluation studies have shown, the 'disturbances' or variegating factors are *usually* so numerous and so strong that the assumptions of policy-makers about what they are achieving, or might reasonably hope to achieve, are impugned. In response to this situation, a whole school of public policy theory has emerged holding that 'top/down control' is undesirable *in principle,* and that 'bottom/up' policy-making is superior both in effectiveness and in participation-value.

However, two other kinds of response are possible. First, it is by no means the case that improvement of policy evaluation and correction in the public sector of a democratic polity is not *technically* feasible. Control is weak partly because the will is weak, partly because several possible methods are not used. Relatively simple planning, forecasting and monitoring techniques (sometimes called 'feed-forward control') can help out of all proportion to the costs involved. The shortcomings of PPBS (Planning, Programing, Budgeting system), PAR (Programme Analysis and Review) and output budgeting generally have all been well publicised; but it has not been demonstrated that these and similar techniques are intrinsically faulty, simply that they are foolishly applied, and/or strongly resisted by those whose interests are affected, and/or overwhelmed by external factors like inflation or world recession.

Second: policy objectives are not the only kind of objectives pursued in the public sector. As already suggested, public sector organizations are expected to be accountable not only for their substantive outputs and results, but also for their procedures, the manner in which they carry out tasks, and their internal processes. Thus, public servants are supposed to operate with economy in the use of resources, and not profligately; with attentiveness and accuracy, not indifference or carelessness; with dispatch and promptness, with no undue delay or laxity; with integrity and probity, without malversation or corruption; with fairness and equity towards all, without favouritism, nepotism or partiality; according to the law of the land, and without exceeding their powers; withal, preserving the amenities of the environment and the well-being of the population; and so on. Civil servants themselves will expect all to be done consonant with maintenance of staff morale, agreements on conditions of work, and the other concomitants of 'being a good employer'.

These 'procedural' objectives are no more mutually-compatible than are policy objectives. For example, economy will often be in competition with accuracy and promptness, equity can be at the expense of amenity, and so on. And it is frequently alleged that staff interests take precedence over all others.

But one feature of 'procedural' norms is a gain, in comparison with policy objectives. By and large, they operate across the whole of the public sector (probity and promptness are as relevant in education as in roads or railways). Secondly, they are relatively constant over time. One might predict, therefore, that evaluation mechanisms for procedural norms will, on average, be more highly developed than those for substantive policy objectives; and so, of course, it proves.

It is a commonplace observation that a government official may take foolish and ineffective decisions all his life without retribution, provided he takes them *properly,* according to due form. In a typical advanced industrial society, controls against *"détournement de pouvoir"*, malversation, nepotism, injury to amenity and other such norms are quite potent. Perhaps it is not quite so demonstrably the case as regards controls against waste, indifference, carelessness, delay, and certain other procedural standards; they exist, but control is often not tight – information is lacking or late, and for sanctions one may have a choice between the trivial and the draconian. And sometimes the will is weak, too.

Judging from this evidence, our societies place a higher premium on control over malversation and favouritism, over excessive use of legal powers, and nowadays over certain environmental matters, than they do over the mundane malpractices of work routine. But undoubtedly the tightest controls of all are maintained over work *conditions* and other domestic matters within the bureaucracy – for fairly obvious reasons.

Checking procedures is clearly something that the variety available in the controlling mechanisms can more nearly cope with than it can the control of substantive policy. It is theoretically more likely, and is indeed empirically more clearly demonstrated, that control in the public sector, *de facto,* is predominantly *procedural* control, control over process.

We earlier eschewed on theoretical as well as practical grounds any notion of *centralised* control, all threads being somehow gathered in one place. So we expect to find procedural control dispersed, carried out by different mechanisms acting more or less independently, in isolation from each other. And so it proves. Indeed, the separateness of the mechanisms is adduced as an additional safeguard.

All modern public sectors (indeed, all ancient ones too) instal a Finance Ministry or Treasury, with contacts or even members located in each other department of government, and looser ties with public sector agencies outside the central government sphere. In each ministry, local authority, or other public sector organisation there is a financial hierarchy, whether or not directly linked with the central Treasury or Finance Ministry, with duties of preparing budgets and monitoring expenditure. This constitutes a control network permeating the whole of the public sector, staffed by people who have had similar training and share a common outlook and motivation, concerned with (and to a great extent *only* with) 'the financial aspects' of all policy questions: provision of finance, economy in the use of financial resources, and accounting for disbursements.

There is also, often, a *distinct* network concerned purely with the accuracy and probity of financial transactions, the 'audit function'. There may be a separate mechanism for 'efficiency audit', or the control of work methods and cost effectiveness, either internal, or by occasional central 'fishing expeditions', or by employing outside consultants.

That is one easily recognisable control mechanism, or group of mechanisms, in the financial resources field. It is usual to find a similar network, of central agency and parallel hierarchies in other ministries and authorities, concerned with the staffing function; often embracing controls over recruiting and training, promotions, retirements and pensions, as well as economy in the use of manpower. Listing the actual distinct datums being maintained in such a network would be a lengthy exercise.

There is commonly a distinct network of legally-qualified persons, for litigation, but also for interpretation of powers, advice on legislative drafting and the like. The collection and collation of government statistics can provide another, slenderer network; and there may be institutionalised control of 'information' or propaganda and public relations, with outposts in larger departments.

Such departments, especially the finance and staffing ministries, are sometimes called 'the central departments', or 'control ministries', precisely because they stand somewhat apart from the other ministries (the 'spending' or 'service' ministries), and have functions that relate to the governing of the public sector itself, rather than the governing of the people.

Control over a second set of procedural norms, in particular over constitutionality and use of powers, and over intrusion into the amenity of the environment, tends to be via a different kind of mechanism: that is, a separate system of courts, tribunals, and public enquiries, not intrinsically ministerial or departmental.

Control over a third set of procedural norms, including those earlier named attentiveness, accuracy, promptness, and to a degree equity, tends to be via a third kind of mechanism, not this time a separate network, but combining external monitoring by disadvantaged citizens and aggrieved clients with sanctions operated through the normal 'line of command' or substantive hierarchy (that dealing with the production of whatever good or service is being provided); that is to say, one's ordinary superiors.

Over a fourth set of procedural norms, those concerned with staff conditions of work and allied matters, control is via an internal mechanism combining monitoring by civil service trade unions and other representative associations of norms set through regular industrial negotiating machinery, or joint consultative bodies, with enforcement through the substantive hierarchy.

Thus we can envisage four different kinds of control mechanism, cutting across substantive policy or production control, each monitoring departure from a large number of procedural standards, all operating simultaneously and largely independently, penetrating the decision-making processes of departments at all levels, every standard at every decisionpoint subject to negative-feedback or other regulatory cycles; somewhat as, in the human organism, action is mediated by the interaction of the circulatory system, the respiratory system, the sensory nervous systems and the muscle motor systems – each of a different *kind*, acting independently by quite different methods, but with concerted outcome.

But that imagery, though apt in some ways, would by no means portray the crucial significance of these crosscutting control networks in public sector organisations, or their importance to overall control of the public sector as a whole. For we have not yet taken into the picture the fact that many of these procedural norms are mutually contradictory, that tight control over one must therefore mean slacker control over some others, and that these priorities are established not centrally but at the point of decision. When we now take these factors into account, we shall perhaps have the clue to how the public sector can be 'steered' and 'tuned' – and it is *not* by the familiar 'negative-feedback' mode.

16.5 The Dynamics of Control in the Public Sector

At the focus of these interpenetrating networks of procedural control is the individual decision-maker – which is to say, virtually every official of any conse-quence in any of the governmental bureaucracies, since it is of the nature of bureaucracy that competence to take decisions is widely distributed, according to the level of generality or specificity of the question (a matter of relative 'horizons', the more exalted officials having wider 'fields of vision'), and according to the expertise required, or the custodianship of the necessary specialised knowledge (on the 'horizontal' plane). If each bureaucracy is to be subject to the several kinds of control mechanism just described, then they must simultaneously and continuously be brought to bear on each decision-maker. In some way, each official's decision environment must contain not only the substantive or 'production' problems and pressures (including problems and pressures from within his or her own command, as well as from lateral colleagues and from superiors), in response to which the decision-maker seeks to come to appropriate decisions; but also the awareness of all these watchdogs and single-minded maximisers in the control branches – finance and accounts, audit, staffing, work methods, law; superiors with the routine procedural goals of accuracy, attentiveness, promptness and so on in mind; the external (sometimes self-appointed) custodians of the environment, or of particu-lar ideological territories; the 'shop stewards' or joint consultative machinery in respect of working conditions; and so on. It is a formidable array of 'ghosts' that looks over the decision-maker's shoulder; and yet it is a quite familiar model of the situation.

Carl Friedrich's 'doctrine of anticipated reactions' (Friedrich 1937: 16) long ago pointed to the conclusion that the great bulk of 'obedience' in an organisation could not be accounted for by responses to specific instructions, but came from a subordinate's awareness of what the superior would want of him in a situation of choice. In an important sense, the superior is only there to reinforce these expectations from time to time, to renew them, guide and change them as circumstances demand. We are adding to this understanding the appreciation that the 'superior' should not be regarded as single, but multiple: alternatively, that the decision-maker is at the centre (from his/her point of view) of a *network* of constraints, not a simple hierarchy of superior/subordinate. So it may be that the 'doctrine of anticipated reactions' will cope with this extension of the model, the control and monitoring agencies simply putting flesh on the 'ghosts' from time to time, reinforcing anticipations, specifying particular standards on request, altering requirements now and again.

But: in any actual decision situation, at least two (and probably many more) of the standards thus personified by these ghosts (if that be possible) will be mutually incompatible. The decision-maker may quite correctly anticipate reactions, and yet will not have a solution to his/her problem. The more the official moves to maintain one standard, the greater the discrepancy on another – the concept of *dilemma* (Hood 1976: 163). A dilemma has only two 'horns' (either/or). If we conceive here of a situation where seven, eight, or seventy-eight standards are to be simultaneously kept to, and several or even *most* of them are mutually incompatible, we get the concept of *polylemma*.

Some commentators on the parallel situation in an industrial manufacturing setting describe it thus:

"Multi-system control implies that there are a number of control criteria which people in an organisation are trying to satisfy at one and the same time. A particular task has to be completed by a predetermined date to satisfy the production controller; it may involve using certain methods to satisfy the work study man; and a limited number of people to satisfy the personnel manager; it has to comply with certain quality standards to satisfy the inspector; it should not involve more than certain costs, to satisfy the cost accountant; and so on. With these control mechanisms operating in parallel, and the different goals not always being compatible with each other, the supervisor's main task is to violate each of the standards as infrequently as possible." (Reeves and Woodward, in Woodward 1970: 51).

But whatever priorities the bureaucratic decision-makers establish in a particular situation, and however they arrive at their judgement, the ghosts are still there. High superiors cannot relieve decision-makers of *polylemma* by establishing over-all priorities among procedural goals, for the simple reason that *all* of them (legality, economy, equity, probity and the rest) are official objectives, none being publicly sacrificeable. A case might be made for sacrificing one in the interest of another in a specific situation, but not *generally*. Decision-makers must therefore be prepared to answer for their choice of priorities among equally-ranked goals: ludicrous though it is, they must show cause for not giving *all* objectives highest priority all the time.

The resultant state of things is a formally-intolerable one where decision-makers are notionally expected to come up to the mark in several contradictory ways at once; but where correction is latent, potential, rather than applied. Polylemma is admissible as a 'fact of life' for the decision-maker. But it is more than that: it plays a crucial role in *control*. For these latent corrections, these potential demands for explanations, create a fabric of tensions, a structure of stresses, a complex of opposed leverages, which provides the mechanism both for 'steering the system' and for 'tuning' the controls to the required strength. In fact, the one turns out to be a concomitant of the other.

Let us examine this within the individual bureaucracy, before we turn to the larger system, the public sector as a whole. Since all of the mutually-incompatible standards are equally approved but their detector and effector mechanisms are held in suspense, superiors can bring *any* of them into play in a particular situation, or for a period; stressing *economy,* perhaps, when under that pressure themselves; emphasising the need for *promptness* another time; or even calling for innovation and fresh thinking on yet another occasion. By these interventions they bias the decision-maker's polylemma, by as it were putting more flesh on one ghost than on his chief rival, or by weakening one of the mutually-opposed watchdogs and encouraging its opponents. None of the goals is abandoned entirely; no one can go too far or too fast in the now-favoured direction without provoking sufficient outcry from controllers whose standards are being outraged to inhibit the excess. But some controls are *de facto* being tightened, some relaxed. Each of the values being maintained in the system will remain within a certain range; but the particular configuration of values, the distribution of the variables, can be chosen within those ranges. And the method of 'steering' is by 'tuning' the relative strength of opposing control mechanisms.

The 'tuning' is itself done by perfectly ordinary and unremarkable means in the individual bureaucracy – which in its *structural* aspects (for present purposes, its hiring-and-firing, promotion, and posting operations) is hierarchical and authoritarian (and accepted as 'under discipline') to a remarkable degree. The latent power to ask for explanations of particular decisions from a subordinate can be activated, and displeasure conspicuously indicated, or approval made very clear. Signals can be hoisted by who gets promoted and posted, and where expansion and contraction is planned. In numerous such ways the climate of expectations can be altered, anticipated reactions recalibrated, priorities biased.

Or, more overtly (and perhaps 'for public consumption' as much as for the organisation itself), superiors can mount a campaign for 'tightening up' on some factor which can be alleged to be getting 'too slack' (without acknowledging that this means tolerating a compensatory shortfall in the relevant counteracting factors). A loophole that has been around for years without anything being done about it will suddenly be closed, with publicity. One bad case of corruption or the like can lead to several new rules being devised, new procedural controls installed, or even a new control agency or watchdog being created.

In such ways are more-or-less-temporary priorities among procedural objectives superimposed upon basic polylemma – until the next 'crisis' or scandal or political necessity brings forth a different set of priorities. But the capacity to do this derives from the ubiquity of polylemma itself, and from another factor, which supplies the effector power: many bureaucrats and groups within the structure are pursuing *official* (and not merely personal) objectives which are mutually incompatible. Each therefore has an official interest in maximising that objective – it is their *duty* to do so; and equally, in trying to prevent that interest being infringed by the maximising of some other official group. This is what produces the field of mutually-opposed tensions which presents itself to individual decision-makers as polylemma.

It is, of course, the wider social system, or culture, which determines what the cross-cutting maximisers are maximising, and the relative intensity with which each operates. Religious or ideological orthodoxy may be significant in some societies, social etiquette in others, 'participation' values in yet others. The control system as such is 'neutral': it is operated in the interests of those who operate it, and set its values; but 'control' itself is simply 'government', no more politically loaded, or directive, than is the idea of government as such. (Of course, there are those who do object to the idea of government.)

Considering now the public sector as a whole, rather than the individual bureaucracy: the basic pattern is the same, of a system comprising self-controlling subsystems. But two things generally differ. First, the boundaries of the system and the strength of the bonds linking the elements of the public sector are less marked than in the individual organisation; and second, the imagery of 'network' rather than 'hierarchy' dominates. Or it may not be realistic to postulate a single 'public sector system' at all; there may be notable differences in the strength of interorganisational links between one subset of organisations (say, Ministries) and other subsets (say, non-ministerial bodies, and public enterprises); with a stronger sense of hierarchical relationship between the first subset and the system-as-a-whole than between the other subsets and the system (i.e. the Government can 'command' the Ministries, or bring them to account, more easily than it can the other public sector bodies).

Lacking hierarchical discipline, central controllers have to look for other ways of mediating the 'biasing' of the tensions between opposing maximisers which represents their steering capacity. Different cultures choose a different mix of methods. One country may rely heavily on a class-based 'clubland' or old-boy-network of peer-group pressures to conform, sanctioned by powers of appointment to governing boards. Another may employ the 'double government' devices of Stalin's USSR (Bendix 1964: 166), where the party nexus exploited mutual incompatibility of objectives. Reigns of terror throughout history have rested on uncertainty about what conduct will be approved.

A third country may extend the mutual-check mechanisms implicit in the single organisation by creating specific counter-organisations for certain agencies, 'adversarial bureaucracy', to recreate tensions at the higher level; another option is to create across-sector control agencies with specific briefs covering not just ministries but all public organisations (applied in some corruption-conscious regimes). Yet another mode is to mimic a 'market' situation as far as is feasible, within the public sector. Lastly, a society may turn to its law courts and treat these as a sector-wide control system, heavily favouring constitutionality and legality against other objectives, with the judges coming under varying degrees of influence from ruling powers. A society may thus determine that its elected Government will *not* be able to steer the control mechanism, or part of it; relieving them of responsibility accordingly.

Since this chapter cannot become a treatise on comparative government, perhaps it will be enough to say that, probably, all advanced industrial countries can be found employing all these methods (and perhaps others) in different combinations. To the cyberneticist they are alternative empirical embodiments of the basic control mode, which employs 'manipulable polylemma', or in Hood's (Ch. 36) terminology, 'interpolable balance'.

To the cyberneticist the analysis is of considerable theoretical interest. The basic state of equilibrium maintained by simultaneously imposing a large number of mutually-incompatible criteria is *not homoeostasis*, the restoration of former equilibrium after disturbance; there is no designated or designed (or 'natural') state of affairs to which the system returns. It is not to be explained, either, by the theory of self-regulating machines or servomechanisms as such, monitoring departures from set standards and taking corrective action – although an extension of that model would accommodate much of the situation: we should imagine the correcting devices of one servomechanism being interfered with by the correcting devices of another, so that neither can correct their respective deviations, and yet neither gives up the attempt, and takes full advantage of any relaxing by the other.

The stability of polylemma seems to derive from the same source as the immobility of Buraam's ass. Equal and opposite attractions (or repulsions) can freeze movement. Either attraction is subject to temporary external inhibition, destabilising the equilibrium. If the inhibition is sustained or permanent, that equilibrium is destroyed; if shortlived, there may be movement, which is arrested when the equilibrium is restored by the removal of the external disturbance. Perhaps the simplest physical model of pair-equilibrium interpolation, or 'manipulable dilemma', is that kind of desk lamp which is mounted on two sets of counteracting springs. Inhibit one of the sets by pushing the shade into a new position, and the *other* set will help your intention; take away your fingers, and the lamp will stay where you put it.

But several other models meet the specification: for instance, the relationship of predator and prey in an ecological system, and a great many of the internal controls in the human organism, already discussed. The motive power of bodily movement is mediated by sets of muscles with contrary functions, very similar to the desk lamp. The water content of the human body is maintained within the quite narrow thresholds which life requires not by homoeostasis, or return to a set quantity, but by a never-ending struggle between two maximisers. The sugar balance, the acidity/alkalinity levels, and a large number of other quantities are maintained by similar processes; as are the operations of the two distinct networks of the autonomic nervous system – one constantly trying to speed things up, the other to slow things down; as also the heart-beat, the breathing rate, and other life-rhythms. It is Nature's typical control mechanism.

Polylemma implies multiple interacting dilemmas or pair-equilibria, and the human body models this also: many of the balances being maintained are interrelated. And the body will also model the 'manipulability', or interpolation, in so far as the organism, by forming intention, can for example engineer movement, steering the positioning of its parts in infinite variety and great precision within their inherent limitations; or, nowadays, in so far as we can, by taking drugs, inhibit one side or the other of some malfunctioning balance in an area inaccessible to intention more directly.

It is a little odd that this ubiquitous natural mode of control has received so little general attention (as compared with controls of the direct sort, or with self-regulating machines) that there is no readily-recognisable name for it, save *balance*: and that not only has the connotation of dilemma only, rather than polylemma, but does not convey the important additional concept of manipulability, or controlled disturbance of balance. Labels like 'selective inhibition of opposed maximisers', while descriptive, are not handy. Hence the resort to coinage: 'interpolable balance', 'manipulable polylemma'.

The fundamental explanation of guidance, evaluation and control in the public sector which this analysis offers, therefore, is as follows. The public sector, *because* 'public', has to be all things to all men. Since this is impossible, and yet must be so, scores of tensions are set up between these contradictory objectives. Largely unconsciously, though occasionally deliberately, those with responsibility for the operation of the whole system, or for any part of it, utilise these tensions by adding their weight one way or the other, as if at the fulcrum of a seesaw (again, 'dilemma' only). Since the ponderosity of bureaucracy is great, such shifts act so slowly that they are normally reversible; that is, the inherent instability of a system of balancing forces can be itself arrested by shifting weight back again – if the built-in cross-checks of polylemma, multiple interacting pair-equilibria, have not already operated to do so. Thus stability of a sort is maintained: a state of equilibrium that cannot be described as 'stable equilibrium'as conventionally understood (e.g. a ball on a concave surface); and yet is not either wholly unstable (e.g. a ball on a convex surface) or indifferent (e.g. a ball on a plane surface, which will run freely in any lateral direction). What we need, apparently, is an image of a ball on a convex surface, held at the apex by elastic threads from many points, and capable also of taking up a position on the surface that is *not* the apex, without immediately falling off; an equilibrium of tensions, inherently unstable, made stable by the very number of ways in which it is potentially unstable.

A model like this implies that political intervention from a higher level of system can in the short term achieve considerable displacements in governing values without completely destabilising the system, and even relatively quickly, if will is strong (e.g. by purges or other draconian measures); but that if political pressure in particular directions is then removed, the system will revert, not to the former state (except coincidentally), but to whatever accommodation of the forces then current is achievable, subject to purely bureaucratic manipulation or interpolation. In the longer term, social and cultural change can alter governing values by allowing some procedural objectives to fall into desuetude, while new ones are introduced. No doubt, too, that sudden and drastic change in governing values *can* be imposed, if sanctions are strong enough; but that *will* destabilise the system, and time will be needed to re-establish control over e.g. the mundane procedural objectives such as economy, promptness, accuracy and so on.

In all this, we are speaking of *procedural* objectives, sector-wide and relatively enduring. Precisely because control over *substantive* or policy-field objectives is comparatively weak, it is relatively easy for political intervention to alter substantive objectives drastically and quickly – this is politics' function. That does not imply that the actual changes made in government operations, or changes made 'in the world', will correspond to what is intended any more than they did under the previous policies; indeed, it is obvious that they are less likely to do so, unless again accompanied by sanctions so strong as to destabilise the system. Most bureaucratic sectors in liberal-democratic countries can cope easily with alternating policy-field programmes deriving from the alternation of parties in office, without any destabilisation, i.e. within the range of interpolation. One can conceive of a 'superflexible' bureaucratic system, incorporating such a set of values and governed with such looseness of control (wide tolerances) that its ability to absorb and respond to political intervention, or other disturbance from outside, was considerably greater than that of another bureaucratic system with less flexibility; the second would have tighter control but less survival-value. But there is no end to such speculations.

References

Ashby, W. R. (1952): *Design for a Brain*. London: Chapman and Hall.

Ashby, W. R. (1956): *An Introduction to Cybernetics*. London: Chapman and Hall.

Beer, S. (1959): *Cybernetics and Management*. London: English Universities Press.

Beer, S. (1966): *Decision and Control*. London: John Wiley.

Beer, S. (1972): *Brain of the Firm: The Managerial Cybernetics of Organization*. London: Allen Lane, Penguin Press.

Bendix, R. (1964): *Nation-building and Citizenship*. New York: John Wiley.

Bennett, S. (1979): *A History of Control Engineering 1800–1930*. Stevenage: Peter Peregrinus. (For Institute of Electrical Engineers.)

Burns, T. and G. M. Stalker (1961): *The Management of Innovation*. London: Tavistock.

Cannon, W. B. (1932): *The Wisdom of the Body*. New York: W. W. Norton.

Cyert, R. M., and J. G. March (1963): *The Behavioral Theory of the Firm*. Englewood Cliffs, N. J.: Prentice-Hall.

Deutsch, K. W. (1963): *The Nerves of Government*. New York: Free Press.

Dunsire, A. (1978): *Implementation in a Bureaucracy*. Oxford; New York: M. Robertson; St Martin's Press.

Dunsire, A. (1978): *Control in a Bureaucracy*. Oxford; New York: M. Robertson; St Martin's Press.

Friedrich, C. J. (1937): *Constitutional Government and Politics*. New York: Harper and Brothers.

Hood, C. C. (1976): *The Limits of Administration*. London: John Wiley.

Kalmus, H. (ed.) (1967): *Regulation and Control in Living Systems*. London: John Wiley.

Kaufman, H. (1973): *Administrative Feedback*. Washington, D. C.: The Brookings Institution.

Kennedy, D. (ed.) (1967): *From Cell to Organism: Readings from Scientific American*. San Francisco: W. H. Freeman.

Kuhn, A. (1974): *The Logic of Social Systems*. San Francisco: Jossey-Bass.

Lindblom, C. E. (1965): *The Intelligence of Democracy: Decision Making Through Mutual Adjustment*. New York: Free Press.

March, J. G., and H. A. Simon (1958): *Organizations*. New York: John Wiley.

Maxwell, J. C. (1868): "On governors." *Proceedings of the Royal Society 1867/68* 16: 270–283; and in Bellman, R., and R. Kalaba (eds.), *Mathematical Trends in Control Theory*, 3–17. New York: Dover (1964).

Mayr, O. (1971): *The Origins of Feedback Control*. Cambridge, Mass.: MIT Press.

Meyer, P. (1973): *Systemic Aspects of Public Administration*. Copenhagen: G. E. C. Gad.

Nathan, P. (1969): *The Nervous System*. Harmondsworth: Penguin.

Rose, R., and B. G. Peters (1978): *Can Government go Bankrupt?* New York: Basic Books.

Shannon, C. E., and W. Weaver (1949): *The Mathematical Theory of Communication*. Urbana, Ill.: Univ. of Illinois Press.

Stanley-Jones, D., and K. Stanley-Jones (1960): *The Kybernetics of Natural Systems*. London: Pergamon Press.

Steinbruner, J. D. (1976): *The Cybernetic Theory of Decision*. Princeton, N. J.: Princeton Univ. Press.

Wiener, N. (1948): *Cybernetics: Control and Communication in the Animal and the Machine*. New York: John Wiley.

Wiener, N. (1950): *The Human Use of Human Beings*. New York: Houghton Mifflin.

Woodward, J. (ed.) (1970): *Industrial Organization: Behaviour and Control*. London: Oxford Univ. Press.

Part 4
Comparing Institutional Modes
of Coordination

17. Markets and Hierarchies

Hans-Günter Krüsselberg

Abstract

The starting-point of this chapter is a warning not to regard all so-called mechanisms of coordination as configurations of similar value structure or of equal objectives – only because ultimately all of them intend to create order (17.1). This has the – often neglected – consequence that they cannot be thought of as working without friction side by side, according to some blue-print (which takes them to be complements). Not to notice this fact may result – as the German tradition of "Ordnungstheorie" rightly stresses – in a state of "point-by-point interventionism" ("punktueller Interventionismus"), a state where contradictory ideas and measures are applied in different parts of the economy and society causing tensions, crisis, and social damage within the system. In order to avoid this the Social Sciences have to develop clear-cut pictures of the crucial differences between order-creating systems. That is the message of this chapter. Thus, in 17.2 the Comparative Systems Analysis is applied to the concepts of markets and hierarchies in order to determine their general traits in relation to the functioning of economic systems. This is an inevitable task as well as that to analyze how different order-creating systems might work in combination.

Subchapter 17.3 tries to get on this way in referring to one outstanding case, to "Hierarchical Organizations in Market Economies". It stresses the human action perspective and its institutional aspects, the process dimension and the importance of specific assets' choices for strategic behavior (against misguiding mechanistic analogies in socio-economic theory). Its result is, nevertheless, that an old message of economics is confirmed: Firms, hierarchial organizations, are compatible with market coordination; *but efficiency solutions depend on highly competitive dynamic markets guarded by a well-established hierarchy of law.*

17.1 Order-Creating Systems – An Introductory Statement

This paper is an endeavor to consider the role of two order-creating systems, usually called coordination mechanisms, in the setting of modern industrial societies, especially the place of hierarchies within markets. We regard it to be part of a series of studies which are designed to improve the explanatory power of theoretical institutionalism, a possibility now being discussed in an affirmative way.

Nearly every social scientist seems to be sure that he or she knows what coordination in society is. But looking at concrete applications of the term one detects a strange vagueness of terminology: Coordination (as well as institution) – I fear – has become an "umbrella" word indicating no more than the presence of some variant of order whatever it may be. In the course of time too many meanings have been attached to the term which has created confusion since a single concept is now used in contradictory ways.

I think that at least four of them have to be distinguished very precisely: market coordination, subordination of activities according to some central plan, hierarchical organization and mutual consistency (of measures) in policy implementation.

Market Coordination

In the beginning (of the Social Sciences) coordination was said to be the result of a functioning "spontaneous order". Thus it was related to the general theory of the market. Some scholars still argue that "the possibility of men living together in peace and to their mutual advantage *without having to agree on common concrete aims,* and bound only by abstract rules of conduct" must be called perhaps the greatest discovery mankind ever made (Hayek 1976: 136, italics H. G. K.). That spontaneous orders are *"co*-ordinated" means there exist series of continuous activities in which people *(getting together)* bargain out of a *common* interest for *mutual* advantage in order to reach *joint* agreements. Coordination is achieved by permanent contracting and re-contracting based on choices constrained only by law.

In this sense the existence of markets for very many goods and services minimizes the necessity to attain public consensus *in detail.* The concept of a market economy (as a spontaneous order) thus presupposes a consensus to tolerate a high degree of heterogeneity: e.g. in skills, personal (occupational and shopping) engagement, in tastes and preferences (as revealed in the offering and accepting prices). It relies on a general consensus on a vast variety of personal accommodations to individual patterns of life. It presumes an agreement to accept singularity up to a point where special demands can be satisfied as soon as demand prices motivate potential suppliers to offer the required goods or services whatever they be and however many of them are asked for. This is basic to a process which informs potential participants about their special wealth-creating capacities (in all their diversity). Presupposed are neither *given ends* nor *given means.* Only an evolutionary process is at stake, reflecting constant changes of demand and supply. Its success (or failure) depends on its chance to deliver valued artifacts which – competing with each other – might be substitutes (or supplements) according to the choice of agreeing people. Measurement of this type of success seems to be a difficult matter.

The experience with market processes posed a totally new task for social and economic theory: to explain the emergence of a system of economic order *through* spontaneously evolving, mutually advantageous processes of reaching agreements between *independent* decision-makers, trying nothing more than to further their own objectives. Order here means a highly productive compatibility of multiple single plans, and the existence of a coherent pattern of the *whole* economic process (Eucken 1950: 88, 125, 141) without any necessity to rely on order-creating decisions of a supreme authority.

Thus, one suitable starting-point for a discussion about markets and hierarchies in the context of the public sector may be the opening statement of Cairncross about "The Market and the State" (1976: 113): "Modern economics can be said to have begun with the discovery of the market . . . the state, by contrast, needed no such discovery". – Let us immediately add that for the purpose of this book we should prefer to say: It is hierarchy which needed no such discovery.

Hierarchy Number I: Subordination of Activities to Some Central Plan

It was Hicks who in his "Theory of Economic History" (1969: 24, 22) explicitly stressed: that the hierarchical organization of economic activities is "the principal background against which the evolution of the market is to be studied". And he hastens to add that although the relevant forms of societies differ, there is "one strictly economic thing" which all of them have in common. "Their central economic nexus is revenue, the tax, or tribute, or land rent . . . to some recognized authority . . . The nearer approach to centralization and command, the more important the revenue will potentially become."

This is especially the case in centrally planned systems where the centralization of decision-making in a political agency is the dominant principle. Their (ambitious) aim is to *organize* economic activity in a "one-firm state", and their crucial regulating instrument is the budget. By centralizing the acquisition of the economic "surplus" of the country those states achieve a maximization of revenue according to their computations in order to *subordinate* all economic activity to the objectives of some central plan. The organizational task is, then, the allocation of given (planned) means to given (planned) ends.

Nevertheless most authors in the area of the theory of socialist economies call this a "coordination" by a central plan, though some make a qualification: "It is a basic principle of socialist planning to guarantee the internal consistency of programs" (Lange 1968: 158–159). The necessity, however, to achieve an *internal consistency of programs* demands that single, *mutually dependent* decisions are *"harmonized"* in order to fulfill the plan. Combined with a central choice of priorities one expects to get an *optimal program* (Brus 1971: 193, 106). The measure of success (or failure) is to state conformity to the plan, a seemingly easy procedure. Much of the fascination which the idea of planning apparently holds for certain scientists and politicians may be explained by this fact.

The far-reaching distinctions between "planning" in market systems and the central planning of whole economic systems are discussed in 17.2, in the section about a comparative systems analysis of centralized and decentralized economies. We think there is no possibility of bridging *the basic gap between hierarchical overall planning*, i.e.: planning the processes for a whole (economic) system as a comprehensive solution of the problem of economic order *and the coordination problem of large numbers of autonomous decision-makers*. The fact that hierarchy is a structural element of organizations cannot be used to deny distinctions between systems which rely on authority centers for whole systems, and other systems that rely upon widely dispersed knowledge coordinated by prices.

The idea of conceiving "optimal programs" by planning seems, however, to be so attractive to scientists that Dahl and Lindblom (1953: 38–39, 26) conclude: "rationality requires *coordination,* when several actions are required to attain goals. . . . The more rational action is also the more efficient action." They are cautious enough to add that "to agree whether one action is more rational than another, observers must agree on the goals involved, their assumptions about reality, and the consequence for goal achievement of certain alternative courses of action given the assumed reality." Thus, their concept refers to given ends-given means relationships, even though they concede that sometimes the ("closed model") language may become "slippery and cumbersome".

This is a reason for taking care and registering the fact that given ends-given means models imply very much: a high degree of consensus about ends and relevant means, and (an almost) complete knowledge of future states of affairs; furthermore, it is necessary to ascertain what kind of consensus is meant and between whom, and whose knowledge is concerned. Slippery language like: "there are 'degrees' of planning", suggesting that planning may be weak, strong, or of middle range (see the critical remarks of Shackle 1968: 241) can only be avoided, if it is concretely known to whom those who plan are responsible, what and for whom they plan, and what degree of coerciveness is involved, and for whom. Only "impartial" observers can generally judge the previously promised rationality and efficiency, and they will have to recognize that given ends-given means concepts always require some hierarchical relationships: at least people who have to imagine and to decide what may be assumed to be given in the plan. But there will also be people who possess rights of disposal over means, who possess the power to allocate resources according to their plans. A combined planning and allocating power creates high degrees of autonomy. – This should be sufficient to propose the following: In order to attain efficiency, the processes of hierarchical planning of the allocation of resources must be submitted to external control.

Hierarchy Number II: Hierarchical Organizations within Markets

If it is true that – historically – hierarchy preceded the market, it is also true that it survived the emergence of markets and is still with us. Of course, essential transformations of it have occurred, some of them associated with a change in the character of the State, others with the development of the modern firm, which will be the subject of later sections of this chapter. How a private enterprise system (of firms) and modern government, *both acting through hierarchical organizations,* work (and function) in market economies will thus have to be discussed in this volume (and partly in this chapter).

Organizations have to be central agents although they are instruments of human design, human artifacts, in which human capital ("know-how"), monetary and real capital are used as assets in order to produce some (planned) output. If *comparative systems analysis* (see 17.2) falls short of a highly sophisticated theory of industrial and governmental organization, it remains a *theory without structure* and will fail to produce a theory of action. Thus, we shall try to sketch some of those elements of the structure of industrial market systems we consider to be important.

Why firms emerge as hierarchical organizations in markets, to what extent they are acting or re-acting units, how they are guided and controlled by external factors, how their activities are coordinated in processes of adaptive efficiency, that is the theme of subchapter 17.3. We shall see that markets and firms (as efficient hierarchical organizations) are complementary.

But as the activities of firms, markets and governments are interrelated, markets and governments in Western societies are complementary to one another, too. No modern analysis will therefore regard the state and the market as "all-or-none" alternatives though the scientific and political problems of today are those of a world showing trends toward greater intervention in economies, relying primarily on the market. Thus, efforts toward carving out a place for market forces in economies, which pride themselves on the achievements of government plannings, efforts which argue about "the only sensible question worth pursuing", that of the division of labor between the state and market (Cairncross 1976: 114), may be rewarding.

Up to now it is still a special trait of Western industrial economies that chains of actions are coordinated by explicit law (rules) and that market evaluations are basic to *all* evaluative activities in the economic field. And the framework for monetary flows which unite decisions being made in numerous types of organization which themselves are hierarchical subsystems of society does rely on markets guided by law as well.

The Need for Mutual Consistency in Policy Implementation

It is crucial for modern industrial systems, as we said before, that there exists a multitude of rather independent decision-makers. This is true also for the governmental subsector of society (a fact discussed in this volume in some of the *following* chapters). Thus "coordination" is thought to be necessary in the field of public policy, too. Therefore, it is important that we are warned about the "fallacy" that economic and governmental policy be regarded as organized in a uniform and central manner. In reality, economic policy is rightly said to be the result of (often) a (very) large number of decision-makers. The conclusion is: the more decentralization of policy is to be found, and the more administrative units will intervene on different levels in the economy and society, the greater will be the urgency of a "coordination" of those policies which will increase enormously (Tuchtfeldt 1983: 107, 109).

Again we encounter the term "coordination" (in a fourth sense), but what is meant is a need to maintain mutual consistency in policy implementation, of principles of actions and acting units legitimized to administer other people's actions within a policy concept that accords with the declarations of the government.

A Conclusion

In Western societies – there is a need for four order-creating systems: for *coordination, subordination, organization and consistency in policy*.

We note that there are very complicated and rather different procedures at stake, and the literature abounds in conflicting points of view. Let us try, then, to indicate some of these conflicting points of view while avoiding those pitfalls which threaten further confusion. This may turn out to be successful, if we refrain from "theorizing in social vacua", remembering the theoretical message of Adam Smith: Economics as a Social Science should seek to discover that societal framework which favors that activation of human and material resources which increases human welfare. Then its task would be "to recommend those institutions which tend to promote the public welfare. . . . The perfection of police, the extension of trade and manufactures, are noble and magnificent objects . . . we are interested in whatever can tend to advance them . . . All constitutions of government, however, are valued only in proportion as they tend to promote the happiness of those who live under them" (Smith 1976: 185).

This comprehensive description by Smith seems to me to be not too remote from this book's definition of the "Public Sector". And his method , i.e. the comparison of institutional arrangements in order to select superior variations (Krüsselberg 1984d: 201–204), corresponds to the ambitions of the present authors.

We believe that much misunderstanding about "coordination" has arisen out of an insufficient analysis of different logics of choice that apply to centralized planning systems, and systems where planning authority is exercised by a multitude of autonomous actors. Thus, we shall start our consideration of Markets and Hierarchies by analyzing their content in the context of economic order.

17.2 Markets and Hierarchies in the Context of Economic Order

Comparative Systems Analysis of Centralized and Decentralized Economies

In economics the core of the market-hierarchy debates is nearly always related to the context: "establishing the economic order as a scientific problem". Hensel justifies the participation of a specialized science like economics in this Social Science debate by stating that economic analysis deals with a "Leitproblem", a central problem of society – the procurement of material means of existence under conditions of scarcity. Economizing appears to be a procedure to further ultimate goals of shaping human life: it is thus intermediary and provisional. It asks for solutions which recognize "the integrative nature of (human) existence". It takes into account that the phenomena of social life are elements in a pattern of comprehensive interdependence. Thus, the alleviation of scarcity (Knappheitsminderung) depends upon a solution of the problem of economic order (Hensel 1965: 181–192; Lowe 1965: 12; Hensel 1974: 15; 1977).

In order to find a solution, we have according to Hensel, "at the same time", to focus on three main problems of all economic activity which are basic to any economic order: the planning problem, the problem of economic performance (evaluation) and the problem of (motivations and) interests. His answer, which may be taken as *a reference system for further analysis*, contains the following arguments:

Economic activity always requires planning; all economies must necessarily be "planned economies". Scarce resources and labor must be arranged, calculated, evaluated and suitably combined – the use of the scarce resources must be planned. Moreover, the use of each commodity must be planned separately in relation to the consumption side of economic relationships. Thus, at least as many individual plans have to be worked out as there are kinds of goods and different uses of goods. In a modern economy there are several million goods and uses of goods. At the same time, many thousand millions of technically possible relationships are conceivable between the millions of different kinds of goods and between the means –

ends relationships. If the scarce means are not to be misdirected and wasted, those must be sought out from among the thousands of millions of technically feasible combinations that are economically useful, and all economic actions and processes must be coordinated as carefully as possible. In planning terms this means that the millions of individual plans must be coordinated to form an overall economic system of plans. In any economic order however organized an overall coordinated economic system of plans must thus be established. Hence the basic *economic* quality of overall economic orders is grounded upon planning systems.

But individual plans – and, along with them, an overall coordinated economic system of plans – can come into being only, if there exist common indicators for planning and coordinating decisions so that the degrees of scarcity of the different kinds of goods in the economy as a whole can be recognized. Therefore there can be as many overall economic planning systems as there are kinds of evaluation which indicate degrees of scarcity.

Degrees of scarcity in an economy may be indicated either by

(a) prices which are established in the *markets* or
(b) quantitative balances resulting from the difference between the *available* and the *required* quantity of the same commodity as computed by *(a planning) authority*.

The level (and structure) of (relative) prices that may be the result of bidding and bargaining procedures (between organizations) as well as of arbitration or of everyday evaluations by autonomous traders (individuals, firms, associations) indicates the degree of scarcity within a market context. Balancing, the primary method of central planning, is used to identify the level of the *missing quantity* as an indicator of shortage. In the *one* case, the authoritative agencies for planning decisions are *all* potential economic actors of a community (public bodies included), whereas in the *other* case, they are only planning bureaus and/or political leaders. In a micro- and macro-perspective two systems, i.e. "civil planning" and "State planning" of the overall process, can be and have been distinguished. Nevertheless, there is a great diversity of orders actually in existence: Economic actions have many constituent elements, and they may be induced by many different motivations and drives. At any time they also depend upon physical, psychological or notional stimuli, and upon controls and implied coercion. It is the basic message of the German "Ordnungstheorie" that these stimuli and controls must be established primarily by the institutional framework of a "Wirtschaftsordnung", an economic order. This requires discovering what kinds of stimuli to action and what forms of control or coercion into action may be based upon economic orders, and how effective they are in relating special interests of individuals, groups, organizations etc. to general interests.

It is assumed by Eucken (1952) and Hensel: With a "civil" ("staats-bürgerliche") planning of the overall process, combined with a system of fundamental rights, private property, competition in the markets, balanced money supply and adequate liability, actions and interests are controlled in two ways – first, in so far as legal prescriptions are concerned, by the state. Secondly, interests are controlled by the interests themselves, apart from the state, i.e. with regard to self-control out of self-interest: control by competitors and, finally, the control of the interests by all consumers will be in operation. Interests become – and this is a very remarkable phenomenon – a regulating force which operates far more widely, more diversely, more rapidly and, above all, much more powerfully than any state controls can.

A social market economy – i.e. an economy based on civil planning and shaped according to social principles – will and *can only be founded* upon these controls of *interests by interests.*

In the case of State planning of the economic process, with state ownership of the means of production, the problem of the control of interests – which here is widespread, too, of course – is a *completely different one.* The centralization of economic planning, away from the members of society to a central planning authority, makes the political leadership the sole legal entity for the formation of economic intent. Although in a central planning system of this kind the intentions and interests of the political leadership are asserted, their realization is dependent upon the people involved in the economic process, and the interests of these have to be stimulated and controlled. The difficulties that this causes for the political leadership are immense and circumscribed by the problems of fulfilling plans, lowering costs, utilizing reserves, realizing profits in excess of planned figures, encouraging technical progress, and so on. The whole of life is and must be economized, the reason being that *State planning and State ownership* of the means of production create interests that are directly opposed to a positive solution of the performance problem. Above all, in an economic order of this kind, the controlling of interests by interests themselves is hardly possible, or possible only with little effect, and so *interests have to be subjected to an all-embracing system of state control and state coercion regarding actions.* In so far as economic efficiency depends upon the efficiency of the controlling system, countries with economic orders involving central planning and State ownership are undoubtedly at a disadvantage.

If by a free society we understand a system in which the formation of the life patterns of its members rests on their own responsibility, this is economically possible only, if the economic process is directed according to the goals of these private patterns of life. But this is so only where the economic overall process is determined by civil planning so that the system of civil planning is the economic condition of "Ordnungstheorie" for a free society.

If, on the other hand, the planning of the economic process of a whole society is centralized by a state planning authority, the formation of intent in all other spheres of life, too, must be centralized and given political character owing to the above-mentioned relationship between the economy and the patterns of life. All formation of intent then proceeds from the political leadership and must proceed from it alone. The totalitarian state is based, economically and in terms of Ordnungstheorie, upon the system of state planning.

This theory is a very clear presentation of crucial differences between a hierarchically organized centralized planning of the whole economic process and processes initiated by autonomous planning of multiple units relying on their special knowledge and expectations. It is a system of thought which is as good as invulnerable against assumptions about convergence. I think that this contribution of the German "Ordnungstheorie" to the discussion of order-creating systems is a fundamental one, even if it did not develop that sophisticated theory of industrial and governmental organization which we need. And many arguments raised against it are refutable.

One objection goes that, in reality, in every economic system prices can be "found" which might be used as planning indicators. But how? Years ago Hensel, the first scholar in the world who developed an *empirically realizable* scheme of central planning as a scientifically closed argument (using the above-mentioned method of quantitative balances), demonstrated in accordance with real procedures in socialist economies that here the (central) planning process is finished long before the authorities fix the prices (Hensel 1954: 187–188).

This is how quantitative (or material) balancing uses monetary expressions of value: they are derived from planning in natural quantities and have to fulfill an accounting function. When experts of the GDR planning staff guess that the necessary number of economic relations to be planned is between two and twenty billion of which five thousand are recognized in the plan of 1982, it is easy to see that there is only a small chance to realize the required conformity of material and financial planning (Knauff 1983: 140–151, 180–185).

Another point of criticism is a pretended deficit in Eucken's and Hensel's institutional analysis. We agree with this, if it means that there is no clear-cut distinction between micro-, meso- and macro-analysis (see Kaufmann 1982: 256–258), no special theory of the firm and the interorganizational relationships in a system where firms of different size interact (see Krüsselberg 1965). Nevertheless, one finds studies for example on labor relations, legal systems and other institutional problems.

Unquestionably Eucken and Hensel used theoretical tools that try to avoid "the point of remaining wholly silent on the identity of the choosing agent." They have "bothered with the difficult issue of identifying properly the entity for whom the defined economic problem exists" (Buchanan 1979: 21). It can be shown that this type of theory corresponds to a "logic of disposal over assets" (Krüsselberg 1980: 29–30; 1984c: 53–58) by agents whose position statement (or action potential) can be recorded in personal or organizational balance sheets. Transactions with that number of assets and liabilities (united in a balance) whose value is accounted for by the socially acknowledged degree of scarcity are basic to economic activity in general, and the "transactions potential", the possibility to change the present form, volume and value of assets, is partly regulated by law, a central instrument of an economic order. But – according to Hensel – this is not sufficient to realize an "economic order of free people". As economic (and social) orders are ethical, legal and "morphological" (institutionalized) systems, it is equally necessary to stress the importance of "ethical spontaneity" (the responsibility for other people), and of those institutional arrangements that rely on controls of interests by interests in mutually advantageous agreements (Hensel 1977: 163, 170).[1]

As far as this *institutional* level is concerned there are at least three building blocks of Western industrial societies which check the appropriateness of Hensel's concept of order. Three institutions can be enumerated which separate market economies from centralized planning systems: 1) the labor market, 2) the capital market, and 3) the governmental financial system which in Western democracies may be called a "revenue (or even a tax) market", not only because of its very strong linkage with the security market (government debts), but also because of the yearly tax bargaining which is enacted between government and the public, and mediated by opposing political parties.

This is the empirical background of Hensel's distinction which is more than a dichotomy. Numerous field studies, especially those undertaken by the Marburg School of Research in Comparative Economic Systems, are based on his categories (see e.g. Cassel and Thieme 1976; Schüller et al. 1983; Hamel 1983; Krüsselberg 1984a; Gutmann 1983).

But there is another subject which has to be discussed in the market-hierarchy debate: some developments within economic theory which are mainly concerned with planning within market economies. This will be the next step in our inquiry.

National Planning

Another crucial factor for arguments raised in the modern debate about markets and hierarchies is an aspect of economic theory which – I think – has so far been neglected: the (neoclassical) concept of equilibrium which favors a logic of planning (re. the following cf. Krüsselberg 1969: 13–26). Equilibrium is regarded here generally as the best position. This theory suggests that in order to reach the state of equilibrium in perfect markets it suffices to know the conditions which the optimal solution of the problem of a rational economic order must satisfy. Economists like Lange and Taylor (1938) thought that this market equilibrium is discovered by trial and error. They concluded that based on the parametric function of prices it would, or at least could, work much better in a planned economy than in a competitive market. There the Central Planning Board was supposed to have a much wider knowledge of what is going on in the whole economic system than any private entrepreneur could ever have. And Massé (1962), pondering over the problem of optimal investment decisions in market economics, summarized that the Planning Commission, in the future, was going to be a substitute for the market.

This is a far-reaching statement: it proposes a central plan to be a solution superior to market coordination because of its higher level of relevant knowledge – even in Western industrial societies. That is, of course, a fascinating idea for ambitious social engineers (who tend to "think in terms of defined objectives and of specific means", neglecting the task of " searching among available alternatives for some optimal solution, and the study of the behavior of persons as they carry out such search" – cf. Buchanan 1979: 128). Thus, the implication of the ideas discussed above must be made clear.

This perspective rests on a "logic of choice" which deals "almost entirely with choices between certainties, largely ignoring all uncertainty and attitudes of uncertainty". In addition it draws a clear "frontier-line between the duties of the expert and the functions of the political authority responsible for policy". The prerogative of citizens and statesmen is assumed to be valuations and different objectives whereas the technical expert has to pronounce on predictions of the consequences of different policies and the suitable means to realize preferences (Hutchison 1964: 17–19). – Of course, such a model of applying given means to given ends is highly convenient to attain a planning answer.

Planners are politicians in power, top administrators in planning institutions.

Political leadership decides on general guide-lines. The task of government and administrative staff is to transform those guide-lines into operative objectives and ascertain their inner compatibility. Planning units have to design the plans, and to choose the procedures and means thought capable of achieving these objectives in the most appropriate manner; and the members of those planning units are experts, professionals. This is the pattern of analysis which concentrates on the technical aspects of planning, the organizational set-up, and on forecasting and data collection methods. This concept of hierarchical planning relies on foresight, and instructions in a vertical structure of organizations. It is the *prototype of a perfect hierarchy*.[2]

It is a reliable result of research in comparative economic systems that this concept of central planning is inadequate because plan implementation contains elements of conflict, inefficiency and waste. Examples of waste in plan implementation are slack plans, wasteful criteria, instability of plans, rationing of producer goods, sellers' markets, misallocating prices, personal consumption problems, difficulties with innovation and diffusion of new techniques, very long construction and running-in periods for new plants, and bureaucratization.

Scholars who compare this planning approach with reality in Western democracies detect a "complete denial of any ideological element". They quote a sentence of Dahl and Lindblom (1953: 6): "In economic life the possibilities for social rational action, for planning, for reform – in short, for solving problems – depend . . . largely upon choice among particular social techniques". This argument must – they suppose – refute the central planning "myth (or the new ideology)". "Myth" means here "that the technical solutions of an economic development plan can be applied equally in a communist, socialist or capitalist system, as well as under different planning systems – comprehensive or partial, compulsory or indicative". Instead they propose as "a point for investigation a different hypothesis: in every instance of national planning, it is necessary to find the belief systems and ideologies behind the social action or technique adopted, as well as to identify the values (or value-images) of the planners themselves" (see Bilski and Galnoor 1980: 91, 79–81, 84–85).

All political belief systems are said to have similar functions: the guidance and justification of organized social action. In this definition the "ideological system" covers the entire system of political belief in two dimensions of argumentation – *fundamental* ideology presents the "great vision", the final goals, and the ways and means for their achievement, *operative* ideology justifies technical prescriptions (as that which is done).

In the practical application this concept reveals itself to be largely true: This is easy to see, when one considers (and analyzes) the most hierarchical way of planning as in the case of the Soviet Union. Here the specific principles are the partyline, a directive character, one-man management, scientific analysis, balance method, the principle of plan fulfilment, the priority principles and the principle of economic accounting (see again especially Hensel 1954, 1965, 1977; Bress and Hensel 1972 or Ellman 1979). Priority as a cornerstone of planning shows its (political) importance in the notion of priority sectors where the whole is dealt with in terms of priorities. By establishing a priority scale, a decision to range one attainment of goals over others will lead to the neglect of non-priority sectors. But it is an open question whether deliberately neglected non-priority sectors do not have a vital role in the functioning of the whole system (Manor 1980: 46–47).

Thus one might take this result of empirical research about planning systems as a truly important message: "the many difficulties encountered in launching a planning process that includes plan preparation, execution and feedback changes (and the few successes in this endeavor) call for attention to the possible influence of the ideological component on every stage of the process and the possibility of using values and ideologies for consensus building or even as a coordination device" (Bilski and Galnoor 1980: 97).

Whenever the debate reaches this stage it is surely *inadequate* to conclude as Conn (1983: 69) does, i.e. that science succeeded in developing an appropriate framework for the study of economic systems. It does *not* suffice to assume, that economic institutions are very complex characterized by aspects referred to as the structure of decision-making, information, motivation (or incentives), and coordination. To consider that a system, described by an *identified specification of these structures*, acts on a *given* environment (population base, resources, preferences, technology etc.) to produce actions which yield outcomes, boils down into (nothing more than a discretionary variant of thinking about systems:) a formal pattern of structure without dynamics, a pattern quitting the crucial elements of an institutional framework and the forces enacting structural changes. It is "theorizing in a social vacuum" (Krüsselberg 1983b: 56–63) without ethical, legal and "morphological" content, without any "great vision" of the direction of potential constitutional reform.

The issue remains that the Comparative Systems Analysis' task is to ask for the best way of "planning our common affairs": Under what conditions e.g. is it "better that the holder of coercive power should confine himself in general to creating conditions under which the knowledge and initiative of individuals are given the best scope so that *they* can plan most successfully;" and when does a rational utilization of our resources require *"central direction and organization of all our activities according to some consciously constructed 'blueprint'"? (Hayek 1978: 234)*

This question can, of course, only be answered if a consensus can be reached about: The Use of Knowledge in Society. This topic is of central concern to Hayek. Thus, it seems useful to consider his arguments. They are central to the market-hierarchy debate.

Decentralized Decision-Making Processes

Like the central planning protagonists Hayek starts his argument with reflections about the equilibrium concept (see Hayek 1949: 33–56, 77–91):

(1) All propositions of equilibrium analysis – he points out – are propositions about the relations between actions. His correct feeling was that what generally is presented as an equilibrated position can only have a *precise* meaning when it is confined to the analysis of the action of a *single* person and *not* to a *group of independent* individuals. Actions of a person, however, can be said to be in equilibrium as far as they can be regarded as part of *one plan*.

(2) Thus, there are decisive differences between a situation in which a *single* person has reached a state of equilibrium and another one in which *several independent* persons have achieved an equilibrated nexus in their interactions.

(3) Originally the concept of equilibrium was meant to describe the existence of some sort of balance between the actions of different individuals, a state of coordination. But what is the content that is crucial for a term *not* related to the *interdependence of the diverse actions of one person?* When may the same term be applied to the problem of consistence between the plans of more persons than one each of whom may have a different perspective of external events and thus divergent expectations? Merely under this aspect: "Since some of the data on which any one person will base his plans will be the expectation that other people will act in a particular way, it is *essential for the compatibility of the different plans* that the plans of the one contain exactly those actions which form the data for the plans of the other" (Hayek 1949: 38).

Hayek demonstrates how by disregarding this fact an inconspicuous change of meaning in the term "datum" has brought confusion into the debate: the decisive difference between the "data" concept in the subjective interpretation of a single mind and a "data" concept suggesting the existence of objective facts being the same for all people is cancelled.

(4) The main problem, however, to be solved is why data in the subjective sense should ever come to correspond to the objective data. The question to be asked is about those conceivable sets of external events which will allow all people to carry out their plans and not cause any disappointments. In a world of non-perfect foresight such states of correspondence can only occur by accident, if there is no *explanation of the way* in which *people learn by experience* and *acquire the knowledge* that drives the coordinating process toward the compatibility of individual plans. Further, it has to be determined what knowledge is relevant to bring about equilibrating activities.

(5) Hayek regards it as a fact of social life that there exists some *division of knowledge.* This – he thinks – has been nearly completely neglected in Social Science explanations. Nevertheless, it might be the "really central problem of economics as a Social Science". If empirical observations demonstrate that, for instance, in reality there is a tendency that prices correspond to costs (which is consistent with a compatibility of plans), coordination is nothing but a consequence of the fundamental fact that people get to know how the different commodities can be obtained and used, and under what conditions they are actually obtained and used. From *dispersed information* a pattern of coordination can emerge, if independently deciding actors are allowed to mediate between uncoordinated single plans by trading economic goods (information and commodities). We repeat (a sentence from the Introduction to this paper): Market coordination implies an agreement to accept singularity and diversity of decisions in a process leading to a state which informs all participants about their special possibilities.

(6) Nevertheless, this state of coordination is under permanent threat; it will normally be exploded by every new human thought, by every new idea to combine available resources; it will be changed by every invention, every innovation. Hayek correctly states: any change in the relevant knowledge of a

person, that is, any change which leads him to alter his plan, *disrupts* the equilibrium relation between his actions taken before and those taken after the change in his knowledge, – and, of course, the equilibrium state of the whole system.

In this world of inevitable change the economic problem of society is that of rapid adaptation to changes "in the particular circumstances of time and place". Only by attaching to each kind of scarce resource (according to its availability at given times and places) a numerical quantity containing in condensed form its value and its significance in view of the whole means-ends structure, ultimate decisions can be left to those people who are familiar with the relevant circumstances, who know the most (which is possible) of relevant changes and of the resources implied. To ensure this, autonomy is needed – it is needed for efficiency –, and a price system as well that can coordinate the separate actions of different people (in the same way as subjective values help the individual to coordinate the parts of his plan).

These arguments – I think – are apt to lead an unprejudiced analyst of economic systems toward the core of the so-called coordination problem. Starting on the assumption that real-world conditions are in accordance with the characteristics of what Shackle named "evolutionary time", Hayek has rejected the idea that much insight into economic life can be gained by solving systems of equations in search for a state of equilibrium. He insists that "nothing is solved when we assume everybody knows everything". The real problem is how it can be brought about "that as much of the available knowledge as possible is used." This raises the special question of coordination in free societies: "Not how we can 'find' the people who know best, but rather what institutional arrangements are necessary in order that the unknown persons who have knowledge suited to a particular task are most likely to be attracted to that task?" (Hayek 1949: 95). Shackle (1965: 194, 188) thought that this line of reasoning brought into light "a central strand in all economic problems and explanations (. . .) the question of what knowledge or *knowledge-substitutes* can be possessed by those who choose one action out of many available".

This state of the debate causes Kirzner (1973: 30 ff.) to propose a mental experiment in order to separate human actions according to their *decision-making* and *economizing* aspects. Though all this may occur in a single mind, this distinction allows us to introduce into the analysis of activities two different perspectives which apply to reality: One looking only toward pure economizers using known possibilities to reach optimized results against the background of assumed dates; the other recurring to an element "not comprehensible with the narrow conceptual limits of economizing behavior", an element he calls entrepreneurship.

In Kirzner's point of view, which should be considered in organizational analysis as well, it is a matter of fact that real life implies a situation of inherent disequilibrium. Always there are to be found opportunities for desirable change generated by the imperfection of knowledge on the part of market participants (for a similar approach see Krüsselberg 1969: Part I). Ignorance is the basis on which absence of coordination can happen: Sellers might have sold for prices lower than the price which may in fact be obtainable; buyers bought for higher prices than necessary, in particular because resources were used which were more costly than other resources capable of yielding comparable commodities.

Absence of coordination causes welfare losses: inefficiency is to be found where unexploited, mutually beneficial exchange opportunities between human beings can be discovered. Each party's situation can be improved by agents competent to unfold those bits of knowledge which enable the reaping of mutual benefits hidden up to now. Kirzner (1973: 216–217) is firmly convinced that "it is possible to evaluate the success of a system of social organization in promoting the coordination of the decisions of its individual members without invoking any notion of social welfare at all." As long as uncoordinated bits of information are scattered throughout the economy "successful coordination of these bits of information cannot fail to produce coordinated activity-exchange benefiting both parties". The dynamics of the market process are evidence for successful entrepreneurship identifying more and more uncoordinated situations, and at the same time spreading the information perceived among ever wider circles of the market.

This crucial element – so Kirzner insists – is nearly always neglected when comparisons are proposed between efficiencies of government and market decision-making in terms of transaction costs: What are the institutional arrangements which ensure that available opportunities are brought to the attention of government decision-makers? What substitutes for the profit incentive are available under government direction in the absence of omniscience – "not merely to spur the exploitation of socially desirable opportunities, but to direct attention to their very existence." What is actually under debate is the issue of potential mobilization of information (Kirzner 1973: 230–231).

Again: not only the generating of a tendency toward equilibrium, but also the discovery and correcting of discordant individual plans and decisions are central tasks of modes of coordination. It is necessary that both be accomplished by human actions – in market systems as well as in organizations surrounded by markets. Optimum conditions cannot be assumed to exist in every day's patterns of action. Thus there is always room for changes in patterns of activities in any given state of affairs. But who knows what is desirable about the direction of change? Kirzner proposes that the elimination of uncoordination be the yardstick for measuring the desirability of such change of patterns. This is a plea for institutional analysis!

If an observer finds that there might be a chance (or an occasion) to overcome a given constellation, he should be urged first to try to answer the question of what might be the reasons for change not having occurred. Every situation in which people are clustered in a certain configuration of relationships seems to present benefits to some and costs to others. But without any signs of a struggle for a re-ordering of relationships are there any sure signals indicating other mutually beneficial pattern of coordination?

I guess the answer of transaction-costs-analysts would be: yes! Transaction costs reducing configurations are the moving force of evolution. – Some other economists (like me) would say: perhaps – or better: it depends on . . . This possibility will thus have to be examined in some detail. Applied to the theory of the firm it is the theme of the following part of this paper.

17.3 Transactions, Firms, and Markets

Coase and the Transaction-Costs Paradigm

Much of the interest in the debate about markets and hierarchies centers – I am sure – around the dictum that "the study of markets and hierarchies expressly attempts to assess the efficiency properties of alternative contracting modes" (Williamson 1975: XI). This interest will, of course, be enhanced, if the field of inquiry is extended to cover all those institutional arrangements which serve to increase efficiency, "whether governmental or voluntary" (North and Thomas 1973: 5–6). And it will reach a climax when, finally, an explanation of the fundamental transformation of the structure of the economy in the past century is attained. What is of concern is "the mix of economic decision-making between households, voluntary organizations, government, and markets", – in a world where markets are not perfectly competitive, where "a large percentage of economic decisions are made outside markets by households, firms, trade unions", and by governments that spend "almost 33 percent of GNP" (North 1978: 964–965).

In order to study the changing constraints under which economic choices are now made, theoretical premises and limitations which call for new tools must be considered (North 1978: 974–975). The study of *transaction costs* seems to offer real advantages in the explanation of changes in economic organization over time. The development of a new set of political controls over *property rights* requires more fundamental theorizing about the nature of governance. Finally, a systematic analysis of reasoning in the *sociology of knowledge* might be essential to further enlightenment of the changing political and judicial relationships that occur over time.

We agree and shall discuss elements of these scientific efforts. What North has in mind, what is at stake is nothing more than a theoretical system suited to explain the macro-organization of the economy *and* public administration, and the choice of relevant forms of organization in both fields (Schenk 1981: 1–4). There is no doubt that in this discussion households, firms, associations, and governments are regarded as "hierarchies".[2] Their existence is the result of micro- and macroforces as well, forces to which they themselves react in order to influence or to structure these forces. The immediate reference systems of this cluster of behavior are the economy, the nation, the society in which these hierarchies exist.

Thus there is certainly a need to discover criteria which allow us to distinguish among hierarchies and to classify them (Schenk 1981: 90). But with regard to the state of theory it is perhaps reasonable to listen to St. N. S. Cheung who warns that the issues surrounding what was initiated by Coase almost a half century ago "are far from resolved" (Cheung 1983: 2).

Usually the publication of Coase's paper on "The Nature of the Firm" (1937, see now 1952: 331–351) is taken as the beginning of the transaction-costs paradigm. Coase's "penetrating insight" (Alchian 1977: 86) was that markets do not operate without cost. His central proposition is that the higher the cost of transacting across markets, the greater will be the comparative advantage of organizing resources within a firm. Thus his basic explanation of the existence of firms is the cost of using markets *to form contracts*. *Ceteris paribus,* this proposition will be neither objectionable nor refutable. But there seems to be some tendency to conclude that this idea will suffice to explain an evolutionary force creating the modern cluster of organizational hierarchies within Western societies – market-directed ones like firms as well as constitutionally founded ones like governmental entities.

How far this claim is justified will be scrutinized in this subchapter. Its type of argument convincingly highlights the dynamics of markets out of which "islands of power" (firms) emerge on efficiency grounds. But it does not explain why governmental agencies are a common characteristic of Western societies.

To understand the issues involved, it is necessary to quote R. H. Coase's initial formulation in his paper on "The Nature of the Firm". There the central thesis was presented, "that differences in the cost of operating institutions (transaction costs) lead to the emergence of a firm to supersede a market" (Cheung 1983: 3). This choice is made to reduce transaction costs. Within firms market transactions are "eliminated, and in place of the complicated market structure with exchange transactions we have the entrepreneur-co-ordinator who directs production" (Coase 1952: 333). The "distinguishing mark of the firm" is said to be "the supersession of the price mechanism", its replacement, though "the amount of 'vertical' integration, involving as it does the supersession of the price mechanism, varies greatly from industry to industry and from firm to firm" (Coase 1952: 333–334).

This is a rather puzzling starting-point for an approach which is meant to explain how hierarchically structured organizations evolve in a market context, out of a network of relative prices and costs. Coase concedes that they are "related" to it. Nevertheless, he "assumes" that they *supersede* the price mechanism. It is necessary, then, to discover the exact nature of this relationship between firms and markets, and he is content to say (with Dobb) that the entrepreneur plans and organizes consciously inside each firm, though in his relations with the rest of the economic world outside his immediate sphere he plays a mainly unconscious role. Thus, coordination is the work of the price mechanism in *one* case, and that of the entrepreneur in the *other*.

In the same paper, however, Coase stresses that there is a problem involved in "discovering what the relevant prices are". That raises a problem: Who can discover it, if not the entrepreneur? And: Who will act within that field, if not the entrepreneur? In the business world it is he who agrees to accept an external price offer for inside use. But also he may not accept, thus confirming or refuting an external estimation of value by an inside computation. This act is a crucial signal to commodities, services, and securities of what they might be worth for interested demanders. This essential feature of a market process to agree or not to agree with the prices (in all levels of economic activity – commodities markets, labor markets, capital markets) that suppliers hope to realize, creates a potential for choice and differential evaluation. This possibility, however, confirms the efficiency of the least-cost way of producing any output. In regard to the functioning of a market economy it is extremely important to see that costs of production are inevitably linked to *market-revealed values;* values which are detected in a competitive "discovery process" (Hayek). Thus firms are the mirror images of knowledge of individual minds about particular productive opportunities dependent on information supplied by the market about which kinds of supply are wanted, and how urgently they are wanted. It is this rule of the game that finally determines

"that whatever is being produced will be produced by those people who can do so more cheaply than (or at least as cheaply as) anybody who does not produce it (and cannot devote his energies to produce something else even more cheaply), and that each product is sold at a price lower than that at which anybody who in fact does not produce it could supply it" (Hayek 1978: 184–185).

This is the criterion for "public interest" in a competitive market system; and it derives from the effect of competitive pressure in reducing profits and increasing consumer surplus. Privately owned firms will survive only, if they can provide services that the public wants at a competitive price. They are "a source of public services" whatever the purposes of the decision-makers might be (Alchian 1977: 137). Markets as institutional arrangements meet the criteria for being public facilities, i.e. they are subject to joint use in the absence of exclusion (Ostrom 1983: 141, 150).

In a free market, prices are regulated by negative feedback. Thus, they are always a consequence of ongoing processes of evaluation and revaluation by suppliers *and* demanders. In this process firms are usually the most active agents. Only in a world where the "parametric function of prices" is used as a dictatorial device to steer production units according to the preferences of a central planning board, can the Coasean "assumption" hold. The same may be theoretically justified by having recourse to an equilibrium state of perfect competition in which prices are "data" (see above). The world of markets, however, is one of active participants who are invisible only to those who create static models.

But the trouble goes further! Some economists take this "steady state" to be one in which "coordination is essential" to the management of the firm. Even the usual vagaries ("all with stochastic regularity"), minor shifts in demand and similar disturbing influences of a transitory nature require – that is the argument – the requesting of the relevant data, the processing of the information supplied, and the providing of the appropriate *instructions and direction* (Williamson 1967: 125). Others (see especially the convincing arguments of Penrose 1980: 16–21, 31–37), however, though granting that the firm is always to be regarded as an administrative organization – rely on the fact that the techniques for decentralizing administrative organization have been developed "to a fine point". Therefore, the central management is "apparently not one of attempting to comprehend and run the entire organization". As soon as an established firm succeeds in creating optimum administrative procedures and framing an optimum set of policies the administrative problem is thought to have been solved. Then, it can operate successfully "without any overt acts of central management at all", i.e. without "coordinating" activities.

The solution of the whole riddle is now coming into sight. There is a crucial distinction to be made: on the one hand we have the problem of "administrative coordination" as "authoritative communication" being related to the *execution* of entrepreneurial ideas and proposals, instructions and directions, and to the *supervision of existing operations*. This needs the presence of managerial services. On the other hand there is some need for market coordination that must rely on entrepreneurial services: It is entrepreneurship which is the connecting link between the administrative organizational system of the firm and its environment (Krüsselberg 1965: 22, 98–112).

Entrepreneurial decisions relate to the introduction and acceptance on behalf of the firm of new ideas with respect to products, locations, changes in technology, acquisition of managerial personnel or capital, and expansion. In a certain way they are "macrodecisions" (Perroux) intended to change the structure of the environment in the interest of the firm; though *in a competitive system of markets* they are the forces which tend to create and establish an efficient system of a dynamic order. To define firms in a market context without reference to the entrepreneurial element in decision-making means to reduce them to an anonymous cell in an overall planned economic system. Only here is the market superseded by hierarchy.

This critique does not imply that there is nothing important in Coase's problem. But: language is treacherous, and misunderstandings may cumulate. Our endeavor has been to state the planning problem in Coase's approach as clearly as possible in order to stress the adequacy of an institutional framework and the necessity to differentiate among "coordination"-mechanisms which are neither on a continuum nor suited to be mixed, i.e. they are mutually exclusive. To get an evaluation system that allows citizens to express their values freely is "almost impossible without a market that registers their choices" (Cairncross 1976: 115). As long as the hierarchy within markets, the firm, allocates its resources within the firm in competition with other firms, it uses the pricing mechanism in a conscious, though autonomous planning. The "Nature of the (Coasean) Firm" is that of a very special institution of the market economy (Krüsselberg 1972: 183–187). I am sure, Coase never intended to deny that.

Thus, ultimately Coase did not ask about the "nature" of the "FIRM" in all different types of economic order; instead he wanted to know "why a firm emerges at all in a specialized *exchange* economy." The main reason for that – he supposes – is that there is "a cost of using the price mechanism". "Organizing" *production* obviously requires the discovery of the relevant prices (costs of information). In addition there are "the costs of negotiating and concluding a separate contract for each *exchange transaction* which takes place on the market". "*Contracts* are *not eliminated* when there is a firm, but they are *greatly reduced*" (Coase 1952: 336; italics by H. G. K.). Every exchange transaction involves a contract. To increase efficiency in production by employing productive resources, contracts must constantly be made, and thus, transaction costs are to be taken into account.

This concept evidently focusses on the costs of operating institutions. Though no consent has been achieved about a standardized terminology, nevertheless, transaction costs are usually described as costs that arise in search of advantageous contractual arrangements for gathering the information needed to concretize their potential benefits and risks in bargaining, value accounting and control (e.g. Schüller 1983: IX).

Time, resources and effort – that is the key message – are used to prepare and perform transactions: Transactions, to recall the argument of Commons (1968: 1–19), occur at points in time. They serve to guide the behavior on the present, but originate in the purposes of people and their plans for the future. They coordinate the future-oriented activities between two or more people at given moments.

Transactions comprise a "meeting of wills", a transfer of goods and/or services, and a determination of prices.

Contracts, Employment, Central Agencies

This is the point where institutions where law come into the analysis (see the subsequent part on the legal regime in market chains of transactions). Thus I welcome Cheung's interpretation of the Coasean approach, published in 1983, which unmistakably describes its market economy basis as "contractual". In his opening remarks Cheung relates Coase's "firm" paper to the choice of contracts which imply transfer of goods and/or services *after* a determination of their prices. He mentions that it was Coase himself who asked Cheung to be aware of the significance and relevance of the *measurement* problem in contractual arrangements: In every transaction some attributes must be measured, whether the deal is between a) an agent and a customer, b) an agent and an input owner, or c) an input owner and a customer.

Market transactions involve products or commodities; the price is paid on the basis of a direct measurement of their consumption or production contribution – cases a) and c). – Factor owners may produce commodities autonomously, guided by the continual reference to the market prices of those outputs which their activity may produce. In such a case product markets and factor markets coincide.

Firm transactions involve the organization of production on the basis of contractual arrangements with the owners of factors of production. But there are costs of measuring and pricing performance in an organizational context where the productive contribution or activity is *not directly* priced. The growth of a firm may thus be viewed as the *replacement of a product market by a factor market,* resulting in a saving in transaction costs. This, however, is Coase's central thesis according to Cheung who admits that "this thesis might not be easy to understand". It must be stressed that the crucial distinction is therefore that between commodities and factor services. Both are acquired by payment, but prices are paid for a definite transfer in the first, and only for a temporary one in the second case which brings in the time component as an additional, separate characteristic: an interplay between law and money, a transfer of use rights against cash. Factor prices are the monetary compensation for a limited set of use rights, a set which essentially contains the right to *direct* the whole of a given productive capacity (of a person or machine etc.) during a concretely fixed time. Not being obliged to pay a price for each singular activity saves transaction costs.

A delimited set of use rights is surrendered in exchange for an income, under a form of contract that binds the input owner to follow directions instead of determining his own course. The message is: Agents *acquiring factor services* from their owners by a promise to pay them, *expecting to receive payments* from their customers for the products they supply have to deal with *two very different sets of measurement*. And: firms are those special agencies that organize activities under contractual arrangements that *differ* from those of ordinary product markets.

The *employment relationship* is the basic element in a firm. Of course, in principle, all contributions of input owners, as well as the services of the coordinator, can be separately priced and sold to customers by directly measuring various attributes of each contribution, if this can be identified as a special product. But even where producers (and middlemen) immediately experience the preferences of a certain clientele, price signals transmitted to the suppliers are only sufficient, if the product demanded is of a measurable quality. The less explicitly the transmitted price indicates consumer preferences or product specifications, the more direction will be needed in the production process.

In production lines where many special components are used, component workers are given specifications (and – perhaps – deadlines for delivery). In cases where models often change significantly between orders or unique products are required, or in cases where relative contributions of workers are difficult to distinguish, piece rate wages will give way because it becomes less costly to measure work contributions by proxies under the arbitration of an agent.

Thus, it can be summarized:

"A proxy such as an hour or a day is easily measured; it does not change as components or contributions do; it can be separately measured for each worker; and it can embrace a host of activities to be performed by each worker, some of them too trivial to be subject to contracting. . . . But a unit of time in itself contributes no productive value; it merely represents what a worker presumably can perform. More stringent monitoring and direction are thus required under a wage contract because the activity itself is not directly priced." (Cheung 1983: 15)

What is essential is this: pricing by measurement of a proxy incurs extra costs of management and increased chance of decision errors; these costs rise as the price signals transmitted contain less information, and this requires greater control over the use rights delegated by input owners. And it is evident that management and decision-error costs are higher in pricing a proxy which presents the benefit of a reduction in the costs of discovering prices! This paradox implies that (strong) tensions are inherent in the organization of firms.

Wherever arrangements favoring proxy-pricing in wage contracts gain importance for the supply of goods and services, *product market transactions* decline; they will partly be superseded by *factor-market contracts*. If Coase's paper relates to the choice of contracts, his argument, that one effective way to reduce the costs of discovering prices is to *substitute* some device other than the direct and separate pricing of activities, is cogent. And Cheung is right, too, in arguing that this substitution may be as simple as the use of the piece-rate contract or as complex as the establishment of a communist regime. But it is also important when Cheung, in his excellent analysis, concludes that "it is *not* quite correct to say that a 'firm' supersedes 'the market'. Rather, one type of contract supersedes another. Coase's main concern is with the type of contract in which an input owner surrenders a delimited set of rights to use his input in exchange for income" (Cheung 1983: 10).

This means: to consider hierarchies implies looking at employment relationships. Where a proxy has to be chosen for measurement instead of a concrete, quantitative result of individual effort, the problem of guidance and control is to be resolved by deciding whether to rely upon management controls in light of the potential transaction costs inherent in alternative arrangements. The conclusion of all this for a theory of efficient (cost-reducing) production can be summarized as follows:

(1) Where cooperation between input owners is necessary, a substitute for their mutual contracting might be an arrangement of that type: Every factor owner bargains with a central agent, not with every potential participant. That central agent employs each owner according to special conditions and sells the final product at his own discretion. This greatly reduces the number of transactions.

(2) A consumer cannot be expected to know the value of each component part of a commodity. For a component which by itself has no readily identifiable value, efficient price bargains will evidently occur between specialists and input owners.

(3) In the case of factor inputs the main item of the required services cannot usually be stated in advance. Thus, the transfer of use rights for a (longer) period against payment for proxies is more efficient than casual short-term employment bargains.

(4) The contribution of each of a number of input owners working in collaboration may not be easily delineated; this requires an *agent* to hire them on a proxy basis instead of paying for the contribution itself.

To avoid these costs means using agents who function as directors, monitors, and entrepreneurs. Thus hierarchies arise out of the endeavor to save the costs of discovering prices and entering into and enforcing contracts. Costs will grow in size as long as the agency costs do not cover savings.

These four general reasons may be taken to be the basic activities of a central agency called a "firm". The following systematic presentation (see Fig. 1) might be useful as a scheme of reference in comparative organizational studies.

I hope that this presentation is clear enough in describing a firm's activities. But it should be seen that it introduces a new accent into the Coase-Cheung argument as contained in the formulation: storage of human and non-human capital which turns the transaction-cost paradigm into a "Vermögen" (a right of disposal) paradigm (Krüsselberg 1980; 1984b, c). Its kernel are assets. What Commons (1968: 12–22, 156–157) and Boulding (1950: 26–45) said about "intangible property" as assets needs to be urgently rediscovered today for organizational analysis: Without a balance sheet, without any visible capital structure, without debts, and with the assumption of a simultaneous purchase of inputs and sale of outputs at constant rates the firm – and every other organization as well – is nothing but a strange bloodless creature (Boulding).

Assets include physical commodities, cash, deposit accounts, contracts, stocks, bonds, even goodwill. It is useful to remember with Commons that modern economic theory began with the commodity as its ultimate scientific unit, i.e. a static point of view, shifted to feeling ("utility"), and then discovered transactions as the basic element of its dynamic problem. Transaction is a "relation between two or more persons looking toward the future". The "purposes of the future" reveal themselves "in rules of conduct governing transactions which give rise to rights, duties, liberties, private property, government, and associations" (Commons 1968: 4–5). Assets mean the expected exchange value of anything in any transactions of modern business that enables one to obtain an income. It is *not* the present ratio-of-exchange which is essential, but the relationship of the present right to a *future* ratio of exchange.

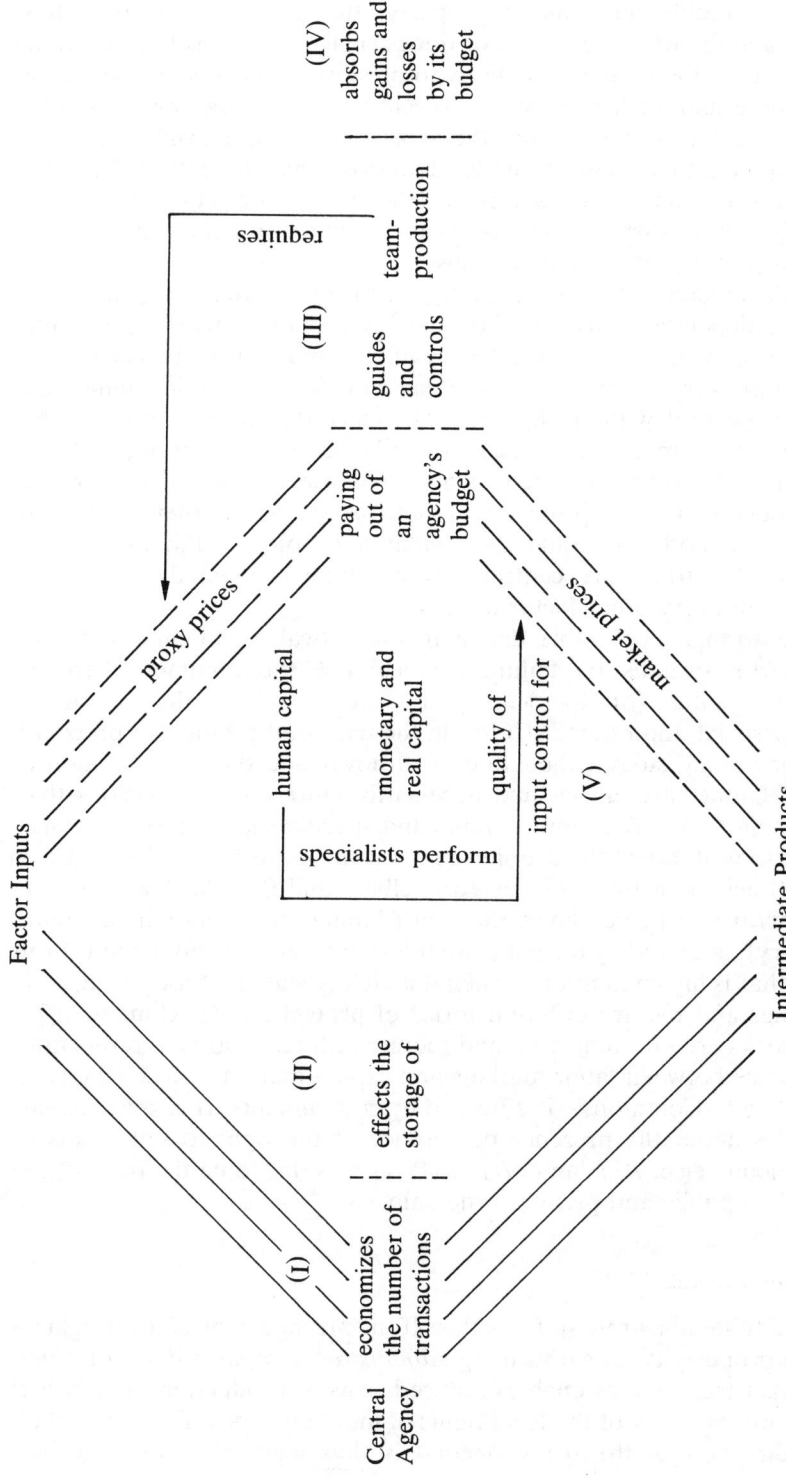

Fig. 1: Basic Activities of a Business Firm (Enterprise)

Thus there is a double meaning of property: things owned (commodities, physical objects) and the exchange value of things (marketable assets). The value of assets depends upon their supposed ability to produce "social-use-values" measured by expectations and realizations on the *commodity and money* markets, all in terms of exchange value or price. But "the substance of capitalism" is that the meaning of property and economic rights of disposal had to extend from the expected use in production and consumption (the static dimension) to expected transactions on the markets where one's assets and liabilities are determined by the ups and downs of prices (the dynamic dimension).

"Capitalism" developed a system of multiple control in order to gain overall efficiency: an interdependent process of controlling economic activities by independent evaluations, in the *commodity, factor, money* and *security* markets. "If it were asked what discovery has most deeply affected the fortunes of the human race it might probably be said with truth – that discovery that a debt is a saleable commodity", to quote Commons (1968: 21, 24). It is the discovery of *negotiability*, the recognition that contracts between owners and users as a set of promises embodied in a document, i.e. promises of one person to another potentially convertable into commodities, could be bought and sold on the *money* and *securities* markets. Contracts are central – where time is implied – in capital markets as well as in every other factor market.

But there is a strange deplorable deficit in theoretical arguments about the functioning of market systems: the failure to reveal a central asymmetry between factor markets as "capital" (or stock) markets and commodity ("flow") markets according to their social importance. "It lies in the nature of productive processes that decisions concerning stocks, their rate of turnover and their composition at different points of time, are always and necessarily more crucial decisions than decisions concerning flows. The more durable and specific capital goods become, the heavier the responsibility of the decision-makers, the more crucial the nature of their decisions" (Lachmann 1979: 75; see Krüsselberg and Brendel 1980: 88–89).

Our firm's activities' scheme shows that both human and non-human capital (real and monetary), acquired by the firm, are relevant stocks for production. Both are concerned – that is my contention – when it is rightly stated: "Stocks and flows are different things and require different forms of protection" (Lachmann 1979: 77). However, stocks are different, too, and require different forms of protection: that is the difference between labor markets and capital markets. Accessibility to markets – according to Commons – is enforced by governments. It is government, too, which decides about the presence or absence of the right to sell shares of ownership to someone else. Alchian (1977: 138) regards this to be the basis of the differences between public and private ownership.

Firms in Dynamic Markets

What I have tried to demonstrate so far is this: If the arrangement of legal rights is that of a private property type, substituting *administrative organizations* or *"hierarchies"* for market transactions enables reduced costs of production to be achieved. The acquisition of a part of the legal rights of input owners in firms (and their use under the direction of the firms' agents) is thus legitimized on efficiency grounds (see also Coase 1968: 435). Can this result be strengthened by looking at other studies of the internal organization type?

Another type of theory can be used here which regards the firm as the central actor in markets (Krüsselberg 1969: 203–213), and explains the development of the large modern corporation in a market context. The basic assumption is that a firm has an incentive to select the resources that are the most valuable for its specialized activities. This fund of specialized, heterogeneous assets is the action potential of the firm: a firm is basically a collection of resources, and of assets (see Penrose 1980: 71–80; Krüsselberg 1965: 82–92). The possibility of using assets changes with changes in knowledge. Thus the significance of resources to a firm and the productive services they can yield are functions of knowledge. And firms are blocks of constantly changing, *complementary* interaction schemes between material and human resources.

Entrepreneurship means the ability to select only those combinations of assets which grant at least constant, but generally increasing returns (Krüsselberg 1967: 284, 290). Entrepreneurship is specialization in expert knowledge concerning market analysis in both factor and product markets. In order to handle uncertainty (which cannot be reduced to zero) contractual arrangements are used to secure relative calculability of those heterogeneous factors at the disposal of firms. These contractual arrangements are the means to absorb the uncertainties coupled with the phenomenon of input, particulary those specific factors which are of strategic value in the supply of the firm (Krüsselberg 1969: 291, 208–213, 284). Firms are specialized market institutions "for collecting, collating and selling input information". They serve as "highly specialized surrogate" markets. To ignore that a shifting of resources within firms *is market competition* implies careless analysis (see Alchian 1977: 105, 241).

Alchian and Demsetz (1972: 777–795) concluded, that on account of informational and other functional inseparabilities, firms are needed to exploit the advantages of team-work. Since in teams, however, the incentive to give the best performance is not always guaranteed, and shirking by consuming leisure on the job is possible, monitors are required to control the team. The problem of economic organization, the economical means of metering productivity and rewards, is that productivity does not automically create its reward. But: the specific system of rewarding which is relied upon stimulates a particular productivity response. If the economic organization meters[3] poorly, with rewards and productivity only loosely correlated, productivity will be smaller; but if the economic organization meters well, productivity will be greater. Team production – like all other production processes – requires an assessment of marginal productivities, if efficient production is to be achieved. Non-separability of the products of several differently owned, joint inputs raises the cost of assessing the marginal productivities of the resources or services of each input owner. Monitoring or metering productivities to match marginal value of productivities with costs of inputs and thereby reduce shirking can – the authors assume – be achieved more economically in a firm (than by across-the-market bilateral negotiations among inputs).

The contractual structure arises as a means of enhancing efficient organization of team production. In particular, the ability to detect shirking among owners of jointly used inputs in team production is enhanced (detection costs are reduced) by this arrangement, and the discipline (by revision of contracts) of input owners is made more economic.

Alchian (1977: 76–77, 108–109) and Demsetz conclude:

"As a consequence of the flow of information to the central party (employer), the firm takes on the characteristic of an efficient market in that information about the productive characteristics of a large set of specific inputs is now more cheaply available. Better recombinations or new uses of resources can be more efficiently ascertained than by the

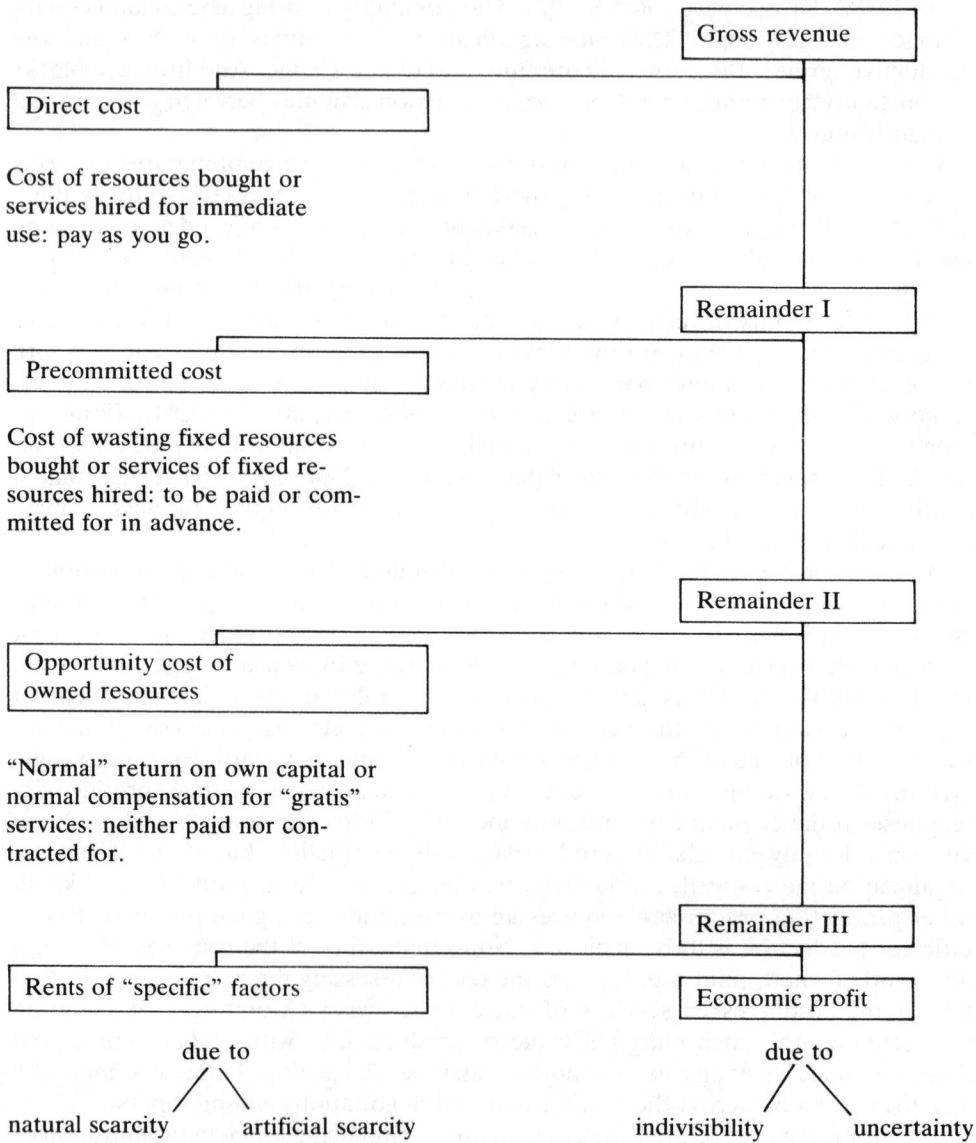

Fig. 2: The Distribution of Total Revenue
       Source: Machlup 1952: 257.

conventional search through the general market. In this sense inputs compete with each other within and via a firm rather than solely across markets as conventionally conceived. Emphasis on *interfirm* competition obscures *intrafirm* competition among inputs. Conceiving competition as the revelation and exchange of knowledge or information about qualities, potential uses of different inputs in different potential applications indicate that the firm is a device for enhancing competition among sets of input resources as well as a device for more efficiently rewarding the inputs."

Efforts to discover variants of the performance of firms in dynamic market processes can rely on an old-fashioned cluster developed in microeconomics. It contributes an useful device to theory to inform the action perspective (or the activities required).

Hidden behind the components of Machlup's (1952) Remainder III in the distribution of total revenue: rents of "specific" factors (which are nothing else than the special inputs selected for special firm's activities), indivisibility and uncertainty (see Figure 2), we discover the basic structure which in a world of change causes firms to become very special agents, very heterogeneous "acting personalities": the necessity to combine specific assets, under the risk of failure, in patterns of complementarity which cannot easily be dissolved in the short run.

This has consequences for the concept of industrial organization. Dynamics in markets leave no room for an "optimum size of the firm" nor for an equilibrium of equal actors. How different firms' positions may arise can easily be made clear if life cycles of production are taken into account.

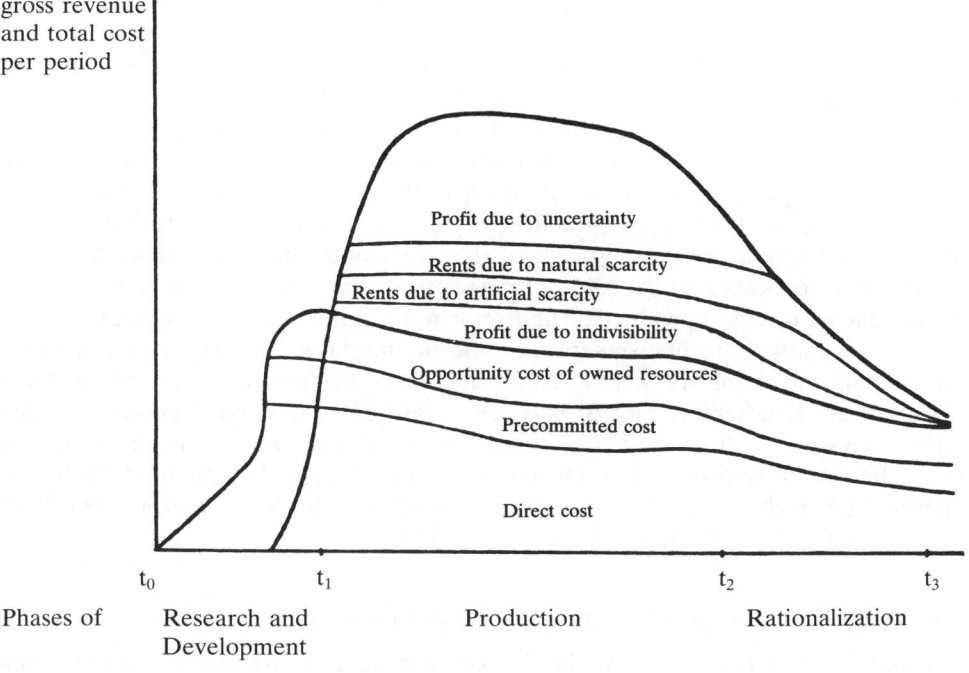

Fig. 3: Life Cycle of Product or Industry
Source: Krüsselberg 1969: 282.

In competitive markets, all firms should anticipate an erosion of profit on their way from t_1 to t_3 (see figure 3). But there will be no uniform decisions to dispense with older product lines and to initiate product innovating activities. Thus, a structure of firms with rather unequal programs (and profit levels) existing side by side will evolve embodying a wide variety of supplied commodities and services – a merit of dynamics in markets.

This insight supports the theoretical messages of J. A. Schumpeter, W. J. Baumol, E. H. Chamberlin that it is the general structure of market arrangements which achieves efficiency in dynamics. Heterogeneity of supply is to be seen as an independent ideal of welfare. Efficiency of market systems means their ability to perform differentiation of functions *and* coordination in the structure of markets.

The competitive process is effective, if guidance and control of processes in the creation and development of products as well as guidance and control of changes in technical procedures result in a maximization of the number of those diverse cost minima that are concretely available in a historical setting (Krüsselberg 1983a: 75–97). The strength of a competitive process is its adaptive efficiency as the result of continuous adaption of activities to new and different initiatives within the whole system of potential actors that influence and transform given structures. Adaptive efficiency, rightly interpreted, implies an urgent regard to allocative, productive, and X-efficiency (Marris and Mueller 1980: 33). Thus, hierarchies cannot supersede markets on efficiency grounds because only evaluations in competitive markets do elucidate what efficiency of a firm's behavior means exactly. This is so when firms face competition in both factor and product markets.

This is more than just a semantic issue: A firm is a market-mediated structure of transactional relationships – as Alchian and Demsetz have stated. I myself agree with what H. Albach has summarized as the central point of view in the development of German business economics (1981: 717–722): The modern firm is *not* primarily the result of market failure. It is an input-output system that forms an *integral* part of the allocative system of the economy. It is a *necessary* institution in society that improves the overall efficiency of the allocative system by overcoming the inadequacies of special factor markets. It is also a searching institution – a place where competition drives a process of discovery and innovation (Hayek) – that *creates* new markets and coordinates mass production and differentiated demand by producing branded products. The firm is not a simple hierarchical input-output system: its control mechanisms include internal markets, but external controls for monitoring the monitors include credit and share markets (see also Krüsselberg 1980: 20–23; Krüsselberg and Brendel 1980: 83–109). These conditions imply that the firm is *not simply an institution that competes with the market* (as an instrument for efficient allocation). "On the contrary: the firm is complementary to the market" (Albach 1981: 721). – And one should add: both are complementary to the public sector, and the public sector to them!

The Legal Regime in Market Chains of Transactions

At that stage of reasoning we should consider Bilski's and Galnoor's important hypothesis (see 17.2: National Planning) that in every instance of national planning (we prefer to say, in every conscious effort to participate in constitutional reform), "it is necessary to find the belief systems and ideologies behind the social action or technique adopted": Political belief systems are thought to guide and justify organized social action. The ideological system covers – by definition – *fundamental* ideology ("the great vision", the final goals and the ways and means for their achievement) and *operative* ideology (the justification of technical prescriptions).

The message of the German *"Ordnungstheorie"* is that it is *the general legal regime which enables decentralized systems of economic decision-making* to select efficient mechanisms. Authors like Miksch and Eucken insist that the modern degree of division of labor and a novel rationalization of all economic events through sophisticated accounting methods led to the emergence of an economic system which can only function in a satisfactory manner within the *framework of a constitution*. According to them a constitution is necessary because there is not only an interdependence of all economic relationships, but an interdependence of each specified economic order with all other potential orders of human life: a pattern of interconnected interrelations between morals, law, economy and polity. Because of this complexity such systems react to all inconsistencies in coordination procedure "with utmost sensitivity" (Eucken 1952: 11).

Authors like Rüstow (1950: 28, 50; 1971: 26) deplore that there is a serious deficiency in many debates about markets which causes trouble: they are sociologically blind (Rüstow 1950: 28, 50–67). They insist that markets function within an ultra-economic legal framework, mainly set by governments. But this framework should be created according to a clear "planning conception", not in uncoordinated ad-hoc steps. Planning social policy is only one important requirement in this context. What is required, too, is a form of government motivated to plan its own activities for longer periods in advance, thereby making government action more predictable (Hayek 1978: 244).

According to Eucken, the primacy of monetary policy, open markets, private property, freedom and enforceability of contracts, liability (responsibility for damages done to others), and constancy of economic policy are the constituting principles of a competitive order – none of which are dispensible. And he hastens to add (in the manuscript of his unfinished book published after his death) that this competitive order is only part of a more comprehensive system of social order (Eucken 1952: 369–371).

Consistent adherence to principles, or at least a search for consistency are thought to be guiding virtues of the constitutional process. Here consideration has to be given to the minimal number of ethical provisions capable of generating consensus among people. Not only Rüstow, but Müller-Armack (1966) as well, register the sociological necessity to frame the market by integrative structures of other kinds in order to create a counterweight against the lack of integrative power of competitive processes. They repeatedly stress the inevitable need to attend to the idea of rights that must be guaranteed to safeguard basic human needs ("vital rights") and to rely on solidarity-establishing institutions *beyond* the market system (see e.g. Rüstow 1950: 50–56).

Of crucial importance to all these conceptual efforts is the unrestrained dictum that as far as the "bonum commune", the public interest, is concerned politics has an essential claim: "more important than the economy are all forms of social integration." Accordingly, one should be willing to make economic sacrifices in order to have an economic system which is preferable because of its ultra-economic benefits. Human values are to be defended, if necessary, by prohibitive laws which are used to safeguard other values (Rüstow 1960: 7–16), employing the "forces of natural liberty" to introduce new social structures which, ethically and politically, are more to the satisfaction of society at large. Both reciprocity and exchange are necessary to the integration of a modern economic system which cannot rely only upon the presumably integrative potential of a competitive order (see also Boulding 1981).

These authors generally insisted that for a systematic analysis of the interrelationships between "historically given" institutions and the economic processes of "every day", especially the analysis of the organizational patterns of firms and of the monetary and financial (sub-)systems is indispensable. Let us follow their advice and see how the organizational patterns of firms are structured by the institutions of money and law intending to create a "good working order". That means it has to be shown how the legal system, nothing but a configuration of working rules of going concerns, invades the economic domain to structure markets via legal institutions. But only by disaggregation can economics demonstrate how far the regulative force of law permeates economic transactions, and why market economies are rightly named contractual economies. We think that, above all, reference to the assets and liabilities in the balance sheet of a firm is apt to concretize the relationships which are at stake.

Assets enlarge, liabilities limit the field of initiatives; they are the basic units of economic activities. They circumscribe "one's faculty, ability, capacity or potency to act". The potential and the possible, however, constitute "in the future – the world of imagination and the world of value – the place where man lives". And: "it is in view of the potential and possible that the act or transaction has its value" (Commons 1968: 78–81).

Thus, I propose to test in institutional studies the following idea: *Assets are the crucial target of institutionalization.* I guess, history taught societies to learn that their (members') decisions concerning stocks, that means: human and real assets, determine their long-run welfare position – because of their expected capacity to create "social-use-values" in the future. This is a matter of "public interest". Accordingly societies will conceive that assets require (different degrees and forms of) protection and control (remember the argument in: Contracts, Employment, Central Agencies – above –). Institutions, "arrangements for interdependent decision making in reciprocal and joint efforts" (Ostrom 1976: 841), are needed. Two of them are the institutions of money and law.

To rationalize the image of the future the institution of money proves to be indispensable. It serves to keep an account of all transactions in their immense variety and multiplicity. It enables every transaction to be related to every other in terms of time and place and expresses values in terms of a common unit of accounting. In market systems, however, the total monetary value of assets is closely linked with contractual claims, with liabilities that are a variant of debt. Both are subject to exchange and transformation. Yet transactions with assets and debts are seldom related to each other, it is only money, the medium of accounting, which is suitable for *recording* them in balances as equivalent. Claims as convertible debt are an institutional innovation of a far-reaching character: in order to expand this area of choice potential actors draw resources from a great many other potential actors. In most cases the traders never meet; the resources are conveyed to them through very different channels and intermediate instances. Manifold chains of transactions and interactions transport resources to those places where they become the most valued assets. In market economies their evaluative counterpart are records in vast nets of intercontractual claims – the financial mirror image of the interconnections of real wealth in the processes of production, distribution and consumption. Assets and liabilities are crucial elements in a multi-dimensional mechanism of mutual control within intermediate marketing processes. That this device creates efficiency in an order that utilizes the separate knowledge of nearly everyone of its members to perform coordination and adaptation in dynamic environments (Krüsselberg 1984b: 5–8; 1984c: 41–44, 53–58), was already understood by Mises in 1932.

To state the controlling power of the markets' evaluations of assets and liabilities does not mean that market controls must be (or are) sufficient. Thus, in real systems, there is no variant of economic activity which is not guided by custom, morals or law. It is a fact surprisingly seldom recognized in economic paradigms that the legal system is *never neutral* with regard to the structures, processes and performances in an economic system (Mishan 1967a; 1967b; Krüsselberg 1973: 444–445; 1976: 168–192; 1977: 299–308).

What can be done to reveal the belief systems' elements in every conscious social action or technique adopted? With the help of Figure 4 (see page 380) we try to pave the way. It gives evidence to the fact that all assets and liabilities are linked with specific markets, all of them embedded in a framework of (often very detailed) legislature: Domestic and foreign markets, commodity and labor markets, various financial markets, and even "tax (and social security) markets"! There is no market of any social importance which is not controlled by strict rules of the game, and it is this fact which attaches social importance to all assets and liabilities as well.

Thus, I propose to regard law as that instrument by which societies "attach" different social ranks to different markets. Law shapes the markets' preconditions and transforms industrial systems into heterogeneous configurations of an assemblage of politico-economic subsystems. All markets are "politicized" by special laws. It is a striking, though rarely reflected trait of Western industrial societies that the degree of regulation and institutionalization increases massively along the way, starting from commodity markets through financial markets to labor markets, and what I have called "tax-markets". There are clear hierarchical patterns, marked by composition and decomposition, in framing markets which reveal the extent to which societies react to what they consider legitimate grievance regarding the markets' performance and, thus, reveal the political content of the economic "constitution" of a society.

Unfortunately, the Social Sciences do not seem to be very conscious of these intricate relationships. Even economists do not care much of the basic truth that law is the stuff upon which the social cost calculus depends. If societies assign civil and personal rights to persons they assign social standing to be taken into account in a social cost calculus. When people cannot be made against their will to do a specific work, when they are free to choose from alternatives, the costs of

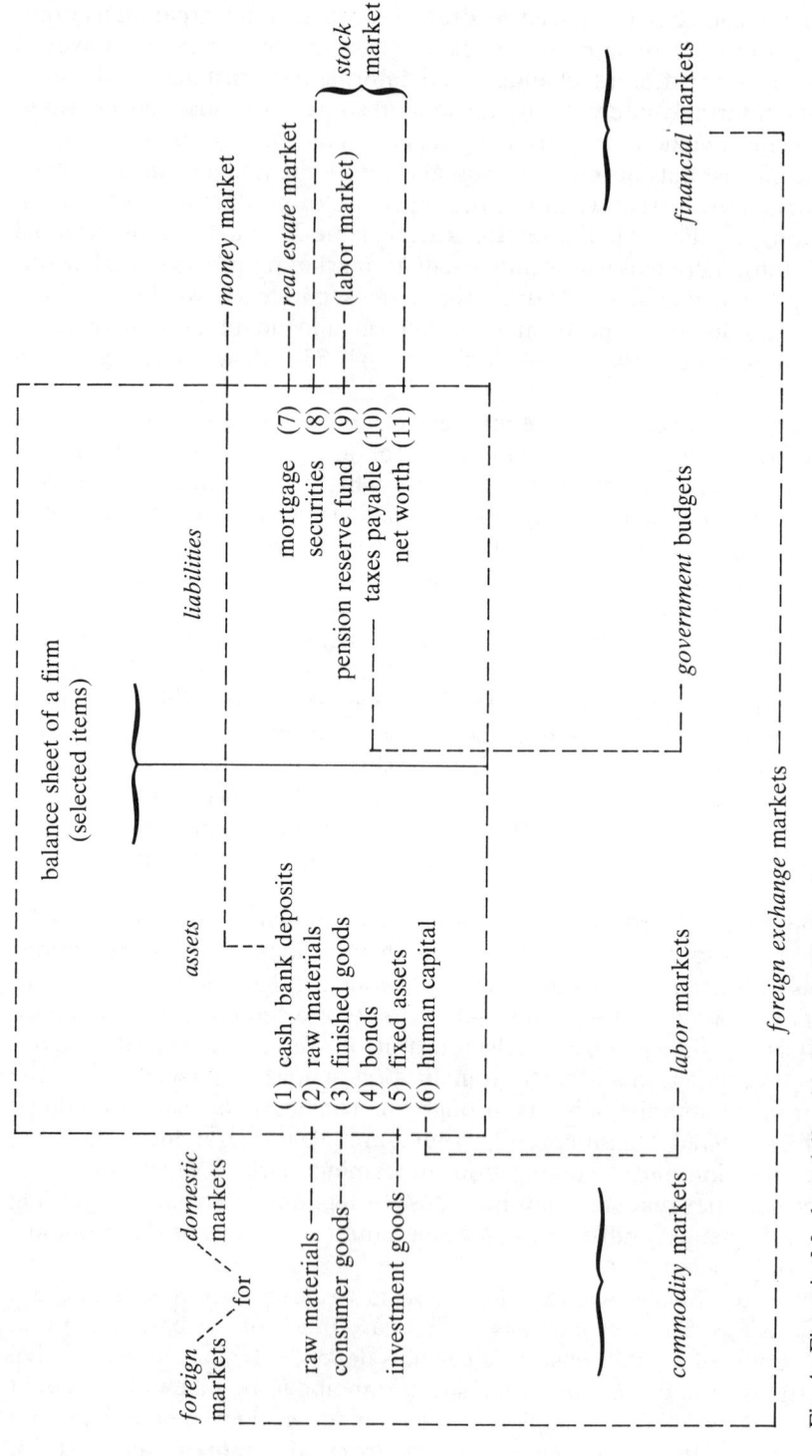

Fig. 4: Firms in Markets (all guided by specific laws)

employment change. To prohibit employment of younger or older people would mean an intervention in the calculation of social cost. The same is the case when legislation forbids the production of certain goods or the use of certain tools. Law is crucial for the determination of incomes – through taxes, subsidies, price regulations and controls, and a huge volume of public expenditure. Law is never neutral in respect of allocation: it determines the pattern of the output set as well as the magnitude of the costs necessary to realize that pattern. Law can never be neutral because it generally has to decide in cases of conflicting interests whether the burden of reaching "optimal" arrangements, i.e. arrangements reached by mutual consent, is to be placed on this or that party.

Law may be permissive in the sense that people can agree to exempt themselves from existing freedoms to act, when they are paid a minimum compensatory sum. Law may be prohibitive; the impact of prohibitive law is that in order to act within the generally-forbidden realm people are forced to bargain (and compensate) hoping to get free, though they may try in vain.

To illustrate the importance of that distinction let us regard the case of "amenity rights", (see Mishan 1969: 255–281; 1967a: 71–73), legal rights freely to enjoy a particular environmental amenity. Without any doubt they are a substantial source of welfare to an individual. But from the point of view of this individual the minimally acceptable compensation for its withdrawal may far exceed the largest sum he can afford to pay in order to retain it. Legislation recognizing

"the citizen's rights to amenity – the right to such once free goods as quiet, fresh air, natural beauty – and putting the burden of compensation squarely on the incidental destroyers of amenity without exception", would – so Mishan – not only "be equitable in itself, it would promote a wider range of choices than is offered under the present dispensation . . . In the absence of comprehensive sanctions against trespass on the citizen's amenity, existing institutions . . . place the burden of reaching agreement on the person or group whose interests have been damaged. . . . Though all existing law acts to prevent calculated blackmail and victimization, there is still this hiatus in the law that enables incidental damage – though frequently severe and lasting damage – to be inflicted on people unless they can find the means to bribe the perpetrators." (Mishan 1967b: 278–279)

This conflict of interests is not symmetric in all relevant respects, and the question of which of the parties ought, if possible, to compensate the other, is to be decided by law, by principles involving ethical standards. Thus, in accordance with the liberal maxim, the freedom of any man to choose what he chooses can be conceded – but with the crucial proviso that his choice does not reduce the freedom of others. A conflict of interests does not arise from reciprocal effects or imply equal culpability. Conflict arises from the damage inflicted by one of the parties on the other, or by both upon each other.[4]

It follows that if the law provides comprehensive safeguards, e.g. of the citizen's rights to certain fundamental amenities, the range of voluntary agreements that are, or might be, entered into within the existing legal framework, will be enlarged. And it is an essential hypothesis of welfare economics that whenever the choice index of a person expands, his welfare will increase. Law decisively shapes the content of that which is implied in the social cost calculus. Thus, there are no unguided markets in Western market economies, and law is an essential medium of social control.

17.4 Some Final Remarks

We see: into each private transaction "a government factor" is introduced as an additional variable. Regulations or laws affect private transactions in order to impact that "volitional" change of ideal states which – according to Boulding – best deserves the name of "policy". The behavior of government in all of its many branches encompasses regulations *and* transactions, both under "policy" – aspects. Its activities must be distinguished to be either related to law or to money; though it is more exact to say: transactions of government (exchanges and transfers) always involve some kind of *redistribution of assets* between government and private persons and organizations (by tax payments, subsidies, pensions sales or purchases), while its laws and regulations set the framework within which private persons and organizations transact.

All this has consequences for the "Ordnungstheorie" as a theory of comparative systems. W. Eucken (1952: 314–324) regarded the activities in the field of Social Policy as complementary to activities in the field of competitive markets: social security is seen side by side with market dynamics, both combined in a comprehensive system of economic *and* social policy. From this perspective the problem of guidance and control of the public sector is a problem of multiple control. In order to reach timely optima between integration and disintegration, security and freedom, order and change (Krüsselberg 1978: 302–308), a complex mechanism of complementary, supplementary and overlapping control must work in a pattern of interdependencies. It is to be hoped that the most crucial of them are described in this volume. But we should remember what Alchian (1977: 149) once uttered: The greater "the extent to which *'society' reduces risks* that must be *individually* borne, and instead has them *borne by society* at large – thus reducing the correlation between choice of action and consequences for people as individuals – the *greater is the extent of public property*. How much this depends upon a choice to socialize certain risks, and how much reflects the voting and decision-making process are questions I cannot answer" (Italics by H. G. K.).

Acknowledgement

I am very grateful for a very active and helpful communication with Elinor and Vincent Ostrom and Franz-Xaver Kaufmann.

Notes

1 I am sure that Hensel would agree, if he was asked whether these "levels" of order-creating systems are indispensable to "fashioning a shared community of understanding" in a "free democratic society" (see e.g. V. Ostrom 1974: 97, 132). He would, I think, say that this is the core of the message about the interdependency of all partial orders.

2 I do not object to Simon's proposal to distinguish different forms of hierarchy. But I hesitate (like Shackle in the case of "degrees of planning") to regard "systems in which there is no relation of subordination among subsystems" as some variant of "hierarchy". – The superior solution by far seems to me to be V. Ostrom's attempt to identify "shared communities of interest" within human orders, his terminology referring to "polycentricity", as well as his emphasis on crucial differences in the composition of social systems

according to their institutional arrangements, and to their capacity to rely on self-organizing structures (Ostrom 1983: 125–127).

3 The authors mention that "meter" means to measure and also to apportion (control), they use "meter" to denote both relating to output.

4 I agree with V. Ostrom's supplementary statement which thus should be added here: "Conflicts may also arise in the tragedies of the commons where limited resources and overuse of resources cause people to impose harmful actions upon each other. The source of the tragedy may not even be initially known until the consequences have reached proportions of serious damage or injury, necessitating modifications in the structure of property rights or institutions for the collective management of the commons. The language at this point needs to be sensitive to conflicts that arise from the tragedy of the commons as against the circumstance where someone accidentally or intentionally harms another" (cf. Ostrom 1974: 56–58, 62, 64).

References

Alchian, A. A., and H. Demsetz (1972): "Production, Information Costs and Economic Organization." *American Economic Review* 62/5: 777–795.

Alchian, A. A. (1977): *Economic Forces at Work*. Indianapolis: Liberty Press.

Albach, H. (1981): "The Nature of the Firm – A Production-Theoretical Viewpoint." *Zeitschrift für die gesamte Staatswissenschaft* 137/4: 717–722.

Bilski, R., and I. Galnoor (1980): "Ideologies and Values in National Planning." In Bilski, R. (ed.), *Can Planning replace Politics? The Israeli Experience*. 77–98. The Hague–Boston–London: Nijhoff.

Boulding, K. E. (1950): *A Reconstruction of Economics*. New York: Wiley. (Repr. 1962. New York: Science Editions).

Boulding, K. E. (1981): *Evolutionary Economics*. Beverly Hills–London: Sage.

Bress, L., and K. P. Hensel (eds.) (1972): *Wirtschaftssysteme des Sozialismus im Experiment. Plan oder Markt*. Frankfurt: Fischer.

Brus, W. (1971): *Funktionsprobleme der sozialistischen Wirtschaft*. Frankfurt: Suhrkamp.

Buchanan, J. M. (1979): *What Should Economists Do?* Indianapolis: Liberty Press.

Cairncross, A. (1976): "The Market and the State." In Wilson, Th., and A. S. Skinner (eds.), *The Market and the State. Essays in Honour of Adam Smith*, 113–134. Oxford: Clarendon Press.

Cassel, D., and H. J. Thieme (eds.) (1976): *Einkommensverteilung im Systemvergleich*. Stuttgart: Fischer.

Cheung, St. N. S. (1983): "The Contractual Nature of the Firm." *Journal of Law and Economics* 26/1: 1–21.

Coase, R. H. (1952): "The Nature of the Firm." In Stigler, G. J., and K. E. Boulding (eds.), *Readings in Price Theory*, 331–351. London: George Allen and Unwin.

Coase, R. H. (1968): "The Problem of Social Cost." In Breit, W., and H. M. Hochman (eds.), *Readings in Microeconomics*, 423–456. New York: Holt, Rinehart and Winston.

Commons, J. R. (1968): *Legal Foundations of Capitalism*. Madison–Milwaukee–London: Univ. of Wisconsin Press.

Conn, D. (1983): "Comparative Economic System Theory: Progress and Prospects." *The Aces Bulletin* 25/2: 61–80.

Dahl, R. A., and Ch. E. Lindblom (1953): *Politics, Economics, and Welfare*. New York–Evanston–London: Harper & Row.

Ellmann, M. (1979): *Socialist Planning*. Cambridge: Cambridge Univ. Press.

Eucken, W. (1950): *Die Grundlagen der Nationalökonomie* (2nd ed.). Berlin–Heidelberg–New York: Springer.

Eucken, W. (1952): *Grundsätze der Wirtschaftspolitik*. Tübingen: Mohr.

Gutmann, G. (1983): *Das Wirtschaftssystem der DDR*. Schriften zum Vergleich von Wirtschaftsordnungen 30. Stuttgart–New York: Fischer.

Hamel, H. (1983): *Bundesrepublik Deutschland – DDR. Die Wirtschaftssysteme* (4th ed.). München: Beck.

Hayek, F. A. von (1949): *Individualism and Economic Order*. London: Routledge & Kegan Paul.

Hayek, F. A. von (1976): *Law, Legislation and Liberty* (Vol. 2: *The Miracle of Social Justice*). London–Henley: Routledge & Kegan Paul.

Hayek, F. A. von (1978): *New Studies in Philosophy, Politics, Economics and the History of Ideas*. London–Henley: Routledge & Kegan Paul.

Hensel, K. P. (1954): *Einführung in die Theorie der Zentralverwaltungswirtschaft*. Stuttgart–New York: Fischer.

Hensel, K. P. (1965): "Establishing the Economic Order as a Scientific Problem." *The German Economic Review* 3/3: 181–192.

Hensel, K. P. (1974): *Grundformen der Wirtschaftsordnung* (2nd ed.). München: Beck.

Hensel, K. P. (1977): *Systemvergleich als Aufgabe*. Schriften zum Vergleich von Wirtschaftsordnungen 26. Stuttgart–New York: Fischer.

Hicks, J. (1969): *A Theory of Economic History*. Oxford: Clarendon Press.

Hutchison, T. W. (1964): *Positive Economics and Policy Objectives*. London: George Allen & Unwin.

Kaufmann, F. X. (1982): "Wirtschaftssoziologie I: Allgemeine." In *Handwörterbuch der Wirtschaftswissenschaft (HdWW)* Vol. IX, 239–267. Stuttgart–New York: Fischer; Tübingen: Mohr; Göttingen–Zürich: Vandenhoeck & Ruprecht.

Kirzner, J. M. (1973): *Competition and Entrepreneurship*. Chicago–London: Univ. of Chicago Press.

Knauff, R. (1983): "Die Funktionsmechanismen der Wirtschaftssysteme." In Hamel, H. (ed.), *Bundesrepublik Deutschland – DDR* (4th ed.), 116–198. München: Beck.

Krüsselberg, H. G. (1965): *Organisationstheorie. Theorie der Unternehmung und Oligopol*. Berlin: Duncker & Humblot.

Krüsselberg, H. G. (1967): "Profite, externe Vorteile und wirtschaftliche Entwicklung." In *Theoretische und institutionelle Grundlagen der Wirtschaftspolitik*. Theodor Wessels zum 65. Geburtstag, 217–297. Berlin: Duncker & Humblot.

Krüsselberg, H. G. (1969): *Marktwirtschaft und ökonomische Theorie*. Freiburg i. Br.: Rombach.

Krüsselberg, H. G. (1972): "Enterprise". In *Marxism, Communism and Western Society. A Comparative Encyclopedia* (Vol. 1), 183–187. Freiburg–Basel–Wien: Herder.

Krüsselberg, H. G. (1973): "Die Wiederentdeckung der Politischen Ökonomie – Betrachtungen zum gegenwärtigen Stand der Diskussion über die Beziehung zwischen Wirtschaft und Gesellschaft." In Albrecht, G. et al. (eds.), *Soziologie. Sprache, Bezug zur Praxis, Verhältnis zu anderen Wissenschaften*, 434–453. Opladen: Westdeutscher Verlag.

Krüsselberg, H. G. (1976): "Wirtschaftswissenschaft und Rechtswissenschaft." In Grimm, D. (ed.), *Rechtswissenschaft und Nachbarwissenschaften* (Vol. 1, 2nd ed.), 168–192. München: Beck.

Krüsselberg, H. G. (1977): "Wissenschaft im Test." In Mück, J. (ed.), *Politische Ökonomie*, 280–320. Frankfurt–New York: Campus.

Krüsselberg, H. G. (1980): "Die vermögenstheoretische Tradition in der Ordnungstheorie." In Krüsselberg, H. G. (ed.), *Vermögen in ordnungstheoretischer und ordnungspolitischer Sicht*, 13–32. Köln: Otto A. Friedrich-Kuratorium.

Krüsselberg, H. G. (1983a): "Paradigmawechsel in der Wettbewerbstheorie?" In Enke, H., W. Köhler, and W. Schulz (eds.), *Struktur und Dynamik der Wirtschaft*. Beiträge zum 60. Geburtstag von Karl Brandt, 75–97. Freiburg i. Br.: Haufe.

Krüsselberg, H. G. (1983b): "Property Rights-Theorie und Wohlfahrtsökonomik." In Schüller, A. (ed.), *Property Rights und ökonomische Theorie*, 45–77. München: Vahlen.

Krüsselberg, H. G. (ed.) (1984a): *Vermögen im Systemvergleich*. Schriften zum Vergleich von Wirtschaftsordnungen 34. Stuttgart–New York: Fischer.

Krüsselberg, H. G. (1984b): "Vermögen im Systemvergleich – die Problemstellung." In Krüsselberg, H. G. (ed.), *Vermögen im Systemvergleich*, 1–17. Stuttgart–New York: Fischer.

Krüsselberg, H. G. (1984c): "Vermögen, Kapital, Eigentum – Schüsselbegriffe der Ordnungstheorie?" In Krüsselberg, H. G. (ed.), *Vermögen im Systemvergleich*, 37–60. Stuttgart–New York: Fischer.

Krüsselberg, H. G. (1984d): "Wohlfahrt und Institutionen: Betrachtungen zur Systemkonzeption im Werk von Adam Smith." In Kaufmann, F. X., and H. G. Krüsselberg (eds.), *Markt, Staat und Solidarität bei Adam Smith*, 185–216. Frankfurt–New York: Campus.

Krüsselberg, H. G., and H. Brendel (1980): "Innovationsfinanzierung, Kapitalmärkte und Kontrolle des Unternehmensverhaltens." In Krüsselberg, H. G. (ed.), *Vermögen in ordnungstheoretischer und ordnungspolitischer Sicht*, 83–109. Köln: Otto A. Friedrich-Kuratorium.

Lachmann, L. M. (1979): "The Flow of Legislation and the Permanence of the Legal Order." *ORDO, Jahrbuch für die Ordnung von Wirtschaft und Gesellschaft* 30: 69–77. Stuttgart–New York: Fischer.

Lange, O., and F. M. Taylor (1938): *On the Economic Theory of Socialism*. New York: McGraw-Hill.

Lange, O. (1968): *Einführung in die Ökonometrie*. Tübingen: Mohr.

Lowe, A. (1965): *On Economic Knowledge*. New York–Evanston: Harper & Row.

Machlup, F. (1952): *The Economics of Sellers Competition*. Baltimore: The Johns Hopkins Press.

Manor, Y. (1980): "Conceptions of National Planning: A Tentative Model." In Bilski, R. (ed.), *Can Planning replace Politics? The Israeli Experience*, 29–58. The Hague–Boston–London: Nijhoff.

Marris, R., and D. C. Mueller (1980): "The Corporation, Competition and the Invisible Hand." *Journal of Economic Literature* 23/1: 32–63.

Massé, P. (1962): *Optimal Investment Decisions: Rules for Action and Criteria for Choice*. Englewood Cliffs, N. J.–New York: Prentice Hall.

Mishan, E. J. (1967a): *The Costs of Economic Growth*. London: Staples Press.

Mishan, E. J. (1967b): "Pareto Optimality and the Law." *Oxford Economic Papers* 19/3: 255–282.

Mishan, E. J. (1969): *Welfare Economics. An Assessment*. Amsterdam: North-Holland Publishing Company.

Müller-Armack, A. (1966): *Wirtschaftsordnung und Wirtschaftspolitik*. Freiburg: Rombach.

North, D. C., and R. P. Thomas (1973): *The Rise of the Western World*. Cambridge: Cambridge Univ. Press.

North, D. C. (1978): "Structure and Performance: The Task of Economic History." *Journal of Economic Literature* 16/3: 963–978.

Ostrom, V. (1974): *The Intellectual Crisis in American Public Administration* (2nd ed.). Alabama: Univ. Press.

Ostrom, V. (1976): "John R. Common's Foundations for Policy Analysis." *Journal of Economic Issues* 10/4: 839–857.

Ostrom, V. (1983): "Reflexions on Public Administration in Europe." In European Institute of Public Administration (ed.), *The Development of Research and Training in European Policy Making*, 121–169. Maastricht: EIPA.

Penrose, E. T. (1980): *The Theory of the Growth of the Firm* (2nd. ed.). Oxford: Basil Blackwell.

Perroux, F. (1973): *Pouvoir et économie*. Paris–Bruxelles–Montréal: Dunod. (German ed. 1983: Wirtschaft und Macht. Bern: Haupt).

Rüstow, A. (1950): *Das Versagen des Wirtschaftsliberalismus* (2nd ed.). Godesberg: Küpper.

Rüstow, A. (1960): "Wirtschaft als Dienerin der Menschlichkeit". In Aktionsgemeinschaft Soziale Marktwirtschaft (ed.), *Was wichtiger ist als Wirtschaft,* 7–16. Tagungsprotokoll Nr. 15. Ludwigsburg: Martin Hoch.

Schenk, K. E. (1981): *Märkte, Hierarchien und Wettbewerb*. München: Vahlen.

Schüller, A. (1983): "Einführung." In Schüller, A. (ed.), *Property Rights and ökonomische Theorie,* VII–XXI. München: Vahlen.

Schüller, A., H. Leipold, and H. Hamel (eds.) (1983): *Innovationsprobleme in Ost und West*. Schriften zum Vergleich von Wirtschaftsordnungen 33. Stuttgart–New York: Fischer.

Shackle, G. L. S. (1965): *A Scheme of Economic Theory*. Cambridge: Cambridge Univ. Press.

Shackle, G. L. S. (1968): *Economics for Pleasure*. Cambridge: Cambridge Univ. Press.

Smith, A. (1976): *The Theory of Moral Sentiments*. Ed. by Raphael, D. D., and A. L. Macfie. Oxford: Clarendon Press.

Tuchtfeldt, E. (1983): *Bausteine zur Theorie der Wirtschaftspolitik*. Bern–Stuttgart: Haupt.

Williamson, O. E. (1967): "Hierarchical Control and Optimal Firm Size." *Journal of Political Economy* 75/2: 123–138.

Williamson, O. E. (1975): *Markets and Hierarchies: Analysis and Antitrust Implications*. New York–London: Free Press.

18. Solidarity and Markets

Klaus Gretschmann

Abstract

In the following chapter solidarity as a principle of socio-economic control based on non-selfish, cooperative behavior is compared with the market mechanism built on self-interest and competition. It will be shown that from a guidance theory perspective it is the real entrepreneurial performance of the market rather than its theoretically modelled (general equilibrium) advantages which only can serve as the yardstick for a comparison with the solidarity principle.

As far as the latter is concerned, a pure economic explanation of solidarity according to the rule of utility maximizing behavior under uncertainty and risk, as supposed in choice-logic models, is inadequate. We, therefore, interpret solidarity, from an extended public-choice perspective, as the voluntary renunciation of taking the free-rider attitude in cases where this would be economically rational: Solidarity implies the voluntary respect for the concern of others as a general principle of action.

According to such a concept solidarity not only supports the functioning of both state and market but can possibly serve, as will be demonstrated, as a general principle of guidance of a new socio-economic order, based on "need-orientation" instead of acquisition as well as on cooperation instead of competition. The steering capacity of these is, however, insufficient to replace the market performance as a whole, but is nevertheless able to control a whole series of societal functions especially at the small scale level of communal organizations.

18.1 Coordination: Workable Mechanisms and Functions to Be Fulfilled

For Schumpeter it was an element of the so-called "schützenden Schichten", Durkheim interpreted its disappearance as a cause of alienation and anomia, and Sombart thought it to be the double precondition for both the existence and the transformation of the market system.

What we are talking about is the phenomenon of solidarity, a kind of personal orientation towards the commonweal close to the German category of *Gemeinsinn* (common spirit), which – in small groups on the one hand or society-oriented on the other – reaches far beyond pure self-interest, which traditionally represents the actor's motivational basis on the stage of the market system.

In view of the orthodox polar case of market versus state as the predominant though too abstract modes of coordination, solidarity today seems to indicate a renaissance of unorthodox thinking about how to coordinate and harmonize actions beyond hierarchies and markets.

Indeed, the differentiation between only two types of coordinating mechanics, namely state and market, as we can find them in most textbooks of economics and public finance, is much too narrow (see Gretschmann 1983a).

If one boils the problem down, however, from the abstract state-market level to more concrete mechanisms of coordination and allocation – as the economist would call it – a whole range of coordination principles can be pointed out, f.e. hierarchies and orders, votes and vetoes, markets and prices, mutual adjustment and consensus by "discourse", persuasion and arbitration, trust, responsibility and last but not least solidarity.

Some of these are more or less autonomous or basic mechanisms, for example the price mechanism, while others, such as responsibility or persuasion, are more lateral or supportive. All of them, however, imply the existence of special property rights, differ in their processes, transactions and transaction costs (see Krüsselberg: Ch. 17) and outcome (for a comprehensive set of comparative criteria see: E. Ostrom: Ch. 24).

These different mechanisms are expected to fulfil a whole set of functions indispensable to the task of coordination itself.

Kaufmann (1983) has indicated as the most basic and prominent conditions that coordination mechanisms must deliver a binding standard of judgement for behavior (1), that they must guarantee mutual adjustment of actors by presenting transaction and interaction rules (2), and, finally, that they must incorporate criteria for evaluating success and failure setting incentives for learning by feedback processes (3). From a more detailed perspective the following functions can be added:

– to secure and reinforce motivation for actions;
– to provide information about others' interests, plans and activities;
– to guarantee adequate standards of information and communication;
– to indicate demands;
– to create incentives for production;
– to allocate scarce resources efficiently and effectively;
– to minimize negative external effects and maximize the positive ones;
– to distribute output according to generally accepted criteria;
– to minimize transaction costs while maximizing transaction benefits;
– to reduce complexity, uncertainty, and risk;
– to secure social integration, settle conflicts and make compromises workable;
– to guarantee personal freedom;
– to reduce power and to reinforce participation;
– to ensure responsibility and control.

Since it is self-evident that none of the above mentioned coordination mechanisms can perform all these tasks equally well, we will have to clarify in this chapter the actual performance capacity of solidarity versus markets against the background of the functions listed above. We must specify e.g. under what circumstances solidarity works, which types of relation, such as constituency, correction, substitution, competition or complement, exist between solidarity and other kinds of coordination what the effects of market or state action on solidarity are, what standards of success and control are used and which fields of practical experience can be demonstrated.

18.2 The Market as a Self-Regulating System

Social Aspects of the Market Order

According to Max Weber "the market" is the perfect archetype of rational social behavior (Weber 1976: 489). Markets are generally defined in economics as "places" or institutional arrangements for a meeting of the supply of and the demand for homogeneous goods at a certain point in time. This abstract definition of markets and – more generally – of market *systems* has as its object a relational composite of varied economic interaction patterns with uncertain content, far more than, for example, anthropological market categories, as they are found in the model of the barter market (for example in Polany's works).

In the composite the regulating network is constructed of individuals who are "neither more nor less" than a preference order equipped with certain property rights (Vogt 1979: 391) and whose relations are regulated by the equivalence principle under the pressure of competition, while in traditional markets the barter element based on reciprocity dominates, without regards to competition or equivalence. The decisive economic and regulating difference is that in the latter prices do have no feedback effects on production decisions under conditions of scarcity; reciprocity as a principle thus means nothing more than "mutuality".

"Market societies exist neither naturally nor are their basic institutions agreed upon; however, they are products of human action." (Berger 1978: 330). The social market theories from Smith and Mandeville to Hayek and Eucken take as their subject the unplanned and nevertheless allegedly optimal results of autonomous individual actions, which do not end in chaos but rather guarantee order. Historically, personally based communalization *(Vergemeinschaftung)* is thus replaced by the development of an anonymous society *(Vergesellschaftung)* based on markets. For this reason the important thing in the market controlled "simple system of natural liberty" is no longer the restraint of "selfish passions" earlier considered reprehensible. Such passions are rather – if they are placed in a structure such as that of the market – not only compatible with the requirements of social integration but also socially and economically vital.

The most important feature of this market mechanism is the possibility to calculate benefits and scarcity individually and to allocate them according to self-interest without the divergence of the persons' and system's welfare optima in the ideal case of a perfect market. For this reason one can operate with a small decision capacity and in border-line cases without communication (Luhmann 1972: 190). Individual actions and decisions do need as their only point of orientation nothing more than a few anonymous data and the personal preferences of the agents. Interaction and social behavior, which are thought to be generally necessary for economic processes, become dispensable (Seidl 1980).

Through price and quantity signals, which regulate exchange relationships, communication is, on the one hand, universalized and, on the other hand, reduced to mere information. The resulting simplification makes possible the easy control of concentrated and complicated interaction. The communication dimension of the market in this way loses its social content to the extent that individual decisions about buying and not buying, production or nonproduction are made using abstract cost-benefit-calculations and not by means of social discourse about quantity and quality of production and consumption. For this reason, theory and practice of the market development lack the quality of solidary interaction and communication – e.g. in free and open discussions – which characterizes the "Solidarbürger" (socially conscious citizen) who embodies the phrase "liberty, equality, fraternity" and who represents, as will be shown below, a constitutive element of an economy regulated by solidarity.

Economic Performance: Entrepreneurial Economy versus General Equilibrium

In contrast to the social and integration theory aspects of markets outlined above within the framework of a theory of institutional arrangements, the *pure* theory of the market, as the incarnation of economic control or allocation dynamics, models a simultaneous determination of the economic variables "price" and "quantity" on the basis of a specific supply and demand calculus. This calculus represents – roughly speaking – the basic type of economic rational behavior. The pure theory thus follows the way from the classical theory of value creation by means of socio-economic regulation through markets to the abstract equilibrium models of market price formation and related efficient allocation. According to this thesis, markets on the basis of choice-logic calculations are the best and perhaps even the only control mechanisms appropriate to both the economic principle and the system's requirements. Its control function consists in the allocation of scarce resources.

The transformation from micro- to macro-relationships originating within the market itself optimizes the state of the entire system and guarantees a Paretian welfare optimum (for a critique see Sen 1980).The optimizing process takes place only through the price signals provided by the market, which themselves relieve exchange relationships of information and transaction costs. In the ideal Walrasian market model – an exact imitation of the stock exchange – the auctioneer collects the supply and demand quantities at certain prices and revises these constantly until a market clearing price-quantity equilibrium is reached. In this process information and transaction costs are neglected because immediate adjustment, complete information, and logic rationality are assumed as axiomatic.

In such pure market models, however, neither the existence of initial endowments nor the production function and preference theory basis of regulation are explained. The only goal is the deducing of a general equilibrium, which determines quantities and prices and is based on the utility theory approach. This presupposes that in principle a market equilibrium is conceivable for all extraeconomic, e.g. externally determined, data, a condition in which all markets are simultaneously balanced through equilibrium prices. Changes of the data cause, however, short run disequilibria, which in turn effect adjustments, as long as the price mechanism is permitted to function undisturbed. Thus, external shocks always result in new equilibria (relative stability/ultrastability) in so far as economic expectations are not too far removed from the respective general equilibrium, assuming sufficient price flexibility.

Above all in the most highly developed economic theories, such as the extremely formalized welfare economic theories, on the one hand, or the Arrow-Debreu-models on the other, the mechanics or automatics forces of the market have crowded out the real acting subjects.

Particularly when considered from the point of view of real regulation, as Streissler (1980) points out, the advantages of the market justified by purely static and allocational arguments, such as those in the general equilibrium theory, are less significant than the entrepreneurial, dynamic performance aspects, such as innovation potential, learning ability, flexibility, feedback through price sanctions, etc.

The distorted neoclassical picture of markets is, however, not able to explain precisely the related control capacity stressed above all by the (neo-)Austrian school. The assumptions of the model and the restrictive structure of neoclassics – the assumed free preferences, the perfect information, the absence of uncertain expectations, the neglect of institutions and the role of the entrepreneur, the rejection of *historical* time and effect sequence – play an important role (for criticism see Krelle 1973; Ostleitner 1981). The advantages of a market-based entrepreneur economy result, however, from the fact that in the real world information is limited, preferences fluctuate, and imponderables exist; that time sequences contain action sequences, etc. (Streissler 1980; Röpke 1980).

This implies that the following discussion of solidarity must be compared less with the market abstractions of neoclassics and the Paretian welfare economy than with the empirical control capacity of (imperfect) markets, if a nirvana comparison is to be avoided. Moreover, questions must be asked, as Kaufmann (1984) has already done, about the goal determining, information, coordination, learning, and feedback function of solidarity.

Markets, Solidarity and Economics

Self-interested economic man, as the basic axiom of neoclassical microeconomics as well as of modern welfare economics, dominates the textbooks. We have learned that the self-interest of economic agents, interacting within he context of a market structure, constitute a mechanism of social choice which guarantees the "bonum commune" as the optimal final outcome (Thiemeyer 1980: 265). Consequently, the market model does not incorporate some central agency responsible for goal setting, process monitoring or outcome evalution. According to theoretical claims, the market system's mechanics work on the basis of individualistic, self-interested patterns of action and thus are supposed to lead to a theoretically proven completion of personal action and the system's equilibrium. In reality, however, we not only find self-interested people but numerous phenomena based on non-selfish action, such as labor grants, transfers, charity, the care for future generations, the voting in favor of poor people concerns, or men who drown in trying to rescue a child. Undoubtedly, it is a truism that beyond the limits of neoclassics, a whole range of refined hypotheses on the plurality of (non-selfish) interests, on the multi-dimensional motivation of human action and so forth can be demonstrated and even modelled (Collard 1978). But then we are faced with the problem that these hypotheses cannot guarantee any closed axiomatic general equilibrium system of allocation as it can be decuded from neoclassical assumptions (see Mackscheidt 1980: 81 ff.).

Against this background we can easily understand the intensive involvement of a whole academic discipline in the study of the steering capacity of markets. At the same time, there are very few scholarly works on solidarity in economics as well as in the other social sciences.

This is all the more surprising when we take into account the fact that, despite the merits of theory, market failure can both be demonstrated by empirical evidence and be proven theoretically (Bator 1958; Mackscheidt and Steinhauser 1977, 4–5). But the transfer of social tasks and responsibilities to state bureaucracies as a result of such market failures must also be treated with the utmost scepticism because of *inter*organizational as well as *intra*organizational problems (Hanusch 1983). It is this scepticism and bad experiences which make necessary the search for other forms of allocation and modes of control. As such an alternative we can interpret solidarity, representing – as will be demonstrated below – an independent logic of action as well as a monistic and systemic structure of guidance, performance and control.

Opposed to solidarity as a *motivational basis* we can find the concept of self-interest. As for the *logic of coordination,* solidarity implies *cooperation* in contrast to *competition,* and as far as the suitable *institutional arrangements* are concerned, solidarity is less favorable to a *market economy* but rather constitutes a *social or cooperative economy* ("Gemeinwirtschaft"). Even in the well-known writings on types of guidance and control, these aspects of solidarity are not discussed: they are neither mentioned in the screen of the Dahl-Lindblom (1963) alternatives, as are pricesystems, hierarchies, polyarchies, and bargaining, nor are they covered by Münnich's (1980) polarization of exchange versus transfer. Until quite recently solidarity was of interest only from the viewpoint of the history of economic and social thought or the "archeology of economics". This neglect is still typical of the situation in present day societies.

The reason for this neglect may be that solidarity, which in former times was a means of internal integration *and* realization of interests in the social environment for societal groups and social movements (extended families, guilds, co-operatives, settlement movements etc.) as well as a possibility of jointly producing socio-economic output (neighborhood help, mutualities etc.), not only was crowded out and destroyed by the welfare state's "Bonapartism" (for the term see Horn and Schülein 1976) and the commercialization of private associations and everyday life, but it was also discredited by the Nazis and their concept of the "solidarity of the national community" (Volksgemeinschaftssolidarität).

18.3 Solidarity as Type of Action

Let us start with a look at solidarity as a pattern of action underlying the guidance-theory aspects of solidaristic contextual situations. We will have to clarify two more or less contradictory lines of arguments: The first can be called the economistic point of view interpreting solidarity as the motivational basis of action "in a specified field of social organization prepared for the cooperation of self-interested and monadic actors" (Vanberg 1978); the second perspective may be termed "idealistic" and conceptualizes solidarity as a form of cooperative orientation and as an independent pattern of action strictly opposed to self-interest (Weisser 1954).

The Orthodox Economist's View

In traditional neoclassics, solidarity can be modelled on the basis of assuming homogeneous preferences, common values, interdependent utility functions, that is the assumption that personal utility functions contain interpersonal arguments, and non-separable production functions. In this context solidarity may be derived directly from (non-selfish) utility maximizing behavior. It can either be interpreted as an investment which will yield future benefits or as a rewarding act in itself. As Rothschild points out, it is the fact of "interpersonal connected utilities which makes in some cases non-selfish collective action yield better welfare results than individual purchasing acts" (1980: 33). People may gain a higher degree of personal satisfaction from non-selfish giving to peers, neighbors and others than from making a profit. Quite similarly John Rawls argues in favor of solidarity basically from the viewpoint of gaining personal utilities from interpersonal structures by putting the question: "What sort of world would you choose to be born into, were you yet unborn and had no idea about your skills, defects and so forth?" Under the condition of risk aversion people are expected to choose a world organized on the principle of solidarity. Moreover, individuals – and this is neglected by neoclassics – not only value the outcome of actions but also the *means and processes* affecting outcome. They may accept lowered income, decreasing profits or losses in output, when they can derive satisfaction from, for example, a production process with highly personal commitment and communication between co-producers. In such cases there are not only transaction costs but also *transaction benefits* (see Gretsch-mann 1983b) involved.

Without a closer look at social value systems which in the last instance determine the (non-)hedonistic and (non-)selfish behavior of individuals (see Kaufmann: Ch. 10), in the economic conception of rational individualism solidarity is permitted to enter only – e.g. by implicit exchange – through the narrow gate of the utility function. Even if this model fits choice-logic economic theory well, the problem of explaining why solidarity succeeds in one context and not in the other remains.

As for public choice theory, the economist's perspective can be understood in relation to the so called free-rider problem. Free-riding means preferring that others give their efforts, input and money to perform some outcome, while the free-rider himself wants to receive the resulting benefits at no cost. This calculus of action is normally restricted to the type of collective goods characterized by externalities and non-excludability.

From this point of view solidarity has to be understood as a selfish strategy of action, the realization of which depends upon

(1) the relation between individual contributions and expected benefits,
(2) the probability of gaining the expected utility even without solidarity, coopera-tive endeavors and sacrifices, and finally

(3) the opportunity costs. Solidarity will occur only if total benefits exceed total costs.

In this conception, however, the "homo cooperativus" is reduced to a modification of the "homo oeconomicus", practising solidarity only to obtain personal advantages. Such a concept of solidarity as a variety of the utility maximizing rule (Wesche 1979:42 ff.) is characteristic of the rationalist-utilitarian view. Considering the European context of the last two centuries, the latter is formulated too much individualistically and too far removed from historical experience because it denies the existence of a genuine, communitarian and binding type of solidarity. Cooperative behavior is, at least, said to be highly improbable because of the basic risk involved: If you cannot rely upon the solidarity of others, you will be worse off acting solidarily than selfish (Vogt 1979: 387). This type of "prisoners dilemma" line of argument, however, presupposes again the axiom of self-interest as being preexistent. Self-interest, however, is only one side of the coin, but never the whole!

The Other (Extended) Perspective

Opposed to the concept sketched above, solidarity can also be thought of economically, the other way round, as a (voluntary) constraint on the utility maximizing rule of the homo oeconomicus type of action. This way of coping with the problem of what really is characteristic can again be related to the free-rider: Solidarity can be interpreted as the voluntary renunciation of taking the free-rider attitude in cases where the latter would be 'rational'.

Solidarity in this context reaches beyond utility maximizing or even satisfying behavior; *it means the voluntary respect for the concern of others as a principle of action!* This becomes true, for example, when for the sake of future generations we refuse to waste scarce and exhaustible resources, when we, in the role of employees, accept voluntary wage restraints for the purpose of creating jobs for the unemployed or when we support others going on strike, even if this has negative effects on us. Such cases can be reinterpreted into analytical categories by using certain types of collective goods as standard of reference, such as f.e. "existence goods", meaning goods which are valued highly even by people who never won't use them; "option goods", that is goods which should be present in case of need, even if one does not desire them at the moment (e.g. police or medical care), and "future goods", which are not to be used at the present but are to be kept for coming generations (see Krutilla 1967).

In our times when *nobody's* actions can be restricted in their effects to the private sphere, in times of ever increasing and all-embracing externalities produced even by private goods' production and consumption – for example when we install air conditioning, we cool the rooms inside, but we heat up the environment outside, or when we fly from Frankfurt to New York the plane produces bad air for others – solidarity in the sense of *non-free-riding* is becoming more and more important for the functioning of the economy and society as a whole. As Kaufmann has stressed recently (1984), "solidarity as guidance is a characteristic feature in such social domains where the interpersonal action relations take into account not only the persons' own interests but also the specific interest of third parties and other groups, implying that the criteria for evaluating action represent an all over balance between differing norms and interests."

What we need to encourage solidarity, is a binding ethic which – especially in the public sector – should add to the "being responsible *for*" the "being responsible *to*". This must not be confused with "altruism". While the latter may cause paradoxial welfare results, for example the "after you-problem", arising when two altruists interact, each trying to make the other use first certain goods or services, solidarity represents the "together-solution". Hence, following Boulding who once defined economics as "knowing the value of nothing but the price of everything", we in turn can define solidarity as acting according to common values and duties while neglecting the price. This however implies certain steering theory consequences, as will be demonstrated below!

The use of solidarity as a means of coordination and a tool for allocation can be legitimized by the consequences of actual solidary behavior. Acting together may imply spillovers to others, inducing the willingness on their part to take over costs for the community. The probability for this increases the more individual action and group action differ in their outcome.

As especially pointed out by Marx and Lukacs, solidarity represents in historical retrospective a collective means of coping with and overcoming the physical and psychological difficulties resulting from the given type of economic system ("Wirtschaftsweise"): The only chance for the poor and weak in societies is in solidarity with others within a given social system and in striving to promote new institutional arrangements which may lead to a change in self-consciousness and social differentiation and a better chance of satisfying wants and needs (Hondrich 1975: 75).

Moreover, it is solidarity alone, the principle of joint responsibility – one for all and all for one – which guarantees for the individual a solid basis for his personal development. Solidarity offers the best prospect for self-management and self-realization of individuals in collectives.

Hence, cooperation stands beside competition as a real alternative, replacing it, when individual autonomy falls below internalized and institutionalized standards of material or psychological well-being (Brentano 1980). Solidarity, therefore, can be justified bilaterally, "wertrational", i.e. by the rationality of social or personal values, on the one hand, and "zweckrational", i.e. by the rationality of means and ends, on the other. It may be conceded that the calculus of economic utility is not far from that, nevertheless solidarity lacks the quality of profit-making as a market driving force. Instead, it incorporates the acceptance of mutual conflicts and interests, with the aim of compromising, and the consideration of social and interpersonal obligations (Neumann 1973: 60).

Dangers in Solidarity

Following the line of thought sketched above, we must agree with Hirschmann, who relates solidarity to the category of loyalty: In his opinion practising solidarity means:

(1) remaining within a social group even if one suffers losses,
(2) not showing dissatisfaction by exit, and

(3) accepting disadvantages within certain limits by putting aside personal interest
     (Hirschmann 1979: 66).

Moreover, Hirschmann's categories "exit" *and* "voice", which represent the basic
principles of human reaction to unpreferred changes in the organizational and
institutional environment of individuals, can be used to draw a relatively clear line
of distinction between "positive" forms of "true" (face-to-face) solidarity, on the
one hand, and the "negative" ideological use of an abstract, anonymous solidarity
as a general means of political power and control. It is above all the conveyance of
the normative components of solidarity from the level of small group activities
involving short "chains of action" to that of large latent groups, big organizations
or even nations which can produce dangerous consequences: Socio-political systems often use solidarity actively as the binding ideological cement in order to
guarantee the coherency of the system, to stabilize power and to prevent from
unfavorable criticism. The historical forms of artificially created class-solidarity,
national solidarity, religious solidarity and their misuse by political agencies sheds
some light on the dangers involved.

   Therefore, the difference between cases of small group, interactive solidarity
and the call for a non-personal, politically reduced general solidarity by power
elites can be clarified by introducing Hirschmann's "voice" as an important
element of solidary action: Whereas, in the former case "voice" (instead of exit)
plays a crucial role as an expression and reflection of the individuals' responsibility
to and for his group fellows, in the latter case scrutiny and responsibility are
dispended and replaced by blind dependence or even serfdom in the name of
solidarity. We can find this in some forms of "new populism" in forms of "corps
spirit" and, last but not least, in an exaggerated colleagual loyalty.

   Another problem with solidarity is the tendency of solidary structured groups
(and collectivities) to isolate themselves against environmental influences. At the
economic or business level this is clearly represented by cartels which are going to
circumvent competitive market structures in the name of what they call business
solidarity.

   Even if voluntary self-restraints of and personal obligations between actors in
order to create social balance and integration by means of mutual help and non-
selfish grants etc. typify the basic axiom of "true" solidarity (Engelhardt 1980:
1130), we have to be aware of the problems outlined above. Nevertheless, the hard
core of true solidarity is the consciousness of the fact of interpersonal interdependencies. Any explanation of human behavior which reduces this consciousness to
purely economic arguments is inadequate because it ignores the major characteristics of solidarity discussed above!

Solidarity, Public Choice and Some Constitutional Considerations

A concept of solidarity developed in this way has not only the advantage that it can
be used in connection with sociological, policy science, and economic theories; it
also has its logical basis in the fundamental contract theory ideas of the "public
choice" school. In particular, reflections about the change from the preconstitutional state of nature to the constitutional state of society suggest the crucial question

of how and why individuals are prepared to renounce their personal sovereignty – within limits – in favor of a political authority like the absolute sovereign, or a constitutional law based on a covenant (see V. Ostrom: Ch. 5; Hettlage 1979).

If one wants to accept economic, i.e. utility approach explanations based on methodological individualism, to analyze the transfer of sovereignty, one immediately becomes entangled in theoretical snares. According to the utility approach, the renunciation of personal and political sovereignty is a result of the calculation that under the condition of risk aversion it is useful for an individual to renounce some of his sovereignty in order to obtain security guarantees – based on constitutional law – from others. Since the contract state is, however, itself a public good proper, i.e. when it is once established no one can be excluded from its advantages (non-excludability), it would be logical, according to the self-interest rationality assumptions of economic theory, for individuals to attempt to enjoy the advantages free, i.e. without giving up any sovereignty. They would thus not join the social contract but would participate in its benefits as free-riders. This means that under the conditions of public goods and economic behavior, a social contract would have no chance to be concluded. One must, therefore, agree with V. Ostrom that it is a "combination of introspection, taking the perspective of others, discounting partialities, and aspiring to impartiality (which) provides the key for making interpersonal comparisons about standards of value that apply to human social relationships" (V. Ostrom: Ch. 11). Particularly the setting of norms by the communication community (Kommunikationsgemeinschaft) of the people concerned – corresponding approximately to the Habermas discourse model (Habermas 1976: 102 ff.) – who determine and examine the acceptance claims of norms as participants in a practical discourse, requires a "sympathy feeling", i.e. the "walk a mile in my shoes", as a precondition for the possibility of a normative consensus! An exclusive utility approach explanation will necessarily be inadequate. The change from the preconstitutional level of society to a constitutional state requires, therefore, non-utilitarian elements (Buchanan 1979: 117 ff.). Rules for a constitutional order must consequently be chosen on another level, by another process, and with other behavioral assumptions than is the case with decisions made later within the framwork of such rules. This means – if one agrees with Krüsselberg (1983: 76) – that there is a value orientation which is independent of immediate needs and material interests and is, as it were, above the economic action system based on the one-dimensional, self-interest concept of choice-logic.

If, therefore, neither self-interest nor a list of voting rules – which have yet to be determined – is able to explain a non-violent normative consensus and thus a voluntary renunciation of sovereignty, a basic element of human action must be considered which explains the renunciation of free-rider behavior. This means that in order to reach a consensus in the form of a general will or a general interest, every individual must look beyond his own, purely subjective interests and consider in addition those of other persons. A nonviolent consensus regarding norms is only possible if every individual gives the same considerations to the interests of other persons as he does to his own. This principle can be called the *solidarity rule*. A universal solidarity thus is in the end the only possibility of achieving a nonviolent consensus regarding the existence of norms.

If, however, the existence of "solidarity" as a type of behavior beyond self-interest can be proven conclusively in the transition of a preconstitutional to a social contract state, the question is justified as to whether economic self-interest is the only behavior orientation present in a constitutional state, i.e. whether solidarity has been lost. Logically convincing answers are lacking. But it seems not only justified but quite necessary from the point of constitutional considerations and public choice to recognize the existence of solidarity in the sense of a voluntary renunciation of "free rider" behavior.

18.4 Guidance Theory Aspects of Solidarity

According to Wilhelm Weber, solidarity is "first of all a collective social coordination and integration principle" (Weber 1980: 1470) which combines economic factors and aspects of social control.

Durkheim was also of this opinion (1977). He saw in the evolutionary change from segmentary to functional differentiation in societies a latent social tension in the area of "solidarity": The "mechanical" solidarity of small communities with clear standards and roles for their members cannot be replaced totally and everywhere by "organic solidarity" which should carry out the functions necessary for the variability of social relationships. As a result of the evolutionary break caused by a replacement of the "conscience collective" by individual self-interest, alienation and anomia develop, particularly in economic areas.

Building on these arguments, Hondrich (1976) above all has stressed how important it is today in many areas to replace the dominant but inadequate organic solidarity with forms of mechanical solidarity.

The Significance of Solidarity

With regard to economics, this means that the social integration of monadic individuals by market forces, individuals whose relations ideally are controlled by price signals and quantity reactions, must again be enriched by the social, common and cooperative determination of economic processes (allocation and distribution decisions). Thus, ideas are becoming increasingly significant which aim at establishing solidarity as a motive structure (action determining), as a form of economic activity with certain social goals (need-oriented economy), as a concept of supporting agencies (joint responsibility or liability), as a task orientation (organization goal), as a collective form of individual initiative (the primacy of social networks), and finally as an economic subsystem (alternative economy). In a society which tends to promote superficial, rapidly changing partial identity at the expense of a deeper forming of the personality because of increasing differentiation of social reference systems, solidarity helps to link economic and social behavior.

In such cases solidarity has the task of securing the supply of data and information about cooperation and also the creation of communication structures that guarantee cooperation (Freitag 1974: 213). The former strengthens the ability to act, the latter the will to act.

Furthermore, solidarity is often the critical point in the functioning of markets and hierarchies, where both producers and consumers, bureaucrats and clients are guided by self-interest: "The price system would work less well . . ., were it not that the economic agents . . . in fact display a decent regard for the interest of those with whom they exchange and for society as a whole" (Phelps 1975: 3).

Arguments for the economic efficiency and control capacity of solidarity indeed go much further: While neoclassical economics assume that all actors involved in the market process are well-equipped with *all* information necessary for perfect foresight, in the non-Walrasian real world of imperfect foresight, uncertainty, and risk, actions of both *ego* and *alter* are much more predictable when we can assume that the others will act with a sense of solidarity. Information, bargaining, and transaction costs will be reduced. In extreme cases government regulation, enforcement, and control costs can be cut when voluntary corporate responsibility and solidarity are favored as substitutes.

The more areas of economic activity are structured cooperatively, the less markets and hierarchies must direct and control. Since solidarity is able to integrate social systems, force or material incentives become unnecessary to a considerable degree, just as they conversely become more important to the extent that solidarity is lacking.

The Organizational Setting

As demonstrated above, the general problem is not to encourage people to act cooperatively, but to provide them with an institutional framework, allowing them to do so. The special reason for this is, as Hägerstrand (1970) has shown, that the existing institutional environment makes certain types of action impossible, destroys motivation, and reduces non-selfish behavior.

The principle of solidarity as an alternative idea of socio-economic control has largely lacked an institutional and economic foundation such as the private, profit-making firms represent for the market or the hierarchical bureaucratic agencies for the state. If, therefore, an economy based on solidarity is to be tried or developed, the individual economic and organizational preconditions have to be examined which make cooperative control and the resulting cooperation achievements possible. This institutional option refers empirically and theoretically to the differentiation or creation of small organizations marked by a mixture of economic goals and activities, which are intended and institutionally organized for the benefit of the members as well as for other large and small collectives. Such social systems are structured in an egalitarian-friendly way; completely self-administered; usually strive for autonomy; collectively perform tasks proposed from outside or arising internally largely with their own resources, and distribute the rewards of their efforts according to common interests. They are polyvalent in that they do not have any strictly formalized roles, produce high, but varying participant intensity, their interactions aim at broad goals, their motivation is not related to particular aims, and their technology is universally oriented (Geser 1980: 205). From the point of view of organization theory such solidarity organizations are, to be sure, extremely inefficient because of their "problematic preferences", unclear process technology, changing object of attention, the uncertain participation of the members, and the often compulsive need for consensus and interpretation of the goals and means

(Ridder 1979: 258), and carry the classic concept of organization to the point of absurdity.

Let us supplement this description from an economic point of view: Voluntary cooperation for the purpose of achieving a goal, maximal creative freedom, and personal development in and through one's work are practiced on the basis of economic and personal ties. The collective risk, which is covered by "social capital" (common property), corresponds to the common work. Unlike other forms of economic organization, solidarity organizations are based on the equality of the members, whereas market enterprises are based on a proportionality of both capital participation and the rewards for the investors. The economic purpose of solidarity organizations is, finally, to cover expenses; this means that they are largely need and not profit-oriented.

If such an institutional foundation with the corresponding incentives can be created, solidarity can certainly become an independent social and economic force. This can be explained by the mobilization of unused resources, above all the readiness of the members or sympathetic outsiders (experts, scientists) to perform voluntary and/or poorly paid work and by the identity of workers and users, which solidarity implies, and which promotes quality consciousness and the saving of time and materials.

Thus in addition to the social need for solidarity, there is also the need for efficiency.

Solidarity as a General Principle for a New Socio-Economic Order: Possibilities and Restraints

What is said above does not explain anything about the extent and value of solidarity in the total social context. Whereas the "extent" refers to the number of persons and their social distribution as well as the range of their fields of activity with cooperative emphasis, the term "value" refers to the question of whether solidarity is a primary or a subordinate type of action, that is, whether it only occurs in cases where other types of action fail or it functions as a basis for other types. Moreover, the two terms "extent" and "value" can be described more specifically in respect to whether solidarity implies partial changes or extensive reforms with the goal of creating new systems of action. These questions, in an economic context, are discussed below.

The concept of "solidarism" is characterized by the idea of a comprehensive plan of multiple centered social control. This is the economic-political maximum program of Gide's French "cooperativism". Here solidarity receives a constructive as well as a regulative value for the organization of the economy. Based on the early socialist ideas of Proudhon, Fourrier, Louis Blanc, Buchez and others, individual companies and competitive markets are to be replaced by associations and federations in which private initiative is combined with mutual help; need oriented economies with the goal of an integrated system of production, consumer, credit, and agricultural cooperatives are to eliminate economic structures based on acquisition; common profits are not to be used privately, but rather collectively distributed; economic coordination is to be achieved not through the price signals of the market, but through a system of solidarity agreements. The goal seems to be an associative federalism, a federation of cooperatives: "Economic solidarity is thus, that social systems . . . require an organization of the economy corresponding to the solidarity principle." (Bauer 1926: 504). The two basic elements seem to be the *need-orientation* and the *operation by agreements*. Nonprofit satisfaction of needs means first of all only a negative separation from the market: Goods are not produced *a priori* for markets, but rather for organized consumption. The term "need orientation" refers to an institutional arrangement of the whole economy "in which the need-oriented allocation of resources is given priority over the individualistic production and distribution based on acquisition (Weuster 1980: 167).

This arrangement is supposed to minimize "slack", eliminate profit speculation, and reduce insecurity, since production will not be for risky markets but for real needs. The profit motive is eliminated as a mechanism for regulating production.

In my opinion the second essential element of solidarity as an overall principle of economic guidance is the idea of an economy based on agreements. In his fundamentally important article, Weippert showed this system to be a logical third, largely neglected control system in addition to markets and plans. With the help of an agreement, which is not to be confused with possible previous bargaining, such questions can be answered as, for example, what goods are to be produced and how, which qualities and quantities are desired and necessary, whether production should be expanded or cut, and what should be distributed according to which guidelines. Weippert also stressed "that agreements can operate where the market mechanism, the automatic formation of prices, is unable to function" (1974: 174). To be sure, he also conceded that strict control in accord with coordination theory, as is guaranteed by price-quantity planning for the market, is not possible in an agreement system: "Since behavior is neither based on prices nor regulated by a central plan, uncertainty generally prevails."

Whereas in the market information is transmitted indirectly – communication about needs, organization and performance is replaced by price-quantity indicators – information in a solidarity economy is conveyed discursively. As a result, decisions in markets are based on price information, and the room for decision is limited by income size (the budget constraint). In addition, decisions are made by individual units engaged in competition. In contrast, information about needs, which has not passed a price filter, plays a role in decisions in the solidarity economy. The budget constraint is more flexible because redistribution considerations are also included in solidarity decision processes. Finally, in the markets the monitoring of results is reduced to monetary "numéraires" with which profit and loss are evaluated and which are expressed in household and company incomes and indicate the success or failure of economic action. In the solidarity sector the monitoring of results is more direct – in collective discussion of use value and common utility of the work performed. Considerations of efficiency are supplemented by effectiveness comparisons. This is, on the one hand, a relatively low-cost procedure as far as only small groups are concerned, whereas, on the other hand, we must expect relatively high costs if solidarity is to control the society as a whole.

Therefore, the comparative advantages or even the superiority of solidarity as a means of steering socio-economic and political processes seem to be restricted to areas of clearly structured small social networks within which individuals act in a face-to-face context being fully aware of the possible implications and effects of their activities on others. According to Kaufmann (1984), such areas are characterized by the existence of "short chains of action". This also implies that the crucial precondition for the working of solidarity to control such areas are homogeneous interests of the group members.

This may be a good reason for the assumption that for purposes of an overall guidance of hypher-complex socio-political systems solidarity is not adequate.

Measured by the size of systems, markets provide relatively better control for information, coordination, and determining results in fragmented, interdependently structured large systems. But in turn, they provide too much control for small social systems and thus destroy their natural forces of integration!

Solidarity, on the other hand, is able to regulate small social systems by means of discursive integration, and even if it does not produce the maximum of possible output, it is *process optimal*. A number of connected preference systems are optimized. A steering of the total economy using solidarity is, however, questionable because prices in such a system represent concentrated communal value estimates and are only slightly influenced by scarcity. Prices function only as indicators of social significance. Solidarity would, therefore, be inadequate to control large economic systems; one reason for this is that given n-goods in a market expressed in monetary terms correspond to exactly n-prices while in a pure barter or bargaining situation the exchange complexity rises according to the well known numerical formula $n\,(n-1)/2$.

This does not mean that solidarity as a pattern of action could not – in part – replace regulation, competition or control, because in some areas the latter may be helped to perform their tasks with a greater degree of reliability when supported by solidarity. For example, in the well-known Buchanan-Tullock model (1967), where the optimality in a decision situation is dependent on the number of participants and mechanisms of choice from which follow both the costs of achieving a consensus and so-called external (acceptance) costs, the optimal solution can be made cheaper by solidarity, which lowers the former and reduces latter.

In this sense, social needs and concerns can be met efficiently, cheaply, and with great effect when action strategies are carried out by solidarity agencies, for example local networks etc.

For state agencies this necessitates, at least in part, a change in their self-image, from being agencies of first and full responsibility to being catalysts supporting solidary private, communal and nonprofit organizations. This may reduce the state's involvement in all of society's concerns, but it will not simultaneously take away the social responsibility of the state for the weak and the poor.

18.5 Conclusion

Considered functionally, the development of cooperative (solidarity) economic patterns contains elements of socio-cultural systems independent of the state, or, considered historically, a pre-state system of socio-cultural control. As Kaufmann (1983) has pointed out recently, solidarity implies not only a common definition of action arenas by the actors but also the acceptance of common norms and thus is regulated primarily by "social control", or the other way round, a highly moral gratification value is causal for solidary behavior. Nevertheless, solidarity has in the past been described more by a negation of the structural elements of the other two systems, hierarchies and markets, than by a positive definition of its own elements. Thus, it can function for the time being only as an indication of the often mentioned possibilities and realities of cooperative action, until now insufficiently understood and generally ignored because of the predominance of one-sided theories.

References

Bator, F. M. (1958): "The Anatomy of Market Failure." *Quarterly Journal of Economics* 72/3: 351–379.

Bauer, Th. (1926): "Solidarismus." *Handwörterbuch der Staatswissenschaften*, 503–507. Jena: Gutav Fischer.

Berger, J. (1978): "Intersubjektive Sinnkonstitution und Sozialstruktur – Zur Kritik handlungstheoretischer Ansätze der Soziologie." *Zeitschrift für Soziologie* 7/4: 327–334.

Brentano, D. von (1980): "Die Bedeutung der Solidarität in Genossenschaften und bei genossenschaftlichen Gründungsvorgängen." *Archiv für öffentliche und freigemeinnützige Unternehmen* 12: 11–31.

Buchanan, J. M. (1979): *What Should Economists do?*, Indianapolis: Liberty Press.

Buchanan, J. M., and G. Tullock (1967): *The Calculus of Consent*, Michigan: Univ. Press.

Collard, D. (1978): *Altruism and Economy*, Oxford: M. Robertson.

Dahl, R. A., and C. E. Lindblom (1963): *Politics, Economics and Welfare*. New York: Harper & Brothers.

Durkheim, E. (1977): *Über die Teilung der sozialen Arbeit*. Frankfurt a. M.: Suhrkamp.

Engelhardt, W. W. (1980): "Selbsthilfe." In *Evangelisches Soziallexikon*, 1130–1132. Stuttgart–Berlin: Kreuz-Verlag.

Freitag, F. O. (1974): "Integration und Kommunikation bei Genossenschaften." *Zeitschrift für das gesamte Genossenschaftswesen* 24/3: 209–220.

Geser, H. (1980): "Kleine Sozialsysteme: Strukturmerkmale und Leistungskapazitäten." *Kölner Zeitschrift für Soziologie und Sozialpsychologie* 32/2: 205–239.

Gretschmann, K. (1983a): "Cooperative Self Management of Public Services: Possibilities for and Limitations of a Reduction in Public Expenditure." In Pfaff, M. (ed.), *Public Transfers and Some Private Alternatives During the Recession*, 196–211. Berlin: Duncker & Humblot.

Gretschmann, K. (1983b): *Wirtschaft im Schatten von Staat und Markt*. Frankfurt a. M.: Fischer.

Habermas, J. (1976): *Legitimation Crisis*. London: Heinemann.

Hägerstrand, T. (1970): "What about People in Regional Science." *Papers of the Regional Science Association* 26: 1–27.

Hanusch, H. (ed.) (1983): *Anatomy of Government Deficiencies*. Berlin: Springer.

Hettlage, R. (1979): *Genossenschaftstheorie und Partizipationsdiskussion*. Frankfurt a. M.– New York: Campus.

Hirschmann, A. O. (1979): *Abwanderung oder Widerspruch*. Tübingen: Mohr.

Hondrich, K. O. (1975): *Menschliche Bedürfnisse und soziale Steuerung*. Reinbek: Rowohlt.

Hondrich, K. O. (1976): *Solidaritätsprobleme in modernen Gesellschaften*. Bochum (Mimeogr.).

Horn, K., and J. A. Schülein (1976): "Politpsychologische Bemerkungen zur Legitimations-krise." In Kielmansegg, P. Graf (ed.), *Legitimationsprobleme politischer Systeme*, 123–178. Opladen: Westdeutscher Verlag.

Kaufmann, F. X. (1983): "Steuerungsprobleme im Wohlfahrtsstaat." In Matthes, J. (ed.), *Krise der Arbeitsgesellschaft*, 474–490. Frankfurt a. M.–New York: Campus.

Kaufmann, F. X. (1984): "Solidarität als Steuerungsform – Erklärungsansätze bei Adam Smith." In Kaufmann, F. X., and H. G. Krüsseberg (eds.), *Markt, Staat und Solidarität bei Adam Smith*, 158–184. Frankfurt a. M.–New York: Campus.

Krelle, W. (1973): "The Dynamics of the Utility Function." In Hicks, J. R., and W. Weber (eds.), *Carl Menger and the Austrian School of Economics*, 92–118. Oxford: Univ. Press.

Krüsselberg, H. G. (1983): "Property Rights-Theorie und Wohlfahrtsökonomik." In Schül-ler, A. (ed.), *Property Rights und ökonomische Theorie*, 45–77. München: Vahlen.

Krutilla, J. V. (1967): "Conservation Reconsidered." *American Economic Review* 57/4: 777–786.

Luhmann, N. (1972): "Geld, Knappheit und die bürgerliche Gesellschaft." *Jahrbuch für Sozialwissenschaft* 23/2: 186–210.

Mackscheidt, K. (1980): "Der Entfaltungsspielraum bei dezentraler Steuerung." In Dett-ling, W. (ed.), *Die Zähmung des Leviathan*, 81–106. Baden-Baden: Nomos.

Mackscheidt, K., and J. Steinhausen (1977): *Finanzpolitik II. Grundfragen versorgungspoli-tischer Eingriffe*. Tübingen–Düsseldorf: Mohr-Werner.

Münnich, F. E. (1980): "Gesellschaftliche Ziele und Organisationsprinzipien." In Streissler, E. and Ch. Watrin (eds.), *Zur Theorie marktwirtschaftlicher Ordnungen*, 162–196. Tübingen: Mohr.

Neumann, M. (1973): "Konflikt- oder Harmonietheorie der Genossenschaften." *Zeitschrift für das gesamte Genossenschaftswesen* 23/1: 46–62.

Ostleitner, H. (1981): "Logik und Systematik von Reformschritten." In Meissner, W., J. Kosta, and J. Welsch, *Für eine ökonomische Reformpolitik*, 119–142. Frankfurt a. M.:EVA.

Phelps, E. S. (1975): *Altruism, Morality and Economic Theory*. New York: Russell Sage Foundation.

Ridder, P. (1979): "Prozesse der Machtbildung in selbstverwalteten Vereinigungen." *Köl-ner Zeitschrift für Soziologie und Sozialpsychologie* 31/2: 256–266.

Röpke, J. (1980): "Zur Stabilität und Evolution marktwirtschaftlicher Systeme aus klassi-scher Sicht." In Streissler, E. and Ch. Watrin (eds.), *Zur Theorie marktwirtschaftlicher Ordnungen*, 124–154. Tübingen: Mohr.

Rothschild, K. (1980): "Kritik marktwirtschaftlicher Ordnungen als Realtypus." In Streiss-ler, E. and Ch. Watrin (eds.), *Zur Theorie marktwirtschaftlicher Ordnungen*, 13–37. Tübingen: Mohr.

Seidl, Ch. (1980): "Die Individual- versus die Kollektiventscheidung: Freiheit in marktwirt-schaftlichen Ordnungen." In Streissler, E. and Ch. Watrin (eds.), *Zur Theorie marktwirt-schaftlicher Ordnungen*, 386–435. Tübingen: Mohr.

Sen, A. K. (1980): "Personal Utilities and Public Judgement: Or what is wrong with Welfare Economics." In Roskamp, K. W. (ed.), *Public Choice and Public Finance*, 19–41. Paris: Cujas.

Streissler, E. (1980): "Kritik des neoklassischen Gleichgewichtsansatzes als Rechtfertigung marktwirtschaftlicher Ordnungen." In Streissler, E. and Ch. Watrin (eds.), *Zur Theorie marktwirtschaftlicher Ordnungen*, 38–69. Tübingen: Mohr.

Thiemeyer, Th. (1980): "Das öffentliche Interesse in der ökonomischen Theorie." *Archiv für öffentliche und freigemeinnützige Unternehmen* 12: 263–281.

Vanberg, V. (1978): "Markets and Organizations – Towards an Individualitsic Theory of Collective Action." *Mens en Maatschappij* 53/3: 259–281.

Vogt, W. (1979): "Politische Ökonomie." In Habermas, J. (ed.), *Stichworte zur geistigen Situation der Zeit.* Vol. 1, 381–407. Frankfurt a. M.: Suhrkamp.

Weber, M. (1976): *Wirtschaft und Gesellschaft.* Tübingen: Mohr.

Weber, W. (1980): "Solidarität." *Handwörterbuch des Genossenschaftswesens,* 1468–1476. Wiesbaden: Deutscher Genossenschaftsverlag.

Weippert, G. (1974): "Vereinbarung als drittes Ordnungsprinzip." In Jürgensen, H. (ed.), *Gestaltungsprobleme der Weltwirtschaft,* 167–178. Göttingen: Vandenhoeck & Ruprecht.

Weisser, G. (1954): "Genossenschaft und Gemeinschaft." *Gemeinnütziges Wohnungswesen* 7/12: 565–572.

Wesche, E. (1979): *Tauschprinzip, Mehrheitsprinzip, Gesamtinteresse.* Stuttgart: Klett-Cotta.

Weuster, A. (1980): *Theorie der Konsumgenossenschaftsentwicklung.* Berlin: Duncker & Humblot.

19. Solidarity and Hierarchy: Institutional Arrangements for the Coordination of Actions

Friedhart Hegner

Abstract

Problem-processing is conceived as a set of actions requiring cooperation between individual and collective actors. Cooperation depends on the coordination of actions and objects being in the hands of the actors. The organized coordination of actions, outside of price-determined markets, is based on two factors: (a) generalized behaviour dispositions, that is, intra-individual guidelines for cooperative behaviour (e.g. altruism, loyalty); and (b), structural arrangements referring to the social symmetry between actors with regard to the willingness, ability or obligation to contribute (e.g. reciprocity, solidarity). The stability of the coordination of a (large) number of individual and collective actors depends on encompassing institutional arrangements which guarantee the accommodation of generalized behaviour dispositions, structural arrangements and situational contexts. Three types of institutional arrangements are distinguished: solidaric reciprocity, hierarchic redistribution, and price-determined markets. Solving a specific problem will require identifying the components – economic and social – and then searching through possible institutional arrangements to discover the best combination.

19.1 Introduction

In recent years, many political party leaders, representatives of big corporations and governmental speakers have made an appeal to "solidarity" (Kirsch 1983). For example, some (former) apologists of the modern welfare state have rediscovered such archaic institutions as self-help and mutual-aid in the context of the household, the neighbourhood or private charities. "Solidarity" is encouraged in the forms, e.g. of unpaid work and free help to the disadvantaged. Why? Because public redistribution demands an enormous increase of expenditure, bureaucracy and professionalism *while* remaining inadequate in meeting people's wants for material and sociopsychic well-being. From a completely different viewpoint, the apologists of market society and business civilisation strongly support these assumptions and suggestions. They, too, underline the importance of social organizations and transactions outside the state, – and the market. They appeal to the "solidarity" of those who are in the labour market with those outside it, arguing that the "solidaric" forgoing of wage increases will help to create additional work places. They appeal to the "solidarity" of welfare recipients, arguing that the forgoing of (increased) benefits will help to secure the stability of the welfare state for the sake of future generations. They speak in favour of "solidaric" fighting against the growing tax burden, being a prerequisite for the stabilization of the competitive position of the national economy in the world market. Paradoxically, the apologists of the welfare state and the market society are outflanked by their critics in their appeals to "solidarity". For example, the latter appeal to the "solidarity" of the rich nations with the poor nations, arguing that the "convivial austerity" (Illich) of the better-off is a prerequisite of the well-being of all.

How has it happened that an old-fashioned concept like solidarity has entered the forefront of discussion in the 70s and 80s? One answer could be the growing awareness of the negative effects of state and market provision of goods and services (Marien 1978). Behind these criticisms lies the assumption that inadequate living-conditions and social inequality could be better alleviated by reciprocity and solidarity than by public redistribution and private market exchange (Hoefnagels 1979). The assumption claims a need for either: (1) the substitution of hierarchic redistribution within the public sector and price-determined exchange within the market by reciprocity and solidarity; or, (2) new modes of combination of the various types of institutional arrangements (hierarchic redistribution; price-making markets; reciprocity/solidarity). The implications require elaboration.

In Section 2, the psychic and social bases of the coordination of inter-individual cooperation are outlined. Section 3 deals with two types of generalized behaviour dispositions (altruism, loyalty) which stabilize cooperation. In Section 4, two types of structural arrangements (reciprocity, solidarity) are described, both being prerequisites for continuous cooperation outside the market and the state. Section 5 summarizes the arguments by introducing three types of institutional arrangements (solidaric reciprocity; hierarchic redistribution; price-determined markets). In Sections 6 and 7, a basis for a comparison of institutional arrangements as well as some illustrations are presented.

19.2 The Bases of Inter-Individual Cooperation: Individual Behaviour Dispositions and Social Coordination Mechanisms

At first glance, giving help at the scene of an accident seems to be an example of purely spontaneous coordination of individual actors. The helpers are passers-by who have never met before, that is, they have to coordinate their individual actions according to the specific requirements of the situation. How does this coordination work?

The actions are *guided* by four mechanisms: (a) a general norm – in the FRG, anchored in the criminal code – obliging people to give help to others in emergency situations; (b) a feeling of compassion or sympathy towards those who are in urgent need of help; (c) the assumption that the helper of today may be the helpless of tomorrow being, then, in need of the help of others; and (d) more or less precise ideas on the adequacy of actions based on personal or reported experiences with similar situations. These guidelines for action can be reinforced and specified by face-to-face communication between the helpers. The *control* of actions is grounded on the following mechanisms: (a) the reactions of the help-needing victims (whether they seem to feel better or worse due to the helper's actions); (b) the reactions of other helpers and observers who comment on the help given; and (c) the intra-individual comparisons drawn between present actions and reminiscences of former actions in similar situations. The *evaluation* of performance partly coincides with the situational control mechanisms and is partly postponed to the later judgements of experts (e.g. the staff of an arriving ambulance). To sum up: the cooperation between helpers is due to spontaneous coordination based on discourse as well as on pre-defined norms, given experiences, and a common understanding of the situation.

Similar mixtures of coordination mechanisms can be found in modern family households. It is the coexistence of sympathy, common experience, customary reciprocity, and legal obligations which coordinates the actions of family members. In his *Theory of Moral Sentiments,* Adam Smith notes with regard to sympathy:

"Every man feels his own pleasures and his own pains more sensibly than those of other people. . . . After himself, the members of his own family, those who usually live in the same house with him, . . ., are naturally the objects of his warmest affections. They are naturally and usually the persons upon whose happiness or misery his conduct must have the greatest influence." (Smith 1853: 321)

The warmest affections can be conceived as an intra-personal mechanism guiding benevolent actions towards other persons. If the others are guided by corresponding feelings, benevolence and sympathy can work as coordination mechanisms for ongoing cooperation (Boulding 1978). As the family members "usually live in the same house", a direct inter-personal control of actions is possible. Each member is confronted with the effects of his own actions on others, that is, he or she can observe whether the actions induce "happiness or misery". As Maurice Halbwachs (1925: Ch. 5) noted, inter-actions between household members are not exclusively guided and controlled by affections and sentiments, but also by (a) common habits and routines resulting from living together for a long period and (b) the possibility of developing common situational definitions resulting from the permanent exposure to a specific natural and social environment. These factors enable each family member to anticipate the feelings and actions of other members and to direct his or her behaviour towards these anticipations.

The aforementioned intra-personal, inter-active and situational coordination mechanisms guarantee stable cooperation only as long as three conditions are present (Ferguson 1773: 16–92): (a) sympathy and benevolence prevail over antipathy and selfishness; (b) the number of participants is small enough to enable continuous face-to-face interaction; and (c) the common exposure to a limited natural and social environment (e.g. resources, role sets) guarantees homogeneous situational definitions rendering possible the tacit accommodation of actions. Given the weakening or disappearance of these conditions, there emerges a need for additional coordination mechanisms (Durkheim 1967: Ch. V–VII). Intrapersonal, inter-active, and situational guidance and control have to be outflanked by general rules (norms) and generalized individual behaviour dispositions.

19.3 The Outflanking of Interactive Coordination Mechanisms by Generalized Individual Behaviour Dispositions: Altruism and Loyalty

With regard to the sociopsychic bases of the coordination of actions by solidarity and hierarchy, two gneralized behaviour dispositions deserve special attention: altruism and loyalty. Both work as intra-personal guidelines of cooperative actions, but differ from "warmest affections" in two respects: (a) They are directed towards a large variety of other actors, that is, not only towards those others for whom one has "warmest affections" (e.g. love, friendship). (b) They are aimed at a large variety of situations, that is, not only at those situations to which the participants are continuously and encompassingly exposed. Undoubtedly, altruism and loyalty can be found in primary and other small groups, but their scope is not at all limited to them.

Altruism

August Comte opposes altruism to egoism and assumes that the first symbolizes collectivism whereas the second represents individualism (Comte 1969: 26; 1956: 145–157, 237 f.). People who are guided by altruistic behaviour dispositions postpone their own interests in favour of the interests of others. They contribute to the want satisfaction of others without insisting on the satisfaction of their own wants. They give without receiving (cf. Durkheim 1967: 237 ff.).

At first glance, there seems to be a purely one-sided and asymmetrical relation between the one who gives and the one who receives (one-way transaction). But this onesidedness is only true if the focus of attention is limited to observable objects changing hands on any one occasion. Taking into account the unobservable objects as well as the encompassing institutional framework, the one-way grant can be conceived as being parallelled by two-way transactions. First, the altruist experiences non-material want satisfaction by observing the growing well-being and the gratitude of the receiver, both of them inducing positive feelings. From this perspective, altruism may be conceived as a form of hedonism (Baumann et al., 1981). Secondly, there is the feeling of having done something good. This feeling depends on a social environment which honours altruistic giving. This may be done directly (e.g. through the explicit approval of bystanders) or indirectly (e.g. through ethical premises or religious promises which have been internalized by the giver). (Spencer 1961: 161–168; Durkheim 1967: 245 f., 262 ff.)

To summarize: The coordination of actions by generalized altruistic behaviour dispositions functions when the one-way grants of means of want satisfaction are parallelled by non-material responses from the recipients (e.g. gratitude) or of a third party (e.g. social esteem from reference groups). Under these conditions, altruism guarantees the inclination of actors to contribute without expecting a benefit of the same kind.

Loyalty

The same is true with loyalty. Here, again, the guidance and control of actions is based on a mixture of affections and norms (Parsons 1964: 77–78). Generally speaking, a loyal person keeps faith with another person, or a group of persons, without economically weighing the advantages and disadvantages of that behaviour step-by-step. Within a more or less precisely defined "zone of indifference", or "acceptance" (Barnard 1938: 169; Simon 1945: 12), faith with the other(s) is not broken even if the behaviour of the other(s) implies risks, dangers and even concrete disadvantages for the loyal person. Hirschmann (1970: 76–105) notes that loyal members of a collectivity forgo the option of exit even if the membership – at least, momentarily – does not grant a favourable balance of advantages (benefits) and disadvantages (costs, obligations).

Behind this behaviour lies a wide variety of motives: ranging from affections (e.g. love, benevolence, devotion) through adherence to norms (e.g. feudal duties, obligations between superiors and subordinates) to the grounded experience and expectation that the others (will) behave loyally, too. This expectation is not primarily based on personal trust in the benevolence of the others. Above all, it is grounded on the socially stabilized trust in the working of a common sense of duty or obligation (*"esprit de corps"*, cf. Merton 1968). The reliance on the common sense of duty results from involvement in a collectivity the members of which (a) are confronted with similar problems and (b) adhere to the same norms.

Undoubtedly, there is an element of altruism in actions guided by loyalty. Nevertheless, loyalty differs from altruism in two respects: (a) loyal actions are directed toward specific objects, that is, to a limited set of actors and rules which form a collectivity of which the loyal actor is a member. (b) The temporarily experienced imbalance of advantages and disadvantages goes hand in hand with the experience-based generalized expectation that loyalty – at least, in the long run – is more favourable than breaking faith with the collectivity. This expectation corresponds to "the sense of a common destiny of all those who work together" (Merton 1968: 254).

19.4 The Outflanking of Generalized Behaviour Dispositions by Structural Arrangements: Reciprocity and Solidarity

In the long run, the continuous functioning of altruism and loyalty needs to be outflanked by structural arrangements referring to the social symmetry between actors. Two of them deserve special attention: reciprocity and solidarity.

Reciprocity

Following Marcel Mauss (1969: 18–20), reciprocal behaviour is organized along a general pattern of *"do ut des"* (I give in order that you may give). Similarly to altruism and loyalty, there is a temporary forgoing of advantages. But this forgoing is parallelled by the expectation that the other(s) are willing, able, and obliged to respond in some way in the future. Behind reciprocal behaviour, there is the notion of *social symmetry* between giver and receiver with regard to willingness, ability or obligation (Polanyi 1957).

Presenting a gift (for example, a Christmas gift) to someone implies the expectation that the other will respond by presenting a gift, too. In contrast to contractual obligations, the expectation of reciprocation may be unspecific and non-obligatory. Nevertheless, there is an expectation – otherwise, the transactions are not reciprocal but altruistic (Kennett 1980).

The stabilization of coordination by reciprocity is reached through the generalization of the *"do ut des"* -principle. Generalization implies two sets of rules: (a) The obligation to respond to a giving-act in some way in the future is normatively extended to *all* recipients of the gift(s), irrespective of whether they have positive feelings for one another or not. This is possible only if reciprocity is accepted as a widely-shared guideline of behaviour and if there are social means for controlling and enforcing its observation. (b) The *long-term* balance of present giving and future receiving is made obvious to all members of a collectivity by setting common standards of well-being. With the help of widely shared standards, every member can control whether the present forgoing of individual benefits is parallelled by similar actions of other members, both of them improving the situation of all participants.

The success of generalizing the expectation of reciprocation depends on several factors: (a) It is easier in small collectivities where all members can – at least, from time to time – directly control whether even those with whom they are not linked by positive affections do respond in an adequate way to acts of giving. (b) it is less difficult in homogeneous collectivities where members share similar living-conditions and common customs, both of them rendering possible the emergence of widely shared standards of well-being. (c) In large and heterogeneous collectivities (e.g. formal organizations with several departments, inter-organizational networks) the success of the generalization of reciprocation depends on the development of differentiated (multiple) standards by which different kinds of reciprocal expectations can be specified (Weisser 1954; Thompson 1967: 51–82).

Solidarity

Reciprocity, loyalty, and altruism can be conceived as aspects of solidarity. Solidaric actions are along the general pattern of "one for all and all for one" (von Brentano 1980). Taken in isolation, the *"one for all"*-principle seems to be an accentuated mode of altruism and loyalty (Spencer 1961: 157 f., 165 ff.; Durkheim 1967: 407 f.). The accentuation lies in the fact that solidaric altruism and solidaric loyalty are directed towards the collectivity as a whole. That is: (a) the actions of giving without expecting a corresponding response are directed to "any" other member and (b) the individual forgoing of the option of exit is extended to "any" requirement imposed by the collectivity. Pure solidarity comes close to complete self-negation, and, in turn, complete absorption of the individual by the collectivity. But this is only half the truth. The other half is represented by the *"all for one"*-principle. Here, the individual's wants are taken as the focus of giving-actions from the side of "any" other member and the collectivity as a whole. The individual readiness and disposition to self-negation is outbalanced by the social-ized confidence that the collectivity will always guarantee the willingness, ability or obligation of a response from other members (Weber 1964: 278–282; Parsons 1964: 97–98).

The obligation to respond to a giving-act is not confined to the receiver, but to all those who could be receivers. In the case of solidaric reciprocity, the response of the other(s) is not necessarily postponed to the future, but can be expected and implemented at once – depending on the urgency of the need for contribution. Urgent cases of want satisfaction and problem processing typically necessitate quick responses and contributions from "any" member being near at hand. That is the reason why solidarity is conceived as a coordinating mechanism well-suited to collectivities which are permanently or repeatedly exposed to situations of risk and danger (Vierkandt 1972: 706). The repeated exposure of a collectivity to risky situations requires stable modes of cooperation being independent of time-consuming processes of individual cost-benefit-calculations and inter-individual bargaining (Thompson 1967: 52–56).

The institutionalization of the "one for all – all for one"-principle guarantees quick collective actions. This is conclusive as long as all members feel threatened by similar risks or can be induced, by force or moral obligation, to behave as if they were. It is the differentiation of risks, that is, the exposure of members and sub-collectivities to heterogeneous risks and requirements which may undermine the working of solidarity as a coordination mechanism (Weber 1964: 293–301; Weber 1924).

Three reactions to this situation can be observed: (a) the overall replacement of solidarity by other coordination mechanisms guiding and controlling the actions of *all* members of the collectivity; (b) the limitation of solidarity to *specific* sub-collectivities and requirements of problem processing – the "one for all and all for one"-principle, then, outflanked and parallelled by a *"quid pro quo"* (exchange), a *"do ut des"* (reciprocity) or an *"oboedio dominum"* (hierarchy); and (c) the inability of the collectivity to develop one or more coordination mechanisms which are suited to the differentiation outside and inside the collectivity, that is, disorganization and disintegration.

19.5 The Interplay Between Coordination Mechanisms and Institutional Arrangements: Solidarity, Hierarchy, Market-Exchange

Given the differentiation of wants, problems, and modes of problem processing nowadays, the coordination of actions exclusively based on solidarity is confined either to small groups, e.g. mutual-help groups, sometimes embedded in large collectivities, e.g. informal work-groups within formal organizations, or to specific situations of problem processing, characterized by urgency or/and high uncertainty, e.g. fire-brigades in action; professionals confronted with contingencies. It is the mix of coordination mechanisms which is characteristic of institutional arrangements in modern societies (Dahl and Lindblom 1963: 171–365; Boulding 1973; Galbraith 1975: 233–343; Ouchi 1980).

Figure 1 gives an overview of three fundamental coordinating mechanisms: solidarity, hierarchy, and market-exchange. The three are anchored in individuals

	Solidarity	Hierarchy	Market exchange
Individual Level	Feeling of common risk sharing	Sense of common duty or obligation	Belief in the common positive effects of competition
Personal Systems	Sympathy for other persons	Respect towards role incumbents	Interest in the goods of others
	Loyalty to other persons	Loyalty to position holders	Loyalty to abstract rules of equivalence
	Altruism/ Cooperativeness	Conformism/Rule obedience	Selfishness/Orientation to individual advantages
Inter-individual Level	Reciprocal transaction	Redistributive transaction	Price-regulated exchange
Social Systems	Longterm balance of benefits and duties	Legalized (at least, legitimated) short-term imbalance of benefits and obligations combined with the announcement of a longterm balance	Formally stated or factual short-term equivalence of values/ goods given and received
– Micro-social Level (small groups) – Meso-social Level (formal organizations)	De facto or proclaimed social symmetry of participants	De facto social asymmetry of participants	Abstract, or formal, social symmetry of participants (the aspect of symmetry is reduced to specific and ephemeral transactions)
– Macro-social Level (societal subsystems, societies)	Exposure of all members of a social system to common risks	Exposure of all members of a social system to common obligations and rules	Exposure of participants to the competitive actions of other participants

Fig. 1: Coordinating mechanisms and actors to be coordinated

(personal systems) as well as in collectivities (social systems). To fit the interplay between these two levels of system formation, specific institutional arrangements are needed (Polanyi 1957): solidaric reciprocity, hierarchic redistribution, and price-making markets.

Elements of Institutional Arrangements

On the 'individual level', the three coordination mechanisms can be classified according to the quality and the objects of behaviour dispositions. With regard to the quality, there is a differentiation between (a) the feeling of common risk-sharing, combined with sympathy, (b) the sense of common obligation or duty, combined with respect, and (c) the belief in the positive effects of competition, combined with interest. The objects of behaviour dispositions are: (1) other persons, irrespective of their social rank and economic potential; (2) role incumbents, irrespective of their personality; and (3) economic 'goods' (means of want satisfaction) which are in the hands of others.

It is assumed that no coordination mechanism can work without a minimal level of feelings of loyalty. They may be addressed to other persons, combined with cooperativeness, to incumbents of positions, combined with rule obedience, or to abstract rules of equivalence, combined with the assumption that contractual fidelity guarantees the balance of selfish advantages for all participants.

The intra-individual coordination mechanism (behaviour dispositions) are outflanked by inter-individual (collective) patterns of action coordination, both of them being part of institutional arrangements. The concept of arrangement indicates that there is a need for (a) the coordination of actors and actions as well as (b) the coordination of actors and material objects (material means of want satisfaction like instruments, goods, and money). The concept of institution indicates that the arrangements are not only grounded on spontaneous agreements between persons, but also on predefined social rules (norms) patterning the transactions (supplying people with the means of want satisfaction) and the status-relations (allocating social positions, roles, and prestige).

The pre-defined transactions and status-relations result from a historic process of institutionalizing rules and behaviour expectations. Institutionalization has two aspects (Berger and Luckmann 1969): (a) the emergence and establishment of rules and patterns which are accepted by, or enforced on, all members of a collectivity as guidelines of behaviour continuously re-enforced and re-shaped by inter-action; (b) the internalization of the rules and patterns during lifelong socialization whereby new generations adopt the given arrangements and 'old' generations learn to handle them with regard to varying situational requirements.

Solidarity, hierarchy, and market-exchange work as coordination mechanisms embedded in specific institutional arrangements. In Figure 1 (below the double line), the institutional arrangements are characterized with regard to four aspects: (1) the mode of transactions (reciprocal, redistributive, price-determined); (2) the balancing of benefits and costs or obligations within collectivities (long-term versus short-term; expected versus legalized versus formally, or abstractly, stated); (3) the status-relations between the actors (social symmetry versus social asymmetry); (4) the kinds of prevailing common experiences to which all members of a collectivity are exposed (risks, obligations and rules, competitive actions of others).

Solidaric Reciprocity

Institutional arrangements based on solidarity are characterized by: (a) reciprocal transactions between participants, that is, two-way transfers of 'goods' being not necessarily based on a one-to-one equivalence of the 'goods' exchanged; (b) the expected long-term balance of benefits and obligations (costs), that is, the commonly shared expectation that there will be – in the long run – a balance of giving and receiving without a specific contractual obligation; (c) symmetrical status-relations between the participants, that is, the commonly shared concrete experience or/and accepted belief that there is no inequality of status with regard to the willingness, ability, and obligation of giving and receiving; (d) the exposure of all participants to similar risks, that is, the prevailing experience that there are urgent problems which cannot be solved without advance-contributions from every participant disposing of the means needed at the moment.

For a certain time period, the aforementioned prerequisites of solidaric actions may exist only in the 'minds and hearts' of the actors, being only reminiscences of a former situation not completely corresponding to observable present-day reality (von Brentano 1980). That is, solidarity may work as a coordination mechanism without being outflanked by an adequate institutional arrangement. But this discrepancy between belief and reality will – sooner or later – induce the collapse of cooperation based on solidarity. Then, additional or substitutional coordination mechanisms are needed.

Hierarchic Redistribution

One of those additional mechanisms may be hierarchy. Institutional arrangements based on hierarchy are chracterized by: (a) redistributive transactions, that is, one-way transfers pre-supposing the organized differentiation between the collection of 'goods' which is based on acts of giving and the reception of 'goods' which results from distribution; (b) the legalized – or, at least, formally legitimized – short-term imbalance of benefits and obligations combined with the binding announcement of an authoritatively guaranteed long-term balance; (c) the social asymmetry of 'distributors' and receivers, that is, the organized differentiation between actors who are part of the allocative centre in the collectivity and actors who are obliged to contribute and entitled to receive; (d) the prevailing experience that all members of a collectivity are exposed to a common set of explicitly – or even formally – defined rules and obligations which work as guidelines and control mechanisms for behaviour.

The willingness to contribute and the expectation of receiving are based on the common experience that the allocative centre, e.g. the government, has the means to enforce rule obedience. This works rather well as long as hierarchic coordination can rely on a limited variety of wants and means of want satisfaction. Given the necessity of accommodating a large variety of wants and means, purely hierarchic coordination becomes too cumbersome. There is a growing need either for the specification and differentiation of rules and control mechanisms, leading to intransparency and the enlargement of the allocative centre, or for very generalized rules, leaving room for discretion and arbitrariness (Hegner 1978). These failures of hierarchy can be counteracted by institutionalizing a minimum of solidarity or an additional coordinating mechanism.

Price-Determined Markets

Additional to, or substituting for, hierarchy and solidarity, price-determined exchange can guarantee the coordination of actors aiming at the accommodation of wants and means of want satisfaction. The differentiation and refinement of wants and means as well as the scarcity of 'goods' require an institutional arrangement which renders possible the coordination of a large variety of actors who belong to divergent collectivities and who live in distant places (Polanyi 1957). Institutional arrangements based on market-exchange are characterized by: (a) price-determined two-way transactions, that is, the locational and appropriational movement of 'goods' is based on the assumption of the supplier that the 'goods' offered will produce a favourable price and on the assumption of the buyer that his demand for 'goods' will be met at as favourable price level; (b) the formally (abstractly) stated or de facto short-term equivalence of 'goods' exchanged, that is, the exchange produces, at once, a gain which is as favourable to each party as he can make it; (c) a formal (abstract) social symmetry between seller and buyer, that is, the equal freedom of both parties to take part in the exchange process, or not, the equal obligation of the participants to practice contractual fidelity, and the equal ability of each party to make the exchange as favourable to himself as possible, irrespective of inequalities resulting from status-relations outside the act of exchange; (d) the prevailing experience of the participants that each of them is exposed to the competitive actions of others, that is, to antagonistic relationships between the parties of the market system.

At first glance, there is a contradiction in terms between the element of antagonism and the coordination of actors by price-determined exchange. This inconsistency is resolved by two circumstances, both of them correlates of the differentiation of wants and means of want satisfaction (Ferguson 1969: 301–426; Hegel 1970: 346–360, 382–398):

(1) The participants in price-determined transactions are dependent on one another only with regard to a very limited range of 'goods' (means of want satisfaction). Their interdependence is confined to specific objects of transaction. Therefore, the antagonistic relationships do not lead to widespread hostility, but only to specific conflicts (Coser 1956).

(2) Even in a market system, antagonistic competition is parallelled by the coordination of actions through hierarchy and solidarity. There are, for example, hierarchically structured formal organizations of buyers and of sellers, inducing the participants to accept binding rules. They go hand in hand with redistributive transactions as well as with small work groups practising solidaric reciprocity on an informal basis. There are public authorities guaranteeing competition as well as the termination of conflicts. There is also cooperativeness and loyalty rendering possible exchange processes in situations of high uncertainty and different degrees of buyer's and seller's knowledge (Arrow 1975). This is based on the common belief that the long-term well-being of participants depends on the solidaric defence of contractual fidelity (Hirschman 1982).

Coordination by solidarity, hierarchy or market exchange can be found on all levels of social system formation (small groups, formal organizations, inter-organizational networks, societies). Nevertheless, as was pointed out, there are specific structural prerequisites for coordination at the different levels of system formation. They imply either dominance by one of the three corrdination mechanisms or a mix of different types (Matzner 1982). The relative weight of the three coordination mechanisms depends on the kinds of problems which have to be processed on the different levels of system formation.

19.6 The Focus for a Comparison of Institutional Arrangements: The Problems to Be Solved and the Actors Concerned

Any comparison between institutional arrangements needs, if it is not arguing from ontological premises, a specific focus. The focus of the comparison between hierarchic redistribution, price-making markets, and reciprocity/solidarity lies with two problems and the ways of their processing: the improvement of living-conditions and the reduction of social inequality. The first can be conceived as a set of economic problems, the second as a set of social problems (Polanyi 1944: Pt. 3).

Economic and Social Problems

The notion of 'improvement of living conditions' (economic problem) implies that there is some insufficiency in the goods and services which are perceived as means of want satisfaction. The notion of the 'reduction of social inequality' (social problem) implies that some people are insufficiently included in, or are not sufficiently participating in, the provision for the means of material or non-material want satisfaction.

These notions are based on the assumption that a discrepancy exists between (1) observable economic and social deficiencies, and (2) defined standards of good living-conditions and desired social equality (Merton 1971; Albrecht 1977). The coincidence of economic and social discrepancies forms the fundamental problem of social policy (Heimann 1929/1980). Due to this coincidence, the area of social policy is characterized by a large spectrum of varieties of problem-mixtures. Following from this, divergent types of coordination mechanisms are needed (Robson 1976; Kaufmann 1982, 1983; Matzner 1982).

Speaking of economic and social problems does not make sense without answering the following questions: (1) With regard to the provision for satisfying wants, which means are lacking? (2) For which means is there an unequal inclusion of people? (3) Which individual and collective actors are affected by economic or social problems?

Means of Want Satisfaction

With regard to the first question, a "one-eyed view of economies" (Marien 1978) prevents an unbiased definition of the means of want satisfaction. The widespread notion of economic means, nowadays, is restricted to money, wages, cash income, monetary consumer expenditures, savings, etc. (Luhmann 1972). This notion is not limited to the provision of means by the market, but it also applies to hierarchic redistribution by the state (consider, for example, transfer payments, monetary subsidies, cash benefits, grants, etc. (Boulding and Pfaff 1972). The provision for satisfying wants is, by definition, restricted to the market and the state. Non-monetary means, that is, means which are not calculable, or not calculated, on a money basis are left aside as a *quantité négligeable*. Consequently, provision processes which are not guided and coordinated by the mechanisms of price-making markets and hierarchic redistribution are put to the 'backstage' of economic discussions. To overcome this one-eyed view, a broader concept of the means of want satisfaction is needed (Landshut 1969; Burns 1975; Scitovsky 1976).

Starting from a broader concept of the economy, a large variety of means can be observed: ranging from material or tangible goods (e.g. finished products) to goods-centered services (e.g. repair, transport) and person-centered services (e.g. education, nursing). The latter include intangible means for satisfying non-material wants.

Non-material wants cannot be as easily standardized as material wants, – both being often mixed and linked to *individual* (personal) emotions, motivations, expectations and situational definitions. Consequently, the standardization of means for the satisfaction of non-material wants is, by far, more difficult than the standardization of the satisfaction of material wants. Therefore, only a small proportion of intangible means and non-material wants can be provided for and dealt with by price-determined markets and hierarchic redistribution (Gross 1983). Additional institutional arrangements for the coordination of actions which aim at the provision of intangible means (e.g. personal services) are needed. The same proves true for the provision of tangible goods and goods-centered services if want satisfaction can only be reached by their adaption to the particularities of individual cases (Scitovsky 1976: 63–145).

Chains of Means-End(Want) Relationships

The chain of progression from the provision of means to the satisfaction of wants, that is, the chain of actions which links means to ends and ends to means can be short or long. There can be few or many intermediate steps and actions which may form simple or complex networks of transactions (Elias 1976, II: 331–341; Parsons 1968: 229–241). Some material or non-material means (e.g. clothing, nursing) contribute directly to the satisfaction of wants (final consumption). In contrast to this, others contribute only indirectly. They can be conceived as intermediary means (e.g. cloth, nurse training) which have to be processed or transformed in order to render possible final want satisfaction. The differentiation between final and intermediary means is parallelled by a diversification and refinement of wants which requires complex sets of means. The complexity of the chains of means-end(want) relationships is symbolized by the variety of intermediary means which are needed to facilitate the processes of exchange between the actors who take part in the provision and consumption of goods and services.

Two types of intermediary means deserve special attention: money and legal entitlements (Luhmann 1981). Both render possible long and complex chains of means-end relationships which require calculative rationality, individual discipline, systematic planning, formal organization, and standardized evaluation.

Money can be conceived as an abstract 'all-purpose' means of indirect want satisfaction (Polanyi 1957: 264–265). In a market economy, unsatisfied wants for goods and services normally result from a lack of money (before all, wage earnings). Inequality in the capacity of disposing of money forms one of the bases of social inequality.

The same is true for legal entitlements. Where there is neither a direct or money-mediated access to goods and services nor a legal entitlement guaranteeing the disposition of means of want satisfaction, inadequate living-conditions and social inequality may result. In contrast to money, legal entitlements are not 'all-purpose' means of want satisfaction, but they are confined to *specific* purposes, that is, they guarantee access to pre-defined classes of material and non-material 'goods'. In contrast to the provision of concrete services and goods, legal entitlements are *abstract* means of want satisfaction guaranteeing a high degree of freedom with regard to the quality of objects used, the suppliers contacted, the time of use preferred, and the pecularities of consumption taken.

Undoubtedly, money and legal entitlements form important components of the chains of means-end relationships in both the market economy and the welfare state (Luhmann 1981). But, being intermediary means, they cannot form the final point of the provision for satisfying wants. They only facilitate the transaction of goods and services, especially of those goods and services which can be standardized and calculated. With regard to the provision of intangible goods (e.g. personal services) and of those tangible goods which lead to want satisfaction only if they are adapted to the particular situation of the needy, additional transaction processes are needed before final consumption can take place. The coordination of these final transaction processes is often done outside of price-determined markets and hierarchic redistribution (e.g. in private households or self-help groups).

Problems to be Processed and Actors Involved

It is assumed that the mode of coordination required depends on the characteristics of the means needed. Furthermore, it is assumed that the mode of coordination also depends on the actors involved. Involvement of actors in economic or social problems has two aspects: (1) the problem to be solved, that is, being affected by the lack of means or insufficient inclusion in the provision for means; and (2) the solving of the problem, that is, being actively engaged in the process of problem-processing.

In Figure 2, there is a differentiation between two types of actors: individual actors (personal systems) and collective actors (social systems). The problems to be solved are related to the types of actors involved. In addition to the foregoing outline of economic and social problems, both are specified with regard to types of means of want satisfaction.

Referring to the differentiation between concrete means of want satisfaction (tangible goods, services) and abstract means (money, legal entitlements), economic problems are seen as substantive or formally stated (catallactic). Behind this differentiation, there are two meanings of "economic" resulting from different institutional arrangements, that is, from a barter economy and a market economy (Burns 1975; Chapman 1972):

"The substantive meaning of economic derives from man's dependence for his living upon nature and his fellows. It refers to the interchange with his natural and social environment, in so far as this results in supplying him with the means of material want satisfaction . . . The formal meaning of economic derives from the logical character of the means-ends relationship, as apparent in such words as 'economical' or 'economizing'. It refers to a definite situation of choice, namely that between the different uses of means induced by an insufficiency of those means. If we call the rules governing choice of means the logic of

Problems to be solved / Actors concerned	Economic problems		Social problems	
	Substantive economic problems	Formally stated economic problems	Basic social problems	Derived social problems
Individual actors	Unsatisfied wants for goods and services	Inadequate choices of means (goods, services) in relation to ends (wants)	Insufficient inclusion or participation in the production or/and consumption of goods and services needed for want satisfaction	Insufficient participation in political decision processes and cultural integration processes
Personal systems	Lack of means for want satisfaction	Lack of purchasing power or/and application power		
Collective actors Social systems – small groups – formal organizations – inter-organization networks – societies	Social definitions of unsatisfied wants for goods and services Socially defined lack of means for want satisfaction Collectively experienced lack of means for want satisfaction	Inadequate collective choices of means in relation to socially defined ends (wants) Deficiency of the price system or/and of authoritative decisions with regard to the production and distribution of goods	Inequality of members of a social system with regard to the inclusion in the production and distribution of goods and services Exclusion of some members from the participation in the labour market and the goods market	Inequality of members with regard to the participation in political decision processes and cultural integration processes Exclusion of some members from political decision making and cultural integration

Fig. 2: Problems to be processed and actors involved

rational action, then we may denote this variant of logic . . . as formal economics." (Polanyi 1957: 243).

The definition of economic problems in catallactic terms (lack of purchasing power or/and application power) fits very well to the provision of standardized 'goods' by market exchange and hierarchic redistribution but not necessarily to the provision of personal services by face-to-face transactions (Gross 1983: 50–85; Fauri 1978). It also fits well to specific types of actors, for example, formal organizations, but is less well accommodated to small groups, for example, family households (Hegner 1982). Therefore, a substantive definition of economic problems forms a prerequisite for the analysis of coordination mechanisms like reciprocity and solidarity.

To make explicit the links between economic and social problems, Figure 2 distinguishes between basic and derived social problems. *Basic* social problems (e.g. poverty, unemployment) are linked to economic problems insofar as they refer to the insufficient inclusion of actors in the provision of means of want satisfaction, resulting in relative deprivation on the labour-market or the goods-market (Runciman 1972: 222–287).

Problems like poverty, unemployment, bad housing conditions etc. often result from market-failure (Mishan 1969). Most of the basic social problems, nowadays, are processed by the state, that is, by hierarchic redistribution (e.g. social security systems). Modern forms of hierarchic redistribution are characterized by long and complex chains of means-end relationships which require money and legal entitlements as well as professional (paid) work and formal – sometimes bureaucratic – organization (Luhmann 1981; Kaufmann 1983).

Derived social problems, too, imply inequality, but, here, the focus is on insufficient inclusion in (a) processes of political decision-making and (b) the provision for cultural means of non-material want satisfaction. As political decision processes imply the authoritative allocation of means for want satisfaction, exclusion from political participation may induce economic deprivation (Olson 1965). As insufficient cultural integration – that is, deficiencies in socialization (e.g., education, professional training) – leads to a lack of fitness, talent, skills, and sociopsychic abilities, cultural deprivation may result in exclusion from political participation *and* economic provision.

With regard to the processing of derived social problems, the provision of personal services, nowadays, often lies with the welfare state. There has been an enormous expansion of publicly financed or organized people-processing activities (e.g. in the areas of child rearing, education, social work, psychiatric treatment) (Hegner 1983). The coordination of actions is based on the combination of hierarchic redistribution through formally organized public agencies with elements of – proclaimed and de-facto – cooperativeness between professionals and clients (Fauri 1978). Some of the public services are outflanked – and sometimes even replaced – by self-help and mutual-help groups relying on altruism, reciprocity and solidarity (Hegner 1979: 80–110; Badura 1980).

19.7 Co-Relations Between Problems to Be Solved, Institutional Arrangements and Levels of Social System Formation

The durable working of institutional arrangements depends on the fit between the coordination mechanisms used and two sets of factors: (a) the characteristics of the problems to be solved and (b) the characteristics of the collectivities (social system) which are involved in problem processing. To put it briefly: first, no coordination mechanism is suitable for all kinds of problems (economic and social deficiencies); second, no coordination mechanism is suitable for all kinds of social system formation (small groups, formal organizations, interorganizational networks); third, no level of social system formation is suitable for all kinds of problem processing (short and long, or simple and complex, chains of progression from the provision of means to the satisfaction of wants). Figure 3 presents an overview of the components of the puzzle which is used for the estimation of coordination mechanisms and institutional arrangements.

Institutional arrangements structuring the guidance, coordination and performance evaluation of individual or/and collective actors		
Solidarity	Hierarchy	Market Exchange
Within small groups – primary groups (e.g., family, household) – self-help and mutual-help groups – work groups forming part of formal organizations	Within small groups – primary groups – self-help and mutual-help groups – work groups forming part of formal organizations	Barter Gift Exchange
Between small groups – kinship networks, household networks – self-help and mutual-help group networks – work group networks	Between small groups – kinship networks, household networks – self-help and mutual-help group networks – work group networks	Trade Gift Exchange
Within formal organizations – bureaucratic org. – professional org.	Within formal organizations – bureaucratic org. – professional org.	Within formal organizations – bureaucratic org. – professional org.
Bargaining Interest Pooling	Between formal organizations – bureaucratic org. networks – professional org. networks	Between formal organizations – bureaucratic org. networks – professional org. networks
	Within societies – within societal subsystems (within economic, political, cultural subsystems) – between societal subsystems	Within societies – within societal subsystems – between societal subsystems
	Between societies – betweeen subsystems of different societies – between nations and states	Between societies – between subsystems of different societies – between nations and states
	Within "world society"	Within "world society"

Fig. 3: Focus of analysis: Types of institutional arrangements and actors involved

Levels of Social System Formation

In Figure 3, the assumed co-relations between institutional arrangements (including coordination mechanisms) and levels of social system formation (ranging from small groups to societies) are made explicit by the framed boxes. It is assumed, that the coordination of actions by solidarity plays a dominant part in small groups (e.g.

family households) and in transaction processes between small collectivities (e.g. self-help group networks). Within formal organizations (e.g. firms, agencies), solidarity may be present alongside of hierarchy, thereby guaranteeing durable cooperation in work groups (for example, in work groups confronted by performance ambiguities and risky tasks; Ouchi 1980). Coordination by hierarchic redistribution only plays a minor part in small collectivities, but is not necessarily absent (see, for example, the role of the "pater familias" in household families and the role of the "leader" in self-help groups).

Hierarchic redistribution of goods, e.g. materials, information, forms the dominant coordination mechanism in formal organizations, for example, in private firms and public agencies. It may be parallelled by reciprocity over time, that is, by deferred two-way transfers, e.g. from one department to another within the framework of a common 'budget', as well as by "bargaining processes" and "interest pooling" (Dahl and Lindblom 1963). With regard to the transactions *between* formal organizations, hierarchic redistribution may even be subordinate to the coordination of actions by bargaining and interest pooling. This proves true, particularly, for transactions between public agencies and private firms and, for example, between trade unions and employers' associations. Additionally, or substitutively, the relations between formal organizations may be based on price-determind exchange, which encompasses cooperation as well as competition.

Price-determined marked exchange is assumed to be one of the dominant coordination mechanisms on the level of modern industrialized societies where the economic subsystem is differentiated from the political and the cultural system (Parsons 1951). It also renders possible repeated and relatively durable transactions *between* societies. Alongside market exchange, transactions within societies may be coordinated by reciprocal solidarity (e.g. between individual and collective actors of the same class) and hierarchic redistribution (organized by the government, that is, by the actors of the political subsystem). In pre-industrial societies (of the tribal or archaic type), price-determined exchange may be subordinate to hierarchic redistribution and reciprocation, both being combined with "gift exchange" (Mauss 1969), "barter" (Chapman 1972) and "trade" (Polanyi 1957). But barter and trade can also be found in, and between, small groups (outside of and within formal organizations), forming part of highly industrialized societies.

Due to lack of space, the co-relations between coordinating mechanisms and levels of social system formation cannot be elaborated in greater detail. Nevertheless, we must give a preliminary answer to the question, *why* the aforementioned co-relations are assumed to be true. To answer this question, we have to refer to the co-relations between types of problems to be solved, ways of problem-processing, and actors involved.

Ways of Problem Processing

It is assumed that formally organized collective actors as well as inter-organizational networks play a dominant part in the provision of those means of want satisfaction (a) which can be standardized and calculated and (b) which require long, or complex, chains of means-end relationships. Due to their bureaucratic or/ and professional character, formal organizations, normally, fit the requirements of hierarchic redistribution and price-determined market exchange very well. With the help of division of labour and organizational departmentalization, they may even succeed in providing standardized *and* non-standardized means of want satisfaction, at the same time. For example, within welfare agencies, there may be specific departments for the delivery of standardized benefits in cash and in kind, being parallelled by departments for the delivery of personal services. Despite departmentalization, formal organizations often do not succeed in adapting the delivery of intangible goods (e.g. personal services) to the particular problems and wants of the clients. This failure is due, partly, to legal constraints and budgetary restrictions and, partly, to the dynamics of bureaucratization and professionalization (Grunow and Hegner 1980; Gross 1983: 124–160).

A growing number of critics decries the deficiencies of the delivery of means of want satisfaction by formal organizations (in the public as well as in the private (market) sector). Their criticisms focus on (a) the – assumed, or observed – lack of transparency and rigidity of complex chains of means-end(want) relationships, (b) the deficiencies of the provision of intangible goods (e.g. personal services), and (c) the standardization of delivery processes which prevents the adaption of material and non-material means to particular situational contexts (von Ferber 1983). Alongside these criticisms, there is the assumption that neither hierarchic redistribution nor price-determined market exchange are able to meet people's wants for particular treatment, personal commitment, cooperativeness, community, and – solidarity (Schumpeter 1970: 121–163; 205–218, 417–418; Boulding 1973).

Seen against this background, the current search for alternatives to "the welfare state" and "the market economy" becomes understandable (cf. Hoefnagels 1979). Nevertheless, the question has to be raised, whether altruism, reciprocity and solidarity can really work as alternative, or substitutional, coordination mechanisms, or whether they have to be seen as additional, or complementary, social mechanisms. Because of the specific sociopsychic and structural prerequisites for their working, which have been outlined in Sections 3–5, it is assumed that they, nowadays, primarily form complements to hierarchic redistribution and market exchange. Their functioning depends on the possibility of breaking into pieces long, or complex, chains of means-end(want) relationships. The segmentation, or differentiation, of complex chains renders possible the combination of different types of coordination mechanisms (Hegner 1979: 76–110).

Modern households, neighbourhood networks, self-help and mutual-aid groups as well as certain types of work groups within formal organizations make obvious that the provision of goods and services can be based on reciprocity and solidarity (Illich 1973). But, normally, they succeed in providing for want satisfaction only if they focus on the provision of means which can be produced, distributed and consumed within short and simple chains of progression (e.g. do-it-yourself, self-service, gardening). In addition, they may play a dominant part in the final stages of those long chains of provision which are based on the use of money, legal entitlements, and large-scale equipment: for example, groups of young people who engage in the remodeling of a youth centre. Finally, coordination of actions based on altruism, reciprocity or solidarity may be of use with regard to the provision of personal, or human, services. For example, self-help groups of (former) patients who need more than medicaments, surgical skill, and technical perfection provided by a formally organized private or public hospital.

19.8 Summary and Conclusion

In Section 1, the question was raised: How has it happened that the wide-spread criticisms of market failure and state failure are parallelled by the rediscovery of "solidarity"? The preliminary answer to this question was that there seems to be a discrepancy between existing problems to be solved and prevailing institutional arrangements. To eleborate this global answer a bit more, two typologies were outlined: a typology of institutional arrangements and a typology of problems to be solved and actors involved.

Problem-processing is conceived as a set of actions requiring cooperation between individual and collective actors. Cooperation depends on the coordination of actions and of objects being in the hands of the actors. The organized coordination of actions, outside of price-determined markets, is grouned on two bases: (a) generalized behaviour dispositions, that is, intra-individual guidelines for cooperative behaviour (e.g. altruism, loyalty); and (b), structural arrangements referring to the social symmetry between actors with regard to the willingness, ability or obligation to contribute (e.g. reciprocity, solidarity). The stability of the coordination of a (large) number of individual and collective actors depends on encompassing institutional arrangements, which guarantee the accommodation of generalized behaviour dispositions, structural arrangements and situational contexts. Three types of institutional arrangements are distinguished: solidaric reciprocity, hierarchic redistribution, and price-determined markets.

Solving a specific problem will require identifying the components – economic and social – and then searching through possible institutional arrangements to discover the best mix for a solution. Given the circumstances at our present point in time, these solutions are going to require some consideration in matching the problem to an optimum combination of hierarchy, market and reciprocity/solidarity. The goodness-of-fit of this matching will determine the success of any specific solutions.

Acknowledgement

My thanks go to Mirzda M. Troemel who helped to bring the text into better English and to clarify some of my arguments.

References

Albrecht, G. (1977): "Vorüberlegungen zu einer 'Theorie sozialer Probleme'." In Ferber, Chr. v., and F. X. Kaufmann (eds.), *Soziologie und Sozialpolitik*, 143–185. Opladen: Westdeutscher Verlag.
Arrow, K. J. (1975): "Gifts and Exchanges." In Phelps, E. S. (ed.), *Altruism, Morality and Economic Theory*, 13–28. New York: Russel Sage.

Badura, B. (1980): "Self-help Groups as an Alternative to Bureaucratic Regulation and Professional Dominance in the Human Services." In Grunow, D., and F. Hegner (eds.), *Welfare or Bureaucracy?*, 199–212. Cambridge, Mass.: Oelgeschlager, Gunn & Hain; Königstein/Ts.: A. Hain.

Barnard, Ch. I. (1938): *The Functions of the Executive.* Cambridge, Mass.: Harvard Univ. Press.

Baumann, D. J., R. B. Cialdini, and D. T. Kenrick (1981): "Altruism as Hedonism." *Journal of Personality and Social Psychology* 40/6: 1039–1046.

Berger, P., and T. Luckmann (1969): *Die gesellschaftliche Konstruktion der Wirklichkeit.* Frankfurt: S. Fischer. (first publ. 1966)

Boulding, K. E. (1973): *The Economy of Love and Fear.* Belmont, Calif.: Wadsworth.

Boulding, K. E. (1978): "Réciprocité et échange." In Michel, A. (ed.), *Les femmes dans la société marchande,* 21–37. Paris: P. U. F.

Boulding, K. E., and M. Pfaff (eds.) (1972): *Redistribution to the Rich and the Poor.* Belmont, Calif.: Wadsworth.

Brentano, D. von (1980): "Die Bedeutung der Solidarität in Genossenschaften und bei genossenschaftlichen Gründungsvorgängen." *Archiv für öffentliche und freigemeinnützige Unternehmen* 12: 11–31.

Burns, S. (1975): *Home, Inc.: The Hidden Wealth and Power of the American Household.* Garden City, N. Y.: Doubleday.

Chapman, A. (1972): "Barter as an Universal Mode of Exchange." *L'Homme* 20/3: 33–83.

Comte, A. (1956): *Discours sur l'esprit positif* (Ed. by I. Fetscher). Hamburg: Meiner 1956. (first publ. 1844)

Comte, A. (1969): Système de politique positive, Vol. II. In Comte, A., *Sociologie, Textes choisis* (Ed. by J. Laubier). Paris: P. U. F. (first publ. 1851–54)

Coser, L. (1956): *The Functions of Social Conflict.* London: Routledge & Kegan.

Dahl, R. A., and C. E. Lindblom (1963): *Politics, Economics, and Welfare.* New York–London: Harper & Row; The Univ. Library. (first publ. 1953)

Durkheim, E. (1967): *De la division du travail social.* Paris: P. U. F. (first publ. 1893)

Durkheim, E. (1967): *Le suicide.* Paris: P. U. F. (first publ. 1897)

Elias, N. (1976): *Der Prozeß der Zivilisation* (2 Vols.). Frankfurt: Suhrkamp. (first publ. 1936)

Fauri, D. P. (1978): "Public Service as a Service to Clients." *American Behavioral Scientist* 21/6: 859–879.

Ferber, Chr. von (1983): "Laienpotential, Patientenaktivierung und Gesundheitsselbsthilfe." In Ferber, Chr. von, and B. Badura (eds.), *Laienpotential, Patientenaktivierung und Gesundheitsselbsthilfe,* 265–293. München–Wien: Oldenbourg.

Ferguson, A. (1969): *An Essay on the History of Civil Society.* Farnborough, Hants.: Gregg. (Repr. of the ed. of 1773)

Galbraith, J. K. (1975): *Economics and the Public Purpose.* Harmonsworth: Penguin (first publ. 1974)

Gross, P. (1983): *Die Verheißungen der Dienstleistungsgesellschaft.* Opladen: Westdeutscher Verlag.

Grunow, D. and F. Hegner (eds.) (1980): *Welfare or Bureaucracy?* Cambridge, Mass.: Oelgeschlager, Gunn & Hain; Königstein/Ts.: A. Hain.

Halbwachs, M. (1925): *Les cadres sociaux de la mémoire.* Paris: P. U. F.

Hegel, G. W. F. (1970): Grundlinien der Philosophie des Rechts (1821). In Hegel, G. W. F., *Werke in zwanzig Bänden.* Theorie Werkausgabe. Vol. 7, §§ 182–208; 230–256. Frankfurt: Suhrkamp.

Hegner, F. (1978): *Das bürokratische Dilemma.* Frankfurt–New York: Campus.

Hegner, F. (1979): *Bürgernähe, Sozialbürgerrolle und soziale Aktion.* Bielefeld: Kleine.

Hegner, F. (1982): "Arbeiten, Herstellen und Handeln in familialen Haushalten." In

Hegner, F. and D. Freiburghaus, *Private Haushalte und Erwerbsneigung*. IIM/LMP 82–83. Wissenschaftszentrum Berlin.

Hegner, F. (1983): "Public Personal Services." In König, K., H. J. von Oertzen, and F. Wagener (eds.), *Public Administration in the FRG*, 149–162. Antwerpen et al.: Kluwer-Deventer.

Heimann, E. (1980): *Soziale Theorie des Kapitalismus*. Frankfurt: Suhrkamp. (first publ. 1929)

Hirschman, A. O. (1970): *Exit, Voice, and Loyalty*. Cambridge, Mass.: Harvard Univ. Press.

Hirschman, A. O. (1982): "Rival Interpretations of Market Society." *Journal of Economic Literature* 20/4: 1463–1484.

Hoefnagels, H. (1979): *Die neue Solidarität*. München: Kösel.

Illich, I. (1973): *Tools for Conviviality*. London–Boston: Calder & Boyars.

Kaufmann, F. X. (1982): "Elemente einer soziologischen Theorie sozialpolitischer Intervention." In Kaufmann, F. X. (ed.), *Staatliche Sozialpolitik und Familie*, 49–86. München––Wien: Oldenbourg.

Kaufmann, F. X. (1983): "Steuerungsprobleme im Wohlfahrtsstaat." In Matthes, J. (ed.), *Krise der Arbeitsgesellschaft*, 474–490. Frankfurt–New York: Campus.

Kennett, D. A. (1980): "Altruism and Economic Behavior. I, II." *American Journal of Economics and Sociology* 39/2;4: 183–198; 337–352.

Kirsch, G. (1983): "Ein Deckmantel kollektiven Zwangs." *Frankfurter Allgemeine Zeitung* 66: 15. (March 19, 1983)

Landshut, S. (1969): "Der Begriff des Ökonomischen." In Landshut, S., *Kritik der Soziologie und andere Schriften zur Politik*, 131–175. (Ed. by W. Hennis, and H. Maier). Neuwied–Berlin: Luchterhand.

Luhmann, N. (1972): "Knappheit, Geld und die bürgerliche Gesellschaft." *Jahrbuch für Sozialwissenschaft* 23: 186–210.

Luhmann, N. (1981): *Politische Theorie im Wohlfahrtsstaat*. München: Olzog.

Marien, M. (1978): "Toward a Devolution of Services." *Social Policy* 9/3: 26–35.

Matzner, E. (1982): *Der Wohlfahrtsstaat von morgen*. Frankfurt–New York: Campus.

Mauss, M. (1969): "La cohésion sociale dans les sociétés polysegmentaires (1931)." In Mauss, M., *Oeuvres*, Vol. 3: 11–27. (Ed. by V. Karady, 3 Vols.). Paris: Ed. de Minuit.

Merton, R. K. (1968): "Bureaucratic Structure and Personality (1940)." In Merton, R. K., *Social Theory and Social Structure*, 249–260. New York: The Free Press.

Merton, R. K. (1971): "Social Problems and Sociological Theory." In Merton, R. K., and R. N. Nisbet (eds.), *Contemporary Social Problems*, 697–737. New York: Harcourt. (3rd ed.)

Mishan, E. J. (1969): *The Costs of Economic Growth*. Harmondsworth: Penguin. (first publ. 1967)

Olson, M. (1965): *The Logic of Collective Action*. Cambridge, Mass.: Harvard Univ. Press.

Ouchi, W. G. (1980): "Markets, Bureaucracies, and Clans." *Administrative Science Quarterly* 25/1: 129–141.

Parsons, T. (1968): *The Structure of Social Action* (2 Vols.). New York: The Free Press. (first publ. 1937)

Parsons, T. (1964): *The Social System*. New York: The Free Press. (first publ. 1951)

Polanyi, K. (1944): *The Great Transformation*. New York: Van Nostrand.

Polanyi, K. (1957): "The Economy as Instituted Process." In Polanyi, K., K. M. Arensberg, and H. W. Pearson (eds.), *Trade and Market in the Early Empires*, 243–270. Glencoe, Ill.: The Free Press.

Robson, W. A. (1976): *Welfare State and Welfare Society*. London: Allen & Unwin.

Runciman, W. G. (1972): *Relative Deprivation and Social Justice*. Harmondsworth: Penguin. (first publ. 1966)

Schumpeter, J. A. (1970): *Capitalism, Socialism and Democracy*. London: Unwin Univ. Books. (first publ. 1942)

Scitovsky, T. (1976): *The Joyless Economy*. Oxford et al.: Oxford Univ. Press. (Paperback 1978)

Simon, H. A. (1945): *Administrative Behavior*. New York: MacMillan. (Paperback 1965)

Smith, A. (1853): *The Theory of Moral Sentiments*. London: H. G. Bohn. (Repr. of the 6th Ed. of 1789).

Spencer, H. (1961): *The Study of Sociology*. Ann Arbor: The Univ. of Michigan Press. (first publ. 1873)

Thompson, J. D. (1967): *Organizations in Action*. New York et al.: McGraw-Hill.

Vierkandt, A. (1972): "Solidarität." In Bernsdorf, W. (ed.), *Wörterbuch der Soziologie* (3 Vols.), 704–706. Frankfurt: Fischer. (first publ. 1969)

Weber, M. (1924): "Zur Geschichte der Handelsgesellschaften im Mittelalter (1889)." In Weber, M., *Gesammelte Aufsätze zur Sozial- und Wirtschaftsgeschichte*, 312–443. Tübingen: Mohr.

Weber, M. (1964): "Typen der Vergemeinschaftung und Vergesellschaftung in ihrer Beziehung zur Wirtschaft (1921)." In Weber, M., *Wirtschaft und Gesellschaft* (2 Vols.), Vol. 1, 275–301. (Ed. by J. Winckelmann) Köln–Berlin: Kiepenheuer & Witsch.

Weisser, G. (1954): "Genossenschaft und Gemeinschaft." *Gemeinnütziges Wohnungswesen* 7/12: 565–572.

20. Votes and Vetoes

Roberta Herzberg and Vincent Ostrom

Abstract

Votes and vetoes serve to authorize, constrain, and create essential linkages in the way that decision structures are related to one another in the governance of societies. Special attention is given to electoral systems based upon single-member constituencies and at-large constituencies with proportional representation and how these structures affect the articulation of opinion, the representation of interests, and the basic linkages that establish the grounds for governmental actions.

20.1 Introduction

A critical factor in the constitution of a democracy is the use of voting to take collective decisions and the use of vetoes to interpose limits in the exercise of authority. The laws that apply to the exercise of suffrage are of fundamental constitutional importance in any democratic society whether or not such laws are formulated in a specific document identified as the "constitution". A democratic republic is that form of government where the people of a republic exercise basic prerogatives of government. Voting as a way of signalling choice is necessary for people to participate in the taking of collective decisions; and laws of suffrage are one of the most fundamental elements in the constitution of democratic republics (Rae 1967: 3–7).

People cannot, however, discharge all of the prerogatives of government while acting in a collective capacity. Different institutional arrangements are necessary for assigning different decision-making responsibilities to officials who exercise a fiduciary responsibility in the discharge of political responsibilities in relation to the larger community of people in a democratic republic. Linkages that establish patterns of accountability are expressed in structures that reflect dependencies, autonomy, limits, and interdependencies. Patterns of dependency require those who exercise authority to be accountable to others. The exercise of discretion, however, always implies some degree of autonomy. Those who have the responsibility to exercise discretion on the behalf of the larger community of people must have an autonomous authority to do so. Where complex divisions of labor occur in the exercise of governmental authority, limits can either be formally specified or informally exercised. Limits are manifest as vetoes and express the way that authority is shared among diverse decision structures. Patterns of interdependencies are reflected by the way that dependent, autonomous, and limited relationships get linked together.

Some political systems make explicit use of vetoes as an exercise of constitutional prerogative. The American system of checks and balances is a complex structure of authorizations and vetoes to both distribute the power of government and establish conditions for the separable and joint use of those powers. The withholding of essential capabilities in the operation of society may also function as a veto mechanism. A strike by labor unions or a general suspension of regular activities as an expression of solidarity by a population as a whole can be used as vetoes to place limits upon the authority of governments.

Processes of collective decision making depend upon elucidating information both about preferences that are held by people in the larger society and the means-ends calculations that apply to collective endeavors that are being taken to affect the joint welfare that members of a society share with one another. The communication of preferences through voting mechanisms is an essential way for people to inform one another about what is valued and how to establish priorities as among different possibilities that are the objects of collective action. Seeking public office and voting for candidates to public office provides the occasion for a dialogue in democratic societies about basic priorities in public life.

Beyond establishing priorities in public life there is a problem of fashioning mutual understandings about what is to be done and how the burdens and benefits of collective action are to be shared among members of a society. Whatever is done involves costs. To pursue some possibilities forecloses other possibilities. To gain best advantage of the opportunities that are created often requires intelligent use of public services and public facilities on the part of citizens and ordinary members of a society as well as public servants. Only when there is a reciprocal understanding among producers and consumers of public goods and services can best advantage be taken of the opportunities that are made available. Good performance depends upon proportioning the supply of public services to effective demand in a way that yields a good fit between what is produced and how that which is produced is used or enjoyed by people in the larger society.

Many essential public services are intermediate products that enter effectively into the economic life of a society only if properly used by members of the larger society. Those members of that larger society become essential coproducers of many public services. Teachers cannot produce education alone. Education requires the coproductive efforts of students and their parents as well as the efforts of teachers. The dialogue between candidates for public office and voters can be an occasion then for fashioning mutual understandings that pertain to the way that public endeavors are organized and operated and how the reciprocal responsibilities of officials, voters, taxpayers, those who render public services, and those who use public services relate to one another in mutually interdependent chains of actions. Votes and vetoes, thus, shape the conditions of entrepreneurship in the public sector and provide a way that voters can hold officials accountable for the discharge of their offices as a public trust.

Electoral arrangements are fashioned in different ways in different societies. The method of the vote, the nature of the election, who is subject to election, and under what circumstances, in turn, have profound effects upon the nature of the dialogue that occurs between voters and candidates for public office in different societies. The way in which a democracy performs is, thus, significantly influenced by patterns of suffrage, structure of electoral arrangements, and how elections are linked to other decision structures in the organization of a system of government.

20.2 Comparing Votes and Vetoes in Different Electoral Systems

Given the limitations and constraints upon human communication in collective decision making, institutions are designed to relate citizen preferences to political action. Voting and veto mechanisms are ways of transmitting information about citizen interests for the purpose of political order. To understand the degree to which official channels of political action provide citizen input, we concern ourselves with three aspects of the process. First, we examine the way that different voting arrangements structure communication and affect the way that preferences are articulated and aggregated. Second, we consider how deliberations inform decisions, and finally, we outline how the consequences of decisions impinge upon those who are subject to collective decisions. Comparisons will be limited to two different types of competitive electoral arrangements: the single-member constituency where one representative is elected from each of a series of geographically-defined constituencies and the at-large constituency where all representatives are elected from the same constituency in proportion to the votes received in an election. Most democratic systems include some form or variation of these two basic types of electoral arrangements. In concentrating on these two basic types, we hope to isolate some general conclusions regarding the effect of electoral rules on the linkages between popular preferences and public decisions. Constraining the analysis to these two forms makes it difficult to capture the diversity of forms included in each of the basic types. Only in this general framework, however, can we examine the impact of these electoral rules apart from the other factors of particular importance in determining linkages in each nation.

Elections usually involve the selection of someone to function in some collective decision structure. Elections are, thus, always linked in critical ways to other decision structures. We assume voters base their electoral decisions on expected policy outcomes at later stages in the decision-making process. Thus, electoral support can play an important part in the difficulty or ease with which future governmental decisions are made. These linkages always imply that those who are subject to selections are players in a series of simultaneous and sequential games where a move in any one game potentially affects the opportunities that are available in the other linked games. The electoral connection between voting and decision structures can be expected to affect the structure of decisions made by representatives and elected officials in particular ways. The strong regional perspective of members of the U.S. Congress can be attributed, in part, to the electoral structure that designates representation on the basis of specific geographical constituencies and the interests of those constituents. Voters reward representatives for making policies that take their regional interests into account (Mayhew 1974; Arnold 1979). To the extent that voters select representatives within smaller geographical boundaries, they can protect local interests that might otherwise be lost in the broader, national arena. The cost of regional protection, however, may be conflict and stalemate with regard to truly national policy objectives if there is some fundamental antithesis between local and national interests.

Elections serve to regularize patterns of citizen input in the decision-making process so as to limit other forms for participation, such as political protest or mass demonstrations (Ginsberg 1982). The frequency and multiplicity of electoral opportunities provide electors with mechanisms to both channel and constrain collective choices in relation to the different communities of interest that are related to different units of government. If interests are not being served by currently elected representatives, voters may indicate their displeasure and throw them out. Thus, elections act as a crude veto mechanism over collective decisions.

The effectiveness of this veto relates to the rules and structure of the electoral system. Major electoral losses are strong ways of informing officials of citizen discontent with existing policies. The effectiveness of this veto mechanism depends, in part, on how direct the relationship is between the electoral decision and the formation of a government. In a single-member district system where structure drives the process towards two parties, a single party has the potential for exercising leadership in particular decision structures or in a government as a whole. A major electoral loss for the majority party is a clear message of discontent with leadership policies. In a proportional representation system, voters may be less clear about how to use their vote to indicate concern about the policies of a coalition government. In this latter case, voters may depend on protest movements and mass demonstrations in the interim between elections. More generally, veto opportunities arise whenever decisions in one context function as constraints on decisions in other contexts. Vetoes exist as a negative expression of electoral opportunities, but may also occur when one set of public decision makers constrains the actions of another set. Voters exercise an indirect veto whenever they are able to elect government officials to separate positions in the decision process so that those officials act as a check on the actions of others. Citizens, thus, participate in the exercise of both direct and indirect veto actions on collective decisions.

20.3 Single-Member Constituencies

Electoral arrangements that rely upon single-member constituencies require a process of apportionment where constituencies are assigned by some specifiable criteria. The most common criterion is one of equal proportions so that each constituency contains an approximately equal population. Other criteria may apply that take account of the boundaries of other political jurisdictions. In many federal systems of government the assignment of constituencies in the national legislature, for example, takes account of cantonal, provincial, or state boundaries. The mechanism for determining constituency boundaries affects the relative equality of political representation (Dixon 1968).

Most single-member-constituency electoral systems function under a plurality rule that designates the candidate who receives the largest number of votes as winner. Alternatively, simple majority rule would require a run-off election between the two leading candidates when no single candidate has received a majority of the total votes. Strict majority rule variations are relatively rare: the candidate, receiving the largest vote, wins.

Designating the winner as the one receiving the largest number of votes yields certain anomalies for political systems relying upon single-member-constituency electoral systems. If four candidates stand for election, the minimum winning vote would be one fourth of the total votes plus one. A minority of the population can, under that circumstance, successfully elect a representative for that constituency. If similar circumstances existed in each other constituency, a minority of the aggregate population might be successful in electing a majority of members to a legislature.

Although the above example is possible, it is highly unlikely for a number of reasons that significantly ameliorate such tendencies. First, since only the largest number of votes counts, there is an incentive for voters to shy away from any candidate whose chance of winning is not strong. Unless your candidate receives the greatest margin of support, you stand among the losers. Second, since only majority support can guarantee a victory, incentives exist for candidates to take positions that appeal to the greatest number of voters. These incentives reduce the probability of a four-way split.

When two candidates run for an election in a single-member constituency, each has a relatively equal chance of winning. When a third candidate enters the race, more complex calculations arise. The appeal of a third candidate is likely to detract more heavily from one of the two principal contending candidates than the other. The votes gained by the third candidate are likely to be at the cost of that candidate who is most closely associated with the appeal being made by the third candidate. Two scenarios are possible. First, inclusion of a third-party candidate may split the vote of a potential majority coalition and contribute to victory of the least preferred candidate. Alternatively, the minority coalition may be split resulting in a landslide for the winning candidate. The latter may be less serious with respect to outcome, but it can have the effect of justifying serious underrepresentation of fairly sizeable minorities. Voters may, thus, fear the consequences of voting for a third candidate. Only if a candidate has a serious chance of being one of the two major contenders are voters likely to give their support.

When national elections are organized into single-member districts, parties with support spread evenly across all districts may be seriously underrepresented in the seats-to-votes ratio while parties with concentrated regional strength may be greatly overrepresented in the national arena (Tufte 1973). The potential for underrepresentation in single-member constituencies was most recently indicated by the electoral fate of the Liberal/Social Democratic Parties' Alliance in Great Britain. Gaining 26.1 percent of the popular vote nationally, the Alliance captured only 23 seats in Parliament compared to Labour's 209 seats with 28.3 percent of the vote. The Alliance suffered from its consistent and strong second place finish in districts won by the Conservative majority. Unlike Labour with its regional strongholds, the Alliance could not depend on "safe" districts. To be advantaged in a single-member constituency arrangement, electoral support must be sufficiently concentrated to result in winning votes in particular districts.

The tendency towards underrepresentation of mainstream third parties accounts for the strong bias toward a two-party system in electoral systems that rely upon single-member constituencies. To maintain national support and attention requires being kept in the public eye. With only 23 seats, it is unlikely that the Alliance will be able to turn broad electoral support into a highly visible place in parliamentary proceedings. Regional concentration of support is a necessary condition for maintenance of third parties in a single-member system.

There is, however, another tendency at work in single-member constituencies that requires attention. If the constituency shares preferences so that the largest portion of the population is clustered around a median between two extremes, the contending candidates will have incentives to make their principal appeal to the median voter (Black 1958; Downs 1957). This yields a tendency for the contenders to make appeals that are not easily distinguished from one another. Voters are presented with a choice between two candidates who advocate much the same program.

When such circumstances arise and there is little risk of voter abstention, incentives exist for third candidates to enter electoral contests. This, in turn, creates incentives for the two leading candidates to differentiate their appeal to the electorate. Concern about throwing away one's vote once the two leading candidates have differentiated their appeal contributes to a lack of viability for a third candidate. This, in part, explains why third parties often are important in raising new issues but are virtually powerless in gaining electoral victories. They may create sufficient public concern for new issues to be placed on the agenda of public deliberations, but the rules of the electoral system seriously constrain their chances for electoral success (Mazmanian 1974). They affect the agenda of collective action without being able to win office and sponsor legislation. Single-member-constituency systems are thus marked by tendencies toward two leading contenders, but with recurrent entry of third contenders who maintain only short-term viability. Such a system biases appeals to voter preferences that reflect central tendencies in a population, but leads to a challenge by other contenders whenever the appeal of leading contenders fails to provide distinguishable options.

In summary, single-member-constituency systems place major emphasis on maximizing relative vote totals and in so doing limit the potential for minority representation. The policy focus expected from such a system is towards more broad, and sometimes ambiguous, positions. To the extent that support must be broad, each individual voter exercises less power in potentially vetoing public programs. Only if the margin of support changes significantly are changes in representatives and policy likely to occur.

The working out of these tendencies is significantly influenced by the linkages to political parties, interest groups, and the relevant decision structures of government. Incentives exist to gain the advantage of teamwork by forming a joint slate of candidates who cooperate in making a joint appeal to the electorate and in getting out the vote on election day. Information dissemination, where the party acts as a signalling device, is an important factor in single-member constituency elections. The slating of candidates affects the options that are available to voters. The availability of ways and means to appeal to voters and get out the vote has an effect upon who wins and who loses. Who wins and loses elections in turn affects how governmental prerogatives are exercised in taking of collective decisions. The relationship between candidates and later decisions is affected by the degree of party cohesion with respect to issue positions. Party may be a meaningful force in electoral considerations, but far less effective in structuring the remainder of the decision process. The way these structures are linked establishes who and what is taken into account in making collective decisions (Ostrogorski 1964). If party discipline is strong, as in Great Britain, electors vote for candidates who reflect a party position and the linkage between an electoral decision and policy decisions is directly associated. Control over the government goes to the majority party in Parliament. Alternatively, where parties serve as electoral tags, but individual candidates control their own issue positions and future policy decisions the linkage associated with party is less clear (Crotty and Jacobson 1980).

When party, for whatever reason, fails to provide strong links between elections and decisions, interest groups may assume this role. The difficulty with interest groups providing the link between citizens and official representatives is their tendency to concentrate on specialized policy decisions without concern for the broader interests and support necessary to win elections in single-member constituencies. Rather than giving coherence to the linkage process, interest groups may generate conflicting signals that confound the voting decision and its relation to future governmental decisions. When such groups are powerful forces in politics, interests may be well-protected at the cost of collective action. Such groups may gain access to official agendas and control key points where they exercise veto power over decisions that threaten their specific interests.

Success in future elections requires representatives in single-member constituencies to place emphasis upon the demands and interests of constituents. Each representative faces the multiple realities of constituency, party organization, and a voice in the formal structure of government. Wherever there are independent opportunities to affect outcomes, a potential veto-point exists. The structure of linkages establishes the potential combination of votes and vetoes and the incentives that people have to either support or constrain choice in linked structures of votes and vetoes.

In the British Parliamentary system, control over both legislative policy and over the executive apparatus of government accrues to the leadership that maintains a voting majority in the House of Commons. This creates strong incentives to maintain a disciplined coalition that will vote together on legislative matters. Its future success depends in turn upon maintaining a strong organization that is capable of slating candidates, conducting a campaign, and getting out the votes in a few week's notice when the timing of an election is usually determined by the leadership of the majority party or coalition.

The structure is organized to facilitate dominance by majority leadership that can preempt consideration of policy issues during its tenure in office. Opportunities to influence policy must await a new election when a similar preemptive advantage accrues to the new majority leadership. The absence of vetoes within the government itself means that the creation of veto potentials depends upon a realignment of parties, a modification in the constitution of particular parties to constrain the dominance of parliamentary leadership, ways to withhold essential economic services, or a combination of all three strategies. The implicit negotiation of what might be referred to as "social contracts" then serves as constraints upon the "unlimited" power of Parliament.

The American system of government is marked by many different structures that are linked by explicit veto mechanisms internal to the structure of government. The legislative process in the national government is organized by reference to three

different decision structures that rely upon quite different constituency relationships. The House of Representatives is elected from 435 single-member constituencies. The members of the Senate are elected from states that constitute single-
member constituencies for any particular senatorial election. The President is
elected through a mechanism in which each state votes as a constituency to elect
presidential electors equal to the number of representatives and senators for that
state, and these electors, in turn, elect the President.

Enactment of legislation depends upon the concurrence of the House of Representatives, the Senate, and the President. A veto by the President can be overrid-
den by a two-thirds majority in the House of Representatives and the Senate. The
electoral arrangements mean that the national constituency is aggregated in three
different ways and that legislation requires the concurrence of those who represent
three different types of constituency relationships to the same population. The
institutional rules of each of these bodies of government reflect the different
constituency basis of each branch. The smaller the base of constituency concerns,
the less centralized official decision mechanisms are. Although each deals with
national interests, the differences in electoral structure create different conditions
for the consideration of these national issues. As constituency size is altered, some
change in the agenda is likely to occur. Redundancy in deliberation occurs by
taking account of different communities of interests shared by the same population.

The organization of political parties in the United States is largely controlled by
state laws. Open primary elections have increasingly replaced the old party caucus
as a closed selection process. Under primary election procedures, any party
member is free to challenge any other party member in a publicly conducted
election for a party's nomination to a particular office. Slating under these rules is
primarily controlled by the party members in each constituency. Party leadership
exercises only weak influence in establishing party slates and in how individual
representatives vote in making collective decisions.

The competence of the judiciary to consider the constitutional standing of
legislation and the discharge of governmental prerogative in accordance with
constitutional due process means that courts can also interpose potential vetoes.
Since courts act only on the initiative of those who seek redress of a grievance, the
exercise of judicial vetoes is potentially available to any aggrieved party. Factors
such as education and wealth of the individual or the calendar of the courts may
limit the degree to which a veto through the judiciary is available to any one
individual. However, controlling for resource constraints, any person (and that
person need not be a citizen) has potential access to veto capabilities in relation to
collective decisions.

20.4 At-Large Constituencies with Proportional Representation

Parliamentary systems of government in continental Europe have traditionally
relied upon some form of at-large constituencies with proportional representation.
In its most simple form, a nation-state forms a single constituency. The voter's
choice in that simple form is a choice among the parties that submit lists of

candidates standing for election. The proportion of votes cast for each party is used to determine the proportion of representatives that are elected to the national legislative assembly. The organization of government follows the parliamentary tradition of assigning political leadership to those who can gain and maintain majority support.

In the traditional party-list system, the slating of candidates is done by a national party organization. Although formally the national party controls final lists, regional and local party officials may in fact play a major part in recruitment and in determining the general content of the list. The extent to which regional officials influence the selection process will influence how important regional considerations may be in the strategy of electoral politics. The order in which the names of candidates is listed is of critical importance. The higher on the list, the greater the probability of election.

Since success depends, in large part, upon an appeal to a national constituency in relation to identifiable communities of opinion, each political party has an incentive to articulate an appeal that differentiates its supporters from other communities of opinion. Unlike the single-member district system in which parties were required to establish some regional basis for their support, this is not *necessary* in the proportional representation system unless separate regional slates are used in structuring at-large constituencies. This does not imply that regional factors are unimportant in organizing coalitions in these systems. Any party that can maintain support from a differentiable community of opinion based on any of a number of factors – language, religion, class, etc. – can be assured of success in proportion to the size of that community of opinion. Even a small identifiable community of opinion assures success for some small fraction of representatives elected to a legislative assembly so long as their aggregate vote exceeds the minimum ratio for representation.

The structure of incentives in an at-large electoral system with proportional representation yields a party system that places greater emphasis upon ideological differentiation of diverse communities of opinion. The rules of the electoral structure do not require diverse interests to compromise or soften their particularized interests to gain seats in a representative body except to the extent that those interests surpass an established minimum. The appeal to diverse communities of opinion yields a tendency toward multiple parties. Governing, however, still requires the formation of larger groups that may soften the intensity of conflict in the at-large system. There exists a tension in proportional representation systems between the rules that apply to electoral contests and the rules of government formation (Katz 1980). In essence, electoral incentives promote greater ideological differentiation, while incentives of governance require room for compromise within the programs of the different parties.

The formation of coalitions that are capable of maintaining majority support typically occurs in negotiations among parties since any one party is not likely to command majority support from the larger national constituency. Bargaining among party leaders becomes an essential process in the formation of a government. Bargaining power is not proportioned directly to the votes received from the electorate, but to the value of each party in forming a coalition. Representatives of the marginal party forming a governing coalition exercise greater weight in establishing a coalition's program than an equivalent number of representatives of the most numerous party in the coalition (Dodd 1976). Although the party with the largest number of representatives is most likely to gain the major governing positions, their share of positions will be proportionately less than those granted the marginal party or parties. The power exercised by each coalition member is a function of their contribution to the majority status of the coalition and the availability of acceptable alternative coalition partners. Parties may be constrained in the formation of coalition governments by ideological distance between potential coalition partners (Grofman 1982).

If no ideologically acceptable alternative coalition members exist, the marginal party will have an even greater degree of bargaining potential in the formation of the new government. Failure on the part of the marginal party to go along may result in the collapse of the government requiring a new election. In this instance, the marginal party can demand a much higher proportion of the political advantage from other coalition members.

Success in future elections depends upon the maintenance of the continued support for distinguishable communities of opinion by the leadership of each party. When essential interests of any one party are threatened, it is capable of exercising a veto. Unless an oversize coalition exists, withdrawal of a party's support means the collapse of the majority coalition and the necessity to either form a new coalition or call a new election. Potential veto positions can be exercised by any party in a coalition, but they may be very costly to the party exercising the veto. If the veto attempt fails to result in a weakened position for the major parties in the coalition, the vetoing party may be excluded from future positions of government or be punished in the resulting electoral contest. Thus, we would expect coalition members to use their veto only when *essential* interests are in question.

Processes of government are bounded by combinations of votes and vetoes. The viability of small splinter parties representing extreme opinions exposes a political system relying upon an at-large electoral system with proportional representation to the formation of parties that use electoral processes and parliamentary processes of government to attack those institutions and to obstruct efforts to seek deliberative solutions to common problems. Although obstruction is possible by splinter parties, proportional representation systems maintain some level of consensual support by punishing parties that promote extreme conflict by excluding them as potential governing partners. A party that continually proposes extreme positions unacceptable to a majority of the population may by that strategy exclude itself as an unacceptable coalition partner. Without the potential for governing power, extreme parties may find it difficult to maintain their electoral position, particularly if voters base their choices on expected policy decisions as we assume.

The basic justification of the at-large electoral system with proportional representation is to provide an accurate reflection of public opinion in the councils of government. With regard to deliberations in the representative body this may be true. However, in terms of governmental decisions, the operation of such a system yields counterintuitive results. Extensive veto capabilities and significant bargaining power to those who represent relatively minor positions among the population creates the potential for underrepresentation of major interests in society. In essence, the potential for underrepresentation in the single-member constituency system may simply be moved to the post-election governing stage in the proportional representation system.

Post-World-War-II European constitutions have significantly modified at-large electoral systems by disqualifying splinter parties receiving less than a specified fraction of the vote, the use of regional lists as a substitute for or as a supplement to national lists, and the use of voter preferences to establish priority among candidates on any one list. Some elements of the single-member-constituency electoral system have also been introduced as complements to at-large electoral systems with proportional representation to yield mixed electoral systems.

An even greater concern than the question of underrepresentation present in each of the systems is the problem associated with the indecisiveness of election outcomes for government formation in proportional representation systems. When the decision of government formation is made separate from the electoral contest, it is difficult for the individual voter to know how that vote will be translated into government action. A party with issue positions of great distaste to the voter may, in fact, be a part of the governing coalition their vote is used to support. At the time of voting, the voter may be unaware of what positions and issues will be traded to other parties in an effort to establish a majority coalition. Their vote for one party may have been based on the party platforms along the issue dimensions that are now largely controlled by ministers of an opposing party. Although voters may have some information regarding possible coalition partners prior to the election, the exact balance and distribution of positions and control will depend on the final vote totals and thus, not be available at the time of the vote. This presents a serious problem in proportional representation systems. Guidance of government decisions by voters becomes difficult when they are unsure of how those votes will be translated into policy. The extent to which voters are able to exercise control over governmental decisions, in large part, rests on the ability of parties to practice a veto within the coalition over issues of importance to the voters. If parties are effective when essential interests are concerned, voters may exercise a voice with reference to essential interests.

20.5 Conclusion

No electoral system will permit the "Voice of the People" to prevail. Any electoral system permits people to exercise some voice in collective decisions. The nature of that voice does *not* turn upon the fact of election per se, but the way that elections are linked to the diverse processes of government in a society. Whoever is elected to some office serves as a link between those who do the electing, those who assist in the election, and the decision-making structure in which the office is embedded. Meeting the requirements of these diverse structures is a limiting condition that bounds the strategic opportunities for anyone who aspires to an elective office.

Electoral processes provide participants with opportunities to speak and be heard. The nature of the communication, the matters that are addressed, the positions taken, and the nature of the response are significantly affected by the way that electoral processes are structured. The single-member constituency yields quite different results than at-large electoral arrangements with proportional representation.

Participating in electoral processes enables citizens to compare their circumstance with the assessments and proposals advanced by candidates. Candidates learn about the problem, preferences, and responses of constituents. But, the opportunities to act depend upon meeting the conditions of choice both in authorizing and implementing collective decisions. A multitude of others are involved. Limits to human knowledge, constraints upon opportunities to have a say, and self-serving distortions of information mean that collective choice is plagued by propensities for errors. The problem is how to limit those propensities to err and to provide human beings with constructive opportunities to develop their potentials and take account of one another.

In devising appropriate decision-making arrangements, no simple arrangement will suffice. If everyone were required to agree to any course of collective action, then each person would be in a position to veto collective action. Under those circumstances, each person would become the judge of his or her own interest in relation to the interest of others. Once a rule of unanimity is relaxed to allow for some form of majority or plurality decisions, then an opportunity is created for some to exploit others. Such possibilities can be constrained only as anyone is capable of interposing a veto whenever his or her essential interests or rights are jeopardized. This is the ground for establishing judicial remedies to interpose limits upon official discretion.

Authority to act always needs to be viewed in relation to correlative limits upon authority to act. But votes and vetoes are necessary complements to one another in establishing appropriate boundaries to the exercise of human discretion and to create a structure of incentives to search out mutually productive resolutions to joint problems. The way structures become linked together through mechanisms like elections has an important effect upon the rule-ruler-ruled relationship. Linkages can create bonds of reciprocity in human societies; or they can align elements in a society to war upon one another.

There is no perfect mode of election. Elections cannot provide mandates for action without regard for the interests of others. Elections always need to be viewed in the way that they link structures together to take account of diverse interests and diverse sets of consideration. They provide occasions for dialogue and deliberation among the elected about what is in the joint interest of those who elect.

The dialogue between candidates for public office and voters and the relationship of this dialogue to who wins and who loses serves as a mechanism for targeting legislative deliberations and collective action. Veto mechanisms serve to bound or constrain the realm of feasible collective action. By both targeting and bounding the realm of public discourse and collective action, votes and vetoes perform an important function in steering processes of collective action along channels that establish the scope of what is politically feasible.

Acknowledgement

Theo Toonen was especially helpful in his critique of an earlier draft of this paper. What we say needs to be appropriately qualified in addressing the characteristics of particular electoral systems, and the way they are linked to structures of government and to the longer-term cultural heritage and patterns of settlement that have established the basic cultural and spatial patterns in different societies.

References

Arnold, R. D. (1979): *Congress and The Bureaucracy*. New Haven, Conn.: Yale Univ. Press.

Beyme, K. von (1982): *Parteien in westlichen Demokratien*. München: Piper.

Black, D. (1958): *Theory of Committees and Elections*. Cambridge, Mass.: Cambridge Univ. Press.

Crotty, W., and G. Jacobson (1980): *American Parties in Decline*. Boston: Little, Brown.

Dixon, R. (1968): *Democratic Representation*. New York: Oxford Univ. Press.

Dodd, L. (1976): *Coalitions in Parliamentary Government*. Princeton, N. J.: Princeton Univ. Press.

Downs, A. (1957): *An Economic Theory of Democracy*. New York: Harper and Brothers.

Duverger, M. (1954): *Political Parties*. New York: John Wiley and Sons.

Farquarson, R. (1969): *Theory of Voting*. New Haven, Conn.: Yale Univ. Press.

Ginsberg, B. (1982): *The Consequences of Consent: Elections, Citizen Control and Popular Acquiesence*. Reading, Mass.: Addison-Wesley.

Grofman, B. (1982): "A Dynamic Model of Proto-Coalition Formation in Ideological N-Space." *Behavioral Science*, 29/1: 77–90.

Katz, R. (1980): *A Theory of Parties and Electoral Systems*. Baltimore, Md.: John Hopkins Univ. Press.

Lawson, K. (ed.) (1980): *Political Parties and Linkage: A Comparative Perspective*. New Haven, Conn.: Yale Univ.Press.

Mayhew, D. (1974): *Congress: The Electoral Connection*. New Haven, Conn: Yale Univ. Press.

Mazmanian, D. (1974): *Third Parties in Presidential Elections*. Washington, D. C.: Brookings Institution.

Michels, R. (1962): *Political Parties*. New York: The Free Press.

Milnor, A. J. (1969): *Elections and Political Stability*. Boston: Little, Brown.

Neimi, R., and H. Weisberg (eds.) (1976): *Controversies in Voting Behavior*. San Francisco: Freeman.

Ostrogorski, M. (1964): *Democracy and the Organization of Political Parties*. Garden City, N. Y.: Doubleday.

Page, B., and R. Brody (1972): "Policy Voting and the Electoral Process: The Vietnam War Issue." *American Political Science Review* 66/3: 979–995.

Rae, D. (1967): *The Political Consequences of Electoral Laws*. New Haven, Conn.: Yale Univ. Press.

Riker, W. (1962): *The Theory of Political Coalitions*. New Haven, Conn.: Yale Univ. Press.

Riker, W. (1982): *Liberalism Against Populism*. San Francisco: Freeman.

Rokkan, S. (1970): *Citizens, Elections, Parties*. New York: D. McKay.

Sartori, G. (1965): *Democratic Theory*. New York: Fr. A. Praeger.

Sorauf, F. (1980): *Party Politics in America*. Boston: Little, Brown.

Tufte, E. (1973): "Relationship Between Seats and Votes in Two Party Systems." *American Political Science Review* 62/2: 540–554.

21. Mutual Adjustment by Debate and Persuasion

Giandomenico Majone

Abstract

Interdependent activities may be coordinated in the absence of a central coordinator if each individual in a group adjusts himself to the state of affairs resulting from the actions of other individuals in that group. Such coordination by mutual adjustment can assume different forms: competitive adjustments, as in the market; persuasion, as in an adversary process; consultation, as in a collegium. This chapter focuses on the last two types of mutual adjustment. Persuasion is shown to be as important in achieving social consensus on policy as in resolving conflicts among experts over technical issues with public policy implications. The collegium is discussed as a distinct principle of coordination based on consultation and persuasion, rather than on competitive adjustments or administrative rules. When cognitive complexity is high, outcomes ambiguous, and quality difficult to evaluate, the collegium has definite advantages over alternative modes of coordination and control. Hence, it is proposed that collegiality, rather than hierarchy, should be the main organizing principle for highly technical activities of public administration such as environmental and safety regulation. The chapter concludes by noting the role of persuasion in bridging the gap between policy formulation and implementation, and in creating a context in which social learning can take place.

21.1 Introduction

An important reason for the difficulties presently experienced by policymakers is the shifting focus of public programs from activities limited in scope and simple enough to be organized by traditional administrative methods to activities involving great cognitive complexity, idiosyncratic rather than standardized tasks and, above all, a multiplicity of actors and long chains of actions (cf. Kaufmann: Ch. 10). This shift has become increasingly noticeable during the last two decades, and is exemplified by the transition from old-style economic regulation, which tends to be confined to specific sectors of the economy and concerned with such tangible issues as prices of products, entry conditions, and licenses and quotas, to the new social regulation dealing with problems like environmental protection, occupational health and safety, consumer ignorance, technological risks, and unfair employment practices. Because these problems are so pervasive, social regulation extends to many more industries and affects many more workers, consumers, and other citizens than the old kind of regulation. It also affects much more directly the conditions under which goods and services are produced, often rasing scientific and technological questions for which no unambiguous answers are yet available.

Public concern with environmental externalities, consumer ignorance, risk, or discrimination is usually justified by the argument that such problems cannot be handled by the voluntary exchange mechanisms of private markets. It is not possible, or too costly, for individuals to rely on private markets to buy clean air and water, protection from toxic chemicals, insurance against the risk of catastrophic nuclear accidents, or a more satisfying working environment. On the other hand, experience has shown that bureaucratic regulation in these and similar areas is intrinsically rigid, often ineffective, and has a built-in tendency to become obsolete quickly.

The simultaneous occurrence of "market failure" and "bureaucratic failure" presents an insoluble dilemma as long as social science research is guided by the implicit assumption that the price system and bureaucracy are the only practically important forms of social organization, at least when large numbers are involved. Fortunately, as the preceding chapters have shown, the pool of available modes of coordination and control is a good deal richer than traditional theory would lead one to believe. If in the past the same standard solutions have been proposed again and again, today's problems require a greater willingness to experiment with variants whose merits may be as yet unjudged in the context of public policy.

This chapter discusses certain forms of coordination by mutual adjustment whose importance in specialized settings such as the law, scientific research, or professional organizations, has long been recognized but which, it will be argued, could also be usefully applied on a larger scale in the public sector.

21.2 Coordination by Mutual Adjustment

Coordinating large numbers of people is a key problem which every social organization must somehow solve. Bureaucratic organization is one important method by which a relatively small number of people can coordinate the activities of large numbers of individuals. Indeed, it is widely assumed that a hierarchy of authority is essential for coordination in all complex organization. Hierarchical coordination implies, *inter alia,* that the solution of every new problem that arises between different individuals or organizational units is delayed until relevant information has been transmitted up the hierarchy and a decision has been made and sent down again.

But as Blau and Scott (1962) have shown, in the very organizations where interdependent activities are most pronounced, and hence the need of coordination most acute, coordination is not achieved by hierarchical methods. Instead, two alternative mechanisms are used: prior design of the production process (e.g., the arrangement of work stations on the conveyors), and horizontal, rather than vertical, communication among peers. Thus, in the spinning department studied by Richard Simpson (1959), most contacts of first-line foremen for the purpose of coordinating their interdependent sections were not with superiors or subordinates, but with other foremen of their own level.

These two mechanisms correspond to the two basic forms of social coordination discussed by Kaufmann in Chapter 10, namely, coordination by rules and coordination by interaction. In fact, the informal pattern of communication among first-line foremen examplifies a method of interactive coordination which, following Polanyi (1951) and Lindblom (1965), we shall call coordination by mutual adjustment. A characteristic feature of this method is that each individual (or institutional actor) in a certain set adjusts himself to a state of affairs resulting from the actions of other individuals or actors in the same set. A competitive market is the paradigm example of a system whose parts are coordinated by a series of spontaneous adjustments, but as Polanyi (1951: 162–167) has shown, the coordination of buyers and sellers in a market is only a special case of a more general mechanism which also operates in such disparate fields as the law (particularly Anglo-Saxon common law) and science.

A judge deciding a difficult case refers not only to legal sources, precedents, and doctrine, but to the entire contemporary trends of opinions and societal values. In this way, coordination is achieved by a sequence of adjustments between succeeding judges, guided by a parallel interaction between the judges and the general public. The social order thus generated differs profoundly from the spontaneous order of a competitive market: "While an economic system of spontaneous order coordinates individual actions merely to serve the momentary material interest of its participants, an orderly process of judicature deposits a valid and lasting system of legal thoughts" (Polanyi 1951: 163).

Unlike the judge, the scientist is not given a case to decide, but selects his own research problems. Still, in attempting to solve his chosen problem, he resembles the judge in accepting a great deal of previously established knowledge, while also taking into account the whole trend of current scientific opinion. What is common to scientists and judges is the particular method used to achieve coordination by mutual adjustments. This is a process of *consultation* which stands in marked contrast to the *competitive adjustments* through which a spontaneous order is established in the market.

A debate between advocates of different opinions provides another example of mutual coordination. Each advocate adjusts his arguments to what has been said before, and thus all the different aspects of a case are in turn revealed, and the audience is eventually persuaded to accept one opinion and reject the others. Polanyi classifies this type of coordination separately as a system of spontaneous order based on *persuasion*.

In Chapter 10, four levels of the coordination problem have been identified: intraindividual coordination, interindividual coordination, intraorganizational coordination, and interorganizational coordination. Mutual adjustment has been mostly discussed in the literature at the level of interindividual and interorganizational coordination, but it is also important in intraorganizational, and even intraindividual (Perelman and Olbrechts-Tyteca 1958; Festinger 1957), relations. Chester Barnard, for example, recognizes that persuasion ("changing states of mind") is important for reducing the incongruence of goals that is present in every organization.

"An organization can secure the efforts necessary to its existence, then, either by the objective inducement it provides or by changing states of mind. It seems to me improbable that any organization can exist as a practical matter which does not employ both methods in combination." (Barnard 1968; 141).

This is especially true in the case of peer or collegial groups, professional organizations, and other types of "organic associations" (Durkheim 1933) which, lacking a hierarchical coordinator and monitor, must rely on social control and mutual adjustments to coordinate the activities of their members. The effectiveness of such indirect methods is shown by the fact that these associations can achieve great regularity of relations and tolerate levels of ambiguity in performance that would baffle bureaucratic as well as market mechanisms of control (Ouchi 1980).

Spontaneous methods of intraorganizational coordination deserve special attention at a time when the influence of professionalism in government is rising sharply, and "government by administrators", typical for example of the American New Deal, makes for "government by professionals" (Mosher 1968: 105; Porter 1980). For this reason and because, as noted, the literature on coordination by mutual adjustment has largely ignored questions of internal organization, coordination in collegial groups receives separate treatment in this chapter. On the other hand, methods of mutual adjustment that operate by altering the benefits or costs of various courses of action, like bargaining and negotiation, are not discussed here. While such methods have been carefully investitgated by a number of scholars (e.g. Dahl and Lindblom 1953, 1976; Schelling 1960; Neustadt 1960; Lindblom 1965, 1976 and Chapters 23, 24, and 25 in this volume), much less is known about coordinating actions by debate and persuasion.

21.3 Partisan Debate

The notion of "government by discussion", conceived as a cooperative search for the best course of collective action, is as old as Aristotle and plays a central role in the classical theory of parliamentary democracy (Bagehot 1956). However, the importance of *partisan* discussion in bringing about an uncoercive kind of coordination among policy actors has been recognized only recently. Lindblom (1965: 220–222 and *passim*) demonstrates the extraordinary potential of partisan debate by contrasting it with cooperative discussion, where the various participants are assumed to share common criteria adequate to distinguish between right and wrong, or correct and incorrect decisions. Participants in a cooperative discussion are not free to modify or abandon values and criteria that are supposedly shared by the group. Thus, cooperative discussants may remain frozen on what each understands to be common values, while advocates are free to shift values that impede agreement. Connected with the rigid adherence to general principles is a tendency of cooperative discussion to become abstract and ideological. By contrast, participants in a partisan debate tend to proceed pragmatically, letting their values emerge implicitly from the policy positions they take, and acknowledging legitimate differences in interests and opinions. Again, participants in cooperative discussion cannot proceed until they find a set of values on which they all can agree, while advocates do not require any such prior agreement.

It is also worth noting that the range of permissible arguments is much more restricted in cooperative discussion where persuasion is limited to appeals to empirical evidence that certain proposals do not, in fact, produce the consequences which the group is supposed to prefer (Lindblom 1965: 221). Partisan arguments, on the other hand, may be directed to disagreements about values and preferences, as well as to disagreements about matters of fact. Thus, advocates can engage in a fruitful interplay between facts and values and explore possibilities of agreement that are largely precluded to people committed to a closed set of principles.

In recent years, partisan debate has played an increasingly important role in specialized areas of public policy previously entrusted to the responsibility of recognized experts. This development is closely related to the expansion of the area where science, technology and public policy meet, the consequent growth of "regulatory science", and the emergence of powerful movements demanding a social assessment of new technologies and greater environmental and consumer protection. Under such conditions, obtaining and coordinating expert opinion in fields like nuclear power, environmental protection, or occupational health and safety has proved to be a much more difficult problem than the early advocates of governmental regulation could imagine. Expert A disagrees with the conclusions of expert B but finds it difficult or impossible to disprove specific points in B's arguments. The same data, differently interpreted, lead to divergent policy recommendations. Factual arguments are practically inseparable from subjective considerations having to do with the plausibility of the opponent's assumptions, his selection of the evidence, or choice of methodology. And because there often is no objective way of verifying the correctness of the technical conclusions, the credibility of the expert becomes as important as his competence.

Actually, the issues over which expert disagreement is most serious are, in Alvin Weinberg's terminology, "trans-scientific" rather than strictly scientific or technical. Trans-scientific issues are questions of fact that can be stated in the language of science but are, in principle or in practice, unanswerable by science (Weinberg 1972). The determination of the health effects of low-level radiation is an example. It has been calculated that in order to determine by direct experimentation, at the 95% confidence level, whether a level of X-ray radiation of 150 millirems would increase the spontaneous mutation in mice by ½ percent, would require about 8 billion mice. Time and resource constraints make such an experiment practically infeasible. Hence, radiation standards cannot be based on a firm foundation of scientific knowledge, but involve a good deal of extra-scientific judgment. The same is true of analyses attempting to determine the risk of extremely unlikely events like catastrophic reactors accidents, since the data presently available do not allow any direct verification of the calculations.

Where the issues to be resolved are trans-scientific, disagreement among experts is to be expected. In the nature of things, conflicting opinions can be legitimately held and fruitfully debated by equally reputable scientists. Such a state of affairs suggests that partisan debate among technical experts, modeled on the adversary procedures of law courts, may be an effective method of dealing with controversial scientific issues of public policy. As physicist Weinberg argues, an adversary process "undoubtedly has considerable merit in forcing scientists to be more honest, to say where science ends and trans-science begins, as well as to help weigh the ethical issues which underlie whatever choices the society makes between technological alternatives" (1972: 214).

However, the notion of partisan debate is foreign, when not abhorrent, to modern science. It will be recalled that Descartes considered "almost as false whatever was only probable", and disagreement a sure sign of error. In a famous passage of the *Regulae ad Directionem Ingenii* he writes: "Every time two men make a contrary judgment about the same matter, it is certain that one of them is mistaken. What is more, neither of them possesses the truth, for if one of them had a clear and precise view of the truth, he would be able to expound it to his opponent so as to force the latter's conviction" (1913: Regula II).

Historically, the ideal of a cooperative search for truth has been as important in the development of modern science as the notion of "government by discussion" –as a cooperative search for the best course of collective action – in the development of the liberal theory of the state (Barker 1958: 228–231). For this reason, the average scientist still views adversary procedures as cognitively inadequate and alien to his tradition. For him, high-level advisory panels and commissions of recognized scientific experts are the appropriate method for resolving controversial scientific issues with policy implications.

Such elite groups of consultants are supposed to evaluate the scientific evidence, draw conclusions and, if necessary, suggest questions that require further investigation. In principle, the experts would operate with the same criteria that are normally used by scientists to evaluate academic research. However, these methods have often failed to work well in the policy arena. On the one hand, the reports of high level advisory bodies tend to be consensus documents that avoid dissenting opinions in order not to detract from the aura of objectivity of the report and thus reduce its political effectiveness (Primack and von Hipple 1974). On the other hand, scientists with a special expertise in a given area are likely to have predetermined opinions and vested interests in the way issues arising in that area are settled. This disqualifies them as partial judges; yet they could play useful roles as advocates directing their best arguments at each other and at a panel of sophisticated scientific referees. The disputants themselves are in the best position to display the strengths of their own arguments and to probe the weak points of opposing positions, thus providing an effective antidote to the tendency of advisory bodies to camouflage important differences of opinion as well as vested interests and biases.

Legislative and other public hearings are another method frequently used in an attempt to coordinate conflicting expert opinions. However, in the hearings opposing witnesses often fail to speak to each other's conclusions while differences in assumptions may be mistaken for disagreements about facts. Adversarial procedures, on the other hand, are specifically designed to bring out unstated assumptions, differing interpretations, and gaps in logic or in the factual evidence.

In sum, the advantages of adversary procedures over more conventional methods of handling conflicting opinions about (trans-) scientific issues are strictly analogous to the advantages of partisan debate in coordinating different values and policy positions. The real question then, is not whether debate and persuasion should be used in policymaking, but how they can be used so that their potential for coordination may be fully realized. Like other forms of interactive problem solving, debate and persuasion to be productive require shared understanding and common rules (Kaufmann: Ch. 10; Ostrom: Ch. 22). But they also need, in addition, an interactive structure or framework, a forum where divergent viewpoints confront each other directly, and mutual criticism is conducive to learning (cf. van Gunsteren: Ch. 13). Fora of debate can assume a variety of institutional forms, from law courts and scientific journals to peer groups and professional organizations.

21.4 Mutual Adjustment in Peer Groups

A peer group differs fundamentally from a bureaucracy in that it operates with no hierarchy and a minimum of formal rules. Lacking by design a central coordinator, the members of a peer group must coordinate their actions by direct observation and evaluation of each other's performance. In professional peer groups mutual adjustment is the product of consultation, competition, and persuasion. In scientific research, for example, coordination is achieved by each scientist taking note of the published results of other scientists; by the competitive struggle of ideas; and by using all the available means of communication in order to persuade scientific opinion of the originality and significance of one's conclusions (Ziman 1968). In a collegium or organization of fellow craftsmen, Freidson writes, "the work is coordinated by the workers themselves, using functional criteria mediated by the authority of expertise and its qualities of persuasive demonstration" (1975: 93).

The basic strength of the collegial or peer group with respect to both market and hierarchy is the ability to coordinate and control its own activities on the basis of information that is often too ambiguous and qualitative to form the basis of a system of prices or of administrative rules. The price system (or any other output-dependent mode of coordination) can perform adequately only when certain conditions are satisfied. First, it must be possible to evaluate the output unambiguously. Second, prices should be "sufficient statistics" with respect to all the relevant aspects of the activity, i.e., they should contain all the information required for effective monitoring and control. Also, in the case of joint or highly interdependent activities it should be possible to evaluate separately the individual contributions to the final outcome. Finally, in some situations it may be necessary to distinguish results that are due to chance from those that can be attributed to foresight.

Different types of "market failure" appear when one or more of these conditions are not satisfied. For example, most professional services cannot be carried out exclusively on the basis of an impersonal cash-for-service exchange, as in pure market transactions, because of (a) the ambiguity of the outcome – there may be no obvious relationship between what the doctor does and the outcome in an illness of any complexity; (b) the difficulty, due to consumer ignorance, of distinguishing chance from foresight or skill; and (c) the phenomenon of "co-production" – the final result is determined by the joint efforts of the professional and of his client – which in some cases makes it difficult to distinguish their separate contributions (cf. Ostrom: Ch. 22; Wirth: Ch. 35).

In such cases there is, as Kenneth Arrow writes,

"an expectation of personal responsibility, of fidelity and trust; physician and patient behave in many ways more like co-workers in the same organization than like a large manufacturer and his remote and unseen customers. Similar relations are typical of labor services, agents, and in general, of transactions involving goods or services where quality standards are significant and not easily verified in detail by the purchaser" (Arrow 1978: 83–84).

Thus, the peer group embodies a principle of social organization – the collegium – that is qualitatively different both from price-mediated and from hierarchical modes of coordination. The market achieves coordination *(ex post)* by the unplanned compatibility of the quantities supplied and demanded by individuals engaged in exchange on the basis of rational calculation of self-interest. The coherence of a hierarchical organization stems from the deliberate *(ex ante)* planning and control of work on the part of a limited group of central coordinators. In the collegium, work is coordinated by the workers themselves. Coordination is achieved by direct observation of each other's performance and by the kind of subtle readings of signals that is possible among co-workers sharing a body of knowledge and a specialized language (Freidson 1975: 90–94).

To these three different principles for organizing work there correspond three different conceptions of work:

"Whereas the thrust of work in the free market is toward a *gainful* product, and the thrust of work in a disciplined organization is toward a *standardized* product, the thrust of work in the collegium, or organization of fellow craftsmen, is toward a *qualitative* product. The intrinsic value of the product can be legitimately judged only by the collegium, not by the customer or the manager, for it is claimed that only the collegium possesses sufficient knowledge and skill to do so" (Freidson 1975: 93; Freidson's italics).

Because of its emphasis on quality, the collegium has a natural tendency to learn, to constantly refine and specialize skills, independent of client demand. The commitment to knowledge and skill for its own sake breeds hostility toward bureaucratic standardization of work, and indifference to practical consideration of cost. This may create a serious problem for public policy, since the danger of "Cadillac only" medicine, education, or artistic production arises as soon as it is accepted that neither budgetary preoccupations nor rigid adherence to administrative norms should be allowed to interfere with the search for professional excellence.

It is doubtful, however, that the problem can be resolved by strengthening external bureaucratic controls. Where cognitive complexity is high, outcomes ambiguous, and quality difficult to evaluate there seems to be no satisfactory alternative to collegial control.

"If the essential criteria of work are qualitative, emphasizing discretion to better serve individual patients, then *direct* observation and control are essential. The collegium, organized collaboratively in a division of labor, has far more potential for undertaking the routine, direct observation of its own performance than does any device of administrative supervision. It is possible for the collegium to exercise supervision as part of its normal work activity. Furthermore, it can do so directly, in the same qualitative terms as work takes place, without the distorting use of administrative artifacts" (Freidson 1975: 256; Freidson's italics).

It is of course true that, historically, professional discretion has often been used as a thinly disguised argument for professional privilege, and that the rules of professional etiquette have seriously impeded mutual observation and evaluation of performance. Moreover, the frontier of professional research and experience is continuously expanding, leaving behind large areas of practice where standardization of methods and procedures is possible. The norms and customs of a hallowed tradition are not sufficient to justify the continued existence of certain forms of professional autonomy. The conditions under which professionalism, as a specific type of occupational control centered on the collegium, is socially and ethically desirable must therefore be submitted to constant verification (Majone 1984).

The fact that the collegium, like all social institutions, is vulnerable to corruption and abuses is not a valid reason for ignoring its great potential for coordination in situations where other methods have been tried and found wanting. In particular, it appears that some of the most difficult tasks facing public administrations today may be adequately performed only by nesting the professional model inside the traditional bureaucratic framework.

21.5 Professional versus Bureaucratic Administration

The tendency, which goes back to Max Weber, to regard rational administration as identical with bureaucratic administration has been called into question by several studies showing that professionalization can be an alternative method of institutionalizing rationality. Stinchcombe's comparative analysis of construction and mass-production industries, for example, shows that the professionalized work force in the construction industry serves as an alternative to bureaucratization for assuring the rational organization of production. This author found that

"decisions, which in mass production were made outside the work milieu and communicated bureaucratically, in construction work were actually part of the craftsman's culture and socialization, and were made at the level of the work crew . . . Contracts contained specifications of the goals of work and prices; they did not contain the actual directives of work, which, it seemed to us, did not have to be there because they were already incorporated in the professionalized culture of the workers" (Stinchcombe 1959: 180).

The replacement of bureaucratic by craft administration in the construction industry is explained by economic instability, due to seasonal fluctuations in the level of activity, which makes it uneconomical to maintain permanent bureaucratic structures. Complexity of the services to be performed is another reason for replacing bureaucracy by professionalism. Activities like research, teaching, or medical care are too unstandardized and idiosyncratic to be broken down into routine specialized tasks. Hence, professional judgments, rather than strict adherence to rules, inform the task structure – the coordination and control of work – of the organization. Even when the services are provided in a bureaucratic context, professionals claim the power to disregard administrative rules and regulations if the interest of the client, as they define it, so requires.

Two important dimensions of task complexity have been identified by Perrow: the frequency with which an organization faces exceptions, and the availability of a body of standardized knowledge from which precise solutions of key problems can be derived. Where an organization faces many exceptions and lacks such a cognitive basis, structural arrangements approximating a professional model (egalitarian, flexible, allowing discretion) tend to replace bureaucracy. Where these two conditions are reversed, a bureaucratic type of organization is expected (Perrow 1965; Benson 1973).

Perrow's taxonomy is relevant to issues of public regulation in areas like nuclear safety, pollution control, and occupational health and safety. As already noted, the intensity of partisan debate in these areas is directly related to the lack of a reliable scientific basis from which unambiguous solutions could be derived, and to the unique features of each regulatory problem. While physicists and other natural scientists deal with homogeneous classes of objects – every hydrogen atom is identical to every other hydrogen atom – environmental and health regulators must deal with highly heterogeneous situations. Each individual has a unique genetic composition and life history, and thus a unique response to environmental pollutants. Hence, standards developed for statistically "normal" individuals must be adjusted to protect sections of the population at high risk. Similarly, major technological risks tend to be heterogeneous and incomparable. Every technology generates its own characteristic risks, and there is no obvious way of mapping one structure of risks onto another, or of expressing both on a common scale. Because of the heterogeneity of the situations to be controlled, regulators face problems that cannot be satisfactorily resolved with the existing scientific and technical tools.

The more uncertain the scientific basis of regulation, the more unique the nature of the problems to be solved, the greater the need for flexibility, adaptability, and discretion in the interpretation of technical norms. But rigid bureaucratic regulation sets narrow limits to professional judgment. Bureaucratic regulation tends to focus attention on a small set of permissible values and approved practices, at the expense of more comprehensive assessments of the overall quality of ambient or workplace environment. The logic of statutory controls is such that it is difficult to differentiate between the important and the trivial, between form and substance. With no formal place for discretion in technical interpretations, the situation becomes one of either compliance or breach.

A possible solution of this dilemma consists in stressing professionalism rather than hierarchy as the main organizing principle of regulatory agencies. A professional model does not presuppose the existence of a firm body of standardized knowledge from which regulators could derive ready-made solutions. On the contrary, codes of professional behavior have been developed to deal with situations where the provider of a service must rely, to a greater or lesser extent, on idiosyncratic information and "tacit" knowledge. As was noted above, when knowledge becomes standardized, professional principles can be replaced by bureaucratic or managerial modes of coordination and control.

The practical meaning of this suggestion may be illustrated by reference to the field of occupational health and safety. The main task of a professionally organized health and safety inspectorate would not be, as it is at present, that of ensuring compliance with minimum legal requirements. Rather, inspectors would be concerned with the broad aspects of safety and health at the workplaces they visit, as much as with those narrow aspects which may have been the subject of detailed regulation. The provision of skilled and impartial advice and assistance would become one of their most important functions. Rigid and uniform legal rules could then be replaced by standards and behavioral norms developed by industry itself (jointly by workers and management), and by independent research institutions and professional organizations. Thus, a professional model of regulation would rely less on laws and more on voluntary self-regulation at the industry and plant level. In this system the inspectors would enjoy a considerable degree of auto-

nomy, and the internal organization of the regulatory agency would use a minimum
of hierarchical control, relying instead on intense consultation and peer review.
Incidentally, somewhat similar proposals have been made in 1972 by the British
Committee on *Safety and Health at Work* (Robens Committee), and have found
wide acceptance in the Health and Safety at Work Act of 1976.

The organization of the British Alkali and Clean Air Inspectorate may be quoted
as a further example of a professional model ensuring a considerable degree of
autonomy and collegiality. In the words of the *Annual Report of H. M. Alkali and
Clear Air Inspectorate for 1973:*

"The Chief Inspector, with the help of his deputies, lays down the broad national policies
and provided they keep within their broad lines, inspectors in the field have plenty of
flexibility to take into account local circumstances and make suitable decisions. They are
given plenty of autonomy and are trained as a team of decision-takers with as much
responsibility and authority as possible" (Hill 1983: 90–91).

The Inspectorate uses very few legal standards, but "presumptive limits" or
guidelines have been developed for a considerable number of emissions. The
setting of presumptive standards is entirely at the discretion of the Chief Inspector.
Also the British Nuclear Installations Inspectorate has developed a style of
consultative regulation and inspection with participative overstones which is in
antithesis to control by statutory regulations (Critchley 1978).

The proposed professional model of regulation shifts the emphasis from legal
enforcement to the provision of information and high quality advice. In turn, this
presupposes greater reliance on self-regulation, but also on public participation in
the regulatory process. In the case of occupational health and safety, major
responsibility for developing locally adequate rules would rest with management
and employees (or their representatives). In other fields, such as the environment,
various interest groups should be provided with relevant information and given the
possibility of challenging in the courts or at public inquiries proposals with adverse
environmental effects, or to comment on draft laws and regulations to protect the
environment. Such a combination of professionalism and partisan debate could
significantly increase the rationality as well as the legitimacy of public policy.

21.6 Persuasion and Policy Development

Our analysis of mutual adjustment would be incomplete if, before concluding this
chapter, we failed to mention the important role of persuasion in policy development. The discussion so far, like most writing on coordination by mutual adjustment, has been implicitly confined to the initial stages of policymaking: deliberation and policy formulation. But to reach agreement on policy is not enough; the
policy must be accepted and executed by many people who did not contribute to its
formulation. The process of justification and legitimation depends heavily on
persuasive arguments to explain the chosen course of action, to give it a convincing
intellectual basis, to elicit assent and anticipate criticisms.

The role of justificatory arguments in the policy process may be compared with
that of judicial opinions in the legal process. A judge may decide a case on the basis
of his subjective notion of fairness, a hunch that a particular decision would be

right, while realizing at the same time that considerations of this kind do not count as justifications for rendering a binding legal decision. Hence, he frames his opinion in the objective categories of legal argument, and any subsequent developments in the case (for example, an appeal) will be based on the published opinion, not on the actual process followed by the judge in coming to his conclusion. Thus, the opinion becomes a key element in the process of mutual adjustment among legal actors, while conflicting legal arguments drive the judicial process and sustain the development of legal doctrine. Similarly, partisan arguments, criticism, counterproposals, and indeed the entire debate following the first formulation of a policy, become an integral part of the process of policymaking and provide the essential stimulus to further developments.

The use of persuasion for the purpose of policy justification has often been criticized as mere "rationalization", i.e., as an attempt to explain or justify a policy *a posteriori* by means of rational motives rather than by the "real" ones. Indeed, one of the recurrent criticisms of policy analysis is that it provides "pseudoscientific rationalizations" for politically or bureaucratically determined positions. But it is not necessarily dishonest or merely "rationalizing" to use arguments based on considerations different from those that led to the adoption of a certain position.

As Karl Weick argues, rationality is better understood as an *ex post* than as an *ex ante* occurrence:

"Rationality makes sense of what has been, not what will be. It is a process of justification in which past deeds are made to appear sensible to the actor himself and to those other persons to whom he feels accountable. It is difficult for a person to be rational if he does not know precisely what it is that he must be rational about. He can create rationality only when he has available some set of actions which can be viewed in several ways. It is possible for actors to make elaborate, detailed statements of their plans. However, the error comes if we assume that these plans then control their behavior. If we watch closely, it will become clear that the behavior is under the control of more determinants than just the vocally stated plan. And at the conclusion of the actions, it will never be true that the plan as first stated will have been exactly accomplished. But something will have been accomplished, and it is this something, and the making sense of this something, that constitute rationality" (Weick 1969: 38).

The legal analogy suggests similar conclusions. Most legal systems allow the opinion stating the reasons for a judicial decision to follow rather than precede that decision. Also, different judges may agree on a decision, but disagree about the best way to justify it; in the American system, for example, they are given the opportunity to present their positions in separate arguments.

Such procedural rules seem absurd to anybody who assumes that a judicial opinion must be an accurate description of the process followed by the judge in coming to a decision. If, however, the opinion is viewed as a report of justificatory procedures employed by the judge, then the appeal to legal and logical considerations which possibly played no role in the actual decision process, becomes quite understandable (Wasserstrom 1961). In fact, the judge's opinion is not the premise of a syllogism which concludes in the decision. Rather, it is a means of increasing the persuasive force of the decision and exercising rational control over conclusions that may be suggested by extralegal considerations.

Like the judicial decision, a policy is a conclusion in search of a premise. Partisan debate and persuasion are often needed to discover the premises that make the policy internally consistent, and convincing to the largest possible audience. The ability to persuade has always been recognized as an important attribute of political leadership, and this recognition acknowledges the fact that much of politics consists of efforts to redirect attitudes by argument and persuasion. This ability is even more necessary today, when the success of public programs often depends on affecting the attitudes and behaviors of millions of individuals and thousands of organizations.

21.7 Conclusion

In a democracy, persuasion can be effective in the long run only as a two-way communication channel. Democratic legitimacy involves consent and support, and these are more likely to be forthcoming if the people responsible for implementing policies and those affected by them have a voice in formulating and developing these policies. Partisan discussion articulates interests and perspectives that are bound to emerge in subsequent stages of the policy process. Hence, debate and persuasion bridge the gap between decision and implementation by creating a context for policymaking that reflects the political forces it will later have to engage (Porter 1980: 241–247).

They also create a context that makes social learning possible. In a polity, as in a peer group, people can coordinate their activities by mutual adjustment only if they share some common understanding of the nature of the problems to be solved. When the problems are complex and constantly changing, the community of understanding is always in danger of disintegrating and must continually be recreated. Experience shows that new understanding emerges more naturally in open fora of debate than by suppressing contrasting viewpoints and incongruent interpretations of reality in the name of efficiency and logical consistency.

References

Arrow, K. (1978): "Organizational Goals and Control Systems: Internal and External Considerations." In Preston, L. E. (ed.), *Research in Corporate Social Performance and Policy,* 79–97. Greenwich, Conn.: JAI Press.

Bagehot, W. (1956): *Physics and Politics.* Boston: Beacon Press (first ed. 1867).

Barker, E. (1958): *Reflections on Government.* New York: Oxford Univ. Press. (first ed. 1942)

Barnard, C. I. (1968): *The Functions of the Executive* (30th anniversary ed.). Cambridge, Mass.: Harvard Univ. Press.

Benson, J. J. (1973): "The Analysis of Bureaucratic-Professional Conflict: Functional versus Dialectical Approaches." *The Sociological Quarterly* 14/3: 376–394.

Blau, P. M., and R. W. Scott (1962): *Formal Organizations.* San Francisco: Chandler.

Critchley, O. H. (1978): "Aspects of the Historical, Philosophical and Mathematical Background to the Statutory Management of Nuclear Plant Risks in the United Kingdom." In British Nuclear Energy Society (ed.), *Radiation Protection in Nuclear Power Plants and the Fuel Cycle,* 11–20. London: BNES.

Dahl, R. A., and Lindblom, C. E. (1976): *Politics, Economics, and Welfare.* Chicago: The Univ. of Chicago Press. (first ed. 1953)

Descartes, R. (1913): *Oeuvres de Descartes* (Ed. by Charles Adam and Paul Tannery), Vol. 10. Paris: Léopold Cerf.

Durkheim, E. (1933): *The Division of Labor in Society*. New York: The Free Press.

Festinger, L. (1957): *A Theory of Cognitive Dissonance*. Evanston, Ill.: Row, Peterson.

Freidson, E. (1975): *Doctoring Together*. New York: Elsevier.

Hill, M. (1983): "The Role of the British Alkali and Clean Air Inspectorate in Air Pollution Control." In Downing, P. B., and K. Hanf (eds.), *International Comparisons in Implementing Pollution Laws*, 87–106. Boston, The Hague: Kluwer-Nijhoff.

Lindblom, C. E. (1965): *The Intelligence of Democracy*. New York: The Free Press.

Majone, G. (1984): "Professionalism and Nonprofit Organizations." *Journal of Health, Politics, Policy and Law* 8/4: 639–659.

Mosher, F. C. (1968): *Democracy and the Public Service*. New York: Oxford Univ. Press.

Neustadt, R. E. (1960): *Presidential Power*. New York: Wiley and Sons.

Ouchi, W. G. (1980): "Markets, Bureaucracies, and Clans." *Administrative Science Quarterly* 25/1: 129–141.

Perelman, C., and L. Olbrechts-Tyteca (1958): *Traité de l'argumentation. La nouvelle rhétorique*. Paris: Presses Univ. de France.

Perrow, C. (1967): "A Framework for the Comparative Analysis of Organizations." *American Sociological Review* 32/3: 194–208.

Polanyi, M. (1951): *The Logic of Liberty*. London: Routledge and Kegan Paul.

Porter, R. B. (1980): *Presidential Decision Making*. Cambridge, Mass.: Cambridge Univ. Press.

Primack, J., and F. von Hipple (1974): *Advice and Dissent*. New York: Basic Books.

Schelling, T. (1960): *The Strategy of Conflict*. Cambridge, Mass.: Harvard Univ. Press.

Simpson, R. L. (1959): "Vertical and Horizontal Communication in Formal Organizations." *Administrative Science Quarterly* 4/1: 188–196.

Stinchcombe, A. L. (1959): "Bureaucratic and Craft Administration of Production: A Comparative Study." *Administrative Science Quarterly* 4/1: 168–187.

Wasserstrom, R. A. (1961): *The Judicial Process*. Stanford, Calif.: Stanford Univ. Press.

Weick, K. E. (1969): *The Social Psychology of Organizing*. Reading, Mass. Addison Wesley.

Weinberg, A. M. (1972): "Science and Trans-Science." *Minerva* 10/2: 209–222.

Ziman, J. (1968): *Public Knowledge*. Cambridge, England: Cambridge Univ. Press.

22. A Method of Institutional Analysis

Elinor Ostrom

Abstract

This chapter provides an initial framework for analyzing all types of institutional arrangements. A key conceptual unit is identified – called an action arena. Action arenas include a model of an action situation and a model of the actors in that situation. A model of the action situation can be characterized using eight clusters of variables: (1) participants, (2) positions, (3) outcomes, (4) action-outcome linkages, (5) information, (6) control exercised by participants, (7) costs and benefits assigned to outcomes and actions, and (8) the number of iterations of the situation itself. A model of the actor must include assumptions about the resources that an actor brings to a situation; the evaluation actors assigned to states of the world and to actions; the way actors acquire, posess, retain and use information, and the process the actors use for selecting particular courses of action. Analysts predict and explain behavior using the working parts of these two component models of an action arena.

Underlying the way analysts model action arenas are implicit assumptions about the rules individuals use to order relationships, about attributes of the states of the world and their transformations, and about the nature of the community within which the arena occurs. Rules are viewed as contextual, prescriptive, and followable linguistic entities. A primary focus is placed on working rules in use by participants in action arenas. A method for developing a meaningful classification of a set of rules affecting action arenas is presented and then illustrated in Chapter 24.

22.1 Introduction

A general theme running through previous chapters is that most analysis of institutional arrangements concentrates on a limited set of idealized institutional arrangements such as markets, hierarchies, or majority voting schemes. Markets and hierarchies are frequently presented, for example, as fundamentally different institutions or "pure types" of organization. Not only are the types of institutional arrangements perceived to be different but each requires its own explanatory theory. Scholars who attempt to explain behavior within markets must use economic theory while scholars who attempt to explain behavior within hierarchies must use sociological theory. Such a view precludes a more general explanatory theory which could be used to predict and explain behavior in all types of institutional arrangements. Such a view also forecloses comparative analysis across different types of institutional arrangements.

The authors of previous chapters, however, see the world as being composed of a much richer set of institutional arrangements none of which exist in isolation from others. Solidaristically organized work teams may exist within hierarchically organized firms that operate in competitive markets made possible through the operation of courts and the exercise of police powers in a general system of law. Hegner (Ch. 19), for example, describes the emergence of solidaristic cooperation combined with hierarchical redistribution and competitive market exchange.

The theme of these chapters poses a fundamental problem for those who are interested in questions of guidance, control, and evaluation of diverse institutional arrangements. If a wide diversity of institutional forms exist not only side by side but nested within one another, behavior cannot be explained, nor guided, controlled and evaluated, through reliance on any limited sets of pure theories. We need to ask whether similar conceptual characteristics underly all hierarchies, markets, courts, electoral contests, collegial fora, and solidaristically organized communities. Is there a common set of variables that can be used to analyze all types of institutional arrangements? If such a common set of variables exists, then many differences in surface reality can be expected to result from the way these variables are assigned different values and are combined with one another. A set of such variables would provide a framework for comparing institutional arrangements as different as hierarchies and markets or as similar as monopolistic and oligopolistic markets. Such a framework would identify the major types of structural variables present to some extent in all institutional arrangements, but whose values differ from one type of institutional arrangement to another.

This chapter is an attempt to provide the beginning of such a framework and to do so in several steps. The first step is the identification of a conceptual unit – called an *action arena* – that can be utilized to analyze, predict, and explain behavior within institutional arrangements. Action arenas include a model of an *action situation* and a model of the *actors* in that situation. A model of the action situation can be characterized using eight clusters of variables – *participants, positions, outcomes, action-outcome linkages, information, the control participants exercise, the costs and benefits assigned to outcomes and actions, and the number of iterations of the situation itself*. A model of the actor must include assumptions about four clusters of variables: the *resources* that an actor brings to a situation; the *valuation* actors assign to states of the world and to actions; the way actors acquire, process, retain, and use *information*; and the processes actors use for *selection* of particular courses of action. Using these assumptions made about the situation and the actor, the analyst predicts actions and results.

Analysts do use these variables to identify classic types of situations which may occur in any and all types of institutional arrangements. For example, a particular combination of values for these variables yields an action situation which has variously been called a "Commons Dilemma situation," a "Prisoner's Dilemma situation," or a "Free Rider situation." Once an action situation is identified as having the structure of a Commons Dilemma situation, predictions about likely behavior can be made no matter whether the participants are relating to an ocean fishery, an overcrowded bridge, a meadow owned in common, or the electromagnetic spectrum. Unless participants have worked out an implicit or explicit contract for allocating the use of the commons, an analyst would predict that each will be led to adopt a strategy that leads all of them to overuse the commons (Hardin 1982).

Once an analyst understands the structure and likely consequences of a Commons Dilemma situation, the analyst can utilize the same model for explaining behavior and results which occur in such different types of organizations as: (1) a hierarchy (e.g., the problem of keeping gunners at their posts to cover a retreating army), (2) a small community relying upon traditional legal systems (e.g., the problem of overgrazing on a commons), or (3) a family (e.g., the problem of keeping a room clean where two brothers sleep, study, and play). Formal theorists have identified other action situations, such as "Chicken" or the "Battle of the Sexes," whose structure can also occur within any of the more traditionally viewed institutional arrangements. Theorists who have taken a less formal and more dramaturgical perspective have also identified classic situations whose structure occurs in many guises throughout all organized life (Harre and Secord 1972; Garfinkel 1967; Burke 1966).

Action arenas are thus identified as an initial conceptual unit of importance for explaining behavior in diverse types of institutional arrangements. Two additional steps are the "natural" outgrowth of this approach. One step digs deeper and inquires into the factors which themselves affect the structure of an action arena. From this vantage point the action arena is viewed as an intermediate conceptual unit. The values of the variables in an action arena are now viewed as dependent upon other factors. These factors include three clusters of variables: (1) the rules used by participants to order their relationships, (2) the attributes of states of the world which are acted upon in these arenas, and (3) the structure of the more general community within which any particular arena is placed (see Kiser and Ostrom 1982).

Often the rules, states of the world, and structure of the community are implicitly assumed in models of action arenas. The mid-section of this chapter will focus on an explanatory level which explicitly examines how shared understandings of rules, states of the world, and nature of the community affect the values of the variables characterizing action arenas. The first two levels of explanation examined in this paper are schematically represented in Figure 1.

The last step in this endeavour moves outward from action arenas to consider methods for explaining complex structures that link sequential and simultaneous action arenas to one another. In the "real world" few action arenas exist totally isolated from other arenas. Thus, enhancing the usefulness of the methodology described in this chapter depends upon methods of analysis which focus on linkages among action arenas rather than solitary action arenas.

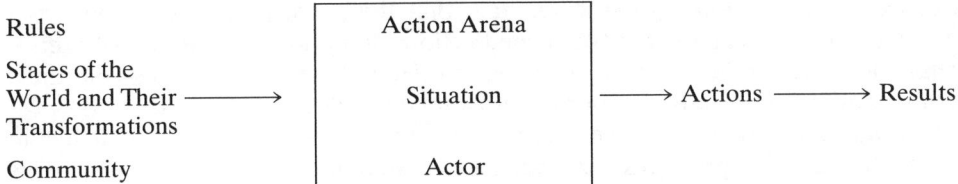

Phenomena to Be Explained
Explanation Within Frame of an Action Arena
Explanation Viewing Action Arenas as Intermediate Conceptual Units

Fig. 1: Levels of Explanation Used in Institutional Analysis

22.2 Explanation Within the Frame of an Action Arena

The term *action arena* refers to a complex conceptual unit containing a set of variables called an *action situation* and a set of variables called an *actor*. One needs both components – the situation and the actors in the situation – to derive predictions about likely behavior and results.

The Action Situation

The term *action situation* is used here to refer to an analytic concept that enables an analyst to isolate the immediate structure affecting an action process of interest to the analyst for the purpose of explaining regularities in human actions and results. Examples include models of formal games, of social situations, of markets, of committees and legislatures, of supervisor-subordinate interactions in a hierarchy, and of bargaining processes between a bureau chief and a sponsor. Rawls (1968) used the term "practice;" Commons (1957) used the term "transaction;" Weick (1969) used the term "double interact;" Newell and Simon (1972) used the term "task environment;" Popper (1967) used the term "logic of the situation;" and Harre (1974) used the term "well-defined social episode" to refer to the same type of analytical concept.

A common set of variables used to describe the structure of an action situation include: (1) the set of participants, (2) the specific positions to be filled by participants, (3) the states of the world which can be affected (outcomes), (4) the set of allowable actions and their linkage to outcomes, (5) the level of control each participant has over choice, (6) the information available to participants about the structure of the action situation, (7) the costs and benefits assigned to outcomes and actions, and (8) the number of times an action situation will be repeated. How these variables are used to model electoral and bargaining arenas is illustrated in Chapter 24.

These elements are necessary and sufficient to describe the structure of most simple but interesting action situations in the public sector. The number of participants may vary, but there must always be participants in positions to have any structure to analyze. Similarly, there must be sets of potential actions that actors are authorized to take. This set of actions represents the resources made available to the participants by the structure of the situation. Information about the situation may vary, but all participants must share some information about the situation before an analyst can even state that the participants are *in* an action situation. The costs and benefits assigned actions and outcomes can be thought of as the incentives and deterrents in a situation. How these affect actions, and thus, results, depend also on the resources and valuation patterns of participants.

Not only can action arenas be characterized by these variables, but a change in any of the variables produces a *different* action situation. Thus, three participants trying to arrive at a single decision affecting all three individuals is different than two persons making the same decision. Possibilities for coalition structure are created that do not exist in a two-person situation. Changing the set of alternative actions or the information conditions also fundamentally alters the structure of a situation.

When explaining actions and cumulated results within the framework of an action arena, these variables are the "givens" that one works with to describe the structure of the situation. One assumes that the actors within a situation cannot change the structure of the situation in the short run. Within a particular situation, a participant can only attempt to act in light of the opportunities and constraints of that situation and the actor's resources and values.

The Actor

The *actor* in a situation can be thought of as a single individual or as a group functioning as a corporate actor. In order to derive inferences about the likely behavior of each actor in a situation (and, thus, about the pattern of joint results that may be produced), the analyst must make assumptions about what and how participants value, what resources and information they have, their information processing capabilities, and the internal mechanisms they use to decide upon strategies. The term "action" refers to those human behaviors for which the acting individual attaches a subjective meaning (Weber 1947; Kaufmann: Ch. 10; Schutz 1967).

At the most general level, the analyst puts himself into the position of each of the actors in a situation and tries to reason through the objectives that the actor would pursue, what resources they would bring to the situation, how much knowledge they would have, how they might learn from experience over time, and what type of calculation process they would adopt. Having done this, the analyst infers the likely behavior of different participants and how they would or would not be led to stable results. These assumptions about the actor become the components of an analytical engine that gives "motion" (i.e., is a moving part) in a model of an action arena, and enables an analyst to predict the actions of participants and how these cumulate to produce a set of likely results.

The most fully developed, explicit model of an actor is the extreme rational choice model which has evolved over time in microeconomic theory and in game theory. Even though this model makes "unrealistic" assumptions about the information processing capabilities of individuals, and about the evaluation and calculation processes, it has been useful in helping analysts to generate predictions of specific results in a variety of tightly constrained decision situations. Those predictions have been empirically useful for predicting aggregate behavior in "real-world" situations which come closest to approximating the tight constraints of the models. Given the simple structure of some highly repetitive situations, the limited capacity of human beings to code (develop appropriate language structures), store, and process information may not be exceeded. In such situations, it is analytically useful to assume that individuals have complete information relative to the task at hand and the way the action processes are organized.

Many scholars feel, however, that the extreme rational choice model used in much of formal theory is an inadequate behavioral model for applications to more complex and interesting action situations than a perfectly competitive market (see, for example, Heiner 1983). No need exists to limit institutional analysis to the use of any single pre-defined model of the actor. Considerable work in cognitive psychology, experimental gaming, and management science is proceeding with models of the actor involving different assumptions about information processing capabilities and valuation procedures than the extreme rational choice models. No one can predict which of the many different approaches will prove to be the most useful for institutional analysis of more complex and open action arenas. This is an era of intellectual ferment and experimentation with diverse approaches, none of which should be ruled out on *a priori* grounds.

The Prediction of Results

Depending upon the analytical structure of a situation and the particular model of the actor used, the analyst makes strong or weak inferences about results. In tightly constrained action situations, under conditions of little or no uncertainty, where participants are strongly motivated to select particular strategies or chains of actions which jointly lead to stable equilibria, an analyst can make strong inferences and specific predictions about likely patterns of behavior and outcomes. Many situations, however, are not so narrowly constrained. Within these situations, participants may adopt a broader range of strategies, and change their strategies over time, as they learn about the results of past actions. The institutional analyst examining these more open, less constrained, situations makes weaker inferences and predicts the patterns of outcomes that are relatively more or less likely to result from a particular type of situation. Even weak inferences have an importance in specifying general tendencies. Predicting what will not occur may be all that an analyst can do, but such predictions are still useful.

A variety of useful analytical techniques have been developed in formal approaches which aid analysts in generating predictions about expected results in specifiable action arenas. A key to these methods is finding a simple way to represent the situation. Inferring an equilibrium involves potentially complex sequences of operations on an already highly abstracted representation of an action arena. The more general the form of representation selected, the more the institutional detail generating the structure of the initial action arena fades from the consciousness of the analyst. This has the advantage of producing highly general theoretical results, but the process takes analysts away from many practical problems related to institutional analysis and institutional design.

22.3 Explanation Viewing Action Arenas as Intermediate Conceptual Units

Underlying the way analysts model action arenas are implicit assumptions about the *rules* individuals use to order their relationships, about attributes of *states of the world and their transformations*, and about the *nature of the community* within which the arena occurs. Analysts tend to make more explicit assumptions about states of the world than they make about rules or the nature of the community. This is particularly the case when analysts wish to contrast behavior related to goods and services considered to be private goods (exclusion is feasible and consumption is divisible) with behavior related to goods and services considered to be collective goods (exclusion is not feasible and consumption is joint) (see V. Ostrom and E. Ostrom 1977). But even assumptions about attributes of the states of the world are frequently left unstated and ambiguous.

The extreme positivist stand of many social scientists during the last half-century placed efforts to base explanations on mental constructs – such as the concept of rules – outside the boundaries of scientific explanation. However, the effort to explain complex human behavior in action arenas without any reference to shared cognitive systems, which affect the way individuals relate to one another and to the world, has not succeeded. As Searle (1969) has so vividly recounted, it is possible to describe the behavior of teams playing American football as a succession of circular, linear, and interpenetrating forms. But, without knowing the rules of football, and that individuals are organized into opposing teams each of which is trying to win a game, one cannot explain the game of football in any meaningful sense. Nor, could one try to guide any organized sport – as do various associations governing teams that play against one another – without a fundamental awareness of how rules about behavior and about physical properties (type of ball, size and surface of fields, equipment, etc.) interact to produce games which are more or less fair, exciting, and safe.

The Concept of Rules

Rules, as used in this chapter, are linguistic entities (Ganz 1971; V. Ostrom 1980; Commons 1957) that refer to prescriptions about what behaviors (or states of the world) are *required, prohibited, or permitted*. Weber (1947: 124) identified the set of rules to which actors had reference in selecting actions as the order which underlies a field of social action. Weick (1969: 62) defines organizing as:

". . . the set of rules by which elements interact in predictable fashion with predictable results. Organizing is the grammar by which the vocabulary of elements in an organization is made meaningful."

All rules are the result of implicit or explicit efforts to achieve order and predictability among humans by creating classes of persons (positions) who are then required, permitted, or forbidden to take classes of actions in relation to required, permitted, or forbidden states of the world. As Atkins and Curtis (1969: 217) so aptly phrased it, "rules of every sort share at least one common property: They all may be said to rule in something or other, while ruling out something else."

Rules are linguistic entities that are *contextual, prescriptive, and followable* (Shimanoff 1980). They are *contextual* in the sense that they apply to a general set of action arenas but do not apply everywhere. The rules of chess apply *only* to situations in which participants wish to play chess, but they apply in *every* instance in which individuals want to play chess. The game of chess provides the context for the application of its rules. The formal and enforced laws of a jurisdiction apply to all action arenas occurring within a domain. Rules against stealing a chess piece or assaulting the other player exist almost everywhere chess might be played even though these rules stem from a formally existing legal system rather than from the specific rules of chess. The jurisdiction provides the context for rules against stealing or assault.

Rules are *prescriptive* in the sense that "those who are knowledgeable of a rule also know that they can be held accountable if they break it" (Shimanoff 1980: 41). They may be "held accountable" by fellow participants who call them to task for breaking a rule (what Weber called "convention") and/or by officials who monitor behavior and can impose punishment on those whose behavior is found inconsistent with a set of rules (what Weber called "law"). Rules provide information about the actions an actor "must" perform *(obligation),* "must not" perform *(prohibition),* or "may" perform *(permission)* if they are to avoid the possibility of sanctions being imposed.

Considerable dispute exists among scholars who have dealt with the concept of rules over the prescriptive force of "permission." Ganz (1971) and Shimanoff (1980) argue that prescriptive force is restricted to "obligation" and "prohibition" and does not include "permission" while Commons (1957), von Wright (1968), and Toulmin (1974) overtly include "permission" in their conception of rules. Viewing rules as affecting the values of variables in an action situation, rather than as directly controlling behavior, helps one to understand how rules can be prescriptive while defining a set of permissible actions. Permitted actions are the *set* of actions available to participants within an action situation. For example, most highway laws define an upper limit to the permitted speed in particular zones and may define a lower limit. A driver is then permitted to drive any speed within the "allowable" set which remains. Drivers can be sanctioned under a rule defining a set of permissible actions, but sanctions are imposed for actions outside the full set of permissible acts.

Rules are *followable* in the sense that it is possible for actors to perform obligatory, prohibited, or permitted actions as well as it is possible for them not to perform these actions. In other words, it is physically possible for actors to follow or not to follow a rule. This distinguishes *actions* that are explained by reference to *rules,* from *behavior* that is explained by *scientific laws.*

Rules can be divided into two classes: *working rules* and *formal rules.* Working rules are the rules in use by participants in on-going action arenas. They are the set of rules to which participants would make reference if asked to explain and justify their actions to fellow participants. While following a rule may become a "social habit," it is possible to make participants consciously aware of the rules they are using to order their relationships. Individuals can consciously decide to adopt a different rule and change their behavior to conform to such a decision. Over time, behavior in conformance with a new rule may itself become habitual (see Shimanoff 1980; Toulmin 1974; Harre 1974). The capacity of humans to use complex cognitive systems to order their own behavior at a relatively subconscious level makes it difficult for empirical researchers to ascertain what the working rules are for an on-going action arena. An empirical researcher cannot just assume that individuals are following a set of written rules or that it is easy to discover the rules in use in on-going arenas.

Formal rules are self-consciously enacted or declared rules that may be formulated endogenously or exogenously to a community of participants (Pejovich 1982). In a community with legitimate "law makers" who themselves follow constitutional rules about their own behavior, formal rules are an important source of the working rules used by participants in coordinating their activities with one another.

The relationship between working rules and formal rules varies from one action arena to another and one time and place to another. But the relationship between working and formal rules can be theoretically and empirically examined.

Rule following or conforming actions are not as predictable as biological or physical behavior explained by scientific laws. All rules are formulated in human language. As such, rules share all the problems of lack of clarity, misunderstanding, and change that typifies any languaged-based phenomenon. Words are "symbols that name, and thus, stand for classes of things and relationships" (V. Ostrom 1980: 312). Words are always simpler than the phenomenon to which they refer.

The stability of rule-ordered actions is dependent upon the shared meaning of the words used to formulate a set of rules. If no shared meaning exists when a rule is formulated by some authority, confusion will exist about what actions are required, permitted, or forbidden. Regularities in actions cannot result if those who must repeatedly interpret the meaning of a rule within action situations arrive at multiple interpretations. Because "rules are not self-formulating, self-determining, or self-enforcing" (V. Ostrom 1980: 312), it is human agents who formulate them, apply them in particular situations, and attempt to enforce performance consistent with them. Even if shared meaning exists at the time of the acceptance of a rule, transformations in technology, in shared norms, and in circumstances more generally, change the events to which rules apply. "Applying language to changing configurations of development increases the ambiguities and threatens the shared criteria of choice with an erosion of their appropriate meaning" (V. Ostrom 1980: 312).

Analysts frequently make a simplifying assumption in analytical theories that participants in an action arena will only take lawful actions (e.g., "Let us assume law and order"). This assumption helps the analyst proceed to examine important theoretical questions not related to how well rules are understood, agreed to, and enforced. Using this assumption, the analyst can posit what results are likely to follow if all the participants were to carefully follow a particular set of rules. When rules are clear, accepted as legitimate and fair, and actively enforced, this is a reasonable assumption to follow. But, it may well be appropriate in explaining behavior in some situations to overtly model an action situation in which illegal behavior is included in action sets and payoff rules are conceptualized as a compound probability of being caught and of having particular levels of sanctions imposed. If these probabilities are low – a behavioral assumption of a model – and if illegal behavior can produce highly desired outcomes, then one would predict a high level of illegal activity.

The Multiplicity of Rules in Use

But what rules are important for institutional analysis? A myriad of specific rules are used in structuring complex action arenas. All too many scholars interested in legal structure have been overwhelmed in their work by the volume of discrete rules used in various public settings and the lack of a guiding set of questions to help sort the essential from the trivial. Scholars have been trapped into endless cataloguing of rules not related to a method of classification most useful for theoretical explanations. But classification is a necessary step in developing a science. As Langer (1953: 23) described the process:

"Whenever we may truly claim to have a science, we have found some principle by which different things are related to each other as just so many forms of one substrata, or material, and everything that can be treated as a new variation belongs to that science."

In reflecting upon Langer's work, Boynton (1982: 40) identifies the first aspect of a scientific principle as "nothing more than defining a set," but he points out that the "real trick is the intuition that defining these particular elements or occurrences as a set will lead one to a very general, ordered set of relationships." Anyone attempting to define a useful typology of rules must be concerned that the classification is more than a method for imposing superficial order onto an extremely large set of seemingly disparate rules. By asking how rules affect the structures of action situations, we can hopefully begin to develop a useful way to cluster rules that can serve as a first step in a theory about how rules relate to the structure of action situations, affecting thereby the way individuals act and results are produced.

Rule Configurations

A first step toward identifying the working rules, can be made, then, by examining how working rules affect specific variables in an action situation. The elements of an action situation as stated above are: participants, positions, outcomes, action-outcome linkages, control over actions at a node, information sets, benefits and costs assigned to actions and outcomes and the number of iterations. A set of working rules about these variables should constitute the minimal but necessary set of working rules that one would need to offer an explanation of actions and results based on the working rules used by participants to order their relationships within an action arena. Since states of the world and their transformations and the nature of a community also affect the structure of an action situation, working rules alone never provide both a necessary and sufficient explanation of the structure of an action situation.

Tab. 1: Configuration of Working Rules

1. *Boundary rules* set the entry, exit, and domain conditions for individual participants.
2. *Scope rules* specify which states of the world can be affected and sets the range within which these can be affected.
3. *Position rules* establish positions, assign participants to positions, and defined who has control over tenure in a position.
4. *Authority rules* prescribe which positions can take which actions and how actions are ordered, processed, and terminated.
5. *Information rules* establish information channels, state the conditions when they are to be open or closed, create an official language, and prescribe how evidence is to be processed.
6. *Aggregation rules* prescribe formulae for weighting individual choices and calculating collective choices at decision nodes.
7. *Payoff rules* prescribe how benefits and costs are to be distributed to participants in positions given their actions and those of others.

Adopting this view of the task, seven types of working rules can be said to affect the structure of an action situation. These are: *boundary rules, scope rules, position rules, authority rules, information rules, aggregation rules, and payoff rules*. They are each defined on Table 1. The cumulative effect of these seven types of rules affect the structure of an action situation (setting the values of the variables that structure an action situation). Thus, boundary rules affect the number of *participants*, their attributes and resources, whether they can enter freely, and the conditions they face for leaving. Scope rules delimit the *outcomes* that can be affected and working backwards, the actions linked to specific outcomes. Position rules establish *positions* in the situation. Authority rules assign sets of actions that participants in positions at particular nodes must, may, or may not take. Authority rules, combined with the scientific laws about the relevant states of the world being acted upon, determine the shape of the decision tree – the *action-outcome linkages* and the *number of iterations*. Information rules affect the *information sets* of participants. Aggregation rules affect the level of *control* that a participant in a position exercises in the selection of an action at a node. Payoff rules affect the *benefits and costs* that will be assigned to particular combinations of actions and outcomes and establish the incentives and deterrents for action.

Table 2 illustrates how an action situation of a competitive market can be structured by a rule configuration. The simple statement, "let us assume a highly competitive market," presumes that participants act with reference to a complex rule configuration similar to that suggested by the list of rules shown in Table 2.

Tab. 2: Working Rules of Competitive Markets

Boundary Rules

1. Buyers and sellers may enter and exit at their own initiative.
2. Licensing requirements for sellers or buyers are minimal.
3. Buyers and sellers must own or borrow resources to enter.
4. Exit is forced on sellers if long-run profit is less than zero and on buyers if they do not have sufficient funds to buy.

Scope Rules

1. Participants can exchange their own or borrowed resources and goods, but not resources owned by others.
2. Participants are limited in terms of costs they can externalize on others – rules regarding what is an allowable externality vary from market to market.

Position Rules

1. Positions of owner, seller, buyer, employer, police, judge, and jury are defined.

Authority and Procedure Rules

1. Seller authorized to decide how much to offer for sale at what price.
2. Buyer authorized to decide how much to offer to buy at what price.
3. Police authorized to arrest those suspected of unlawful use of resoures and goods owned by others.
4. Judges authorized to determine rights and obligations of buyers and sellers in civil proceedings and of suspects in criminal proceedings.

Tab. 2 continued

Information Rules

1. Prices of current offers to sell and buy are available to all participants.
2. No participant is authorized to force information from other participants concerning preferences or costs.
3. Seller may have to provide specific information on content of goods.

Aggregation Rules

1. Whenever any two participants agree to an exchange, that transaction is authorized.
2. Police can make an arrest on their own initiative.
3. Aggregation rules for judges and juries vary depending on type of case.

Payoff Rules

1. Seller retains profit, if any, after payment for input variables, taxes, and interest.
2. Buyer retains consumer surplus, if any, after payment for goods.
3. Suspects pay fines, or spend time in jail, if judged guilty of criminal acts.
4. Buyers and/or sellers pay damages and costs to other parties if ordered to do so by judge.

Substantial changes in any one of these rules affects the structure of a market and the resulting inferences that can be made about equilibria and market performance. Changes in only a few key variables, and one would no longer call the action situation a market at all. A change in the aggregation rule, for example, allocating goods to consumers based only on choices made by officials, transforms the resulting action situation into something other than a market. (This is the rule that the military uses to assign uniforms to recruits!) Changes in boundary rules affect the number of participants who enter and exit and determine whether the resulting market is competitive, oligopolistic, or monopolistic. By affecting the structure of the market, changes in boundary rules eventually affect predictions concerning the price at which goods will be sold, the quantity to be sold, and the relative distribution of producer and consumer surplus.

The set of working rules is a *configuration* in the sense that the effect of a change in one rule depends upon the other rules in use. A change in scope rules, such as increasing the standards for smoke stack emissions, may lead to the elimination of many firms if boundary rules require them to face competition from firms not subject to the same regulation. However, if boundary rules protect such firms from "external" competition, the prices of the goods manufactured will rise, but the number of producers may stay relatively constant after such a change in scope rules.

Similarly, the effect of a change in aggregation rules depends upon the boundary rules and the number of resulting participants. The marginal decision-making costs resulting from the use of a unanimity rule may not be very high if restrictive enty rules keep the size of the group small. But under nonrestrictive entry rules, the number of participants may become large. If so, the use of unanimity rules will lead to high decision-making costs. Buchanan and Tullock (1962: 279–280) point out that effects of allowing vote-trading in legislative bodies is dependent upon the aggregation rules in force. They posit that an authority rule allowing vote-trading combined with an aggregation rule of unanimity, leads to Pareto optimal results.

Vote-trading combined with simple majority rules will not necessarily lead to Pareto optimal results.

The seven types of working rules specified here provide initial guidance to the analyst concerning the types of working rules which need to be specified in order to make explicit the underlying structure. A rule configuration can be produced as a result of a series of questions asked about the rules which affect each element in the action situation as conceptualized. In regard to the number of participants, for example, one is led to ask: Why are there N participants? How did they get there? Under what conditions can they leave? Are there costs, incentives, or penalties associated with entering or exiting? Are some participants forced into entry because of their residence or occupation? A similar set of questions about each of the elements of an action situation yields a set of working rules that affects the structure of the situation.

States of the World and their Transformation

While the rule configuration affects all of the elements of an action situation, some of the variables of an action situation are also affected by attributes of the states of the world and their transformation. What outcomes can be produced, what actions are physically possible, how actions are linked to outcomes, and what is contained in the information sets are affected by the world being acted upon in a situation. The same set of rules may yield entirely different types of action situations depending upon the types of events in the world being acted upon by participants. How individual actions are linked to outcomes and the divisibility of outcomes will be affected by whether a work team, for example, is producing divisible consumer goods in a factory versus producing jointly consumed local police services for a city.

The attributes of states of the world and their transformation are explicitly examined when the analyst self-consciously asks a series of questions about how the world being acted upon in a situation affects the outcomes, action sets, action-outcome linkages, and information sets of the situation. Several key questions about outcomes help to pinpoint the difference in action situations related to exchange, production, and use of goods and services that are called *pure private goods* from situations related to *collective goods*. Asking whether the total outcome of a situation is divided among a set of participants or whether all receive the same outcome identifies a situation characterized by divisible consumption in the first case and joint consumption in the second (Samuelson 1954; 1955). Asking whether a set of actors will receive valued outcomes, whether or not they act in a manner conducive to the production of these outcomes, identifies situations characterized by feasibility of exclusion. The configuration of rules underlying a market situation yields different action situations depending upon whether the outcomes are jointly or individually consumed and on whether exclusion is feasible or not. When no participant can be excluded from positively valued outcomes, whether or not they take costly actions to help produce those outcomes, participants will not be motivated within an arena to contribute to nor to reveal their true preferences for outcomes. An analyst would predict that many participants would adopt a free-rider strategy in action situations so characterized.

Asking explicit questions about action-outcome linkages also identifies important attributes of these transformations important in explaining the structure and results of action arenas. Do the individual actions of specific participants *separably* contribute to the amount of outcome or is the effect on the amount of outcome dependent on the interaction between the amount of inputs contributed by several participants (separability of production functions)? (Alchian and Demsetz 1972; Parks et al. 1981). The same rules used to produce outcomes with a separable production function will operate differently if used in situations with an inseparable production function (Schwartz 1983). Similarly, the predictability and complexity of action-outcome linkages affects the structure of action arenas. As Majone (Chapter 21) indicates, rules used to create situations which yield effective and efficient results, when combined with simple and predictable production functions, yield entirely different results when combined with complex and uncertain production functions. Problems are even more difficult when the outcomes themselves are difficult to measure.

The relative importance of the rule configuration and states of the world in structuring an action situation varies dramatically across different types of action situations. The rule configuration almost totally constitutes some games, like chess, where physical attributes are relatively unimportant. There is little about the size of a chess board or the shape of the pieces that contributes to the structure of a chess game. Chess is played on computer screens, in formal gardens, and with a wide variety of different boards and pieces. This is not the case in regard to many other games. Imagine, for example, switching the balls used in American and European football. The strategies available to players in these two games, and many other sports, are strongly affected by the physical attributes of the balls used, the size of the field, and the type of equipment.

The relative importance of working rules to attributes of the world also varies dramatically within action situations considered to be part of the public sector. A legislature is closer in many respects to chess than to football. Rules define and constrain voting behavior inside a legislature more than attributes of the world. Voting can be accomplished by raising hands, by paper ballots, by calling for the ayes and nays, by marching before an official counter, or by installing computer terminals for each legislator on which votes are registered. In regard, however, to organizing communication within a legislature, attributes of the world strongly affect the available options. The principle that only one person can be heard and understood at a time in any one forum strongly affects the capacity of legislators to communicate effectively with one another (see Ostrom: Ch. 5).

The Community

A third set of variables that affect the structure of an action arena relates to the community within which any action situation and set of actors occurs. The attributes of a community which are important in affecting the structure of an action arena include the norms of behavior generally accepted in the community, the level of common understanding potential participants share about the structure of particular types of action arenas, the extent of homogeneity in the preferences of those living in a community, and the distributions of resources among those affected. The term "culture" is frequently applied to this bundle of variables.

Scholars who have tried to change outcomes in developing countries by introducing institutional rules, which have proved successful in highly developed countries, have frequently found that the same set of rules operates with perverse consequences when placed into a different cultural context. Exactly how rules and general cultural norms interact when simultaneously related to a particular type of problem in the world is not well understood. Given space limitations, I can do little more than to point to this important set of variables. I have chosen to focus primary attention on the nature of institutional rules since these variables have been so little examined of recent times and to refer the reader to other efforts to focus on the nature of the community (see Ostrom: Ch. 11; Majone: Ch. 21; Bates 1981; Popkin 1979).

22.4 Linking Action Arenas

In addition to analysis which digs deeper into the factors affecting individual action arenas, an important development in institutional analysis is the examination of linked arenas. While the concept of a "single" arena may include large numbers of participants and complex chains of action, most of social reality is composed of multiple arenas linked sequentially or simultaneously. An adequate analysis of the results likely to be produced within a single arena is frequently an extremely difficult task and one needs to be cautious about venturing too far in analyzing even more complex linkages among multiple arenas. Some relatively simple arenas have already been examined and we know they are linked in the world. The next logical step is to address the results likely when particular types of arenas are linked together. This topic is addressed in several other chapters of this volume and thus can only be mentioned here. Herzberg and Ostrom (Ch. 20) examine the linkage between electoral arenas, party organization, legislatures, and the organization of governments. In Chapter 24, I analyze the results of the linkage between electoral arenas and the bargaining arena between elected officials and bureau chiefs. Shubik (Ch. 28) engages in an even more ambitious effort to examine the results of a series of sequentially played games. And, in Chapter 5, Ostrom analyzes the constitutional structure of government systems whose underlying designs require a basic separation of governmental powers into relatively autonomous arenas each of which is linked to the others and acts to regulate the results achieved in other arenas.

22.5 Conclusion

The public sector is composed of many different types of situations in which individuals are differentially led to engage in highly productive or, at times, grossly counterproductive and destructive actions. Institutional analysis provides some of the tools needed for guiding and controlling at least some aspects of the complex chains of action which compose the public sector. No guidance or control is possible without an understanding of how complex systems work. Identifying the key "working parts" of action arenas provides the first step in a systematic effort to predict the likely pattern of results to be obtained by individuals in particular types of arenas.

When humans wish to intervene to change the structure of incentives and deterrents faced by participants in socially constructed realities to guide (or control) participants toward a different pattern of results, they do so by attempting to change the rules individuals use to order their interactions within particular types of action arenas. How rules affect behavior and results has not, however, been a question at the forefront of intellectual inquiry in political science, public administration, policy sciences, organization theory, and the other disciplines that study the public sector. This chapter has attempted to provide a brief overview of a method of institutional analysis that can be used to examine the question of how rules, in combination with other variables, affect the structure of action situations and through this transformation affect the incentives and deterrents faced by individuals, the actions they select, and the cumulated results produced. An application of this method is pursued in Chapter 24.

References

Alchian, A., and H. Demsetz (1972): "Production, Information Costs, and Economic Organizations." *American Economic Review* 62/5: 777–795.

Allport, F. H. (1962): "A Structuronomic Conception of Behavior: Individual and Collective." *Journal of Abnormal and Social Psychology* 64/1: 3–30.

Ashby, W. R. (1962): *An Introduction to Cybernetics*. New York: Wiley & Sons.

Atkins, J. R., and L. Curtis (1969): "Game Rules and the Rules of Culture." In Buchler, I., and H. Nutini (eds.), *Game Theory in the Behavioral Sciences*, 213–234. Pittsburgh: Univ. of Pittsburgh Press.

Bates, R. H. (1981): *Markets and States in Tropical Africa*. Los Angeles, Calif.: Univ. of California Press.

Boynton, G. R. (1982): "On Getting From Here to There: Reflections on Two Paragraphs and Other Things." In Ostrom, E. (ed.), *Strategies of Political Inquiry*, 29–68. Beverly Hills: Sage.

Buchanan, J. M., and G. Tullock (1962): *The Calculus of Consent: Logical Foundations of Constitutional Democracy*. Ann Arbor: Univ. of Michigan Press.

Burke, K. (1966): *Language as Symbolic Action*. Berkeley, Calif.: Univ. of California Press.

Commons, J. R. (1957): *Legal Foundations of Capitalism*. Madison, Wis.: Univ. of Wisconsin Press.

Crozier, M. (1964): *The Bureaucratic Phenomenon*. Chicago: The Univ. of Chicago Press.

Ganz, J. R. (1971): *Rules: A Systematic Study*. The Hague: Mouton.

Garfinkel, H. (1967): *Studies in Ethno-Methodology*. Englewood Cliffs, N. J.: Prentice-Hall.

Hardin, R. (1982): *Collective Action*. Baltimore, Md.: The John Hopkins Univ. Press.

Harre, R. (1974): "Some Remarks on 'Rule' as a Scientific Concept." In Mischel, T. (ed.), *Understanding Other Persons*, 143–184. Oxford: Blackwell.

Harre, R., and P. F. Secord (1972): *The Explanation of Social Behavior*. Oxford: Blackwell.

Harsanyi, J. C., and R. Selten (1982): *A General Theory of Equilibrium Selection in Games*. Institute of Mathematical Economics, University of Bielefeld. (Working papers for Chapter 1–5.)

Heiner, R. A. (1983): "The Origin of Predictable Behavior." *American Economic Review* 73/4: 560–595.

Kiser, L., and E. Ostrom (1982): "The Three Worlds of Decision Making: A Metatheoretical Synthesis of Institutional Approaches." In Ostrom, E. (ed.), *Strategies of Political Inquiry*, 179–222. Beverly Hills, Calif.: Sage.

Langer, S. (1953): *An Introduction to Symbolic Logic* (2nd Ed.). New York: Dover.

Newell, A., and H. A. Simon (1972): *Human Problem Solving*. Englewood Cliffs, N. J.: Prentice-Hall.

Ostrom, V. (1980): "Artisanship and Artifact." *Public Administration Review* 40 (July/August): 309–317.

Ostrom, V., and E. Ostrom (1977): "Public Goods and Public Choices." In Savas, E. S. (ed.), *Alternatives for Delivering Public Services. Toward Improved Performance*, 7–49. Boulder, Color.: Westview Press.

Parks, R. B., P. C. Baker, L. L. Kiser, R. Oakerson, E. Ostrom, V. Ostrom, S. L. Percy, M. B. Vandivort, G. P. Whitaker, and R. Wilson (1981): "Consumers as Coproducers of Public Services: Some Economic and Institutional Considerations." *Policy Studies Journal* 9/7: 1,001–1,011.

Pejovich, S. (1982): "Karl Marx, Property Rights, and Social Change." *Kyklos* 35: 383–397.

Popkins, S. (1979): *The Rational Peasant: The Political Economy of Rural Society in Vietnam*. Los Angeles, Calif.: Univ. of California Press.

Popper, K. R. (1967): "La Rationalite et le Statut du Principle de Rationalite." In Classen, E. M. (ed.), *Les fondements philosophiques des systèmes économiques: Textes de Jacques Rueff et essais rédigés en son honneur 23 août 1966*, 145–150. Paris: Payot.

Rawls, J. (1968): "Two Concepts of Rules." In Care, N. S., and C. Landesman (eds.), *Readings in the Theory of Actions*, 306–340. Bloomington, Ind.: Indiana Univ. Press. (Orig. printed 1955 in *Philosophical Review* 4.)

Samuelson, P. A. (1954): "The Pure Theory of Public Expenditure." *Review of Economics and Statistics* 36 (November): 387–389.

Samuelson, P. A. (1955): "Diagrammatic Exposition of a Theory of Public Expenditure." *Review of Economics and Statistics* 37 (November): 350–356.

Schütz, A. (1967): *The Phenomenology of the Social World* (Tr. by G. Walsh, and F. Lehnert). Evanston, Ill.: Northwestern Univ. Press.

Schwartz, T. (1983): *"Policy and Compliance: The Lesson of Dr. Krankheit and A Monster Who Eats Babies."* Austin, Tex.: The University of Texas at Austin, Department of Government, Working Paper 19, Working Papers on Institutional Design and Public Policy.

Searle, J. R. (1969): *Speech Acts. An Essay in the Philosophy of Language*. Cambridge: Cambridge Univ. Press.

Shimanoff, S. B. (1980): *Communication Rules. Theory and Research*. Beverly Hills, Calif.: Sage.

Toulmin, S. (1974): "Rules and Their Relevance for Understanding Human Behavior." In Mischel, T. (ed.), *Understanding Other Persons*, 185–215. Oxford: Basil Blackwell.

Weber, M. (1947): *The Theory of Social and Economic Organization* (Tr. by A. M. Henderson and T. Parsons). New York: The Free Press.

Weick, K. E. (1969): *The Social Psychology of Organizing*. Reading, Mass.: Addison-Wesley.

Wright, G. H. van (1968): "The Logic of Practical Discourse." In Klibansky, R. (ed.), *Contemporary Philosophy*, 141–167. Rome: La Nuava Italia Editrice.

Part 5
Coordination in Interorganizational Relationships

23. Interorganizational Arrangements and Coordination at the Policy Level

Hans-Jürgen Franz

Abstract

The article starts from the assumption that even government agencies in the strict sense, i.e. the administrative bodies within the federal system, are no longer coordinated by pure principles of hierarchy. Instead the various forms of interlevel collaboration within the three-tier-system are discussed. The analysis concentrates on the types of coordination which emerge from interrelations among the administrative agencies of the three institutional levels. The point of departure is that the increase of governmental activities makes the process of policy making more complex. These more complex forms of coordination are analyzed within a theoretical framework, which is based on organization theory and interorganizational analysis. The key argument is that the federal administrative system represents an interorganizational arrangement determined by its interorganizational relationships. This increased problem of policy coordination will be considered in the change of interorganizational relationships within the federal system.

23.1 Introduction

As other sections have shown (see part 2) the modern public sector corresponds neither to the classical public/private dichotomy nor to the traditional and very influential concept of a hierarchical and unitary system guided by one decision centre at the top, – the key argument of the Weberian idealtype of bureaucracy (see Weber 1976: 125–130). Insofar as public and private organizations interact within various interorganizational arrangements, the "reality" of the sector is generated by an interplay of highly organized actors with separate interests, goals, and strategies (see Scharpf 1978: 347). Thus the concept of a homogeneous sector governed by uniform rules, often denoted as "the state," has to be replaced by the model of "organized complexity" which is characterized by an increased number of components, their relative variety and differentiation, and the degree of interdependence among them (see La Porte 1975).

The notion of "organized complexity" not only indicates another sophistication of the academic discussion. It takes into account the fact that the existence of a plurality of organized actors and of organizational forms prevents reliance on pure types of coordination to ensure the proper functioning of the public sector. The assumption, that even government agencies in the strict sense (i.e. administrative bodies of ministries) are coordinated by hierarchy and its essential nexus of legitimate command and obedient execution has become more and more relative when confronted with various forms of collaboration among governmental and non-governmental organizations comprising relationships of exchange, competition, mutual adjustment, or bargaining. Although the legal authority to enforce government decisions still constitutes the core of any political process, as scholars of sociological systems theory point out (see Parsons 1969: 320; Luhmann 1970), the various institutional arrangements due to organizational growth and differentiation within the public sector have generated more complex forms of coordination. Therefore this chapter will deal with two questions; namely: what are the conditions for the emergence of such complex arrangements, and how do they operate?

The process of policy making within a three-tier-system represents a long chain of action where processes of coordination between the different institutional levels and among the units of one institutional level occur. Although the critique of a bureaucratic system is the core idea of federal systems, the analysis of policy making within federal systems has often presumed that the centre's objectives have to be perceived as the only standard of correct and effective policy making. The interdependence of processes of policy making and the coordination of the administrative agencies were recognized only to the extent, to which the often implicit assumptions of central guidance became obviously insufficient in the face of the complexity of public policies.

In this chapter we will consider federal systems within a sociological framework developed in terms of organization theory which perceives the federal administrative system as a specific interorganizational arrangement, the coordination of which depends on the structural properties of that arrangement and the strategies of the people involved in its organizations[1].

The analysis of the configuration of coordinating mechanisms at the policy level has to take into account, that differing national historical developments and cultural traditions affect the conceptualization of the public sector. Although federal systems represent the theoretical alternative to unitary systems, the degree to which they are analyzed in a top-down perspective which presumes some "centre", depends on different cultural traditions of conceptualizing public policy. As Nettl (1968) points out, the concept of a unitary "state" is contingent on random historical developments, intellectual traditions and cultural orientations of a generalized cognition of state by the people. These variables constitute different degrees of "stateness" in different countries. Therefore the complaints about problems of coordination in the German federal system refer to a higher degree of stateness than the debate about policy coordination in the federal system of the USA.

23.2 Coordination and the Problem of Interdependence

Different academic approaches to analyzing the public sector take "interdependence" for granted and apply the term to different kinds of coordination problems. So some studies from the field of implementation research concentrate on the question, to what extent executant organizations are capable of distorting the goals set by legislative authority (e.g. Pressman and Wildavski 1973, Bardach 1977). On the other hand, scholars of the policy sciences are interested in the conditions for coherent policy formation and operation within a fragmented decision structure (e.g. Scharpf 1973). On the level of concrete service delivery the performance of joint programs by formally independent organizations is perceived as problematic (e.g. Aiken and Hage 1968; Warren et al. 1975). These few examples illustrate that 'interdependence' and 'coordination' among organizations seem to be key words for the understanding of the modern public sector. In this chapter we do not define coordination as a quest for more central control[2], but use an institutional analysis based on the premise that different institutional solutions are possible.

As Elazar (1974) pointed out with regard to the American federal system there is no reason to assume a rational centre and a chaotic jungle of executive organizations. Instead, an institutional analysis of coordination problems has to prove what kind of interdependence affects the structure of the federal system in such a way that coordination becomes problematic. From an analytical point of view any institutional arrangement is characterized by some independence and interdependence among its components. For example, even the ideal competitive market compromises both; the independence of actors to decide voluntarily about their separate transactions and the interdependence of these actions dictated by price mechanisms. On the other hand, the hierarchically structured public administration is characterized by a formalized control of internal interdependence through the distribution of responsibilities. But there are also certain degrees of independent decision making on the different hierarchical levels due to the process of growth and internal differentiation.

The formal structure of a federal system is determined by constitutional law ensuring the interdependence of governmental actions as well as the relative autonomy of the three institutional levels (see Friedrich 1968). Since the late sixties this concept of a coordination by law has been criticized, because the assumption of a well-functioning (i.e. balanced) relation between independence and interdependence became insufficient in front of the increased interdependence of decisions increasing more complex forms of coordination than law. Although the theory of federalism traditionally emphasizes the variability of institutional arrangements, the separation of power and the independence of public decisions which should be directed to the community, who are affected by these decisions (see Hamilton et al. n. d.; Friedrich 1968: 11–30), the debate about federal policy making oftenly reduced federal systems to the formal structure set by law. This theoretical reduction of the theory of federalism indicates, how much the scientific discussion of coordination problems was bound to the implicit premises of a centralistic top-down perspective of a unilateral guidance through law.

This concept sees the process of policy making as a *system of independencies* in which the principle of a separated, and thereby balanced, power admits independent political operations within a constitutionally determined realm. From this point of view the three institutional levels need not consider each other in their day-to-day operations, because the compatibility of the decisions is guaranteed by the constitutionally distributed legal authority. Communication between government organizations are few and restricted to single interactions. As to interlevel cooperations within the three-tier-system some interlevel collaboration is quite normal. But it is restricted to efforts to gain some degree of re-integration, which does not change the intergovernment relations ruled by law (see Kisker 1971).

Like any other social system the federal system is embedded in the evolutionary process of an increased functional differentiation. Using modern sociological systems theory (Luhmann 1976) one can say that the components of a system increase their autonomy which constrains central control and is contrained by it. This "relative autonomy" (Gouldner 1959: 255) is subject to an enduring tension between the component's effort to maintain or extend its independence and the system's need to ensure some internal coherence and to control the components. In the federal system the quantitative and qualitative change in public policies due to the increased government responsibilities for economic growth and some standard of social welfare sharpens this tension and makes intergovernment relations more complex.

If the development of the federal institutional arrangement is considered with reference to the qualitative change of public policies, then the process of administering federal systems has to be discussed. According to the concept of coordination by law two structural options for effecting policies are possible. On the one hand, there are the United States and their system of direct administration offering the federal government all the merits and demerits of centralization; i.e. the chances of strong and direct influence and the risks of resistant executive organizations (see Friedrich 1968: 70–76). On the other hand, there is the system of delegated administration in West Germany where the federal government does not have administrative bodies of its own but depends on the capacities of the Laender and the communities (see Johnson 1973). By depending only on the formal, legally-defined structure, both types of administrations manifest the assumption that constitutionally destributed legal authority determines policy coordination.

Although the federal system is still based on the formal structure set by constitutional law the increase of government activities has induced a change of conceptualizing policy processes which, for example, is described as a shift from "regulatory" to "distributive and redistributive politics" (Lowi 1969) or as a transition from "reactive policies" to "active policy making" (Mayntz and Scharpf 1975). The growth of federal grants-in-aid in the United States (see MacMahon 1972: 83–107; Staats 1974) and West Germany (see Kisker 1971: 40–52) on the one hand, and the enhanced chances of the lower institutional levels to resist or modify the operation of policies set by the centre on the other, has induced the empirical conversion of the two types of administration (see Friedrich 1968: 75). The interlevel coordination is no longer clearly determined by legal authority alone. Intergovernment relations correspond neither to the model of partnership (delegated adminitration) nor to the centre/agent relation of direct administration (see MacMahon 1972: 27).

Rhodes (1980) points out that existing intergovernment relations do not fit the models of 'partnership' or 'centre/agent', because neither a reciprocity of influences nor a superiority of the federal (central) government can be taken for granted. By contrast there is a wide range of relations comprising interlevel agreements or "memoranda of understanding" among administrators (MacMahon 1971: 185), advisory commissions, and forms of institutionalized cooperation and joint decision making. The outcomes of these arrangements are not completely determined by legal authority, but legal authority has become more related to other interorganizational linkages. In this context the typology of linkages within the public sector, which Hood developed in Chapter 9 with reference to the variety of para-governmental organizations, is useful for our analysis of arrangements constituted by the organizations of the federal system. Legal authority has become relative to the opportunity for the executive organizations to monopolize information ("nodality"), their technical capacity (stock of buildings, personnel) to realize public policies ("organization") and the budget ("treasure").

It is not assumed by this that "power" is totally replaced as the ultimate basis for political decisions but that it is more involved with the other interlevel linkages. In so far as the use of legal authority as the core structure of the three-tier-system is more and more affected by these other linkages, coordination at the policy level is contingent on variable arrangements of interorganizational relationships. As they only concentrated on a formal, legally-defined structure, the dominant assumptions about the analysis of problems of coordination have proved insufficient.

Therefore we can specify the kind of interdependence which induces problems of coordination at the policy level. It is the variety of intergovernmental relations due to the complex and variable structures of the positional resources given by authority, information, organization, and treasure, which enlarge the criterion of 'legal/illegal' by strategic calculi. According to these considerations we will analyze the three-tier-system from the point of view that contributions from the field of organization and interorganization theory provide. "The unit of analysis of this discussion is large-scale pluralistic systems consisting of networks of formally autonomous, functionally interdependent organizations" (Metcalfe 1978: 39).

23.3 The Federal System as Interorganizational Relationship

In specifying the problem of interdependence and coordination at the policy level with regard to the qualitative change of the interlevel relationships within a three-tier-system, the system is not perceived as a centre-ruled actor but as an institutional arrangement defined by its interrelations.[4] The disaggregation of the federal state into its component organizations and their relationships emphasizes the processes of conflict and change. As mentioned above, intergovernmental relations were often defined by the structure set by legal authority, although the classical theory of federalism as well as the reality of federal systems does not prescribe such a structure. In contrast, the integration of the key arguments of organization and interorganization theory offers a theoretical framework which is more adequate to the changed, i.e. more complex, interlevel relationships.

According to the traditional assumptions of the top-down perspective and its centralistic premises, the two structural options of federal administration imply interlevel relationships which are determined by the unambigously distributed legal authority. But neither concept fits the variety of informational, organizational, and financial linkages any longer. In the model of direct administration the basic dilemma is "how to achieve goals and objectives that are established by the national government through the actions of other governments, state and local, that are legally independent and may even be politically hostile" (Sundquist 1969:

12). Clear superior-subordinate relations are replaced by intergovernment bargaining (see Rhodes 1980; Ingram 1977). On the other hand, the pre-assumed partnership within the system of delegated administration (see Kisker 1971; Friedrich 1968), is replaced by various forms of interlevel influence from centralization through federal grants-in-aid to a monopoly of executive capability by state and local organizations.

The more intergovernment linkages exist the more the single organization gains some degree of autonomy as to its interorganizational behaviour. By perceiving the different agencies of the federal, state, and local level of policy making as *organizations* we transfer the *organization/environment nexus* of organization theory to the federal system in order to bring to bear the strategies of the federal agencies and the structure of their interorganizational relationships. Accordingly we have to relate the main features of the modern sociological theory of organizations.

Despite a lot of controversy there is a minimal agreement among scholars of organization theory that an organization has to be seen with explicit reference to its environment. Starting from systems theory the organization as a whole represents the unit of analysis and is defined as an "open system", the characteristics of which are ongoing exchange relations with its environment (see Katz and Kahn 1966). These environmental relations of exchange are based upon the properties of an organization as a "resource-getting-system" (see Yuchtman and Seashore 1967). In considering the organization/environment nexus it is possible to distinguish two theoretical perspectives, which differ in the extent to which "uncertainty" or "dependency" is defined as the main environmental problem of organizations (see Aldrich and Mindlin 1978).

Although a detailed discussion of the methodological differences of these concepts is outside the ambit of this paper, one can say with regard to our subject, namely the interorganizational arrangement of the federal system, that "uncertainty" and "dependency" are not incompatible but supplementary concepts. On the one hand, *"dependency"* is defined with regard to the *structural conditions* of the organization's operations as e.g. size, amount of autonomously disposed resources, availability of alternative resources (see Cook 1977). On the other hand, *"uncertainty"* stresses the *behavioral level* of decision makers' perceptions, their information processing, and choices.

Neither perspective excludes the other. The organization as an open system does not act like a natural person but depends on the behavior of individuals which is largely determined by the conditions of membership, career structures, and formalized tasks. Individuals play behavioral games, choose environmental strategies (e.g. Child 1972), and manage informational complexity (see March and Simon 1958) under specific structural constraints. As Astley and Van de Ven (1983) point out the discussion of this methodological pluralism, albeit innovative, bears the risk of compartmentalization that needs a re-integration.

In the analysis of intergovernment relations within the federal system this chapter starts from a systems-theoretical point of view that is concerned with the organization as a whole. In this the importance of individual behavior is not denied, but it is assumed that this behavior is largely structured by the formalization of membership and the standardization of work (see Luhmann 1976). Thus one can say that any agency of the federal, state, and local level represents an organization which is involved in exchange relations with the other organizations of the federal system. The general notion of the "organizational environment" becomes more precise when it is considered to be constituted by other organizations producing the constraints, contingencies, and opportunities the organization has to deal with (see Thompson 1967; 24). In so far as any organization of the three-tier-system is confronted with precedent, parallel, and consequent decision the degrees of uncertainty and dependency characterizing its interorganizational relationships constitute the environmental complexity.

As mentioned above, the discussion of coordination problems, concentrated on the idea that the formal structure set by the distribution of legal authority minimizes uncertainty and fixes dependency to a balance of power. Interlevel collaboration is assumed either to be ruled by law or to be a re-integration of the distributed responsibilities. According to these assumptions the environment of the organizations is not very complex. As qualitative policy change emerges, the interorganizational relationships are no longer coordinated only by law but linkages with information, organization, and treasure become more complex.

The structural change of the federal system from a system of independencies supplemented by infrequent interactions among its elements to a system of high interdependence that stems from the variety of interorganizational linkages can be analyzed as an increase in environmental complexity. Emery and Trist (1965) developd a typologoy of organizational environments that differentiates several levels of complexity in the interrelations among organizations. They distinguish randomized, clustered, disturbed reactive, and turbulent environments. The degrees of complexity range from no interrelations among organizations to a system of richly joint elements (see Metcalfe 1974). Within the federal system the degree of complexity changes from the low level of clustered, i.e. law ruled interconnections to the turbulence of richly joint elements, the interrelations of which depend rather on configurations of different interlevel linkages than on constitutional law alone.

A new kind of interorganizational relationship is developed. The system of normal cooperation created by interactions among the legally independent organizations becomes a system of high interdependence, the joint decision making of which is characterized by strategic interdependence. The dependency on the other organizations' resources, – their capacities to change laws, to monopolize information, to perform and to finance public policies –, and the uncertainty about their autonomous decision making generate this complexity. Pennings (1981: 433) defines strategic interdependence "by the similarity of organizations' input or output disposal. Strategically interdependent organizations are aware that such behaviors are contingent on the behavior of the other organizations." It is a consequence of this high degree of complexity that all the interorganizational relationships based on legal authority, information, organization, and treasure are closely linked so that any policy decision within the federal system affects these four kinds of linkages or is affected by them. Faced with the uncertainty that stems from the environment of the other organizations every federal agency, like any other organization, seeks to cope with this problem by creating some kind of a "negotiated environment" (see Cook 1977: 65).

The aim of any organization to gain some kind of a negotiated environment and to reduce the interorganizational complexity promotes different forms of interlevel collaboration and coordination. As mentioned above, informal memoranda of understanding among administrators, formal interlevel agreements and institutionalized processes of joint decision making represent solutions to the problem of increased interdependence. The forms of collaboration differ in the degree of obligation imposed by the decisions made by the organizations. Under conditions of low complexity based on a few clustered interrelations among the organizations informal processes of interpersonal adjustment and some formal agreements, supplementing the core structure set by constitutional law, are sufficient to ensure the compatibility of decisions. By contrast the complexity of multiple interrelations induced by linkages other than legal authority transcends the informal nature of processes of adjustment and exceeds the manageable number of agreements.

For the single organization decision making is no longer manageable, if the organization has to anticipate all the decision's consequences and potential reactions to it. This is the reason, why organizations of the three-tier-system establish arrangements that reduce the variety of interorganizational strategies to a manageable level of complexity.

Strategic interdependence imposes on organizations very high costs of coordination in terms of time required and computational expense. What Williamson (1979) calls the transactional costs overload organizations if to prevent disadvantageous consequences any organization that might be affected by a decision has to be considered. Furthermore, these interorganizational relations meet the condition of Litvak and Hylton (1961), that a conflict of interests replaces the rule of an overall authority. The distribution of legal authority, the strategic use of grants-in-aid and of information, and the legally independent disposal of organizational resources represent a network the coordination of which depends on varied strategical constraints and opportunities.

The concept of an "interorganizational network" emphasizes that the interorganizational relationships consist of properties which cannot be derived from the components' actions (see Turk 1970: 1). In so far as the federal systems as a whole have changed in their internal complexity, which we defined by the increase of interorganizational relations, coordination depends on the structure of the network of organizations. Coordinated decisions of the different organizations are no longer predictable from the formal structure set by constitutional law, but they are the result of an interorganizational bargaining between the representatives of those organizations involved in the network. The outcome of this process is contingent on the variable configurations of constraints and opportunities which the network offers. An organization at federal government level, for example, which is concerned with regulatory policies or with the budgeting of policies, has greater opportunity to effect its interests vis-à-vis the executive organization than an organization dealing with problems of local service delivery, where the subordinate organizations can monopolize executive responsibilities.

Following White (1974) we perceive a network as an emergent phenomenon and discard an interorganizational analysis which only extends the intra-organizational perspective to the level of networks. The interorganizational networks within the federal system can be considered as a political economy. Benson (1975) points out, that a network represents a political economy to the extent to which the component organizations are concerned with the distribution of the two scarce resources of money and authority. 'Authority' and 'money' refer to the legal legitimacy of activities and the disposal of resources. Access to strategically relevant resources and the disposal of them depends on the location of the organization within the network. The more central an organization is within the network and its resource flows, the more its bargaining power is enhanced vis-à-vis the peripheral organizations (see Cook 1977). It is this structure of opportunities and constraints which influences the decisions organizations make about the application, combination, or mere threat of their interorganizational strategies.

In general there are four types of strategies to distinguish (see Benson 1975: 241–245). Cooperative strategies are used in relationships where neither party is totally powerless in relation to others, whereas disruptive strategies are based on a substantial power imbalance, so that one organization can threaten the resource basis of others. Manipulative strategies can be interpreted as an influencing over time and finally authoritative strategies depend on legal power. The sequential, combined, or only threatened use of these strategies generates a high degree of complexity, which goes far beyond the computational capacity of the representatives of the organizations. But the interorganizational network it not a situation of an "once for all" decision, which some game theoretical considerations might suppose, but lasts over time.

In the long run the network gains some degree of stability. The problem of radical uncertainty is restrained by the existence of organizational domains which define the scope and responsibility of an organization's tasks according to its location in the network (see Warren et al. 1973). As Braito et al. point out, any interorganizational network depends on a certain degree of domain consensus, because the organizations "may be highly committed (self definition of domain) to the reduction of a specific problem, but unless they receive support from other organizations in their environment (domain consensus) they will have little success in working with other organizations in this problem area" (Braito et al. 1972: 183). The domain consensus of the organizations' spheres of activities, the ideological consensus of the definition of problems and the means to resolve them, positive mutual evaluation in working together, and earlier experiences of effective collaboration (see Benson 1975: 235) enhance the equilibrium within the network. Thus the wide range of possible interorganizational strategies is constrained by the requirements of a durable collaboration.

We can say that the coordination of the federal system, although it is still directed towards the legal distribution of responsibilities, is not determined by law. Instead there are various interorganizational networks dealing with different policy areas. The interlevel coordination of the organizations of the federal system depends on the specific structure of the network, which comprises various interorganizational linkages due to the characteristics of the policy area. As mentioned above, it is important for the structure of a network and the organizations' strategies, whether the network deals with regulatory or investment policies offering a large opportunity for central influence, or whether it deals with problems of social service delivery offering the executive organizations more opportunity to exercise their interests. These differences constitute different forms of interlevel coordination, so that the federal system comprises a wide range of coordinative

modi. Centralization and some kind of grass-root coordination among executive
organizations represent only the margins of this wide range of forms.

In order to analyze the coordination of the federal administrative system one has
to consider seriously that this "system" is differentiated into various specialized
interorganizational networks. The distribution of interorganizational resources like
legal authority, information, organization, and treasure, the degree of conflict and
of domain consensus among organizations, and finally interorganizational bargaining within the network produce more complex forms of coordination than the
assumptions of constitutional law suggest. In the next section we will demonstrate
the development of an interorganizational network with reference to the empirical
example which the interlevel cooperation within the German "Politikverflechtung"
offers.

23.4 The Interorganizational Network of the German "Politikverflechtung"

The so-called *"Politikverflechtung"* in the Federal Republic of Germany is a good
illustration of the structure of an interorganizational network at the policy level and
the specific outcomes of interorganizational coordination. The meaning of the
notion *Politikverflechtung* is that the three institutional levels of the federal
government, the Laender, and the communities are linked by joint decision
making within specialized intergovernment commissions. As mentioned above, the
federal system of the FRG is based on delegated administration, which is characterized by a highly differentiated decision structure and a very high degree of joint
decision making (see Mayntz and Scharpf 1975; Johnson 1973).

Interlevel cooperation is not a new phenomenon within the German system of
delegated administration, because there were cooperative actions before the
formalized structure was established. As in any other federal system the federal
government cooperated with the subordinate levels and vice versa, when a policy
required a re-integration of the constitutionally separated areas of responsibility.
This interlevel cooperation bound to constitutional law was assumed to be a natural
complement to delegated administration (see Kisker 1971: 303). But the cooperation was restricted to interactions, which were coordinated by legal authority
namely certain amendments of the laws. Within this system of delegated administrative interaction among the three institutional levels was based on the interests
of the legally independent organizations. If one of the Laender had to operate a
policy that transcended its capacities, it looked for assistance from the federal
government, which could decide independently, too. On the other hand, the
federal government was able to induce some specific changes in one Land without
taking the others into account. A consequence of this structure was the generation
of a variety of independent policies with the increased risk of conflicting effects.

In the late sixties the so-called incremental process of policy making characterized by a great number of independent programs and by singly interactions among
the organizations of the different levels was seen to be unsatisfactory when
confronted with the qualitative change of policy objectives. Increased government

responsibility for economic growth and for the compensations or even prevention of negative social effects required policies recognizing the interdependence of these problems. It was argued that the fragmentation of responsibilities and the dispersion of resources prevented adequate solutions to the problems, because the limited perceptions of different organizations and the negative coordination among them, i.e. their aim to ensure their domains, produced sub-optimal outcomes (see Mayntz and Scharpf 1975; Scharpf 1976: 20)[5]. As a result of discussion on the qualitative change of public objectives a new article of contitutional law was passed intitutionalizing a process of interlevel joint decision making. These joint decisions were explicitly restricted to decisions of the federal government and the Laender and they included policy problems such as urban renewal, highway planning, planning of education and science, and regional economic aid (see Marnitz 1974).

In this chapter we leave aside the discussion on the assumptions of political planning namely their bias towards centralization, which constituted the 'background' of the 'Politikverflechtung'. Instead we will look at the changes in the interorganizational network, which the new article 91a of the German constitution evoked. The network changed from numerous single interactions towards a bilateral or coalitional cooperation, still subject to legal authority alone. The coordination of these richly joint, strategically independent organizations depended on the interorganizational resources of legal authority, information, organization, and treasure. Article 91a of the German constitution enacted this kind of a network into law, so that the interlevel relationships became highly complex and the legally independent strategies of the organizations had to shift from tactics of maximal short run success to long run optimization.

Under the conditions of low complexity within 'normal cooperation' each of the government organizations tried to solve its environmental problems by means of direct influences on the other organization, i.e. source of uncertainty and dependence. These actions were guided by the organization's interest of maximal success. By contrast, the strategically interdependent organizations of the network have to develop more complicated strategies, because any other organization that might be affected by a decision has to be taken into account. Thus tactics of maximal short-run success have to be replaced by optimization strategies calculating the opportunities and constraints which a decision and the reactions to it may generate in the long-run. Because of this complexity each of the organizations involved in the network favours a decision structure which prevents any violation of the established domains. Therefore, the federal government as well as the Laender, which had to agree to the constitutional amendment of the article 91a, accepted only the principle of unanimity within the network. On the basis of this decision structure each organization is able to ensure at any time a veto-position in favour of its own domain. But this aim of minimizing uncertainty generates additional constraints for interorganizational coordination not derived from any "natural" interdependence, but depending on the organizations' self-interests.

If one perceives the process of coordination at the policy level as a result of interorganizational networks characterized by strategic interdependence, then the different interests of the organizations and their conflicts have to be discussed, because these networks are not determined by an overall power but by various conflicts of interests (see Litvak and Hylton 1961). By this it is not assumed that there are symmetrical power relations, but that the four interorganizational resources we mentioned above generate a situation where neither party is power-less in relation to others (see Benson 1975; Cook 1977). Within the network of institutionalized interlevel collaboration in the FRG the organizations on the level of federal government are interested in preventing any distortion of their goals through the behavior of the executive organizations, and they seek opportunities for central control. On the other hand, the Laender are able to use their executive resources of information and organization to influence the outcome of coordina-tion according to their own interests.

F. W. Scharpf and his colleagues (Scharpf et al. 1978) developed a theoretical framework for the analysis of these networks. The joint tasks which the organiza-tions have to perform according to article 91a of the German constitution are large scale investment policies. Thus the network is concerned with the allocation, amount, structure, and side-effects of public investments. Scharpf (1976: 27) argues that a decision structure of legally decentralized responsibilities and inde-pendence generates four types of coordination problems:

(1) fixing the size of the investment
(2) the optimal structure of the investment
(3) allocating investments to different sectors
(4) externalities and their interdependence.

Because of the legal independence of the organizations and the heterogeneity of their interests the capacity of the network to coordinate depends on its structural ability to resolve conflicts and to cope with informational complexity (see Scharpf 1973: 36–40). The principle of unanimity, the result of organizations interest to secure their domains, enhances the demand for conflict resolution.

There are four possible modes of conflict resolution within such a network. First of all each organization can try to carry its interest into effect by *sanctions,* but no sanctions are given by the structure of the network. Strategies of *consensus building* become irrelevant faced with the complexity of issues and interests affected by large scale investment policies. Finally, *information strategies* as well as strategies of *convincing* the other organizations impose transactional costs that prevent any decision (see Scharpf 1973: 55–90). Therefore, conflict avoidance has become the dominant mode of coordination within the network of the "Politikver-flechtung". If an organization has to prove in advance any possible consequence of a decision, then the complexity of the coordination process transcends any compu-tational capacity[6]. The principle of negative coordination, and decision rules that minimize conflicts are favoured, so that established organizational domains are not changed.

The network that was established in order to gain well-coordinated policies and to reduce the complexity of interorganizational interdependence to a manageable level has had the opposite effect, namely coordination at the lowest level of agreement i.e. the maintenance of the status quo. As some studies of policies that were coordinated by this network show (see Bentele 1979, Garlichs 1980), this institutional arrangement is only capable of solving quantitative problems but fails with regard to qualitative problems which require a violation of the established domains. The development of the "Politikverflechtung" illustrates that the highly organized actors at the policy level, i.e. the organizations of the three institutional levels, produce situations, in which their particular interests increase the costs of coordination to such a high degree that only sub-optimal outcomes are possible.

23.5 The Risks of Coordination by Constraints

There are a lot of interpretations of the interorganizational network which the "Politikverflechtung" represents. Scharpf (1976: 66) speaks of a dangerous inactivity in the political system due to the very low level of coordination. Some other comments correspond to this negative appraisal by emphasizing the ineffectiveness of such a "bureaucratic oligarchy" (Kisker 1971: 305) which undermines parliamentary control (see Lehner 1979). The unsatisfactory outcomes of this network challenge the idea of a coherently functioning public sector and the behavior of the self-interested actors at the policy level accertuates the fact that standard setting and standard using represent the key problem of guidance (see Kaufmann: Ch. 10).

But the development of the public sector is not determined by some unavoidable "fate". As Schleicher (Ch.: 25) shows, there is no "one-best-way" of organizing the public sector. Instead, several organizational forms are possible. This gives rise to the question, why such an ineffective structure as the German network of interlevel collaboration is established, although all the organizations and the politicians involved complain of its ineffectiveness (see Schnabel 1980). As in any other modern federal system policy making in the FRG has to a large extent become the responsibility of administrative organizations (see Häussermann 1978). Thus, highly specialized administrative organizations prepare and perform the majority of policies which the elected officials can only ratify. It is this trend of replacing political decisions by adminitrative ones, which Schnabel (1980) refers to in speaking of "politics without politicians". The emergence of the German policy network illustrates very well the thesis of March (1981) that organizational change is ongoing and pragmatically oriented but also restricted by the limited rationality of self-interested organizations. The organizations of the German federal system adapted themselves to the problem of interdependence only when their domains seemed to be affected. Therefore, their strategies to ensure their domains gave rise to conflict avoidance as the dominant mode of coordination. With regard to the organizations' aims to reduce uncertainty and to control contingencies, which the complexity of the interorganizational relationships generates, one can say that the actors at the policy level prefer "security" to the abstract standard of "effectiveness".

Finally, we can conclude that the federal system is differentiated into specialized interlevel networks of administrative organizations. Their coordination depends on the interorganizational resources of legal authority, information, organization, and treasure. The example of the German interorganizational network demonstrates that the organizations are primarily interested in ensuring their domains. This pragmatic and self-interested orientation fosters the maintenance of a very low level of coordination and stability. But this stability of the highly organized process of policy making bears the permanent risk that policies are not responsive to the interests and needs of the people affected by them. The analysis of the negative effects resulting from the principle of unanimity within this network of policy making must be the basis of any quest for institutional alternatives.

Notes

1 The theoretical framework of this article, which is based on sociological contributions to modern organization theory and interorganizational analysis represents an alternative approach to the public choice theory proposed by E. Ostrom in Chapter 22.

2 The assumption of a rational centre which is capable of planning and coordinating the public sector from an all-inclusive and objectively "best" level is very ideological. The centre's quest for control (see van Gunsteren 1976) is not neutral but determined by the specific self-interest of the organizations at the top.

3 Further consideration of the core principles of federal systems is not the subject of this chapter. A detailed discussion of the nationally differing concepts of organizing federal institutional arrangements is given by V. Ostrom in Chapter 5.

4 In addition to sociological organization theory other academic disciplines contribute to interorganizational analysis. The economic theory of market structures, for example (see Kandwalla 1981), discusses relationships among economic organizations. But within the federal system of administrative organizations there is no equivalent to prices and exchange relations are more complex. Therefore, the framework of organization theory seems to be more adequate.

5 The problems of political planning, which were implied by the discussion about an "active-policy making", are the subject of other contributions to this volume (see Ch. 27).

6 The complexity of the interorganizational network is a problem that the representatives of the organizations have to deal with. This behavioral level of the problem of complexity is discussed by scholars who discuss the "boundary spanning persons" of an organization (e.g. Adams 1976).

References

Adams, J. St. (1976): "The Structure and Dynamics of Behavior in Organizational Boundary Roles." In Dunnett, M. D. (ed.), *Handbook of Industrial and Organizational Psychology*, 1175–1199. Chicago: Rand McNally.

Aiken, M., and J. Hage (1968): "Organizational Interdependence and Intra-Organizational Structure." *American Sociological Review* 33/4: 912–930.

Aldrich, H., and S. Mindlin (1978): "Uncertainty and Dependency: Two Perspectives on Environment." In Karpik, L. (ed.), *Organization and Environment*, 149–170. London: Sage.

Astley, W. G., and A. H. Van de Ven (1983): "Central Perspectives and Debates in Organization Theory." *Administrative Science Quarterly* 28 (June): 245–273.

Bardach, E. (1977). *The Implementation Game*. Cambridge, Mass.: MIT-Press.

Benson, K. J. (1975): "The Interorganizational Network as a Political Economy." *Administrative Science Quaterly* 20 (June): 229–249.

Braito, R., S. Paulson, and G. Klonglon (1972): "Domain Consensus: A Key Variable in Interorganizational Analysis." In Brinkerhoff, M. B., and P. R. Kunz (eds.), *Complex Organizations and their Environment*, 176–193. Dubuque: Brown.

Child, J. (1972): "Organizational Structure, Environment and Performance: The Role of Strategic Choice." *Sociology* 6/1: 2–21.

Cook, K. S. (1977): "Exchange and Power in Networks of Interorganizational Relations." *The Sociological Quaterly* 18 (Winter): 62–82.

Elazar, D. (1974): "The New Federalism: Can The States Be Trusted?" *The Public Interest* 35 (Spring): 89–103.

Emery, F. E., and E. L. Trist (1965): "The Causal Texture of Organizational Environments." *Human Relations* 18/1: 21–32.

Friedrich, C. J. (1968): *Trends of Federalism in Theory and Practice*. New York–London: Praeger.

Garlichs, D. (1980): *Grenzen staatlicher Infrastrukturpolitik: Bund-Länder Kooperation in der Fernstraßenplanung*. Königstein/Ts.: Athenäum.

Gouldner, A. (1959): "Reciprocity and Autonomy in Functional Theory." In Gross, L. (ed.), *Symposium on Sociological Theory*. New York: Harper & Row.

Gunsteren, H. van (1976): *The Quest of Control*. London: Wiley.

Hamilton, A., J. Madison, and J. Jay (n. d.): *The Federalist*. New York: The Modern Library.

Häussermann, W. (1978): *Die Politik der Bürokratie*. Frankfurt/M.–New York: Campus.

Ingram, H. (1977): "Policy Implementation Through Bargaining: The Case of Federal Grants-In-Aid." *Public Policy* 25/4: 499–527.

Johnson, N. (1973): *Government in the Federal Republic of Germany*. Oxford: Pergamon Press.

Katz, D., and D. L. Kahn (1966): *The Social Psychology of Organizations*. New York: Wiley.

Khandwalla, P. N. (1981): "Properties of Competing Organizations." In Nystrom, P. C., and W. Starbuck (eds.), *Handbook of Organizational Design* (Vol. 1), 409–432. Oxford: Oxford Univ. Press.

Kisker, G. (1971): *Kooperation im Bundesstaat: Eine Untersuchung zum kooperativen Föderalismus in der BRD*. Tübingen: Mohr.

LaPorte T. R. (1975): "Organized Social Complexity: Explication of a Concept." In LaPorte, T. R. (ed.), *Organized Social Complexity: Challenge to Politics and Policy*, 3–39. Princeton: Princeton Univ. Press.

Lehner, F. (1979): "Politikverflechtung: Institutionelle Eigendynamik und politische Kontrolle." In Matthes, J. (ed.), *Sozialer Wandel in Westeuropa*, 611–629. Frankfurt–New York: Campus.

Litwak, E., and L. F. Hylton (1961): "Interorganizational Analysis: A Hypothesis On Coordinating Agencies." *Administrative Science Quarterly* 6 (June): 395–418.

Lowi, T. J. (1972): "Four Systems of Policy, Politics and Choice." *Public Administration Review* 32 (July): 298–311.

Luhmann, N. (1970): "Soziologie des politischen Systems." In Luhmann, N., *Soziologische Aufklärung* I, 154–177. Opladen: Westdeutscher Verlag.

Luhmann, N. (1977): *Zweckbegriff und Systemrationalität*. Frankfurt/M.: Suhrkamp.

MacMahon, A. (1972): *Administering Federalism in a Democracy*. New York–London: Oxford Univ. Press.

March, J. G. (1981): "Footnotes to Organizational Change." *Administrative Science Quaterly* 26 (Dec.): 563–577.

March, J. G., and H. A. Simon (1958): *Organizations*. New York: Wiley.

Marnitz, S. (1974): *Die Gemeinschaftsaufgaben des Artikels 91a des Grundgesetzes als Versuch verfassungsrechtlicher Institutionalisierung der bundesstaatlichen Kooperation*. Berlin: Duncker & Humblot.

Mayntz, R., and F. W. Scharpf (1975): *Policy Making in the Federal Republic of Germany*. New York–Amsterdam: Elsevier.

Metcalfe, L. (1974): "Systems Models, Economic Models and the Causal Texture of Organizational Environments." *Human Relations* 27/3: 639–665.

Metcalfe, L. (1978): "Policy Making in Turbulent Environments." In Hanf, K., and F. W. Scharpf (eds.), *Interorganizational Policy Making*, 37–56. London: Sage.

Nettl, J. P. (1968): "The State as a Conceptual Variable." *World Politics* 20/4: 559–593.

Parsons, T. (1969): "The Concept of Society: The Components and their Interrelations." In Parsons, T., *Politics and Social Structure,* 5–33. New York: Free Press.

Pennings, J. M. (1981): "Strategically Interdependent Organizations." In Nystrom, P. C., and W. Starbuck (eds.), *Handbook of Organizational Design* (Vol. 1), 433–456. Oxford: Oxford Univ. Press.

Pressman, J. L., and A. Wildavsky (1973): *Implementation.* Berkeley: Univ. Press.

Rhodes, R. A. W. (1980): "Analysing Intergovernmental Relations." *European Journal of Political Research* 8/3: 289–323.

Scharpf, F. W. (1973): "Komplexität als Schranke der politischen Planung." In Scharpf, F. W., *Plannung als politischer Prozeß,* 73–114. Frankfurt: Suhrkamp.

Scharpf, F. W. (1976): "Theorie de Politikverflechtung." In Scharpf, F. W., B. Reissert, and F. Schnabel, *Theorie der Politikverflechtung,* 13–71. Kronenberg/Ts.: Athenäum.

Scharpf, F. W. (1978): "Interorganizational Policy Making: Issues, Concepts and Perspectives." In Hanf, K., and F. W. Scharpf (eds.), *Interorganizational Policy Making,* 345–371. Beverly Hills: Sage.

Scharpf, F. W., B. Reissert, and F. Schnabel (1978): "Policy Effectiveness and Conflict Avoidance in Intergovernmental Policy Formation." In Hanf, K., and F. W. Scharpf (eds.), *Interorganizational Policy Making,* 57–115. London–Beverly Hills: Sage.

Schnabel, F. (1980): "Politik ohne Politiker." In Wollmann, H. (ed.), *Politik im Dickicht der Bürokratie,* 49–71. Opladen: Westdeutscher Verlag.

Staats, E. B. (1974): "Intergovernmental Relations: A Fiscal Perspective." *The Annals* 416 (Nov.): 32–40.

Sundquist, J. L. (1969): *Making Federalism Work: A Study of Programm Coordination at the Community Level.* Washington: Brooking.

Thompson, J. D. (1967): *Organizations In Action.* New York: McGraw-Hill.

Turk, H. (1970): "Interorganizational Networks in Urban Society." *American Sociological Review* 35/1: 1–18.

Warren, R. L. (1973): "The Interactions of Community Decision Organizations." In Negandhi, A. R. (ed.), *Modern Organizational Theory,* 145–160. Ohio, Kent.: Univ. Press.

Weber, M. (1976): *Wirtschaft und Gesellschaft.* Tübingen: Mohr.

White, P. E. (1974): "Intra- and Interorganizational Studies: Do They Require Separate Conceptualizations?" *Administration and Society* 6/1: 107–152.

Williamson, O. E. (1981): "The Economics of Organization: The Transaction Cost Approach." *American Journal of Sociology* 87/3: 548–578.

Wright, D. S. (1974): "Intergovernmental Relations: An Analytical Overview." *The Annals* 416 (Nov.): 1–17.

Yuchtman, E., and S. E. Seashore (1967): "A System Resource Approach to Organizational Effectiveness." *American Sociological Review* 32 (2)/6: 891–903.

24. Multiorganizational Arrangements and Coordination: An Application of Institutional Analysis

Elinor Ostrom

Abstract

Two linked action situations are examined in this chapter using the method of institutional analysis previously described in Chapter 22. The first arena is the one in which public officials are elected. The most influential model of this arena was developed by Anthony Downs. The second arena is the one in which elected officials bargain with the heads of administrative agencies (sponsors) over the amount of the budget to be allocated and the amount and type of goods or services to be produced. William Niskanen developed an important model of this process. The central question addressed in this chapter is how multiple organizations, competing according to sets of rules, tend to enhance the responsiveness of public officials and bureau chiefs to the preferences of the citizens they serve in both of these arenas. Empirical evidence supporting the proposition that competition among potential producers of a public good will enhance performance is presented related to the provision of solid waste removal services in American cities.

24.1 Introduction

Some interesting and important institutional arrangements for coordinating complex chains of actions among large numbers of actors involve multiple organizations competing with one another according to a set of rules. Markets are the most frequently studied institutional arrangements that achieve coordination by relying primarily on rule-governed competitive relationships among organizations. Rule-governed competition among two or more political parties is considered by many analysts to be an important requisite for a democratic polity (see Frey 1982). Less studied, but potentially as important a means for achieving responsiveness and efficiency in producing public goods and services, are arrangements that allow rule-ordered competition among two or more potential *producers* of public goods and services.

Most of the efforts to analyze the effects of institutional arrangements in the public sector have focused primarily on single arenas such as elections, legislatures, administrative agencies, courts, etc. A complex series of processes must be channeled through many simultaneous and sequential action arenas, however, for citizens to receive bundles of public goods and services. Thus, the public sector does not consist of only an election, a legislature, an executive, or a court as isolable units, but as separable structures that function in relation to one another in complex interrelationships. Citizens receive and pay for bundles of goods and services as a result of actions taken in a series of linked action arenas.

Both theory and research are usually confined to examining a single action arena. Models of legislative choice, for example, have most frequently pursued the question of which legislative decisions are likely to result and be stable. Models of elections have focused on predicting the type of proposed policies that winning candidates will pursue. Models of the bargaining process between elected officials and bureau chiefs have focused on the budget to be allocated to the bureau. When these action arenas are linked, however, strategies adopted by participants in one arena may strongly affect the resulting strategies and outcomes in several simultaneous and linked action arenas. A legislator may vote for a bill in a legislature and: (1) affect the future policies that administrative agencies will be expected to enforce, (2) affect the legislator's own power position inside the legislature, and (3) affect the legislator's own potential for re-election. The same vote is a move that simultaneously affects outcomes in at least three action arenas.

In this chapter I will examine two linked action arenas. The first arena is the one in which public officials are elected and has been modeled in an influential book by Anthony Downs (1957). The second is the arena in which these elected officials bargain with the heads of administrative agencies over the amount of the budget to be allocated and the amount and type of goods or services to be produced. William Niskanen (1971) developed an important model of this process. Many others have based their own analysis of the public sector on the Downs and/or Niskanen models. The first part of this chapter will examine the working parts of Downs's and Niskanen's original models of these linked action arenas and of the modifications in structure proposed by other analysts. Substantively, I will examine how multiple organizations competing according to sets of rules tend to enhance the responsiveness of public officials and bureau chiefs to the preferences of the citizens they serve in both of these action arenas. In addition to the substantive content, this chapter illustrates the method of institutional analysis described in Chapter 22.

24.2 Electoral and Budgetary Bargaining Arenas

The Actor

Both Downs and Niskanen rely upon a *rational choice model of the actor*. Downs provides a clear overview of this model:

"A rational man is one who behaves as follows: (1) he can always make a decision when confronted with a range of alternatives; (2) he ranks all the alternatives facing him in order of his preference in such a way that each is either preferred to, indifferent to, or inferior to each other; (3) his preference ranking is transitive; (4) he always chooses from among the possible alternatives that which ranks highest in his preference ordering; and (5) he always makes the same decision each time he is confronted with the same alternatives. All rational decision-makers in our model . . . exhibit the same qualities." (Downs 1957: 6)

Each of the specific actors in these linked situations are assumed *to maximize an externally objective function.* This enables the analyst to derive specific predictions about results and eliminates the tautology of assuming that individuals maximize whatever they maximize. Elected officials are assumed by Downs to maximize the probability of their being re-elected. Voters are assumed to maximize the difference between the flow of expected net benefits from future policies plus positive values they receive from voting minus the costs of voting.[1] Bureau chiefs are assumed by Niskanen to maximize the budget of their bureau.

The Situations and Predicted Results

Downs assumes a situation containing two types of participants – politicians and voters. Politicians form themselves into two teams that function as political parties and are modeled as corporate actors. One team holds the position of being the government and the other team holds the position of being the opposition. In his initial model, Downs assumed that both parties had full information about citizen preferences. While Downs later changes to an assumption of uncertain information, most of the models based on Downs's work use his initial assumption of certainty. I will continue to assume that politicians have full information about voters' preferences and voters have full knowledge of both politicians' promises and their past performance since Niskanen and others discussed below rely entirely on Downs's initial model in this regard.[2] Downs models each of the political parties as offering platforms containing alternative sets of policies to voters. Voters then vote for one party or the other based on their evaluation of the estimated net sum of future benefits and costs flowing from the alternative sets of policy proposals. The party that gains a majority commands public bureaus to produce the policy outcomes preferred by that party in its efforts to obtain re-election. Downs does not overtly include the administrative chiefs of public bureaus as participants. They are modeled as a mechanism that carries out the commands of the governing party with efficient precision.

From his theory, Downs concludes that electoral procedures based on plurality vote will constrain a governing party to select (and therefore produce) the output/cost combination most preferred by the median voter within a community. Downs describes his own process of inference in the following way:

"According to our hypothesis, governments continue spending until the marginal vote gain from expenditure equals the marginal vote loss from financing. The determinants of vote loss and vote gain are the utility incomes of all voters and the strategies of opposition parties. Thus governments are engaged in political warfare as well as maximization problems.

Under conditions of certainty, a government's best strategy is to adopt choices which are favored by a majority of voters. Before making any expenditure, it takes a hypothetical poll to see how voters' utility incomes are affected by the expenditure and the necessary financing. If it fails to adopt the majority's views, its opponents will do so and will fight the election on this issue only, thereby insuring defeat for the incumbents." (Downs 1957: 73)

The Downsian model predicts an optimal equilibrium in terms of responsiveness (allocative efficiency). Movements away from these results would enable the other party to win the next election by offering a policy package with the optimal combination of outputs and costs. Downs' prediction of optimal performance results from his analysis of the behavior of elected officials under the threat of being voted out of office by a competing party. It is the presence of a competitor ready to snatch any advantage that pushes the government party toward constant attention to what citizens prefer.

When Niskanen examines how bureaucracy affects the linkage between citizen preferences and government performance, he focuses on the process of bargaining between the team of elected officials (called the *sponsor* by Niskanen) and *bureau chiefs* assigned the responsibility to direct agencies producing the desired goods and services. Voters are now modeled as a mechanism that would only oust a government if the marginal budget assigned to a bureau *exceeded* the benefits received minus the cost of that level of output. In Niskanen's model, not only are voters left out as active participants but they are no longer viewed as trying to obtain the maximal difference between benefits and costs. Niskanen assumes that a bureau chief attempts to obtain as large a budget as possible for a bureau in order to secure the most private gain and to produce the most goods and services for a community. Niskanen's elected officials, like Downs's, know the preferences of the citizens that elect them. So do the bureau chiefs. However, elected officials do not know the production costs of the bureau. Nothing exists to require bureau chiefs to reveal costs or provide information on alternative budget-output combinations.

The *bargaining process* is initiated in Niskanen's model by the bureau chief offering to produce the maximum output that is just sufficient to produce a small marginal benefit for the median voter. This is a "take it or leave it" offer. Niskanen presumes that elected officials are forced to accept this offer since it is slightly better than no output at all. The equilibrium predicted by the model is not responsive to citizen preferences since more than optimal levels of output are produced. On the other hand, Niskanen assumes that the bureau is able to produce this greater than preferred level of output at the least possible cost. The result is thus technically efficient, but unresponsive to the preferences of those served.

The difference between the optimal performance predicted by Downs and the nonoptimal performance predicted by Niskanen is illustrated in Figure 1 using a simple model of a three-person community. Voters A, B, and C are represented as having varying levels of utility for a budget devoted to producing a particular public output. Voter C places a higher value on this output at every budgetary level than either B or A, while Voter B is uniformly more positive than A. Each utility curve intersects the horizontal axis at the level of utility that a voter derives from a zero budget allocated to the production of this good. All of the utility curves initially rise as more budget is devoted to this good and then fall when diminishing marginal returns for this good occur. B_2, B_3, and B_6 represent the optimal level of the budget devoted to this output from the perspective of each of the three voters.

In this arena, Voter B is the *median voter*. Downs *predicts* that the representation process would lead a government team to offer and deliver the budget-output combination (B_3) most preferred by the median voter. Niskanen predicts that the bureau chief would demand a budget just to the left of B_5. The difference between B_3 and B_5 is the amount of budget allocated to the production of a good beyond the optimal level. This budget is barely preferred by the median voter to the situation of having *no* budget allocated to the production of this good. In this nonoptimal world, the median voter is only a constraint on the size of the budget demanded by the bureau chief, while in the Downsian model, the predicted result is exactly the median's voter's most preferred position.

Despite their differences, both Downs and Niskanen see the *electoral and bargaining arenas as intertwined in mutual interdependence*. The outcome of an

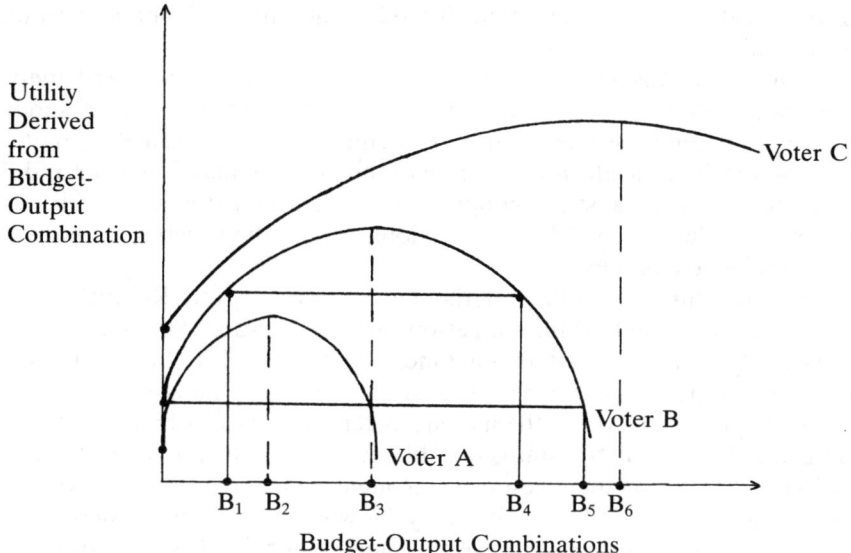

B$_3$ – Budget-output combination predicted by Downs.
B$_5$ – Budget-output combination predicted by Niskanen.
B$_4$ – Budget-output combination predicted by Romer and Rosenthal if status quo budget is
      B$_1$ and reversion rule is status quo.

Adapted from Mackay and Weaver (1978: 147).

Fig. 1: Predicted Budget-Output Levels Derived From Models of Downs, Niskanen, and
        Romer and Rosenthal

election affects the level and type of goods and services that elected officials try to
provide to citizens through their relationship with producing agencies. The success
that elected officials have in their bargaining with bureau chiefs affects their
chances of re-election. Downs succinctly expressed this mutual dependence in
commenting that "votes depend upon actions, and actions depend upon votes"
(Downs 1957: 73).

Niskanen also tried to include both action arenas in his analysis. Niskanen
viewed his book as "an attempt to match a now conventional theory of the demand
for government services in a representative government with a new theory of
bureaucratic supply" (Niskanen 1975: 617). Despite an electoral arena that yields
relatively optimal results, Niskanen predicts nonoptimal results because of the
control that bureau chiefs are posited to have over information and their capacity
to dominate the agenda for bargaining with sponsors.

The Niskanen model has been strongly criticized by scholars who adopt diverse
perspectives (Goodin 1982; Breton and Wintrobe 1975, 1982; Mique and Belanger
1974). The model does, however, capture enough of what many scholars perceive
to be essential elements of the bargaining process between elected officials and
bureau chiefs that a rich literatue has evolved based on the Niskanen formulation.

More recent work has attempted to modify the initial assumptions to make them more realistic.

Romer and Rosenthal (1978) argue, for example, that Niskanen used an unrealistic assumption about what would happen to the budget if no agreement was reached. Niskanen assumed that bureau chiefs could threaten elected officials with *no* output if the officials did not agree to the initial demand. Romer and Rosenthal argue that a more realistic assumption is that the budget would revert to the status quo budget (the one used for the previous year) if the officials did not agree to the initial budgetary request.

Changing this assumption in the model, Romer and Rosenthal continue to predict that the equilibrium budget-output combination represents a nonoptimal, over-supply. Their predicted outcome is, however, less than that predicted by Niskanen. If the status quo were B_1, for example, the equilibrium budget would be just to the left of B_4 where the median voter receives slightly more utility than the status quo budget. If the status quo budget were relatively close to the optimum preferred by the median voter B_3, Romer and Rosenthal predict an outcome similar to that originally predicted by Downs. Additional models developed by Mique and Belanger (1974), Breton and Wintrobe (1975), Niskanen (1975), Mackay and Weaver (1978), Denzau and Mackay (1977), Orzechowski (1977), and Miller (1977) all change assumptions to a greater or lesser extent leading to derivations that vary somewhere between the extremes predicted by Downs and by Niskanen.

The most dramatic change in assumptions is made by McGuire et al. (1979) who introduce a second bureau to compete with the monopoly bureau chief in the bargaining arena.[3] Whatever offer is made by one bureau can then be challenged by the second bureau. Over time the offers will approach the same optimal level as predicted by Downs. If one agency proposes too high a budget, the other will be motivated to make a counteroffer of a more optimal budget-output combination. As the number of agencies increases beyond two, the pressure on all potential agencies to offer an optimal budget-output combination also increases.

23.3 Inferring the Factors Affecting the Action Arena

The above models have focused directly on the structure of the action arenas and only indirectly on the rule configurations, events in the world, or nature of the community yielding that structure. Niskanen does not specify why he models the bargaining arena presuming that the budget would revert to zero if no agreement were reached. This assumption, however, is part of what leads to his conclusion of nonoptimal performance. Equally important is his assumption that only one bureau can bargain with elected officials. Romer and Rosenthal challenge the first assumption and presume that most jurisdictions would renew the previous budget level of a bureau if no agreement were reached. McGuire et al. challenge the second assumption and show how competition among bureaus would drive the process toward more optimal results.

Without *explicit* analysis of the rules and other factors affecting the structure of an arena, *implicit* assumptions underlying the overt analysis may be the most important assumptions generating predicted results. If one wants to *use* the analysis at the action situation level to guide behavior in public sector situations toward better, rather than worse, performance, one needs to make explicit these implicit assumptions. One needs to know what rules create the structure as modeled and what implicit assumptions have been made concerning the attributes of events and their transformation and about the community. The first factor – rules – may be changed through legislation and enforcement. The other factors – attributes of events (goods) and the community – represent potential constraints on the type of situations in which a particular rule configuration may work.

Events and Community

Assumptions about rules, events or goods, and community were largely left unspecified by Downs and by Niskanen, and by those building on their models. My effort to examine explicitly how these factors affect the structure and results within the linked arenas must identify what implicit assumptions are consistent with the Downs and Niskanen models specified at the action arena level. Both Downs and Niskanen presume their models would apply to a wide range of goods and services. Both conceptualize outputs as varying in small, incremental units. *Step-goods* (Hardin 1982), including most public works like bridges, dams, and some modern weapon systems, do not fit their models. Nor would *pure public goods,* where exclusion is difficult and citizens jointly consume outputs, fit the way they model citizens' demand. Both Downs and Niskanen appear to presume that the technology for producing an output is known – at least by the bureau chief – and that a determinate and measurable output can be produced.

In regard to norms held within the broader community, both presume a high level of cutthroat competition is acceptable. Downs carefully states that the team of politicians currently in office is prohibited by constitutional rules from directly eliminating its rival and from infringing on free speech. Downs presumes that within these rules, each party is expected, however, to pursue any opportunity ruthlessly and take advantage of any error made by its opposition. Likewise, Niskanen models the bureau chief as a relentless negotiator pushing his agenda control advantage to the limit allowed by the rules.

Rules

In regard to the underlying rule configuration, it seems reasonable to presume that Downs, Niskanen, and the other analysts discussed above hold *similar,* implicit assumptions about three types of rules: (1) *scope rules* specifying the amount of public goods and services to be produced and the budget to be allocated to this production; (2) *position rules* defining the positions of elected officials, voters, and bureau chiefs; and (3) *payoff rules* rewarding teams of politicians for winning elections and bureau chiefs in relation to the size of a bureau's budget.

Thus, we will assume that three sets of rules are similar in all of the models. A fourth set of rules – boundary rules – are obviously different. Niskanen originally presumed that potential competitors were ruled out of the bargaining process.

McGuire et al. (1979) adopted a different assumption and overtly modeled the bargaining arena with multiple producers. Niskanen's model is based on implicit boundary rules that protect the monopoly position of a producing agency while McGuire et al. had to presume a different boundary rule allowing multiple agencies to enter the bargaining arena.

A major portion of the aggregation rules underlying the linked situations are similar. A plurality formula for equally weighted voters is assumed in the electoral arena and an unanimity rule is assumed between elected officials and bureau chiefs. But the default or reversion rule implicitly assumed by Niskanen for what happens if the bureau chief and elected officials do *not* agree is different from the explicit assumption made by Romer and Rosenthal. Niskanen presumed that a zero budget would occur in the absence of agreement while Romer and Rosenthal assumed that the status quo budget would continue.

So far, inferring the underlying rule configuration has been relatively simple. Information and authority rules remain to be specified and this step is not as easy as the prior steps.

We know that the information condition in the action arena differs in the Downs and Niskanen models. In his initial model, Downs presumes that elected officials had full information. Niskanen presumes that bureau chiefs have complete information about costs of production while elected officials are ignorant of production costs. This difference in information available to participants could simply be the result of a *span-of-control problem* (a transformation of one state of the world into another in which information is consistently lost or biased). Elected officials running a government may have so many bureaus to supervise and activities to accomplish that they simply cannot know the production costs of all the bureaus with whom they must bargain.

Without either information rules or authority rules (or both) giving bureau chiefs additional control over information limiting the capability of elected officials to act so as to obtain information, span-of-control problems alone do not seem to be a reasonable base for making such a strong assumption about information conditions in the action arena. Niskanen models the process in the bargaining arena as a single, "take it or leave it" offer. Thus, he had implicitly to assume that the bureau chief is authorized by the rules to control the agenda, to take a first, pre-emptive move, and to end negotiations after one round.

On the other hand, for Downs to have presumed that those who win an election can produce what they promise to the voters, he had to conceptualize the authority rules differently than Niskanen. The *authority rules* in a rule configuration underlying a Downsian analysis could not give bureau chiefs strong restrictive powers over what budget-outcome combinations would be considered. To derive his initial conclusions, Downs had to presume all potential budget-outcome combinations could potentially be placed on the agenda. As Ladha et al. (1982: 32) speculate in a footnote:

> "Although usually not explicitly specified, implicit in [the 'median voter' framework] is the assumption of open or competitive agendas, with no restrictions on access to the agenda."

Thus, I presume that the authority rules related to agenda control differ substantially in the Downs and Niskanen models. The difference in information levels can be accounted for by a combination of the span-of-control problem and the difference in authority rules. Thus, we can presume that information rules are similar in all of the models.

Consequently, I assume that four types of rules are similar for the entire set of models discussed above (position, scope, payoff, and information rules). Boundary rules, the default aspect of the aggregation rule, and the agenda control aspect of the authority rules vary across models. The differences in the underlying rule configuration are represented in a matrix shown in Figure 2. The conclusions concerning predicted results in the action arenas are entered in the cells.

The models developed by Niskanen and by Romer and Rosenthal both give the bureau chief the capacity to make a "take it or leave it" offer. Thus, both of these models assume the same authority rule giving the bureau chief full control over the agenda. But these models differ in regard to the default specified in the aggregation rule – the rule controlling the budget-outcome level if no agreement is reached between the bureau chief and the elected officials. Niskanen presumed this rule would allow the budget to revert to zero. No agreement – no funds! Romer and Rosenthal argued that this was "unrealistic." Instead, they think a more reasonable rule would be to continue the budget in effect for the previous year. No agreement – continuance of the status quo! The difference in the structure of action arenas and resulting equilibria as modeled first by Niskanen, and then by Romer and Rosenthal, can thus be thought of as the result of a rule configuration that holds all rules constant except the aggregation rule concerning the budgetary reversion level.

If we speculate about the way Downs was thinking about the relationships between the party in power and government bureaucrats, we would place the Downsian model in the upper left cell – making a similar assumption about reversion level as Romer and Rosenthal, but differing in regard to agenda control from both Romer and Rosenthal and Niskanen (see Downs 1957: 69). Consequently, the difference in the results predicted by Downs, by Niskanen, and by Romer and Rosenthal can be related to changes in authority rules and aggregation rules without changes in the remaining rule configuration.

McGuire et al. accepted the Niskanen presumption that the reversion level was zero while introducing a change in the boundary rules allowing other producers to enter the bargaining process. This change in boundary rules generates a different situation leading to a prediction of relatively optimal performance as contrasted to Niskanen's prediction of nonoptimality. The change in boundary rules opens up a new column of potential action situations under varying conditions of authority rules. An effort that Parks and Ostrom (1981) made to examine the effect of multiple producers in metropolitan areas upon the efficiency of public agencies is closely related to the rule conditions specified in the upper right-hand cell. The implications of the action situations created by the other combinations of rules represented in the second column have not yet been explored.

The diversity of results predicted by these theorists can be viewed in two quite different ways. One approach is to develop the *one* correct model that is most predictive of experience in the world. This is the dominate way the debate about these different models and their results are presented in the literature.

The second way of viewing these different models and their results – and, the

Authority Rules	Boundary Rules	
Aggregation Rules	Entry to Bargaining Process Restricted to One Bureau	Allow Multiple Bureaus to Enter Bargaining Process
Open Agenda Reversion Level is Status Quo	Downs (1957) Equilibrium is the most preferred budget/output combination of the median voter. Thus, preferences of median voter dominate decision.	Parks and E. Ostrom (1981) Even if no direct competition between two producers serving same jurisdiction, presence of comparison agencies in same urban area will reduce costs of monitoring and increase pressure toward an equilibrium producing the highest net value for the community.
Reversion Level is Zero Budget	No model yet developed for this combination of rules.	No model yet developed for this combination of rules.
Restricted Agenda Controlled by Bureau Chief Reversion Level is Status Quo	Romer and Rosenthal (1978) Equilibrium is the highest budget/output combination that provides the median voter with at least as much value as the status quo.	No model developed for this combination of rules, but given McGuire, Coiner, and Spancake (1979) status quo reversion level can only enhance tendency of equilibrium to move toward highest net value for the community.
Reversion Level is Zero Budget	Niskanen (1971; 1975) Equilibrium is the largest budget/output combination capable of winning majority approval in an all-or-nothing vote. Preference of median voter is only a constraint.	McGuire, Coiner, and Spancake (1979) Equilibrium tends over time toward budget/output combination producing the highest net value for the community.

Fig. 2: Predicted Equilibrium Budget/Output Combinations Under Different Rule Configurations

way I prefer to think about them – is to illustrate the differences in predicted outcomes that are derived from different configurations of rules. Instead of one reality, there are many "realities" that humans can potentially create. Self-consciously and explicitly examining how a rule configuration affects the structure and results of an action situation enables analysts to see how a family of models are affected by key changes in assumptions about underlying rules. Families of models provide powerful thought experiments for specifying variable factors in both institutional analysis and institutional design.

24.4 Empirical Significance

Effective thought experiments about the impact of different combinations of rules on the incentives faced by participants in action arenas, their consequent actions, and cumulative results, also provide the basis for well-designed empirical research. When dramatically different results are predicted in arenas structured by different rule configurations, an opportunity exists for testing competing conjectures if empirical instances similar to those examined in ,the theory can be found.[4] An interesting, substantive relationship is between boundary rules affecting competition and enhanced performance. An empirical test of how this change in a rule configuration affects performance depends upon finding instances of legal rules that meet two essential characteristics.

First, the rules must assign authority to elected officials for determining the amount of good to be provided and the budget that will be allocated to a bureau. In other words, the authority to *provide a good or service* must be vested in the officials elected for the purpose of representing the aggregated interests of a community (see Ostrom et al. 1961). These officials function as *providers* in representing a community as potential consumers of jointly consumed goods or services. This condition needs to be met in all of the empirical settings examined. Secondly, among those arenas meeting the first condition, empirical instances of two types of rules must exist. In one type of empirical setting, boundary rules should allow multiple agencies (bureaus) to compete against one another in the bargaining process with elected officials, but preclude the actual entry of competitors once a budget has been determined for a fixed period of time. The budget would be written in the form of a contract between an elected government and one production bureau (which might be public or private). In the second type of empirical setting, boundary rules should preclude entry of potential producers in the bargaining process as well as in the production process.

A major research effort exploring the effect of different institutional arrangements for service delivery in metropolitan areas on efficiency and responsiveness has located empirical instances of just these combinations of rules. A research team directed by E. S. Savas (1977) conducted a study of institutional arrangements for the provision and production of refuse-collection services in American cities. Savas identified a variety of different types of arrangements between locally elected public officials and bureaus that produced refuse-collection services. Three of these arrangements were present in sufficiently large numbers that the researchers could obtain accurate data about the annual costs (per household) that citizens pay for a defined level of service (once-a-week, curbside refuse collection). Savas called the three types of institutional arrangements: "municipal", "contract", and "private". The "municipal" and "contract" arrangements meet the two conditions specified above. The "private" arrangement is an interesting empirical variant not considered in the theoretical formulations discussed above, but frequently confused with the contract arrangements.

Under both the municipal and contract arrangement, locally elected officials are assigned the authority for determining the amount of goods to be produced and the budget to be assigned to a production agency. A *municipal* arrangement in the Savas study is one where locally elected officials bargain annually with one and only one municipal bureau charged with the responsibility for producing refuse collection within a municipality. The Niskanen model is of this type of arrangement. A *contract* arrangement is one where locally elected officials bargain annually with one or more agencies (public or private) who are interested in obtaining a contract with the city for a defined period to produce services for the city and where no exclusive relationship is presumed to exist. Under a contract arrangement, boundary rules permit multiple producers to anticipate counteroffers in the bargaining process. This is the type of arrangement that McGuire et al. modeled. The *private* arrangement is one in which locally elected officials did *not* have authority to make provision for a community. Every household made its own arrangements with private producers. Since elected officials were not involved in this arrangement, it is entirely different than those modeled by either Niskanen or by McGuire et al. However, since private agencies may be involved in *contract* arrangements and private agencies are definitely involved in private arrangements, casual commentaries have sometimes treated both of these arrangements as the same. The popular term *privatization* has unfortunately been attached to both of these distinctly different institutional arrangements.

As discussed in Chapter 22, one would expect more than just a rule configuration to affect the structure and results of an action arena. In particular, one would expect the structure of events and their transformations to have a considerable effect. The frequency of service provided (weekly or bi-weekly), transformations used (curbside or alley pick-up), the quantity of service (tons of refuse collected), and weather also affect cost. Savas found that a number of physical attributes of the communities being served affect the cost of refuse collection. Size of community is related to cost of production in a curvilinear fashion. The highest costs are found in very small towns (under 3,000 population). Costs are lowest in small- to medium-sized towns (15,000 to 30,000) and slowly rise for larger towns and cities as diseconomies-of-scale are reached. Recognizing the multiple factors affecting outcomes, Savas estimated the annual cost of waste collection per household for each of the three types of institutional arrangements under study – municipal, contract, and private – holding constant factors such as wage rates, amount of refuse per household, residential density, service level, and weather conditions (see Figure 3).

The results of the Savas study are consistent with the predictions made by McGuire et al. Contract arrangements are more cost effective than the municipal arrangements and particularly so in larger cities. Thus, competition in the bargaining arena appears to enhance the strength of locally elected officials to choose producers who will charge taxpayers less than municipal monopolies protected from such competition. In its important to note that direct competition among producers – the private arrangement – does not enhance performance. This arrangement is consistently the most expensive form of refuse collection in all of the cities studied. Considerable economies of location in refuse collection exist that are captured when a local government arranges for one producer to serve a location and are lost when private agencies bargain directly with each household and several producers consequently serve the same neighborhood. Recent policy interest in "privatization" has at times confused these two types of arrangements presuming that all efforts to increase competition among agencies enhance performance. The poor performance record of direct competition in production compa-

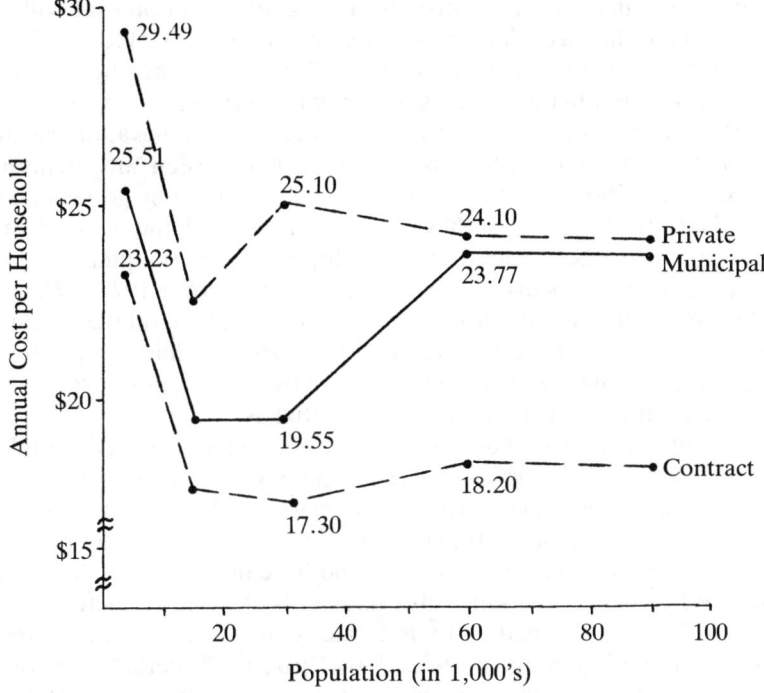

Adapted from Savas (1977: 133).

Fig. 3: Annual Cost for Private, Municipal, and Contract Arrangements by City Size

red with the higher performance achieved by competition in the bargaining process should highlight the need to make careful, theoretically-based distinctions among the myriad of specific types of arrangements that can actually be established in local, regional, and national public sectors.

24.5 Implications for Guidance and Control of the Public Sector

This chapter has demonstrated how guidance, control, and performance in the public sector can be enhanced by a fuller understanding of the method of institutional analysis presented in Chapter 22. As discussed in Kaufmann (Ch. 1), economic theory has enabled analysts to understand how direct competition among producers of private goods (homogeneous, divisible goods where exclusion is feasible) enhance guidance, control, and evaluation of multi-actor systems. Political theory suggests how direct competition among political parties enhances guidance, control, and evaluation of electoral and representation processes in the public sector. The actions of political leaders are more sensitive to public preferences when there are at least two parties competing for office. Elected members of a party know that they must take actions having general support, or members of the other party will be able to offer a proposed program of action that will win more electoral support in the next election. Citizens can control elected officials to some extent by a threat to "throw the rascals out of office" if their actions do not produce what citizens want. Evaluation occurs at regular intervals.

Current theories accepted by many political scientists, public administrators, and organization theorists, have not, on the other hand, seen any benefits in the possibility of competition among potential *producers* of public goods and services. A major reform tradition in both western Europe and the United States has consistently called for the elimination of multiple and overlapping producers that are essential to such a process (see Sharpe: Ch. 8; Ostrom 1972). The efforts of theorists to model the effects on performance of different rule configurations as they affect the structure of action arenas, have shown that competition among parties in electoral arenas tends to make elected officials want to produce a bundle of output-cost combinations most desired by citizens.

Examining only the electoral arena may, however, lead to a false confidence that competition among parties is a sufficient guiding and controlling mechanism leading to optimal performance in the public sector. Niskanen's examination of the linked arenas – the electoral arenas as Downs originally modeled it *plus* the bargaining arenas between elected officials and bureau chiefs – led him to different conclusions. When facing a monopoly bureau, Niskanen predicted that elected officials would be handicapped in their capacity to guide the bureau toward the output-cost combination most preferred by citizens. Several variations of the Niskanen analysis have been discussed above. The most important variant for thinking about guidance, control, and evaluation in the public sector is the model developed by McGuire et al. who introduce competition in the bargaining arena between multiple bureau chiefs and elected officials. Strong empirical support for their conclusions has been provided by studies of local arrangements for refuse collection.

By focusing on the rule configuration underlying several analytical models of action arenas, this chapter also illustrates how the method of institutional analysis briefly described in Chapter 22 can relate seemingly disparate analytical results stemming from a family of models represented by specific variations in a rule configuration. Analyzing variations in rule configurations is a more explicit and precise method than efforts to dichotomize the universe of institutional arrangements into a dichotomy of public or private arrangements. Precision is particularly important in efforts to design new institutional arrangements or reform existing ones. The current intellectual fad of identifying "privatization" as a "cure" for bureaucratic "ills" has not made a careful distinction between governmental provision of services using contracts with private or public bureaus as contrasted with individual households contracting with competing vendors. Empirical findings show that reforms based on inaccurate conceptions of critical institutional variables can lead to worse, rather than better, performance.

Notes

1   A major controversy exists in the literature over the proper specification of the "objective function" for a voter. Downs's original formulation led to a prediction that no

one would vote unless they received more utility from a sense of duty about voting than the costs of voting. This meant that the decision to vote was not dependent upon the policies of the incumbent government even though the decision concerning which party to vote for would be so based.

2 I personally share Downs's own strong sense that imperfect information is a better assumption to be used in modeling these arenas, but my effort here is to examine several already constructed models rather than to construct my own.

3 Niskanen had himself suggested that an important structural change that could be made to his model would be to increase competition among bureaus in the supply of the same or similar services.

4 Romer and Rosenthal, with a series of colleagues, have explored the empirical signifi- cance of variations of institutional arrangements in referendum elections closely related to the rules posited here. See Ladha et al. (1982), Romer and Rosenthal (1982), and Filimon et al. (1982).

References

Breton, A., and R. Wintrobe (1975): "The Equilibrium Size of a Budget-Maximizing Bureau." *Journal of Political Economy* 83 (February): 195–207.

Breton, A., and R. Wintrobe (1982): *The Logic of Bureaucratic Conduct.* Cambridge: Cambridge Univ. Press.

Denzau, A., and R. Mackay (1977): *Some Aspects of Bureaucratic Discrimination.* New Orleans: Tulane Univ.

Downs, A. (1957): *An Economic Theory of Democracy.* New York: Harper and Row.

Frey, B. (1982): "Schumpeter, Political Economist." In Frisch, H. (ed.), *Schumpeterian Economics,* 126–142. New York: Praeger.

Filimon, R., T. Romer, and H. Rosenthal (1982): "Asymmetric Information and Agenda Control: The Basis of Monopoly Power in Public Spending." *Journal of Public Economics* 17 (February): 51–70.

Goodin, R. E. (1982): "Rational Politicians and Rational Bureaucrats in Washington and Whitehall." *Public Administration* 60 (Spring): 23–41.

Hardin, R. (1982): *Collective Action.* Baltimore, Md.: The John Hopkins Press.

Ladha, K., T. Romer, and H. Rosenthal (1982): "If At First You Don't Succeed: Budgeting by a Sequence by a Referenda." Pasadena, Calif.: California Institute of Technology, Social Science Working Paper No. 449, October.

Mackay, R. J., and C. L. Weaver (1978): "Monopoly Bureaus and Fiscal Outcomes: Deductive Models and Implications for Reform." In Tullock, G., and R. Wagner (eds.), *Policy Analysis and Deductive Reasoning,* 141–165. Lexington, Mass.: Lexington Books.

McGuire, T., M. Coiner, and L. Spancake (1979): "Budget Maximizing Agencies and Efficiency in Government." *Public Choice* 34 (Issue 3/4): 333–359.

Miller, G. T. (1977): "Bureaucratic Compliance as a Game on the Unit Square." *Public Choice* 29 (Spring): 37–52.

Mique, J., and G. Belanger (1974): "Toward a General Theory of Managerial Discretion." *Public Choice* 17 (Spring): 27–43.

Niskanen, W. A. (1971): *Bureaucracy and Representative Government.* Chicago: Aldine- Atherton.

Niskanen, W. A. (1975): "Bueaucrats and Politicians." *Journal of Law and Economics* 18 (December): 617–643.

Orzechowski, W. (1977): "Economic Models of Bureaucracy: Survey, Extensions, and Evidence." In Borcherding, T. (ed.), *Budgets and Bureaucrats: The Souces of Govern- ment Growth,* 229–259. Durham, N. C.: Duke Univ. Press.

Ostrom, E. (1972): "Metropolitan Reform: Propositions Derived from Two Traditions." *Social Science Quarterly* 53 (December): 474–493.

Ostrom, V., C. Tiebout, and R. Warren (1961): "The Organization of Government in Metropolitan Areas: A Theoretical Inquiry." *American Political Science Review,* 55 (December): 831–842.

Parks, R., and E. Ostrom (1981): "Complex Models of Urban Service Systems." In Clark, T. (ed.), *Urban Policy Analysis: Directions for Future Research,* 171–199. Urban Affairs Annual Reviews, Vol. 21. Beverly Hills, Calif.: Sage.

Romer, T., and H. Rosenthal (1978): "Political Resource Allocation, Controlled Agendas, and the Status Quo." *Public Choice* 33/4: 27–43.

Romer, T., and H. Rosenthal (1980): "An Institutional Theory of the Effect of Intergovernmental Grants." *National Tax Journal* 33/4: 451–458.

Romer, T., and H. Rosenthal (1982): "Median Voters or Budget Maximizers: Evidence from School Expenditure Referenda." *Economic Inquiry* 22/4: 556–570.

Savas, E. S. (1977): *The Organization and Efficiency of Solid Waste Collection.* Lexington, Mass.: Lexington Books.

25. Building Coordination Structures

Heinz Schleicher

Abstract

The view is expressed that any economic and social policy is based on coordination structures. A coordination structure is defined as a structure (a set of decision centers which are interrelated either in a mechanistic or strategic manner) where the decision centers are linked by one or several coodinating mechanisms in order so solve one particular policy problem. Coordinating mechanisms may be the decentralized price mechanism, negotiation, arbitration, mediation, voting, auctioning, etc.

One particular policy problem, river water pollution control, is analyzed in some detail (French River Basin Agencies, the "Ruhrgenossenschaften", the Ohio River Water Sanitation Compact). These examples show that for a given economic policy problem there exists in general more than just one solution in terms of coordination structures which functions satisfactorily. Their variety will depend on already existing legal and constitutional frameworks, behavioral patterns and time (urgency of the policy problem).

25.1 Prologue

Generally the relationship between a worker-consumer-saver-citizen-voter, in short a citizen and the state is that of an individual, seeking, in a very large sense, direct or indirect help. For a centralized planning system[1] this amounts to a tautology as any consumer demand is satisfied by the state itself or by a state owned organisation. The underlying hypothesis of the subsequent sections will be that of a *mixed economy,* to use a rather imprecise term.

Very generally, the citizen may seek *direct* "help" or support by monetary transfers or in kind. He may ask for *indirect* "help" through legislative action, i.e. protecting him from an "offensive" neighbour, seeking legal constraints to bar free entry into markets etc. The "fuzzy" term "help" may be sharpened by looking at the most common ministries of comtemporary democracies. there are generally at least 8 departments:

(1) Economy, finance, foreign trade (France), industry, transport, commerce, and agriculture, (2) Social affairs, work, social security, health, environment, (3) Education, universities, (4) Culture, (5) Justice, (6) Interior, (7) Foreign affairs, (8) Defence.

What are the most important goods and services demanded by citizens and which department does provide them? This question may easily be answered for (6) and (8); i.e. the department of interior provides internal security, the department of defence provides external security etc. This concerns public services. There are also laws, like drug control, which interdict the consumption of goods. The good or right to employment often can only be offered indirectly (not so if government employs directly a public servant) by an appropriate budgetary and monetary policy. The right to employment may thus be provided by a package of indirect government (and possibly central bank) measures. Thus one may look at government help either as monetary transfers, goods and services, or as functions: such as allocation, stabilization, redistribution, and growth (Musgrave and Musgrave 1983).

As far as publicly provided goods and services are concerned: they need not all be public goods and services, in the sense of being indivisible and nonexcludable. They may be privat goods. Also they may be produced by private or public enterprise. Not even the decisionmaking on the provision of these good need generally be governmental (in a very large sense). On the contrary the borderline between public decisionmaking and private action in at least part of these areas is variable and thus the subject of the subsequent discussion. In fact, a government may choose to provide goods and services directly by its administration, or indirectly, that is it creates intermediate authorities with some autonomy, or leaves it to a private entity. A great variety of coordination structures or organizations are conceivable and do exist in various countries. One may thus ask the value loaded question: Given a mixed economy, how much government interference in the private sector is necessary and voluntary or desirable, to comply with the demands for government actions by individual or groups of citizens?

25.2 The Problem

It ist probably impossible to give a general answer to the preceding question. There are special cases, and may be classes of cases within which some generalization may by present. One may retain 5 important criteria which influence the extent of government action: (1) The nature of the transfer, good or service demanded; (2) the constitution and the simple laws referring to (1); (3) the administrative situation; (that is: is an existing administration legally endowed and factually able to cater to new demands by citizens); (4) the economic situation; (5) the political situation. As these constituent parts vary within a country at different times, and, particularly, between countries, one may expect a great variety of solutions to particular demands for public intervention. There is worthwhile research to be done on how given countries at different times, or different countries at the same time, have solved particular problems of guidance, control, and performance evaluation in the public sector.

In the subsequent sections one particular problem will be analyzed in some detail: The question of *river water pollution*. River water pollution is an external diseconomy for all downstream water users. In heavily industrialized regions (Ohio river, Seine river, Ruhr river), or countries (France, Germany, U.S.A., etc.), water pollution may become a serious economic and social (health-) problem which demands private, public or intermediate solutions. The externality of river water pollution (pollution from here after) is well defined. One knows in general the polluter and the point of pollution, one knows the direction of flow and thus the recipients (pollutees). All the participants of the activity are known in general.

Polluters (households, municipalities, industries) and pollutees act within a legal and constitutional framework. That is, if one or several participants think their rights are violated, they may seek arrangements among themselves, and, if not possible, due to free-rider behaviour or the non-existence of the core Schleicher 1980), compensation for damages by court action. This may be costly, time consuming, and finally unsuccessful. The next step in seeking to internalize pollution may be a call for administrative help if some agency or several agencies are competent in that matter. However, administrative slowness and also local, or, regional jurisdictional incompetence may call for government intervention by new legislation. The problem then becomes political (Schleicher 1982b). In fact, all these stages are apparent at some point in water quality management in France, Germany, and the U.S.A. (and possibly other countries) which will be dealt with in the following in more detail.

To summarize, given a river water pollution problem, the main actors are: The *polluter,* the *pollutee,* the *courts,* the *administration,* and the *politician.* These actors function within a given institutional and legal framework in the short run and a changing legal and maybe institutional framework in the medium and long run. The whole process of pollution control can be represented in a stylized way as a 4-stage game (Fig. 1).

At the start of the policy making process one may imagine a situation with little legal structure with respect to decisionmaking in pollution control. *Consider a laisser-faire economy* where polluters risk little court action on pollution abatement because industrial activity is deemed more important to society than environmental problems (Stage 1) (Cleary 1967:127). Then pollution may only be curbed by bilateral or multilateral agreements between polluters and pollutees (Schleicher and Selten 1982). However, free-rider behavior may make it impossible to reach a regional agreement where all polluters and pollutees along a river are members. Then *certain members may go to court* to reach a court injunction. (Stage 2) This procedure is often costly and time consuming to the plaintiffs and to the defendants. Moreover court action may be limited by competence and also geographically which can complicate the matter such that – if constitutionally possible – *administrative action* is demanded. (Stage 3) Limitation by competence means that there are different administrations for different kinds of pollutants and geographical limitation means that an administration is only competent for part of a river bed or river system. A necessary consequence is *government intervention* to permit or to form regional units such as the Ohio River Valley Water Sanitation Compact (Orsanco), the Ruhrgeossenschaften or the French River Basin Agencies, or to impose national anti-pollution policies, such as effluent charges, effluent standards or outright control of pollution (Stage 4).

After each stage the game is over if an agreement is reached between the participants. If not, the game continues at the following stage. The game ends with stage 4 where government intervenes to solve the problem in some "strong" way. The final result may be a regional, national, or trans-national anti-pollution policy.

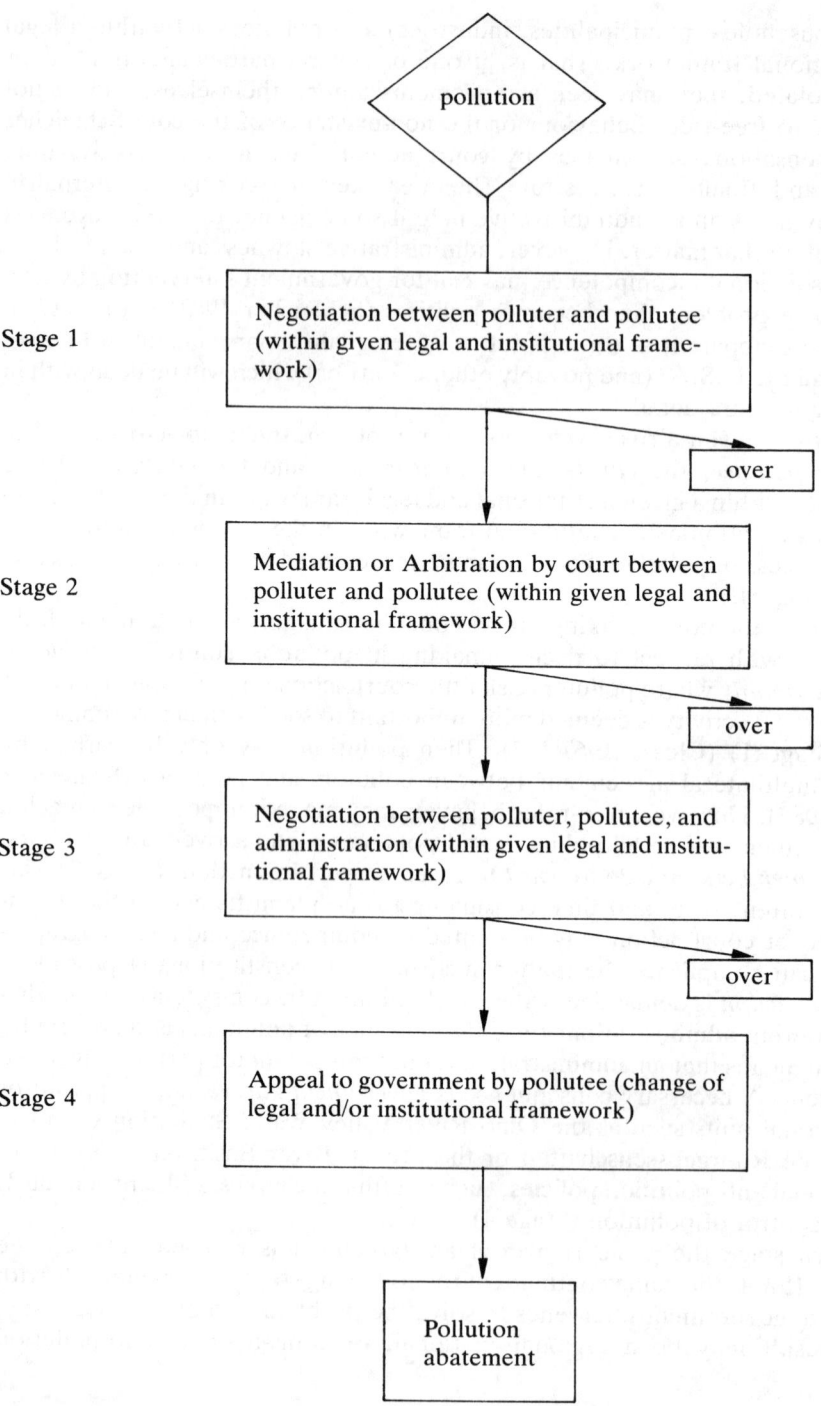

Fig. 1: River water pollution control as a 4-stage game

25.3 Definitions

The pollution problem, as other problems of public policy, may be regarded as an allocation problem. Contemporary (institutional) economics provides many mechanisms which may be helpful in solving those types of problems (Arrow 1963; Shubik 1970). Market Exchange, Bargaining, Auctioning, Arbitration, Voting, by Fiat, Solidarity and Fraud (illegal behavior).

Any economic and social policy implies at least 3 types of actors: The *decisionmakers,* the *middlemen* (those who act as catalytic agents between the decisionmakers and those who should be catered to, or whose behavior should be influenced by economic and social policy), and the *potential recipients.*

The decisionmakers act via the above mentioned allocation (or coordinating) mechanisms on the potential recipients and vice versa to produce a desired policy result. In reality, not only one particular but, generally, a mix of *coordinating mechanisms* is present. One may thus talk of *configurations of coordination mechanisms.* To be more specific in the subsequent sections the following terms will be defined: *institution, structure, coordination structure* and *organization.* These definitions are by no means absolute but merely an attempt to best capture the flavor of the subsequent pages.

Definition 1

An *institution* is a legal or constitutional framework within which decisionmakers, middlemen, and addressees, are free to act. Sometimes the domain of freedom of action may be constrained by custom and habit. However, this strategy set, to use a game theoretic term, is normally contained within the legal and constitutional set. If not, the framework of action is enlarged to illegal actions (see above: fraud as an allocation mechanism). *Remark:* We do not use institution synonymous with organisation.

Definition 2

A (static) *structure* (or system) is a stylized description of a state, that is a set of decision centers (actors, groups of actors) which are interrelated either in a mechanistic or strategic manner. The set of strategies of each decision center is determined by the institutional framework. One may call the description of changing states of a structure a dynamic structure.

Definition 3

A *coordination structure* (or system) is a structure where the decision centers are linked by one or several coordinating mechanisms to solve one particular policy problem.

Definition 4

A coordination structure in action is called an *organization.*

25.4 Solutions

Economic and social policy is very often regarded as *national* economic and social policy. Exceptions are regional policy and fiscal federalism (Oates 1972). Stabilization, growth, and redistribution are deemed to be inherently national goals, whilst the allocation function is generally seen to be better solved regionally or locally. The reason for national policies are considerations of equity (unemployment should be dealt with nationwide) and a belief among many economists and politicians that it suffices to set policy parameters on a national scale to obtain the desired policy results. For the allocation branch to work smoothly (Oates 1972), one wants policies to conform as close as possible to individual or group preferences. These viewpoints originate in part from wishful thinking and in part from factual circumstances (i.e. the decentralization policy in the Federal Republic of Germany led to ballooning local expenditures and debt due to politically desirable but economically wrong decisions). In order to attain first best or second best economic and social policy, policy objectives and the results, after all stages of the policy making process have been passed, should converge. In a free society, with a large extent of individual freedom of action, this to happen, policy goals and personal and group interests of the different actors should tend to converge, too. (This may be a sufficient condition for success, but not always a necessary one. Pure altruism or strict obedience to orders may do the same job. However, these two conditions may be difficult to find in modern, complex societies.) Assuming that actors in a national economy act like members of a team (Marschak and Radner, 1972) may be wishful thinking. Individual and group interests are assumed to be identical. However, reality shows that this may be true only occasionally. Consider legal avoidance, evasive and fraudulent behavior occur in taxation, unemployment, and sickness insurance. Free-rider behavior, moral hazard, or simply lying seems to be at least partially present whenever collective action is to be taken. Freeriding and holdout strategies may also occur within the institutional processes of government themselves (Crozier 1967).

The extent of such socially obnoxious behavior depends, from an economic policy point of view, largely on the degree of freedom of action in a society and the will and means to practice law enforcement. The more individual freedom of action prevails and/or the less rigorous law enforcement is the more serious obstacles will exist to practice what may be called *classical macropolicy*.

Economic and social policy may be conceived in a most simplified way as a cyclical process (Fig. 2) evolving in time. The basic structure is composed of four decision centers: the citizen (C), the government (G) and the middlemen (M) (parties, professional organizations, administrations, etc.). The citizen demands according to his preferences goods, services, and possibly institutions; and the government supplies them via a coordination structure either satisfactorily, complying with demand, or not. In the first case the circle is closed and the problem is solved. In the second case there may be a new demand for a change of the coordination structure and a new cycle begins.

The initiative for economic and social policy may come from, C, G or M and go in both directions. That is the citizen may demand clean river water via his local representative or address himself directly to the local or regional health administra-

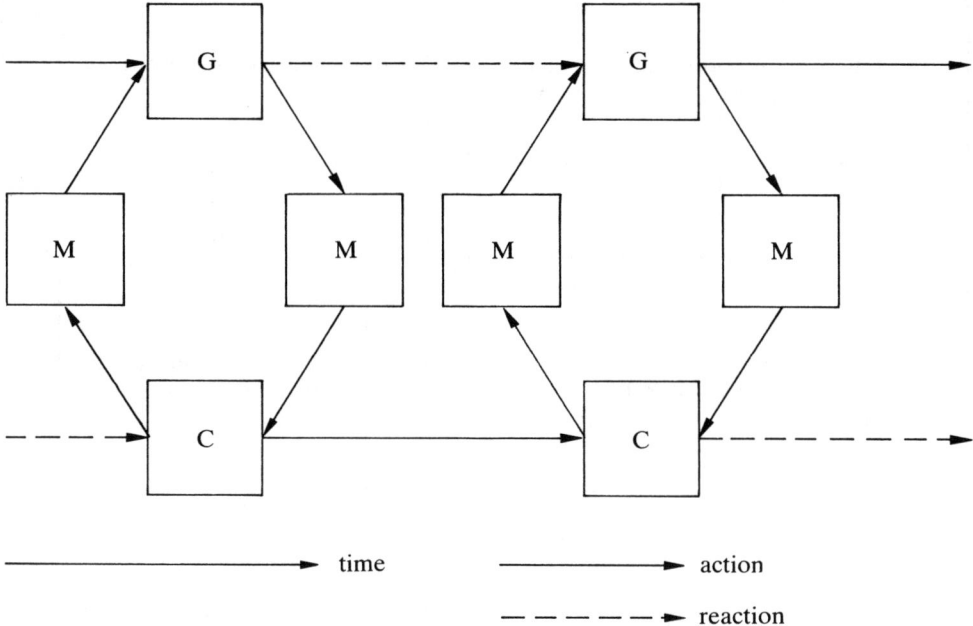

time   action

─ ─ ─ ─ ─ ►   reaction

Fig. 2: Economic and social policy as dynamic coordination structures

tion. Within the basic cyclical policy process one may distinguish, in a very abstract manner, three different approaches to economic and social policy making. (1) *Classical macropolicy,* (2) *intermediate macro-micropolicy,* and (3) *micropolicy.* Each one of these policy approaches stresses the particular position of the actor who takes the initiative in the policy making process.

(1) *Classical macropolicy* can be regarded as a policy making process decomposed into 4 elements (Fig. 3). The basic idea is that of a given coordination structure (an econometric model) within which a government may manipulate parameters to approach or reach fixed goals (Johansen 1978) (desired inflation-, unemployment-, growth rate, balance of payments surplus or deficit etc.). This policy approach may also be called the *centralized planning approach* or the *deductive method.* For ideological reasons this (Keynesian) method is often adopted by social-democratic, or socialist governments (i.e. contemporary France). One of the most serious flaws of this approach seems to be its mechanistic view, that is the neglect of strategic behavior among economic agents. A country is not normally a team in the sense of Marschak-Radner (except in times of outside attack), especially if economic policy implies sacrifices from some individuals or groups of citizens and not others. Classical macropolicy is based on highly aggregated models where institutions and thus the strategy spaces of the actors become merely parameters (i.e. income tax parameter).

(2) *Intermediate macro-micropolicy* takes account of the effects of individual behavior on economic and social policy goals. The general idea is to design institutions (implementation problem, Malinvaud 1967; Hurwicz 1973; Hurwicz et

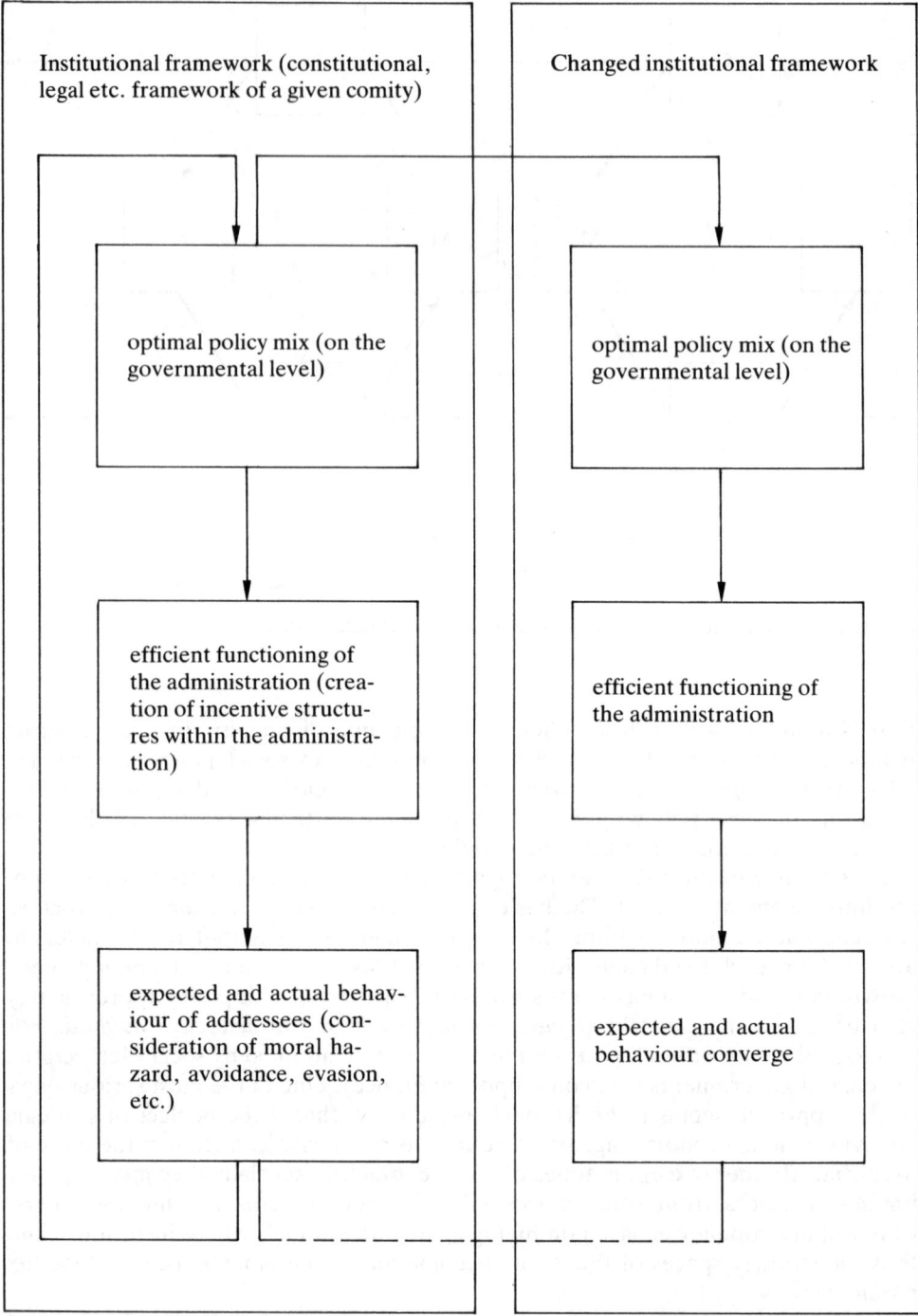

Fig. 3: Macropolicy

al. 1978) in a manner such that government policy objectives and individual rational behavior converge. (Nash solutions of noncooperative games). This is sometimes called the *axiomatic method*. The policy making process may be decomposed into 3 basic elements under this approach (Fig. 4).

Intermediate macro-micropolicy has one point in common with classical macropolicy. The ultimate center of decisionmaking is on the (national) governmental

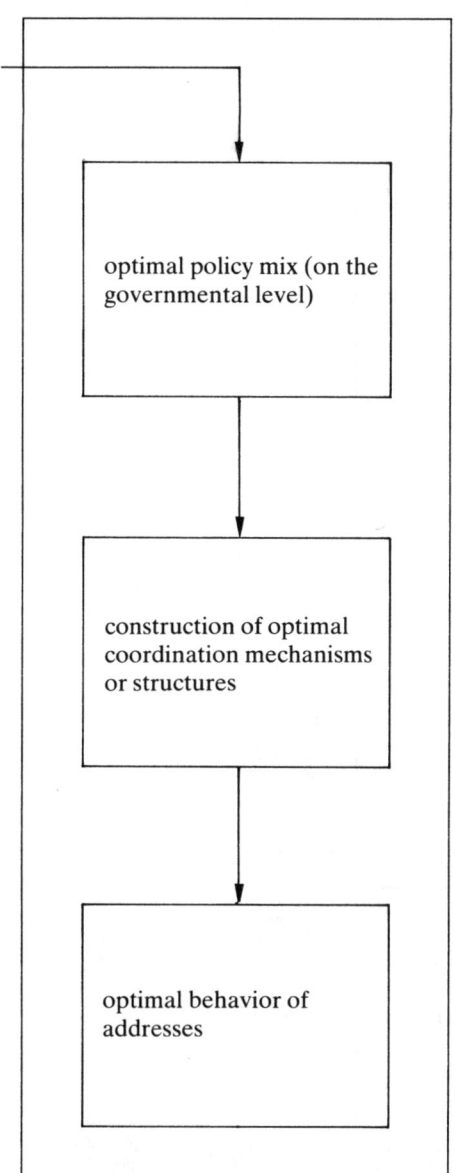

Fig. 4: Intermediate macro-micropolicy

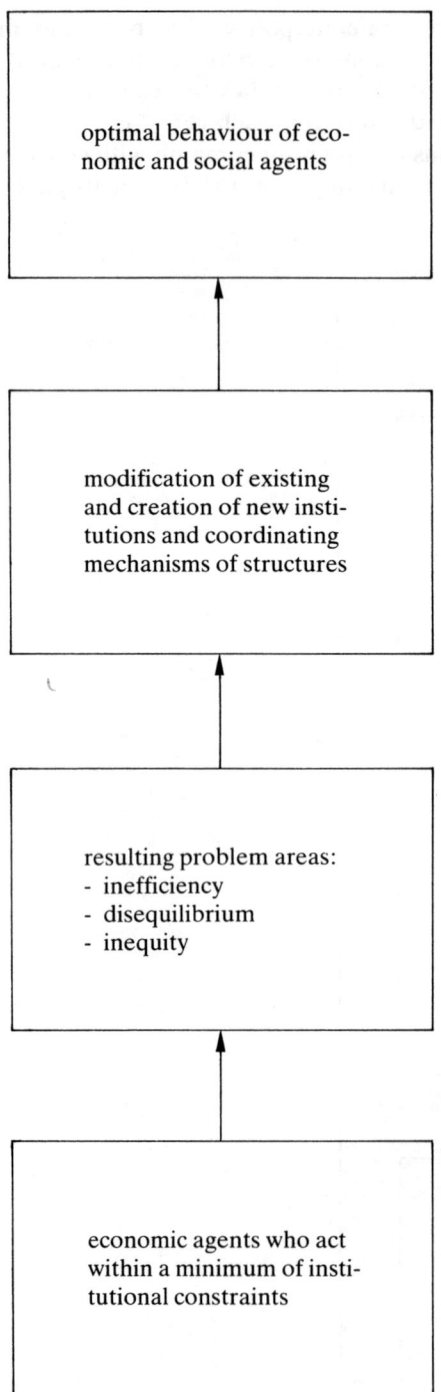

Fig. 5: Micropolicy

level. The national government fixes the goals and, for intermediate macro-micropolicy, the optimal institutions and coordination mechanisms or structures within which the economic agents act freely. The design of optimal institutions and coordination mechanisms or structures may be workable for well defined problems, but their application to nationwide economic and social policy does not yet seem operational.

(3) *Micropolicy* is a grass-roots approach to economic and social policy. It may also be called the *inductive method*. One may start from a situation with a very low degree of government interference with individual behavior (which may be hypothetical), or, more realistically, with a given well defined institutional framework which acts as constraint to individual and group action. One then asks the question: What are the institutions and coordinating mechanisms or structures necessary to successfully solve the economic or social problem as experienced by citizens. The chain of causality of the policy making process is inverted. The starting point is now the citizen. The ultimate center of decisionmaking may be more or less close to those who need help. One may distinguish four basic elements of this policy approach (Fig. 5).

In general micropolicy seems to be a persuasive approach to many specific economic and social policy problems. Consider the example of river water pollution control (see Fig. 1). In fact Figure 1 is a specification of Figure 5 for the case of river water pollution control. It may be interesting and useful to go into more detail and to survey how in reality the problem of river water pollution was solved in three different cases: Ohio River Valley Water Sanitation Compact (Orsanco), Ruhrverband-Ruhrtalsperrenverein (RV-RTV), and the French River Basin Agencies.

Ohio River Valley Water Sanitation Compact (Orsanco)[2] (Cleary 1967)

Pre-Orsanco period

1924: Informal agreement among health authorities – in several states to act in concert for control of phenol discharges from by-product coke plants (in general there existed declarations on cooperation without legal status on special areas). Uncoordinated efforts by interests related to sanitation, real estate, garden club, school, church, and civic betterment.

1935: Local legislative actions (Indiana: to strenghten legal compulsions and to allow municipalities greater freedom in financing sewage works with revenue bonds).

1935: Cincinnati Camber of Commerce took leadership in regional cooperation in pollution control.

Two possible approaches:

1. Macropolicy approach (federal action) industry was opposed, conservation groups were favorable

2. Micropolicy apporach (state action) industry was still opposed, but if a all necessary, then state action

Within Macro- or micropolicy approach two possible policies

1. Outright prohibition or control with heavy penalties	2. "Reasonable" legislation with provision for grants-in-aid, and for promotion of public education, research, and industrial incentives to stimulate action.

1948: Cincinnati Stream Pollution Committee advocates and chooses "reasonable" micropolicy approach[3]. Federal legislation on *Orsanco* was passed. Approval by industrial interests was obtained by "threat" of federal action and "physical urgency" (30 public sources of water supply were endangered by pollution of the Ohio River).

Orsanco period members

Eight member states (New York, Pennsylvania, West Virginia, Ohio, Indiana, Illinois, Kentucky, Virginia); the governor of each state appoints three commissioners (generally of Public Health Commissioner, an engineer, a staff member of the Fish and Wildlife Service of the Department of Interior); the President of the United States appoints three federal commissioners (without voting right in enforcement actions). Total members of commission: 27.

Budgetary process

Commission sends budget proposals to state governors who screen it and convey their views to state legislature which adopt it amended. Various cost sharing schemes were discussed (normative rules, such as equal cost sharing, for more recent views on the matter see (Schleicher 1978, 1980). Adopted was a politically feasible rule: Costs are allocated with respect to the size of the drainage area and the population without mentioning industry. Reason: "We would not want industry represented because they are potential violators, and we do not want them in to vote against enforcement of regulation against themselves" said one negotiator (Cleary 1967: 49).

Establishing Pollution Control Standards

Minimum requirements to be easily controllable were set; i.e. primary treatment was demanded with respect to sewage discharges of communities, for the rest flexible policy (education, moral suasion etc.).

Enforcement Authority

An issuance of an order requires
1. a majority of 5 states, where at least two commissioners of each state vote for the order, and
2. a majority of a least two commissioners of the state affected by the order.

Orsanco policy on financing municipal projects	1. Selffinancing by mortgage revenue bonds became possible for municipalities, with repayment guaranteed by service charge based on a percentage of the water bill.

Orsanco policy
on financing
municipal projects

1. Selffinancing by mortgage revenue bonds became possible for municipalities, with repayment guaranteed by service charge based on a percentage of the water bill.
2. Federal-aid program (retarded in some cases the construction of municipal facilities as beneficiaries waited for federal help. This implied injustice to those who proceeded without federal subsidies. Inflation hampered this wait-attitude). To stimulate the realization of economies of scale of bigger facilities cooperative ventures obtained bigger grants.
3. State-aid program.
4. Embargo on sewer extensions without construction or extension of waste water treatment plants.

Conclusion. Orsanco is clearly a micropolicy approach. The structure was the Ohio Valley with its industrial interests, municipalities, and citizens. The institutional framework put very little constraints on polluters. Coordination mechanisms were mediation and arbitration by courts, but especially bargaining among municipalities, municipalities and industrial interests, the states and federal government. The resulting coordination structure was the interstate compact Orsanco. Within this organisation bargaining and voting were the predominant allocation mechanisms.

The Ruhrgenossenschaften (RV-RTV) (Kühner and Bower 1981)

1913 Ruhr River
Pollution Control
Law

Foundation of *Ruhrverband* (RV), and on the same day the *Ruhrtalsperrenverein* (RTV) was made a public corporation.
1. The purpose of the RV is to keep good water quality in the Ruhr River and its tributaries.
2. RV and RTV are awarded the authority to make mandatory contributions from their members.
3. RV is "to build, maintain, and operate the facilities that are required to prevent pollution of the Ruhr and its tributaries by the individual members" of the association.
4. Kind and number of facilities, as well as their alterations and expansions, are subject to the approval of the responsible minister (Ministry of Nutrition, Agriculture and Forestry of Northrhine-Westfalia).
The purpose of the RTV is to replace the water that has been withdrawn from the Ruhr river system to its detriment (water consumed) and to improve the utilization of the hydropower potential of the river system.
1. The purpose of the RTV is to build and operate its own reservoirs,
2. to support construction and operation of reservoirs not owned by the RTV,
3. to build and operate facilities to obtain water from the River, and
4. to build and operate other necessary facilities.

Members of RV (Compulsory membership)	1. Industries 2. Municipalities 3. RTV
Members of RTV (Compulsory membership)	1. Waterworks and other withdrawers of ground-water and surface water from the Ruhr River and its tributaries (withdrawal must exceed 30000 m³/year). 2. Users of the Ruhr River system's hydropower.
Budgetary process	A policy is defined and then the implied probable total costs are assessed. Total cost is shared according to amount and use of water withdrawn.
Water Quality Management inside the RV area Establishment of Pollution Control Standards	State level: The Ministry of Agriculture, Nutrition and Forestry oversees all activities of lower agencies (implementation of laws and regulations), distributes grant money for construction of water quality management facilities to municipalities, water agencies and other eligible entities. *Regierungspräsidium* level: The Regierungspräsidium 1. establishes effluent requirements and pretreatment requirements for individual dischargers, 2. the Institute of Hygiene (state level agency) agrees to set pretreatment specifications for industrial facilities discharging into municipal sewers and then into RV facilities (industrial indirect dischargers). 3. the Regierungspräsidium reviews, discusses and agrees to effluent specifications of RV facilities to be constructed in a formal hearing.
Authorization procedure	Regierungspräsidium 1. issues, changes, and withdraws discharge permits for lst order receiving waters. 2. It issues, changes, and withdraws water withdrawal licenses for all surface waters and groundwater. 3. It levies fees for licences (withdrawal of water) and permits (discharge of liquid residuals).
Enforcement authority	Monitoring is done by the Institute of Hygiene (state level administration), RV, and state agency for water and solid waste (Stawa) (county level). Inspectors of these agencies have free access to all waste water generation and waste water treatment facilities. Sanctions for non compliance are with state agencies.
Federal Law regulating the establishment of water agencies (1937)	There exist 15000 water and soil conservation agencies based on this law in Germany. Only 9 water resources authorities were established under special laws (all in Northrhine-Westfalia).

Framework Law on Water (Wasserhaushaltsgesetz, 1957)	This law fixes water quality management under the responsibility of the state.
Sewage Water Law (Abwasserabgabengesetz, 1981)	It introduces a nationwide effluent charge.

Conclusion. Establishing RV-RTV as an association with compulsory membership is intermediate macro-micropolicy. (The coordination mechanism was hierarchy.) Coordination mechanisms within RV-RTV are bargaining and voting as far as budgeting and the construction of treatment facilities are concerned. Establishing pollution control standards, authorization procedures, and enforcement authority are done by hierarchical decisions. The nature of RV-RTV as a purely regional solution necessitates complementary macropolicy measures: a nationwide effluent charge.

The French Financial Basin Agencies (Barre 1981)

Pre-Law-on-Water period	1. Civil code and rural code: These codes define the rights and duties of land owners regarding the waters which are on or adjacent to their properties. The rural code gives police powers on water to the administrative authorities, and defines the limits of the property rights and obligation of maintenance.
	2. Code of Public Health and Departmental Sanitary Regulations: These define protected areas around intakes for drinking water, norms for waste water discharged into the sewers and general conditions for sewage systems.
	3. The Classified Establishment Law. It is the Fundamental Law to control nuisances (more than 400 activities are classified establishments). One distinguishes between 2 categories: Activities to be declared to the prefect and the classified establishment service and activities, permitted prior to their starting or modifying.
National Law on Water (1964)	Sets the general framework for modern water management in France.
Ambient water quality	1. Defines ambient water quality (objectives, procedure). A national ambient water quality inventory is instituted by law.
Discharge regulations	2. Specifies waste water discharge regulations (procedures for establishing local standards and for authorizing discharges). Authorization procedures with respect to wastewater discharges involve the following actors: the prefect, the discharger (municipality or industrial activity), the departmental services (agriculture, environment, classified esta-

blishment service) and sometimes the public. Consensus among all of them produces prefectoral decree.

Definition of standards case by case but also minimum standards, i.e. no algae or floating objects, no fish mortality 50 m beyond discharge point, definition for special standards for industrial dischargers if to be accepted by a municipal sewage system.

Rule exists, accepted by all parties, concerning the relative effort water users have to make on the same water course from upstream to downstream.

Controls and penalties

Inspectors of Classified Establishment Service may inspect freely whether standards are met.

1. Administrative procedures: in case of violation temporary closing of plant until requirements are met.
2. If there is a complaint by a pollutee: legal procedure with inspection. If requirements have not been met, then legal action based on violation of authorization conditions, or nonadherence to discharge standards, or infraction of rural code.

Bargaining among actors does not normally lead to court action (cost, time and "judicial record" favor private agreement).

Basin agencies (1964)

These are public administrative establishments (government agencies) which

1. elaborate multi-year programs of intervention (approved by the prime minister),
2. have a technical function (advisory with respect to planning, development and operation of the projects of which the program exists), and
3. have a financial function by levying charges and granting subsidies and loans to achieve their programs.

Actors (national versus basin balance of power)

Director, Executive Board of the agency (one half of members representatives of government, one half elected from Basin Committee, the members of which are constituted by one third government agents, one third from water users, and one third elected officials), Basin Committee (approves the level of effluent charges). Delegated Basin Commission and Interministerial Mission on Water.

Actors (institutional balance of power)

1. Basin agency
2. Technical ministries (agriculture, environment, industry)
3. Ministry of economy and finance
4. Industries in basin
5. Municipalities in basin

Budgetary process and financial policy

Elaboration of five year plan with definition of objectives on water quality; degree of treatment to be achieved plus amounts of financial aid determine total cost which has to be allocated by effluent charges on different pollutants. Capital costs of treatment facilities are financed by (1) loans and grants from relevant Basin agencies, (2) municipal budgets, (3) grants from regional and departmental budgets (which come from national budget).

Operation and maintenance are financed by (1) sewage tax, (2) the premium (based on the amount of pollutants removed in treatment), (3) superpremium (in case where sewage treatment plant is efficient).

Conclusion. Institutions in France prior to the Law on Water were insufficient to curb river water pollution. The national problem (macropolicy) was solved by the Law on Water. The existing institutional framework and power areas of political hierarchies allowed very little space to build new coordination structures. The resulting *basin agencies* (intermediate macro-micropolicy) have only some financial power and are narrowly controlled by the administration. In general major decisions are taken within the administration which is represented at each level of the decision making process. River water pollution control in France is a mix of hierarchial decisions, bargaining, and voting. The underlying coordination structure is very complex and highly centralized.

25.5 Conclusion

The preceding examples show that, for a given economic policy problem, there exist *in general many possible solutions* represented by coordination structures. It will often be difficult to judge which one will be the most acceptable according to some criterion, such as economic efficiency, equity, promptness of execution or level of conflict. The pollution problem lends itself to a game theoretic analysis as there are actors with equal or opposite interests. Cooperation among actors in this particular policy field is certainly desired, but does not always come about due to behavioral (freeriding) or legal and constitutional constraints (local or regional jurisdiction). *If cooperation takes place* then, in fact, many possible outcomes (cost sharing schemes) are possible and this within a given legal and constitutional framework (Core, Aumann-Maschler Bargaining Set, Shapley Value, Nucleolus, Harsanyi-Selten solution, etc.). A change in the legal and constitutional framework affects in general the number of coordination structures.

According to the aforementioned solution concepts of cooperative game theory each participant knows in advance what his share in total group benefits or costs will be. The outcomes are in general pareto efficient. *If cooperation does not take place voluntarily,* then local, state or national government may intervene weakly (by moral suasion, monetary transfers or threat) or strongly (compulsory membership) to impose de facto cooperation. The coordination mechanism chosen will depend on behavioral patterns (bargaining is very common in the United States, subsidies work quite well in France).

Voluntary cooperation may be time consuming, however least costly to government and society if the resulting extent of cooperation is large. An agreement may imply all the following functions: Authorization of intakes and discharges, financial autonomy, design, construction and operation of facilities, establishment of pollution control standards, enforcement authority (see Table 1). Free-riding and administrative cost may be low when the members of the agency are responsible for all costs. On the other hand monetary transfers to foster cooperation may be inequitable and costly due to moral hazard. The positive short term effects of having poor municipalities participate may be outweighed in the longer run by low efficiency. Despite such possible adverse effects, voluntary and compulsory cooperation (micropolicies and intermediate macro-micropolicies) may be more efficient than nationwide macropolicies which rely on governmental resolution but may have the advantage of being more quickly put in place. A government may thus choose to levy nationwide damage or *effluent charges* (macropolicy approach). The *principle of causality* where the polluter has the choice between compensation of damages and waste water treatment, and the institution of a nationwide *effluent standard* or the *outright control of pollution* (i.e. every polluter must treat its discharges) are macropolicies (Majone 1976; Schleicher 1982a). In reality these policies are often intermingled. The reason is simply that policies evolve in time. I.e. RV-RTV are public corporations with financial autonomy, but still have to pay a national effluent charge.

Tab. 1: Functions of Pollution Control Agencies

	Orsanco	Ruhrgenossen-schaften	French Basin Agencies
Authorization of intakes and discharges	not applicable	no	no
Financial autonomy	yes restricted	yes	yes levies charges
Design, construction and operation of facilities	no	yes	no
Establishment of pollution control standards	yes	partially	no
Enforcement authority	yes	partially	no

25.6 Epilogue

The preceding sections were variations on a common theme: The extent of government intervention to control river water pollution. The final statements of the analysis were conditional, depending on legal and constitutional frameworks, behavioral patterns and time (urgency). All three examples (configuration structures) of river water pollution control seem to work satisfactorily. Incentives seem to play an important role (cost sharing schemes, subsidies, threats) in this result.

Can these conclusions be generalized to other areas intermediate between the public and the private sector? That is, may the same coordination structures be implemented to solve different economic and social policy problems. This may be so in all fields where groups of well defined actors and well defined externalities are present as in the field of old age insurance, health insurance, accident insurance, professional organisations. However, each particular problem should be analyzed in depth within a given environment (country). Generally professional advice (economists, lawyers, administrative scientists, sociologists, political scientists, fieldworkers) will be necessary before any satisfactory coordination structure may be proposed. Further research will help to clarify the way that different configurations of coordination structures can be used to solve different economic and social policy problems.

Acknowledgement

The author would like to thank Vincent Ostrom for helpful editorial advice.

Notes

1 The problems of guidance, control, and performance evaluation are present in such a system as they are in a mixed economy. Public servants or state employees need to be guided, that is instructed, controlled, that is motivated, in an analogous manner in both systems. Rational use of scarce resources to attain social policy objectives should lead to the evaluation of policy results, that is to the specification of payoffs to individual actors and to society as a whole. However, all problems related to a centrally planned economy shall be disposed off. A comparative study of guidance, control, and performance evaluation of the public sector in a mixed and a centrally planned economy may be worthwhile and interesting in itself.

2 "A compact is a unique instrumentality made available for the conduct of cooperative undertakings among states" (Art. I, Section 10, Class 3, Constitution of the United States).

3 "We should not have to run to Washington every time we want to flush the toilet". Statement of Hudson Biery, Chairman of the Committee on Stream Sanitation of the Cincinnati Chamber of Commerce, in "Pollution of Navigable Waters", Hearings of Committee on Rivers and Harbors, House of Representatives, 79th Congress, 1st session, Nov. 1945, p. 183.

References

Arrow, K. J. (1963): *Social Choice and Individual Values*. New York: Cowles Foundation.
Barre, R. (1981): Water Management in France, with Special Emphasis on Water Quality

Management and Effluent Charges. In Bower, B. T. et al. (eds.), *Incentives in Water Quality Management, France and the Ruhr Area,* 31 ff. Resources for the Future. Inc., Research Paper R-24, Washington, D. C.

Cleary, E. J. (1967): *The Orsanco Story: Water Quality Management in the Ohio Valley under an Interstate Compact.* Baltimore: John Hopkins Press.

Crozier, M. (1967): *The Bureaucratic Phenomenon.* Chicago: Univ. of Chicago Press.

Hurwicz, L. (1973): "The Design of Mechanisms for Resource Allocation." *American Economic Review* 63 (2): 1–30.

Hurwicz, L., A. Postlewaite and E. Maskin (1978): *On the Feasibility of Allocation Mechanisms. Paris (Mimeogr.).*

Johansen, L. (1978): Lectures on Macroeconomic Planning. Amsterdam: North-Holland Publishing Company.

Kühner, J., and B. T. Bower (1981): "Water Quality Management in the Ruhr Area of the Federal Republic of Germany, with special emphasis on Charge Systems." In Bower, B. T. et al. (eds.), *Incentives in Water Quality Management, France and the Ruhr Area,* 213 ff. Resources for the Future, Inc. Research Paper R-24, Washington, D. C.

Majone, G. (1976): "Choice Among Policy Instruments for Pollution Control." *Policy Analysis* 5/3: 589–613.

Malinvaud, E. (1967): Decentralized Procedures for Planning. In Malinvaud, E., and M. O. L. Bacharach (eds.), *Activity Analysis in the Theory of Growth and Planning,* 170–211. London: Macmillan.

Marschak, J., and R. Radner (1972): *Economic Theory of Teams.* New Haven: Cowles Foundation.

Musgrave, R. A., and P. B. Musgrave (1973): *Public Finance in Theory and Practice.* New York: McGraw Hill.

Oates, W. E. (1972): *Fiscal Federalism.* New York: Harcourt, Brace, Jovanovich Inc.

Schleicher, H. (1978): *Classes of Core Configurations of Three-Person Convex Cost Games and Equivalent One-Point Solution Concepts.* Groupe de Recherche en Economie Publique et Calcul Economique, 78.01. Université Paris (XII) Val-de-Marne.

Schleicher, H. (1980): "Techniques de répartition des coûts dans l'évaluation des investissements publics: une analyse par la théorie des jeux." In Vallee, R., and H. Schleicher (eds.) *Théorie des systèmes et théorie des jeux, économies et sociétés.* Série: Economie Mathématique et Econométrie , 1415–1468. Paris ISMEA.

Schleicher, H. (1982a): *A Note on River Pollution Control: Alternative Institutional Approaches.* Center for Interdisciplinary Research, Bielefeld, Preprint Series No. 20.

Schleicher, H., and R. Selten (1982a): *The River Basin Game: A Noncooperative Analysis of Cooperation.* Center for Interdisciplinary Research, Bielefeld, Preprint Series No. 22.

Schleicher, H. (1982b): *Effizienz in der Wasserwirtschaft durch Kooperation: Vier Beispiele.* Groupe de Recherche en Economie Publique et Calcul Economique, 82.05. Université Paris (XII) Val-de-Marne.

Shubik, M. (1970): "On Different Methods for Allocating Resources." *Kyklos 23/2: 332–337.*

26. Associations and Coordination

Hans-Jürgen Franz, Bernd Rosewitz and Hartmut Wolf

Abstract

Through a historical view it is shown that associations can no longer be regarded as 'input factors' of political processes. Today they have become an integral part of the complex political system and are also engaged in the public performance. The analysis focuses on the question of how governmental and associational processes of decision making are coordinated in view of mutual independence of the various organizations. The strategic uncertainty within the interorganizational network constituted by public and associational organizations is analyzed as the key factor to processes of coordination.

26.1 Introduction

As other sections of the volume have shown, the modern public sector consists of a plurality of organizational forms which does not fit the classical idea of an unambiguous distinction between public and private spheres of society. Instead the public-private dichotomy is withering because governmental as well as non-governmental (private) organizations are involved in the functioning of the modern public sector (see Hood: Ch. 9; Kaufmann: Ch. 6). In this chapter we will discuss how the private actors called "associations" are involved in the public sector and how they affect the proper functioning of the latter.

The analysis of associations, usually perceived as private organizations of collective voluntary action in behalf of commonly shared interests, has to deal with a multifaceted and heterogeneous phenomenon (see Sills 1968). We are confronted with a variety of organizational forms, internal structures, goals, and nationally differing societal roles ascribed to the associations. Informal linkages among actors for the provision of mutual aid, voluntary service organizations in the field of welfare work, and large scale organizations of business and labour interests are examples of the wide range of associational action. Therefore we have to proceed from a general analytical point of departure and definition which perceives associations as voluntary unions of actors in order to promote *commonly shared interests*. The definition's emphasis of "voluntary action" and "common interests" is twofold, because these features are analytically the points of reference for the various forms of associations and they characterize the historical sources of associations namely the traditions of *interpersonal charitable work* following the historical line of stewardship and personal caring and help and the historical line of *free association* for mutual help. The commonly shared interest in mutual aid and/or charitable work constituted the bases of local self-help groups, the voluntary service organizations in the USA or their German equivalent the welfare associations (Wohlfahrtsverbände), and political interest organizations as for example labour unions. So far we can distinguish two axes or dimensions along to which associations have developed. On the one hand, there is the dimension of internal structure including solidaristic orientations within associations for mutual aid as well as formalized procedures and apathic members within large-scale organizations. The other dimension refers to the relationship between government and associations, which have changed from a strict separation between government and absolutely independent (i.e. private) self-help groups to a mutual interpenetration of public agencies and para-governmental associations providing public services in the field of social welfare.

As to the relationships between government and associations the latters were thought of as "intermediary agencies" whose functions were held to be the promotion of mutual aid in civil life and the political articulation, aggregation and implementation of citizens' interests vis-à-vis the government. Traditionally, associations were perceived as instruments for the attainment of commonly shared interests and as a necessary constraint of government authority. Tocqueville's (1948 II: 106–110, 115 ff.) extensive discussion of civil and political associations as vital elements of a democratic system has substantially influenced the theory of pluralism which analyzes the relationship between associations and government by the concept of "pressure group politics" and defines a multitude of associations, competing with each other for political influence, as necessary restraint of power and input-factor of a responsive political system (see Kariel 1968).

The classical pluralist assumptions have become relative, because the increase of welfare properties of the public sector and, along with this development, the emergence of large-scale associations providing public services and, thus, attaining a para-governmental status led to a public-private mix within certain policy areas. The discussion of "neo-corporatism" (see Schmitter and Lehmbruch 1979) places emphasis on the interlocking structures between government and associations. The partnership of public agencies and a few large scale associations characterizes the corporatist arrangements which induce symbiotic public-private relationships within certain policy areas affecting both, the structure of the interorganizational relationship between government and associations and the internal structures of the latter. The formerly input-factor of government becomes its partner of policy making and thus, target of direct government influence. Along with this development, the organizational growth and the para-governmental status affect the members' behavior by a formalization of procedures and the complexity of mixed interests (i.e. of members and government).

The approach of "neo-corporatism" is concentrated on the relations among government and the associations of corporations and labour or, in other terms, of labour and capital. It is argued, that the two groups of the socio-economic production are the most important and privileged associations, because their behaviors directly affect the fiscal basis of government (see Offe 1981: 138–140; Lehmbruch 1979b: 149). However important the relationships between associations of corporations and labour are, the sketched plurality of associational forms illustrated that the public-private mix within the modern public sector goes far beyond the classically economic issues and is contingent on nationally differing traditions.

The nationally differing socio-political conditions of the United States of America and Europe are important for the analysis of the public-private mix in modern public sectors. Scholars of corporatism (see for example Schmitter 1979; Panitch 1979; Cawson 1978) refer to the European development of associations and its high degree of centralized bargaining power and unification of structural forms. As to the American context, Turkel (1982) demonstrates by the example of the 1980 "Chrysler Loan Guarantee" act, that the USA represent no full-blown corporatism. Since neither corporations nor labour have a sufficiently centralized bargaining power at their disposal, major corporatist structures emerge only in times of national crisis and remain reactive and seldom (see Turkel 1982: 170). By contrast, the German "concerted action" of government, corporations and labour and the Austrian advisory bodies for economic issues represented durable arrangements for the anticipation and long-run management of crises.

Another example for the nationally differing forms of a public-private mix in the public sector is the field of social welfare. In the USA, the so called "voluntary service organizations" (VSOs) are rather more important for the provision of social services than public bureaucracies. Kramer (1979: 2) speaks of a volunteer-service field which consists of over 30 federal programs involving 3 millions volunteers. The US government extensively uses voluntary agencies in the field of welfare by direct grants for private services. Kramer (1981) pointed out, that 90% of the incomes of VSOs are public funds and the formally non-governmental organizations governed by an elected board of directors have become paragovernmental organizations. The changed organizational environment of the VSOs in the USA (i.e. more federal funding) also affects their internal structure. A general trend of increased formalization, specialization and interdependence among the VSOs and between them and public agencies induces the emergence of large-scale organizations (see Kramer 1973: 63 ff.) characterized by an entrepreneurial behavior vis-à-vis government and a strive for political influence. It has to be noticed, that the increase of public funding did not lead to an bureaucratic overregulation or "loss of autonomy". Kramer (1979: 8–10) found little evidence for the thesis of a "loss of autonomy" and he noticed, that VSOs mostly have scarce resources at their disposal and the highly fragmented federal system in the USA offers them a diversity of income sources. The relationship between government and VSOs is, thus, characterized by mutual dependency.

The German welfare associations represent a good contrast. Although they also provide social services in the public sector and are mostly funded by government, their organizational forms are quite different. The welfare associations have a rather more centralized bargaining power at their disposal than the VSOs, because they constituted federations or peak federations on the national level in order to strengthen their position vis-à-vis government. Furthermore the relations among public and associational agencies are ruled by law (i.e. the legal principle of "subsidiarity"), so that the relationships are more formalized, and associations have become recognized partners of policy making in the field of welfare (see Wegener 1978). A final difference refers to the self-help groups on the community level. Whereas, in the USA, self-help groups often remain informal although providing relevant social services, the German "local association" (Verein) is officially registered and submitted to laws which impose certain internal procedures and ascribe the status of a "legal personality" to the association (i.e. a separate sphere of rights).

So far, we placed emphasis on the heterogeneity of the multifaceted phenomenon "associations". In the following sections our considerations proceed from the assumption, that there is much evidence for the common trend of increased interpenetration of public (governmental) and associational action on the level of policy making and service delivery in the modern public sector. The long chains of action characterizing the modern public sector (see Kaufmann: Ch. 10) are thus determined by interorganizational fields constituted by public and associational organizations. According to nationally differing organizational structures, the arrangements vary in the degree of their formalization, but despite these differences more complex forms of coordination among the organized actors of government and associations have become inevitable.

The general trend of a public-private "blurring" or "interpenetration" affects both, the internal structure of associations and the interorganizational relationships between government and associations. In order to clarify, how government and associations are interlinked on the level of policy making and public service delivery and what are the intra- and interorganizational consequences, we will discuss the historical example of the German associations and their development. The changes of the internal structures of associations will be dealt with next. Finally we consider the characteristics of coordination within and among associations as well as between them and government agencies.

26.2 The Historical Development of Associations

In medieval feudal society associations had the character of an important social group. Membership determined the fate of the members (cf. Mayntz 1963: 18) since the individuals were integrated into these "compulsory associations" on account of their status. At the same time, these associations were part of the social order.

During the process of social differentiation a separation of the two spheres 'state' and 'society' occured (cf. Tenbruck 1981), which had previously been thought of as one and the same.

Lorenz von Stein (1869) showed, that the societal sphere became a counterpart of the state. Free individuals founded unions as an intermediary institution between individual and state. These unions constituted themselves on the base of the former "compulsory associations" (Herder-Dorneich 1972: 75). At first, the aims of unions were not always considered to express legitimate interests. They were frequently suspected of subversive activities potentially dangerous to the state. General acceptance by state was attained only very gradually.

This was shown mainly by the rather different use of the freedom of association. In Germany, the foundation of local associations started in the second half of eighteenth and the first half of nineteenth century. A freedom of trade-act passed in Prussia in 1810/11 meant the end of the association-abolition at the same time.

Impressed by the political development in England and France the Prussian State suspended freedom of association in 1845. In 1850 the Prussian 'Union-Law' was passed which abolished the aggregation of political unions. In 1869 the freedom of association was made possible again but with limiting conditions.

Structure and Functions of Unions

Initially a main task of these unions was to offer a degree of security to those groups of persons who had been deprived of their former social ties.

The unions were structurally constituted as a union of formally free citizens who joined together on the basis of free will. People were able to place common, collectively shared interests within an organizational framework. This feature of a union provided the opportunity for a flexible adaptation of objectives and means to the common interests of the members. Also membership could be combined with specific interests and expectations.

In terms of the internal structure of unions, this meant the necessity to relate member's actions directly to the aims of the union. This was also an impediment to the "break down" of the aims and objectives of the unions according to a variety of specialized susidiary aims and to dealing with them in bureaucratic and hierarchic manner (see Teubner 1979: 41). Given that the union is a social system, the limiting conditions of such a close link between membership and organizational purpose implies that a system of this kind can function successfully only while the members engage in frequent social interaction and jointly harmonize their aims. The environment of the social system 'union' remains apparent to all the members.

From our perspective two main sociological functions of unions can be distinguished. First, there ist the internal cohesion which makes this social system different from other forms of organization. By their common aim members are joined together in a kind a mechanical solidarity (Durkheim 1933). There is a distinct normative consensus extended to all members (Coyle 1930). In the type 'union' the cohesive function is limited to the agreed aims. The solidary character of the union also means that all external activities are bound to the general ideas shared by the members. This contains a reference to the second main function of unions which we call transformation. Unlike the medieval association the union aims to strengthen the interests shared by many individuals and make them valid in society. According to Kirberger (1978: 31f.) "the individual citizen who wants to realize effectively his or her personal ideas, is dependent on a union like-minded individuals in an organization equipped with financial means and personnel, for the purpose of spreading more effectively the personal ideas of these individuals". A constant link with the interests of the individual members has to be guaranteed. With this type of union, we note patterns of cohesion and transformation which are characterized by a close reciprocal relationship. This also means that the social structures cannot serve to develop a diverse, outwardly directed activity.

Union and Federation

The union model described above does not correspond with the associational structures in our time. They grew to flexible and complex organized social systems. An important structural development took place, which let the unions join together. Unions interlocked on a translocal level and became members of federations. These federations can be seen as a second main associational structure which we want to discuss further.

The main task of the federation is to pursue a specific policy according to the aims of the union-members. While in the local unions the face-to-face communication is the prevailing form of interaction between the union-members, the federation mainly performs service functions for the unions and not for its personal members. With the foundation of federations it became necessary, for specialized people to actively pursue the aims of the federation in the name of all other members. The clearly defined purpose of the federation made such a division of activities possible. As a result it was no longer necessary for the members to concern themselves with the policy of federation's administrative bodies, since the latter were bound by their purpose and could thus be controlled nor did the administrative bodies need to make membership, i.e. beyond the fulfilment of the purpose, seem particularly attractive since the purpose itself enabled a clear distinction (see Luhmann 1968: 154). By and by the specialized honorary persons became fully paid officials. This resulted from an increased attractiveness for potential members on the one hand and the increased importance of the federations in the political system. At the same time, the internal structure of the federations continued to divide into hierarchically or functionally specialized subunits.

As a further structural development we can identify the unification of several federations engaged in the same field. But also federations with different aims and interests can join together and builds a new associational structure named here 'Peak-Federation' (in Germany "Spitzenverbände"). This level of emergence has been reached in Germany by a multitude of associations, e.g. employers and workers, the cities and counties and the welfare associations. The foundation of 'peak-federations' became necessary because the decision level for important political subjects moved to central, often national areas. This required a 'peak-federation', that represented the organized interests on the central platform. In the following we want to discuss some common features of unions, federations and 'peak-federations'. In order to avoid misunderstanding we shall speak of associations, if all forms are meant.

Unions and their personal members

Generally speaking, the differentiation of internal associational structures leads to a situation in which the cohesive function is becoming less significant. Specialized functions developed out of the former union-structure. The representation of interests vis-a-vis other social institutions tends to be less closely linked to the interests of all members.

The gradual disappearence of cohesive patterns in associational social systems in favour of a maintenance or extension of transformation is of significance in relation to many phenomena which have been discussed in the relevant literature. For instance, the apathy of a large majority of association members described by Barber (1950) can be more easily understood in these terms. By contrast, the organizational aim of a federation or 'peak-federation' is frequently defined in a more formal manner and independently of the direct motivation of the members.

Geiger (1928: 67) regards an federation based on common interests as a organizational form in which transformation has become a dynamic force of its own to an extent where it can be manipulated by the top echelons of an organization – the cohesive function of membership is turned into a farce: It is now hardly or not at all concerned with the individual. One joins such associations, perhaps without ever coming into contact with its organs and the other members except by correspondence. In any case, such groups are not interested in the personalities of their members, only in whether they share the interests of the association which they are not even expected to confirm. For many such associations, the main point is that, when putting their case, they can refer to a large number of members who 'back them up'.

In spite of the increasing formalization of the membership of an association, the members remain an essential force in the operation of an association. A further possible consequence of this development is that an additional, specialized function emerges within an association because the latter attempts to keep its members together, i.e. because it wants reassurance that members are loyal to its policy.

The factor of ideological consensus is significant in this respect. An ideological consensus between officials and members can help to overcome difficulties in the relationship of members to their association. Finally, a high degree of loyalty also strengthens the impact of the representatives of an association vis-a-vis other social institutions which, in case of decreasing or lack of support on the part of the members, would soon be at risk.

In the case of interactive social groups, it is possible to ensure cohesion through certain rituals which, at least on an emotional level, strengthen the associative ties which Coyle (1930: 144f.) has described the lulling of the critical faculties and the heightening of suggestibility by the chants, incense and candles have always contributed to the emotional fusion of individuals which, when directed to that end, creates cohesion in the organization. Since most contemporary associations rarely invite their members to meetings, the officials have use alternative methods to ensure the loyalty of the members. Speeches and articles conveyed to them via the mass media enable the officials to exert an influence on members without contacting them personally.

In his work on the ideology of associations, Hondrich has shown how associations secure a uniform, socially effective creation and concentration of interests by ideological means. The members are told what is in their interest and what is not: the ideology of the associations serves to make manifest interests which are latent (Hondrich 1963: 152).

From our historical discussion we can conclude, that in contemporary associations cohesion and transformation no longer carry the same weight. Rather the function of transformation has been extended while cohesion is often formally undermined and merely fulfils the special function of safeguarding members' loyalty. Through the differentiation of special functions within the structures of associations, the internal complexity has grown and, at the same time, the capacity for action has increased.

What we have in fact described is a specific characteristic of the present-day social system 'association': an increasing divergence between the organizational purpose and the motivations of members (Teubner 1979).

The trend to generalized motivation

Extension beyond the local sphere, which had been necessary to represent the interests of an association more effectively, and the resulting increase in membership were accompanied by a differentiation of the internal structure of the association. There is a direct connection between the increasing differentiation of the relevant environments of associations, which will be explained in detail below, and the divergence between the aims of members and the organizational purpose. As opposed to concrete motivations, associations now have to establish generalized motivations for the purpose of attracting potential members by offering a wide range of organizational objectives. This assumption is also borne out by Beyme (1974: 49) who found that an association tends to be less successful in conducting general policies as interests become more specialized.

The aggregation of federations, previously active only on a regional level, into supra-regional associations leads to sudden increases in the number of members to be represented and, consequently, to an enlarged range of demands and statements to be put forward on various problems. The individual association is thus faced with a twofold task of co-ordination since it has to co-ordinate the activities within the organization itself as well as vis-a-vis other organized units (Kaufmann et al. 1979: 21).

Against this background of increased complexity in the two environments relevant to the system, growing tendencies towards an internal structural differentiation and an increased bureaucratization within the associations can be found. Luhmann (1964: 79) regards this internal structural differentiation as a process through which the whole system in trying to solve the problems of its environment by transmitting them into the interior.

26.3 The Modern Organization of Associations

After having shown the historical development of associational systems by discussing three main types in form of the union, the federation and the 'peak-federation' we want to focus systematically on the structural variation of associational systems. According to Weber (1977: 79) we refer to three general dimensions pertaining to the associational type of social organization.

The first dimension is the degree of organization, especially the kind of potential membership of an association. If all potential members are organized, there is, though it is dependent on the degree of loyalty, a strong possibility of an effective activity vis-a-vis the politico-administrative system. A different situation occurs if only some of the potential members are organized in the association. Other associations may work in the same field and constitute a competitive situation between the associations. This also entails a weakening of the representative's position in relation to the politico-administrative system.

The second dimension is that of organizational levels. Many associations have passed through a process of hierarchical differentiation resulting in the formation of associational substructures on the local, the regional and the national level. In this perspective the historical development described above in the main types of union, federation and 'peak-federation' is also a definition of a process of organizational differentiation. While the union works exclusively on the local level and with face-to-face communication-channels, the federation is organized on a regional level and also shows formalizaton and bureaucratization. The 'peak-federation' is a product of the increased process of organizational differentiation. At the same time it works on a higher, generally a national level. The process of organizational differentiation also leads to an increased pressure for adaptation and co-ordination. But this differentiated organizational form is the only one that enables an association to act competently and effectively at all important levels.

The third dimension is that of the organizational form. In the union, formal rules prescribed how members are to be integrated in the organizational structure and how they can participate in the process of decision-making. The organizational form also determines which official tasks and positions are to be created within an association and the range of their influence. But as associations are relatively autonomous in determining their organizational form the real influence of the members may vary. It often happens, that member's rights are rather restrictive by and that member's meetings are convened only at long intervals. As already stated the members of federations are often not people but organizations. This is also an important fact for the organizational form.

The 'peak-federation' shows an organizational form that is oriented more to the politico-administrative system and desired effects than to the internal membership.

Now we want to focus on the last aspect and look to the situational constraints that enable the federation and especially the 'peak-federation' to intervene effectively in the politico-administrative system.

Associations in the politico-administrative system

Weber (1977: 219) describes the influence of interest groups on politics and administration as the result of a wellfunctioning bureaucratic apparatus, the permanence of its leadership and the continuity of its object-related-strategies. This statement refers to the fact that an association is engaged in seeking both an effective and lasting influence in the politico-administrative system. For this reason, the social interactions between the associations and the administration consist of regular consultations rather than sensational actions. A constant aim of 'peak-federations' is the safeguarding of agreements which have been reached. Another one is the initiation of new laws or the amendment of existing legislation. These aims lead to a certain adaptation of the 'peak-federation' to the procedures of public administration (Weber 1977: 218). They already contain a considerable measure of the 'logic of administration' as described by Donaldson and Warner (1974). It can be concluded that a 'peak-federation' which has many officials (specialization), keep more files (formalization) tends to apply more routine procedures (standardization) and is characterized by a high degree of hierarchy (centralization).

These processes of structural development can lead to the establishment of stronger relations with the environment. In an analysis which we conducted of a large number of 'peak-federations' in the Federal Republic of Germany, the presence of this effect could be underlined. We generally found, that a high degree of internal structural differentiation exists in those 'peak-federations', which worked in a highly differentiated field and had to transform problems of their environment to the interior. The actual organizational structure has two causes: on the one hand they are differentiated according to the ferderal states in Germany and on the other hand according to the fields of their activity. The organizational development can be interpreted as a process of adjustment to the constitutional structure of the Federal Republic of Germany and a process of adjustment to the structure of membership. By this we conclude an adaptation of the 'peak-federation' to two important organizational environments: the politico-administrative system and the members.

In order to guarantee the continuing activity of the 'peak-federation' a further differentiation took place by a specialization of the executive organs as departments and committees, some of them staffed by experts. The continuity of the function could be influenced by elections of those officials, who represent the 'peak-federation'. But sometimes these elections are held only at six-year intervals and re-election makes long terms in office common (cf. Rosewitz and Wolf 1981: 189 f.). The increase in the power of the officials (cf. Bethusy-Huc 1976: 225) means that the participation of members in neutralized, if not impossible. The politico-adiministrative system initially served as a sort of legal superstructure according to the liberal concept of a minimal state and the societal 'free play of forces'. In the course of social change the politico-administrative system became a 'provident institution'. It intervened in all social spheres (Weber 1977: 219; Kaufmann 1977: 37) by means of welfare measures and support and regulation. With the transition from a state characterized by the order-principle to a welfare-state, the politico-administrative system extends its control to an increasing number of societal subsystems. The extension of state intervention coincides with a rise in the level of social claims. Therefore in a pluralistically structured society, the politico-administrative system is easily overloaded.

The increasing state intervention necessitates the availability of relevant information from the social subsystems to ensure appropriate decisions. But the politico-administrative system is often unable to gain the relevant information and therefore turns to 'peak-federations'. In the Federal Republic of Germany the attempts of the 'peak-federations' to aquire political influence were interpreted and criticized as government's loss of power and function in the fifties (cf. Beyme 1979: 204; Kaiser 1956). Since then 'peak-federations' are increasingly accepted as an important element of the political infrastructure (Narr and Naschold 1971: 204).

A situation occurs in which certain non-government factors ('peak-federations', Interest groups), although they do not participate in the constitutionally organized executive power, nevertheless take part in political decision-making, i.e. in a legally defined way (Böckenförde 1976b: 466).

Corporate Structures

The growing participation of the 'peak-federations' and their integration into the process of the politico-administrative decision-making is currently interpreted in terms of the 'corporatism model' or 'neo-corporatism' in political science. The contemporary discussion on 'neo-corporatism' focuses on the integration and functional representation of 'peak-federations' in this system (Heinze 1979: 162). Heinze sees the main issue in the attempt to overcome the prevailing concept of "pressure group politics".

The 'corporatism model' places more emphasis on the interlocking structures which have formed a kind of symbiosis. The starting-point of these considerations is a change in emphasis within the institutions of the politico-administrative system (Offe 1981). The importance of parliamentary institutions in determing political decision-making is diminishing. At the same time the importance of the administration increases. Both institutions increasingly surrender some of their tasks to negotiating and decision-making bodies in specific policy areas (Wiesenthal 1979: 171).

The concept of 'neo-corporatism' was developed for the specific development in Great Britain before being generalized in the discussion on the crises and ungovernability of the western capitalist industrial societies. It has to be taken into account, that the situation in the several western countries is quite different. In the United States of America formal corporate structures are not of central importance (see Turkel 1982: 165ff.).

In Western Europe the integration and functional representation of 'peak-federations' is central to the discussion on neo-corporative structures (Heinze 1979: 162). In his important article "Still the century of corporatism?" Schmitter (1979) describes conditions for the detachment of pluralistic, socio-political systems by a 'societal corporatism'.

Offe (1981: 136) argues that corporatism is a concept that does not describe a situation, but an 'axis' of development. In other words, political systems can be more or less corporatist, more or less advanced in the process of corporatization, depending upon the extent to which public status is attributed to organized interest groups. Cawson (1978: 196f.) remarks about the different areas in which corporate strategies are applied: "Apart from the need to regulate the economy, the trend towards corporatism can be observed in land-use planning, local government, health administration, water supply, education, and in many other areas of established public policy". This interlocking between the 'peak-federations' and the state offers advantages for both sides. For the state greater capacity for guidance, for the 'peak-federations' a guarantee of their own continuance and an effective reinforcement of their interests (see Heinze 1979: 168). 'peak-federations' are used as instruments for the guidance-activities of the state. By this the 'peak-federations' act not only as partial interest-organization as in the pluralistic system. They are also integrated into the political process and are part of the formulation and enforcement of political guidance.

This kind of structure is typical of the area of public welfare and welfare organization in the Federal Republic of Germany. A strong net of welfare organizations produces an important part of social policy measures. They are involved in the field of legislation as well as in the local service delivery (cf. below). The 'Konzertierten Aktionen' (concerted actions) in the Federal Republic of Germany are another example (Beyme 1979; Wiesenthal 1979; Lehmbruch 1979).

We can state, that the 'peak-federation' is able to take over four main functions for and within the political system. They are: 1. the articulation of social demands; 2. the provision of information relevant for decision-making; 3. the availability of the necessary resources; 4. to safeguard legitimacy (see Rosewitz and Wolf 1981: 98). The fact that 'peak-federations' are so closely interconnected with the politico-administrative system means that they have a para-governmental status according to the typology of C. Hood (Ch. 9).

The first function, the articulation of social demands or the articulation of relevant interests to the politico-administrative system need an aggregation and selection of interests in the 'peak-federation'. This internal clarification ensures that the communication-channels of the political system (Easton 1965: 117) are not overloaded. 'peak-federations' frequently hold a monopoly of information for the subjects they represent. By providing information relevant to decision-making they can ease the strain on the politico-administrative system. Since they also have access to resources the 'peak-federations' rather than the politico-administrative system are capable of discharging services in many spheres. 'peak-federations' can reduce the task of the government or share its burdens (Kirberger 1978).

Since various policy areas are administered by self-governing bodies, the politico-administrative system is largely absolved from both actively intervening and taking responsibility for policy outcomes. The fourth function of 'peak-federations' can be named 'safeguarding of legitimacy'. This means, that the association has a capacity to control the reaction of its members according to the decisions made.

A further interesting question is which channels of influence are preferred by the associations. Scharpf (1973) argues that problem-solving occurs mainly on the lower levels of departmental administration and its sections (Abteilungen, Referate). Higher levels of administration cannot initiate programs based on their own problem-solving activities without the lower-level organizations as the departmental administration is characterized by a high degree of decentralization. The tasks of departmental sections are divided according to groups of the population, economic sectors or other aspects.

Such a rigid assignment of tasks to the lower levels leads to a permanent specialization in specific subjects and problems. It also leads to a stabilization of objectives and adherence to well-established networks of personal contact and communication. Given this structural situation 'peak-federations' find it easy to maintain contact with the various departments and establish fruitful co-operation. The political system may profit from concentration of attention in specific areas and a high sensibility towards problems in the relevant areas.

In a highly organized society such as the Federal Republic of Germany approximately 70% of new legislation is prepared by the departmental administration. Since its own ability to absorb and process information is rather restricted, the departmental administration considers the 'peak-federation' as an important supplier of information.

In practice, 'peak-federations' are directly included in the legislative process. They are asked to comment and they are invited to attend meetings of the various departments (see Neysen 1968: 12). The so-called 'Beiräte' (advisory bodies) can be seen as the most advanced form of institutionalized influence exercised by interest groups on the departmental administration. As the 'peak-federation' is represented in these advisory bodies, its influence on the departmental administration becomes more obvious. To some extent it also becomes more controllable (Weber 1977: 277), because the influence results in a commitment to act and make decisions which can expect concrete support by private actors (see Wiesenthal 1979: 181).

26.4 Associational Coordination

The previous discussion of the historical development and structural changes of associations which led to three differing and still existing structural forms of local unions, federations organized on a regional or national level and peak federations made it even more clear that the blurring of the public-private dichotomy stems not only from public (i.e. governmental) interventions in the private sphere of the "market" but also from a high level of intertwinement between the "state" and the other – often neglected – dimension of the private sphere of society which is the social domain of voluntary associations.

Since the federations no longer in a *piecemal way* affect solely the input-side of the political process through "demands" and "supports" (see Easton 1965; Almond and Powell 1966), but also constitute *permanently* to the availability of relevant informations and discharge autonomously services in the public sector, the relations between the organizations of government and federations are no longer clearly regulated and 'self-evident' as far as their coordination is concerned. The organizational plurality of the modern public sector aggravates the problem of guidance, control and performance evaluation, because numerous as well as structurally differing organizations[1] generate on the basis of their legal and institutional independence the long chains of decisions and actions which characterize the functioning of the public sector (see Ch. 10). The interplay of governmental and associational decisions in nearly all sectors of public performance turns their mutual coordination into a problem insofar as the institutionally differentiated, pure forms of coordination which are, on the one hand, hierarchical control based on the governmental authority of power and obligation and, on the other, associational self-coordination of actors on the basis of elective processes must relate to each other in order to achieve certain public performances.

To the extend to which federations and peak federations have become an integral part of the political system the question is raised how processes of associational coordination affect the relationship between government and federations and thereby the crucial problems of a well functioning public sector.[2] Therefore we shall now examine the three basic features of associational coordination.

1. processes of internal coordination within unions and federations
2. coordination among unions and federations
3. coordination between federations and government.

For the analysis of associational coordination, it is important to know in which way the co-operative actors "association" and "federations" cause their members to act collectively and what consequences on the combined effect of governmental and associational decision originate from this internal processes of organizing which comprises all the three structural forms of local unions, federations and peak federations.

The internal coordination of *unions* is generally characterized by a voluntary association of individual actors with a view to collective acting in accordance with a set of statutes, which lay formally down specific rules on the participation in decision-making. Hence unions are primarily based on a procedural guidance which is largely bound to a purpose-related consensus among the associated actors about the aims of collective actions. It is decisive that both, individual decisions and the statutory rules, can, in principle, be influenced by members and their options of "exit" or "voice" (see Hirschman 1970). On the structural level of associations any collective action is bound to specific goals which have to be reconciled with the personal motives and interests of the members. Therefore the internal coordination of unions is characterized by solidaristic features like common shared and defined interests, values and goals which are based on the principally possible chances of a face-to-face communication among the associated actors. As pointed out above, modern *federations* are no longer in line with this model of a free association of joint and local interests, but represent large-scale organizations, whose realms of activities have been expanded to such a high degree that the multiplicity of specific personal interests of the members no longer is instructive for collective actions on the more aggregated level of federations and are replaced by a generalized motivation of membership. In this case, the federation can no longer be regarded as the "sum" of the associated personal interests of its members. The structural difference between an "union" and a "federation" is due to three developments, which are the emergence of a separate legal sphere constituting an organized actor, the replacement of solidaristic elements through a formal membership role guiding the behaviors of members and more formalized procedures of participation. These trends generate the differentiated organizational structure of modern federations.

The process that federations as organized actors attain extensive freedom of choice, can be illustrated by the legal construction of the juristic person of organizations. The fact that federations required of a professionalized staff and officials to ensure the relevant objectives of the organization as a whole which are a durable and effective external representation and internal stability based on dues and the loyalty of the members, is not only a consequence of the problem of organizing large interest groups, as stated by Olson (1965). The attribution of rights and legal status to the federation as a whole rather defines the quality of a modern organization than its mere size.

Max Weber (1966) pointed out, that the problem of an unambigous determination of the significance of every action of every member and every official of an organization had to arise in consequence of the growing exchange economy. As the advanced process of differentiation and appropriation among and within the various organizations, as individuals can be simultaneously members of several organizations and as, finally, contracts both of individuals and between the organization as a whole and outsiders became more frequent, a clear determination of the actions of individuals and of organizations respectively their officials became necessary.

"The technical legal solution of this problem was found in the concept of the juristic person. (...) The most rational actualization of the idea of the legal personality of organizations consists in the complete separation of the legal spheres of the members from the separate constituted legal sphere of the organization. While certain persons designated according to rules are regarded from the legal point of view as alone authorized to assume obligations and acquire rights for the organization, the legal relations thus created do not affect the individual members and their property and are not regarded as their contracts, but all these relations are inputed to a separate and distinct body of assets." (Weber 1966: 156–157)

The fact that the officials tend to become a separate force and the specific interests of members respectively the heterogeneity of them are standardized by the conditions of a membership role which guides the members in accordance with generally defined goals and formalized procedures (see Luhmann 1975: 41), has repeatedly been criticized from normative and democratic points of view because the advanced differentiation and formalization of federations increase the tangible and intangible costs of "voice" which the individual member has to bear in order to promote *his personal interests* (see Hirschman 1970).[3]

With regard to the political system as a whole, where the modern large scale federations reduce the complexity of the citizens' demands by its internal processes of selection and aggregation of successful issues, the procedural intra-organizational guidance offers the officials a high degree of autonomy, bound to certain democratic rules, in order to formulate and to carry into effect specific aggregated interests. Thus, processes of associational coordination within federations occur on a higher level of aggregation than that of the individual member, owing to the change from a purpose-related self-coordination within a "free union" to a coordination by the officials of a federation.

As to the empirical extent to which bureaucratization is realized we have to distinguish between two options of structuring a federation. Whereas so-called *mass federations* (Massenverbände) like, e.g. the General German Automobile Club (ADAC), are highly centralized because they are not based on relatively autonomous local associations but on millions of members for whom participation is too costly, other *federations* function as *aggregation of local unions* and this structure restraints the trends of formalization and bureaucratization. We previously mentioned that most of the modern large scale federations were created by unions in order to concentrate the similar interests of members and to expand their domains. Therefore the internal coordination of federations rest upon processes of information and negotiation among the representatives of the local unions.

The decisions of the top echolons about issues (i.e. the selection of successfull interests) and appropriate strategies of realizing them are not only bound to the procedural control of members assemblies respectively their delegates, but they are dependent on the services as well as on the individual members of the relatively autonomous unions.

The internal differentiation of complexity of the modern federation can now be described more precisely, by stating the diversity of the local interests of associations is internally aggregated, by equally specialized representatives, generating the aggravated problem of coordination. Whereas *social cohesion* represents the crucial problem of coordinating actors on the local level of unions federations have to deal with longer chains of voluntary action which necessitate more complex forms of coordination in order to meet the requirements of a *transformation* of interests into successful forms of influence within the public sector.

In accordance with the structural change the internal coordination of federations comprises the general problems of guidance, control and evaluation as they were theoretically explored in this volume by Kaufmann (Ch. 10) and Ostrom (Ch. 12). In order to cause the members (i.e. individuals and legal persons) to act collectively federations have to set standards by selecting and aggregating successful issues, to control the members' behaviors according to the standards and to respond to the members' evaluations of "success" or "failure". Therefore federations are subject to a high internal pressure of coordination, where, from an analytical point of view, the organizational environment constituted by the members has to be reconciled with the environment of the political system. The compatibility of the two environments represents a permanent problem for the federations (see Teubner 1979).

The problem of compatibility is aggravated on the highest level of aggregation which is the so-called *peak federation*. The structural characteristic of an peak federation is its primary orientation towards the political system. Analogously to federations, the peak federation functions as a specific kind of aggregation of associational actions (i.e. the actions of federations). The factual relevance of peak federations depends on the extent, to which they obtain the legitimacy to represent the organized members and, along with this, the means of obligation according to their decisions. A variety of organizational forms exists which comprises coordinative agencies operating as advisory bodies without any competence for autonomous decisions as well as peak federations functioning as separate and distinct decision units.

With regard to the general problem of coordination all peak federations functioning as advisory bodies or distinct units have to deal with long chains of actions and a highly organized decision process. The specific and to some extent differing or even competing interests of the member federations must be harmonized with the requirements of an effective impact on the political system which necessitates both, the realization of the members' interests and the cooperation with the government agencies. In this process, the top echelons have to take into consideration the interests of their "co-operative members" insofar as these – just as individual members – are provided with the strategic options of "voice" and "exit" as well as informations relevant to decisions, and their chances to mobilize their individual members.

A solution of these problems of complexity can be seen in the internal fragmentation of decision and, along with this, in the differentiation of levels of decision. Comparatively autonomous strategies and specific demands can be developed on the three levels of associational aggregation, confronting the top echolons with the problem of re-integrating this highly differentiated structure. The main point of reference for the activities of peak federations is the function of transformation, which necessitates some assimilations of the peak federations according to the interests of their partners of the political system, and generates the symbiotic relationships between the state and federations characterizing the modern corporatist arrangements (see Lehmbruch 1979a; Panitch 1979).

Lehmbruch (1979b: 64–66) pointed out that a sufficient central guidance through the dicisions of peak federations is a necessary pre-condition for the modern corporatism. For example, the American peak federations of labour, i.e. the AFL/

CIO and the National Association of Manufactures suffer from the notoric problem, that they cannot oblige the several member federations to a certain behavior. In contrast, the German peak federation, the DGB, is authorized to decide autonomously and these decisions set standards for the member federations. Lehmbruch (1979b) concluded, as other authors of corporatism (see e.g. Schmitter 1979; Panitch 1979: 139–143), that a strong and autonomous top echelon organized as peak federation is both the necessary condition for the emergence of corporatist patterns and the source of its instability. The instability of the corporatist arrangements depends on the fact that unions, federations, and peak federations are ultimately based on *voluntary action* and the necessary competences of central guidance must be balanced with the members' interests. How the peculiarity of associational processes of coordination affects the functioning of the public sector can be illustrated by the example of the welfare associations in the FRG. The entire spectrum of welfare work in the FRG is the domain of six peak federations.[4] The legal status of theses charitable institutions is that of registered associations. The structural change from a "free union" to a modern large-scale federation and peak federation also applies to their historical development. The multitude of local unions were aggregated on the level of federations according to certain statutes and subject to the authority of the six peak federations (see Bauer 1978; Wegener 1978). With regard to the process of coordination we find elements of solidarity, democratic representation and central control. On the level of local unions, solidaristic elements are still important, because the honorary activities of members contribute to the various services delivered by the union. On the level of federations, processes of negotiation and information among the member unions generate the problem of compatibility which is aggravated on the peak level.

The German welfare federations attained a para-governmental status because they are privileged by the government and vested with a monopoly of representation. Therefore welfare federations correspond to some of the characteristics of corporatist arrangements which Schmitter (1979: 13) defined by a *limited number* of *singular, compulsory, non-competitive, hierarchically ordered* and politically *recognized* associations (see also Heinze and Olk 1981). As a study of the reform of the institutions of elementary education (i.e. the "Kindergartenreform") showed (see Domscheit and Kühn 1984), departments of the public administration and the welfare federations generated symbiotic relationships on the basis of mutual dependence.

As the departments of educational matters planned the integration of the elementary education into the school boards, the domains of both, the bureaucrats of the social welfare departments and the welfare federations were threatened, so that they concentrate their efforts in order to reform "their" kindergarten by themselves. In this case the peak federations were able to realize the intended structural reform even on the level of service delivery, because they had the necessary resources of reorganization at their disposal (see Domscheit and Kühn 1984: 74–79).

Finally we can say that associational coordination fits neither the model of self-coordination nor hierarchy but represents an ongoing process of balancing the two organizational environments constituted by the members (individuals, legal persons) and the government agencies. In the following we shall have to analyze the way in which associational and government actions in the public sector are coordinated.

26.5 Co-Ordination of Interorganizational Relations Between Government and Associations

As explained above, the relationship between government, administrative, and associational agencies is characterized by a factual interplay of public and private decisions and symbiotic forms of collaboration. As the associations become an integral part of the political system by providing the latter with information relevant to decision-making, legitimation and a sharing of burdens, by providing autonomously services in the public sector, they gain continual, partly privileged and comprehensive political influence in relation to the governmental agencies. Scholars of 'neo-corporatism' denote this process as an "intimate mutual penetration of state bureaucracies and large interest organizations" (Lehmbruch 1979a: 150) which determines the processes of policy formation and implementation. In this section we will consider how this mutual penetration is patterned with regard to the problem of coordination. Federations and administrative agencies become subject to a mutual quest for cooperation which lead to specific constraints of their actions. The formal authority of governmental agencies to alter the relationship with the associations unilaterally through legal regulations and constraints, is restricted in fact, on the one hand by its dependence on information and, on the other, by its interest in support by or a reduction of governmental tasks through the to some extent para-governmental activities of the federations. Thus, an interrelationship exists between governmental agencies and associations, in which formally independent organizations are dependent on each other and need to co-ordinate their activities in the area of public performance.

Again the policy of public welfare work in the FRG represents a good example. Administrative agencies are involved in stable relationships with the compulsory six peak federations, so that they have to deal with a quite transparent environment of relevant actors sharing the burden of public responsibilities. But any decision of government is constraint by the federations' mandate of an autonomous provision of services (see Bauer 1978; Domscheit and Kühn 1984). The peak federations on the other hand are highly dependent on public funding in order to maintain their domains. The mutual dependence necessitates "consensus building" as the dominant and necessary mode of coordination. In the following, we shall analyze the co-ordination within the interrelationship between the government and the associations by way of sociological approaches of interorganizational analysis, as this perspective is adequate for this specific level of "organized actions". A general starting point for the many diverse interorganizational approaches[5] is the fact that organizations co-operate voluntarily on the basis of certain mutual interdependences which are not necessarily symmetric. As these relations are not determined by an overall authority, they are characterized by conflicts of interest and contingent outcomes of these conflicts (see Litwak and Hylton 1961).

On the analytical level of the individual organization, government and associational agencies are to be regarded as "resource getting systems" (Yuchtman and Seashore 1967: 892) which interact with their environment. According to Thompson (1967: 24), these interactive relations can be characterized by

(1) constraints which the organization must face
(2) contingencies which the organization must meet, and
(3) variables which the organization can control.

As pointed out in Chapter 23, *uncertainty* in relation to environmental changes and *dependency* on resources which are at the disposal of the other organizations constituting the environment, are thus considered to be the crucial problems of any organization. Because of the uncertainty regarding its dependence on governmental decisions the modern federation seeks to reduce this risk by means of stable interorganizational relations based on the principle of an exchange. In a similar way, governmental agencies seek to influence their informational problems and dependence on the services provided by the associations.

As the stable and established interactions between administrative bodies and federation show, the stability of these interorganizational relations means that the network of manifold interrelationships develops emergent characteristics in the form of codes for decision-making and procedure which have to be analyzed in terms of the concept of an *'interorganizational network'*. The analytical focus has thus shifted from individual organizations to the structure of the relationships between them. With reference to Turk (1970) one can define a network in terms of those structural features which do not relate to the characteristics of the network components, but emerge from the internal network processes, i.e. the joint decision making and negotiations among the organizations involved.

The framework of a sociological analysis of interorganizational relations developed in Chapter 23 is also applicable to the network formed by government and associations. The power of being authorized to make binding decisions in the public sector, as well as the material resources for the provision of services, determine the relationship of administrative and associational organizations. The internal structure of the network is dependent on the different bargaining powers of the organizations so that the interorganizational relationships do not remain in a state of equilibrium, but are the subject of comprehensive strategies. Generally one can distinguish four types of interorganizational strategies operating sequentially, in a combined form or as a mere threat. The four strategic options are cooperation, manipulation, disruption and authoritative efforts.

In principle, the general uncertainty as to which strategy will be used is found in the networks constituted by governmental and associational organizations as well as in the administrative networks analyzed above (see Ch. 23). The fact that the negotiations are not a "unique" event or constantly being re-staged, but form part of durable interactions, offers the possibility of reducing this factor of uncertainty through forms of an "ideological consensus" on the definition and solution of problems, of a consensus on the domains of the organizations involved, and of a mutual and positive co-ordination of experience and tasks. The formalization of decision-making processes as, for example, in committees and advisory bodies (Beiräte) and the emergence of commonly shared orientations among the respective representatives also contribute to the stability of the network.

The structural stability of the administrative-associational network does not imply, however, that predictable outcomes can be expected. Since such a network is highly dependent on the processes of consensus formation initiated by the negotiating parties, a differentiation of numerous specialized systems of negotiation is necessary in order to arrive at objectives which are transparent and capable of consensus, by way of a selective fragmentation of problems.

This implies, though, that the co-ordination between the government and the associations, since it is the result of a larger number of structured networks of negotiations, does not enable a uniform and central guidance free from contradiction, but is in fact a complex system of minimally interrelated, interorganizational networks which are characterized by those very emergent network structures which defy a central and direct guidance on the part of governmental as well as associational agencies. We have already stated that the individual organizations respond to each increase in environmental complexity with an internal structural differentiation by trying to optimize restrictions, uncertainties and possibilities of control (see Thompson 1967: 70).

With respect to governmental and associational organizations, this means that, in view of the high degree of internal differentiation, the top echelons are now able to co-ordinate their operations on the aggregate level only by determining premises of decision-making, e.g. budgetary distribution or rules of procedure, while the majority of actual services in terms of information and decision-making is directly provided by the administrators and specialized representatives of the association (Scharpf 1973: 79–83; Luhmann 1968). To the extent that the relations between government and associational organizations develop from being occasional contacts into being lasting and structured relations with the environment, these relations adopt the emergent quality of interorganizational networks.

The characteristic of co-ordination in an interorganizational network is that the common interests of the various organizations have to be reconciled with the individual interests of these organizations by way of a co-ordination of negotiating parties which also have their own interests (see Franz 1982: 137). The fact that organizations cannot act directly like an individual actor, but require the action of a representative for the mediation and effective realization of their interests, generates the specific problems of interorganizational co-ordination. It is the representative of organizations, the so called boundary-spanning person who effect co-ordination between organizations. "The interrole relationships between the boundary role persons of two or more organizations are ... the vital linkages and binding forces between the organizations" (Adams 1980: 331). As research on the sociology of organizations regarding the problematics of the boundary role has shown (see Katz and Kahn 1966; Adams 1976), that such persons find themselves in the dilemma, on the one hand, of being instructed to carry out specific strategies in order to attain "power" and "money", the vital resources in a network, and, on the other hand, of being part of a negotiation which has a strategic and dynamic character of its own and may involve certain deviations from the instructions.

The dynamic force inherent in situations of interorganizational negotiations is due to the double contingency, characterizing every interaction, which Parsons (1968: 436) has formulated thus: "The actor is knower and object of cognition, utilizer of instrumental means and mean, emotionally attached to others and an object of attachment, evaluator and object of evaluation..." The representatives of an interorganizational network are faced with the specific problem of having to act on the level of organized action and being thus exposed to both the influence of their immediate counterparts in the negotiations and that of their own organization (see Adams 1980: 330). Accordingly, the co-ordination within an interorganizational network is also characterized by a doubly contingent interrelationship of organized actions since the interests of the organizations involved may vary in respect of themselves, and the actions of the representatives may vary vis-à-vis their organizations (Rosewitz and Wolf 1981: 81; Franz 1982: 125).

The question as to which strategies are employed by an organization within a network to attain specific goals, whether cooperative, disruptive, manipulative or authoritative (see Ch. 23), can thus not be answered only on the basis of structural factors, e.g. a varying dependence on the processes of interchange within a network. Rather, it is the dynamic force inherent in processes of interorganizational negotiations which decides on the outcomes; and a co-ordination effected by the "organized actors", such as governmental and associational agencies, is characterized by precisely this strategic uncertainty.

This *strategic uncertainty* found in an interorganizational network, however, does not entirely fit the notion of complete incalculability regarding the strategies of the other side(s) and the effectiveness of an organization's own tactics as some game theoretical models suggest, since the well-established negotiations, sometimes formalized through advisory bodies and committees, lead to a certain calculability of the negotiating situation.[6] The recurrence of negotiations in the interorganizational network of government and associations can be dealt with analytically by referring to the negotiation model of Walton and McKersie (1965). Walton and McKersie distinguish four types of processes which can be usefully applied to interorganizational processes.

(1) Distributive bargaining for an effective realization of interests.
(2) Integrative bargaining for an indentification of common interests.
(3) Attitudinal structuring to influence the atmosphere of negotiations.
(4) Intraorganizational bargaining for the harmonization of the results of negotiations and the interests of the organizations represented.

The contingencies of the four subprocesses of interorganizational coordination pose the problem of reconciling intra- and interorganizational demands within the action arena of the negotiating representatives. Since neither the instructions of the represented organizations nor the self-interests of the representatives solely determine the negotiation common orientations become relevant. The recurrent experiences of being both "actor" and "target of action" reinforce solidary elements. The actors share the burden of highly contingent negotiations by role-taking and common orientation. The coordination between government and federations, thus, depend on the interactive processes among representatives, who have to reinforce solidary elements of interpersonal "sympathy", "trust" and "understanding" in order to cope with the contingencies of the negotiation (see Kaufmann 1984).

We can thus conclude that the co-ordination within a network made up of governmental and associational agencies is dependent on the negotiating parties reaching decisions which both demand of their organizations only those concessions which are inevitable and do not endanger the negotiating situation as a whole. The high degree of contingency which occurs in this situation, prevents the development of a comprehensive network of government and associations. *Government and federations thus do not form a unified "system" which would approach the vision of a "megastate".* Since processes of negotiation are highly dependent on processes of consensus formation, both on account of mutually dependent relationships between the organizations and the pecularities of the negotiation process within a network, a differentiation is required of specialized, limited, and largely decentralized systems.

Notes

1 Despite the actual interplay of public and private actions, the structural difference remains important, namely that, contrary to the case of associations, public decisions become collectively binding decisions on the basis of their constitutionally guaranteed and monopolized right to use obligation in the case of conflict (see Parsons 1969; Luhmann 1970: 158; Weber 1976: 15).
2 Kaufmann (Ch. 10) pointed out that the key problem of the modern public sector is the coordination of its long chains of action. As these chains of action increasingly consist of the formally independent actions of federations, guidance, control and evaluation are no longer the internal problems of state bureaucracy but of interorganizational relationships.
3 We cannot discuss here how an intra-associational democracy can be secured, e.g. by insitutionalized protest (Hirchman 1970).
4 The six German welfare federations are organizations for social relief actions which were established by the Catholic Church, the Protestant Church, the Red Cross, the labour movement, the association of German Jews and the association of ideologically independent organizations (see Lampert 1980; Bauer 1978).
5 For the variety of interorganizational approaches, see Negandhi 1975; Evans 1978. Here we discuss sociological approaches to the analysis of interorganizational relations; contributions from economics, e.g. oligopoly theory, would go beyond the limits of this chapter.
6 The game theoretical model of the "Prisoners' Dilemma", for example, has been applied to problems of policy coordination (see Metcalfe 1978; Scharpf 1978), but without sufficient consideration of the factors of "time" and "experience". For a critique of the very abstract premises of the PDG-model, see Buckley et al. 1974.

References

Adams, J. St. (1976): "The Structure and Dynamics of Behavior in Organizational Boundary Roles." In Dunnett, M. D. (ed.), *Handbook of Industrial and Organizational Psychology*, 1175–1199. Chicago: Rand McNally College Publ.
Adams, J. St. (1980): "Interorganizational Processes and Organizational Boundary Activities." In Staw, B. M. (ed.), *Research in Organizational Behavior,* 321–355. Greenwich, Conn.: Jai Press.
Almond, G. A., and G. B. Powell (1966): *Comparative Politics.* Boston: Little, Brown and Co.
Babchuk, N., and C. K. Warringer (1965): "Four Types of Voluntary Associations", *Sociological Inquiry* 35/2: 138–148.

Barber, B. (1950): "Participation and Mass Apathy in Associations." In Gouldner, A. W. (ed.), *Studies in Leadership*, 477–504. New York: Harper and Brothers.

Bauer, R. (1978): *Wohlfahrtsverbände in der Bundesrepublik Deutschland*. Weinheim: Beltz.

Bethusy-Huc, V. Gräfin von (1976): "Vorschläge zur Kontrolle des Verbandseinflusses im Parlamentarischen Regierungssystem." In Dettling, W. (ed.), *Macht der Verbände – Ohnmacht der Demorkatie?*, 231–236. München: Olzog.

Beyme, K. von (1974): *Interessengruppen in der Demokratie* (4. Aufl.). München: Piper.

Beyme, K. von (1979): *Das politische System der Bundesrepublik Deutschland*. München: Piper.

Böckenförde, E.-W. (1976a): "Lorenz von Stein als Theoretiker der Bewegung von Staat und Gesellschaft zum Sozialstaat." In Böckenförde, E.-W., *Staat, Gesellschaft, Freiheit*, 146–184. Frankfurt/M.: Suhrkamp.

Böckenförde, E.-W. (1976b): "Die Bedeutung der Unterscheidung von Staat und Gesellschaft im demokratischen Sozialstaat der Gegenwart." In Böckenförde, E.-W., *Staat und Gesellschaft*, 395–431. Darmstadt: Wissenschaftliche Buchgemeinschaft.

Buckley, W., T. Burns and L. D. Mecker (1974): "Structural Resolutions of Collective Action Problems." *Behavioral Science* 19/3: 277–298.

Coyle, G. (1930): *Social Process in Organized Groups*. New York: Richard Smith.

Domscheit, S., and M. Kühn (1984): *Die Kindergartenreform: Fallstudie bundesdeutscher Sozialpolitik*. Frankfurt/M. – New York: Campus.

Donaldson, L., and M. Warner (1974): "Structure of Organizations in Occupational Interest Associations." *Human Relations* 27/8: 721–738.

Durkheim, E. (1933): *The Division of Labor in Society*. New York: Macmillan, (org. 1897).

Easton, D. (1965): *A System Analysis of Political Life*. New York: Wiley.

Franz, H.-J. (1982): *Steuerungsprobleme der Sozialpolitik und das Beziehungsgeflecht zwischen Staat und Verbänden*. (Diplomarbeit an der Fakultät für Soziologie der Universität Bielefeld). Bielefeld.

Geiger, T. (1928): *Die Gestalten der Gesellung*. Karlsruhe: Braun.

Heinze, R. G. (1979): *Neokorporatistische Strukturen im politischen System der Bundesrepublik?*. (Dissertationsschrift). Bielefeld.

Heinze, R. G., and T. Olk (1981): "Die Wohlfahrtsverbände im System sozialer Dienstleistungen." *Kölner Zeitschrift für Soziologie und Sozialpsychologie* (KZfSS) 33/1: 94–115.

Herder-Dorneich, P. (1972): *Wirtschaftssysteme*. Opladen: Westdeutscher Verlag.

Hirschman, A. O. (1970): *Exit, Voice, and Loyalty: Response to the Decline of Firms, Organizations, and States*. Cambridge, Mass.: Harvard Univ. Press.

Hondrich, K. O. (1963): *Die Ideologie von Interessenverbänden*. Berlin: Duncker und Humblot.

Kaiser, J. H. (1956): *Die Repräsentation organisierter Interessen*. Berlin: Duncker und Humblot.

Kariel, H. S. (1968): "Pluralism." In Sills, D. (ed.), *International Encyclopedia of the Social Sciences*. Vol. 12, 164–168. New York: Macmillan and Free Press.

Kaufmann, F. X. (1977): "Sozialpolitisches Erkenntnisinteresse und Soziologie." In von Ferber, Ch., and F. X. Kaufmann (eds.), *Soziologie und Sozialpolitik* (Sonderheft 19 der Kölner Zeitschrift für Soziologie und Sozialpsychologie), 35–76. Opladen: Westdeutscher Verlag.

Kaufmann, F. X., and P. Schäfer (eds.) (1979): *Bürgernahe Sozialpolitik*. Frankfurt/M.: Campus.

Kaufmann, F. X. (1984): "Solidarität als Steuerungsform – Erklärungsansätze bei Adam Smith." In Kaufmann, F. X., and H. G. Krüsselberg (eds.), *Markt, Staat und Solidarität bei Adam Smith*, 158–185. Frankfurt–New York: Campus.

Kirberger, W. (1978): *Staatsentlastung durch private Verbände*. Baden-Baden: Nomos.

Kramer, R. M. (1973): "The Future of the Voluntary Service Organization." *Social Work* 18/6: 59–69.

Kramer, R. M. (1979): "Public Fiscal Policy and Voluntary Agencies in the Welfare States." *Social Service Review* 53/1: 1–15.

Kramer, R. M. (1981): *Voluntary Agencies in the Welfare State*. Berkeley. Cal.: Univ. of California Press.

Lampert, H. (1980): *Sozialpolitik*. Berlin: Springer.

Lehmbruch, G. (1979a): "Liberal Corporatism and Party Government." In Schmitter, P. C., and G. Lehmbruch (eds.), *Trends Towards Corporatist Intermediation*, 147–185. London: Sage.

Lehmbruch, G. (1979b): "Wandlungen der Interessenpolitik im liberalen Korporatismus." In Alemann, U. v. and R. G. Heinze (eds.), *Verbände und Staat*, 50–71. Opladen: Westdeutscher Verlag.

Lippold, K. W. (1974): *Ansatzpunkte zur systemtheoretischen Betrachtung des Verbandes. Ein Beitrag zur Verbandstheorie*. Berlin: Duncker und Humblot.

Litwak, E., and L. F. Hylton (1961): "Interorganizational Analysis: A Hypothesis on Coordinating Agencies." *Administrative Science Quarterly 6* (June): 395–418.

Luhmann, N. (1964): *Funktion und Folgen formaler Organisation*. Berlin: Duncker und Humblot.

Luhmann, N. (1968): *Zweckbegriff und Systemrationalität*. Tübingen: Mohr (Paul Siebeck).

Luhmann, N. (1970): "Soziologie des politischen Systems." In Luhmann, N., *Soziologische Aufklärung I*, 154–177. Opladen: Westdeutscher Verlag.

Luhmann, N. (1975): "Allgemeine Theorie organisierter Sozialsysteme." In Luhmann, N., *Soziologische Aufklärung II*, 39–51. Opladen: Westdeutscher Verlag.

Mayntz, R. (1963): *Soziologie der Organisation*. Reinbek b. Hamburg: Rowohlt.

Metcalfe, L. (1978): "Policy Making in Turbulent Environments." In Hanf, K., and F. W. Scharpf (eds.), *Interorganizational Policy Making*, 37–56. London: Sage.

Narr, W.-D., and F. Naschold (1971): *Theorie der Demokratie Band III*. Stuttgart: Kohlhammer.

Neysen, W. (1968): *Die Beteiligung von Interessenverbänden an der Gesetzesvorbereitung durch die Bundesregierung*. Bochum. (Dissertationsschrift).

Offe, C. (1981): "The Attribution of Public Status to Interest Groups: Observations on the West German Case." In Berger, S. (ed.), *Organizing Interests in Western Europe: Pluralism, Corporatism, and the Transformation of Politics*, 123–158. Cambridge: Cambridge Univ. Press.

Olson, M. (1965): *The Logic of Collective Action*. Cambridge: Cambridge Univ. Press.

Panitch, L. (1979): "Development of Corporatism in Liberal Democracies." In Schmitter, P. C., and G. Lehmbruch (eds.), *Trends Towards Corporatist Intermediation*, 111–147. London: Sage.

Parsons, T. (1968): "Interaction: Social Interaction (Art)." In Sills, D. L. (ed.), *International Encyclopedia of the Social Sciences*, 429–440. New York: Macmillian, Free Press.

Parsons, T. (1969): "The Concept of Society: The Components and Their Interactions." In Parsons, T., *Politics and Social Structure*, 5–33. New York: Free Press.

Rosewitz, B., and H. Wolf (1981): *Struktur und Funktion von Verbänden – eine systemtheoretische Perspektive*. (Diplomarbeit an der Fak. f. Soziologie d. Univ. Bielefeld). Bielefeld.

Scharpf, F. W. (1973): "Komplexität als Schranke der politischen Planung." In Scharpf, W., *Planung als politischer Prozeß*, 73–113. Frankfurt/M.: Suhrkamp.

Scharpf, F. W. et al. (1978): "Policy Effectiveness and Conflict Avoidance in Intergovernmental Policy Formation." In Hanf, H., and F. W. Scharpf (eds.), *Interorganizational Policy Making*, 57–115. London: Sage.

Schmitter, P. C. (1979): "Still the Century of Corporatism?" In Schmitter, P. C., and G. Lehmbruch (eds.), *Trends Towards Corporatist Intermediation*, 7–53. London: Sage.

Sills, D. L. (1968): "Voluntary Associations: Sociological Aspects." (Art.) In Sills, D. L. (ed.), *International Encyclopedia of the Social Sciences*. Vol. 16, 362–379. New York: Macmillan and Free Press.

Tenbruck, F. (1981): "Emile Durkheim oder die Geburt der Gesellschaft aus dem Geist der Soziologie." *Zeitschrift für Soziologie* 10/4: 333–350.

Teubner, G. (1979): "Neo-korporatistische Strategien rechtlicher Organisationssteuerung: Staatliche Strukturvorgaben für die gesellschaftliche Verarbeitung politischer Konflikte." *Zeitschrift für Parlamentsfragen* 10/4: 487–502.

Thompson, J. D. (1967): *Organizations in Action*. New York: McGraw Hill.

Tocqueville, A. de (1948): *Democracy in America* (2 Vols.). Bradley, P. (ed.). New York: A. A. Knopf.

Turk, H. (1970): "Interorganizational Networks in Urban Society: Initial Perspectives and Comparative Research." *American Sociological Review* 35/1: 1–18.

Turkel, G. (1982): "Situated Corporatist Legitimacy: The 1980 Chrysler Loan Guarantee." In Spitzer, S., and R. J. Simon (eds.), *Research in Law, Deviance and Social Control: A Research Annual*. Vol. 4, 165–191. Grennwich, Conn.: Jai Press.

Walton, R. E., and R. B. McKersie (1965): *A Behavioral Theory of Labor Negotiations*. New York: McGraw Hill.

Weber, J. (1977): *Die Interessengruppen im politischen System der Bundesrepublik Deutschland*. Stuttgart: Kohlhammer.

Weber, M. (1966): *Max Weber on Law in Economy and Society*. Rheinstein, M. (ed.), Cambridge, Mass.: Harvard Univ. Press.

Weber, M. (1976): *Wirtschaft und Gesellschaft* (5th ed.). Tübingen: Mohr (Paul Siebeck).

Wegener, R. (1978): *Staat und Verbände im Sachbereich der Wohlfahrtspflege*. Berlin: Duncker und Humblot.

Wiesenthal, H. (1981): *Die Konzertierte Aktion im Gesundheitswesen: Ein Beispiel für Theorie und Politik des modernen Korporatismus*. Frankfurt/M.: Campus.

Yuchtman, E., and S. E. Seashore (1967): "A System Resource Approach to Organizational Effectiveness." *American Sociological Review*. Vol. 32.2/6: 891–903.

27. Planning and Organizational Intelligence

Jürgen Reese

Abstract

In revising the older concepts of political planning, it will shown that in spite of many sophisticated methods there remain two main problems of societal decision making: the coordination of many divergent interests and the detection and consideration of risky developments. Therefore, the organization centered planning concept is reformulated in favor of a task-oriented concept of organizational intelligence. It is argued that a decentralized knowledge production in the private and the semipublic sector is indispensible for a successful "authoritive allocation of values" by the government. Governments do not necessarily have to produce the information needed by themselves and even decision-making should be done in a more consensual way by collaboration of the actors and groups mainly interested and affected. But the governments have to play an active part organizing these processes according to the changing societal tasks. Thus, a more modest function of politics in conjunction with a skillful activity in organizing consensus – building processes seems to be a more promising concept for the future.

27.1 Introduction

Traditional social and educational structures proved to be inadequate in many industrialized countries during the sixties. As these facilities belong to the public infrastructure a prospective planning which would also cope with future political demands was requested by many people. In the midst of the seventies – after poor results of the whole planning movement – this vocal request for long range political planning diminished. Was it resignation or did it follow from the change of priority of political tasks?

The following arguments are based on the thesis that political tasks have not diminished but rather grown and that the resignation of the planning movement can be explained as an overestimation of centralized planning organization. Therefore we will have to revise the prevailing concept of planning in favour of an organization of societal action which is more related to specific situations, problems, and cases.

Such a claim might appear overstated and unrealistic against the background of the phenomena of bureaucratization as analyzed by Grunow (Chapter 2). In fact, not only the type of hierarchical coordination which has spread over more and more societal tasks but also the inflexibility and immobility of bureaucracies, both public and private has increased the scepticism about this kind of coordination.

On the other hand organizational reality cannot accurately be described in terms of either market or bureaucracy. There is a growing "gray zone" of organized coordination which is neither public nor private, neither bureaucratic nor market, neither official nor voluntary. It comprises all these factors. In Chapter 6 Kaufmann focuses on this "gray zone" when he speaks about the public/private mix. For instance, the discussion about quasi governmental organizations (Quagos) as well as about quasi non-governmental organizations (Quangos) has pointed out this issue for about 15 years (Levitt 1973). In addition, there is an increasing competition and collaboration among organizations within the public sector, as analyzed by Franz (Ch. 23) above, and between state organizations on the one hand and Quagos and private organizations on the other (see Sabatier: Ch. 15, Franz et al.: Ch. 26).

It seems evident that this jungle of interconnected organizations is a challenge to social scientists. E. Ostrom (Ch. 22) shows the possibilites of a more descriptive analysis, adapted to the "polluted" organizational landscape, and Majone (Ch. 21), Schleicher (Ch. 25) and Shubik (Ch. 28) elucidate forms of coordination beyond the monolithic bureaucratic structure without simply reverting to the market. All these approaches can be interpreted as attempts to improve public policy making and emphasize the questions we have to ask: are government organizations able and willing to learn from such concepts? Can we hope that the traditional planning concept of bounded rationality can be supplanted by a concept of situational design and implementation of different institutional arrangements? (see Williamson 1975).

These questions will be elaborated in the following. But this will not be done in general. Instead we will concentrate on the traditional concept of planning which is much less successful than it was supposed to be. We will subject it to a dimensional analysis, using the criteria of coordination and time. In this way we develop the thesis that a concept of actively designing intra- and interorganizational coordination is the most appropriate one. *We call it the concept of organizational intelligence.*

27.2 The Planning Movement Reconsidered

Deficient prognosis of future market developments can lead to the bankruptcy of a business firm, especially in cases of great capital investments. In general there exists an additional rule which says that the flexibility or adaptability of organizations declines with their growing size. Both factors – capital risk as well as organizational inflexibility – compel large enterprise to long term prognosis and to strategic planning. Political decisions often tie up much more capital than business decisions, and compared to business administration the organization of public administration is rather less flexible. This economical and organizational irreversibility is further strengthened by the binding effects of laws and administrative rules. Due to these characteristics the planning of public activities is evidently more important than it is for private firms. An optimization of scare resources and political effects requires a far reaching prognosis of problems and public tasks as well as a comparison of different means for dealing with them.

But this brief outline of the planning problem shows the conceptual confusion of the planning discussion within the last twenty years. Political planning was, and is, often conceived of in contrast to market relations. Such a concept of planning corresponds to the antagonism between public and private management of societal problems (see Kaufmann: Ch. 6). But there is also a completely different conception of planning which aims at the coordination of different activities and the estimation of their long term effectiveness. Our position here is close to the second concept. When government and public administration act, they shall do so in a rational and coordinated way, taking into consideration secondary effects and (future) advantages and disadvantages as well as possible.

Particular problems impede this planning task within the public sector:
(a) The goals and criteria for success of governmental action are often vague and controversial.
(b) Government programs often disturb latent social functions, with the consequence that unforeseen impacts call for additional programs.
(c) Public programs call for a hard and time-consuming coordination of different autonomous actors. Because political power is shared.
(d) The competition among different political parties directs the politicians interests to the next election. Thus, they are more interested in prompt results than in political risks and chances in the far future.

These four limits of reasonable planning can be mitigated to some degree by changing government organizations, but they will never disappear (see Etzioni 1968; Merton 1957; Scharpf 1973; Schumpeter 1942).

The capability of using organizational and informational resources in order to achieve more rational planning shall be called *organizational intelligence*. This term is broader as it not only covers the meaning of planning, but also includes the role of government in the establishment of public/private mixed cooperation. There is quite a lot of evidence that a mitigation of the limits of reasonable planning depends on the *effective use of mixed forms*.

The concept of organizational intelligence is wider than that of organizational learning as developed, for instance, by Sabatier (1983). Organizational learning means adaptability to a changing environment or changing perceptions or goals. It is centered on the structure of the "learning organization", and it does not focus on the boundary between the organization and its environment. In contrast, organizational intelligence is centered on tasks which are mainly articulated and defined by various groups or organizations in the society as demands for (central) decision-making.

All organizations and individuals in a society are subject to the structuring impetus of organizational intelligence. At an extreme point the organizational intelligence may come to the conclusion that the best "organization" of a well-defined public task is just non-organization as, for instance, the growth of self-help. But even this extremely decentralized procedure would have to be confirmed as a convenient solution for a societal task.

During the last twenty years planning theory has criticized a deficient organizational intelligence particularly in long range planning in fields like education, traffic and health services (see Kaiser 1965; Jantsch 1969; Dror 1968). An overestimation of consensus building capacities within democratic political systems as well as a belief in technocratic solutions of knowledge and coordination problems led to an incredible trend of planning staffs, planning divisions or even whole planning ministries. Many theorists and practitioners connected normative claims with these organizational reforms, but most of them were disappointed (for instance PPBS). Where planners only strived to assemble information, as for example in indicative planning (e.g. the planification française) large scientific and administrative organizations grew, but their utility remained controversial.

In terms of the theoretical development the disillusion has led to different consequences according to the identified causes of the deficiencies. Rational planners have made their choice among many different ways, for instance: policy analysis (Sharkanski 1970), implementation analysis (Pressmann and Wildavsky 1973), or marxist analysis of the capitalistic state (Miliband 1969).

All these "lessons" stem from one single paradigm of rationalistic planning, which presupposes an extensive political potential for goal oriented societal change by using means-ends-chains and centralized administrative structures.

The rationalistic paradigm tends to reduce planning problems to information and implementation lags. Whether the lags seem to be manageable or not depends, then, only on the readiness to more or lesser expenditures for information production and implementation structures. Ideas like technology assessment, social indicators, and advocacy planning point in this direction. Partial success of these movements cannot be denied and it would be foolish to dispense completely with them simply because they root in technocratic thinking. In face of both the failure of strategic planning and the remaining need for more adequate policies we should ask whether the whole potential of organizational intelligence has already been exhausted with the model of centralized planning functions.

This question has some tradition in the recent political science, too. One should remember the discussion between Charles Lindblom and Yehezkel Dror (1964) on incrementalism or the contest between pluralism and the theory of democratic elites (see Scharpf 1970). With regard to the empirical essence of such theories there is undoubtedly more evidence for the assumption of many competing decision centers as it is conceived more or less in all previous chapters of this book. This might explain the delay and faint-heartedness of so many decisions as well as the failure of centralized planning concepts. The failure results from disharmony between a centralized planning organization and a decentralized political power structure. Accordingly a more successful organizational intelligence should be interested in higher correspondence between the two structures. And organizational intelligence itself should be conceptualized as a moderating function of the government with the intention of coordinating the right people with the right agenda at the right time.

What does it mean: the right people, the right agenda, the right time? Obviously it is not easy, perhaps not even possible to give a general answer to these questions. We will turn back to them after some explanatory work about the essential planning problems of early problem identification, or definition, and of successfull management of the recognized problems today.

27.3 Problem Sensibility in Developed Democracies Today

In the following we will differentiate between problem pressure, problem identification or problem analysis, and political pressure. *Problem pressure* is a very subjective category and emerges in many different contexts. For instance, it can be the result of a substantial need as well as of the insight into a causal connection between, say, feeding habits or air pollution on the one hand and illness on the other. Sometimes it emerges in an organized group, sometimes in a greater number of individuals in similar life situations, and sometimes it is the result of a new recognition or explanation by a scientist when he discovers a link between needs and collective behaviour.

If the definition of decision making requirements is solely concerned with problem pressure, the option of a creative policy with far reaching perspectives will be lost. Politics would then be conceived of only as a reaction to emergencies. Such a concept does not fit into the societal framework of affluent societies. Therefore, we extend our concept of "problem pressure" to include regret stemming from missed choices about alternative futures. The ideological commitment of intellectual groups can be ascribed to that as well as the demand for high technology which underlay the space race between the USA and the USSR. The expectation of many people in Great Britain of a reconquest of the Falklands it also a kind of problem pressure which has nothing to do with substantive needs. In all such cases the problem pressure results from demands which rest a large part on ideologies.

The crucial incentive for political action as well as for political planning within the government agencies is very often an external demand. But ideologically oriented thinking and acting happens also within public administration. Perhaps we had better say that the goal setting function cannot be witheld from the administration. The administration itself makes policies and formulates political demands far beyond its vital interest in wages, organization structure, careers, and so on. For instance, it can enforce demands of persons or groups from the political system's environment, it can suppress weak signals or diminish them. Using David Easton's (1965) framework one should keep an eye on the throughput function of a political system when discussing the problem sensibility in a society. Research on "representative bureaucracy" and on the administrative "culture" elucidates that there are more relevant political factors within the administrative or planning organization (see Maier and Nigro 1975; Putnam 1976).

These political factors become increasingly important the more the administration establishes explicit look out functions, for instance, in the form of "heuristic staffs". Such staffs should look for hidden problems which have not yet been articulated by interest groups or others. Their task is a kind of early warning function, by which negative impacts of today's policies as well as inconsistencies in different political programs can be detected. Nowadays such problem detection seems to be indispensable particularly in the field of technological change, and the Congress Office of Technology Assessment with its work about impact forecasting is an exact institutionalization of that function (see Kasper 1972; Medford 1973).

To summarize, first, we differentiate two kinds of problems which can be identified without special institutional arrangements simply because of their inherent problem potential:

– objective risks like environment pollution, unemployment and so on;
– subjetive, but collective problem or goal identifications.

Second, we assume the existence of problems which are not collectively articulated as an element of political pressure (e.g. many social problems). Nevertheless, under changing conditions they might become disruptive. Therefore, a complex society needs institutional arrangements for the identification of such problems. Below, we shall look more closely at this function of problem identification.

All efforts to increase society's problem sensibility with artificial administrative organizations lead sometimes to political conflicts, and very many *problem identifications* of early warning groups have been ignored or rejected by politicians in the past. The jobs in such groups are certainly not the most favored ones which in turn means that they often recruit outsiders. What is the reason for all this? As we will see there is more than one reason for the difficulties, some of them being quite manageable others posing hard challenges to responsible politicians and administrators.

In the following we shall examine three important functions of future-oriented politics which can be added to the look-out function. They belong to a more technical or methodological level of successful policy-making. The basic question, here, is, how can we design an optimal policy *after* having recognized the problem? From the government administration's point of view this question encourages examining a) the knowledge of future developments and causal relationships (predictability), b) the range of common evaluations of means and goals (evaluation) and c) the costs of knowledge production in these fields (information economy).

(a) *Predictability*. Planning as a future oriented activity necessitates reliable information about the future development of the political system's environment (status quo prognosis) as well as about the consequences of political actions. A reliable prognosis enables politicians to reformulate their policies so that cumulative negative impacts can be avoided. The basic idea of this strategy is the conviction that the costs of compensatory trouble shooting can be minimized by using the most appropriate concept at a very early stage of political action. In his analysis of the development of a very complex technology Robert F. Coulam (1975) called it "the importance of the beginning".

It is important, for instance, to have an exact estimation of future needs for hospital beds before hospitals are planned, or to establish a legal structure for the private economy which prevents dangerous or unpleasant externalities such as environmental pollution. After high investments in technical infrastructure of industrial plants, institutional changes are extremely expensive and are opposed to well-articulated and strong interests. Thus, time or chronological order itself is an important factor. Very early action implies a much broader range of alternatives than late action, and anticipatory action offers better payoffs than simple reactions. But whether or not these payoffs can be realized depends on correct information and reliable prognosis. That is the crucial point.

The planning movement in the sixties motivated the development and testing of methods for prognosis. Simple trend extrapolation was improved, analytic prognosis was invented, followed by simulations, econometric models, and delphi technique. To feed the methodological thinking with appropriate data, more and more data banks were established and statistical programs were extended. However, the success fell short of most expectations. The projection of the GNP for just one year is still very inexact, the forecast of city development is not better (see Forrester 1969), and the whole environmental policy continues to be based on more or less arbitrary assumptions (Global 2000: 1980). On the other hand, the installation of extended scanning systems on the earth and in space combined with extremely sophisticated computer programs and communication networks have improved weather forecasting significantly. Substantial progress can also be perceived in the micro-simulation of the outcomes of different welfare policies in terms of transfers (see Schmidt and Schips 1980). No doubt, prognosis in a complex world is terribly difficult, but with our methodological knowledge and technical equipment we are making progress.

(b) *Evaluation.* Since attitudes, interests, and values are an essential part of politics, projections are also subject to judgements and to political conflicts. This is true in a double sense: first, the prognosis situation can hardly be imagined by many people. How shall they compare different possible futures? How can they choose between an option with rewards for today and an option with imagined and only potential rewards for tomorrow? The lack of information about our own preferences in the future is the main obstacle to a rational choice. Second, all politics are directed to the future. But the longer the range of a prognosis is, the greater the chances of possible manipulation are possible not only by group pressure, but also by finagling of information. By so doing a demand for government action can be created or suppressed, and the choice between alternative policies can be influenced in a very secret way.

The influence on politics by manipulating prognosis is common. Groups with a higher education rate and organizations with their own analysts have a better chance at such political influence than the simple citizen. Therefore, the disproportion of political power increases with the time horizon of planning. Planners have developed methods which should help to correct this: advocacy planning, for instance, is such an approach. But whatever professional planners do in favour of more transparency and more participation, the asymmetry of political influence grows with the planning range.

Here we are very close to an explanation of distrust towards and conflicts about "look-out staffs". Well established and strongly organized interests have made up their minds about future-oriented policies and they furnish the political system and the public with information which is most advantageous to them. Every independent problem detection function within the government administration is a potential threat to their scenarios and policies. This threat can be amplified when other interests are seriously taken into account. The imperative of well established and powerful interest groups is consequently a destruction of competing information centers within the political system, especially if they gain autonomy. The strategies are manifold: reports, doubts about the experts' competence, indirect political pressure. One of the most instructive fields for studying the battles about information is the social indicator movement. (see Olson 1969; Zapf 1972).

(c) *Information Economy.* Organized information production is expensive. Thus, from the theoretical point of view the pay-off of each marginal information unit has to be estimated before a decision about the gatherging of additional information will be made. In practice there are very few useful decision rules in the information economy, and this is all the more true of political decision making. The estimation of the use of some potential information is simply impossible in the field of complex policies. Nevertheless, public administrations look for information about future developments and produce them all the time. Why do they do it and what are the underlying rules of their information habits?

There are two models of explanation. First, we assume the administrator to behave in a rational way. He tries to calculate the costs of a wrong decision (return costs) and the probability that his decision turns out to be wrong. Then he optimizes his search for information until the marginal information costs reach the marginal benefit in terms of risk reduction. Second, we assume the administrator to behave in a pragmatic way. Instead of the disadvantages of a wrong decision for the community he is only interested in his personal liability. His criterion is the objective judgement about whether or not one could have known the negative consequences of a decision. There is only one definite failure possible in his achievement. That is the correct prognosis of somebody else, another administration, an interest group, a scientific institute. Therefore, the second case of a risk-minimizing strategy implies very careful observation of the politically relevant information production in the entire society.

In his book "The Active Society" Amitai Etzioni (1968) analyzes the role of the intellectuals as a sort of a countervailing power and he insists on their function for societal change. They look for new data as well as for new interpretations (contextual framework) whereas the power elite tends to reject new contextual frameworks. There ist no doubt about this conservative bias of politics, information politics included. On the other hand in democracies the government administration has to be very sensitive to competing information production centers. Problem sensibility of government agencies does not so much depend on special long term planning staffs, look-out groups, etc., as it does on the challenge presented by competing information producers.

As a consequence we should keep in mind that at least the problem sensibility of political institutions does not necessarily correlate with the degree of centralization of the information production. On the contrary, decentralized competitive information production seems to be a better guarantee of early problem detection and rapid learning. Nevertheless, the produced information or knowledge has to be available and utilized in the decision making centers of the political system. Therefore, the best way to organize information production is a very redundant, decentralized system with large overlapping competences combined with a centralized function of information gathering within public administration.

27.4 Problem Solving in Developed Democracies Today

Suppose a problem is well defined and the need for government action is obvious and admitted by the majority. What is the action framework in terms of more or less planned behaviour? Here we have to differentiate between two scales:

– Along the coordination scale we distinguish actions with an increasing number of agencies involved. In addition, the collaboration can be limited to the public administration of one government. But it can also be extended to the administrations of different governments (federal, state or international collaboration) or even to private business (see Franz: Ch. 23)

– Along the time scale there are action courses with different ranges, for instance, short, medium, and long range planning. Problems which can be solved with little improvements, little money, and little administrative expenditure need only short range planning, whereas for very expensive solutions perhaps with a complex social, organizational, and technical infrastructure, medium or long range planning (up to 15 years) is more appropriate.

If we look at the political scene in Western democracies today we face a growing fragmentation of the formal decision making structure as well as the achievement in favour of more internationally coordinated action. The scale from very little units to very large units, both with rather limited competence, is becoming more and more extended. (For instance in West Germany, additional subregional representative bodies were installed at the same time as new coordination groups on the European level began their work.) The growing pyramid of regional decision making units shows the increasing importance of coordination as a consequence of economic and social interdependence in the world. Parallel to its vertical growth the pyramid has also widened, because additional political tasks have emerged on all levels and lead to new administrative units.

From a liberalistic standpoint this development looks threatening, since a nearly ubiquitous political system seems to constrain individual freedom more and more. But this assumption is not necessarily true. Above all the sheer inflation of the political system is just a reaction to the increasing need for coordination in a world of increasing interdependence. Private business firms behave in the same way when they grow to almost larger production and administration systems, often with an internationalization of their own. As long as the growth of social systems is accompanied by their internal fragmentation, their implementation power is constant or even diminished despite their potentially increased coordination abilities. This is one of the reasons for the call for the centralization of political decision making.

The ongoing change of the political and administrative structure can not cope with all coordination problems, especially not with those which stem from new policy areas (broadening of the pyramid). Specialization overtaxes the coordination power of hierarchies. Thus, new forms of coordination are established. There is a long list of such forms, ranging from timely limited teams and coordination conferences to new systems of fiscal coordination (e.g. PPBS, Zero-based Budgeting). The organizational intelligence seems to be well developed in this field. On the other hand empirical facts nurture the suspicion that there is little efficiency beyond the formal coordination structure. Obviously the division of labour within administration corresponds with political interests, and the re-coordination of separate goal functions or programs is always a power play, too. Here the efficiency of non-hierarchial coordination must remain limited.

At the beginning of this essay we noticed the lack of correspondence between the *planning organization and the political power structure*. Now we will return to this question. Against the background of our argument it seems understandable that so many theorists and practitioners of political planning favoured a re-hierarchization of political administrations. All planning organization of the social-liberal coalition in the Brandt area, for instance, was a lifting of coordination functions within the hierarchy with the intention of increasing the attention of political and administrative leaders to coordination needs. But as we know the partial interests proved stronger, and the ingeniously constructed coordination network broke down just after its promoters had resigned (Schatz 1978; Mayntz and Scharpf 1975). That is ten years ago now, and nobody has initiated another attempt, probably with good reason.

Whenever a strategy fails we have to look for better strategies. But we do not want to fail again. The starting point must be a careful analysis of the failure. Did we pursue the wrong goal or were circumstances disadvantageous? The latter reason can be excluded, since different political systems in the western world have made similar efforts with nearly the same outcome (for instance PPBS in the United States). Why are there such persistent obstacles to more systematic coordination?

Effective coordination presupposes early mutual information about planned programs so that in cases of interdependent policies or actions active coordination in the sense of common optimization can take place. Within the mentioned pyramid from the local level to the international level there are at any point in time thousands of programs in preparation. If only ten of them are interdependent it is nevertheless necessary to check through all potential combinations, which go into millions. Clearly, most of these combinations can be excluded a priori because they aim at completely different object areas. But the remaining number is still too large for active coordination. The rationalistic model of effective and optimal coordination is just utopian (see Scharpf 1973).

In reality, coordination works quite reasonably within the different branches of the pyramid, where the most related policies are linked under the same hierarchy. Even beyond the borders of the formal hierarchy there exist many contacts between planners with an informal coordinating effect. High personal continuity together with an individual organizational culture guarantees a medium and obviously satisfying level of coordination. Every enforcement of more systematic coordination forms results in a diminishing capacity for problem solving activities on the specialist's level.

The situation becomes aggravated according to the time scale of political action. (We should remember that a well defined problem of some minimal complexity is presupposed here, so that our attention is again directed to the problem solving strategy.) First, let us look at the dimension of this problem today:

For instance, air and water pollution have dangerous consequences for the oceans and for vegetation, especially for the woods. In central Europe almost the whole fir-pine wood and large parts of the leafy woods will die within the next ten years. The problem has been recognized, and some political answers, as well. But the decisions will possibly come too late. Even if the emissions of sulfur dioxide were dramatically reduced at once the wood is given up by many experts.

Never before have the risks of short-sighted politics been so threatening for the whole world than today, and there is a lot of evidence that the risk will further increase. The problem is all the ongoing ecological developments, many of which have already been sufficiently analyzed.

This is only an example. There are many other problems which are still in a kind of incubation period, but with analytical methods the breakdown of ecological systems can be better foreseen. When a technique with some pollution effects is already widely implemented, the decrement caused by its prohibition seems too expensive. There is an economic, sometimes even technical, irreversibility of very large technical projects like power plants or of the manifold individual use of less complex and less expensive inventious such as the automobile. Generally there is no point of no return but the way back takes about the same amount of time as was invested to get there. If we accelerate the retreat, people will compare the accruing costs to the individual damages stemming from the technique in terms of pollution. If external effects release on ecological "crash down", people will probably be willing to pay these costs. Free rider problems aggravate the problem (see Olson 1965).

As long as the electorate neglects the "way back" so will the politicians. It seems even crazy to expect them to warn and to inform the public since they will be made responsible for the expensive dead-end journey. Thus, the only reasonable chance for a solution of the problem of cumulative negative impacts seems to be an authoritative setting of action frameworks which protect the potentially affected values as early as possible. The crucial point is that externalities (negative impacts of production) must not get the status of property rights within a still wide frame of technical standards and laws.

An early structuring of action frames within potentially endangered environments presupposes prompt information of negative developments. To this extent we have reached the same point as in our discussion of problem pressure and problem identification, and arrive at the same conclusion concerning the organization of information production. But the specific kind of problem which is posed here draws our attention to an additional crucial point:

The many competing actors (firms) in a market economy try to exploit all relevant advancements, e.g. in the field of externalities, and they do it secretely to secure for themselves a better competitive position as long as possible. Information about the negative impacts of these externalities would not be given to the public even if the single "polluter" was aware of the cumulative effects of his and the others' actions. The whole problem can be focussed to the question of how the critical information can be *independently* produced. Here we have to think about established forms of official licencing in cases of technical changes as well as new forms like the privacy protection officer within the private firm. In other words: Where the growing need of an action frame has not yet been recognized, organizational intelligence can switch to a lot of different and more smooth forms of early control and information production.

27.5 A Final Remark: The Possibility of Non-Hierarchical Coordination

A look at all the technical coordination which has been done by mixed commissions of individual and government representatives shows high efficient coordination forms. A large number of problems have been managed on this level before they entered a public forum, and many of them would have grown to giant dimensions if they had not been solved at a very early stage. There are hundreds of teams even on the international level which elaborate standards for the industry. The secret of this effectiveness is the feeling of *responsibility*. All these coordinators know that it is up to them whether technical problems constrain their firm's competitiveness within the near or far future. They are interested in succesful coordination.

In contrast, hierarchical coordination depends on legal norms which have to be created before coordination becomes effective. But with the legislative bodies the whole political machinery starts working, with all its heaviness and its incalculability. The process gets out of hand, and that is possibly the main reason for the then defensive behaviour of industrial interest groups. They do not even have the responsibility for poor results since the government has put the problem on the agenda.

It seems more reasonable to leave the responsibility where power and effective self-control can be presupposed. So the free bargaining of wage contracts works well, and it seems unimaginable that the government could reach similar results in this field. For good reasons nearly all governments in Western democracies behave very reservedly on this issue. But why don't they extend the use of those coordination forms by publicly defining coordination tasks or, if it is unavoidable, by taking the role of a promoter in public/private mixed coordination teams? In rare cases a government could also threaten a legal regulation for failing self-coordination. For example, the Japanese government acts in this way on many issues. When it becomes aware of any important and possibly disruptive development, it brings together the most influential actors, under the leadership of the governmental administration. In many cases this consensus strategy has proved extremely successful. This is one example of how organizational intelligence of political planning could be further developed.

References

Coulam, R. F. (1975): "The Importance of the Beginning: Defense Doctrine and the Development of the F-111 Fighter-Bomber." *Public Policy* 23/1: 1–39.

Dror, Y. (1964): "Muddling Through – 'Science' or Inertia?" *Public Administration Review* 24/3: 153–157.

Dror, Y. (1968): *Public Policymaking Reexamined*. San Francisco: Chandler.

Easton, D. (1965): *A Framework for Political Analysis*. Englewood Cliffs, N.J.: Prentice-Hall.

Etzioni, A. (1968): *The Active Society: A Theory of Societal and Political Process*. London: Collier-McMillan; New York: Free Press.

Forrester, J. W. (1969): *Urban Dynamics*. Cambridge, Mass. and London: The M.I.T. Press, Mass. Institute of Technology.

Global 2000 (1980): *The Global 2000 Report to the President*. Council on Environmental Quality and Ministry of Foreign Affairs (ed.). Washington: U.S. Government Printing Office.

Jantsch, E. (1969): *Perspectives of Planning*. Organization for Economic Co-Operation and Development (OECD). Paris.

Kaiser, J. H. (1965): *Planung* (Vols. I–VI). Baden-Baden: Nomos (1965–1972).

Kasper, R. G. (1972): *Technology Assessment – Understanding the Social Consequences of Technological Applications*. New York–London–Washington: National Academy of Public Administration.

Levitt, Th. (1973): *The Third Sector: New Tactics for Responsive Society*. New York: Free Press.

Lindblom, C. E. (1959): "The Science of 'Muddling Through'." *Public Administration Review* 19/2: 79–88.

Mayntz, R., and F. W. Scharpf (1975): *Policy Making in the German Federal Bureaucracy*. Amsterdam: Elsevier.

Medford, D. (1973): *Environmental Harassment or Technology Assessment*. Amsterdam–London–New York: National Academy of Public Administration.

Meier, K. J., and L. G. Nigro (1975): "Representative Bureaucracy and Policy Preferences: A Study in the Attitudes of Federal Executives." Paper presented to the Annual Meeting of the American Political Science Association, San Francisco, Sept. 5, 1975.

Merton, R. K. (1957): *Social Theory and Social Structure*. Glencoe, Ill.: Free Press.

Miliband, R. (1969): *The State in Capitalist Society*. London: Wiedenfeld and Nicolson; New York: Basic Books 169.

Olson, M. (1968): *The Logic of Collective Action*. Cambridge: Harvard Univ. Press.

Olson, M. (1969): "Social Indicators and Social Accounts." *Socio-Economic Planning Sciences* 2: 335–346.

Pressman, J. L., and A. Wildavsky (1973): *Implementation. How Great Expectations in Washington are dashed in Oakland*. Berkely: Univ. of California Press.

Putnam, R. D. (1976): *The Comparative Study of Political Elites*. Englewood Cliffs, N.J. Prentice Hall.

Sabatier, P. A. (1983): Toward a Strategie Interaction Framework of Policy Evolution and Learning. Davis, Calif. (Unpubl. paper).

Scharpf, F. W. (1970): *Demokratietheorie zwischen Utopie und Anpassung*. Konstanz: Scriptor.

Scharpf, F. W. (1973): "Komplexität als Schranke politischer Planung." In Scharpf, F. W. (ed.), *Planung als politischer Prozeß*, 73–113. Frankfurt: Suhrkamp.

Schatz, H. (1978): "Regierungs- und Verwaltungsreform im politisch-administrativen Spannungsfeld." Studien zur Reform von Regierung und Verwaltung. *Schriftenreihe des Vereins für Verwaltungsreform und Verwaltungsforschung*, 9–20. Bonn.

Schmidt, H, and B. Schips (eds.) (1980): *Verknüpfung sozioökonomischer Modelle*, Frankfurt a. M.: Campus.

Schumpeter, J. A. (1942): *Capitalism, Socialism and Democracy*. New York: Harper and Brothers.

Sharkanski, I. (1970): *Policy Analysis in Political Science*. Chicago: Markham.

Williamson, O. E. (1975): *Markets and Hierarchies: Analysis and Antitrust Implications*. New York: Free Press; London: Collier Macmillan.

Zapf, W. (1972): "Social Indicators: Prospects of Social Accounting Systems." *Social Science Information* 11/3, 4: 279–285.

28. The Games Within the Game: Modeling Politico-Economic Structures

Martin Shubik

Abstract

The different social sciences are directed towards studying aspects of human behavior which are manifested over different lengths of time. The time spans of prime concern to psychologists investigating the senses, to economists concerned with consumer behavior or investment, to sociologists concerned with group solidarity or to anthropologists investigating the rise and decline of culture are considerably different.

The formal modeller in the social sciences must recognize that depending upon the time span being investigated there are games within the game. Economic political and societal events are interlinked but it is critical to understand the way the different time scales intermesh if one is to understand the relationship between the phenomena. This paper represents a first attempt to formalize this interrelationship.

28.1 Preamble

This paper attempts to provide a sketch of an approach to socio-politico-economic modeling in a manner consistent with both optimizing and evolutionary behavior. Much of economic theorizing has stressed optimization within the rules of a given game. Yet in a complex evolving society the givens and the rules for one set of individuals may be the variables for another. Man is a rule creating and a rationalizing animal. A key problem in political science and in law is how to describe and justify the evolution of constitutions and law in an open society.

The emphasis in short term economic theory has been upon more or less rational individuals pursuing more or less well defined goals in a fixed environment. Yet the sociologist, psychologist and psychiatrist all see a creature of habit, with internal conflicts, limited perceptions and lack of clarity of goals.

The sensitive historian spins a tale with many, not one chain of causality. The microdynamics which determine the direction of development of a society are seen even by the most perceptive, after the event, if they are seen at all.

Formal methods and mathematical models can be simultaneously tools for precise analysis and straightjackets which limit our attention to apparently well defined problems set in the context of an overly constrained and simplified environment.

An attempt is made here to use the methods of the theory of games intermixed with an approach to limited rationality to provide a basis for the construction and analysis of politico-economic and bureaucratic models of behavior. The goal of this approach is to construct bridges among economic, political and sociological modes of thought, yet maintain a relatively high level of formal analytical structure. The purpose is not merely methodological but stems from a belief that our ability to start to comprehend the dynamics of the development of the modern mixed public sector, private sector nation state calls for an explicit attempt to construct multidisciplinary models even though the early attempts to do so have and will undoubtedly continue to show the special disciplinary biases of the authors.

Before sketching the model, a few general observations concerning my beliefs in the power and limits of formal economic analysis are in order. The model of utilitarian man maximizing some given goals is highly attractive and powerful because of parsimony and its successes both apparent and real in explaining many diverse phenomena in the economy. Yet the very successes of microeconomic analysis lead to a type of "economic theory imperialism" which confuses models of optimizing human behavior with economic behavior. The discipline of economics has no monopoly on the concepts of goal oriented optimization. It is the relevance and realism of the description of the economic setting that provides the economist with a class of problems which can be fruitfully analyzed by the methods of optimization. Game theoretic extensions of economic models have shown that even if we confuse the world of the microeconomist for the larger world of the political economy, basic problems both in methodology and empirical description appear. Economic motivation alone may not be enough to provide a complete dynamics. Other ingredients are needed, and depending upon the problem at hand, may easily dominate the economic factors.

The game theoretic basis for the modeling described is given elsewhere (Shubik 1982) as is a discussion and set of bibliographical references to the work of Downs, Niskanen, Kramer, Breton, Ordeshook, McKelvey, Williamson and others all of whom have built mixed models involving economics, politics and bureaucracy (Shubik 1984).

In spite of the apparent modernity of the topic, it appears to me that much of this approach has as its basis both of the great works of Adam Smith (1976a, 1976b). The *Wealth of Nations* provides the context of political economy, but the *Theory of Moral Sentiments* raises the more difficult psychological and phisophical problems of how a society evolves its codes and laws which provide the operating environment.

28.2 The Approach Adopted

Is it possible to take steps towards formalizing the qualitative considerations stressed in the great writings on politics and sociology or will any attempt to do so be forced to yield to a utilitarian format with human capital, justice, trust or progress as the commodities?

It is suggested here that it is possible to start to reconcile politics, and sociology with the formal structures of mathematical economics and political science. But the cost of doing so involves setting the economic considerations in an appropriate perspective. An overstressing of economic motivation and costs in political economy can be compared with trying to explain the behavior of the Catholic church by choosing to concentrate on the records of the church's cost accountants rather than on the motivation and acts of members of the college of cardinals.

The approach outlined in the subsequent sections calls for a set of "games within games" where institutions and organizations are regarded as rules of the game. Their members are the players and their behavior is locally rational. But when viewed as a whole the political process of formulation and execution of policy followed by reformulation (elections and legislation) and changes in the rules of some of the games (constitutional reform, legal process and other forms of institutional and organizational change) should be considered as a social process in which the values of the society are simultaneously progressively perceived and implemented.

28.3 A Descriptive Model of a Socio-Economic System in the Short Run

The model sketched here is designed to encompass economic factors, political structure and bureaucracy. Furthermore, it is explicitly game theoretic involving a sequence of games with different actors. The model is based more on the United States political structure than elsewhere. However, it should be regarded more as representative of class of models rather than a statement of the specific importance of a single structure.

It is argued in section 3 that a key factor in the reconciliation of the roles of social, political and economic man is the understanding that limited rationality, perceptions and capacity for action call for differentiated functions, training, sensitivity of perception and goals.

The actors in economic theory are virtually all the same. The consumer, producer and manager are minor variants of *homo oeconomicus*. The actors in political and sociological theory involve others with different perceptions and purpose. Without attempting to explain how in the long run elites are formed, what is the dynamics of recruitment or why specialists specialize, we may take the differentiation as given in the short term. With this differentiation a rich short term theory of process can be constructed. If the only justification of this endeavour were to understand better the interaction of political, economic and bureaucratic forces in the generation of effective demand and supply for public goods and services, it would be worthwhile. Beyond that, however, the attempt to extend our models of man may help in our understanding of the operational meaning of limited rationality.

Individual Actors and Institutions

The individual actors considered are (1) the citizen-voter-consumer-worker; (2) active political party members; political office holders and candidates; (3) the business elite; (4) the elite other than the politicians and businessmen; (5) the politically appointed controllers and other members of the bureaucratic elite; (6) the non-elite members of the governmental bureaucracy.

A slightly more ambitious model would include (7) the elites in other not-for-profit institutions (including organized pressure groups, unions, universities, the church); (8) the members of these institutions; (9) the other members of corporate bureaucracies; (10) entrepreneurs; (11) the elite of the financial establishment; and (12) other members of the financial bureaucracies.

The approach adopted here is that institutions in the short run (say up to four or five years) may be taken as given and more or less unchanging (clearly there are exceptions especially in times of great social, political or economic stress). The institutions may be described then as part of the rules of the game. The behavior of an institution is to be explained as the output of the joint strategies of the members of the institution, in other words, it is the result of the interactions of the real players manifesting their activities in the strategies of the institutional players. These institutional players provide the context for the subgames that are played.

The institutions to be considered directly in the model are (1) the political parties, (2) the government, (3) the governmental bureaucracies.

In the more ambitious version it would be of interest to add (4) corporations, (5) unions, (6) the armed forces, (7) religious institutions, (8) financial institutions and (9) formally organized pressure groups. But at this time the first three are adequate for a model sufficiently complex to characterize much of the overall behavior which would be still manifested even with further complications.

Products and Programs

The utility function much used in expositions of microeconomic theory has, in general, a finite number of arguments usually interpreted as specific quantities of goods or services. The classical model of an exchange economy is phrased in terms of n individuals trading in m goods where each individual i is presumed to have an initial endowment of resources of the form $(w_1^i, w_2^i, \ldots, w_m^i)$. Large firms often sell each other and governments not products or services but whole systems or programs. Governments in general are concerned with programs not products or even individual services. The number of categories needed to provide a good macro socio economic picture of government programs is around fifteen to thirty. As a first cut most of the headings in the Statistical Abstract of the United States or other national statistics handbooks will do. A sample list is suggested here.

Defense	Employment, Working Conditions
Justice and Safety	Science and Technology
International Relations	Communications and Transportation
Population	Cultural Activities
Immigration	Agriculture
Health	Basic Resources
Education	Manufacturing
Welfare	Environment
Housing	Finance
Social Security	Taxation

Each one of these calls for relatively high level establishment of policy and none of these items appears to enter directly into the type of utility function exposited in conventional consumer choice theory.

Behind each policy choice there has to be an implementation plan and a budget. The budget will contain a listing of line items such as the number of police cars, revolvers, two-way communication systems and so forth required by the police to carry out a law enforcement program. But the list of physical inputs alone does not describe the quantity or quality of the outputs. Yet both government and voters propose and vote upon policies and programs not lists of products.

Where are the public goods? Most of them appear as part of the program packages. On occasion a specific item such as a special hospital in an individual's district appears as of direct concern to the individual who is in a position to take direct action such as to vote on a bond issue, but this is the exception not the rule at the federal level and covers only a fraction of state and city expenditures.

Preferences and Values

The valuation of goods and direct services as well as the social and political value systems must all be manifested in the individual's system of preference structures. The view adopted here is to regard the individual as a collection of cooperative agents each used for a different type of decision and each operating on a different configuration or aggregation of all information. Thus, Figure 1, without pretending to particular rigor suggests a structure for the individual may be regarded as a single rational player represented in agent form, where the player's agents may be required to act on aggregated or limited information on part of the set of decisions faced by the individual.

The interpretation of Figure 1 is as follows. We may consider the individual to operate in at least economic, political and social modes. Where different types of individuals lay different emphasis upon different routines. The symbol $\boxed{D}$ stands for the presence of many detailed subroutines. $\boxed{M}$ indicates the presence of a middling number of subroutines; whereas $\boxed{H}$ indicates the presence of a set of subroutines many of which may be wholly or heavily dependent on habit and other forms of socialization.

Commencing first with the structure of economic decisions a division into investment and entrepreneurship; employment and personal finance is suggested. As was observed by Keynes (1936) and many others, investment and saving are not the same activities. Most individuals are neither entrepreneurs or investors. Their resources which may reach investment activities do so for the most part via financial intermediaries which are used for saving.

Those individuals in society distinguished as investors or entrepreneurs or both would have highly developed subroutines for such activities. Of central concern to many individuals and an item which occupies much of an adult's available time is his employment. The concern with permanency of jobs, tenure, seniority, mobility, promotion prospects, pensions and unemployment appear to vary with both personal and societal attitudes and mores. Most individuals appear to have at least some conscious and habitual subroutines dealing directly with their employment.

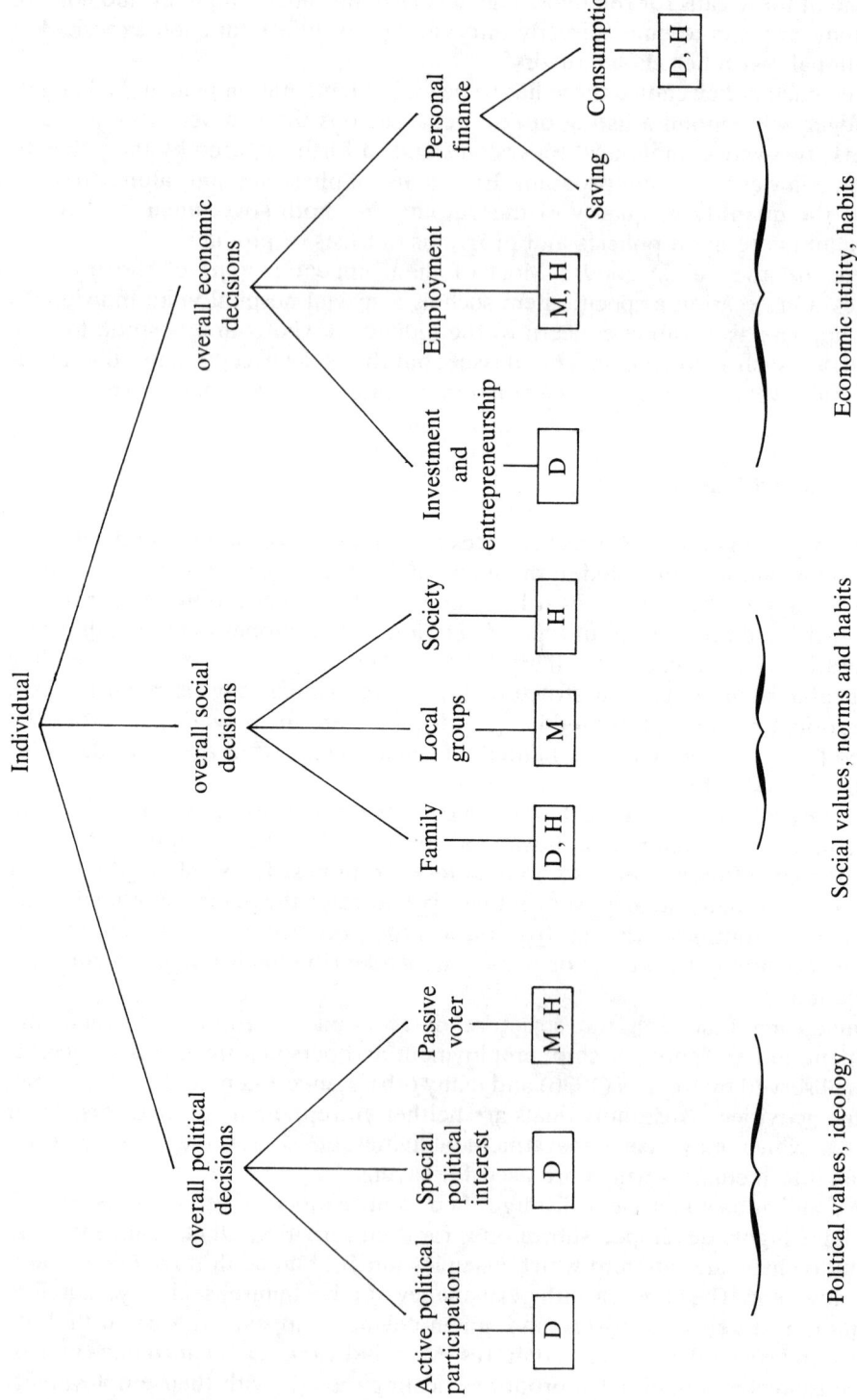

Fig. 1

Personal finance includes both saving and consumption. Beyond the earning of income and possibly the area where most of the economic choices of the individual have to be made is personal finance. Especially in consumption the individual appears to have detailed sets of consciously followed and habitual routines. Shopping for bargains; being an expert on automobiles; knowing where are the best stores; recognizing different gradations in quality are all manifestations of these routines.

Dahl's perceptive work on political activity (1961) suggests that we should at least distinguish the politically active and professionals from the more or less passive voters and the pressure groups or lobbyists. At one extreme we have the dedicated professional politician whose life and employment is politics. All working hours are directed to politics and it may be that politics are dreamt as well. At the other extreme there is the individual who scarcely even bothers to vote, let alone invest time in obtaining information needed for rational political decisionmaking.

Three divisions are suggested. The professional politicians who in general include officeholders, officeseekers and active party workers. They will have many politically oriented subroutines and sociopolitical factors such as power, position, prestige and ideology may figure high in their preference structures.

The ordinary voter may have a poorly developed or even a well developed preference structure over configurations of policies but nevertheless may not manifest political activity much beyond voting, the occasional petition and a certain amount of conscious and habitual data gathering, processing and evaluation.

An individual with no particular other interests in the political process or its control may, nevertheless, find himself with deep interests in some particular aspect of the political programs which effect him and which at least call for actions within his strategic scope such as lobbying, making political donations or joining formally or informally organized special purpose groups. Thus, gun lobbies, antiabortion groups, environmental protection groups, social, religious and economic special interest organizations may be designed to enlarge the strategic possibilities for those whose political interests and other political activities are otherwise minimal.

In this work, little detailed consideration is given to the more sociological aspects of individual conscious and habitual behavior. Much of the activity at this level is devoted to longer run factors than are dealt with here. Changes in customs, modifications of institutions, evolution of norms and of social structures are for the most part on a time scale far different from two or even three elections. In Figure 1 the relatively crude division suggests a division of the social individual's attention and activities into immediate family, local groups with whom interaction is frequent and at first hand and society as a whole, where social values and mores may be inchoate, dimly perceived, but also important.

The approach adopted here is that for consumption of private goods and for saving, the standard utility function structure offers a fruitful description. The voter when confronted by an election involving overall socio-political and economic issues collapses the dimensionally of his economic activity into one, or in special interest situations, into two or three dimensions. They are money, his job or his business activity. The money – without specifying details on income, exposed or hidden wealth – provides a one dimensional measure for general economic well-being. When the ordinary voter votes, he is not concerned with political or bureaucratic power or status or entrepreneurial or other inventive activity, his preferences are described on a structure of around 20 to 30 programs (as indicated in Table 1) together with one dimension for how his overall wealth is effected and in some instances an extra dimension if his particular job or other economic activity is under direct attack. More appropriately, his choice must be based not merely upon what he has in the way of services delivered – but he must take into account and evaluate that which is being promised to him by the parties. This involves an appropriate description of how expectations are formed which discount promised programs.

Many aspects of political platforms are broad statements loosely connected to physical specifics and to cost-benefit analysis. The costs are at most loose constraints. When confronted with two or three programs, the individual voter in general makes a comparison among the programs proposed and not a large set of alternative programs. At most the voter and even most politicians conceptualize no more than five to ten *qualitatively* different programs. They are primarily the ones being offered the previously proposed and enacted programs and one or two other sufficiently conceptualized programs that they can meaningfully be considered as perceived operational alternatives.

It is suggested that aspects of political purpose and public programs which deal with those qualitative features of policy such as the quality of justice, equity, the tone of foreign policy are not fruitfully dealt with by the same type of intellectual apparatus as pure public goods, toll highways or other physically reasonably well defined items. Furthermore, it is suggested that the concept of the Pareto optimal surface is not the most fruitful construct for describing the strivings of the vote seekers or the choices of the voters. The politicians and the voters know that even if their feelings are strong, as they are not all philosophers, their conceptualization and ability to verbalize their concepts of freedom or justice or other qualitatively critical concepts is limited.

In general, most individuals can distinguish which of several programs is of greatest appeal to them in particular. Furthermore, this perceptual exercise utilizes all the help or hinderance obtained from philosophers, news commentators, poets and politicians. For some the conceptual filters may depend heavily on sausages and circuses and for others on Socrates and Adam Smith or the Federalist papers.

Rather than describe Pareto optimal surfaces defined in a vacuum, it is suggested that our concern for formalization be directed towards process. Thus, our concern must be with who selects policies and programs and how individuals vote on the programs over which they have a direct or indirect say.

It is the task of the political scientist, sociologist and moral philosopher to specify the mechanisms of program generation, the domain of choice, the special properties of the domain (such as its mathematical structure) and the choice rules of the individuals. By default the economist can do so in many ways with ease – for example, we may assume that all programs can be mapped onto a single dimension "wealth" – that all individuals have a preference ordering over wealth which can be represented by a continous utility function and that the choice operator is maximization of utility.

28.4 The Strategy Sets and Preferences of the Players

In the remainder of this paper, a sketch of a politico-economic process set in a social context is given. The time span selected is the space between two elections in a heterogeneous democracy such as the United States. The reason for making this specification is more to illustrate how to construct a model of this type than to stress the particular model.

The Games within the Game

A cycle is described which begins before the selection of political candidates to run in an election and ends before the selection for the next election. Figure 2 shows the flow diagram of the process. It can be viewed as a set of (six, seven or eight) "local interest games" each to be played by the appropriate subgroup of players (or agents) directly concerned.

Initial conditions include the population of all voter-consumer-workers which is assumed to be very large; the politically active may be some few thousands; the elite some tens of thousands and the lower and middle bureaucracy is assumed to be large. As data are also the current officehoulders, the program promised by the winning party, the program delivered by the winning party and the position of the electorate prior to the last election. This includes not only its private endowments, but the public program delivered before the previous selection of candidates.

In order to build a full local interest game at this level, we would have to present a relatively detailed candidate competition model. For simplicity, we assume that incumbents run again and that there is a two party system where a candidate is selected at random from the politically active.

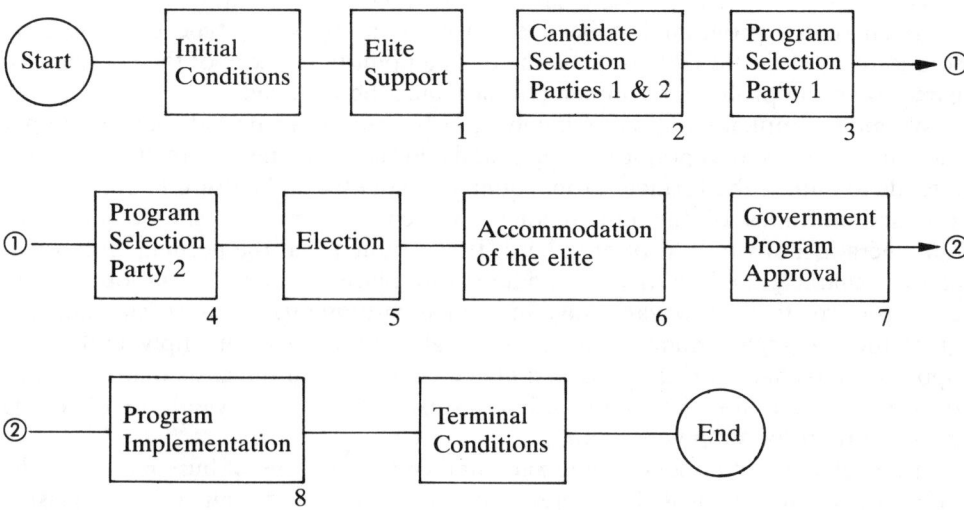

Fig. 2

By the above simplification the candidate selection game has been avoided and replaced by a relatively simple choice mechanism.

The next step in the process calls for other interested members of the elite (of all sorts including corporate presidents, lawyers, union leaders, preachers and professors) to make their bargains and place their bets. The coin they may pay in may be money, time, talent, propaganda or other items such as promises to take care of a losing politician with positions such as affiliations "of counsel" to large law firms or special advisor to investment houses and so forth. The coin they will be paid in if their ship comes home will be appropriate positions in the high administrative but politically controlled governmental structure, or in influence on policy.

The first task of all candidates is to select a party platform which we can represent by a set of social programs and taxation. The probability for each candidate being elected depends on the voter in his district, thus chances for each vary with overall policy. At a slightly more detailed level, we might wish to consider a list of local public goods.

As a function of how well he does and his party does, a politician gains or loses a set of positions in the top bureaucracy which he can fill from the nonelected elite. In practice, many top businessmen, professors, generals, lawyers and others are available and they will have indicated their availability by services already rendered. At a later point *quid pro quo* in the form of government contracts, ideological constraints or modified programs may appear.

When the election is over, the winners have the opportunity to remove some of the previous administrators and to replace them with their own (note: we are not attempting to describe at this level of generality the many different rules for bureaucratic tenure and the variations in the *quid pro quo* that exist between politicians and those who they are in a position to appoint). This step may be regarded as a payoff for support rather than a new game.

Given the disaggregation to individual elected members of an assembly, we may treat the actions of the government as a whole, as the outcome of a multiperson game where the vote is not necessarily decided along party lines.

Given that a program has been decided upon, by some type of bargaining solution, say characterized as the value or as a point in the core of the cooperative game, then the problem of implementation must be resolved.

We model implementation as involving a bargaining game between the upper bureaucracy viewed as politically appointed and the permanent bureaucracy which intends to outlast the former. From country to country and culture to culture, the size and attitudes of the bureaucracy vary considerably. A simple model of bureaucratic motivation is offered here. It is assumed that the permanent bureaucracy is characterized by those individuals who place a high value on job security and upon relatively low variability in their environment. Security, size and the quiet life are high among goals to be sought. This does not imply unthinking opposition to change. But opposition may be generated if the costs that they must bear to provide for flexibility and adjustment to change yield no offsetting compensation for supplying them.

A key element in understanding and appreciating the role of bureaucracy in the public or private sector is the appreciation of the costs and limits on any decision process. All but the most elementary of organisms or organizations are complex information aggregating and disaggregating devices. The locus of attention changes and one set of detail disappears to be replaced with another. Williamson (1975), Nelson and Winter (1982) and many others have stressed the underlying rationale that in many instances calls for hierarchies and bureaucracies where the conditions for the operation of a market as an efficient alternative are not present. Indivisibilities, fewness in numbers; need for highly specialized nonmarketable information; the need for highly differentiated routines, location or environment, or specific activities are but a handful of the factors calling for structured differentiated organizations to perform that which the market does badly or cannot do at all.

In the process outlined here, the input to the final game is the agreed upon program and the output is the program as implemented. The cycle is complete and the public now has the data to update its expectations for the next nominations and elections.

If we endow the public with a reasonable amount of scepticism, then although there is no need for budgets to balance or expected costs, promised costs and actual costs to be the same, the larger is the gap between that which is promised and that which is delivered, if it is unfavorable, the larger will be the inclination to chance votes.

A Playable Game

In the remainder of this paper, a mixed verbal and diagrammatic representation of the overall game and the local interest games is presented. In projected work three further steps remain. The first is to use simple specific mathematical forms to construct a playable game. The use of gaming-simulation such as the various business games used in teaching, training and experimentation (see Shubik 1975; Shubik with Levitan 1980) or teaching games in sociology such as Gamson's Simsoc (Gamson 1966) can be of considerable value in forcing rigor of thought in model building while maintaining more flexibility than is usual in straight mathematical model building and analysis. Careful use of gaming-simulation especially for interdisciplinary work provides a procedure for uncovering and making clear difficulties in formulating logically consistent, complete and believeable models. It is a methodological device of considerable importance as an aid in modeling.

The second step which remains to be done is to provide some empirical evidence for the relationship used in a simple model and to actually define and calculate solutions. The third step is to present a more generalized model. Although these steps are not carried out here, it is important to stress that by adopting a game theory, gaming, simulation approach a stress in approach is proposed that is different from both the essay style of much of social science and the predominant type of static mathematical analysis characteristic of much of modern microeconomic theory. The stress is on the modeling and on process.

28.5 The Game and Local Interest Games

Ideally a full process description of the system and its subsystems would provide the most satisfactory model. In general, this goal is difficult to attain without being swallowed in special institutional detail.

The tradeoff between detail and modeling methods, between modeling methods and solution concepts is one that is central to the applications of game theory. The extensive strategic and cooperative forms of representation of a game are used at different levels of abstraction. The solution concepts associated with each of them are different (See Shubik 1982). In particular, associated with the extensive form (and variants which include games without a specified beginning or termination) are behavioral solutions and other dynamic solutions. The strategic form drops much of the detail concerning information and the specifics of moves. It concentrates on strategic description and the predominant solution concept is the noncooperative equilibrium of Nash (1951). When we constrain our modeling to relatively well defined economic situations, the Nash equilibrium coincides with that of Cournot (1897) and other economic solutions suggested for the study of oligopolistic structure. The cooperative form presents the most aggregated viewpoint of a strategic situation. Detail concerning moves, information and mechanisms is surpressed. The solutions associated with the cooperative form are several. Some of which are highly non-unique in their delimitation of outcomes. Von Neumann and Morgenstern proposed a *stable set solution* based upon an idea of social stability; the *core,* in essence, delimits a set of outcomes impervious to countervailing power; the *value* can be used to select a set of outcomes which may, from a certain point of view, be regarded as sociologically neutral.

The Game as a Whole and Limited Rationality

In the model in this section, the subgames are described in different levels of detail, thus different forms and solution concepts are suggested.

The model formalized is shown in Figure 3 with four local interest games and a general equilibrium system.

Local Interest Game 1: Elite Support

Players	Candidates and the elite
Game Form	Cooperative resource bargaining
Resources	Expected positions, skills of the elite, own money, "other peoples money", programs, expected contracts.
Solution	The core
Outputs	(1) Candidates with support, (2) bounds on programs, (3) commitments or promises for positions and (4) contracts.

Local Interest Game 2: Program Selection and Elections

Players	The candidates; the electorate is modeled as a behavioral mechanism (or several mechanisms to reflect blocks such as the bureaucracies or unions)
Game Form.	Extensive form with the incumbent party naming its program first, followed by the opposition. Then the voters voting. The selection of the party programs can be regarded as cooperative subgames by the party candidates.

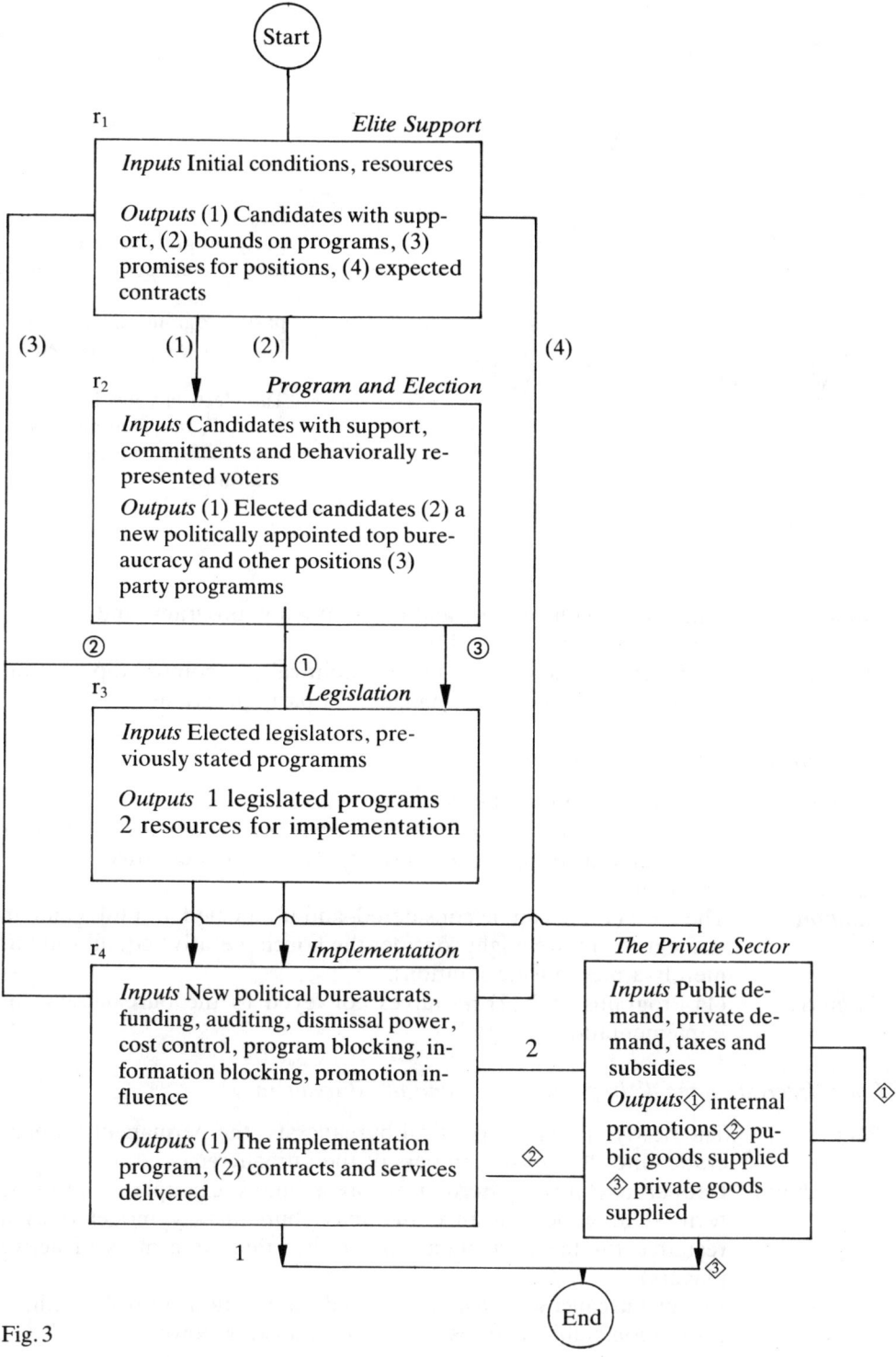

Fig. 3

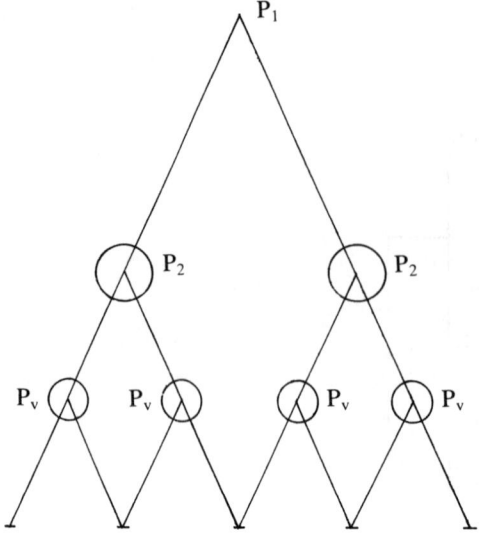

r_{2a} party program selection by
        party 1 a cooperative game

r_{2b} party program selection by
        Party 2 a cooperative game

The election votes by all
voters P_v modeled here as
a mechanism triggered by the
programs.

Fig. 4

Resources   Candidates with support and commitments, programs and votes.
Solution   The noncooperative equilibrium.
Outputs   (1) Elected candidates, (2) a new politically appointed top bureau-
               cracy and other position changes, (3) party programs.

Local Interest Game 3: Legislation

Players   The elected representatives.
Game Form   Cooperative form (with both strategic form and a mechanism–or
               precommited strategies–as an easily described alternative).
Resources   Programs
Solution   The core (value can be considered–and if modeled as a full game in
               strategic form, we might consider the noncooperative equilibrium or
               merely a mechanistic solution).
Outputs   (1) Programs and (2) resources conveyed to the bureaucracy for
               implementation.

Local Interest Game 4: Implementation and the Bureaucracy

Players   The newly appointed political bureaucrats, the permanent bureau-
               cratic elite; the mass members of the bureaucracy.
Game Form   Cooperative form (alternatively as a simple example, a strategic
               form – in either instance the mass bureaucracy modeled as a
               resource for the permanent elite rather than as a mass of active
               players).
Resources   Lower bureaucracy, cost control and information control, funding,
               promotions, ability to dismiss, audit, blocking power.

Solution   The core (alternatively a noncooperative equilibrium).
Outputs   (1) The implemented program; (2) promised contracts or services delivered.

Local Interest Game 5: The Private Industrial Sector

The private sector is modeled here as a general equilibrium system rather than as a game. If we were to fully reflect the oligopoly elements of the private sector, its bargaining possibilities on government contracts and private prices, we would need a full game here. Taxes are given exogenously to this local interest game. It is assumed that prices and the vector of goods and services to the bureaucracy have been contracted for with the following conditions that one or two parameters provide measures of a transaction costs and organizational slack (see Selten 1982).

Consider two government contracts. The first is for a space shuttle and the second for army flashlights. The first will call for original Research and Development; the breaking of the budget into hundreds of thousands of line items with overheads tucked in everywhere and with many of the items from a sole source supplier to a sole sink demand. In contrast, the order for flashlights could be filled by many different firms and at most (given that mechanisms such as a governmental audit exists) a price differential can only be maintained by appeals to the special qualities of durability or other features which can be defended as forms of product variation enough to justify a price spread from "ordinary private sector flashlights."

Reported profits may play an important role in the internal promotion system of the private sector. Thus, even though the correlation between some form of expected profit maximization and the career pattern of a member of the industrial elite may be less than 1, it may nevertheless be high.

The games described above are regarded as played more or less sequentially with the outputs from one serving as inputs to others. In order to be able to separate the strategic behavior of many of the agents, we have introduced the *Dei ex Machina* in the form of estimations of how the expected results from future games might feed back on the local game about to be played. Clearly, in some instances, the forecasts must be about future games and *ex post* the forecast will have changed the outcome. To those more comfortable with equilibrium analysis, we could look for self-fulfilling prophecies, "rational expectations" and steady states. But our view is that socio-political choice takes place in a system in which the problems of moral philosophy are not only posed and refined, but the implementation of programs and the clarification of values take place in constant interaction. Thus, it is more natural to conceive of the normal state of the system being in disequilibrium "the grail is in the seeking not the cup". In spite of this view paradoxically the approach suggested is via a sequence of subgames each played and analysable in terms of some form of statics and limited rationality, but all linked together dynamically by hope or expectations.

Subsolutions and the System as a Whole

Although the local interest games and the system as a whole have not been formalized to the level at which strict game theoretic analysis can be performed on all local interest games, nevertheless, it is possible to make some comments about the parts and the system as a whole with varying degrees of formality.

In particular, without conditions which might be regarded as particularly restrictive, for any set of expectations and any expost random events, the local interest election game will have a unique (up to inessential degeneracy) equilibrium point. Under some circumstances all the other local interest games will have cores. It is conjectured that under reasonable circumstances there will be a considerable indeterminacy in the system which can be demonstrated by showing that strategy with a point in the core of the first local interest game generates a noncooperative equilibrium in the second; the set of all noncooperative equilibria so generated leads to a class of local interest games at the next stage many of which will have cores. Any point in any of these cores may be considered as feeding into the last stage and many of these will also have cores.

The meaning of this conjecture is that the system is considerably underdetermined even though its economic aspects are fully described – unless one adopts the view that the missing political, sociological and psychological detail can all be explained by economics.

It must also be stressed that in this formulation, it is the individuals not the institutions who are the players. They have free will and they play strategically on a limited stage.

The higher the level of activity of the individuals, the more likely it is that their strategies consist of "environment setting" for others. A move of one player may amount to limiting the domain of the moves of another.

In the sketch of the model, legislation has been noted and legislation may take the form of changing rules, thus modifying the local interest games by changing the institutions and organizations. At a longer run and more profound level, we would also wish to contemplate constitutional change and change in overall societal mores such as in religion. But it is precisely as we move to the higher order features of society such as the evolution of the concept of freedom and the institutions which operationalize the concept that the simpler variables and techniques of the economist are of limited use.

All of the analysis in this argument has been based directly upon individual optimization. But goal-seeking strategic behavior is far more than economic optimization. An attempt to explain freedom or say war as manifestations of an economic determinism is to ignore history and to replace a multivariate evolving system with only its simplest and most quantifiable local interest game.

28.6 Local Optimization and Global Evolution

Mechanisms, Process and Optimality

An attempt has been made to sketch a closed system with local maximization via a limited scope of strategic activity, where the institutions appear as special rules of the game.

No claim is made of the empirical accuracy of the particular model. Nor are casual political conclusions to be quickly drawn. On the contrary, it appears that the performance of the system will depend considerably upon the specifics of the power of the elites and the bureaucracy and it is not easy to make generalizations *a priori.*

In models of human behavior with no costs or limits to decisionmaking, the institutional arrangements do not matter as we may assume that rules can be costlessly created and changed at will. The simplifying assumptions made by von Neumann and Morgenstern (1944) to describe the cooperative stable set solution exemplify this approach. All coalition formulation and communication costs are left out of the game and do not effect the set of optimal outcomes. Similarly, choice theory and general equilibrium theory are process free. Hence, in all of these theories the Pareto optimal set is fixed in advance and is independent of institutional arrangements, bargaining costs and implementation systems.

If we adopt the view that at any point of time, institutions and other rules of the game are given and that changing the rules of the game is costly and takes some time to do so, then the feasible set of outcomes will be constrained by the resources utilized in resource allocation. Thus, optimality must be defined as dependent on the allocation mechanism.

When we contrast the long view with the short and contemplate individual conscious behavior, the paradox of local rationality and societal evolution begins to be resolved. Much of the time of most individuals is spent acting in short run well structured situations with the rules given and the expense of either changing the rules or learning how to play in a different game too high to be risked. The charismatic leaders, the saints, heros, innovators, the mad, the misfits, the poets and preachers advocate or acutally attempt to change the rules of the game; even at the cost of poor performance in the well specified local interest games. Professors of politics are, in general, not as powerful as professional politicians, professors of economics are not as rich as investment bankers or others fully dedicated to money making. In general, those who worry overly much about meaning and values inhibit themselves and others in taking decisive action on the many smaller stages of everyday life.

The optimality of the economist is optimality in an extremely limited context. The design of self-policing systems in which there are criteria whereby we may judge the evolution of better rules in the local interest game is probably feasible in a limited context. But *a priori* once the openness of the economic system to sociopolitical and other forces is recognized, the limitations to our being able to define global good or efficiency must be accepted.

On Public Goods Delivery Systems

Without becoming too deeply philosophical and worrying too much about the general problems of when is societal change progress, the domain of more immediate operational application of the type of model presented here is in the examination of the nature of the wants manifested and public goods supplied constraining ourselves to the more prosaic of the entries in Table 1. The fundamental difference between this approach and conventional welfare economics is that no attempt is made to define a social welfare function. It is the outcomes of the processes of playing the local interest games which generates the demand and triggers the supply.

The more we wish to consider imponderables such as the quality of justice, the more difficult it becomes to produce convincing models. But staying closer to more convential criteria of physical, economic and societal welfare, the type of model sketched here appears to be feasible and worthwhile.

Communism, Democracy and Limited Rationality

It is suggested that Lindblom's (1977) attempt to contrast democratic and primarily market oriented societies with communist societies can be considered in the context of the variants of game theoretic analysis.

Viewed in their most favorable light, both democratic market oriented theories of human socio-political welfare and communist theories appear to be concerned with the welfare of all individuals. However, taking the emergence of the people's democracy and the final withering away of the state, as a serious operational problem, it appears that implicit in this view is a philosophical position shared with utopian utilitarians on the perfectability of the human being. In contrast, the democratic models tend to be based upon a view which not merely stresses individual motivation but also implicitly or explicitly assumes limitations on individual capabilities.

We may adopt at least three models of human governance (1) Humans are and will in all probability remain with limited perceptual, conceptual and coordinating capabilities and will persist in maintaining individual differences in abilities, values and preferences (2) Humans may maintain individual differences in abilities, values and preferences but they can be considered to be striving towards perfect individual rationality, (3) In the ultimate perfect state, education, indoctrination and individual realization of social identity will yield a rule-free, institution-free rational cooperation.

The first model is not only closest to much of the spirit of political theorizing on representative government but is also allied with much of market economy theorizing from Adam Smith onward. Even more recently the developments in economic thought have turned towards formalizing the concepts of limited rationality. This includes limitations on perception and computation, routines for search with only limited conscious strategic choice in selecting routines and limitations on the perceptions of choice and preference formation. The impetus to this approach was given by work at Carnegie Institute of Technology (now Carnegie Mellon University) exemplified by that of Simon (1979) and Cyert and March (1963), and more recently by Nelson and Winter (1982).

Most of the work on game theory except for some attempts to devise behavioral or myopic solutions for dynamic games has been based upon fully rational models of man. One of the still open and centrally difficult problems is how to reconcile a learning theory or for that matter other behavioral theories with game theory. The suggestion here is that a potentially satisfactory way to achieve a theory with an intermix of behavioral components and strategic futures is to consider that organization, information, communication and evaluation costs are all sufficiently high that it is optimal to have the short run delegation of decisions to agents who will perform local or parochial optimizations.

The game theoretic approach based upon a view of the individualistic rational actor gives rise to two distinct viewpoints of the social system and solution theory. In particular, the main thrust of the work of Harsanyi which may be described as "rule utilitarian," had been the search for a single equilibrium point which can be calculated as the appropriate outcome to any strategic situation which can be specified. In contrast with this resolutely philosophical viewpoint, another approach is reflected in the work of Shapley, Shapley and Shubik, Shubik, Selten, Schmeidler, Aumann and Maschler and others where a pluralistic willingness to entertain many different solution concepts is manifested.

In part, the pluralistic view comes from a somewhat pragmatic and special purpose orientation of the uses of game theory in application to special models built for a variety of purposes. The model and solution concept to be used may both vary with the nature of the questions to be answered.

Crude solution concepts such as the core may be used in solutions where the modeling does not even supply enough detail to specify the game mechanism in detail. But technically the model may offer a description of the cooperative form without ever specifying the strategic form.

A justification of the eclectic approach is that our models are invariably simplifications and aggregations of the phenomena we wish to study. Thus, for example, the crudeness of a solution concept such as the core may indicate that the model cannot be expected to yield a more determinate solution without adding further detail concerning psychological, social, political or other factors.

The third game theoretic approach suggested here is to try to blend limited rationality and strategic individualism.

A priori the methodology of game theory provides no rules or axioms concerning the correlation of the preferences or values of the individuals. Team theory does – all individuals are agents serving a higher purpose. Costs and difficulties in communication make the problem of coordination and joint optimization difficult, but goal orientation or social cohesion is supplied by axiom. Thus, it appears that game theoretically a perfect communist or other utopian state requires both unlimited rationality and a sense of "brotherhood" or correlation of individual concern. Identity of interest along with costly communication and limited rationality offers only a limited utopia where the state does not wither away as organizations and institutions are still needed to supply the guidance in the form of rules of the game to direct the socially cooperative but less than perfectly rational members of a potential utopia.

Economics, Politics and Sociology

The problems of social and political control of public programs do not stand in opposition to price systems be they either controlled economies or competitive markets.

The progressive refinements of microeconomic theory have produced at a high level of abstraction and with minimal institutional description an economic theory of markets and prices. The increasing precision in the specification of prices, goods, services and markets was paid for at the cost of a virtually complete separation of economics from political economy. The analytical benefit in doing so has been highly beneficial in exploring the technical conditions for the existence of systems which can be efficiently decentralized by prices.

The very power of the general equilibrium analysis suggests that the time is ripe to take two steps beyond this analysis in terms of scope of the questions to be asked and problems to be investigated. The first step has been taken up to a point in the last few years. It involves considering the effects of taxation, subsidies and the supply of public goods upon the general equilibrium system.

The introduction of the control levels imposed exogeneously by the socio-political system can be analysed to see what influence they will have on the economic engine of society.

A socio-politico control system must be connected with the economic engine. It is suggested that such an interconnection opens the way to the analysis of mixed sociopolitical and economic systems in a manner which simultaneously attempts to separate out the considerations of economics, politics, administration, bureaucratic structures and powers of the elite (to mention a few items); together with trying to formalize a specification of their interconnections and feedbacks.

Acknowledgement

The author is indebted to Vincent Ostrom, Elinor Ostrom, Reinhard Selten, Heinz Schleicher and Franz-Xaver Kaufmann for many useful discussions.

References

Cournot, A. A. (1897): *Researches into the Mathematical Principles of the Theory of Wealth.* (Transl. from the French by N. T. Bacon, orig. 1838). New York: McMillan.

Cyert, R. M., and J. G. March (1963): *A Behavioral Theory of the Firm.* Englewood Cliffs, N.J.: Prentice-Hall.

Dahl, R. A. (1961): *Who Governs? Democracy and Power in an American City.* New Haven: Yale Univ. Press.

Gamson, W. A. (1966): *Simsoc: A Manual for Participants.* Ann Arbor, Mich.: Compus.

Keynes, J. M. (1936): *The General Theory of Employment Interest and Money.* London: McMillan.

Lindblom, C. E. (1977): *Politics and Markets.* New York: Basic Books.

Nash, J. F. jr. (1951): "Noncooperative Games." *Annals of Mathematics* 54/3: 286–295.

Nelson, R., and S. Winter (1982): *An Evolutionary Theory of Economic Capabilities and Behavior.* Cambridge, Mass.: Harvard Univ. Press.

Neumann, J. von, and O. Morgenstern (1944): *The Theory of Games and Economic Behavior.* Princeton: Princeton Univ. Press.

Selten, R. (1982): *Elementary Theory of Slack Ridden Imperfect Competition.* Institute of Mathematical Economics, University of Bielefeld. Working papers, No. 117 Bielefeld. (mimeogr.)

Shubik, M. (1975): *Games for Society, Business and War.* Amsterdam: Elsevier.

Shubik, M. (1980): *Market Structure and Behavior.* Cambridge, Mass.: Harvard Univ. Press. (with R. E. Levitan).

Shubik, M. (1982): *Game Theory in the Social Sciences* (Vol. I). Cambride, Mass.: M.I.T. Press.

Shubik, M. (1984): *Game Theory in the Social Sciences* (Vol. II). Cambridge, Mass.: M.I.T. Press.

Simon, H. A. (1979): *Models of Thought.* New Haven: Yale Univ. Press.

Smith, A. (1976a): *An Inquiry into the Nature and Causes of the Wealth of Nations.* Campbell, R. H., and A. S. Skinner (eds.), W. B. Todd (textual editor). Oxford: Clarendon Press. (3rd ed. of 1784).

Smith. A. (1976b): *The Theory of Moral Sentiments.* Raphael, D. D., and A. L. Macfie (eds.). Oxford: Clarendon Press. (orig. ed. 1759).

Williamson, O. E. (1975): *Markets and Hierarchies: Analysis and Antitrust Implications.* New York: Free Press.

Part 6
Accountability, Performance Evaluation and Control in Public Administration

29. Control in Public Administration: Plurality, Selectivity and Redundancy

Wolfgang Wirth

Abstract

Institutional modes of coordination in the public sector and more or less institutionalized controls in public administration are closely related. This chapter tries to link the issue of coordination at the policy level discussed in the preceding section with the following papers that analyze particular instruments and devices of evaluation and control as well as their impact on the executive's performance. It emphasizes the fact that all specific modes of control are selective and at best of only partial influence in multidimensional action situations. A discussion of various analytical aspects of selectivity and some related basic problems that are more or less common to the functioning as well as to the efficiency and effectiveness of all concrete controls illustrates the importance of mixtures, systems and networks of multiple or interrelated controls in complex administrative action arenas and performance processes. Pointing further to the limits and difficulties of systematic design and coordination of controls in terms of ensuring universal bureaucratic accountability and conformity to politically set standards, it is finally concluded that the existence of a redundancy of controls becomes necessary in order to keep potentially insufficient, deficient or even dysfunctional effects of (inappropriately applied) selective controls, at least to some extent, within tolerable limits.

29.1 Introduction

It is one of the central arguments of this volume that problems of coordinating the actions of a multiplicity of more or less organized, relatively autonomous but nevertheless interdependent actors have to be analyzed with respect to the three dimensions of *guidance, control* and *evaluation*. Kaufmann (cf. Ch. 10) argues that there is a need for some fit or consistency in the operating of these three functions in order to establish a coordinated interplay among various relevant actors in terms of linked actions which is considered to be necessary for the satisfactory achievement of some desired outcome of higher complexity. Coordination may take place in various forms by means of a plurality of devices and instruments, but is always related to specific action arenas (which are characterized by specific action situations and specific actors in those situations; see E. Ostrom: Ch. 22) to which specific forms may be more or less appropriate. In addition, the relevant actors involved have to coordinate their own behavior and activities by establishing adequate internal chains of action and exchange relationships with their external environment. We can distinguish institutional coordination by configurations of rules, and operational coordination by interaction and mutual adjustment, intraorganizational (or intra-actor) and interorganizational coordination. It is a problem of institutional or organizational design to develop arrangements of "pure" or mixed types of coordination which are appropriate to the relevant action arenas and the nature of the goods and services to be produced.

We have discussed the resulting problems of coordination in the preceding section with regard to the public sector, dealing primarily with state, para-state and private actors' activities that are of importance to more or less complex processes of policy-making. It has been demonstrated that there are in fact many different mechanisms of coordination operating. Moreover, the existence of a multiplicity of forms of coordination was regarded as necessary, since single forms can only be partially effective due to the polycentric structure of the public sector and the complexity of problems to be solved here. This explains at the same time the relatively high contingency and unpredictability of policy decision-making processes and their results.

The present part 6 of this volume deals with problems of accountability, performance evaluation and control in public administration. The single chapters of this section refer to a more practice-oriented level of analysis dealing with the working, the relative efficiency and the potential effectiveness of more or less *institutionalized controls in public administration* instead of *institutional modes of coordination in the public sector*. Nevertheless, both the functions of coordination and control and the conceptual units "public sector", "public administration" or "public bureaucracy"[1] are intimately linked, and the problems involved as well as the conclusions to be drawn show many similarities.

29.2 Coordination in the Public Sector and Control in Public Administration

To some extent, control in public administration can be considered to be a reduced mirror image of the problem of coordination in the public sector and, at the same time, an important "subgame" for its solution. There are at least four reasons that support this argument.

First, control is defined by Kaufmann (cf. Ch. 10) as a function of information and motivation for intelligent conformity to a system of interrelated actions that are guided by more of less commonly accepted standards set for the performance of the actors involved. Hence, *control is a central part of the coordination problem*. It links the functions of guidance and evaluation. Effective control is needed to ensure conformity to standards, to realize coordination and to achieve the desired results in any performance context.

Second, *public administration is a central part of the public sector*. According to the separation of powers in democratic societies, public administration can be analyzed as a highly aggregated institutional *actor* who is expected to execute public tasks in compliance with standards set by politics. This refers to the issue of accountability that in its broadest sense links democracy and bureaucracy (see Lipsky 1980: 160). As part of the coordination problem control refers to the interrelatedness of actions. But *control is also part of the accountability problem* that refers to the interrelatedness of actors who are in a position to set standards and legitimated to exercise control and those who are expected to behave in accordance with these standards, thus being subject to such control. Control can then also be considered as an attempt to ensure that public administration, being responsible for the performance of specific tasks within the public sector, is responsive to legitimate sources of authority in fulfilling in these tasks[2].

Traditional theories of bureaucracy assume conformity to set standards and accountability to institutionalized sources of authority like legislature and judiciary as a more or less self-evident matter of fact. But modern approaches emphasize that the public at large and the political system must be considered as relevant environments of the public administration (and vice versa) in terms of being *both* influential sources of authority and areas of bureaucratic intervention; i.e. that public administration has become a relatively autonomous, expanded system which fulfills not only executive tasks but is also engaged in processes of standard setting at various stages and levels of policy-making (see Luhmann 1981). Hence, (external) control *over* public administration must not only address the operational solutions of exogenously defined tasks, but also the performance of guidance and control functions *by* public administration itself in exchange relationships with other actors in the public sector. Moreover, it has to include the (internal) processes of control *in* public administration which in turn have most important consequences for the nature and quality of the outputs of administrative action and their effects on third parties.

Thirdly, it would hence be too simplistic a way of dealing with the problems we are interested in, if we analyzed public administration only in terms of being one unitary actor who is interdependent with other actors in the public sector. Public administration must also be considered in terms of being an *action arena* of its own with a highly differentiated internal structure. Public administration itself consists of a multiplicity of more or less organized acting units or actors (e.g. agencies and bureaucrats) who are responsible for the performance of a variety of different tasks and expected to be accountable to multiple internal and external sources of authority. In fact, the multiplicity of actors who are operating in the public sector pursuing differential interests confront public administration(s) with numerous claims, demands and pressures that are coordinated internally more or less consistently. Häussermann (1977: 65ff. and 97ff.) argues that societal pluralism is reproduced in a kind of bureaucratic pluralism as well as in a pluralism of bureaucracies.

Hence, public administration can also be regarded as a system of interrelated actions, but it is not a "closed" one, although it has of course narrower and more visible boundaries than the public sector and is – at least formally – characterized by more precisely defined rule-ordered relationships. *Hierarchy* as an institutional mode of coordination is usually used as a synonym for bureaucracy. Indeed, hierarchical structure is an essential characteristic of public administration. But there are exchange relationships within as well as between administrative units that may also be coordinated by other means. Administrative actors are not only linked along vertical but also along horizontal, functionally interdependent and informal lines. They have, to a variable extent, potentials for self-regulation and may also interact both in terms of cooperation and conflict within various levels and stages of performance processes. For example, in a case of conflict between two agencies there is not necessarily a third, superior administrative actor who is in a position to make appropriate directive decisions. Bargaining or mutual adjustment by debate and persuasion (see Majone: Ch. 21) may be the only possibility of solving such conflicts. However, relative autonomy even of formally subordinate and dependent units varies with the complexity of tasks they have to fulfill and is especially high, if standards set by superiors remain ambiguous or vague and are subject to wide degrees of interpretation by the different actors involved. If this is the case, it is frequently necessary to specify and modify such standards *in* processes of program implementation or street-level performance. But on the other hand, there is also the danger that guiding goals and rules will be misinterpreted and even ignored; that bureaucracies might become unaccountable to specific sources of legitimate authority. Control in public administration in terms of securing accountability to multiple sources of authority and of ensuring conformity to various standards resulting from an often poorly coordinated interplay at the policy level becomes a *multidimensional* problem that cannot be sufficiently solved by means of hierarchy and related control mechanisms alone. However, the demand for bureaucratic accountability seems to be one of the few issues that are – as a normative principle – not contested in contemporary democracies. But in reality accountability has as many "faces" as there are different interests in the political arena. As a consequence, a lot of different controls are operating in public administration. This leads to our last point.

Fourthly, there is in fact a *plurality* of more or less institutionalized forms of control to be found in the modern public administration that reflect the polycentric structure of the public sector but also its above mentioned problems. There are controls conducted exclusively by specific actors, others that are exerted by different actors simultaneously, but answering diverse purposes or representing various interests. There is, for example, judicial control exercised by law courts, financial control by audit courts, management control by administrators and bureau-chiefs, political control by parliaments and interest groups, performance or quality control in a general sense by all of them and by professional colleagues, external advisors, citizens and so on. Who ever is in a position to exercise control may do this by using a plurality of devices (see Malinowski and Münch 1975: 77 ff.). Available instruments are innumerable and differ considerably in terms of applicability and complexity. Financial control, to use an actual example, may be conducted by a variety of different auditing techniques that range (in alphabetical order) from relatively simple methods of traditional "Accounting" in terms of legality and regularity of expenditures to the relatively complicated procedures of "Zero-Based Budgeting".

Other forms of control may include formal and institutional oversight as well as informal bargaining. They may be pursued by means of establishing authority relationships and responsibility structures as well as strategic sanctioning and rewarding within given structures, spontaneous protests and complaints or inspections that leave official channels aside. As with regard to the problem of coordination in the public sector, we can also in this context distinguish an institutional (control by structure building), an operational (control by interaction), an intra-actor (internal control) and an inter-actor (external control) perspective.

Of course, not all available forms of control are accessible to all relevant actors. The various controllers within and around public administrations are usually only exerting influence on specific aspects, elements and phases, on limited dimensions and segments of performance. Moreover, there are considerable differences with regard to the functioning, efficiency, effectiveness and impacts of applied controls. *The plurality of controls coincides with a selectivity of the single forms.* Wittkämper (1982: 192ff.) argues that "pure" forms of control which are performed by institutionally fragmented actors are always selective in terms of time, locus, substance and criteria and in terms of the (social) effects of their own functioning. Hence, in view of the general demand for accountability and the frequently multidimensional nature of public tasks, selectivity and the related limits of single controls require and have resulted in the design and emergence of *systems of mixed controls* of different kinds and size. According to the characteristics of the relevant performance arrangements, various forms and instruments of control have to be linked or must be interrelated in order to take into account the complexity of problem structures and political programs as well as the variety of relevant demands and standards of performance modern public administrations are confronted with. Control is therefore not only part of the overall coordination problem, but is, in an operational sense, at the same time *subject to coordination.*

The specific advantages and benefits as well as the weaknesses and costs of some important concrete devices and systems of control will be discussed in the following chapters in more detail, although there will and cannot be an attempt to discuss their vast number exhaustively.[3] This chapter will discuss, first, on an intermediate level of analysis, aspects of selectivity related to some basic theoretical modes and dimensions of control. We will then address some central problems that are more or less common to the implementation, coordination, functioning and success of all concrete controls, and consequently are of essential importance to almost all scientific and practical approaches which deal with the issue of control in and over bureaucracy. Against this background, we will finally argue that there is a need for the existence of multiple and redundant controls and try to show how the given plurality of controls is in fact interrelated within the complex action arena called "public administration".

29.3 Selectivity of Various Modes of Control

We can now put Kaufmann's above-mentioned definition of control more concretely: Control in public administration refers

- to the monitoring and assessing of administrative decisions, procedures and outputs,
- to preventive or corrective interventions with the aim to enforce rules and to avoid or rectify intolerable deviations of administrative activities or their (unintended) results from relevant goals and standards, and
- to the adjustment or modification of such standards, goals or rules in view of changed or potentially changing problem situations.

Hence, realization of control requires an evaluation of procedures and outcomes as well as the mobilization and application of powers to ensure compliance for the purpose of achieving some desired results. However, strict compliance with fixed rules ("work to rule") often turns out to be ineffective and sometimes impossible or even counterproductive. This will inevitable happen, if goals are ambiguous or not clearly formulated, or if standards are not appropriate to the relevant action situations. It then becomes important to feed the knowledge derived from such evaluations back into processes of standard setting or processes of choice and utilization of means in subsequent performance. Hence, control links rulers, rules and the ruled, directive and operative actors, decisions and outputs, and it addresses problems of political and organizational learning in terms of linking standard setting and standard using within and among various levels and stages of politico-administrative performance. Control is the link between the dimensions of guidance, accountability and evaluation, but it itself must be discussed in terms of various analytically separable dimensions in order to demonstrate appropriately the problems related to the plurality and selectivity of existing controls.

One important dimension of selectivity refers certainly to the *standards of control*, and hence to the criteria and measures of evaluation that are available for the gathering, processing and assessment of information and for the provision of feedback with regard to quality and quantity of performance. The selectivity of controls is of course to a large extent a consequence of selective performance measures or of evaluation techniques and instruments that are not necessarily compatible with complex procedures and outputs to be evaluated and controlled. Since other contributions in this volume discuss the usefulness and limitations of evaluation research (cf. Hellstern: Ch. 14), performance evaluation (cf. Arvidsson: Ch. 30) as well as of criteria and standards for evaluation and control (cf. Grunow: Ch. 31), we will not deal with these issues here in detail[4]. Nevertheless, they are implicit in the following discussion of modes of control.

The term "modes of control" refers to techniques, methods, substance and scope of control. It takes into account that it is impossible to control all relevant dimensions of administrative performance as a whole and suggests the choice of one dimension out of many to exercise control. Therefore, "modes of control" are always related to a specific way of achieving compliance, conformity and accountability with regard to specific aspects of performance. Management by exception, by delegation of responsibility, by objectives or by breakthrough as well as control by programming, by budgeting, by recruitment or by results, and many more could serve as concrete examples. However, we will use the term on a more general level referring to characteristic approaches or styles rather than to elaborate devices of control. We will first consider *how* or *through which* intermediaries or means the control intentions of various actors may become realized. We will then turn to the question of *what* substantial aspects of performance can be controlled and finally ask *when* such modes of control may be applied.

Controlling How?

The question of how or by which means compliance, conformity or accountability can be achieved cannot adequately be discussed without raising the additional question of *who* is in a position to exercise control, i.e., of the structure of authority relationships. The most widespread view is that performance in hierarchically structured organizations is controlled from the top. Superiors are considered to initiate downward information flows by giving instructions to subordinates, and to ensure compliance with administrative directives by strict formal oversight and sanctioning. Of course, formal authority structures and the classic bureaucratic forms of control that have already been described by Max Weber in the twenties (see Weber 1972) are still evident and dominant in contemporary public administrations but this does not mean that there is necessarily effective control from above; formal accountability is not necessarily factual accountability.

Successful control needs access to information, evaluative competences and above all *power* which can be defined as the ability of actor A to get actor B to do that which he would not otherwise have done (see Pfeffer 1982). But power can also be defined as being the ability of actor B to resist doing what actor A wants him to do. In any event, power is a function of resources such as knowledge, money, time, force, etc. Such resources are not equally distributed. Of course, due to the institutionalization of rules, ranks and roles in public administrations each superior has a more or less wide span of control and more or less fixed formal devices or resources related to his authority position in order to exercise control over his subordinates. There is no doubt that most formal power *is* at the top – but its application, may be more or less, or not at all, successful. Hierarchical or legal controls are neither sufficient to ensure accountability or compliance in complex performance contexts, nor sufficient to explain by what means and by which actors performance is actually influenced and controlled. Control in public administrations as well as in other organizations is not simply identical with the perspective "from the top looking down" in terms of surveillance and sanctioning of subordinates' performance. There are also forms of control related to the pespectives "from the bottom looking up", "from the inside looking around" and "from the outside looking in" (McKinlay 1975: 341).

Superiors cannot supervise and control everything their subordinates do, and it is frequently very difficult, if not impossible for them to gain sufficient information from the lower levels of bureaucracy about what is really going on there, as Simon, Smithburg and Thompson (1950) have already shown. Since not only the capability to sanction but, inter alia, also the availability of information serves as a power base, asymmetries of formal power may be useless, if there are opposite asymmetries of information.

Moreover, Dunsire (1978) argues that almost all office holders in bureaucracies have both a superior and a subordinate and are at the same time decision-makers and problem solvers having more or less discretion due to the substantial characteristics of the tasks they have to fulfill. One may assume that bureaucrats at the bottom of a hierarchy have the least degree of relative autonomy, but Lipsky (1980) has demonstrated very clearly that especially street-level bureaucrats, for example in schools, police, lower courts and welfare departments, have considerable discretion in fulfilling their jobs, and cannot be effectively controlled from above by means of management directives and formal oversight. They are, moreover, frequently in a position to resist or ignore managers' orders and instructions. McKinlay concludes from considerable field research that in reality, formal organizations are influenced and partially controlled from the bottom, as well as, or instead of, from the top. He argues that lower employees within formal organizations and also clients or inmates wield considerable power and influence not associated with their formal position (see also Wirth: Ch. 35). "Such participants may be said to have informal personal power, but little formal authority" (McKinlay 1975: 349).

Complex administrations provide examples of a great variety of internal control structures and processes, but they are at the same time subject to external control[5] also along both horizontal and vertical lines. In fact, external actors such as formally insitutionalized control agencies and legislators, but also interest groups, colleagues in functionally related agencies, citizens, etc., influence performance at *all* levels of public administration. However, the effectiveness of external controls is also to a large extent dependent on internal (formal and informal) transformation processes (see Grunow: Ch. 31), and the success of attempts at "looking in from the outside" depends heavily on the cooperation of the "insiders". Many studies have shown that the principles and practice of secrecy and confidentiality frequently impede access to internal information for outsiders and may defend or protect administrative bodies from unpopular external control (see Øyen 1982).

However, different actors are affected differently by confidentiality and secrecy. According to the resources at their disposition they have more or less access to three main modes of control in terms of achieving compliance with procedural standards, conformity to substantive goals or accountability to specific demands and claims. These modes can be called "duress", "exchange" and "identification" (Dunsire 1978: 35ff.), or "coercive", "utilitarian" and "normative" (Etzioni 1975: 118ff.) respectively. *Duress* and *coercion* imply achievement of compliance by threat or use of force and penal sanctions including the withholding of rewards, and rest on people's fear of not conforming. The *utilitarian* or *exchange* mode is based on complementary interests, on interdependencies between superiors and subordinates, on the necessity of the latters' agreement on the tasks they are expected to fulfill and on their ability to use countervailing powers. Conformity or cooperation is achieved by means of bargaining, negotiating or contracting with the aim to assure material or immaterial rewards for actual performance. *Normative* controls or *identification* are based on common norms and shared values and refer to conformity as a result of internalization of controls, ethical or occupational codes by socialization, training, persuasion or indoctrination.

Not only are these modes of control available to various actors to a variable extent, but also more or less applicable or appropriate to concrete action situations. Dunsire argues that duress is more likely to be appropriate and successful where substantive discretion is narrow and uncertainty low; exchange, where discretion is relatively broad but uncertainty still low; and identification, where uncertainty is high, regardless of the scope of discretion. Etzioni argues that the limits of each mode are determined by the relevant underlying goals to be achieved: Symbolic goals are most likely to be achieved by normative controls which entail the least amount of compliance costs in terms of induced alienation and resistance. The use of utilitarian controls would be less effective in this context since it undermines identification with symbolic goals and standard-setting actors by bringing about an individualistic orientation of maximizing self-interests. Such controls are, in turn, most appropriate to goals that refer to the production of concrete goods and of services which cannot – in terms of economic rationality – be achieved with the same effectiveness by normative or coercive controls. Normative controls are less precisely applicable in specialized production processes that require precise and easily measurable rewards and sanctions, and coercion would be insufficient or even detrimental, if initiative and flexibility of the controlled is required. Etzioni emphasizes that coercion in this context may only be effective with regard to standardized procedures. Coercion, in a legal sense, is primarily applied to maintain internal order and avoid deviant behavior. However, it produces the highest amount of compliance costs, which may cause controllers to apply normative and utilitarian controls as well to achieve such goals. There is frequently a mix of all three modes of control in concrete performance arrangements, although one of them is usually predominant.

We can conclude that all these modes of exercising control are selective in terms of their availability and accessibility to specific actors, their applicability to specific performance contexts and their successful functioning. However, subjective definitions of the situation may cause specific actors to consider single modes of control to be appropriate to specific action situations, although they are not necessarily compatible with the real characteristics and elements of the performance that is to be controlled. This leads to the question of *what* can be controlled by the various actors.

Controlling What?

Viewed analytically, there are only three elements or dimensions of performance that can be controlled: inputs, throughputs – by which inputs are transformed into outputs – and the resulting end states. Referring to Majone (1981/82) we thus distinguish three basic modes of control that each have specific limitations as well: control by *inputs,* by *process* or *behavior* and by *outputs*.

Since administrative agencies like organizations of any other type have been established to effect something, they are of course confronted with questions such as: "Have the goals been reached?" "Have the problems been solved?" "Do results justify expended resources?" "And what has to be done if not?" Output control is most important in order to answer such questions appropriately.

Majone argues that output control is feasible, if there are unambiguous, reliable and generally accepted measures of desired results available; if these measures capture all significant dimensions of performance and contain all the information required for full evaluation; if single or individual contributions to final outputs can be measured separately in case of complex, joint or interdependent activities; and if results that are due to chance can be distinguished from those which can be attributed to foresight. One can expect output control to operate successfully, if these conditions are given, e.g. with regard to a bureaucrat's performance whose only and clearly defined task is to produce some kinds of material outputs, the nature and amount of which is predictably determined by the application of standardized procedures, and can be evaluated completely and appropriately in quantitative terms. Output control would then be at least the most efficient or least costly way to assess performance, to detect deviations from relevant goals or standards, and hence to provide a sufficient basis for corrective interventions, since it only requires comparatively little information that can moreover be easily gathered and processed.

However, evaluation and control of outputs is *always* a requisite for enabling a sophisticated gauging of the success or failure of performance, but by itself does not necessarily ensure adequate performance. Output control will become very difficult, its effectiveness is likely to be seriously endangered, and its transaction costs may become excessive when one or more of the above conditions are not satisfied. For example, relying on purely quantitative evaluations of results may divert the attention of the controllers and the controlled from other significant dimensions of performance which may even be important for the final achievement of quantitative goals, but cannot themselves be standardized (see the study of Blau (1963) as an example). Such an evaluation may be positively misleading, if desired results themselves are of a qualitative nature. Moreover, all output controls are problematic, if objectives and intended results are poorly defined in advance, or if it is difficult to find agreement on actual results which depend on variable internal and external inputs and hard-to-measure qualities. This is especially characteristic of medical, educational or personal social services, where discharge of tasks has to be considered mainly in terms of qualitative, more or less discretionary *processes*. McDermott (1977: 138) expresses these difficulties with regard to a physician's performance:

"Much, perhaps most of what a physician does must be categorized as process, and process not even calculated to affect outcome. Indeed, in many cases, whether or not a particular process was initiated is the only true "outcome" that can be measured."

To some extent, this is true of all human services. In such contexts, it may even be destructive to pursue control strategies that *only* rely on results especially in terms of preset artificial quantitative output goals. Failing control in this sense may result in performance that does not meet the substantive problems to be solved. Moreover, if only results count, although their achievement is relatively unpredictable, performance "at all costs", i.e. an operational ideology that the end justifies the means, may be the consequence. Comparatively "cheap" output control may then result at least in inefficient or wasteful use of resources.

Limits of output control call for the establishment of other or additional control mechanisms. Control of process or behavior, periodical or permanent monitoring of the use and transformation of resources may be applied to ensure accountability and a specific nature or quality of performance. Usually, organizations of all kinds apply more than one mode of control. Nevertheless, specific modes may prevail with regard to particular types of organizations. There is no doubt that especially in public bureaucracies which, by definition, do not work according to principles of maximizing outputs or profits, procedural control of performance processes is the prevailing formal mode of control exercised primarily by means of surveillance of behavior through direct observation of activities or through review of records on the basis of formal rules and standards.

In general, process control may be informative and flexible in terms of evaluating and ensuring desired activities, but it may also suffer from subjective distortions with regard to perception, interpretation and assessment of observed behavior – again unless criteria of evaluation and principles of judgment are unequivocal and accepted. It may help to detect and correct *causes* of program failure in qualitative and quantitative terms – but only if the relevant *"production function"*, i.e. the causal relationship of activity and outcome is sufficiently known, and, of course, only if undesired outputs are due to internal, manageable aspects of performance and not to environmental conditions, uncontrollable inputs or subsequent transformations of outputs into impacts that are not accessible to the relevant controllers' influence. Formal rules and regulations may, if clearly defined, restrict the opportunities of actors to behave arbitrarily or to use available resources in intolerable ways, and lead to regularity and standardization of performance[6]. If formal rules and standards provide clear measures for evaluation, deviations may easily be identified and rectified. Nevertheless, compliance with formal rules and standards is not necessarily identical with or appropriate to the achievement of substantial goals. Sometimes, considerations of efficiency and effectiveness may even suggest deviations. Moreover, attempts to apply process control equally and consistently at all levels and functionally different stages of administrative actions would be extremely costly and time-consuming. If at all applicable to performance processes that transcend various hierarchical and functional lines, comprehensive process control may even over-proportionally expend resources that are urgently needed for appropriate service delivery. We will return to such problems later, but can conclude, again with reference to Majone (1981/82), that process control may be useful with regard to homogeneous segments of organizations' activities, but cannot be expected to perform well on an organization-wide scale.

When output control and process control fail or appear to be inapplicable, infeasible or too expensive, superiors and managers in public administration usually apply mechanisms of input control to restrict or enlarge possibilities and alternatives for action. Controlling inputs means defining and allocating means and resources available for performance, earmarking them for specific purposes, and specifying the permitted ways of dealing with them. Material (e.g. financial) or symbolic outputs of performance at one level of the administrative system may become relevant inputs for performance at another level. Hence, rules and instructions, defined standards and objectives can also be considered as inputs from superior actors or functionally preceding "production processes". Insofar, there is a kind of overlap with or basis for procedural control. Moreover, input control may be performed, for example, by recruitment and distribution of staff in order to have appropriately qualified personnel – as a human resource – where it is needed. Yet, input control is primarily discussed in terms of influencing performance by means of the budget; i.e. to allot funds for specific purposes or, especially in the face of fiscal scarcity, to freeze, limit or cut down budgets and reduce current or projected expenditures. Indeed, reducing the available amount of resources and the potential variety of options for their utilization as well as limiting possiblities of choice to substitute one input for another, diminishes the opportunities for discretionary behavior and may eliminate waste. But it may, of course, also have negative impacts on the quality and effectiveness of administrative service delivery. This is obviously the case when budget cuts and "money saving" aggravate goal attainment. However, any kind of input control may become responsible for poor performance, if one does not sufficiently know which resources are really required at different times and places to achieve the desired outputs, or when such knowledge is not sufficiently taken into account. Hence, if input control is to be successful in the long run in terms of ensuring appropriate performance under conditions of potentially rapidly changing (environmental) conditions, it needs feedback concerning the actual course of subsequent activities and their results.

Controlling When?

Feedback is the basis for learning from failure or success of performance *and* its controls and thus refers to a dynamic perspective of control. Dynamic problem structures need dynamic administrations (see König 1977) and also dynamic controls. Up to now, our perspective of control has been a relatively static one. The differentiation between input, throughput and output refers to an analytical reconstruction of performance processes and addresses mainly targets and objects of control but not explicitly the dimension of time in dynamic processes. We have to note that every mode of control can be applied at all *stages* of politico-administrative processes which include the phases of definition of problems and goals, formulation and implementation of programs and their concrete delivery and final outcome, as well as at various, although not necessarily all *points in time* within each of such more or less interrelated phases or stages.

For example, output control can take place *directly* when outputs are achieved, at the *end* of each phase, however this may be defined, or *retrospectively* at some time in the *future,* but may nevertheless *indirectly* influence the subsequent performance. There are diverse and variable inputs entering performance processes *all the time.* Input control may consequently be applied at the *beginning* or *during* running processes. Both process control and the activities to be controlled may occur *at the same time,* but behavior can also be controlled *subsequently* by a review of records. Such control need not *always* take place, but the possibility of its application *after* actual performance has finished may make bureaucrats perform correctly *here and now.*

However, a specific administrative activity may have multidimensional implications, but each single mode of control focusses only on a specific aspect and does obviously not ensure a *comprehensive control* of all dimensions. Moreover, administrative performance processes may be lengthy and consist of various functionally connected, temporally limited or continuing, sequential or overlapping elements and acts, but the various relevant controls are not necessarily linked together or sufficiently interrelated in order to bring about a kind of *systematic longitudinal control.* Such control would of course be most easily understood in terms of an *accompanying* control that is exercised continuously by one unitary actor or by various cooperatively interacting controllers. But one controlling actor could at best be in a position to control short and relatively standardized performance processes effectively in this way. We have already indicated that complex, long and far-reaching chains of action cannot be completely controlled by one unitary actor alone – not to speak of the enormous costs he would have to pay in terms of time and money. In reality, such processes are usually controlled by a variety of actors *simultaneously* and or *subsequently* with each one focussing only on specific parts or segments, but, as the preceding sections of this volume have shown, *these actors are not necessarily interacting cooperatively.* Possibilities and resources for a systematic accompanying control over longer periods of time are thus usually lacking. But apart from this, (potential) controllers frequently consider such a control to be dispensable or undesirable, either because of its danger of reducing flexibility or because all relevant aspects and dimensious of performance are expected to be controlled sufficiently by *ex ante* or *ex post* control.

Ex ante control refers to problems of finding alternatives and priorities in the formation of goals and shaping of programs. Its main intention is to minimize risks and to increase certainty of performance processes before these begin. It is closely related to planning (see Reese: Ch. 27) as well as to research and prognosis in terms of social, economic or technological forecasting, assessment of potential risks and impacts, and so on; i.e. to the discovery of unknown or the definition of supposed "production functions" with regard to the implementation of new projects or the future development of established procedures and activities. If it succeeds in prognosticating, explaining or designing such production functions, it may not only help to allocate means adequately, but also to supervise their transformation into outputs appropriately and, consequently, to avoid that performance becomes too expensive or fails. Effective ex ante control of this kind is of course most likely to be achieved in action arenas that include a defined set of actors and few factors with relatively limited variability which determine the range of potential action situations. Nevertheless, if potential failures of planned activities – already without careful ex ante control – can be expected not to result in intolerable damages, exactly such performance conditions suggest relatively high chances of corrective intervention and may cause controllers to prefer a less systematic (and therefore less expensive) incremental strategy.

However, the chance of ensuring or predicting the achievement of specific goals by means of ex ante control with sufficient certainty diminishes in fact considerably, if the fulfillment of relevant tasks requires complex processes of interactive exchange with a variety of relatively autonomous actors in the political or social environment of public administrations. In such situations, hypotheses are manifold and prognoses are usually contestable issues, due to the complexity, variability, self-dynamics and relative contingency of such processes, so that risk-taking within accepted boundaries may become inescapable.

Nevertheless, ex ante control is not superfluous, despite its limits and problems. It may even be irresponsible to neglect it, e.g. with regard to the implementation of dangerous projects that may have destructive or even irreparable effects in case of accidents or failure.[7] Even if unable to define and establish exactly those conditions that have to be satisfied in order to ensure successful performance according to given objectives, ex ante control may at least be effective in terms of identifying the nature of potential risks, and in this way improve precautions and standards for procedural control aiming at risk avoidance, or increase the likelihood of being prepared to react appropriately and to minimize damages, if they should become reality.

In any case, the effectiveness of ex ante control depends to a large extent on the quality and appropriateness of the available *generalized knowledge* of causal relationships between intended actions and desired results. If, as often happens, programs are initiated that have been designed to exist over longer periods of time, although errors of preceding assessments and mistaken projections are possible or even probable due to complex or variable circumstances and a comparatively poor "state of the art", the required knowledge must be updated in time to ensure, also at future dates, the best possible ex ante control for subsequent continuation or further development of performance. One may, for instance, enlarge or improve a given range and quality of information by consulting various external, e.g. scientific sources which may have generated potentially useful findings about empirically observed causal relationships between specific actions and their actual results in the same or related performance contexts, but in fact, in most cases the generalized knowledge has to be made more specific by analyzing the actually relevant performance processes and their results *a posteriori* – of course only as long as the implied risk-taking strategy does not become an inadmissible option. Hence, ex ante control needs to be linked to ex post control that can be considered as the classic form of evaluating the success or failure of performance, and as a necessary instrument to explain it.

Of course, the results of ex post evaluation and control are frequently controversial, too, as long as there are no integrated theoretical frameworks or sufficiently reliable methodological instruments to cope with complex problems and phenomena (for more details see Arvidsson: Ch. 30; Hellstern: Ch. 14). In any case, they are often of transitory instrumental utility with regard to administrative tasks that will continue to exist in problem contexts and action arenas which are changeable in the course of time, for, in analytical terms, concrete ex post controls, like ex ante controls, are then necessarily applied only temporarily at a specific point *within* the continuum of time of a running program. They are always designed to evaluate retrospectively the activities and results of a defined and frequently only partial period or sequence of administrative performance that has itself not necessarily been terminated or completed. Hence, the effectiveness of ex post controls in terms of providing a basis for learning and, if necessary, successful corrective intervention increases with repeated use.

However, simply knowing what went wrong and even why it did is not enough to ensure correction or adaptive change, unless experience or knowledge becomes translated into running performance by means of controlling powers and the modes of control discussed above. In order to achieve or enhance bureaucratic accountability, appropriate information must not only be gained from, but also transmitted to relevant actors, if necessary across various horizontal and vertical lines. Moreover, these actors must be capable of receiving and understanding it correctly, and they must also be motivated to consider, process and transform it adequately in the course of subsequent processes of action or interaction. In this context, those actors who try to evaluate and influence administrative performance, time and again come up against some central problems and difficulties that they have to overcome or avoid in order to carry out their control intentions or functions successfully, and that are hence subject to numerous, more or less sophisticated, influential and promising reflections and analyses in administrative practice as well as in academic discussion.

29.4 Heterogeneous Worlds of Ideas and Homology of Problems

Relevant scientific "knowledge production", i.e. theories and research on bureaucracy and public administration reflect the multiple dimensions of their subject. There is a large number of approaches and perspectives on the issue of controlling administrative performance which are closely connected, but not necessarily unified. Subsequent to the work of Max Weber, sociologists, political scientists, behaviorist psychologists and economists, scholars of law and public finance, and many others have studied the issue theoretically and empirically, though partly making different assumptions, focussing on different aspects, and arriving at results and judgments that frequently differ and are often inconsistent as well. But there are also interrelated and overlapping findings that have been produced in various scientific contexts under different labels and on different levels of analysis and aggregation.

There are, for instance, the classic studies of *control in bureaucracy* (see Blau 1963; Downs 1967), classifying approaches of different forms of *control in administration* (see Eilon 1966; Hood 1976), the traditional literature on *control in organizations* (see March and Simon 1958; Tannenbaum 1968) as well as the vast body of modern literature on *management control* in various settings (see Miringoff 1980; Self 1975). Some authors are dealing explicitly with *internal* bureaucratic processes and relationships (see Dunsire 1978; Simon et al. 1950). Others are more concerned with questions related to *control by* and *control over* bureaucracy or with the related *inside-outside* interactions (see Grauhan 1971; Ellwein 1971; Peters 1977/78). Some prefer a *system-oriented* perspective rather than an *actor – oriented* approach for dealing with the control problem (see Derlien 1980), while others focus mainly on *institutional* or *constitutional* and *action-oriented* frameworks of control (see various contributions in the preceding sections). Finally, there are the detailed catalogues of formalized *legal controls* (see for example Schwartz and Wade 1972), but also contributions that challenge central rule approaches from a theoretically broader *political perspective* (see van Gunsteren 1976).

The above list of references is, of course, not exhaustive, but detailed and thorough treatment of all the relevant lines of inquiry, of their differences as well as similarities and overlaps is beyond the scope of this paper. However, we will try to give a brief generalized illustration of the range and heterogeneity of some influential foci in the theoretical discussion of the subject, and subsequently point to some core problems which – despite heterogenous ways of defining, classifying and handling them – are of central importance to all relevant approaches.

Some Important Foci of Analysis

As Christopher Hood demonstrates in the last chapter of this section, we can distinguish two alternative theoretical conceptions or ways of thinking about control in public bureaucracy: Control as *"Comptrol"* and as *"Interpolable Balance"*. "Comptrol", defined as self-conscious oversight exercised by institutionalized actors with regard to officially set standards on the basis of formal authority, presupposes a direct, asymmetric relationship between controllers and the controlled. The latter are considered to be monitored, supervised and dominated by the overseers in a strict sense. "Interpolable balance" refers rather to the implications of having something kept within acceptable bounds, as a result of the continuing interplay of existing self-balancing processes and forces. It is argued that complex systems cannot be completely controlled by the precisely defined and overt "comptrollers" alone – a position that is strongly supported by our discussion of the selectivity of particular modes of control.

Nevertheless, the concept of "interpolable balance" also includes direct "comptrolling" as well as the possibility of intentional control that operates indirectly through intervention in that given balance of competing forces by manipulating self-policing to reach or maintain a desired state. Such control is not necessarily exercised from or in some fixed place in the system, but implies shifting seats and balances and a multiplicity of separate, overlapping, redundant and complementary checking mechanisms. Consequently, the direct relationships between controllers and the controlled may be relatively loose, and the latter are considered to have variable degrees of relative autonomy. Improvement of bureaucratic accountability then does not only imply remedying deficits of specific controls by means of improving the overseers' resources and power in order to achieve a better oversight, as the "comptrol-" approach almost exclusively suggests, but also designing institutional and organizational systems and networks that strengthen immanent mutual control and self-control.

Of course, such a wide concept of control complicates the explanation of control processes, but it is by no means a mere theoretical pastime in the "ivory tower" of the social sciences, although practitioners and managers especially in bureaucratic organizations usually have a narrower concept of control that focusses primarily on the *formal* control competences, tasks and relationships, on certain formally established units, devices and processes of control, and on specific institutionalized feedback channels within single agencies or public administration as a whole.

Although these *structural* factors play an important role, control systems typically extend beyond the boundaries of a single organization and even of "the" public administration. Majone (1981/82) argues that structure is not identical with control, although the traditional literature on organizational control does not clearly distinguish between control and structure. He also points to the fact that structural approaches largely ignore the wealth of concepts and evidence from the literature on *evaluation* and *learning* which have to be taken into account in order to understand properly the *functions* of control. Moreover, explanation of the success or failure of administrative performance as a function of its control also requires a careful analysis of non-structural and non-formal factors that influence performance by motivating some actors to exercise specific forms of control and others to comply with set standards or not. Hence, we have to focus our attention also on the *functional relevance of the "human factor"* for the effectiveness of control and performance. This includes the motives, interests and intentions, the personal resources, skills and cognitive, communicative and interactive competences, and the spontaneous actions or strategic behavior of individual members of organizations, regardless of their formal position. It further includes intentional, routinized or contingent *informal interaction processes* and, of course, also situations in which formal controllers are *informally* controlled by or to some extent dependent on their subordinates because the latter are the experts who possess the information the superiors need to exercise their tasks effectively.

There is no doubt that all the above-mentioned aspects and perspectives have something substantial to contribute to the adequate identification and explanation of the basic problems which may affect the functioning and success of more or less all efforts of control in public administration, and which have to be discussed at least with regard to three dimensions:

- the difficulties of implementation and exercise of controls that arise from barriers and resistance to control on the side of those who are to be controlled,
- insufficient applicability and usefulness of control as a consequence of inherent limitations of selective forms of control, and
- the potentially resulting dysfunctional effects of exercised controls.

Some Central Problems of Control

Infeasibility, high costs, insufficient efficiency or effectiveness and counterproductive effects of control are interrelated and constitute a dialectic pattern of core problems: in general, obstacles to control stem from the cause of its existence, and pathologies of bureaucracies may stem from the bureaucratic exercise of control. Of course, control is not per se problematic, ineffective and counterproductive. Just as there are specific conditions that have to be satisfied for specific modes of control to be feasible and successful, concrete occurrence and specific nature of such problems depend on a variety of factors that are characteristic of the relevant action arenas and situations. However, from an analytical point of view, we can identify some basic common roots.

Problems and negative effects of control may be a consequence of shortcomings as well as of the exclusive or too extensive and intensive use of specific controls that are only partially compatible or even totally inadequate for the potentially multidimensional conditions and nature of performance. For example, in areas where predictability, reliability and uniformity of administrative performance are possible and regarded to be necessary for the sake of equity, control with the aim to achieve compliance with a defined set of rules and regulations may fail because of the insufficient enforcement powers of the controller, but also their inappropriate utilization. Exaggerated emphasis on hierarchical and standardized control, or on coercion and punishments in the case of rule violations may in many cases not only be of limited usefulness, but also result in pathological phenomena which have been described by various authors (see Crozier 1964; Merton 1940; Türk 1976) in terms of *overcontrolled, overstabilized* and *overcomplicated* performance arrangements as well as with regard to the emergence of *bureaucratic personalities*.

An overcontrolled, or in Hood's terminology an "overcomptrolled" bureaucracy, may be out of control in a broader sense. If too much time and energy is spent on internal tasks and processes of bureaucratic control in relation to the direct and substantial activities of achieving the underlying program objectives, the effectiveness of regular performance is likely to be reduced. Control then becomes counterproductive. Flexible cooperation of concerned actors that, in the light of conditions of environmental complexity and change, has frequently proven to be indispensable for successful performance is then seriously impeded. But nevertheless, there are some contradictory tendencies inherent in this issue. Realization of flexible performance requires relative autonomy and discretion for the performing actors and is frequently also related to a relative incalculability of results. This may be an unavoidable consequence of the characteristics of the goods and services to be produced, but also of inadequate, insufficient or mistaken activities of the relevant actors. This in turn constitutes one of the essential reasons for the necessity of control and at the same time creates serious problems for its efficiency and effectiveness, which may finally result again in countervailing processes of bureaucratization and standardization.

However, *problems of control may also result from difficulties in information gathering and processing,* especially if controls seek to achieve intelligent conformity to a complex and changeable system of actions instead of blind compliance with some fixed formal rules. Such problems are of course related to the already mentioned conditions of goal ambiguity, lack of knowledge of production functions, acceptable and reliable measures for desired outputs, and so on. But they are also related to the tendency of individual and corporate actors to manipulate and withhold information for the sake of "turf protection" and strategic or even opportunistic self-seeking that illustrates again the importance of control in general.

Hence, the necessity of control, the obstacles to its implementation, and the problems related to its effective and successful functioning are to a large extent derived from the same set of underlying conditions: *bounded rationality, complexity and uncertainty with regard to the tasks to be performed and the problems to be solved, selectivity of controls and their inappropriate use, and opportunism.* This is particularly true of the difficulties potential controllers may have in gaining the required information from the relevant actors. Williamson (1975: 31 ff.) links some of these conditions in his *"organizational failures framework"* by the concept of *"information impactedness"* that – as a derivative condition – arises mainly because of uncertainty and opportunism, but also involves bounded rationality.

Information impactedness "... exists in circumstances in which one of the parties to an exchange is much better informed than the other regarding underlying conditions germane to the trade, and the second party cannot achieve information parity except at great costs – because he cannot rely on the first party to disclose the information in a fully candid manner" (Williamson 1975: 14).

He shows that an exchange between two or more actors – however they may be formally related to each other – is very likely to be subject to hazards under such conditions.

In fact, individuals usually do not want to be controlled by anyone, least of all by someone from outside. Control is regarded as a lack of trust in their abilities, reliability and willingness, as a reduction of autonomy and discretion. Consequently, they look for means and techniques to evade control and develop strategies of *control avoidance* which are of course the more easy and successful to pursue, the more standardized, already known or reasonably predictable, in a word, the more "bureaucratic" the potential controls are with regard to their application, functioning and consequences. Large and complex bureaucracies in particular, dealing with multidimensional tasks, usually provide many opportunities for such efforts – in spite of or sometimes just because of their highly differentiated structure and formalized devices of control. Nevertheless, this problem of control avoidance, too, often provokes a call for the strengthening of bureaucratic control forces which may again lead to costly, but inefficient, ineffective or even counterproductive over-use of administrative rules and regulations. However, administrations and the quality of their performance may finally suffer so much from an increasing intricacy, unintelligibility and fruitlessness of overcomplicated formalizations that deregulation becomes an issue of its own (see Voigt 1980).

On the other hand, although comprehensive formal regulation and standardization obviously does not make control avoidance impossible for the members of administrative agencies, it nevertheless may, in the long run, already have created bureaucratic personalities that need regulation as well as continuity. Formalized laws and rules are the only basis of occupational action for a "pure-type bureaucrat". Good service records and undisturbed advancement according to special, fixed career paths are the basis of his motivation. Avoidance of risks and mistakes in his greatest problem. In the light of experienced or anticipated controls of superiors, or of sanctions in the case of rule violations, he works almost absolutely predictably and reliably – *as long as rules remain stable and unequivocal!* However, steadily growing and ultimately overcomplicated systems of rules may confront him, too, with serious problems. But deregulation may have similar consequences for him. After years of bureaucratic performance he may judge himself to be performing optimally, but actually he is extremely inflexible and skeptical about *any* kind of change that affects his routine and working techniques. If there is any new task or prescription that does not fit into a given, internalized frame of orders and rules, and especially if such a frame itself is deemed less important by superiors or has even become outdated, he may "collapse" or take no notice of the formally changed situation. He may ignore it unconsciously, for example, if the understanding and processing of new tasks and rules is beyond his intellectual capacities and instrumental skills, or consciously, for example, if he sees no other possibility of maintaining his traditional bureaucratic identity. In any case, he would not question authority frankly. There are thus silent mechanisms of displacements of goals, when routine activities and habitual behavior tend to substitute the "new"-professed goals or standards.

Closely related to such phenomena is the occurrence of dysfunctional effects of control as a consequence of one-sided assessments and judgments of the procedures and outputs to be controlled. Such biased controls and evaluations reflect a specialized "tunnel view" of the relevant actors and are based on criteria and indicators that reflect a dominant operational philosophy, but are of partial validity, reliability and usefulness at best. Indeed, this is not only related to the performance of more or less "pure-type bureaucrats" who may focus primarily on formal standards such as legal correctness or economy. It is also observable with regard to the special scientific disciplines or paradigms of professionals in bureaucratic agencies. Especially in the case of biased recruitment other criteria or professional perspectives than those that are dominant in the specific arena will always tend to be ignored, neglected or underestimated. This tendency affects the perception of reality and may result in a critical consolidation of a specific, but not necessarily appropriate way of defining and handling problems as well as in the generation of outputs that are inadequate with regard to the problems to be solved. It may finally also restrict the capacities, abilities and readiness to recognize and correct mistakes and failure in due course.

29.5 Interrelation and Redundancy of Controls

In principle, controls of any kind are confronted with the problems analyzed above, although to a variable extent in differently structured action arenas. The described insufficiencies and pathologies are not a function of the plurality of various forms, but of the immanent selectivity and shortcomings of specific forms of control and their inadequate application in specific arenas as well as of their over-use that may weaken or override complementary or compensatory potentials of control. Effects of control vary with the relative compatibility of controls with the nature of tasks, goals and conditions of (administrative) action. If standards and production processes are multidimensional, single, unidimensional controls may produce more harm than good, if there are no supplementary and balancing controls operating. Relying only on the relatively simple strategy of alternatively increasing or reducing density, extensiveness or intensity of the application of specific formal control types in cases of perceived ineffectiveness or dysfunctional effects may result in a vicious circle. Such a strategy does not necessarily solve the related problems, but may even reinforce them, or reproduce them on another level. Hence, the problem is finding those *mixtures of controls* from the available plurality of modes and instruments that promise to fit the specific characteristics of the relevant action arenas and performance processes in an optimum way.

Systematic Coordination of Controls – A Theoretical Ideal?

The task of linking selective modes and forms of control appropriately in order to achieve satisfactory results of administrative performance is closely related to the problems of institutional and organizational design discussed in various chapters of this volume (e.g. E. Ostrom: Ch. 22; Kaufmann et al.: Ch. 37) Indeed, efforts to devise and implement control systems or evaluation systems and management information systems that mix and coordinate "pure" forms of control in specific performance contexts or in administrative agencies of various kinds and size are numberless.[8] There are doubtless many examples of the successful operation of intentionally planned management control systems, although failure of many efforts of this kind show that effective management control is far more difficult in public agencies than in private, profit-oriented organizations, since there is not necessarily a commonly accepted goal like the profit objective (see Steiss 1982). Arrow (1978: 82) argues that the design of control systems in large organizations is already a formidable task, but several orders of magnitude simpler than a control system for a government where a single utility function is replaced by a variety of utility functions of the different groups responsible for political pressures of various kinds in the political system.

This points to the limits of systematic design and establishment of systems and networks that promise *perfect* control in public administration. Even if one succeeded in designing control systems that were as complex as the relevant systems to be controlled, but tried to institutionalize them formally in terms of determining definitively inducements, contents, criteria, means, procedure and times of control, they would still be subject to "the law of inevitable selectivity of controls" (Wittkämper 1982: 192) in view of rapidly changing environmental conditions. Morever, it is plain that total and perfect control, if at all feasible, need not be socially desirable, if one thinks, for example, of the oppressive effects of total control exercised by an omnipotent authority in George Orwell's well-known science fiction novel "Nineteen-Eighty Four" (see Wirth 1984).

However, returning to scientific analysis, we have to state that there is no political power center in the public sector possessing total steering capacity with regard to public administration; that there is no omnipotent authority center within the public administration that could control all aspects of performance of its parts; and, finally, that there is *no best way* to coordinate various controls systematically in order to render them appropriate to all circumstances and effectively operable or at least predictable in *all* kinds of situations. And especially, if the fulfillment of a *specific* task is not only multimensional, but also derived from goals and standards that are immanently ambiguous or contradictory, perfect control will be quite *impossible*. Hence, not only the functioning and effects of established controls, but also the possibilities and chances for systematic creation and successful implementation of (new) forms, systems and networks of control depend heavily on the size and quality of performance arrangements and on the nature of the goods to be produced under them.

Problems of coordinating controls in public administration reflect the problems related to the coordination of actions of the more or less organized actors that operate in the public sector. We have to realize that mixtures of controls must not be stable and durable, if problem structures, environmental conditions and political demands are variable; that controls of any kind cannot be unequivocal, if goals and standards set at the policy level are ambiguous; that there cannot be a common understanding of accountability, if there is no common agreement on tasks (see Lipsky 1980: 159ff.). Control that should nevertheless be effective in terms of ensuring intelligent conformity of administrative action to such standards as well as accountability to a variety of legitimate sources of authority, must be flexible and itself open to adaptive changes on the basis of experienced failure. Hence, it requires multidimensional information on procedure, outputs and impacts of performance to be controlled *and* sufficient feedback with regard to its own functioning. If controls cannot be coordinated systematically and effectively by one unitary actor or a set of cooperatively interacting actors in a way that is commonly accepted and perfectly compatible with the nature, complexity and variability of relevant action situations, interests involved, goals to be achieved and goods to be produced, the actually exercised, more or less selective controls must then be subject themselves to other controls in order to keep dysfunctional effects within acceptable bounds. Elling (1983: 88) argues in this context that "... effective systems to ensure bureaucratic accountability are those which are redundant such that certain means at least partially compensate for deficiencies of others."

While this argument refers mainly to the *means* and *processes* for ensuring or enhancing bureaucratic accountability, Kaplan Daniels (1975: 331) puts more emphasis on the necessity of balancing all the legitimate (control) interests and demands of relevant *actors* together in a joint review system. She supposes that "... no accountability system can ever be really effective without a check and balance system permitting all those affected by the professional service to have a voice in its evaluation and manner of transmittal"[9]. Moreover, a redundancy of controls refers not only to the normative issue of assuring bureaucratic accountability, but also to the substantial or "technical" issue of having sufficient information to achieve successful performance in terms of the solution of multidimensional problems. The ability of administrations to adapt to environmental complexity and change, to minimize errors and to avoid program failure will be increased by the creation of redundancy, since this "... greatly increases the likelihood of the right information being available in the right place at the right time, if it exists in the system at all." (Dunsire 1978: 9).

Not relying on the pure and strict hierarchic-rational conceptions and models, such a plea for redundant controls operating within open and reflexive systems of checks and balances, of course, also poses a challenge to institutional and organizational design. However, achievement and effects of redundancy in the administrative reality are not without problems, either, and a given redundancy does not mean that available information and the various existing modes, forms and systems of control are *always* appropriately interrelated.

The Answer of Reality: A "Cobweb" of Control

To summarize, redundancy refers to multidimensional information, to multiple forms of control as well as to the various actors who may apply them[10]. Hence, the achievement of redundancy implies the generation of information on the same aspects of performance by various different actors, from several sources, in different forms and its passage via many different channels, many times and in many different ways. It may thus be a consequence of informal interaction processes among bureaucrats and/or external actors that are interested in or affected by their performance; of inputs from associations, parties, mass media or interest groups, of external professional advice, collegial debate, inter- or multidisciplinary scientific evaluations or consumer feedback that reaches the relevant administrative actors directly or indirectly with variable intensity in a periodical, occasional or incidental way; and last but not least, also of various forms of formally institutionalized political, legal or administrative oversight, and so on. Hence, deliberate achievement of redundancy of controls and information would, of course, be facilitated by the institutionalization of various feedback and communication channels, by the creation of overlapping jurisdictions and by the establishment of various controlling and monitoring bodies on hierarchical as well as on horizontal lines within the relevant action arena (see Downs 1967: 147).

The following chapters on performance analysis, internal control in public administration, audit control, parliamentary and judicial control and control by publics give ample evidence that there *are* many such channels, institutions and mechanisms, that there *is* a redundancy of controls within and around public administration. However, the existing plurality of more or less selective forms, instruments and systems of control that may influence administrative performance at various levels and stages is not balanced within a rationally planned system. Instead of assuming an artificial, logically consistent lattice of control, we should rather use the image of a very complex "cobweb" of control relationships within the public administration and around its single units with various points of contact with its environment through which outputs from the inside but also the various and partly conflicting external control inputs are passed. But there are also numerous internal ramifications, nodes, rows, circles and transformation points through which the different internal and external controls move toward their targets (which they eventually hit or miss) and through which they may be linked in manifold ways more or less appropriate to the relevant action situations. Many parts of this network have grown in an unplanned way, but there are many others that have – although often independently of each other – been systematically designed and implemented. In addition to the more or less accidentally emerging and rapidly changing informal control relationships, there are various relatively autonomous, functionally differentiated and specialized controlling actors and institutions within public administration that evaluate and control the performance of other administrative actors or institutions as representatives of the public on the basis of specific standards (e.g. "legality" by courts, "economy" by audit offices). Almost all controlling actors are at the same time subject to the control of other agencies focussing on other, but equally specialized aspects and standards of performance (e.g. the performance of audit offices may at the same time be controlled in terms of legality by other actors), and each has its own internal control units with equally specialized tasks and competences that reflect externally set standards and exercised controls at a lower level.

Hence, there is a strong division of labor not only in the public sector, but also in public administration both in terms of pursuing specific substantial goals through the performance of specific agencies *and* in terms of controlling specific aspects of this performance on the basis of particular standards. Such controls are each only of partial virtue and to a variable extent able to overcome control resistances. Each of them may take place periodically and regularly with regard to a limited range and specific segments of performance processes, but their linkage within and across several more complex, functionally and structurally interrelated levels of performance is usually relatively *fortuitous*. There are some examples where redundancy *and* interrelatedness of different controls is predictably achieved by formal regulations[11], but exercise and functioning of multidimensional control, as of any other task of higher complexity, can neither be ensured nor sufficiently explained by means of hierarchy and law alone.

Many formally established control institutions need (formal) inputs in terms of complaints, suits, requests etc., to address specific aspects of the performance of specific administrative agencies, and are, moreover, dependent on the cooperation of the latters' internal controlling units to fulfill their task successfully. They may be activated by inputs of a variety of different actors such as other formal controllers operating within public administration, more or less organized actors operating in the public sector, individual citizens and so on. However, not all control interests have the same chance to be appropriately taken into account, and not all factually exercised controls are to the same extent influential on processes and results of administrative performance in particular action situations. Not all relevant actors affected by or legitimately interested in administrative performance possess sufficient information, resources and (often bureaucratic) competences needed to activate formal representative controls. Realized redundancy of controls exercised by various actors in a specific action situation implies the possibility that there are controls that support and complement each other, but also that there are mutually incompatible controls that neutralize or obstruct the deficient as well as successful functioning of others. Hence, activated controls, whether formal or informal, whether from the top, from the bottom or from the periphery of a given action arena, may be frustrated by countervailing powers that represent stronger control interests. Consequently, even if there are regular and routinized internal control procedures, there is a relatively high *incalculability for administrative actors* in terms of what external controls may be exercised by whom and at what time, if there is more than only one legitimate source of authority that may choose to enter the game or not. But on the other hand, there are also *considerable imponderabilities for external controllers* with regard to the results and success of their endeavor to influence administrative performance.

If administrations are confronted with many demands and inputs from outside, there is of course a redundancy of available *information* given, but this implies the possibility of relevant and correct as well as of unintelligible, unreliable, false and obscure information getting through. To ensure the solution of multidimensional problems, if at all possible, there is still a need for appropriate perception, interpretation, understanding and operationalization at the receiving end and of appropriate transformation through various internal channels, e.g. from the bottom to the top or vice versa. Dunsire (1978: 71) argues that the main problem in any large communication network "... is accurately to sort out the real message from the noise." However, what is the irrelevant "noise" that could be neglected or ignored in the case of a given redundancy of *controls* (not only of information); when various actors monitor and evaluate administrative performance on the basis of specific standards and intervene with the aim to induce corrections, improvements or change, especially if there are partly conflicting or totally incompatible, but nevertheless legitimate control interests involved? In such situations, administrations or their members are confronted with a dilemma or even "multilemma"[12], i.e. the achievement of universal accountability to all relevant actors and of conformity to all relevant standards becomes an unsolvable task for any single agency or its internal controllers. Although all standards such as legality, economy, efficiency, effectiveness or responsiveness might be judged to be of equal value and importance, priority decisions are unavoidable. But since any change in favor of one demand or standard is at least partially at the expense of another (see Hegner 1978), every decision (or non-decision) will cause one or more affected external actor(s) to accuse the public administration of being unaccountable, ineffective, inefficient or whatever.

To sum up, the empirically evident redundancy of controls within the administrative system as a whole does, on the one hand, not necessarily ensure a redundancy of controls operating at any level, at any given time and with regard to any aspect of bureaucratic performance. In fact, specific performance processes and activities are to a variable rather than to an equal extent subject to multiple, differential or redundant, and more or less consistently interrelated controls. However, a given redundancy of controls and a given redundancy of information does, on the other hand, not necessarily ensure a generally satisfactory compliance, conformity and accountability of single administrative actors (whether agencies or their members) and their actions. Moreover, it does not necessarily exclude the internal over-use of specific selective controls on the basis of formal standards that may be inadequate for the fulfillment of substantial tasks. Hence, a redundancy of controls and information cannot guarantee a perfect solution, but in situations where it is lacking, goal displacements, insufficient performance, unintended, dysfunctional or pathological side-effects of performance and its control are much more likely to remain undetected or uncorrected, and subjective distortions – whether they are wilful or not – of controlling and controlled participants with regard to their perception of reality are much more likely to result in deficient decisions and actions. By contrast, a redundancy of controls will offer opportunities for different actors and interests to strengthen various standards of administrative behavior and output, and hence contribute to an "interpolable balance of control". Innovations and adaptive change, even if only slow and ponderous, to potentially rapidly changing political and social environments on the basis of experienced success or failure of performance will be facilitated and are more likely to take place.

29.6 Conclusions

The public administration, their agencies and individual members have to justify their performance and give an account of what they have done to a variety of legitimate sources of authority. There is a plurality of modes, forms and devices of control available that may be applied by various more or less institutionalized actors within and around public administration and its numberless single units with the aim of ensuring bureaucratic accountability and conformity of administrative performance to politically set standards. However, the various controls are always selective and more or less compatible with specific action situations. They have specific advantages and benefits, but also weaknesses and deficiencies. In any case, they are, each of them, at best of only partial influence and limited effectiveness in complex performance arrangements, but some may remain without any impact, and others may even produce dysfunctional effects and subvert service quality, especially if they are exclusively and too intensively applied, in spite of being not or only partially compatible with the nature of the underlying public tasks to be fulfilled.

Over-use of selective controls may result in pathological phenomena, if there are no compensatory or balancing controls operating at the same time. Hence, the absolute certainty of avoiding such problems – if at all possible – would require systematic coordination of controls, but this has turned out to be extremely difficult and frequently even impossible in public agencies due to the changing, ambiguous and partly conflicting environmental demands and politically set standards with which public administrations are expected to comply. There is no perfectly regulated apparatus as the ideal-type picture of hierarchy may suggest; no smooth running machinery that controls public administration effectively in every respect, but a redundancy of multiple controls which may interact successfully, but also with considerable frictional losses. The single controls may, focussing on specific standards, partly operate with calculable regularity, but they are linked with a relatively high contingency across various levels and lines of more or less interrelated performance processes.

There is a widespread tendency among practitioners in public administration – but not only there – to characterize such a redundancy of controls in terms of an *expensive overcontrol.* Indeed, a redundancy of controls may be very costly, inefficient and ineffective in terms of economic rationality. But such a perspective does not sufficiently take the political dimensions of public administration in contemporary democratic societies into account. Hence, we support the opposite position: *administrative performance suffers more from the over-use of specific controls than from a supposed overcontrol in terms of multiple and redundant controls.*

The existence of a plurality and redundancy of more or less selective internal and external controls in public administration is the necessary consequence of the existence of a plurality of only partially influential mechanisms of guidance in the public sector. It may aggravate the security needs of public officials and contribute to their suffering because of work. However, a given unpredictability of controls in administrative action arenas operates in a similar way to the competitive forces in the market mechanism; it creates uncertainty in order to improve performance (cf. Krüsselberg: Ch. 17).

Effective control in terms of political rationality requires a redundancy of controls that keeps insufficiencies and deficiencies of single controls at least partially within acceptable limits and takes into account the polycentric structure of the public sector, the variety of legitimate interests, the multidimensional character of political programs and the complexity of problem structures in rapidly changing environments – although, or perhaps even because it reflects countervailing trends and contradictory impulses of society, uncertainties and conflict. However, the problem of control(s) in public administration will always be a contested issue to the same extent as the underlying politically set goals or standards are contested, too.

Acknowledgements

I am grateful to Franz-Xaver Kaufmann and Giandomenico Majone for their constructive comments on a previous draft of this article. Moreover, I am indebted for instructive insights of various kinds to Jürgen Reese and some of his discussion papers. The exacting work Jean Randigh and Adelheid Baker have done in terms of improving the English style of this contribution deserves my special thanks.

Notes

1   Our usage of the terms "public administration" and "public bureaucracy" refers to different perspectives of dealing with the problems under discussion. The term "public

administration" is used in an empirical sense, referring to the *concrete* subject of analysis, i.e., to the formally institutionalized system of administrative units or actors that – from a general legalistic point of view – have been established in order to implement public policies and to carry out political programs. However, administrative agencies are usually considered to fulfill their tasks in a more or less "bureaucratic" way (for a discussion of the issue of bureaucratization see Grunow: Ch. 2 and 1982). Hence, the term "public bureaucracy" is, of course, also appropriate in this context, but it implies a more theoretical dimension and is used here primarily to indicate a relevant *analytical* type of performance arrangement (see Weber 1972: 126ff.).

2   We are referring here to the definition of Gates (1980: 65): "When organizations, programs, and organizational actors are responsive to legitimate sources of authority and influence, it is said that their behavior is *accountable*. ... Although sometimes used interchangeably, the terms *accountability* and *responsibility* are not the same and should not be confused. Whereas the organizational actor may be responsible *for* the performance of a task, the actor may also be accountable *to* some group or individual possessing legitimate authority over its performance. Accountability, then, explicates a specific source of power, authority, or influence." Such sources of authority and influence may be, for example, courts, parliaments, media, citizens, internal superiors, administrators, etc.

3   There are, of course, also structural and functional differences that have to be taken into account with regard to different countries. There will be an illustrative demonstration of such differences with regard to audit control, parliamentary control and judicial control in Chapters 32, 33 and 34.

4   With regard to evaluation and control in public administration, especially Arvidsson and Grunow discuss problems related to measurement and appropriateness of criteria and standards such as *legality* (compliance with law), *economy* (money saving), *efficiency* (ratio of output per input unit, referring to productivity), *effectiveness* (ratio of outputs achieved in comparison with politically set goals), *impact* (external, intended or unintended effects on third parties) and *responsiveness* (degree of consideration or inclusion of substantial environmental needs, problems and demands of a diverse clientele), which all together reflect the "many faces of accountability."

5   The definition of "internal" and "external" depends, of course, upon the conceptual unit or action arena one chooses to analyze. Very complex systems of checks and balances may be considered as referring to internal control within public administration as a whole, but the controlling agencies institutionalized within this arena become external controllers of other agencies which are, of course, also internally controlled. Finally, their internal control procedures are external controls for single bureaucrats who, in turn, may have more less *internal*ized them.

6   This may be of essential importance particularly in situations where there is no sufficient knowledge of production functions with regard to the solution of substantial problems that serves as a kind of "natural" guide-line for action. Formal rules may then represent an "artificial" production function with regard to specific aspects of performance by determining the transformation of inputs into desired outputs according to formal standards. For example, legality *is* certainly and reliably achieved by compliance with formal law.

7   This may be the case, for example, with regard to safety and potential hazards of nuclear energy production. Nuclear plants are in Germany at least partially under state control and administered by bureaucratic agencies. The implementation and operation of such plants after initial political decisions have been made require careful ex ante control in view of potential accidents that could lead to catastrophic disasters, but also in view of risks associated with exposure to radioactive materials at the workplace and continual release of low-level radiation. Such risks cannot be obviated by ex ante

control alone. But relying, for example, on a trial-and-error strategy would be inexcusable.

8   The terminological difference between forms and systems of control is introduced here merely to distinguish different levels of analysis. However, there are similarities and overlaps of meaning since the issue of linking or mixing the basic, analytical separable *modes* of control described above is of central importance to design at both levels. *Forms* of control refer to the existing plurality of concrete devices and procedures that are the result of the manifold ways in which the analytical "building stones" of control may be linked at the lowest level. (For example: input control exercised by an internal superior at the beginning of each year by means of allocating money). A deliberately planned and implemented, interrelated set of various forms, a bundle of established control procedures constitutes more or less complex *control systems* that are expected to fulfill specific tasks in specific action arenas. Finally, *networks of control* which will be discussed in the next paragraph refer to the more or less accidental linkage of diverse forms and systems of control as well as of internal and external controlling actors within action arenas of higher complexity across various functional and hierarchical lines and levels.

9   Kaplan Daniel's argumentation refers primarily to the performance of professionals in formal organizations providing welfare services. Nevertheless, her conclusion that welfare systems need to be monitored by clients as well as by professional colleagues, administrators, legislators and regulatory agencies as representatives of the public to ensure accountability, can, of course, also be drawn for the issue of bureaucrats' performance in administrative agencies.

10 For more detailed references to the relevant literature dealing with the concept of "free information" and related issues see Andrew Dunsire's book "Control in a Bureaucracy", published in 1978.

11 This is the case, for example, with regard to periodical, politically motivated, financial control exercised by parliaments in terms of effectiveness and financial control in terms of efficiency and economy exercised by audit courts which may have to submit their results to parliaments and their commissions (see the contributions of Arvidsson and Sigg in Chapter 34 and also of Hellstern in Chapter 33).

12 The issues of "dilemma", "multilemma" or "polylemma" with which administrations may be confronted have been discussed by various contributors to this volume in more detail: see Dunsire: Ch. 16; Grunow: Ch. 31; Hood: Ch. 36; and also Hegner in his 1978 published book "Das bürokratische Dilemma".

References

Arrow, K. J. (1978): "Organizational Goals and Control Systems: Internal and External Considerations." In Preston, L. E. (ed.), *Research in Corporate Social Performance and Policy,* Vol. 1, 79–97. Greenwich, Conn.: Jai Press.

Blau, P. M. (1963): *The Dynamics of Bureaucracy* (2nd ed). Chicago: Univ. of Chicago Press. (first edition 1955).

Crozier, M. (1964): *The Bureaucratic Phenomenon.* Chicago: Univ. of Chicago Press.

Derlien, H. U. (1980): "Zur systemtheoretischen Fassung des Kontrollproblems in der öffentlichen Verwaltung." In Hauptmann, H., and K. E. Schenk (eds.), *Anwendungen der Systemtheorie und Kybernetik in Wirtschaft und Verwaltung,* 195–224. Berlin: Duncker & Humblot.

Downs, A. (1967): *Inside Bureaucracy.* Boston: Little, Brown.

Dunsire, A. (1978): *Control in a Bureaucracy.* New York: St. Martin's Press.

Eilon, S. (1966): "A Classification of Administrative Control Systems." *Journal of Management Studies* 3 (Feb.): 36–48.

Elling, R. C. (1983): "Bureaucratic Accountability: Problems and Paradoxes; Panaceas and (Occasionally) Palliatives." *Public Administration Review* 43/1: 82–89.

Ellwein, T. (1971): "Kontrolle der Bürokratie oder Kontrolle durch die Bürokratie?" In *Probleme der Demokratie heute,* 170–179. Sonderheft 2 der Politischen Vierteljahresschrift. Opladen: Westdeutscher Verlag.

Etzioni, A. (1975): *Die aktive Gesellschaft. Eine Theorie gesellschaftlicher und politischer Prozesse.* Opladen: Westdeutscher Verlag. (Orig. ed.: *The Active Society.* A Theory of Societal and Political Processes. London: Collier McMillan; New York: Free Press. 1968).

Gates, B. L. (1980): *Social Program Administration: The Implementation of Social Policy.* Englewood Cliffs, N. J.: Prentice Hall.

Grauhan, R. R. (1971): "Kontrolle der Bürokratie oder Kontrolle durch die Bürokratie." In *Probleme der Demokratie heute,* 165–169. Sonderheft 2 der Politischen Vierteljahresschrift. Opladen: Westdeutscher Verlag.

Grunow, D. (1982): *Bürokratisierung und Debürokratisierung im Wohlfahrtsstaat. Soziologische Analysen eines gesellschaftlichen Problems.* Habilitationsschrift. Bielefeld.

Gunsteren, H. R. van (1976): *The Quest for Control.* London: Wiley.

Häussermann, H. (1977): *Die Politik der Bürokratie.* Frankfurt/Main – New York: Campus.

Hegner, F. (1978): *Das bürokratische Dilemma: Zu einigen unauflöslichen Widersprüchen in den Beziehungen zwischen Organisation, Personal und Publikum.* Frankfurt/Main – New York: Campus.

Hood, C. C. (1976): *The Limits of Administration.* London: Wiley.

Kaplan Daniels, A. (1975): "Professionalism in Formal Organizations." In McKinlay, J. B. (ed.), *Processing People,* 304–338. London – New York – Sydney – Toronto: Holt, Rinehart, Winston.

König, H. (1977): *Dynamische Verwaltung.* Stuttgart: Bonn aktuell.

Lipsky, M. (1980): *Street-level Bureaucracy: Dilemmas of the Individual in Public Services.* New York: Russell Sage Foundation.

Luhmann, N. (1981): *Politische Theorie im Wohlfahrtsstaat.* München: Olzog.

Majone, G. (1981/82): "Modes of Control and Institutional Learning." Preprint No. 17 of the Research Group an Guidance, Control and Performance Evaluation in the Public Sector. Bielefeld. (mimeogr.).

Malinowski, P., and U. Münch (1975): *Soziale Kontrolle.* Neuwied: Luchterhand.

March, J. G., and H. A. Simon (1958): *Organizations.* New York: Wiley.

McDermott, W. (1977): "Evaluating the Physician and His Technology." In Knowles, J. H. (ed.), *Doing Better and Feeling Worse,* 135–157. New York: Norton.

McKinlay, J. B. (1975): "Clients and Organizations." In McKinlay, J. B. (ed.), *Processing People,* 339–378. London – New York – Sydney – Toronto: Holt, Rinehart, Winston.

Merton, R. K. (1940): "Bureaucratic Structure and Personality." *Social Forces* 18/4: 560–568.

Miringoff, M. L. (1980): *Management in Human Service Organizations.* New York: Macmillan.

Ouchi, W. G. (1977): "The Relationship between Organizational Structure and Organizational Control." *Administrative Science Quarterly* 22/1.

Ouchi, W. G. (1979): "A Conceptual Framework for the Design of Organizational Control Mechanisms." *Management Science* 25/9: 833–848.

Øyen, E. (1982): "The Social Functions of Confidentiality." *Current Sociology,* Confidentiality: Theory and Practice, 30/2: 1–42.

Peters, B. G. (1977/1978): "Insiders and Outsiders. The Politics of Pressure Group Influence on Bureaucracy." *Administration & Society* 9/2: 191–218.

Pfeffer, J. (1982): *Power in Organizations.* Marshfield, Mass. Pitman.

Schwartz, B., and H. W. R. Wade (1972): *Legal Control of Government*. Oxford: Clarendon.

Self, D. (1975): *Econocrats and the Policy Process: The Politics and Philosophy of Cost-Benefit Analysis*. London: Macmillan.

Simon, H. A., D. A. Smithburg, and V. A. Thompson (1950): *Public Administration*. New York: Knopf.

Steiss, W. (1982): *Management Control in Government*. Lexington, Mass.: D. C. Heath.

Tannenbaum, A. S. (1968): *Control in Organizations*. New York: McGraw Hill.

Türk, K. (1976): *Grundlagen einer Pathologie der Organisation*. Stuttgart: Enke.

Voigt, R. (ed.) (1980): *Verrechtlichung*. Königstein/Ts.: Athenäum.

Weber, M. (1972): *Wirtschaft und Gesellschaft*. Grundriß der verstehenden Soziologie (Fifth ed.). Tübingen: Mohr (Siebeck) (first ed. 1921).

Williamson, O. E. (1975): *Markets and Hierarchies: Analysis and Antitrust Implications*. New York: Free Press; London: Macmillan.

Wirth, W. (1984): "Der öffentliche Sektor 1984: Wissenschaft und Fiktion – ein futuristischer Epilog auf ein interdisziplinäres Forschungsprojekt." Preprint No. 24 of the Research Group on Guidance, Control and Performance Evaluation in the Public Sector. Bielefeld. (mimeogr.)

Wittkämper, G. W. (1982): "Die politische Kontrollproblematik der öffentlichen Verwaltung." In Hesse, J. J. (ed.), *Politikwissenschaft und Verwaltungswissenschaft*, 191–204. Sonderheft 19 der Politischen Vierteljahresschrift. Opladen: Westdeutscher Verlag.

30. Performance Evaluation

Göran Arvidsson

Abstract

The starting point for this chapter is three widely held opinions: performance evaluation in public administration is necessary, difficult and seldom used. In order to explain what *performance evaluation is, several aspects or dimensions, are identified: object, time perspective, criterion, management – accountability – knowledge perspective, evaluator, user, intended use and type of activity. Measurement problems and quality dimensions are discussed with the use of a schematic production model. The problem of multiple, non-comparable goals in noted. Four "ethics" are identified: economic, democratic, legal and professional. Examples of indicators related to these ethics are given. Four design considerations are then treated at some length: the users, intended uses, types of activities and evaluators. For each there is a discussion of* how *different situational factors could be considered in the design of performance evaluation. Finally, the importance of active public officials is pointed out.*

30.1 Introduction

There are three widely held views concerning performance evaluation in public administration:

- "Performance evaluation is necessary."
- "Performance evaluation is difficult."
- "Performance evaluation is seldom used."

The purpose of this chapter is to throw some light on these arguments and to summarize a number of observations, experiences and conclusions concerning performance evaluation in practice. It is based both on international experiences and on my own personal experiences of development and implementation of performance evaluation in Sweden's central government administration.

Let us look a little more closely at the arguments.

Performance evaluation in necessary. Citizens and taxpayers require that public programs be properly examined and the politicians and public officials be held accountable. This argument has also long been advanced by analysts and budget experts, but politicians and managers of public programs have shown little interest or have responded negatively. Politicians do not wish to be informed of previous mistakes or inadvertencies in their decisions. They want to look forward and concentrate on future activities which may receive support from the public. Managers have been used to competing for additional resources. Under such circumstances there is little motivation for scrutinizing past or present activities.

Recently, however, the emphasis in public budgeting has shifted from resource addition to resource allocation or – rather – re-allocation.

Where new requirements cannot be met due to lack of additional resources, reconsideration of past obligations and ongoing programs becomes necessary. Savings, cut-backs, productivity improvement, privatization, etc. have come into focus. In view of this situation both politicians and managers are asking for more and better information: they need performance information as a basis for their intervention. There is now a clear demand for performance evaluation among stake-holders who were clearly reluctant only a few years ago.

Performance evaluation is difficult. Indeed it is. Especially where aims are high. Many approaches have been introduced and many have failed. There seems to be a rather widely held view that a search for general models is in vain. General models fail to yield what is needed in the varying applications. Also, many methods and techniques are too difficult to comprehend for practitioners with limited time and interest in "managerial" or "scientific" tolls.

This means that the supply of more or less refined techniques and studies has not met the practitioners' demands for simple tools and relevant information. The analysts have not been sufficiently aware of the needs of the decision-makers and the latter have not acted in their own interests when rejecting methods and information offered to them.

Performance evaluation is seldom used. (Many decision-makers would say that it is seldom usable.) There are at least two inferences here. One is that performance evaluation is not made at all. The other is that performance information is gathered and analyzed but not used – for whatever reason. Both statements are relevant to many public systems. The danger is that vicious circles can and do occur. The principal actors in the system learn that performance evaluation is of little use. Consequently, they do not introduce it in new contexts or in modified versions.

The above account of the present "state of affairs" may lead to quite different conclusions. The remainder of this treatise starts from the following premises:

(a) Since performance evaluation is needed and demanded, methods should be developed and implemented. This should be done with regard to the users' needs and the organizational and managerial context.

(b) Since performance evaluation is difficult of application there should be an emphasis on developing and introducing administratively efficient methods, i.e. they should not cost more to apply than they yield in the form of better public activities.

(c) Since performance evaluation is seldom used – and seldom considered as sufficiently usable – the emphasis in methods development should be on applicability and validity rather than on completeness or technical refinement. "It is better to be vaguely right than exactly wrong." This means that is seems important to study what kinds of approaches are most administratively efficient in different kinds of public activities and for different purposes.

Before going into the question of *how* to design and implement "useful" performance evaluation it is necessary to briefly discuss and make clear *what* it is.

30.2 What is Performance Evaluation?

It is not the purpose of this chapter to present and argue for a precise definition of performance evaluation. Nor is the purpose to go into a concept analysis. The intention is to "problematize": to identify and to some degree penetrate what I consider to be major aspects of performance evaluation. For this purpose it is sufficient – at this stage – to state that *performance evaluation means to find out and appraise how well an activity, a program or an agency fulfills or has fulfilled its objectives.*

With this definition we have already distinguished three aspects of performance evaluation: *Object, time perspective* and *criterion.* We are interested in the performance of undertakings – not of people per se. We restrict our interest to past or present performance, to facts – and exclude pre-valuations e.g. appraisals made in policy analyses. And, thirdly, we consider performance as an expression of results related to objectives. If the objectives are multidimensional, then performance is a multidimensional concept.

There are several other aspects of performance evaluation which should be observed.

The *perspective* may vary. With a *management* perspective, performance evaluation is likely to be regarded as an integral part of the management control system of a public institution. Its usefulness for internal planning, monitoring and decision making processes are of primary interest (cf. Grunow: Ch. 31).

With an *accountability* perspective, the focus is on the relation between the "principal" and the "agent": Did the agency accomplish what was expected from it, did the public institution perform responsibly and in accordance with rules and regulations, etc.? (see Wirth: Ch. 29 and 35; Hellstern: Ch. 32 and Ch. 33; Arvidsson and Sigg: Ch. 34).

With a knowledge perspective, performance evaluation is seen as a way to acquire new or better insight into an activity, its effects, management procedures etc. This is, of course, something quite different from control in its narrow sense of supervision.

Another important aspect is the *evaluator's position.* External evaluation and internal evaluation often have basically different purposes. The types of aspects studied and the methods of analysis differ. The roles of politicians, managers, staff specialists and clients are important to identify and analyze if one wants to understand the "dynamics" of performance evaluation. Evaluation often involves both conflict and co-operation between interest groups. Therefore, bargaining, manipulation of information, persuasion, threats, etc. may be important features of an evaluation.

Since performance evaluation usually has an operational purpose, i.e. its purpose – at least indirectly – is to improve operations, there is another important aspect to observe: how it is *related to policy making and managerial decision making.* To whom is the information presented? How detailed is it? How is the timing? What are the forms of presentation? Etc.

Several other aspects could easily be identified, but this is not necessary. The point so far is that *performance evaluation is an activity with many dimensions.* To understand its conditions it is necessary to know that its objects may vary, that the criteria are not self-evident, that there aree different perspectives, that different interests are involved, etc. – and that these factors matter. In order to show the implications of this I will proceed from a simple production model. Successively, more aspects will be added.

30.3 A Simple Production Model

A public program, or an agency, can be described as an input-throughput-output-impact system. "Inputs" are resources used in operations where they are transformed (as "throughputs") into outputs.

The "outputs" are the direct results of the activity, i.e. goods and services supplied by the agency. The "impacts" are the effects of the output on individuals or groups of people (or at least on a social "problem"). Within this frame-work – and with a management perspective – performance evaluation would mean studying and assessing past or ongoing activities in order to determine future activities. This, in turn, means that performance analysis necessarily contains assessments of outputs and their impacts as well as of costs and non-economic sacrifices. It also contains attempts of determine whether certain qualities are good or bad and to explain why.

Even though the problem of acquiring a fair estimation of the inputs and how they are used should not be underestimated, it is evident that the outputs and impacts create the major problems in performance evaluation.

Traditionally, the benefits arising out of most public activities were only assessed intuitively, but for several years determined efforts have been made to measure outputs and impacts. In many instances, however, it has not proved meaningful to quantify outputs or impacts. In other cases quantitative data have been useful but not sufficient. Both quantitative and qualitative descriptions are usually needed to get an adequate picture. This means that it is more appropriate to talk about *output description* than about output measurement. Also, different parties tend to have contradictory opinions on the objectives of public activities and their benefits – and thus may value the same results differently. This means that the measures must be consistent with the frame of reference through which the activity is viewed. It also means that condensing output information into one or more aggregate measures may be undesirable. (cf. Ridgway 1966.) A multidimensional description may be the only relevant method of representation.

In measurement centered approaches outputs are usually regarded as "producing" or "causing" impacts. However, impacts may be realized only step by step, in a long chain of consequences. Therefore, a description of outputs is not a sufficient basis for performance evaluation.

Having a chain of outputs and impacts means that the focus of output and impact description may be either closer to the activity or to the objectives (see figure 1). Where to focus depends on the intended use of the description. If a budgetary decision within the school system concerns the mixture of lectures and laboratory work within a specific line of vocational training, a description of classroom hours, exams passed, etc. may be most appropriate. If the decision concerns the dimensioning of the enrollment of students one would have to seek more "ultimate"

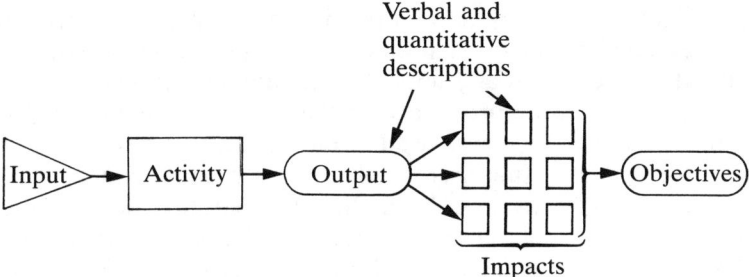

Fig. 1: A traditional Production Model

impact descriptions. Also, routine decisions require routine information. There is little time for specific studies. Thus for routine decisions one would have to be content with production and output statistics in addition to cost accounting information and intuitive impact judgements. Strategic decisions require and can "afford" deeper analyses.

One common criticism of the usefulness of impact assessments is that the impacts of one activity cannot be isolated from the effects of other government activities and other changes in society. Though a serious problem, this should not be a reason for not undertaking otherwise desirable impact studies.

Now, let me turn to the multidimensional aspect of performance description and analysis. In order to avoid technicalities, I will restrict myself to some aspects of political and administrative relevance.

30.4 Multidimensional Performance Evaluation

In many western industrialized countries, program budgeting ideas were introduced in the mid-sixties. One important feature of this new paradigm of public planning and budgeting was the emphasis laid on economic rationality, effectiveness and efficiency. (See e.g. Lee and Johnson 1973; Lyden and Miller 1982). This and other PB-ideas strongly influenced the concept of "good" ministerial and agency planning and budgeting during the first half of the seventies. In many countries considerable advancements were made. Modernizing a government budget system, however, is no easy task. Many implementation problems were underestimated (see Arvidsson 1980). Among many politicians the ideas were felt to be too far removed from what was described as political rationality. In Sweden a common argument run: "Public activities cannot – and should not – be run by using control systems appropriate to factories. Public activities have intrinsic values which cannot be expressed in terms of economic effectiveness or rationality."

There were also other objections. Unions of civil service employees, people in personnel departments and others felt that the stress placed on effectiveness and efficiency was in conflict with basic values of employee participation, personal development, working conditions etc. Others questioned how economic rationality should be balanced against professional standards.

Program budgeting never became what its most optimistic proponents had hoped for. The actual behavior of politicians and public administrators did not conform with the models. Goals, impacts, outputs and processes could not be measured and analyzed in accordance with the requirements of the PB-systems, etc. However, many elements were used in the subsequent development.

In Sweden, for example, the discussions led to a broader concept of effectiveness. Since the 1960s effectiveness in public administration had been associated with goal achievement in relation to resources used, i.e. with economic rationality. The broader concept encompassed additional aspects: A government agency performs effectively if it reaches its objectives

– whilst husbanding its resources
– with due regard to demands for public service, public disclosure and due process
– and with regard to the employees' need for job satisfaction, good working environment, job security and possibility to codetermination and personal development.

This definition was officially established in 1979 at an agreement between the National Agency for Government Employers and the central unions of civil service employees.

In comparison with the PB-concept of effectiveness this definition makes overall impact assessments more complicated. Husbanding of resources is not defined as more crucial than the other goals; the latter may not be seen simply as restrictions. (However, in the last few years husbanding of resources has – again – come into focus in public debate as well as in budgetary directives.)

This means a formal acceptance of multidimensional goal structures and, consequently, multidimensional standards for performance evaluation. Attempts by analysts to make goal functions more clear-cut by optimizing only efficiency in achieving production goals have not been accepted by politicians and managers. However, the loss in clarity for professional evaluators may have been offset by gains in terms of opportunities for communication between politicians, administrators, analysts, the public, and other interest groups.

This development does not entail going back to pre-PB-notions of public performance with obscure policies concerning the desired qualities of public activities. Instead, there is now a new frame of reference for impact studies and performance evaluations.

This development is not peculiar to Sweden. Similar approaches may be found in e.g. American literature. Fried (1976) has a similar frame of reference. In an effort to show that the traditional concept of performance is too narrow, he distinguishes three equally important aspects of "bureaucratic performance", namely

– effectiveness, corresponding to the "work ethic"
– responsiveness, corresponding to the "democratic ethic"
– liberalism (or due process), corresponding to the "legal ethic".

Fried also discusses what further dimensions each of these incorporate. The personnel aspect belongs, for example, to the democratic ethic.

Clearly, the relative importance of these ethics has shifted over time. Also, at each point in time it differs from policy area to policy area and from country to country. *Distinguishing between different ethics seems to be one important aspect to consider in understanding the deeper meaning of performance.* The use of these concepts has, however, led me to add a fourth ethic: the professional ethic. The medical, military, teaching, legal, scientific, cultural and other professions have their own ethics or standards. These may be seen as a specific kind of work ethic but they are seldom economic in character. On the contrary, professional standards are often strongly defended against economic arguments in times of cut-backs and re-allocation of resources. It seems appropriate to distinguish between the foll-owing major dimensions – or ethics – of performance:

(1) economic ethic
(2) democratic ethic
(3) legal ethic
(4) professional ethic.

The ethics[1] are, of course, too general by themselves to serve as yard-sticks for evaluation purposes. A battery of indicators for each ethic is needed. Some *examples* are:

- Economic ethic: cost per product, time per case handled, variance from budget, criticism by auditors
- Democratic ethic: treatment in political assemblies and public debate, new "movements", legitimacy crises
- Legal ethic: complaints, appeals, verdicts by administrative courts, criticism by ombudsmen and legal inspectors
- Professional ethic: opinions expressed by leading professionals, research find-ings, statements by professional associations, violation of professional standards where such exist.

These examples of "indicators" illustrate a general problem of performance evaluation of public activities: the difficulty in finding indicators which are both relevant and operational. This concerns all four ethics but especially the democrat-ic and professional ethics. The consequence is that performance can seldom be expressed in a meaningful way by quantitative data only. To a great extent, analysis of performance has to be based on qualitative descriptions and statements. This, in turn, means that subjective elements are unavoidable. My own experience is that *explicit reference to the ethics facilitates performance discussions* of e.g. program managers and evaluation staff. Identifying the ethics and their significance helps them to discern important, sometimes conflicting values governing decisions concerning the program. It also facilitates understanding the behavior of different protagonists. It may even make it easier to reach agreements about the actual as well as desired balancing of the four ethics as far as a certain program is concerned.

The ethics can also be used to analyze – or to actively build in – counter-vailing powers in agencies or programs. Different "actors" may represent different ethics. Legal staff and financial controllers are two relatively clear examples. How political appointees, general managers and project leaders act with respect to the ethics is, on the contrary, often not at all clear. To study how priorities and outcomes are affected by the attention paid to the different ethics by key actors may be an important task for performance evaluators.

If we widen the perspective and include the perceptions and intentions – whether articulated or not – of the persons engaged in performance evaluation there is another aspect to consider. Do they represent different ethics and, if so, what does this imply for the design and implementation of performance evaluation? Finding answers to this question is one way of addressing the "old" problem of non-use of evaluation results (see e.g. Weiss 1966).

30.5 Performance in an Expanded Production Model

The ethics concern the outputs and their quality as well as the quality of the production processes. Another way of looking at performance is to relate it to production goals and organizational goals.

The *production* (or external) *goals* concern the production of goods and services to the customers, clients, beneficiaries etc. They represent the short and long range societal functions of the activity.

The *organizational* (or internal) *goals* represent the interest in maintaining and developing the agency's financial, material and intangible resources, i.e. the basis for future action. Certain activities may be directed primarily to the fulfillment of these goals. Labour on budget requests, office maintenance and recruitement of staff are a few examples. Others may affect them indirectly, as for example public relations activities and support to educational institutions.

Elaborating on the production model in figure 1 is one way of illustrating the wider concept of performance. See figure 2.

A production model of this type can be a good starting point for the design and planning of performance evaluation. Depending on the purpose of the evaluation the emphasis may differ.

In order to clarify what type of qualitative aspects should be regarded in performance analyses – and how they should be described or measured – a pilot project was undertaken in the Swedish Central Government Administration. Its first phase was limited to four aspects of agency administration, namely planning, rationalization, personnel administration, and personnel training. Indicators were developed and tested with some success. The study confirmed, however, that indicators are not meaningful if not developed for use in clearly specified contexts. It was, for example, quite evident that indicators developed for internal planning use, were in all but a few cases considered unusable on aggregate levels, e.g. as indicators in reports to superior authorities. Development of useful methods for description and measurement thus presupposes that a judgment has been made of what aspects different stake-holders should be informed about.

The conflict between relevance and measurability was a permanent dilemma. It was difficult to find measures that were convincingly related to policy goals. Another problem was the agencies' varying definitions of basic concepts. Without uniform concepts – and uniform formats for registration of basic data – there is no strong foundation on which to develop general indicators for use in different

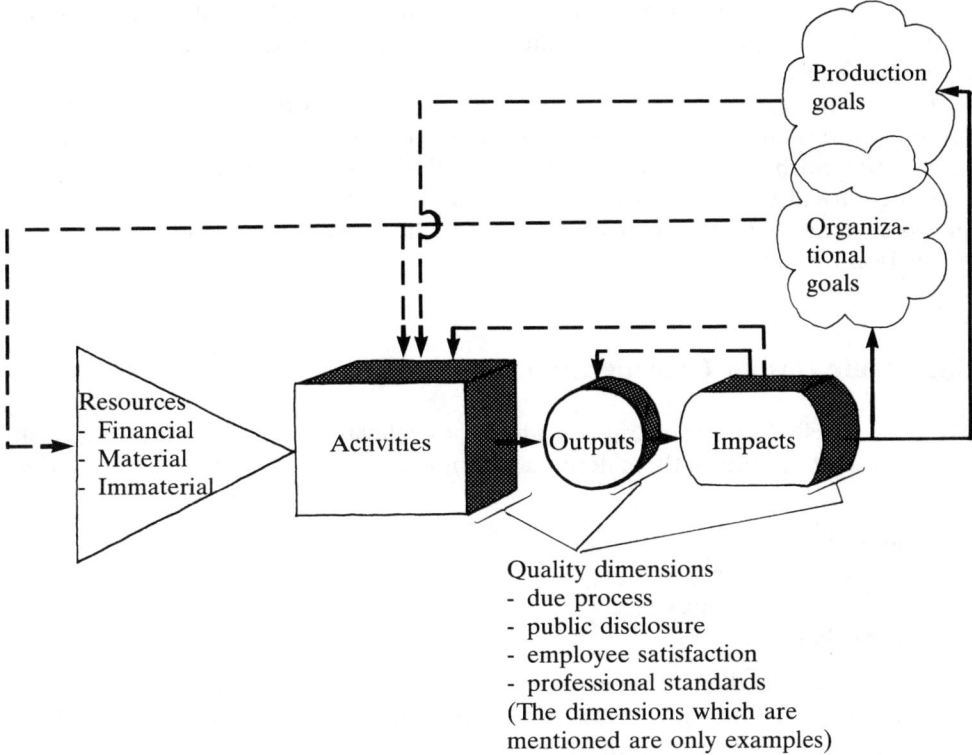

Fig. 2: An expanded production model

settings, e.g. for comparisons between different agencies (see Riksrevisionsverket et al. 1979).

One advantage of basing the design of performance evaluation on a model of the type illustrated in figure 2 is that it clarifies the relationship between different steps in the production process. Measurement of productivity, activity levels, cost per produced item etc are examples of approaches based on a production perspective.

There are, however, situations where a production oriented approach may be misleading or at least not very useful. One example is cases where clients' participation is a necessary condition for the whole activity. In education and rehabilitation programs – to mention two areas – the quality of the clients' participation is a major determinant of the overall performance. In such cases of co-production other, "consumer oriented" models focusing on relations between the program and the behavior, knowledge, attitudes, well-being, etc. of the clients may be more relevant.

Also, instead of viewing an activity as a matter of producing outputs which "cause" impacts – in a one way flow – one can talk conceptually about producing "outputs" which are consumed by the participation of different groups resulting in new outputs which in turn are consumed, ad infinitum. This way of looking at an activity or an agency as an open system interacting with its clients is necessary if an evaluation is to include questions of e.g. responsiveness and strategic adaptation. Ultimately, the "quality of life" of different groups in society are involved as well as equity issues.

The point here is that it is necessary to *decide where in the production/ consumption chain the evaluation should be made and what stake-holders should be recognized.* Such decisions are often made without a clear specification of a) who is supposed to use the performance data, b) in what situation and c) for what purpose. Failure to do so seems to be a major reason for the under-use of evaluation results.

30.6 Four Design Considerations

We have touched upon several considerations relevant for the design of performance evaluation. Four of them deserve a somewhat more thorough treatment. They concern:

(1) The users
(2) The intended uses
(3) The types of activities
(4) The evaluators.

Before we turn to them it seems appropriate to make the central concepts more precise and formulate a few theses as a starting point for the subsequent discussion, which will have a normative character.

– *Performance description* means to identify and express benefits and sacrifices of an activity in quantitative and qualitative terms.
  Thesis: Based on the interests of legitimate stakeholders the relevant aspects – or dimensions – of performance should be identified, and for each aspect one should try to find valid, reliable and unbiased measures or other modes of description.
– *Performance analysis* is to relate performance description data to each other, to standards of performance, to the objectives of the activities etc.
  Thesis: The analysis may be made within a follow-up or evaluation frame-work. The frame-work should be an important determinant of the depth and regularity of the data collection and analysis.
– *Follow-up of performance* means to compare actual performance data (cost, output and impact data) to budgets or other standards, consider the findings and draw conclusions for managerial decisions. (Cf. Wholey 1979: 117, who labels this "performance monitoring".)
  Thesis: The emphasis in the analysis should be on decision support within the control and monitoring systems of the organization.
– In *performance evaluation* cost, output and impact data are related to political and other objectives of the activity in question. Estimation of the effectiveness of the activity in producing desired results may be one purpose. Another would be to study how observed impacts are caused by the activity. (Cf. Wholey 1979: 149, who discusses what he calls "intensive evaluation".)

Thesis: The emphasis should be on support to strategic decision making – not only at the top level but also at program and project levels.

The follow-up and evaluation frame-works are, of course, overlapping. The point here is that e.g. data collection, form of analysis and reporting could – and probably should – vary considerably depending on whether the findings are being used in regular managerial decision making or in strategic or ad-hoc decision situations.

Now, let us turn to the four "design considerations". My experience is that these four, and the ethics, are the crucial ones to consider. They should be dealt with before interest is turned to the question of measurement and the method of analysis.

30.7 Users of Performance Evaluation

The motive for spending time and effort on performance analysis is that the feedback it gives is expected to contribute to effective and efficient operations: "Without follow-up and performance evaluation, planning and budgeting become meaningless." "Performance evaluation is necessary in order to determine whether an activity corresponds to requirements." "We need performance evaluation so that we can set the right priorities in the budget process." "How can we know that an agency is properly run if its performance isn't analyzed?"

There are many good reasons for performance evaluation, but their interrelationship is often obscure in practice. One way to gain some clarity is to find out what different users want from the analyses.

Internal users seek performance data to support their control of the system. Key issues seem to be follow-up of plans and budgets, organizational learning, search for evidence supporting the activity (e.g. arguments to be used in the budget process), use of indicators for monitoring purposes and quantity, quality and cost control.

External users want performance information for decisions as to whether or not to intervene in the system. Politicians and Budget Examiners want to know which social needs are not yet satisfied and how much money to put into each activity. Superior authorities want to know how task delegation works and to what extent subordinate units are effective and efficient. Taxpayers want to know that their money is properly spent. Interest organizations want information about service levels, effects of regulations and other quantitative and qualitative aspects of the activities which are important to them as consumers, objects of public intervention etc.

Evidently, the interests of internal and external users often conflict. "Knowledge is power." The establishment of audit offices and institutes for independent evaluation shows that external parties recognize this fact. They do not want to depend solely on internal performance evaluations.

One conclusion would be that the role of the user must be recognized when designing performance analysis models and when actually undertaking such studies. Also, the control situation and the user's decision capacity must be considered.

If the results of performance evaluation do not matter – in the sense that they do not affect future behavior – *then they are of no value from a decision point of view* (though they may have a value as historical records). Failure to address decision makers' "real" problems and bad timing in the presentation of results account for many of the fiascos in this field.

30.8 The Intended Uses

Two types of application of performance data have already been identified: follow-up data in managerial decision situations and evaluation results in strategic decision making and in special situations where deeper analysis is desired.

This is not to say that problem is to find potential fields of application for different kinds of measurements and analyses. On the contrary. The need for information for guidance and control purposes should govern the choice of methods for performance description and analysis. Information which cannot be used – or is not used – should not be gathered and reported. The characters of the planning and decision situations decide what type of information is appropriate. For monitoring purposes accessibility, regularity, coverage, intelligibility, unambiguity, low cost and prima facie acceptance ought to be more important than completeness, depth, thought provocation and option generation. When it comes to performance information for use in political debate, strategic planning, redesigning of programs or choice of working methods, it ought to be the other way around. There are many practical examples illustrating that this was not considered when the follow-up or evaluation methods were implemented.

Another observation is that the decision maker and the evaluator (if they are not identical) have often different opinions on the intended use of the findings. In many cases they are not aware of this; in others they openly disagree. A common feature is that concepts for clarifying the intentions are missing. Discussions in terms of the management, accountability and knowledge perspectives may be helpful. If the perspective is determined from the outset it is probably easier to agree on how and by whom the results should be utilized.

Another useful categorization of intentions is:

1 supervision
2 validation
3 innovation.

If the interest of the "principal" is *supervision* (of an agency or a program), then he wants to know whether the behavior of the supervised object is in accordance with rules, stated goals or other expectations. He is generally not interested in receiving studies questioning basic policies and suggesting new ones. He is probably most happy if the evaluation shows that all is in order (given that it actually is in order). If not, he is probably ready to take corrective action, but this is something quite different from being prepared to initiate policy changes. Failure to realize this is one reason for why creative performance auditors or inspectors are sometimes frustrated.

If *validation* is the purpose, then the principal wants to test the rationale of a program, examine hypotheses of cause-effect relationships, know if aspiration levels are reasonable, etc. In this case he wants analysis, not mere descriptions or statements that goals are fulfilled or that no criticism is warranted. He is probably more interested in acquiring a better knowledge of the existing program than in receiving new options.

If, on the other hand, *innovation* is the motive, then the principal is expecting new ideas based on the evaluation. He is probably already convinced that "something should be done" and is hoping that the evaluation will generate ideas for further action. If the evaluators do not "deliver" this, there will at least be disappointment on the part of the principal.

It should be clear that it is important that decision-makers ("principals") decide and communicate to the evaluators the real purpose of an evaluation. If this is not done, conflicts and troubles are bound to appear – except under fortunate circumstances.

30.9 The Types of Activities

Public activities are of many kinds. Classifications may be made in numerous ways. If the interest concerns methods for performance evaluation, the character of the "production process", the outputs and impacts are more important than the policy area.

Three main categories may be identified, namely *regulation, reallocation* and *production*. Within each category a subdivision may be made according to the types of processes and outputs. Also, a distinction may be made between the *governing* and the *executive functions* within each type of system.

One design problem is to find out what types of performance analyses would be most adequate for each control level in each type of activity. The research evidence is limited but I will summarize some views based on field work in the area.

Regulation

A characteristic of the regulating function of the public sector is its purpose to influence actors outside the sector, i.e. individuals, business firms etc. Regulation also exists within the public sector. Central government regulates activities by local government, even though the latter is not subordinate to the former.

The regulatory activities in a certain policy area are often organized in a hierarchy with the political system at the top followed by regulatory bodies, who in turn supervise inspecting and controlling bodies. The supreme political decision-makers frequently restrict themselves to broad policy decisions (e.g. "frame-work laws") leaving considerable freedom to central agencies to specify the norms in detail.

Performance evaluation can be undertaken at different system levels. At a higher level, important questions would concern the change in needs for regulation, the balance between strict norms and recommendations and between the issuing of norms and the control of the enforcement and observance of them. Performance evaluation aiming at the system's effectiveness would thus imply a number of considerations of both political and analytical character. The design would have to be of a non-standardized format and use methods like cost/benefit analysis, quality of life surveys and policy studies.

Performance evaluation of the regulatory bodies could be more stuctured. Regular follow-ups would monitor adherence to time-schedules, budgets, etc. More intermittent but still relatively standardized analyses would concern changes in the demand, coverage and observance of the norms. The results of such analyses could for example be reported regularly within the budget process. A third kind of analysis comprises evaluations of the consequences of the norms for different stakeholders, studies of the influence of the regulations on actual behaviour etc. Assessment of spill-over effects into other areas and the degree of reversibility of new regulations would belong to this category. Such studies require unique designs. There is unfortunately a lack of good examples of this kind of analysis.

Inspection and control activities are often of a recurrent character. Performance analyses can therefore be undertaken according to a certain format and include the use of data from standardized information systems such as cost accounting and inspection statistics. Productivity measurement is often adequate. It should be complemented with intermittent studies of the dimensioning of different control functions and of the quality of the inspections. Estimations of the impacts should be compared with costs.

Thre are many good examples of these types of analyses in e.g. police departments and customs offices. Comparative studies could be made on the basis of such cases. It is much more difficult to evaluate performance when the object of supervision is a broad social function such as environmental protection or culture. Supervision is more abstract and often combined with support efforts in these cases.

Reallocation

Large portions of government budgets consist of the reallocation or transferring of purchasing power. Transfers to low income households, subsidies to agriculture, social insurance and taxation are some examples. Transfers also exist within the public sector, e.g. from central to local government and from rich to poor regions.

Performance evaluation in such systems becomes extremely difficult as soon as one leaves the disbursing processes and tries to get insight into the system's effectiveness. Assessing the effects of the transfers in relation to stated objectives and implicit values of the people poses several challenges to the analyst. How should the system be defined? How can information on the flow of money be acquired? How do different transferring systems affect the individual recipient? How do they interact as information processing systems?

As in the case of regulation, performance evaluation could focus on the effectiveness of the reallocation system as a whole or directed to specific funtions in the system. There is a planning and regulating function governing the transfer system. This function can be divided between political bodies and administrative units. Performance analysis in this function should be concentrated on the adequacy of eligibility rules, aggregate impacts of related transfer systems as well as studies of factors influencing the amount of resources transferred, e.g. index rules, population growth, business cycles etc. The administrative costs of alternative transfer systems are also worth studying.

The activities of the disbursing units are to a great extent repetitive. Follow-up of productivity and service levels and security checks are examples of important areas for performance studies.

Models as well as examples of performance analysis of transfer systems are still scarce.

Production

Production of public goods and services is in many respects easier to describe and analyze. The processes and outputs are more visible than is the case in regulation and reallocation. Here we find a broad spectrum of approaches to performance analysis ranging from descriptions of the production process to broad evaluations of the social effects of the activity.

The quality of performance analysis seems to be generally better in production systems than in regulation and reallocation systems. This is not to say that the situation is satisfactory. There is a growing tendency to put more emphasis on comparing ambitions and quality demands with costs and on finding alternative production structures. There is seldom adequate performance data to support such reviews.

In comparison with the other two types of activities the importance of traditional managerial control seems to be much greater. (See for example Anthony and Young 1984.)

30.10 Evaluation by Whom?

There are different ways of addressing the question of who should carry out performance description, analysis and evaluation. One aspect is the institutional: the roles of internal and external control and evaluation units. Since this is discussed by Hood (Ch. 36), I will restrict myself to the question of "expertise" in performance evaluation, undertaken or at least initiated by the institution itself.

There is a tendency to see performance description and analysis as a business for experts. And indeed it should be. The question is: what sort of experts?

For the sake of simplicity I will distinguish between three types of experts.

The *first* kind are experts on "methods", i.e. statisticians, sociologists, economists, operations researchers, implementation researchers, political scientists, etc. In certain types of studies such expertise is indispensable. Also, when designing systems for production statistics, reporting, cost accounting and so on there is an obvious need for this type of expertise. Scarcity of such experts is often used as an argument for not undertaking performance studies and discussions, even in cases where they are not at all necessary for achieving good quality in the evaluation. There is also the opposite problem: the experts play too dominating a role. Experts of this type often fail to communicate adequately with the potential users of the analyses. The users may not comprehend what the analysts are saying or they may reject their findings and conclusions because these do not correspond with their own experience and convictions. In such situations the question is seldom one of "right" or "wrong". Different aspects may be stressed. Expectations of the level of performance may differ. Validity may have different meanings to analysts and users. Their conceptions of the four ethics previously discussed may vary as well as the relative importance attached to them.

The *second* type encompasses those engaged in the activity. Even if external evaluation may be necessary in order to induce major changes in public programs and even if methodological expertise may be needed in some stages of internal performance studies, my experience is that the main burden of performance description and analysis must be carried by the people in charge of the activity. They have the best insight into it and they will live with the activity even when the study is finished. (Cf. Grunow: Ch. 31) Conservatism, unwillingness to open up one's own business to criticism and other barriers to reconsideration and change could be decreased by consciously involving the managers and other personnel in not only discussions on the results of performance analysis but also in the stages of formulating the aspects of performance to study, fact finding, analysis and formulating conclusions. Continuous change in response to new demands presupposes that the managers on all levels have the main responsibility for adjustments in their operations. This responsibility is hard to live up to if one does not actively engage oneself in performance description and analysis.

The *third* category of expertise are those for whose benefit the activity is conducted. In some respects they are represented by the politicians. Political considerations are, of course, the best example. But there are many aspects of performance of interest to the beneficiaries which are not treated best in a political context. Detailed questions about the design of services to different categories of "customers" are of this kind. This means that "experts" on the demands and desires directed at public activities should also have a voice in performance evaluation. Their contribution may vary, from being interviewed and filling in questionnaires to taking part actively in evaluation projects and similar activities. (Cf. Wirth: Ch. 35).

I noted earlier that output and impact description could be made close to either the activity or the objectives. On this scale it seems natural that performance evaluation conducted close to the activity would be a main task for the managers while analysis close to the ultimate goals would be an important task for political and public scrutiny. Governmental, parliamentary and independent evaluation units can perform those independent analyses which in many cases are necessary for identifying the need for major policy changes.

However, in both types of evaluation methodological experts are needed. The design of data collection routines and of specific evaluations demands professional competence as do specific types of cost/benefit calculations and other types of analyses. A necessary but not sufficient condition regarding performance analyses is therefore that they be technically of high quality. If one believes in striving toward more rational decision making, the value of scientifically based analyses is obvious.

Ambitious, creative and dedicated professional evaluators, however, often create problems. They tend to intrude into the other parties' domains. This means that they may "relieve" the managers from part of their responsibility, namely self-criticism and the task of suggesting better ways of fulfilling political goals. It is easy to find examples of this. In some cases managers even hire evaluation experts as an excuse for not engaging themselves in follow-up and evaluation activities. This may also be done in order to postpone uncomfortable but necessary decisions having negative consequences for e.g. their own staff.

Another observation is that managers of public organizations resent attempts by "outsiders" to interfere, to define and apply performance criteria to "their" programs. Performance descriptions that do not comply with their own self-image and their desired public image tend to be rejected. Participation in making the description would promote acceptance. If participation is not feasible, care should be taken to explain what the descriptions tell – and what they do not tell.

The methodological experts may also draw the politicians' and the public's attention to aspects of relatively subordinate interest. Experts on quantitative methods may concentrate upon economic aspects, and particularly upon those which are easy to measure in numbers, at the expense of democratic, legal and other qualitative aspects. Reporting low efficiency may even induce *lower* performance, since otherwise useful programs, which do not yield tangible or immediate results, may be crippled or abandoned. Also, there is a risk that focusing on outputs and identifiable results may cause broader goals to be displaced by various indicators supposed to measure good performance.

Awareness of these dangers is necessary if methodological experts should be able to play a constructive and useful role together with managers and political and other principals.

30.11 Will Performance Evaluation Contribute to Improved Public Activities?

In this chapter performance evaluation has been treated as an administrative tool. Its benefits are related to its ability to contribute to better decisions and more effective and efficient operations. Its costs consist of the time and money spent on it and any negative impacts it may have on actual performance.

One reason for the fact that performance analyses are often not undertaken or not used in decision processes is that they do not fulfil reasonable requirements of administrative effectiveness and efficiency. In such cases they are not worth carrying out or taking into consideration. The main emphasis here has been on explaining this situation and to indicate what could be done to make performance analyses more useful. However, it is not enough to solve the situational design problem, the acceptance problem and the problem of linking performance evaluation to the formal decision processes. If performance information is to be of real significance, there must also be a willingness on the part of decision-makers to draw conclusions from what they see, and to act.

In the design and application of models for "rational decision-making" it is usually presupposed that the problem is given and it is merely a question of making the right choice. What is needed is a goal function, relevant data on resources, restrictions etc., analyses of alternatives and their consequences and finally an "optimal" solution. This is all very well, but often the crucial aspect is whether a decision is taken at all and, of course, whether it is implemented.

If the willingness to make changes is lacking, performance evaluation may seem meaningless. But this is a static way of looking at it. Serious and technically skilled performance descriptions and analyses may very well have their main value in that they encourage change in the public administration. With facts to face, it is difficult for even the most conservative public officials to resist motivated changes. If responsiveness, flexibility and initiatives are required of the public institutions, one good strategy would be to engage key people in evaluation and discussion of performance to determine what could and should be done in the light of this information.

Such a strategy could very well be the most effective weapon against one of the "deadly sins of public administration" pointed out by Drucker (1980) and formulated as the fifth of six prescriptions for *non*-performance: "Make sure that you will not learn from experience".

Note

1 The issue of ethics in the public sector or with regard to bureaucratic performance has been discussed in detail in various chapters of this volume; see Ostrom: Ch. 11, Selten: Ch. 12 and van Gunsteren: Ch. 13

References

Anthony, R. N., and D. R. Young (1984): *Management Control in Nonprofit Organizations* (Third ed.). Homewood, Ill.: Richard D. Irwin.
Argyris, C. (1970): *Intervention Theory and Method – A Behavioral Science View*. Reading, Mass.: Addison-Wesley.
Arvidsson, G. (1980): "Budget Reform as an Instrument for Change." In *Strategies for Change and Reform in Public Management*, 155–169. Paris: OECD.
Drucker, P. F. (1980): "The Deadly Sins in Public Administration." *Public Administration Review* 40/2: 103–106.
Fried, R. C. (1976): *Performance in American Bureaucracy*. Boston, Mass.: Brown.
Lee, R. D. Jr., and R. W. Johnson (1973): *Public Budgeting Systems*. Baltimore, Md.: University Park Press.
Lyden, F. J., and E. G. Miller (eds.) (1982): *Public Budgeting: Program Planning and Evaluation*. Chicago, Ill.: Rand McNally College Publishing Company.
Ridgway, V. F. (1966): "Dysfunctional Consequences of Performance Measurements". In Rubinstein, A. H., and C. J. Haberstroh (eds.), *Some Theories of Organization*, 569–575. Homewood, Ill: Irwin.
Riksrevisionsverket, Statens Personalnämnd, Statens Personalutbildningsnämnd and Statskontoret (1979): *Kvalitetsaspekter på myndigheternas internadministrativa verksamhet* (Quality Aspects of the Internal Administration in Government Agencies). Stockholm (mimeogr.)

Weiss, C. H. (1966): "Utilization of Evaluation: Toward Comparative Study". Repr. 1971 in Caro, F. G. (ed.), *Readings in Evaluation Research,* 136–142. New York, N. Y.: Russell Sage Foundation.

Wholey, J. S. (1979): *Evaluation: Promise and Performance.* Washington, D. C.: The Urban Institute.

31. Internal Control in Public Administration

Dieter Grunow

Abstract

This contribution is based on the following assumption: although forms and results of external control of public administration (especially scandals) are more visible and receive more scientific attention, they are less *important for the effective functioning of the public sector than* internal *control processes. It is argued that external control is only effective if it is transformed into decision processes within the administrative organization – either through anticipation of control demands, through incremental learning, or through ex-post revisions of (wrong) decisions taken.*

The main emphasis of the contribution is placed upon the description of different forms of internal control, starting with personal self-control and ending with interdepartmental control. This analysis not only shows the diversity of internal control measures but also the restricted applicability of each single measure and the contradictions between different elements of them. An explanation for this is given with reference to the incongruence of general goals of public administration (i.e. legality, economy, effectiveness, responsiveness) and to the subsequent lack of precise definitions of functions and tasks.

31.1 Definitions and Forms of Internal Control

Control is a basic element in the living world and especially in the social world (for a general discussion see Wirth: Ch. 29). In simplest terms the process of control includes the "behavior" of a social entity and the examination/evaluation of this "behavior" according to a yardstick (i.e. qualitative and quantitative standards of "behavior"). In an extended concept of control, one can also include the (re)action to the examined "behavior", in terms of *effecting* change, and the demands on this "behavior", in terms of guidance. In the extended concept, one can speak of having a certain "behavior" *under control*. At a more general level yet, the standards may be revised (if found inadequate, outdated, too costly, etc.).

This basic model can be applied to social phenomena on different levels of aggregation, ranging from a *single interaction process* taking place between superior and subordinate (for instance a tax official has a long telephone conversation with his wife while a client is waiting and therefore is criticized by his superior) to a *complex control system* such as in tax administration (e.g. computer checks of taxation procedures). These examples not only indicate the broad scope and the far-reaching interdependencies of control processes, but also make us aware of the *arbitrariness* of selecting specific fields of control for academic analyses. In the literature on "control in organizations" (see, for example, Etzioni 1965; Lawler

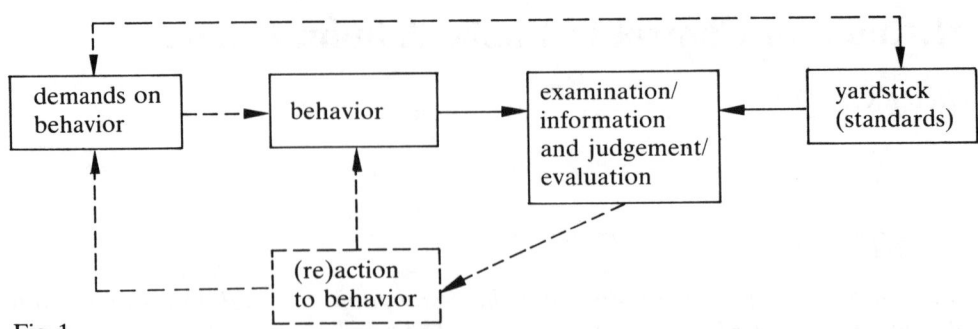

Fig. 1

1976; Dunbar 1981; Kerr and Slocum 1981), this problem is not discussed because organizational boundaries are seen as "natural delineations" of control processes. This view is not adequate for our present purpose, which is internal control in public administration, where we have to acknowledge external control as a contrasting form of control and where organizational boundaries are not necessarily the limits of the control processes under study.

In the following, we select a specific *subset* of control processes: *internal control* in public administration, which is not identical to control in the public sector. We only consider those organizations of the public sector which produce a certain output or which show a performance (whether it is law enforcement, planning, service delivery or whatever) that does *not* basically consist of the control of other public institutions. In this context, control constitutes an internal *tool* for improving performance. Control is not the primary goal of organizational "behavior" as when the object is to control institutions within (e.g. judicial control) or outside the public sector (e.g. union control). This selection of a field for analysis still leaves us with many different forms of control in public administration

- individual *self*-control in an organization
- interpersonal, mutual control within the, more or less, bureaucratic organization
- control structures as part of the basic design of the organization
- control among organizations in the public sector which are not basically control institutions (but cooperatively produce goods, services, etc.).

The organizations under study constitute the *productive basis* of the public sector; external control agencies or institutions only play a derived role because their very existence depends on the pre-existence of "production" and "delivery" processes. Even if control institutions are in a position to revise decisions or actions taken by the "production organizations", they cannot implement the corrected action: they do not put somebody into jail; they do not pay the increased welfare benefits. Thus if control processes are primarily designed to improve the output or the performance of public administration, *internal control* (in the sense defined above) is the most important part of all control efforts from within or without the public sector. External forms of control are the more effective the more they are adapted to internal control processes: the cost of external control depends on the functioning of internal control processes. This interdependence between internal and external control indicates the basic tasks and problems arising in the structuring of internal control processes. They have to *integrate* very different (functionally specific) external control demands. The questions for our further analysis can be derived from this basic problem: To what extent is the integration of control processes possible or at least realized in public administration? On which level of "behavior" is the integration of control to be organized: individual, group, organization, interorganizational network? How are control processes combined with processes of performance evaluation and management and which techniques, tools and resources are used to fulfill this task?

These are some of the basic questions which are discussed in the literature on "control in organizations". They cannot and should not be quoted at length in this chapter. In the context of the present chapter it might be of interest, though, to ask about the *special conditions of internal control* in public administration. This issue has been infrequently discussed (see, for example, Morstein-Marx 1965). In general, very little distinction has been made in the description of control processes in first-, second- or third-sector organizations (Gebert 1974); this might be a consequence of ambiguities in the delimitation of these "sectors". More precisely, it can be argued that the *multiplicity* of control processes and control structures is similar in these three sectors. But, on the other hand, there are also indications that not all modes of control can be applied equally in these three sectors: in public administration, there are problems in implementing MbO techniques and PPBS controls; in private enterprise, the scope for using coercive power to correct "false behavior" is limited; in voluntary organizations, there are limits to the use of interpersonal control on the basis of positional power (instead of personal power). Thus, in spite of the diversity of control processes and structures in public administration and the many similarities with control processes in non-public organizations, there must be special conditions (and restrictions) for internal control in public administration.

Although most of the arguments – put forward with regard to these special conditions – might only indicate differences *in degree* (instead of differences in the principal mode of control), they still allow conclusions about the quality of performance in the public sector:

(1) Internal control in public administration is strongly influenced by external control. Characteristic is the control of "production" *procedures,* which, eventually, become more important than output control. This control feature is a central aspect in the construction of legitimate power application (in the extreme: coercive power) by the state: scrutiny, control (especially legal) and the opportunity to change actions authorized by the state have been seen as the basic protection of the freedom of the citizen. Although state/public administration is increasingly producing and delivering goods and services to citizens, the principles of *procedural control* are still dominant.

(2) Because of the expansion of its tasks public administration is confronted with different objectives and thus with different "logics of control". Although this might be seen as a general feature of open systems acting in a complex environment, the specifics of the public sector can be described as the difficulty or even impossibility of *ordering* these different logics of control because they are all (at least partially) based on laws.

(3) Because it very often has to act upon very diffuse goals and programs – which are a product of multiple political compromises – public administration often lacks the basic prerequisites of internal control: no demands on behavior and, thus, no yardsticks for the examination and evaluation of that behavior are available.

(4) Some of the special restrictions of internal control can be seen in the importance of purely or partially symbolic politics – which also includes or affects public administration because it has to contribute to the overall legitimacy of the politico-administrative system. If no practical and manifest results are sought by administrative action, the question of control is more or less redundant: it is difficult to address non-decision making as an objective of internal control.

In the following, these arguments are not used to demonstrate differences between the public sector and the other sectors in society. They are used to characterize options as well as problems of internal control in public administration. As a first step, we ask for modes of control which are *required* by different objectives and standards guiding the "production" and "performance" of public administration. As a second step, we analyze more closely the functioning of different forms of control within public administration. Here we will look at the *combination* of (organizational) criteria and control procedures from two different perspectives: (a) from each basic criterion and (b) from each control device. In doing so we refer mainly to *German* public administration. There is no space to draw comparisons with other countries. But it can be expected that the differences are not too great. The only point we want to mention in this context is the overemphasis on a formal legal basis for public administration in the "Prussian" state perspective. This accounts for the importance of the *procedural* orientation of administrative action and legal control. It will be different in the less "etatistic" politico-administrative systems of other countries (for instance, the United States).

31.2 Options for and Restrictions on Internal Control in Public Administration

Although control processes take place everywhere and at all times in an organization, they do not automatically lead to coordinated paths of action and adherence to organizational goals or fixed procedures. It is a characteristic of any formal and bureaucratic organization that it develops *written instructions* about control units, techniques and procedures. These arrangements have to be non-contradictory, applicable and not too costly. This is a very difficult task if we deal with organizations as open and probabilistic systems of action in a changing environment. Thus, it cannot be expected that this task can be fulfilled by a simple and unitary model of control arrangements – as, for instance, a strictly hierarchical model of command and control. Many different devices have to be used and are used for the organizing (ordering) of control processes. Some general alternatives at hand shall be described next.

(1) Although we are now dealing with devices of control which are introduced *formally* into chains of action in the organization, *informal processes* of control still take place. For any design of complex control systems, this fact has to be

acknowledged or even anticipated by a conscious review of formal control arrangements. Thus it is left to the members of the organization to operate a formal but
abstract control principle in the context of everyday activity. (2) This can be related
to the *differentiation between long and short circuits* of control. In general, one can
expect formally defined control processes to be applied to long circuits of action,
i.e. to multiple steps and many participants. The informal ones are often the only
way to influence short circuits of action. (3) But the selection of formal or informal
control procedures is also dependent on the object and the subject of control: *Who/
what controls what/whom?* Is the application of the "yardstick" done by people or
by technical devices (e.g. computers)? Are individual actions or machine work the
objects of control? In general, the large-scale short-circuit control most probably
include technical devices. A continuous *interpersonal control* is possible only in a
few situations (of simultaneous presence, etc.) and it is very time consuming. (4) If
interpersonal control takes place, short circuits of control are only possible if
people are working closely together. Thus, control processes might be more
plausible along *horizontal* lines (among colleagues) than along vertical lines
(control from above and control from below). (5) These types of interpersonal
control are related, but not equivalent, to the question of the authority bases of
control. The control power can be derived from formal (line) authority, from
special (functional) expertise, or from informal prestige. (6) The resources and
knowledge needed for control depend on the selection of the main aspects of the
action chain: Are controls focused on procedures, on outputs, or on impacts (in the
environment)? Are these controls applied continuously (mainly in short circuit
control) or at particular points of the action process? (7) As has been mentioned
above, the opportunities for control are not only dependent on the precision of the
yardstick used but also on the strength of the demand for action formulated in
advance. Control devices, thus, have to adapt to different forms of goal definition
and program specification.

The formulation of general goals and specific tasks for public administration is very
difficult for many reasons:

- The process of policy formation and codification is very complicated and time
  consuming; task and goal definitions must either anticipate correctly subsequent
  problem developments or remain very general to leave room for situational
  specification.
- The principle of uniformity of public administration requires a general applicability of task prescriptions and operative procedures.
- There are heterogeneous demands on the performance of public administration
  which cannot be summarized by costs and/or profits considerations; many such
  (especially political) demands are ambivalent because they are the result of
  bargaining and compromises.

As a consequence of this situation, there is not yet a satisfactory theoretical
conceptualization of public tasks or of the tasks of the public sector (Ellwein and
Zoll 1973) which can be related to specific principles of determination or selection
and to the existing accumulation of such tasks. The development of public tasks is
an incremental and partially chaotic process within the stream of bureaucratization

– which has many sources and causes. Thus, the "definition" of public tasks consists in an enumeration of the tasks fulfilled by public institutions or by public finance.

Internal control in public administration very often presupposes self-definition or at least specification of task structures within each organization. This of course differs according to the precision of formal description within laws and administrative regulations at hand: There is less discretion on the executive level in tax administration than in a federal ministry. This does not automatically lead to a less strenuous control procedure, though. In the ministry, the coordination of individual actions toward a common goal might be very important, whereas in tax administration the uniformity of rule application requires a tight control system. In other words: there are generalized standards or procedures to be pursued which may differ in their relevance for each organization of the public sector; but they may involve the same control costs (as an important part of transaction costs).

Besides the task structure (program structure) of a public organization which formally defines the problems which have to be solved by the organization and the instruments that have to be applied for task fulfillment, there are general standards or criteria specified for the public sector: *legality; effectiveness; economy* (in Germany, this means the minimizing of costs rather than economic efficiency) and *responsiveness* to the demands and needs of society. It is quite clear that these general standards are purely formal (i.e. without content) and do not lead to any solution of problems or provision of services without a complementary task formulation. But even if such a task structure is available, there might be a competition or even a contradiction between the paths of action demanded by formal and substantive standards. This divergence might be the consequence of influence exerted by external control processes. As these *formal* standards are the main preoccupation of external control, they might be determined more by (external) control specialists than by the organization which has a primary task of solving problems or providing services, and so forth. Anticipated external formal controls (according to the standards described above) eventually become internalized measures of self-control which might not be compatible with the primary task structure of the respective organization. Another source of ambivalence or divergence can be seen in the fact that the four general standards are not even compatible among themselves. As there is *no hierarchical order* among them, they represent a "magical goal square". None of them can be maximized without restricting the fulfillment of the other ones.

These "multilemmas" of standards and tasks in public administration lead to difficulties within the control arrangements we can observe and describe in many forms and on different levels of analysis. If one looks for evidence of the deficiencies of public organization structures and management, most of it is related to the "multilemmas" described above (Töpfer 1982). As long as the goal and task structures contain so many inconsistencies, these will also be characteristic of the control arrangements within public institutions. Thus, we find different measures of control with incompatible demands on behavior and conflicting "yardsticks" of evaluation.

Forms of Control related to Different Standards of Performance in Public Administration

The major forms of internal control of public institutions are listed in the following chart; the dominant types are indicated by black triangles. Some explanation of the chart is necessary, the following are the main standards of internal control:

(a)*Legality*: Control processes for ensuring the legality of actions taken in the public sector are, in general, the dominant ones. Traditionally, this is the attempt to protect the citizen against state authority and state intervention: all such actions are subject to judicial inquiry. But this criterion is also important because it does not just refer to law but also to the many thousands of rules and regulations guiding the decision making process in the public sector. Moreover, legality often also implies a claim of legitimacy and seeks for uniformity and reliability in public administration. The criterion of legality is already reinforced *by the possibility* of judicial control which requires a detailed documentation of the decision procedures. Thus, individual, interindividual, technical, and interorganizational devices of control are implemented in the public sector to ensure compliance to rules and regulations. The personnel is trained to fulfill such a function – in part by internalizing rule-oriented perspectives. The interpersonal control by a chain of superior – subordinate relationships has different techniques at its disposal: the superior might reserve the right to sign all reports and decisions prepared by the subordinates; the superior might review files and cases; he might ask for special reports, and so on. In a more generalized form, superiors report on staff performance which is often defined as rule conformity (see for example, Grunow 1976). In general, the emphases and precision of formally defined demands on behavior allow different options for control processes: structure, procedure or substance (Dunsire 1978). As the definition of tasks or *substantive* goals (e.g. justice in the taxation system) is often ambiguous, the main focus of legality control is *procedural* in nature. This criterion is also supported by technical control processes. They are increasingly used in organizations that have to deal with large numbers of clients (e.g. tax administration; income maintenance; unemployment agencies; etc.). With the assistance of information processing technology, control processes become as impersonal as Weber described them in his ideal type of bureaucratic organization (e.g. error statistics for each employee in tax administration). These forms of control are dependent on a detailed description of procedure; or in other words: control by legality depends on the computer compatibility of rules and regulations.

Internal control by legality is not confined to a single organization and to the hierarchical distribution of control functions. Legal inspection is one of the tasks of higher-level bureaucracies (e.g. on regional, state or national levels). It aims at uniformity of rule application and tries to clarify, or formally decide controversies in the interpretation of laws, rules and regulations. For this purpose, jurisdictional specialists/special branches within the organizations of public administration are also available. They are not only responsible for the application of extremely difficult and complex legal "yardsticks" to paths of action, but they also have to ensure correctness in the (anticipated) way of judiciary control and revision.

(b) *Economy:* Such processes are – at least in comparison with the preceding

Chart 1: Major Forms of Internal Control

forms of control \ standards	legality	economy	effectiveness	responsiveness
individual self-control	rule-oriented, procedure-oriented perspective	cost awareness		
interpersonal control – from above	control signature; file check; report on performance	reservation of costly decisions to superiors	management by objectives; report on performance; reports about task attainment	
– from colleagues			competition among colleagues; case review	case review
– from below		suggestions for improvement	suggestions for improvement	information transfer about boundary experience
– from boundary transactions			accumulation of clients' needs and problems	register of client protest or objection
control by specialists in special branch	jurisdictional specialists	internal cost accounting; budget planning and control	evaluation studies	survey of clients' interest and client satisfaction
technically assisted control	computer-based random test (check)	computer-based monitoring	computer-based models of micro-simulation	
interdepartmental & interorganizational control – from above	legal inspection		task-oriented inspection	
– from equivalent units		contracting within and outside the public sector	bounded competition among public institutions	bounded competition among public institutions
– from below		demand for coordination and clarification	demand for coordination and clarification	
– from special branches	clearing unit; ombudsman	cost accounting unit	implementation & evaluation studies; organiz. development	

standard of legality – marginal in the context of public administration. One major reason for this is the fact that economy and legality (in the broad sense defined above) are not fully compatible: control processes and/or law enforcing procedures are continued even if the costs of the actions might be higher than the fine collected from "the offender". Thus, often control on behalf of economy is just a side-effect of the control of legality. If the laws, rules and regulations of the procurement of material are followed (e.g. to ask for three different bids) or if the rules are adopted correctly for the payment of different staff members, money might be saved. But this is, of course, not necessarily the case because 'economy' is not the predominant "yardstick" and demand on behavior. Although each organization in public administration has to plan and justify its annual budget as well as to control the spending of the budget, the budgetary process (especially in Germany) makes it very difficult to apply standards of efficient administration. Depending on the yearly rhythm, the large proportion of legally fixed expenses and the organization of the budget items leaves (at least in the German budget law) little room for special emphasis on "economic behavior". Even more important is the fact that – due to the system of public finance and budgeting processes – it is very difficult to decide/anticipate which decisions might be "economic" (in terms of money saving and/or in terms of efficiency) in their *final effect*. As long as costs are not calculated or at least assessed on the basis of *alternative paths* of action to be followed, it is vain to demand cost awareness and accompanying control procedures. Consequently, there are very few control strategies on behalf of economy "in the hierarchical line": superiors might reserve costly decisions to themselves or even pass them on to their superiors; there are opportunities for subordinates to make proposals for the organization of task fulfillment to save money in the public sector. It is quite plausible that new developments can be observed in the design of special positions and organizational units which have to develop internal forms of cost accounting. They cooperate closely with units which are responsible for personnel and organization planning and for the preparation of new budget demands. This task is supported by computer technology which allows a centralized and real-time monitoring of the spending process. The function of this tool might be to ensure that the budget has been completely spent at the end of the period and *not* to save money. But it can also be used to ensure maximal output in relation to the available budget. Another strategy (which is increasingly used) relies on competition within the public sector or between public institutions and private contract partners. For example, a computer-assisted comparison of cost developments in comparable units (tax bureaus; local administration units) might stimulate control processes on behalf of economy. This is even more efficient if organizations outside the public sector are included: competitive offers can be used to reduce costs, and so forth. But clear-cut evidence of such economic controls by contracting are very few: statistics on reprivatization strategies show (KGSt 1976) that only in very few cases had a cost comparison been made before deciding on a contract.

(c) *Effectiveness:* To a certain degree, the definition of "economical behavior" is independent of the question of whether a relevant societal task is fulfilled. Parkinson's example of the growing administration of navy ships which have been scrapped does not exclude the claim that the organization has worked according to the "rules of economy". The abstract criterion of economic paths of action means minimizing the cost of these actions; control can be formally addressed to waste in public spending, to slack resources in the budgets of public institutions. It is much more difficult – if not impossible – to formulate such abstract and empty goals with reference to effectiveness. A precise definition of tasks is necessary to place control processes in the context of measures of effectiveness. In the paragraphs above we have already mentioned that one of the major deficiencies of public institutions is their lack of precise task description: political goals are often a vague product of compromises; and in addition, they might be changed quite rapidly; even if the goals are clear and definite, there is no certainty about the effective (operational) way to attain these goals: as implementation studies have often shown, plans for the realization of the programs – even if they are formulated as laws – are only wishful thinking and a normative short-cut through complex interdependencies (Mazmanian and Sabatier 1981). But, of course, there are laws, rules and regulations which not only define goals but also prescribe realistic paths for implementation. The effect of their realization (including unintended effects, etc.) might still be incomprehensible. This is partially the result of changing environmental demands and expectations or even of unexpected protest and severe counteraction. Under these conditions the forms of internal control mentioned on the chart are approaches to the problem but not effective solutions. If one ignores the specification of tasks as a primary necessity for control processes in this context, the departure from a predominantly procedural orientation of interpersonal control is most important. Management by objectives; reports about progress in problem solving or service delivery (instead of a description of legal procedures applied to address the problem); report and communication about the performance of each staff member on the basis of substantive task fulfillment (instead of the confirmation of non-deviant behavior): these are attempts made to organize control processes for effectiveness. They are most likely in a situation of goal-oriented programming and action processes (e.g. social work), but at least as important in a situation of conditional programming (e.g. paying unemployment benefits). The more open and uncertain the demands on action paths are, the more important are short circuits of control and the more colleagues and "subordinates" have to be included in the exchange of information and decisions; competition and team cooperation among colleagues and subordinates are relevant devices for monitoring the action paths for effectiveness. As this criterion has to take environmental conditions into account in a much more complex way (as the goals discussed on the preceding pages), coordination of the actions of different public institutions (and even beyond the public sector) are necessary as well. Hierarchical devices of formal task-oriented inspections *(Fachaufsicht)* are only a small part of the control requirements. They are very selective, and long circuits of control are typical. Thus, there are additional forms of effectiveness control: internal evaluation studies dealing with the structural and procedural arrangements of task fulfillment (realized by organizing specialists and others); this is also a form of long circuits control but more complex and reliable than hierarchical inspections. The usage of teamwork or project groups (mixing staff members from different task fields and different hierarchical levels – also in the sense of matrix organizations –) as well as elements of competition between staff members and between organizational units might increase possibilities of short circuits of control for effectiveness. This way of self-monitoring step by step action is central in a situation of goal ambivalence and low operational quality of task structures: often enough each single person in a basic unit of a ministry has to define his task himself – by trying to get a "feeling" of what might be of interest to superiors or to the environment.

(d) *Responsiveness to problems, needs, and demands of clienteles.* This generalized standard of public administration is a novel one; before the mid-seventies the relevant textbooks did not mention such a criterion or generalized performance measure for public administration. Now it is an accepted part of such books (e.g. Joerger and Geppert 1976) and a field of administrative activity. Responsiveness is a necessary supplement to measures of effectiveness because it has to consider the substance (and not just the formal or financial circumstances) of demands from the environments of public administration. This is even more important if not just an adaptation to the environment is sought but a *coproduction* between organization and environment is seen as necessary. In additon, it has become quite clear during the last decades that exchanges between public administration and its publics are an important source for the acquisition of *legitimacy* for public action. (Political parties and parliamentary institutions are not adequately fulfilling this task). But, of course, the introduction of such a general standard is a slow and time-consuming process: it requires major shifts in the overall organization of public institutions and in control processes as well. *It implies a shift toward guidance and control from the periphery* (rather than from the center) or from the street level instead from the top of hierarchy. Problems with such "alternative" forms of control not only stem from the opposition of those who are afraid of losing their authority position but also from the necessity to observe the *impact* of public action more closely. This necessitates more contacts with the public, possibly more data collection, and so on. In the first place, however, existing internal resources of control for responsiveness can be used. Information and experiences collected in boundary or outreach positions of public administration can be helpful for decision making and control circuits on the higher levels of hierarchy. In addition, large-scale and systematic surveys are being made to learn more about the reaction of the clientele – which very often is not identical with reactions of pressure groups. The major deficiency of the *practical* actions toward the criterion of responsiveness is their *one-off* character. There are not yet examples of a repetitive or even continous control effort on behalf of responsiveness. This would be of central importance, though, if one acknowledges changes in environmental demands as an important catalyst for changes in paths of action in the public sector. Especially in a situation where task definitions of the political institutions are diffuse and/or changes by revision of the law are too slow, public administration has to react directly to environmental changes. As a necessary contribution to this process, there are credible attempts made to reduce the number of rules and regulations and to enable more flexible reactions to situational changes. (As far as legally defined entitlements are among those regulations to be abolished, it might also result in a less responsive reaction of public administration).

Levels of Internal Control and their Potential for the Integration of Diverse Task- and Goal Structures

Internal control in public administration is the most important prerequisite of a functioning public sector because these are the institutions which are supposed to solve problems, plan new programs, administer service delivery or enforce compliance to the law. External controls primarily detect errors, but do not directly effect "better" paths of action. Internal control is the more effective the more it anticipates and even internalizes measures of external control. But as these measures do not necessarily include an operational description for (new/better) demands on organizational action, the orientation toward these "yardsticks" may lead to contraproductive results: avoidance of risk, non-decision making, refusal of responsibility and accountability and so forth. This unintended effect is the more likely, the more ambivalent the substantive task descriptions are and the more paths of actions are controlled on the basis of formal and empty goals (i.e. performance measures) as described above.

Although we were able to describe a long list of devices for control in public administration, they are not equally distributed and relevant for influencing paths of action. As long as the problems with the definition of substantial tasks of public institutions prevail, the formal criteria of legality and economy will be dominant. They are not as dependent on substantive task descriptions as the standards of effectiveness and responsiveness. This does not imply, though, that in cases with a relatively precise task structure the four formally defined standards might be equally fulfilled. The chart of the forms of control quite clearly shows that there are conflicting demands for instance in the field of interpersonal control. Strictly hierarchical control procedures on behalf of legality have to be combined with horizontal control processes as well as with control from below – if one tries to pursue other general standards as well. Management by objectives, teamwork, case review systems or other task-oriented short circuit control devices are hardly compatible with the traditional forms of procedural compliance as the main focus of control from above. This also holds true if control from the periphery has to be given more weight to be able to react to environmental changes.

The main task and greatest problem in designing internal control procedures in public administration can be seen in a *differential combination* of tasks/goals with specific forms of control. Whereas external control institutions can be very selective with regard to their targets, internal control processes have to be coordinated, that is related to different types of control demands simultaneously. Whereas in theory or in dogmatic legal formulation the formal criteria (for performance) are of the same relevance to public administration as a whole, there are de facto differences according to the tasks to be fulfilled and the types of administrative institution (e.g. national, state or local). Whereas each formal criterions (as described above) might be judged as equally important (compared to the other ones), priority decisions have to be made – for instance, with regard to the specific goals of organizations, to changing demands in society (as of now, the "book-keepers" seem to dominate), to changing political priorities, and so on. *Thus, the analysis and the design of internal control has to cope with the heterogeneous organizational forms of public administration* and cannot restrict itself to typical *simplifications* of traditional scientific analysis (e.g. Luhmann 1964; Niska-nen 1971; v. Hayek 1978). The most problematic simplification is the identification of public administration with "some principle of hierarchy" – as if there had been no development since the *"Polizey-Wissenschaft"*[1] more than two hundred years ago. In the succeeding discussion we want to stress the fact that there are already many different modes of internal control available for public administration but that their applicability to and/or compatibility with the existing organizational structures is not yet sufficiently understood.

(a) *Individual self-control in public administration:* One of the most important functions of control in an organization is to keep its members in accord with the general standards and the procedural rules of cooperative production and delivery of decisions, goods and services. The more people with different tasks contribute to goal attainment and the more contingent the conditions for task fulfillment are, the more complicated and costly is the control effort. It can be reduced, though, if the personnel shows a high degree of *adequate* behavior (which is not necessarily the same as conformity). In this case, the control process is "placed" on the individual: awareness of demands on behavior, self-observation, self-evaluation and self-monitoring are the devices applied to realize adequate paths of action on the basis of internalized short-circuit control (for a summary see Koch 1982; Bosetzky 1982; Lawler 1976). The basic methods of implementing this type of control are formal training, selection and socialization (in the organization). Whether individual self-control is effective, depends on the conditions which govern these three processes. In public administration, we find (in many countries) very formal training and selection – even with features of professionalization. Much less is known about socialization processes and effects – although there are some attempts to classify "bureaucratic personalities" which basically do not fit into the "self-control model" (Bosetzky and Heinrich 1980). As self-monitoring is quite demanding of competence and (especially intrinsic) motivation it seems to be most suitable for professionals/specialists in public administration (Hartmann 1968; Scott 1966; Hebal 1961) – with relatively high degrees of autonomy and discretion in a context of predominantly goal-defining "purposive programs". As can be seen from organization charts, this personnel is very often excluded from the line system of guidance, coordination and control. This implies that some of the basic problems of internal control are *not* covered by individual self-control: (1) no integration of different control demands (e.g. from the different formal standards); typically, we have *different* groups of experts for different formal standards (i.e. legality, economy, etc.); (2) no coordination of different tasks to be fulfilled at the same time and/or cooperatively; only in very small groups/teams does this seem to be possible on the basis of self-control; (3) no effecting of uniformity in procedure and output, where the same tasks are fulfilled by large numbers of personnel (e.g. tax officials working on income declarations). Although individual self-control is an important part of the total control effort – because it allows a reduction of other forms of control to more or less selective, one-off interventions – only in extreme cases (of professional teamwork, etc.) does it cover the whole control demand for adequate paths of action. Even with a further improvement of training, selection and socialization this situation will hardly be changed because of the rapid changes in environmental demands, the (often) incomplete knowledge of the "production function" for decisions, goods and services, and because of the internal complexity of the cooperative system in public bureaucracies.

(b) *Interpersonal control in public administration:* Some of the limitations of self-control can be overcome by the different forms of interpersonal control. In the first place, this type of control is identified with a hierarchical line of superior-subordinate-relationships. It is the task of the superior to formulate or specify the demands on behavior, to collect information for evaluation and to effect changes in the behavior of subordinates (if necessary). There are many informal and more or less formalized modes of interpersonal hierarchical control which have been mentioned already in the last paragraph. Here the question has to be raised of whether this control mode fulfills its functions, especially the coordination of actions toward task fulfillment and integration of different formal standards of public administration. Both functions are related to the extent of control (see, for example, MacKenzie 1978: 117ff.) which is given to the superior and to his management competence (Steinbach 1982; Lauxmann 1971). As many studies show (for a summary of the German situation see Becker and Krüger 1981) these managerial qualifications in public servants are "underdeveloped". This is not only a consequence of inadequacies in formal training but also an effect of the *low autonomy for managerial decisions:* (1) the superior has always to keep in mind that he is also a subordinate within the hierarchical line: his coordination and integration efforts might not be understood/supported by his superior; (2) principles of internal organizing and of personnel management are as formalized as the "production" processes; management functions are relegated into specialist units of the organization. Thus, public servants are often reluctant to exert "leadership" within the organization. This will increase the diversification of tasks and types of personnel necessary to fulfill these tasks. The myth of the generalist (trained as lawyer) who can be appointed to any position in public administration is losing credibility. As far as superiors are not able to observe and judge the performance of their subordinates adequately, they are forced to give up some of their control functions – either by reducing their control span or by seeking alternative modes of control. Control among peers, mutual control in teamwork or even "control" from below are some of the alternatives in interpersonal control. Project groups and matrix organization are the structural forms for the implementation of these alternatives. Although they might be necessary preconditions of any attempt to integrate the four general goals into the paths of action, they are especially important in cases of complex tasks and an almost unknown "production function". In addition, these modes of control are more adequate for contingent situational conditions of task fulfillment and/or in a context with a high degree of discretion for the personnel which is closely engaged in interaction with the clientele: Case reviews, supervision and even "outside control" by the community of professionals are special forms of interpersonal control.

(c) *Organizational structure as control structure in public administration:* It has been mentioned already that internal control in public administration (especially in Germany) depends very significantly on formalized structural and procedural provisions. They allow the avoidance of interpersonal and especially of interactive control and are nowadays increasingly supported by devices of information technology. Although there is – as described above – a large variety of public tasks, the dominant and still unifying principles of formal control structures are directed to the *bureaucratic* administering of masses of similar and well-defined cases (such as in tax administration; see, for example, Tannenbaum and Cooke 1979). The control becomes more impersonal and procedural in nature; by using technical devices (i.e. information technology) it is not confined to long circuit control (e.g. output control), but can be applied as a continuous monitoring procedure. Even if we acknowledge that this dominant model of an internal control system can only be applied to a specific task structure (e.g. a widely known "production function"), the same critical questions about its functions have to be raised as for all other modes of control. The first problem arises from the necessity to make different subsets of the control process compatible: especially the systems of performance observation, performance evaluation, rewards distribution (incentive structure), and sanctions distribution (enforcement structure). As the procedural control system builds upon *extrinsic* motivation for task fulfillment, these three components of control (see the model in the first part of the paper) must be structurally adapted to allow effective control processes. Although it is very difficult to make generalizations about the configurations of whole control systems, it can be argued that such a compatiblity is not the rule but the exception: the realization of more suitable paths of behavior seems to be especially difficult in a situation where there is almost no opportunity for sanctioning a bad performance and where the opportunity for offering rewards is decreasing. In addition, the distribution of these components is partially or even mainly dependent on the decisions of *subdivisions* within the organization: *specialists* for organizing, for personnel selection and allocation, for performance evaluation principles, for budgeting, and so forth are responsible for the design of the formalized control system. This leads to even more complications of the second function with regard to integration/coordination: How are differential control processes according to different formal standards integrated into the internal control structure? As much as they are formalized, they are kept apart, functionally differentiated into subdivisions or special branches within the organization. In this way, they reproduce external control institutions and perspectives without contributing to an *integration* of internal control strategies. On the organizational level we find basically independent and partially incompatible control systems (see Dunsire 1978) which – at best – can be activated separately at different times and for special tasks/issues and which – at worst – can restrict or eliminate each other simultaneously.

With this further example of inadequate coordination of internal control demands we can conclude that there are good reasons for speaking of an expensive overcontrol of public administration which is not even effective and thus does not make any external control superfluous. This might also help to answer the question as to why – under such a diffuse control configuration – public administration does not function anarchically. Although there are examples of anarchic behavior (see Klages 1982; Bosetzky 1982) its diffusion is limited by the innumerable implicit or explicit, informal or formal, cumulative or antagonistic controlling factors influencing "the behavior" of public administration. As long as the organization is seen, and is practically managed, as an open system, this "shifting balance" may be maintained. It should be also kept in mind, however, that many consequences of ineffective control might have been "paid away" by rising budgets in the public sector. As much as we experience the fiscal crisis (in public budgets), the deficiencies and the high costs of uncoordinated control devices in each organization will become more visible – and possibly contribute to the general understanding of control in the public sector.

31.3 Conclusions

Although some of the major difficulties of internal control in public administration have been mentioned within the explanation of the vertical and horizontal lines of the chart (see above), the main focus of our argument has been to *describe* existing devices of control. But their existence does not imply effective functioning. In this last section, we want to summarize the limitations of internal control in the form of some theses which concentrate on the basic dilemmas between the structural arrangements of the public sector and the necessary components of an effective control system (again mainly with reference to the German system):

(a) There are many different devices of control which follow only partially compatible formal goals, but there is *no balanced system* of control in public administration. There is a tendency to overcontrol the economy and legality of procedures; there is a lack of control for effectiveness and responsiveness. No attempt is made to combine or integrate different forms of control – partly because the respective preconditions for functioning are not known or not acknowledged by those in charge of designing control systems. The dominance of procedural controls is inadequate for a situation of changing environments and not completely calculable paths of action toward goal fulfillment. The dominant devices of control are relics of classical models of bureaucratic organization which are no longer typical of large parts of the public sector.

(b) For large parts of the public sector (except financial transfer payments and similar *conditional program* implementation) there is not even a detailed description of substantive tasks to be fulfilled by each staff member to reach the overall goals of the organization. Although it is a well-known fact that such a "masterplan" does not exclude individual interpretations and situational deviations, it is an important prerequisite for control and learning processes. Members of public bureaucracies complain that they do not know what their tasks are; they do not know *why* they are following certain paths of action. During performance evaluation of staff members it becomes quite clear that superiors and subordinates *do not have a common understanding* of the task to be fulfilled. This is (in part) also a consequence of the paucity of connections drawn between the four formal standards of performance in the public sector: legality, economy, effectiveness, responsiveness.

(c) For a growing part of the public sector, the lack of task description is not just a fault or an omission. It is the unavoidable consequence of dependence on changing environments and the result of complex problem structures which do not allow deterministic models or procedures of problem solving. Goal setting programs with corresponding (high) degrees of discretion in the realization of those substantive goals demand short circuit team control of paths of action. This means of individual self-control and social self-monitoring is, as a rule, *not* supported by structural and personnel arrangements in public administration. There is a remarkable lack of managerial competence among high-ranking officials. And there is a general tendency toward risk avoidance – which is especially unsuitable under conditions of uncertainty in organizational decision making.

(d) Even if there are fields with a relatively precise task description (= demands on behavior) and simultaneously a yardstrick for control, the results of performance evaluation will often not lead to practical consequences. It is almost impossible to "enforce" proposals for improving performance. Unless illegal actions are taking place, staff members with tenure positions are almost "immune" from the effects of control. In the past, this problem has been alleviated by offering incentives during times of staff expansion and growing budgets. It is much more difficult nowadays: top officials in public administration complain that they cannot motivate their subordinates because they have no extra qualifications to offer. The regular (and regularly increasing) income is somehow taken for granted; it does not promote attempts to control and improve performance of public administration. As one reaction to this situation, a new emphasis on a non-financial incentive system can be observed. An inflation of titles or of symbolic promotions as well as small-scale privileges in everyday activities might be the result of such a development. It is not at all clear whether this can provide a new basis for effective and efficient control processes.

These propositions demonstrate quite clearly that the problems of internal control in public administration are not just a matter of the specification of yardsticks and demands on behavior. Control processes and their functioning are dependent on very broad and complex (often legally defined) structural and procedural arrangements in public institutions. A greater efficacy of control processes – especially for effectiveness and responsiveness in the public sector – requires large-scale revisions of such structural and procedural arrangements (e.g. in terms of organizational development) – probably including changes in the forms and major aims of external control as well.

Note

1   "Polizey-Wissenschaft" is the original term for the scientific analysis of public administration in general.

References

Becker, U., and B. Krüger (1981): "Personalverwaltung und Personalführung." In König, K., H. J. v. Oertzen, and F. Wagener (eds.), *Öffentliche Verwaltung in der Bundesrepublik Deutschland*, 337–358. Baden-Baden: Nomos.

Bosetzky, H. (1982): "Systemimmanente Grenzen einer planvollen Verwaltungsführung." In Remer, A. (ed.), *Verwaltungsführung*, 219–230. Berlin – New York: de Gruyter.

Bosetzky, H., and P. Heinrich (1980): *Mensch und Organisation. Aspekte bürokratischer Sozialisation*. Stuttgart: Kohlhammer.

Dunbar, R. L. M. (1981): "Designs for Organizational Control." In Nystrom, P. C., and W. H. Starbuck (eds.), *Handbook of Organizational Design. Vol. II: Remodeling Organizations and Their Environments*, 85–115. Oxford: Oxford Univ. Press.

Dunsire, A. (1978): *The Executive Process*. London: Robertson.

Ellwein, T., and R. Zoll (1973): *Zur Entwicklung der öffentlichen Aufgaben in der Bundesrepublik Deutschland.* Baden-Baden: Nomos.

Etzioni, A. (1965): "Organizational Control Structures." In March, J. G. (ed.), *Handbook of Organizations,* 650–677. Chicago: Rand McNally.

Gebert, D. (1974): *Organisationsentwicklung. Probleme des geplanten organisatorischen Wandels.* Stuttgart: Kohlhammer.

Grunow, D. (1976): *Personalbeurteilung. Empirische Untersuchung von Personalbeurteilungssystemen in Wirtschaft und Verwaltung.* Stuttgart: Enke.

Hartmann, H. (1968): "Arbeit, Beruf, Profession." *Soziale Welt* 19/3: 193–215.

Hayek, F. A. von (1978): "Die Entthronung der Politik. In Frei, D. (ed.), *Überforderte Demokratie?,* 17–30. Zürich: Schulthess.

Hebal, J. J. (1961): "Generalist Versus Specialist in the Bureau of Indian Affairs." *Public Administration Review* 21/1: 16–22.

Joerger, G., and M. Geppert (1976): *Grundzüge der Verwaltungslehre* (2nd enl. ed.). Stuttgart: Kohlhammer.

Kerr, St. and J. W. Slocum (1981): "Controlling the Performances of People in Organizations." In Nystrom, P. C., and W. H. Starbuck (eds.), *Handbook of Organizational Design. Vol. II: Remodeling Organizations and Their Environments,* 116–134. Oxford: Oxford Univ. Press.

KGSt (Kommunale Gemeinschaftsstelle für Verwaltungsvereinfachung) (1976): *Privatisierungsmaßnahmen. Bericht über eine Umfrage.* Köln.

Klages, H. (1982): "Grenzen der Organisierbarkeit von Verwaltungsorganisationen." In Remer, A. (ed.), *Verwaltungsführung,* 197–218. Berlin – New York: de Gruyter.

Koch, R. (1982): "Berufsethos und Rollenausführung öffentlicher Bediensteter – Zur Bedeutung einer beruflichen Basismotivation für die Verwaltungsführung." In Remer, A. (ed.), *Verwaltungsführung,* 355–374. Berlin – New York: de Gruyter.

Lauxmann, F. (1971): *Die kranke Hierarchie. Not und Hoffnung der öffentlichen Verwaltungen.* Stuttgart: Deutsche Verlagsanstalt.

Lawler, E. E. (1976): "Control Systems in Organizations." In Dunnette, M. D. (ed.), *Handbook of Industrial and Organizational Psychology,* 1247–1291. Chicago: Rand McNally.

Luhmann, N. (1964): *Funktionen und Folgen formaler Organisation.* Berlin: Duncker & Humblot.

MacKenzie, K. D. (1978): *Organizational Structures.* Arlington Heights, Ill.: AHM Publishing Corporation.

Mazmanian, D., and P. A. Sabatier (eds.) (1981): *Effective Policy Implementation.* Lexington, Mass.: Heath.

Morstein-Marx, F. (1965): *Verwaltung. Eine einführende Darstellung.* Berlin: Duncker & Humblot.

Niskanen, W. A. (1971): *Bureaucracy and Representative Government.* Chicago: Aldine-Atherton.

Scott, R. W. (1966): "Professionals in Bureaucracies. Areas of Conflict." In Vollmer, H. M. (ed.), *Professionalization,* 265–275. Englewood Cliffs, N. J.: Prentice-Hall.

Steinbach, H. (1982): "Die Bedeutung hierarchischer und monokratischer Strukturen in den öffentlichen Verwaltungen für die Gehorsamspflicht und das Führungsverhalten." In Remer, A. (ed.), *Verwaltungsführung,* 181–196. Berlin – New York: de Gruyter.

Tannenbaum, A. S., and R. A. Cooke (1979): "Organizational Control. A Review of Studies Employing the Control Graph Method." In Lammers, C. J., and D. J. Hickson (eds.), *Organizations Alike and Unlike,* 183–210. London: Routledge & Kegan Paul.

Töpfer, A. (1982): "Organisationsprinzipien und Führungsgrundsätze in der öffentlichen Verwaltung." In Remer, A. (ed.), *Verwaltungsführung,* 109–140. Berlin – New York: de Gruyter.

32. When Courts Intervene: Judicial Control in a Comparative Institutional Perspective

Gerd-Michael Hellstern

Abstract

In recent years an increased awareness of judicial intervention into administrative policies has given rise to an intense debate on the proper role and control-functions of the courts and on the need for reform of the courts, of the legislation preparing rules and statutes and for the administration in exercising procedures in most developed countries. The rise of alleged excessive amount of disputing and administrative litigation has raised the question of over-legalislation and of hyperlexology, the incapabilities of the courts to give effective relief and dissolve effectively disputes, yet simultaneously extent their reach into areas beyond both their competency and legitimacy. The question centers mostly on two issues: on the capacity of the courts to work efficiently and on the legitimacy of the courts to create laws and shaping administrative and executive decisions and behaviour.

There are strong institutional differences between the European Roman law and the Common law countries as to the organisation of the judicial control of administration as well as to the underlying conceptions of law and of the public domain. The widening of the functions of government and the growing complexity of administrative issues however lead to similar problems in all developed countries and one can observe trends of convergence also concerning the institutional solutions for such problems.

32.1 Introduction

The judicial control of public administration has been developed into different forms in different countries, and it seems inappropriate to deal with that subject unless to take into consideration the constitutional and institutional differences in the embodiment of the legislative, the executive and the judiciary function. In order to keep our subject within the limits of a single chapter we have, however, to restrict the focus to a problem which seems to challenge the judiciary function in nearly every political system, i.e. the impact of court resolutions in far-reaching controversial policy conflicts. The crucial role the judiciary commands in processing disputes in the public spheres has focused professional debate and sensitive public attention in the last years (National Academy of Sciences 1980, American Bar Association 1983, Buiren, Ballerstedt and Grimm 1982, Goehlert 1983, Harlow and Rawlings 1984, Papier 1979).

The classic function of the judiciary with respect to public administration is the protection of individual rights of the citizen against administrative interventions.

Following the different traditions of European continental and common law countries there is a distinctive form of judicial control of public administration (Verwaltungsgerichtsbarkeit)[1] only in the continental state tradition (cf. Grimm: Ch. 4). Here public interventions in the rights and liberties of the citizens must be based on public law, and administrative action is assumed to be determined fully by written regulations which serve as standard for the litigation of the case.

Whereas this model fits rather well to the classical functions of government, i.e. maintaining peace and order and raising taxes, it becomes too simple with respect to the technological economic and welfare functions of modern states. Administrative action becomes here more goal-oriented, less fully determined by conditions set by law (Luhmann 1972: 228 ff.). Moroever the effects of public decisions often do not concern specific inividuals only but have a lasting and often not predictable impact upon the life situation of a not yet defined group of individuals. Thus courts have become concerned more and more with discretional decisions of public administrations, from the location of large-scaled public facilities (e.g. airports, motor-ways, waste-disposal) the setting of standards on safety (e.g. concerning nuclear plants, environmental protection or occupational health) to the distribution of benefits (e.g. social services, commercial subsidies). Thus the growth of the judicial power partly reflects the growing role of governmental institutions and at the same time the increasing interdependencies of modern societies (Auby and Drago 1984, Grohm 1982, Summers 1983).

The multifacetted engaged discussion in which legal scholars, constitutional lawyers and judges disagree on a series of specific questions on legal control by courts may be somewhat unjustifiedly narrowed to two opposing streams of reasoning with differing underlying assumptions and conceptional models: Critiques of alleged judicial expansion tend to argue, as the 'least democratic institutions', the courts have to exercise – using Felix Frankfurter's famous phrase – *'judicial self-restraint'* limiting judicial controls to individual protection of human (or natural and constitutional) rights and allowing the administration, the executive and legislative branches the right of actions and latitude in exercising discretion as far as possible. Apart from concern of the *legitimatorial basis* of the courts as a democratic institution, *efficiency considerations* lead to ask for judicial constraints. Their knowledge base is limited and their information-processing capacity by procedural rationality institutionally constrained. Expanding their power beyond their traditional judicial role would intrude into the working of the other institutions and undermine the trust and credibility of the courts.

Partly against this view *'expansionists'* derive the credibility and the legitimacy of courts from the courts' contribution to (social) justice and emphasize their contribution to social problem-solving (Summers 1983). The legitimacy of courts is judged by their external function and outcome and by the social and political impacts of their decisions. Whereas the former stress the limits and adherence to the internal and processual rationality of adjudication and judicial decision-making, the latter counter with the quest for a receptive and responsive law reflecting what society needs (Nonet and Selznick 1976).

Those competing views on the core functions of the judiciary and the claimed impacts of a potential transformation of the judicial institutions have raised interest into the empirical working of the existing legal institutions. In section 2 we shall sketch the changing role of the courts and their impact on the other constitutional institutions. By considering different legal systems the historical differences of the institutionalization of judicial control in public administration becomes obvious (section 3). The comparison of the different institutional solutions may illuminate the limits of the judicial contribution to social and political problem solving and help to specify the conditions of a new equilibrium among courts responsibility and political and administrative accountability (section 4).

32.2 The Growing Impact of the Judiciary

The impact of alleged judicial expansion has focused attention on two intermingled questions:

(1) On the *legitimacy* of the judiciary to exercise their power and their proper role:
   a) Are courts allowed to transcend the scope of their traditional jurisdiction? (Davis 1969)
   b) Where are the limits to the intensity of their scrutinies? (Bertossa 1984)
(2) On the efficiency and effectiveness of courts, more specifically the *cost* involved especially in respect to the political and managerial needs to upkeep an effective administration of public policies (Dimock 1980) considering:
   a) *unintended effects* of judicial decisions on the behaviour of the administration (Kadish and Kadish 1973),
   b) the *unknown consequences* from the implementation of the judicial decision (Johnson and Canon 1984).

The Changing Role of Courts

In most nations the institutionalization of judicial or even constitutional review powers on administrative and legislative decisions have been conceived as a protection device against potential institutional failures of the other branches, balancing their mutual inherent operational deficits (Cappoletti 1971, Schermers 1983). Judicial powers were considered as exercising a negative control on excessive administrative and legislative acts operating sporadic, on demand and expost. It seems naturally that the rise of administrative laws and instruments increased the need for remedial actions and spawned judicial growth (see Davis 1969, Debbasch 1974, Jaffee 1965, Smith 1973). Civil Right protesters have pointed to the need for the protection of substantive individual rights, implementation researchers have drawn attention to the facts of non-compliance in multiorganizational hierarchical setting and the frictions which are created in translating the rules through the administrative hierarchical layers.

In a certain sense, reasoned argumentation by two parties, following procedural rules rooted in the rule of law, resting on precedent cases and legal enactments form the basis for authoritative determination of controversary questions between parties by courts. Adherence to this procedural and formal rationality requires neutrality and an independent status of the courts. But judicial judgements on administrative decisions may often differ from the conflict-resolution adversary model, as often the third party may be understood as part of the one side in the conflict, thus not mediation between parties, but one-sided adjudication may dominate in the realm of public law, if not institutional constraints operate. Indeed, the decision situations in administrative courts are by far more complex. When questions of public interests and social utility have to be weighted against individual rights as in modern social policies and planning, the bipolar conception breaks.

Conflict about the correct interpretation among the multiple interested parties and even among governmental institutions becomes part of the disputes. The constituency of the differing sources of rules intended to govern behaviour not only between policy fields but also in the assumed hierarchy of constitutional laws, federal and state statutes and even internal non-statutory rules may bread controversies. This merging complexity in polycentric, dynamic decision-situations is further enhanced by the increasing pace of social, economic and technological change. It requires adaption of rules to fit the changing conditions to societies' understanding of fairness and justice and involves the courts in the dispute of complex technical and economic facts for establishing evidence on the effects of governmental decisions (Buiren, Ballerstedt and Grimm 1982). Those cases require not only reconstructing past events and interpreting legal facts, but predicting future risks and consequences and understanding social facts (Horowitz 1977).

The Costs

This new situation seems to unbalance or at least to shift the precarious equilibrium among the judiciary and the other powers. On the one hand agencies may orient their behaviour and their decisions too extensively to the alleged jurisdictional decisions, thus becoming subject to 'judicial finality' (Charlesworth). On the other hand the judiciary is suspected to dress political, social and economic questions into legal problems and to impose by their 'creative decisions' uncontrollable costs upon different segments of society (Glazer 1975, Schmidt 1978).

In response to court actions, officials tend to have recourse to an elaborated tool-kit of defensive, self protective tactics; build a record, fortification resulting in inaction, delay, formalism and procedural concern, whose costs – the neglectance of outcomes – have to be paid by the public. Ritualistic performance to bureaucratic rules and procedures and a preoccupation with possibilities of threats raise transaction costs and lead to implementation failures. In favor of *'judicial minimalism'*, judicial realists argue that under the condition of modern democratic systems, traditional functions of the constitutional branches have been transformed, giving rise to an administrative bureaucracy responsible for societal risk-management and anticipative planning, balancing public and private interests, limiting negative impacts of uncertainties for the future and diminishing the negative consequences of technological and economic decisions for third parties. Judicial activism paralyzes administrative responsibilites. As most plausible consequences *risk avoidance* and *judicalizations* of the administrative procedures may emerge, at best local coping strategies attempt to achieve some level of *informal justice* to accommodate the conflicting demands from many sources (clients, professionals, the community etc.) versus the set law. Against those views some defend the judicalization and claim that reenforcing formal bureaucratic culture and the judicalization of the administration contain some benefits. The tactics of personal risk-minimization, inactions, delay, formalism and decisional transformations are not unmitigated evils. They help to eliminate imprudent conduct, they may even yield more prudent, more careful considered, more accurate and balanced decisions enjoying broader consensus.

Courts emerged in history as ultimate arbiter of litigated disputes utilizing established principles and precedents. Traditionally the conventional functions of the courts have been (1) to identify the governing rules, by which the disputed actions should be judged, (2) to establish the facts which have to meet the requirements of the rules, and (3) to device a decision which enforces action following the rule. Insofar as administrative action is only partially determined by established rules, the traditional criteria and doctrines of legal reasoning become less well apt to solve disputes (Debbasch 1974, Nonet/Selznick 1978, Satta 1978, Buiren, Ballersted, and Grimm 1982). Features that may overtax the traditional model of litigation are mainly

- the involvement of multiple parties, some of them may even not be represented in the litigation of the case
- consequences of decisions that transcend the case in question by the dynamic nature of the issue involved
- problems which need for their clarification a substantial amount of technical expertise and where experts do not agree upon.

To assess complex issues of natural and social science dimensions to solve disagreement on the meaning of law and on the interpretation of facts approaches the limits of the judicial capacity. Reliance on past statements and prefabricated (legislated) laws becomes questionable when uncertain future impacts and the management of potential risks indicate noncorrespondence of issues and mandate a more complex reasoning. One has to ask therefore which constitutional actors may be in the best position to decide in these controversial matters and under which institutional arrangements the risks of one-sided or uninformed decisions may be minimized.

Despite divergent opinions among scholars, judges, lawyers and politicians on the proper role of the courts, on the kind of questions the courts may properly adjudicate and how far their decisions may reach, few disagree, that the courts have extended their judicial power, impacting by their decisions the administration of educational systems, hospitals, planning agencies, welfare and other public institutions, thus transforming their traditional role. Despite this broad agreement there are substantial differences in the explanation of this 'hyperlexological syndrom'. Is it the result of a litigous citizenry, of overlegislation induced e.g. by the dominance of the legal profession in all branches of government or is it simply caused by the insufficient problem-solving capacities in the executive and the legislation? Some hint at dramatic changes operating between the various societal actors, the division of labour arriving at a critical threshold in complexity where the elaboration of rules cannot cope anymore with the increase of organizational interdependencies and the risks of an artificial and technical society (Nelkin 1981).

In discussing courts' role so far neither the *complementary* character of judicial control in relation to other forms of (e.g. managerial, financial and political) control nor the differential and multifunctional nature of the impacts have been considered. If one relates the problem to the wider context of guidance and control (cf. Kaufmann: Ch. 10), a broader differentiated picture of courts' control embedded into the whole political and social context may arise. The rich variety of institutions that operate under the term of judicial controls are themselves part of a wider system of control in which legislative and executive institutions as well as professionalized experts, a critical public opinion and individual citizens take part (cf. Wirth: Ch. 29). The open question is how this manyfold forms of control many stimulate mutual social learning processes where nobody knows in advance the best solutions.

In this broader political and social context a comparative evaluation of different institutional arrangements shows, that it is difficult to decide "what courts do better" in an abstract functional analysis. Their double function i.e. to correct deficits in other institutions and to protect individual rights may be institutionalized in various ways and following pragmatic solutions within a given historical and constitutional context.

32.3 Comparing Legal Systems

A fruitful strategy to gain a better understanding of the potentials and limits of judicial review is the systematic comparison of the experience with judicial review in different countries. The variety of mixes, in which judicial review of administrative actions occur, may help to get a deeper understanding of the differential legal instruments available depending on the legal system and its political, cultural and historical contexts [2] (Schermer 1983, Scharpf 1966, National Institute 1977, Cappelletti 1971). Courts' impacts onto the administration or in broader sense on different public policy fields *differ*. The relationship between the administration and judicial control is not a fixed constellation, but rather a contingent dynamic continuum with a range of problems and processes differing in respect to different dimensions and various conditions. The interplay between administration and courts has to be understood as one of dynamic change, in which a set of different variables have to be investigated: The kind of judicial control closely related to the type of bureaucracy or constitutional order a country possess, their types of institutions and historical roots, the role and type of rules and procedures shaping the extent of control and discretion. Each of these variables may differ from one country to another, and those variables are not only unrelated, but their interconnected systems and rules are closely knit into the social fabric of a particular country.

But differences in historical traditions, peculiar concepts, principles, rules, institutions and judicial techniques evolving should not hinder to see the broader cultural forces working in different systems into the same direction or producing equivalent results. Even if law is seen as serving different functions like being a conservative force in the sense that it satisfies reasonable expectations based on the past experience in a country, or being used as instrumental technique to achieve some kind of social progress, it may turn out that results achieved and techniques developing are closely related (Hart 1961, Summers 1983).

Different Roots

Many observers trace the concept of judicial review back to the famous decision *"Marbury vs. Madison"* (1803) by the US Supreme Court under Chief Justice Marshall. From a more comparative and analytical viewpoint, this celebrated decision seems to be rather a culmination of differential historical experiences and political struggles as Cappelletti (1971: 25) noted. "The american version of judicial review was the logical result of centuries of European thought and colonial experience . . ."

Among other nations, scope, intentions, organization and procedures of judicial control vary mirroring the often byzantine governmental administrative structures, evolving out of a complex and varied mixture of traditionally inhereted institutions, guiding principles, historical experience and political struggles and adhoc improvements and fine-tuning. Careful comparison of the manifold institutional, procedural and instrumental mixtures lead to two types of mutually dependent functions which finally determine what kind of shape judicial review takes on:

(1) Some countries stress the *individual protection* of subjective rights of a citizen;
(2) other stress the *objective control* of the working of the institutions.

In a certain view the building of special institutions for administrative control as a means of citizen protection is historically weaker in those states, in which democratic principles have a long tradition. At one extreme, Sweden and Switzerland seem to rely far more on cultural style than on (court-)institution building. In Sweden the understanding of personal administrative responsibility – even independent from his superior – and the working of the (informal) power of the Ombudsman may outweigh alleged organizational deficits. On the other side, in those nations which have had a long struggle against absolute forms of sovereignty, protection of the citizen ("Rechtsstaat") and binding of the administration to the law ("Gesetzesbindung") became a primary concern. Both principles in controlling administration do not contradict each other. To protect the rights of a person requires a fair and effective administration; the aim of an efficient and legally oriented administration should further a just outcome. The dual split between the task to ensure legal behaviour in the bureaucracy and the subjective protection of individual rights emerge in such a view not as alternatives but rather as different sides of the same coin.

It may even turn out that rising legal complexity needs both principles for judicial decisions. The growth of norms and the hierarchy between different (constitutional, legislative, administrative) norms and inavoidable contradictions between norms in different policy fields or simply the informational deficit or political unability to establish in advance clear rules and conditions may require a careful balancing for which both principles are needed. But the different priority given to those principles led to eminent consequences in the organization and conduct of administrative control. Thus comparison yields a bewildering institutional picture far more complex in organization, definitions and techniques than to be outlined here.

Some countries use the ordinary court system for administrative control like in the USA, in some countries redress against administrative wrongs can be obtained mainly through the administrative hierarchy (cf. Sweden), others like France have special administrative courts inside or – as in the Federal Republic – independent from the administration, in other nations like Britain some types of specialized institutions (administrative tribunals) emerged beside the ordinary courts. History explains some of those differences. The strength and vigourous judicial activism of the courts in the USA compared to England may stem from the different functions the court has played in history. In the USA courts served from the early beginning as control – to check the (British) parliament –, later the Federalists were concerned to establish multiple bounds and checks on any possible over-arching authority. In France, the ordinary court system, seen as potential source for anti-revolutionary backlashes, led to an unique interpretation of the separation of power doctrine understood as a rule to prevent judicial interference into the execution of parliamentary enacted laws. To enforce proper execution – to control the administration for it – became so naturally a task of the administration. In Germany a compromise emerged from an interest to protect citizens from abuses of authority and an interest to minimize outside interference into the administration, whereas in Britain the early victory of the parliament and the concern with parliamentary sovereignity led to a longstanding reservat for Crown privileges and to the safety-door of creating an ever-increasing number of seperate administrative tribunals with quasi-judicial functions to control administration.

Each chosen organizational decision produces consequences which differ stretching from access to actions till the implementation of court decisions into the administration. It affected the extent of administrative control by the courts, the procedures used before the court and the variety of remedial instruments available. Those differences may even influence the rise of a peculiar bureaucratic culture as a response to court rulings effects and dominate the cognitive understanding of the functions of legal rules. Some nations which seem to lack a superior system of judicial ex-post-facto control frequently developed other extra-judicial (institutional and informal) safeguards against potential abuse or misuse of public power. More informal advisory norms e.g. in connection with permits and licences like in Britain may exist or public hearing may serve as ex-ante control. A parliamentary *Commissioner of Administration* or *Ombudsman* may reduce complaints and narrow the gulf between the administered and the administration.

Some caveats are necessary for a comparative evaluation of different control tools, techniques and instruments, as differences have to be accounted for before appraising control outcome.

- the *factual situations* in which jurisdiction may be envoked and conducted,
- *the purpose* for which jurisdiction must or may be used,
- *the forms of proceedings* in which courts decide,
- the *nature, characteristics and effects of the remedies* and sanctions courts may award,
- *the conditions* which must be satisfied before any form of juridical relief or particulars remedies and sanctions are obtainable, may differ.

Obviously, nature and extent of judicial review of administration as well as the institutions by which it is undertaken vary.

History, politics and constitutional theories and legal concepts played a part in the determination of the position court-control attained. In common law countries like Great Britain, Australia, New Zealand, Ireland, Israel and former dependent nations like India and Canada, the ordinary courts are responsible for legal control of the administration. In those countries the separation of functions is understood to require an independent and undivided judiciary. But even those systems have developed special instruments and procedures like prerogative orders (certiori, prohibition, mandamus) to deal with the special situation the administration of public interests demands. In addition, many systems have developed additional institutions who engage next to other tasks in adjucationary activities and mediation. A movement which may be traced back to the Interstate Commerce Act (1887) in the USA and the creation of the Interstate Commerce Commission to control and regulate railways and other carriers.

Despite basic similar patterns even the common law countries differ due to contextual and historical factors. In England a long tradition of extensive state intervention has been accepted by courts, in the USA the courts resisted and government stayed for a long time limited. The American judiciary – established by written constitution – commands about other legitimatory sources than the inherited and successively altered English institute. The byzentine structure of the British system with its numerous semi-autonomous agencies and heavy reliance on local government developed a different kind of judicial control compared to the USA with its multipurpose regulatory agencies, the strong emphasis on constitutional rights and on federal principle.

Evading the Limits of Judicial Controls? – The English System

The most dominant feature of English public law is like in all common law countries that the limits of the powers of public authorities are determinated not by a special administrative court but by the ordinary courts of justice (Robson 1951). From a traditional view, the British system is still minted by Diceys and Duguits suspicion that the institutionalization of separate administrative courts would serve to protect governmental interests and that therefore all cases should be dealt with in private (ordinary) courts. This tradition had the consequence that the British system is primarily concerned with remedies and procedures and less with the substance of law. In court procedures, it is rather the party and not the court who has to take the initiative. The doctrine of precedents (case law) aims to secure the use of 'cumulative wisdom' based on experience, and by stretching its binding forces from the supreme court ("The House of Lords" through the Court of Appeal and the High Court of Justice). Uniform application in legal rules and certainly should prevail (Smith 1973, Schwartz and Wade 1972, Wade et al. 1984).

Organization. England possesses no special courts for public law questions and no special corps of public lawyers, but has developed some rules and remedies with special application to public law in the courts (Halsbury). But besides the ordinary courts which for England and Wales consist of the Magistrates' Courts (deriving from the 14th century with the Justices of Peace), county Courts (for minor civil disputes) and the High Court of Justice (comprising the Queens Bench Division, The Chancery Division and the Family Division), the highest court being the House of Lords (by convention without the lay peers), around 2000 *tribunals* determine claims of the citizens against public authorities (e.g. Agricultural Tribunals (8), Consumer Credit Tribunals (5), Industrial Tribunals (16), National Health Service Tribunals (490), Weal Valuation Courts (64), Revenue Tribunals (429) etc.).

Laws has been held upright to exclude review (Smith vs. East Elloe R. D. C. (1956) A. C.

736) and no principle like the due process clause in the 5th and 14th amendments of the USA Constitution or the German Art. 19 section 4 of the Basic Law allows to bring administrative acts under review. The current tendency to force a more open concept and to give up some of the past traditions like the concern for governmental secrecy may reduce legal certainty, in the absence of a constitution and a bewildering maze of laws judges' discretion may rise, even creating some kind of unfairness (Smith 1973).

There are signs of change, the traditional distinction to hold jurisdictional issues for reviewable and limit jurisdictional decisions to cases of 'errors' of law or 'fact on record' has been blurred. By-laws are increasingly judged by applying the principle of reasonablessnes. The 'audi alteram partem rule' (that the other is to be heard) is less often dismissed in public litigations. Even principles have risen to test administrative discretion ('improper purpose, irrelevant considerations, unreasonablessnes').

But still public services are held responsible like private citizens. Even, if at the same time the fair treatment principle is applied, in many respects, no rights exist to protect effectiveness against potential administrative dominance (cf. licence procedures). The interfusion of private and public law has delayed the development of adequate tools to challenge administrative decisions. Far more it seems that court rulings still lack to shape general principles (or they remain rather hidden). The unity brought forth by codification and constitutional rights in other countries is not developing through ad-hoc decisions. Such public law is still dominated by interest in remedies, loosing out of sight the results of acts. The unifying force of Supreme (Constitutional) Court rulings is lacking. The wide range of similar but separately enacted acts of parliament with slightly different languages are further complicated by differentiated reasoning in case-laws. The creation of quasi-judicial procedures (ex-ante): Hearings. Inquiries and ex-post Tribunals (in 1958), Parliamentary Commissioner of Administration (1967) cannot fully cover the loss in effectiveness and consistency in developing judicial control.

The Law Commission (Law Commission Act 1965) with its aim of systematic development and reform, and the continuous concern of the Council of Tribunals (cf. Annual Reports) to shape and foster more coherent rulings may have changed the climate even rising a sporadic concern to provide for a more systematic protection and guidance of individual rights by a future constitution.

The Limits of Procedural Fairness – the US System

It has often been pointed out that the American constitution is characterized by two opposing principles, the separation of powers and checks and balance. Whereas the first principle gives the three branches their independence, the second works as their cooperative mechanism. This furthers the distinctive features of the American system of judicial control, its reliance on *procedure*. In this, the judge is seen as an umpire who decides on the evidence of the facts and the presentation of arguments of law, but the conduct of the case ist not his task, but that of the parties, even witnesses are examined by the parties. He aims to resolve disputes between parties in controversy whose legal rights and interests are in collision ('case and controversaries' doctrine of Art. III).

In judicial control the purpose of the courts is to guard the maintenance of the constitution, to see that powers are lawfully vested in public agencies and to maintain the constitutional, statutory and common law rights of persons by controlling the lawful exercise of powers. On a more general level stressing present activities, their purpose is to reconcile private and public interests and to build democratic safeguards and standards of fair play within the effective conduct of government. As a process to solve disputes, to establish 'peace and order', the procedure rests on the model of a two party conflict, on the use of past conflict-solutions (case law) and a close connection between remedies and rights. Although the legal system had always allowed for broad access, the *'American rule'* (each party covers its own expenses) deterred from using one's own rights and kept the level of litigation rather low till the legal service reforms in the late sixties and early seventies. In addition, a peculiar system of regulation and adjudication developed outside the courts by commissions and boards.

Today, the traditional model seems in transition. Since the seventies more public law litigation and structural reform cases have (in the aftermath of the activist Warren court from the fifties on) led to the evolution of a new more active court caused by the amorphe or polycentric structure of (interested) parties, loosening strict requirements of *locus standi;* from personal subjective involvement making the parties representative of broader target groups (class suits) and by raising awareness of future impacts and risks as well as the implementation consequences of such polycentric disputes.

Organization: The judicial control of the legality of administrative measures is exercised by the same courts as of any civil or criminal law case. Only for suits against the government exist special 'Claim Courts'. The judicial branch consists of the 'Supreme Court', 11 'Courts of Appeal', 90 'District Courts' and special courts like the US 'Tax Court', US 'Court of Claims', the US 'Customs Court', the US' Court on Customs and Patent Appeals'. All federal are appointed by the President for life time. The organs of the states are shaped similar to the federal level. Each state has its own system of courts, determined by the state constitutions. The large states have three tiers, the smaller a two level system (Mezines et al. 1983, Warren 1980).

Access, especially to the higher courts or the Supreme Court, is quite limited, reducing the number of written opinions on merit to some 120 cases a year. Like other federal systems the mass of administrative control is exercised by state courts except for cases of ratione materiae (federal laws) or ratione personae (e.g. in case of diverse citizenships) (Davis 1978).

Purpose and Principles. Subject to control by the judicial branch are the legality of all acts by the administration, included are all administrative matters handled by special boards and commissions like the Atomic Energy Commission or the Civil Aeronautics Board. Excepted from control are certain political questions and Presidential actions in the conduct of armed force and foreign affairs (Scharpf 1966, Jaffee 1965). In addition the courts may invalidate any legislation which violates the constitution, especially those which violate the Bill of Rights in the Constitution (free speech, press, religion, of assembly, equal protection, fair trial etc.). The flexibility of those provisions allowed the court a far-reaching political role, although this had been understood in contrast to the positive role of the administration and the legislation as a 'legative one' (Jowell 1975). Although the body of statutory law has grown steadily, the role of the courts as law creators has not been diminished. The courts exercise their control on three ways:
1) in the control of the constitutionality of legislation
2) in the interpretation of written laws,
3) in the reformulation of unwritten (common) law (Davis 1969).

Quite frequently, this power of the Supreme Court has been under close scrutiny by critiques. In some cases the Congress' rejoinders to the Court's decision resulted in amendments to the constitution like in Chisholm vs. Georgia and the Dread Scott case, in other situations the Supreme Court seemed to be wise enough to change its attitude as it happened during the New Deal legislation, when the court held up nearly all legislations by ruling the enacted laws as unwise – not fitting precedent cases or even the constitution – till President Roosevelt reacted with a 'Court-Package Bill' threatening the Supreme Court[3]. But more often the tendency of Supreme Courts' decisions seemed to favour uniform rulings supporting federal activism and unification, although many facets of the administrative law are still quite different from one state or another (e.g. Water laws of the Eastern States differ from the rules in the arid West).

In general, the state decisions doctrine of the common law seems to be more limited in the USA. Confined partly by the existence of constitutional rights, partly by the courts sensitivity to political requirements, not least due to the political nomination process which has produced mixed results: a combination of judicial longevity and partisan tenacity led as a rule to retartation and slowing down of political changes. Especially since the Warren court precedents have often been overruled. Part of the trend of overruling has been the growing recognition and influence of the Law Schools who emphasized against a once conservative Supreme Court the need for adaptation, for recognition of realistic situations and for social needs and demands (Sociological Jurisprudence) (Pound 1911). In addition, the American Bar Association worked in stressing uniform laws and rulings.

In court proceedings the state is just one party, but the similarity of the court systems for administrative and civil cases should not hide that the main procedures and remedies differ. Most techniques used in controlling the administration are channelled to questions of the jurisdiction of the administration, sometimes court orders, alternative mandamus, in which officials must give causes and prerogative writs, in which the court directs the administration, more often restraining injunctions are given. Damage suit are often selected to prevent the administration to act.

Perhaps more than elsewhere the courts in the U.S. have forced the administration to develop procedures in order to remain controllable (see table 1).

Tab. 1: Principles of 'Due Process'

Adequate Notice
Speedy Justice
Discovery (Right of Information)
Opportunity to be heard
Compulsory Process
Representation
Confrontation
Cross-Examination
Strict and relevant Evidence
Public Participation
Decision-rules (impartiality, evidence in record, standards to proof in writing, reason)
Appeal Rights

It seems not incidental, that the Administrative Bar Association had been founded the same year as the New Deal legislation started the fight for an Administrative Procedure Act, which took shape in 1946, containing:

(1) adequate protection of private rights, interests, privileges, and benefits; (2) notice, hearing, and prompt decision; (3) publication of all delegations and prohibition of decision-making by officers who have not personally examined the evidence; (4) representation by counsel; (5) admission and debarment of attorneys by administrative tribunals; (6) prohibition of unnecessary disturbance of persons.

At the Brink of Centralized Administrative Self-Judicalization: France

In the past, the French model of judicial control has been oriented to a spirit of close, but (in its aim to preserve the *'mission de service public'*), cooperative, administrative control. Recruitment pattern and political culture as well as legal doctrine seemed to support the model of a highly systematic and centralized court decision system. In addition, French law has become famous for its extended codifications and successful implementation of court decisions. The reliance on a system of internal administrative courts and the broad advisory functions of the *Conseil d'Etat* contributed to the strength of the French system covering in its jurisdictional scope more than most other systems (Debbasch 1981, Lâubadère 1982, David 1982). Today controversial political decisions have weakened the top advisory function and the centralized system seems to fit less complex judicial control requirements on the local base and shows shortcomings to cut through the complex maze of different legal enactments. Thus the old top-down model seems to decline, a new more situative along generalized principles taking shape.

Organization. The French system consists of three Supreme Courts: The 'Cour de Cassation' for ordinary courts' questions dealing with civil law cases, commercial, social and criminal appeals; the 'Conseil d'Etat' with appelate jurisdiction over the (regional) administrative councils (dealing with the droit administratif), the drafting of legislation for the cabinet; advisory opinions on legislative and executive matters and the supervision of rules of public administration; in addition, the 'Conseil constitutionnel' controls legislation in advance (concerning organic laws) judging disputes between the constitutional organs checking appointments of high officials, financial bills and over conflicts of procedures in constitutional organs. the 'Tribunal des Conflits' decides on jurisdictional questions between ordinary and administrative courts. Lower level courts are the 31 tribunaux administratifs (Anby and Drago 1984, Debbasch 1981).

Purpose and Principles. The French Conseil d'Etat (Ordonance No 45-1708; 31.7.45, last modified in Decret No 81-29; 16.1.81) at the top of administrative courts is one of the most powerful administrative court in Europe and served as pacemaker for other courts (David 1982). There are a number of other principle bodies of special jurisdiction (jurisdiction d'attribution) for which on legal issues the Conseil d'Etat serves as a board of appeal like the Cour des Comptes, the Conseil Superior de l'Education Nationale and the Commission Centrale d'Aide Sociale. the Conseil d'Etat is an advisory body on legislation and also the Supreme Administrative Court of the country. The Conseil d'Etat has the right to call government's attention to fields where legislation seems desirable, the Conseil must be consulted on ordinances of general application.

Individuals have no access to the Constitutional Court, but easy access to the administrative courts compensates for this constitutional deficit. Considering the concern with the 'mission de service public', the past concern with effective working of the administration seems to be more dominant than narrow control by definite principles (Lâubadère 1982). At the same time the citizen had few means to stop governmental actions, but many (and easy access e.g. no costs involved, broad definition of right to actions), if he feels an interest is violated. In the ruling of access not his right of action is judged, but the objective legality of action and convenient means for compensation.

More than any other nation the French administration rests on a conglomerate of different types of enacted laws and court-decisions (David 1982, Debbasch 1974). Constitutional provisions governing the organisation and functions of public authorities and in the 'preambel' the enumeration of fundamental rights influence decisions by the Conseil d'Etat, whereas administrative courts refer next to the constitutional und legal provisions to these decisions. The lack of internal coherence between the different types of enacted ordinary law, which the règlements of different rank and the manifold kinds of arrêts necessitates the judges to fill the lacunae. This creative role of the judges is reinforced today, the law has to be adapted more often to new circumstances and applied in unforseen situations by the legislators. Thus judges have begun to exercise wide discretion sometimes even taking refuge to scientific research (Anby and Drago 1984). This has been taken place despite courts' recognition of the administrations broad latitude in exercising discretion. The courts have begun to elaborate principles like equity, relativity of rights, ordre sociel to guide their decisions. But the administration may still take the concept of public interest or public policy as an escape from close control.

The fact that the system of the administrative courts is closely embedded into the administration allows for a sensitive understanding of the wide range of different administrative actions and helps to develop corresponding remedies and workable decisions. Despite the broad access the protection of the individual citizen remains however limited because the system is lacking suspensive rights against the enforceable administration.

Powerful, yet limited – the German Verwaltungsgerichte

The German system of administrative control is probably the most comprehensive and coherent one, but insofar as the pursue of legal action is bound on the *violation of individual rights,* access is more limited and the range of issues to be discussed in courts is more limited than in most other legal systems. Despite some inconsistencies the constitutional and administrative courts are well cooperating and coordinated. The power of relief is awarded – e.g. suspension and relief rights – so powerful as to cause often concern of the administration and politicians (Investment jam). Administrators and politicians are well aware to take into account courts rulings or potential rulings even with such precautions necessary that a rising number of scholars are asking for legal enactment for explicit discretion to allow the 'more democratic legitimated' government to act. The extensive strict rulings have led to administrative preemption of court rulings and widespread amplification of judicial procedure in the administration. Intense consideration for unified administrative procedures and trends for codification and unification of the eminent administrative laws e.g. in the field of social policy and planning, seem the natural outcome of this limited but effective judicial control system.

Organisation. In contrast to the previous system the German judiciary evolved around three set of systems to solve litigious disputes. The public law disputes (öffentlich-rechtliche Streitigkeiten) are separated from disputes in civil and criminal matters (bürgerliches Recht und Strafsachen) and from constitutional disputes (Verfassungsrechtsfragen). The ordinary courts are confined to private and criminal law jurisdiction. For constitutional (Verfassungsgerichtsbarkeit) and for administrative jurisdiction (Verwaltungsgerichtsbarkeit) separate courts exist. Judicial Control of the administration is exercised by general administrative courts (Verwaltungsgerichte) and special administrative courts for financial (Finanzgerichtsbarkeit), social security (Sozialgerichtsbarkeit) and patent jurisdiction (Patentgerichtsbarkeit). Two special courts for disciplinary jurisdictions of civil servants and the military have to be named as well. The system is even further complicated as the lower courts belong to the states. The Federal Constitutional Court (Bundesverfassungsgericht) has extensive rights to consider the constitutional validity of any federal or land statute, as well as to rule on disputes among the branches of government. Any person can directly complain to the

Constitutional Court if he feels violated in his basic rights (Grundrechte). The general administrative courts are since 1960 organized on three levels (Verwaltungsgerichte, Oberverwaltungsgerichte und Bundesverwaltungsgericht), whereby the tax courts and the social security courts remain separate organization and possess their own procedures.

Function and Principles. The scope of jurisdiction is allcomprehensive. Art. 19.4 GG (Basic Law) permits judicial control of measures of the administration. The precondition for taking actions before the courts is a claim for individual protection bound to the violation of subjective rights. An action before the administrative courts is only permitted "when the plaintiff asserts that his rights have been violated by the implementation, refusal or omission of an administrative act" (§ 42, 2 VerwGO (Administrative Court Code)). The main task involved in the control of the administration by the courts is the protection of individual subjective rights. Public law-suits are excluded. Unlike in France or the USA, on principle, it is not possible for associations or citizens' initiatives to assert their interests against the administration by calling on the courts, as long as they are not affected as individuals. To effect individual protection the courts often leads the court to decisions which are no longer oriented along the strict control of the legality of action, but deriving at conclusions preempting administrative decisions. As a consequence in case of a new law the administration is often waiting till the courts have taken the responsibility for concretisizing the law. Such a tendency has been supported by the rise of general clausel esp. regarding risk estimations (safety, planning, environment) e.g. terms like "Gefahr" (§ 5 Nr. 1 BImSchG (dangerous risk) Federal Immission Protection Law), state of technology (§ 5 Nr. 2 BImSchG), state of science and technology (§ 7 II Nr. 3 AtG (Nuclear Law).

Similar questions arise in the exercise of administrative discretion e.g. in planning laws. To some degree the courts tended to develop principles of procedural fairness, enforcing participatory rules and ask for weighing differing interest in a reasoned manner.

For exercising discretion a net of principles have been developed, which narrows the action-space of the administration (Willkürverbot, Übermaßverbot, Gebot einer gerechten Abwägung, Vertrauensschutz).[4]

It has been recognized for a long time that the legislator can only regulate complex matters by using indefinite legal concepts and broad general clauses. Regulative difficulties of the legislators in economic, ecological or technical areas imposed on the administration and the administrative courts often the burden of having to take the responsibility for decisions in individual cases without precise legal guidance.

Political difficulties, narrow parliamentary majorities or the complexity of areas, in which the technical and economic experience on which the legislature needs to base its decisions is lacking and fear that legal statute by parliament could put an end to the necessary process of clarification and discussion, require more often today recourse to general clauses and 'empty' terminological comprises. The statement that administrative decisions should not be anticipated is not uncommon practice in the legislative.

A particular contribution to the stabilization of administrative decisions is the instrument of an abstract control of norms (§ 47 VerwG (Code of the Administrative Courts)). It enables to test the validity of legal ordinances below the level of federal or state laws (Police regulations, bye-laws, development plans) even when they have not been put into effect in individual cases as means of preventive legal protection to avoid individual cases in technically and legally complicated administrative acts (planning), in which administrative decisions interlock and require coordination. Here judicial control of norms stabilizes coherent administrative decision-making.

But the system is not all comprising; some leaks of major importance are:

– The awarding of government contracts. In the German legal system this is an area of civil law and not of public law. Consequently, lawsuits – for example those filed by persons whose tenders have been ignored – fall under the jurisdiction of the civil courts and not of

the administrative courts. However, the civil courts are less experienced in dealing with administrative decisions; furthermore, the means of instituting proceedings provided for by the Code of Civil Procedure of 1877 are not really suitable for such cases. Consequently, the administration is less sharply controlled in this area than elsewhere.
- The civil service code. In this area political patronage has, unfortunately, increased greatly in the last few years. Nevertheless, such biased decisions are seldom subject to control by the courts. In this case, an applicant who had been discriminated against would have to bring an action. But the dominant doctrine does not (yet) acknowledge this kind of action of competitors under the civil service code.
- Public lawsuits as often asked for by environmentalists to allow for a cost-efficient prototype process.

32.4 Assessment

Control over the administration may be exercised by many forces. The main emphasis in most constitutions is on controls exercised by the legislative branch and by the executive, less attention is paid to the controls exercised by the judicial branch. Many view courts as a kind of semi-detached monitor who calls the other branches to account their decisions according to the principles and maxims which are stated directly by the constitution and the statute, or which are intrinsically part of the precedent jurisdictional history. For many the judge is the last final voice, as he judges according to natural or positive law, his rulings are definitive. As judges are deciding on other branchs activities, a special responsibility is allocated to them.

While the control of the administration by the legislature and by the executive is quite easily to understand out of democratic and economic reason, the concept of judicial finality is a concept more difficult to understand. It assumes that this institution is rather a reference and protector, not a leader and master, and in the past it often assumed as source of its wisdom and a suprahuman and changeless law.

Judicial and other controls

From a comparative institutional point of view the question arises, what is the performance of the judiciary? In a still pathbreaking article Scharpf (1966) pointed to the limits of judicial power. In issues requiring flexibility, secrecy and special expertise a judicial system cannot work, foreign affairs, military issues – the classical political questions – have to be decided by other institutions.

The judiciary possesses a reliable competence in the protection of rights, on controlling procedures, it seems less reliable in deciding on many substantive issues. This seems particularly true when there are decisions at stake whose consequences are a matter not of legal but e.g. technical, economic or social standards and where experts disagree. In this cases the amount of subjective appraisal and opinion is particularly high (Buiren, Ballerstedt and Grimm 1982: 52), and it seems questionable if judges are in a better position to decide about such matters than administrators with specialized experience or politicians which are assigned to make decisions under conditions of uncertainty. The task of the courts then is to watch over the appropriateness of procedures rather than of results.

This assessment is an application of a more general insight: Judicial, political and administrative decision making differ, and institutional analysis has started to build a better understanding of the different functions appropriate to the various systems (cf. also Ch. 31 and 33). Issues of social and political reality may under dynamic conditions become so varied and subtle that their regulation by broad principles seems inadequate, at least until sufficient experience has been made with various tentative solutions. Often these have to rely on the interplay of many different factors, and an adversary formal procedure would undermine those issues.

Often institutions have been built on different features:

- Judges may have life tenure, whereas legislatures to ensure care and responsibility to their voters have shorter tenure.

- The decision structure differs significantly in the political and administrative arena. In taking decisions, the administrative official must shape reality not just at certain points, but on the basis of a vast range of possible administrative actions. The law provides the framework or the constraints, but goals and standards of his acts often stem from completely different areas, they are, for example, economic efficiency, financial considerations and political expediency.

- Both possess two different ways of looking at things. The comprehensive task-oriented approach of the administrators contrasts the rule-oriented approach of the judges. The judge does not have to pass judgement on an overall situation but only on those aspects of a situation which are causing the lawsuit. The judge acts after the event and is not under pressure; he observes exclusively legal standards and works in accordance with the procedures of legal doctrine. The specifically legal treatment of the case is the source of his legitimation. The nature of the law as a generally accepted standard prevents irregular behaviour and guides decision, but is is not the only source for the administrator or politician.

- The political branches can initiate issues and determine which issue they address, a judge cannot. A legislative and administrative system may have manifold sources of information and can express to some degree its freedom how to use this information. A judicial system usually is limited to the information available by the advocates and litigants, and judges search only for information immediately relating to the case. Thus the flexibiliy and scope of the courts is – compared to other institutions – severely limited. Therefore the operational conditions for the courts are rather different.

Besides the protection of individual rights the main task of judicial control of administration results from failures of the particular mechanism of guidance relevant to particular decisions, e.g. market failures or political failures. the identification of flaws in the legislative process or in the executive and administrative management becomes the task of the judiciary. E.g. as organizational research often demonstrates, there is a tendency of public organization to goal displacements. The interests of particular organizations (or even of persons within these organizations) may interfere with the stated or implicit goals of political measures, thus distorting the implementation process. Courts then may serve to control for those organizational trends with respect to legal duties. They may also redefine operational procedures (e.g. just procedure, voting rights tec.), if certain groups like religious, racial or ethnic minorities are at disadvantage under majority rule following one-sided interest.

The correctional function of the courts to take account of possible defects of other institutions has its standard in the conception of the proper functioning of those institutions. This however is not always recognizable in an unequivocal way by the stated law. The view that value judgements and substantial decisions should be made in the political and administrative processes and that the role of the judiciary is to police the implementation of legal enactments in order to correct political malfunctions often falls short of the problem at stake. The differentiation between procedure and substance is too simple. Many decisions the courts have been concerned with in the last decade were related to procedural issues, but they could not be resolved without taking refuge to substance. Political institutions are not only a body of procedural regulations to arrive at decisions but most constitutions contain also some distinctive decisions already set out, e.g. concerning human rights. In situations where courts have to judge about the possible consequences of legislative or administrative decisions a recourse to substantial concerns seems unavoidable.

Judges can be guardians because they are set up as outsiders, but it seems not that the malfunction does always require court corrections. Often the systems themselves may produce reforms. Political stereotypes and prejudices may be corrected through the political process, as the political process is itself a complex mutually-controlled process by parties, by elections, by federalism.

As far as the organization of internal administrative control is specifically concerned, trust in the effectiveness of legal protection through the courts may conceal the fact that other controls are necessary. Recourse to the administrative judge is sometimes inadequate because it demands judicial control of the administration even in areas where such control is systematically out of place (e.g. on managerial issues or supervision of the reports of the courts of audit). Often forms of internal controls may be more adequate and less rigid and detrimental (cf. Arvidsson: Ch. 30 and Grunow: Ch. 31). The questions courts have to decide are not only declaring the right, but as well to define the remedy. Sometimes like in the famous Brown vs. Board of Education 347 U.S. 483 (1954) it declined to specify the remedy with a result that lower courts had difficulty later when administrators obstructed desegregation.

Unlike other institutions, the legal training and professionalization often serves for perceptual homogenity between administrators and courts. This may be one of the reasons why judges prefer procedures and tend to require the administration to take over some of their procedures. This may be a two-sided process as the administration tries to apply rules which do not fail the test of the courts or even limit their action to those activities where court approval already has been achieved, and avoid cases of legal doubts or uncertainty. There are deficits, the judicial information is often poorly equipped to receive information on the desires and preferences of the public, and judges are not able to weight the larger conflicting interests in a case context (cf. Wirth: Ch. 35). Sensitivity to issues which a larger public concern often fail in the court and the impacts of the court decision may undermine the trust of the public in its fairness and understanding.

Often remedies and changes come from the political process and it is the judiciary that is unwilling to allow for corrections. The problem is that the judiciary should be excluded from some range of activity and the legislative process from a range of other activities, but where is the boundary to be drawn? The need for disinterested, contemplative and neutral judicial decision-making is often contrasted with the passionate, self-interested hurly-burly of the legislative process, where moral and principled inquiries are assigned to the judiciary and policy or expedient questions to the political process. Politicians in such a view react as reflexive decision-makers to the desires and preferences of their constituents – desires and preferences that do not necessarily accord with moral principles. Policies are short-term and narrowly focused, more expedient and more responsive to the needs of the moment. But this division seems to be questionable, there are few questions which who are not dealt with in the courts and there are few questions which are not dealt in legislatures. In addition, making policy processes more contemplative, introducing more reason, may require to loose public will, desire and commitment available in the legislative process. Far more, the intentions and motivations of the actors may provoke unintended results. It is a common analytical fallacy that intentions and motives already account for aggregate effects. Passion, self-interest and short-sightness may provide helpful tools to achieve justice in the long run, whereas the opposite may become as well true.

The political process may have imperfections, but it may be still superior to other alternatives. The principle on which decisions are made, either on longterm or on short term predictions about such immediate practical consequences of a decision on the behaviour of individual actors, does not immediately favor judicial (personal) argumentative inspection reliant on legal doctrines over societal decision-making.

Public Law and its Consequences

European legal doctrine distinguishes between private and public law, which governs the affairs of the communities and the acts of governmental authorities: "publicum ius est quod ad statum rei Romanae spectat". Despite much learned discussion the distinction is still blurred and quite differently applied in different systems. The medieval law even did not know a public-private distinction. Landrecht (territorial law), Lehnrecht (feudal law), Hofrecht (manorial law), Dienstrecht (servitary law), Stadtrecht (town law) and even the royal power were coined in private law terms (contracts, obligations etc.), which applied to private relationships. It was only with the emergence of the modern nation-state that die private-public law distinction gained momentum: The formation of a modern state bureaucracy, the concentration of power by the sovereign, the differentiation and diversification of an administrative state organization and the advancement of a legally trained bureaucracy bound to execute a public will favored the growth of two separate systems. Legal rules as channeling action in the public interest and controlling its exercise became more widespread. Conceptually the division between 'puissance exécutrise' and 'puissance de juger' in Montesquieu's *De L'Esprit des Lois* provided the conceptual foundation of a dual court system. In France administrative controversies were entrusted to the administrative bodies (Decree of 6–11. Sept. 1790) and later to a superios administrative tribunal, the Conseil d'Etat. This model, which trusts the control-function to the administrative body spread from France to Belgium, Luxemburg, the Netherlands, Portugal und Greece. To some degree the Swedish and the Swiss conceptions may be understood as related models, although their peculiar organizational arrangements and principles deserve separate treatment. In Germany, a distinction developed between the justice system and the 'policy' system. The policy system acted at the discretion of the prince by decree (Verordnung), and the justice system served to check legality enactments. It was an early compromise between the liberals favoring the ordinary court model and the conservatives insisting on internal control which led to the emergence of special administrative courts, an organizational device which countries most notable, Italy and Turkey, followed with similar independent administrative courts for public law cases.

Although the distinction between public and private law is firmly established on the continent, comparative analysis demonstrates that the boundaries are far from evident. The increased governmental expansion into all spheres of social and economic life led to an intermingling of both spheres and hybrid situations. Some public law as in Germany is part of the jurisdiction in the ordinary courts.

Even in constitutional law differences between the Roman law countries exist. In France, the protection of the fundamental rights of a citizen is not considered to the constitute law. In Germany they form a substantial part of it. With regard to organizational questions, some have established overarching constitutional courts, others not. Access and jurisdiction again differ.

In most countries the legislative rules give wider discretion to the agencies and their courts than in provision of law given to the ordinary courts. In most civil law fields the parties are free to set their own rules by contract. In public law however the authorities have to apply the codes and laws. Judges in the public law have more discretion, especially in Germany the prevalance of indefinite legal concepts (unbestimmte Rechtsbegriffe) like public goods, public order, public security, danger, risk etc. permit a considerable latitude for court decisions. As result it has often become the task of the courts to define principles to be applied by the administration in exercising discretion.

In France, administrative law concerning 'organizational proper' is mainly written down, but not 'administrative proper' rules which rely mainly on judicial precedents. In Germany, administrative law has been divided between general and special law (Allgemeiner und Besonderer Teil). The latter may be subdivided according to subject matter in police law, trade law (Gewerberecht), social service law (Fürsorgerecht), building law (Baurecht), educational law (Schulrecht) etc. The question, whether in those fields similar procedures and principles should apply, is subject to intense discussion.

Professional training may play an important role. In France and Italy, the judges are specially trained (in France mainly from the Ecole Nationale d'Administration), in Italy selected from the Higher Civil Service, whereas in the Federal Republic they have received ordinary training like all judges according to the Richtergesetz (Law of Judges).

In both countries, France and Germany, the increasing duties of government in the field of social services, has partly increased the load on the administrative courts, but at the same time has led to an opposing tendency: the flight of public administration into the private law, meaning *the performance of public function under the rule of private law*. But the encroachment of public law into the field of private relations has been eminent as well. Exercise of certain professions and trades are subjected to licenses, administrative acts may limit the property rights, affect the law of contract and the law of associations. In planning law compulsory purchase, the concept of eminent domain, the use of property in zoning laws, the limitations of building permittance and other regulations have crept into private rights. Holders of concession in public utilities may be limited in their contract freedom. The validity of private contracts may become depending on public approach (Genehmigung, authorisation). Considering in addition the numerous administrative regulations relating to trade, public health, public safety and social services of professional activities, the inroads in public law from citizen protection into public interest protection became obvious. Concurrently public authorities tried to evade the strict rules of public law regulations by turning to private law institutions and means.

In France, the régie under direct administrative control integrated into the public service and subject to budgetary and administrative accounting methods has given more and more way to public concessions. In addition, new hybrid organizations have emerged like the établissement public and mixed economy companies (cf. also Hood: Ch. 9). Furthermore, the concession may fall as an administrative act under public law, but the relation between the concessionnaire and the user under private law. Nationalized 'enterprises publique' are mainly under the jurisdiction of ordinary courts, moreover in the field of social security entrusted to private organizations (e.g. caisses de sécurité sociale) are subject in the relation of the users and the offices to private law. Sometimes like in the important professional organizations of the doctors their acts of public nature (admission or expulsion) are subject to administrative law and their internal organization to private law.

In Germany, the traditional distinction between hoheitlich (based on administrative governmental power) and fiscal (fiskalisch) (activities of public authorities by private law) has been blurred and various theories (subordination, subjects involved, interests served) have dedeloped to distinguish which court has jurisdiction. Especially the rich context of German public authorities, who have considerable freedom to choose the kind of legal form they wish, has given rise to difficult problems concerning the question which principles habe to be applied from public or private law. It seems difficult for outsiders to understand that users of the federal railways (Deutsche Bundesbahn) are in private law relations, those of the federal mail service (Bundespost) are in public law relations. Choosing private forms, public authorities may often be able to evade restriction of political control or attempt to increase managerial flexibility or control over their employees. Subvention laws provide a special rich area of those intermingling problems.

Differences and Convergence

Despite historic, textual, technical and philosophical principled differences between the Anglo-American conception of administrative law and that which
prevails in civil-law countries heated discussion on standards and limits of administrative discretion about the pathological features of a litigious society and the
inherent weaknesses of the basic concepts of legal reasoning and theorizing point to
similar problems on both sides. Changes in the patterns of governmental activity,
the reorganizing of legal work and the concern for individual rights protection and
access have given rise in all countries to an increase in legal activities.

Traditionally a great contrast has been seen between Roman Law countries and
Common Law countries, between the Code Law Systems and Case Law Systems
(Goodnow 1893, David 1982). Till 1800 the difference was far less marked.
Reporting and discussion of precedent cases, being already an important feature in
the English legal system, dominated judicial decisions and professional discussion
to some degree in both systems, and most legal systems emphasized already
procedural aspects of judicial decision-making to ensure fairness and impartiality.
Historical reasons, political and social forces enhanced the process of codification
in the 18th and 19th century on the continent and the absence of it in England
resulted in its placing differential emphasis on legal schools and in the English
system of judges in establishing legal techniques and procedures (Hart 1961,
William 1982). Common Law 'architecture' seemed to serve as a helpful tool to
limit and resist royal absolutism. The common law procedures provided for all its
complexity and costs sufficient remedies. Its intricacies and pecularities were of
high political value since they impeded the total exercise of executive power, such
in Common Law countries the political and economic interests rather urged against
codification. In continental countries codification was first often part of the
political struggle for national unity and absolute sovereignity, later it became part
of the political strive to prevent further extension of governmental power and
interference. In France the exclusion of administrative and governmental controls
from the ordinary court control was seen as necessary to allow effective governmental actions. The differential historical constellations gave rise to different
responses. In the English system emphasis was laid on the enactment of (partial
and specific) statutes to provide for governmental acts, in judicial decisions on the
virtue of exhistorical experience rather than on abstract logic and principles in
search for a rational structure of the whole system.

Despite such divergent starting points, it seems a historical irony that later the
continental system often had difficulty to develop out of general principles coherent and consistent judicial decisions, whereas from the casuistic judicial decision
process systematic case-reporting and digesting proved to be subtle instruments to
achieve unification of judicial decision-making. Thus on the continent judicial
'creative' rule-making rised to bridge the gap between principles and decision-
needs or to adapt dysfunctional codes by justifiable reinterpretation, while at the
same time Common law countries developed more general criterias and principles
well established in the continental systems. Thus in both systems evolved elements
of systematic continuity and coherence and creative discretionary judgements. To
some degree it may be even argued that traditions have been reversed. Comparing

the US and the German system, one may tend to note the rising importance of judicial rule-making and opinion-forming and the relative decline of academic theories and doctrines, whereas in the USA the law schools emerged beside the Bars as powerful and influential institutions (Schermers 1983, Sutta 1978, Debbasch 1974).

The traditional distinction is still alive, it is demonstrated in the intense interest, especially in the USA, on processes and on judicial opinions and behaviour and impacts of courts' decisions and in the more dogmatic interests in the continental countries (Johnson and Cannon 1985). But the vivid discussion on the 'line of decisions' shows the importance of more principled reasoning in the case law countries as well. Creative judgment may be exercised by elaborating the principle, by the continuation and enlargement the scope of its appliance (the grammer of principle). Judgements may even occur in facts-plus-order approaches as the precedent cases are reconstructed and some facts are ruled 'obiter'. Therefore wide choices exist in the operation. This gives the judges discretion and flexibility to broaden or narrow an application of some principle (Davis 1961, Dworkin 1977, Harlow and Rawlings 1984).

Sometimes the nature of legal relations has been considered to serve as a material basis for the distinction between private and public law, one party has been thought to be inferior (Subjektivitätstheorie) or a public law has been conceived as containing 'coercive' (zwingend) rules. Others emphasize a 'public interest' concept or conceive of public law as shaped by 'special rights' (Sonderrechte), but all formal logical distinction seems to be insufficient to explain fully why some legal fields are classified public laws and others not. Likewise even the distinction of jurisdiction between administrative and ordinary courts seems to follow no clear principles. In Germany, a litigation is considered of public law if it concerns a legal relation between a state (or another public authority, public establishment, public corporation or the church) and a subordinated individual, but not in liability suits. In France, the principle of public service ('service publice') favoured by Hariou seems to be applied in a highly opportunistic manner.

A mix of national history and adherence to different conceptual theories may best explain the fundamental distinctions. Such in France, the law of 16.–24. Aug. 1790 forbade interference by the judiciary in administrative matters. In the French conception of 'separation of power' one institution should not check the other institution, but rather each institution should limit itself to its own kind of reasoning and decision-making process. Administrative acts should be within the exclusive competence of administrative courts, finally with the Conseil d'Etat Administrative. Thus, whereas all acts of the administration (décisions exécutoires and opérations administratives) are subject to control, administrative jurisdiction has been assigned to the tribunaux administratifs and the Conseil d'Etat. Just as an appeal to the court leads to a higher court, an appeal from one administrative authority should rest with an higher administrative authority. Only this would secure the true separation of power. Two principles should guide the judicial control of the administration the protection of the individual and the concept of public service. To adjudicate conflicts which may rise between the administration and the courts Napoleon set up a special Court 'the Conseil d'Etat'. The Conseil conceived as part of the administration. Therefore he had possessed advisory functions to the government. Today a special 'Tribunal des Conflicts', consisting out of five judges from the 'Cour de Cassation' (highest civil court) and the 'Conseil de Etat' administers jurisdictional conflicts. The minister of justice possessing the tie-breaking vote as 'garde des sceaux'.

Organizational arrangements do not determine the effectiveness in protecting the individual. A court system to protect may provide more limited access and prove effectiveness. At the same time, an inbuilt administrative system like in Sweden may be quite flexibel and provide easy access and immediate remedies. Especially in cases where planning invervenes, the aftergoing court protection may be quite insufficient and more informal means like tribunals and inquiry systems prove to be more effective.

The French system, despite broad access, limits decision to ex post remedies in most cases; in Germany, where an extend right ('vorläufiger Rechtsschutz') is provided, the access is more limited, yet more effective.

Nonlegal mechanisms like self-control (Switzerland, Sweden) have to be taken into account as well as the importance of parliamentary constituency policies (USA) or of press and public pressure groups.

To consider interest and purpose of the law as guidance principle in the interpretation of law seems at least today an insufficient remedy, as the protection of interest and the achievement of a purpose the legislatures tried to attempt are often rather a compromise, a delicate balancing of different interests. In today's situation, the continental judge may be confronted with the same situations as the American or the English judge. *Convergence* seems to become dominant.

Still some remarkable *differences* exist. The Roman system tries to build rules the citizen can rely on, which protect him in the case of his affairs, and the Anglo-American system concentrates on litigious situations and conflicting interactions. However, as more and more rules begin to dominate private and public life, there seem to be trends of convergence, even here.

The two types of courts have evolved different procedures, but in Common Law countries we find a tendency to take procedures from the civil law system and adapt them to the evolving public law system, whereas in the continental system we find a rising tendency to develop independent procedures and instruments. Although both systems emphasize administrative procedures, it seems that the traditional emphasis of Common Law countries derived its power from the larger influence of natural law thinking into the court decisions. The rule 'audi alteram partem' has led to the form of hearings, public inquiries, on which the common law system became famous for. Full and fair hearing is an important aspect of Common Law countries, increasingly gaining recognition in continental countries as well. Whereas in Common Law countries consolidation of judgements have been an important issue, in Roman-Germanic countries, due to their wide variations in local customs, codification seemed to be the historical convenient mode to achieve fair justice. This explains the importance academic law schools played in the late 19th century in the Roman-Germanic countries and the importance of court decisions in the Anglo-German systems. But today we may note a reversion, the judges and practicioners gaining influence in the Civil Code countries, and in Common Law countries law schools as they train and bring forth evidence and discuss cases. On a first glance, Common Law countries seem to have an advantage insofar as the jurisdiction seems far more unified, for the courts can deal with all justiciable matters. Secondly, they seem far more adaptable as the system grows bit by bit. The costs are a lack of form and symmetry. Thus, common law seems to be more pragmatic, more concerned with function than style. Academic lawyers and theories play less a role, but the situation has changed: in the United States law schools and the Bars have emerged as powerful sources to produce codes of conducts and unify. In England even a discussion is entering about the need for a constitution, and some years ago a law commission has been established to give shape to the growing disparaties in the legal system.

32.5 Conclusion

In recent times the continental and the common law system of judicial control have become confronted with similar problems. As a consequence of their marked differences the typical shortcomings revealed by this new problems are also different. One can observe, however, that the basic trend in the two systems becomes reversed: the Common Law countries tending more and more to codification and systematization whereas the continental systems attempt to stress the situational contingencies and the need for differentiation into more informal justice, emphazising administrative procedures, hearings, participative mechanisms etc. It seems, therefore, that the new types of problems created by technological and welfare state developments are acting towards more convergence in the procedures of judicial control in public administration.

As to be effective protection of the citizens the comparative perspective makes clear, that there is no optimal institutional arrangement per se which solve that problem. Judicial agencies and institutions of legal protection may be less effective than internalist systems of protection. Protection may come from institutions like the Ombudsman in Scandinavia of the petition committees in parliaments. Sweden without a well developed protection and control by courts may be more effective in protecting the rights and claims of citizens by institutionalizing self-responsibility of the officials in whose decisions the immediate cannot interfere. Therefore an appeal in the institutions may be more effective than the complicated process through which independent courts operate, and public assess.

To evaluate the effectiveness of the institutions they have to be understood in the context of their surrounding institutional networks and the working of those institutions has to be taken into account.

Notes

1 Legal terms in any language take their coloration and meaning in considerable measure from the legal system in which they are used. Expressions from the European continent most often take quite a different meaning in common law countries, some terms are simply unknown. In the United States are 'interlocutary decisions' decisions, which not finally determine a case; in France 'jugement interlocutoire' refers to decisions on procedures; procedures of review are called 'appel' in France, 'Berufung' in Germany, 'apello' in Italy, in higher courts in France 'pourvoi', in Germany 'Revision'. As a rule,

where misunderstanding may have emerged, the technical term is set in parenthesis in the original language.

2 Comparing legal systems in the past has been undertaken mostly as a kind of transnational learning and borrowing. More recently, especially in European countries, unifying trends have become more urgent as national laws become interdependent under the rule of the EEC and the national legislatures loose part of their dependence and have to take into consideration the legal implications onto other systems.

3 Considerations to curb judicial power has often been undertaken. Interest to curb the power of the Supreme Court in the United States during the 1820s in Marshall Courts year emerged because the ruling was conceived as favoring centralization. later, because of his conservative and obstructive attitude, in Roosevelt's days, during the Warren-Court period, some bills have claimed that the court neglects national security and favors subversive elements and social issues like abortion. His decision on school praxis and busing let the public discussion not die till today.

4 The kind of reasoning is well illustrated by the criteria of 'Systemgerechtigkeit', playing a leading role during administrative reform: Administrative reorganization-measures have to orientate themselves along models of reorganizations. Those models may be reviewed. At the same time the model approved has to be followed, that means that the decisions criteria are not to be changed during the process, and political values are not all allowed to change, they may be applied contingent to a situation, but not in a different way (BVerfGE 13, 331/340. 18 367/382).

References

American Bar Association (1983): *Administrative Law Review*, Vol. 35, Chicago: Rothman.

Auby, J. M. and R. Drago (1984): *Traité de Contentieux Administratif*, Paris: L.G.D.J.

Berger, J. (1977): *Government by the Judiciary*, Cambridge, Mass: Harvard University Press.

Berle, A. A., JR. (1917): The Expansion of American Administration Law. *Harvard Law Review*. Vol. 30 (March): 430–448.

Bertossa, F. (1984): *Der Beurteilungsspielraum*, Abh. zu schweizerischem Recht. N. F. 489, Bern: Haupt.

Brohm, W. (1982): Die Verwaltungsgerichtsbarkeit im modernen Sozialstaat. *Die öffentliche Verwaltung*, Vol. 35/1: 1–10.

Buiren, Sh. van, Ballerstedt, E. and D. Grimm (1982): *Richterliches Handeln und technisches Risiko*, Baden-Baden: Nomos.

Cappelletti, M. (1971): *Judicial Review in the Contemporary World*, Indianapolis: Bobbs Merrill Law.

David, R. (1982): *Les grands systèmes de droit contemporains*. Droit comparé, Paris: Dalloz.

David, R., Egawa, H., Graveson, R., Knapp, V., Mehren, A. T. v., Noda, Y., Razmaryn, S., Tschichradze, V. M., Valladao, H., Yntema, H. and Zweigert, K. (1975 ff.): *International Encyclopedia of Comparative Law*, Vol. 1–12, Tübingen: Mohr, The Hague: Mouton, New York: Oceana.

Davis K. C. (1969): *Discretionary Justice: A Preliminary Inquiry*, Baton Rouge: Louisiana State University Press.

Davis, K. C. (1969): *Administrative Law Treatise*, 4 Vols., St. Paul, Minn.: West.

Debbasch, Ch. (1974): *Le Droit Administratif Face à l'Evolution de l'Administration Francaise*, Paris: Waline.

Debbasch, Ch. (1981): *Contentieux Administratif*, Paris: Dalloz.

Debbasch, Ch. (1982): *Des Institutions et Drois Administratifs*, Paris: Dalloz.

Dicey, A. V. (1975): The Development of Administrative Law in England. *Law Quarterly Review,* Vol. 31/1: 148–153.

Dimock, M. E. (1980): *Law and Dynamic Administration,* New York: Praeger.

Dworkin, R. (1977): *Taking Rights Seriously.* Cambridge, Mass.: Harvard Univ. Press.

Frankfuter, F. (1927): The Task of Administrative Law. *University of Pennsylvania Law Review.* Vol. 75 (May): 614–621

Glazer, N. (1975): Towards and Imperial Judiciary, *The Public Interest,* Vol. 41, Fall 1975: 104–123.

Goehlert, R. (1983): *Policy Studies on Judicial Processes,* Monticello, Ill.:

Goodnow, F. J. (1893): *Comparative Administrative Law: An Analysis of the Administrative Systems, National and Local of the United States, England, France and Germany,* 2 Vols. New York: Putnam.

Harlow, C., Rawlings, R. (1984): *Law and Administration,* London: Weidenfeld and Nicolson.

Hart, H. L. A. (1961): *The Concept of Law,* Oxford: Clarendon Press.

Horowitz, D. L. (1977): *The Courts and Social Policy,* Washington DC: Brookings Institution.

Jaffe, L. L. (1965): *Judicial Control of Administrative Action,* Boston: Little, Brown.

Johnson, Ch. A. and B. C. Canon (1984): *Judicial Policies, Implementation and Impact,* Washington DC: Congressional Quarterly Inc.

Jowell, J. L. (1975): *Law and Bureaucracy: Administrative Discretion and the Limits of Legal Action,* Port Washington. N. Y.: Dunellen.

Kadish, M. R. and S. H. Kadish (1973): *Discretion to Disobey: A Study of Lawful Departures from Legal Rules,* Stanford, Ca.: Stanford University Press.

Kommers, D. P. (1976): *Judicial Politics in West Germany.* Beverly Hills, Calif.: Sage.

König, K., Oertzen, J. J. von and F. Wagener (eds.) (1983): *Public Administration in the Federal Republic of Germany,* Deventer; Kluwer Press.

Krawietz, W. N. (1983): *Metatheorie juristischer Argumentation,* Berlin: Springer.

Lâubadère, A. de (1982): *Manual de Droit Administratif,* Paris: Dalloz.

Luhmann, N. (1972): *Rechtssoziologie. 2 Vols.* Reinbek: Rowohlt.

Mezines, B. J., Stein, J. A. and J. Gruff (1983): *Administrative Law,* New York: Matthew Bender.

Mosler, E. ed. (1962): *Constitutional Review on the World Today,* Heidelberg: Springer Verlag.

National Acadmy of Sciences (1980): *Forecasting the Impact of Legislation on Courts,* Washington DC: National Academy Press.

National Academy of Sciences (1983): *Risk Assessment in the Federal Government,* Washington DC: National Academy Press.

National Institute for Law Enforcement and Criminal Justice (1977): *Comparative Analysis of the Statistical Dimensions of the Justice Systems of Seven Industrial Democracies,* Washington DC: GPO.

Nelkin, D. (1981): *Problems and Procedures in the Regulation of Technological Risk,* Ithaca N. Y.: Cornell University Press.

Nonet, Ph., Selznick, Ph. (1978): *Law and Society in Transition: Toward Responsible Law,* New York, Hagerstown, San Francisco, London: Harper and Row.

Papier, H. J. (1979): *Die Stellung der Verwaltungsgerichtsbarkeit im demokratischen Rechtsstaat.* Berlin, New York: de Gruyter.

Perrot, R. (1983): *Institutions judiciaires,* Paris: Dalloz.

Pound, R. (1910): Law in Books and Law in Action, *American Law Review* Vol. 44: p. 12–36.

Robson, W. A. (1951³): *Justice and Administrative Law,* Westport: Greenwood Press.

Rotelli, E. (1981): *Constituzione e Amministrazione dell' Italia Unita,* Bologna.

Saks, M. J. and Baron, Ch. H. (eds.) (1980): *The Use-Nonuse-Misuse of Applied Social Research in the Courts,* Cambridge, Mass.: Abt Books.

Satta, F. (1978): *Principi di Giustizia Amministrativa,* Padova: Cedam.

Summers, R. D. (1983): *Pragmatischer Instrumentalismus und amerikanische Rechtstheorie,* Freiburg/München: Karl Alber GmbH.

Scharpf, F. W. (1966): Judicial Review and the Political Question: A Functional Analysis, *Yale Law Journal,* Vol. 75/4: 517–568.

Scharpf, F. W. (1970): *Die politischen Kosten des Rechtsstaates.* Tübingen: Mohr.

Schermers, H. G. (3) (1983): *Judicial Protection in the European Countries,* Deventer: Kluwer Law.

Schmidt, G. (1978): Die Verwaltungsgerichtsbarkeit an den Grenzen des Verwaltungsrechtsschutzes. *Neue Juristische Wochenschrift.* Vol. 31 (36): 1769–1776.

Smith, S. A. (1973): *Judicial Review of Administrative Action.* London: Stevens.

Scholz, G., Schmidt, D. and G. Assmann (1977): *Verwaltungsverantwortung und Verwaltungsgerichtsbarkeit,* Bd. 34, Berlin, New York: Walter de Gruyter.

Tribe, L. (1978): *Constitutional Law.* New York: Praeger.

Ule, C. H. (1983): *Verwaltungsprozessrecht,* München: Heymann Verlag.

US Office of the Federal Registrar, National Archives and Record Services, General Services Administration (n. d.): *Codex of Federal Regulations,* Washington, D. C.: GPO.

US Senate, Committee on the Judiciary (1981): *Constitutional Restraints upon the Judiciary: Hearings Before the Subcommittee on the Constitution of the Senate Committee on the Judiciary,* 97th Congress, 1st Session. Washington, DC: GPO.

Wade, E. C. et al. (1984): *Constitutional and Administrative Law,* London: Longman.

Warren, K. F. (1980): *Administrative Law in the American Political System,* St. Paul, Minn.: West.

Weber, M. (1922): *Max Weber on Law in Economy and Society* (edited in 1954 by M. Rheinstein), Cambridge, Mass.: Harvard University Press.

Wraith, R. E. and P. G. Hutcheson (1973): *Administrative Tribunals.* London: RIPA.

William, C. C. (1982): *The American Law School and the Rise of Administrative Government,* Madison, Wisc.: The University of Wisconsin Press.

33. Unwilling to Bark, not Able to Bite? Theories and Realities of Parliamentary Control

Gerd-Michael Hellstern

Abstract

The inverse relationship between the rise of power of the modern intervention state and the perceived decline in the ability of parliaments to control the executive branch and to implement their legislative goals has given rise to a rich variety in constitutional and parliamentarian reform efforts *across many nations during the last decade. This movement reflects the felt need to keep the complicated fabric of* checks and balances *in modern states alive to ensure that governments and their bureaucracies can be held* accountable, responsive *and* productive.

There has been little progress in achieving these reform goals by institutionalizing new techniques, or gaining additional resources and powers. Partly, empirical systematic research and evaluation is missing, partly the theoretical understanding *of the oscillating and fragile control-relationship between legislatures and the executive is still oriented along traditional mechanical* division of power models.

Dynamic multidimensional *models explaining the constant changes in formal and informal uses or non-uses of controls are emerging mainly from comparative research.* Comparing constitutional arrangements *may provide the best source to learn what parliamentary control can mean, what the costs (and advantages) of different forms of institutional arrangements are, and what kind of arrangements and techniques provide for the best* opportunity structure *to activate and keep parliamentary* control alive *as well as minimizing control costs.*

33.1 Past Problems, Continuing Concern[1]

Failed Innovations

Whenever reformers felt the necessity to improve the working of representative institutions in society, the quest for effective control of those who rule claimed prime attention (Mill 1861; Bagehot 1867; Weber 1917/18). In the seventies this search for tighter parliamentarian control in many nations became equated with:

- an expansion of parliamentary resources and capacities, bringing professional advice and knowledge into the parliamentarian *"review" process,*
- the remolding of the structure and organizational procedures of the representative institutions, stressing the work of *"oversight" and "select" committees* to supervise the enforcement of control,
- the advance in new sophisticated tools and techniques for oversight, most notably in:

(a) the installment of computer-based *information systems* often linked to *sunset-ting*-like procedures for reporting and investigating,
(b) the explosive demands for *evaluation research* and the tendency to insert *impact and risk assessment clauses* in new laws,
(c) the extensive use of *evaluative hearings* and *commissions* vested with investigative powers,
(d) the innovative application of legislative techniques like the use of *appropriation riders* and *legislative vetos* (see Harris 1964; Ogul 1976; Rieselbach 1978; Aberbach 1979; Zweig 1979).

This gradual expansion of resources, institutional technology and legal tools has slowed down since the beginning of the eighties. In the USA it came to a sensational halt when the Supreme Court overruled the application of a congressional veto against the expulsion of a young East Indian from the USA in 1983 (Immigration and Naturalization Service vs. J. Chadha, June 23, 1983). This controversial decision affecting 207 veto provisions in a total of more than 126 laws drastically symbolized the resurgence of executive of executive power and the limits set for the congress (Congress. Research Service 1983):

"In the decision, following Chief Justice Burger's deliberate reasoning, the Supreme Court attempted to restore the traditional *balance of power* between Congress and the Presidency as it had been designed by the Founding Fathers, stressing the strict separation of the powers to legislate and to execute the law, a principle which guides most modern constitutional systems of Western democracies (Congress. Quarterly 1983: 125). The Brookings Institution's Director for Government Studies considered the ruling to contain an element of *"irony"* as the legislative veto was actually designed to prevent the loss of check and control which the Founding Fathers had foreseen:

"If it violated the Constitution's language, it actually served to reinforce the very constitutional principle the Chief Justice chose to cite in striking it down" (Sundquist 1983: 16).

Supporting the landmark decision, leading lawyers argued against the *"intrusive"* access of parliamentarians into executive decisionmaking processes. The unconstitutional legislative "participation" and "arbitrary" *overcontrol* in the execution of laws would and had undermined the governability and clear pattern of accountability in modern governments (Bruff and Gellhorn 1977: 1373). In its reports on governmental waste the monumental and powerful *Presidential Grace Commission* (privately financed) even held the power of Congress to be responsible for much of the 195.4 billion Dollar budget deficit in the fiscal year 1983 (Presidential Commission 1984). Like many reforms, the aggressive attack on the part of legislators to tighten control, curb bureaucracy and counter governmental discretion or supposed crime in critical issues *(Watergate, CIA, MAD)* seemed to have produced questionable effects, resulting in less control, more fragmented policies and increased irresponsiveness.

Many nations which have set up parliamentary or constitutional reform commissions (i.e., *Scandinavia, Switzerland,* and *West Germany*) often linked to exhaustive hearings and comprehensive reports as in the *USA* and in *Great Britain,* seemed in the end to be content with minor changes speeding up procedures, improving the information capacity and streamlining the parliamentarian organization but evading the sensitive and crucial decisions about *how* control should be exercised in specific fields of government action and at which point in time.[2] The most vexing questions such as

- the perennial, nagging weaknesses in *budgetary controls,*
- the issues arising about *political planning control,*
- the controversial use of the executive rights for *secrecy and discretion*

(highlighted in the data-protection and war-power issues) remained unsolved. Should in those fields governmental discretion and parliamentary self-constraint prevail, at least in the execution phase when irreversible facts are established? How powerful is a parliament which is left with the difficulties of ex-ante deliberations and preventive measures in uncertain decision – situations or a symbolic ex-post action in situations in which facts can no longer be reversed? Overwhelmed by the myriad of governmental tasks and functions and administrative actions, effective control would need to co-equal governmental bureaucracy by maximizing parliament's information processing capacities, even under rapidly changing technological conditions, an uneconomical, if not politically infeasible solution. Despite all improvements in parliamentary information systems, the expansion of staff and advisory resources and the assured rights to have open access to governmental performance records, strategies for parliamentarian controls have to accept the limited information capacities of the parliament. If parliaments aimed to catch up, they would have to create a similar bureaucracy, to rely on even more professional knowledge, building a "hidden government" of policy advisers and interest groups (Nader 1973), a questionable prospect. Thus most parliamentarians have tacitly given in to the old *"Executive Force Theory"* again, admitting the executive should act and the parliament should react, ratify and selectively exercise controls to provide legitimation and obviate the need for ex-post justification of governments (Ogul 1976). In critical evaluation of the parliamentary zeal for control, the past demands for increased parliamentary power may be due to turbulent external events and the loss of trust in governability in the seventies rather than reflect the interests and demands of overworked and time-pressured legislators. The brief period of parliamentary revival seems in the beginning of the eighties to be giving way again to a longterm drift towards executive domination over those who by many are supposed to possess the legitimating authority to rule and watch the execution of the rules. Considering the differing alternatives open to parliamentarians it seems more often to be a less risky undertaking for them to leave decisions to governments as long as they still can have some hope of possessing some power to intervene in governmental affairs when they see a need for it (when there is some advantage to be gained[3]).

A Reformulated Perspective

If conscious efforts to reshape substantially formal institutional structures and procedures to achieve effective comprehensive control of the executive in the early seventies have failed, how can one expect that parliamentarians can sufficiently take into account the still excessive expectations to curb supposed governmental excesses in the eighties? If parliamentarians seem to be not able or unwilling to exercise the full range of their demanded control-functions, how can the essential constitutional principle of *checks and balances* be upheld to tame the Leviathan in modern Western democracies?

Probably a more realistic answer avoids instrumental trapping questions and views the shifting relations between the branches of government from a *multidimensional system view* (Loewenstein 1938), in which control flows from a multiplicity of forces, and the institutional patterns or procedures are only the opportunity structures from which external events, public pressures, and interest group activities intermingle with the historical and evolutionary understanding of changing utilizations of the potential operational means. It may emerge that reshaping the conceptual understanding of the functions of control as inherent in a diverse set of activities may turn out to be the most promising step for improving the working of the system of checks and balances. Such an approach necessitates

(1) concentrating on the broader political context and climate to correlate the functions of the parliaments and the executive to changes in the whole society and the working of the whole institutional and political system,
(2) investigating the whole complex of interactions between parliament, administration and the executive as we may find in many actions unwritten, informal means of control and as in view of changing needs and perceptions of it – last not least due to the constantly members' turnover – narrow understandings of control functions have to be replaced by a larger view on the purposes of control as some kind of evolutionary, gradual learning process,
(3) taking the broad variations of configurations in means and uses to be found throughout time and in different nations, to gain in indiosyncratic understanding and operational knowledge for improved usage. To render such a perspective possible the following considerations try to shed some light on current parliamentarian control function in different nations. By reviewing some major governmental systems, differing in their basic elements and assessing the uses of their differing instruments we may learn about the potential feasibility for institutional rearrangements and about the use of alternative control instruments whose working may depend on some factors outside the considerations of past reform attempts.

33.2 Constitutional Arrangements: A Comparative View on the Control Nets

The Model

Few constitutions contain an explicit norm stating a control function for the parliamentary body. Art. 85.11 of the Swiss Federation (Schweizerische Bundesverfassung), the long list contained in the detailed Indian constitution and the insertion of procedural rules into the French Constitution of 1958 are remarkable exceptions. Most detailed prescriptions regulating the exercise of controls are contained in legislative organization acts like the one in the USA from 1947 which, following the New Deal and the Second World War, prescribes *"continuous watchfulness"* over the activities of the executive agencies, or in fiscal organization acts like the *Congressional Budget and Impoundment Control Act of 1974* which involved the Comptroller General in congressional control over the President's authority to impound funds. Even more common is the practice of the British House of Commons and the German Bundestag to use their agreed on standing and sessional orders to operationalize the control function, often supplemented by unwritten rules of practice deriving in Britain from the rules given by the Speaker or in Germany from the Elderly Council.

The constitutional power to legitimate the exercise of parliamentary controls can be inferred rather implicitly from the principle of *separating the functions of the legislation and execution* of laws to be found in the basic articles of the US Constitution of 1787 (Art. I, II, III) or in the Art. 20,2 of the Basic Law in Germany (Grundgesetz, GG). Richard Neustadt (1960: 33) has realistically redefined the principle as a separation of institutions sharing powers; Barthelemy (1934: 248) found in reviewing the principle that "C'est une recette d'art politique que chacun interprète à sa manière"; Loewenstein (1957) asked to reconsider the principle using it as a rather pragmatic device which helps to distribute governmental power horizontally and vertically among different actors to fit the function of policy determination, policy execution and policy control. All actors may share in the use of the functional powers, the inter- and intra-institutional distribution of those powers, and their vertical distribution (relating those powers to societal forces) allows the best mutual control. As for many constitutional norms, the power as divided and fixed in the constitution may differ according to legal interpretations in real terms and there may be a further difference between the potential laid down in the constitution and the real powers exercised (Sundquist 1981).

But even if the exercise of mutual control is understood as a continuous process, constantly reshaped by enacting and reacting between different constitutional actors, the difference in constitutional arrangements will still shape the potential effectiveness of control.

The existing legal structure may be understood as the opportunity structure, the legal capacity to act. Despite a rich legal tradition of research on constitutional design, little is actually known about how different *configurations* of control mechanisms work, what inventories of tools are made available by different constitutions and how they operate in different political and cultural settings based on national-historical experiences. Understanding the impact of the interaction of the different forces constituting the control framework requires comparing the different constitutional conditions under which parliamentary controls must operate. By taking the differences between systems in Western democracies as a point of departure, we may not only find varying legal instruments, but also more important differences in the environment, the electoral system and the internal organizational arrangements of institutions which influence the extent, the need and the content of control.

By explaining differences in the control behaviour as a flow from external events channelled through interest groups and by the work of the electoral system which influences dispositions, interests in and ambitions for control efforts by parliaments may help to understand the peculiar shifts and dynamic "viscosity" of control combinations, which aim to achieve a balance of control measures. As we will find that on a general level most systems provide for similar instruments such as removal of government (vote of confidence, impeachment), committee hearings, investigations, parliamentary questioning, the use of legislative and budgetary power or special forms of communication with the citizenry (through ombudsman, constituency work or petition rights) and the administration (through party channels, direct access rights, citation rights), only the different combination and the varying degree in utilizing those instruments can help to gain a systematic view of the different instruments, and thus to dissociate them meaningfully from their context, separate them analytically and recombine them without loss in their synergetic power.

The Elements of Five Systems

The working of different systems of control could probably best be explored in concentrating on the two most popular versions, the *presidential system* as it is embodied in the *US Congress* and the *French Assembly* and the representative *parliamentarian system,* of which the *House of Commons* is often seen as the prototype with the German *Bundestag* as a variant of it. Different from both the *Swiss system* may be seen as a stimulating deviant case, containing many elements which are lacking in the other systems, elements which may be relevant to analyze for a reform or modernization of the systems (cf. Price 1943, 1944 and Laski 1944).

The USA
Among all legislatures the *US Congress* certainly stands out in respect of size and importance. In many respects the American Constitution is very explicit in its attempts to balance powers by mutual checks and balances. The Constitution put all legislative powers into the hands of the Congress. As in most other systems, there is a second chamber, the Senate, which originally had been devised to balance (or control) the power of the popularly elected representatives, giving each state the same weight in the Senate. As the President is elected separately by popular vote, he can rely on his own electoral (and legitimating) base, being less dependent on the majority in the Congress than the head of the executive in other systems. More often than not he even differs in his party affiliation from the majority in the House, providing additional incentive for members to exercise tight controls and oversight. At the same time the House is rarely successful in agreeing on a coherent control policy. Due to the open competition in the nominating system, the party machinery is not able to enforce unity and coherence. Intensified by the short reelection cycle to the House of Representatives, *constituency work* and personal campaign finance are important tasks for the individual member of the House. Whereas those features promote personal interest in control and oversight, the same reasons often account for the lack of ability to make control effective by joint actions and in broader policy fields or worse, may lead to biased and arbitrary control interventions (having led to an ethics code more recently). With the exception of *case-work* (for the constituency), control is exercised mostly by committees who establish *subcommittees for oversight,* the weaknesses of which are counterbalanced by the collegial structure of those committees. Informal fraction building, continuous bargaining and the feeble experiments in caucus

Tab. 1: Factors Influencing the Composition of the Parlamentarian Control System

Environment	Electoral System	Political System in parliament	outside parliament	relation to the executive
External Events – agenda: domestic internatio- nal – arena: regulatory distributive – issue: visible latent	*Nominations* – Party – Consti- tuency (influences nomina- tions)	*Organizational Structure* – bicameral system – committee structure – plenary procedures	*Intergovern-mental System* – unitarian – federal	*Presidential System* (independent power)
Public Opinion mass (participation) elite (gatekeeper) media (ownership)	*Voting System* – representa- tive (pro- por- tional) – majority rule	*Instruments* – budget rights – legislative rights (ex- tent) – authority to question – rights to sanction, to investi- gate etc.	*Judicial Sys-tem* – constitutio- nal court – administra- tive courts	*Collegial Sys-tem* (separated pow- ers)
Interest Groups – public bodies – private interests – non-profit organiza- tions		*Staff Resour-ces* – institutional – personal	*Implementa-tion Structures* – centralized – delegated – self-govern- ment – independent units (agencies)	*True Parlia-mentary Sys-tems* (shared power, majority party, opposition buil- ding inside par- liament)
Political Culture – history (tradition) – elite system (selec- tion) – socialization (con- sensus)		*Behavioral Pattern* – fragmented, indivduali- stic, multi- stable, is- sue-orien- ted, bargai- ning and lo- grolling – fractions and disci- pline, party leadership		

forming are similar signs of attempts to overcome fragmentation by a *collegial form of decision-making*. In addition, the modernization of the committee system in the mid-seventies helped to reintegrate the individualized control system supported by what is probably the most extensive system for *information support* in the world. Those trends helped to transform the individualistic and dispersed oversight interests into a manageable joint force. At the same time, Congress weakness may even be interpreted as its strength, giving individual members more power to control than in other systems, and making the Congress more responsive to a broad range of interests and grievances, tendencies which are reemphasized by the rather frequent *public hearings* and the close connections to the *press*. If members thus still favor individualistic usages of pinsticking control instruments, publicity and enforced collegiality may provide for a minimum of self-control and coordination to be effective.

France

As in the United Stated the President and the parliament, the *National Assembly,* are elected separately (and in different years as well). The second, less powerful chamber is elected by regional bodies. But unlike the US constitution, only limited legislative power is given to the National Assembly (enumerated in Art. 34), leaving many far-reaching decisions to the "reglement" of the Prime Minister, who is not elected by the Assembly, but selected by the President. A President, who in M. Debrè's formulation is the *'pouvoir politique'*, the politically responsible Prime Minister being only the *'pouvoir administratif'*. The legislative power may be challenged by the Prime Minister by calling the *Conseil Etat* to set limits to the decisions of the parliaments. As so far all Presidents could command over a majority in the National Assembly, clashes between the executive and the legislative body could always be resolved. The power is not as Duverger once commented totally *'dictatorial'* or outside any control of the National Assembly. The majority in the Assembly can implement a vote of confidence and reject presidential proposals as happened in the past. Even the *referendum,* used as an additional check on parliament (to circumvent the parliament), may lead to a reinforced check of the executive as De Gaulle's defeat in 1969 demonstrated.

Switzerland

For many constitutional and political scientists the Swiss federation presents a unique case. *Popular control mechanisms* are deeply embedded into the system, regarded as working only in the special situation Swiss society enjoys *(social consensus, small size, relative high income)*. As in France and in the United States, the executive and the parliament, the *Federal Assembly,* are kept strictly separate. The executive being a collegium *(Bundesrat)* elected by the Joint National Assembly (of both chambers) for four years without the possibility of being overthrown. This has lessened party control and party cohesion in the parliament in the past all the more as the members of the executive collegium are selected in light of regional variations and through application of a *"golden formula"*, first used in the election of the executive in 1959. This has led to frequently changing coalitions on political issues the *participative mode* is reinforced as most control is organized through Commissions (the most important for control being the *Geschäftsprüfungskommis-*

sion). Even the *referenda,* increasingly used by the losing party as an instrument of last resort favors such participatory, informal controls. Although the immediate consequences of a referendum are less significant (esp. as the participation rate is usually low and popular referenda are rarely successful), its function as a potential sword of Damocles influences decision-making process in favour of bargaining and compromise. Last but not least, prevented the threat of referenda the Swiss parliament from giving up its unique (only reimbursed not paid) lay *(Miliz)* parliament. This has provoked serious concern about the composition of the parliament, since members of public organizations (supposed to be controlled) have more spared time (and interests) to set aside. The remarkably intense constitutional reform discussion is not least due to the discontent felt about the special features of nonprofessional laycontrol and the joint circles reproduced in participative decision-making. The highly probably small reform steps following the longlasting discussion attempt to re-emphasize the special feature of the system, working through joint comissions.

West Germany

The *German Bundestag*, like the US-Congress, is often described to be a *working house* operating mainly through its *committees.* Unlike the presidential systems of France and the USA, the executive power is shared with the majority party in parliament giving rise to conciliate power showed between the executive and the majority in parliament. The *opposition parties* are conceived to constitute the basic controlling elements. In the system members are selected partly on constituency base, partly through the state lists, giving the *party* strong power to control members' behaviour. As the majority in the Bundestag can preside over the election of the Chancellor, the party cohesion works against intense public scrutinization of the government. Although no Chancellor can govern against the will of the majority, the binding of the *vote of confidence* (Art. 67 Basic Law) to the possibility to dissolve parliament gives him power to control his party. Indeed the quest for control in state and federal parliaments has always been raised mainly by the *opposition party,* who can command about special rights, who may ask questions, ask for public debates and even demand investigations. The strong power of the parties (and the fraction leadership) has given rise to a replication of the committee system in fraction committees *(party working groups)* which in many respects may be regarded as the true agenda setting bodies, the controlling governing party's working groups exercising (hidden) control on the government. Those tendencies have led to factions in the major parties and intense discussion on the *internal democracy* of the parties. As one party rarely achieves an absolute majority, the need for *coalitions* among ruling parties may be regarded as an additional powerful restraint on the exercise of governmental power. Two further checks have to be mentioned. Unlike the French but like the US system, West Germany is a *federal system* with tremendous power – even restricting the legislative power of parliament-given by the Basic Law to the states which administer and implement most laws. In the state chamber *(the Federal Council)* the state governments appoint the members, who can exercise suspensive or absolute vetos in all legislative matters, and who exercised those vetos in critical decisions, having successfully crushed major reform zeals in the seventies and imposing an unvolun-

Tab. 2: Comparing Systems of Control Configurations (Power Base, Limits, Style)

	Electoral System	Selection of Executive	Political Responsibility
France	districts absolute majority party nominations	President by separate vote, President nominates Primeminister	only Prime minister (vote of confidence not binding)
USA	districts, majority [open primaries]	President by separate vote	impeachment rights
Switzerland	majority	Bundesrat by the joint assembly (proportional rule since 1959)	vote on issues only
West Germany	representational (districts and list) partynomination	Chanceller by the parliament (Bundestag, coalition)	Restricted vote of confidence
Great Britain	districts absolute/relative majority party nomination	Primeminister by the parliament (House of Commons, majority)	unlimited vote of confidence

	Main instruments used for Control	Dissolution of parliaments	Upper Chamber legitimation (Election)
France	Questions, Debate	full discretion by the executive	by regional bodies (distorted proportional)
USA	Subcommittees, Hearings, Investigations Oversight	no right	by states (equal in numbers)
Switzerland	Commissions, Issue-Committees, Minority Rights	no right	by states (equal in numbers)
West Germany	Opposition Rights, Investigations, Questions	within limits (no confidence vote)	by state government (adjusted numbers)
Great Britain	(Select) Committees Questions, Opposition Rights	unlimited	appointed and heredity

	Judicial Influences	Citizenry rights	Characteristic Style
France	Conseil Constitutionel	referendum by executive decision	legitimation challenge to the liberal dictatorship by debate
USA	Supreme Court	(Case work)	diffused individualistic and bargained committee control

Tab. 2 continued

	Electoral System	Selection of Executive	Political Responsibility
Switzerland		issue and popular referendum	joint collegial control
West Germany	Constitutional Court	(petitions)	intergovernmental (bureaucratic) and party control
Great Britain	Administrative Tribunals	referendum, Administrative Commissioner	adversary party control

tary self-constraint on the parliament in cases when the political majority in power differs from the political majority in the Federal Council. This has reinforced the emergence of a tight intergovernmental *(administrative)* system, largely outside parliament and its controls. As in the US, the *Constitutional Court* plays an important role in limiting and forcing the parliament to act.

Great Britain
In the British system the *House of Commons* as the main representative body is elected on constituency base. This has led to the concentration on a two party system with some, more recent, variations. The House of Commons elects the Prime Minister, who is political responsible to the parliament. Unlike the German system, the Prime Minister may be voted out of office at any time, this leading to new elections. If he resigns without formal censure, the majority party may replace him. The upper chamber *(the House of Lords)* has mainly delaying power reinforcing the reconsideration of a bill. Control, as in the German system, rests mainly with the *opposition,* which rarely succeeds in rejecting bill or refusing money requested. Often characterized as a debating club dominated by the party leaders, the *question time* deserves special interest. All members irrespective of party participate and priority is accorded to them in Departments of Government. The more recent changes in 1979 with the establishment of 14 *selected committees* to "scrutinize the expenditure, administration and policy" of the main government departments are beginning to strengthen the control function of parliament. In addition, some older control committees such as the *Public Accounts Committees* which examine governmental appropriations and the *Joint Select Committee* which scrutinizes the propriety of statutory instruments in delegated legislation have gained in power. Maladministration may in addition be challenged by the *Commissioner for Administration* (the parliamentary ombudsman) who independently investigates complaints by citizens. Those changes have led to better scrutiny of the bureaucracy, without however challenging the strong, steadily rising power of the prime minister.

Obviously, as the review of the five systems suggests, the specific constitutional features are important to how control systems operate. Parliamentary controls do not operate in a void. In federal systems decisions about the distribution of power among the levels influence the kind of power parliament may exercise. This is especially true for Germany, where the state governments may decisively influence the outcome at the national level. This may even be true in the unitarian systems, depending there on the power and kind of electoral system chosen for the second chamber. Selective control may be strengthened by the influence of the electorate, which may lead, as in the United States, to intense case work for the constituency. Mass behaviour and public reactions may prove to be decisive even in those systems, where the control instruments, such as in France, seem to be weak as the legitimating power has proved to be more than once not only a symbolic barometer. What emerges from the mapping of the different constitutional systems is that most single instruments can only be understood by taking into account the more complex pattern and net of control mechanisms and the diverse historical situations, emerging from their working.

At a more abstract level some integrative features emerge, in the USA, for example, with the great *dispersal of control interests* clustered together in committee hearings with intense intelligence support. Given the wide diversity, the collegial committee system resting on sporadic individualistic exercise of control measures supported by a rational and systematic intelligence clearing machinery may produce much oversight information yet achieve little broad impact. The French system still has not experienced the possible deep clashes between Assembly and President, and the constitutional stalemate feared by observers may be unrealistic as long as the President can command over a majority in the Assembly. The concern for *"broad general (and symbolic) control"* and the neglect of detailed and effective policy controls seems to continue. The Swiss system stressing *joint collegial control* mechanism backed up by *popular control mechanism* if its exposure to special interests does not break down the system and if it learns to overcome the lack of professionalization and secrecy surrounding the commissionary work may well provide examples for innovative elements.

In the German system parliament may be effective in *detailed control* due to the close, informal, cooperative character, but drive out oppositional forces, responsible for basic governmental control. Recent experimentation with special public commissions (Enquete- and Investigative Commissions) and Hearings may rebalance this need for broader forms of controls. The renewed British system may be able to put strong pressure on the administration without gaining in control against the executive, still leaving the individual member in parliament with little effective influence on the control agenda except during Question time for single issues concerning personal/community grievances with the Government. If the aim of controlling government and its bureaucracy is to make them sensitive, responsible and accountable, the constitutional powers have been put to use. Obviously in presidential systems open clashes are to be expected more often, yet they are only effective if in the parliament some agreement can be achieved. This makes the increased use of commissions, of committees and bargaining in the US Congress understandable instruments the French Assembly largely lacks. In parliamentary systems, the sharing of power implies that controls need the rights of minority for access to information and rights to put their views on the agenda. In addition effective control may depend on the ability of the majority in the parliament to exercise some form of "hidden" control operating through the internal democratic process and the factions inside the party. Whereas in the presidential system parliaments may have strong incentives to ask for legislative clauses in the law to exercise control and monitor continuously the implementation of the laws, party controlled parliaments may hesitate to push their government into the public responsibility, yet the web of the party may help to ensure that parliamentary actions will not disperse and be lost by numerous sporadic activities but bound together and put into effect, if the party itself is working and responsive. Thus, from the various systems different opportunities for exercising controls arise, which produce differential impacts and consequences for the executive (see Table 3). The parliamentary system may have more power to impact governments, although mutual dependencies may prevent parliaments from exercising those powers in the open, and controls therefore tend to be rather invisible and diffused. Often the executive and the administration try to take control impacts into consideration before controls can be enacted to avoid the high cost linked to control measures. The presidential systems with usually strong leadership in the executive are more prone to conflicts, controversies and public forms of control, even if control measures may fail, but controls may have less impact except for cases, where detailed regulations provide for explicit statutory power. Likewise a unitarian system may possess simpler forms of control than the highly complex and politically sensitive fabric in a federal system with more institutions exercising controls sometimes with countercurrent effects. Yet, any such interpretation is subject to concrete historical situations; political events influence the probability that certain institutional opportunities can and will be transformed into actions (see Table 3).

Tab. 3: Control Impacts in Different Constitutional Arrangements

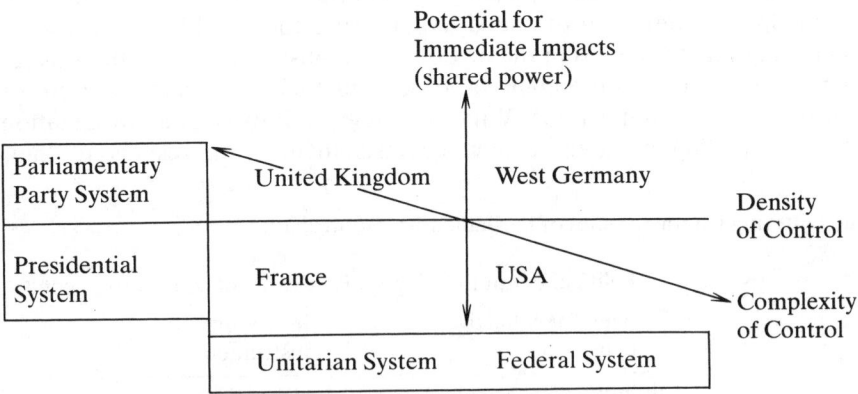

33.3 Applying Instruments: A Mismatch Between Uses and Needs

Despite continuing cries for improved controls, evidence is emerging that most parliaments can command a broad range of tools to be applied to exercise control. Any list of instruments like the one given here for a presidential system (the USA) and a parliamentary system (West Germany) may end up to be insufficient to document the broad range of instruments available for the legislature to exercise control (see Table 5). The strategy of the past years to develop new instruments like new forms of earmarking expenditures, developing sun-setting procedures, applying evaluation clauses and impact assessment and improving the information collection capacities by new staff and resources and inviting external advice has certainly helped to adapt the control system to fit better the needs to oversee and control the complex programs and problems the members are held responsible for. It is less certain if the impacts of those controls are understood. This would demand a political engineering on the part of the parliaments, exploring the risks of the instruments and their impact on the controlled policy field and whether the political feasibility of the formal instruments is available to ascertain the application of the instruments. Obviously for some instruments to be effective agreement between the parliamentarians has to be reached, which requires coordination and some degree of consensus on the goals which should be achieved. Other instruments may be used individualistically and may often be viewed as following special interests or being intrusive with negative effects compared to comprehensive, coordinated controls. A further division relates to the impacts of the instruments on government and the bureaucracy, some of which may lead to immediate actions having larger implications on the execution and implementation of laws, others being rather symbolic or adhoc corrections of single issues. Those unconventional dividing lines classifying instruments according to political feasibility and potential impacts may help to understand the need for differing and flexible use of instruments and may highlight the gaps in the mix of control instruments and their usage in parliament (see Table 4). Like many other instruments, some may be used for different purposes (or even misused). What the table exhibits is an approximation stressing the compelling need to review the instruments with respect to their

Tab. 4: The Differing Characteristics of Parliamentary Control Tools

		Political Feasibility (legislative degree of consensus needed)	
		need for collective consensus	individualistic instruments
Significance of Impacts	high	*authoritative control* e. g. sunsetting, program reviews	*single issue voting* e. g. legislative veto
	low	*policy guidance* e. g. debate and some types of interpellations	*constituency policy* e. g. petitions, casework, questions

Tab. 5: List of Exemplary Modes of Oversight

British House of Commons

---

 (1) Question time
 (2) Debates (motion for the adjournment of the house or substantive motions)
 (3) Opposition day debates (19 days when business is selected by official Opposition)
 (4) Budget sanctions
 (5) Scrutiny of expenditures (by committees and Auditor General)
 (6) Control of Statutory (delegated) legislation by joint select committees
 (7) Reports
 (8) Debates on nationalized industries
 (9) Parliamentary Commissioner or Administration
(10) Vote of no confidence

German Bundestag

---

 (1) Questions (interpellation rights)
 (2) Debate (Aktuelle Stunde)
 (3) Cabinet information (Right to receive information on cabinet meetings)
 (4) Citation right
 (5) Minority and Opposition rights
 (6) Investigation rights (by commissions)
 (7) Enquete commissions and hearings
 (8) Reporting requirements
 (9) Budget rights (riders etc)
(10) Budget auditing
(11) Petitions
(12) Ombudsman (for military and data-protection)
(13) Participation in supervisory bodies of public institutions
(14) Vote of disapproval
(15) Vote of no-confidence

US Congress

---

 (1) Personal visits and phone calls to bureaucrats (constituency care work)
 (2) Use of third parties such as prestigious clients to communicate a congressional view
 (3) The release of studies, committee reports to the public
 (4) The use of hearings esp. during the budget process
 (5) Request of evaluation studies by outside agencies (the GAO, CRS, CBO)
 (6) Statutory changes dissolving or influencing the program of an agency
 (7) Legislative clauses
 (8) Legislative vetos
 (9) Reporting requirements
(10) Defense of budget requests
(11) Exercising selective control in the appropriation and authorization of budget items
(12) Confirmation of key personnel decisions (key branch officials) (only the Senate)
(13) Impeachment

---

political usefulness and demonstrate the need to take political feasibility into account. As we may expect, those control measures applied more frequently are to be found in the field of low significance involving a minimal need for cooperation. Those instruments which depend on the institutional performance of the legislature are probably more difficult to administer and the task ahead may well be to relate the individualistic tools to accomplish the aims of the more collectivistic instruments or transform the results of the less significant instruments to the impacts achieved with the more powerful instruments. Each constellation shall be highlighted by focusing on one typical, innovative or eminent instrument.

Legislative Oversight: High Impacts – Need for Collective Actions

Much attention has been paid in the more recent past to legislative oversight procedures. In the beginning some have argued to include all control activities and -techniques open to parliament under those terms, prohibiting an adequate understanding of the new character of such procedures.

In a historical perspective it is more reasonable to define oversight by limiting it to those evaluative activites by parliament which involve the provision of systematic information about probable effects and outcomes of policies, either by systematic studies through suppporting agencies like the *General Accounting Office, the Congressional Budget Bureau* and the *Congressional Research Service* in the USA or outside experts or by devising participatory forms of building evidence by hearings and commissions. Systematic attempts like program review systems in the United Kingdom or sunset legislations may for those purposes be less effective since the pursuit of comprehensive oversight could prove selfdefeating.

Nevertheless the implementation of legislative clauses to allow for selective systematic and comprehensive review may be a first step towards providing better conditions for continuous learning. Oversight activities require some statements on whom, what and when such reviews should be conducted. Such decisions are more easily reached than the often pushed requests for explicit goals and clear objectives in the legislation. As most representatives tend to satisfy divergent goals and possess a multiplicity of controversial priotities, such requirements can rarely be satisfied. What does emerge from past oversight activities is the need for institutional incorporation of review activities into the work of special committees as exemplified by the work of the oversight subcommittees attached to major committees in the USA or the select committees in the United Kingdom, and the need for taking a long-term perspective which may even overcome an adhoc partisan split in the long run and avoid the adhoc evidence often prevalent in hearings and meetings held out of pressing political reasons. Last but not least it needs an institution like the GAO in the USA, which watches and cares about the quality of the oversight activities and provides methodological assistance to enable a process of learning from past oversight and hearings.

Legislative Veto: High Impact – Individualist Check

Many legislative hopes were connected with the exercise of the *legislative veto* which requires that an agency must reach agreement with the parliament if actions

Tab. 6: Reporting Requirements for Oversight by Departments and Congressional Committees having Jurisdiction in 1980 (US Congress) (only main departments and main committees)

Department Reportings

Agency	Number of Requirements
Department of Defense	174
Department of Health, Education and Welfare (includes both Dep. of Educ. and Dep. of Health and Human Services)	144
Department of the Interior	126
Department of State	83
Department of Agriculture	75
Department of Commerce	75
Department of Energy	75
Department of Transportation	57
Department of Justice	56
Department of Labor	52
Department of the Treasury	50
Veterans Administration	51
General Accounting Office	57

The total number of submitted reports are 2,039 comprising statutory, non-statutory and voluntary reports, but not one-time reports.

Congressional Committees having Jurisdiction

Senate	Number of Requirements
Committee on Governmental Affairs	386
Committee on Labor and Human Resources	199
Committee on Appropriations	193
Committee on Energy and Natural Resources	169
Committee on Armed Services	164
Committee on Commerce, Science and Transportation	159

House	
Committee on Government Operations	303
Committee on Appropriations	252
Committee on Armed Services	164
Committee on Interstate and Foreign Commerce	151

Joint	
Joint Committee on Printing	293

Source: US General Accounting Office, Analysis of Requirements for Recurring Reports to the Congress (PAD-80-72), Washington, DC 1980

Tab. 7: Overview on the Use of Questions in Different Parliamentarian Systems

Country	France	Germany F. R.	Switzerland	United Kingdom
Cons. Regul.	Art. 48.2 French Const. Art. 133 ff. GONA	Art. 40.1 GG §§ 105–111 GO BT	Art. 85 z 11 Art. 30–25, 54, 70, 71 a GR	no written Constitution Standing Orders N 8,9
Allocated Time	one session during each session week	two question hours á 90 minutes per session week	one session of 90 min. in the second and third week of a session	daily in session time
Types of Questions	*Questions Ecrites* – written questions – every member	*Schriftl. Frage* – written – a maximum of two per session	*Einfache Anfrage* – written – every member	*Written (Unstarred) Questions* – written answer – every member
	Questions Orales sans Débate – written application – President decides	*Kurze mündl. Anfrage* – oral question during the "Question Hour" – a maximum of two question per member – two supplementary quest.	*Interpellations* – with written answers – with oral answers – with debates following the answers	*Oral (Starred) Questions* – daily – a maximum of two per member – supplementary questions allowed
	Questions Orales avec Débate	*Große Anfrage* – support by 26 members required (minimum fraction size) – written answer becomes a topic on the agenda for a debate *Kleine Anfrage* – support by 26 members required – written answer – no debate		
	Questions au Gouvernement (before 1974 Questions d'Actualite) – each session week – on wednesday	*Dringliche Anfragen* – urgent questions – President decides	*Einfache dringliche Anfrage* – with consent of the president – a question may be declared urgent	*Private Notice Questions* – Speaker decides on urgency

Tab. 7 continued

Country	France	Germany F.R.	Switzerland	United Kingdom
Types of Questions		*Aktuelle Stunde* – open debate – support by 26 members required – no longer than one hour (except government makes extensive use of right to speak)	*Dringliche Interpellation* – If in a three week session on at least the second day questions are asked to be answered in the session the fractions presidents'conference can agree to call them as urgent.	
Remarks	For most questions gov. can refuse answers (rarely)		Questions are in most cases answered in the following session period	

are to be taken. It was first applied in 1933 (preventing at that time the reorganization of the executive). More recently controvarsy has arisen over the war-power-veto forcing the president to withdraw troops 60 days after an intervention unless the congress approves of his actions. The use of vetoes has risen since 1977, applied mainly to issues like environmental decisions, energy problems and educational issues. Its rise may be closely related to the lost trust of represenatives that delegated power may be used according to legislative intentions. As it is argued that fair representation in the administrative agencies is often difficult to achieve, the legislative veto allows for correcting biased decisions and avoiding the establishment of non-recursive facts. Opponents have argued forcefully that the veto not only provides for the arbitrary intrusions of representatives to serve special interests, but also may delay needed executive actions and prevent flexible administrative and governmental actions. Obviously the above decision by the Supreme Court to rule the veto as unconstitutional may result in the search for alternative instruments like the appropriation riders ("No funds should be under this act," imposing a large list of restrictions) and attempts at more restrictions on allowances for administrative discretion[4].

A similar device may be seen in the *confirmation procedure* influencing the selection of top executives. Those checks allow for precontrol measure. In most nations confirmations by parliaments of government appointments are limited to the election of the prime minister or less often to the selection of ministers. In Germany as in other nations the members of the higher courts are partly nominated with the help of the parliament, a special select committee. Procedures like the constitutional mandated confirmation in the US Senate (Constitution of the US,

Article LL, Sec. 2) are rare. In Germany even the Comptroller General is not confirmed by the parliament. In contrast the US Senate confirms in two years of a congress more than 100,000 (e.g. in 1973–1974, 131,254 nominations, in 1977–1978 124,730 appointments) selections, yet most of them are military promotions which do not require special care. Only some twenty thousand are political nominees and of these only 50 are more careful scrutinized with some 10 to 15 usually take under oath and very few rejected.

But informally all parliaments take great care to review personnel decisions e.g. the Wörner Affair in the West German Bundestag had its root in the decision by the Defense Ministry to replace one of the highest generals, a right he may exercise independent of parliament. Some critics have pointed to the danger of partisanship arising with parliamentary approved appointees e.g. in the selection of judges for the Highest Court. Still unsettled is the basic aim of those procedures: is the Senate for example, allowed to control and affect policies or is its task to weed out unqualified and corrupt persons?

Interpellation: Low Impact – Mixed Uses

The most extensively used instruments in parliament are *questions;* only the US-Congress has substituted these rights by committee hearings. The questions may serve as an attempt to exercise political control, are a visible form of voter service or try to influence the building of an agenda. Often it is only through questions that access to measures taken in the administration can be enforced.

Most representative systems allow for a large degree of differentiation in the emphasis of the questions. As the general trend (see Table 8) indicates, there is a tendency in the parliaments to have more individual questions put forward and reduced numbers of broader more sweeping oral questions with debates. Still the number and content of those debates are registered as signs of increasing tensions. By forcing debate, publicity is ensured and the subject brought onto the political agenda, often serving as a first step for further actions (see Table 7).

Constituency Work: Low Impact – Individualistic Usage

The handling of constituency complaints and the protection of constituency interests is gaining in importance, especially in those countries where the election systems provide a strong incentive for constituency casework. This applies to the United States where the representatives depend on a clear recognition of their efforts and can expect some electoral rewards for their work. In representational systems, such as the West German one, little gain may be expected by the representative by engaging in extensive constituency casework. Indeed more activities and interest is to be found in countries like Britain and the USA where the representative depends on a direct election by his constituency, which applies especially for marginal seats and for newly elected representatives. Likewise the effects may differ. Intruding the bureaucracy by representatives is violating the code of ethics and any form of bargaining with lower echelon bureaucrats is (officially) forbidden in West Germany. The only recognized means available to the representative are questions in the parliament and the provision of information

Tab. 8: Trends in the Unse of Questions as Instruments in Different Parliaments

Country	Type of Questions	Year 1950	1960	1970	1980
France (Assemblee)	*Questions Ecrites*	4134	4330	6039	6277
	Questions Orales			235	113
	sans debat	–	105	250	3
	avec debat	247	139		
	Questions Au Gouvernement (till 1974 Questions d'actualité)	–	–	359	181
Germany F. R. (Bundestag)	*Oral Questions Inquiries*	98	384	5867	3691
	small	89	103	108	190
	large (with debate)	80	12	11	10
	Debate	0	0	3	0
Switzerland (Nationalrat)	*Questions*	–	–	198	191
	Interpeliations	43	35	44	131
	Motions	–	–	39	87
	Postulates	–	–	94	95
United Kingdom (House of Commons)	*Oral Questions* (or starred)	7971	10161	4547	8175
	Written Questions (or unstarred)	1890	3310	24007	22688

Sources: France: Assemblée Nationale, Annual Tables Chronologiques provided by the Service de la Séance, Paris from the Journal Officiel Germany: P. Schindler, Datenhandbuch zur Geschichte des Deutschen Bundestages, Bonn Deutscher Bundestag 1983; Switzerland: Information provided by the Parlamentsdienste, Bern; United Kingdom: D. Butler and A. Sloman, 1980, British Political Facts, London: Macmillan and unpublished figures provided by The journal Office, House of Commons.
Comments: Figures are computed for session periods commencing in the dated year e.g. 1980–1981. The figures for Germany F. R. and Switzerland are computed by dividing the total election period by the number of years corresponding (except for Debates and Inquiries, where actual number has been available).

for the citizens. The *petition rights* may be conceived as a substitute for the constituency case work. Some opposition leaders have discovered its potential use as the number of petitions increased. The still individualistic handling of those petitions and only limited analysis of their systematic trends has prevented providing for a broader impact on government and its bureaucracy. Arguments for petition rights and constituency casework are primarily coming from the rise in awareness of the individual needs in the modern welfare state. To handle individual complaints and avoid biased intrusion into the administrative institutions, the model of an administrative *ombudsman* as in Britain may be more attractive. Similar institutions have been set up in West Germany for military complaints and for data-protection. He provides the parliament with a yearly systematic report, less often acted on, but creating pressure through its publication.

Tab. 9: Protection of Citizens Interests – Ombudsman – Petitions – Constituency Work

Ombudsman cases in Great Britain (Annual Report)
(Parliamentary Commissioner for Administration, established 1967)

Year	1967	1968	1969	1970	1971	1972	1973	1974	1975	1976	1977	1978
Cases completed	849	1,181	790	651	516	596	536	653	916	863	846	1,305

Petitions in election periods in Germany F. R. (Report)

Period	1949–1953	1953–1957	1957–1961	1961–1965	1965–1969	1969–1972	1972–1976	1976–1980
Number (excluding mass-petitions)	27,200	33,000	29,559	29,993	23,232	23,793	49,204	48,846

Casework-handling in the US Congress (Gallup Congressional Election Study 1978)

Received Numbers per week	∅	less than 20	21–40	40–60	61–80	81–100	over 100	Missing
Congressmen Percentage	102	9%	28%	18%	6%	12%	16%	10%

Main topics (listed according to rank)

Germany F. R.	Great Britain	USA
Social Security	Social security	Social security
Internal Problems	Housing	Military/Veterans Benefits[1]
(contains environmental, guest-worker issues etc)	Taxes	Immigration
	Immigration	Unemployment Benefits
Civil Service	Health Care	Internal Revenue Service (Tax)
Penal Law	Military service[1]	Health Care
Unemployment	Education	Civil Service
Legal Justice	Planning Permits	Housing
Public Utilities	Public Utilities	Black

[1] Military Complaints are dealt with in Germany F. R. by a special Ombudsman (number of cases in 1981 7 265)

33.4 Parliamentary Control: Missed Opportunities or Glimmering Options?

There is broad agreement that most parliaments have sufficient control provisions for exercising control. Conventional wisdom often suggested that lack of incentives and rewards seem to hinder successful control measures. Lawmaking and more representative functions in parliament seem more promising for a political career than the issue of control. In Germany the opposition usually stresses the creation of alternatives and not of detailed control and oversight. Part of the problem is the understanding of control. For many politicians the degree of difference in opinion to the government influences their perception and judgement about lack of control. If they disagree with certain policies, the quest for parliamentarian control and oversight arises. Their political perception determines what kind of problems are important and what control questions need to be answered.

The greatest demand is therefore not for creating new arms of control but in understanding the utilization of the different tools available for control. The need is for a theory of control that would enable understanding the behaviour of the parliamentarians and the different effects of control under different constitutional conditions and in diverse political situations. A less ambitious aim is to draw a conceptual map of the different institutions and uses made of control. Despite the massive volume on congressional research little is actually known about the difference in organizations, procedures and political powers used for control. Systematic evidence is rare and the increasing tendency to build large information systems on parliamentary activities (Germany, Great Britain, USA) seems a reasonable yet insufficient step towards a massing elementary knowledge still lacking on how even formal processes of legislative control are working. The rich inventories of possible control instruments has then to be related to the differing political structures and cultural styles.

Control questions have to be understood in relation to the electorate. The influence of constituency mass behaviour and public reactions is an important to understanding the process of control as is the discoverance of the institutional variances between constitutions.

Last but not least, measures to evaluate parliamentary controls are lacking. There are no agreed criteria by which to judge the effectiveness of a parliamentary control system. Quantitatively there exists no clear consensus about how to measure control activities. Undercounting may occur. Part of the problem is that control actions are so closely interwoven with other activities that any count of identified separate control measures may neglect the manifold informal continuous control actions carried through in the daily work of the representatives. Almost any committee devoting its energy to new legislation pays considerable attention to past experiences, reviewing past experiences, past failed implementations and potential risks of the new legislations. Qualitatively there are no easy available criteria by which to judge effective control. Members may differ on how to judge the effectiveness of control on a particular issue. When representatives claim a lack of control they often simply mean that their particular views has been not accommodated by the implementation of a new law. Those who cry are often those who failed to put their view through in the legislative process, and those who succeeded often shy away to avoid any public repercussion of their protected law.

Critiques finding control actions as sporadic, selective, unsystematic, symbolic and unsustained develop this perspective often from a very limited understanding of the working of the more complex system which needs to allow for flexible responses, selectivity, sporadic actions and symbolic rituals to accommodate for the rich variety met in political reality.

Much of the work on control is based on an assumption resting on a mechanical understanding of action and control. It may be argued that most control is exercised smoothly by informal means. As executive and administrative reactions to the parliaments are geared to build consensus, many dissenting voices are taken into account by internalizing expectations. The danger stems rather from the how and by what means the parliamentary system is able to discern special interests from common interests and identify iron triangles composed out of parliaments, administrative agencies and public interest groups, protecting their mutual interests.

The fragmented and highly diverse set of members may serve an essential function by integrating and controlling for those special interests rather better than the specialized rationality of the professional advisers and the administrative agency. The "irrational" tactical considerations and bargaining procedures may provide for necessary accommodation of divergent control needs. For such a function the ability of the minority to voice and find their interests taken care of by the parliamentary process and the continuous search for transparency may be as relevant as the search for more effectiveness as the main aim of many rational control efforts.

The creation of information capacities may help to serve as a check on the politicians own coherence and continuity. The existing fear that parliamentary control agencies may enlarge the hidden force of a policy community network which outplays the politicians (Heclo 1978) would only emerge if those agencies didn't concenrate on the needs of the representatives, who demand beyond analysis better information on the feasibility and necessity of actions which respond to the grievances and complaints stemming from diverse unsatisfied interests in their constituencies. The policy analysts as information brokers on the needs and the gap between programs and needs may prove essential for the survival of those members in the parliament who engage in the battle on the floor.

The past tendency to draw a line between legitimate, ex-post evaluations and exante assessment and (continuous watchfulness) participative control may wane. As most human actions are irreversible, arguments against participative control-means, which mesh executive and legislative functions, are inappropriate. Due to the need for policy discretion and to uncertainty about the effects of planning, attempts at forward control by detailed legislation will continue to fail as ex-post controls in the past have been insufficient. Most governmental systems have recognized the need for an interactive control-mix to acquire for their discretionary powers the legitimation and the sensitivity which only the representative body commands. If a loss of control has developed despite extension of processual oversight functions, this may be rather true to new structural trends shaping government actions, for which a lack exist in the traditional control system:

(1) In the United States regulatory commissions are *outside the immediate control of parliaments;* in West Germany new institutions to allow for the explicit incorporation of diverse interests e.g. of trade-unions' and employers' organizations or between the federal and state governments are developing. Those quasi- and intergovernmental institutions regulate public actions invisibly without traditional parliamentary control. New third party organizations are emerging which carry out public programs whose implementation are difficult to control.

(2) *The control of the parliament* may prevent effective control. In Germany the

state governments may to some degree exercise more control on governmental programs than most parliamentarians can do. The rise of international institutions like the EEG or the IMF may interfer with proper control. In many respects taken together with the tight reins governments can exercise over the majority party, parliament may find itself under pressure to avoid control measures due to a conglomerate of either supraparliamentarism powers, interest group pressures or reelection interests.

(3) *The uncontrollable part of the budget,* that part of the budget outlays which cannot be controlled in an annual budget seems to continue to grow. The Office of Management and Budget (OMB) in the USA estimated it to have grown due to entitlement programs (social security, medicare, unemployment trust funds), net interests and other longterm commitments from 59 percent in 1967 to 76 percent. The quest for trust in past decisions, the concern for longterm stability and the need for equity and legality prevent any annual infringements. Developing tools like fiscal impact statements or multi-year finance planning can only be made effective if adequate controls can be designed which have a longer time horizon in mind by exercising them.

In most countries parliaments are now better equipped to understand those pressures, having better access to information and having managed to develop a net of different control strategies. Still as analysis shows, for the enacting of control measures parliaments rely on external events. The political situation, the existing party structure and the inner-party democracy and cohesion are crucial to the exercise of control. The selective use – as long as systematic use is infeasible – may still possess an uncontrolled system bias. Moreover, as the power of committees and individual members as in the USA is growing, a more systematic and cross-program control to integrate the centrifugal interests may be in demand.

Changes in the parliament have to differ due to the different culture and institutional arrangements. They have to differ most certainly between presidential and parliamentary systems. Whereas in the presidential system the legislature may be asked to take steps towards an effective interplay between the main plenary body, its committees and oversight/subcommittees, the parliamentary system probably needs to strengthen the role of the opposition parties as the majority parties are too closely interlinked with the ruling government and may be disinterested in direct control.

Those searching for structural changes will be disappointed. Those searching for limited progress building on

(1) improving the learning from oversight for improved legislation,
(2) meshing more diverse professional evaluation research with parliamentary oversight functions,
(3) translating constituency casework into legislative knowledge, and
(4) combining legal and financial control instruments with broader and flexible policy controls

may see a glimmer of changing perceptions and views, forcing the representatives' priorities to serve the interest of crucial aspects in the society, and to improve the exercise of parliamentary control to make the representative accountable. As the varied controls will continue to be exercised by piecemeal and episodically, the understanding of the complex system of controls needs continous attention.

Notes

1   In this chapter I follow the common usage in applying the terms "parliament, parliamen-
    tarians" for all representative and legislative bodies. If I concentrate on the distinctions
    between different forms of "representative legislatures," I use the term parliamentarian
    government for those bodies in which the parliament chooses the head or the members
    of the executive and presidential government for the separate election of the executive.
    The "vote of confidence" functions as a crucial criterion for distinction. The potentially
    useful analytical distinction which developed out of the work of the Iowa Center between
    the active and reactive parliaments seemed to me US-biased (see Mezey 1979), and most
    of the other distinctions end up with single case categories (e.g. Loewenstein 1957).
2   Unfortunately there is no full source reviewing parliamentary reform efforts (e.g. Judge
    1983; Kornberg 1973). Still the best solution is to turn to the publications and proceed-
    ings of the different reform commissions. As it is not possible to document here the full
    range of commissionary work on parliamentary reform, the two volume bibliographic
    reference by the Interparliamentary Union may serve as a substitute Interparliamentary
    Union 1983. For Europe, Oberreuter (1981) has edited a review on parliamentary
    reform. For an especially sensitive discussion of reform possibilities see the Swiss reports
    on constitutional reform (Studienkommission 1978).
3   More recently there have been a number of studies on the perception of the parliamen-
    tarian's role in the USA, Great Britain and Germany. What emerges from those data,
    gathered mostly in the late sixties and early seventies, is a split in the perception of the
    members in parliament between the perceived need and the perceived actions. Espe-
    cially in Germany and the USA control is viewed to nearly equal the legislative task, yet
    the time alloted to it is considerably less. Reviewing more personal qualitative state-
    ments, the deficit seems to stem mainly from the interpretation of what constitutes
    control. The perception and understanding of what control means varies, and in many
    cases it is the shaping of the bureaucracy according to the members' (and not the
    parliament's) will, in others only formal functions delegated to a committee are con-
    ceived as control.
4   The need for government and administrative discretion has been increasingly recognized
    not only out of technical reasons (impossibility of detailed conditioning for the future by
    law) but more so by the recognition that only discretionary governments can be held
    responsible.

References

Aberbach, J. D. (1979): "Changes in Congressional Oversight." *American Behavioral Scientist* 22/5: 493–515.

Arnold, D. (1979): *Congress and the Bureaucracy*. New Haven: Yale Univ. Press.

Bagehot, W. (1867): *The English Constitution*. Oxford: Oxford Univ. Press.

Barthélemy, J. (1934): *Essay sur le travail parlementaire et le système des commissions*. Paris: Dalloz.

Blondel, J. (1973): *Comparative Legislatures*. Englewood Cliffs, N. J.: Prentice-Hall.

Bruff, H., and E. Gellhorn (1977): "Congressional Control of Administrative Regulation: A Study of Legislative Vetoes." *Harvard Law Review* 90/7: 1369–1440.

Butler, D., and A. Sloman (eds.) (1980): *British Political Facts 1900–1979* (5th ed.). London: Macmillan.

Congressional Quarterly (1983): *Current American Government*. Washington: Congressional Quarterly.

Congressional Research Service (1983): *Legislative Vetoes*. Washington, DC: Library of Congress.

Dodd, L. C., and B. I. Oppenheimer (eds.) (1977): *Congress Reconsidered*. New York: Praeger.

Dodd, L. C., and R. L. Schott (1979): *Congress and the Administrative State*. New York: Wiley.

Duverger, M. (1978): *Institutions politiques et droit constitutionel* (15th ed.). Paris: PUP.

Fenno, R. F. (1978): *Home Style: Representatives in their Districts*. Boston: Little Brown.

Harris, J. (1964): *Congressional Control of Administration*. Washington, D. C.: The Brookings.

Heclo, H. (1978): "Issue Networks and the Executive Establishment." In A. King (ed.), *The New American Political System*, 87–123. Washington, DC: American Enterprise Institute for Public Policy Research.

Herman, V. (ed.) (1976): *Parliaments of the World*. London: Macmillan.

Inter-Parliamentary Union (IPU) (ed.) (1983): *World Directory of Parliaments*. Geneva: IPU.

Judge, D. (ed.) (1983): *Politics of Parliamentary Reform*. London: Heineman.

Laski, H. J. (1944): The Parliamentary and Presidential System. *Public Administration Review* 4/4: 347–359.

Kornberg, A. (1973): *Legislatures in Comparative Perspective*. New York: McKay.

Loewenberg, G., and S. C. Patterson (1979): *Comparing Legislatures*. Boston: Little, Brown and Co.

Loewenstein, K. (1938): "The Balance between Legislative and Executive Power." *University of Chicago Law Review* 5/4: 566–608.

Loewenstein, K. (1957): *Political Power and the Governmental Process*. Chicago: Univ. of Chicago Press.

McMurty, V. (1979): *Sunset Laws: Establishing Systematic Oversight Procedure*. Washington: Congressional Research Service.

Mezey, M. L. (1979): *Comparative Legislatures*. Durham, NC: Duke Univ. Press.

Mill, J. S. (1861): *Consideration on Representative Government*. London: Longmans.

Nader, R. (1973): *The Hidden Government*. New York: Doubleday.

Neustadt, R. E. (1960): *Presidential Power*. New York, London: Wiley.

Oberreuter, H. (ed.) (1981): *Parlamentsreform in westlichen Demokratien*. Passau: Passavia Universitätsverlag.

Ogul, M. S. (1976): *Congress Oversees the Bureaucracy*. London: Univ. of Pittsburg Press.

Ornstein, N. J. (ed.) (1982): *Vital Statistics on Congress*. Washington: Congressional Quarterly.

Presidential Commission on Waste in Government (Grace Commission) (1984): *Diverse Reports*. Washington, DC: GPO.

Price, D. K. (1943): The Parliamentary and Presidential System. *Public Administration Review* 3/4: 317–335.

Price, D. K. (1944): A Response to Mr. Laski. *Public Administration Review* 4/4: 360–364.

Rieselbach, L. N. (ed.) (1978): *Legislative Reform and Public Policy*. Lexington, Mass.: Lexington Books.

Schindler, P. (1983): *Datenhandbuch zur Geschichte des Deutschen Bundestags*. Bonn: Deutscher Bundestag.

Studienkommission der Eidgenössischen Räte (1978): "Zukunft des Parlaments." *Bundesblatt* II: 966.

Sundquist, J. L. (1981): *The Decline and Resurgence of Congress*. Washington, DC: The Brookings Institute.

Sundquist, J. L. (1983): "The Legislative Veto: A Bounced Check." *The Brookings Review,* Fall: 13–16.

US Congress (1976): *Legislative Oversight and Program Evaluation:* A Seminar sponsored by the Congressional Research Service, 94th Congress, 2nd sess., Washington: GPO.

US Congress. House, Rules Committee (1980): *Recommendations on Establishment of Procedures for Congressional Review of Agency Rules.* 96th Congress, 2nd sess. Washington: GPO.

US General Accounting Office (GAO) (1980): *Analysis of Requirements for Recurring Reports to the Congress.* Washington, DC: PAD-80-72.

Weber, M. (1958): "Parlament und Regierung im neugeordneten Deutschland." In *Weber, M. Gesammelte politische Schriften* (2nd ed.), 294 ff. Tübingen: Mohr. (first published 1917/1918)

Wolff, H. W. (1978): *Intelligence Community: Congressional Oversight.* Washington: Congressional Research Service.

Zweig, F. M. (ed.) (1979): *Evaluation in Legislation.* Beverly Hills, London: Sage.

34. Audit Control

Wolfgang Sigg and Göran Arvidsson

Abstract

In view of the fiscal scarcity in most modern states, financial control of administrative performance has become an issue of crucial importance. Against the background of stagnant economic growth rates, and of the changed and expanded tasks public administrations are expected to fulfill in welfare states, the question of what are the "right" audits is debated time and again in political, scientific and public contexts. Should the activities of audit offices be restricted to their traditional functions of supervising the legality of expenditures, the regularity of accounts and economy in performance? Or should they in addition evaluate and assess the efficiency of government operations or even the effectiveness of political programs? Moreover, how can such audits be done "right" in order to ensure the – frequently contested – effectiveness of auditing and financial control itself?

Such problems are dicussed in the first part of this chapter by way of a case study of the tasks, organizational structure and working of the financial control by audit courts in the Federal Republic of Germany. The discussion is continued in the second part, by emphasizing that the constitutional roles, the functions and the scope or contents of auditing vary from country to country. The range of trends and options concerning the choice of audit strategies is demonstrated and it is argued that there seems to be no generally accepted "right" type of audit. The impacts of different kinds of audit depend on a variety of factors including the quality of the personnel, of strategic and tactical choices in different arrangements as well as the interplay with other controls. However, the conclusion is that there may be no alternative to certain traditional functions of auditing, but many alternative actors or institutions who could perform the extended forms of audit.

Part A. Tasks, Organization and Current Problems of Financial Control in the Federal Republic of Germany

Wolfgang Sigg

34.1 The Structure and Functions of Budget Control

Financial control of administrative performance in the Federal Republic of Germany is exercised at various levels and by various actors in the politico-administrative system. With regard to the functions and structure of *audit control* we have to distinguish between external budget control carried out by formally autonomous *audit courts,* and internal budget control performed by *pre-audit offices* within administrative institutions[1].

In accordance with the federal structure of the Federal Republic of Germany *external budget control* of the federal administration is exercised by the Federal Court of Audit (Bundesrechnungshof) and control of the federal state administrations by the courts of audit of the federal states (Landesrechnungshöfe) self-administring corporate bodies are only partly subject to scrutiny by the audit offices. The local authorities, for example, make use, for the most part, of the so called courts of audit for local communities (Gemeindeprüfungsanstalten).

The audit offices are independent institutions guaranteed by the constitution. They are not subject to directives either from the government or from parliament. Their activities serve both to control the administration by the head of the administration (the government) – so-called administrative control- and the government by parliament – so-called governmental or constitutional control. The audit offices have, therefore, a twofold function.

From an historical point of view, the courts of audit began as bodies which simply assisted the monarchs and their cabinets in the control of the administration. It was only after parliament archieved sovereign control of the budget that the courts of audit also acquired the function of supporting parliament in its control of governmental implementation of the budget. The struggle for the direct access of parliament to the reports of the Federal Court of Audit ended only in 1969 with a change in Article 114 of the German Basic Law. This explicitly entitled both the executive *and* the legislative to receive the audit reports. Before the change, the reports first had to be presented to the Federal Minister of Finance who then passed them on to parliament together with a statement of his own.

The Federal Court of Audit consists of the president, the vice-president and the necessary number of directors and high-ranking officials. The latter, however, must be explicitly nominated. In accordance with Article 114, Paragraph 2 of the Basic Law the members of the Federal Court of Audit enjoy judicial independence. The civil servants assigned as auditors to the Federal Court of Audit are bound by the directives of their superiors.

The Federal Court of Audit consists of eight departments, each containing six auditing areas[2]. The heads of the departments are directors, the heads of the auditing areas and the departmental section high-ranking officials. Auditing officials are assigned to the auditing areas and competent officials to the departmental section. The auditing areas correspond fairly precisely to the structure of the administration which is subject to control by the Federal Court of Audit.

Because of the judical independence of the individual members, the internal structure of the Federal Court of Audit is determined above all by the *principle of collective competence*. In auditing procedures the Federal Court of Audit takes all decisions collectively. As a rule, the high-ranking officials as heads of the auditing areas and the directors as heads of the auditing departments take the decisions together for their spheres of competence.

In exceptional cases, provision is made for decisions by the senate, the full senate or a combined senate consisting of members of the Federal Audit Office and of the audit offices of the states (Länder). The president and the vice-president of the Federal Court of Audit are proposed for office by the Minister of Finance and appointed by the Federal President with the countersignature of the Minister of Finance. The Minister of Finance procures the approval of the cabinet for his proposal.

The financially important processes controlled by the Federal Court of Audit are subject to preliminary examination by the administrative authorities, who employ a so-called pre-audit office for this purpose. In contrast to the Federal Court of Audit, which can be regarded as an external body of control, the pre-audit offices exercise *internal administrative controls*. As their name implies, they prepare the ground internally for the subsequent auditing of the Federal Court of Audit, by searching for and remedying errors, ambiguities and incomplete entries in the books and records. As all accounts must, as a matter of principle, be examined first by these offices, the Federal Court of Audit can restrict its activities to sample audits. The tasks of the pre-audit offices are analogous to those of the Federal Court of Audit. This means that they also control the *adequacy, orderliness, technical correctness, legality, efficiency* and *economy* of administrative performance. Their organizational position constitutes a special phenomenon (see Damkowski 1977). Although they are, as has been said, internal units of the public administration, they are subject to a twofold control: on the one hand, they are under the general supervision of the head of the administrative department within which they have been established; on the other hand, they are subject to the special supervision by the Federal Court of Audit, an external body. This ambiguous position creates considerable problems, It leads to complicated demarcations of areas of competence and, as a result, to uncertainty in the behavior of the members. These difficulties are aggravated by the subordination to an external authority, which certainly does not facilitate co-operation between the superior within the civil service hierarchy and the outside expert with supervisory powers. Because of these problems, there have been various proposals to take the pre-audit offices out of the administration and to place them directly under the offical supervision of the Federal Court of Audit.

34.2 The Staffing of Budget Control

The qualifications of the staff is of decisive importance for the quality of the auditing carried out by the *audit offices.*

Today, the courts of audit are still a domain of the administrative lawyers who occupy all positions within the audit offices. The auditing activities are for the most part carried out by promoted officials who have advanced from the middle to the upper grades of the civil service. These civil servants mostly come from the administrative fields which they are to audit later. It seems questionable, therefore, whether such officials possess the independence necessary for their dealings with their former spheres of activity. There is, moreover, a danger that civil servants who are no longer completely suitable for employment can be eased out of the administration in this way (see Karehnke 1969/70).

Whereas officials in the upper grades must have a university degree, those in the middle grades (and those promoted to the upper grades) come from the polytechnics and professional colleges. In this context it must be noted that the training of officials in the upper grades is primarily a legal one, and although that of the officials from the middle grades is also legally oriented, the emphasis of their studies and of the experience they have gathered is, above all, on the field of book keeping.

The social background of the civil servants of the Federal Court of Audit is identical with that of the administration as a whole, i.e., there is a relatively high degree of social mobility.

If the status of the staff of the Federal Court of Audit is measured by income, a certain advantage over the rest of the administration can be clearly recognized. The president of the Federal Court of Audit enjoys a salary comparable to that of a minister, the other posts are on average better paid (and at a higher level) than posts in the normal administration. For the middle grades, in particular, there are good opportunities for promotion. However, it cannot be said that a position in the Court of Audit is in general regarded as desirable within the administration. The main reason is, probably, that the activities of the Court of the Audit are looked upon as the work of "pedants and misers" because the emphasis is still largely upon the control of the adequacy, orderliness and thrift of administrative activities.

If one surveys the fields in which the courts of audit operate, the main problem seems to be that there is scarcely any suitably trained staff available for areas such as the supervision of economic efficiency or organization, i.e., for areas which are becoming more and more important. The increasing complexity of state activities requires, above all, that more of supervision than hitherto should be taken over by academically trained, specialized personnel (economists, graduate engineers), and that the work should not be left almost entirely to auditing officials of middle grade or to those promoted to the upper grades. However, applicants who are not career civil servants, for example those with a training in economics, are only occasionally appointed.

Advisors from the private industry sector of the economy are seldom called upon to assist in auditing. For the reform of the staff structure of the Federal Court of Audit it is proposed, above all, that the choice of personnel, which has hitherto been more or less the product of chance, should in future be carried out in accordance with a planned staffing system. This would include the appointment of specialized applicants, particularly persons with economic training. New tasks require the appointment of the corresponding personnel.

The staff of the *pre-audit offices* consists in the main of civil servants of the middle grade with a training in book-keeping or with professional specialization in this field. These officials also come for the most part from the administrations they have to audit, and their careers are similar to those of "normal" administrators. In the case of the pre-audit offices there is an even greater danger that less qualified personnel will be appointed. Of all the places to which a head of department might appoint highly qualified personnel, the position of internal auditing control is probably the last. The Federal Court of Audit has no legal means of influencing appointments to the pre-audit officies. Its views are heard only in connection with the appointment of the head of the pre-audit office.

34.3 The Tasks and Working Methods Involved in Financial Control

The Federal Court of Audit is required to control all budgetary and economic acitivities of the Federal Government, including its special assets and enterprises (see Sigg 1983: 28 ff.). The entire financial policy is the subject of auditing – in accordance with the so-called principles exclusivity and completeness of auditing competence (similar regulations also apply to the auditing offices of the federal states).

The standards of control are:

(1) The adequacy, orderliness and technicall correctness of accounting (rechnungs-technische Ordnungsmäßigkeit)
(2) Legality (Rechtmäßigkeit)
(3) Efficiency and Economy (Wirtschaftlichkeit und Sparsamkeit)

Technical correctness, adequacy and orderliness of accounting means the justification and documentation of income and expenditure and the correct statement of accounts for the household and assets. The auditing is, therefore, a matter of measuring the accounts in accordance with the generally valid rules of accounting.

In controlling the legality, the Federal Court of Audit Office does not restrict itself to examining to what extent the financial activities of the administration agree with the budget law and the budget. It goes further and examines executive actions in the light of all legal provisions, including, for example, the constitution.

Whereas the first two standards are essentially unproblematical, the standards of efficiency and economy have still not been sufficiently clarified. On these points the lack of a consistent set of goals is particularly evident (see Rürup 1971: 15 ff.). The expenditure set out in the budget does not represent the costs of a program designed for the achievement of a certain goal; it is simply a set of isolated items of expenditure. The budget reveals only the input of resources without explaining or clarifying the desired output of performance. In spite of these difficulties, demands have even been made recently for a control of effectiveness and success through the Federal Court of Audit (see below). The Federal Court of Audit has not acceded to these demands as yet: it restricts itself essential to the control of efficiency in a narrow economic sense and the "philosophy" of its auditing is primarily based upon technical correctness, adequacy and orderliness in the running of the household in the sense mentioned above.

The techniques of control are restricted basically to checking the book-keeping and to argumentation based on common sense. Formal methods of analysis (such as, for example, cost-benefit analysis or cost-effectiviness analysis) are scarcely ever applied.

The courts of audit base their work largely on the auditing activities of the pre-audit offices. Because of the scope of the material to be audited and the limited staffing capacity, they have to restrict themselves to sample audits. The courts of audit are free in the choice of the subject matter they control. Control can be initiated for various reasons, for example reports in the press or an unusual increase in the budget of a particular department, etc. The activities of the courts of audit are restricted on principle to *a posteriori control*.

The control procedure ends with a report of the results to the heads of the department concerned. These must then comment on the report within a fixed period of time. Such reports can also be sent to other bodies, in particular to boards of control.

In so far as they are important for the formal approval of government policy in regard to the household and to the administration of assets, the final results of the audit are summarized in the so-called "comments" (Bemerkungen), a report to parliament (Bundestag) and the Federal Council (Bundesrat), which is also sent to the Federal Government. This report by the Federal Court of Audit is intended to be a final statement, based on thorough examination, of the accounting period under review. This single, concluding statement is the only means provided for by the constitution through which the Federal Court of Audit can influence the procedures connected with the approval of government policy. The Federal Court of Audit has no legal means at its disposal to enforce its decisions on the bodies it has audited. Its comments are not legally binding.

Proposals for the improvement of the auditing activity of the Federal Cout of Audit point, above all, toward a more extensive use of the modern techniques of economic analysis[3].

34.4 Performance Evaluation of Policy Decision-Making by the Courts of Audit

With the aid of concepts such as program evaluation, control of effectiveness and success and task criticism, politicians and academic experts have in the last few years intensified their efforts to come to grips with the control of policy decision-making (see Derlien 1976; Bohne and König 1976; Dieckmann 1980). More limited resources and, in particular, the long-term lock-ups and uncritical up-dating of old programs have proved to be a serious restriction on the reform policies which have been pursued particularly since 1969. These policies involve new social tasks which can only be met by the provision of substantial means. Extensive planning systems have been developed at a federal and state level and the administrations have had to implement a great variety of political programs. The implementation presented no problems as long as the growth of the economy guaranted steadily growing budgets. But when the financial room for maneuver grew smaller as a result of the relative stagnation of growth rates, the problem of choice and of deciding on priorities among the various programs arose.

The Need for Performance Evaluation

The precondition for a rational choice is, above all, the analysis of the effectiveness of programs. There has, therefore, been a growing demand for performance evaluation as a counterpart to policy decision-making. However, in the opinion of the *"Kommission für den wirtschaftlichen und sozialen Wandel"* (1977), there are numerous indications that the extension of the duties of the state has not been accompanied by a corresponding growth in the controlling capacity of the instances which are required to examine the effectiveness with which administration master their tasks and reach their set goals. The absolute increase in state activity has, therefore, been paralleled by a relative decrease in performance evaluation.

It is hoped that with the aid of intensified performance evaluation, ineffective programs and inefficient program elements will be discovered and that this will in turn provide a political legitimation and justification for a redistribution of resources in favour of new or existing effective programs.

Methodological Difficulties in Performance Evaluation

The first difficulty presented by performance evaluation involves the standards of control. Unfortunately, there is as yet no uniform terminology in this field. There is complete confusion in the use of concepts such as effectiveness, efficiency and success. A starting-point for the following considerations is the definition of the two most important concepts of efficiency and effectiveness as already mentioned in the preceding chapters. Effectiveness is meant in the sense of a target-output relationship, i.e. a relationship between political goals and results. It compares targets and performance in terms of the goal set and the results actually achieved. The concept of efficiency, on the other hand, is reserved for the characterization of economic input-output relationships; it is concerned therefore, with the relationship between expenditure and return (see Reinermann 1974: 2 f.). This terminological distinction can be justified, firstly, by the fact that the concepts of effectiveness and efficiency can be assigned to clearly demarcated areas of control. Secondly, statements about the relationship between targets and performance, on the one hand, and ends and means, on the other, refer to different features of a program. Thirdly, the other concepts used, such as impact and economy can partly be understood as sub-concepts of efficiency and effectiveness.

But are both effectiveness and efficiency standards for the evaluation and control of success or failure of performance? Aderhold (1973: 246), for example, when speaking of the control of success means only control of effectiveness. Others place the standards of both efficiency and effectiveness in the category of evaluation (e.g. Bohne and König 1976: 27). In my opinion, only the latter is correct. Performance evaluation is designed, above all, to enable comparison and choice between different programs. For this purpose, however, a control of effectiveness alone is not sufficient. It is quite possible that two programs are equally effective in reaching the same goal, i.e. that their degree of goal accomplishment is identical, but that one of the programs is substantially more efficient, i.e. its relationship of expenditure and returns is much better. But a decision on this point is precisely what performance evaluation should make possible. It is, of course, clear that a comparison of the efficiency of different programs only makes sense, if and when the effectiveness of each program has already been confirmed.

Apart from the establishment of the terminology and the standards of evaluation, methodological difficulties in connection with performance evaluation arise, above all, in the following ways:

– Because of the lack or inadequacy or operationally defined program goals, indicators of effect have to be developed after the event. Such indicators may only partially correspond to the intentions which determined the original development of the program, or they may cover only incompletely the unforeseen positive and negative side-effects of a project.
– The effects cannot always be measured because the necessary data in the form of official statistics or of data collected after completion of the program are not available and can only be procured with difficulty in subsequent inquiries.
– Even when it is possible to measure the effects of a program a clear-cut causal attribution of these effects to the program concerned can frequently not be made because of the lack of experimental program instructions. As a result, it cannot be excluded that, for example, external factors neutralize positive effects or create negative effects (on this point see, above all, Derlien 1978: 52 ff.).

However, these difficulties do not make performance evaluation completely unfeasible. There is no substitute for the control of success through evaluation. In spite of all the sources of error listed, a methodologically clear evaluation study will always provide more scientifically validated results than the otherwise customary subjective, intuitive, informal and anecdotal assessments of programs (see Steinberg 1976: 208).

The Institutionalization of Performance Evaluation in the Courts of Audit

In the Federal Republic of Germany performance evaluation has, in the past, been initiated mostly as a result of political criticism of a program or conflict within the administration. In comparison with the United States, for example, a political or legal obligation to evaluate programs has, up to now been the exception. However, evaluations initiated ad hoc are often resisted by the units responsible for the programs. It is, furthermore, difficult to secure the methodological preconditions for the optimal implementation of a program, it they have not already been included in the planning when the program was developed. It appears, therefore, that there is an urgent need to institutionalize program evaluation in the form of a legal obligation to carry out analyses of effect. In this context, the all-important question is to decide who should implement it, i.e. which body inside or outside the executive should take on this task.

On this point a series of proposals have already been made. The creation of expert planning committees with a corresponding organizational basis has been suggested. These "should provide an objective basis for the control of program implementation" (Harnischfeger 1969: 134). Harnischfeger has also proposed that the government be required to issue official reports subject to supervision by parliamentary delegates. Rürup (1971: 147 f.) suggests that control of success should be placed in the hands of the Federal Statistical Office. Other plans assume that the task of evaluation will be located in the executive or legislative (see Steinberg 1976: 209; Derlien 1976; Bohne and König 1976: 38).

Some authors suggest that the courts of audit should bear the responsibility for the political control of success (see Rürup and Seidler 1981; Greifeld 1981).

"For the Federal Republic of Germany there appears to be a real chance that the institutions of external financial control – the courts of audit and the auditing offices (Rechnungsprüfungsämter) – could widen their competence beyond their present functions of financial control to include a more extensive political control of success" (König 1977: 36).

The reason given for this viewpoint is that above all, the body responsible for such a political control must be independent, which, in the case of the Federal Court of Audit, is constitutionally guaranteed by the Basic Law (the situation is similar for the federal state courts of audit). Moreover, the courts of audit are in an ideal position to control success or failure because of their unique knowledge of the administrations they supervise. "No other body has such intimate knowledge of the object of control at its disposal." (König 1977: 38). The authors of these proposals realize, of course, that an institutionalization of such performance evaluation within the courts of audit assumes substantial changes in all control procedures and supervisory activities.

An extension of the financial control of the courts of audit to include standards of effectiveness and success would involve the introduction of qualitatively new tasks for the courts of audit from a number of points of view.

It is true that the courts of audit no longer just look for orderliness and technical correctness of administrative acts, but also check their economic efficiency and thrift. However, this is not a control of success in the real sense of the word, as has already been shown. Moreover, the control of economy and economic efficiency is located at a different level than the evaluation and control of effectiveness. Control of economic efficiency takes place at a micro-economic management level, whereas the evaluation of political success or failure is carried out at the macro-economic level. If one follows Brümmerhof and Wolff's (1974: 484) division of planning into strategic, tactical and operational areas, the control of economic efficiency by the courts of audit would be located at the operational level, the level of direct implementation. Strategic and tactical questions, such as, for example, the examination of the legitimacy of a certain policy or of the competition between different goals or the establishment of certain preferences in planning decisions are matters of political performance control. This is something different from the supervision of budgetary correctness and orderliness and the management of funds on a rational input-output basis, as carried out by the Federal Court of Audit.

A broader concept of political performance evaluation and control would open up new dimensions of supervision activity by the courts of audit, especially because they would inevitably become controllers of parliaments. – Financial control would be extended to include parliament. In implementing such a performance evaluation the courts of audit would, for example, also have to examine whether the programs approved by parliament are realizable, whether they will achieve the desired goals and whether there are conflicts between the goals of the different programs. It is not, therefore, a question of controlling implementation, but of controlling the programs themselves. In the German case, this would presumably exceed the constitutionally established duties of the courts of audit.

Moreover, such performance evaluation is "an eminently political business because its standards are value-loaded" (Aderhold 1973: 256). Entrusting of such enlarged control tasks to the courts of audit could involve them in the arena of political conflict, which is not compatible with their "neutral" position between the executive and the legislative. The independent position of the courts of audit was deliberately conceived to place them above conflicting political interests. If the control of success or failure is institutionalized in the courts of audit, there is a risk that they will impose their own standards of value and political conceptions, which have not been democratically legitimated, on the bodies they control, and, furthermore, they can do this to an even greater extent than would be possible for parliament when it approves the funds. As long as all state activities are not guided by concrete political planning of goals or goals systems, the Federal Court of Audit would have to rely on its own standards of performance evaluation and control. But not even the budget contains such concrete planning statements of an operational kind. The task of political performance evaluation should, therefore, not be entrusted on the Federal Court of Audit (the same is true of the federal state courts of audit).

However, it seems worthy of consideration to accord the Federal Court of Audit the right to make proposals for the implementation of specific controls in terms of effectiviness or success. A realistic alternative might be to permit the Federal Court of Audit, in accordance with the auditing duties stated in § 90 of the Federal Budget Regulations (Bundeshaushaltsordnung), to indicate the areas and the measures which require evaluation which would then, however, be carried out by the government (see Derlien 1978: 55). But Derlien's view that evaluation and control should be restricted to the government alone seems questionable. This could then very easily degenerate into an instrument of justification. The implementation of effective controls would place the government in the risky position of uncovering errors in the planning and realization of programs. As a result, the evaluation reports might be "doctored". To prevent such a dangerous development, evaluation units should be established within the administration for the purpose of political control of the administration by the government, and alongside these should also be external institutions for the political conrol of effectiveness, success and impacts which should, above all, do the preliminary work for parliament.

34.6 The Effectiveness of Financial Control by the Federal Court of Audit – a Need for Reform?

Although the Federal Court of Audit does not have at its disposal legal sanctions to ensure the acceptance of its ciriticisms, its activities do have a substantial influence on the activities of the administration and on political processes, at least according to the self-assessment of its members (see the various statements by its presidents Schafer 1976 and Wittrock 1978). The steadily growing tendency of administrative officials to call up "their" auditors at the Federal Court of Audit, as a precautionary measure, before taking problematic decisions, indicates that this self-assessment is not entirely false. The ministries also often include the Federal Court of Audit in decision-making processes at an early stage, for example in the drafting of laws.

This "influence" of the Federal Court of Audit can be attributed mainly to the following factors (see Sigg 1983: 76 ff.):

In order to ensure acceptance of its criticisms by the executive bodies it controls, the Federal Court of Audit can apply a means of proved effectiveness, i.e. it can threaten to report back to the heads of the government or to the parliamentary bodies.

A further "weapon" in the hands of the Federal Court of Audit is the publicity given to the results of its auditing. The duty to publish them arises from the position of the Federal Court of Audit as the representative of the interests of the general public. Parliament by and large fails to fulfil its duties in the sphere of financial control. The "Remarks", for example, are only dealt with long after their publication, so that the immediate political relevance is lost. Consequently, a public discussion of defects and errors "when the iron is still hot", often has greater controlling force than the parliamentary supervision of finance. Moreover, the supervision of parliament is largely a matter for the opposition, i.e. for the minority. But a minority whose control remains restricted to the inner pathways of parliament without finding a wider echo in public, largely remains without power and influence.

Hence, audit courts play an important role in terms of controlling public administrations, but the success or failure of their efforts to exercise effective financial control, i.e. only to detect mismanagement, waste or insufficient use of resource etc., but also to correct such failures and deficiences and improve future performance, is to a large extent dependent on supportive activities or adequate reactions of other, more or less institutionalized controlling actors such as parliaments, parties, the press and so on. This may be one reason why there is still – in spite of the reform of 1971 – a tendency in the political, scientific and public debate to consider public financial control a deficient and imperfect business that needs improvement.

However, criticism must address the parliamentary budget control rather than the organization and working methods of the audit courts, although there are some pragmatic proposals for reform which could improve the effectiveness of financial control by audit courts. These include, inter alia,

– periodical submitting of provisional reports on inadequate administrative perfor-

mance to parliaments and shortening of the time-lag between the publication of
the "comments" of the audit courts, and the final approval of government policy
or the decision-making concerning the new budget;
- the improvement of personnel in audit officies in order to achieve a better
  quality of auditing and counselling activities; or
- the improvement of the system of pre-audits with the aim to avoid conflicts that
  may emerge from the pre-audit offices' ambiguous formal position.

There is no necessity to re-organize the structure and functioning of the German
courts of audit completely. Rather, in view of the constitutional basis and limitia-
tions of the formal position of audit in the Federal Republic of Germany, there is a
need to reinforce parliamentary control, and to strengthen the connecting links or
intensify the interactions or cooperation between parliaments and audit courts in
order to improve the effectiveness of financial control. However, under changed
conditions, or in other countries one may prefer modified or alternative strategies
for the development of financial control. In fact, there are various trends and
options of audit control to be found in the modern democratic states as the
following part of this chapter will demonstrate in greater detail.

Part B. Audit Control – Trends and Options

Göran Arvidsson

In comparison with most other forms of control in the public sector audit is relatively well defined. According to Geist (1981: 3), who has reviewed audit practices in a number of countries, state audit "is or ought to be independent; it deals with problems at a high level of state administrations; it reviews from the outside and with objectivity the activities of the state administration and various public organs; it has – or ought to have – unlimited access to the accounts, files and personnel of all public organizations subject to its scrutiny. The aim of state audit can be defined as the collection of data on the activities of the organization it inspects and their comparison to norms in order to induce the correction of shortcomings and improve public administration."

34.7 Developments in Public Sector Audit

Within this general frame-work, the constitutional role, functions, scope and contents of government auditing vary from country to country as do the organization, personnel policies and auditing methods.

Despite these differences, however, it seems quite clear that the professional discussions among government auditors in most countries have changed in the same direction: while the problems of "doing the audits right" are still pertinent more and more emphasis is put on "doing the right audits". Sigg's discussion above is one example of this.

What, then, are "the right audits"?

The traditional functions of government audit are supervision of the *legality* of expenditures and the *regularity* of accounts and financial statements. "Compliance audit" and "financial audit" are commonly used terms.

In several countries traditional functions now also include assessments of *economy* and *efficiency* in government operations. This is sometimes called "value for money" audit.

In some countries the audit has been extended to encompass also program audit (or effectiveness audit). At the same time functions of internal control of accounting and disbursement systems have often been defined away from the area of auditing. (Review of internal control system is, however, clearly an audit function.)

The *traditional scope* of central government audit is usually restricted to payments connected with the operations of ministries, departments and central government agencies. Expenditures in the form of grants to local authorities, support to private or semi-private institutions (e.g. in the areas of education, culture, health and transportation) are traditionally not audited once they have been paid out from the government. In some countries, however, auditors at federal, state and local levels are now institutionalizing joint audit. Financial support in the forms of tax reductions and similar subsidies are clearly outside the scope of traditional auditing. In very few countries have these types of non-budgetary expenditures caught the auditors' interests. Other areas with hidden costs are regulatory functions and the "infra-structure" of the government administration.

There is certainly money in this, but what can and should auditors do? Must there be payments or accounts for auditors to consider a function or an area to be "auditable"? How should priorities be set in the audit offices? Is it enough to stick to the old functions?

Several supreme audit institutions (SAI) around the world have already answered "no" to this question. Certain tendencies can be observed in their activities:

(1) More emphasis on auditing for matters of economy and efficiency and, in some countries, effectiveness.
(2) Delegation of financial auditing from the SAI to local audit offices supervised by the SAI.
(3) Strengthening of the SAI's independent status.
(4) Widening of the scope of audits to grants, subsidies etc.
(5) More emphasis on the follow-up of previous audits.
(6) Widening of the SAI's functions from merely auditing to e.g. advice on financial and economic matters to parliament and/or government, responsibility for central accounting systems, training of government officials in financial and economic administration, aid to budget officials in the budget process etc.
(7) Recruitment of professionals also from other fields than accounting and law, e.g. business administration, economics, sociology, technology.
(8) Emphasis on training programs for the auditors and development of professional standards for government auditing.
(9) Deliberate actions to increase the relative status of government auditors.

There are similar tendencies in local government audit.

Clearly, there will be problems when audit goes into new areas:

– Can program audits, where the purpose is to evaluate program results, really be carried out without going into political decision making?
– How and when should the results of such audits be reported?
– Can auditors really go into advisory functions without losing their independence?
– Can the extended type of audits be carried out within the traditional audit institutions or are new organizational set-ups necessary?
– Is it possible to train financial auditors to these new tasks or it is necessary to change recruitment policies and salary levels in order to attract and keep staff with skills in qualified analytical work?
– Is it really advisable to decrease financial audit in times of fiscal crisis and move into new types of audit with rather uncertain effects on the public purse?

The design of public sector audit is evidently a question of strategic choice. A few factors which seem to be important in this context will be pointed out and discussed in the remainder of this chapter.

34.8 The Role of Audit

The role of an audit institution is a function of many variables. Its formal position, the tasks it is instructed to fulfill and its freedom in the choice of field of activity and audit methods, the financial management systems, its own competence, its "competitors" (other "controllers" executing alternative or complementary forms of control) and its learning record (successes and failures) seem to be the most important ones.

The formal status of the major state audit institution varies between different countries. In the Federal Republic of Germany, for example, The Federal Audit Court (Bundesrechnungshof) is formally an autonomous body independent of both Government and Parliament. In the United States The General Accounting Office (GAO) reports to the Congress. In Sweden there are both elected Parliamentary Auditors with a small staff of some twenty auditors/evaluators and a National Audit Bureau (Riksrevisionsverket) formally reporting to the Cabinet but in practice free to choose where and what to audit in central government administration (except the ministries which are relatively small policy-making staff units to the Cabinet).

The formal status of an audit institution has to do not only with to whom it reports. Most important is probably that the formal status implies – explicitly or implicity – what the audit institution has to do, what it ought to do and what it is allowed to do. The status affects the area of strategic choice. It seems reasonable to assume that the formal status is in practice closely related to the scope and emphasis of the audit. To give an example: It is probably not a coincidence that *"der Bundesrechnungshof"* has put great emphasis on compliance types of audits, that the GAO has a long record of evaluation types of audits and that *"Riksrevisionsverket"* has concentrated on management audits.

34.9 Audit Strategies

An audit institution considering widening its scope beyond the traditional areas as described above has several options. Condensing the option into a few strategic concepts facilitates the discussion. These concepts should be so broad as to encompass most "new" approaches and at the same time so specific that they highlight basic differences between different approaches.

One strategic concept which is close to the traditional function of audit is *accountability promotion*. With such a strategy the auditors would concentrate on describing and analyzing the congruence of objectives and actual performance. This means investigating how managers on different levels fulfill their tasks within the boundaries set by superior goals, existing regulations and their own budgets.

With an accountability perspective the type of budgets will have a decisive influence on the design of audits. With detailed line item budgets leaving little freedom to local managers in the choice and use of different resources it becomes logical to undertake compliance audits and irrelevant to audit with an effectiveness perspective. With program budgets the opposite approach becomes more appropriate. (This is probably one of the major explanations of the differences between the court-type relatively formalistic "continental" audit and the more performance oriented audit in e.g. Canada, Israel, Sweden and The United States.)

Even in more performance oriented "accountability audit" the auditors would, however, still have a control perspective (in the narrow sense of the word "control"). The working style would be mainly formal, inspector-like and the "back-bone" of the audits would be delegation rules, budgets, instructions governing the audited entity etc.

Like the traditional forms this type of audit could be classified as *corrective*. The underlying idea is to promote better management by scrutinizing how public managers run their activities and holding them accountable for both successes and good management – on one hand – and failures, neglections and other forms of mismanagement on the other.

Another strategy could be labelled *decision support*. The audits would be designed to yield "better information" to decision-makers. So, for example, could one function be to find and present other – and possibly more correct – information about the costs, effects and administration of public programs than the picture given by the responsible managers.

The perspective would not be "control" but rather "knowledge seeking" and "informing". The working style would be neutral, objective, "scientific". By finding out and informing about how things really are, the idea is that the audits should contribute to more informed and therefore better decision-making in government. If the results of such audits are communicated openly, they could in several respects come very close to qualified investigative journalism or empirical social science research. Especially if the auditors communicate primarily by exhaustive written reports, this strategy could be called a *report strategy*.

A third strategy is to participate more actively in the policy-making and decision-making processes. Following this strategy, *change promotion,* the auditors would work in close contact with politicians and/or public managers on adequate levels. Their main functions would be to ask questions (without necessarily reporting the answers openly), reason and suggest changes. The style would be informal, educational, supportive, non-threatening, perhaps – but not necessarily – confidential.

To influence by criticism, new knowledge or reasoning are three quite different approaches which an expansive audit institution may adopt. Obviously, they demand different skills of the auditors. Also, it is no easy task to convert a traditional audit office to e.g. a knowledge-seeking, "research" organization. Nor is it easy for auditors trained in accounting to become policy evaluators or discussion partners to senior officials.

34.10 Choosing Audit Strategies

Choosing a new strategy for an audit institution – or rather developing supplementary strategies – involves several considerations. Beside the ones already mentioned, the strategic problems of the public sector and the alternatives to auditing seem to be of major importance.

In many countries the size, role and effectiveness of the public sector is a matter of great concern. Critics ask for more and better control, increased responsiveness, more information, less bureaucracy, more flexibility, reduction of inefficient and ineffective programs, better management etc. One answer to such demands is the activation of the audit function. The audit institutions assume the role of "effectiveness agents" beside their traditional functions. In this situation one of their major cncerns will be: How can audits most effectively contribute to better performance in different public systems? A simple model may help to illustrate how the choice of audit approach may be made with regard to the perceived "problem" in the system to be audited.

Suppose that the audit office is considering how to contribute to the improvement of a system like, for example, child care, housing support or traffic safety. The meaning of "improvement" must be defined, e.g. reducing costs with given outputs, eliminating sub-optimization by structural change, increasing flexibility and adaptability or adjusting priorities to changed demands. Since actors others than the audit office decide about and manage the "system" their behavior and ways of influencing the system must be considered. Key factors seem to be *freedom of action* (discretion), *knowledge* and *motive powers*. The existence and quality of each of these factors are probably crucial to the extent to which desired changes will actually be realized.

In figure 1 the factors are further exemplified and brought together in a simple change model. A brief discussion may show how such a model can be used for analyzing the prospects of different audit strategies.

If those responsible for a certain system – including its managers – are energetic and competent to act while their problem awareness is considered to be inadequate, then a knowledge seeking audit may yield considerable effects. A report strategy aiming at supplying decision-makers with information relevant to their

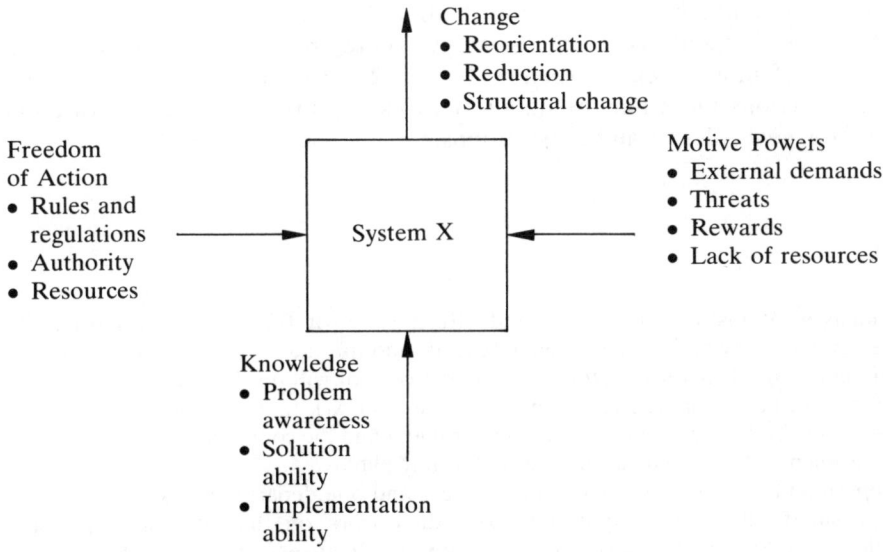

Fig. 1: A Change Model

decisions would consequently seem appropriate. If, on the other hand, the ability to solve existing problems is lacking, then the best revenue of the audit may be gained if it is mainly aimed at suggesting action programs.

In another system there may exist knowledge and motive powers, while the freedom of action is limited due to tight regulations. In such a case the most effective audit could be one aimed at analyzing and affecting the rules surrounding the system. If, on the other hand, change is difficult to bring about due to lack of "movable" resources for e.g. change projects, then an audit of budgetary rules and procedures might be the most appropriate.

In a third system the decision-makers may, for some reason, be unwilling to decide on modifications even though there are many good reasons for changes. In this case it would seem appropriate for the auditors to estimate their prosepcts of influencing the motive powers. A report strategy intended to supply "more valid information" would hardly be very effective. Instead, a persuasive strategy might be worth considering.

In conclusion, there seems to be no "right" type of audit. The impact of different kinds of audits depends on factors like the ones just treated. This means that an audit institution widening its scope outside the traditional areas has to make both strategic and tactical choices. The strategic choices include decisions on what type of audits to include in the repertoire and to build and staff a suitable organization. The tactical choices concern what approach to use in each situation. To a large extent it seems as if the question of doing "the right audits" boils down to finding out

– where and what the problems are which can be influenced by audit
– the probability of success, in these cases, of different audit approaches
– the alternatives to audit.

Top officials in audit institutions tend to consider most social problems to be at least in principle auditable, i.e. possible to affect by audit. Even if this is true, it may not be true that audit is the best strategy. There are many alternatives to the extended type of audits as can be seen in chapters 29–36 of this section. For certain traditional functions there may be no alternatives. This is sometimes forgotten in the search for new roles of audit institutions.

Notes

1   Our analysis of tasks, organization and effectiveness of financial control primarily addresses the activities of these audit courts and pre-audit offices. Although the functioning and effects of parliamentary budget control will not be dealt with in detail (see the contribution of Hellstern (Ch. 33) in this context), there will be a discussion of the relationships between parliament or government and the courts of audits as well as of some problems of the political role the latter may play.
2   In Department VII there are five auditing areas and one departmental section.
3   The pre-audit offices are required to base their work on the same standards and techniques as the audit courts. The problems which arise from their activities are, consequently, the same as those of the audit courts.

References

Aderhold, D. (1973): *Kybernetische Regierungstechnik in der Demokratie*. München–Wien: Olzog.

Bohne, E., and H. König (1976): "Probleme der politischen Erfolgskontrolle". *Die Verwaltung* 9/1: 19–38.

Brümmerhoff, D., and H. Wolff (1974): "Aufgabe und Möglichkeit einer Erfolgskontrolle der staatlichen Aktivität." *Zeitschrift für die gesamte Staatswissenschaft* 130/3: 477–493.

Damkowski, W. (1977): "Funktion und Problematik der verwaltungsinternen Haushaltskontrolle und Möglichkeiten ihrer Verbesserung." *Die öffentliche Verwaltung* 30/3: 81–85.

Derlien, H.-U. (1976): *Die Erfolgskontrolle staatlicher Planung*. Baden-Baden: Nomos.

Derlien, H.-U. (1978): "Organisatorische Aspekte der Programmevaluation", *Verwaltung und Fortbildung* 6/2: 51–61.

Diekmann, R. (1980): "Schwierigkeiten mit der Erfolgskontrolle in der öffentlichen Verwaltung." *Die öffentliche Verwaltung* 33/20: 737–744.

Geist, B. (1981): "State Audit: An Introduction." In Geist, B. (ed.), *State Audit – Developments in Public Accountability*, 3–22. Hongkong: MacMillan.

Greifeld, A. (1981): *Der Rechnungshof als Wirtschaftlichkeitsprüfer*. München: Ch. Beck.

Harnischfeger, H. (1969): *Planung in der sozialstaatlichen Demokratie*. Neuwied–Berlin: Luchterhand.

Karehnke, H. (1969/1970): "Die Bedeutung der Personalarbeit für die Arbei der Rechnungshöfe." *Der öffentliche Haushalt* 10: 78–82.

König, H. (1977): *Kritische Analyse des Managements finanzieller, personeller und materieller Resourcen in der öffentlichen Verwaltung*. Verwaltungswissenschaftliche Informationen, Sonderheft 3. Bonn: Dt. Sekt. der Internat. Inst. f. Verwaltungswiss.

Kommission für den wirtschaftlichen und sozialen Wandel (ed.) (1977): *Wirtschaftlicher und sozialer Wandel in der Bundesrepublik Deutschland*. Gutachten der Kommission. Göttingen: Schwartz.

Reinermann, H. (1974): *Wirtschaftlichkeitsanalysen*. Handbuch der Verwaltung (Vol. 4.6). Köln: Heymann.

Rürup, B. (1971): *Die Programmfunktion des Haushaltsplans*. Berlin: Duncker & Humblot.

Rürup, B., and H. Seidler (1981): "Von der fiskalischen Haushaltskontrolle zur politischen Erfolgskontrolle." *Die Verwaltung* 14/4: 501–519.

Schäfer, H. (1976): "Finanzkontrolle und parlamentarische Demokratie." *Bulletin der Bundesregierung* 128: 1225–1233.

Sigg, W. (1983): *Die Stellung der Rechnungshöfe im politischen System der Bundesrepublik Deutschland, zugleich ein Beitrag zur Finanzkontrolle der Universität*. Berlin: Duncker & Humblot.

Steinberg, R. (1976): "Evaluation als neue Form der Kontrolle final programmierten Verwaltungshandelns." *Der Staat* 15/2: 185–210.

Wittrock, K. (1978): "Unsere Kritik wird ernst genommen." *Das Parlament* 46: 8. (v. 18. 11. 1978).

35. Public Administration and Publics: Control of Bureaucratic Performance by Affected Citizens

Wolfgang Wirth

Abstract

Does the perspective of publics get lost in public administration or can citizens control and influence bureaucratic peformance? The paper analyzes the various roles that citizens who are affected by bureaucratic activities may play in politico – administrative performance processes as well as the opportunities they have of ensuring administrative accountability and controlling the quality of services. Particular chances and limitations of control by publics are discussed with regard to three different, but interrelated levels of analysis: the constitutional level, the policy level and the street level of administrative reality. Formally institutionalized control instruments and feedback channels which are in principle available and accessible to all members of the citizenry *in order to indirectly influence public administration in general are considered as well as opportunities for political participation of specific, more or less organized* target groups *of administrative programs, and, especially, the more informal devices for direct control exercized by individual* clients *in bureaucratic encounters. However, it is shown that the utilization and succes of all these instruments and devices for control is highly selective and confined within relatively narrow limits of institutional, organizational, individual and situational factors.*

35.1 Introduction

How can *public* administration be controlled by *publics?* How can citizens who are affected by bureaucratic decision-making and activities control administrative agencies? The issue of accountability and responsiveness necessarily calls for the *inclusion of the citizens' perspective* in evaluating and controlling bureaucratic performance in democratic societies. In this context, control by publics has to be discussed primarily in terms of, first, *avoidance or correction of inadequacies, mistakes or malpractice in the use of bureaucratic power or discretion;* and second, *attainment or maintenance of successful performance with regard to citizens' needs, demands and problems.*

This raises the question of what opportunities and possibilities citizens have to supervise and check administrative processes of decision-making and performance for legal compliance and accuracy, to evaluate given outputs in terms of relevance, appropriateness, effectiveness and impact on the solution of problems and satisfaction of needs, and on this basis, to participate in influencing or shaping administrative performance in terms of initiating, maintaining, correcting or improving specific activities and resulting outputs[1].

However, citizens are usually considered to be the most powerless and passive players in this game. This corresponds to a dominance of a *bureaucratic, provider – based perspective* in the theory and practice of control in public administration: obviously, there is a bias toward those forms of control which are exercised by bureaucratic or professional experts. Citizens often seem to be objects of bureaucratic rules and regulations rather than active controllers of administrative actions. In fact, this view has all too often proved to be well-founded, but it is nevertheless too general. It tends to simplify the range and complexity of the tasks public administration is expected to fulfill, the various ways in which citizens may be affected by, and the heterogeneity of factual roles they may play in bureaucratic performance processes.

Of course, administrative agencies to a large extent fulfill explicit regulatory and control functions over various aspects of public and private life, but many of them also, or primarily, provide support and services to citizens. Especially in the seventies, there has been an enormous expansion of public service delivery. Today, there are few areas of everyday life that are not touched by administrative activities; we all are, in one way or another, affected by or sometimes actually dependent on bureaucratic performance (see Katz el al. 1977: 5ff.), but not necessarily all to the same extent or with the same consequences. Citizens may be affected *directly* by the activities of service or control agencies or *indirectly*, as agencies regulate economic, ecological or social policies that affect the conditions of life[2]. Moreover, citizens are not necessarily "outsiders" in bureaucratic performance processes. They may be involved as clients in concrete bureaucratic encounters or participate as members of more or less organized target or interest groups in administrative decision-making processes. Finally, appropriate, successful or legitimate bureaucratic performance is dependent on various inputs or reactions of citizens, e.g. on adequate information about (social) problems and needs, consensus on goals, acceptance of rules or utilization of services. In many areas, the quality and impact of service delivery is to a high degree dependent on active support or cooperation of those "public reference groups" to which performance is primarily addressed.

Public administration is – according to the analytical level of aggregation and on the nature, generality and "public reach" of performance – confronted with various "publics" being of a distinct nature, too, and representing various (control) interests. This creates problems for the appropriate discussion and practical inclusion of control by publics in terms of affected citizens. Just as the type and the method of administrative performance influences the nature of impact and the need for control, so the corresponding relationships between public administration and citizen, the latter's role, formal involvement and functional importance influences the availability, accessibility, applicability and appropriateness of specific instruments and devices for control. These factors need to be examined with reference to differently structured and aggregated, but nevertheless interdependent operational contexts of administrative performance. Hence, the issue of control by publics has to be specified and discussed by means of a multilevel analysis with regard to the conceptualization of bureaucracy and performance arrangements, nature of the goods or services to be produced and affected publics. Taking this into account, we will analyze the various particular opportunities for and devices of control citizens may use

- *as members of the citizenry* with regard to accountability and responsiveness of public administration in providing public goods in general (constitutional level),
- *as members of target groups* for specific programs in collective decision-making and relevant administrative planning processes (policy level), and finally,
- *as members of particular agencies' clientele* with regard to the operational production and delivery of concrete goods and services in bureaucratic encounters (street level of administrative reality).

These three levels of analysis point, inter alia, to different dimensions and stages of politico-administrative performance processes that each have more or less universal (e.g. in the case of pure public goods) or selective (in the case of specific programs and single activities) impacts on publics[3]. Nevertheless, they are of course interrelated. Clients are usually at the same time members of target groups and also of the citizenry (not necessarily vice-versa). Service production in bureaucratic encounters is part and a consequence of existing political programs which are themselves part of efforts to provide or achieve more general public goods like public security or welfare. It will be shown that various *levels of "affectedness"* correspond to various *roles* citizens may play in public administration and to the various opportunities they may have to control and influence bureaucratic performance more or less directly – but also that control exercised at one level of administrative reality is to a variable extent influential on the procedures and results of performance at other levels. However, in this context, we are primarily interested in problems and potential consequences of control at the street level which in most cases is only insufficiently taken into consideration. Coordination and control at the constitutional and at the policy level of analysis have already been discussed in detail in the preceding sections. But to elaborate the importance of the street level for the theory and practice of public administration appropriately, it is nevertheless necessary to illustrate first, comparatively briefly, the chances and limits of utilization and success of some important formal and institutionalized control instruments available to the citizens through the constitution as well as of the effects of more or less informal efforts of interest groups to participate at the policy level.

35.2 Control by the Citizenry

It is the essential principle of democracy that decisions and actions of the administrative state must be rendered accountable to its sovereign, the people. Administrative accountability to the citizenry claims that bureaucratic performance is shaped in accordance with the public interest and is based upon such standards as justice, liberty and general welfare. The *public at large* becomes a legitimate source of authority to which the exercise of bureaucratic power should be responsive. But the constitutional issue of accountability to the citizenry seems to be most starkly posed when misguided or even illegal bureaucratic action has a direct and adverse impact on *individual citizens,* as Rosenbloom (1979: 70) argues. Furthermore, accountability refers also to the issue of assuring responsiveness in supplying public goods and services in relation to consumer needs, preferences and well-being. This points to the importance of individual satisfaction as a legitimate criterion of evaluation (see Katz et al. 1977: 190f.) – especially with regard to social services which are usually delivered with the explicit aim of improving the living conditions of individuals or social groups. Thus, public interest *and* individual welfare are cited as operational guides for the provision of these services (see Kaufmann 1982: 63ff.). However, ensuring responsiveness to specific needs and accountability to the citizenry may pose major problems for public agencies.

Public interest and individual interests do not necessarily coincide and citizens may evaluate performance differently and may also have different preferences and expectations which are not automatically recognized in the course of administrative decision-making processes. On the one hand, lack of relevant information impedes the necessary task of planning and implementing policy programs, involving the risk of losing the perspective of individual citizens, social groups or the general public (see Kaufmann et al 1982: 9ff.). On the other hand, where information is sufficient, goal conflicts may call for normative political decisions which may hurt particular interests for the sake of some more general interests. What are then the constitutional remedies that enable citizens as individuals to have effective re-course against those considered to be responsible in order to initiate corrections or improvements?

Not all dimensions of administrative performance are similarly open to direct public control and influence, although they may affect citizens directly and seriously. The more the elements of a general collective significance dominate, the less possible the succesful exercise of informal, individual control becomes. In this context, attention needs to be directed to the indirect and formally *institutionalized feedback channels* and to the *representative control institutions* established to operate on behalf of the citizenry (see Marmor and Morone 1980: 132ff.), though their appropriate functioning frequently presupposes formal inputs from individual citizens, too.

The creation of legal sources of accountability by the separation of power and the institutionalization of periodical elections are fundamental to the idea of representative democracies. Both are considered necessary for the adjustment of conflicting interests, for citizens to participate in public decisions and for the binding of the exercise of state prerogatives to the interests of the citizenry. This points to the establishment of mechanisms and criteria of performance to ensure that each branch of government behaves in accordance with accepted principles. Bureaucracy is regarded as being accountable primarily to elected representatives and to the courts which apply the rule-of-law doctrines.

Voting, the heart of democratic decision-making processes, is seen as a mecha-nism for revealing citizens' needs and preferences and influencing and sanctioning political performance (see Herzberg and Ostrom: Ch. 20). Elections are considered to be necessary in order to obtain and preserve desired standards of behavior on the part of elected officials. However, actual political deliberations and especially the implications of bureaucratization and centralization (see Grunow: Ch. 2, Sharpe: Ch. 8), indicate some objections to these assumptions. Periodical elections for parliamentary representatives, especially on highly centralized levels are of limited value in terms of issue voting in the absence of referenda. Indeed, we find, at least in Germany, a relatively high rate of participation in federal, state and also local parliamentary elections, but because of the high level of formalization and the inherent time-lags we cannot consider formal voting as an appropriate means of articulating either individual preferences or satisfaction and dissatisfaction with regard to *specific* programs. But even if that were the case, the control function of voting has limited bearing upon bureaucratic performance, since public bureaucracies – due to the growing scope and complexity of tasks to be fulfilled by government and administration – have

"emerged as major power centers of their own, exercising authority independently of the elected branches and being relatively uncontrolled by them. Consequently, in the modern administrative state, holding the elected accountable does not guarantee that government as a whole will be accountable" (Rosenbloom 1979: 69).

The traditional, elected representative bodies (of control) are dependent on the competences and capacities of the non-elected public administrators to recognize, judge and process external problems. In many cases, these are the officials who actually decide which problems need what government intervention and which should be left to their own devices. We find such a partial *reversion of control* not only with regard to government, but also with regard to parliament since we are faced with a growing "legislative" activity of bureaucracy in enacting administrative rules and regulations (see Treutner 1982: 147ff.).

However, even in such cases, processes of parliamentary control with regard to specific aspects of administrative performance may be (re-)activated by affected citizens who try to assert their concerns toward bureaucracy; for example if they present petitions to parliaments and ombudsmen, or if they address complaints or requests to their member of parliament. But, of course, the effectiveness of these additional instruments for a more "problem-centered", but nevertheless indirect public control is – apart from inherent shortcomings[4] – also affected by the limits of parliamentary control, which are described by Hellstern (see Ch. 33) in more detail.

Especially in areas where access to sufficient *information* that is under the control of public bureaucrats cannot be guaranteed, all the formally institutionalized instruments which should enable citizens or their representatives to evaluate and control bureaucratic performance may fail to a considerable degree. We must note the tendency of bureaucracies to pursue a tactic of *control prevention* and *resistance* by making relevant information inaccessible to the outside evaluator. Although democratic constitutions prescribe administrative accountablility to the citizenry, and although citizens usually possess legal remedies, e.g. suit and grievance, in case of malpractices or damages, there is not necessarily a judicially enforcable right to be supplied with information from public administrations about bureaucratic files or activities. This may, of course, vary for different countries and is also dependent upon the type of problem involved and on the type of jurisdiction. The U.S. Right to Information legislation, for example, gives far greater access to information than the German administrative law ("Verwaltungsrecht") does (see Scherer 1978). However, Rosenbloom (1979: 67ff.) shows that Supreme Court decisions actually provide an ample constitutional basis for bureaucratic secrecy from which the citizen has little recourse. The citizen's "right to know" often depends on the administration's willingness to supply information or on the possibility of it being accidentally or even illicitly obtained and perhaps disseminated by the press or other mass media, which of course fulfill a central public control function. Given the bureaucratic penchant for secrecy, this factually limits the opportunity of citizens to mount legal challenges to the use of bureaucratic discretion and authority.

However, this may be considered less important, if citizens could base a suit or grievance on provable personal experience of insufficiencies or illegal performance in bureaucratic encounters. But to grant rights to citizens which entitle them to utilize legal remedies or aid in this context does not guarantee the assertion of these rights. Legal jargon for example proves to be a serious barrier in this regard. The successful utilization of judicial remedies conceded to citizens to hold public administrations accountable requires specific knowledge of the relevant legal claims or rules and their applicability in the single case as well as the general *formal competences* that are necessary to activate courts. Since court dockets are often overloaded and proceedings frequently costly and protracted, time and money are also very important necessary *resources*. Such competences and resources are not equally distributed in society, and there is much evidence that (consequently) especially the poor and less educated (also) lack the necessary motivation to take legal steps. Bruinsma (1980: 359), for example, describes this phenomenon as follows: "In the eyes of the poor the law and its officials cause more problems than they solve, and therefore it is better to stay as far away as possible."

But Bruinsma also shows that there are in general only a few conflict situations where the assertion of rights is called for, and that most people, having made a simple, individual cost – benefit analysis, try to settle their special problems with public organizations outside the lawyers' offices and court rooms. There are many serious public, social or individual problems that cannot be solved and often not even formulated adequately in the language of law. Most judicial remedies are post hoc by definition and necessarily bound to the formal criterion of legality and legal compliance, usually neglecting criteria of responsiveness and success of performance. This means that courts, if activated by citizens, are mainly concerned with decisions on specific cases of compensation or of restoring persons or things to a former condition. Ex ante remedies or judicial rulings that refer to the shaping of future administrative performance may – like parliamentary standard-setting – at best provide (procedural) rules about decision rules and decisions about desired behavior and equitable (re-)action sets of bureaucratic actors and affected citizens (see Kiser and Ostrom 1982: 207 ff.)

However, just as the establishing of entitlements does not guarantee their assertion, the formulation of judicial decisions or legislative standards does not guarantee their application, especially if courts and legislative bodies cannot or can only partly control the subsequent implementation and consideration of their decisions themselves. Specific rules may get lost in the abundance of existing and sometimes conflicting regulations; more general regulations are often vague and leave much room for further bureaucratic discretion and interpretation. Hence, the constitutionally granted formal feedback mechanisms and the institutionalized indirect control channels that may be activated by all citizens of a (national) state or community are, of course, necessary for the fundamental issue of ensuring legitimate politico-administrative decision-making and standard-setting (at least in terms of a basic *contextual guidance* of bureaucratic performance at various levels), for the legal binding of "the" public administration's activities and, thus, for governmental accountability to "the" citizenry in general. But there is an important need for some additional, sustaining, decision-enforcing, rule-interpreting and performance-shaping controls within and around public bureaucracy in order to ensure the expedient and successfull fulfillment of specific public tasks more directly.

The production of public goods in modern welfare states is typically based on the assumption of a public interest that demands the assignment of legal responsibility to governmental actors for the general well-being of all (individual) members of a society. However, the realization of such a normative, abstract and universal goal requires the implementation of many specific political programs and administrative interventions which are usually fragmented, more or less well coordinated and affect different (groups of) people in different ways and degress of intensity. Such programs are often – as in social policy – explicitly addressed to *specific target groups*, i. e. to those members of society who are considered to have personal or to cause social problems and who are therefore defined as the intended "recipients" of specific administrative performance.

Since the appropriateness and effectiveness of selective programs is also at least partly dependent on specific problem-related inputs or policy-related reactions of those affected[5], and since taking legal proceedings or voting (and the working of the respective representative control institutions) are not necessarily sufficient, but frequently too general or formal, too inflexible or incomplete for ensuring success and responsiveness of particular public policies with regard to the needs and problems of their target groups, the question is: Which other, more informal, but also more direct opportunities and instruments do the members of these groups have – in *addition* to those that are linked to their formal belonging to the citizenry – for controlling and enhancing the quality of administrative performance at the policy level.

35.3 Control by Target Groups

During the last decade, few issues in public administration have generated more practical and theoretical interest than *direct participation* by affected citizens which has frequently and intensively been claimed to be the key to the solution of the problem of accountability and control. Despite some differences in the use of the term, participation in this context has to be considered as an instrument for citizens to influence specific administrative *decision-making processes* concerning the (future) provision or production of concrete goods and services, i.e. to influence directly *processes of planning, implementation, regulation and allocation on the policy level*[6].

With regard to the differentiation of public administration, judiciary and legislative at the constitutional level of analysis, we can consider "the" public bureaucracy in general as being in a position to shape its performance to a relatively large extent in accordance with its administrative convenience. In principle, this also holds for the policy level, but there is some variety in terms of the scope single administrative units have for autonomous action. We have to bear in mind that public administration is not a monolithic actor, having a defined set of goals and interests and pursuing them in isolation from "outside" actors (see Wirth: Ch. 29). Rather, we have to consider public administration as consisting of a complex network of *organized actors,* charged to fulfill different tasks, more or less dependent on "public inputs" and, hence, more or less open to citizen participation. This implies that participation – according to different degrees of centralization which correspond to different "distances" to individual needs and problems – may take place at the federal level, the state level, the local level and also in single agencies[7], and requires at each level an adequate degree of organization of interests.

Such structural and local differences explain the "practical" variations in the use of the term and also the variety of different models of participation under discussion. Inter alia, participation has been connected with issues like "decentralization", "citizen action", "community control", "community action", "community development", "neighborhood organization", "consumer feedback systems", and many others[8]. The multiplicity of different models of participation points again to the fact that this kind of public control must always be seen as a procedure which involves groups of actors with different goals and interests.

However, proposals for more participation are always based on the criticism of internal administrative decision-making behind closed doors. This is seen to result in ineffective, unresponsive and unsatisfactory administrative performance. Likewise, one can describe the essential advantages that proponents consider participation to have briefly as follows: *In general:* improvement of the democratization of society; realization of the ethical value of democratic self-determination; improvement of the legitimacy of state or administrative action. *With regard to citizens:* better representation of and responsiveness to citizens' needs, preferences and problems; improvement of information transfer to citizens. *With regard to administrations:* avoidance of conflicts caused by unsatisfactory performance which could delay or impede the fulfillment of administrative tasks, generation of capability and motivation of affected citizens to behave in accordance with fixed goals and norms.

It is obvious that forms of organized "citizen action" like public protest, citizen initiatives or "new" interest groups, etc., which exercise, more or less successfully, informal political pressure upon governments and administrations have grown enormously during the last decade. The demand for participation has gained support in theory and administrative practice and even – with regard to specific policy areas – in laws or programs: in the United States, for example, Title XX of the Social Security Act, the Older Americans Act, the Rehabilitation Act, the Housing and Community Development Act, and so on. Moreover, the incorporation of formal "outsiders" as well-accepted partners in administrative decision-making processes has proved to be practicable and also unavoidable in many cases as we can learn from the example of the more traditional interest groups, associations and lobbies, representing organized private or social interests (see Franz et al.: Ch. 26). Nevertheless, public administrations often try successfully to resist progress towards direct *"citizen involvement"* – again by means of selective or restrictive information transfer and control. Opposition to citizen participation is usually supported by the formal argument of participation's incompatibility with the principles of representative democracy and by pointing to the potentially negative aspects of the proponents' arguments, especially in terms of economic criteria: citizens are considered to lack the appropriate special knowledge and, hence, to influence decision-making processes negatively instead of improving them; participation is feared to be abused by unqualified, but militant groups, to create avoidable conflicts and to generate only a small increase in effectiveness in terms of achieving a program's substantial objectives or politically set goals, but a large decrease in purely economic efficiency.

It is evident that economic criteria, political, legal or judicial criteria and criteria of citizens' satisfaction may compete or conflict (see Grunow: Ch. 31). Given this fact and, moreover, taking the various proposed forms of participation into account, it seems fairly impossible to make an unequivocal judgment of participation success in general or to propose one model as the best for solving all the problems under discussion. History shows that many models collapsed pretty soon and that others have been institutionalized and operated with good results in special policy arenas for longer periods of time (see Janowitz 1978). But this does not mean that the latter would be similarly succesful in all politico-administrative arenas.

Hence, citizen participation has important advantages, but may also create problems. Therefore, it has to be considered not as a substitute for, but only as an additional, supplementary instrument to the constitutional mechanisms of preference articulation and control, aiming at compensation of their insufficient sharpness and flexibility, but finding its limit where they become deteriorated instead of supported. Appropriate implementation of citizen participation in public administration requires a detailed consideration of the particular case in terms of the relevant nature of goods and services to be produced. Analyses of what can and cannot be accomplished by participation in detail require proper specification of the kind of problems to be solved by the specific administrative performance in order to be sufficiently informative. However, although this is beyond the scope of this chapter, we must note, on a more general level, that the structure and tasks of public organizations are important determinants for success and failure of participation (for more details, see Kweit and Kweit 1981). For example, control agencies are naturally much more resistant to participation of affected citizens than service agencies: the more coercive or legalistic bureaucracies are, the less likely direct citizen participation becomes (see Giordano 1977: 35).

However, looking principally at citizens' needs and problems, especially with regard to the target groups for social services, participation must be considered as a *necessary condition* for improving the responsiveness and impact of administrative planning and decision-making (see footnote 5). But besides the difficulties of realization caused by bureaucratic resistance, there are some basic problems common to most of the models of participation, pointing to the fact that even participation cannot be regarded as a *sufficient condition* for the responsive (street-level) production or delivery of concrete goods and services within given policies or programs.

Active participation and its success is again highly selective and closely connec-ted to the availability of resources like power and information or knowledge (see

Etzioni 1975). Since decision-making processes concerning the shaping of political programs in the public sector have increasingly become a matter of organized actors in terms of *collective or interorganizational bargaining*, there are only a few opportunities for successfull direct participation available to *individual* citizens. The entry qualifications for playing a part in these bargaining processes have grown so high that usually only concentrated interests are likely to meet them (see Marmor and Morone 1980: 161). However, opportunities increase with decreasing sizes of administrative systems and diminishing distances between the place of decision and citizens' concrete problems. This explains why most of the citizen involvement models refer to the local level. But also in this area – and not only at the state level – we have to note that collective forms of participation have greater prospects of succeeding than individual ones (see Petterson 1978: 142). This fact points to another aspect of participation selectivity which could be called the "white-collar bias". Of all citizens or members of target groups affected by administrative decisions those with relatively high social status and level of formal qualification are over-represented in terms of organized participation. Members of lower classes and especially of marginal groups appear comparatively seldom. The well-known fact that "the poor say less"[9] is linked to these groups' lesser ability and readiness to define and articulate their needs and problems collectively in facing public administrations, to organize their interests actively and address them to the formally appropriate authority or agency. Thus, lacking the requisite *organizational competences* and resources, these "... groups cannot successfully compete in the battle for social benefits" (Øyen 1980: 46). Many organized interest groups are fighting this battle. The intended recipients of bureaucratic welfare services are usually the weakest party in this context. The preferences of stronger parties which dispose of necessary support and power are likely to be emphasized over others. The interests of non-participants are likely to be ignored.

Blaming the insufficient inclusion of these groups as being one of the central causes leading to injustice in the distribution of goods and services and to unresponsiveness or failure of administrative performance resulted in the social movements of the sixties – especially in the United States – which aimed at obtaining "maximum feasible participation" by political program target groups in planning processes. "Community action" and "advocacy planning" have been the issues closely connected to the American "War on Poverty" and especially to the Economic Opportunity Act of 1964 which has been the government's official attempt to make welfare efforts accountable to the poor, to encourage and to help them to participate actively with the aim of improving administrative decision-making processes and their outputs. But the result were disappointing[10]. Gates (1980: 78f.) describes the actual situation as follows:

"The reality, as the welfare amendments, the Economic Opportunity Act, and Title XX amply demonstrate, is indeed that participation is an integral part of the processes surrounding both policy making and implementation. But even if provided with a forum and substantial resources, it is not the ordinary folk, participating in structured "participatory processes", who will influence the key decisions. These decisions have already been influenced and made by "blue ribbon" committees of experts, and interest group spokesmen in the upper echelons of the federal implementing organizations, in the budgetary recommendations submitted by the President, the Governors and the mayors; and by the congressmen, legislators and council members who must authorize public expenditures".

This again points to the problem that rights granted will not necessarily be asserted. But we have to argue in addition that even in cases of realized citizen participation at the policy level, responsiveness and impact of the actions that flow from these decisions at the operational level will not necessarily be improved. The existence of multiple constituencies and interest groups with differential interests and powers, all exercising more or less influence over a limited range of decisions at different levels of policy making, with varying concreteness and specific time limits may even threaten the integrity of resulting programs (see Gates 1980: 61 ff.).

Indeed, money is allocated – but often without clear definition of purpose; rules are formulated and laws are enacted – but often with vague contents and in unprocessable multiplicity; and programs or plans are implemented – but, especially in social policy, seldom stated clearly. The results of collective bargaining processes are often characterized by complexity, instability, uncertainty and ambiguity and still leave much room for administrative discretion. But the nature and scope of administrative actors' discretion varies according to their position in the network of organized actors. Assuming, for reasons of simplicity, an administrative system that is "only" hierarchically structured across several functional and structural levels, one can conclude that each bureaucratic unit is, on the one hand, dependent on the outputs (money, decisions, regulations, etc.) of the next higher or functionally preceding unit, but retains, on the other hand, a more or less wide margin for action. *The scope of discretion that operative units have in relation to directive units, administrative units on the state level in relation to federal decisions and regulations, local units in relation to state units and single field agencies in relation to their community administration reduces in absolute terms at each lower level of analysis and performance, but – looking upon horizontal lines and including here also the external constituencies and target groups of the relevant domain – remains relatively constant with regard to the corresponding, associated or affected bureaucratic or non-bureaucratic actors operating or interacting at the same level.*

Hence, administrative actors are at least partly in a position to define their specific domains and to structure their activities themselves. Performance, then, is to a large extent directed primarily to organizational self-interests and not necessarily to the needs and problems of target groups or clients. Maximization of resources, maintenance and enlargement of autonomy and domain have priority (see Greenley and Kirk 1973). Responsiveness may then be defined in terms of a specific administrative "operating ideology" (cf. Sharpe: Ch. 8), but at the risk that such provider-dominated performance will no longer be accountable to the intended clientele. But if participation at the policy level cannot be regarded as a guaranteed solution to this problem either, what other opportunities do citizens, especially after they have become individual clients of administrative agencies, have to control bureaucrats' performance?

35.4 Control by Clients

Administrative discretion should not always be regarded as a *regrettable result* of imperfectly coordinated processes of planning and decision-making. It points, in addition, to another, very important aspect: discretion, defined as the relative autonomy of (administrative) actors to make a choice among possible courses of action or inaction, is also an *inescapable condition* for the successful handling and solving of many tasks which are too complex to be adequately directed and controlled "from the top" by use of the traditional instruments of *law, hierarchy* and *money* or, to put it more generally, by centralized guidance, control and performance evaluation (see Luhmann 1981: 143). Gotthold (1983: 258ff.) argues that every administrative agency charged with tasks of not unequivocally programmable interventions into its public environment is forced to procure or obtain necessary inputs like relevant information, knowledge and consensus by its own means and devices in interaction with other relevant actors, especially target groups and clients in order to be capable of fulfilling its tasks successfully. The actual definitions and formulations of modalities, nature and goals of *specific* administrative activities are frequently fixed during these interaction processes by using the media of *cooperation* and *contract*. This has often proved to be the case on the policy level where detailed program goals are often designated only in the course of implementation processes (see Mayntz 1980). But it also turns out to be true with regard to the decentralized, operational level of administrative action carried out during everyday contacts or encounters between representatives of public administrations and individual citizens (see Grunow 1978, Katz et al. 1977). Many public policies are only concretely "produced" at this "*street-level*" of bureaucratic performance, as Lipsky calls it.

"I argue that the decisions of street-level bureaucrats, the routines they establish, and the devices they invent to cope with uncertainties and work pressures, effectively *become* the public policy they carry out. I argue that public policy is not best understood as made in legislatures or top-floor suites of high-ranking administrators because in important ways it is actually made in the crowded offices of daily encounters of street-level workers. I point out that policy conflict is not only expressed as the contention of interest groups, but is also located in the struggles between individual workers and citizens who challenge or submit to client-processing" (Lipsky 1980: XII).

Here, *citizens necessarily participate personally in processes of administrative performance.* Bringing their needs and problems, as applicants, to the attention of an agency or being, as clients, already involved in performance processes which they had voluntarily demanded or which had been initiated by the agency, they directly experience public policy. In the course of these encounters problems and needs are articulated or defined, objectives are fixed, procedures and instruments to realize given goals are chosen and applied, and hence, output, result and individual satisfaction, but especially the program's real utility for its recipients are determined. This also implies that inputs are needed from both bureaucrats (or professional experts) *and* citizens in order to initiate or maintain performance, to handle and solve specific problems successfully, to satisfy individual needs and so on. This is true – although with some variability in the nature of inputs required – for agencies performing regulatory and control functions by directly placing constraints on citizens, for correctional agencies wanting to change non-conformity of citizens' behavior, for public relief agencies offering payments in cash and in kind on the basis of application or means-testing procedures, and, finally, for personal social services offering individualized, need-oriented help to citizens. Production and delivery of all such goods and services always require a more or less pronounced cooperative relationship. Moreover, the quality and impact of service delivery in terms of satisfied needs and solved problems is to a large extent dependent on service providers' and users' ability and motivation for cooperation.

This argument has its origin in various approaches concerning the development of the service economy or the service society and has recently been taken up under the key word of *"coproduction of services by clients"* in the German discussion on social policy[11]. Pointing to the fact that personal social services, usually of an immaterial nature like education or counseling, are produced and consumed *simultaneously* ("uno-actu-principle"), Badura and Gross (1976: 68ff.) have shown that these services are *client-intensive,* because they require direct communicative and interactive participation of clients in terms of definition and articulation of needs and problems, perception and processing of information obtained in performance processes and its transformation into activities suitable for treatment in order to achieve the goals of service delivery. They conclude that improvement of service delivery always means improvement of cooperation between formal "producer" and client. But clients' behavior is also of central importance with regard to the more traditional, material goods and services, offered by administrative agencies "only" for consumption. Supply alone does not satisfy needs or increase welfare. These goods also need to be demanded and used. The nature and appropriateness of consumers' choice and "technology of consumption"[12] is of fundamental importance. Citizens' capability for meeting their own preferences, needs and goals by choosing appropriate goods, but also the way they are able and ready to use received goods – both dependent on information and knowledge about the characteristics of the goods as well as on skills to finally consume or handle them – are central factors in determining the impact of goods and services on consumers' welfare.

But applying these two arguments to street-level bureaucracies in general, we have to recognize that cooperation in this sense means only that clients *always* contribute *somehow* within or subsequent to *every* bureaucratic encounter to performance, output or impact. The coproduction argument is of purely analytical value by pointing to the theoretical importance of citizens' behavior, to clients' important *functional role* concerning the impact and success of services – regardless of this behavior's actual nature and quality. Consequently, the argument must not be misinterpreted in terms of suggesting a symmetrical partnership between two actively cooperating actors having mutual control over performance processes. This is, of course, not excluded, but cooperation in terms of providing necessary, but variable inputs within interaction processes may also refer to asymmetric relationships including the possibility of one actor being expected to behave more passively in compliance with the other actor's orders or prescriptions. The range of possible forms of cooperation may include aspects of coercion as well as voluntary bargaining and contract. Since the theoretical coproduction argument, however valid, does not give sufficient information about the actual *social roles* clients may play in various performance arrangements, questions as to which forms of cooperation and coproduction exist, how they are initiated and maintained and who really dominates or controls them, are of central importance.

Now, in the ideal case, bureaucrats and professionals in service agencies respond to the individual needs or characteristics of the people they serve according to their professional norms and ethics. But it is well known that this is not always the case. Clients' characteristics, their *communicative competences* and the inputs they (are able and ready to) give may differ considerably. The needs and problems they have are often complex and difficult to handle. The expectations and demands they articulate vis-à-vis street-level bureaucrats are very heterogeneous and often conflict with the views of the "experts" on appropriate performance. Thus bureaucratic encounters often seem to consist of "two persons ostensibly playing the same game, but adhering to rules that are private" (Mayer and Timms 1969: 3). All these problems create *uncertainty* for bureaucrats and clients.

On the other hand, demands often exceed resources and work requirements prohibit individual service. However, the street-level bureaucrat controls scarce resources needed by clients. Lipsky's second main thesis is that street-level bureaucrats develop informal techniques and models of practice which are at variance with service ideals in order to reduce complexity, maximize efficiency and minimize the negative conditions of their work. Since the nature of needs and problems to be handled and the vagueness of given rules and goals allows street-level bureaucrats in many areas to perform largely outside the regulation and scrutiny of the agency, i.e. its management, they, too, "... have considerable discretion in determining the nature, amount and quality of benefits and sanctions provided by their agencies" (Lipsky 1980: 13).

Hence, bureaucrats or professional experts in street-level agencies have gained institutional power and authority on the basis of instrumental knowledge or coercive capacity. The more discretion the bureaucrat has, the greater is his potential power over the client (see Gummer 1979: 215). The potentially emerging, more or less intended dominance of the bureaucrat's (personal) perspective may tend to pay little or even no attention to those "specifics" of clients' problems, orientations and expectations which are inappropriate to standardization, or even to develop strategies of *performance avoidance* in relation to difficult and "unpopular" clients (see Wirth 1982: 133 ff.) This may of course compromise the effective attainment of politico-administrative goals as well as the succesful solution of citizens' serious problems. In performance arrangements, where central aspects of encounters between staff and citizens that are of importance in this context, cannot be monitored sufficiently from above or from outside, the necessity for supplementary evaluation and control from below, exercised by the institutionally weaker, directly affected clients becomes obvious.

However, this is not an argument against the necessity for public bureaucracies' selectivity and the related power of their representatives as "gatekeepers". Nor is it the intention to bring professional expertise which is based on instrumental knowledge or specific skills and necessary in solving clients' problems into discredit. It reflects "only" the insight that improvement of accountability, quality and impact of administrative performance demands direct inclusion of the "clients' perspective" (Giordano 1977). This refers to bureaucratic encounters in practice, but also to academic analyses which try to explain and evaluate the functioning of administrative performance processes and to identify opportunities for enhancing their quality: the (initial) inputs of clients are frequently the only basis for concrete administrative activities, the (subsequent) behavior of clients essentially influences service programs' impact, and clients, (finally) benefitted or harmed by bureaucratic performance, are a necessary source of information for professionals to correctly assess the consequences of administrative service delivery with regard to the achievement of goals, reduction of problems and individual well-being.

Emphasizing its supplementary function, active control by clients should be considered useful and opportune in terms of initiating, ensuring or improving *correctness of selectivity* in intake and performance processes, *appropriateness of procedure* and *impact of results* with regard to needs and problems. Concerning individual citizens, control of correctness refers to the issue of protection from errors, injustice or even illegality of any kind of administrative action (see Handler 1979). Control of appropriateness and impact, in this context, refers to improvement in the quality of performance in terms of effectiveness, responsiveness and individual satisfaction. The latter criteria of control by clients relate primarily to those aspects of service delivery which are legitimized by their aims to improve individual living conditions or increase individual opportunities for action. Bureaucratic control functions which aim at defining the conditions, procedures and limits of service delivery or at directly prescribing or restricting behavior of citizens and bureaucrats are usually more explicitly performed on behalf of a more general public. Nevertheless, here, too, effectiveness and success is largely influenced by the cooperative behavior of those affected, but primarily in terms of acceptance of duties or adherence to rules[13]. If there are clear, standardized and legally binding procedural rules for performance, individual control by directly and perhaps negatively affected citizens may then – for the sake of uniformity of performance, equity or justice – necessarily address only criteria of legal compliance or correctness, Clients may monitor and examine street-level bureaucrats' observance of regular laws, administrative rules or organizational regulations, if they are aware of them. They may even effect correction of rule violation or omission by direct informal intervention – at least in the case of unintended errors or faults. Otherwise, they would have to make appeals to courts, mobilize proxies such as the press and organized interest groups, or address complaints to a bureau chief in order to activate internal processes of control and sanctioning. This again seems to be more likely and promising in smaller administrative agencies with obvious and direct hierarchical linkages where the responsible chief is easily found and has fewer problems in directing and controlling his street-level bureaucrats. However, this refers to the formal criterion of correctness. Control of administrative control or service performance in terms of influencing definition, change or improvement of underlying program decisions concerning the selectivity and procedure of performance or the position of clients and bureaucrats may happen only at the policy level. Only where the results of policy-making or standard setting by institutionalized and organized representative actors leave some room for discretion at the operational street level, *direct* control by individual clients in terms of intentional and active influencing of performances' quality – including definition of problems, goals and application of appropriate means – seems to be adequate and possible, although street-level bureaucrats' position and behavior may often thwart this.

Unfortunately, we know relatively little about the opportunities for direct control clients have in diverse contexts of bureaucratic performance, since most research in this area has been and is still based on an organizational "provider"-

perspective that takes for granted the often merely superficial portrayal of clients as being hardly influential and passive objects of administrative action. I do not want to deny that clients in public administrations are usually in a dependent position and that they very frequently, if not in most cases, seem to take or to be pushed into the role of a passive participant. But to be the structurally weaker party in administrative performance does not necessarily imply passivity and absolute powerlessness, and does not mean that there are no opportunities for control at all. We have to assume that the structure of interaction situations, the degree and intensity of dependency, the positions of relative power and autonomy, administrators' discretion and citizens' behavior in street-level bureaucracies are influenced by various factors which have not yet been systematically studied in terms of their effects on the realization and success of active control by clients, and which can only be briefly suggested here: task-related factors reflecting the nature of the problem to be solved or the goods and services to be produced; institutional factors like intake and procedural rules or professional ethics guiding administrative selectivity and performance; organizational factors like size and hierarchical structure of the agency affecting internal communication and control processes; and personal factors which characterize social status, individual competences, resources and motivations of participants. In other words, just as we cannot talk of *the* public bureaucracy, we will not find *the* street-level bureaucrat and certainly not *the* bureaucratic encounter or *the* client. For example, the sentenced inmate of a prison is more dependent than a fee-paying patient in a communal hospital. The stigmatized recipient of welfare transfers is in a different position from the middle-class client of a service center, and there are also differences between the happy bride in the registry office and the lamenting tax payer in the revenue office, etc.

However, differences in (formal) executive power and the power of definition on the part of bureaucrats or administrators point to their varying *potentials* to dominate clients and to ignore their interests. But, the mere existence of a potential power base does not necessarily mean that the administrator will choose to exploit it (see Gummer 1979: 215). Whether he does or not depends essentially on his own personality and on the (informal) incentives, rewards and punishments he may additionally get or at least expect – from his agency and also from his clients. *Hence, the range of discretion bureaucrats dispose of in connection with their formal power or authority, may be the source of unresponsive performance, but is at the same time an inescapable condition for the successful fulfillment of complex tasks and thus, also offers a chance for clients to have their specific needs and interests incorporated in performance processes.* In this sense, clients are, of course, not in a position to change the underlying administrative programs which provide the essential groundwork for bureaucracies' opportunities to act successfully and responsively and which also define the structural limits of active cooperation and control, but they may influence the frequently broad opportunities for a program's interpretation which determines concrete performance, results and impact to a large extent.

We can conclude that performance takes place in differently structured bureaucratic encounters in which different types of "providers" and "recipients" interact. It takes place within different institutional and organizational rule arrangements which define more or less strictly different sets of alternatives for action and which may enhance or limit the power of recipients to control administrative actors and vice versa. The nature and quality of specific performance processes and their results depend on the exploitation of the potentials for control and coproductive action by *both* actors; on choice and application of control instruments and on realization of behavioral patterns in anticipation of or reaction to the counterpart's behavior in specific interactive situations. Hence, one should – *ceteris paribus* – not only speak of the correlation: different clients = different outcomes (see Rees and Wallace 1982), but also: different clients = different performance = different outputs = different impact. On the one hand, we have to recognize the important *functional role* of (affected) citizens' (re-)actions for the (successful) production of public goods and services in general. On the other hand, it is necessary to differentiate specific, institutionally based *structural positions* with regard to the relative autonomy and power of clients and the diverse *social roles* they are expected, allowed, able and motivated to play in terms of more or less active cooperation in bureaucratic encounters. The development of a typology of clients on the basis of an analytical spectrum of ideal-type roles representing various degrees of clients' active incorporation within performance processes may help to learn more about their opportunities to control performance directly at the street level. Due to limits of space in this chapter, a proposal can only be outlined here. Thus, taking the general coproduction argument as given with regard to the *impact* of performance in any case, we can distinguish the following analytical, but nevertheless empirically founded social roles on the basis of different, although in principle always relatively weaker structural positions of clients.

Clients as Objects of Control

Bureaucrats are in control of the situation and of the client. They dominate encounters by defining the cause and procedure of bureaucratic intervention. Clients show passive or retiring behavior and act in compliance with orders or prescriptions. In case of conflict with their own needs and problems, they react with "acquiescence" or "flight" (Bruinsma 1980: 361), if there is any "exit option" (see Hirschman 1970) at all. Direct control by clients tends toward zero.

This role is most likely to be found in control and correctional agencies, in total institutions (see Goffman 1973), where street – level bureaucrats are in a position to use strong measures of coercion and where formal rights granted to affected citizens to directly control and influence performance or to gain access to relevant information may be limited most easily.[14]

Clients as Cases to be Administered

Different from the above role, performance in this context *may* also be initiated by clients. This includes, at least theoretically, a limited steering potential. But with regard to subsequent concrete performance, clients do not exercise any active influence, either. Again they take or are pushed into the passive parts concerning definition of performance goals and decision on application of means to reach them. This role is most likely to be found in service arrangements both

- where relevant bureaucratic actors or professional experts possess a monopoly position, where performance is highly standardized and routinized, that is to say, where there exists a relatively high indifference to the person and "specifics" of individual needs and problems (e.g. "the client of file" (Bäuerle 1970) in the case of universal transfers or payments in cash); and
- where specific personal characteristics of the clients or particular attributes of their "life space" are fundamental to performance, but evoke at the same time discriminating stigmatization or competence-denying by the "formal" experts (as it often – although not necessarily – takes place, for example, in social casework practice; see Maluccio 1979: 104), or where such individual characteristics really and directly impair clients' capacity for active cooperation and control, hence promoting the development of asymmetric dependence relationships (e.g. in the case of seriously handicapped or apathetic clients in nursing homes).

However, formal rights and formally conceded opportunities to appeal and to revise procedure and outputs may be more extensive in this context and point to a comparatively better structural position of clients.

Clients as Consumers

This role includes a more active behavior and is based on a greater relative autonomy of the client, although it does not contest street-level bureaucrats' executive power and authority in general. There is still a clear distinction between "producers", "providers" or "sellers" who offer or apply their specific skills, instruments and knowledge to exercise performance or to create desired outputs and consumers who more or less effectively and successfully "demand", "buy" or "utilize" these outputs for their own benefit or satisfaction (see McKinlay 1980: 119f.).

Hence, the consumer plays a passive role in the performance or production process itself, but he induces administrative activities *in any case* by giving initial inputs in terms of his intentional demand. Clients as consumers are in a position to react to satisfactory or unsatisfactory performance with renunciation, retrenchment or extension of consumption and demand. By this, consumers may, at least in the long term, exercise indirect influence on decisions, for example at an agency's management level, concerning (future) performance – especially where service providers are to some extent dependent on the demands of those they should serve; where consumers may have influence on agencies' funding by paying directly (fees) or indirectly (vouchers); where "payments" for services thus depend at least partly on recipients' satisfaction. From consumers' opportunities for reaction there accrues a potential base of bargaining or negotiating power which the individual client may use vis-à-vis individual bureaucrats to actively and directly control the nature and quality of goods and services to be performed or delivered *for* him.

Thus, this role requires non-monopolistic performance arrangements in which the client has the opportunity to choose among several performance offers of similar or even substitutive type. It is most likely to occur when alternative sources of necessary or demanded services, benefits, help or support are in principle available and accessible to the client. Such sources may be other agencies (or at least other bureaucrats in one agency) and providers in the private market sector as well as within the informal social networks of more or less intimate traditional "lay-referral-systems" (Freidson 1960: 377) and modern self-help groups.

Clients as Active Coproducers

Here, the distinction between consumer and producer becomes blurred also with regard to actual performance processes and concrete outputs – which both may be identical – and thus not only in terms of services' impact. In this context, the client must be considered as an *intentionally active consumer and producer* of services at the same time.

Clients do not only make initial inputs and then remain objects to be worked *on* or persons bureaucrats work *for*, but they become actors who actively cooperate *with* bureaucrats or professionals. Clients participate personally in performance processes and communicate with administrative actors during all phases of service delivery. Both interactively transform inputs into outputs, and both jointly influence the nature and quality of performance and results. Thus, clients' activities and behavior include a qualitative *productive* component; bureaucratic encounters consequently tend to have the character of negotiations or bargaining processes with the aim of reaching joint acitivities or compromise agreements over procedures to be applied and outputs to be performed.

Such agreements may be most easily achieved where some kind of normative consensus about the domain and activity of bureaucrats exists, where mutual reciprocal relationships may emerge from common or overlapping interests or where, in case of different, but complementary interests, cooperative behavior is expected to be of advantage to both actors and/or the agency – i.e. to increase clients' satisfaction and positively affect their evaluation of the quality and responsiveness of performance, and (simultaneously or subsequently) to improve the achievement of agencies' objectives and thus maintain or enlarge their domain and position vis-à-vis rival "producers" or service providers, to ensure continuous and possibly growing flows of resources from supporters or sponsors, to reduce uncertainty and (especially psychological) costs for bureaucrats and to promote their career or status. The clients may promote or ensure such agreements by means of friendly discussions and confident bargains, by giving constructive support or informal incentives and rewards in terms of positive sanctions and motivating control. But in case of performance and "domain discrepancies" (Greenley and Kirk 1973: 72) when different preferences, priorities and criteria exist with regard to performance or goals, when clients are frustrated because their expectations have been disappointed and needs have not been satisfied, cooperation may also include some conflicting bargaining and clients may react with persuasive arguments or vetoes as well as with various pressure tactics. Of course, Hirschman's (1970) "voice" – alternative which is the articulation of dissatisfaction ranging from faint grumbling to vigorous and aggressive protest is more likely to be successful, if the client is in a position to reinforce his concern with reference to the possible utilization of formal, legal instruments of control and sanctioning or with more or less organized political support at other levels. However, political and administrative movements toward decentralization can be seen to strengthen voice on the street level as well as the introduction of competition or the insertion of elements of choice into the administrative system can be seen to strengthen the exit option of clients (see Young 1971: 429 ff.).

The role of the active coproducer seems most likely to be realized in personal social services which usually require repeated face-to-face interactions offering opportunities for learning for the parties concerned on the basis of mutual personal experience over time; in performance arrangements in which bureaucrats have no coercive or punitive power to exercise over the client, but "only" authority based on their professional knowledge combined with client-oriented professional ethics, and where performance is only to a limited extent dictated by standardized operational procedures or procedural decision rules. Here we can find the best opportunities for clients to directly control and influence performance in public bureaucracies. Nevertheless, the client is still, although to a less serious extent, in the weaker structural position, since bureaucrats or professional experts within public administrations may, in principle, have the "last word" in the actual encounter at the street-level.

35.5 Conclusions

Control of administrative performance by affected citizens in terms of ensuring or improving bureaucratic accountability, responsiveness and impact of public service delivery is a necessary supplement to the classic forms of control in public administration. There are various mechanisms and instruments which may enable citizens to exercise control. They all have specific advantages and limitations and are variously appropriate and applicable to distinct administrative contexts or "action arenas". There are institutionalized formal and indirect devices and feedback mechanisms granted by the constitution such as the utilization of legal remedies and voting; partly formal and indirect strategies like activating the media or participating in organized interest groups at the policy level; and informal, direct opportunities for individual control by clients in bureaucratic encounters at the street-level of performance including spontaneous reactions as well as strategic actions in terms of mobility- or articulation-related activities (see Specht 1979: 58 ff.) like voting by feet, bargaining, motivating cooperation, etc.

But utilization and success of all these action sets and instruments is highly selective. They are not equally feasible within all performance contexts, and citizens are not always able and motivated to apply control strategies or devices. So, affected citizens are not necessarily voters or – in the case of inadequacies, mistakes or malpractice – plaintiffs; members of target groups do not necessarily organize their interests in order to influence politico-administrative decision-making, and individual clients do not necessarily try to exercise active control in street-level performance, although their behavior usually appears to be of central importance to its success and impact. Some may fear the costs of doing so in terms of getting worse instead of better service afterwards, others may lack knowledge of formal and informal instruments of control as well as the resources and competences to use them. But even if this is not the case, successful control by "publics" may be impeded or even frustrated by counterpoising institutional, organizational or motivational characteristics of public administration, single agencies or their representatives. There is much evidence that administrative actors are frequently not ready to accept clients as active coproducers; they often tend to prevent and avoid control by affected citizens. Such unresponsive strategies are especially apparent in performance arrangements which are or have been subject to far-reaching trends of bureaucratization, centralization, standardization, routinization and technological rationalization.

However, there is also good reason to believe that administrative performance is *not always* as inflexible as is generally maintained, and that affected citizens, especially in direct street-level encounters, may exercise supplementary control functions and thus contribute to the maintenance or improvement of the correctness of agencies' selectivity in intake processes, to the appropriateness of procedure, and to the quality, effectiveness and responsiveness of resulting outputs. Of, course, the type and quality of underlying policy programs, the financial and legal basis, and the institutional and organizational framework of street-level performance, its contextual guidance and more or less bureaucratic control "from above" are essential roots of its functioning, success or failure – also for the reason that these factors set structural limits to clients' opportunities to cooperate and control. The design of these context-shaping conditions, their change or improvement is usually not open to direct individual control and influence by affected citizens, but requires political participation at the policy level via institutionalized feedback mechanisms and/or collective bargaining by institutional or organized representative actors. However, this does not render control by individual clients in bureaucratic encounters unnecessary as the issue of agencies' and bureaucrats' discretion with regard to the fulfillment of their tasks during everyday contacts with citizens frequently shows.

But there is another reason for looking closely at the street-level. Experience of successful active cooperation and control at this lowest level of administrative performance may, especially with regard to social service delivery, enhance citizens' capability and motivation to support, join or initiate efforts of participation at the less "visible" policy level. So, *active coproduction* and *political participation* must also be considered as interdependent and supplementary mechanisms for the realization of the principle of *inclusion* which is regarded as fundamental to modern welfare states (see Kaufmann 1982; Luhmann 1981). But we still know very little as to where, when and under which conditions clients may play such active and productive roles in bureaucratic encounters, and what institutional and organizational arrangements or feedback mechanisms are the best to promote active coproduction and to facilitate the inclusion of the client's perspective.

Acknowledgements

I am very much indebted especially to Elinor and Vincent Ostrom and to Giandomenico Majone for detailed comments on earlier drafts of this paper and for their permission to incorporate their very thoughtful and constructive criticism. Moreover, I would like to thank Else Øyen and Göran Arvidsson for their helpful hints and proposals. Last, but not least, I am grateful to Gillian Hood who "polished" my very German style of writing in English.

Notes

1 This broad concept of control combines elements of control and evaluation by considering evaluation as a part or even a necessary condition for goal-oriented, intentional control which operates by providing initial or feedback inputs. For more details see Wirth: Ch. 29.

2 Citizens may be affected personally by administrative performance, but may be processed differently with regard to the specific problems to be solved or tasks to be fulfilled. Citizens may also be affected by the results of bureaucratic performance without having had any direct contact with administrative agencies, just by reason of their membership in specific social groups or communities. For instance, intendend recipients of social services affected by the political shaping and implementation of programs; members of occupational groups by administrative decrees on specific rights and duties; town dwellers by municipal authorities' plans for urban development, or most generally citizens who have to pay taxes for the realization of all these purposes. Hence, different performance affects different people differently. But also the same performance may have diverse consequences for different people and even for one particular person. So people may in the case of rule violation experience official intervention directly by being imprisoned on behalf of a more general public interest; individuals as consumers of public goods, e.g. social security or clean air, may indirectly benefit from direct bureaucratic control of private or public organizations or business firms. Specific regulations and restrictions may be imposed on motorists who may benefit at the same time, like the less directly affected pedestrians, from resulting road safety, etc.

3 Elaborating a complex metatheoretical synthesis of institutional approaches, Larry Kiser and Elinor Ostrom (1982) distinguish three similar levels of analysis: *"the world of constitutional choice"* where decisions about decision rule are made. These rules are considered to govern *"the world of collective choice"* where collective decisions are made to determine, enforce, continue or alter actions within institutional arrangements. These decisions are plans for future action at the *"operational level"*, i.e. the only *"world of action"* where activities in the physical world flow directly from a decision, where individuals either take direct action or adopt a strategy for future behavior, depending on expected contingencies. With regard to our subject and with reference to Michael Lipsky's book on "Street-Level Bureaucracy" (1980), we call this the "street-level of administrative reality". Here, the more or less discretionary actions of public employees in bureaucratic encounters with individual citizens determine access to government rights and benefits, or *are* the benefits and sanctions of government programs. In our terminology, these programs themselves are shaped at the "policy level" in the course of collective decision-making processes – again more or less in accordance with those institutionalized rules that have been set (and may be changed) at the "constitutional level."

4 Committees or ombudsmen who are responsible for the processing of petitions are often overburdened, provided with insufficient rights and not attractive to most members of parliament. Length of time for petition processing and success in terms of activating parliamentary control are thus frequently unsatisfactory for petitioners and commissions.

5 Kaufmann (1982) describes the functioning and effects of socio-political interventions in terms of the improvement of living conditions of specific (groups of) individuals, and points to the importance of *(intended) recipients* with regard to policies' impact. However, members of *target groups* are not necessarily actual *clients*. But utilization of social services is, inter alia, a necessary precondition for a program's success, and there is much evidence that the motivation to accept and utilize such services increases the

more the needs and preferences of target groups are included in processes of program planning and implementation.

6   This includes attempts to influence processes of finding, structuring and decomposition of problems by articulating needs and preferences as well as processes of formulation of goals and implementation or administration of programs by introducing specific interests.

7   With regard to single agencies we can distinguish a management level and a lower performance level, where the "man at the desk" or the professional expert serves individual clients. Participation, as it is defined here, refers to the management level in this context.

8   Within the German context we can find issues like *"Repräsentative Bürokratie"*, *"Selbstverwaltung"*, *"Bürgernahe Verwaltung"*, *"Bürgerinitiativen"*, *"Bürgerbefragung"*, *"Planungszelle"* and so on.

9   Elinor Ostrom (1983) indicates that this may vary with the size of a community, too. The poor may "say more" in smaller communities. Moreover, administrative agencies in big communities seem to be in a better position to hide internal inefficiencies and thus to avoid pressure from the community.

10   Various factors have been held responsible for the failure of the War on Poverty which cannot be discussed appropriately in this paper (for more details see the discussion in Gates 1980: 74ff.). However, one of the most influential interpretations is that the program was primarily intended to serve covert interests other than those that were formally expressed in the officially declared goals. Daniel Moynihan, in his well-known "Maximum Feasible Misunderstanding" (1969), argues in this context that maximum feasible participation was included in the act only to ensure the federal government's influence on those communities that used the funds for relevant welfare programs.

11   For problems of service economy and service society see, inter alia, Fuchs 1969 or Gartner and Riessman 1974. The beginning discussion on *"coproduction"* in the United States is reviewed in Brudney and England 1983. There are some additional aspects discussed in the British (see Stacey 1982) and German (see Gross 1983) context.

12   The economic term *"consumption technology"* is taken from the work of Kelvin Lancaster who points to some parallels of economic theories of consumption and production. He argues (1979: 21f.) that consumers' welfare, attained from a given set of resources, depends on the preferences of individuals, the consumption technology which determines the collection of characteristics that can be obtained by consumers from a given collection of goods of specified design, the production technology and the choice of number and types of various goods to be used as a transfer mechanism between production and final consumption. This implies that welfare can be improved by giving more information to the consumer – as a basis for effective choice, for "consumer efficiency" and, as I would like to add, for control.

13   These rules are defined and fixed at the policy level. The resulting performance may be appropriate and effective with regard to the underlying, more general public interests, but may be in conflict with needs of individual actors and correspondingly valued less by them. Attempts by affected clients or bureaucrats to change this situation and improve individual well-being or satisfaction which violates or neglects legal rules or regulations beyond granted spheres of discretion must be called malpratice, collusion or corruption. This illegal form of "cooperation" has nothing in common with our understanding of "active coproduction" which refers to improvement of performance quality in terms of policy effectiveness *and* responsiveness to individual needs and problems. Nevertheless, corruption may be found at the policy level *as well as* at the street-level of bureaucratic performance, as Rose-Ackerman (1978) shows in detail.

14   Such structural factors contribute primarily to defining the position of clients which alone is not sufficient to predict the social role they play. They are introduced only to

illustrate the performance contexts in which the relevant roles are most likely to occur. However, different roles may be played in the same context and the same role may be played in different contexts. Clients of "open" personal services may behave passively, inmates of prisons, perhaps engaged in social therapeutic programs, may cooperate actively. Since cooperation and control by clients seems to depend on a complex combination of a variety of factors, this typology is intended to be of heuristic value.

References

Badura, B., and P. Gross (1976): *Sozialpolitische Perspektiven. Eine Einführung in die Grundlagen und Probleme sozialer Dienstleistungen*. München: Piper.

Bäuerle, W. (1970): *Sozialarbeit und Gesellschaft* (2nd ed.). Weinheim – Berlin – Basel: Beltz. (1rst ed. 1967).

Brudney, J. L., and R. E. England (1983): "Toward a Definition of the Coproduction Concept." *Public Administration Review* 43/1: 59–65.

Bruinsma, F. (1980): "The (Non-)Assertion of Welfare Rights: Hirschman's Theory Applied." *Acta Politica* 15/3: 357–383.

Etzioni, A. (1975): *Die aktive Gesellschaft. Eine Theorie gesellschaftlicher und politischer Prozesse*. Opladen: Westdeutscher Verlag. (Orig. ed.: *The Active Society. A Theory of Societal and Political Processes*. New York: Free Press 1968).

Freidson, E. (1960): "Client Control and Medical Practice." *American Journal of Sociology* 65/1: 374–382.

Fuchs, V. R. (1965): *The Growing Importance of the Service Industries*. New York: Columbia Univ. Press.

Gartner, A., and F. Riessman (1974): *The Service Society and the Consumer Vanguard*. New York: Harper & Row.

Gates, B. L. (1980): *Social Program Administration: The Implementation of Social Policy*. Englewood Cliffs, N. J.: Prentice Hall.

Giordano, P. C. (1977): "The Clients' Perspective in Agency Evaluation." *Social Work* 22/1: 34–39.

Goffman, E. (1973): *Asyle. Über die soziale Situation psychiatrischer Patienten und anderer Insassen*. Frankfurt/Main: Suhrkamp. (Orig. ed.: *Asylums*. Chicago: Aldine, 1961).

Gotthold, J. (1983): "Privatisierung oder Entbürokratisierung kommunaler Sozialpolitik?" In Voigt, R. (ed.), *Abschied vom Recht?*, 249–271. Frankfurt/Main: Suhrkamp.

Greenley, J. R., and S. A. Kirk (1973): "Organizational Characteristics of Agencies and the Distribution of Services to Applicants." *Journal of Health and Social Behavior* 14/1: 70–80.

Gross, P. (1983): *Die Verheißungen der Dienstleistungsgesellschaft*. Opladen: Westdeutscher Verlag.

Grunow, D. (1978): *Alltagskontakte mit der Verwaltung*. Frankfurt/Main – New York: Campus.

Gummer, B. (1979): "On Helping and Helplessness: The Structure of Discretion in the American Welfare System." *Social Service Review* 53/2: 214–228.

Handler, J. F. (1979): *Protecting the Social Service Client*. Legal and Structural Controls on Official Discretion. New York: Academic Press.

Hirschman, A. O. (1970): *Exit, Voice and Loyality*. Cambridge, Mass.: Harvard Univ. Press.

Janowitz, M. (1978): *The Last Half Century: Social Change and Politics in America*. Chicago: Chicago Univ. Press.

Katz, D., B. A. Gutek, R. L. Kahn, and E. Barton (1977): *Bureaucratic Encounters*. Ann Arbor: Univ. of Michigan.

Kaufmann, F. X. (1982): "Elemente einer soziologischen Theorie sozialpolitischer Intervention." In Kaufmann, F. X. (ed.), *Staatliche Sozialpolitik und Familie,* 49–86. München – Wien: Oldenbourg.

Kaufmann, F. X., A. Herlth, K. P. Strohmeier, and W. Wirth (1982): *Verteilungswirkungen sozialer Dienste. Das Beispiel Kindergarten.* Frankfurt/Main – New York: Campus.

Kiser, L. L. and Ostrom, E. (1982): "The Three Worlds of Action: A Methatheoretical Synthesis of Institutional Approaches." In Ostrom, E. (ed.), *Strategies of Political Inquiry,* 179-222. Beverly Hills, London and New Dehli: Sage Publications.

Kweit, M. G., and R. W. Kweit (1981): *Implementing Citizen Participation in a Bureaucratic Society: A Contingency Apprach.* New York: Praeger.

Lancaster, K. (1979): *Variety, Equity and Efficiency.* New York: Columbia Univ. Press.

Lipsky, M. (1980): *Street – Level Bureaucracy: Dilemmas of the Individual in Public Services.* New York: Russell Sage Foundation.

Luhmann, N. (1981): *Politische Theorie im Wohlfahrtsstaat.* München: Olzog.

Maluccio, A. N. (1979): *Learning from Clients.* Interpersonal Helping as Viewed by Clients and Social Workers. New York: Free Press.

Marmor, T. R., and J. A. Morone (1980): "Representing Consumer Interests: Imbalanced Markets, Health Planning and the HSAs." *Milbank Memorial Fund Quarterly* (Health and Society) 58/1: 125–165.

Mayer, J. E., and N. Timms (1969): "Clash in Perspective Between Worker and Client." *Social Casework* 50 (Jan.): 32–40.

Mayntz, R. (ed.) (1980): *Implementation politischer Programme.* Empirische Forschungsberichte. Königstein/TS.: Athenäum, Hain, Scriptor, Hanstein.

McKinlay, J. B. (1980): "Professionalism and the Imbalance Between Client's Needs and the Organization's Interest." In Grunow, D., and F. Hegner (eds.), *Welfare or Bureaucracy?,* 109–129. Cambridge, Mass.: Oelgeschlager, Gunn & Hain; Königstein/Ts.: Hain.

Moynihan, D. (1969): *Maximum Feasible Misunderstanding.* New York: Free Press.

Øyen, E. (1980): "Structural Rationing of Social Service Benefits in a Welfare State." In Grunow, D., and F. Hegner (eds.), *Welfare or Bureaucracy?,* 45–58. Cambridge, Mass.: Oelgeschlager, Gunn & Hain; Königstein/Ts.: Hain.

Ostrom, E. (1983): "Relative Inequalities and Metropolitan Fragmentation." Paper presented at the International Workshop on "Analytical Models and Institutional Design in Federal and Unitary States", Rotterdam, June 27–30.

Petterson, U. (1978): "Control and Participation in Swedish Public Welfare." *International Journal of Contemporary Sociology* 15/1–2: 115–144.

Rees, S., and A. Wallace (1982): *Verdicts on Social Work.* London: Arnold.

Rose – Ackerman, S. (1978): *Corruption.* New York: Academic Press.

Rosenbloom, D. H. (1979): "Constitutional Perspectives on Accountability and Evaluation: The Citizen vs the Administrative State in Court." In Hyde, A. C., and J. M. Shafritz (eds.), *Program Evaluation in the Public Sector,* 67–82. New York: Praeger.

Scherer, J. (1978): *Verwaltung und Öffentlichkeit.* Baden-Baden: Nomos.

Specht, G. (1979): *Die Macht aktiver Konsumenten.* Stuttgart: Poeschel.

Stacey, M. (1982): "Who are the Health Workers? Patients and Other Unpaid Workers in Health Care". Paper for the ISA Mexico 1982 Conference,

Treutner, E (1982): *Planende Verwaltung zwischen Recht und Bürgern.* Zur Interdependenz von Bürger- und Verwaltungshandeln. Frankfurt/Main – New York: Campus.

Wirth, W. (1982): *Inanspruchnahme sozialer Dienste. Bedingungen und Barrieren.* Frankfurt/Main – New York: Campus.

Young, D. R. (1971): "Institutional Change and the Delivery of Urban Public Services" *Policy Sciences* 2/4: 425–438.

36. Concepts of Control over Public Bureaucracies: "Comptrol" and "Interpolable Balance"

Christopher Hood

Abstract

This paper contrasts two different styles of thought about 'control' over the public sector. One, termed 'comptrol', denotes the conception of control as self-conscious oversight, on the basis of authority, by defined individuals or offices endowed with formal rights or duties to inquire, call for changes in behaviour and (in some cases) to punish. The other, termed 'interpolable balance', denotes the conception of control as the management of balancing processes which serve to keep the state of some system within acceptable bounds. It is important to stress that what is being contrasted are styles of thought, not necessarily substantive types of control. After drawing this contrast, the paper explores and discusses the implications of each style of thinking for 'stepping up' control over public sector bureaucracies. 'Comptrol'-style thinking looks to improvements in the powers, scope, standards and institutional base of the system of formal oversight as central elements of its recipe for 'better control'; 'interpolable balance' thinking stresses manipulated self-policing processes, system redesign to build immanent control into the institutional fabric, and the need for a 'redundant' network of complementary and overlapping detectors and effectors. Such ideas are implicit in many of the earlier contributions of the book. These two styles of thinking about control are at best 'ideal types', and the dichotomy has been artificially sharpened for the purpose of exposition. Both are pervasive in contemporary discussions of 'control' over bureaucracy; but for those accustomed to think about control in one style, the switch to the other style requires a major shift of mental orientation.

36.1 Introduction

As previous chapters show, the term 'control' figures large in discussions of how public sector bureaucracies operate, or ought to operate. As has likewise been shown, the word is an elusive one and there are many possible ways of itemizing substantive forms of control. For instance, types of control can be distinguished in terms of placing in a production process (input, output and throughput as control 'sites') or a decision sequence (*ex ante* and *ex post* control); of institutional levels or types (management, audit, legislative...) or the substantive implements used for control (judicial, financial, physical...); and so on through the whole gamut of *quis, quid, ubi, quibus auxillis, cur, quomodo, quando* (Kassem and Hofstede 1976: 136), taking such dimensions severally or in combination (see Wirth: Ch. 29).

But it is not the business of this chapter to go over that ground again. Rather than itemizing *substantive types* of control, the aim here is to juxtapose two different *styles of thought* about control as a generic concept. Like all dichotomies, this doubtless over-simplifies; and two styles of thinking which in reality often merge with one another will here be contrasted as starkly as possible in order to bring out their differences. The distinction is merely an heuristic: it does not spring from any particular philosophical 'worship of tidy-looking dichotomies' (Austin 1962: 3).

One way of thinking about 'control' which is commonly applied to public sector bureaucracies is the ancient notion of 'comptrol' or *contra-rotulus* (Hood 1976: 121, f.n. 17). This denotes the periodic checking and examination of the activities of public officials by external actors possessed of formal or constitutional authority to investigate, to grant *quietus* or to censure, and in some cases even to punish. The words *contrôle* in French and *Kontrolle* in German still possess this fairly specific connotation in relation to government, and in that sense have retained more of their classical purity than the word 'control' in modern English usage. Stipulatively, the term 'comptrol' will here be extended well beyond its rather specific origins, to denote any conception of 'control' as self-conscious oversight, on the basis of authority, by defined individuals or offices endowed with formal rights or duties to conduct inquiries, to call for changes in behaviour where performance is unsatisfactory and perhaps also to punish miscreants. This mode of thinking about control can be applied to a variety of institutional settings and levels, within and among organizations. In the case of control over public bureaucracies, formal self-conscious oversight is exercised by institutions such as legislatures, audit offices and 'adversary bureaucracies' of various sorts; and 'comptrol' is the definition of 'control' usually employed by those who look at the public sector from the point of view of such institutions.

This can be contrasted with a quite different way of thinking about 'control' which embraces both immanent, self-balancing processes which may not be conscious or under any over-arching direction and conscious, purposeful actions for the attainment of desired goals. Any system in art or nature can be said to be 'under control' if its state is maintained within some sub-set of all its possible states by 'balancing' processes of some sort. Balance is a mechanical metaphor to denote the existence of forces which may come into play to throw their weight against the tendency of a system to take up certain states. This way of thinking about control also has classical origins, but it has been sharpened up since the 1940s by the development of cybernetics, which provides a common terminology for analyzing such balancing processes as they occur in very diverse contexts (cf. Wiener 1948; Ashby 1956).

Moreover, a cybernetic understanding of 'control' in this broad sense leads to two important conclusions, already sketched out by Dunsire (Ch. 16). First, complex systems cannot be controlled by overt or self-conscious 'controllers' alone; such systems are largely 'self-controlled' and cannot be otherwise. Second, and consequently, those who wish to import conscious direction to such systems must find ways of *interpolating* in an immanent or built-in balance of forces – manipulating that balance to steer the system toward the desired sub-set of its possible states. Hence the term 'interpolable balance' used here (for want of a better) to denote control as understood in this way.

Some aspects of 'interpolable balance' as a way of thinking about control are familiar in social theory, in terms of a number of related but not quite interchangeable ideas. For instance, 'equilibrium' has been a powerful idea in all the social sciences since their beginning (Russett 1966), appearing in guises such as the 'hidden hand' negative feedback processes perceived by Adam Smith and 'balance-of-power' ideas in political science, as applied both to international and to domestic politics (in the latter case, with Madison's famous dictum in *Federalist 51* that government and other social structures should be so contrived that 'ambition must be made to counter ambition'). Relatedly, the exercise of 'social control' by immanent peer-group pressures and the like – 'no hands' control, as it were – has been recognized at least as far back as Aristotle (*Rhetoric*, Book Z.6: 1384a). Modern social science almost takes it for granted that formal social control depends in practice on personal norms of self-discipline or on 'self-policing' mechanisms, either physically embedded in building layouts (Newman 1972; Sennett 1977: 15) or built in to social situations, such as the mutual balancing of peer-group rivalry in encapsulated communities (Hague et al. 1975: 22; Bailey 1969). Ideas of this kind will quickly surface in any social science discussion of 'control'.

What is relatively new, however, is the juncture of 'interpolation' with control understood as immanent balance: the notion that the point at which a complex system 'settles down' can be altered by deliberate 'interference' with such balances. Some of this may be implicit in older ideas about balance of power; but not until Dunsire's (1978) *Execution Process* was the idea explicated to any extent for public bureaucracies. Interpolable balance is not to be equated with immanent social control: it is a *manipulative* or *interventionist* way of thinking about control.

Both of these styles of thought pervade discussions of 'control' over public bureaucracies. The first, classical way of understanding control is deeply embedded in the European tradition of constitutional (limited) government and formal public accountability in financial affairs. Traditions and institutions embodying the 'comptrol' form of thinking date back at least to medieval times in Europe, for example in the long history of the evolution of public audit offices form their original form as appendages of royal government to independent or legislature-based institutions (Normanton 1966: 13–21). And in most countries, well-backed arguments are advanced for augmenting 'comptrol', by adding to the legal powers, scope or capabilities of those exercising formal oversight, in order to match the growth in government activity to be overseen. Analogous arguments can be found in a wide variety of institutional levels and contexts.

Seen from the viewpoint of 'interpolable balance', however, the discussion of control over public sector bureaucracies in the language of 'control' can be questioned as stereotyping the problem within too narrow a frame (Beer 1966: 50). From this viewpoint, it can be argued that there are severe inherent limitations to any vision of 'control' as a formalized and routinized process seated in some fixed and specialized position in the political system. Any 'control' system conceived in these terms is bound to be narrowly constrained by intractable technical (Beer 1972: 54), organizational and constitutional/political factors. Moreover, it can be argued that the 'interpolable balance' conception of control enables us to 'see' ways in which public authorities can be (brought) 'under control' which are not so easily perceived through the spectacles of 'comptrol'.

The two sections which follow develop these points. The first explores the implications of thinking about control over public bureaucracies in terms of 'comptrol'; the second section looks at the implications from the viewpoint of 'interpolable balance'. Before embarking on that, it may be useful to offer a summary of some of the main differences between the two ways of understanding 'control' which are being contrasted here. These differences can be schematically portrayed as follows:

	Control as 'Comptrol'	Control as 'Interpolable Balance'
Detection of problems	By *regular* or *ergodic, self-conscious* checking and evaluation	'Problems' identifiable only *ex post facto* from actors' behaviour; 'issues' raised irregularly, opportunistically, through 'redundant' channels.
Setting of standards	Defined official norms	Tensions among contradictory principles, pressures, goals
Achievement of compliance	By 'authority' – possibly backed by sanctions	By *any* process of tension serving to keep behaviour within limits
Control operatives	Defined official overseers manning a permanent 'control room'	Variable (whomever it many concern at the time); heavily dependent on system 'insiders' (for 'information-impactedness' reasons)
Recipe for 'stepping up' control	Strengthen official authority or sanctions; expand or change comptrollers; redefine or tighten up formal procedures	Re-think the wider system so as to augment self-policing mechanisms already in the structure or to build them in

36.2 Control Conceived as 'Comptrol'

If the problem of control over public bureaucracies is posed in terms of recognizing and checking waste and mismanagement in such bureaucracies for those outside, the 'comptrol' style of thinking offers a well-established set of prescriptions. Among those prescriptions for improving 'control' are the following:

(1) expand the scope, legal powers and resources of those in formal authority as 'comptrollers';
(2) devise more clear-cut standards by which behaviour can be judged;
(3) strengthen the institutional base of official oversight, in terms of some or all of
(a) better 'men' (b) better 'measures' (c) better 'structures'.

Such recipes are standard, familiar, bred-in-the-bone. They can be confidently predicted to appear in any institutional context where a 'control deficit' is perceived: they are the 'reflex response' of the 'comptrol' style of thinking to such a situation. They are, however, inherently limited and may even be self-defeating if pressed too far.

All Power to the Comptrollers?

To call for expansion and augmentation of the official authority and resources of the formal overseers is a natural consequence of the 'comptrol' style of thinking. Technically, this will only meet the 'requisite variety' requirement for a 'variable' control system (Ashby 1956: 206–8; Beer 1966: Ch. 11; 1972: 135) at the point where the comptrol apparatus can match the variety of the public bureaucracies which are to be monitored. Carried to its logical conclusion, this may require an overseer for every potential wrong-doer (Beer 1974 and 1975); and that in turn sparks off the potentially infinite regress of *quis custodiet ipsos custodes?* Reliance on formal oversight alone, with no element of unofficial 'selfpolicing', is thus almost infinitely expensive as an administrative operation; *but* as soon as any element of self-policing appears in the overall control system, there ceases to be any guarantee that augmentation of the formal comptrol apparatus will produce a net increase in requisite variety. It depends on the reaction of the 'clients' to such change. In some circumstances, aggrandizement of the official overseers may thus be ineffective or even counter-productive – for example, if it triggers off Downs' (1967) 'Law of Counter Control' in bureaucracies (Hood 1976: Ch. 5).

Quite apart from the technical problems of producing a net increase in requisite variety by concentrating on the formal apparatus of oversight, there are constitutional questions to consider. Any discussion of 'comptrol' in a traditional sense will quickly cut to fairly basic constitutional issues of who may do what to whom. By whose authority is policy to be made and judged? To what extent can, or should, formal oversight be exercised in a fashion which is neutral or impartial among the various contenders for power – particularly as between incumbents and challengers? For instance, those who claim to be 'independent' oveseers *vis-a-vis* government – such as judges or auditors – must be cautious of taking up contentious issues over which a government and an opposition party are sharply divided if they do not wish to provoke challenge from those with rival claims to be the tribunes of the people.

Constitutional issues of this kind limit the effective scope for expansion of oversight from such sources. It has to be recognized that the degree of political consensus within a polity is what fundamentally determines the extent to which it is possible to develop independent oversight over government by bureaucrats, permanent professionals or out-of-office politicians. Where that consensus is low, it is unlikely to be possible to carry such oversight beyond very narrow concerns with legality and procedural correctness.

Even if there were no constitutional issues to be addressed in relation to a call for aggrandizement of a 'comptrol' apparatus, there are what may be termed 'situational constraints' which are built into any conception of control as something exercised by defined individuals in a fixed and permanent location in an institutional system, and which will not necessarily diminish as the scale and scope of 'comptrol' increases. That is, whatever their size as a unit and however they are constituted, the overseers have to live permanently with their 'clients'. Frequent rotation of office is the traditional response to that situation as faced by 'comptrollers' within government administration, but that leads to dilemma (polylemma?) of how to balance speed of rotation, cumulativeness of oversight experience and propensity to 'go native' (that is, seeing the world wholly from the clients' point of view). Even when individual overseers are rotated in office, there are permanent *institutional* relations between clients and overseers as a group to be considered.

Therefore, in such a conception of control, zealotry by the overseers must always be tempered by consideration of the consequences (such as reduced co-operation or political challenge) that may follow from an attempt to 'go for broke'. Publicity, for example, is a weapon which has to be used somewhat circumspectly in the context of any continuing relationship; it may be risky to carry dramatic *exposés* or medias 'sensationalism' to the point where the access, standing and personal relations of the overseers with their clients may be seriously weakened in the future. This phenomenon is very familiar in the discussion of business regulation (cf. Mitnick 1980: 34–78), and it is not likely to be affected by the formal powers possessed by overseers or by the paper qualifications which they hold.

Better Standards?

If expansion of the power, scope and resources of overseers flows naturally as a prescription for 'better control' from the 'comptrol' style of thinking, so does the focus on improving the way that official standards are defined (by broadening, tightening or otherwise modifying them). Fundamental to the 'comptrol' vision of control is the framing of clear-cut formal standards against which behaviour can be checked. Such thinking forces us to confront the hard choices involved in moving from vague expressions of preference to hard-and-fast, narrowly-construable standards.

The problem, of course (as has been shown earlier in this volume) is that there are important circumstances in which this task is not merely difficult, but impossible. It is not easy to reconcile the 'comptrol' style of thinking with circumstances in which defined standards cannot or do not exist.

Moreover, a concern with raising or tightening up standards must address the question of the 'compliance costs' which the imposition of official standards (particularly reporting requirements) impose on their targets. 'Compliance cost' is a concept which is familiar, if difficult to pin down in practice, in the discussion of business regulation (see Gatti 1981: 95–129; Breyer 1982: 2), and exactly the same issue is raised in relation to control in and over, rather than through, government. It is a common enough complaint, for example, that over-emphasis on 'regularity audit' may discourage experiment, initiative and adaptation; may result in vastly expanded and costly record-keeping, and encourage an 'alibi consciousness' among those subjected to such scrutiny (cf. National Staff Side 1979: 4). More 'sophisticated' or 'up-to-date' versions of oversight will have different 'compliance costs' and skew the behaviour of the scrutinees in other ways. 'Compliance costs' are inextricably tied up with 'compliance benefits' in the imposition of any external standards.

Improving the Overseers' Institutional Base: Men, Measures, Structures

Apart from a preoccupation with raising official standards and augmenting the power, scope and resources of formal overseers, the 'comptrol' style of thinking will also direct attention to ways in which the institutionalization of formal oversight may be improved. To use the classic triad of administrative analysis, this may mean a search for better 'men', better 'measures' and better 'structures'. However, to search for the 'ideal' in any of these elements is to assume away the possibility that there may be sharp trade-offs or dilemmas to be faced in any choice of alternative structures or systems (cf. Blau and Scott 1962: 242–50; MacLaren 1982); and in fact awkward trade-offs cannot be avoided in organizing (or reorganizing) any system of formal oversight. A brief discussion must suffice.

First, 'men'. Even a social engineering approach which puts heavy emphasis on the importance of 'getting the machinery right' rather than the ancient slogan of 'men not measures' (Sennett 1977: 104f.) must address the question of *who* should exercise oversight and what would constitute 'improvement'. As soon as one passes beyond such cloudy (and perhaps dubious) sentiments that '... there should be men in office who love the state as priests love the church' (Sir Arthur Helps, quoted in Schaffer 1973: 39), hard choices must be faced. For example, a lifetime career model of the classic bureaucratic type – recruiting overseers in their early youth for continuous service, with a pension on retirement – pays for the (no doubt considerable) advantages of long experience with the obvious dangers of ossification and of 'going native'. Staffing on the alternative basis of 'in-and-outers', temporaries and 'parachutists' will have different costs and benefits. The problems include lack of continuity, endless 'reinventions of the wheel' and potential conflicts of interest, in relation to the positions from which such overseers may come, and to which they may subsequently depart; among the advantages are new perspectives, fresh thinking and outside contacts. Similar dilemmas attend the question of what 'basket' of skills and backgrounds those serving as overseers ought to have. What should be the balance of 'insiders' and 'outsiders', those from 'political' and those from 'professional' backgrounds, those with traditional or conventional 'comptrol' skills (law, accountancy) and those with other kinds of skills (operations research, social-science evaluation)? To raise such questions is to enter a debate about the proper training of government elites which goes back to Plato, and in which a number of well-known and quite contradictory lines of argument can be advanced.

When one turns from 'men' to 'measures' and considers the means by which oversight may be exercised, other very familiar dilemmas arise. One very well known example is the problem of whether to lay the main emphasis on *ex ante* or *ex post* oversight. *Ex ante* checks have the potential for 'stopping things before they start' and for nipping costly mistakes in the bud. The price is paid in the form of slowing up the administrative workings of the scrutinee, even in circumstances where speed may be of the essence, and in the possible blurring of responsibility for failure, with the overseers under such a system running the risk of being a party to what may subsequently turn out to be embarrassing errors – or worse (UN/INTOSAI 1980: 62). On the other hand, *ex post* checking may permit speedier administrative action and keep responsibility for mistakes more clear-cut, but naturally is vulnerable to the charge of 'shutting the stable door after the horse has gone', which tends to be the fate of expensive forensic inquiries.

This is only one example of problems of choice concerning 'measures' for effective formal oversight. Similar dilemmas surround other options – for instance, as between 'active' and 'passive' oversight and as between 'hawkish' and 'dove-ish' approaches to the treatment of offenders (using 'influence' and 'pressure' to correct behaviour as against a 'big stick' crime-and-punishment approach).

There are also 'structural' matters which present hard choices for those aspiring to design better systems of formal oversight. These include such familiar dilemmas as the extent and mode in which overseeing institutions should be specialized, and the constitutional location of independent 'comptrol' institutions (for instance, in the choice of an independent, legislative or executive basis for a public audit office). Dilemmas of this kind are inherent in the organization of formal oversight in and through government as well as over it (compare, for example, the dilemmas of 'classical' business regulation as against other ways of influencing business behaviour, which have been ably laid out by Breyer (1982: Chs. 2–8)).

It is, of course, in the nature of dilemmas that they cannot be 'solved' (Hood 1976: 152). One can move from one position to another, thus choosing successively to enjoy (and suffer) mixes of benefits and costs that cannot be enjoyed (and suffered) simultaneously. Indeed, the act of moving from one less-than-perfect recipe to another can have both costs and benefits of its own ('disruption' costs, 'honeymoon' benefits, for instance). What cannot be escaped in those circumstances is the fact that in preferring one design principle to another, advantages are foregone as well as gained; and this limits what 'comptrol' prescriptions for 'stepping up control' over public bureaucracies can be expected to deliver, even under the best of circumstances. Indeed, when one begins to probe the diagnoses, value-premises and behavioural assumptions embedded in those prescriptions, one starts to move from a no-nonsense world of taken-for-granted 'common-sense' ideas into an altogether less certain universe.

36.3 Interpolable Balance: An Alternative Conception of Control

By contrast with 'comptrol', the conception of control as 'interpolable balance' starts from different assumptions, raises different questions and suggests different directions that developments in 'control' over public bureaucracies might take. An 'interpolable balance' perspective takes as its starting-point a need to identify 'self-policing' mechanisms which are already present in any system, and to build on those; may point to the need to redesign government in a way which will strengthen immanent control rather than taking the existing structure as given and seeking to strengthen formal oversight; and does not assume that 'control' is necessarily to be exercised from any fixed place in an institutional system, but can contemplate a network of complementary and overlapping detectors and effectors (that is, 'redundant channels', in information-processing language), with mobility – even lability – in the seat of the checking mechanism. Such ideas – self-policing, redundancy, structures with designed-in control features – are implicit in much that has gone before in this volume. Some of the implications of this style of thinking about control will be briefly discussed below.

Manipulated Self-Policing

The 'interpolable balance' style of thinking takes it as axiomatic that complex systems can only be brought 'under control' by manipulated self-policing. Indeed, it is important to stress that, from this viewpoint, the distinction between control 'over', 'in' and 'through' government, which is convenient to make for some purposes (cf. Dunsire 1978: VII) cannot be sharply drawn, however awkward that may be to reconcile with conventional constitutional doctrines. Both control 'through' and control 'in' must provide most of the ingredients for control 'over'.

This is because the interpolable balance approach looks to a sub-structure of immanent or self-acting controls to provide the requisite variety that formal oversight alone must inevitably lack and which are invisible to those who see 'control' only in terms of official checking-up activities by those in authority. Cybernetics, social control theory and an older tradition of 'divide-and-rule' statecraft (cast more in the form of 'maxims' than elaborate theories) are bodies of ideas leading to the expectation both that immanent controls can be found to exist in any complex system and that there is no way of controlling such systems from the outside except by 'working with Nature' to manipulate their balance by what Dunsire (1978: 225) terms the 'selective inhibition' of forces in opposition.

Some of these ideas have existed for a long time, though Dunsire's (1978) concept of 'managed equilibrium' in bureaucracies is a major innovation. Since the 1960s, social scientists have been feeling their way to an understanding of control over government couched in 'interpolable balance' terms. In the early 1970s, for example, the Anglo-US Carnegie Corporation study of 'Accountability and Independence in the Contract State' (Smith and Hague 1971; Hague et al. 1975) looked at the problem of 'control over the public sector' in terms not very different from those of the 1981–2 Bielefeld group. The argument, too, ran along similar lines. Hague et al. (1975: 21–2) recognized the formal constitutional structure of public accountability as 'still a necessary myth and to that extent a reality', and saw it as capable of development and modernization by the employment of 'new' evaluative techniques; but argued that, even so, that structure alone could never be capable of securing effective public accountability of government in modern conditions. Rather, it was necessary to understand, develop and institutionalize 'self-policing' capabilities if modern government was to be 'under control' in anything but a formal sense.

Fundamental to the 'interpolable balance' style of thinking is a structure of managed 'politics', in the sense of competition for power in a political arena. Wherever there is competition for power, challengers have some incentive to act as 'controllers', by detecting and exposing mistakes in order to discredit those in office. Hence the familiar arguments at 'macrolevel' for strengthening facilities or access rights of opposition parties or groups, or means by which office-holders at one level of government can challenge the incumbents at another level by directly addressing each others' constituencies.

But it is not only 'formal' competitive politics to which this kind of analysis can apply; micro-political arenas may also contain competition for power and thus offer opportunities for 'interpolable balance' to citizens or public officials. Public bureaucracies, and networks of such bureaucracies, are arenas within which disputes break out and competition for power takes place, often serving to bring what would otherwise be private quarrels into the public arena. For example, bureaucracies often compete for policy space, locking horns with one another where jurisdictions overlap, objectives clash or services are provided by one agency for another. Similarly, conflicts may well arise within any single bureaucracy over the use of that bureaucracy's resources and over the tactics to be pursued in relation to budget expansion or cutbacks.

An 'interpolable balance' approach to control over the public sector will seek to harness and develop such immanent tendencies, on the assumption that any affective control over public bureaucracies must largely operate in and through such bureaucracies, whether through a bureaucratic ethos that will serve to check deviations from accepted standards, or by a system of institutionalized and managed conflict. A very similar argument, of course, is advanced by those who favour the 'dove-ish' philosophy of government regulation of business, which stresses self-policing rather than external policing (cf. CMND. 5034 1972; an ingeniously modified version of the same argument in advanced by Stone 1975).

A different style of harnessed conflict can be illustrated by the way that a 'consumer interest' can be generated by transparent and visible financing of government operations. Niskanen (1971) has advanced the now very well-known argument that if government services are 'transparently' financed, in the sense that they are paid for directly by users, those users will always have some interest in limiting waste and extravagance, and that bureaucracies financed by user charges will tend to be subjected to a much stronger 'efficiency lobby' than bureaucracies financed by block budgets. The argument may be plausible: empirical evidence is hard to find.

'Visibility' stands for a slightly different way of charging 'openly' for what bureaucracies do. It denotes financing of government operations by irregular, high-profile and perhaps earmarked charges rather than by the means which are conventionally seen as the epitome of 'good' taxation, namely the contriving of apparently 'painless' charges, concealed in deduction-at-source mechanisms or in invisible percentages on retail transactions (Hood 1976: 118). Where charges are 'visible' in this sense, the pain of payment on the part of citizens will be keenly felt, and political anti-waste campaigns may more readily mobilize than in circumstances where taxation is smooth, continuous and hardly noticeable to the casual observer.

Thus it may be no accident that taxes on real estate – which have the characteristics of 'lumpiness' and high visibility – have been one of the most powerful spurs to 'taxpayer revolts' and anti-government waste movements in Britain and the USA, where there is a high degree of owner-occupation in housing. Indeed, where taxes are highly 'visible' in this sense *and* go to pay for bureaucratic services that larger or influential sections of the taxpayer community do *not* use – for example, low-rent housing in Britain – the anti-waste mobilization potential may be very high indeed. The incidence of such activity may well spread during a period of inflation combined with low economic growth (and consequently stagnant or falling real incomes among the bulk of taxpayers), for three reasons. First, the expansion or even maintenance of government activities under such circumstances necessarily involves sharp tax increases, some at least of which may be highly 'visible' (cf. Rose and Peters 1978). Second, the progressivity of tax structures has the effect (especially under inflation) of sweeping more citizens into the role of direct taxpayers, thus transforming bureaucratic waste into a mass issue rather than a marginal one affecting only a small disgruntled elite. Third, fiscal crisis may prompt more general resort to 'transparent' user charges, thus increasing the incidence of self-acting 'customer controls', especially for those services where pure 'exit' (in Hirschman's (1970) terms) is not a practicable option for the bulk of consumers.

These immanent self-policing processes in public bureaucracies are just two examples of possible sites for 'interpolable balance' thinking about control – thinking which runs on lines very different both from the 'comptrol' style of thinking and also from much conventional thought about the design principles of 'good government'.

For instance, the notion of bureaucratic conflict as a control mechanism leads us away from conventional arguments for vertical integration and clear lines of responsibility in government bureaucracies towards the idea of positive encourage-ment of a redundant or 'untidy' bureaucratic structure, with overlapping and cross-cutting jurisdictions, conflicting objectives and inter-agency linkages of a complica-ted kind. It also leads to thinking about how to 'open up' bureaucracies to outside scrutiny or, if that is unattainable, about ways of protecting 'moles' and 'whistle-blowers' in government bureaucracies as a counterweight to the official departmen-tal 'line'.

Again, the idea of control potential being built in to certain kinds of financing methods leads us away from conventional ideas about the merits of 'general fund' financing of government, so widely developed since the French Revolution, the virtues of 'invisible' taxes and the transactions-cost disadvantages of individualized user charges. Looked at from an 'interpolable balance' viewpoint, highly visible taxes, transparent user charges and even earmarked non-user charges may have the effect of building 'self-policing' tendencies into the wider government system.

Overlap agency jurisdictions? Tax non-users? To think about 'control' over public bureaucracies in these kinds of terms is to move far outside the conventional agenda within which the 'control problem' is discussed, and raises awkward and heretical questions which can conveniently be left on one side in a 'comptrol'-oriented discussion. But that is precisely what the interpolable balance approach to control leads one to do, by observation of self-policing processes which are already at work within a system.

System Redesign versus Stricter Oversight

Closely related to the idea of examining and building upon existing 'self-policing' processes is a second way in which an 'interpolable balance' conception of control may serve to alter the perspective in which the problem appears. As has already been indicated, if 'control' is conceived as 'comptrol', the way to step it up or to remedy 'control deficits' is to strengthen the numbers or powers of the overseers. Looking at control as interpolable balance, on the other hand, may shift the discussion of stepping up control into the realm of broader questions about the design of government bureaucracy. That is, instead of taking the current frame-work of government as given and trying to encompass it with oversight, one may think instead of redesigning whole systems in such a way that self-policing processes are strengthened and become more pervasive, built in to the structure.

Once thinking about 'control' over the public sector goes on to this tack, the focus moves somewhat away from issues such as the numbers, skills and formal powers of overseers and evaluators, and design features such as bureaucratic reward structures, rules of legal standing and budgeting strategies bulk larger in the discussion. Space permits only a brief and highly selective illustration of this style of thinking.

First, bureaucratic reward structures. Inherent in any attempt to control large bureaucracies from the outside is the problem of 'information-impactedness' (Williamson's (1975) term for a requisite variety deficit by outside overseers). One way of countering information-impactedness is by appointment and other strategies which deliberately seek to turn bureaucratic 'poachers' into 'gamekeepers'. A case in point from Britain is the appointment of Sir Christopher Hinton, formerly of the UK Atomic Energy Authority, as head of the Central Electricity Generating Board in 1957 (Williams 1980: 21 and 25). This put for the first time at the head of the CEGB a nuclear scientist who was thoroughly conversant with the affairs of the CEGB's monopoly supplier of nuclear generating plant: that appointment served to bring detailed discussion of the cost and technical options of the nuclear electricity programme into the public domain for the first time in the 1960s. Many similar examples might be cited, and there are other ways in which poachers may turn gamekeepers; but a 'design' approach would consciously seek to contrive 'poacher-turned-gamekeeper' situations as a regular and pervasive feature of the operation of public bureaucracies, rather than merely being pleased when this happens spontaneously (as it periodically does).

Designed-in incentives for poachers to turn gamekeeper illustrate how challenges to the practices of public bureaucracies may be built up from the 'inside'. Additionally, design for interpolable balance control might focus on ways to give 'clout' to those with an interest in challenging the conduct of such bureaucracies from the outside. One example of how this might be done is the framing of rules of legal standing in such a way that public agencies can be relatively easily challenged in law courts by pressure groups (cf. Mazmanian and Sabatier 1981: 14). The broader the rules of legal standing that are adopted, the more easy it will be for citizen pressure groups to bring questions relating to the general policy of government authorities to court, illustrating another way in which interpolable balance control can be 'designed-in' to the general fabric of the public sector.

A third example of designing interpolable balance into the structure is the deliberate use of fiscal pressure on agency budgets as a control device. The widespread phenomenon of 'incremental' budgeting in the recent past – with each agency being assured of its budgetary 'base' and then struggling to secure an increment of 'real new money' on top of that (Wildavsky 1964: Ch. 3) – might almost have been designed for confining inter- and intra-bureaucratic argument to the tip of the budgetary iceberg (the increment). The huge bulk of spending (the budgetary 'base') glided effortlessly along, conveniently cushioned from rancorous who-gets-what arguments. Efforts to counter this tendency by means such as 'zero-based' budgets were relatively unsuccessful in challenging the system (Hammond and Knott 1980). But the climate of fiscal crisis which set in for most governments in the 1970s (cf. O'Connor 1973; Rose and Peters 1978; Hood and Wright 1981) has the effect of putting incrementalism into reverse for at least some public sector bureaucracies, and may do so for a sustained period.

Sustained fiscal pressure of this type may in some circumstances provide a site for interpolable balance control by bringing conflict about the use of government resources more into the open (cf. Greenwood, et al. in Wright 1980). It will not do so in *all* circumstances. For instance, budget cuts which are not large enough to provoke immediate major change in an agency's operations and which are seen as temporary (that is, likely to be reversed when the 'good times' come back) will almost in their nature call forth perverse strategic responses from public bureaucracies, typically in the direction of making operations much less efficient and much less responsive to outside demand or change. Familiar examples of this everywhere are 'tactical' cuts in high-profile or popular activities and hiring freezes which distort and ossify resource use. There is a kind of rationality, albeit a perverted one, about such responses (see Hood and Wright 1981: 216).

Such responses are much less likely to occur when the time horizon is different, in that fiscal pressure is sustained over a period, so that expectations of a quick return to base-protecting budgeting diminish and behaviour alters accordingly (cf. Hartley in Hood and Wright 1981: Ch. 6). Similarly, massive budget cuts – say, of fifty per cent – cannot but provoke major changes in bureaucratic operations. Neither kind of fiscal pressure can long be accommodated by the familiar 'maintenance-cuts-and-hiring-freeze' reflex, and tactical cuts in output may under these circumstances become counter-productive. Sooner or later agency officials confronted with across-the-board cutbacks have to face up to hard choices of priorities and arguments about value for money in bureaucratic operations. Something in the nature of peer-group accountability (Hague et al.: 1975) may come into play, as bureaucrats struggle to keep their units in existence in the face of cost-saving reviews designed to find out what is essential and what is unnecessary in their activities.

Moreover, intra-bureaucratic conflict may well come increasingly to spill over into the public domain in these circumstances, still further strengthening the 'interpolable balance' that fiscal pressure creates. For example, during budgetary 'hard times', public sector jobs at least are likely to be scarce and the disgruntled are thereby more likely to use 'voice' rather than 'exit' (Hirschman 1970) to express their discontent with the organization for which they work. Under such circumstances, the activity of bureaucratic 'moles' – those individuals who anonymously 'leak' information about the controversial activities or decisions of their colleagues or employers to the news media – may well increase. The same may apply to 'whistle-blowers' Nader's (1972) term for employees who act as common informers), who openly denounce their fellows or superiors in public, since a period of bureaucratic standstill and spending cuts may create a body of frustrated middle-level officials with no promotion prospects, who may be tempted to retire early or to take voluntary severance and 'blow the whistle' on their bosses or colleagues in a way which may offer rewards and new opportunities.

These are just three examples of ways in which the wider structure of government could be redesigned so as to develop possibilities of interpolable-balance control. None of them is a panacea and it is important to stress that these cases are illustrative of this style of thinking, *not* an exhaustive account of all redesign possibilities.

Permanent Comptrol versus Redundant Channels and Shifting Balances

A third way in which an 'interpolable balance' conception of control over bureaucracy may differ from thinking of control as 'comptrol' is that the former does not necessarily view control as something exercised from or in some fixed place in an institutional system. This view may lead us to pursue the idea of control through 'redundant' channels – that is, the use of a multiplicity of separate, overlapping, complementary checking mechanisms – rather than leading us to put very much weight on any single one (cf. Beer 1966: Ch. 9; 1972: 260 f.). Multiple redundant channels are typically important to the way that natural systems are kept under control (see Stanley-Jones 1960), and the notion is in fact pervasive in the way that control over the public sector has been depicted in this volume. It suggests an 'opportunistic' conception of how a variety of different monitoring and influence processes can be available for mobilization in relation to public bureaucracy, so that the 'heat of the action' (in the sense of where the critical development in checking waste and inefficiency are taking place) can shift quite quickly, 'flaring up' in first one place and then another.

As has already been pointed out, an 'opportunistic', redundant-channels, multiple-seat, shifting-balance conception of 'control' does not admit of rigidly separating the discussion of 'control in' and 'control over'; and it likewise cuts across distinctions between 'formal' and 'informal' and 'governmental' and 'extra-governmental' detection and checking processes. Indeed, what is important from this viewpoint is that there be a number of bases around which the flame may flicker (to pursue the 'heat of the action' metaphor).

The requisite-variety limits of control conceived as formal oversight provides the basic argument for redundancy and complementarity, especially in complex institutional systems (for instance where multi-national communities of interest or multi-organizational arenas are involved) of the kind that are often alleged to be 'ungovernable'. There are, moreover, three somewhat more specific possible grounds for arguing that if we want controls over bureaucracy to be *efficient* and not merely *dignified* (to use Bagehot's (1877) well-known terminology), we should not focus only on *single* institutions of 'control', and we should not expect the locus of 'control' to stay fixed. The first reason is the commonplace observation that the efficacy of fixed control systems and defined standards tends to diminish over time whenever conflicting actors capable of strategic behaviour are involved (cf. Steinbruner 1974: 40). In such circumstances, control 'targets' inevitably learn avoidance strategies, 'honeymoon effects' wear off, the overall state of the world changes in ways which may reduce the efficacy of the control system. After a point, the 'running-repairs' capability of the overseers and the vitality of their support may be so eroded that it may be easier to set up another 'comptrol' apparatus, with different people, in a different place, than to keep 'patching' the original system.

A second reason for suggesting that a redundant, shifting-seat conception of control over public bureaucracy may be politically 'efficient', in Bagehot's terms, is that looking at 'control' in this way makes it possible to tap into the political needs of those in elected or managerial office as well as those in opposition or adversarial positions, and thus to mobilize another kind of 'efficiency lobby'. Institutions which may be re-tailored or created anew will attract the attention of each new generation of incumbents in office, because the political need to place a particular 'stamp' on the government system can be served in this way. For example, ambitious politicians in office who take an interest in finding waste will want to employ methods or institutions which look new – even if that novelty is in reality quite spurious. They will be less likely to work placidly through institutions set up by political enemies or predecessors in office. In Britain, the 'efficient' locus of government-inspired efforts to cut waste out of the central bureaucracy has shifted quite markedly from one point to another in Whitehall over the past forty years, from the Treasury-based reviews of the 1940s (Lee 1977) to 'Policy Analysis and Review' in the (now defunct) Civil Service Department in the early 1970s (Heclo and Wildavsky 1974); ten years later, it was the Cabinet Office which was in the front line, with the waste-finding 'Rayner' scrutinies (HC 360-V 1980-l).

Typically, of course, the fossilized remains of the 'change agents' used by an earlier generation of office-holders linger on long after their original political thrust has disappeared. Frequently, too (and perhaps inevitably), it turns out that proclaimedly 'new' techniques for discovering waste and promoting efficiency are not new ideas at all – they are the same trite old ideas that have been tried before by different protagonists in different contexts (cf. Caiden 1970: 78; Caiden in Leemans 1976: 142). What is new is the rhetorical idiom in which they are cast and the political base from which they are advanced. These elements are typically more important in determining the effectiveness of control schemes than the technical details of the methods used, and the ability to vary them might be argued to be very important for maintaining the political 'efficiency' of controls over the bureaucracy by incumbents in office.

To an 'interpolable balance' way of thinking, such 'fickleness' is not necessarily to be deprecated. It suggests instead that we abandon that bureaucratic style of thinking which expects to find the 'control room' tidily located in some single fixed and permanent place in the political system. If we think in terms of 'redundant channels', we can contemplate quite large shifts in the seat of effective control with the changing configuration of power in a political system without necessarily concluding that public bureaucracy is 'out of control'. Indeed, for some at least of the redundant channels in the system, it is desirable to look for ways in which the form, title and locus of waste-finding and efficiency-searching machinery can be most easily changed in order to catch every shift of the political wind, match the attention-grabbing needs of the politicians and 'put the action wherever the power is'.

A third argument for 'redundancy' is that important kinds of control may work through particular manifestations which rise and fall quickly – indeed, which burn themselves out by their very activity. But such 'self-destruct' phenomena may be highly effective as ways of bringing bureaucracies under control, partly because the individuals involved (unlike formal overseers) *can* afford to go for broke on a single issue. A case in point mentioned earlier, is the bureaucratic 'whistle-blower' – the individual who chooses publicly to expose waste, mismanagement or wrong-doing in the agency for which he or she is working. Unlike the 'mole' (who gives information anonymously, protecting his 'cover'), the whistle-blower necessarily exposes and identifies himself by his action, and that in many cases (organizations being what they are) is likely to be the end of his career in the bureaucracy in question.

Such activities are self-terminating, irregular, unofficial and fairly rare, and may thus be almost invisible to those who think of control as 'comptrol'. From a wider 'interpolable balance' perspective on control, however, the product of one effective whistle-blower may be worth years of regular official scrutinies. To see such activities as 'control' is to raise uncomfortable issues. For instance, is it desirable to take steps to protect the social'habitat' of potential whistle-blowers, in order deliberately to encourage this kind of activity? It might be designed-in to some extent by severance arrangements aimed at reducing the cost to the individual of 'coming out', or by the creation of opportunities for a second career as poacher-turned-gamekeeper in 'public interest' research groups.

On the other hand, many would fear the socially corroding effect of measures designed to create a community of publicity-seeking 'sneaks' and informers. An alternative to such measures, it might be argued, is to create a strong ethos of bureaucratic rectitude, such that 'mole-worthy' scandals are less likely to occur. Or again, it could be argued that if bureaucracies were made more open to the wider community, on the American 'sunshine' principle, the need for moles and whistle-blowers would diminish.

A redundant-channels perspective does not require that an overall view be taken on such matters; rather, it would suggest that *each* of these courses be pursued, without putting all the control eggs in a single basket. The idea of 'redundant channels' and shifting seats of activity is not peculiar to cybernetic thinking; it appears, for example, in the idea of multiple-channel legal systems (such as the classical Greek, Roman, German, English (Schaffer and Lamb 1981: 11f.)). But a 'shifting seat' conception of control, when it is pushed very far, presents something of a challenge to the 'comptrol' conception, with its vision of public bureaucracy being overseen from a permanent, official, relatively depoliticized 'control room'.

Closely related to the idea of redundancy, but not identical with it, is the idea of moving the perspective on control from public bureaucracies in the singular to bureaucracies in the plural. This idea has already been briefly alluded to in the discussion of bureaucratic conflict over jurisdictions and the like. It means contemplating networks of bureaucracies so arranged that the network *itself* operates as a control, for instance in quasi-market structures, structures analogous to the 'invisible college' of science (such as any kind of 'league table') or in other adversarial balances. Such ideas formed an important theme of the earlier parts of this volume.

36.4 Conclusion

The two styles of thinking about 'control' which have been contrasted here are at best 'ideal types'. The aim in drawing such a contrast is heuristic (as in McGregor's (1960) famous distinction between 'Theory X' and 'Theory Y' in management). That is, it is a means of comparing broad styles of thought, not of categorizing every real-life control system into one or the other box. To dichotomize in this way is certainly to run the risk of caricature; it has been artificially sharpened for the purpose of exposition. Nevertheless, there are some very different conceptions of the 'public sector control problem' which confusingly (in English, at least) employ the same terminology. For those accustomed to talk one language of 'control', the switch to the other language requires a major shift of mental orientation.

It is not necessarily suggested that 'comptrol' represents the dominant way that we think now about control over the public sector, and that 'interpolable balance' represents the way that we ought to think; at least, that would be an exaggeration. Indeed, in one sense, the 'comptrol' approach is a more 'down-to-earth' one. It appeals more readily to common-sense ideas about what 'control' is like; it is firmly located in authority and constitutional tradition, on the basis of which a powerful case can always be made for crowding on more 'comptrol' canvas; and it is powerfully backed by professional interest groups arguing that 'better control' over public bureaucracy can be equated with more of whatever they have to offer – such as legislative inquiry, judicial review, audit scrutiny, social-science evaluation.

The 'interpolable balance' approach takes a more panoramic view and does not advance the interest of any particular organized group – which is both its weakness and its strength. But in another sense, this approach has its feet more firmly planted on the ground than the 'comptrol' approach. By starting with the 'universals' – that is, what is basic to any system which can be said to be 'under control' – it can help us to understand some of the inherent limitations of the 'comptrol' approach; lead us to be wary of stereotyped and 'labelling' solutions for improving control over bureaucracy (Thompson 1976: 48; Edelman 1977: Ch. 5); and also raises more fundamental (or at least different) questions about what 'stepping up control over public bureaucracies' might mean from a broader perspective on 'control'. These have a very direct bearing on the issues about the design of institutional arrangements in the public sector which have been raised throughout this book.

Some of the implications of the 'interpolable balance' view – a few of which have been sketched out here – can, of course, be uncomfortable ones. Control as the ability to intervene in the balance of opposed forces may have heavy 'energy costs' in the building and maintenance of such balances, even in mechanical systems. And in social systems, the necessary balances must be built from a structure of human conflict, or at least the potential for such conflict. This is never likely to be uncontroversial or depoliticizable: there will always be arguments over the point at which the advantages of more outside 'controllability' over public bureaucracies are balanced by the 'energy costs' (to put it neutrally) of reduced political momentum and potential for deadlock. But if 'control' were all that mattered – if you really wanted to put the capacity for 'turning public bureaucracies on a sixpence' into the hands of outsiders – the 'interpolable balance' approach offers one way of thinking about it.

To discuss 'control' over the public sector intelligently requires either that the two approaches sketched out here be kept apart or that they be self-consciously combined, to join the analytical cutting edge of the 'interpolable balance' approach with the traditional constitutional and political 'bottom' of the 'comptrol' approach, without destroying the essential features of either. Much of the discussion in this volume represents an attempt to integrate these two styles of thinking.

Acknowledgements

This is a much-altered version of a paper which originally discussed these questions in the narrower context of 'audit reform'. That paper went through three drafts while I was at ZiF, and I was subsequently encouraged by my colleagues there to broaden the argument. The approach borrows heavily from the writings of Andrew Dunsire: I am grateful to all my colleagues at ZiF for the many stimulating comments offered on earlier drafts of this paper, and in particular to Franz-Xaver Kaufmann, Vincent Ostrom, Jim Sharpe, Andrew Dunsire and Göran Arvidsson, who took the trouble to comment on previous drafts in detail and generously allowed me to incorporate their suggestions.

References

Ashby, W. R. (1956): *An Introduction to Cybernetics.* London: Chapman and Hall.
Austin, J. L. (1962): *Sense and Sensibilia.* Oxford: Clarendon.
Bagehot, W. (1877): *The English Constitution and Other Political Essays.* New York: Appleton.
Bailey T. (1969): *Stratagems and Spoils.* Oxford: Basil Blackwell.
Beer, S. (1966): *Decision and Control.* London: Wiley.
Beer, S. (1972): *Brain of the Firm.* London: Allen Lane.
Beer, S. (1974): *Designing Freedom.* London: Wiley.
Beer, S. (1975): *Platform for Change.* London: Wiley.
Blau, P. M., and W. R. Scott (1963): *Formal Organizations.* London: Routledge and Kegan Paul.
Breyer, S. G. (1982): *Regulation and Its Reform.* Cambridge, Mass.: Harvard Univ. Press.
Caiden, G. E. (1970): *Administrative Reform.* Allen Lane.
CMND. 5034 (1972): *Report of the Robens Committee on Safety and Health at Work.* London: HMSO.
Downs, A. (1967): *Inside Bureaucracy.* New York: Wiley.
Dunsire, A. (1978): *Control in a Bureaucracy.* Oxford: Robertson.
Edelman, M. (1977): *Political Language: Words That Succeed and Policies That Fail.* New York: Academic Press.
Gatti, J. (ed.) (1981): *The Limits of Government Regulation.* New York: Academic Press.
Hammond, T. H., and J. H. Knott (1980): *A Zero-Based Look at Zero-Based Budgeting.* Eastbourne: Holt-Sanders.
Hague, D. C., W. J. M. MacKenzie, and A. Barker (1975): *Public Policy and Private Interests.* London: Macmillan.
HC 360-V (1980–1): Treasury and Civil Service Committee, Efficiency and Effectiveness in the Civil Service. *Minutes of Evidence.* London: HMSO.
Heclo, H., and A. Wildavsky (1974): *The Private Government of Public Money.* London: Macmillan.
Hirschman, A. O. (1970): *Exit, Voice and Loyalty.* Cambridge, Mass.: Harvard Univ. Press.
Hood, C. C. (1976): *The Limits of Administration.* London: Wiley.
Hood, C. C., and M. Wright (1981): *Big Government in Hard Times.* Oxford: Robertson.
Kassem, M. S., and G. Hofstede (1976): *European Contributions to Organization Theory.* Assen: Van Gorcum.
Lee, J. M. (1977): *Reviewing the Machinery of Government 1942–52.* London: Birkbeck College.
Leemans, A. F. (1976): *The Management of Change in Government.* The Hague: Nijhoff.
McGregor, D. (1960): *The Human Side of Enterprise.* New York: McGraw-Hill.
McLaren, R. I. (1982): *Organizational Dilemmas.* Chichester: Wiley.

Mazmanian, D. A., and P. A. Sabatier (1981): *Effective Policy Implementation*. Lexington: Lexington Books.

Mitnick, B. M. (1980): *The Political Economy of Regulation*. New York: Columbia Univ. Press.

Nader, R., P. Petkas, and K. Blackwell (1972): *Whistle Blowing*. New York: Grossman.

National Staff Side (1979): *"Accountability and Efficiency in the Civil Service". (Mimeogr.)*

Newman, O. (1972): *Defensible Space*. New York: Macmillan.

Niskanen, W. A. (1971): *Bureaucracy and Representative Government*. Chicago: Aldine Atherton.

Normanton, L. (1966): *The Accountability and Audit of Governments*. Manchester: Manchester Univ. Press.

O'Connor, J. (1973): *The Fiscal Crisis of the State*. New York: St. Martin's Press.

Rose, R., and B. G. Peters (1978): *Can Government Go Bankrupt?* New York: Basic Books.

Russett, C. E. (1966): *The Concept of Equilibrium in American Social Thought*. New Haven: Yale Univ. Press.

Schaffer, B. (1973): *The Administrative Factor*. London: Cassell.

Schaffer, B., and G. Lamb (1981): *Can Equity Be Organized?* Farnborough: Gower.

Sennett, R. (1977): *The Fall of Public Man*. Cambridge: Cambridge Univ. Press.

Smith, B. L. R., and D. C. Hague (1971): *Accountability and Independence in the Contract State*. London: Macmillan.

Stanley-Jones, D. and K. Stanley-Jones (1960): *The Kybernetics of Natural Systems*. London: Pergamon.

Steinbruner, J. (1974): *The Cybernetic Theory of Decision*. Princeton: Princeton Univ. Press.

Stone, C. D. (1975): *Where The Law Ends*. New York: Harper and Row.

Thompson, V. A. (1976): *Bureaucracy and the Modern World*. Morristown, N. J.: General Learning Press.

UN/INTOSAI (1980): *Public Auditing Techniques for Performance Improvement*. New York: UN.

Wiener, N. (1948): *Cybernetics*. New York: Wiley.

Wildavsky, A. (1964): *The Politics of the Budgetary Process*. Boston: Little Brown.

Williams, R. (1980): *The Nuclear Power Decisions*. London: Croom Helm.

Williamson, O. E. (1975): *Markets and Hierarchies*. London: Collier Macmillan.

Wright, M. (1980): *Public Spending Decisions*. London: Allen and Unwin.

Part 7
By Way of Conclusion

37. Experience, Theory and Design

Franz-Xaver Kaufmann, Giandomenico Majone and Vincent Ostrom

Abstract

The editors summarize the thrust of the present volume. It combines current approaches in the American social sciences with European traditions of thought in order to assess the impact of the still ongoing differentiation of government and its growing interdependence with nongovernmental public and private bodies. By analyzing characteristic patterns of coordination as institutional arrangements, a way has been opened to the search for institutional design. Taking into account the constraints of rational decision making, standards for institutional design should give more prominence to the possibilities of feedback and learning, i.e., to the social processes of evaluation than to the rational processes of calculation.

37.1 Specialization and Coordination of Effort

The experience of different peoples, who have shared an active role in the development of modern civilization, has been one of rapidly expanding knowledge and technologies. Advances have been especially marked in the physical sciences with new sources of energy and new forms of technology that have greatly amplified human productive potentials. The variety of goods and services available for human use and enjoyment has increased with a radical expansion in both the variety and scale of tools that can be used as instruments of production to yield still other goods and services. The craftsman who carries his tools to work can be contrasted to the workman whose place of work is a large assemblage of tools housed in factories.

These developments have been accompanied by an increasing division of labor in many different types of human endeavors. Teamwork makes it possible for human beings actings jointly in teams and in teams of teams to accomplish tasks that cannot be accomplished by the same individuals acting alone. The jointness and interdependence of teamwork, in turn, depends upon complex structures of shared understanding where relationships are organized by working rules in many different types of going concerns (Commons 1924). The great number and variety of organizations reflects the way that rule-structured relationships in one enterprise or another is coordinated with the instruments and processes of production to yield a great variety of artifacts and artifactual states of affairs that shape the conditions of human livelihood.

The levels of achievement attained through joint endeavors and hence long chains of actions are always exposed to potential threats where some individuals have opportunities to function as free-riders by shirking in the performance of their efforts and yet hoping to share in the aggregate yield achieved by teamwork. But shirking has an adverse affect upon yield; and joint productivity in teamwork suffers unless performance can be monitored to maintain appropriate levels of achievement. Threats also arise from the exercise of differential claims to shares in the return from joint productive efforts and the way that responsibility is differentially allocated for determining how each individual shares in that return from joint productive efforts. Some exploit opportunities for increased productivity through joint effort by free-riding, or what might more aptly be called easy-riding; others exploit opportunities by dominating collective decision structures and deriving disproportionate returns from the joint endeavor. Problems of rule-ordered relationships abound in the organization of joint enterprise requiring elaborate patterns of coordination.

These problems are even more critical in the public sector where the nature of the goods or services being supplied typically pose difficult problems of measurement, and where the desired levels of achievement may depend upon the coproductive efforts for those who are being served (Wirth: Ch. 35). Under such circumstances, proximity to the community of people being served, their conditions of life and preferences, are variables that are of importance in achieving and assessing performance.

Where conditions of joint use or enjoyment of goods and services occur among communities of people, similar problems to those that arise in organizing joint production are faced in organizing joint consumption. Where exclusion is infeasible or difficult to achieve, individuals may have incentives to take advantage of whatever is made available without assuming a commensurate responsibility for contributing to the joint provision of the collective good or service. Free-riding occurs among communities that make joint consumptive use of collective goods and services. Free-riding among a community of service users on the consumption side of a public economy occurs under much the same circumstances where the yield of producers is difficult to measure. Commensurate opportunities for shirking exist in both the production and consumption of public goods and services.

The challenge is how to avoid the circumstances where joint use of common-pool resources and common facilities works its way through to tragic consequences, and how to facilitate and maintain patterns of reciprocity among people linked by long chains of action. How can they be kept in mutually productive communities of relationships? This requires differential assignment of authority and patterns of accountability in interdependent decision structures whenever substantial division of labor or specialization of efforts occurs. Achieving constructive ways of organizing patterns of supply to meet desired levels of service and creating complementary patterns of use among communities of users requires complex patterns of organization among the communities of people who are involved.

Commensurate division of labor and differentiation of efforts has occurred in the exercise of the basic prerogatives of government. Patterns of governance in all Western societies have been marked by a differentiation of legislative and judicial functions from the exercise of executive functions. A close examination of legislative bodies reveals an extraordinary complex structure of teams of teams organized predominantly as collegial work-groups in a manner that is characteristic of mutual adjustment by debate and persuasion (Majone: Ch. 21). In turn, different systems of courts, each court in its own operation, and the relationship of any one court to other courts represent complex patterns of teamwork in both joint and adversarial relationships.

The differentiation of rule formulation from rule implementation implies that rules have a potential for a publicness of meaning so that communities of people have shared standards of reference in ordering their relationships to one another. The publicness of standards is reinforced by requiring the concurrence of judicial authorities before criminal sanctions can be mobilized and used by executive instrumentalities of government. Law as a medium for the ordering of human relationships acquires a publicness that accrues from contestation about the meaning of law in the context of prospective (legislative), concurrent (executive), and retrospective (judicial) assessments.

The reciprocal processes of specialization and coordination of effort occur within processes that are marked by varying patterns of symmetry and nonsymmetry in human relationships (see the contributions of Ostrom and Shubik in Ch. 11). Where patterns of exchange and reciprocity occur among equals, substantial degrees of symmetry can exist in human relationships. But many relationships, including the rule-ruler-ruled relationships, depend upon nonsymmetries such that some are assigned authority that can impose limits and enforce rules in relation to others. No one, among human beings, is omniscient; and each depends upon the knowledge and skill exercised by others. Nonsymmetries in knowledge and skill occur in different patterns of relationships than those that apply to the exercise of authority.

While nonsymmetries are a fundamental and necessary feature of relationships in human societies, there remains the possibility that nonsymmetrical relationships can be linked in ways that yield increasing degrees of symmetry among nonsymmetrical structures. When such occurs, those who exercise the essential prerogatives of rulership, for example, may be linked in decision structures that make them dependent upon collective decision processes that are exercised by those who are, in some circumstances, their subjects. Those who are subjects, in some circumstances, are citizens, in other circumstances, where they exercise important prerogatives of rulership over those who are governmental officials. By rotating the nonsymmetrical assignments of authority through time, communities of people may come to share a symmetry of understanding about the more general community of relationships implied in the structure of nonsymmetrical relationships. The linking of nonsymmetrical patterns of relationships in ways that yield increasing symmetry implies that larger patterns of interdependency are created in the nexus of human relationships.

37.2 Institution Building as Condition for the Lengthening of Chains of Action

The division of labor and the fragmentation of power as basic features of modern societies from the starting point for our inquiry to explain the operation of what is conventionally called "the public sector." It has been shown in Part 2 that traditional differentiations of economic and political theory such as state/society, public/private, or policy/economy lose their accepted meaning because they are far too simple to explain what goes on in organized public life. We are, therefore, aiming at a more complex and abstract approach which should enable us to deal with issues of public policy in terms of an interaction between public and private actors or – in more sophisticated terms – an interpenetration of political, economic, and social systems. The growing public sector has, therefore, to be conceived as a multibureaucratic structure rather than a megabureaucratic structure. A multiplicity of organized bodies are interacting within more or less loosely coupled networks, and their interactions are only partially (and to a variable extent) regulated by law. This multiplicity of organizations is built upon structures that are of a formally public or formally private status. Legislatures, for example, are formally public; but in many societies political parties as well as "peak-associations" (see Franz et al.: Ch. 26) are formally private. Yet, they both assume essential roles in organizing the processes of government. To conceive formally private organization as belonging to "the public sector" means that their performance depends upon the exercise of governmental prerogatives and, therefore, implicate some kind of public interest. The public sector cannot be conceived as a boundary maintaining system. Rather, it is an integrating arrangement for multifarious and multidimensional areas of society that are considered in the common perspective of being influenced by associated governmental activities (cf. Gretschmann: Ch. 7; Shubik: Ch. 28). In a more substantive perspective, one should speak rather about public sectors in the plural in order to state the problem correctly. It consists mainly of a variety of interorganizational networks that are focused on specific policy areas. These interorganizational networks are described in e.g. Chapters 8 and 9 and are analyzed more generally in Part 5 (see e.g. Franz: Ch. 23).

If the public sector cannot be conceived as a single "system" in order to account for the high variability of contested issues, types of organization, patterns of interaction, and modes of coordination, how then is the basic problem to be conceived that allows for an unifying approach? The basic idea with which this volume starts is the problem of coordination of a multiplicity of actors. These (individual or organized) actors are conceived as having a potential for self-regulation, as having resources and interests, as being able to act, to know, and to learn in light of performance within their social environment. All these features are given as variables, i.e., there is no equality assumed among the actors, their relative strengths and potentials are matters of fact. It is, however, assumed that every actor has potentials to react to the behavior of other actors so that agreement or disagreement, cooperation or conflict, affects the costs of particular actions.

Coordination of a multiplicity of actors cannot mean that *all* the actions of these diverse actors are coordinated by a single central steering mechanism. Such an utopian approach neglects the need for self-regulation within multiple actors and underestimates, therefore, the costs of conformity and the losses of adaptive potentials present within the various actors. Hierarchic coordination by a center is, of course, an important mode of coordination; but it is a specific form of coordination that never relates to all the actions of an actor. We therefore conceive the coordination problem as related to actions and not to actors. Coordination happens, insofar as different actions of various actors become linked to constitute *chains of actions*.

Considering the multifarious and multidimensional structure of relationships within the public sector, it becomes obvious that most actors are engaged in a multiplicity of chains of action and that there is a constant striving on the part of the different actors to reconcile the demands from various parts of their social environment with their own resources and interests. There also exists, therefore, a problem of internal coordination within actors in order to behave efficiently. If we focus upon internal coordination, we have to consider separate actors as self-regulating systems. Our main focus is, however, upon the inter-systemic relationships that are conceived here as a problem of establishing extended chains of actions.

If we consider that for most purposes within the public sector the establishment of the relevant chains of action necessitates the cooperation of more than two actors, it becomes obvious that the issues involved here cannot be conceived exclusively as a problem of interaction between two systems. The chains of action, which are of interest, have, so to speak, a large number of links among various systems and we have to explain therefore the establishment of longer chains of actions that transcend the realm of direct interactions. This has led us to distinguish operational coordination (i.e., in the immediate context of actions and interactions) and institutional coordination as the establishment of configurations of rules with coordinative power among multiple action arenas. Operational coordination can be improved substantially when it takes place in the context of rules that are known to the actors concerned.

Our concern in this volume is, however, not with all sets of rules that may ease operational coordination – it is hard to imagine rules that might not produce this effect in particular circumstances. We are only concerned with configurations of rules that are related in a systematic way to the improvement of coordination processes among actors. We, therefore, had to analyze the coordination problem in terms of guidance, control, and feedback. From an analytic perspective, coordination depends upon solutions to three problems: (1) the problem of guidance, i.e., standard-setting such that the actions of particular actors may be evaluated in terms of their reference to third parties; (2) the problem of control, i.e., the motivation and the information of the actors in order to promote the complementarity of their actions; and (3) the problem of feedback, i.e., to enable evaluations including those made by third parties to be taken into account in modifying further actions (cf. Kaufmann: Ch. 10). Insofar as institutional coordination is concerned, the rule configurations are not necessarily efficient in guiding, controlling, and evaluating particular actions as such, but in establishing frameworks that provide for procedures in deviant cases and for promoting regularities and reliabilities among actors and chains of actions.

37.3 Causes, Norms, and Reasons: The Interplay of Analytic and Normative Inquiry

The aim of this volume has been to provide empirical evidence, theoretical foundations, and conceptual tools for better understanding the operations that take place within what is conventionally called the public sector. This is an analytical as well as a normative task. Insofar as activities have to be considered as belonging to the public domain, one cannot judge them primarily in the perspective of individual interests, but one has to assume that they serve a public interest – whatever this means. The substance of what is referred to as being of public interest as well as the scope of the public domain are always contested issues in democratic societies. Under these circumstances, scientific work has to be concerned mainly with the conditions and procedures which, despite the contestability of nearly every issue of public interest, allows for an assessment of patterns of development in relation to standards of performance (cf. Hellstern: Ch. 14).

Given the great variety of political theories, constitutional provisions, institutional arrangements, and administrative cultures among Western societies, it is very difficult to ascertain common patterns of regulation that apply to the public sector. The thrust of the research group consists, therefore, in an attempt to find conceptual tools that account for both common features and differences in the problem and functions of public sector activities.

In trying to draw general conclusions from our inquiries, one has first to record that guidance, control, and feedback within the networks of multiple actors in the public sectors cannot be explained by reference to a single pattern of institutional arrangements. There is not a comparably elegant theory to market theory for explaining coordination among private enterprises. The fit of standard setting, control of producers, and provision for the needs of citizens/taxpayers/consumers can by no means be taken for granted in public services. This is due mainly to the fact that public services are expected to serve a variety of different goals and are evaluated by a multidimensional set of standards (e.g., legality, economy, effectiveness, responsiveness) that cannot be reduced to a unidimensional standard of cost or utility. The reason why the production of goods and services is of public interest is to be seen in their impact upon political, cultural, or social aspects of life. If – as in market theory – the mechanism of competition and floating prices for commodities is judged to be a convenient form of coordination, this amounts also to the acceptance of money, as a medium of exchange, as, simultaneously, an appropriate measure of utilities and interests.

Standard setting and standard using (evaluation) is therefore necessarily a *multidimensional* issue in the realm of public interest. This fact complicates the problem of coordination as well as the problem of understanding the nature of the public realm. The operating ideologies of practitioners (and often also of scientists in close association with some policy area) tend to emphasize particular dimensions of a policy problem and to neglect others. Thus, there necessarily seems to be conflict among different interests that cannot be readily settled by established rules of law or by cost-benefit analysis.

Practical solutions to this multi-goal and multi-standard problem have occurred within particular national traditions. One finds, however, a common feature: Particular organizations are created to pursue specific goals, and particular organizations are charged with evaluation and control with reference to particular standards or criteria (e.g., law courts for legality and auditing courts for economy, cf. Part 6). In other words, a strong division of labor within the public sector occurs with reference to tasks to be accomplished or criteria to be applied. But, there is no "common denominator" (such as market prices) that facilitate the necessary bargains and transactions in accommodating extended chains of actions. The public sector is necessarily fragmented, and so are the operating controls. This, however, does not mean that control lacks regularity. Rather, one may ascertain various patterns of control linked to specific standards and accessible to specific monitoring arrangements (cf. Dunsire: Ch. 16; Wirth: Ch. 29). From a political point of view, then, the question is inevitable which interests have access to what forms of control and to what extent the standards used fit the needs and interests of those involved in the larger configurations of relationships in human societies. This leads not only to questions of ethics (cf. Chs. 11 and 13) but also to issues of institutional design as have been sketched in Part 4.

From a more analytic point of view, our problem can be stated as follows: How can such a multiplicity of actors with particular interests coordinate their actions in order to produce outputs that are consistent with the interest of third parties? As has been shown, this can be explained only by using a multilevel approach to issues of guidance, control, and feedback, and by distinguishing various types of institutional coordination with specific strengths and weaknesses. Moreover, one has to assume a redundancy of control structures in order to hold deficiencies within reasonable limits. This approach may disappoint both those who believe in the possibilities of rational policymaking and those who are convinced of the evils of public intervention. There is no easy way to political ideologies from the framework just sketched.

Our inquiry is normative insofar as it is concerned with the coordination problem. We, therefore, assume that it is worthwhile to search for the common features of institutional arrangements that support the integrative function of a shared understanding, while also allowing for flexibility and responsiveness to diverse problems requiring collective decisions. This kind of normative reasoning has to face two standard objections: First, that it is impossible to *prove* the desirability of normative standards. And, second, that even if there were substantial agreement about the issues there may still be serious impediments to institutional reforms.

Insofar as the first objection is concerned, we want to deal with it as a feature of shared experience below the level of philosophical speculations. Any normative standard – to facilitate or ease coordination – is general and open to different specifications. Coordination is possible through conflict as well as by cooperation. Both may lead to the establishment of extended chains of actions under specific institutional arrangements.

Rivalry in competitively constrained circumstances among political parties, interest groups, and bureaucratic organizations, for example, can yield coordinated chains of actions of as great or greater complexity than those attained through conscious cooperation (cf. E. Ostrom: Ch. 24). Specific arrangements and their alleged properties and consequences become a part of a larger awareness in the contestation of political debate.

Moreover, the standard by which we propose to evaluate the coordinative capacity of institutional arrangements is not taken from personal convictions, but emerge in the course of analytic inquiry about modes of coordination, i.e., by analyzing empirical evidence and theoretical explanations of coordination in the economic and political domain. Specific norms accrue from an awareness of problems that every actor has in interaction with other actors.

The general quality of institutional arrangements that ease coordination can be described as follows: Given the limited rationality of all actors and the contestability of all political issues, institutional arrangements provide possibilities for learning among all of the actors concerned. Learning implies the experiencing of successes and failures. In order to enable coordination to occur with other actors, it is, however, necessary that successes and failures are related to the evaluations of those who are concerned with particular actions. This cannot be performed by market mechanisms alone, but depends upon various other institutional arrangements as well.

One should add perhaps some reflections concerning the image of man that underlies this presentation. Man is conceived here neither as exclusively selfish nor as being bound only to the pursuit of material self-interest (as in economic theories), nor as motivated exclusively by fear and pleasure (as in theories of dominance), nor as bound primarily by societal values and committed to internalized norms (as in sociological structuralism). Each of these simplifying approaches emphasizes a particular aspect of human potentialities and of the possible impacts of institutional ordering. Moreover, we would emphasize a fourth aspect, namely the capacity of man for sympathy, for a fellow-feeling and a sense of propriety and of justice as described first by David Hume in his moral philosophy, and by Adam Smith in his theory of moral sentiments. It is plausible to assume that in anonymous relationships as they are characteristic for highly organized market situations, men orient themselves primarily by what they conceive to be in their self-interest. The cognition of what is in one's own interest, however, depends crucially on the institutional arrangements that govern the situation. Moreover, men are capable of assessing not only their present situation but also how institutional arrangements, the configurations of norms themselves, affect those situations. It is in this respect that one may assume that a sense of justice and propriety is operative as standards of judgment applicable to diverse circumstances. Under conditions of relative equality, nobody knows whether he will eventually be among winners or losers if the rules of the game favour one-sided outcomes (cf. Rawls 1971; Buchanan and Tullock 1962). Incentives exist to strive for fairness of outcomes, given essential equalities among all concerned.

This last argument also provides some answer to the second objection to an inquiry into the possibilities of institutional design. It is, of course, undeniable that institutional reform is facilitated and hampered by contested interests, whatever its scope and content may be. And there are many examples of a resistance to changes that seem to be impenetrable to better arguments. But the veil of ignorance often makes it more difficult to assess one's own interest with respect to institutional arrangements than to operational arrangements with known payoffs. This provides oportunities to pursue institutional reforms where operational arrangements yield perverse consequences. There is enough evidence that existing modes of coordination yield perverse effects at operational levels to require further attention to problems of institutional analysis and design.

37.4 Institutional Analysis and Design

A major question that we face at this juncture in history is whether we have the rudiments of knowledge to undertake the design of human institutions and what limits apply to such design capabilities. The problem must be approached with caution because several different levels in the ordering of relationships are involved. One level is the order of relationships that accrues through patterns of mutual adjustment among human beings as they act with reference to one another. We find strong emphasis in the work of F. A. Hayek upon the patterns of mutual adjustment that are the source of endogenous change in human societies. Human institutions are marked by an evolving social order that Hayek contrasts with a planned or directed order. To speak of analysis and design is to have reference to planning, at least in some sense.

Hayek's warnings about a planned or directed order are more aptly applied to an operational level of analysis where the question is what government, organized as a monopoly of power, should do. A planned order is then a directed order subject to a centralized structure of command. Hayek has also recognized that, "the possibility of men living together in peace and to their mutual advantage without having to agree on common concrete aims, and bound only by abstract rules of conduct, was perhaps the greatest discovery mankind ever made" (Hayek 1976: 136). Rules of just conduct can apply as much to the ordering of actions as means as they can to the purposes or outcomes as ends. There is a level, then, where planning might occur in the design, creation, and alteration of rule configurations for the governance of human societies.

Alexander Hamilton, in this sense, raised, in the opening paragraph of Federalist 1, the question of "whether societies of men are really capable or not of establishing good government from reflection and choice or whether they are forever destined to depend for their constitutions upon accident and force" (Hamilton, Jay, and Madison n.d.: 3). "Good government" presumably is that type of arrangement that would be capable of reasonably high levels of performance. Reflection and choice, however, has reference to principles of organization that are not limited to a *directed* order. Montesquieu enunciates a principle of using power to check power in the design of institutions appropriate to the constitution of liberty. Madison also referred to a principle of design "where the constant aim is to divide and arrange the several offices in such a manner that each may be a check upon the other" (Hamilton, et al. n.d.: 337).

The design principles formulated by both Montesquieu and Madison presume that it is possible to design human institutions that manifest equilibrating tendencies among multiple centers of power. Planning, as applied to institutional analysis and design, need not be confined to direct command and control by a central directorate. The design of institutions based upon using rule-constrained power to check rule-constrained power through opposite and rival interests depends critically upon shared communities of understanding about the normative standards to be used to assess individual and aggregate levels of performance and to specify diversely structural processes for ordering relationships in human societies consistent with those general norms. No single form of organization is appropriate to all circumstances. Human societies require recourse to diverse modes of organization.

This circumstance permits people to learn from the experiences that are accrued in establishing institutions that enable them to cope with problems that have plagued peoples in all societies.

At a level of interpersonal relationships, where human beings learn to relate to one another in the immediate exigencies of life, distinctions accrue in routines that are appropriate to family life, play, care for others and for things, work, accomplishments, and how to relate to others in diverse circumstances. Many of the problems of sharing, exchange, reciprocity, teamwork, joint use of common facilities, rule setting, rule applying, and rule enforcing occur in the microcosm of family, neighborhood, and community relationships that are experienced from earliest childhood and throughout life.

While the microcosm of life as experienced by individuals has reference to habituated routines and relationships reflected in a wide range of human institutions, the problems of crossing the thresholds from experience to theory, and from theory to design in the larger context of human societies, is plagued with difficulties. What is bound up in complex patterns of specific relationships to particular individuals and circumstances must be transformed into generalized structures that distinguish, simplify, and specify essential elements and relationships. This is required in translating from the world of experience to the communicable symbols of human language.

Distinctions need to be made among institutions. The basic elements and relationships implicated in distinguishable sets of institutions must be indicated so that the relationships of conditions and consequences can be specified to allow theoretical inferences to be drawn. If patterns can be generalized, the generalized structure of relationships should be replicable in similar circumstances that also have their distinct individualities or uniquenesses. Efforts to distinguish, generalize, and represent are plagued with serious potential for error when removed from the context of the discrete exigencies of life. But, this is the burden of translating from what is experienced into what is knowable.

The larger configurations of relationships in human societies that go beyond the bounds of personal knowledge become more dependent upon formalized relationships that rely explicitly upon rules and systems of governance that pertain to rule-ruler-ruled relationships. The primacy of interpersonal relationships of an informal character gives way to the primacy of formally-structured relationships of a more impersonal nature. Yet, the possibility remains that generalized patterns of relationships applicable to different types of institutional arrangements, and to generalized tasks associated with each type of institution, can be specified as essential conditions pertaining to the design of human institutions.

A theory of human institutions implies that the terms and conditions can be specified and can be used as a basis for creating institutions in different societies. These may be grounded in different presuppositions, rely upon different design characteristics and imply that people would relate themselves to one another in different ways. Yet, the question remains whether different peoples might learn from one another's experience to draw upon different conceptions and explore their potential usefulness for ordering relationships in human societies in more just, reliable, or productive ways. Tocqueville once observed, in his *Recollections*, that "what are called necessary institutions are only insitutions to which one is accustomed and that in matters of social constitution the field of possibilities is much wider than people living within each society imagine" (1970: 76).

Development of theoretical models, variations in models, and their use in design of both simple and complex organization arrangements have the potential for yielding experience that can be used to accumulate increasing design capabilities and a greater critical awareness about potentials for the design of human institutions. Democratic societies, in particular, depend upon acquiring a sufficient level of experience and knowledge to have a critical self-awareness about standards of performance than can reasonably be expected from the way that human beings relate themselves to one another in different institutions. Perfection cannot be expected on the part of fallible creatures. Thus, errors and misfortunes can be expected to occur. But, human institutions should enable those involved to learn from experience. Where errors and misfortunes persistently reoccur so that actions depart from acceptable standards of performance, people in a democratic society need to have diagnostic capabilities for identifying the "cause of their wretchedness," as Tocqueville has put it (1948: I,231), and explore the availability of possible remedies. When people are "unable to discern the causes of their wretchedness,... they fall a sacrifice of the ills of which they are ignorant" (Tocqueville 1948: I,231).

Institutional analysis and design need not be confined to decisions about what the "government" or the "state" should do, but about how institutions of governance should themselves be organized. Some of the most extreme perversities including the grossest injustices and the most extreme cruelty and oppression occur on the part of those who exercise the prerogatives of governance. The myth of the state, as Ernst Cassirer (1946) has indicated, will yield recourse to social magic and to the drama of the magician's rituals unless people in democratic societies are prepared to extend their inquiries about human institutions to the institutions of government and learn how to specify the appropriate terms and conditions so that authority can be exercised on behalf of their shared interests, but subject to limits consistent with the proper exercise of a public trust.

When conditions in the habitual routines of daily life are raised to a level of critical awareness so that essential distinctions, specifications, and relationships yield theories of human institutions, and such theories generate critical discourses about institutional analysis and design, we have circumstances where the organization of human societies is amenable to "reflection and choice." Processes of governance and processes of making decisions about the institutions of human governance might then be organized to facilitate the use of "reflection and choice" in human affairs rather than placing primary reliance upon "accident and force."

It is in this context that Montesquieu's principle of using power to check power in the context of Madisons's opposite and rival interests can be viewed as the foundations not for stalemate and war but as occasions for people to come together and explore the underlying community of interests that is shared by opposite and rival interests. When the fundamental structure of interdependencies that generate opposite and rival interests is raised to a level of critical awareness, human beings have the potential for coming to a level of understanding about how their particular interests relate to the interests of others, and how their interdependence of interests relate to their shared public interests.

Life in democratic societies is grounded in a faith that particular interests, if properly understood, are compatible with public interests and that shared communities of interest are the proper foundations of human societies. Where the rule-constrained exercise of power is used to check rule-constrained power, human beings can come to a resolution of how to relate to others in properly constituted communities of interest so that power is shared among the diverse interests that constitute larger communities of interests. Conflict provides the energy that drives the use of human intelligence toward resolution. It is conflict and the quest for conflict resolution that enables human beings to transcend what is and to consider what might be. We can but inquire, explore, attempt to understand, in light of contestation, and then to engage in social experiments grounded in rules of just conduct and critically informed by reflection and choice.

Shared communities of understanding that provide the foundation for extended chains of actions characteristic of modern society depend upon translating the world of experience into symbolistic representations articulated in language and then using those symbolic representations to reconstitute the reality of social experience. *The translation of experience into theoretical knowledge, and the use of theoretical knowledge to alter the relationships that are constitutive of experience, are integral aspects of human cultural evolution.* Whether the course of events revealed by history yields new achievements in human cultural evolution depends in some significant degree upon the relationships of experience and knowledge to institutional analysis and design that are properly disciplined by processes of contestable argumentation, reflection, and choice that are, in turn, bounded by rules of just conduct. In some general sense, we presume that standards of truth, justice, and well-being are compatible with one another in ordering relationships in human societies. Assessments indicating conflict between values of human life do not per se contest the compatibility of standards but define situations as challenges for improvement.

37.5 The Larger Context of Inquiry

The discriminating reader will have detected at many points in this book an affinity between our approach and other methods of analysis that have a recognized place in the social science literature. The approach of this book is interdisciplinary and hence it draws heavily on contributions from disciplines ranging from law to sociology, and from economics, game theory, and moral philosophy. Our emphasis on the multiplicity of social processes of coordination and control has an important antecedent in Dahl and Lindblom's *Politics, Economics and Welfare* (1976); even though our analysis of specific modes of coordination (for example, in Chapters 18 (Gretschmann) and 19 (Hegner) on solidarity), and in the chapters of Part 5 on coordination in interorganizational relationships goes considerably beyond the scope of their treatment.

Similarly, our interest in processes of mutual adjustment and social interaction owes much to such works as Michael Polanyi's *The Logic of Liberty* and Lindblom's *The Intelligence of Democracy*. However, we stress the fact that interactive problem solving always presupposes some shared meaning and common rules, i.e., elements that set the context of particular action situations. The theory of public choice, and the market-failure, the bureaucratic-failure, and the government-failure literature are other important antecedents for many of the issues discussed in the preceding chapters.

Perhaps the most pervasive influence on the present work is that of the new institutional economics, and in particular of the transaction costs or "organizational failures" approach associated with Armen Alchian, James Buchanan, Ronald Coase, Mancur Olson, Gordon Tullock, and Oliver Williamson. Market failure is only a special, albeit important, case of institutional failure. If it is advantageous, under some circumstances, to shift transactions from the market to hierarchical organization; the reverse movement can also advantageously take place. Hence, markets and hierarchies are alternative methods for carrying out related sets of transactions. The reasons for organizing some transactions internally, by administrative methods, rather than across markets, by sales contracts, have ultimately to do with uncertainty and differential costs of negotiating, writing, executing, and policing contracts.

The key behavioral assumptions of the organizational-failure approach are bounded rationality and opportunism. The notion of bounded rationality is familiar from the writings of Herbert Simon. It relates to physical limits on the ability of individuals to receive, store, retrieve, and process information, as well as to linguistic limits on the ability of individuals to articulate their knowledge, experience, and preferences by the use of symbols (words, numbers, pictures) that may be unambiguously interpreted by others.

Given perfect foresight and information, it would be possible to foresee every possible contingency, and hence to draft and enforce complex sales contracts in a world of private goods and services at negligible transaction costs. However, as Williamson (1975) points out, the cognitive constraints set by bounded rationality are binding only if the environment exhibits a high degree of uncertainty and complexity. The same point can be put in different terms. The price system has considerable advantages over other institutional arrangements *provided* that the transactions are simple enough so that prices convey the needed information to all concerned parties. Obviously, this condition does not always hold. In many human services, for example, information is asymmetrically distributed between supplier and user (doctor and patient, teacher and student, social worker and welfare recipient); outcomes are ambiguous; and the nature of the transactions is such as to involve hard-to-measure aspects of quality, trust, and confidentiality. In such cases price signals do not carry sufficient information, and exclusive reliance on market arrangements leads to less than optimal results. Williamson neglects the universe of collective goods, common-pool resources, and common facilities that are of critical importance in the public sector. The failure of exclusion and jointness of use or consumption forecloses direct reliance upon price signals and requires other mechanisms to articulate demands, arrange supply, proportion supply to demand, and regulate patterns of use among communities of users. But, diverse options remain available.

Opportunism, as the term is used by Williamson, extends the traditional economic assumption of self-interest to include *deceitful* seeking of self-interest: withholding or distorting information, making false promises, misrepresenting one's preferences and intentions, and so on. The assumption is not that all agents are given to opportunism, but that *some* may behave opportunistically, and that it is impossible or very costly to differentiate *ex ante* between honest and opportunistic agents, or *ex post* between honest and dishonest behavior.

From a comparative viewpoint, opportunistic behavior is an important factor in understanding why certain institutional arrangements are not viable, or are less developed than they might be on purely technical grounds: why it is difficult to get certain types of insurance, to get jobs for which one is intellectually qualified but has no acceptable school certificate to prove it, or why the presence of people who wish to sell defective products as good products will tend to drive out legitimate businesses. In these and many other similar cases, the transaction costs of distinguishing between honest and dishonest behavior tend to be high. Unless alternative institutions arise to counteract the effects of opportunism and the consequent lack of trust, transactions will be difficult and expensive, slowing down or impeding opportunities for development (the correlation between lack of trust and economic backwardness has been pointed out by E. C. Banfield (1961) and several other scholars).

Just as bounded rationality raises institutionally interesting problems in connection with a relatively high level of uncertainty or complexity, so the significance of opportunism is particularly greater when small numbers of actors can collude to exploit large numbers of others. For example, in a truly competitive market (a large-number situation, by definition) the opportunistic inclinations of some sellers will be usually checked by the competitive behavior of many other sellers. Collusions, cartels, and other secret agreements for deceitful purposes are, in general, viable only under conditions where small numbers of sellers can exploit large numbers of buyers.

Because relationships among members of an organization tend to be more frequent and long-lasting than market relations, opportunistic behavior is more easily exposed and subjected to sanctions. Internal auditing and control can rely on more extensive information (e.g., on quality of inputs and on production processes) than is usually available in market transactions (cf. Arvidsson: Ch. 30; Grunow: Ch. 31; Arvidsson and Sigg: Ch. 34). Again, the benefits gained by opportunistic behavior may not be so easily and fully appropriated by the employees of an organization as they are by independent agents in a market. Problems still remain in monitoring performance to constrain that form of opportunism that Alchian and Demsetz (1972) have identified as shirking, i.e., the appropriation of on-the-job leisure. Information asymmetries in large-scale bureaucracies may yield systematic filtering and distortion of information that increases proneness to error and shortcomings in performance (Tullock 1965).

Compared to the organizational failures framework outlined here, our approach reveals important similarities as well as significant differences. Like Coase, Simon, Tullock, and Williamson, we appreciate the enormous significance of bounded rationality for the *genesis* and *modus operandi* of social institutions. We also stress that cognitive constraints become especially binding in situations of uncertainty and complexity. In the public sector this means an extensive division of labor among governmental, semi-public, and private actors, long chains of actions, and a multiplicity of more or less loosely coupled networks. Finally, as our extensive discussion of methods of internal coordination, control, and evaluation shows, we agree that attention to internal organization is essential for understanding broader, system-wide questions of structure, guidance, and performance.

On the other hand, we believe that the minimization of transaction costs, while obviously important, is not a decisive criterion for choosing among alternative institutional arrangements in the public sector. In the conditions prevailing here, *the capacity to learn from one's own actions seems to us to be much more important than trying to specify least-cost decisional structures in advance.* Hence, the behavioral assumption of bounded rationality is expanded to include subjective limitations on memory and attention, and especially, instability of preferences. Correspondingly, the environment is characterized not only in terms of this uncertainty/complexity but also of structural and transactional features (e.g., recurrent vs. one-time exchanges) that may facilitate or impede learning (cf. Kaufmann Ch. 10) in relation to a range of goods and services that do not carry specifiable price tags (cf. Ostrom: Ch. 23).

The second behavioral assumption of the organizational failures model – opportunism – plays a relatively minor role in our discussion (but see van Gunsteren: Ch. 14 and Wirth: Ch. 29). This should not be taken to imply that, in our opinion, opportunistic behavior is not a serious problem in organizations and in the relationships between citizens and officials. The very asymmetry of roles between principals and agents, superiors and subordinates, rulers and ruled in a polity or hierarchically structured organization, produces conflicts and hence, powerful incentives to follow opportunistic and "suboptimizing" strategies. The few can easily collude within the structure of governmental institutions to exploit the many. We recognize this, but at the same time we point out that solidarity, trust, and "sympathy" in the sense of Adam Smith's *Theory of Moral Sentiments* (cf. Kaufmann 1984) are crucial for productive social interaction and a necessary basis for enduring social arrangements. For this reason, we have chosen to devote more attention to an exploration of the capabilities and limitations of solidarity as an alternative mode of guidance and control (cf. Chs. 18, 19 by Gretschmann and Hegner). That our emphasis on solidarity is a necessary complement to the study of the organizational and social implications of opportunism, rather than an alternative behavioral hypothesis this is shown by the fact that transaction-cost economists have recently begun to recognize the importance of factors like the valuation humans place on dignity and "due process" (cf. Williamson 1983). The problem is how to extend the bonds of trust to larger communities of relationships and avoid the perverse forms of "solidarity" that arise among the few who collude to exploit the many.

Despite these newer concerns, the organizational failures approach remains rather narrowly focused on economic efficiency, measured in terms of the transaction-cost criterion. On the other hand, broader issues of citizen participation, quality evaluation, and loyalty play a key role in Hirschman's *Exit, Voice, and Loyalty*. Not surprisingly the influence of the exit-voice framework is apparent in a number of chapters of the present book. While Hirschman's approach does not lead to a definite prescription for some optimal mix of exit and voice (and it is unlikely that one could specify an efficient mix of the two that would be stable over time), it does show that it is possible to determine, at any given time, whether there is a deficiency of one or the other of the two modes of response to quality decline. This is very much in the spirit of the present work which is directed to make the reader sensitive for situations of imbalance or poor fit among different methods of coordination and control, rather than to advocate some allegedly optimal combinations.

Our efforts go beyond concerns with exit, voice, and loyalty within the confines of existing institutional arrangements and begin to explore questions of how alternative types of institutional arrangements affect opportunities for the articulation of demand through both voice and exit. Perhaps the most important opportunity for the exercise of voice in human societies pertains to institutional analysis and design, and the critical assessment of performance through alternative institutional arrangements.

As we extend the range of our inquiry into problems of institutional analysis and design, the relationship of the modes of inquiry being developed in the new institutional economics, public choice theory and game theory (cf. Shubik Ch. 28) suggest a close kinship to scholarship in the German traditions of *"Ordnungstheorie"* and the Austrian traditions of political economy. *Ordnungstheorie* has focused predominantly upon the comparative study of economic systems as being embedded in different institutional systems, K. Paul Hensel (1972: 9), for example, observes that, "The order in which we live are the foundations of our existence and way of life." The conditions of those order, Hensel suggests, determine the way that social relationships are organized in human societies. He concludes in the opening paragraph of his foreword with the observation: "The imperative of political education is to be acquainted with the possible orders, gain the clearest picture of them, and how they condition, influence, and imprint different patterns in our lives" (Hensel 1972: 9). Scholars in the *Ordnungstheorie* tradition are drawing both upon the earlier traditions of German institutionalism and the new institutional economics to extend their understanding of economic orders as ways of life (Schüller 1983). Our efforts have been to extend the type of inquiries pursued by scholars in *Ordnungstheorie* to an explicit consideration of the public sector.

At the same time, contemporary scholars in the new institutional economics and public choice traditions, like Bruno Frey (1982), are indicating the importance of recognizing the earlier contributions of J. A. Schumpeter and other scholars, like F. A. Hayek, in the Austrian traditions of political economy. Other European traditions in economics, jurisprudence, philosophy, political theory, and sociology as reflected in the works of Cassirer, Durkheim, Luhmann, Pareto, K. Polanyi, M. Polanyi, Popper, and M. Weber help set the frame for many of our efforts.

As we extend our reflections about the study of human institutions, it becomes apparent that Europe has maintained a multidisciplinary and multinational community of scholarship from the enlightenment to the present which is concerned with the nature and constitution of order in human societies. Hobbes, Rousseau, Montesquieu, Hume, Smith, Kant, Hegel, Tocqueville, Marx, and many others all make their potential contributions to a continuing inquiry about problems associated with the nature of order in human societies. Contending arguments and potential contradictions abound in many of these formulations. Many different levels of analysis are implicated. Too often words have been used pejoratively to war upon one another. The task of fashioning contestable arguments that can be translated into a common language of discourse remains as a challenge to enlightened discourse. The use of theory to design new institutions and to transform societies has occurred in one form or another among all of the countries of Europe and North America. We, in this volume, have variously drawn upon different traditions of social theory, social science research, and social experience; but we have also tried to repay our debts by contributing to the continuity of that multidisciplinary, multinational community of scholars concerned with the nature and constitution of order in human societies.

References

Alchian, A. (1950): "Uncertainty, Evolution and Economic Theory." *Journal of Political Economy* 58/3: 211–221.

Alchian, A., and H. Demsetz (1972): "Production, Information and the Allocation of Resources of Invention." *American Economic Review* 62/5: 777–795.

Banfield, E. C. (1961): *Political Influence*. Glencoe: Free Press.

Buchanan, J. M. (1968): *The Demand and Supply of Public Goods*. Chicago: Rand McNally.

Buchanan, J. M., and G. Tullock (1962): *The Calculus of Consent*. Ann Arbor, Mich.: Univ. of Michigan Press.

Cassirer, E. (1946): *An Essay On Man: An Introduction to a Philosophy of Human Culture*. New Haven: Yale Univ. Press.

Coase, R. (1937): "The Nature of the Firm." *Economica* 4/16: 386–405.

Commons, J. R. (1951): *Institutional Economics: Its Place in Political Economy*. New York: MacMillan.

Commons, J. R. (1924): *Legal Foundations of Capitalism*. New York: MacMillan.

Dahl, R. A., and C. E. Lindblom (1976): *Politics, Economics and Welfare* (2nd ed.). Chicago and London: Univ. of Chicago Press.

Hamilton, A., J. Jay, and J. Madison n.d. *The Federalist*. Oxford: Blackwell. (1948)

Hayek, F. A. von (1976): *Law, Legislation and Liberty*. Vol. 2: The Mirage of Social Justice. London: Routledge & Kegan Paul.

Hensel, K. P. (1972): *Grundformen der Wirtschaftsordnung: Marktwirtschaft, Zentralverwaltungswirtschaft*. München: Beck.

Hirschman, A. O. (1970): *Exit, Voice, and Loyalty*. Cambridge, Mass.: Harvard Univ. Press.

Kaufmann, F. X. (1984): "Solidarität als Steuerungsform – Erklärungsansätze bei Adam Smith." In Kaufmann, F. X., and H. G. Krüsselberg (eds.), *Markt, Staat und Solidarität bei Adam Smith*, 158–184. Frankfurt – New York: Campus.

Lindblom, C. E. (1965): *The Intelligence of Democracy*. New York: Free Press.

Olson, M. (1965): *The Logic of Collective Action*. Cambridge, Mass.: Harvard Univ. Press.

Polanyi, M. (1951): *The Logic of Liberty*. London: Routledge & Kegan Paul.

Rawls, J. (1971): *A Theory of Justice*. Cambridge, Mass.: Harvard Univ. Press.

Schüller, A. (ed.) (1983): *Property Rights und ökonomische Theorie*. München: Beck.

Tocqueville, A. (1948): *Democracy in America* (2 Vols.). New York: Knopf.

Tocqueville, A. (1970): *Recollections*. Garden City, New York: Doubleday.

Tullock, G. (1965): *The Politics of Bureaucracy*. Washington: Public Affairs Press

Williamson, O. E. (1965): *The Economics of Discretionary Behavior*. Englewood Cliffs, N. J.: Prentice-Hall.

Williamson, O. E. (1975): *Markets and Hierarchies: Analysis and Antitrust Implications.*
    New York and London: Free Press, MacMillan.
Williamson, O. E. (1983): *The Economics of Governance: Framework and Implications.*
    Univ. of Pennsylvania, Center for the Study of Organizational Innovation. Discussion
    Paper No. 153 (July).

List of Contributors

Dr. *Göran Arvidsson*
Audit Director
The Swedish National
Audit Bureau
Box 34 105
S-10026 Stockholm
Sweden

Prof. *Andrew Dunsire*
Professor of Politics and Head of the
Department of Politics, University of York,
Department of Politics
University of York
Heslington, York
England Y 015DD
Great Britain

Dipl.-Soz. *Hans-Jürgen Franz*
Research Fellow
Institute for Population Research and Social
Policy (JBS)
University of Bielefeld
Postbox 8640,
D-4800 Bielefeld 1,
Fed. Republic of Germany

Dr. *Klaus Gretschmann*
European University Institute
Department of Economics
Badia Fiesolana: Via dei Roccettini 9
I-50016 San Domenico di Fiesole
(Firenze)
Italy

Prof. Dr. *Dieter Grimm*, LL. M. (Havard)
Professor of Law
Faculty of Law
University of Bielefeld
Postbox 8640
D-4800 Bielefeld 1
Fed. Republic of Germany

Prof. Dr. *Dieter Grunow*
Professor of Public Administration
Gesamthochschule Kassel
Fachbereich 7,

Monteverdistr. 2
D-3500 Kassel
Fed. Republic of Germany

Prof. Dr. *Herman R. van Gunsteren*
Professor of Political Theory
University of Leiden
Faculty of Law
Hugo de Grootstraat 27
NL-2311 XK Leiden
Netherlands

Dr. *Friedhart Hegner*
Senior Research Fellow
International Institute of Management
Wissenschaftszentrum Berlin
Platz der Luftbrücke 1–3
D-1000 Berlin 42
Fed. Republic of Germany

Dr. *Gerd-Michael Hellstern*
Scientific Assistant
Freie Universität Berlin
Zentralinstitut für Sozialwissenschaftliche
Forschung (ZI 6)
Sarrazienstr. 11–15
D-1000 Berlin 41
Fed. Republik of Germany

Prof. *Roberta Herzberg*
Professor of Political Science
Indiana University
Political Science Department
Woodburn Hall
Bloomington, Indiana 47405
USA

Christopher C. Hood
Lecturer
Glasgow University
Department of Politics
Adam Smith Building
Glasgow G 12 8 RT
Scotland
Great Britain

Prof. Dr. *Franz-Xaver Kaufmann*
Professor of Sociology and Social Policy and
Director of the Institute for Population Re-
search and Social Policy
University of Bielefeld
Faculty of Sociology
Postbox 8640
D-4800 Bielefeld 1
Fed. Republic of Germany

Prof. Dr. *Hans-Günther Krüsselberg*
Professor of Economics and Director of the
Institute for Social- and Family-Policy
Philipps University Marburg
Department of Economics
Am Plan 1
D-3550 Marburg
Fed. Republic of Germany

Prof. Dr. *Giandomenico Majone*
Professor of Public Management
Harvard University
John F. Kennedy School of Government
79 John F. Kennedy Street
Cambridge, Mass. 02138
USA

Prof. *Elinor Ostrom*
Professor of Political Science and
Co-Director of Workshop in Political
Theory
and Policy Analysis
Indiana University
Workshop of Political Theory and Policy
Analysis
513 North Park
Bloomington, Indiana 47405
USA

Prof. *Vincent Ostrom*
Arthur F. Bentley Professor of Government,
Professor of Political Science and
Co-Director of Workshop in Political
Theory and Policy Analysis
Indiana University
Workshop in Political Theory and Policy
Analysis
513 North Park
Bloomington, Indiana 47405
USA

Prof. Dr. *Jürgen Reese*
Professor of Economics
Gesamthochschule Kassel
Fachbereich 7
Monteverdistr. 2
D-3500 Kassel
Fed. Republic of Germany

Dr. *Bernd Rosewitz*
Scientific Assistant
Max-Planck-Institut für Gesellschafts-
forschung
Lothringer Str. 75
D-5000 Köln 1
Fed. Republic of Germany

Prof. *Paul A. Sabatier*
Professor and Chairman of the Division of
Environmental Studies, University of
California
University of California, Davis
Division of Environmental Studies
Davis, CA. 95616
USA

Prof. Dr. *Reinhard Selten*
Professor of Economics
Department of Law and Economics
University of Bonn
Adenauerallee 24–42
D-5300 Bonn
Fed. Republic of Germany

Prof. Dr. *Heinz Schleicher*
Professor of Economics
Université Paris XII
U.E.R. de Sciences Economiques et de
Géstion
58, Ave. Didier
F-94210 La Varenne St.-Hillaire
France

Lawrence J. Sharpe
University Lecturer in
Public Administration and Fellow
Nuffield College,
Oxford, OX1
England

Prof. *Martin Shubik*
Seymour H. Knox Professor of
Mathematical Institutional Economics
Yale University
Cowles Foundation for Research in
Economics and School of Organization and
Management
Box 2125 Yale Station
New Haven, CT 065260
USA

Dr. *Wolfgang Sigg*
Second Mayor of the City of Friedrichshafen
Tannenriedweg 14
D-7900 Friedrichshafen 24
Fed. Republic of Germany

Dipl.-Soz. *Wolfgang Wirth*
Research Fellow
Institute for Population Research and Social
Policy (IBS)
University of Bielefeld
Postbox 8640
D-4800 Bielefeld 1
Fed. Republic of Germany

Dr. *Hartmut K. Wolf*
Scientific Assistant
Technische Universität Berlin
Fachbereich 22, Sekr. 4–4
Franklinstr. 28–29
D-1000 Berlin 10
Fed. Republic of Germany

Index of Authors

This index indicates only the pages of the references made at the end of the 37 chapters of this volume.

Index of Subjects

de Gruyter Studies in Organization

An international series by internationally known authors presenting current research in organization.

The Japanese Industrial System

By *Charles J. McMillan*
2nd revised edition
1985. 15,5 x 23 cm. XII, 356 pages. Cloth DM 88,–.
ISBN 3 11 010410 5

Political Management

Redefining the Public Sphere
By *Hall Thomas Wilson*
1984. 15,5 x 23 cm. X, 316 pages. Cloth DM 98,–.
ISBN 3 11 009902 0

Limits to Bureaucratic Growth

By *Marshall W. Meyer* in Association with *William Stevenson* and *Stephen Webster*
1985. 15,5 x 23 cm. X, 228 pages. Cloth DM 88,–.
ISBN 3 11 009865 2

International Business in the Middle East

Edited by *Erdener Kaynak*
1985. 15,5 x 23 cm. XVI, 274 pages. Cloth DM 114,–.
ISBN 3 11 010321 4

The American Samurai

Blending American and Japanese Managerial Practice
By *Jon P. Alston*
1986. 15,5 x 23 cm. Approx. 390 pages. Cloth approx. DM 98,–.
ISBN 3 11 010619 1

Forthcoming Title:
Management in China

By *Oiva Laaksonen*
1986. 15,5 x 23 cm. Approx. 290 pages. Cloth approx. DM 88,–.
ISBN 3 11 009958 6

Prices are subject to change without notice

WALTER DE GRUYTER · BERLIN · NEW YORK

ORGANIZATION STUDIES

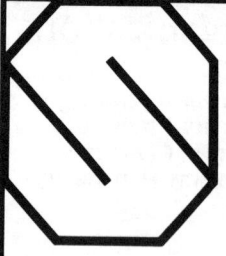

An international multidisciplinary journal devoted to the study of organizations, organizing and the organized in, and between societies

Editor-in-Chief: David J. Hickson, University of Bradford

Co-Editor: Alfred Kieser, Mannheim

Managing Editor: Susan van der Werff

Editorial Board: F. Agersnap, Copenhagen; K. Azumi, Newark; G. Benguigui, Paris; S. Clegg, Queensland; P. Coetsier, Gent; F. Ferraresi, Turin; J. Hage, Maryland; B. Hedberg, Stockholm; F. Hegner, Berlin; B. Hinings, Alberta; G. Hofstede, Arnhem; J. de Kervasdoué, Paris; C. Lammers, Leiden; B. Mannheim, Haifa; R. Mayntz, Cologne; G. Morgan, Toronto; I. Nonaka, Tokyo; J. Olson, Bergen; J. Padioleau, Florence; J. Pennings, Pennsylvania; G. Salaman, Milton Keynes; B. Stymne, Stockholm; A. Teulings, Amsterdam; H. Thierry, Amsterdam; J.-C. Thoenig, Fontainebleau.

Organization Studies is a supranational journal, based neither on anyone nation nor on collaboration between any particular nations. Its aim is to present diverse theoretical and empirical research from all nations, spanning a broad view of organizations and organizing. Its current Editorial Board is drawn from thirteen nations, and its contributors are worldwide.

O. S. is published in English because that language is the most widely read in this field of research. But manuscripts in other languages can be reviewed in those languages prior to translation. O. S. reviews books published in languages other than English to bring them before its international readership, and News and Notes cover conferences and research in many countries.

O. S. has published papers by authors from sociology, political science, management and public administration, psychology and economics. Some among the range of titles are listed overleaf. O. S. is not only about the study of "the organization", though that is central. It is also about the processes of organizing people, whether in business, public services, or public administration and government; and it is about the response of "the organized". It is not only about the contemporary scene, especially differences around the world, but also about the historical developments which have led to that scene.

Subscription rates 1986

Per volume of four issues. Libraries and institutions **DM 118,–**/approx. US $ 43.70. Individuals (except FRG and Switzerland) **DM 59,–**/ approx. US $ 21.85 (DM-prices are definitive, $-prices are approximate and subject to fluctuations in the exchange rate).

Published in collaboration with the European Group for Organizational Studies (EGOS) and the Maison des Sciences de l'Homme, Paris by

WALTER DE GRUYTER · BERLIN · NEW YORK

Verlag Walter de Gruyter & Co., Genthiner Straße 13, D-1000 Berlin 30, Tel.: (0 30) 2 60 05-0
Walter de Gruyter, Inc., 200 Saw Mill River Road, Hawthorne, N. Y. 10532, Tel.: (914) 747-0110